The Editor

GEORGE GIBIAN was Goldwin Smith Professor of Russian and Comparative Literature at Cornell University. His honors included Fulbright, Guggenheim, American Philosophical Society, and Rockefeller Foundation fellowships. He is the author of *The Man in the Black Coat: Russia's Lost Literature of the Absurd, The Interval of Freedom: Russian Literature during the Thaw,* and *Tolstoj and Shakespeare.* He is the editor of the Norton Critical Editions of Dostoevsky's *Crime and Punishment,* Gogol's *Dead Souls,* Tolstoy's *War and Peace,* and of the Viking Penguin *Portable Nineteenth-Century Russian Reader.* Professor Gibian's articles appeared in the *Wall Street Journal, The New Republic,* the *Christian Science Monitor,* and *Newsday,* among others.

ANNA KARENINA

THE MAUDE TRANSLATION

Revised by George Gibian

BACKGROUNDS AND SOURCES
CRITICISM

SECOND EDITION

A NORTON CRITICAL EDITION

Leo Tolstoy

ANNA KARENINA

THE MAUDE TRANSLATION
Revised by George Gibian

BACKGROUNDS AND SOURCES

CRITICISM

SECOND EDITION

Edited by

GEORGE GIBIAN

LATE OF CORNELL UNIVERSITY

W • W • NORTON & COMPANY • *New York* • *London*

Printed in the United States of America

The text of this book is composed in Electra
with the display set in Bernhard Modern.
Composition by PennSet, Inc.
Manufacturing by Courier.

Library of Congress Cataloging-in-Publication Data
Tolstoy, Leo, graf, 1828–1910.
[Anna Karenina. English]
Anna Karenina : backgrounds and sources, essays in criticism / Leo
Tolstoy ; the Maude translation ; edited by George Gibian.—2nd ed.
p.   cm.—(Norton critical edition)
Includes bibliographical references.
1. Adultery—Russia—Fiction. 2. Russia—Social life and
customs—1533–1917—Fiction. I. Maude, Aylmer, 1858–1938.
II. Gibian, George. III. Title.
PG3366.A6   1995
891.73'3—dc20   94-25857

ISBN 0-393-96642-9

W. W. Norton & Company, Inc., 500 Fifth Avenue, New York, N.Y. 10110
www.wwnorton.com

W. W. Norton & Company Ltd., Castle House, 75/76 Wells Street,
London W1T 3QT

3 • 4 • 5 • 6 • 7 • 8 • 9 • 0

Contents

Preface to the
Second Norton Critical Edition

The first Norton Critical Edition of Tolstoy's *Anna Karenina* met with generous, persistent interest. In the quarter century since the first edition was prepared, however, many fine new studies of Tolstoy's works have appeared in Russia, the United States, and other countries. A new edition is clearly called for.

I have included a variety of new critical and scholarly essays. The ideas of Mikhail Bakhtin have spread from Russia outward and have influenced and stimulated responses on the part of innumerable students of literature; I have included a brief piece by a foremost specialist in Bakhtin's writings, Caryl Emerson. A school of thought stressing the "prosaics" of fiction is represented here by Gary Saul Morson's provocative study of *Anna Karenina*. Morson places the temporal dimension of *Anna Karenina* against other elements of its structure—fate, beginnings, closures, and foreshadowings. He brings out the importance of details and ordinary, undramatic moments in the novel. Morson discusses fatalism and the film of the book starring Greta Garbo, which, he shows, gives its viewers Anna's Anna, rather than Tolstoy's Anna. Literary studies of the roles of women, and by women, have become increasingly important. We have chosen three essays by women scholars, Caryl Emerson, Lydia Ginzburg, and Donna Tussing Orwin. Caryl Emerson applies Bakhtin's conceptions of polyphony to Tolstoy, showing that in Tolstoy multiplicity is more linear and temporal than in Dostoevsky, studying his "obsession with timing," and demonstrating that Tolstoy was "a master of mapping the ways in which people are *not* free." The close studies in the history of ideas—moral, philosophical, and psychological—by Donna Tussing Orwin and by the Russian critic Lydia Ginzburg round off the new materials. Orwin analyzes thoroughly Tolstoy's attitudes toward nature, as embodied in children and peasants, in *Anna Karenina*, and in a second study, his relationship toward Schopenhauer and Rousseau. Ginzburg, whom Edward J. Brown has called "one of the most distinguished and original minds to have worked on the nature of verbal art," contrasts Tolstoy's characters' psychology with Dosteovsky's. She illustrates the fluidity of the ego in Tolstoy and analyzes the characters' conditioned existence and their various defensive maneuvers. I have also reached into Russia for a sample of the writing of Eduard Babaev, which exemplifies the best of succinct, level-headed Russian scholarly writing. Babaev reveals the pattern wrought in the novel by three scenes in which characters view paintings of Anna, and he explains how these scenes embody Tolstoy's theory of art.

Some of the critical essays included in the first edition seem less illuminating from our present perspective and have been dropped. I have brought the Selected Bibliography up to date, supplied new explanatory footnotes to the text of the novel, as well as to the critical materials, expanded others, and made corrections of typographical and other mistakes that had crept into the first edition. The translations (both of the novel and of the critical essays) have been emended in many places. Many of the new footnotes and corrections to the text of the novel are indebted to the information supplied by Babaev in his notes to volumes 8 and 9 in the Russian collected works of Tolstoy in twenty-two volumes (Moscow, 1982).

Tolstoy's novels continue to be read, enjoyed, and admired by millions of readers all over the world. Tolstoyan criticism and scholarship are flourishing. I hope this new edition will bring the established, traditional canon of Tolstoyan criticism, as well as modern and contemporary approaches, close to the readers and students of our age. I am very grateful to those of my students, friends, and colleagues who over the years have suggested desirable additions and corrections, particularly to students in my course on the Russian novel at Cornell University, Joseph Read, Daniel Blumenthal, and Thomas Kim, and to the late Edgar Lehrman, who sent me a list of ten emendations, which I have been able to incorporate in this edition.

George Gibian
Ithaca, New York

List of the Principal Characters[*]

Agatha Mikháylovna, Lévin's housekeeper
Annushka, Anna's maid
Chírikov, best man at Lévin's wedding
Cord, the English trainer
Dunyásha, Kitty's maid
Goleníshchev, a friend of Vrónsky's
Karénin, Alexéy Alexándrovich, Anna's husband
Karénin, Sergéy Alexéyich ('Serëzha,' 'Kútik'), Anna's son
Karénina, Ann Arkádyevna ('Anna')
Katavásov, Theodore Vasílyevich, a professor
Koznyshëv, Sergius Ivánich ('Sergéy'), Lévin's half-brother
Krítsky, an acquaintance of Nicholas Lévin's
Lévin, Constantine Dmítrich ('Kóstya')
Lévin, Nicholas, Constantine's brother
Linon, Mlle, governess at the Shcherbátsky's
Lvov, Prince ('Arsény')
Lvóva, Princess Nataly Alexándrovna, Prince Shcherbátsky's second
    daughter
Lydia Ivánovna, Countess, Karénin's friend
Mary Nikoláevna ('Másha'), living with Nicholas
Mikháylov ('Sásha'), a Russian painter
Mikháylova, Mikhaylov's wife
Nástya, Sviyazhsky's sister-in-law
Nórdston, Countess
Oblónskaya, Princess Dárya Alexándrovna ('Dolly'), Oblónsky's wife;
    eldest daughter of Prince Shcherbátsky
Oblónskaya, Princess Barbara, Anna's aunt
Oblónsky, Prince Stephen Arkádyevich ('Stiva')
    Alësha and Nikólenka, Oblónsky's younger children
    Grísha, Oblónsky's son
    Tánya, Oblónsky's daughter
Petrítsky, Lieutenant, Vrónsky's friend
Petróv, an invalid artist

[*] Russians are not given middle names but patronymics—derivatives of the first name of the person's father. Hence all siblings will have the same patronymic. The masculine and feminine forms differ slightly. Alternate forms of the names are enclosed in parentheses.

Petróva, Anna Pávlovna, Petróv's wife
Serpukhovskóy, General Prince
Shcherbátskaya, Princess
Shcherbátskaya, Princess Catherine Alexándrovna ('Kitty'),
        Shcherbátsky's youngest daughter
Shcherbátsky, Prince Alexander
Shcherbátsky, the young Prince Nicholas
Shilton, Baroness
Sorókina, Princess, a friend of Vrónsky's mother
Stahl, Mme
Sviyázhsky, Nicholas Ivánich, a Marshal of the Nobility
Tverskáya, Princess Elizabeth Fëdorovna ('Betsy')
Tverskóy, Prince
Várenka, Mlle
Veslóvsky, Vásenka, a second cousin of the Shcherbátskys
Vrónskaya, Countess, Vrónsky's mother
Vrónsky, Count Alexéy Kirílich
Yáshvin, Captain Prince, Vrónsky's friend

List of Russian Words

Arshín, 28 inches.
Chétvert, about 5¾ bushels.
Desyatína, about 2¾ acres.
Great Morskáya, one of the chief streets in Petrograd.
Izvózchik, a public conveyance corresponding to our cab. The word
        was also used for the man who drove it.
Kópek, about a penny; the one-hundredth part of a rouble.
Kvas, a nonalcoholic drink made out of bread.
Sázhen, 7 feet. Firewood is usually sold by the square sázhen. The logs
        are laid on one another to a height of one sázhen, the depth
        being 21 inches, which is the length of each log.
Tarantás, a large four-wheeled vehicle with leather top. It rested on long
        wooden bars instead of springs and was specially adapted for
        use where roads were bad.
Verst, ⅔ of a mile.
Zémstvo, nearly equivalent to County Council, a unit of local self-
        government.

The Text of
ANNA KARENINA

Translated by Louise and Aylmer Maude
Revised by George Gibian

BOOK I

'VENGEANCE IS MINE; I WILL REPAY.'[1]

Part I

Chapter I

All happy families resemble one another, but each unhappy family is unhappy in its own way. *Is there such a thing as a happy family?*

Everything was upset in the Oblonskys' house. The wife had discovered an intrigue between her husband and their former French governess, and declared that she would not continue to live under the same roof with him. This state of things had now lasted for three days, and not only the husband and wife but the rest of the family and the whole household suffered from it. They all felt that there was no sense in their living together, and that any group of people who had met together by chance at an inn would have had more in common than they. The wife kept to her own rooms; the husband stopped away from home all day; the children ran restlessly about the house; the English governess quarrelled with the housekeeper and wrote to a friend asking if she could find her another situation; the cook had gone out just at dinner-time the day before and had not returned; and the kitchen-maid and coachman had given notice.

On the third day after his quarrel with his wife, Prince Stephen Arkadyevich Oblonsky—Stiva, as he was called in his set in Society —woke up at his usual time, eight o'clock, not in his wife's bedroom but on the morocco leather-covered sofa in his study. He turned his plump, well-kept body over on the springy sofa as if he wished to have another long sleep, and tightly embracing one of the pillows leant his cheek against it; but then suddenly opened his eyes and sat up.

'Let me see—what was it?' he thought, trying to recall his dream. 'What was it? Oh yes—Alabin was giving a dinner-party in Darmstadt—no, not in Darmstadt but somewhere in America. Oh yes, Darmstadt was in America,—and Alabin was giving the party. The dinner was served on glass tables—yes, and the tables sang "*Il mio tesoro*"[2] . . . no, not exactly "*Il mio tesoro*," but something better than that; and then there were some kind of little decanters that were really women.' His eyes sparkled merrily and he smiled as he sat thinking. 'Yes, it was very nice. There were many other delightful things which I can't just get hold of—can't catch now I'm awake.' Then, noticing a streak of light that had made its way

---

1. A quotation from Paul's Epistle to the Romans 12.19, which reads, "Vengeance is mine, I shall repay, says the Lord." This in turn is a reference to a longer passage in Deuteronomy 32.35.
2. "My treasure."

in at the side of the blind, he gaily let down his legs and felt about with his feet for his slippers finished in gold kid (last year's birthday present, embroidered by his wife); and from nine years' habit he stretched out his arm, without rising, towards where his dressing-gown usually hung in their bedroom. And then he suddenly remembered that he was not sleeping there but in his study, and why. The smile vanished from his face and he frowned.

'Oh dear, dear, dear!' he groaned recalling what had happened. And the details of his quarrel with his wife, his inextricable position, and, worst of all, his guilt, rose up in his imagination.

'No, she will never forgive me; she can't forgive me! And the worst thing about it is, that it's all my own fault—my own fault; and yet I'm not guilty! That's the tragedy of it!' he thought. 'Oh dear, oh dear!' he muttered despairingly, as he recalled the most painful details of the quarrel. The worst moment had been when, returning home from the theatre merry and satisfied, with an enormous pear in his hand for his wife, he did not find her in the drawing-room nor, to his great surprise, in the study, but at last saw her in her bedroom with the unlucky note which had betrayed him in her hand.

She sat there: the careworn, ever-bustling, and (as he thought) rather simple Dolly—with the note in her hand and a look of terror, despair, and anger on her face.

'What is this? This?' she asked, pointing to the note. And, as often happens, it was not so much the memory of the event that tormented him, as of the way he had replied to her.

At that moment there had happened to him what happens to most people when unexpectedly caught in some shameful act: he had not had time to assume an expression suitable to the position in which he stood toward his wife now that his guilt was discovered. Instead of taking offence, denying, making excuses, asking forgiveness, or even remaining indifferent (anything would have been better than what he did), he involuntarily ('reflex action of the brain,' thought Oblonsky, who was fond of physiology)[3] smiled his usual kindly and therefore silly smile.

He could not forgive himself for that silly smile. Dolly, seeing it, shuddered as if with physical pain, and with her usual vehemence burst into a torrent of cruel words and rushed from the room. Since then she had refused to see him.

'It's all the fault of that stupid smile,' thought Oblonsky. 'But what am I to do? What can I do?' he asked himself in despair, and could find no answer.

Chapter II

Oblonsky was truthful with himself. He was incapable of self-

---

3. Oblonsky is thinking of I. M. Sechenov's extremely popular materialistic-physiological book *Reflexes of the Brain*, published in 1853.

deception and could not persuade himself that he repented of his conduct. He could not feel repentant that he, a handsome amorous man of thirty-four, was not in love with his wife, the mother of five living and two dead children and only a year younger than himself. He repented only of not having managed to conceal his conduct from her Nevertheless he felt his unhappy position and pitied his wife, his children, and himself. He might perhaps have been able to hide things from her had he known that the knowledge would so distress her. He had never clearly considered the matter, but had a vague notion that his wife had long suspected him of being unfaithful and winked at it. He even thought that she, who was nothing but an excellent mother of a family, worn-out, already growing elderly, no longer pretty, and in no way remarkable—in fact, quite an ordinary woman—ought to be lenient to him, if only from a sense of justice. It turned out that the very opposite was the case.

'How awful! Oh dear, oh dear, how awful!' Oblonsky kept repeating to himself, and could arrive at no conclusion. 'And how well everything was going on till now—how happily we lived! She was contented, happy in her children; I never interfered with her but left her to fuss over them and the household as she pleased. . . . Of course it's not quite nice that *she* had been a governess in our house. That's bad! There's something banal, a want of taste, in carrying on with one's governess—but then, what a governess!' (He vividly pictured to himself Mlle Roland's roguish black eyes, and her smile.) 'Besides, as long as she was in the house I never took any liberties. The worst of the matter is, that she is already . . . . Why need it all happen at once? Oh dear, dear, dear! What am I to do?'

He could find no answer, except life's usual answer to the most complex and insoluble questions. That answer is: live in the needs of the day, that is, find forgetfulness. He could no longer find forgetfulness in sleep, at any rate not before night, could not go back to the music and the songs of the little decanter-women, consequently he must seek forgetfulness in the dream of life.

'We'll see when the time comes,' thought Oblonsky, and got up, put on his grey dressing-gown lined with blue silk, tied the cords and drawing a full breath of air into his broad chest went with his usual firm tread toward the window, turning out his feet that carried his stout body so lightly, drew up the blind and rang loudly. The bell was answered immediately by his old friend and valet, Matthew, who brought in his clothes, boots, and a telegram. He was followed by the barber with shaving tackle.

'Any papers from the Office?' asked Oblonsky, as he took the telegram and sat down before the looking-glass.

'They're on your table,' answered Matthew with a questioning and sympathizing glance at his master—adding after a pause with a sly smile: 'Some one has called from the cab driver's.'

Oblonsky did not answer, but glanced at Matthew's face in the looking-glass. From their looks, as they met in the glass, it was evident that they understood one another. Oblonsky's look seemed to say: 'Why do you tell me that? As if you don't know!'

Matthew put his hands into the pockets of his jacket, put out his foot, and looked at his master with a slight, good-humoured smile.

'I ordered him to come the Sunday after next, and not to trouble you or himself needlessly till then,' said he, evidently repeating a sentence he had prepared.

Oblonsky understood that Matthew meant to have a joke and draw attention to himself. He tore open the telegram and read it, guessing at the words, which (as so often happens in telegrams) were misspelt, and his face brightened.

'Matthew, my sister Anna Arkadyevna is coming to-morrow,' he said, motioning away for a moment the shiny plump hand of the barber, which was shaving a rosy path between his long curly whiskers.

'The Lord be thanked!' said Matthew, proving by his answer that he knew just as well as his master the importance of this visit: namely, that Anna Arkadyevna, Stephen Arkadyevich's favourite sister, might help to reconcile the husband and wife.

'Is she coming alone, or with Mr. Karenin?'

Oblonsky could not answer as the barber was busy with his upper lip; but he raised one finger, and Matthew nodded to him in the glass.

'Alone. Would you like one of the upstairs rooms got ready?'

'Ask Darya Alexandrovna.'

'Darya Alexandrovna?' Matthew repeated, as if in doubt.

'Yes, tell her. Give her the telegram, and see what she says.'

'You want to have a try at her?' was what Matthew meant, but he only said: 'Yes, sir.'

Oblonsky was washed, his hair brushed, and he was about to dress, when Matthew, stepping slowly in his creaking boots, re-entered the room with the telegram in his hand. The barber was no longer there.

'Darya Alexandrovna told me to say that she is going away. "He may do as he pleases"—that is, as you please sir,' he said, laughing with his eyes only; and, putting his hands in his pockets with his head on one side, he gazed at his master. Oblonsky remained silent, then a kind and rather pathetic smile appeared on his handsome face.

'Ah, Matthew!' he said, shaking his head.

'Never mind, sir—things will shape themselves.'

'Shape themselves, eh?'

'Just so, sir.'

'Do you think so?—Who's that?' asked Oblonsky, hearing the rustle of a woman's dress outside the door.

'It's me, sir,' answered a firm and pleasant woman's voice, and Matrena Filimonovna, the children's nurse, thrust her stern pock-marked face in at the door.

'What is it, Matrena?' asked Oblonsky, going toward her.

Although he was entirely guilty and was conscious of it, almost every one in the house—even the nurse, Darya Alexandrovna's best friend—sided with him.

'What is it?' said he mournfully.

'Won't you go and try again sir? By God's grace you might make it up! She suffers dreadfully; it's pitiful to see her, and everything in the house is topsy-turvy. You should consider the children! Own up, sir—it can't be helped! There's no joy with-out . . .'

'But she won't admit me!'

'Do your part—God is merciful. Pray to Him, sir, pray to Him!'

'All right—now go,' said Oblonsky, suddenly blushing.

'I must get dressed,' said he, turning to Matthew, and he resolutely threw off his dressing-gown.

Matthew blew some invisible speck off the shirt which he held ready gathered up like a horse's collar, and with evident pleasure invested with it his master's carefully tended body.

Chapter III

When he was quite dressed Oblonsky sprinkled some scent on himself, pulled down his cuffs, and as usual distributing in different pockets his cigarette-case, matches, pocket-book, and the watch with its double chain and bunch of charms, he shook out his handkerchief, and feeling clean, sweet, healthy, and physically bright in spite of his misfortune, went with a slight spring in each step into the dining-room where his coffee stood ready. Beside the coffee lay letters and papers from the Office.

He read the letters, one of which impressed him unpleasantly. It concerned the sale of a forest on his wife's estate, and came from a dealer who wanted to buy that forest. This forest had to be sold; but until he was reconciled with his wife the sale was quite out of the question. What was most unpleasant was that a financial consideration would now be mixed up with the impending reconciliation. The idea that he might be biased by that consideration, might seek a reconciliation in order to sell the forest, offended him. Having looked through his letters, Oblonsky drew the Departmental papers toward him, and turning over the pages of two files made a few notes on them with a big pencil; then pushing them aside, began to drink his coffee.

At the same time he unfolded the still damp morning paper, and began reading. Oblonsky subscribed to and read a Liberal paper—not an extreme Liberal paper but one that expressed the opinions of the majority. And although neither science, art, nor politics specially interested him, he firmly held to the opinions of the majority and of his paper on those subjects, changing his views when the majority changed theirs,—or rather, not changing them —they changed imperceptibly of their own accord.

Oblonsky's tendency and opinions were not his by deliberate choice: they came of themselves, just as he did not choose the fashion of his hats or coats but wore those of the current style. Living in a certain social set, and having a desire, such as generally develops with maturity, for some kind of mental activity, he was obliged to hold views, just as he was obliged to have a hat. If he had a reason for preferring Liberalism to the Conservatism of many in his set, it was not that he considered Liberalism more reasonable, but because it suited his manner of life better. The Liberal Party maintained that everything in Russia was bad, and it was a fact that Oblonsky had many debts and decidedly too little money. The Liberal Party said that marriage was an obsolete institution which ought to be reformed; and family life really gave Oblonsky very little pleasure, forcing him to tell lies and dissemble, which was quite contrary to his nature. The Liberal Party said, or rather hinted, that religion was only good as a check on the more barbarous portion of the population; and Oblonsky really could not stand through even a short church service without pain in his feet, or understand why one should use all that dreadfully high-flown language about another world while one can live so merrily in this one. Besides, Oblonsky was fond of a pleasant joke, and sometimes liked to perplex a simple-minded man by observing that if you're going to be proud of your ancestry, why stop short at Prince Rurik and repudiate your oldest ancestor—the ape?

Thus Liberalism became habitual to Oblonsky, and he loved his paper as he loved his after-dinner cigar, for the slight mistiness it produced in his brain. He read the leading article, which explained that in our time it is needless to raise the cry that Radicalism is threatening to swallow up all Conservative elements and to maintain that the Government should take measures to crush the hydra of revolution; for, on the contrary, 'in our opinion the danger lies not in an imaginary hydra of revolution, but in an obstinate clinging to tradition which hampers progress,' etc. He also read the finance article in which Bentham and Mill were mentioned and hits were made at the Ministry. With his natural quickness of perception he understood the meaning of each hit, whence it came, for whom it was meant, and what had provoked it, and this as usual gave him a certain satisfaction. But to-day the satisfaction was marred by the memory of Matrena Filimonovna's advice, and the fact that there was all this trouble in the house. He went on to read that there was a rumour of Count Beust's journey to Wiesbaden; that there would be no more grey hairs; that a light brougham was for sale, and a young person offered her services; but all this information did not give him the quiet, ironical pleasure it usually did.

Having finished the paper, his second cup of coffee, and a buttered roll, he got up, flicked some crumbs off his waistcoat, and, expanding his broad chest, smiled joyfully, not because there was anything specially pleasant in his mind—no, the smile was but the result of a healthy digestion. But that joyful smile at once brought everything back to his mind, and he grew thoughtful.

Then he heard the sound of two childish voices outside the door, and recognized them as the voices of his eldest daughter, Tanya, and of his little boy Grisha. They were dragging something along, and had upset it.

'I told you not to put passengers on the roof,' the girl shouted in English. 'Now pick them up!'

'Everything is disorganized,' thought Oblonsky; 'here are the children running wild—' and going to the door he called them in. They left the box, which represented a train, and came to their father.

The girl, her father's pet, ran boldly in, embraced him, and hung laughing on his neck, pleased as she always was, to smell the familiar scent of his whiskers. Having kissed his face, flushed by stooping and lit up by tenderness, the girl unclasped her hands and was going to run away, but he held her back.

'How's Mama?' he asked, passing his hand over his daughter's smooth delicate little neck, as he smilingly said 'Good morning' in answer to the little boy's greeting.

He was conscious of not caring as much for the boy as for the girl but did his best to treat them both alike. The boy felt this and did not respond to his father's cold smile.

'Mama? She's up,' said the girl.

Oblonsky sighed.

'That means that she has again not slept all night,' he thought. 'Yes, but is she cheerful?' he added.

The girl knew that her father and mother had quarrelled, and that her mother could not be cheerful, and also that her father must know this, so that his putting the question to her so lightly was all pretence, and she blushed for him. He noticed this and blushed too.

'I don't know,' she said. 'She said we were not to have any lessons, but must walk with Miss Hull to Grandmamma's.'

'Well, you may go, my little Tanyakin. . . . Oh, wait!' he said, still holding her and stroking her delicate little hand.

Taking a box of sweets from the mantelpiece where he had put it the day before, he chose two sweets which he knew she liked best, a chocolate and a coloured cream.

'For Grisha?' she asked, holding out the chocolate.

'Yes, yes,' and stroking her shoulder he kissed the nape of her neck, and let her go.

'The carriage is ready,' said Matthew, 'and there is a woman waiting to see you on business.'

'Been here long?'

'About half an hour.'

'How often must I tell you to let me know at once when anyone is here?'

'But I must give you time to finish your coffee,' answered Matthew in his friendly rude tone, with which it was impossible to be angry.

'Well, ask her in at once,' said Oblonsky, his face wrinkling with vexation.

The woman, widow of a petty official named Kalinin, was petitioning for something impossible and absurd, but nevertheless Oblonsky, with his usual politeness asked her to sit down and heard her attentively to the end, gave her full instructions how and to whom to apply and even wrote briskly and fluently in his large, graceful and legible hand a little note to a personage who might be of use to her. Having dismissed her, he took his hat and paused to consider whether he had forgotten anything. He found he had forgotten nothing but what he wanted to forget: his wife.

'Oh yes!' his head dropped, and his handsome face became worried.

'To go, or not to go?' he asked himself; and his inner consciousness answered that he ought not to go: that it could only result in hypocrisy; that it was impossible to restore their relations because it was impossible to render her attractive and capable of exciting love, or to turn him into an old man incapable of love. Nothing except hypocrisy and falsehood could now result—and these were repugnant to his nature.

'Nevertheless it will have to be done sooner or later. After all, things can't remain as they are,' he said, trying to brace himself. He expanded his chest, took out a cigarette, lit it, took two whiffs, then threw it into a pearl-shell ash-tray, and crossing the drawing-room with rapid steps, he opened the door which led to his wife's bedroom.

Chapter IV

Darya Alexandrovna was there in a dressing-jacket, her large frightened eyes made more prominent by the emaciation of her face, and her once beautiful and luxuriant hair done up in a knot. The room was littered with scattered articles, and she was standing among them before an open wardrobe, sorting things out. Hearing her husband's step she stopped and looked at the door, vainly trying to assume a severe and contemptuous expression. She felt that she was afraid of him and afraid of the impending interview. She was trying to do what she had attempted ten times already during those three days, to sort out her own and her children's clothes to take to her mother's; but she could not bring herself to do it, and said again, as she had done after each previous attempt, that things could not remain as they were—that she must do something to punish and humiliate him, and to revenge herself if only for a small part of the pain he had caused her. She still kept saying that she would leave him, but felt that this was impossible. It was impossible because she could not get out of the habit of regarding him as her husband and of loving him. Besides, she felt that if here, in her own home, it was all she could do to look after her five children properly, it would be still worse where she meant to take them. As it was, during these three days the youngest had fallen ill because they had given him sour broth, and the others had had hardly any dinner yesterday. She felt that it was impossible for her to leave; but still deceiving herself, she went on sorting the things and pretending that she really would go.

On seeing her husband she thrust her arms into a drawer of the wardrobe as if looking for something, and only looked round at him when he had come close to her. But instead of appearing stern and determined as she intended, her face expressed only perplexity and suffering.

'Dolly!' he said in a soft, timid voice. He bowed his head, wishing to look pathetic and submissive, but all the same he shone with freshness and health. With a rapid glance she took in his fresh and healthy figure from head to foot. 'Yes, he is happy and contented,' she thought, 'but what about me? . . . And that horrid good-nature of his which people love and praise so, how I hate it!' She pressed her lips together and a cheek-muscle twitched on the right side of her pale nervous face.

'What do you want?' she said quickly in a voice unlike her usual deep tones.

'Dolly,' he repeated unsteadily, 'Anna is coming to-day.'

'What's that to do with me? I can't receive her!' she exclaimed.

'But after all, Dolly, you really must,' said he.

'Go away, go away, go away!' she cried, as if in physical pain, without looking at him.

Oblonsky could think calmly of his wife, could hope that 'things would shape themselves' as Matthew had said, and could calmly read his paper and drink his coffee, but when he saw her worn, suffering face, and heard her tone, resigned and despairing, he felt a choking sensation. A lump rose to his throat and tears glistened in his eyes.

'Oh, my God! What have I done? Dolly—for heaven's sake! . . . You know . . .' He could not continue. His throat was choked with sobs.

She slammed the doors of the wardrobe and looked up at him.

'Dolly, what can I say? . . . Only forgive me! Think, nine years. . . . Can't they atone for a momentary—a momentary . . .'

Her eyes drooped and she waited to hear what he would say, as if entreating him to persuade her somehow that she had made a mistake.

'A momentary infatuation, . . .' he said, and was going on; but at those words her lips tightened again as if with pain, and again the muscle in her right cheek began to twitch.

'Go away—go away from here!' she cried in a still shriller voice, 'and don't talk to me of your infatuations and all those horrors!'

She wished to go away, but staggered and held on to the back of a chair to support herself. His face broadened, his lips swelled, and his eyes filled with tears.

'Dolly!' he said, now actually sobbing, 'for heaven's sake think of the children—they have done nothing! Punish me—make me suffer for my sin! Tell me what to do—I am ready for anything. I am the guilty one. I have no words to express my guilt. . . . But Dolly, forgive me!'

She sat down and he could hear her loud, heavy breathing. He felt unutterably sorry for her. She tried again and again to speak and could not. He waited.

'You think of our children when you want to play with them, but I am always thinking of them, and I know they are ruined now,' she said, evidently repeating one of the phrases she had used to herself again and again during those three days.

But she had spoken of 'our children,' and looking gratefully at her he moved to take her hand; but she stepped aside with a look of repugnance.

'I do think of the children, and would do anything in the world to save them; but I do not know how to save them—

whether by taking them away from their father, or by leaving them with a dissolute—yes, a dissolute father. . . . Tell me, do you think it possible for us to live together after what has happened? Is it possible? Say, is it possible?' she repeated, raising her voice. 'When my husband, the father of my children, has love affairs with his children's governess?'

'But what's to be done?—what's to be done?' said he, in a piteous voice, hardly knowing what he was saying, and sinking his head lower and lower.

'You are horrid and disgusting to me!' she shouted, getting more and more excited. 'Your tears are—water! You never loved me; you have no heart, no honour! To me you are detestable, disgusting—a stranger, yes, a perfect stranger!' She uttered that word *stranger*, so terrible to herself, with anguish and hatred.

He looked at her and the hatred he saw in her face frightened and surprised him. He did not understand that his pity exasperated her. She saw in him pity for herself but not love. 'No, she hates me; she will not forgive me,' he thought. 'It is awful, awful!' he muttered.

At that moment a child began to cry in another room, probably having tumbled down. Darya Alexandrovna listened, and her face softened suddenly.

She seemed to be trying to recollect herself, as if she did not know where she was or what she had to do. Then she rose quickly and moved toward the door.

'After all, she loves my child,' he thought, noticing the change in her face when the baby cried; '*my* child—then how can she hate me?'

'Dolly, just a word!' he said, following her.

'If you follow me, I shall call the servants and the children! I'll let everybody know you are a scoundrel! I am going away to-day, and you may live here with your mistress!'

She went out, slamming the door.

Oblonsky sighed, wiped his face, and with soft steps left the room. 'Matthew says "things will shape themselves,"—but how? I don't even see a possibility. . . . Oh dear, the horror of it! And her shouting—it was so vulgar,' he thought, recalling her screams and the words *scoundrel* and *mistress*. 'And the maids may have heard it! It is dreadfully banal, dreadfully!' For a few seconds Oblonsky stood alone; then he wiped his eyes, sighed, and expanding his chest went out of the room.

It was a Friday, the day on which a German clockmaker always came to wind up the clocks. Seeing him in the dining-room, Oblonsky recollected a joke he had once made at the expense of this accurate baldheaded clockmaker, and he smiled. 'The German,'

he had said, 'has been wound up for life to wind up clocks.' Oblonsky was fond of a joke. 'Well, perhaps things will shape themselves—"shape themselves"! That's a good phrase,' he thought. 'I
must use that.'

'Matthew!' he called, 'will you and Mary arrange everything for
Anna Arkadyevna in the little sitting-room?' he added when
Matthew appeared.

'Yes, sir.'

Oblonsky put on his fur coat, and went out into the porch.

'Will you be home for dinner, sir?' said Matthew, as he showed
him out.

'I'll see. . . . Oh, and here's some money,' said he, taking a
ten-rouble note out of his pocket-book. 'Will it be enough?'

'Enough or not, we shall have to manage, that's clear,' said
Matthew, closing the carriage door and stepping back into the
porch.

Meanwhile Darya Alexandrovna after soothing the child returned
to her bedroom, knowing from the sound of the carriage wheels
that her husband had gone. It was her only place of refuge from
household cares. Even now, during the few minutes she had
spent in the nursery, the English governess and Matrena Filimonovna had found time to ask some questions that could not be
put off, and which she alone could answer. 'What should the
children wear when they went out? Ought they to have milk?
Should not a new cook be sent for?'

'Oh, do leave me alone!' she cried; and returning to her bedroom she sat down where she had sat when talking with her
husband. Locking together her thin fingers, on which her rings
hung loosely, she went over in her mind the whole of their
conversation.

'Gone! But how did he finish with *her*?' she thought. 'Is it
possible that he still sees her? Why didn't I ask him? No, no! It's
impossible to be reunited. . . . Even if we go on living in the
same house we are strangers—strangers for ever!' she repeated,
specially emphasizing the word that was so dreadful to her. 'And
how I loved him! Oh God, how I loved him! . . . How I loved—
and don't I love him now? Don't I love him more than ever?
The most terrible thing . . .' She did not finish the thought,
because Matrena Filimonovna thrust her head in at the door.

'Hadn't I better send for my brother?' she said. 'After all, he
can cook a dinner;—or else the children will go without food till
six o'clock, as they did yesterday.'

'All right! I'll come and see about it in a moment. . . . Has the milk been sent for?' and Darya Alexandrovna plunged into her daily cares, and for a time drowned her grief in them.

Chapter V

Oblonsky's natural ability had helped him to do well at school, but mischief and laziness had caused him to finish very low in his year's class. Yet in spite of his dissipated life, his unimportant service rank, and his comparative youth, he occupied a distinguished and well-paid post as Head of one of the Government Boards in Moscow. This post he had obtained through Alexis Alexandrovich Karenin, his sister Anna's husband, who held one of the most important positions in the Ministry to which that Moscow Board belonged. But even if Karenin had not nominated his brother-in-law for that post, Stiva Oblonsky, through one of a hundred other persons—brothers, sisters, relations, cousins, uncles or aunts—would have obtained this or a similar post with a salary of some 6000 roubles a year, which he needed because in spite of his wife's substantial means his affairs were in a bad way.

Half Moscow and half Petersburg were his relations or friends. He was born among those who were or who became the great ones of this world. One third of the official world, the older men, were his father's friends and had known him as a baby, he was on intimate terms with another third, and was well acquainted with the last third. Consequently the distributors of earthly blessings, such as government posts, grants, concessions, and the like, were all his friends. They could not overlook one who belonged to them, so that Oblonsky had no special difficulty in obtaining a lucrative post; he had only not to raise any objections, not to be envious, not to quarrel, and not to take offence—all things which, being naturally good-tempered, he never did. It would have seemed to him ridiculous had he been told that he would not get a post with the salary he required; especially as he did not demand anything extraordinary. He only wanted what other men of his age and set were getting; and he could fill such an office as well as anybody else.

Oblonsky was not only liked by every one who knew him for his kind and joyous nature and his undoubted honesty, but there was something in him—in his handsome and bright appearance, his beaming eyes, black hair and eyebrows, and his pink-and-white complexion, that had a physical effect on those he met, making them feel friendly and cheerful. 'Ah! Stiva Oblonsky! Here he is!' said almost every one he met, smilingly. Even if conversation with him sometimes caused no special delight, still the next day, or the next, every one was as pleased as ever to meet him.

It was the third year that Oblonsky had been Head of that Government Board in Moscow, and he had won not only the affection but also the respect of his fellow-officials, subordinates, chiefs, and all who had anything to do with him. The chief qualities that had won him this general respect in his Office were, first, his extreme leniency, founded on a consciousness of his own defects; secondly, his true Liberalism—not that of which he read in his paper, but that which was in his blood and made him treat all men alike whatever their rank or official position; thirdly and chiefly, his complete indifference to the business he was engaged on, in consequence of which he was never carried away by enthusiasm and never made mistakes.

Having arrived at his destination, Oblonsky, respectfully followed by the door-keeper bearing his portfolio, entered his little private room, put on his uniform, and came out into the Office. The clerks and attendants all rose and bowed with cheerful deference. Oblonsky walked quickly, as was his wont, to his place, shook hands with the Members, and sat down. He chatted and joked just as much as was proper and then turned to business. No one could determine better than he the limits of freedom, simplicity, and formality, necessary for the pleasant transaction of business. The secretary came up with the papers, cheerfully and respectfully like everybody in Oblonsky's office, and remarked in the familiarly Liberal tone introduced by Oblonsky:

'After all, we've managed to get that information from the Penza Provincial Office. Here—will you please. . . .'

'Got it at last?' said Oblonsky, holding this paper down with his finger. 'Well, gentlemen . . .' and the sitting commenced.

'If they only knew,' he thought, bowing his head gravely as he listened to a Report, 'how like a guilty little boy their President was half-an-hour ago! . . .' and his eyes sparkled while the Report was being read. Till two o'clock the business was to continue uninterruptedly, but at two there was to be an adjournment for lunch.

It was not quite two when the large glass doors suddenly swung open and some one came in. All the Members sitting beneath the Emperor's portrait or behind the Mirror of Justice, glad of some distraction, looked toward the door; but the door-keeper at once turned out the intruder and closed the glass doors behind him.

When the report had been read, Oblonsky rose, stretching himself, and by way of tribute to the Liberalism of the times, took out a cigarette before leaving the Office to go to his private room. Two of his colleagues—Nikitin, an old hard-working official, and Grinevich, a Gentleman of the Bedchamber—followed him out.

'We shall have time to finish after lunch,' said Oblonsky.

'Plenty of time,' said Nikitin.

'He must be a precious rogue, that Fomin,' said Grinevich, referring to one of those concerned in the case under consideration.

Oblonsky made a face at these words, thereby indicating that it is not right to form an opinion prematurely, and did not reply.

'Who was it came in?' he asked the door-keeper.

'Some man came in without permission, your Excellency, when I wasn't looking. He asked for you. I told him, "When the Members come out, then. . . ."'

'Where is he?'

'Perhaps he has gone out into the hall; he was walking about there just now. That's him,' said the door-keeper, pointing to a strongly-built broad-shouldered man with a curly beard, who, without taking off his sheep-skin cap, was running lightly and quickly up the worn steps of the stone staircase. A lanky official, going down with a portfolio, stopped, with a disapproving look at the feet of the man running upstairs, and then glanced inquiringly at Oblonsky, who was standing at the top of the stairs. His kindly face, beaming over the gold-embroidered collar of his uniform, grew still more radiant when he recognized the man who was coming up.

'Why, it's you, Levin, at last!' he said scrutinizing the approaching Levin with a friendly mocking smile. 'How is it you deign to look me up in this *den*?' he asked; and not contented with pressing his friend's hand, he kissed him. 'Been here long?'

'I've only just arrived, and am very anxious to see you,' answered Levin, looking round with constraint, and yet crossly and uneasily.

'Well then, come into my room,' said Oblonsky, who knew his friend's self-conscious and irritable shyness; and seizing him by the arm he led him along as if past some danger.

Oblonsky was on intimate terms with almost all his acquaintances, men of sixty and lads of twenty, actors, Ministers of State, tradesmen, and Lords in Waiting, so that a great many people on familiar terms with him stood at the two extremes of the social ladder and would have been much surprised to know that they had something in common through Oblonsky. He was on familiar terms with everybody he drank champagne with, and he drank champagne with everybody. But when in the presence of his subordinates he happened to meet any of his 'disreputable pals,' as he jocularly called them, he was able, with his innate tact, to minimize the impression such a meeting might leave on their minds. Levin was not a 'disreputable pal,' but Oblonsky felt that Levin imagined he might not care to show their intimacy in the presence of his subordinates, and that was why he hurried him into his private room.

Levin and Oblonsky were almost of the same age; and with
Levin, Oblonsky was on familiar terms not through champagne
only. Levin had been his comrade and friend in early youth, and
they were fond of one another as friends who have come together in
early youth often are, in spite of the difference in their characters
and tastes. Yet, as often happens between men who have chosen
different pursuits, each, while in argument justifying the other's
activity, despised it in the depth of his heart. Each thought that his
own way of living was real life, and that the life of his friend
was—illusion. Oblonsky could not repress a slightly sarcastic smile
at the sight of Levin. How many times he had already seen him
arriving in Moscow from the country, where he did something,
though what it was Oblonsky could never quite understand or feel
any interest in. Levin came to Moscow always excited, always in a
hurry, rather shy and irritated by his own shyness, and usually with
totally new and unexpected views about things. Oblonsky laughed
at all this, and yet liked it. Similarly, Levin in his heart despised
the town life his friend was leading, and his official duties which he
considered futile and ridiculed. But the difference was that
Oblonsky, doing as every one else did, laughed with confidence
and good-humour, while Levin laughed uncertainly and sometimes
angrily.

'We have long been expecting you,' said Oblonsky entering his
private room and releasing Levin's arm, as if to show that here all
danger was past. 'I'm very, very glad to see you!' continued he.
'Well, how are you, eh? When did you arrive?'

Levin looked silently at the faces of the two strangers, Oblonsky's
colleagues, and especially at the hands of the elegant Grinevich,
who had such long white fingers and such long yellowish nails
curving at the points, and such large glittering sleeve-links, that
evidently his hands occupied his whole attention and deprived him
of freedom of thought. Oblonsky at once noticed Levin's look and
smiled.

'Oh, of course! Let me introduce you,' he said. 'My colleagues:
Philip Ivanich Nikitin; Michael Stanislavich Grinevich,' then turning to Levin, 'Constantine Dmitrich Levin, an active member of
the Zemstvo, one of the new sort—a gymnast who lifts a hundredweight and a half with one hand, a cattle-breeder, a sportsman,—my
friend, and a brother of Sergius Ivanich Koznyshev.'

'Very pleased . . .' said the old official.

'I have the honour of knowing your brother, Sergius Ivanich,'
said Grinevich, holding out his narrow hand with the long finger-
nails.

Levin frowned, shook hands coldly, and immediately turned to

Oblonsky. Though Levin had great respect for his step-brother, an author known throughout Russia, he hated to be regarded not as Constantine Levin but as a brother of the famous Koznyshev.

'No, I am no longer on the Zemstvo—I have quarrelled with the lot of them, and don't attend their meetings any more,' said he, addressing his friend.

'Quick work!' said Oblonsky, with a smile. 'What was it all about?'

'It's a long story—I'll tell you some other time,' said Levin, but began telling it at once. 'To put it in a nutshell, I have come to the conclusion that there is, and can be, no such thing as Zemstvo work,' he said, speaking as if some one had just offended him. 'On the one hand it's simply playing! They play at being a parliament, and I am neither young enough nor old enough to amuse myself with toys. On the other hand . . .' he hesitated, 'it is a means of getting pelf for the provincial *coterie*! We used to have guardian-ships and judgeships as soft jobs, and now we've Zemstvos—not bribes, but unearned salaries!' he went on as warmly as if he had just been contradicted.

'Aha! I see you've reached another new phase—a Conservative one this time!' said Oblonsky. 'However, we'll talk about that later.'

'Yes, later! . . . But I want to see you,' said Levin, gazing with aversion at Grinevich's hand.

Oblonsky's smile was hardly perceptible.

'Didn't you tell me you would never again put on Western European clothes?' he asked, surveying Levin's new suit, evidently made by a French tailor. 'That's it! You're in a new phase.'

Levin suddenly blushed, not as grown-up people blush who hardly notice it themselves, but as boys blush who are aware that their shyness is ridiculous and therefore feel ashamed of it and blush still more, almost to tears. It was so strange to see that intelligent manly face in such a childish plight that Oblonsky left off looking at him.

'Where shall we see one another? You know it is very, very important for me to have a talk with you,' said Levin.

Oblonsky seemed to consider: 'Well—suppose we go to lunch at Gurin's and have a talk there? I am free till three.'

'No,' said Levin, after a moment's consideration; 'I have to go somewhere else.'

'Well then, let's dine together.'

'Dine? But I've nothing particular to say—only a word or two . . . to ask you something! We can have a talk some other time.'

'Well, tell me the word or two now, and we'll talk at dinner.'

'The two words are . . . however, it's nothing particular,' said

Levin, and his face became almost vicious in his efforts to overcome his shyness.

'What are the Shcherbatskys doing? All going on as usual?'
Oblonsky, who had long known that Levin was in love with
his, Oblonsky's, sister-in-law Kitty, smiled very slightly and his eyes
sparkled merrily.

'You spoke of two words, but I can't answer in two because
. . . . Excuse me a moment. . . .'

The secretary came in, familiarly respectful, though with a
certain modest consciousness (common to all secretaries) of his
superiority to his chief in knowledge of business affairs, approached
Oblonsky with some papers, and on the plea of asking a question
began to explain some difficulty. Oblonsky, without hearing him
to the end, put his hand in a kindly way on the secretary's sleeve
and, softening his remark with a smile, said:

'No; please do it as I said,' and having in a few words explained
his view of the matter, he pushed the paper away and said finally:
'Yes, please do it that way, Zachary Nikitich!'

The secretary went out, abashed. Levin, who during Oblonsky's
talk with the secretary had quite overcome his shyness, stood
leaning both arms on the back of a chair and listening with ironical
attention.

'I don't understand it at all!' he remarked.

'What don't you understand?' asked Oblonsky with his usual
merry smile, as he took out a cigarette. He expected Levin to say
something eccentric.

'I don't understand what you're doing' said Levin, shrugging
his shoulders. 'How can you do it seriously?'

'Why not?'

'Because there's nothing to do!'

'That's how it seems to you, but really we're overwhelmed with
work.'

'—On paper! Ah well! you've a gift for that sort of thing,' added
Levin.

'You mean I'm deficient in something?'

'Perhaps!' said Levin. 'But all the same I admire your dignity and
am proud that my friend is such a great man! But all the same
you've not answered my question,' he added, making a desperate
effort to look Oblonsky straight in the face.

'All right! All right! Wait a bit, and you'll be in the same position yourself. It's all very well for you, who have three thousand
desyatins [4] in the Karazin District, and such muscle, and are as
fresh as a twelve-year-old girl! But still, you'll be joining us yourself
some day! . . . Now, about what you were asking: nothing has
changed, but it's a pity you've stopped away so long.'

4. About eight thousand acres.

'Why?' asked Levin in alarm.

'Oh, nothing—' answered Oblonsky. 'We'll talk it over later on. But what has brought you here specially?'

'We'll talk about that too later on,' said Levin and again blushed to his very ears.

'All right, that's natural enough!' said Oblonsky. 'Well, you know, I'd ask you to come to us, but my wife is not very well. Let's see,—if you want to meet them, you'll be sure to find them in the Zoological Gardens from four to five. Kitty skates there. Go there, and I'll call for you and we'll dine somewhere together.'

'Splendid! Well then, *au revoir!*'

'Mind you don't forget! I know you—you may rush off back to the country!' shouted Oblonsky after him.

'That'll be all right!' said Levin and left the room, only recollecting when already at the door that he had not taken leave of Oblonsky's colleagues.

'He seems a very energetic man,' said Grinevich when Levin was gone.

'Yes, my dear fellow,' said Oblonsky, shaking his head, 'and he's a lucky man! Three thousand desyatins in the Karazin District, his life before him, and such freshness! Not like some of us!'

'What have you to complain of, Stephen Arkadyevich?'

'Oh, things are wretched, miserable!' said Oblonsky, and sighed heavily.

Chapter VI

When Oblonsky asked Levin his reason for coming to town, Levin had blushed and been angry with himself for blushing, because he could not answer: 'I have come to propose to your sister-in-law,' although he really had come solely for that purpose.

The Levins and the Shcherbatskys were two old aristocratic Moscow families that had always been on intimate and friendly terms. Their ties were drawn still closer during Levin's University days. He had prepared for and entered the University together with young Prince Shcherbatsky, Dolly's and Kitty's brother. At that time Levin often visited the Shcherbatskys, and fell in love with the family. Strange as it may seem, it was the whole Shcherbatsky family—especially the feminine half of it—that Levin was in love with. He could not remember his mother, and his sister was much his senior, so that in the Shcherbatskys' house he saw for the first time the family life of a well-educated and honourable family of the old aristocracy—a life such as he had been deprived of by the death of his own father and mother. All the members of that family, especially the women, appeared to him as though wrapped in some mystic poetic veil, and he not only saw no defects in them, but imagined behind that poetic veil the loftiest feelings and every possible perfection. Why these three young ladies had to speak French and English on alternate days; why at a given time they played, each in her turn, on the piano (the sound of which reached their brother's room where the students were at work); why those masters of French literature, music, drawing, and dancing came to the house; why at certain hours the three young ladies accompanied by Mademoiselle Linon were driven in a calèche to the Tverskoy Boulevard, wearing satin cloaks (Dolly a long one; Nataly a somewhat shorter one; and Kitty so short a cloak that her shapely little legs in their tight red stockings were quite exposed); why they had to walk up and down the Tverskoy Boulevard accompanied by a footman with a gilt cockade in his hat,—all this and much more that happened in this mystic world he did not understand; but he knew that everything done there was beautiful and he was in love with the very mystery of it all.

In his student days he very nearly fell in love with the eldest daughter, Dolly; but a marriage was soon after arranged between her and Oblonsky. Then he began falling in love with the second daughter. He seemed to feel that he must fall in love with one of the sisters, but he was not sure with which. But Nataly too, as soon as she came out, married the diplomat, Lvov. Kitty was still a child when Levin finished at the University. Young Shcherbatsky who entered the navy was drowned in the Baltic; and after that, in spite of his friendship with Oblonsky, Levin's intercourse with the Shcherbatskys became less frequent. But when he had come to Moscow early in the winter of this year and met them, he knew at last which of the three sisters he was really fated to love.

It would seem that nothing could be simpler than for him, a man of good family, rich rather than poor, and thirty-two years of age, to propose to the Princess Shcherbatskaya. In all likelihood he would have been considered quite a suitable match. But Levin was in love, and therefore Kitty seemed to him so perfect in every respect, so transcending everything earthly, and he seemed to himself so very earthly and insignificant a creature, that the possibility of his being considered worthy of her by others or by herself was to him unimaginable.

Having spent two months in Moscow, living as in a fog, meeting Kitty almost every day in Society which he began to frequent in order to meet her, he suddenly made up his mind that it was impossible, and returned to the country.

Levin's conviction that it was impossible rested on the idea that from her relatives' point of view he was not a good or suitable match for the delightful Kitty, and that Kitty herself could not love him. From her parents' standpoint (it seemed to him) he had no settled occupation or position in the world. He was thirty-two, and while his former comrades were already colonels, aides-de-camp, Bank and Railway Directors, or Heads of Government Boards like Oblonsky, he (he knew very well what others must think of him) was merely a country squire, spending his time breeding cows, shooting snipe, and erecting buildings—that is to say, a fellow without talent, who had come to no good and was only doing what in the opinion of Society good-for-nothing people always do. Of course the mysterious, enchanting Kitty could not love a plain fellow, such as he considered himself to be, a man so ordinary and undistinguished. Moreover, his former relation to Kitty had been that of a grown-up man towards a child whose brother's friend he was, and this seemed an additional obstacle in love's path. He thought a plain kindly fellow like himself might be loved as a friend, but to be loved with the kind of love he felt for Kitty, a man must be handsome, and above all remarkable.

He had heard that women often love plain ordinary men but he did not believe it, because he judged by himself and he could only love beautiful mysterious exceptional women.

But after spending two months alone in the country, he became convinced that this time he was not in love as he had been when quite young—for his present feelings gave him not a moment's rest—and that he could not live unless the question whether she was to be his wife or not were decided; also that his despair had been the outcome of his own fancy, and that he had no proof that he would be rejected. So he had now come to Moscow determined to propose to her, and to marry her if he was accepted. Or . . . but he dared not think what would happen if she refused him.

Chapter VII

Having reached Moscow by a morning train, Levin went to stay at the house of his half-brother Koznyshev, who was older than he, and after changing his clothes entered his brother's study, intending to tell him why he had come and to ask his advice. But his brother was not alone. A well-known professor of philosophy was with him, who had come specially from Kharkov to settle a dispute that had arisen between them on an important philosophical question. The professor was engaged in a fierce polemic against the materialists, and Sergius Koznyshev, who followed this polemic with interest, on reading the professor's last article had written to him reproaching him with having conceded too much to the materialists; and the professor had come at once to talk the matter over. The question was the fashionable one, whether a definite line exists between psychological and physiological phenomena in human activity; and if so, where it lies? [5]

5. A heated polemic was raging between K. D. Kavelin's and I. M. Sechenov's followers concerning the degree of materialistic-physiological causation of psychological phenomena.

When Levin entered, Sergius Ivanich greeted him with the coldly affable smile he bestowed on everybody and, having introduced him to the professor, went on with the discussion.

The small spectacled man with the narrow forehead interrupted the conversation a moment to say, 'how do you do' to Levin and, paying no further attention to him, went on talking. Levin sat down to wait till the professor should go, but soon became interested in the subject of their conversation.

He had seen in the papers the articles they were discussing, and had read them because they interested him as a development of the bases of natural science—familiar to him as he had studied in that faculty at the University; but he had never connected these scientific deductions as to man's animal origin,[6] reflex actions, biology and sociology, with those questions concerning the meaning to himself of life and death, which had of late more and more frequently occurred to him.

Listening to his brother's conversation with the professor, he noticed that they connected the scientific question with the spiritual and several times almost reached the latter, but every time they approached this, which seemed to him the most important question, they at once hurriedly retreated and again plunged into the domain of fine sub-divisions, reservations, quotations, hints and references to authorities; and he found it difficult to understand what they were talking about.

'I cannot admit,' said Koznyshev with his usual clear and precise expression and polished style, 'I cannot on any account agree with Keiss that my whole conception of the external world is the outcome of impressions. The most fundamental perception—that of existence—is not received through the senses, for there is no special organ to convey that perception.'

'Yes, but they (Wurst and Knaust and Pripasov) will tell you that your conception of existence results from the collective effect of all your sensations and is therefore a result of sensations. Wurst actually says that without the senses there can be no perception of existence.'

'I would maintain the opposite . . .' began Koznyshev.

But here again it seemed to Levin that having reached the most important matter they avoided it; and he made up his mind to ask the professor a question.

'Consequently, if my senses are destroyed, if my body dies, no further existence is possible?' he asked.

The professor, vexed and apparently mentally hurt by the interruption, turned to look at this strange questioner, who resembled a barge-hauler rather than a philosopher, and then looked at

6. Charles Darwin's book on human evolution was published in Russian translation in 1871. Tolstoy's friend N. N. Strakhov wrote articles critical of Darwinism.

Koznyshev, as if asking, 'What can one say to this?'

But Koznyshev, who did not speak with anything like the same effort, or as one-sidedly, as the professor, and had room in his head for an answer to his opponent as well as for comprehension of the simple and natural point of view from which the question arose, smiled and said:

'That question we have as yet no right to decide. . . .'

'We have not the data . . .' added the professor and went back to his arguments. 'No,' said he; 'I point out that if, as Pripasov definitely states, sensation is based on impressions, we must still carefully distinguish between these two perceptions.'

Levin listened no longer but sat waiting for the professor to go.

Chapter VIII

When the professor had gone, Koznyshev turned to his stepbrother.

'I am very glad you have come. Are you here for long? How do you get on with your farming?'

Levin knew that farming did not interest his elder brother and that the question was merely a concession; therefore he replied generally as to the sale of wheat and money matters. He wanted to tell his brother of his intended marriage and to ask his advice. He had even firmly made up his mind to do so, but when he saw his brother and heard his conversation with the professor, and afterward noticed the involuntarily patronizing tone in which he asked him about the business of their estate (this estate which they had jointly inherited from their mother had not been divided, and Levin was managing the whole of it), he felt that something prevented him from beginning to speak to his brother about his intention to marry. He felt that his brother would not look at the matter as he wished him to.

'Well, and how is your Zemstvo getting on?' asked Koznyshev, who took a keen interest in the rural administration and attached great importance to it.

'I really don't know.'

'What? But you are a Member?'

'No, I am no longer on it. I resigned,' answered Levin, 'and don't attend the Meetings any more.'

'That's a pity!' said Koznyshev, and frowned. To justify himself Levin began to relate what used to happen at the Meetings in his district.

'There now! It's always the same,' interrupted Koznyshev. 'We Russians are always like that. It may be a good trait in us—this capacity to see our own faults—but we overdo it, and comfort ourselves with sarcasm, which is always ready on our tongues. I can only tell you, that with such rights as we have in our rural institutions, any other European nation—the English or the Germans—would have secured their freedom, while we only jeer at our Zemstvos!'

'But what is to be done?' said Levin guiltily. 'That was my last attempt. And I tried with my whole soul. . . . But I can't do it! I'm incapable.'

'Incapable!' said Koznyshev. 'No, you don't look at it from the right point of view.'

'That may be,' said Levin mournfully.

'Do you know that our brother Nicholas is here again?'

Nicholas was Constantine Levin's elder brother, and Koznyshev's half-brother. He was a ruined man who had squandered the greatest part of his fortune, mixed with the strangest and worst society, and quarrelled with his brothers.

'You don't mean to say so!' cried Levin, horror-struck. 'How do you know?'

'Prokofy met him in the street.'

'Here, in Moscow? Where is he? Do you know?' Levin rose from his chair as if meaning to go at once.

'I am sorry I told you,' said Koznyshev, shaking his head at his brother's excitement. 'I sent to find out where he is living, and forwarded him a note of hand he had given to Trubin, which I had paid. And this is the answer I received.'

Koznyshev took a note from under a paper-weight and handed it to his brother.

Levin read the note, written in a curious but familiar hand:

'I humbly beg you to leave me alone. That is all I demand of my dear brothers.—Nicholas Levin.'

When Levin had read the note he remained standing in front of Koznyshev holding it in his hand, without lifting his head.

A struggle was going on within him between the desire to forget his unfortunate brother for the present, and the consciousness that this would be wrong.

'He evidently wants to offend me,' continued Koznyshev, 'but he cannot do that. I wish with all my heart I could help him, but I know it can't be done.'

'Yes, yes,' said Levin, 'I understand, and appreciate your attitude toward him; but personally I shall go to see him.'

'Go if you like, but I don't advise it,' said Koznyshev. 'That's to say, I'm not afraid of it on my own account, he will not make mischief between us, but on your account I don't advise it. You had better not go. It's impossible to help him. However, do as you please!'

'It may be impossible to help him, but I feel—especially at this moment . . . but that's a different matter—I feel that I cannot be at peace. . . .'

'Well, I don't understand that,' said Koznyshev. 'But what I do understand is a lesson in humility. I have begun to look differently, more leniently, at what is called rascality, since brother Nicholas became what he is. Do you know what he has done?'

'Ah, it's dreadful, dreadful!' Levin repeated.

Having got the address from Koznyshev's footman Levin thought of going at once to see his brother; but, on reflection, decided to put off the visit till the evening. To obtain peace of mind it was necessary first of all to decide the business that had brought him to Moscow. He therefore went to Oblonsky's office, and having received news of the Shcherbatskys he drove to the place where he was told he could see Kitty.

Chapter IX

At four o'clock that afternoon Levin, conscious that his heart was beating rapidly, got out of the hired sledge at the Zoological Gardens and went down the path leading to the ice-hills and skating lake, sure of finding Kitty there, for he had noticed the Shcherbatskys' carriage at the entrance.

It was a clear frosty day. Carriages, private sledges, sledges for hire, and mounted police stood at the entrance. Well-dressed people, their hats shining in the sunlight, crowded at the gates and thronged the clean-swept paths between little houses built with carved eaves in Russian style. The bushy birch trees in the Gardens with all their branches weighed down by snow seemed attired in new festive garments. He walked along the path leading to the skating lake, and kept repeating to himself: 'I must not be excited. I must be quiet! . . . What are you doing? What's the matter? Be quiet, stupid!' he said to his heart. But the more he tried to be calm, the more laboured grew his breath. He met an acquaintance who called to him, but Levin did not even notice who it was. He approached the ice-hills and heard the clanking of the chains by which the sledges were being pulled up, their clatter as they descended the hills, and the sound of merry voices. A few more steps brought him to the skating lake, and among all the skaters he at once recognized her. He knew she was there by the joy and terror that took possession of his heart. She stood talking to a lady at the other end of the lake. There seemed to be nothing striking in her dress or attitude, but it was as easy for Levin to recognize her in that crowd as to find a rose among nettles. Everything was lit up by her. She was the smile that brightened everything around.

'Can I really step down on to the ice, and go up to her?' he thought. The spot where she stood seemed to him an unapproachable sanctuary, and there was a moment when he nearly went away, he was so filled with awe. He had to make an effort and reason with himself that all sorts of people were passing near her and he himself might have come just to skate. He stepped down, avoiding any long look at her as one avoids long looks at the sun, but seeing her as one sees the sun, without looking.

On that day of the week and that hour, people belonging to the same set and acquainted with one another, met on the ice. Among them were masters of the art of skating showing off their skill, and beginners with timid and awkward movements holding on to the backs of chairs fitted with runners; boys, and old men skating for hygenic reasons; and they all seemed to Levin to be fortune's favourites because they were here near her. Yet skaters appeared quite calmly to gain on her, to catch her up, and even speak to her, and quite independently of her to amuse themselves enjoying the excellent ice and the fine weather.

Nicholas Shcherbatsky, Kitty's cousin, in a short jacket and tight trousers, with skates on his feet, was sitting on a bench, and seeing Levin, called out to him.

'Hullo, you Russian champion skater! When did you come? The ice is splendid—put on your skates!'

'I haven't any skates,' answered Levin, wondering at such boldness and freedom of manner in her presence, and not losing sight of her for a moment although not looking at her. He felt the sun approaching him. She was turning a corner, her little feet, shod in high boots, kept close together, and she was skating timidly toward him. A little boy dressed in Russian costume, violently swinging his arms and stooping very low, was overtaking her.

She was not very firm on her feet. Having drawn her hands from the muff that hung by a cord from her neck, she held them out and looking at Levin, whom she had recognized, she smiled at him and at her fears. Having turned the corner, she pushed off with an elastic little foot, glided straight up to Shcherbatsky, and catching hold of him with her hand, nodded smilingly to Levin. She was more beautiful than he had imagined her.

When he thought about her he could vividly picture to himself her entire person, and especially the charm of her small, fair-haired head, so lightly poised on the shapely girlish shoulders, and the childlike brightness and kindness of her face. In that childlike look, combined with the slim beauty of her figure, lay her special charm; and this he thoroughly appreciated, but what always struck him afresh as unexpected was the expression of her eyes—mild, calm, and truthful,—and above all her smile, which carried him into a fairyland where he felt softened and filled with tenderness—as he remembered feeling on rare occasions in his early childhood.

'Have you been here long?' she said, shaking hands with him. 'Thank you,' she added as he picked up the handkerchief she had dropped from her muff.

'I? No, not long—since yesterday . . . I mean to-day . . .' replied Levin, in his excitement not quite taking in her question. 'I wanted to come and see you,' he went on, and then, remembering the reason why he wanted to see her, he became abashed, and blushed. 'I did not know that you skated, and so well.'

She looked attentively at him as if wishing to understand his confusion.

'Your praise is valuable. There is a tradition here that you are the best skater,' she said, flicking off with a small black-gloved hand some hoar-frost crystals that had fallen on her muff.

'Yes, I used to be passionately fond of skating. I wanted to be perfect at it.'

'You seem to do everything passionately,' she remarked with a smile. 'I should so like to see you skate. Put on a pair and let us skate together.'

'Skate together! Can it be possible?' thought Levin looking at her.

'I'll go and put them on at once,' he said, and went to hire some skates.

'You've not looked us up for a long time, sir,' said one of the attendants as, holding up Levin's foot, he bored a hole in the heel of his boot. 'Since you left we have had no gentleman who is such a master at it as you! Is that right?' he added, pulling the strap tight.

'Yes, that's right, that's right! Please be quick!' answered Levin, trying to restrain the happy smile which appeared on his face. 'Yes, he thought, 'this is life—this is joy! She said, "Together: let us skate together"! Shall I tell her now? But that's just why I'm afraid of speaking. Now I am happy, if only in my hopes—but then? . . . But I must . . . I must . . . I must . . . ! Away with this weakness!'

He stood up, took off his overcoat, and having given himself a start on the rough ice near the shelter, glided down to the smooth surface of the lake, increasing and diminishing his speed and shaping his course as if by volition only. He approached Kitty timidly, but her smile again tranquillized him.

'She gave him her hand and they went on together, increasing their speed, and the faster they went the closer she pressed his hands.

'I should learn quicker with you; for some reason I feel confidence in you,' she said.

'And I am confident of myself when you lean on me,' he

answered, and was immediately frightened of what he had said, and blushed. And in fact, as soon as he had uttered these words her face lost its kind expression—as when the sun hides behind a cloud—and Levin noticed that familiar play of her features which indicated an effort of mind: a wrinkle appeared on her smooth forehead.

'Has anything unpleasant happened . . . ? But I have no right to ask,' he said hurriedly.

'Why? . . . No, nothing unpleasant has happened,' she answered coldly, adding immediately: 'You have not seen Mlle Linon?'

'Not yet.'

'Go to her then, she is so fond of you.'

'What does she mean? I have hurt her. Help me, O Lord!' thought Levin, hastening toward the old Frenchwoman with the grey curls, who sat on one of the benches. She welcomed Levin as an old friend, showing her set of false teeth in a smile.

'Yes, you see we grow up,' she said, indicating Kitty with a glance, 'and grow old. "Tiny Bear" is grown up!' continued the Frenchwoman, laughing and reminding him of his old joke when he called the three young ladies the Three Bears of the English fairy tale. 'Do you remember when you used to call her so?'

He had not the faintest recollection of it, but she was fond of the joke and had laughed at it for the last ten years.

'Well, go—go and skate! Our Kitty is beginning to skate nicely, isn't she?'

When Levin returned to Kitty her face was no longer stern and her eyes had their former truthful, kindly look; but he thought there was an intentionally quiet manner in her affability and he felt sad. Having spoken about her old governess and her peculiarities, she asked him about his way of life.

'Do you really manage not to feel dull in the country in winter?' she said.

'I don't feel at all dull, I am very busy,' he answered, conscious that she was subduing him to her quiet tone, from which—as had happened at the beginning of the winter—he would not be able to free himself.

'Have you come for long?' asked Kitty.

'I don't know,' he answered, without thinking of what he was saying. The idea that if he accepted her tone of calm friendliness he would again go away without having settled anything occurred to him, and he determined to rebel.

'You don't know?'

'I don't. It all depends on you,' he said, and was at once terrified at his own words.

Whether she had not heard his words or did not wish to hear

them, anyhow, after slightly stumbling and striking her foot twice against the ice, she skated hurriedly away from him toward Mlle Linon, said something to her, and went toward the little house where the ladies took off their skates.

'My God! What have I done? O Lord, help me and teach me!' prayed Levin, and, feeling at the same time a need of violent exercise, he got up speed and described inner and outer circles.

Just then a young man, the best of the new skaters, with a cigarette in his mouth and skates on, came out of the coffee-room, and taking a run, descended the steps leading to the lake, clattering with his skates as he jumped from step to step. He then flew down the slope and glided along the ice without so much as changing the easy position of his arms.

'Oh, that's a new trick!' said Levin, and at once ran up to try that new trick.

'Don't hurt yourself—it needs practice!' Nicholas Shcherbatsky called out.

Levin went up the path as far back as he could get up speed, and then slid downwards, balancing himself with his arms in this unaccustomed movement. He caught his foot on the last step, but, scarcely touching the ice with his hand, made a violent effort, regained his balance, and skated away laughing.

'Good! Dear man!' thought Kitty who at that moment was just coming out of the little house with Mlle Linon, looking at him with a smile of gentle tenderness as at a dear brother. 'Can I really be guilty—have I really done anything wrong? They say it's coquetting. . . . I know it's not him I love, but still I feel happy with him, he is so charming! Only why did he say that?' she thought.

When he saw Kitty who was going away, and her mother who had met her on the steps, Levin, flushed with the violent exercise, stood still and considered. He then took off his skates and overtook mother and daughter at the gates of the Gardens.

'Very pleased to see you,' said the Princess. 'We are at home on Thursdays, as usual.'

'And to-day is Thursday!'

'We shall be glad to see you,' said the Princess coldly.

Kitty was sorry to hear that cold tone and could not resist the desire to counteract her mother's coldness. She turned her head and said smilingly:

'Au revoir!'

Just then Oblonsky, his hat tilted on one side, with radiant face and eyes, walked into the Gardens like a joyous conqueror. But on approaching his mother-in-law he answered her questions about Dolly's health with a sorrowful and guilty air. After a few words with her in a subdued and mournful tone, he expanded his chest and took Levin's arm.

'Well, shall we go?' he asked. 'I kept thinking about you, and am very, very glad you've come,' he went on, looking significantly into Levin's eyes.

'Yes, yes! Let's go,' answered the happy Levin, still hearing the voice saying: 'Au revoir!' and still seeing the smile with which it had been said.

'The Angleterre, or the Hermitage?'

'I don't care.'

'Well then, the Angleterre,' said Oblonsky, choosing the Angleterre because he was deeper in debt to that restaurant than to the Hermitage, and therefore considered it wrong to avoid it. 'Have you a sledge? . . . That's a good thing, because I've sent my coachman home.'

The two friends were silent all the way. Levin was considering what the change in Kitty's face meant; now persuading himself that there was hope, now in despair, seeing clearly that such hope was madness; but yet feeling an altogether different being from what he had been before her smile and the words 'Au revoir!'

Oblonsky during the drive was composing the menu of their dinner.

'You like turbot, don't you?' he asked, as they drove up to the restaurant.

'What?' said Levin. 'Turbot? Oh yes, I am *awfully* fond of turbot!'

Chapter X

When they entered the restaurant Levin could not help noticing something peculiar in his friend's expression, a kind of suppressed radiance in his face and whole figure. Oblonsky took off his overcoat, and with his hat on one side walked into the dining-room, giving his orders to the Tartar waiters, in their swallow-tail coats, with napkins under their arms, who attached themselves to him. Bowing right and left to his acquaintances who, here as elsewhere, greeted him joyfully, he passed on to the buffet, drank a glass of vodka and ate a bit of fish as hors-d'œuvre, and said something to the painted Frenchwoman, bedecked with ribbons and lace, who sat at a little counter—something that made even this Frenchwoman burst into frank laughter.

Levin did not take any vodka, simply because that Frenchwoman —made up, as it seemed to him, of false hair, powder, and toilet vinegar—was offensive to him. He moved away from her as from some dirty place. His whole soul was filled with Kitty's image, and his eyes shone with a smile of triumph and happiness.

'This way, please your Excellency! This way—no one will disturb your Excellency here,' said a specially officious waiter, an old white-headed Tartar, so wide in the hips that the tails of his coat separated behind.

'If you please, your Excellency,' he said, turning to Levin and as a mark of respect to Oblonsky paying attention to his guest. In a moment he had spread a fresh cloth on a round table already covered with a cloth beneath a bronze chandelier, moved two velvet chairs to the table, and stood with a napkin and menu awaiting the order.

'If your Excellency would like a private room, one will be vacant in a few moments. Prince Golitzin is there with a lady. We've some fresh oysters in, sir.'

'Ah—oysters!' Oblonsky paused and considered.

'Shall we change our plan, Levin?' he said, with his finger on the bill of fare and his face expressing serious perplexity. 'But are the oysters really good? Now be careful . . .'

'Real Flensburg, your Excellency! We've no Ostend ones.'

'They may be Flensburg, but are they fresh?'

'They only arrived yesterday.'

'Well then, shall we begin with oysters and change the whole plan of our dinner, eh?'

'I don't mind. I like buckwheat porridge and cabbage-soup best, but they don't have those things here.'

'Would you like *Buckwheat à la Russe?*' said the Tartar, stooping over Levin like a nurse over a child.

'No,—joking apart, whatever you choose will suit me. I've been skating and I'm hungry! Don't think that I do not appreciate your choice,' he added, noticing a dissatisfied look on Oblonsky's face. 'I shall be glad of a good dinner.'

'I should think so! Say what you like, it is one of the pleasures of life!' said Oblonsky. 'Well then, my good fellow, bring us two—or that will be too little, . . . three dozen oysters, and vegetable soup . . .'

'*Printanier,*' chimed in the waiter.

But Oblonsky evidently did not wish to give him the pleasure of calling the dishes by their French names.

'. . . vegetable, you know. Then turbot with thick sauce; then . . . roast beef (and mind it's good!); and then capon, shall we say? Yes. And stewed fruit.'

The waiter, remembering Oblonsky's way of calling the items on the French menu by their Russian names, did not repeat the words after him, but afterwards allowed himself the pleasure of repeating the whole of the order according to the menu: '*Potage printanier, turbot, sauce Beaumarchais, poularde à l'estragon, ma-*

cédoine de fruits . . .' and immediately, as if moved by springs, he put down the bill of fare in one cardboard cover, and seizing another containing the wine-list held it out to Oblonsky.

'What shall we have to drink?'

'Whatever you like, only not too much. . . .Champagne!' said Levin.

'What, to begin with? However, why not? You like the white seal?'

'*Cachet blanc*,' chimed in the waiter.

'Yes, bring us that with the oysters, and then we'll see.'

'Yes, sir, and what sort of table wine?'

'*Nuits* . . . no, let's have the classic *Chablis*.'

'Yes, sir. And your special cheese?'

'Well, yes—parmesan. Or do you prefer some other kind?'

'No, I really don't care,' said Levin, unable to restrain a smile.

The Tartar darted off, his coat-tails flying; and five minutes later rushed in again, with a dish of opened oysters in pearly shells and a bottle between his fingers.

Oblonsky crumpled his starched napkin and pushed a corner of it inside his waistcoat, then, with his arms comfortably on the table, attacked the oysters.

'Not bad,' he said, pulling the quivering oysters out of their pearly shells with a silver fork, and swallowing one after another. 'Not bad,' he repeated, lifting his moist and glittering eyes now to Levin, now to the Tartar.

Levin could eat oysters, though he preferred bread and cheese. But it gave him more pleasure to watch Oblonsky. Even the Tartar, who having drawn the cork and poured the sparkling wine into the thin wide glasses was straightening his white tie, glanced with a smile of evident pleasure at Oblonsky.

'You don't care much for oysters?' said Oblonsky, emptying his fine wide-lipped champagne glass—'or perhaps you're thinking of something else. Eh?'

He wanted Levin to be in good spirits. But Levin, if not exactly in bad spirits, felt constrained. The feelings that filled his heart made him ill at ease and uncomfortable in this restaurant with its private rooms where men took women to dine. Everything seemed offensive: these bronzes, mirrors, gaslights and Tartar waiters. He was afraid of soiling that which filled his soul.

'I? Yes, I am preoccupied—and besides, all this makes me feel constrained,' he said. 'You can't imagine how strange it all seems to me who live in the country,—like the nails of that gentleman I saw at your place.'

'Yes, I noticed that poor Grinevich's nails interested you greatly,' said Oblonsky.

'I can't help it,' replied Levin. 'Put yourself in my place—look at it from a country fellow's point of view! We try to get our hands into a state convenient to work with, and for that purpose we cut our nails and sometimes roll up our sleeves. But here people purposely let their nails grow until they begin to curl, and have little saucers for studs to make it quite impossible for them to use their hands!'

Oblonsky smiled merrily.

'Yes, it is a sign that rough work is unnecessary to him. He works with his mind . . .'

'Possibly; but still it seems to me strange that while we country people try to get over our meals as quickly as we can, so as to be able to get on with our work, here you and I try to make our meal last as long as possible, and therefore eat oysters.'

'Well, of course,' said Oblonsky. 'The aim of civilization is to enable us to get enjoyment out of everything.'

'Well, if that is its aim, I'd rather be a savage.'

'You are a savage as it is. All you Levins are savages.'

Levin sighed. He remembered his brother Nicholas and frowned, feeling ashamed and distressed; but Oblonsky started a subject which at once distracted his thoughts.

'Well, are you going to see our people to-night? The Shcherbatskys, I mean,' he said, pushing away the rough and now empty oyster shells and drawing the cheese toward him, while his eyes glittered significantly.

'Yes, certainly I shall go. Though the Princess appeared to ask me rather unwillingly.'

'Not a bit of it! What humbug! It's just her manner. . . . Come, bring us the soup, my good fellow! . . . It's her *grande dame* manner,' said Oblonsky. 'I shall come too, but I must first go to a musical rehearsal at the Countess Bonin's. What a strange fellow you are, though! How do you explain your sudden departure from Moscow? The Shcherbatskys asked me again and again, just as if I ought to know all about you. Yet all I know is that you never do things as any one else does!'

'Yes,' said Levin slowly and with agitation. 'You are right, I am a savage. Only my savagery lies not in having gone away then, but rather in having come back now. I have now come . . .'

'Oh, what a lucky fellow you are!' interrupted Oblonsky, looking straight into his eyes.

'Why?'

  ' "Fiery steeds by" *something* "brands
    I can always recognize;

> Youths in love at once I know,
> By the look that lights their eyes!" ' [7]

declaimed Oblonsky. 'You have everything before you!'

'And you—have you everything behind you?'

'No, not behind me, but you have the future and I have the present; and even that only half-and-half!'

'Why?'

'Oh, things are rather bad. . . . However, I don't want to talk about myself, and besides it's impossible to explain everything,' said Oblonsky. 'Well, and why have you come to Moscow? . . . Here, take this away!' he shouted to the Tartar.

'Don't you guess?' answered Levin, the light shining deep in his eyes as he gazed steadily at Oblonsky.

'I do, but I can't begin to speak about it,—by which you can judge whether my guess is right or wrong,' said Oblonsky, looking at him with a subtle smile.

'Well, and what do you say to it?' asked Levin with a trembling voice, feeling that all the muscles of his face were quivering. 'What do you think of it?'

Oblonsky slowly drank his glass of Chablis, his eyes fixed on Levin.

'There is nothing I should like better,' said he, 'nothing! It is the best that could happen.'

'But are you not making a mistake? Do you know what we are talking about?' said Levin, peering into his interlocutor's face. 'You think it possible?'

'I think so. Why shouldn't it be?'

'No, do you really think it is possible? No, you must tell me all you really think! And suppose . . . suppose a refusal is in store for me? . . . I am even certain . . .'

'Why do you think so?' said Oblonsky, smiling at Levin's excitement.

'Well, sometimes it seems so to me. You know, that would be terrible both for her and for me.'

'Oh no! In any case there's nothing in it terrible for the girl. Every girl is proud of an offer.'

'Yes, *every* girl, but not she.'

Oblonsky smiled. He understood that feeling of Levin's so well, knew that for Levin all the girls in the world were divided into two classes: one class included all the girls in the world except her, and they had all the usual human failings and were very ordinary girls; while the other class—herself alone—had no weaknesses and was superior to all humanity.

---

7. The lines quoted by Oblónsky are from Púshkin's translation of Anacreon's 55th Ode.

'Wait a bit: you must take some sauce,' said Oblonsky, stopping Levin's hand that was pushing away the sauceboat.

Levin obediently helped himself to sauce, but would not let Oblonsky eat.

'No, wait, wait!' he said. 'Understand that for me it is a question of life and death. I have never spoken to any one about it, and can speak to no one else about it. Now you and I are quite different in everything—in tastes and views and everything—but I know you like me and understand me, and so I am awfully fond of you. But for God's sake be quite frank with me!'

'I am telling you what I think,' said Oblonsky smiling. 'And I'll tell you something more. My wife is a most wonderful woman . . . .' He sighed, remembering his relations with his wife; then after a minute's pause he continued: 'She has the gift of clairvoyance. She sees people through and through! But more than that, she knows what is going to happen especially in regard to marriages. For instance, she predicted that the Shahovskaya girl would marry Brenteln. No one would believe it, but as it turned out she was right. And she is—on your side.'

'How do you know?'

'In this way—she not only likes you, but says that Kitty is sure to be your wife.'

At these words a sudden smile brightened Levin's face, the kind of smile that is not far from tears of tenderness.

'She says that?' he cried. 'I have always thought her a jewel, your wife! But enough—enough about it!' and he got up.

'All right, but sit down!'

But Levin could not sit still. He strode up and down the little cage of a room blinking to force back his tears, and only when he had succeeded did he sit down again.

'Try and realize,' he said, 'that this is not love. I have been in love but this is not the same thing. It is not my feeling but some external power that has seized me. I went away, you know, because I had come to the conclusion that it was impossible—you understand? Because such happiness does not exist on earth. But I have struggled with myself, and found that without that there's no life for me. And it must be decided . . .'

'Then why did you go away?'

'Wait a moment! Oh, what a crowd of ideas! How many things I have to ask! Listen. You can't imagine what you have done for me by saying what you did! I am so happy that I'm acting meanly. I've forgotten everything. I heard to-day about my brother Nicholas . . . he's here, you know . . . and I forgot all about him. It seems to me as if he too were happy. It is like madness! But there is one awful thing about it. You, who are married, know the feeling . . . it is awful that we—who are comparatively old and have pasts . . . not of love but of sin . . . suddenly we come into close intimacy with a pure innocent being! That is disgusting, and therefore one can't help feeling oneself unworthy.'

'Well, there haven't been many sins in your past!'

'Ah, but all the same,' said Levin, 'looking back at my life, I tremble and curse and bitterly regret. . . . Yes!'

'What's to be done? That's the way the world is made,' said Oblonsky.

'My one consolation is that prayer that I like so much: "Not according to my deserts but according to Thy loving kindness!" And she too can only forgive me that way.'

Chapter XI

Levin emptied his glass and they were silent for a while.

'There is one thing more that I must tell you,' began Oblonsky. 'You know Vronsky?'

'No, I don't. Why do you ask?'

'Another bottle!' said Oblonsky, turning to the Tartar, who was filling their glasses and hovering round them just when he was not wanted.

'The reason you ought to know Vronsky is this: he is one of your rivals.'

'What is he?' asked Levin, the expression of child-like rapture which Oblonsky had been admiring suddenly changing into an angry and unpleasant one.

'Vronsky is one of Count Cyril Ivanovich Vronsky's sons, and a very fine sample of the gilded youth of Petersburg. I met him in Tver when I was in the Service there and he came on conscription duty. Awfully rich, handsome, with influential connections, an aide-de-camp to the Emperor, and at the same time very good-natured—a first-rate fellow. And he's even more than a first-rate fellow. As I have got to know him now, he turns out to be both educated and very clever—a man who will go far.'

Levin frowned and was silent.

'Well, so he came here soon after you left, and as far as I can make out is head over ears in love with Kitty; and you understand that her mother . . .'

'Pardon me, but I understand nothing,' said Levin, dismally knitting his brows. And at once he thought of his brother Nicholas and how mean he was to forget him.

'You just wait a bit, wait!' said Oblonsky, smiling and touching Levin's arm. 'I have told you what I know, and I repeat that, as far as anyone can judge in so delicate and subtle a matter, I believe the chances are all on your side.'

Levin leant back in his chair. His face was pale.

'But I should advise you to settle the question as soon as possible,' Oblonsky continued, filling Levin's glass.

'No, thanks! I can't drink any more,' said Levin pushing his glass aside, 'or I shall be tipsy. . . . Well, and how are you getting on?' he continued, evidently wishing to change the subject.

'One word more! In any case, I advise you to decide the question quickly, but I shouldn't speak to-day,' said Oblonsky. 'Go to-morrow morning and propose in the classic manner, and may heaven bless you!'

'You have so often promised to come and shoot with me—why not come this spring?' said Levin.

He now repented with his whole heart of having begun this conversation with Oblonsky. His personal feelings had been desecrated by the mention of some Petersburg officer as his rival, and by Oblonsky's conjectures and advice.

Oblonsky smiled. He understood what was going on in Levin's soul.

'I'll come some day,' he said. 'Ah, old chap, women are the pivot on which everything turns! Things are in a bad way with me too, very bad, and all on account of women. Tell me quite frankly . . .'

He took out a cigar, and with one hand on his glass he continued: 'Give me some advice.'

'Why? What is the matter?'

'Well, it's this. Supposing you were married and loved your wife, but had been fascinated by another woman . . .'

'Excuse me, but really I . . . it's quite incomprehensible to me. It's as if . . . just as incomprehensible as if I, after eating my fill here, went into a baker's shop and stole a roll.'

Oblonsky's eyes glittered more than usual.

'Why not? Rolls sometimes smell so that one can't resist them!'

> ' "Himmlisch ist's, wenn ich bezwungen
>   Meine irdische Begier;
> Aber doch wenn's nicht gelungen
>   Hatt' ich auch recht hübsch Plaisir!" ' [8]

Oblonsky repeated these lines with a subtle smile and Levin himself could not help smiling.

'No, but joking apart,' continued Oblonsky, 'just consider. A woman, a dear, gentle, affectionate creature, poor and lonely, sacrifices everything. Now when the thing is done . . . just consider,

---

8. 'It is heavenly when I have mastered my earthly desires; but when I have not succeeded, I have also had right good pleasure!' Oblónsky is misquoting Heine: *Liebeslieder*, 24

should one forsake her? Granted that one ought to part with her so
as not to destroy one's family life, but oughtn't one to pity her and
provide for her and make things easier?'

'As to that, you must pardon me. You know that for me there are
two kinds of women . . . or rather, no! There are women, and
there are . . . I have never seen any charming fallen creatures, and
never shall see any; and people like that painted Frenchwoman with
her curls out there by the counter, are an abomination to me, and
all these fallen ones are like her.'

'And the one in the Gospels?'

'Oh, don't! Christ would never have spoken those words had he
known how they would be misused! They are the only words in the
Gospels that seem to be remembered. However, I am not saying
what I think, but what I feel. I have a horror of fallen women. You
are repelled by spiders and I by those creatures. Probably you never
studied spiders and know nothing of their character, and it's the
same in my case!'

'It's all very well for you to talk like that—it's like that gentleman in Dickens, who with his left hand threw all difficult questions
over his right shoulder.⁹ But denying a fact is no answer. What am I
to do? Tell me, what am I to do? My wife is getting old, and I am
full of vitality. A man hardly has time to turn round before he feels
that he can no longer love his wife in that way, whatever his regard
for her may be. And then all of a sudden love crosses your path, and
you're lost, lost!' said Oblonsky with despair.

Levin smiled.

'Yes, I am lost,' continued Oblonsky. 'But what am I to do?'

'Don't steal rolls.'

Oblonsky burst out laughing.

'Oh, you moralist! But just consider, here are two women: one insists only on her rights, and her rights are your love, which you cannot give her; and the other sacrifices herself and demands nothing.
What are you to do? How are you to act? It is a terrible tragedy.'

'If you want me to say what I think of it, I can only tell you that
I don't believe in the tragedy. And the reason is this: I think love,
both kinds of love, which you remember Plato defines in his "Symposium"—both kinds of love serve as a touchstone for men. Some
men understand only the one, some only the other. Those who understand only the non-platonic love need not speak of tragedy. For
such love there can be no tragedy. "Thank you kindly for the
pleasure, good-bye," and that's the whole tragedy. And for the platonic love there can be no tragedy either, because there everything
is clear and pure, because . . .' Here Levin recollecting his own
sins and the inner struggle he had lived through added unexpectedly, 'However, maybe you are right. It may very well be. But I

9. Podsnap in *Our Mutual Friend*.

don't know, I really don't know.'

'Well, you see *you* are very consistent,' said Oblonsky. 'It is both a virtue and a fault in you. You have a consistent character yourself and you wish all the facts of life to be consistent, but they never are. For instance you despise public service because you want work always to correspond to its aims, and that never happens. You also want the activity of each separate man to have an aim, and love and family life always to coincide—and that doesn't happen either. All the variety, charm and beauty of life are made up of light and shade.'

Levin sighed and did not answer. He was thinking of his own affairs and not listening to Oblonsky.

And suddenly both felt that though they were friends, and had dined and drunk wine together which should have drawn them still closer, yet each was thinking only of his own affairs and was not concerned with the other.

Oblonsky had more than once experienced this kind of acute estrangement instead of union following a dinner with a friend, and knew what to do in such a case.

'The bill!' he shouted and went out into the dining-hall, where he immediately saw an aide-de-camp of his acquaintance, and entered into conversation with him about an actress and her protector. And immediately in conversation with the aide-de-camp Oblonsky felt relief and rest after the talk with Levin, who always demanded of him too great a mental and spiritual strain.

When the Tartar returned with a bill for twenty-six roubles odd, Levin quite unconcernedly paid his share, which with the tip came to fourteen roubles, a sum that usually would have horrified his rustic conscience, and went home to dress and go on to the Shcherbatskys' where his fate was to be decided.

Chapter XII

Princess Kitty Shcherbatskaya was eighteen, and this was her first season. Her success in Society was greater than that of her two elder sisters, and greater even than her mother had expected. Not only were nearly all the youths that danced at the Moscow balls in love with Kitty, but two serious suitors presented themselves for her that very first winter: Levin and, immediately after his departure, Count Vronsky.

Levin's arrival at the beginning of the winter, his frequent visits and evident love for Kitty gave rise to her parents' first serious deliberation as to her future, and to disputes between them. The Prince took Levin's part and said he desired nothing better for Kitty. The Princess with a woman's way of talking round the question said that Kitty was too young, that Levin had not shown that his intentions were serious, that Kitty was not in love with him, and so on; but she did not say the most important things, namely that she expected a better match for her daughter, and that she did not like Levin and did not understand him. When he suddenly left, the Princess was pleased and triumphantly said to her husband, 'You see, I was right!' When Vronsky appeared she was still more pleased and was strengthened in her opinion that Kitty ought to make not only a good but a brilliant match.

In the mother's eyes there was no comparison between Levin and Vronsky. She did not like Levin's strange and harsh criticisms, his awkward manner in Society which she attributed to pride, and what she considered his strange way of life in the country, occupied with cattle and peasants; in particular she did not like the fact that when he was in love with her daughter he came to the house for six weeks as if waiting and looking out for something, afraid of doing them too great an honour by making an offer of marriage, and that he did not understand that, if he visited at a house where there was a marriageable girl, he ought to declare his intentions. And then suddenly he left without proposing!

'It's a good thing he is so unattractive, and that Kitty has not fallen in love with him,' thought her mother.

Vronsky satisfied all the mother's desires: he was very rich, clever, distinguished, with a brilliant military career before him, a position at Court, and altogether was an enchanting man. Nothing better could be desired.

Vronsky was openly attentive to Kitty when they met at balls, danced with her, and came to the house, so there could be no doubt as to the seriousness of his intentions. But in spite of this the mother was in a dreadful state of anxiety and agitation all that winter.

When the Princess herself had married, more than thirty years before, the match had been arranged by an aunt. Her *fiancé* about whom everything was known beforehand came, saw his intended bride, and was seen by her people; then the matchmaking aunt learnt what was thought on each side, and passed on the information. All was satisfactory. Afterwards at an appointed time and place the expected proposal was made to, and accepted by, her parents. Everything was done very easily and simply. At least so it seemed to the Princess. But in her daughters' case she experienced how far from easy and simple the apparently easy business of marrying off a daughter really was. What anxiety she had to suffer, how many questions to consider over and over again, how much money to spend, how many encounters with her husband to go through, when her two elder daughters Darya and Nataly were married! Now that her youngest daughter had come out she was living through the same fears and doubts, and having even worse disputes with her husband than on her elder daughters' account. Like all fathers, the old Prince was extremely punctilious where his daughters' purity and honour were concerned; he was unreasonably jealous especially about Kitty, his favourite, and at every step reproached the Princess with compromising her daughter. The Princess had grown used to this in respect to her elder daughters, but now she felt that her husband's punctiliousness had more justification. She could see that lately social customs had changed very much and a mother's duties had become still more difficult. She knew that girls of Kitty's age formed societies of some sort, went to courses of lectures, made friends freely with men, and drove alone through the streets; many no longer curtsied, and above all every one of them was firmly convinced that the choice of a husband was her own and not her parents' business. 'Nowadays they don't give us away in marriage as they used to!' said these young girls, and even the old people said the same. But how marriages are now arranged the Princess could not find out from anyone.

The French way, of parents deciding a daughter's fate, was not accepted, and was even condemned. The English way, of giving a girl perfect freedom, was also rejected, and would have been impossible in Russian Society. The Russian way, of employing a professional match-maker, was considered monstrous, and was laughed at by everybody, including the Princess herself. But how a girl was to get married, or how a mother was to get a daughter given in marriage, no one knew. Everyone with whom the Princess discussed the subject said the same thing: 'Well, you know, in our days it is time to give up obsolete customs. After all it's the young people who marry and not their parents, therefore they must be left to arrange matters as they think best.' It was all very well for people who had no daughters to talk like that, but the Princess knew that intimacy might be followed by love and that her daughter might fall in love with some one who had no intention of marrying or was not fit to be her husband. And whatever people might say about the time having come when young people must arrange their future for themselves, she could not believe it any more than she could believe that loaded pistols could ever be the best toys for five-year-old children. That is why the Princess was more anxious about Kitty than she had been about her elder daughters.

And now she was afraid that Vronsky might content himself with merely flirting with her daughter. She saw that Kitty was in love with him, but consoled herself with the thought that Vronsky was an honest man and therefore would not act in such a way. At the same time she knew that the freedom now permitted made it easy for a man to turn a girl's head, and knew how lightly men regarded

an offence of that kind. The week before, Kitty had repeated to her
mother a conversation she had had with Vronsky while dancing the
mazurka with him. This conversation had partly reassured the
Princess; but she could not feel quite at ease. Vronsky had told
Kitty that he and his brother were so used to comply with their
mother's wishes that they never made up their minds to take an
important step without consulting her. 'And I am now especially
happy looking forward to my mother's arrival from Petersburg,' he
had said.

Kitty had narrated this without attaching any special meaning to
the words. But to her mother they appeared in a different light. She
knew that the old lady was expected any day, and would approve of
her son's choice; and though she thought it strange that he should
delay proposing for fear of hurting his mother, she so desired the
marriage, and especially relief from her own anxiety, that she believed it.

Hard as it was to see the misfortune of Dolly, her eldest daughter
(who thought of leaving her husband), the Princess's anxiety as to
her youngest daughter's fate, now about to be decided, entirely
absorbed her. Levin's arrival that day gave her further cause for
anxiety. She was afraid that her daughter who had once seemed to
have a certain affection for Levin might be led by an exaggerated
feeling of loyalty to reject Vronsky, and she feared that in general
Levin's arrival might cause complications and delays in matters
now so near conclusion.

'Has he been back long?' asked the Princess when they got home,
referring to Levin.

'He arrived to-day, Mama.'

'There is one thing I want to say . . .' the Princess began, and
from her serious look Kitty guessed what was coming.

'Mama,' she said flushing and turning quickly toward her
mother, 'please, please, say nothing about it! I know, I know quite
well.'

Her wish was the same as her mother's, but the motive under-
lying her mother's wish offended her.

'I wish to say that having given hopes to one . . .'

'Mama, dearest, for Heaven's sake don't speak. It is so dreadful to
speak about it!'

'I won't,—only this, my darling,' said the mother, seeing tears in
her daughter's eyes, '. . . you promised not to have any secrets
from me and you won't, will you?'

'Never, Mama, never at all,' answered Kitty blushing as she
looked her mother straight in the face. 'But I have nothing to say
at present . . . I . . . I . . . if I wished to, I should not know
what to say or how . . . I don't know . . .'

'No, she could not possibly tell an untruth with such eyes,' thought the mother smiling at her agitation and joy. The Princess smiled to think how immense and important what was going on in her own soul must appear to the poor girl.

Chapter XIII

During the interval between dinner and the beginning of the evening party, Kitty experienced something resembling a young man's feelings before a battle. Her heart was beating violently and she could not fix her thoughts on anything.

She felt that this evening, when those two men were to meet for the first time, would decide her fate; and she kept picturing them to herself, now individually and now together. When she thought of the past, she dwelt with pleasure and tenderness on her former relations with Levin. Memories of childhood and of Levin's friendship with her dead brother lent a peculiar poetic charm to her relations with him. His love for her, of which she felt sure, flattered and rejoiced her, and she could think of him with a light heart. With her thought of Vronsky was mingled some uneasiness, though he was an extremely well-bred and quiet-mannered man; a sense of something false, not in him, for he was very simple and kindly, but in herself; whereas in relation to Levin she felt herself quite simple and clear. On the other hand when she pictured herself a future with Vronsky a brilliant vision of happiness rose up before her, while a future with Levin appeared wrapped in mist.

On going upstairs to dress for the evening and looking in the glass, she noticed with pleasure that this was one of her best days, and that she was in full possession of all her forces, which would be so much wanted for what lay before her. She was conscious of external calmness and of freedom and grace in her movements.

At half-past seven, as soon as she had come down into the drawing-room, the footman announced 'Constantine Dmitrich Levin!' The Princess was still in her bedroom, nor had the Prince yet come down.

'So it's to be!' thought Kitty and the blood rushed to her heart. Glancing at the mirror she was horrified at her pallor.

She felt sure that he had come so early on purpose to see her alone and to propose to her. And now for the first time the matter presented itself to her in a different and entirely new light. Only now did she realize that this matter (with whom she would be happy, who was the man she loved) did not concern herself alone, but that in a moment she would have to wound a man she cared for, and to wound him cruelly. . . . Why? Because the dear fellow was in love with her. But it could not be helped, it was necessary and had to be done.

'Oh God, must I tell him so myself?' she thought. 'Must I really tell him that I don't care for him? That would not be true. What then shall I say? Shall I say that I love another? No, that's impossible! I'll go away. Yes, I will.'

She was already approaching the door when she heard his step. 'No, it would be dishonest! What have I to fear? I have done nothing wrong. I'll tell the truth, come what may! Besides, it's impossible to feel awkward with him. Here he is!' she thought, as she saw his powerful diffident figure before her and his shining eyes gazing at her. She looked straight into his face as if entreating him to spare her, and gave him her hand.

'I don't think I've come at the right time, I'm too early,' he said, gazing round the empty drawing-room. When he saw that his expectation was fulfilled and that nothing prevented his speaking to her, his face clouded over.

'Not at all,' said Kitty and sat down at the table.

'But all I wanted was to find you alone,' he began, still standing and avoiding her face so as not to lose courage.

'Mama will be down in a minute. She was so tired yesterday . . .' She spoke without knowing what she was saying, her eyes fixed on him with a caressing look full of entreaty.

He glanced at her; she blushed and was silent.

'I told you that I did not know how long I should stay . . . that it depends on you.'

Her head dropped lower and lower, knowing the answer she would give to what was coming.

'That it would depend on you,' he repeated. 'I want to say . . . I want to say . . . I came on purpose . . . that . . . to be my wife!' he uttered hardly knowing what he said; but feeling that the worst was out he stopped and looked at her.

She was breathing heavily and not looking at him. She was filled with rapture. Her soul was overflowing with happiness. She had not at all expected that his declaration of love would make so strong an impression on her. But that lasted only for an instant. She remembered Vronsky, lifted her clear, truthful eyes to Levin's face, and noticing his despair she replied quickly:

'It cannot be . . . forgive me.'

How near to him she had been a minute ago, how important in his life! And how estranged and distant she seemed now!

'Nothing else was possible,' he said, without looking at her, and bowing he turned to go. . . .

Chapter XIV

But just at that moment the Princess came in. An expression of terror appeared in her face on seeing them alone together and noticing their troubled looks. Levin bowed to her and said nothing. Kitty sat with downcast eyes.

'Thank Heaven she has refused him,' thought the mother, and her face brightened into the usual smile with which she greeted her visitors on Thursday evenings. She sat down and began questioning Levin about his life in the country. He too sat down until the arrival of other guests should enable him to get away unnoticed.

Five minutes later Kitty's friend the Countess Nordston, who had married the year before, came in.

She was a thin, sallow, nervous, ailing woman with shining black eyes. She was fond of Kitty, and her affection showed itself as the affection of a married woman for an unmarried one generally does, in a desire to get Kitty married according to her—the Countess's—own ideal of conjugal bliss; and she wished to see her married to Vronsky. She always disliked Levin, whom at the beginning of the winter she had often met at the Shcherbatskys. Her constant and favourite amusement was to make fun of him.

'I love it when he looks down at me from the height of his dignity, or breaks off his clever conversation because I am too stupid, or when he shows his condescension toward me. I do love it. His condescension! I am very glad he hates me,' she used to say with reference to him.

She was right, because Levin really could not bear her and despised her for the very thing she was proud of and regarded as a merit, that is, her nervousness and refined contempt and disregard for all the rough and common things of life.

Between the Countess Nordston and Levin relations had grown up such as are not infrequently met with in Society, when two people outwardly remaining in friendly relations despise each other to such an extent that they cannot treat each other seriously, or even be offended with one another.

The Countess at once attacked Levin.

'Ah, Mr. Levin! So you have returned to our depraved Babylon!' she said, holding out her tiny yellow hand and repeating the words he had used early in the winter when he had called Moscow 'Babylon,'—'Has Babylon improved or have you deteriorated?' she added, and turned toward Kitty with a sarcastic smile.

'I am much flattered that you remember my words so well, Countess,' replied Levin who had had time to recover his self-possession, resuming immediately and by force of habit his banteringly hostile relation with her. 'They evidently produced a strong impression on you.'

'Why, of course, I always write them down. Well, Kitty, have you been skating again?'

She began to talk with Kitty. Awkward as it would have been for

Levin to leave just then, he would have preferred doing so to remaining in the house for the rest of the evening in sight of Kitty, who now and then glanced at him but avoided catching his eye. He was about to rise, when the Princess noticing his silence turned toward him and said:

'Have you come to Moscow for long? But I believe you are on the Zemstvo and cannot stay away long?'

'No, Princess, I am no longer on the Zemstvo,' he answered, 'I have come to Moscow for a few days.'

'Something out of the common has happened to him,' thought the Countess Nordston, scrutinizing his stern and serious face; 'why does he not start on one of his discourses? But I'll draw him out, I do love to make a fool of him when Kitty's about, and I will.'

'Mr. Levin,' she began, 'explain to me, please, you who know everything, how it is that at our Kaluga estate the peasant men and women have drunk everything they had, and never pay anything they owe us. What is the explanation? You always praise the peasants so much.'

At that moment another lady entered the room and Levin rose.

'Excuse me, Countess, but really I know nothing about it, and can't tell you anything,' he said, and as he turned he saw an officer who had come into the room behind the lady.

'That must be Vronsky,' he thought, and looked at Kitty to make sure. She had already glanced at Vronsky and then turned toward Levin. And by the look of her eyes which had involuntarily brightened Levin realized that she loved this man, realized it as surely as if she had told it him in so many words. But what kind of man was he?

Now, rightly or wrongly, Levin could not but remain. He had to find out what sort of a man it was that she loved.

There are people who when they meet a rival, no matter in what, at once shut their eyes to everything good in him and see only the bad. There are others who on the contrary try to discern in a lucky rival the qualities which have enabled him to succeed, and with aching hearts seek only the good in him. Levin belonged to the latter sort. But it was not difficult for him to see what was good and attractive in Vronsky. It struck him immediately. Vronsky was a dark sturdily-built man of medium height, with a good-natured, handsome, exceedingly quiet and firm face. Everything about his face and figure—from his black closely-cropped hair and freshly-shaven chin to his wide, brand-new uniform—was simple and at the same time elegant. Having stepped aside to let a lady pass, Vronsky approached first the Princess and then Kitty. When he moved toward her his fine eyes brightened with a special tenderness, and carefully and respectfully bending over her with a scarcely perceptible, happy, and (as it seemed to Levin) modestly-triumphant smile, he held out to her his small broad hand.

Having greeted and spoken a few words to every one else, he sat down without having once looked at Levin, who had not taken his eyes off him.

'Let me introduce you,' said the Princess indicating Levin. 'Constantine Dmitrich Levin, Count Alexey Kirilovich Vronsky.'

Vronsky rose and looking cordially into Levin's eyes pressed his hand.

'I was to have dined with you earlier this winter,' he said with his simple frank smile, 'but you unexpectedly went away to the country.'

'Mr. Levin despises and hates the town and us townspeople,' said Countess Nordston.

'My words must make a deep impression on you for you to remember them so long,' said Levin; then recollecting that he had said this before he blushed.

Vronsky glanced at him and at the Countess, and smiled.

'And do you always live in the country?' he asked. 'Isn't it dull in the winter?'

'No, not when one is busy: nor need one be dull in one's own company,' replied Levin abruptly.

'I am fond of the country,' said Vronsky, noticing, but pretending not to notice, Levin's tone.

'But I hope, Count, you would not consent always to live in the country,' said the Countess Nordston.

'I don't know, I never tried it for long. I have experienced a curious feeling,' he went on. 'Nowhere have I felt so homesick for the country, our Russian country, with its peasants in bast shoes, as when I spent a winter with my mother in Nice. Nice in itself is dull, you know. And Naples and Sorrento are pleasant only for a short stay, and it is there that one thinks of Russia, and longs especially for the Russian countryside. They seem to . . .'

He was addressing both Kitty and Levin, his quiet and friendly glance passing from the one to the other. He was evidently speaking quite sincerely and frankly.

Noticing that the Countess Nordston wished to say something, he stopped without finishing what he was saying, and listened attentively to her.

The conversation did not flag for a moment, so that the old Princess who always had in reserve, in case of need, two heavy guns (classical versus modern education, and general conscription), had no need to bring them forward, and the Countess Nordston had no opportunity to tease Levin.

Levin wished to join in the general conversation, but found it impossible, and kept saying to himself, 'Now I will go,' yet he did not go, but waited for something indefinite.

The conversation touched on table-turning and spiritualism, and the Countess Nordston, who believed in spiritualism, began relating miracles she had witnessed.

'Ah, Countess, you must really take me there. For goodness' sake take me to them! I have never seen anything supernatural though I always look out for it,' said Vronsky smiling.

'Very well, next Saturday,' replied the Countess Nordston. 'And you, Mr. Levin, do you believe in it?' she asked, turning to him.

'Why do you ask me? You know very well what I shall say.'

'But I want to hear your opinion.'

'My opinion is that this table-turning proves that our so-called educated class is on the same level as the peasants. They believe in the evil eye and spells and witchcraft, while we . . .'

'Well then, you don't believe?'

'I can't believe, Countess!'

'But if I have seen it myself?'

'The peasant women tell how they have seen the goblins with their own eyes.'

'Then you think I am not telling the truth?' and she laughed mirthlessly.

'Oh no, Masha, Mr. Levin only says he can't believe . . .' said Kitty, blushing for Levin, and Levin understanding this became still more irritated and wished to answer, but Vronsky, with his bright and frank smile, came at once to the rescue of the conversation, which was threatening to become unpleasant.

'You don't admit that it is even possible?' he asked. 'But why not? We admit the existence of electricity, which we don't understand, why can't there be other forces which we do not yet know, but which . . .'

'When electricity was first discovered,' Levin hurriedly interrupted, 'only the phenomena were observed, their cause and its effects were unknown. Centuries passed before any one thought of applying it. But the Spiritualists on the contrary began by the tables writing for them and the spirits coming to them, and they only afterwards began to say that it was an unknown force.'

Vronsky listened attentively to Levin as he always listened, evidently interested in what he was saying.

'Yes, but the Spiritualists say, "We do not yet know what force it is, but it exists and these are the conditions under which it acts. Let the scientists discover what the force is." No, I do not see why it should not be a new force, if it . . .'

'For this reason,' Levin again interrupted him, 'that with electricity, you need only rub a piece of resin against wool, and you will always produce a certain phenomenon, but this other does not always act, so it is not a natural force.'

Probably feeling that the conversation was becoming too serious for a drawing-room, Vronsky did not reply, but in order to change the subject he smiled gaily and turned toward the ladies.

'Let us try now, Countess,' he began, but Levin wanted to finish saying what he thought.

'I think,' he continued, 'that this attempt of the Spiritualists to explain their wonders by some kind of new force is most unsuccessful. They speak definitely of a spiritual force, and yet want to subject it to a material test.'

Everybody waited for him to finish and he was conscious of it.

'I think you would make a splendid medium,' said the Countess Nordston; 'there is something ecstatic about you.'

Levin opened his mouth to reply, but blushed and said nothing.

'Let us try table-turning now, Princess Kitty, please do,' said Vronsky. 'May we, Princess?' he said to her mother and he rose and looked round for a suitable table.

Kitty rose to fetch a table, and as she passed Levin their eyes met. She pitied him with her whole soul, especially because she herself had caused him to suffer.

'If you can forgive me, please do,' pleaded her look. 'I am so happy.'

'I hate everybody, including you and myself,' answered his eyes; and he took up his hat. But he was not fated to go yet. Just as the others began settling round the table and Levin was about to go, the old Prince came in, and having greeted the ladies he turned to Levin.

'Ah!' said he heartily. 'Been here long? I did not even know that you had arrived; very glad to see you.'

He embraced Levin, and speaking to him did not catch sight of Vronsky who rose and stood quietly waiting until the Prince should notice him.

Kitty was conscious that, after what had taken place, her father's cordiality oppressed Levin. She also noticed how coldly her father at last responded to Vronsky's bow, and with what good-natured perplexity Vronsky looked at him, trying, but failing, to understand how it was possible not to be friendly disposed toward him, and she blushed.

'Prince, release Mr. Levin for us as we want to try an experiment,' said the Countess Nordston.

'What experiment? Table-turning? Excuse me, ladies and gentlemen, but in my opinion playing at hunt the ring is more amusing,' said the old Prince, looking at Vronsky and guessing that he had started the thing. 'After all there is some sense in "Hunting the ring." '

Vronsky's unflinching eye glanced in astonishment at the old
Prince, and slightly smiling he at once began talking to the Countess Nordston about the ball that was to take place the next week.

'I hope you will be there,' he said to Kitty.

As soon as the old Prince had turned away from him Levin went
out unobserved, and his last impression was Kitty's happy smiling
face as she answered Vronsky's question about the ball.

Chapter XV

After the guests had gone Kitty told her mother of her conversation with Levin, and in spite of all her pity for him she was pleased
by the thought that she had had a proposal. She did not doubt that
she had acted rightly, yet for a long time she lay in bed unable to
sleep. One image pursued her relentlessly. It was Levin's face with
his kind eyes looking mournfully from under his knit brows as he
stood listening to her father and glancing at her and at Vronsky,
and she felt so sorry for him that tears rose to her eyes. But she immediately remembered for whom she had exchanged him. She
vividly pictured to herself that strong manly face, that well-bred
calm and the kindness toward everybody he always showed: she
remembered the love the man she loved bore her, and again became
joyful and with a happy smile put her head on her pillow. 'It is a
pity, a pity, but I am not to blame,' she said to herself, but an
inner voice said something different. Whether she repented of
having drawn Levin on or of having rejected him she did not know,
but her happiness was troubled by doubts.

'Lord have mercy, Lord have mercy, Lord have mercy,' she repeated to herself till she fell asleep.

Meanwhile below in the Prince's little study her parents were
having one of their frequent scenes about their favourite daughter.

'What? I'll tell you what!' shouted the Prince, flourishing his
arms and immediately again wrapping his squirrel-lined dressing-
gown around him. 'You have no pride, no dignity, you disgrace and
ruin your daughter by this vile idiotic match-making.'

'For goodness' sake, Prince, what in heaven's own name have I
done?' said the Princess almost in tears.

After her talk with her daughter she had come in, happy and
contented, to say good-night to the Prince as usual, and though she
did not intend to speak to him about Levin's proposal and Kitty's
refusal she hinted to him that she thought the matter with Vronsky was quite settled and would probably be definitely decided as
soon as his mother arrived. And when she said that, the Prince
suddenly flared up and began to shout rudely: 'What have you
done? Why this: first of all you *entice* a suitor. All Moscow will

talk about it and with reason. If you give a party invite everybody and not only selected suitors. Invite all the young puppies,' so the Prince called the Moscow young men, 'have a pianist and let them dance; but don't have the sort of thing we had to-night—these suitors and this pairing off. It makes me sick to see it, simply sick, and you have had your way and have turned the child's head. Levin is a thousand times the better man. This one is a little Petersburg fop. They are machine-made by the dozen, all to one pattern, and all mere rubbish. But even if he were a Prince of the blood my daughter does not need him.'

'But what have I done?'

'Just this . . .' exclaimed the Prince angrily.

'I know this much,' the Princess interrupted him, 'that if I were to listen to what you say we should never see our daughter married, and we had better go and live in the country.'

'So we had!'

'Wait a bit! Do I draw them on? No, certainly not, but a young man and an excellent young man falls in love with Kitty, and she too seems . . .'

'Seems indeed! And suppose she really falls in love with him while he intends to marry about as much as I do. . . . Oh, I wish my eyes had never seen it. . . . "Ah spiritualism! Ah how nice! Ah the ball!" ' And the Prince imagining himself to be impersonating his wife curtsied at each word. 'And then if we really ruin Kitty's happiness, if she really gets it into her head . . .'

'But why do you suppose such a thing?'

'I don't suppose, I know! We have eyes for those things, and women haven't. I can recognize a man who has serious intentions—such as Levin—and I can see through a weathercock like that popinjay who only wishes to amuse himself.'

'Oh well, when you once get a thing into your head . . .'

'And you'll find it out, but too late, just as with poor Dolly.'

'All right. All right, don't let's talk,' said the Princess, interrupting him and remembering the unfortunate Dolly.

'Very well then, good-night.'

And having made the sign of the cross over one another and kissed, feeling that each of them retained their individual opinions, the couple separated for the night.

The Princess had been at first firmly convinced that this evening had decided Kitty's fate and that there could be no doubt as to Vronsky's intentions; but her husband's words disturbed her, and when she reached her room, in terror of the uncertainty of the future, she mentally repeated, just as Kitty had done: 'Lord have mercy, Lord have mercy, Lord have mercy!'

Chapter XVI

Vronsky had never known family life. His mother in her youth had been a brilliant Society woman, and during her married life and especially in her widowhood had had many love affairs, known to everybody. He hardly remembered his father, and had been educated in the Cadet Corps.

On leaving that Corps as a very young and brilliant officer he at once joined the swim of the wealthy military Petersburg set. Though he occasionally went into the highest Petersburg Society, all his love interests lay outside it.

In Moscow, after this luxurious course of Petersburg life, he experienced for the first time the delight of intimacy with a sweet, innocent Society girl who fell in love with him. It never entered his head that there could be any wrong in his relations with Kitty. At balls he danced chiefly with her and he visited her at her home. He talked with her the usual Society talk: all sorts of rubbish, but rubbish into which involuntarily he put a special meaning for her. Though he never said anything to her which could not have been said before everybody he was conscious that she was becoming more and more dependent upon him, and the more he felt this the pleasanter it was, and the more tender became his feelings toward her. He did not know that his behaviour toward Kitty had a name of its own, that it was decoying a girl with no intentions of marrying her, and is one of the evil actions common among brilliant young men like himself. He thought he was the first to discover this pleasure and he enjoyed his discovery.

If he could have heard what her parents said that night, if he could have known her family's point of view and learnt that Kitty would be unhappy if he did not marry her, he would have been much surprised and would not have believed it. He would not have believed that what gave so much and such excellent pleasure to him, and—what was more—to her, could be wrong. Even less could he have believed that he ought to marry.

Marriage had never presented itself to him as a possibility. Not only did he dislike family life, but in accordance with the views generally held in the bachelor world in which he lived he regarded the family, and especially a husband, as something alien, hostile, and above all ridiculous. But although Vronsky had no suspicion of what Kitty's parents were saying, he felt, as he left the Shcherbatskys' house that night, that the secret spiritual bond which existed between him and Kitty had so strengthened during the evening that some action ought to be taken. But what this should or could be he could not imagine.

'That's what is so delightful,' he thought as he left the Shcherbatskys' house, carrying away from there, as usual, a pleasant feeling of purity and freshness (partly due to the fact that he had not smoked at all that evening) and deeply touched by a new sense of tender joy in the consciousness of her love for him. 'That is what is so delightful, that nothing was said either by me or by her, yet we so well understand one another in that subtle language of looks and tones that to-day more plainly than ever she has told me that she loves me. And how sweetly, simply, and above all trustfully! I feel myself better and purer, I feel I have a heart and that there is much that is good in me. Those dear loving eyes when she said, "and very much!"'

'Well, and what of it? Nothing, of course. It's pleasant for me and for her,' and he considered where he should finish his evening.

He passed in review the places he might go to. 'The Club: a game of bezique, a bottle of champagne with Ignatev? No, I won't go there. Chateau des Fleurs? There I should find Oblonsky, French couplets, the cancan. No, I am sick of it. That's just what I like about the Shcherbatskys', that I myself become better there. I'll go home.' He went straight to his rooms at the Hotel Dusseaux, had supper, and after undressing had hardly laid his head on his pillow before he was fast asleep.

Chapter XVII

At eleven o'clock next morning Vronsky drove to the Petersburg railway station in Moscow to meet his mother, and the first person he saw on the steps of the large portico was Oblonsky, who was expecting his sister by the same train.

"Hallo, your Excellency!' exclaimed Oblonsky. 'Whom are you after?'

'My mother,' replied Vronsky, shaking hands and smiling (as everybody did when meeting Oblonsky) as they went up the steps together. 'She is coming from Petersburg to-day.'

'I waited for you till two last night; where did you go from the Shcherbatskys'?'

'Home,' replied Vronsky. 'To tell you the truth I felt in such a pleasant mood when I left the Shcherbatskys' that I did not care to go anywhere else.'

> ' "Fiery steeds by" *something* "brands
> I can always recognize;
> Youths in love . . . " '

declaimed Oblonsky, just as he had done to Levin.

Vronsky smiled with a look that seemed not to deny the implication but he immediately changed the subject.

'And whom have you come to meet?' he asked.

'I? A lovely woman,' answered Oblonsky.

'Dear me!'

'*Honi soit qui mal y pense!*[1] My sister Anna!'

'Oh! Mrs. Karenina!' said Vronsky.

'I expect you know her?'

'I think I do. But perhaps not. . . . I really can't remember,' answered Vronsky absent-mindedly, the name Karenina suggesting to him some one stiff and dull.

'But you are sure to know Alexey Alexandrovich Karenin, my famous brother-in-law. All the world knows him.'

'Yes, I know him by repute and by sight. I know he is clever, learned, and by way of being religious, but you know it is not my . . . *not in my line,*' he added in English.

'Oh yes, he is a very remarkable man, a bit conservative, but a splendid fellow,' said Oblonsky, 'a splendid fellow.'

'Well, so much the better for him,' and Vronsky smiled. 'Ah, you are here!' he went on, turning toward his mother's old footman who was standing by the door. 'Come in here.'

Besides liking Oblonsky, as everybody did, Vronsky latterly had felt still more drawn to him because he was connected in his mind with Kitty.

'Well, are we to give a supper for the *diva* next Sunday?' he asked smilingly, taking Oblonsky's arm.

'Certainly, I will collect subscriptions. I say, did you make the acquaintance of my friend Levin last night?' asked Oblonsky.

'Of course. Only he left very early.'

'He is a splendid fellow,' continued Oblonsky. 'Don't you think so?'

'I don't know how it is that all Muscovites, present company of course excepted,' Vronsky put in jokingly, 'are so abrupt. They are always standing on their hind legs getting angry, and seem to want to act on your feelings . . .'

'Yes, there is some truth in that,' said Oblonsky, laughing merrily.

'Shall we have to wait much longer?' asked Vronsky, turning to a porter.

'The train is signalled,' said the porter.

The train's approach was made more and more evident by the preparatory bustle on the station, the rush of porters, the appearance of gendarmes, and the arrival of people meeting the train. Through the frosty mist one could see workmen in sheepskin coats and felt boots crossing the curved railway lines, and hear the whistle of a locomotive and the noisy movements of a heavy mass.

'No,' said Oblonsky who was anxious to tell Vronsky about Levin's intentions concerning Kitty, 'no, you have not judged my Levin rightly. He is a very nervous man, and does make himself un-

---

1. Shame on him who thinks ill of it.

pleasant sometimes, that's true enough; but on the other hand he is sometimes very charming. His is such an honest, straightforward nature, and he has a heart of gold. But yesterday there were special reasons,' continued Oblonsky with a significant smile, quite forgetting the sincere sympathy he had felt for his friend the day before, and now only feeling the same sympathy for Vronsky. 'Yes, there was a reason why he had to be either specially happy or specially unhappy.'

Vronsky stopped and asked him straight out: 'What do you mean? Did he propose to your *belle sœur* last night?'[2]

'Perhaps,' said Oblonsky. 'I seemed to notice something of the kind yesterday. Oh yes, if he left early and was in a bad temper it must be that. . . . He has been in love with her so long, and I am very sorry for him.'

'Dear me! . . . But I should think she may make a better match,' said Vronsky, and expanding his chest he again moved forward. 'However, I don't know him,' he added. 'Yes, it is a painful position! That is why so many prefer women of the *demi-monde*. If you don't succeed in that case it only shows that you have not enough money, but in this case one's pride is in the balance. But here's the train.'

In fact the engine was already whistling in the distance, and a few moments later the platform shook as the train puffed in; the steam spread low in the frozen air, the connecting rods slowly and rhythmically pushed and pulled, the bent figure of the engine-driver, warmly wrapped up, was seen covered with hoar-frost. The engine with the tender behind it moved slowly into the station, gradually slowing down and making the platform tremble still more. Then came the luggage-van in which a dog was whining, and at last the passenger coaches, oscillating before they stopped.

The sprightly guard blew his whistle and jumped off while the train was still moving, and impatient passengers began to descend one after another: an officer of the guards, erect and looking sternly round, a fidgety little tradesman with a bag, smiling merrily, a peasant with a sack over his shoulder. . . .

Vronsky, as he stood by Oblonsky and watched these passengers coming out of the carriages, quite forgot about his mother. What he had just heard about Kitty excited and delighted him. His chest involuntarily expanded and his eyes shone, he felt himself to be a conqueror.

'The Countess Vronskaya is in that compartment,' said the sprightly guard, addressing Vronsky.

His words roused Vronsky from his reverie and reminded him of his mother and of the coming meeting.

In the depths of his heart he did not respect his mother and

2. Sister in law (wife's sister).

(though this he never acknowledged to himself) did not love her, but in accordance with the views of the set he lived in, and as a result of his education, he could not imagine himself treating her in any way but one altogether submissive and respectful, and the more submissive and respectful he was externally, the less he honoured and loved her in his heart.

Chapter XVIII

Vronsky followed the guard to the carriage, and had to stop at the entrance of the compartment to let a lady pass out.

The trained insight of a Society man enabled Vronsky with a single glance to decide that she belonged to the best Society. He apologized for being in her way and was about to enter the carriage, but felt compelled to have another look at her, not because she was very beautiful nor because of the elegance and modest grace of her whole figure, but because he saw in her sweet face as she passed him something specially tender and kind. When he looked round she too turned her head. Her bright grey eyes which seemed dark because of their black lashes rested for a moment on his face as if recognizing him, and then turned to the passing crowd evidently in search of some one. In that short look Vronsky had time to notice the subdued animation that enlivened her face and seemed to flutter between her bright eyes and a scarcely perceptible smile which curved her rosy lips. It was as if an excess of vitality so filled her whole being that it betrayed itself against her will, now in her smile, now in the light of her eyes. She deliberately tried to extinguish that light in her eyes, but it shone despite of her in her faint smile.

Vronsky entered the carriage. His mother, a dried-up old woman with black eyes and ringlets, screwed up her eyes as she recognized her son and her thin lips smiled slightly. She rose from the seat, and giving her hand-bag to her maid held out her small wrinkled hand to her son, then lifting his head which had been bent to kiss it, kissed him on his face.

'You had my telegram? You're well? That's a good thing.'

'Have you had a good journey?' asked her son, sitting down on the seat beside her and involuntarily listening to a woman's voice outside the door. He knew it was the voice of the lady he had met as he entered the carriage.

'All the same I don't agree with you,' the lady was saying.

'Yours are Petersburg views, madam.'

'Not at all, simply a woman's views.'

'Well, allow me to kiss your hand.'

'*Au revoir*, Ivan Petrovich, and please if you see my brother send him to me,' said the lady, closing the door and again entering the compartment.

'Well, have you found your brother?' asked Vronsky's mother, addressing the lady.

Vronsky understood now that this was Mrs. Karenina.

'Your brother is here,' he said rising. 'Excuse my not recognizing you before. Our acquaintance was so slight,' he said with a bow, 'that I am sure you do not remember me.'

'Oh yes, I should have recognized you, especially as I believe your mother and I have talked of nothing but you all the way,' said she, at last allowing the animation she had been trying to suppress to reveal itself in a smile. 'But my brother is not here yet.'

'Go and call him, Alexey,' said the old Countess.

Vronsky went out on to the platform and shouted, 'Oblonsky! Here!'

Mrs. Karenina did not wait for her brother to come in, but, on seeing him, descended from the carriage with a firm light step. As soon as her brother came up to her she threw her left arm round his neck with a movement that struck Vronsky by its firmness and grace, and drawing him to herself gave him a vigorous kiss. Vronsky did not take his eyes off her, and kept smiling, he knew not why. But remembering that his mother was waiting for him he went back into the carriage.

'She is very charming, isn't she?' said the Countess, referring to Mrs. Karenina. 'Her husband put her into the compartment with me and I was very pleased. We talked all the way. And you I hear . . . *vous filez le parfait amour. Tant mieux, mon cher, tant mieux.*' [3]

'I don't know what you mean, *maman*,' the son replied coldly. 'Well, shall we go?'

Mrs. Karenina again entered the carriage to take leave of the Countess.

'There, Countess, you have met your son and I my brother,' she said, 'and I have exhausted my stock of gossip and should have had nothing more to tell you.'

'No, no,' said the Countess holding her hand, 'I could travel round the world with you and not be dull. You are one of those charming women with whom it is nice to talk, and nice to be silent. But please don't fret about your son, you can't expect never to be parted.'

Mrs. Karenina stood very erect and her eyes were smiling.

'Anna Arkadyevna Karenina has a son who, I think, is eight years old,' explained the Countess, 'and she has never before been separated from him and so she is worried at having left him.'

'Yes, the Countess and I have talked all the time—I about my son and she about hers,' said Mrs. Karenina, and a smile brightened

3. Countess Vronsky may have meant, "You are running away from perfect love. All the better, my dear." But the phrase in common French usage means, "You are enjoying a perfect love."

her face, a kind smile on his account.

'I expect you got very weary of it,' he said, quickly seizing in its flight the ball of coquetry she had thrown at him. But she evidently did not wish to continue the conversation in that tone, and turned to the old Countess.

'Thank you very much. I hardly noticed how the time passed. *Au revoir*, Countess.'

'Good-bye, dear!' answered the Countess. 'Let me kiss your pretty face. I'm an old woman and say what I mean, and tell you frankly that I've lost my heart to you.'

Conventional as the phrase was, Mrs. Karenina evidently believed it and was pleased. She blushed, stooped a little, and held out her face for the Countess to kiss, then she stood up again, and with the same smile hovering between her lips and eyes held out her hand to Vronsky. He pressed the little hand, and the firm grip with which she shook his gave him unusual pleasure. She went out with that brisk tread which carried her rather full figure with such wonderful ease.

'Very charming,' said the old lady.

Her son thought so too. He followed her with his eyes as long as he could see her graceful form, and his face retained its smile. Through the carriage window he saw her approach her brother and speak to him with animation about something that evidently had no connection with him, Vronsky, and that seemed to him provoking.

'Well, *maman*, are you quite well?' he said, turning toward his mother.

'Quite, everything is all right. Alexander was very nice, and Varya looks very handsome. She is most interesting.'

And she began to tell about what interested her most, her grandson's christening, for which she had gone to Petersburg, and the special favour the Emperor had shown to her eldest son.

'Here is Lavrenty at last,' said Vronsky looking out of the window. 'We can go now if you like.'

The old major-domo, who had accompanied the Countess on her journey, came in and announced that everything was ready, and the Countess rose to go.

'Come, there is not much of a crowd now,' said Vronsky.

The maid took one bag and the little dog, the major-domo and the porter took the other bags. Vronsky gave his arm to his mother, but just as they were getting out of the carriage several people ran past them with frightened faces. The station-master with his peculiar coloured cap also ran past them.

Evidently something unusual had happened. The people who had left the train were running back to it.

'What? . . . What? . . . Where? . . . Thrown himself under
. . . Run over . . .' shouted the passers-by.

Oblonsky, with his sister on his arm, also turned back, and,
avoiding the crowd, they stood with frightened faces beside the carriage. The ladies re-entered the carriage, while Vronsky and Oblonsky
followed the crowd, to find out about the accident.

A watchman, either tipsy or too much muffled up because of the
severe frost, had not heard a train that was being shunted, and had
been run over.

Before Vronsky and Oblonsky returned the ladies had heard this
from the major-domo.

Oblonsky and Vronsky had both seen the mangled corpse. Oblonsky was evidently upset. His face was puckered and he seemed
ready to cry.

'Ah, how terrible! Oh, Anna, if you had seen it! Ah, how terrible!' he kept saying.

Vronsky remained silent. His handsome face was serious but
perfectly calm.

'Oh, if you had seen it, Countess,' said Oblonsky. 'And his wife
was there. . . . It was dreadful to see her. She threw herself on the
body. They say he was the sole support of a very large family. It is
terrible!'

'Can nothing be done for her?' said Mrs. Karenina in an agitated
whisper.

Vronsky glanced at her and at once went out. 'I will be back
directly, *maman*,' he remarked, turning at the doorway.

When he returned a few minutes later Oblonsky was already
talking to the Countess about the new opera singer, while she was
impatiently glancing at the door in expectation of her son.

'Now let's go,' said Vronsky as he came in.

They went together, Vronsky walking in front with his mother,
Mrs. Karenina following with her brother. At the exit the station-
master overtook them, and said to Vronsky:

'You gave my assistant 200 roubles. Please be so kind as to say
whom you intended it for.'

'For the widow,' said Vronsky, shrugging his shoulders. 'I don't
understand what need there is to ask.'

'You have given it!' exclaimed Oblonsky behind Vronsky, and
pressing his sister's arm he added, 'Very kind, very kind! Isn't he a
fine fellow? My respects to you, Countess,' and he remained behind
with his sister, seeking her maid.

When they came out, the Vronskys' carriage had already started.
The people coming from the station were still talking about the
accident.

'What a terrible death!' said some gentleman as he passed them;

'cut in half, I hear.'

'On the contrary, I think it is a very easy death, instantaneous,' said another.

'How is it that precautions are not taken?' said a third.

Mrs. Karenina got into her brother's carriage, and Oblonsky noticed with surprise that her lips were trembling and that it was with difficulty she kept back her tears.

'What is the matter with you, Anna?' he asked when they had gone a few hundred yards.

'It is a bad omen,' she replied.

'What nonsense!' said Oblonsky. 'You're here, and that is the chief thing. You can't think how my hopes rest on you.'

'And have you known Vronsky long?' she asked.

'Yes. Do you know we hope he will marry Kitty?'

'Yes?' said Anna softly. 'But let us talk about your affairs,' she added, shaking her head as if she wished physically to drive away something superfluous that oppressed her. 'Let us talk of your affairs. I've received your letter and have come.'

'Yes, all my hopes are fixed on you,' said her brother.

'Well, tell me all about it.'

And Oblonsky began his story.

On reaching his house, he helped his sister out of the carriage, pressed her hand, and drove off to his office.

Chapter XIX

When Anna arrived Dolly was sitting in her little drawing-room giving a fair-haired, plump little boy (who already resembled his father) a French reading-lesson. The boy, as he read, kept twisting and trying to pull off a loose button that hung from his jacket. His mother moved his plump little hand away several times, but it always returned to the button. At last she pulled the button off and put it into her pocket.

'Keep your hands quiet, Grisha,' she said, and again took up the rug she was knitting, a piece of work begun long ago, to which she always returned in times of trouble, and which she was now knitting, pulling the wool over the needle with nervous fingers and counting the stitches. Though she had sent word to her husband the day before that she did not care whether his sister came or not, she had prepared everything for her visit and awaited her with agitation.

Dolly was overpowered by her sorrow and was quite absorbed by it. Nevertheless, she remembered that her sister-in-law, Anna, was the wife of one of the most important men in Petersburg, and a grande dame. Thanks to that circumstance she did not carry out her threat to her husband, and did not forget that her sister-in-law was coming.

'After all, it is not in the least Anna's fault,' thought she. 'I know nothing but good about her, and she has never shown me anything but kindness and friendship.'

It was true that, as far as she could remember her visit to the Karenins in Petersburg, she had not liked their house: there seemed to be something false in the tone of their family life. 'But why should I not receive her? If only she does not try to console me!' thought Dolly. 'All these consolations and exhortations and Christian forgivenesses, I have considered them a thousand times, and they are all no good.'

All these last days Dolly had been alone with her children. She did not wish to talk about her sorrow, yet with that on her mind she could not talk about indifferent matters. She knew that, one way or other, she would tell Anna everything, and now it pleased her to think how she would say it, and then she felt vexed to have to speak of her humiliation to her—his sister—and to hear from her set phrases of exhortation and consolation.

As it often happens, though she kept looking at the clock, waiting for Anna, she let the moment when her visitor arrived go by without even hearing the bell.

And when she heard soft steps and the rustle of petticoats already in the doorway, she looked round with an expression not of pleasure but of surprise on her careworn face. She rose and embraced her sister-in-law.

'So you're here already?' she said, kissing her.

'Dolly, I am so pleased to see you!'

'And I am pleased too,' said Dolly with a feeble smile, trying to guess from Anna's expression how much she knew. 'She must know,' she thought, noticing the look of sympathy on Anna's face. 'Come, let me take you to your room,' she went on, trying to put off as long as possible the moment for explanation.

'This is Grisha? Dear me, how he has grown!' said Anna, and having kissed him, she stood with her eyes fixed on Dolly and blushed. 'No, please do not let us go anywhere.'

She took off her shawl and her hat and, having caught it in her black and very curly hair, shook her head to disengage it.

'And you are radiant with joy and health!' said Dolly almost enviously.

'I? . . . yes,' said Anna. 'Why, dear me, here is Tanya! You're just the same age as my little Serezha,' she added, turning to the little girl who had run into the room, and, taking her in her arms, Anna kissed her. 'Sweet girlie! darling! Let me see them all.'

She not only mentioned them all by name, but remembered the years and even the months of their births, their characters, and what illnesses they had had; and Dolly could not help appreciating this.

'Shall we go and see them?' she said. 'It is a pity Vasya is asleep.'

Having looked at the children they returned to the drawing-room and, being now alone, sat down to coffee at the table. Anna took hold of the tray, but then pushed it aside.

'Dolly,' she said, 'he has told me!'

Dolly looked coldly at Anna. She expected now to hear words of insincere sympathy: but Anna said nothing of the kind.

'Dolly dear!' she began, 'I do not wish to take his part or console you; that would be impossible, but, dearest, I am simply sorry for you, sorry from the bottom of my heart!'

Her bright eyes under their thick lashes suddenly filled with tears. She moved closer to her sister-in-law and with her energetic little hand took hold of Dolly's. The latter did not draw back from her but her face retained its rigid expression. She said:

'It is impossible to console me. Everything is lost after what has happened, everything destroyed!'

As soon as she had said it her face softened. Anna lifted Dolly's dry thin hand, kissed it, and said:

'But what is to be done, Dolly, what is to be done? What is the best way of acting in this dreadful position? That is what one has to consider.'

'Everything is at an end, and that's all,' said Dolly. 'And the worst of it is, you understand, that I can't leave him: there are the children, and I am bound. Yet I can't live with him; it is torture for me to see him.'

'Dolly, my darling, he has spoken to me, but I want to hear it from you. Tell me everything.'

Dolly looked at her inquiringly.

Sincere sympathy and affection were visible in Anna's face.

'If you like,' said Dolly suddenly, 'but I'll begin from the beginning. You know how I was married. With the education Mama gave me, I was not merely naïve, but silly! I knew nothing. I know they say husbands tell their wives how they have lived, but Stiva . . .' She corrected herself. 'But Stephen Arkadyevich never told me anything. You will hardly believe it, but up to now I thought I was the only woman he had ever known. In this way I lived for eight years. Only think, that I not only did not suspect him of unfaithfulness, but thought it impossible. I then . . . just imagine, with such ideas suddenly to find out all the horrors, all the abomination. . . . Try to understand me. To be fully convinced of one's happiness and suddenly . . .' continued Dolly, suppressing her sobs, 'to read a letter, his letter to his mistress, my children's governess. No, it is too horrible!' She hurriedly drew out her handkerchief and hid her face in it.

'I could perhaps understand a momentary slip,' she went on after a pause, 'but deliberately, cunningly to deceive me . . . and with whom? To go on living with me as my husband, and with her at the same time . . . it's awful; you cannot realize . . .'

'Oh yes, I do, I do understand, Dolly dear, I do understand,' said Anna, pressing her hand.

'And do you think he realizes the horror of my situation?' continued Dolly. 'Not at all! He is happy and contented.'

'Oh no,' Anna quickly interrupted. 'He is pitiable, he is overwhelmed with remorse . . .'

'Is he capable of remorse?' interrupted Dolly, looking searchingly into her sister-in-law's face.

'Oh yes, I know him. I could not look at him without pity. We both know him. He is kind-hearted, but he is proud too, and now he is so humiliated. What moved me most is . . . (and here Anna guessed what would touch Dolly most) that two things tormented him. He is ashamed of the children, and that, loving you . . . yes, yes, loving you more than anything else in the world,' she hurriedly went on, not listening to Dolly who was about to reply, 'he has hurt you, hit you so hard. He kept saying, "No, no, she will not forgive me!" '

Dolly, gazing beyond her sister-in-law, listened thoughtfully.

'Yes, I understand that his position is dreadful; it is worse for the guilty than for the innocent one,' she said, 'if he feels that the misfortune all comes from his fault. But how can I forgive him, how can I be a wife to him after her? . . . Life with him now will be a torture for me, just because I love my old love for him . . .' Sobs cut short her words.

But as if intentionally every time she softened, she again began to speak of the thing that irritated her.

'You know she is young, she is pretty,' she said. 'You see, Anna, my youth and my good looks have been sacrificed, and to whom? For him and his children. I have served his purpose and lost all I had in the service, and of course a fresh, good-for-nothing creature now pleases him better. They probably talked about me, or, worse still, avoided the subject. . . . You understand?'

And hatred again burned in her eyes.

'And after that he will tell me. . . . Am I to believe him? Never. . . . No, it's all ended, all that served as a consolation, as a reward for my labours, my sufferings. . . . Will you believe me, I have just been teaching Grisha: it used to be a pleasure, and now it is a torment. What is the good of my taking pains, of working so hard? What use are the children? It is terrible, my soul has so revolted that instead of love and tenderness for him I have nothing but anger left, yes, anger. I could kill him . . .'

'Dolly dearest! I understand, but don't torture yourself. You are so deeply hurt, so upset, that you see many things in the wrong light.'

Dolly was silent, and for a moment or two neither spoke.

'What am I to do? Think it over, Anna, help me! I have turned over in my mind everything I could think of, and can find nothing.'

Anna could not think of anything, but her heart responded to every word and every look of Dolly's.

'All I can say is,' began Anna, 'I am his sister and I know his character, his capacity for forgetting everything,' she made a gesture with her hand in front of her forehead, 'that capacity for letting himself be completely carried away, but on the other hand for completely repenting. He can hardly believe now—can hardly understand—how he could do it.'

'No, he understands and understood,' Dolly interrupted. 'And I . . . you forget me. . . . Does it make it easier for me?'

'Wait a bit. When he was speaking to me, I confess I did not quite realize the misery of your position. I saw only his side, and that the family was upset, and I was sorry for him, but now having spoken with you I as a woman see something else. I see your suffering and I cannot tell you how sorry I am for you. But, Dolly dearest, I fully understand your sufferings—yet there is one thing I do not know. I do not know . . . I do not know how much love there still is in your soul—you alone know that. Is there enough for forgiveness? If there is—then forgive him.'

'No,' Dolly began, but Anna stopped her and again kissed her hand.

'I know the world better than you do,' she said. 'I know men like Stiva and how they see these things. You think he spoke to her about you. That never happens. These men may be unfaithful, but their homes, their wives, are their holy places. They manage in some way to hold these women in contempt and don't let them interfere with the family. They seem to draw some kind of line between the family and those others. I do not understand it, but it is so.'

'Yes, but he kissed her. . . .'

'Dolly, wait a bit. I have seen Stiva when he was in love with you. I remember his coming to me and weeping (what poetry and high ideals you were bound up with in his mind!), and I know that the longer he lived with you the higher you rose in his esteem. You know we used to laugh at him because his every third word was, "Dolly is a wonderful woman." You have been and still are his divinity, and this infatuation never reached his soul. . . .'

'But suppose the infatuation is repeated?'

'It cannot be, as I understand . . .'

'And you, would you forgive?'

'I do not know, I cannot judge. . . . Yes, I can,' said Anna, after a minute's consideration. Her mind had taken in and weighed the situation, and she added, 'Yes, I can, I can. Yes, I should forgive. I should not remain the same woman—no, but I should forgive, and forgive it as utterly as if it had never happened at all.'

'Well, of course . . .' Dolly put in quickly as if saying what she had often herself thought, 'or else it would not be forgiveness. If one is to forgive, it must be entire forgiveness. Well now, I will show you your room.' She rose, and on the way embraced Anna. 'My dear, how glad I am you came! I feel better now, much better.'

Chapter XX

The whole of that day Anna remained at home, that is at the Oblonskys' house, and did not receive anybody, although several of her acquaintances who had heard of her arrival came to see her. She spent the earlier part of the day with Dolly and the children, and sent a note to her brother to be sure and come home to dinner. 'Come,' she wrote. 'God is merciful.'

Oblonsky dined at home, the conversation was general, and his wife addressed him familiarly in the second person singular, which she had not done all these days. There was still the same estrangement in their manner to each other, but no longer any question of separating, and Oblonsky saw that explanation and reconciliation were possible.

Immediately after dinner Kitty came. She knew Anna, but only slightly, and came to her sister's not without fear of how she might be received by this Petersburg Society woman whom everybody admired so much. But she noticed at once that Anna liked her. It was evident that her beauty and youth gave Anna pleasure, and before Kitty had time to regain her self-possession she felt not only that she was under Anna's influence but that she was in love with her, as young girls often are with married women older than themselves. Anna was not like a Society woman or the mother of an eight-year-old son. The flexibility of her figure, her freshness, and the natural animation of her face appearing now in her smile, now in her eyes, would have made her look more like a girl of twenty had it not been for a serious and sometimes even sad expression in her eyes which struck Kitty and attracted her. Kitty felt that Anna was perfectly unaffected and was not trying to conceal anything, but that she lived in another, higher world full of complex poetic interests beyond Kitty's reach.

After dinner, when Dolly had gone to her own room, Anna got up quickly and went to her brother who was just lighting a cigar.

'Stiva,' she said to him with a merry twinkle in her eye and making the sign of the cross over him as she indicated the door with a look. 'Go, and may God help you.' He understood, threw down his cigar, and disappeared through the door.

When Oblonsky had gone, she returned to the sofa where she had been sitting surrounded by the children. Whether because they saw that 'Mama' was fond of this aunt, or because they themselves felt her peculiar charm, first the two elder children and then the younger ones, as is often the way with children, had even before dinner begun clinging to her, and now would not leave her side. And they started something like a game which consisted in trying to get as close to her as possible, to touch her, hold her little hand, kiss her, play with her ring, or at least touch the frills of her dress.

'Now how were we sitting before?' said Anna, resuming her seat.

And Grisha again pushed his head under her arm and leaning against her dress beamed with pride and joy.

'And when is the ball to be?' said Anna, turning to Kitty.

'Next week, and it will be a delightful ball. One of those balls which are always jolly.'

'Are there any that are always jolly?' asked Anna with tender irony.

'It is strange, but there are! It's always jolly at the Bobrishchevs' and also at the Nikitins', while it's always dull at the Mezhkovs'. Haven't you noticed it?'

'No, my dear, there are no more jolly balls for me,' said Anna, and Kitty saw in her eyes that peculiar world which was not yet revealed to her. 'There are some that are not as difficult and dull as the rest.'

'How can you be dull at a ball?'

'Why cannot I be dull at a ball?' asked Anna.

Kitty saw that Anna knew the answer that would follow.

'Because you must always be the belle of the ball.'

Anna had a capacity for blushing. She blushed and answered, 'In the first place, I never am: but even if I were, what use would it be to me?'

'Will you go to this ball?' asked Kitty.

'I suppose I shall have to. Here, take this,' she said, turning to Tanya who was drawing off a ring which fitted loosely on her aunt's small tapering finger.

'I shall be very glad if you go. I should so like to see you at a ball.'

'Well, then, if I have to go, I shall console myself with the reflection that it will give you pleasure. . . . Grisha, please don't pull so hard, it is all in a tangle already,' she said, arranging a loose lock of hair with which Grisha was playing.

'I imagine you at that ball in lilac!'

'Why must it be lilac?' asked Anna half laughing. 'Now, children, run away, run away. Don't you hear? There's Miss Hull calling you to tea,' she went on, disengaging herself from the children and dispatching them to the dining-room. 'But I know why you are asking me to go to that ball. You're expecting much from it, and would like everybody to be there and have a share in it.'

'How do you know? Well, yes!'

'Oh yes, it is good to be your age,' Anna continued. 'I remember and know that blue mist, like the mist on the Swiss mountains . . . that mist which envelops everything at that blissful time when childhood is just, just coming to an end, and its immense, blissful circle turns into an ever-narrowing path, and you enter the defile gladly yet with dread, though it seems bright and beautiful. . . . Who has not passed through it?'

Kitty smiled and remained silent. 'How did she pass through it? How I should like to know her story!' thought she, recollecting the unpoetic appearance of Anna's husband Alexey Karenin.

'I know something—Stiva told me and I congratulate you. I like him very much,' Anna continued. 'I met Vronsky at the railway station.'

'Oh, was he there?' asked Kitty, blushing. 'What did Stiva tell you?'

'Stiva let it all out to me, and I shall be very pleased. . . . I travelled yesterday with Vronsky's mother,' she continued, 'and she talked about him all the time. He is her favourite son. I know how partial mothers are, but . . .'

'What did his mother tell you?'

'Oh very much! and I know he is her favourite, but anyone can see he is full of chivalry. . . . For instance she told me that he wished to give all his property to his brother, that already as a boy he had done something extraordinary, saved a woman from drowning. In a word, he is a hero,' said Anna, smiling and remembering the 200 roubles he had given away at the station.

But she did not mention the 200 roubles. For some reason she did not like to think about them. She felt that there had been something in it relating personally to her that should not have been.

'She particularly wished me to go and see her,' continued Anna. 'I shall be glad to see the old lady again, and will go to-morrow. Well, thank heaven Stiva is stopping a long time with Dolly,' she added changing the subject, and she rose, dissatisfied with something, Kitty thought.

'I was first!' 'No, I!' cried the children, who having finished their tea rushed back to Aunt Anna.

'All together!' said Anna laughing and running to meet them, and putting her arms round them she tumbled the whole heap of children—struggling and shrieking joyfully—on to the floor.

Chapter XXI

Dolly came out of her room for the grown-up people's tea. Oblonsky did not appear. He had probably left his wife's room by the other door.

'I'm afraid you will be cold upstairs,' remarked Dolly to Anna. 'I want to move you down, and then we shall be nearer to one another.'

'Oh, please don't trouble about me,' said Anna, scrutinizing Dolly's face and trying to discover whether a reconciliation had taken place.

'It will be too light for you here,' answered her sister-in-law.

'I assure you that I sleep always and anywhere like a dormouse.'

'What are you talking about?' asked Oblonsky, entering the room from his study and addressing his wife.

From his tone both Kitty and Anna gathered that a reconciliation had taken place.

'I want to move Anna downstairs, only the curtains must be changed. I shall have to do it myself, no one else can do it,' Dolly answered addressing him.

'Goodness knows if they have quite made it up,' thought Anna on hearing her tone, which was cold and calm.

'Come now, Dolly! always making difficulties,' said her husband. 'If you like I will do it all.'

'Yes, they must have made it up,' thought Anna.

'I know how you'll do it all,' answered Dolly. 'You will tell Matthew to do something that cannot be done and will go away yourself, and he will muddle everything,' and as she spoke her usual ironical smile wrinkled the corners of Dolly's mouth.

'Yes, a full, a full reconciliation, quite complete. Thank God!' thought Anna, and pleased to have been the means of bringing it about, she went up to Dolly and kissed her.

'Not at all. Why do you so despise Matthew and me?' said Oblonsky, turning to his wife with a slight smile.

All that evening Dolly maintained her usual slightly bantering manner toward her husband, and Oblonsky was contented and cheerful, but not to the extent of seeming to forget his guilt after having obtained forgiveness.

At half-past nine an unusually pleasant and happy family conversation round the Oblonskys' tea-table was disturbed by an apparently very ordinary occurrence which yet struck them all as strange. While they were talking about their mutual Petersburg acquaintances Anna rose suddenly.

'I have her photo in my album,' said she, 'and I'll show you my Serezha's too,' she added with a mother's proud smile.

For toward ten o'clock—the time when she generally said good-night to her son and often put him to bed herself before going to a ball—she felt sad at being so far from him, and, whatever they talked about, her thoughts kept returning to her curly-headed Serezha. She longed to look at his portrait and to talk about him. Seizing the first opportunity she rose and, stepping firmly and lightly, went out to fetch her album. The flight of stairs to her room went up from a landing of the well-heated front staircase. As she was coming out of the drawing-room there was a ring at the door.

'Who can it be?' asked Dolly.

'It is too early for anyone to come for me and it's late for anyone else,' said Kitty.

'Papers from the office for me, I expect,' said Oblonsky.

A footman ran up to announce the new arrival, who stood at the foot of the stairs under a lamp. Anna looked down from the landing where she stood and at once recognized Vronsky, and a strange feeling of pleasure mixed with fear suddenly stirred in her heart.

He stood in his overcoat, feeling for something in his pockets. When Anna was half-way up the top-flight, he lifted his eyes and saw her, and a look of something like embarrassment and fear came into his face. She bowed slightly and went on. She heard Oblonsky's loud voice downstairs asking him to come in, and Vronsky's low, soft voice refusing.

When Anna returned with her album he had already gone, and Oblonsky was saying that Vronsky had called to inquire about a dinner they were giving next day to a celebrity who was visiting Moscow, but that he could not be induced to come in. 'He seemed so queer,' added Oblonsky.

Kitty blushed. She thought that she alone understood why he had come to the house and why he would not come in. 'He has been to our house,' she thought, 'and not finding me in he guessed that I was here. And he would not come in because Anna is here, and he thought it too late.'

They all glanced at one another and said nothing but began examining Anna's album.

There was nothing extraordinary or strange in the fact that a man had called at half-past nine at a friend's house to ask about a dinner they were planning and that he would not come in; but it seemed strange to all of them. To Anna in particular it seemed strange and not right.

Chapter XXII

The ball had only just begun when Kitty and her mother ascended the broad staircase which was deluged with light, decorated with flowering plants, and occupied by powdered footmen in red liveries. From the ballroom as from a bee-hive came the regular sound of movement, and while they were arranging their hair and dresses before a mirror on the landing between the plants, they heard the accurate measured sounds of the orchestra violins just beginning the first waltz. A little old man, who had smoothed the grey hair on his temples before another mirror and who smelt strongly of scent, happened to jostle them on the stairs, and stepped aside in evident admiration of Kitty, whom he did not know. A beardless youth, one of those whom the old Prince Shcherbatsky called *puppies*, with a very low-cut waistcoat, straightening his white tie as he went along, bowed to them and ran past but returned to ask Kitty for a quadrille. She had given the first quadrille to Vronsky and had to give the second to this youth. An officer, buttoning his glove, stood aside at the doorway to make room for them, and smoothing his moustache looked with evident pleasure at the rosy Kitty.

Although Kitty's gown and coiffure and all her other adornments had given her much trouble and thought, she now entered the ball-room in her elaborate dress of white net over a pink slip, as easily and simply as if these bows and laces and all the details of her toilet had not cost her or her people a moment's attention, as if she had been born in this net and lace and with that high coiffure and the rose and its two leaves on the top.

When, just before entering the ball-room, her mother wished to put straight a twisted end of her sash, Kitty drew slightly back: she felt that everything on her must be naturally right and graceful and that there was no need to adjust anything.

It was one of Kitty's happy days. Her dress did not feel tight anywhere, the lace round her bodice did not slip, the bows did not crumple or come off, the pink shoes with their high curved heels did not pinch but seemed to make her feet lighter. The thick rolls of fair hair kept up as if they had grown naturally so on the little head. All three buttons on each of her long gloves, which fitted without changing the shape of her hand, fastened without coming off. The black velvet ribbon of her locket clasped her neck with unusual softness. That ribbon was charming, and when Kitty had looked at her neck in the glass at home, she felt that that ribbon was eloquent. There might be some possible doubt about anything else, but that ribbon *was* charming. Kitty smiled, here at the ball, when she caught sight of it again in the mirror. Her bare shoulders

and arms gave her a sensation as of cold marble, a feeling she liked
very much. Her eyes shone and she could not keep her rosy lips
from smiling at the consciousness of her own loveliness. Before she
had reached the light-coloured crowd of women in tulle, ribbons,
and lace, who were waiting for partners (Kitty never long formed
one of the crowd), she was already asked for the waltz and asked by
the best dancer, the leader of the dancing hierarchy, the famous
dirigeur and Master of the Ceremonies, a handsome, stately married man, George Korsunsky. He had just left the Countess Bonin,
with whom he had danced the first round of the waltz, and looking
round his domain—that is to say, a few couples who had begun to
dance—he noticed Kitty just coming in. He approached her at that
peculiar free and easy amble natural only to Masters of Ceremonies, bowed, and, without even asking her consent, put his arm round
her slim waist. She looked about for some one to hold her fan and
the mistress of the house took it from her with a smile.

'How fine that you have come in good time,' he said with his
arm round her waist. 'It's wrong of people to come so late.'

Bending her left arm she put her hand on his shoulder, and her
little feet in their pink shoes began moving quickly, lightly, and
rhythmically in time with the music, over the smooth parquet floor.

'It is a rest to waltz with you,' he said as he took the first slow
steps of the dance. 'What lightness and precision! it's delightful!'
he remarked, saying to her what he said to almost all the dancing
partners whom he really liked.

She smiled at his praise, and over his shoulder continued to
survey the ball-room. She was not a girl just come out, for whom
all faces at a ball blend into one fairy-like vision; nor was she a
girl who had been dragged from ball to ball till all the faces were
familiar to dullness. She was between those two extremes, and
though elated was able to control herself sufficiently to be observant. She saw that the élite of the company were grouped in the
left-hand corner of the room. There was the beauty Lida, Korsunsky's wife, in an impossibly low dress, and the hostess, and there
shone the bald head of Krivin who was always where the élite were;
youths who had not the courage to approach gazed in that direction,
and there Kitty's eyes found Stephen, and then the lovely head and
beautiful figure of Anna, in a black velvet dress. And *he* was there.
Kitty had not seen him since the day she had refused Levin. With
her far-sighted eyes she recognized him at once and even noticed
that he was looking at her.

'Shall we have another turn? You are not tired?' asked Korsunsky
who was a little out of breath.

'No more turns, thank you.'

'Where may I take you?'

'I believe Anna Arkadyevna Karenina is here, take me to her.'
'Wherever you please.'

And Korsunsky waltzed toward the left of the room, gradually diminishing his step and repeating 'Pardon, mesdames, pardon, pardon, mesdames,' as he steered through that sea of lace, tulle and ribbons without touching as much as a feather, and then turned his partner so suddenly that her delicate ankles in the open-work stockings appeared as her train spread out like a fan and covered Krivin's knees. Korsunsky bowed, straightened his broad shirt front, and offered Kitty his arm to conduct her to Anna. Kitty flushed, and, a little giddy, took her train off Krivin's knees and looked round for Anna.

Anna was not in lilac, the colour Kitty was so sure she ought to have worn, but in a low-necked black velvet dress which exposed her full shoulders and bosom that seemed carved out of old ivory, and her rounded arms with the very small hands. Her dress was richly trimmed with Venetian lace. In her black hair, all her own, she wore a little garland of pansies, and in her girdle, among the lace, a bunch of the same flowers. Her coiffure was very unobtrusive. The only noticeable things about it were the wilful ringlets that always escaped at her temples and on the nape of her neck and added to her beauty. Round her finely chiselled neck she wore a string of pearls.

Kitty had been seeing Anna every day and was in love with her, and had always imagined her in lilac, but seeing her in black, she felt that she had never before realized her full charm. She now saw her in a new and quite unexpected light. She now realized that Anna could not have worn lilac, and that her charm lay precisely in the fact that her personality always stood out from her dress, that her dress was never conspicuous on her. And her black velvet with rich lace was not at all conspicuous, but served only as a frame; she alone was noticeable—simple, natural, elegant and at the same time merry and animated. She was standing among that group, very erect as usual, and was talking to the master of the house with her head slightly turned toward him, when Kitty approached.

'No, I am not going to throw the first stone,' she was saying in reply to some questions, adding, with a shrug of her shoulders, 'although I cannot understand it'; and at once she turned to Kitty with a tender protecting smile. She surveyed Kitty's dress with a rapid feminine glance, and with a movement of her head, scarcely perceptible but understood by Kitty, she signified her approval of Kitty's dress and beauty.

'You even come into the room dancing,' she said.

'She is one of my most faithful helpers,' said Korsunsky, turning

to Anna whom he had not yet seen. 'The Princess helps to make a
ball gay and beautiful. Anna Arkadyevna, shall we have a turn?' he
added, stooping toward her.

'Oh, you know one another?' asked the host.

'Whom do we not know? My wife and I are like white wolves,
every one knows us,' answered Korsunsky. 'Anna Arkadyevna, just
one turn?'

'I don't dance if it is possible not to,' she said.

'But to-night it is not possible,' he rejoined.

At that moment Vronsky approached.

'Well, if it is impossible not to dance to-night, let us dance,'
she said taking no notice of Vronsky's bow and quickly putting her
hand on Korsunsky's shoulder.

'Why is she displeased with him?' thought Kitty, noticing that
Anna had intentionally taken no notice of Vronsky's bow. He came
up to Kitty, reminding her of the first quadrille and regretting that
he had not seen her for such a long time. Kitty, while gazing with
admiration at Anna waltzing, listened to him, expecting him to
ask her to waltz, but he did not do so and she glanced at him with
surprise. He flushed and hurriedly asked her to dance, but scarcely
had he put his arm round her slim waist and taken one step when
the music stopped. Kitty looked into his face which was so near her
own, and long after—for years after—that look so full of love
which she then gave him, and which met with no response from
him, cut her to the heart with tormenting shame.

'Pardon, pardon, a waltz—a waltz,' shouted Korsunsky from the
other end of the room, and seizing the first girl within reach he
himself began dancing.

Chapter XXIII

Vronsky and Kitty waltzed several times round the room and
then Kitty went to her mother, but hardly had she exchanged a
few words with the Countess Nordston before Vronsky returned to
fetch her for the first quadrille. Nothing special was said during
the quadrille: they talked in snatches about the Korsunskys, husband and wife, whom Vronsky very amusingly described as dear
forty-year-old children, and about a projected public theatre, and
only once did the conversation touch her to the quick—when he
asked her about Levin, whether he was still in Moscow, and added
that he had liked him very much. But Kitty had not expected
more from the quadrille, she waited with a clutch at her heart for
the mazurka. It seemed to her that the mazurka would settle everything. That he did not ask her for the mazurka while they were
dancing the quadrille did not disturb her. She was sure that she
would dance the mazurka with him as at previous balls, and she

refused five other partners for that dance, saying that she was already engaged. The whole ball up to the last quadrille was for Kitty an enchanted dream of gay flowers, sounds, and movements. She only stopped dancing when she felt too tired and had to ask to be allowed to rest. But while dancing the last quadrille with one of the youthful bores whom it would not do to refuse, she happened to be *vis-à-vis* [4] to Vronsky and Anna. She had not come across Anna since the beginning of the ball, and now she suddenly saw her again in a different and unexpected light. She noticed that Anna was elated with success, a feeling Kitty herself knew so well. She saw that Anna was intoxicated by the rapture she had produced. She knew the feeling and knew its symptoms, and recognized them in Anna—she saw the quivering light flashing in her eyes, the smile of happiness and elation that involuntarily curled her lips, and the graceful precision, the exactitude and lightness of her movements.

'Who is the cause?' she asked herself. 'All or only one?' And without trying to help her youthful partner who was painfully struggling to carry on the conversation the thread of which he had lost, as she mechanically obeyed the merry, loud, and authoritative orders of Korsunsky, who commanded every one to form now a *grand rond*, now a *chaîne*, she watched, and her heart sank more and more.

'No, it is not the admiration of the crowd that intoxicates her, but the rapture of one, and that one is . . . can it be *he?*'

Every time he spoke to Anna the joyful light kindled in her eyes and a smile of pleasure curved her rosy lips. She seemed to make efforts to restrain these signs of joy, but they appeared on her face of their own accord. 'But what of him?' Kitty looked at him and was filled with horror. What she saw so distinctly in the mirror of Anna's face, she saw in him. What had become of his usually quiet and firm manner and the carelessly calm expression of his face? Every time he turned toward Anna he slightly bowed his head as if he wished to fall down before her, and in his eyes there was an expression of submission and fear. 'I do not wish to offend,' his every look seemed to say, 'I only wish to save myself, but I do not know how.' His face had an expression which she had never seen before.

They talked about their mutual friends, carrying on a most unimportant conversation, but it seemed to Kitty that every word they said was deciding their and her fate. And, strange to say, though they were talking about Ivan Ivanich, who made himself so ridiculous with his French, and how Miss Eletskaya could have made a better match, yet these words were important for them, and

4. Across from.

they felt this as well as Kitty. A mist came over the ball and the whole world in Kitty's soul. Only the thorough training she had had enabled and obliged her to do what was expected of her, that is, to dance, to answer the questions put to her, to talk, and even to smile. But before the mazurka began, when the chairs were already being placed for it, and several couples moved from the small to the large ball-room, Kitty was for a moment seized with despair. She had refused five men who had asked for the mazurka and now she had no partner for it. She had not even a hope of being asked again just because she had too much success in Society for anyone to think that she was not already engaged for the dance. She must tell her mother that she was feeling ill, and go home, but she had not the strength to do it. She felt herself quite broken-hearted.

She went to the far end of a little drawing-room and sank into an easy chair. Her light skirt stood out like a cloud round her slight body; one thin bare girlish arm dropped listlessly and sank into the pink folds of her tunic; the other hand held a fan with which she rapidly fanned her flushed face. But although she seemed like a butterfly just settled on a blade of grass and ready at any moment to flutter and spread its rainbow wings, her heart was crushed with terrible despair.

'But perhaps I am mistaken, perhaps it was nothing of the kind?' And she again recalled all that she had witnessed.

'Kitty, what does this mean?' asked the Countess Nordston, coming up inaudibly over the carpet. 'I don't understand it.'

Kitty's nether lip trembled, and she rose quickly.

'Kitty, are you not dancing the mazurka?'

'No, no,' said Kitty in a voice tremulous with tears.

'He asked her for the mazurka in my presence,' said the Countess, knowing that Kitty would understand whom she meant by 'him' and 'her.' 'She asked, "Are you not dancing with the Princess Shcherbatsky?" '

'Oh! it's all the same to me!' replied Kitty. No one but herself understood her situation, because no one knew that she had only a few days ago refused a man whom she perhaps loved, and refused him because she trusted another.

The Countess Nordston, who was engaged to Korsunsky for the mazurka, told him to ask Kitty instead.

Kitty danced in the first pair, and luckily for her she was not obliged to talk, because Korsunsky ran about all the time giving orders in his domain. Vronsky and Anna sat almost opposite to her. And she saw them with her far-sighted eyes, she saw them close by, too, when they met in the dance, and the more she saw of them, the surer she was that the blow had fallen. She saw that they felt as if they were alone in that crowded ball-room. On

Vronsky's face, usually so firm and self-possessed, she noticed that expression of bewilderment and submission which had so surprised her—an expression like that of an intelligent dog when it feels guilty.

Anna smiled—and the smile passed on to him; she became thoughtful—and he became serious. Some supernatural power attracted Kitty's eyes to Anna's face. She looked charming in her simple black dress; her full arms with the bracelets, her firm neck with the string of pearls round it, her curly hair now disarranged, every graceful movement of her small feet and hands, her handsome animated face,—everything about her was enchanting, but there was something terrible and cruel in her charm.

Kitty admired her even more than before, and suffered more and more. She felt herself crushed and her face expressed it.

When Vronsky happened to knock against her as they danced, he did not at once recognize her, so changed was she.

'A delightful ball,' he remarked, in order to say something.

'Yes,' she replied.

In the middle of the mazurka, performing a complicated figure newly-invented by Korsunsky, Anna stepped into the middle of the room and chose two men and two ladies, one of whom was Kitty, to join her. Kitty, as she moved toward Anna, gazed at her with fear. Anna half-closed her eyes to look at Kitty, smiled and pressed her hand, but noticing that Kitty only responded to her smile by a look of surprise and despair, she turned away from her and talked cheerfully with the other lady.

'Yes, there is something strange, satanic, and enchanting about her,' thought Kitty.

Anna did not wish to stay to supper, but the master of the house tried to persuade her to do so.

'Come, Anna Arkadyevna,' began Korsunsky, drawing her bare arm under his, 'I have such a good idea for a cotillion—*Un bijou.*' [5] And he moved slowly on, trying to draw her with him. Their host smiled approvingly.

'No, I won't stay,' answered Anna, smiling, and despite her smile Korsunsky and the host understood from the firm tone of her voice that she would not stay.

'No, as it is I have danced more in Moscow at your one ball than I danced the whole winter in Petersburg,' said Anna, looking round at Vronsky who stood beside her. 'I must rest before my journey.'

'So you really are going to-morrow?' said Vronsky.

'Yes, I think so,' Anna replied as if surprised at the boldness of his question; but the uncontrollable radiance of her eyes and her smile set him on fire as she spoke the words.

Anna did not stay for supper, but went away.

5. A jewel.

*brother's quest
for spirituality*

Chapter XXIV

'Yes, there is certainly something objectionable and repellent about me,' thought Levin after leaving the Shcherbatskys, as he walked toward his brother's lodgings. 'I do not get on with other people. They say it is pride! No, I am not even proud. If I had any pride, I should not have put myself into such a position.' And he pictured to himself Vronsky, happy, kind, clever, calm, and certainly never placing himself in such a terrible position as he, Levin, had been in that evening. 'Yes, she was bound to choose him. It had to be so, and I have no cause to complain of anyone or anything. It was my own fault. What right had I to imagine that she would wish to unite her life with mine? Who and what am I? A man of no account, wanted by no one and of no use to anyone.' And he remembered his brother Nicholas, and kept his mind gladly on that memory. 'Is he not right that everything on earth is evil and horrid? And have we judged brother Nicholas fairly? Of course, from Prokofy's point of view, who saw him in a ragged coat and tipsy, he is a despicable fellow; but I know him from another side. I know his soul, and know that we resemble one another. And yet I, instead of looking him up, dined out and came here.' Levin went up to a lamp-post and read his brother's address which he had in his pocket-book, and then hired a sledge. On the long way to his brother's he recalled all the events he knew of Nicholas's life. He recalled how despite the ridicule of his fellow-students his brother had lived like a monk while at the University and for a year after, strictly observing all the religious rites, attending service, fasting, avoiding all pleasures and especially women; and then how he suddenly broke loose, became intimate with the vilest people and gave himself up to unbridled debauchery. He remembered how his brother had brought a boy from the country to educate, and in a fit of anger had so beaten the lad that proceedings were commenced against him for causing bodily harm. He remembered an affair with a sharper to whom his brother had lost money, and whom he had first given a promissory note and then prosecuted on a charge of fraud. (That was when his brother Sergius had paid the money for him.) Then he remembered the night which Nicholas had spent in the police cells for disorderly conduct, and the disgraceful proceedings he had instigated against his brother Sergius Ivanich, whom he accused of not having paid out to him his share of his mother's fortune: and lastly, the time when his brother took an official appointment in one of the Western Provinces and was there arrested for assaulting an Elder. . . . . It was all very disgusting, but to Levin it did not seem nearly so disgusting as it must have seemed to those who did not know Nicholas, nor his whole story, nor his heart.

Levin remembered that when Nicholas was passing through his pious stage of fasting, visiting monks, and going to church; when he was seeking in religion for help to curb his passionate nature, not only did no one encourage him, but every one, and Levin among them, made fun of him. He was teased and called 'Noah' and 'monk,' and then when he broke loose no one helped him, but all turned away from him with horror and disgust.

Levin felt that his brother Nicholas, in his soul, in the innermost depths of his soul, despite the depravity of his life, was no worse than those who despised him. It was not his fault that he was born with his ungovernable temper, and with a cramped mind. He always wished to do right. 'I will tell him everything, I will get him to tell me everything. I will show him that I love and therefore understand him,' Levin decided in his mind, as toward eleven o'clock he drove up to the hotel of which he had the address.

'Upstairs, Nos. 12 and 13,' said the hall porter in reply to Levin's question.

'Is he in?'

'I expect so.'

The door of No. 12 was ajar, and from within, visible in the streak of light, issued dense fumes of inferior and weak tobacco. Levin heard a stranger's voice, but knew at once that his brother was there, for he heard him coughing.

As he entered the doorway the stranger's voice was saying: 'It all depends on how intelligently and rationally the affair is conducted.'

Constantine Levin glanced into the room, which was beyond a partition, and saw that the speaker was a young man with an enormous head of hair, who wore a workman's coat, and that a young, pock-marked woman in a woollen dress without collar or cuffs [6] was sitting on the sofa. He could not see his brother, and his heart sank painfully at the thought that Nicholas lived among such strange people. No one noticed him, and, as he took off his goloshes, he overheard what the man in the workman's coat was saying. He was talking about some commercial enterprise.

'Oh, let the privileged classes go to the devil,' said his brother's voice, with a cough.

'Masha, get us some supper and bring the wine if any is left, or send for some.'

The woman rose, came out from behind the partition, and saw Constantine.

'Here is a gentleman, Nicholas Dmitrich,' she said.

'Whom do you want?' said Nicholas Levin's voice angrily.

'It is I,' answered Constantine Levin, coming forward into the

6. At that time better-class women always wore something white round their necks and wrists.

lamp-light.

'Who's I?' said the voice of Nicholas Levin still more angrily.

Constantine heard how he rose hurriedly and caught against something, and then in the doorway before him he saw the familiar yet ever strange figure of his brother, wild, sickly, gigantic, lean, and round-shouldered, with large, frightened eyes.

He was even more emaciated than three years before, when Constantine Levin had last seen him. He was wearing a short coat, and his hands and broad bones appeared more immense than ever. His hair was thinner, but the same straight moustache covered his lips; and the same eyes with their peculiar, naïve gaze looked out at the new-comer.

'Ah! Kostya!' he said suddenly, recognizing his brother, and his eyes lit up with joy. But at the same moment he turned to look at the young man and convulsively jerked his head and neck as if his necktie were strangling him, a movement Levin knew well, and quite another expression—a wild, suffering, and cruel look—settled on his haggard face.

'I wrote both to you and to Sergius Ivanich that I do not know you and do not wish to know you. What is it? What do you want?' He was not at all as Constantine had imagined him. Constantine when thinking of him had forgotten the most trying and worst part of his character, that which made intercourse with him so difficult; but now when he saw his face, and especially that convulsive movement of his head, he remembered it all.

'I do not want anything of you specially,' he answered meekly; 'I have simply come to see you.'

His brother's timidity obviously softened Nicholas, whose lips quivered.

'Ah! You have come just for that?' he said. 'Well, come in, sit down. Will you have some supper? Masha, get supper for three. No, wait a little. Do you know who this is?' he added, turning to his brother and pointing to the man in the workman's coat. 'It is Mr. Kritsky, my friend ever since my Kiev days, a very remarkable fellow. Of course, the police are after him, because he is not a scoundrel.'

And he glanced round at everybody present as was his way. Seeing that the woman in the doorway was about to go out he shouted to her: 'Wait, I told you,' and in the awkward and blundering manner familiar to Constantine, he again looked round at everybody, and began to tell his brother about Kritsky: how he had been expelled from the University because he had started a society to help the poorer students, and also Sunday schools, and how he had afterwards taught in an elementary school, and had been turned out from that too, and had then been tried on some charge or other.

'You were at Kiev University?' Constantine Levin asked Kritsky, in order to break the awkward silence that followed.

'Yes, at Kiev,' Kritsky replied with an angry frown.

'And this woman,' said Nicholas Levin, interrupting him, and pointing to her, 'is my life's companion, Mary Nikolaevna; I took her out of a bad house . . .' and as he said this he again jerked his neck. 'But I love and respect her and beg all those who wish to know me,' he added, raising his voice and scowling, 'to love and respect her. She is just the same to me as a wife, just the same. So now you know whom you have to deal with, and if you fear you will be degraded—there is the door.'

And again his eyes glanced questioningly around.

'Why should I be degraded? I don't understand.'

'Well, Masha, order supper for three, with vodka and wine. . . . No, wait. No, never mind. . . . You may go.'

Chapter XXV

'So you see, . . .' Nicholas Levin continued with an effort, wrinkling his brow and twitching.

He evidently found it hard to decide what to say and to do.

'Do you see . . .' he pointed to a bundle of iron rods tied together with string, in a corner of the room. 'Do you see that? It is the beginning of a new business we are undertaking. The business is to be a Productive Association . . .'

Constantine hardly listened. He kept glancing at his brother's sickly, consumptive face, and felt more and more sorry for him, nor could he force himself to pay attention to what Nicholas was telling him about the Association. He realized that this Association was merely an anchor to save his brother from self-contempt. Nicholas Levin continued speaking:

'You know that capitalism oppresses the workers. Our workmen the peasants bear the whole burden of labour, but are so placed that, work as they may, they cannot escape from their degrading condition. All the profits on their labour, by which they might better their condition, give themselves some leisure, and consequently gain some education, all this surplus value is taken away by the capitalists. And our society has so shaped itself that the more the people work the richer the merchants and landowners will become, while the people will remain beasts of burden for ever. And this system must be changed,' he concluded, with an inquiring look at his brother.

'Yes, of course,' said Constantine, looking intently at the hectic flush which had appeared on his brother's face below its prominent cheek bones.

'And so we are starting a Locksmiths' Association, in which all the products and the profits and, above all, the instruments of production will be common property.'

'Where will the business be?' asked Constantine.

'In the village of Vozdrema, Kazan Government.'

'Why in a village? It seems to me there is plenty of work to do in the country as it is. Why start a Locksmiths' Association there?'

'Because the peasants are still just as much slaves as they used to be, and that is why you and Sergius Ivanich don't like it when anyone wishes to deliver them from their slavery,' replied Nicholas Levin, irritated by Constantine's objections.

Constantine sighed and at the same time looked round the room which was dismal and dirty. The sigh seemed to irritate Nicholas still more.

'I know your aristocratic outlook and Sergius Ivanich's. I know that he uses all the powers of his mind to justify the existing evils.'

'But why talk about Sergius Ivanich?' said Levin with a smile.

'Sergius Ivanich? This is why!' suddenly shouted Nicholas at the mention of the name. 'This is why. . . . But what is the good of talking? One thing only. . . . Why have you come here? You despise it, well, that is all right—then go away. Go, go in God's name!' he exclaimed, rising from his chair. 'Go, go!'

'I do not despise it at all,' Constantine replied meekly. 'I do not even dispute it.'

Meanwhile Mary Nikolaevna had come back. Nicholas gave her an angry look. She hurried up to him and said something in a whisper.

'I am not well and have grown irritable,' said Nicholas, breathing heavily and quieting down. 'And you talk to me about Sergius Ivanich and his article. It is such rubbish, such humbug, such self-deception. What can a man write about justice, who does not understand it?'

'Have you read his article?' he said, turning to Kritsky again, sitting down to the table and clearing away from it a heap of half-filled cigarettes to make room.

'I have not read it,' said Kritsky morosely, evidently not wishing to join in the conversation.

'Why not?' irritably answered Nicholas, still addressing Kritsky.

'Because I consider it unnecessary to waste time on it.'

'What do you mean? May I ask how you knew it would waste your time? That article is incomprehensible to many; I mean it is above them. But it is a different matter with me. I see through his thought, and therefore know why it is weak.'

Every one remained silent. Kritsky rose and took up his hat.

'Don't you want any supper? Well, good-bye. Come to-morrow and bring the locksmith.'

As soon as Kritsky had gone out, Nicholas smiled and winked. 'He also is not much good,' he remarked. 'I can see . . .' But at that moment Kritsky called him from outside the door.

'What do you want now?' said Nicholas and went out into the passage.

Left alone with Mary Nikolaevna, Levin spoke to her.

'Have you been long with my brother?' he asked.

'Yes, it is the second year now. His health is very bad, he drinks too much,' she said.

'Really—what does he drink?'

'He drinks vodka, and it is bad for him.'

'Much vodka?' whispered Levin.

'Yes,' she said looking timidly toward the door, just as Nicholas returned.

'What were you talking about?' he asked frowning and looking from one to the other with frightened eyes. 'What was it?'

'Nothing,' replied Levin in confusion.

'If you do not wish to tell me, do as you please. Only you have no business to talk to her. She's a street girl, and you are a gentleman,' he muttered, jerking his neck. 'You, I see, have examined and weighed everything here, and regard my errors with compassion,' he continued, again raising his voice.

'Nicholas Dmitrich, Nicholas Dmitrich,' whispered Mary Nikolaevna, again approaching him.

'Well, all right, all right! . . . and how about supper? Ah, here it is,' he said noticing a waiter who was bringing in a tray. 'Here, here, put it down here,' he said crossly, and at once poured out a wine-glass full of vodka and drank it greedily. 'Have a drink, will you?' he said to his brother, brightening up at once. 'Well, we've had enough of Sergius Ivanich. I am glad to see you, anyhow. Whatever one may say, after all, we are not strangers. Come, have a drink. Tell me what you are doing,' he continued, greedily chewing a crust of bread and filling himself another glass. 'How are you getting on?'

'I am living alone in the country, as I did before, and I look after the farming,' answered Constantine, observing with horror how greedily his brother ate and drank, and trying not to let it be seen that he noticed it.

'Why don't you get married?'

'I had not the chance,' replied Constantine blushing.

'Why not? For me all that is over. I have spoilt my life. I have said, and still say, that if I had been given my share of the property when I wanted it, everything would have been different.'

Constantine hastened to change the subject. 'Do you know that your Vanyusha is now a clerk in my office at Pokrovsk?' he said.

Nicholas jerked his head and grew thoughtful.

'Yes, tell me what is happening in Pokrovsk. Is the house still standing, and the birch trees, and our schoolroom? And is Philip the gardener really still living? How well I remember the garden-house and the sofa! . . . Mind, don't change anything in the house, but get married soon and set things going again as they used to be. Then I will come to you if you have a good wife.'

'Come to me at once,' said Levin. 'How well we might settle down there!'

'I would come if I were sure I should not find Sergius Ivanich there.'

'You won't find him there. I live quite apart from him.'

'Still, say what you will, you must choose between him and me,' said Nicholas with a timid look at his brother.

His timidity touched Constantine.

'If you want my full confession about it, I will tell you that I take no side in your quarrel with Sergius Ivanich. You are both to blame. You more in external matters and he more in essential ones.'

'Ah, ah! Then you have grasped it, you have grasped it!' joyfully exclaimed Nicholas.

'But personally, if you care to know it, I value your friendship more because . . .'

'Why, why?'

Constantine could not tell him that it was because Nicholas was unfortunate and needed friendship. But Nicholas understood that he meant just that, and frowning, again, took hold of the vodka bottle.

'Enough, Nicholas Dmitrich!' said Mary Nikolaevna, stretching out her plump arm with its bare wrist to take the bottle.

'Let go! Leave me alone! I'll thrash you!' shouted he.

Mary Nikolaevna gave a mild, kindly smile, which evoked one from Nicholas, and she took away the bottle.

'Do you think she doesn't understand?' said Nicholas. 'She understands it all better than any of us. There really is something good and sweet about her.'

'You were never in Moscow before?' Constantine asked very politely, just in order to say something.

'Don't speak to her in that way. It frightens her. No one but the magistrate, when she was tried for an attempt to escape from the house of ill-fame, ever spoke to her so politely. . . . Oh heavens, how senseless everything is in this world!' he suddenly exclaimed. 'All these new institutions, these magistrates, these Zemstvos. . . . What a confusion it all is!'

And he began to relate all his encounters with these new institutions.

Constantine Levin listened to him, and the condemnation of the social institutions, which he shared with him and had often expressed, was unpleasant to him when he heard it from his brother's lips.

'We shall understand it better in the next world,' he said playfully.

'In the next world? Ah, I do dislike that next world,' said Nicholas, fixing his wild, frightened eyes on his brother's face. 'One would think that to leave all these abominations, these muddles (one's own and other people's), would be good, yet I fear death—I fear it terribly.' He shuddered. 'Do drink something. Would you like some champagne? Or let us go out somewhere or other. Let us go to the Gipsies! Do you know I have become fond of the gipsies and the Russian folk-songs?'

His speech began to grow confused and he jumped from one subject to another. With Masha's help Constantine succeeded in persuading him not to go out anywhere, and got him into bed quite tipsy.

Masha promised to write to Constantine in case of need, and to try to persuade Nicholas to go and live with him.

Chapter XXVI

Next morning Constantine Levin left Moscow and toward evening he reached home. On his way back in the train he talked with his fellow-passengers, about politics and the new railway, and felt oppressed, just as in Moscow, by the confusion of the views expressed, by discontent with himself and a vague sense of shame. But when he got out of the train at his station and by the dim light from the station windows saw his one-eyed coachman, Ignat, with his coat-collar turned up, and his sledge with its carpet-lined back, his horses with their plaited tails, and the harness with its rings and tassels, and when Ignat, while still putting the luggage into the sledge, began telling him the village news: how the contractor had come, and Pava had calved,—Levin felt that the confusion was beginning to clear away and his shame and self-dissatisfaction to pass. He felt this at the mere sight of Ignat and the horses; but when he had put on the sheepskin coat that had been brought for him and, well wrapped up, had seated himself in the sledge and started homeward, turning over in his mind the orders he would give about the work on the estate, and as he watched the side horse (once a saddle-horse that had been overridden, a spirited animal from the Don), he saw what had befallen him in quite a different light. He felt that he was himself, and did not wish to be anyone else. He only wished now to be better than he had been formerly. First of all he decided that he would no longer hope for the exceptional happiness which marriage was to have given him, and consequently he would not underrate the present as he had done. Secondly, he would never again allow himself to be carried away by passion, the repulsive memory of which had so tormented him when he was making up his mind to propose. Then, remembering his brother Nicholas, he determined that he would never allow himself to forget him again, but would watch over him, keep him in sight, and be ready to help when things went hard with him. And he felt that that would be soon. Then his brother's talk about communism, which he had taken lightly at the time, now made him think. He considered an entire change of economic conditions nonsense; but he had always felt the injustice of his superfluities compared with the peasant's poverty, and now decided, in order to feel himself quite justified, that though he had always worked hard and lived simply, he would in future work still more and allow himself still less luxury. And it all seemed to him so easy to carry out that he was in a pleasant reverie the whole way home, and it was with cheerful hopes for a new and better life that he reached his house toward nine o'clock in the evening.

A light fell on the snow-covered space in front of the house from the windows of the room of his old nurse, Agatha Mikhaylovna, who now acted as his housekeeper. She had not yet gone to bed, and Kuzma, whom she had roused, came running out barefoot and still half-asleep into the porch. Laska, a setter bitch, ran out too, almost throwing Kuzma off his feet, and whined and rubbed herself against Levin's knees, jumping up and wishing but not daring to put her front paws on his chest.

'You have soon come back, sir,' said Agatha Mikhaylovna.

'I was home-sick, Agatha Mikhaylovna. Visiting is all very well, but "there is no place like home," ' he replied, and went into his study.

A candle just brought in gradually lit up the study and its familiar details became visible: the stag's horns, the book-shelves, the looking-glass, the hot-air aperture of the stove with its brass lid, which had long been in need of repair, his father's couch, the large table on which were an open volume, a broken ash-tray, and an exercise-book in his handwriting. When he saw all this, he was overcome by a momentary doubt of the possibility of starting the new life of which he had been dreaming on his way. All these traces of his old life seemed to seize hold of him and say, 'No, you will not escape us and will not be different, but will remain such as you have been: full of doubts; full of dissatisfaction with yourself, and of vain attempts at improvement followed by failures, and continual hopes of the happiness which has escaped you and is impossible for you.'

That was what the things said, but another voice within his soul was saying that one must not submit to the past and that a man can make what he will of himself. And obeying the latter voice he went to the corner where two thirty-six pound dumb-bells lay and began doing gymnastic exercises with them to invigorate himself. He heard a creaking of steps at the door and hurriedly put down the dumb-bells.

His steward entered and said that, 'the Lord be thanked,' everything was all right, but that the buckwheat had burned in the new drying kiln. This news irritated Levin. The new kiln had been built and partly invented by him. The steward had always been against the new kiln, and now proclaimed with suppressed triumph that the buckwheat had got burnt. Levin felt quite certain that if it had been burnt it was only because the precautions about which he had given instructions over and over again had been neglected. He was vexed, and he reprimanded the steward. But the steward had one important and pleasant event to report. Pava, his best and most valuable cow, bought at the cattle-show, had calved.

'Kuzma, bring me my sheep-skin. And you tell them to bring a lantern. I will go and have a look at her,' he said to the steward.

The sheds where the most valuable cattle were kept were just behind the house. Crossing the yard past the heap of snow by the lilac bush, he reached the shed. There was a warm steaming smell of manure when the frozen door opened, and the cows, astonished at the unaccustomed light of the lantern, began moving on their clean straw. Levin saw the broad, smooth black-and-white back of a Dutch cow. The bull, Berkut, with a ring through his nose, was lying down, and almost rose up, but changed his mind and only snorted a couple of times as they passed by. The red beauty Pava, enormous as a hippopotamus, turned her back, hiding her calf from the new-comers and sniffing at it.

Levin entered the stall, examined Pava, and lifted the red-mottled calf. Pava, becoming excited, was about to low, but quieted down when Levin moved the calf toward her, and sighing heavily began licking it with her rough tongue. The calf fumbled about, pushing its nose under its mother's belly and swinging its little tail.

'Show a light here, Theodore, here,' said Levin, examining the calf. 'Like its mother,' he said, 'although the colour is its father's; very fine, big-boned and deep-flanked. Vasily Fëdorich, isn't she fine?' he said, turning to the steward, and quite forgiving him for the buckwheat under the influence of his satisfaction about the calf.

'Whom could she take after, not to be good? Simon, the contractor, came the day after you left. We shall have to employ him,

Constantine Dmitrich,' said the steward. 'I told you about the machine.'

This one question led Levin back to all the details of his farming, which was on a large and elaborate scale. He went straight from the cow-shed to the office, and after talking things over with the steward and with Simon the contractor, he returned to the house and went straight upstairs to the drawing-room.

Chapter XXVII

It was a large old-fashioned house, and though only Levin was living in it, he used and heated the whole of it. He knew this to be foolish and even wrong, and contrary to his new plans, but this house was a whole world to Levin. It was the world in which his father and mother had lived and died. They had lived a life which appeared to him ideally perfect, and which he had dreamed of renewing with a wife and family of his own.

Levin could scarcely remember his mother. His conception of her was to him a sacred memory, and in his imagination his future wife was to be a repetition of the enchanting and holy ideal of womanhood that his mother had been.

He could not imagine the love of woman without marriage, and even pictured to himself a family first and then the woman who would give him the family. His views on marriage therefore did not resemble those of most of his acquaintances, for whom marriage was only one of many social affairs; for Levin it was the chief thing in life, on which the whole happiness of life depended. And now he had to renounce it.

When he had settled in the arm-chair in the little drawing-room where he always had his tea, and Agatha Mikhaylovna had brought it in for him and had sat down at the window with her usual remark, 'I will sit down, sir!' he felt that, strange to say, he had not really forgotten his dreams and that he could not live without them. With *her*, or with another, they would come true. He read his book, and followed what he read, stopping now and then to listen to Agatha Mikhaylovna, who chattered indefatigably; and at the same time various pictures of farming and future family life arose disconnectedly in his mind. He felt that in the depth of his soul something was settling down, adjusting and composing itself.

He listened to Agatha Mikhaylovna's talk of how Prokhor had forgotten the Lord, was spending on drink the money Levin had given him to buy a horse with, and had beaten his wife nearly to death; he listened and read, and remembered the whole sequence of thoughts raised by what he was reading. It was a book of Tyndall's on heat. He recalled his disapproval of Tyndall's self-conceit concerning the cleverness of his experiments, and his lack of a philosophic outlook. And suddenly the joyous thought came uppermost: 'In two years' time I shall have two Dutch cows in my herd and Pava herself may still be alive; there will be twelve cows by Berkut, and these three to crown all—splendid!' He returned to his book. 'Well, let us grant that electricity and heat are one and the same, but can we substitute the one quantity for the other in solving an equation? No. Then what of it? The connection between all the forces of nature can be felt instinctively without all that. . . . It will be especially good when Pava's calf is already a red-mottled cow, and the whole herd in which these three will be . . . ! Splendid! To go out with my wife and visitors and meet the herd. . . . My wife will say: "Constantine and I reared this calf like a baby." "How can you be interested in these things?" the visitor will ask. "All that interests him interests me . . ." But who is *she*?' and he remembered what had happened in Moscow. 'Well, what is to be done? . . . It is not my fault. But now everything will be on new lines. It is nonsense to say that life will prevent it, that the past prevents it. I must struggle to live a better, a far better, life.' He lifted his head and pondered. Old Laska, who had not yet quite digested her joy at her master's return and had run out to bark in the yard, now came back, bringing a smell of fresh air with her into the room and, wagging her tail, she approached him and putting her head under his hand whined plaintively, asking to be patted.

'She all but speaks,' said Agatha Mikhaylovna. 'She is only a dog, but she understands that her master has come back feeling depressed.'

'Why depressed?'

'Oh, don't I see? I ought to understand gentlefolk by this time. I have grown up among them from a child. Never mind, my dear, as long as you have good health and a clean conscience!'

Levin looked at her intently, surprised that she knew so well what was in his mind.

'Shall I bring you a little more tea?' she said and went out with his cup.

Laska kept on pushing her head under his hand. He patted her a little, and she curled herself up at his feet with her head on her outstretched hind paw. And to show that all was now well and satisfactory, she slightly opened her mouth, smacked her sticky lips, and drawing them more closely over her old teeth lay still in blissful peace. Levin attentively watched this last movement of hers.

'And it is just the same with me!' he said to himself. 'It is just the same with me. What does it matter. . . . All is well.'

Chapter XXVIII

Early in the morning after the ball Anna sent a telegram to her husband to say that she was leaving Moscow that same evening.

'Really I must, I must go,' she said, explaining her altered plans to her sister-in-law in a tone suggesting that she had suddenly remembered so many things she had to do that it was not even possible to enumerate them all. 'Really I had better go to-day.'

Stephen Oblonsky was not dining at home, but promised to be back at seven to see his sister off.

Kitty also had not come, but had sent a note to say that she had a headache. Dolly and Anna dined alone with the children and their English governess. Whether it is that children are inconstant or that they are sensitive and felt that Anna was not the same person to-day as she had been that other day when they had been so fond of her, and that she no longer took any interest in them, at any rate they suddenly left off playing with their aunt and loving her, and were not at all concerned about her leaving. Anna spent the whole morning preparing for her departure: writing notes to her Moscow acquaintances, making up accounts, and packing. It seemed to Dolly that Anna was not at ease in her mind, but in a state of anxiety that Dolly knew well from her own experience, a state which does not come on without a cause, but generally hides dissatisfaction with oneself. After dinner Anna went to her room to dress, and Dolly followed her.

'How strange you are to-day!' said Dolly.

'I? Do you think so? I am not strange, but wicked. It sometimes happens to me. I feel ready to cry. It is very silly, but it will pass,' said Anna hurriedly, and she bent her flushed face over the tiny bag into which she was packing a night-cap and some lawn handkerchiefs. Her eyes shone peculiarly and kept filling with tears. 'I did not want to leave Petersburg, and now I do not want to leave here.'

'You came here and did a good action,' said Dolly, scrutinizing her attentively.

Anna looked at her with her eyes wet with tears.

'Do not say that, Dolly. I have done and could do nothing. I often wonder why people conspire to spoil me. What have I done and what could I do? There was enough love in your heart to forgive . . .'

'But for you, God only knows what would have happened! How lucky you are, Anna,' said Dolly. 'Everything in your soul is clear and good.'

'Every one has a skeleton in their cupboard, as the English say.'

'What skeletons have you? Everything about you is so clear.'

'I have one!' said Anna, and unexpectedly following her tears, a sly, humorous smile puckered her lips.

'Well, at least your skeleton is a funny one and not a dismal one,' said Dolly smiling.

'No, it is a dismal one. Do you know why I am going to-day and not to-morrow? This is a confession of something that oppresses me, and I want to make it to you,' said Anna, determinedly throwing herself back in an arm-chair and looking straight into Dolly's eyes.

And to her surprise Dolly saw that Anna was blushing to her ears and to the curly black locks on her neck.

'Do you know,' continued Anna, 'why Kitty did not come to dinner? She is jealous of me. I have spoiled . . . I mean I was the cause of the ball being a torture instead of a pleasure to her. But really, really I was not to blame, or only a very little,' she said, drawling out the word 'very' in a high-pitched voice.

'Oh how like Stiva you said that,' remarked Dolly laughing.

Anna was annoyed.

'Oh no, no I am not Stiva,' she said frowning. 'The reason I have told you is that I do not even for a moment allow myself to distrust myself.'

But at the moment when she uttered these words she knew they were untrue: she not only distrusted herself but was agitated by the thought of Vronsky, and was leaving sooner than she had intended only that she might not meet him again.

'Yes, Stiva told me that you danced the mazurka with him, and that he . . .'

'You cannot think how queerly it came about. I only thought of arranging the match, and—suddenly it all came out quite differently. . . . Perhaps against my own will I . . .'

She blushed and stopped.

'Oh, they feel that at once!' said Dolly.

'But I should be in despair if there was anything serious in it on his side,' Anna interrupted her. 'I am sure that it will all be forgotten, and Kitty will no longer hate me.'

'Well, do you know, Anna, to tell you the truth, I am not very anxious that Kitty should marry him. It is much better that it should come to nothing if Vronsky is capable of falling in love with you in a day.'

'Oh, my goodness! How stupid it would be,' said Anna, and again a deep flush of pleasure suffused her face at hearing the thought that occupied her mind expressed in words. 'So I am going away having made an enemy of Kitty, of whom I am so fond. Oh, what a darling she is! But you will put it right? Eh, Dolly?'

Dolly could hardly repress a smile. She was fond of Anna, but it was pleasant to find that she too had a weakness.

'An enemy? That is impossible.'

'I should so like you all to love me as I love you; and now I love you still more,' said Anna with tears in her eyes. 'Oh dear, how silly I am to-day.'

She dabbed her face with her handkerchief, and began to dress.

Oblonsky, smelling of wine and cigars, with his face red and happy, came in late, just as she was about to start.

Anna's emotion had spread to Dolly, who as she embraced her sister-in-law for the last time whispered: 'Remember that I love and always shall love you as my best friend!'

'I do not know why you should,' said Anna, kissing her and trying to hide her tears.

'You understood and understand me. Good-bye, my sweet one!'

Chapter XXIX

'Well, that's all over, thank Heaven!' was Anna's first thought when she had taken leave of her brother, who stood to the last moment obstructing the entrance to the railway carriage.

She sat down beside her maid Annushka, and peered round the dimly-lit sleeping compartment. 'Thank Heaven, to-morrow I shall see Serezha and Alexey Alexandrovich again, and my good accustomed life will go on as of old.'

With the same preoccupied mind she had had all that day, Anna prepared with pleasure and great deliberation for the journey. With her deft little hands she unlocked her red bag, took out a small pillow which she placed on her knees, and locked the bag again; then she carefully wrapped up her feet and sat down comfortably. An invalid lady was already going to bed. Two other ladies began talking to Anna. One, a fat old woman, while wrapping up her feet, remarked upon the heating of the carriage. Anna said a few words in answer, but not foreseeing anything interesting from the conversation asked her maid to get out her reading-lamp, fixed it to the arm of her seat, and took a paper-knife and an English novel from her handbag. At first she could not read. For a while the bustle of people moving about disturbed her, and when the train had finally started it was impossible not to listen to the noises; then there was the snow, beating against the window on her left, to which it stuck, and the sight of the guard, who passed through the carriage closely wrapped up and covered with snow on one side; also the conversation about the awful snow-storm which was raging outside distracted her attention. And so it went on and on: the same jolting and knocking, the same beating of the snow on the window-pane, the same rapid changes from steaming heat to cold, and back again to heat, the gleam of the same faces through the semi-darkness, and the same voices,—but at last Anna began to read and to follow what she read. Annushka was already dozing, her broad hands, with a hole in one of the gloves, holding the red bag on her lap. Anna read and understood, but it was unpleasant to read, that is to say, to follow the reflection of other people's lives. She was too eager to live herself. When she read how the heroine of the novel nursed a sick man, she wanted to move about the sick-room with noiseless footsteps; when she read of a member of Parliament making a speech, she wished to make that speech; when she read how Lady Mary rode to hounds, teased the bride, and astonished everybody by her boldness—she wanted to do it herself. But there was nothing to be done, so she forced herself to read, while her little hand toyed with the smooth paper-knife.

The hero of the novel had nearly attained to his English happiness of a baronetcy and an estate, and Anna wanted to go to the estate with him, when she suddenly felt that he must have been ashamed, and that she was ashamed of the same thing,—but what was he ashamed of? 'What am I ashamed of?' she asked herself with indignant surprise. She put down her book, leaned back, and clasped the paper-knife tightly in both hands. There was nothing to be ashamed of. She called up all her Moscow memories. They were all good and pleasant. She recalled the ball and Vronsky and his humble, enamoured gaze, and their relations with one another; there was nothing to be ashamed of. And yet at that very point of her recollections when she remembered Vronsky, the feeling of shame grew stronger and some inner voice seemed to say to her, 'warm, very warm, burning!' 'Well, what of it?' she finally said to herself with decision, changing her position on the seat. 'What does it signify? Am I afraid to look straight at it? What of it? Just as if there existed, or could exist, between me and this officer-lad any relations differing from those with other acquaintances.' She smiled disdainfully and again took up her book; but now she absolutely could not understand what she was reading. She passed her paper-knife over the window-pane, then pressed its cold smooth surface against her cheek and almost laughed aloud, suddenly overcome with unreasoning joy. She felt that her nerves were being stretched like strings drawn tighter and tighter round pegs. She felt her eyes opening wider, her fingers and toes nervously moving, and something inside her stopping her breath, and all the forms and sounds in the swaying semi-darkness around struck her with unusual vividness. Momentary doubts kept occurring in her mind as to whether the train was moving forwards or backwards, or standing still. Was it Annushka who was sitting beside her, or a stranger? 'And am I here, myself? Am I myself or another?' She was afraid of giving way to these delirious thoughts. Something seemed to draw her to them, but she had the power to give way to them or to resist. To get over it she rose, threw off her wrap, and took off the cape of her coat. She came to her senses for a moment, and knew that the lean peasant in the long nankin coat with a button missing who had come into the compartment was the carriage stoker and was looking at the thermometer, and that the wind and snow rushed in when he opened the door; but afterwards everything again became confused. . . .

The peasant in the long coat started gnawing at something on the wall; the old woman began stretching her legs the whole length of the carriage, which she filled with a black cloud; then something squeaked and clattered in a dreadful manner, as if some one was being torn to pieces; then a blinding red light appeared, and at last everything was hidden by a wall. Anna felt as if she had fallen through the floor. But all this did not seem dreadful, but amusing. The voice of a man wrapped up and covered with snow shouted something just above her ear. She rose and came to herself, understanding that they had stopped at a station and that this was the guard. She asked Annushka to give her the cape she had removed and a shawl, and putting them on she moved to the door.

'Are you going out?' asked Annushka.

'Yes, I want a breath of air. It is so hot in here.'

She opened the carriage door. The snow and wind rushed toward her and had a tussle with her for the door. And this too struck her as amusing. She went out. The wind seemed only to have waited for her: it whistled merrily and tried to seize and carry her off, but she held on to the cold door-post and held down her shawl, then stepping on to the platform she moved away from the carriage.

The wind blew boisterously into the little porch of the carriage, but on the platform, sheltered by the train, it was quiet. With enjoyment she drew in full breaths of the snowy, frosty air as she stood beside her carriage looking round at the platform and the lighted station.

Chapter XXX

A blustering storm was rushing and whistling between the wheels of the train and round the pillars and the corners of the station. The railway carriages, the pillars, the people, and everything that could be seen, were covered on one side with snow, and that covering became thicker and thicker. A momentary lull would be followed by such a terrific gust that it seemed hardly possible to stand against it. Yet people, merrily exchanging remarks, ran over the creaking boards of the platform, and the big station doors were constantly being opened and shut. The shadow of a man stooping slipped past her feet and she heard a hammer striking the carriage wheels. 'Let me have the telegram!' came an angry voice from the other side out of the stormy darkness. 'Here, please, No. 28!' cried other voices, while many people muffled up and covered with snow ran hither and thither. Two gentlemen passed her with glowing cigarettes between their lips. She took another deep breath to get her fill of fresh air and had already drawn her hand out of her muff to take hold of the handrail and get into the train, when another man wearing a military overcoat came close between her and the wavering light of the lamp. She turned round, and instantly recognized Vronsky. With his hand in salute, he bowed and asked if she wanted anything and whether he could be of any service to her. For some time she looked into his face without answering, and, though he stood in the shade she noticed, or thought she noticed, the expression of his face and eyes. It was the same expression of respectful ecstasy that had so affected her the night before. She had assured herself more than once during those last few days, and again a moment ago, that Vronsky in relation to her was only one of the hundreds of everlastingly identical young men she met everywhere, and that she would never allow herself to give him a thought; yet now, at the first moment of seeing him again, she was seized by a feeling of joyful pride. There was no need for her to ask him why he was there. She knew as well as if he had told her, that he was there in order to be where she was.

'I did not know that you were going too. Why are you going?' she asked, dropping the hand with which she was about to take hold of the handrail. Her face beamed with a joy and animation she could not repress.

'Why am I going?' he repeated, looking straight into her eyes. 'You know that I am going in order to be where you are,' said he. 'I cannot do otherwise.'

At that moment the wind, as if it had mastered all obstacles, scattered the snow from the carriage roofs, and set a loose sheet of iron clattering; and in front the deep whistle of the engine howled mournfully and dismally. The awfulness of the storm appeared still more beautiful to her now. He had said just what her soul desired but her reason dreaded. She did not reply, and he saw a struggle in her face.

'Forgive me if my words displease you,' he said humbly.

He spoke courteously and respectfully, but so firmly and stubbornly that she was long unable to reply.

'What you are saying is wrong, and if you are a good man, I beg you to forget it, as I will forget it,' she said at last.

'Not a word, not a movement of yours will I ever forget, nor can I . . .'

'Enough, enough!' she cried, vainly trying to give a severe expression to her face, into which he was gazing eagerly. She took hold of the cold handrail, ascended the steps, and quickly entered the little lobby leading into the carriage. But in that little lobby she stopped, going over in her imagination what had just taken place. Though she could remember neither his nor her own words, she instinctively felt that that momentary conversation had drawn them terribly near to one another, and this both frightened her and made her happy. After standing still for a few seconds she went into the carriage and sat down. The overwrought condition which tormented her before not only returned again, but grew worse and reached such a degree that she feared every moment that something within her would give way under the intolerable strain. She did not sleep at all that night, but the strain and the visions which filled her imagination had nothing unpleasant or dismal about them; on the contrary they seemed joyful, glowing, and stimulating. Toward morning Anna, while still sitting up, fell into a doze; when she woke it was already light and the train was approaching Petersburg. At once thoughts of home, her husband, her son, and the cares of the coming day and of those that would follow, beset her.

When the train stopped at the Petersburg terminus and she got out, the first face she noticed was that of her husband.

'Great heavens! What has happened to his ears?' she thought, gazing at his cold and commanding figure, and especially at the gristly ears which now so struck her, pressing as they did against the rim of his hat. When he saw her, he came toward her with his customary ironical smile and looked straight at her with his large tired eyes. An unpleasant feeling weighed on her heart when she felt his fixed and weary gaze, as if she had expected to find him different. She was particularly struck by the feeling of dissatisfaction with herself which she experienced when she met him. It was that ordinary well-known feeling, as if she were dissembling, which she experienced in regard to her husband; but formerly she had not noticed it, while now she was clearly and painfully conscious of it.

'Yes, as you see. Here is a devoted husband; devoted as in the first year of married life,—consumed by desire to see you,' said he in his slow, high-pitched voice and in the tone in which he always addressed her, a tone which ridiculed those who could use such words in earnest.

'Is Serezha well?' she asked.

'And is this all the reward I get,' he said, 'for my ardour? He is quite well, quite well. . . .'

Chapter XXXI

Vronsky did not even try to sleep that night. He sat in his place, his eyes staring straight before him, not observing the people who went in or out; and if previously his appearance of imperturbable calm had struck and annoyed those who did not know him, he now seemed to them even prouder and more self-confident. He looked at people as if they were inanimate things. A nervous young man, a Law Court official, who sat opposite, hated him for that look. The young man repeatedly lit his cigarette at Vronsky's, talked to him, and even jostled him to prove that he was not a thing but a man; yet Vronsky still looked at him as at a street lamp, and the young man made grimaces, feeling that he was losing self-control under the stress of this refusal to regard him as human.

Vronsky neither saw nor heard anyone. He felt himself a king, not because he believed that he had made an impression on Anna—he did not yet believe that—but because the impression she had made on him filled him with happiness and pride.

What would come of it all he did not know and did not even consider. He felt that all his powers, hitherto dissipated and scattered, were now concentrated and directed with terrible energy toward one blissful aim. This made him happy. He knew only that he had told her the truth: that he would go where she went, that all the happiness of life and the only meaning of life for him now was in seeing and hearing her. When he had got out of the train at Bologoe station to drink a glass of seltzer water and had seen Anna, he had involuntarily at once told her just what he was thinking about it. He was glad he had said it to her, and that she now knew it and was thinking about it. He did not sleep at all that night. When he returned to the train, he kept recalling all the positions in which he had seen her, and all her words; and in his imagination, causing his heart to stand still, floated pictures of a possible future.

When he got out of the train at Petersburg he felt, despite his sleepless night, as fresh and animated as after a cold bath. He stopped outside the carriage, waiting till she appeared. 'I shall see her again,' he thought and smiled involuntarily. 'I shall see her walk, her face . . . she will say something, turn her head, look at me, perhaps even smile.' But before seeing her he saw her husband, whom the station-master was respectfully conducting through the crowd. 'Dear me! the husband!' Only now did Vronsky for the first time clearly realize that the husband was connected with her. He knew she had a husband, but had not believed in his existence, and only fully believed in him when he saw him there: his head and shoulders, and the black trousers containing his legs, and especially when he saw that husband with an air of ownership quietly take her hand.

When he saw Karenin, with his fresh Petersburg face, his sternly self-confident figure, his round hat and his slightly rounded back,

Vronsky believed in his existence, and had such a disagreeable sensation as a man tortured by thirst might feel on reaching a spring and finding a dog, sheep, or pig in it, drinking the water and making it muddy. Karenin's gait, the swinging of his thighs, and his wide short feet, particularly offended Vronsky, who acknowledged only his own unquestionable right to love Anna. But she was still the same, and the sight of her still affected him physically, exhilarating and stimulating him and filling him with joy. He ordered his German valet, who had run up from a second-class carriage, to get his luggage and take it home, and he himself went up to her. He saw the husband and wife meet, and with the penetration of a lover he noticed the signs of slight embarrassment when she spoke to her husband.

'No, she doesn't and can't love him,' he decided mentally.

While he was approaching her from behind he observed with joy that she became aware of his approach and was about to turn but, on recognizing him, again addressed her husband.

'Did you have a good night?' he inquired, bowing toward them both, and leaving it to Karenin to take the greeting as meant for himself and to recognize him, or not, as he pleased.

'Yes, quite comfortable, thank you,' she replied.

Her face seemed tired and had none of that play which showed now in a smile and now in the animation of her eyes; but just for an instant as she looked at him he saw a gleam in her eyes and, though the spark was at once extinguished, that one instant made him happy. She glanced at her husband to see whether he knew Vronsky. Karenin looked at him with displeasure, absently trying to recall who he might be. Vronsky's calm self-confidence struck like a scythe on a stone against the cold self-confidence of Karenin.

'Count Vronsky,' said Anna.

'Ah! I believe we have met before,' said Karenin, extending his hand with indifference. 'You travelled there with the mother and came back with the son,' he said, uttering every word distinctly as though it were something valuable he was giving away. 'I suppose you are returning from furlough?' he remarked; and without waiting for an answer said to his wife in his playful manner: 'Well, were many tears shed in Moscow over the parting?'

By addressing himself thus to his wife he conveyed to Vronsky his wish to be alone with her, and turning to Vronsky he touched his hat. But Vronsky, addressing Anna, said:

'I hope to have the honour of calling on you.'

Kàrenin glanced at him with his weary eyes.

'I shall be very pleased,' he said coldly. 'We are at home on Mondays.' Then having finally dismissed Vronsky he said to his wife in his usual bantering tone: 'What a good thing it was that I had just half an hour to spare to meet you and was able to show my devotion!'

'You insist too much on your devotion, for me to value it greatly,' she replied in the same playful tone, while she involuntarily listened to the sound of Vronsky's footsteps following them. 'But what does he matter to me?' she asked herself, and began inquiring of her husband how Serezha had got on during her absence.

'Oh, splendidly! Mariette says he was very sweet. But—I'm sorry to grieve you!—he did not fret after you . . . like your husband! . . . But I must thank you once again, my dear, for having made me the present of a day. Our dear *Samovar* will be in ecstasies.' (He called the celebrated Countess Lydia Ivanovna *samovar* because she was always getting heated and boiling over about something.) 'She was asking after you. And, do you know, if I may advise, you should go and see her to-day. Her heart is always aching about somebody. At present, in addition to all her other worries, she is concerned about the Oblonskys' reconciliation.'

Countess Lydia Ivanovna was Anna's husband's friend, and the centre of that set in Petersburg Society with which Anna, through her husband, was most closely connected.

'But I wrote to her.'

'Yes, but she wants the particulars. Go and see her, my dear, if you are not too tired. . . . Kondraty is here with the carriage for you, and I must be off to the Committee. Now I shan't have to dine alone,' he went on, no longer in a bantering manner. 'You can't think how I have become used to . . .' and with a long pressure of her hand and a special kind of smile he helped her into the carriage.

Chapter XXXII

The first person to meet Anna when she reached home was her son. He ran down the stairs to her regardless of his governess's cries, and with desperate delight called out: 'Mama! Mama!' When he reached her he clung round her neck.

'I told you it was Mama!' he shouted to the governess. 'I knew!' Her son, like his father, produced on Anna a feeling akin to disappointment. Her fancy had pictured him nicer than he was in reality. She had to come down to reality in order to enjoy him as he was. But even as he was, he was charming, with his fair curls, blue eyes, and plump shapely legs in tight-fitting stockings. Anna experienced an almost physical pleasure in feeling his proximity and his caresses, and a moral solace when she met his simple, trustful, and loving gaze and heard his naïve questions. She unpacked the presents which Dolly's children had sent him, and told him that there was a girl in Moscow whose name was Tanya, who could read and even teach other children.

'And am I worse than she?' asked Serezha.

'To me, you are the best in the world.'

'I know,' he said, smiling.

Before Anna had time to finish her coffee the Countess Lydia Ivanovna was announced. The Countess was a tall, stout woman with a sickly sallow complexion and beautiful, dreamy, black eyes. Anna was fond of her, but to-day she seemed to see her for the first time with all her defects.

'Well, my dear! did you take the olive branch?' asked the Countess Lydia Ivanovna as soon as she entered the room.

'Yes, it's all over, but the whole affair was not as serious as we thought,' Anna replied. 'My sister-in-law is, in general, too impulsive.'

But the Countess, who was interested in everything that did not concern her, had a habit of never listening to what interested her, and she interrupted Anna:

'Ah, yes! There is much sorrow and evil in the world, and to-day I am terribly worried.'

'Why! What is the matter?' asked Anna, trying to suppress a smile.

'I am getting tired of breaking lances uselessly in the cause of truth, and sometimes I feel quite unstrung. That Little Sisters' affair' (this was a philanthropic, religio-patriotic society) 'was going splendidly, but to work with those gentlemen is impossible,' continued the Countess Lydia Ivanovna with an ironical air of resignation to fate. 'They took the idea and perverted it, and are now discussing it in such a trivial, petty way! Two or three, your husband among them, understand the full significance of the affair, but the others just drop it. Yesterday I had a letter from Pravdin . . .'

Pravdin was a well-known Panslavist who resided abroad.

The Countess told Anna what he had written.

She then went on to tell her of other unpleasantnesses, and of the underhand opposition to the plan for uniting the Churches, and she went away in a hurry, as she had that afternoon to be at a meeting of another society as well as to attend a Slavonic Committee meeting.

'This is all just as it was before, but how is it that I never used to notice it?' said Anna to herself. 'Or is it that she is specially irritated this morning? But it is really funny; her aim is to do good, she is a Christian, and yet she is always angry and always has enemies—all on account of Christianity and philanthropy!'

After the Countess had left, a friend—a high official's wife—arrived and gave Anna all the Petersburg news. At three she also left, promising to come back to dinner.

Karenin was at the Ministry. Anna, left alone, spent part of the time before dinner in seeing her son have his dinner (he dined apart), in putting her things in order, and in reading and answering the notes and letters that had accumulated on her table.

The feeling of causeless shame she had felt during the journey, and her agitation, had quite vanished. In her accustomed conditions of life she again felt firm and blameless.

She thought with wonder of her state the day before. 'What had happened? Nothing! Vronsky said some silly things, to which it will be easy to put a stop, and I said what was necessary. It is unnecessary and impossible to speak of it to my husband. To speak of it would be to give it an importance that does not belong to it.' She remembered how she had once told her husband about one of his subordinates who very nearly made her a declaration, and how Karenin had answered that every woman living in Society was liable to such things, but that he had full confidence in her tact and would never degrade himself and her by being jealous. 'So there is no need to tell him! Besides, thank Heaven, there is nothing to tell!' she said to herself.

Chapter XXXIII

Karenin returned from the Ministry at four o'clock, but, as often happened, he had no time to go up and see his wife. He went straight to his study to receive some petitioners and sign a few documents brought by his private secretary. At the Karenins' dinners there were usually about three visitors. To-day there were an old lady, a cousin of Karenin's; the Director of a Department; the Director's wife; and a young man who had been recommended to Karenin for a post under him. Anna went into the drawing-room to entertain them. Exactly at five—the bronze clock (Peter I style) had not finished striking—Karenin entered in evening dress with a white tie and two stars on his coat, as he had to attend an official meeting directly after dinner. Every moment of his life was filled up and apportioned, and in order to find time to perform all the tasks allotted to each day he observed the strictest regularity. 'Without haste and without rest,' was his motto. He entered the room, greeted everybody, and quickly sat down, smiling at his wife.

'So my solitude has come to an end. You wouldn't believe how uncomfortable'—he put special emphasis on the word *uncomfortable*—'it is to dine alone!'

At dinner he spoke a little about Moscow affairs with his wife, asking with an ironical smile after Stephen Oblonsky; but for the most part the conversation was general and dealt with Petersburg service and social affairs. After dinner he spent half an hour with his guests, and then, having again with a smile pressed his wife's hand, went away to the Council. That evening Anna went neither to see the Princess Betsy Tverskaya, who having heard of Anna's return had invited her, nor to the theatre, where she had a box for that evening. Her chief reason for not going was that a dress on which she had counted was not ready. Altogether, when, after her visitors had left, Anna busied herself with her toilet, she was much vexed. Before going to Moscow, she—being an adept at dressing on comparatively little money—left three dresses to be altered. She wanted them made up so that they should be unrecognizable, and they were to have been sent home three days ago; but she now found that two were not ready at all, while the third had not been done in the way she wished. The dressmaker came to explain that it was better as she had done it, and Anna lost her temper to such a degree that she afterwards felt ashamed. Completely to regain her composure, she went to the nursery and spent the evening with her son. She put him to bed herself, made the sign of the cross over him, and tucked him up. She was glad she had not gone out that evening but had spent it so pleasantly at home. She felt light-hearted and tranquil, and saw clearly that what in the train had appeared so important had been merely an ordinary and trivial incident of Society life, and that there was no reason for her to feel ashamed, or for anyone to blame her. She sat down by the fire with an English novel and awaited her husband. Exactly at half-past nine there was a ring at the front door, and he entered the room.

'Here you are at last!' she said, holding out her hand to him. He kissed it, and seated himself beside her.

'In general, I see that your journey has been a success,' said he.

'Yes, quite,' she replied, and related everything that had happened from the beginning: her journey with the Countess Vronskaya, her arrival, the accident at the railway station. Then she spoke of her pity, first for her brother and then for Dolly.

'I don't think that one can excuse such a man, even though he is your brother,' remarked Karenin, severely.

Anna smiled. She knew he had said that in order to show that no consideration of kinship could hinder the expression of his sincere opinion. She knew that trait in her husband's character, knew and liked it.

'I am glad it has all ended satisfactorily and that you are back again,' he continued. 'But what are they saying there about the new Statute I carried in the Council?'

Anna had heard nothing about the Statute, and felt ashamed that she had so lightly forgotten what was of such importance to him.

'Here, on the contrary, it has made quite a stir,' he said with a self-satisfied smile.

Anna saw that he wanted to tell her something pleasant to himself about that affair, and by questioning she led him on to tell her all about it. With the same self-satisfied smile he told her about the ovations he had received on account of the enactment of that Statute.

'I was very, very pleased. It shows that at last a clear and reasonable view of the matter is beginning to be firmly held among us.'

Having finished his second cup of tea and cream and his bread and butter, he rose and went into his study.

'And have you not been out anywhere? You must have been dull,' he said.

'Oh no!' she answered, rising and following him through the room to his study. 'And what are you reading now?' she asked.

'I am now reading the Duc de Lille's *Poésie des enfers*,' he replied. 'A very remarkable book.' [7]

Anna smiled, as one smiles at the weaknesses of people one loves and slipping her hand under his arm walked with him to the study door. She knew his habit, which had become a necessity, of reading in the evening. She knew that in spite of his time being almost entirely absorbed by the duties of his post, he considered it incumbent on him to follow everything of importance that appeared in the world of thought. She also knew that really he was interested in political, philosophic, and theological books, and that art was quite foreign to his nature, yet in spite of this—or rather because of it—he never ignored anything that caused a stir in that sphere, but considered it his duty to read everything. She knew that in the sphere of politics, philosophy, and theology, Alexey Alexandrovich doubted and searched; but in questions of art, poetry, and especially music—which he did not at all understand—he held most definite and firm opinions. He liked talking of Shakespeare, Raphael, and Beethoven, and about the importance of the new schools of poetry and music, which in his mind were all classified with very logical exactitude.

'Well, God bless you!' she said at the door of the study, where a shaded candle and a bottle of water had been placed ready for him beside his arm-chair; 'and I will go and write to them in Moscow.'

He pressed her hand and again kissed it.

'After all, he is a good man: truthful, kind, and remarkable in his own sphere,' said Anna to herself when she had returned to her room, as if defending him from some one who accused him and declared it was impossible to love him. 'But why do his ears stick

7. *Poetry of Hell.* Tolstóy seems here in regard to a foreign name to have followed a plan he often adopted with Russian names—namely that of adapting one well known to his readers. He has here probably adapted the name of the well-known French poet, Leconte de Lisle.

out so? Or has he had his hair cut?'

Exactly at midnight, when Anna was still sitting at her writing-
table finishing a letter to Dolly, she heard the measured tread of
slippered feet, and Karenin entered, freshly washed, his hair brushed,
and a book under his arm.

'It's time! It's time!' said he with a significant smile, going into
their bedroom.

'And what right had he to look at him as he did?' thought Anna,
remembering how Vronsky had looked at Karenin.

When she was undressed she went into the bedroom, but on her
face not only was there not a trace of that animation which during
her stay in Moscow had sparkled in her eyes and smile, but on the
contrary the fire in her now seemed quenched or hidden somewhere very far away.

Chapter XXXIV

When he went to Moscow, Vronsky had left his large flat on
the Morskaya to his friend and favourite comrade, Petritsky.

Petritsky was a young lieutenant, not of very aristocratic birth,
and not only not wealthy but heavily in debt, tipsy every evening,
and often under arrest for amusing or improper escapades, but
popular both with his comrades and superiors. Arriving home
from the station about noon, Vronsky recognized a hired brougham
at the front door. When he rang the bell, while still outside, he
heard men's laughter, a woman's lisping voice, and Petritsky shouting: 'If it is one of the villains, don't let him in!'

Vronsky told the servants not to announce his arrival, and softly
entered the first room. Petritsky's friend, Baroness Shilton, with
her rosy little face and flaxen hair, resplendent in lilac satin, sat at
the round table making coffee, and like a canary was filling the
whole room with her Parisian chatter. Petritsky in his great coat,
and Captain Kamerovsky in full uniform probably straight from
parade, sat on each side of her.

'Vronsky! Bravo!' exclaimed Petritsky jumping up and noisily
pushing back his chair. 'The master himself! Baroness, some
coffee for him out of the new coffee-pot. . . . Well, this is unexpected! I hope you are pleased with this ornament to your study,'
he added, pointing to the Baroness. 'Of course, you know one
another?'

'I should think so!' replied Vronsky with a merry smile, as he
pressed the Baroness's small hand. 'Of course: quite old friends.'

'You have returned from a journey?' said the Baroness. 'Oh, I'll
be off home this very moment if I am in the way.'

'You are at home where you are, Baroness,' said Vronsky. 'How
do you do, Kamerovsky?' he added, coldly shaking hands with the

Captain.

'There now! You never manage to say such pretty things,' said the Baroness to Petritsky.

'Oh yes! Why not? After dinner I'll say things quite as good as that.'

'But after dinner there is no merit in it! Well then, I'll give you some coffee. . . . But have a wash and smarten yourself up,' said the Baroness, again sitting down and carefully turning a small screw of the coffee-pot.

'Pierre, pass me the coffee,' she said to Petritsky, whom, not concealing their relations, she addressed by the nickname of Pierre because of his surname. 'I'll put a little more into the pot.'

'You'll spoil it!'

'No, I shan't! And your wife?' the Baroness said suddenly, interrupting Vronsky's conversation with his comrade. 'We here have been marrying you off! Have you brought your wife?'

'No, Baroness. A Bohemian I was born, and a Bohemian I shall die!'

'So much the better! So much the better! Give me your hand.'

And the Baroness, instead of releasing Vronsky, began telling him her plans for the future, interspersing jokes and asking his advice.

'He won't agree to a divorce! Whatever am I to do?' (He was her husband.) 'I want to begin an action. What would you advise? Kamerovsky, look after the coffee, it's boiling over! Don't you see I am occupied? . . . I want to bring an action because I need my property. You see how absurd it is, that because I am supposed to be unfaithful,' she said contemptuously, 'he wishes to have the use of my property.'

Vronsky listened with pleasure to the merry prattle of the pretty young woman, agreed with what she said, and half in fun gave her advice; in a word he immediately adopted his habitual manner with women of her kind. In his Petersburg world people were divided into two quite opposite sorts. One—the inferior sort: the paltry, stupid, and, above all, ridiculous people who believe that a husband should live with the one wife to whom he is married, that a girl should be pure, a woman modest, and a man, manly, self-controlled and firm; that one should bring up one's children to earn their living, should pay one's debts, and other nonsense of that kind. These were the old-fashioned and ridiculous people. But there was another sort of people: the real people to which all his set belonged, who had above all to be well-bred, generous, bold, gay, and to abandon themselves unblushingly to all their passions and laugh at everything else.

Just for a moment Vronsky was staggered, having brought back from Moscow the impression of a totally different world, but immediately, as though he had put his foot into an old slipper, he re-entered his former gay and pleasant world.

The coffee never got made, but boiled over and splashed everybody, effecting just what was required: that is, it gave an excuse for much noise and laughter, staining the valuable carpet and the Baroness's dress.

'Now good-bye, or you'll never get washed, and on my conscience will lie the greatest crime of a gentleman—want of cleanliness. . . . So you advise me to put a knife to his throat?'

'Most certainly, and hold it so that your hand will be near his lips. He will kiss the hand and all will end well!' said Vronsky.

'Then we meet at the French Theatre to-night?' and, her dress rustling, she vanished.

Kamerovsky rose also, and, without waiting for him to go, Vronsky shook hands with him and went to his dressing-room. While he was washing, Petritsky in a few words described his own position in so far as it had changed since Vronsky went away. He had no money at all. His father had said he would not give him any and would not pay his debts. His tailor and another creditor were threatening him with arrest. His C.O. had announced to him that if these scandals continued he (Petritsky) would have to resign. He was sick to death of the Baroness, especially because she was always wanting to give him money; but there was another—he would let Vronsky see her—who was charming, wonderful, of severely Oriental type, in the style of ' "The Slave Rebecca," you know!' He had also had a quarrel with Berkashev, who wished to send his seconds, but of course nothing would come of it. But, in general, everything was first-rate and extremely jolly; and without letting his friend go into the details of his position, Petritsky began telling him all the interesting news. Listening to Petritsky's familiar tales, in the familiar surroundings of the house he had lived in for three years, Vronsky experienced the satisfaction of returning to his customary careless Petersburg life.

'Impossible!' he cried, releasing the pedal of his washstand, which controlled a jet of water under which he was bathing his healthy, ruddy neck. 'Impossible!' he cried, at the news that Laura was under the protection of Mileyev and had thrown up Fertinhof. 'And he is still as stupid and self-satisfied? And what of Buzulukov?'

'Oh, about Buzulukov there is such a tale—splendid!' shouted Petritsky. 'You know his passion for balls? He never misses a single Court ball. He went to a grand ball wearing one of the new helmets—have you seen the new helmets? They're very good, much lighter.—Well, he stood . . . But you are not listening.'

'Yes, I am,' replied Vronsky, rubbing himself with a bath-towel.

'The Grand Duchess passed by with one of the Ambassadors, and as his ill-luck would have it they were discussing the new helmets. The Grand Duchess wishes to show him one of them. . . . She sees our dear Buzulukov standing there'—Petritsky imitated the pose—'The Grand Duchess asks him for his helmet, but he won't let her have it! What can this mean? They wink at him, nod, frown, to make him give it up. . . . No! He stands there more dead than alive. . . . Just imagine it! . . . That—what's his name?—wishes to take it from him, but he won't let go. . . . The other snatches it away and hands it to the Grand Duchess. "Here, this is one of the new ones," said the Grand Duchess, turning it over, and—just fancy!—out tumbles a pear and sweets—two pounds of them! . . . The dear fellow had collected them in his helmet!'

Vronsky shook with laughter, and long after, when he was already talking of other things, he again went off into roars of hearty laughter, showing his compact row of strong teeth, at the remembrance of the helmet.

Having heard all the news, Vronsky, with the help of his valet, put on his uniform and went to report himself. After that he intended to go to see his brother and to see Betsy, and to pay a few calls in order to begin visiting the set in which he could meet Anna Karenina. As usual in Petersburg, he left the house not to return till late at night.

Part II

Chapter I

Toward the end of the winter a consultation was held at the Shcherbatskys' which was intended to ascertain the state of Kitty's health and to decide what should be done to restore her failing strength. She was ill, and with the approach of spring grew worse. Their own doctor prescribed cod-liver oil, then iron, and then nitrate of silver, but as none of them did her any good and as he advised her to go abroad for the spring they sent for a celebrated specialist.

The celebrated specialist, a very handsome man and by no means old, insisted on sounding the invalid.

He, with particular pleasure as it seemed, insisted that a maidenly sense of shame is only a relic of barbarism, and that nothing is more natural than for a man still in his prime to handle a young woman's naked body. He considered this natural because he did it every day, and did not, it seemed to him, either feel or think anything wrong when he did it. He therefore considered a girl's feeling of shame to be not only a relic of barbarism but an insult to him.

They had to submit, for although all the doctors studied in the same schools and from the same books and knew the same sciences, and though some said that this celebrated man was a bad doctor, at the Princess Shcherbatskaya's and in her set it was for some reason assumed that he alone had a quite special knowledge and he alone could save Kitty. After having carefully examined and sounded the agitated invalid, who was stupefied with shame, the celebrity, having carefully washed his hands, stood in the drawing-room talking to the Prince. The Prince frowned and coughed as he listened to the doctor. As a man who had lived in the world and was neither stupid nor ill, the Prince did not believe in medicine, and in his heart was vexed at this farce, especially as he himself was probably the only one who thoroughly understood the cause of Kitty's illness. 'What a windbag,' he thought as he listened to the celebrated doctor's chatter about Kitty's symptoms. The doctor meanwhile found it hard not to show his contempt for the old fellow, and with difficulty descended to the level of his comprehension. He saw that it was waste of time to talk to him, and that the head in this house was the mother. It was before her that he meant to spread his pearls.

Just then the Princess entered the room with the family doctor. The Prince moved away, trying not to show how absurd he thought the whole farce. The Princess was confused and did not know what to do. She felt guilty toward Kitty.

'Well, doctor, decide our fate,' she said. 'Tell me everything . . . . Is there any hope?' she meant to ask, but her lips trembled and she could not utter that question, and only added: 'Well, doctor?'

'In a moment, Princess. I will just have a talk with my colleague, and then I shall have the honour of giving you my opinion.'

'Then we had better leave you?'

'If you please.'

The Princess left the room with a sigh.

When the doctors were alone, the family doctor began timidly to express his opinion, which was that a tuberculous process had begun, but . . . etc. The celebrity listened, but in.the midst of the speech looked at his large gold watch.

'Yes,' said he, 'but . . .'

The family doctor stopped respectfully in the middle of what he was saying.

'We cannot, as you know, determine the beginning of a tuberculous process. As long as there are no cavities there is nothing definite to go by. But we may suspect it; and there are indications —a bad appetite, nervous excitability, and so on. The question is this: When a tuberculous process is suspected, what should be done to nourish the patient?'

'But you know in these cases there is always some hidden moral cause,' the family doctor allowed himself to remark with a subtle smile.

'Yes, that goes without saying,' replied the celebrity, and again looked at his watch. 'Excuse me, has the bridge over the Yauza been repaired, or has one still to drive round?' he asked. 'Oh, it has been repaired! Well then, I can get there in twenty minutes. We were saying that the question is this: How to nourish the patient and strengthen the nerves. The two aims are connected, and we must act on both.'

'How about a journey abroad?' asked the family doctor.

'I am opposed to journeys abroad. You see, if a tuberculous process has begun (which we don't know), a journey abroad will not help the case. Something is necessary which will nourish the patient and do no harm.' And the celebrity explained his plan of a treatment with Soden water, the chief reason for prescribing this evidently being that it could do no harm.

The family doctor listened attentively and respectfully to the end.

'But in favour of a journey abroad I should like to mention the change of habits, and the removal from surroundings which awaken memories. Besides which, the mother wishes it,' said he.

'Ah, in that case let them go, only those German quacks will do mischief. . . . They must obey. . . . However, let them go.'

He again glanced at his watch. 'I must be going!' he said, moving toward the door.

The celebrity informed the Princess (his sense of what was fitting suggested this to him) that he would have to see the patient again.

'What another examination?' exclaimed the mother, horror-struck.

'Oh no, I must only find out a few details, Princess.'

'As you please, doctor.'

And the mother, followed by the doctor, entered the room in the middle of which Kitty was standing. Her thin cheeks were flushed and her eyes were burning after the ordeal she had endured. When the doctor entered she blushed all over and her eyes filled with tears. Her whole illness and the treatment appeared to her stupid and even ridiculous. Her treatment seemed to her as absurd as piecing together the bits of a smashed vase. Her heart was broken. Why did they want to dose her with pills and powders? But she did not want to pain her mother, especially as her mother considered herself to blame.

'Sit down, please, Princess,' said the celebrity.

He sat down opposite to her, smiling, felt her pulse and again began asking tiresome questions. She answered him, but suddenly grew angry and rose.

'Excuse me, doctor, but really this won't lead to anything. You are asking me the same things three times over.' The celebrity was not offended.

'It's only the excitability of an invalid,' he said to the mother after Kitty had gone out. 'And I had finished.'

And to the Princess, as to an exceptionally intelligent woman, the doctor diagnosed Kitty's condition in learned language, and concluded with directions how the unnecessary waters were to be drunk.

In reply to the question whether they should go abroad, the doctor thought deeply, as if solving a difficult problem, and at last he decided that they should go, but should not believe the quacks, and when in doubt should always refer to him.

It was just as if something pleasant had happened when the doctor had gone, and Kitty too pretended to be cheerful. She often now, almost always, had to pretend.

'Really, Mama! I am quite well. But if you wish to travel, let us go!' and trying to appear interested in the journey she began to talk about the preparations for it.

Chapter II

Just after the doctor had left, Dolly came. She knew that there was to be a consultation that day, and though she had only recently got up after a confinement (she had given birth to a daughter at the end of the winter), and though she had many troubles and cares of her own, she left her baby and another little girl of hers who was ill, and called to hear Kitty's fate, which was to be decided that day.

'Well, how is she?' she said, entering the drawing room without removing her bonnet. 'You are all cheerful, so it must be all right!'

They tried to tell her what the doctor had said, but it turned out that though he had spoken very fluently and at great length, it was impossible to reproduce what he had said. The only thing of interest was that it had been decided they should go abroad.

Dolly could not suppress a sigh. Her best friend, her sister, was going away; and as it was, her life was not a bright one. Her relations with her husband after their reconciliation had become humiliating. Anna's soldering had not proved durable, and the family harmony had broken again at the same place. There was nothing definite, but Oblonsky was hardly ever at home, there was hardly ever any money, and suspicions of his infidelity continually tormented Dolly, who tried to repel them, fearing the already familiar pangs of jealousy. The first explosion of jealousy, once past, could not be repeated. Not even the discovery of an act of infidelity could again affect her as it had done the first time. Such a discovery could now only deprive her of her accustomed family life, and she let herself be deceived, despising him, and still more herself, for such weakness. Added to this the care of a large family worried her continually: either something went wrong with the feeding of the baby, or the nurse left, or, as now, one of the children fell ill.

'And how are you all getting on?' asked her mother.

'Ah, Mama, we have plenty of trouble of our own. Lily has fallen ill, and I'm afraid it's scarlet fever. I have come out to-day to hear the news, because I shall not come out at all if (which God forbid!) it really is scarlet fever.'

The old Prince came out of his study after the doctor had gone, and after giving his cheek to Dolly and greeting her he turned to his wife:

'Well, have you made up your minds to go? And what are you going to do with me?'

'I think you should stay behind, Alexander,' replied his wife.

'As you please.'

'Mama, why should not Papa come with us?' said Kitty. 'It would be pleasanter for him and for us too.'

The old Prince rose and stroked Kitty's hair. She lifted her face and, forcing a smile, looked up at him. She always felt that he understood her better than anyone else in the family, though he did not speak much to her. Being the youngest she was his favourite, and it seemed to her that his affection gave him insight. When her gaze now met his kindly blue eyes looking steadily at her, it seemed to her that he saw right through her, and knew all the trouble that was in her. She bent toward him, blushing, and expecting a kiss, but he only patted her on the head and remarked:

'These stupid chignons! One can't get at one's real daughter, but only caresses the hair of expired females. Well, Dolly,' he said, turning to his eldest daughter, 'and what is your prodigal about?'

'Nothing particular, Papa,' answered Dolly, understanding that he referred to her husband. 'He is always out, I hardly see him,'— she could not resist adding with an ironical smile.

'And has he not yet gone to the country to sell the forest?'

'No, he is always preparing to go.'

'Dear me!' said the Prince. 'And so I am also to prepare? I'm all obedience,' he said to his wife, as he sat down again. 'And look here, Kate,' he went on, turning to his youngest daughter: 'You must wake up one fine morning and say to yourself: "Why, I am quite well and happy, and will go out to walk in the frost again with Papa." Eh?'

Her father's words seemed very simple, but they made Kitty feel as confused and flurried as a detected criminal. 'Yes, he knows and understands it all, and in these words is telling me that, though I am ashamed, I must get over my shame.' She could not gather spirit enough to reply. She made an attempt, but suddenly burst into tears and ran away.

The Princess flew at her husband: 'That comes of your jokes. You always . . .' and she began reproaching him.

The Prince listened for some time to her rebukes in silence, but his face frowned more and more.

'She is so pitiful, poor thing, so pitiful, and you don't feel that every allusion to what has caused it hurts her. Oh dear, oh dear, to be so mistaken in anyone!' said the Princess, and from the change in her tone both Dolly and the Prince knew that she was thinking of Vronsky. 'I can't think why we have no laws to punish such horrid, ignoble people.'

'Oh, it makes me sick to hear it!' muttered the Prince gloomily, rising as if he meant to go away, but stopping at the door. 'The laws are there, my dear, and since you have invited it I will tell you who is at fault for it all: you, and you, and no one but you! There always have been and there still are laws against such fellows! Yes, and if nothing had been done that ought not to have been done, I, old as I am, would have challenged him—that fop! Yes, now go and dose her, and call in these quacks!'

The Prince appeared to have much more to say, but as soon as the Princess heard his tone she, as always happened in serious cases, gave in and became repentant.

'Alexander, Alexander,' she whispered, moving nearer and bursting into tears.

As soon as she began to cry the Prince quieted down, and came up to her.

'That will do, that will do! You suffer too, I know. It can't be helped! There's no great harm done. God is merciful . . . thank you . . .' he went on, no longer knowing what he was saying, and after responding to his wife's wet kiss which he felt on his hand, he went out.

When Kitty, in tears, had left the room, Dolly, with her motherly habit of mind, at once saw that here a woman's task lay before her, and prepared to fulfill it. She took off her bonnet and, having mentally rolled up her sleeves, prepared for action. While her mother was attacking her father, she tried to restrain the former as far as filial respect permitted. When the Prince flared up she kept silent, feeling shame for her mother and tenderness toward her father because of his immediate return to kindliness; but when her father left the room she was ready for the chief thing needful, which was to go to Kitty and comfort her.

'I wanted to tell you something long ago, Mama. Do you know that Levin wished to propose to Kitty when he was here last? He told Stephen.'

'Well, what of that? I don't understand . . .'

'Perhaps Kitty rejected him? . . . Did she not tell you . . . ?'

'No, she told me nothing about either—she is too proud. But I know it is all because of that . . .'

'Yes, and just imagine if she refused Levin—and she would not have refused him if it had not been for that other. I know. . . . And then . . . the other deceived her so dreadfully.'

It was too dreadful for the Princess to think how much she was to blame in regard to her daughter, and she grew angry.

'Oh! I can't make anything out! Nowadays girls all want to trust to their own reason. They don't tell their mothers anything, and then . . .'

'Mama, I will go to her.'

'Go. Am I preventing you?' said the mother.

Chapter III

On entering Kitty's little snuggery, a pretty pink room, decorated with *vieux saxe* [1] figures—as fresh, rosy and gay as Kitty herself had been two months before, Dolly remembered how light-heartedly and with what love they two had arranged that room the year before. Her heart grew chill when she saw Kitty sitting on the low chair nearest the door, her eyes fixed on a corner of the carpet. Kitty glanced at her sister, but the cold and rather severe expression of her face did not change.

'I am going home now and shall have to shut myself up, and you won't be able to come to me,' said Dolly, sitting down beside her sister. 'I want to talk to you.'

'What about?' asked Kitty quickly, lifting her face in alarm.

'What but your troubles?'

'I have no troubles.'

'Come now, Kitty. Do you think I can help knowing? I know everything. And believe me it is so unimportant. . . . We have all passed through the same.'

Kitty was silent and her face looked stern.

'He is not worthy of your suffering for him,' continued Dolly, going straight to the point.

'No, because he has despised me,' said Kitty with a shaking voice. 'Don't speak! Please don't speak!'

'But who told you so? Nobody says so! I am sure he was in love with you and is still in love, but . . .'

1. Porcelain (Old Saxony).

'Oh dear! these commiserations are what I dread most of all!' cried Kitty, suddenly flaring up. She turned on her chair, blushed, and began rapidly moving her fingers, pressing now with one hand and now with the other the buckle of a belt she was holding. Dolly knew her sister's habit of fingering something when she was heated, and she knew how apt Kitty was to forget herself when in a passion and to say much that was unpleasant and had better not have been said. She tried to pacify her; but it was too late.

'What do you want me to feel, what?' said Kitty quickly. 'That I was in love with a man who wouldn't have anything to do with me, and that I am dying for love of him? And it is my sister who says that to me. My sister who imagines . . . that . . . that she sympathizes with me! . . . I don't want this commiseration and hypocrisy!'

'Kitty, you are unfair!'

'Why do you torment me?'

'On the contrary, I see you are in distress. . . .'

But Kitty in her excitement did not listen to her.

'There is nothing for me to grieve for or seek comfort about. I have enough pride never to let myself love a man who does not love me.'

'But I am not suggesting it. . . . Only, tell me frankly,' said Dolly, taking her by the hand, 'did Levin speak to you?'

The mention of Levin seemed to deprive Kitty of the last fragments of self-control: she jumped up from her chair, threw the buckle on the floor, and rapidly gesticulating with her hands she began:

'What has Levin to do with it? I don't understand why you need torment me! I have said and I repeat I will never, *never* do what you are doing—returning to a man who has betrayed you and has loved another woman. I can't understand it! You may do it, but I can't.'

Having said these words she looked at her sister and, seeing that Dolly remained silent with her head bowed sadly, Kitty, instead of leaving the room as she had intended to do, sat down by the door, and hiding her face in her handkerchief let her head sink down.

For a minute or two there was silence. Dolly was thinking about herself. The humiliation of which she was always conscious was peculiarly painful when her sister touched on it. She had not expected such cruelty from her, and was angry with her. But suddenly she heard the rustle of a dress and a burst of suppressed sobbing. A pair of arms encircled her neck from below and Kitty was kneeling before her.

'Dolly dear, I am so, so unhappy!' she whispered guiltily. And the sweet tear-stained face hid itself in the folds of Dolly's dress.

As if tears were the necessary lubricant without which the machine of mutual confidence could not work properly between the sisters, after having had a cry they started talking of indifferent matters, and in so doing understood one another. Kitty knew that what she had said in her anger about the unfaithfulness of Dolly's husband and about her humiliation had cut her poor sister to the depths of her heart, but that she was forgiven; while Dolly on her side learnt all that she wanted to know, her suspicions were confirmed and she understood that Kitty's grief, her hopeless grief, was really caused by the fact that Levin had proposed to her and that she had rejected him, and now that Vronsky had deceived her, she was prepared to love Levin and to hate Vronsky. Kitty did not say a word of this; she spoke only of her state of mind.

'I have no troubles whatever,' she said when she had grown calm,—'but can you understand that everything has become horrid, disgusting and coarse to me, and above all I myself? You can't think what horrid thoughts I have about everything.'

'But what horrid thoughts can you have?' asked Dolly smiling.

'The very nastiest and coarsest, I can't tell you. It is not grief, not dullness, but much worse. It is as if all that was good in me had hidden itself, and only what is horrid remains. How am I to tell you?'—she continued, noticing perplexity in her sister's eyes:— 'Papa began to speak to me just now. . . . It seems to me that he thinks that all I need is to get married. Mama takes me to a ball: and it seems to me she only takes me there to marry me off as quickly as possible and get rid of me. I know it is not true, but I can't get rid of the idea. I can't bear to see the so-called eligible men. I always think they are taking my measure. Formerly to go anywhere in a ball-dress was just a pleasure to me. I used to like myself in it; but now I feel ashamed and uncomfortable. Well, what is one to do? The doctor . . .' Kitty became confused; she was going to say that since this change had come over her, Oblonsky had become intolerably disagreeable to her, and that she could not see him without having the coarsest and most monstrous fancies.

'Well, you see, everything appears to me in the coarsest and most horrid aspect,' she continued. 'That is my illness. Perhaps it will pass . . .'

'But don't think . . .'

'I can't. I only feel comfortable with children, only in your house.'

'What a pity you can't come to see us!'

'But I will come. I have had scarlet fever, and I will persuade Mama to let me.'

And Kitty insisted on having her own way, went to her sister's, and nursed the children all through the scarlet fever that really attacked them. The two sisters nursed all the six children success-

fully through the illness, but Kitty's health did not improve, and in
Lent the Shcherbatskys went abroad.

Chapter IV

The highest Petersburg Society is really all one: all who belong
to it know and even visit one another. But this large circle has its
subdivisions. Anna Arkadyevna Karenina had friends and close connections in three different sets. One of these was her husband's
official set, consisting of his colleagues and subordinates, who in
most varied and capricious ways were connected and separated by
social conditions. Anna found it hard now to recall the feeling of almost religious respect she had at first felt for these people. Now she
knew them all as well as the inhabitants of a provincial town know
one another; she knew the habits and weaknesses of each of them,
and where the shoe pinched this or that foot; she knew their relations to one another and to the governing centre; she knew who
sided with whom, and how and by what means each supported
himself, and who agreed or disagreed with whom and about what;
but (in spite of admonitions and advice from the Countess Lydia
Ivanovna) this bureaucratic circle of masculine interests could not
interest Anna, and she avoided it.

Another circle with which Anna was intimate was that through
which Karenin had made his career. The centre of that circle was
the Countess Lydia Ivanovna. It consisted of elderly, plain, philanthropic and pious women and clever, learned and ambitious men.
One of the clever men who belonged to it called it, 'the conscience
of Petersburg Society.' Karenin set great value on this circle, and
Anna, who knew how to get on with every one, had during the first
part of her life in Petersburg made friends in it too. But now, on
her return from Moscow, that circle became unbearable to her. It
seemed to her that she, and all of them, were only pretending,
and she felt so bored and uncomfortable in that Society that she
visited Lydia Ivanovna as rarely as possible.

The third circle with which Anna was connected was Society in
the accepted meaning of the word: the Society of balls, dinner-
parties, brilliant toilettes, the Society which clung to the Court with
one hand lest it should sink to the *demi-monde*, for this the members of that Society thought they despised, though its tastes were
not only similar but identical with their own. Anna was connected
with this set through the Princess Betsy Tverskaya, the wife of her
cousin, who had an income of Rs. 120,000 a year, and who, from
the time Anna first appeared in Society, had particularly liked her,
made much of her, and drawn her into her own set, making fun of
that to which the Countess Lydia Ivanovna belonged.

'When I am old and ugly I will become like that,' Betsy used to say, 'but for you, a young and beautiful woman, it is too early to settle down in that almshouse.'

At first Anna had avoided the Princess Tverskaya's set as much as she could, because it demanded more expense than she could afford; and also because she really approved more of the other set; but after her visit to Moscow all this was reversed. She avoided her moral friends and went into grand Society. There she saw Vronsky, and experienced a tremulous joy when meeting him. She met him most frequently at Betsy's, who was a Vronsky herself and his cousin. Vronsky went everywhere where he had a chance of meeting Anna, and spoke to her of his love whenever he could. She gave him no encouragement, but every time they met there surged up that feeling of animation which had seized her in the train on the morning when she first saw him. She was aware that when they met joy lit up her eyes and drew her lips into a smile, but she could not hide the expression of that joy.

At first Anna sincerely believed that she was displeased with him for allowing himself so to pursue her; but soon after her return from Moscow, having gone to a party where she expected to meet him but to which he did not come, she clearly realized, by the sadness that overcame her, that she had been deceiving herself and that his persecution supplied the whole interest of her life.

. . . . .

A famous *prima donna* was giving her second performance and all high Society was at the Opera House. Vronsky, from the front row of the stalls, seeing his cousin, went to her box without waiting for the interval.

'Why did you not come to dinner?' she said, adding with a smile and so that only he could hear her: 'I am amazed at the clairvoyance of lovers! She was not there! But come in after the opera.'

Vronsky looked at her inquiringly. She nodded, and he thanked her by a smile and sat down beside her.

'And how you used to laugh at others!' continued the Princess Betsy, who took particular pleasure in following the progress of this passion. 'What has become of it all? You are caught, my dear fellow!'

'I wish for nothing better than to be caught,' replied Vronsky with his calm good-natured smile. 'To tell the truth, if I complain at all, it is only of not being caught enough! I am beginning to lose hope.'

'What hope can you have?' said Betsy, offended on her friend's behalf: '*entendons nous!*' [2] But in her eyes little sparks twinkled which said that she understood very well, and just as he did, what hope he might have.

2. Let us understand one another.

'None whatever,' said Vronsky, laughing and showing his close-set teeth. 'Excuse me!' he added, taking from her hand the opera-glasses, and he set to work to scan across her bare shoulder the row of boxes opposite. 'I am afraid I am becoming ridiculous.'

He knew very well that he ran no risk of appearing ridiculous either in Betsy's eyes or in the eyes of Society people generally. He knew very well that in their eyes, the rôle of the disappointed lover of a maiden or of any single woman might be ridiculous; but the rôle of a man who was pursuing a married woman, and who made it the purpose of his life at all cost to draw her into adultery, was one which had in it something beautiful and dignified and could never be ridiculous, so it was with a proud glad smile lurking under his moustache that he put down the opera-glasses and looked at his cousin.

'And why did you not come to dinner?' she said admiringly.

'I must tell you about that. I was engaged, and with what do you think? I'll give you a hundred or a thousand guesses—and you won't find out! I was making peace between a husband and a fellow who had insulted his wife. Yes, really!'

'Well, and did you succeed?'

'Nearly.'

'You must tell me all about it,' she said, rising. 'Come back in the next interval.'

'I can't: I am going to the French Theatre.'

'What? From Nilsson?' asked Betsy, quite horrified, though she could not have distinguished Nilsson's voice from that of a chorus girl.[3]

'It can't be helped, I have an appointment there in connection with this same peacemaking of mine.'

' "Blessed are the peacemakers, for they will be saved!" ' said Betsy, remembering that she had heard some one say something like that. 'Well, then, sit down and tell me about it.'

And she sat down again.

Chapter V

'It's rather improper but so charming that I long to tell it,' said Vronsky, gazing at her with laughing eyes. 'I shan't mention names.'

'So much the better. I shall guess them.'

'Well then, listen: two gay young fellows were out driving . . .'

'Officers of your regiment, of course?'

'I didn't say officers, but just two young men who had been lunching . . .'

3. Christine Nilsson (1843–1921), the celebrated Swedish *prima donna* who had great success in Petersburg and Moscow in 1872–3.

'Translate that "not wisely but too well."'

'It may be. They were on their way to dine with a comrade, and in the highest spirits. They see that a pretty woman in a hired sledge is passing them, looking at them, and laughing and nodding to them—at any rate they think so. Of course off they go after her, galloping full speed. To their surprise the lovely one stops at the door of the very house they are going to. She runs up to the top flat. They only manage to see a pair of red lips under a short veil, and lovely little feet . . .'

'You tell it with so much feeling that I think you yourself must have been one of the two.'

'And what did you say to me just now? Well, the young men go into their comrade's flat. He was giving a farewell dinner. There they may really have drunk rather too much, as always happens at farewell dinners. At dinner they inquire who lives in the top flat. No one knows; but their host's footman, in answer to their question whether "girls" lived there, replies that there are a lot of them thereabouts. After dinner the young men go into the host's study to compose a letter to the fair stranger, and, having written one full of passion and containing a declaration, they carry it upstairs themselves, in order to explain anything that might not be quite clear in the letter.'

'Why do you tell me such horrors? Well?'

'They ring. A maid opens the door; they give her the letter and assure her that they are both so much in love that they will die at once on the doorstep. The maid, quite bewildered, carries on the negotiations. Suddenly a gentleman with sausage-shaped whiskers, and as red as a lobster, appears, announces that no one but his wife lives in that flat and turns them both out. . . .'

'How do you know he had "sausage-shaped whiskers," as you say?'

'You just listen! To-day I went to reconcile them.'

'Well, what happened?'

'This is the most interesting part. It turns out that the happy couple are a Titular Councillor [4] and a Titular Councilloress! The Titular Councillor lodges a complaint, and I turn into a peacemaker—and what a peacemaker! . . . I assure you Talleyrand was nothing to me!'

'What was the difficulty?'

'You shall hear. We duly apologized: "We are in despair; we beg to be forgiven for our unfortunate mistake." The Titular Councillor with his sausages begins to thaw, but also wishes to express his feelings and as soon as he begins to express them he begins to get excited and grows insulting, and again I have to set all my diplomatic talents in motion. "I agree that they acted badly, but

---

4. A modest rank in the Civil Service.

beg you to consider that it was a mistake; consider their youth; besides which the young men had just dined. You understand! They
repent from the bottom of their hearts, and ask you to forgive their
fault." The Titular Councillor again softens. "I am willing to forgive them, Count, but you must understand that my wife, a respectable woman, has been subjected to the rudeness and insults of
these hobbledehoys, these scound . . ." And you must remember
that one of the hobbledehoys is standing there, and I have to reconcile them! Again I set my diplomacy going, and again, just as the
whole business should be concluded, my Titular Councillor flies
into a rage, gets red, his sausages stick out, and again I dissolve into
diplomatic subtlety.'

'Oh, you must hear this!' cried Betsy, laughing and turning to a
lady who was just entering the box. 'He has made me laugh so!'

'Well, *bonne chance!*' [5] she added, giving Vronsky a finger that
was not engaged in holding her fan, and with a movement of her
shoulders making the bodice of her dress, that had risen a little,
slip down again that she might be befittingly nude on returning to
the front of the box into the glare of gas-light and the gaze of all
eyes.

Vronsky went to the French Theatre, where he really had to see
the Commander of his regiment (who never omitted a single performance there) to talk over this reconciliation business which had
occupied and amused him for the last three days. Petritsky, whom
Vronsky was fond of, was mixed up in the affair, and so was young
Prince Kedrov, a first-rate fellow and a capital comrade, who had
lately joined the regiment. Above all, the interests of the regiment
were involved.

Both officers belonged to Vronsky's squadron. Titular Councillor
Wenden had been to see the Commander and had lodged a complaint against the officers who had insulted his wife. His young wife,
so Wenden declared (he had been married six months), had been to
church with her mother, and suddenly feeling unwell as a result of
her interesting condition, was unable to stand any longer and took
the first good sledge she could find. These officers, in their sledge,
raced after her; she became frightened, and feeling still more unwell ran up the stairs to her flat. Wenden himself, having returned
from his office and hearing the front-door bell and voices, went out,
saw the tipsy officers with the letter, and hustled them out. He requested that they should be severely punished.

'No, say what you like,' the Commander remarked to Vronsky,
whom he had invited to his house, 'Petritsky is becoming impossible. Not a week passes without some scandal. That Councillor will
not let the matter rest: he will go further with it.'

Vronsky realized how ungrateful a task it was—that a duel was

5. Good luck!

out of the question, and that everything must be done to soften the Titular Councillor and hush up the affair. The C.O. had called Vronsky in just because he knew him to be honourable and able, and above all a man who valued the honour of the regiment. After discussing the matter, they decided that Vronsky should go with Petritsky and Kedrov to apologize to the Councillor. Both the Commander and Vronsky were aware that Vronsky's name and his badge as aide-de-camp to the Emperor ought greatly to help in softening the Titular Councillor's feelings, and really these things had a partial effect; but the result of the peacemaking still remained doubtful, as Vronsky had explained.

Having reached the French Theatre, Vronsky went out into the *foyer* with the C.O., and informed him of his success or lack of success. After considering the whole question, the Commander decided to let the matter drop; but, for amusement, he asked Vronsky for the particulars of the interview, and could not help laughing for a long time as he listened to the description of how the Titular Councillor suddenly again flared up at the recollection of some incident of the affair, and how Vronsky manœuvred so as to retire just at the last half-word of reconciliation, pushing Petritsky before him.

'A bad business, but most amusing! Kedrov cannot fight that good man! And so he was in a great rage?' repeated the Commander, laughing. 'But what do you think of Clare this evening? Wonderful!' he went on, referring to the new French actress. 'However often one sees her, she is new each day. Only the French can do that!'

Chapter VI

Princess Betsy went home without waiting for the end of the last act. She had scarcely time to go to her dressing-room, put powder on her long pale face and rub it off again, smarten herself up, and order tea to be served in the big drawing-room, before one carriage after another began to arrive at the door of her immense house on the Great Morskaya. The visitors passed beneath the broad portico, and the massive hall porter, who in the mornings read a newspaper behind the glass panes of the front door for the edification of passers-by, now noiselessly opened this enormous door to admit them.

Almost at one and the same time the hostess, her hair rearranged and her face freshened up, entered at one door and the visitors at another of the large, dark-walled drawing-room, with its thick carpets and brightly-lit table, shining in the candle-light with white tablecloth, silver samovar and translucent china.

The hostess sat down beside the samovar and took off her gloves. The chairs being moved by the aid of unobtrusive footmen, the company settled down, separating into two circles: one with the hostess round the samovar, the other, at the opposite end of the room, round the wife of an ambassador, a beautiful woman with black sharply-outlined eyebrows, in a black velvet dress. The conversation in both circles, as always happens at first, hesitated for a few minutes, was interrupted by greetings, recognitions, and offers of tea, and seemed to be seeking something to settle on.

'She is wonderfully good as an actress; one sees that she has studied Kaulbach,' remarked an attaché in the circle round the ambassador's wife. 'Did you notice how she fell . . .' [6]

'Oh, please don't let us talk about Nilsson! It's impossible to say anything new about her,' said a stout, red-faced, fair-haired lady who wore an old silk dress and had no eyebrows and no chignon. This was the Princess Myagkaya, notorious for her simplicity and the roughness of her manners, and nicknamed *l'enfant terrible*. The Princess Myagkaya was seated midway between the two circles, listening to and taking part in the conversation of both. 'This very same sentence about Kaulbach has been repeated to me by three different people to-day, as if by arrangement. That sentence, I don't know why, seemed to please them very much.' The conversation was cut short by this remark, and it became necessary to find another topic.

'Tell us something amusing but not malicious,' said the ambassador's wife, a great adept at that kind of elegant conversation which the English call 'small-talk,' turning to the attaché, who was also at a loss what subject to start.

'People say that is very difficult, and that only what is malicious is amusing,' he began with a smile. 'But I will try, if you will give me a theme. The theme is everything. Once one has a theme, it is easy to embroider on it. I often think that the famous talkers of the last century would find it difficult to talk cleverly nowadays. We are all so tired of the clever things . . .'

'That was said long ago,' interrupted the ambassador's wife, laughingly.

The conversation had begun very amiably, but just because it was too amiable it languished again. They had to return to the one sure and never-failing resource—slander.

'Don't you think there is something Louis Quinze about Tushkevich?' said the attaché, glancing at a handsome, fair-haired young man who stood by the tea-table.

'Oh yes! He matches the drawing-room; that is why he comes here so often!'

This conversation did not flag, since it hinted at what could not

---

6. Wilhelm von Kaulbach (1805–74). Besides his large paintings he illustrated the works of Shakespeare and Goethe, and these illustrations seem to have furnished useful suggestions to Nilsson when she was creating her operatic roles of Ophelia, Desdemona, and Gretchen.

be spoken of in this room, namely, at the relations existing between Tushkevich and their hostess.

Around the hostess and the samovar, the conversation, after flickering for some time in the same way between the three inevitable topics: the latest public news, the theatre, and criticism of one's neighbour, also caught on when it got to the last of these themes— slander.

'Have you heard? That that Maltyshcheva woman also—not the daughter but the mother—is having a *diable rose* [7] costume made for herself?'

'You don't mean to say so! How delicious!'

'I wonder that she, with her common sense—for she is not stupid —does not see how ridiculous she makes herself.'

Every one had something disparaging to say about the unfortunate Maltyshcheva, and the conversation began crackling merrily like a kindling bonfire.

The Princess Betsy's husband, a fat, good-natured man, an enthusiastic collector of engravings, hearing that his wife had visitors, entered the drawing-room before going to his club. Stepping silently on the thick carpet, he approached the Princess Myagkaya.

'How did you like Nilsson?' he inquired.

'Oh, how can you steal on one like that? How you frightened me!' said she in reply. 'Please don't talk to me about the opera—you know nothing of music. I had better descend to your level and talk about your majolica and engravings. Come now, tell me about the treasures you have picked up lately at the rag fair!'

'Shall I show you? But you don't understand them.'

'Yes, let me see them. I have learnt from those—what is their name?—the bankers. . . . They have some splendid engravings. They showed them to us.'

'What? Have you been to the Schuzburgs?' asked the hostess from her place by the samovar.

'I have, *ma chère*. They asked my husband and me to dinner, and I was told that the sauce alone at that dinner cost a thousand roubles,' said the Princess Myagkaya loudly, feeling that everybody was listening. 'And a very nasty sauce it was too, something green! We had to invite them, and I gave them a sauce that cost eighty-five kopeks, and satisfied every one. I can't afford thousand-rouble sauces.'

'She is unique!' said the hostess.

'Wonderful!' said some one else.

The effect produced by the Princess Myagkaya's words was always the same; and the secret of that effect lay in the fact that although she often—as at that moment—spoke not quite to the point, her words were simple and had a meaning. In the Society in which she lived words of that kind produced the effect of a most

7. Shocking pink.

witty joke. The Princess Myagkaya did not understand why her
words had such an effect, but was aware that they did and availed
herself of it.

As while she was speaking everybody listened to her and the
conversation in the circle round the ambassador's wife stopped, the
hostess wished to make one circle of the whole company, and turning to the ambassador's wife, said:

'Will you really not have a cup of tea? You should come and join
us here.'

'No, we are very comfortable here,' replied the ambassador's wife
smiling, and she continued the interrupted conversation.

It was a very pleasant conversation. They were disparaging the
Karenins, husband and wife.

'Anna has changed very much since her trip to Moscow. There is
something strange about her,' said a friend of Anna's.

'The chief change is that she has brought back with her the
shadow of Alexey Vronsky,' said the ambassador's wife.

'Well, why not? Grimm has a fable called "The Man Without a
Shadow"—about a man who lost his shadow as a punishment for
something or other. [8] I never could understand why it was a punishment! But for a woman to be without a shadow can't be pleasant.'

'Yes, but a woman with a shadow generally ends badly,' said
Anna's friend.

'A murrain on your tongue!' suddenly remarked the Princess
Myagkaya, hearing these words. 'Anna Karenina is a splendid
woman. I don't like her husband, but I am very fond of her.'

'Why don't you like her husband? He is such a remarkable man,'
said the ambassador's wife. 'My husband says there are few states-
men like him in Europe.'

'My husband tells me the same, but I don't believe it,' replied
the Princess Myagkaya. 'If our husbands didn't talk, we should see
things as they really are; and it's my opinion that Karenin is simply
stupid. I say it in a whisper! Does this not make everything quite
clear? Formerly, when I was told to consider him wise, I kept trying to, and thought I was stupid myself because I was unable to
perceive his wisdom; but as soon as I said to myself, he's stupid
(only in a whisper of course), it all became quite clear! Don't you
think so?'

'How malicious you are to-day!'

'Not at all. I have no choice. One of us is stupid, and you know
it's impossible to say so of oneself.'

'No one is satisfied with his position, but every one is satisfied
with his wit,' remarked the attaché, quoting some French lines.

'That's it, that's just it,' rejoined the Princess Myagkaya, turning

---

8. There is no tale by the Brothers Grimm about a man without a shadow, but there is a famous
story by the German Romantic, Adalbert Chamisso (1781–1838), *Peter Schlemihl* (1814), on
that theme.

quickly toward him. 'But the point is, that I won't abandon Anna to you. She is so excellent, so charming! What is she to do, if every one is in love with her and follows her about like a shadow?'

'But I don't even think of blaming her!' Anna's friend said, justifying herself.

'If no one follows us about like a shadow, that does not prove that we have a right to judge her.'

Having snubbed Anna's friend handsomely, the Princess Myag-kaya rose with the ambassador's wife and joined those at the table, where there was a general conversation about the King of Prussia.

'Whom were you backbiting there?' asked Betsy.

'The Karenins. The Princess was characterizing Karenin,' replied the ambassador's wife with a smile, seating herself at the table.

'It's a pity we did not hear it!' said the hostess, glancing at the door. 'Ah! Here you are at last!' she added, smilingly addressing Vronsky as he entered the room.

Vronsky not only knew everybody in the room, but saw them all every day, so he entered in the calm manner of one who rejoins those from whom he has parted only a short time before.

'Where do I come from?' he said in reply to the ambassador's wife. 'There's no help for it, I must confess that I come from the *Theatre Bouffe*. I have been there a hundred times, and always with fresh pleasure. Excellent! I know it's a disgrace, but at the opera I go to sleep, while at the *Bouffe* I stay till the last minute enjoying it. To-night . . .'

And he named a French actress and was about to tell them something about her when the ambassador's wife stopped him with mock alarm.

'Please don't talk about those horrors!'

'All right, I won't—especially as everybody knows those horrors!'

'And everybody would go there if it were considered the thing, as the opera is,' put in the Princess Myagkaya.

Chapter VII

Steps were heard at the entrance, and the Princess Betsy, know-ing that it was Anna, glanced at Vronsky. He was looking at the door with a strange new expression on his face. He gazed joyfully, intently, and yet timidly at the lady who was entering, and slowly rose from his seat. Anna entered the room holding herself, as usual, very erect, and without changing the direction of her eyes, approached her hostess, walking with that quick, firm yet light step which distinguished her from other Society women. She shook hands, smilingly, and with the same smile looked round at Vronsky. He bowed low and moved a chair toward her.

Anna responded only by an inclination of the head, though she blushed and frowned. But immediately, nodding rapidly to her acquaintances and pressing the hands extended to her, she turned again to her hostess:

'I have just been at the Countess Lydia's. I meant to come sooner, but could not get away. Sir John was there—he is very interesting.'

'Oh, that missionary?'

'Yes, he was telling us about Indian life. It was very interesting.'

The conversation, interrupted by her entrance, again burnt up like the flame of a lamp that has been blown about.

'Sir John! Oh yes, Sir John! I have seen him. He speaks very well. The elder Vlasyeva is quite in love with him.'

'And is it true that the younger Vlasyeva is going to be married to Topov?'

'Yes; they say it's quite settled.'

'I am surprised at her parents. They say it's a love match.'

'Love match! What antediluvian ideas you have! Who talks of love nowadays?' said the ambassador's wife.

'What's to be done? That silly old fashion hasn't died out yet!' said Vronsky.

'So much the worse for those who follow the fashion! I know of happy marriages, but only such as are founded on reason.'

'Yes, but how often the happiness of marriages founded on reason crumbles to dust because the very passion that was disregarded makes itself felt later,' said Vronsky.

'But by "marriages founded on reason," we mean marriages between those who have both passed through that madness. It's like scarlet fever: one has to get it over.'

'Then some one should invent a way of inoculating love, like vaccination.'

'When I was young I was in love with a chorister,' said Princess Myagkaya. 'I don't know whether it did me any good.'

'No, joking apart, I believe that to understand love one must first make a mistake and then correct it,' said the Princess Betsy.

'Even after marriage?' said the ambassador's wife archly.

'It is never too late to mend!' said the attaché, quoting the English proverb.

'Exactly!' chimed in Betsy. 'One has to make mistakes and correct them. What do you think?' she asked, addressing Anna, who with a scarcely discernible resolute smile was listening to this conversation.

'I think,' replied Anna, toying with the glove she had pulled off, 'I think . . . if it is true that there are as many minds as there are heads, then there are as many kinds of love as there are hearts.'

Vronsky had gazed at Anna and with sinking heart waited to hear what she would say. He sighed, as after a danger averted, when she had uttered these words.

Suddenly Anna addressed him:

'I have received a letter from Moscow. They write that Kitty Shcherbatskaya is very ill.'

'Really?' said Vronsky, frowning.

Anna glanced sternly at him. 'It does not interest you?'

'On the contrary, it interests me very much! What exactly do they write, if I may ask?' he inquired.

Anna rose and went up to Betsy. 'Give me a cup of tea,' she said, stopping behind Betsy's chair.

While Betsy was pouring out the tea, Vronsky went up to Anna. 'What do they write?' he asked again.

'I often think men don't understand honour, though they are always talking about it,' said Anna, without answering his question. 'I have long wanted to tell you,' she added, and, moving a few steps to a side table on which lay some albums, she sat down.

'I don't quite understand your meaning,' he said, handing her the cup.

'I wanted to tell you,' she began again, without looking at him, 'that you have behaved badly, very badly.'

'Don't I know that I behaved badly? But who was the cause?'

'Why say that to me?' she asked, looking severely at him.

'You know why,' he answered boldly and joyously, meeting her look and continuing to gaze at her.

It was not he, but she, who became abashed.

'That only proves you have no heart,' she said. But her look said that she knew he had a heart and that she therefore feared him.

'What you have just referred to was a mistake, and not love.'

Anna shuddered, and said: 'Don't you remember that I forbade you to mention that word, that horrid word?' But then she felt that the one word *forbade* showed that she claimed certain rights over him, thereby encouraging him to speak of love. 'I have long wanted to say that to you,' she went on, looking resolutely into his eyes, her face all aglow and suffused with a burning blush, 'and to-day I came on purpose, knowing I should meet you here. I have come to tell you that this must stop! I have never till now had to blush before anyone, but you make me feel as if I were guilty of something.'

He looked at her, and was struck by the new, spiritual beauty of her face.

'What do you want of me?' he asked, simply and seriously.

'I want you to go to Moscow and beg Kitty's forgiveness,' said she.

'You don't want that,' he replied.

He saw that she was saying what she forced herself to utter and not what she wished to say.

'If you love me as you say you do,' she whispered, 'behave so that I may be at peace.'

His face brightened.

'Don't you know that you are all my life to me? . . . But peace I do not know, and can't give to you. My whole being, my love . . . yes! I cannot think about you and about myself separately. You and I are one to me. And I do not see before us the possibility of peace either for me or for you. I see the possibility of despair, misfortune . . . or of happiness—what happiness! . . . Is it impossible?' he added with his lips only, but she heard.

She exerted all the powers of her mind to say what she ought; but instead she fixed on him her eyes filled with love and did not answer at all.

'This is it!' he thought with rapture. 'Just as I was beginning to despair, and when it seemed as though the end would never come . . . here it is! She loves me! She acknowledges it!'

'Do this for me: never say such words to me, and let us be good friends.' These were her words, but her eyes said something very different.

'Friends we shall not be, you know that yourself; but whether we shall be the happiest or the most miserable of human beings . . . rests with you.'

She wished to say something, but he interrupted her.

'I ask only one thing: I ask the right to hope and suffer as I do now; but if even that is impossible, command me to disappear, and I will do it. You shall not see me if my presence is painful to you.'

'I don't want to drive you away.'

'Only don't change anything. Leave everything as it is!' he said with trembling voice. 'Here is your husband.'

Indeed, just at that moment Karenin, with his deliberate, ungraceful gait, entered the drawing-room.

He glanced at his wife and Vronsky, went up to the hostess, and having sat down with a cup of tea began talking in his deliberate and always clear tones, in his usual ironical way ridiculing somebody.

'Your Hotel Rambouillet is in full muster,' said he, glancing round the whole company, 'the Graces and the Muses.'[9]

But the Princess Betsy could not bear that tone of his: 'sneering' she called it in English: so, like a clever hostess, she at once led him into a serious conversation on universal military service.[1] Kar-

---

9. La Marquise de Rambouillet (1588–1665) formed the first literary *salon* which had considerable influence on literary taste and public opinion.

1. On January 1, 1874, military service was shortened from twenty-five years to six years. The measure had been debated in the press for three years before it was adopted.

enin was immediately absorbed in the conversation, and began defending the new law very earnestly against the Princess Betsy, who attacked it.[2]

Vronsky and Anna remained sitting at the little table.

'This is becoming improper!' whispered a lady, indicating by a glance Vronsky, Anna, and Anna's husband.

'What did I tell you?' replied Anna's friend.

Not these two ladies alone, but nearly all those present in the drawing-room, even the Princess Myagkaya and Betsy herself, several times glanced across at the pair who had gone away from the general circle, as if their having done so disturbed the others. Only Karenin did not once glance that way and was not distracted from the interesting conversation in which he was engaged.

Noticing the unpleasant impression produced on every one, the Princess Betsy manœuvred for some one else to take her place and to listen to Karenin, and she herself went up to Anna.

'I am always amazed at your husband's clearness and exactitude of expression,' she said. 'The most transcendental ideas become accessible to me when he speaks.'

'Oh yes!' said Anna, radiant with a smile of happiness and not understanding a single word of what Betsy was saying; and going across to the big table she joined in the general conversation.

After half an hour's stay Karenin went up to his wife and suggested that they should go home together; but, without looking at him, she answered that she would stay to supper. Karenin bowed to the company and went away.

The Karenins' fat old Tartar coachman, in his shiny leather coat, was finding it hard to control the near grey horse that had grown restive with cold, waiting before the portico. The footman stood holding open the carriage door. The hall-porter stood with his hand on the outer front door, Anna with her deft little hand was disengaging the lace of her sleeve which had caught on a hook of her fur coat, and with bent head was listening with delight to what Vronsky, who accompanied her, was saying.

'Granted that you have not said anything! I don't demand anything,' he was saying, 'but you know that it is not friendship I want! Only one happiness is possible for me in life, the word you so dislike—yes, love . . .'

'Love,' she slowly repeated to herself, and suddenly, while releasing the lace, she added aloud: 'The reason I dislike that word is that it means too much for me, far more than you can understand,' and she looked him in the face. 'Au revoir!'

She gave him her hand, and with her quick elastic step went past

2. An ukase introducing universal conscription on the Prussian model was issued on January 1st, 1874, and was a very general topic of conversation.

the hall-porter and vanished into the carriage.

Her glance and the touch of her hand burnt him. He kissed the palm of his hand where she had touched it, and went home happy in the knowledge that in this one evening he had made more progress toward his aim than he had during the previous two months.

Chapter VIII

Karenin did not see anything peculiar or improper in his wife's conversing animatedly with Vronsky at a separate table, but he noticed that others in the drawing-room considered it peculiar and improper, therefore he also considered it improper, and decided to speak to his wife about it.

When he reached home he went to his study as usual, seated himself in his easy-chair, and opened a book on the Papacy at the place where his paper-knife was inserted. He read till one o'clock as was his wont, only now and then rubbing his high forehead and jerking his head as if driving something away. At the usual hour he rose and prepared for bed. Anna had not yet returned. With the book under his arm he went upstairs; but to-night, instead of his usual thoughts and calculations about his official affairs, his mind was full of his wife and of something unpleasant that had happened concerning her. Contrary to his habit he did not go to bed, but with his hands clasped behind his back started pacing up and down the rooms. He felt that he could not lie down, till he had thought over these newly-arisen circumstances.

When Karenin had decided to talk the matter over with his wife, it had seemed to him quite easy and simple to do so; but now, when he began considering how to approach her, the matter appeared very difficult and complicated.

He was not of a jealous disposition. Jealousy in his opinion insulted a wife, and a man should have confidence in his wife. Why he should have confidence—that is, a full conviction that his young wife would always love him—he never asked himself; but he felt no distrust, and therefore had confidence, and assured himself that it was right to have it. Now, though his conviction that jealousy is a shameful feeling, and that one ought to have confidence, had not been destroyed, he felt that he was face to face with something illogical and stupid, and he did not know what to do. Karenin was being confronted with life—with the possibility of his wife's loving somebody else, and this seemed stupid and incomprehensible to him, because it was life itself. He had lived and worked all his days in official spheres, which deal with reflections of life, and every time he had knocked up against life itself he had stepped out of its way. He now experienced a sensation such as a man might feel who, while quietly crossing a bridge over an abyss, suddenly sees that the bridge is falling to pieces and that he is facing the abyss. The abyss was real life; the bridge was the artificial life Karenin had been living. It was the first time that the possibility of his wife's falling in love with anybody had occurred to him, and he was horrified.

He did not undress, but paced up and down with his even step on the resounding parquet floor of the dining-room, which was lit by one lamp, over the carpet of the dark drawing-room, where a light was reflected only from a recently painted portrait of himself which hung above the sofa, and on through her sitting-room, where two candles were burning, lighting up the portraits of her relatives and friends and the elegant knick-knacks, long familiar to him, on her writing-table. Through her room he reached the door of their bedroom and then turned back again.

From time to time he stopped, generally on the parquet floor of the lamp-lit dining-room, and thought: 'Yes, it is necessary to decide and to stop it: to express my opinion of it and my decision.' Then he turned back again. 'But express what? What decision?' he asked himself in the drawing-room, and could find no answer. 'But after all,' he reflected before turning into her room, 'what is it that has happened? Nothing at all. She had a long talk with him— Well? What of that? Are there not plenty of men with whom a woman may talk? Besides . . . to be jealous is to degrade myself and her,' he said to himself as he entered her sitting-room. But that consideration which formerly had weighed so much with him now had neither weight nor meaning. At the bedroom door he turned back, and as soon as he re-entered the dark drawing-room a voice seemed to whisper that it was not so, and that if others noticed, that showed that there must have been something for them to notice. And again he repeated to himself in the dining-room: 'Yes, it is necessary to decide, and stop it, and express my opinion . . .' And again in the drawing-room, at the turn into her room, he asked himself: 'Decide what?' and then, 'What has happened?' and he replied 'Nothing,' and remembered that jealousy is a feeling which insults a wife; but in the drawing-room he came again to the conviction that something had happened. His mind as well as his body performed a complete circle each time without arriving at anything new. He noticed this, rubbed his forehead, and sat down in her room.

Here as he looked at her table, at the malachite cover of her blotting-book and an unfinished letter that lay there, his thoughts suddenly underwent a change. He began thinking about her: of what she thought and felt. For the first time he vividly pictured to himself her personal life, her thoughts, her wishes; but the idea that she might and should have her own independent life appeared to him so dreadful that he hastened to drive it away. That was the abyss into which he feared to look. To put himself in thought and feeling into another being was a mental action foreign to Karenin. He considered such mental acts to be injurious and dangerous romancing.

'And what is most terrible of all,' thought he, 'is that, just now, when my work is coming to completion' (he was thinking of the project he was then carrying through), 'when I need peace and all my powers of mind, just now this stupid anxiety falls on me. But what is to be done? I am not one of those who suffer anxiety and agitation and have not the courage to look them in the face!

'I must think it over, come to a decision, and throw it off,' he said aloud. 'The question of her feelings, of what has taken place or may take place in her soul, is not my business; it is the business of her conscience and belongs to religion,' said he, feeling relieved at having found the formal category to which the newly-arisen circumstance rightly belonged.

'Well then,' thought he, 'the question of her feelings and so on are questions for her conscience, which cannot concern me. My duty is clearly defined. As head of the family I am the person whose duty it is to guide her, and who is therefore partly responsible; I must show her the danger which I see, warn her, and even use my authority. I must speak plainly to her.'

What he would say to his wife took clear shape in Karenin's head. Thinking it over, he regretted having to expend his time and powers of mind on inconspicuous domestic affairs; but nevertheless the form and sequence of the speech he had to make shaped itself in his mind clearly and definitely, as though it were an official report. 'I must make the following quite clear: First, the importance of public opinion and propriety; secondly, the religious meaning of marriage; thirdly, if necessary, I must refer to the harm that may result to our son; fourthly, allude to her own unhappiness.' And interlacing his fingers, palms downwards, he stretched them and the joints cracked.

That movement—a bad habit of cracking his fingers—always tranquillized him and brought him back to that precision of mind which he now so needed. The sound of a carriage driving up to the front door was heard, and Karenin stood still in the middle of the room.

A woman's steps were heard ascending the stairs. Karenin, ready to deliver his speech, stood pressing his interlaced fingers together, trying whether some of them would not crack again. One of the joints did crack.

By the sound of her light step on the stair he was aware of her approach and, though he was satisfied with his speech, he felt some apprehension of the coming explanations.

Chapter IX

Anna walked in with bowed head, playing with the tassels of her hood. Her face shone with a vivid glow, but it was not a joyous glow—it resembled the terrible glow of a conflagration on a dark night. On seeing her husband she lifted her head and, as if waking from sleep, smiled.

'You're not in bed? What a wonder!' she said, throwing off her hood, and without pausing she went on to her dressing-room. 'Alexey Alexandrovich, it's high time!' she added from beyond the door.

'Anna, I must have a talk with you.'

'With me?' she said with surprise, coming back from the other room and looking at him. 'What is it? What about?' she asked, seating herself. 'Well, let us have a talk, if it is so important. But it would be better to go to bed.'

Anna said what came into her head, and hearing her own words was astonished at her capacity for deception. How simple and natural her words sounded, and how really it seemed as if she were merely sleepy! She felt herself clothed in an impenetrable armour of falsehood and that some unseen power was helping and supporting her.

'Anna, I must warn you,' said he.

'Warn me?' she asked; 'what about?'

She looked so naturally and gaily at him, that one who did not know her as her husband did could not have noticed anything strange either in the intonation or the meaning of her words. But for him, who knew her—knew that when he went to bed five minutes late she noticed it and asked the reason—knew that she had always immediately told him all her joys, pleasures and sorrows —for him, her reluctance to notice his state of mind, or to say a word about herself, meant much. He saw that the depths of her soul, till now always open, were closed to him. More than that, he knew from her tone that she was not ashamed of this, but seemed to be saying frankly: 'Yes, it is closed, and so it should be and will be in future.' He now felt like a man who on coming home finds his house locked against him. 'But perhaps the key can still be found,' thought Karenin.

'I wish to warn you,' he said in low tones, 'that you may, by indiscretion and carelessness, give the world occasion to talk about you. Your too animated conversation to-night with Count Vronsky' (he pronounced the name firmly and with quiet deliberation) 'attracted attention.'

As he spoke he looked at her laughing eyes, which now alarmed him by their impenetrability, and felt the uselessness and idleness of his words.

'You are always like that,' she replied, as if not understanding him at all, and intentionally taking notice only of his last words. 'One day you dislike my being dull, another day my being lively. I was not dull. Does that offend you?'

Karenin started and bent his hands to crack his fingers.

'Oh, please don't crack your fingers! I dislike it so!' she said.

'Anna, is this you?' said he softly, making an effort and refraining from moving his hands.

'But whatever is the matter?' she asked in a tone of comical surprise and sincerity. 'What do you want of me?'

Karenin paused and rubbed his forehead and eyes. He felt that instead of doing what he had meant to do and warning his wife that she was making a mistake in the eyes of the world, he was involuntarily getting excited about a matter which concerned her conscience, and was struggling against some barrier of his imagination.

'This is what I intended to say,' he continued coldly and calmly, 'and I ask you to listen to me. As you know, I consider jealousy an insulting and degrading feeling and will never allow myself to be guided by it; but there are certain laws of propriety which one cannot disregard with impunity. I did not notice it this evening, but, judging by the impression created, all present noticed that you behaved and acted not quite as was desirable.'

'Really, I don't understand at all,' said Anna, shrugging her shoulders. 'It is all the same to him!' she said to herself. 'But Society noticed, and that disturbs him! You are not well, Alexey Alexandrovich!' she added, rose and was about to pass out of the room, but he moved forward as if wishing to stop her.

His face looked plainer and gloomier than she had ever yet seen it. Anna stopped and, throwing back her head and bending it to one side, she began with her quick hands to take out her hairpins.

'Well, I'm listening! What next?' said she quietly and mockingly. 'I am even listening with interest, because I should like to understand what it is all about.'

As she spoke she wondered at her quietly natural tone and at her correct choice of words.

'I have not the right to inquire into all the details of your feelings, and in general I consider it useless and even harmful to do so,' began Karenin. 'By digging into our souls, we often dig up what might better have remained there unnoticed. Your feelings concern your own conscience, but it is my duty to you, to myself, and to God, to point out to you your duties. Our lives are bound together not by men but by God. This bond can only be broken by a crime, and that kind of crime brings its punishment.'

'I don't understand anything. . . . Oh dear! And as ill-luck will have it, I am dreadfully sleepy!' said she, while with deft fingers she felt for the remaining pins in her hair.

'Anna, for God's sake don't talk like that!' he said mildly. 'Perhaps I am mistaken, but believe me that what I am saying I say equally for my own sake and for yours. I am your husband, and I love you.'

For an instant her head had drooped and the mocking spark in her eyes had died away, but the word 'love' aroused her again. 'Love!' she thought, 'as if he can love! If he had never heard people talk of love, he would never have wanted that word. He does not know what love is.'

'Alexey Alexandrovich, I really do not understand,' she replied. 'Explain what you consider . . .'

'Allow me to finish. I love you. But I am not talking of myself. The chief persons concerned are our son and yourself. I repeat— perhaps my words may seem quite superfluous to you; perhaps they result from a mistake of mine. In that case I ask your pardon! But if you feel that there are any grounds, however slight, I beg you to reflect, and if your heart prompts you to tell me . . .'

Karenin did not notice that he was saying something quite different from what he had prepared.

'I have nothing to say. Besides . . .' she added, rapidly, and hardly repressing a smile, 'it really is bedtime.'

Karenin sighed, and without saying anything more went into the bedroom.

When she went there he was already in bed. His lips were sternly compressed and his eyes did not look at her. Anna got into her bed, and every moment expected that he would address her. She was afraid of what he would say, and yet wished to hear it. But he remained silent. She lay waiting and motionless for a long time, and then forgot him. She was thinking of another; she saw him, and felt her heart fill with excitement and guilty joy at the thought. Suddenly she heard an even, quiet, nasal sound like whistling. For a moment the sound he emitted seemed to have startled Karenin, and he stopped; but, after he had breathed twice, the whistling recommenced with fresh and calm regularity.

'It's late, it's late,' she whispered to herself, and smiled. For a long time she lay still with wide-open eyes, the brightness of which it seemed to her she could herself see in the darkness.

Chapter X

From that time a new life began for Karenin and his wife. Nothing particular happened. Anna went into Society as before, frequently visiting the Princess Betsy, and she met Vronsky everywhere. Karenin noticed this, but could do nothing She met all his efforts to bring about an explanation by presenting an impenetrable wall of merry perplexity. Externally things seemed as before, but there intimate relations with one another were completely changed. Karenin, strong as he was in his official activities, felt himself powerless here. Like an ox he waited submissively with bowed head for the pole-axe which he felt was raised above him. Each time he began to think about it, he felt that he must try again, that by kindness, tenderness, and persuasion there was still a hope of saving her and obliging her to bethink herself. Every day he prepared himself to have a talk with her. But each time he began to speak with her he felt the same spirit of evil and falsehood which had taken possession of her master him also, and he neither said the things he meant to, nor spoke in the tone he had meant to adopt. He spoke involuntarily in his habitual half bantering tone which seemed to make fun of those who said such things seriously; and in that tone it was impossible to say what had to be said to her.

Chapter XI

That which for nearly a year had been Vronsky's sole and exclusive desire, supplanting all his former desires: that which for Anna had been an impossible, dreadful, but all the more bewitching dream of happiness, had come to pass. Pale, with trembling lower jaw, he stood over her, entreating her to be calm, himself not knowing why or how.

'Anna, Anna,' he said in a trembling voice, 'Anna, for God's sake! . . .'

But the louder he spoke the lower she drooped her once proud, bright, but now shame-stricken head, and she writhed, slipping down from the sofa on which she sat to the floor at his feet. She would have fallen on the carpet if he had not held her.

'My God! Forgive me!' she said, sobbing and pressing Vronsky's hand to her breast.

She felt so guilty, so much to blame, that it only remained for her to humble herself and ask to be forgiven; but she had no one in the world now except him, so that even her prayer for forgiveness was addressed to him. Looking at him, she felt her humiliation physically, and could say nothing more. He felt what a murderer must feel when looking at the body he has deprived of life. The body he had deprived of life was their love, the first period of their love. There was something frightful and revolting in the recollection of what had been paid for with this terrible price of shame. The shame she felt at her spiritual nakedness communicated itself to him. But in spite of the murderer's horror of the body of his victim, that body must be cut in pieces and hidden away, and he must make use of what he has obtained by the murder.

Then, as the murderer desperately throws himself on the body, as though with passion, and drags it and hacks it, so Vronsky covered her face and shoulders with kisses.

She held his hand and did not move. Yes! These kisses were what had been bought by that shame! 'Yes, and this hand, which will always be mine, is the hand of my accomplice.' She lifted his hand and kissed it. He knelt down and tried to see her face, but she hid it and did not speak. At last, as though mastering herself, she sat up and pushed him away. Her face was as beautiful as ever, but all the more piteous.

'It's all over,' she said. 'I have nothing but you left. Remember that.'

'I cannot help remembering what is life itself to me! For one moment of that bliss . . .'

'What bliss?' she said with disgust and horror, and the horror was involuntarily communicated to him. 'For heaven's sake, not another word!'

She rose quickly and moved away from him.

'Not another word!' she repeated, and with a look of cold despair, strange to him, she left him. She felt that at that moment she could not express in words her feeling of shame, joy, and horror at this entrance on a new life, and she did not wish to vulgarize that feeling by inadequate words. Later on, the next day and the next, she still could not find words to describe all the complexity of those feelings, and could not even find thoughts with which to reflect on all that was in her soul.

She said to herself: 'No, I can't think about it now; later, when I am calmer.' But that calm, necessary for reflection, never came. Every time the thought of what she had done, and of what was to become of her and of what she should do, came to her mind, she was seized with horror and drove these thoughts away.

'Not now; later, when I am calmer!' she said to herself.

But in her dreams, when she had no control over her thoughts, her position appeared to her in all its shocking nakedness. One dream she had almost every night. She dreamt that both at once were her husbands, and lavished their caresses on her. Alexey Alexandrovich wept, kissing her hands, saying: 'How beautiful it is now!' and Alexey Vronsky was there too, and he also was her husband. And she was surprised that formerly this had seemed impossible to her, and laughingly explained to them how much simpler it really was, and that they were both now contented and happy. But this dream weighed on her like a nightmare, and she woke from it filled with horror.

Chapter XII

When Levin first returned from Moscow, and while he still started and blushed every time he remembered the disgrace of the refusal, he had said to himself, 'I blushed and started like this when I was ploughed in physics, and had to remain in the second class; and in the same way I felt myself lost when I made a mess of my sister's affair that had been entrusted to me. And what happened? Now that years have passed, when I remember it, I am surprised that it could have grieved me so much. So it will be with this grief. Time will pass, and I shall become indifferent.'

But three months passed and he had not become indifferent to it, and to think of it still hurt him as it had done in the first days. He could not find peace, because he had so long dreamed of family life and felt so ripe for it, but was still unmarried and further than ever from marriage.

He himself felt painfully what all those around him felt too, that it is not good for a man of his age to be alone. He remembered how, just before leaving for Moscow, he had said to Nicholas, his cowman, a naïve peasant with whom he liked to talk: 'Well, Nicholas, I want to get married,' and how Nicholas had promptly replied, as on a matter about which there could be no doubt: 'And it's high time, Constantine Dmitrich.' But now he was further from marriage than ever. The place was unoccupied, and when in imagination he tried to put one of the girls he knew there, he felt that it was quite impossible. Moreover, the memory of her refusal, and the part he had played in it, tormented him with shame. However much he told himself that he was not at all to blame in that matter, the memory of it, together with other shameful memories, made him start and blush. There had been in his past, as in that of every man, actions which he realized were bad, and for which his conscience ought to have tormented him: but the recollections of those bad actions did not torment him nearly as much as these trivial yet shameful memories. These wounds never closed up. And among these recollections stood the memory of her refusal and the pitiful role he must have played in the eyes of the others that evening. But time and work told. The painful memories became more and more covered over by the commonplace but important events of country life. Every week he thought less and less about Kitty. He waited impatiently to hear that she was married or was getting married soon, hoping that such news, like the drawing of an aching tooth, would quite cure him.

Meanwhile spring had come, a glorious steady spring, without the expectations and disappointments spring usually brings. It was

one of these rare springs which plants, animals, and men alike rejoice in. This lovely spring roused Levin still more and confirmed
him in the determination completely to renounce the past in
order to fashion his solitary life firmly and independently. Though
he had not carried out many of the plans with which he had returned to the country from Moscow, he had held to the most important one, that of living a pure life, and he was not experiencing
the shame which used to torment him when he had fallen, but was
able to look people boldly in the face. Already in February he had
received a letter from Mary Nikolaevna to say that his brother
Nicholas's health was getting worse, but that he would not submit
to any treatment. In consequence of this news Levin went to Moscow, saw his brother, and managed to persuade him to consult a
doctor and go to a watering-place abroad. He was so successful in
persuading his brother, and in lending him money for the journey
without irritating him, that he was satisfied with himself in this
respect. Besides his agricultural pursuits, which required special
attention in spring, and besides reading, Levin had another occupation. He had that winter begun writing a book on agriculture, the
basis of which was that the character of the labourer was treated as a
definite factor, like climate and soil, and that therefore the conclusions of agricultural science should be deduced not from data
supplied by climate and soil only, but from data of climate, soil,
and the immutable character of the labourer. So that in spite of
his solitary life, or rather because of it, his time was completely
filled up; only occasionally he felt an unsatisfied desire to share with
some one besides Agatha Mikhaylovna the thoughts that wandered
through his brain—for even with her he often discussed physics,
agricultural theories, and especially philosophy, which last was her
favourite subject.

The spring had set in late. During the last weeks of Lent the
weather had been clear and frosty. It thawed in the sunshine by
day, but at night the thermometer went down to sixteen degrees
Fahrenheit. The snow was covered with a crust of ice so thick that
carts could pass even where there were no roads. Easter found
snow still on the ground; but on Easter Monday a warm wind began
to blow, the clouds gathered, and for three days and nights warm
stormy rain poured down. On the Thursday the wind fell and a
thick grey mist rose as if to hide the secret of the changes nature
was carrying on. Beneath the mist the snow-waters rushed down, the
ice on the river cracked and moved, and the turbid, foaming
torrents flowed quicker, till on the first Sunday after Easter toward
evening the mists dissolved, the clouds broke into fleecy cloudlets
and dispersed, the sky cleared, and real spring was there. In the
morning the bright rising sun quickly melted the thin ice on the

water and the warm air all around vibrated with the vapour given off by the awakening earth. Last year's grass grew green again and new blades came up like needle-points, buds swelled on the guelder-rose and currant bushes and on the sticky, pungent birch trees, and among the golden catkins and on the willow branches the bees began to hum. The unseen larks burst into song above the velvety fresh green and the frozen stubble, the peewits began to cry above the water brought down by the storm and still flooding the low-lying places and marshes, and high up the cranes and geese flew, uttering their spring call. The cattle, who were just beginning to lose their winter coats, began to low in the meadows; the crooked-legged lambs began to play round their bleating mothers, who were losing their wool; swift-footed children began to run along the quickly-drying paths marked with imprints of bare feet, the merry voices of women who were bleaching their linen began to chatter by the ponds, and the axes of peasants, getting ready their wooden ploughs and harrows, sounded in the yards.

The real spring had come.

Chapter XIII

Levin put on his high boots and, wearing a cloth coat instead of a fur for the first time, went out to attend to his farm. Stepping now on a piece of ice, now into the sticky mud, he crossed the streams of dazzling water.

Spring is the time for making plans and resolutions, and Levin, like a tree which in the spring-time does not yet know in which direction and in what manner its young shoots and twigs (still imprisoned in their buds) will develop, did not quite know what work on his beloved land he was going to take in hand, but he felt that his mind was full of the finest plans and resolutions. First of all he went to the cattle-yard. The cows had been let out there, and, warmed by the sunshine, their glossy new coats glistening, they were lowing to be let out into the fields. After he had for a while admired his cows, all familiar to him to the minutest detail, Levin gave orders for them to be driven into the field and for the calves to be let out into the yard. The cowherd ran away merrily to get ready. The dairymaids, with twigs in their hands, holding their skirts up over their bare white legs, not yet sun-burnt, splashed through the puddles into the yard, driving the calves, who were mad with the joy of spring.

Having gazed with admiration at the exceptionally fine calves born that year—the older ones were as big as peasants' cows, and Pava's three-month-old calf was as big as a yearling—Levin gave orders to bring a trough of food for them and to put some hay into the racks outside. But it turned out that the racks, which had been put up in autumn in the yard and not used during winter, were broken. He sent for the carpenter, who was under contract to be with the threshing-machine, but it turned out that he was mending the harrows, which should have been mended the week before Lent. This was very annoying to Levin. It was vexing that the slovenly farm work, against which he had struggled for so many years with all his might, still continued. He found out that the racks which were not wanted in winter had been taken into the farm-horses' stable, and there had got broken, as they were lightly made, being meant only for the calves. Besides this, it proved that the harrows and all the agricultural implements which he had ordered to be examined and mended in winter, for which purpose three carpenters had been specially engaged, had not been seen to, and that the harrows were now being mended when it was time to start harrowing. Levin sent for the steward, but instead of waiting went at once to look for him himself. The steward, in his astrakhan-trimmed coat, as radiant as everything else that day, was coming from the threshing-ground breaking a bit of straw in his hands.

'Why is the carpenter not with the threshing-machine?'

'Oh, I meant to tell you yesterday that the harrows need mending. It's time to plough, you know.'

'Why wasn't it done in winter?'

'But what do you want with the carpenter?'

'Where are the racks from the calves' yard?'

'I have given orders for them to be put into their places. What is one to do with such people!' said the steward, waving his arm.

'It's not a case of such people, but of such a steward!' said Levin flaring up. 'Tell me what I keep you for!' he shouted; but remembering that this would not help matters, he stopped in the middle of what he was saying and only sighed. 'Well, can we begin sowing?' he asked after a pause.

'It will be possible, beyond Turkino, to-morrow or the day after.'

'And the clover?'

'I have sent Vasily, he and Mishka are sowing. Only I don't know if they will get through, it's very sticky.'

'How many acres?'

'Sixteen.'

'Why not the lot?' shouted Levin.

That they were only sowing sixteen instead of fifty acres with clover was still more annoying. To grow clover successfully it was necessary according to both theory and his own experience to sow it as early as possible, almost before the snow had finished melting, and Levin could never get this done.

'There is no one to do it. What are you to do with such people?

Three have not come. And now Simon . . .'

'Well then, you should have let the straw wait.'

'So I have.'

'But where are the men?'

'Five are making compote' (he meant compost) 'and four are turning the oats over. They might begin sprouting, Constantine Dmitrich.'

Levin understood very well that 'might begin sprouting' meant that the English seed-oats were already spoiling. Here again his orders had not been obeyed.

'Oh dear, didn't I speak about it long ago in Lent. . . .'

'Don't worry, it will all be done in good time.'

Levin waved his hand angrily and went to the barn to look at the oats; then he came back to the stable. The oats were not yet spoilt, but the men were turning them over with shovels whereas they should have let them run down from the loft. Levin ordered them to do this, told off two of the men to help sow the clover, and got over his vexation with the foreman. Indeed, the day was so beautiful one could not long remain angry.

'Ignat!' he called to the coachman, who with sleeves rolled up was washing a carriage at the pump, 'saddle me . . .'

'Which, sir?'

'Oh, Kolpik.'

'Yes, sir.'

While the horse was being saddled Levin again called the steward, who was hanging about within sight, in order to make it up with him, and began to talk about the spring work that lay before them and his plans for the estate.

'Carting manure must be started early so that it should be over before the first hay harvest, and the far field will have to be ploughed continually so as to keep the earth clean. We must hire labour for the hay harvest and not pay in kind.'

The foreman listened attentively and evidently tried to approve of his master's plans: but his face still wore that hopeless and despondent expression so familiar to Levin. This expression seemed to say, 'That's all very well, but it will be as God wills.'

Nothing mortified Levin so much as this manner, but it was one common to all the numerous stewards he had employed. They all took up the same attitude toward his plans, and therefore he now no longer grew angry with them, but he was grieved, feeling all the more stimulated to resist this, so to say, elemental force for which he could find no other name but 'as God wills,' which always obstructed him.

'We'll see if we can manage it!' said the steward.

'Why should you not manage it?'

'We must have at least fifteen more labourers; but you see they don't come. Some came to-day, but they wanted seventy roubles each for the summer.'

Levin was silent. That force was opposing him again. He knew that try as they would they had never managed to get more than from thirty-seven to forty labourers at the proper price. Forty could be hired, but never more than forty. Yet all the same he could not but continue the struggle.

'Send to Sury and to Chefirovka, if they don't come. We must try and find men.'

'I'll send right enough,' said Vasily Fedorich, the steward, despondently. 'But the horses too are getting weak.'

'We will buy some more. But don't I know,' he added laughing, 'that you always want less of everything and worse? However, this year I will not let you have your way. I'll see to everything myself.'

'You don't sleep much as it is, I think. It's always pleasanter for us when the master's eye is on us. . . .'

'Then it's down in the Birch Valley that they are sowing the clover? I'll ride over and see,' said Levin, mounting the little light bay horse, Kolpik, which the coachman had brought.

'You won't be able to cross the streams, Constantine Dmitrich,' the coachman called out.

'Well then, I'll go through the forest.'

And Levin rode across the muddy yard and out of the gate into the field at a brisk amble, his fresh little horse snorting at the puddles and pulling at the bridle.

If he had felt light-hearted in the cattle and farm yards, he felt still more so in the fields. Gently swayed by the ambling pace of his good little horse, and drinking in the warm smell with the freshness of snow and air in it, he rode through the forest over the crumbling sinking snow that melted at each footstep, and rejoiced at the sight of each one of his trees with its swelling buds and the moss reviving on its bark. When he had passed the forest, a vast expanse of velvety green unrolled before him without a single bare spot, and only sprinkled here and there in the hollows with patches of unmelted snow. He was not irritated either by the sight of a peasant's horse and colt treading down the young growth (he told a peasant he met to drive them off), nor by the jeering and stupid answer the peasant, Ipat, whom he happened to meet, gave him in reply to his question:

'Well, Ipat, will it soon be time to sow?'

'We must plough first, Constantine Dmitrich,' said Ipat.

The further he went the happier he felt, and all sorts of plans for his estate, each better than the last, presented themselves to him: to plant rows of willows with a southern aspect on all the fields, so that the snow should not remain long under them; to divide the fields, tilling six and keeping three under grass; to build a new cattle-yard at the further end of the field; to dig a pond, and to make folds for the cattle for manuring purposes. Then he would have three hundred desyatinas of wheat, one hundred of potatoes, and one hundred and fifty of clover, and not a single desyatina exhausted.

Dreaming such dreams, carefully guiding his horse so as not to trample down his young growth, he rode up to the labourers who were sowing the clover. The cart with the seed was standing not on the border but in a field of winter-wheat, which was being cut up by the wheels and trampled by the horse's feet. Both the labourers were sitting on the narrow strip between the fields, probably sharing a pipe of tobacco. The earth in the cart with which the seeds were mixed was not rubbed fine, but was pressed or frozen into lumps. On seeing the master the labourer Vasily moved toward the cart, and Mishka began to sow. This was not right, but Levin seldom got angry with the hired men. When Vasily came up Levin told him to take the cart and horse on to the border.

'It won't matter, sir, the wheat will recover.'

'Please don't argue,' said Levin, 'but do as you are told.'

'Yes, sir,' answered Vasily, and took hold of the horse's head.

'But the sowing, Constantine Dmitrich, is getting on first-rate,' he said making up to the master. 'Only the walking is dreadful. You drag half a hundredweight on your boots.'

'And why has not the earth been sifted?' said Levin.

'Oh, but we crumble it up,' said Vasily, taking a handful and rubbing the earth between his palms.

Vasily was not to blame that they had given him unsifted earth, but still it was annoying.

Having more than once successfully tested a patent remedy for conquering vexation and making all that seemed wrong right again, Levin employed it now. He looked at the strides Mishka took dragging the enormous lumps of earth that stuck to his feet, dismounted, took the seed-basket from Vasily, and prepared to sow.

'Where did you stop?'

Vasily pointed to a mark with his foot and Levin began scattering the seeds and earth as best he could. It was hard walking, and having done a row Levin, wet with perspiration, stopped and gave back the basket.

'Mind, sir, and don't scold me for this row when summer comes,' said Vasily.

'Why? 'said Levin merrily, feeling that his remedy was acting well.

'Oh, you'll see when the summer comes. You'll distinguish it. You just look where I sowed last spring, how regularly I scattered it over. Why, Constantine Dmitrich, I don't think I could try harder if I was working for my own father. I don't like to do things badly myself, and I see that others don't. What's good for the master is good for us too. When one looks over there it makes one's heart rejoice,' said Vasily, pointing to the field.

'A fine spring, isn't it, Vasily?'

'It's a spring such as the old men don't remember. I've been home, and my old father also has sown three measures of wheat. They say it has caught up the rye.'

'And have you been sowing wheat long?'

'Why, it was you who taught us to sow it. The year before last you gave me a bushel of seed yourself. We sowed a quarter of it and sold the rest.'

'Well, mind and rub the lumps,' said Levin, going up to his horse, 'and keep an eye on Mishka, and if the clover comes up well you shall have fifty kopeks for each desyatina.'

'Thank you kindly. We are very grateful to you as it is.'

Levin mounted his horse and rode to the field where clover had been sown the year before, and to another which was deeply ploughed and ready for sowing the spring wheat.

The clover was coming on splendidly. It was already reviving and steadily growing green among last year's wheat stubble. The horse sank into the ground up to his pasterns and drew each foot out of the half-thawed earth with a smacking noise. It was quite impossible to ride over the deeply-ploughed field; the earth bore only where there was still a little ice, and in the thawed furrows, the horse's legs sank right in. The ploughed land was in excellent condition; it would be possible to harrow and sow it in a couple of days. Everything was beautiful and gay. Levin rode back by the way that led across the streams, hoping that the water would have gone down, and he did manage to ford the stream, scaring two ducks in so doing. 'There must be some snipe too,' he thought, and just at the turning to his house he met the keeper, who confirmed his supposition.

Levin rode on at a trot, so as to have dinner and get his gun ready for the evening.

Chapter XIV

As Levin, in the highest spirits, was nearing the house he heard the sound of a tinkling bell approaching the main entrance.

'Why, that must be some one from the station,' he thought. 'They would just have had time to get here from the Moscow train. Who is it? Can it be brother Nicholas? He did say, "Perhaps I'll go to a watering-place, or perhaps I'll come to you." ' For a moment he felt frightened and disturbed lest his brother's presence should destroy the happy frame of mind that the spring had aroused in him. But he was ashamed of that feeling, and immediately, as it were, opened out his spiritual arms and with tender joy expected, and now hoped with his whole soul, that it was his brother. He touched up his horse and, having passed the acacia trees, saw a hired three-horse sledge coming from the station and in it a gentleman in a fur coat. It was not his brother. 'Oh, if only it's some nice fellow with whom one can have a talk,' he thought. 'Ah,' he cried, joyfully lifting both arms, 'here's a welcome guest! Well, I am glad to see you!' he exclaimed, recognizing Oblonsky.

'I shall know now for certain whether she is married or when she will be,' thought Levin.

And on this lovely day he felt that the memory of her did not hurt him at all.

'You did not expect me, eh?' said Oblonsky, getting out of the sledge with mud on his nose, cheek, and eyebrows, but beaming with cheerfulness and health. 'I have come to see you, that's one thing,' he said, embracing and kissing Levin, 'to get some shooting, that's two, and to sell the Ergushevo forest, that's three.'

'That's grand! and what a spring we are having! How did you manage to get here in a sledge?'

'It would have been worse still on wheels, Constantine Dmitrich,' said the driver, whom Levin knew.

'Well, I am very, very glad to see you,' said Levin with a sincere smile, joyful as a child's.

He showed his guest into the spare bedroom, where Oblonsky's things, his bag, a gun in a case, and a satchel with cigars, were also brought, and leaving him to wash and change Levin went to the office to give orders about the ploughing and the clover. Agatha Mikhaylovna, always much concerned about the honour of the house, met him in the hall with questions about dinner.

'Do just as you please, only be quick,' he said and went out to see the steward.

When he returned, Oblonsky, fresh and clean, with hair brushed, and face radiant with smiles, was just coming out of his room, and they went upstairs together.

'How glad I am to have come to you! Now I shall be able to understand what the mysteries you perpetrate here consist of. But, seriously, I envy you. What a house, and everything so splendid, so light, so gay!' said Oblonsky, forgetting that it was not always spring and bright weather there, as on that day.

'And your nurse! quite charming! A pretty housemaid with a little apron would be preferable; but with your severe and monastic style this one is more suitable.'

Oblonsky had much interesting news to tell, and one item of special interest to Levin was that his brother, Sergius Ivanich, intended to come and stay in the country with him that summer.

Not a word did Oblonsky say about Kitty or about any of the Shcherbatskys; he only delivered greetings from his wife. Levin was grateful to him for his delicacy and was very glad of his visit. As usual during his solitude a mass of thoughts and feelings he could not express to those around had collected in his mind, and now he poured out to Oblonsky the poetic joy of spring, his failures, his plans concerning the estate, his thoughts and remarks about the books he had read, and especially the idea of his own book, the basis of which, though he did not notice it himself, was a criticism of all previous works on agriculture. Oblonsky, always pleasant and quick at understanding everything from a hint, was specially pleasant on this visit; there was a new trait in him which Levin noticed and was flattered by—a kind of respect and a sort of tenderness toward him. The efforts of Agatha Mikhaylovna and the cook to make the dinner specially nice resulted only in both the hungry friends sitting down to a snack and having to appease their hunger with *hors d'œuvres* of bread and butter, smoked goose, and pickled mushrooms, and in Levin's ordering the soup to be served without waiting for the pasties with which the cook intended to astonish the visitor. But Oblonsky, though used to very different dinners, found everything delicious; the herb brandy, the bread and butter, and especially the smoked goose and pickled mushrooms, the nettle soup and the fowl with melted-butter sauce, the Crimean white wine— everything was delicious, everything was excellent.

'Splendid, splendid!' he said, lighting a thick cigarette after the joint. 'I seem to have come to you as one lands from a noisy steamer on to a peaceful shore. So you maintain that the labourer should be studied as one of the factors which should decide the choice of agricultural methods? You know I am quite an outsider in these matters, but I should think this theory and its application ought to influence the labourer too.'

'Yes, but wait a bit, I am not talking about political economy but about the science of agriculture. It should resemble the natural sciences and should examine existing phenomena, including the labourer with his economic and ethnographic . . .'

At that moment Agatha Mikhaylovna came in with some jam.

'Ah, Agatha Mikhaylovna,' said Oblonsky, kissing the tips of his plump fingers; 'what smoked goose you have, what herb brandy! . . . But what d'you think, Constantine, is it not time?' he added.

Levin glanced out of the window at the sun which was setting behind the bare trees of the forest.

'High time, high time! Kuzma, tell them to harness the trap,' he said, and ran downstairs.

Oblonsky went down and himself carefully took the canvas cover off the varnished case, opened it, and set to work to put together his valuable gun, which was of the newest type.

Kuzma, already scenting a substantial tip, did not leave Oblonsky for a moment. He put on his stockings and his boots for him, and Oblonsky willingly allowed him to do so.

'Constantine, please leave word that if the dealer Ryabinin comes (I told him to come here to-day) they should ask him in and let him wait.'

'Are you selling the forest to Ryabinin?'

'Yes. Do you know him?'

'Of course I know him. I have had dealings with him, positively and finally.'

Oblonsky laughed. 'Positively and finally' were the dealer's favourite words.

'Yes, he does speak very funnily. She knows where the master is going,' he added, patting Laska, who was whining and jumping round Levin, now licking his hand, now his boots and his gun.

The trap was standing at the door when they went out.

'I told them to harness though it is not far, but if you like we can walk?'

'No, let us drive,' said Oblonsky, stepping up into the trap.[3] He sat down, wrapped a rug round his legs, and lit a cigar. 'How is it you don't smoke? A cigar is such a . . . not exactly a pleasure, but the crown and sign of pleasure. Ah, this is life! How delightful! This is how I should like to live.'

'But who prevents you?' Levin remarked, smiling.

'No—you are a lucky fellow! You have got all you are fond of. You like horses—you have them; hounds—you have them; shooting—you get it; farming—you get it too.'

'Perhaps it is because I am glad of what I get, and don't grieve about what I haven't,' said Levin, thinking of Kitty.

Oblonsky understood and looked at him but said nothing.

Levin was grateful to Oblonsky because, with his usual tact, noticing that Levin was afraid of talking about the Shcherbatskys, he avoided mentioning them; but now Levin wanted to find out about the matter that tormented him, and yet feared to speak of it.

'Well, and how are your affairs?' he asked, recollecting how wrong it was of him to be thinking only of his own concerns.

Oblonsky's eyes began to sparkle merrily.

'But *you* don't admit that one may want a roll while one gets regular rations, you consider it a crime; and I don't believe in life without love,' he answered, understanding Levin's question in his own way. 'How can I help it? I am made that way. And really so

_____

3. The trap was a long vehicle something like a jaunting-car, but with four wheels.

little harm is done to anyone, and one gets so much pleasure . . .'

'Is there anything new then?' inquired Levin.

'There is! Well, you know Ossian's type of woman—such as one sees in a dream? Well, there are such women in reality, and these women are terrible. Woman, you see, is an object of such a kind that study it as much as you will, it is always quite new.' [4]

'In that case, better not study them.'

'Oh, no! Some mathematician has said pleasure lies not in discovering truth but in seeking it.'

Levin listened in silence, but in spite of all his efforts he could not enter into his friend's soul and understand his feeling, nor the delight of studying women of that kind.

Chapter XV

The place where they were going to shoot was not far away, by a stream among young aspen trees. When they had reached the wood Levin got down and led Oblonsky to the corner of a mossy and marshy glade, already free from snow. He himself went to a forked birch on the other side and, leaning his gun against the fork of the lower branch, took off his coat, tightened his girdle, and tried whether he could move his arms freely.

The old grey-haired Laska, following close on his heels, sat down warily in front of him and pricked up her ears. The sun was setting behind the forest, and the little birches interspersed among the aspen trees stood out clearly against the evening glow with their drooping branches and their swollen buds ready to burst into leaf. From the thicket, where the snow had not all melted, the water still flowed in branching streamlets with a gentle rippling sound. Small birds chirped and now and then flew from tree to tree.

In the intervals of profound silence last year's leaves were heard rustling, set in motion by the thawing of the earth and the growth of the grass.

'Just fancy! One can hear and see the grass growing,' thought Levin, as he noticed a wet slate-coloured aspen leaf move close to the point of a blade of grass. He stood listening, and gazing down now on the wet mossy ground, now at the attentive Laska, now at the sea of bare tree-tops stretched out before him at the foot of the hill, and now at the darkening sky streaked with fleecy clouds. A hawk flew leisurely past, high above the distant forest; another followed in the same direction and vanished. In the thicket the birds chirped louder and louder and more eagerly. A tawny owl hooted near by, and Laska started, took a few careful steps, and with her head on one side again listened intently. A cuckoo called beyond the river. It

---

4. Ossian, the legendary Celtic hero and bard under whose name Macpherson in 1762–63 published a collection of poems, the female figures in which are often of a tragic and mysterious type.

called twice in its usual note, then hoarsely and hurriedly and got out of time.

'Fancy a cuckoo already!' said Oblonsky, appearing from behind a bush.

'Yes, I heard,' answered Levin, so reluctant to disturb the silence of the wood that his own voice sounded unpleasant to him. 'They won't be long now.'

Oblonsky's figure again disappeared behind the bush, and Levin only saw the flare of a match, followed by the red glow of a cigarette and a spiral of blue smoke.

Click! click! Oblonsky cocked his gun.

'And what's that screaming?' he asked, drawing Levin's attention to a long-drawn cry like the high-pitched whinny of a colt in play.

'Don't you know? It's a male hare. But stop talking! Listen, they're coming!' Levin almost shouted, cocking his gun.

They heard a shrill whistle in the distance, and after the two seconds' interval so familiar to sportsmen, another followed, and then a third, and after the third whistle came a cry.

Levin looked to the right and to the left, and there before him against the dull light-blue sky, over the lower branches of the aspen tops, appeared the flying birds. They were flying straight toward him; the near sound of their cry—something like the sound made when tightly stretched cloth is steadily torn—seemed close to his ears; the long beak and neck of a bird were quite visible, and just as Levin took aim a red flash came from behind the bush where Oblonsky was standing and the bird descended like an arrow and then fluttered up again. Another flash, followed by a report, and the bird, flapping its wings as if trying to keep up in the air, remained stationary for a moment and then with a heavy thud fell on the swampy ground.

'Can I have missed?' cried Oblonsky, who could not see through the smoke.

'Here it is!' answered Levin, pointing to Laska, who with one ear erect, wagging her fluffy, high-arched tail, stepping slowly as if to prolong the pleasure and seeming almost to smile, brought the dead bird to her master. 'Well, I'm glad you got it,' said Levin, and while he spoke he was already experiencing a feeling of envy at not having killed the bird himself.

'A wretched miss with the right barrel,' replied Oblonsky, reloading. 'Hush . . . coming!'

Indeed, they heard two shrill whistles quickly following each other. Two snipe, playing and racing one another, whistling but not crying, flew almost over the sportsmen's heads. Then there were four reports, the birds took a swift turn like swallows and vanished from sight.

.   .   .   .

The shooting was splendid. Oblonsky brought down two more birds, and Levin brought down two, of which one was not recovered. It began to get dark. Through the young birches, Venus bright and silvery was already shining with her delicate glitter low down in the west, and high up in the east flickered the red fire of the dim Arcturus. Above his head Levin found, and again lost, stars of the Great Bear. The snipe had ceased flying; but Levin decided to stay until Venus, which he could see underneath a branch, should rise above it [5] and all the stars of the Great Bear should be visible.

Venus had risen above the branch and the car of the Great Bear as well as its shafts showed clearly against the dark blue sky, but he still waited.

'Is it not time to go?' asked Oblonsky.

It was quite quiet in the wood, not a bird stirred.

'Let's stay a little longer,' answered Levin.

'As you please.'

They were now standing some fifteen yards apart.

'Stiva!' said Levin suddenly and unexpectedly; 'why don't you tell me whether your sister-in-law is married, or when she will be?'

Levin felt so strong and calm that he thought the answer, whatever it might be, could not agitate him, but he did not at all expect the reply Oblonsky gave him.

'She has not thought, and is not thinking, of getting married, but she is very ill and the doctors have sent her abroad. They are even afraid for her life.'

'You don't mean it!' exclaimed Levin. 'Very ill? What's the matter with her? How did she? . . .'

While they were talking Laska, pricking her ears, kept looking up at the sky and then reproachfully at them.

'What a time they have chosen to talk,' thought she. 'And there it comes flying. . . . Just so, here it is. They'll miss it. . . .'

But at that moment both men heard a shrill whistle that seemed to smite on their ears; they both seized their guns, and there were two flashes and two reports at the same moment. The woodcock that was flying high up instantly folded its wings and fell into the thicket, bending down the thin young shoots.

'That's good! It belongs to both!' cried Levin, and ran into the thicket with Laska to look for the bird. 'Oh! but there was something unpleasant!' he thought. 'Yes, of course, Kitty is ill! But what can I do? I am very sorry,' he thought. 'Found? good dog!' he said, taking the warm bird from Laska's mouth and putting it into his well-filled game-bag.

'We've found it, Stiva!' he shouted.

---

5. Tolstóy seems to have made a slip. Being in the west, Venus would be setting, not rising.

Chapter XVI

On their way home Levin inquired the particulars of Kitty's illness and of the Shcherbatskys' plans, and though he would have
been ashamed to confess it, what he heard was agreeable to him. It
was agreeable because there was still hope for him, and even more
because she was suffering, she who had made him suffer so much.
But when Oblonsky began to speak of what caused Kitty's illness
and to mention Vronsky's name, Levin interrupted him:

'I have no right whatever to know such family details, and frankly
I am not interested in them either.'

Oblonsky gave a scarcely perceptible smile on noticing the quick
change, so familiar to him, in Levin's face, which became as gloomy
as it had been bright a moment before.

'Have you finally settled with Ryabinin about the forest?' asked
Levin.

'Yes, I have. I'm getting a splendid price for it: thirty-eight
thousand roubles; eight at once, and the rest to be paid within six
years. I have been bothering about it a long time. No one would
give more.'

'The fact is you are giving the forest away,' said Levin moodily.

'Why giving it away?' said Oblonsky with a good-natured smile,
knowing well that everything would now seem wrong to Levin.

'Because the forest is worth at least five hundred roubles a desyatina,' replied Levin.

'Oh, you country gentlemen!' said Oblonsky jokingly. 'And your
tone of contempt for us poor townfolk! . . . But when it comes to
getting business done, we do it better than anyone. Believe me, I
have reckoned it all out,' continued he, 'and have sold the forest so
well that I am afraid he may change his mind. You know it's not
timber but, for the most part, only fit for fuel,' said he, hoping by
this remark finally to convince Levin of the injustice of his suspicions. 'And it will not yield more than ten sazhens [6] of wood to
the desyatina . . . and he is paying me at the rate of two hundred
roubles.'

Levin smiled contemptuously. 'I know this manner,' he thought,
'not his only, but all townsmen's, who visit the country two or three
times in ten years, get hold of two or three expressions, use them in
and out of season, and are firmly convinced they know everything.
"Timber," and "yield ten sazhens." He uses these words but understands nothing about the business.'

'I should not try to teach you the things you scribble about at
your office,' he said, 'but in case of need would come to you for advice about them, but you are firmly convinced that you understand

6. Seven feet by 7 feet by 1½ feet, almost 2 face cords (U.S.); a *desyatina* is about 2¾ acres.
The yield will be about 6 cords per acre.

all this forest lore. It is not easy! Have you counted the trees?'

'How can one count the trees?' said Oblonsky, still anxious to
dispel his friend's ill-humour.

> ' "Count grains of sand, and planets' rays,
>   E'en though a lofty mind were able . . ." '

'Well, Ryabinin's lofty mind is able to do it. And no dealer will
ever buy without first counting, unless the forest is given to him for
nothing, as you are doing. I know your forest. I go shooting there
every year, and it is worth five hundred roubles a desyatina cash
down, and he is paying you two hundred on long term. That means
that you have made him a present of about thirty thousand roubles.'

'Come, don't get so carried away,' said Oblonsky piteously. 'Why
did no one offer more?'

'Because he and the other dealers are in league, and he has bought
them off. I have had dealings with them all, and I know them. They
are not genuine dealers, but sharks. He would not consider a deal
which would bring him in ten or fifteen per cent.; he waits till he
can buy at a fifth of the value.'

'Oh, come! You are down in the dumps to-day.'

'Not at all,' said Levin gloomily, just as they drove up to the
house.

At the porch stood a little cart strongly bound with leather and
iron, and to the cart was harnessed a well-fed horse with broad,
tightly-stretched straps. In the cart sat Ryabinin's clerk (who also
performed a coachman's duties), his skin tightly stretched over his
full-blooded face and his belt drawn tight. Ryabinin himself was already in the house and met the two friends in the hall. He was a
tall, spare, middle-aged man, with a moustache, a prominent shaven
chin, and prominent dim eyes. He wore a long-skirted blue coat with
buttons very low down at the back, high boots drawn quite straight
over the calves of his legs and crinkled round the ankles, and over
them he had on a pair of large goloshes. He wiped his face all round
with his handkerchief, and smoothing his coat, which was already
quite in order, smilingly greeted the new arrivals. He held out his
hand to Oblonsky as if he were trying to catch something.

'Oh, so you have come,' said Oblonsky taking his hand. 'That's
right!'

'I dared not disobey your Excellency's commands, though the
roads are quite too bad. I have literally had to walk all the way, but
I have arrived in time. . . .'

'Constantine Dmitrich, my respects to you!' he said turning to
Levin and trying to catch his hand too. But Levin, frowning, pretended not to see the hand, and began taking the snipe out of the
game-bag.

'You have been pleased to amuse yourself with shooting? What kind of bird may that be?' added Ryabinin, looking contemptuously at the snipe. 'Something tasty?' and he shook his head disapprovingly as if much doubting whether this game were worth the candle.

'Would you like to go into my study?' said Levin, frowning moodily, and addressing Oblonsky in French. 'Go into the study, you can talk things over there.'

'That would do very well,—or wherever you like,' remarked Ryabinin with contemptuous dignity, as if to show them that though others might find it difficult to know how to behave with different people, yet for him no difficulty of any kind could ever exist.

On entering the study Ryabinin looked round by force of habit as though to find the icon, but after finding it he did not cross himself. He glanced at the book cupboards and book-shelves with the same look of doubt as he had bestowed on the snipe, smiled contemptuously, and again shook his head disapprovingly, decidedly refusing to admit that this game could be worth the candle.

'Well, have you brought the money?' asked Oblonsky. 'Take a seat.'

'There won't be any difficulty about the money. I've come to see you and to talk matters over.'

'Talk what matters over? But do take a seat.'

'I can do that,' said Ryabinin, sitting down and putting his arm on the back of his chair in a most uncomfortable way. 'You must let me off something, Prince. You're wronging me. As to the money, it is all ready to the last kopek. There will be no delay about the money.'

Levin, who had been putting away his gun in a cupboard, was just going out of the door, but on hearing the dealer's words he stopped.

'As it is you are getting the forest for next to nothing,' he said. 'He came to me too late, else I would have fixed the price.'

Ryabinin rose and smiled silently, surveying Levin from his feet to his head.

'He is very close, is Constantine Dmitrich,' he said, addressing Oblonsky with a smile. 'It's absolutely impossible to buy anything of him. I've been bargaining with him for wheat and offering a good price.'

'Why should I give you what is mine for nothing? I have not found it on the ground nor stolen it.'

'Oh dear no, nowadays it is quite impossible to steal. Absolutely everything nowadays goes before a jury, everything is judged honourably, there's no possibility of stealing. We speak honestly. It's too much for the forest, there's no making any profit on it. I am asking to have something knocked off, if only a trifle.'

'Well, have you settled the business or not? If you have, there's no use bargaining, but if not,' said Levin, 'I will buy the forest myself.'

The smile vanished from Ryabinin's face, which assumed a hawk-like, rapacious, and cruel expression. With his bony fingers he rapidly unfastened his coat, exposing his braided shirt, the brass buttons of his waistcoat, and a watch-chain, and quickly took out a thick old pocketbook.

'If you please, the forest is mine,' he said, rapidly crossing himself and holding out his hand. 'Take your money, the forest is mine. That's the way Ryabinin does business, no fussing about kopeks,' he said, frowning and flourishing his pocket-book.

'If I were you I should not be in a hurry to take it,' remarked Levin.

'What d'you mean?' said Oblonsky with surprise. 'Why, I've given my word.'

Levin went out and slammed the door. Ryabinin looked at it and smiled, shaking his head.

'That's all his youthfulness, his absolute childishness. Why, I am making this purchase, believe me, just for the honour and glory of the thing, so that it should be Ryabinin and not another that has bought Oblonsky's forest. But it's still a question whether by God's mercy I can make a profit. Believe me, before God! Please, sir, the agreement must be written . . .'

An hour later the dealer, with his coat well lapped over, the hooks of his overcoat carefully fastened, and with the agreement in his pocket, seated himself in his little cart and drove home.

'Oh, these gentlefolks!' he remarked to his clerk, while hooking up the leather apron of the cart, 'regular objects!'

'But may I congratulate you on the purchase, Michael Ignatich?'

'Well, well . . .'

Chapter XVII

Oblonsky went upstairs, his pockets bulging with the treasury-bills payable in three months' time with which Ryabinin had paid him. The forest transaction was completed, he had the money in his pocket, the shooting had been fine, Oblonsky was in the best of spirits, and therefore all the more anxious to dispel Levin's ill-humour. He wanted to finish the day at supper as pleasantly as he had begun it.

Levin really was in a bad humour, and in spite of his desire to behave kindly and amiably to his charming guest he could not master himself. The intoxication of the news that Kitty was not married was beginning little by little to take effect on him.

Kitty was unmarried and ill, and ill for love of the man who had slighted her. This slight seemed to rebound on him. Vronsky had slighted her and she had slighted him, Levin. Consequently Vronsky had a right to despise him and was therefore his enemy. But Levin did not think all this. He dimly felt that there was something insulting to him in the affair, and was angry not with what had upset him but with everything that presented itself to him. The stupid sale of the forest, the swindle Oblonsky had fallen a prey to, which had been perpetrated in his house, irritated him.

'Well, have you finished?' he said when he met Oblonsky upstairs. 'Will you have some supper?'

'I won't say no. What an appetite I get in the country, wonderful! Why did you not offer Ryabinin something to eat?'

'Let him go to the devil!'

'Well, really, how you treat him!' said Oblonsky. 'You did not even give him your hand. Why not shake hands with him?'

'Because I do not shake hands with the footman, and the footman is a hundred times better than he.'

'What a reactionary you really are! What about merging the classes?' said Oblonsky.

'Let those who like it merge to their hearts' content, but it sickens me.'

'I see you are quite a reactionary.'

'I have really never considered what I am. I am Constantine Levin, that's all.'

'And Constantine Levin is in a very bad temper,' said Oblonsky, smiling.

'Yes, I am in a bad temper, and do you know why? Because, excuse me, of your stupid sale.'

Oblonsky wrinkled his face good-naturedly, like an innocent man who was being hurt and interfered with.

'Oh don't!' he said. 'When has a man ever sold anything without being told immediately after that it was worth much more? But while he is trying to sell nobody offers him more. . . . No, I see you have a grudge against that unfortunate Ryabinin.'

'Maybe I have. And do you know why? You will again call me a reactionary or some other dreadful name, but all the same it vexes and hurts me to see on all sides the impoverishment of the *noblesse*, to which I too belong and to which, in spite of the merging of the classes, I am very glad to belong. . . . And impoverished not from extravagance. That would not matter so much: to spend like a nobleman is their business—only the *noblesse* know how to do it. At present the peasants around here are buying land—that does not pain me. The squire does nothing, the peasant works and squeezes out the idler. That is as it should be and I am very glad on the peasant's account. But it hurts me to see this impoverishment as a

result of,—shall I call it simplicity? Here a Polish leaseholder buys
for half its value the splendid estate of a lady who lives in Nice.
There land that is worth ten roubles a desyatina is leased to a merchant for one rouble. And now you, without any reason, have presented that scamp with thirty thousand roubles.'

'Then what do you want? Is one to count every tree?'

'Certainly count them! You have not counted them but Ryabinin
has! Ryabinin's children will have the means to live and get an education, while yours may not have!'

'Well, forgive me, but there is something mean in all this counting. We have our occupation and they have theirs, and they have to
make a profit. Anyway the thing is done and there's an end to it.
And here come the fried eggs, just the way I like them best. And
Agatha Mikhaylovna will give us some of that excellent herb
brandy. . . .'

Oblonsky sat down to table and began joking with Agatha Mikhaylovna, assuring her that it was long since he had had such a dinner and supper as that day.

'Well, you appreciate it at least,' said Agatha Mikhaylovna; 'but
Constantine Dmitrich, whatever one gives him, if it were only a
crust of bread, would just eat it and go away.'

Try as Levin would to control himself, he remained morose and
silent. There was one question he wanted to put to Oblonsky, but
could not bring himself to ask, nor could he find the form to put it
in or the moment to ask it. When Oblonsky had gone down to his
room and, after again washing, had put on his frilled nightshirt and
got into bed, Levin still lingered in his room talking about various
trifles and unable to ask what he wanted to know.

'What wonderful soap they make!' he said, examining and unwrapping a cake of scented soap Agatha Mikhaylovna had prepared
for the visitor, but which Oblonsky had not used. 'Just look, it is
quite a work of art.'

'Yes, yes, there are all sorts of improvements in everything now,'
said Oblonsky with a moist and blissful yawn. 'In the theatres for
instance and all places of amusement. . . . Oh, oh, oh!' he yawned.
'Electric light everywhere. Oh, oh!' [7]

'Yes, electric light,' said Levin. 'Yes, by the by, where is Vronsky
now?' he asked, suddenly putting down the soap.

'Vronsky?' said Oblonsky, ceasing to yawn. 'He is in Petersburg.
He left soon after you did, and has not been in Moscow once since
then. And do you know, Constantine, I will tell you quite frankly,'
he said, leaning his elbow on the table by his bed and supporting
on his hand his good-looking, rosy face with its glittering, kind, and
sleepy eyes, 'it was your own fault. You were frightened of a rival.

---

7. Electrical lighting was still a rarity in the early 1870s.

But, as I told you then, I do not know who had the better chance. Why did you not make a dash for it? I told you at the time that . . .' He yawned, but only with his jaw, without opening his mouth.

'Does he, or does he not, know that I proposed?' thought Levin, looking at him. 'Yes, there is something sly and diplomatic in his face,' and feeling himself blush, he gazed in silence straight into Oblonsky's eyes.

'If there was anything on her side at that time, it was only the external attraction,' continued Oblonsky. 'You know his being a perfect aristocrat and his future position in Society had an effect, not on her but on her mother.'

Levin frowned. The insult of the refusal he had had to face burned in his heart like a fresh, newly-received wound. But he was at home and the walls of home are helpful.

'Wait, wait,' he began, interrupting Oblonsky. 'You talk of his being an aristocrat. But I should like to ask you what is Vronsky's or anyone else's aristocracy that I should be slighted because of it? You consider Vronsky an aristocrat. I don't. A man whose father crawled up from nothing by intrigues and whose mother has had relations with heaven knows whom. . . . No, pardon me, I consider myself and people like me aristocrats: people who can point back to three or four honourable generations of their family, all with a high standard of education (talent and intelligence are a different matter), who have never cringed before anyone, never depended on anyone, but have lived as my father and my grandfather did. I know many such. You consider it mean for me to count the trees in my wood while you give Ryabinin thirty thousand roubles; but you will receive a Government grant and I don't know what other rewards, and I shan't, so I value what is mine by birth and labour. . . . We— and not those who only manage to exist by the bounty of the mighty of this world, and who can be bought for a piece of silver—are the aristocrats.'

'But whom are you driving at? I agree with you,' said Oblonsky sincerely and cheerfully, though he felt that Levin ranked him with those who could be bought for silver. Levin's vehemence sincerely pleased him. 'Whom are you driving at? Though much of what you say is not true of Vronsky, I am not speaking about that. I want to tell you candidly that if I were you, I'd come to Moscow now with me, and . . .'

'No . . . I don't know if you knew it or not and I don't care, but I will tell you: I proposed and was refused, and your sister-in-law (Catherine Alexandrovna) is now only a painful and humiliating memory to me.'

'Why? What nonsense!'

'But don't let us talk about it! Forgive me, please, if I have been rude to you,' said Levin. Now that he had spoken out he became once more as he had been in the morning. 'You are not angry with me, Stiva? Please don't be angry,' he said smiling, and took his hand.

'Oh no, not at all! There was nothing to be angry about. I am glad we have had this explanation. And, do you know, the shooting in the early morning is often very good. Should we not go? I would not sleep again after it but go straight from there to the station?'

'A capital idea!'

Chapter XVIII

Though Vronsky's whole inner life was absorbed by his passion, his external life ran unalterably and inevitably along its former customary rails of social and regimental connections and interests. The interests of the regiment occupied an important place in his life, because he was fond of his regiment and still more because the regiment was fond of him. Not only were they fond of him, they respected him too and were proud of him: proud that this man, with his enormous wealth and excellent education and abilities, to whom the road to success of all kinds gratifying to ambition or vanity lay open, had disregarded all this, and of all life's interests had nearest to his heart those of his regiment and his comrades. Vronsky was aware of this attitude of his comrades toward him, and besides liking the life felt bound to justify their view of him.

It goes without saying that he spoke to none of them about his love, nor did he betray himself even in the wildest drinking-bouts (indeed, he never drank so as to lose all self-control). And he silenced any of his thoughtless comrades who tried to hint at the liaison. But in spite of this, his love affair was known to all the town: everybody guessed more or less correctly what his relations with Anna Karenina were. Most of the young men envied him just on account of what was most irksome in the affair, namely Karenin's high rank and the consequent prominence of the affair in Society.

The majority of young women, who envied Anna and had long been weary of hearing her virtues praised, were pleased at what they guessed, and only waited to be sure that public opinion had turned before throwing the whole weight of their scorn at her. They already prepared lumps of mud to pelt her with in due time. Most of the older people and of those highly-placed regretted this impending social scandal.

Vronsky's mother, on hearing of the matter, was at first pleased, both because in her opinion nothing gave such finishing touches to a brilliant young man as an intrigue in the best Society, and also because this Anna Karenina, who had so taken her fancy and who had talked so much about her little son, was after all such as the Countess Vronsky expected all handsome and well-bred women to be. But latterly she had heard that her son had refused a post of importance for his career, merely to remain with his regiment and be able to see Anna Karenina, and that exalted persons were dissatisfied with him for it, so she changed her opinion. She was also displeased because, from all she heard of it, this affair was not one of those brilliant, graceful, Society liaisons which she approved, but a desperate Werther-like passion which might lead him into doing something foolish. She had not seen him since his sudden departure from Moscow, and through her eldest son she sent him word to come and see her.[8]

The elder brother was also dissatisfied with the younger. He did not distinguish what kind of love it was, great or small, passionate or passionless, guilty or pure (he himself, the father of a family, kept a ballet girl, and was therefore lenient in these matters): but he knew that it was a love affair which displeased those whom it is necessary to please, and he therefore disapproved of his brother's conduct.

Besides his military and social interests Vronsky had another one, namely horses, of which he was passionately fond.

That year there was to be an officers' steeplechase, and Vronsky had put down his name, bought an English thoroughbred mare, and, in spite of his love, was passionately, though restrainedly, concerned about the coming races.

The two passions did not interfere with one another. On the contrary he needed an occupation and an interest apart from his love, in which to refresh himself and find rest from the impressions which agitated him too violently.

Chapter XIX

On the day of the Krasnoe Selo races Vronsky came earlier than usual to the regimental mess-room to eat his beefsteak. It was not necessary for him to train very strictly as his weight was just the regulation eleven-and-a-half stone, but he had to be careful not to get fatter and therefore avoided sweets and starchy foods. He sat waiting with his elbows on the table and his coat unbuttoned over a white waistcoat, and while waiting for the beefsteak he had ordered he looked at the pages of a French novel that lay on his plate. He only looked at the book in order not to have to talk to the officers who came in and out of the room while he was thinking.

He thought of Anna, who had promised to meet him after the races. But he had not seen her for three days and, as her husband had returned from abroad, he did not know whether she could keep the appointment to-day or not, and he did not know how to find

8. 'Werther-like passion.' In Goethe's very popular *Leiden des jungen Werthers* the hero kills himself for love of Lotte who was married to his friend.

out. He had seen her last at his cousin Betsy's country house. He went to the Karenins' country house [9] as seldom as possible, but now he meant to go there and was considering how to do it.

'Of course I can say that Betsy sent me to find out if she will be at the race. Yes, of course I will go,' he decided, lifting his eyes from the book, and a vivid sense of the joy of seeing her made his face radiant.

'Send to my house and tell them to harness three horses to the calèche at once,' he said to the waiter who had brought him a beef-steak on a hot silver plate; and drawing the plate nearer to him he began to eat.

From the neighbouring billiard-room came the click of balls, talk, and laughter. Two officers appeared at the entrance door: one with a weak thin face, a young officer who had just joined the regiment from the Cadet Corps; the other a plump old officer with a bracelet on his wrist and small eyes sunk in a bloated face.

Vronsky glanced at them, frowned, and, as if he had not noticed them, turned his eyes on his book and began to eat and read at the same time.

'What? Fortifying yourself for your job?' asked the plump officer taking a seat beside him.

'As you see,' said Vronsky, frowning and wiping his mouth, without looking at the speaker.

'Not afraid of getting fat?' said the other, turning a chair round for the young officer.

'What?' said Vronsky frowning, making a grimace of disgust and showing his regular teeth.

'Not afraid of getting fat?'

'Waiter, sherry!' said Vronsky without replying, and moving his book to the other side of his plate he continued to read.

The plump officer took the wine-list and turned to the young one.

'You choose what we shall drink,' said he, handing him the list and looking at him.

'Suppose we have some Rhine wine,' said the young one, turning his eyes timidly to Vronsky while his fingers tried to catch hold of his just-budding moustache. Seeing that Vronsky did not turn round, he rose.

'Let us go into the billiard-room,' he said.

The plump officer got up obediently and they made their way toward the door.

At that moment Captain Yashvin, a tall man with a fine figure, entered the room, and having given a comtemptuous backward nod

9. It was customary for people who had an occupation in a Russian town in summer to take a country house near the town, where the family could live, while those members of it whose occupation was in town could go back and forth.

to the two officers he came up to Vronsky.

'Ah, here he is!' he exclaimed, and with his big hand gave Vronsky a sharp slap on his shoulder-strap. Vronsky looked up angrily, but his face brightened at once into its characteristic look of quiet, firm kindliness.

'That is wise, Alexey,' said the captain in a loud baritone, 'eat now, and drink one small glass.'

'I don't want to eat.'

'There are the inseparables,' added Yashvin, glancing ironically at the two officers who were just going out of the room. He sat down beside Vronsky, and his legs, encased in tight riding-breeches, being too long for the size of the chair, bent at a sharp angle at the hip and knee-joints. 'Why did you not come to the Krasnensky Theatre last night?'

'I stayed late at the Tverskoys.'

'Ah!' said Yashvin.

Yashvin, a gambler, a rake, a man not merely without principles but with bad principles, was Vronsky's best friend in the regiment. Vronsky liked him both for his extraordinary physical strength, which he chiefly demonstrated by his ability to drink like a fish and go without sleep without its making any difference to him, and for the great mental power which was apparent in his relations with his commanding officers and comrades, who feared and respected him, and in his card-playing when he staked tens of thousands of roubles and, in spite of what he drank, always with such skill and decision that he was considered the best player in the English Club. Vronsky respected and liked Yashvin, particularly because he felt that the latter liked him, not for his name and money but for himself. Among all the people Vronsky knew Yashvin was the only one to whom he would have liked to talk about his love. He felt that Yashvin, though apparently despising all emotion, was the only one who could understand the power of the passion that now filled his whole life. Besides, he felt sure that Yashvin certainly found no pleasure in gossip and scandal, and understood his feeling in the right way— that is, knew and believed that this love was not a joke or an amusement, but something more serious and important.

Vronsky did not talk to him of his love, but was aware that he knew all about it and understood it rightly, and it was pleasant to him to read this in Yashvin's eyes.

'Ah, yes!' he said when he heard that Vronsky had been at the Tverskoys; his black eyes sparkled and he began twisting his left moustache round into his mouth—a bad habit he had.

'Well, and what were you doing last night? Winning?' asked Vronsky.

'Eight thousand. But three of them doubtful. I do not expect he will pay up.'

'Well, then, you can afford to lose on me,' said Vronsky, laughing. (Yashvin had staked heavily on Vronsky.)

'I am sure not to lose. Makhotin is the only dangerous one.' The conversation turned to the forecast of the day's race, the only subject Vronsky could now think about.

'Let us go. I have finished,' said Vronsky, and he rose and moved toward the door. Yashvin rose also and stretched his great legs and long back.

'It is too early for me to dine, but I must have a drink. I will come in a minute. Hallo, wine!' he cried in his loud voice, which was so famous at drill, and here made the glasses tremble. 'No, I do not want any,' he shouted again. 'You are going home and I'll go with you.'

And he and Vronsky went out together.

Chapter XX

Vronsky had his quarters in a roomy, clean, Finnish peasant cottage, divided in two by a partition. Here in camp also, Petritsky lived with him. Petritsky was asleep when Vronsky and Yashvin entered.

'Get up, you've slept enough!' said Yashvin, stepping behind the partition and shaking by the shoulder the dishevelled Petritsky, who lay with his nose buried in the pillow. Petritsky suddenly sprang to his knees and looked round.

'Your brother has been here,' he said to Vronsky. 'He woke me up, devil take him! . . . He said he would come back.' And drawing up his blanket he threw himself back on his pillow. 'Leave me alone, Yashvin!' he said angrily to Yashvin, who was pulling the blanket off him. 'Leave off!' He turned and opened his eyes. 'You had better tell me what to drink! I've such a horrid taste in my mouth that . . .'

'Vodka is better than anything,' said Yashvin in his base voice. 'Tereshchenko! Vodka and pickled cucumbers for your master!' he shouted, evidently enjoying the sound of his own voice.

'Vodka, you think, eh?' asked Petritsky, making a face and rubbing his eyes. 'And will you have a drink? Let us have a drink together! Vronsky, will you have a drink?' he added, getting up and wrapping himself to the arms in a rug of tiger-skin pattern.

He went to the partition door, held up his hands, and began singing in French, ' "There was a king in Thule!" Vronsky, will you have a drink?' [1]

'Get away!' said Vronsky, as he put on the overcoat his servant

---

1. Probably from the opera *Faust* by Charles Gounod (1818–93).

had handed him.

'Where to now?' asked Yashvin. 'Here are the horses,' he added as he saw the calèche drive up to the door.

'To the stables, and then I have to go to Bryansky about the horses,' said Vronsky.

He had really promised to go to Bryansky's, who lived seven miles from Peterhof, and pay him for the horses, and he hoped to make time to call there too. But his friends understood at once that it was not only there that he was going.

Petritsky, still singing, winked his eyes and pouted as if to say, 'We know what sort of Bryansky it is.'

'Mind and don't be late!' was all Yashvin said, and to change the subject he asked, 'Is my roan doing well?' looking out of the window at the middle horse, which he had sold to Vronsky.

'Wait!' shouted Petritsky to Vronsky, who was already going out. 'Your brother left a letter for you and a note. Wait! Where are they?'

Vronsky stopped. 'Well, where are they?'

'Where are they? That is the question!' declaimed Petritsky with solemnity, moving his finger upwards from his nose.

'Come, tell me. This is stupid!' said Vronsky, smiling.

'I have not lighted the fire. They must be somewhere here.'

'Enough of this! Where is the letter?'

'No, really I have forgotten. Or was it a dream? Wait, wait. Why get angry? If you had emptied four bottles a head as we did last night, you would not know where you were lying. Wait a bit, I'll remember it directly.'

Petritsky went behind the partition and lay down on his bed.

'Wait! So I lay, and so he stood. Yes, yes, yes . . . Here it is!' and Petritsky drew the letter from under the mattress where he had put it.

Vronsky took the letter and his brother's note. It was just what he had expected: a letter from his mother reproaching him for not having come to see her, and a note from his brother saying that they must talk things over. Vronsky knew that it all referred to the same subject. 'What business is it of theirs?' thought he, and crumpling up the letters he pushed them in between the buttons of his coat, to be read more attentively on the way. In the passage he met two officers, one of his own and one of another regiment.

Vronsky's quarters were always the haunt of all the officers.

'Where are you going?'

'I have to go to Peterhof.'

'Has the mare come from Tsarskoe?'

'Yes, but I have not seen her since she came.'

'They say Makhotin's Gladiator has gone lame.'

'Nonsense! But how will you manage to ride through such mud?' said the other officer.

'These are the things to restore me!' shouted Petritsky on seeing the new-comers. The orderly stood before him with vodka and pickled cucumbers on a tray. 'Yashvin here has ordered vodka to freshen me up.'

'Well, you did give it us last night,' said one of the new-comers. 'You did not let us sleep all night.'

'Oh, but how we finished up!' said Petritsky. 'Volkov climbed out on to the roof and said he felt melancholy. I said, "Let us have music: a Funeral March!" And he fell asleep up there on the roof to the sound of the Funeral March.'

'Drink, you must drink some vodka and then some seltzer water with plenty of lemon,' said Yashvin, standing over Petritsky, like a mother urging her child to take its medicine. 'And after that a little champagne, about . . . a small bottle.'

'Now that is reasonable! Wait, Vronsky, let us have a drink.'

'No, good-bye, gentlemen. I am not drinking to-day.'

'Why, because of the weight? Well then, we will drink by ourselves. Let's have seltzers and lemons.'

'Vronsky!' shouted some one as Vronsky was already leaving. 'What?'

'You should have your hair cut; it will be too heavy, especially on the top.'

Vronsky was really beginning prematurely to get a little bald. He laughed merrily, showing his compact row of teeth, and drawing his cap over the bald patch, went out and got into the calèche.

'To the stables!' he said, and was taking out the letter to read, but then changed his mind, not wishing to be upset before examining his horse. 'Later will do! . . .'

Chapter XXI

The temporary stable, a wooden structure, had been built close to the racecourse, and it was there his mare was to have been brought the day before. He had not yet been to look at her. During these last days he had not exercised her himself, but had entrusted it to the trainer, and therefore did not in the least know in what condition she had arrived or now was. Hardly had he stepped out of the calèche before his groom, who had recognized it from a distance, had called out the trainer. A lean Englishman in top boots and a short jacket, with only a tuft of beard left under his chin, came to meet him with the awkward gait of a jockey, swaying from side to side with his elbows sticking out.

'Well, how is Frou-Frou?' asked Vronsky in English.

'All right, sir,' came the answer from somewhere inside the

fidgety horse

man's throat. 'Better not go in,' he added, touching his cap. 'I have put a muzzle on her, and she is fidgety. Better not go in, it excites the mare.'

'No, I'll go in. I want to have a look at her.'

'Come along,' said the Englishman frowning and speaking as before without opening his mouth. Swaying his elbows and walking with his loose gait he led the way.

They entered a little yard in front of the shed. A smart, well-dressed lad in a short and clean jacket, with a broom in his hand, met them and followed them. In the shed five horses stood in the horse-boxes, and Vronsky knew that his principal rival, Makhotin's sixteen-hand chestnut, Gladiator, was to have been brought that day and should be standing there too. Vronsky was even more anxious to have a look at Gladiator, whom he had never seen, than at his own mare; but he knew that horse-racing etiquette not only forbade his seeing it, but made it improper for him even to ask about it. As he went along the passage the lad opened the second horse-box to the left, and Vronsky caught sight of a big chestnut horse with white legs. He knew it was Gladiator, but like one who avoids seeing another's open letter, he turned and went to Frou-Frou's box.

'Here is the horse of Mak . . . Mak . . . I never can pronounce his name,' said the Englishman over his shoulder, pointing with his black-nailed thumb to Gladiator's box.

'Makhotin's? Yes, that is my only serious rival,' said Vronsky.

'If you were riding him, I would back you,' said the Englishman.

'Frou-Frou is the braver, but the other is the more powerful horse,' said Vronsky, smiling at the compliment to his riding. 'In a steeplechase everything depends on the riding and on pluck,' said the Englishman.

Vronsky felt that he not only had enough pluck (that is, energy and courage), but, what is much more important, he was firmly convinced that no one in the world could have more pluck than he had.

'Are you quite sure that more training was unnecessary?'

'Quite unnecessary,' said the Englishman. 'Please don't talk loud. The mare is nervous,' he added, nodding toward the closed horse-box before which they were standing, and from which was heard the trampling of hoofs among the straw.

He opened the door, and Vronsky entered the box, which was dimly lit by one small window. In the box stood a muzzled dark-bay mare stepping from foot to foot among the fresh litter. When he had got used to the dim light of the box, Vronsky again instinctively took in at one comprehensive glance all the points of his favourite mare. Frou-Frou was of medium size and by no means free from blemish. She was slenderly built. Her chest, though well arched, was narrow. Her hind quarters tapered rather too much, and her legs, especially her hind legs, were perceptibly bowed inwards. Neither fore nor hind legs were particularly muscular, but on the other hand she was extremely broad in the girth, now that she was lean from her strict training. Seen from the front, her canon bones were very fine and sharp, but unusually wide seen sideways. She appeared all the more narrow in build because so deep in the breadth. But she possessed in the highest degree a characteristic which made one forget all her defects. That was her thoroughbred quality—the kind of blood that *tells*, as they say in English. The muscles, clearly marked beneath the network of sinews, stretched in the fine, mobile skin, which was smooth as satin, seemed hard as bone. Her lean head with the prominent, bright, sparkling eyes, broadened out to her muzzle with its wide crimson nostrils. Her whole appearance, more especially about the head, was spirited yet gentle. She was one of those creatures who seem as if they would certainly speak only if the mechanism of their mouths allowed them to.

To Vronsky at any rate it seemed that she understood all he was feeling while looking at her.

As soon as Vronsky entered, she drew a deep breath and, turning her prominent eyes so that their whites became bloodshot, looked from the other side of the box at the new-comers, shook her muzzle, and stepped lightly from foot to foot.

'There, you see how nervous she is,' said the Englishman.

'Oh, you darling!' said Vronsky, stepping toward the horse and soothing her.

But the nearer he came the more nervous she grew. Only when he reached her head did she suddenly calm down, and the muscles under her fine, delicate coat vibrated. Vronsky stroked her firm neck, adjusted a lock of her mane that had got on the wrong side of her sharply-defined withers and brought his face close to her dilated nostrils, delicate as a bat's wing. Her extended nostrils loudly inhaled and exhaled her breath, and she set back one of her finely-pointed ears with a start, and stretched out her black firm lips toward Vronsky, as if wishing to catch hold of his sleeve. But remembering her muzzle she gave it a jerk, and again began stepping from one of her finely chiselled feet to the other.

'Be quiet, darling, be quiet!' he said, again stroking her flank, and left the box with a joyful conviction that the horse was in the very best condition.

The mare's excitement had communicated itself to Vronsky. He felt that the blood was rushing to his heart, and that he, like the horse, wished to move and to bite; it was both frightening and joyful.

'Well then, I rely on you,' said Vronsky to the Englishman. 'You will be on the spot at half-past six.'

'All right,' said the Englishman. 'And where are you going, my lord?' he asked unexpectedly, addressing him as 'my lord,' which he hardly ever did.

Vronsky raised his head in amazement and looked as he knew how to, not into the Englishman's eyes but at his forehead, surprised at the boldness of the question. But realizing that the Englishman in asking the question regarded him not as an employer, but as a jockey, he replied:

'I have to see Bryansky, but I shall be home in an hour.'

'How often have I been asked that question to-day?' he thought, and blushed, a thing he rarely did. The Englishman looked at him attentively and, as if he knew where he was going, added: 'The chief thing before a race is to keep cool: don't be put out or upset.'

'All right,' said Vronsky smiling, and jumping into the calèche, he told the coachman to drive to Peterhof.

He had not gone many yards before the clouds, which had been threatening since morning, broke, and there was a downpour of rain.

'This is bad!' thought Vronsky, raising the hood of the calèche. 'It was muddy before, but now it will be a swamp.' Sitting alone in the closed calèche he drew out his mother's letter and his brother's note and read them through.

Yes, it was the same thing over and over again. They all, his mother and his brother and everybody, considered it necessary to interfere with his intimate affairs. This interference roused him to anger, a feeling he rarely experienced. 'What business is it of theirs? Why does everybody consider it his duty to look after me? And why do they bother me? Because they see it is something they cannot understand. If it were an ordinary, empty Society intrigue they would let me alone. They feel that it is something different, that it is not a game, and that this woman is dearer to me than life. That is incomprehensible, and therefore it vexes them. Whatever our fate is or may be, we have made it and do not complain of it,' he said, joining Anna and himself in the word 'we.' 'No, they needs must teach us how to live. They have no conception of what happiness is, and they do not know that without love there is no happiness or unhappiness for us, for there would be no life,' he thought.

He was angry with everybody for their interference, just because he felt in his soul that they were right. He felt that the love that united him with Anna was not momentary infatuation, which would pass, as Society intrigues do, without leaving any trace in the lives

of the one or the other except pleasant or disagreeable memories.
He felt all the torment of his and her position, all the difficulties
they were surrounded by in consequence of their station in life,
which exposed them to the eyes of the whole world, obliged them
to hide their love, to lie and deceive, and again to lie and deceive,
to scheme and constantly think about others while the passion that
bound them was so strong that they both forgot everything but
their love.

The recollection of incidents often repeated rose vividly in his
mind, where lies and deceptions revolting to his nature had been
necessary. He remembered most vividly having more than once
noticed her feeling of shame at the necessity for this deception and
lying. And he experienced a strange feeling which since his union
with Anna sometimes overcame him. It was a feeling of revulsion
against something, against Karenin, or against himself, or against
the whole world—he hardly knew which. But he always drove
away this strange feeling. And now too, having given himself a
shake, he continued the current of his thoughts:

'Yes, formerly she was unhappy, but proud and calm; but now
she cannot be calm and dignified, though she still seems so. Yes,
this must be brought to an end,' he decided.

And for the first time the clear idea occurred to him that it was
necessary to put an end to all this falsehood, and the sooner the
better. 'Throw up everything and let us two conceal ourselves
somewhere alone with our love,' said he to himself.

Chapter XXII

The downpour did not last long, and as Vronsky approached his
destination—with his shaft-horse at full trot pulling alone, and the
trace-horses galloping over the mud with the traces loose—the sun
appeared again, the roofs of the houses and the old lime trees in
the gardens on both sides glittered with the moisture, and the
water dripped merrily from the branches and ran down from the
roofs. He no longer thought about the shower spoiling the racecourse, but was glad, because, thanks to the rain, he was sure to
find Anna at home and alone, for he knew that Karenin, who had
recently returned from a watering-place abroad, had not moved
from Petersburg.

Hoping to find her alone, Vronsky, as usual, to attract less attention, alighted before crossing the little bridge that led to the
house and walked on. He did not go straight to the entrance from
the street but passed through the yard.

'Has your master returned?' he asked a gardener.

'No, sir. The mistress is at home. Go in at the front door; the
servants are there and will open it,' replied the man.

'No, I will go through the garden.'

Having made sure that she was alone, and wishing to take her by surprise (he had not promised to come that day and she would certainly not expect him to come before the races), he went, holding up his sword and stepping carefully along the sand-strewn flower-bordered path to the verandah facing the garden. Vronsky had now forgotten all his thoughts on the way, about the hardness and difficulty of his situation. He only thought that he would see her immediately, not merely in fancy, but alive, all of her—as she was in reality. He was already ascending the shallow steps of the verandah, stepping on the whole of his foot so as not to make a noise, when he suddenly remembered what he was always forgetting, the most painful part of his relations with her, namely her son, with his questioning and, as it seemed to Vronsky, inimical look.

That boy was a more frequent hindrance to their relations than anyone else. When he was present neither Vronsky nor Anna allowed themselves to speak about anything they could not have mentioned to every one or even to hint at things the boy would not have understood. They had not arranged this, but it had come about of itself. They would have considered it unworthy of themselves to deceive the child. In his presence they talked as acquaintances. Yet despite this caution Vronsky often noticed the child's attentive and perplexed gaze fixed upon him and a strange timidity and unevenness—now caressing, now cold and bashful—in the boy's manner toward him. It was as if the child felt that between that man and his mother there was some important relation which he could not understand.

And the boy really felt that he could not understand this relation. He tried but could not make out what he ought to feel toward this man. With a child's sensitiveness to indications of feeling, he clearly saw that his father, his governess, and his nurse all not only disliked Vronsky but regarded him with fear and loathing, though they said nothing about him, while his mother regarded him as her best friend.

'What does it mean? Who is he? How should I love him? If I don't understand, it is my fault, I am a silly or a bad boy,' thought the child, and that was the cause of his testing, questioning, and to some extent hostile expression and of the shyness and fitfulness Vronsky found so irksome. The presence of that child always aroused in Vronsky that strange feeling of unreasoning revulsion which had of late come to him. It evoked both in Vronsky and in Anna a feeling such as a sailor might have who saw by the compass that the direction in which he was swiftly sailing diverged widely from the right course but was quite unable to stop, and felt that every moment was taking him farther and farther astray, and that to acknowledge to himself that he was diverging from the right direction was tantamount to acknowledging that he was lost.

This child with his naïve outlook on life was the compass which showed them their degree of divergence from what they knew, but would not recognize, as the right course.

This time Serezha was not at home, and Anna was quite alone, sitting on the verandah waiting for the return of her son, who had gone for a walk and had been caught in the rain. She had sent a man and a maid-servant to look for him and sat waiting. She wore a white dress trimmed with wide embroidery, and as she sat in a corner of the verandah behind some plants, did not hear Vronsky coming. Bowing her curly head she pressed her forehead against a cold watering-can that stood on the balustrade, and both her beautiful hands, with the rings he knew so well, were holding the can. The beauty of her whole figure, her head, her neck, and her arms, always struck Vronsky with new surprise. He stopped, gazing at her with rapture. But just as he was going to step toward her, she felt his nearness, pushed away the can, and turned her hot face toward him.

'What is the matter? Aren't you well?' he said in French as he came up to her. He wished to run toward her, but remembering that there might be others near, turned to look at the verandah door and blushed, as he always did when he felt that he had reason to fear and to be circumspect.

'No, I am quite well,' she said, rising and firmly pressing his outstretched hand. 'I did not expect—you.'

'Oh, heavens! What cold hands!' he said.

'You frightened me,' she said. 'I am alone and was expecting Serezha. He went for a walk; they will return this way.'

But though she tried to be calm her lips trembled.

'Forgive me for coming, but I could not let the day pass without seeing you,' he continued in French. In Russian the word you sounded cold and it was dangerous to say thou, so he always spoke French to her.

'Why "forgive"? I am so glad!'

'But you are ill or in trouble,' he continued without releasing her hand, but bending over it. 'What were you thinking about?'

'Always about the same thing,' she said with a smile.

She spoke the truth. Whenever,—at whatever moment,—she was asked what she was thinking about she could have answered without fail, 'Always about my happiness and my unhappiness.' Just now when he entered she was wondering why, for others, Betsy for instance (of whose secret relations with Tushkevich she knew), it was all easy, while for her it was so tormenting. For certain reasons this thought troubled her more particularly to-day. She inquired about the races. Vronsky answered her, and noticing that she was excited, in order to distract her thoughts began giving her in a very matter-of-fact way particulars of the preparations for the races.

'Shall I tell him or not?' she thought, looking at his calm, caressing eyes. 'He is so happy, so full of his races, that he won't understand it properly, won't understand all the importance of the event for us.'

'But you have not told me what you were thinking about when I came in,' he said, breaking off his narration.

She did not answer, but, slightly bowing her head, looked at him from under her brows questioningly, her eyes shining from under their long lashes. Her hand, toying with a leaf that she had pulled off, trembled. He noticed this, and his face assumed that submissive, slavishly-devoted expression that had such an effect on Anna.

'I see that something has happened. How can I be a moment at peace knowing that you have some sorrow which I am not sharing? Tell me, for heaven's sake!' repeated he entreatingly.

'I cannot forgive him if he does not understand all the importance of it. Better not tell him,—why put him to the proof?' she thought, continuing to look at him in the same way and feeling that her hand with the leaf was trembling more and more.

'For heaven's sake!' he repeated, taking her hand.

'Shall I?'

'Yes, yes, yes . . .'

'I am pregnant,' she said softly and slowly.

The leaf in her hand shook still more violently, but she did not move her eyes from his face, watching to see how he would take it. He grew pale, tried to say something, but stopped, dropped her hand, and bowed his head. 'Yes, he understands its full significance,' she thought, and gratefully pressed his hand.

But she was mistaken in thinking that he understood the importance of the news as she, a woman, understood it. It brought on with tenfold force an attack of that strange repulsion to—he knew not whom, but at the same time he felt that the crisis he had hoped for had now come, that concealment from the husband was no longer possible, and that somehow or other the unnatural situation must be quickly ended. But, besides this, her physical agitation communicated itself to him. He gave her a look full of emotion, humbly kissed her hand, rose, and began silently pacing up and down the verandah.

'Yes,' he said, resolutely approaching her. 'Neither you nor I looked on our union as an amusement, and now our fate is sealed.

We must end'—he went on, looking round—'this falsehood in which we are living.'

'End it? How are we to end it, Alexey?' she said softly.

She was calm now and her face shone with a tender smile.

'By your leaving your husband and our uniting our lives.'

'They are united already,' she replied in a scarcely audible tone.

'Yes, but entirely.'

'But how, Alexey, teach me how?' she said with pathetic irony at the inevitability of her position. 'Is there any escape from such a position? Am I not my husband's wife?'

'There is a way out of every position. One has to take a decision,' he said. 'Anything would be better than the condition in which you are living. Don't I see how you suffer from everything—Society, your son, and your husband?'

'Oh, but not through my husband,' she said with natural irony. 'I don't know him and don't think about him. He does not exist.'

'You are not speaking sincerely. I know you. You suffer from him too.'

'But he does not even know,' she said, and suddenly a vivid flush suffused her face. Her cheeks, her forehead, and her neck turned red, and tears of shame appeared in her eyes. 'Do not let us speak of him.'

Chapter XXIII

Vronsky had tried several times before, though never so definitely as now, to lead her on to a discussion of her position, and had always encountered the same superficiality and lightness of judgment with which she now replied to his challenge. It was as if there was something that she could not, and would not, make clear to herself, or as if, as soon as she began to speak about this matter, she, the real Anna, withdrew into herself and another woman appeared who was strange and alien to him, whom he feared and did not like, and who resisted him. But to-day he decided to speak out.

'Whether he knows or not,' said Vronsky in his usual firm, calm tone, 'that is not our business. We cannot . . . You cannot remain as you are, especially now.'

'What would you have me do?' she asked with the same light irony. She who had so feared that he might take her pregnancy too lightly now felt vexed that he deduced therefrom the necessity of doing something.

'Tell him everything, leave him.'

'Very well; suppose I do so!' she said. 'Do you know what the result will be? I will tell it you all in advance,' and an evil light came into her eyes which a minute before had been so tender. ' "Ah, you love another and have entered into a guilty union with him?" '

(mimicking her husband, she laid just such a stress on the word *guilty* as Karenin himself would have done). ' "I warned you of the consequences from the religious, civil, and family points of view. You have not listened to me. Now I cannot allow my name to be dishonoured . . ." ' my name and my son she was going to say but could not jest about her son . . . ' "my name to be dishonoured" and something else of that kind,' she added. 'In short, he will tell me clearly and precisely in his official manner that he cannot let me go, but will take what measures he can to prevent a scandal. And he will do what he says, quietly and accurately. That is what will happen. He is not a man, but a machine, and a cruel machine when angry,' she added, picturing Karenin to herself with every detail of his figure and way of speaking, setting against him everything bad she could find in him and forgiving him nothing, on account of the terrible fault toward him of which she was guilty. [2]

'But, Anna,' said Vronsky persuasively and gently, trying to pacify her, 'he must be told, all the same, and afterwards our action will be guided by his attitude.'

'What then, run away?'

'And why not run away? I think it is impossible to continue in this way. And not on my account,—I see that you suffer.'

'Yes, run away, and for me to live as your mistress,' she said maliciously.

'Anna,' he murmured with reproachful tenderness.

'Yes,' she continued. 'Become your mistress and ruin my . . . everything.'

She was again going to say 'son' but could not utter the word.

Vronsky could not understand how she, with her strong honest nature, could endure this state of deception and not wish to escape from it; but he did not guess that the chief cause lay in the one word 'son' which she could not bring herself to utter. When she thought about her son and his future relations with the mother who had left his father, she was so terrified at what she had done that she did not reason, but woman-like only tried to comfort herself with false arguments and words in order that everything should remain as before and that she might forget the dreadful question of what would happen to her son.

'I beg you, I entreat you,' said she suddenly in quite an altered tone, sincerely and tenderly, taking him by the hand, 'never to speak to me about that!'

'But, Anna . . .'

'Never. Leave it to me. I know all the degradation, all the horror

---

2. In Russia before the Revolution only an innocent party was allowed to apply for a divorce and it was in any case very difficult to secure one. If obtained, the party found guilty could not remarry and was deprived of the children.

of my position; but it is not so easy to settle the matter as you think. Leave it to me and listen to me. Never speak to me about it. Do you promise? . . . Yes, yes, promise! . . .'

'I promise everything, but I cannot be at peace, especially after what you have told me. I cannot be at peace when you are not.'

'I?' she said. 'Yes, I do suffer sometimes; but it will pass if you never speak to me about it. It is only when you speak to me about it that I suffer.'

'I don't understand . . .' said he.

'I know,' she interrupted him, 'how hard it is for your honest nature to lie and I pity you. I often think how you have ruined your life because of me.'

'I was just thinking the same,' he said; 'wondering how you could sacrifice everything for my sake. I cannot forgive myself for your unhappiness.'

'I unhappy?' she said, drawing near to him and gazing at him with a smile of rapturous love. 'I am like a hungry man to whom food has been given. He may be cold, his clothes may be ragged, and he may be ashamed, but he is not unhappy. I unhappy? No, this is my happiness. . . .' *(p. 182 - beautiful eyes of horse)*

But she heard the voice of her son approaching, and glancing quickly round the verandah she rose hurriedly. Her eyes kindled with the light Vronsky knew so well, and with a rapid motion she raised her lovely hands, covered with rings, seized his head, gave him a long look, lifted her face with parted smiling lips, quickly kissed his mouth and both eyes, and then pushed him away. She was about to go but he held her back.

'When?' he whispered, gazing rapturously at her.

'To-night at one,' she whispered, and with her quick light step went to meet her son.

Serezha had been caught in the rain in the public gardens, and he and his nurse had taken shelter in the pavilion.

'Well, *au revoir,*' she said to Vronsky. 'It will soon be time to start for the races. Betsy has promised to call for me.'

Vronsky looked at his watch and hurried away.

Chapter XXIV

When Vronsky looked at his watch on the Karenins' verandah he was so agitated and so preoccupied that he saw the hands and face of the watch without realizing the time. He went to the high road, stepping carefully over the mud, and made his way to his calèche. He was so full of his feeling for Anna that he did not consider what o'clock it was or whether he still had time to call on Bryansky. He only retained, as often happens, the external capacity of memory which indicated what he had decided to do next. He approached his coachman, who was dozing on the box in the already slanting shadow of a large lime tree, looked with pleasure at the swaying swarms of midgets that whirled above the perspiring horses, and having roused the coachman jumped into the calèche and told him to drive to Bryansky's. Only after going some five miles did he recollect himself sufficiently to look at his watch and to realize that it was already half-past five, and that he was late.

There were to be several races that day: a Life-Guards' race, then an officers' two-verst race, a four-verst race, and then the one for which he had entered. He could be in time for his own race, but, if he called on Bryansky first, he could only just manage it, and the whole Court would already be at the racecourse. That was not the correct thing to do. But he had promised Bryansky to call and therefore he decided to go on, telling the coachman not to spare the horses.

He saw Bryansky, stayed with him five minutes, and drove back at a gallop. This quick drive soothed him. All that was depressing in his relations with Anna, the indefiniteness that remained after their conversation, escaped from his mind. He now thought with enjoyment and agitation of the race, and that after all he would be there in time, and occasionally the expectation of that night's meeting flashed brightly in his imagination.

The spirit of the coming races overcame him more and more as he drove further and further into their atmosphere and overtook carriages making their way to the course from Petersburg and from outlying country places.

When he reached his quarters he found no one there—they had all gone to the races and his valet was waiting at the gate. While he was changing his things, the valet told him that the second race had already begun and that many gentlemen had been to inquire for him, and a lad had run over twice from the stables.

Having changed without hurrying (he never hurried or lost his self-control), Vronsky ordered the coachman to drive him to the stables. From there he could see the sea of carriages, pedestrians, and soldiers surrounding the racecourse, and the stands, which were thronged with people. Probably the second race was just taking place, for as he entered the stables he heard the bell ring. On his way he met Makhotin's white-legged chestnut Gladiator, which in a blue-bordered orange covering, with his ears looking enormous in their blue-trimmed cloth, was being led to the course.

'Where is Cord?' he asked the groom.

'In the stables, saddling.'

In her open box Frou-Frou stood ready-saddled. They were just going to lead her out.

'I am not late?'

[margin note:] unlike Anna

'All right! all right!' answered the Englishman. 'Don't upset yourself.'

Vronsky once again glanced at the beautiful fascinating shape of the mare, whose whole body was trembling, and tearing himself with difficulty from this sight he left the shed. He came toward the pavilions at the very best time to avoid attracting anyone's attention. The two-verst race was nearly over, and all eyes were fixed on an officer of the horse-guards in front and on a hussar officer behind, who were urging their horses to the last limits of their strength as they neared the winning-post. From within and without the ring every one was crowding toward the winning-post, and a group of horse-guards,—officers and men,—with loud shouts were expressing their joy at the expected triumph of their officer and comrade. Vronsky joined the crowd unnoticed, almost at the moment that the bell rang to announce the end of the race, and the tall officer of the horse-guards all bespattered with mud, who had come in first, was bending down in his saddle, loosening the reins of his grey gelding, which was dark with perspiration and panting heavily.

The gelding, planting its feet with effort, reduced the speed of its enormous body, and the guards' officer, like one waking from deep sleep, looked round and forced himself to smile. A crowd of friends and strangers surrounded him.

Vronsky purposely avoided the select and fashionable crowd which moved and chatted with restrained freedom in front of the pavilions. He ascertained that Anna, Betsy, and his brother's wife were there, but in order not to agitate himself he intentionally avoided going near them. But he continually met acquaintances who stopped him, told him about the races that had been run, and asked him why he was so late.

When the winners were called up to the pavilion to receive their prizes and every one was looking that way, Vronsky's elder brother, Alexander, a colonel with shoulder knots, of medium height, as sturdy as Alexey but handsomer and ruddier, with a red nose and a drunken though open countenance, came up to him.

'Did you get my note?' he asked. 'One can never find you.'

Alexander Vronsky, despite the loose and, in particular, drunken life for which he was noted, was quite a courtier.

While speaking to his brother of a matter very unpleasant to him he, knowing that many eyes might be fixed on them, wore a smiling expression, as if he were joking with him about some unimportant matter.

'I received it, but really do not understand what *you* are worrying about,' replied Alexey.

'I am worrying because people have just remarked to me that

you were not here, and that you were seen in Peterhof last Monday.'

'There are things which should be discussed only by those who are directly interested, and the matter you are concerning yourself about is one . . .'

'Yes, but then one should not be in the army, or . . .'

'I beg you not to interfere, that is all.'

Alexey Vronsky's frowning face turned pale, and his prominent lower jaw twitched, a thing that rarely happened to him. Being a very kind-hearted man he seldom got angry, but when he did, and when his chin twitched, then he was dangerous, as Alexander Vronsky knew. Alexander smiled gaily.

'I only wanted to deliver mother's letter. Answer her, and don't upset yourself before the race. *Bonne chance!*' he added smiling and went away.

But just then another friendly greeting stopped Vronsky.

'Won't you recognize your friends? How do you do, *mon cher?*' said Oblonsky, shining here, amid all this Petersburg brilliancy, no less than he shone in Moscow, with his rosy face and glistening, well-brushed whiskers. 'I came yesterday and am very glad that I shall witness your triumph. When can we meet?'

'Come to the mess-room to-morrow,' said Vronsky, and apologetically pressing the sleeve of Oblonsky's overcoat, he went to the centre of the racecourse where the horses were already being led out for the steeplechase.

The perspiring, exhausted horses which had raced were being led away by their grooms, and one by one the fresh ones for the next race were appearing, most of them English horses, which in their hooded coverings and with their tightly-girthed stomachs looked like strange gigantic birds. To the right the slender and beautiful Frou-Frou was being led up and down, stepping as on springs with her rather long elastic pasterns. Not far from her they were taking the horse-cloth off the lop-eared Gladiator. The large, beautiful, perfectly regular shape of the horse, with his wonderful hind-quarters and his exceptionally short pasterns just above his hoofs, involuntarily arrested Vronsky's attention. He wished to go up to his own horse, but was again stopped by an acquaintance.

'Ah, there is Karenin!' said the acquaintance with whom he was talking. 'He is looking for his wife, and she is in the centre of the pavilion. Have you not seen her?'

'No, I have not,' said Vronsky, and without even glancing at the pavilion where Anna was pointed out to him, he went to his horse.

He had not had time to examine the saddle, about which he wished to give some directions, when the riders were summoned to the pavilion to draw their numbers and places. With serious, stern, and in many cases pale faces, seventeen officers assembled at the pavilion and drew their numbers. Vronsky got number seven. The order was given: 'Mount!'

Feeling that he and the other riders were the centre toward which all eyes were turned, Vronsky, in the highly-strung state which generally made his movements calm and deliberate, approached his horse. Cord, in honour of the races, was dressed in his best clothes: a black buttoned-up coat, a stiff starched collar that pressed against his cheeks, a bowler hat, and top boots. He was calm and important as usual, and, standing in front of the horse, was himself holding both its reins. Frou-Frou continued to tremble as if in a fever. Her fiery eyes turned on the approaching Vronsky. Vronsky pushed his fingers under the girths. The mare turned her eyes still further back, showed her teeth, and set back an ear. The Englishman puckered his lip, wishing to express a smile at anyone testing his saddling.

'You'd better mount. You will be less excited.'

Vronsky glanced round at his rivals for the last time. He knew that he would not see them during the race. Two of them were already riding toward the starting-point. Galtsin, one of the formidable competitors and a friend of Vronsky's, was struggling with a sorrel gelding that would not let him mount. A short hussar in tight riding-breeches was galloping along bunched up like a cat in his desire to imitate an English jockey. Prince Kusovlev sat pale-faced on his thoroughbred mare from the Grabov stud farm, which an English groom was leading by the bridle. Vronsky and all his set knew Kusovlev and his peculiarities, which were weak nerves and terrible vanity. They knew he was afraid of everything, even of riding an army horse; but now, just because it was dangerous, because necks might be broken and at each obstacle there was a doctor in attendance, an ambulance wagon with a red cross sewn on it, and a nurse, he had determined to ride. Their eyes met and Vronsky winked at him kindly and approvingly. The only one Vronsky did not see was his chief rival Makhotin on his Gladiator.

'Don't hurry,' said Cord to Vronsky, 'and remember one thing: do not hold back or urge on your horse at an obstacle. Let her have her way.'

'Very well, very well,' said Vronsky taking the reins.

'Lead if you can, but do not despair till the last moment if you are behind.'

The mare had not time to stir before Vronsky with a powerful and agile movement put his foot in the notched steel stirrup and seated himself lightly but firmly on the creaking leather of the saddle. Having got his right foot also in its stirrup he straightened out the double reins between his practised fingers, and Cord removed his hand. As if not knowing which foot to step on first,

Frou-Frou stretched the reins with her long neck, and started as if on springs, shaking her rider on her flexible back. Cord, quickening his steps, followed them. The restive horse tugged at the reins, now to one side, now to the other, trying to deceive her rider, and Vronsky vainly sought by voice and hand to soothe her.

They were already approaching the dammed-up stream on their way to the starting-post. Some of the riders were in front, some behind, when Vronsky suddenly heard a horse galloping through the mud behind him, and Makhotin on his white-legged, large-eared Gladiator went past him. Makhotin smiled, showing his long teeth, but Vronsky looked at him angrily. Vronsky always disliked him and now considered him his most dangerous rival, and he was vexed with him for galloping past and so exciting Frou-Frou. She broke into a canter, gave two leaps, and, angry at the tightened rein, changed back into a jerky trot, jolting her rider. Cord also frowned, following Vronsky almost at a run.

Chapter XXV

Seventeen officers in all had entered for the steeplechase. It was to take place on the large four-verst elliptical course in front of the pavilion. On that course there were nine obstacles: the brook; a barrier nearly five feet high just in front of the pavilion; a dry ditch; a water-jump; an incline; an Irish bank (one of the most difficult obstacles), consisting of a bank with brushwood on top, beyond which there was another ditch which the horses could not see, so that they had to clear both obstacles or come to grief; then two more water-jumps, and another dry ditch. The winning-post was opposite the pavilion. But the start was not in the ellipse, but about 250 yards to one side of it, and the first obstacle, the dammed-up brook seven feet wide, was there. The riders could either ford or jump it at their discretion.

Three times the riders drew up in line, but each time some one's horse made a false start and they had to line up again. Colonel Sestrin, an expert starter, was already getting angry, but at last, at the fourth try, he shouted 'Go!' and the race began.

All eyes and all glasses were turned on the bright group of riders while they were getting into line.

'They have started! They are off!' was heard from every side after the hush of expectation.

Lookers-on, in groups or singly, started running from place to place to get a better view. In the first minute the group of riders began to stretch out and could be seen in twos and threes, and one behind another, approaching the brook. It had looked to the public as if they had all started together, but the riders were aware of a difference of seconds which to them were of great importance.

The excited and over-nervous Frou-Frou lost in the first moment, and several horses started ahead of her, but before reaching the brook Vronsky, who with all his strength was holding back the mare that was tugging at the reins, had easily passed three riders, and ahead of him there was only Makhotin's chestnut Gladiator (whose hind-quarters moved regularly and lightly just in front of him), and in front of all, the exquisite Diana, carrying Kusovlev, who was more dead than alive.

In the first moments Vronsky was master neither of himself nor of his mare. Up to the first obstacle, the brook, he could not control her movements.

Gladiator and Diana approached the stream together, and almost at the same moment rose above it and flew across to the other side; lightly as if on wings Frou-Frou rose up behind them; but at the moment when Vronsky felt himself raised in the air he suddenly saw, almost under his horse's feet, Kusovlev, who was floundering on the other side of the stream with his Diana (Kusovlev had let go of the reins at the jump and the horse fell, throwing him over her head). These particulars Vronsky learned later, now he only saw that Diana's head or legs might come just where Frou-Frou had to alight. But Frou-Frou, like a falling cat, made an effort with her legs and back while in the air, and clearing the other horse rushed on.

'Oh, you darling!' thought Vronsky.

After crossing the brook Vronsky had the mare quite under control, and held her in, intending to cross the big barrier behind Makhotin and then to try and pass him on the flat 300 yards before the next obstacle.

The big barrier was right in front of the Imperial Pavilion. The Emperor, the whole Court, and crowds of people were all looking at them—at him and at Makhotin, who was a full length ahead of him when they approached the Devil (as the solid barrier was called). Vronsky felt eyes directed toward him from all sides, but he saw nothing except the ears and neck of his mare, the ground racing toward him, and Gladiator's hind-quarters and white legs rapidly striding before him, and keeping always the same distance ahead. Gladiator rose without touching anything, swished his short tail, and disappeared from Vronsky's sight.

'Bravo!' shouted a single voice.

Just then the boards of the barrier flashed close before Vronsky's eyes. Without the least change in her action his mare rose under him; the boards disappeared, only behind him there was a knock. Excited by the fact that Gladiator was in front, the mare had risen at the barrier a little too soon and had struck it with a hind hoof. But her pace did not change, and Vronsky, hit in the face by a lump of mud, realized that he was again at the same distance behind Gladiator. He again saw before him that horse's hind-quarters, short tail and flashing white legs, no farther away.

At the very moment that Vronsky thought it time to pass Makhotin, Frou-Frou, understanding what was in his mind, without any urging, considerably increased her speed and began to draw nearer to Makhotin on the side where it was most advantageous to pass him—the side of the rope. Makhotin would not let her pass that side. Vronsky had just time to think of coming up on the outside, when Frou-Frou changed her legs and started to do so. Frou-Frou's shoulder, which was already growing dark with sweat, was on a level with Gladiator's hind-quarters. They ran side by side for a few strides, but before the obstacle they were approaching, Vronsky, not to lose ground, gave the mare her head and just on the declivity passed Mahkotin. He caught sight of his mud-bespattered face, and even thought he saw him smile. He passed, but felt that Makhotin was close behind him, and continually heard just behind his back the regular beating of hoofs and the short, still fresh breathing of Gladiator's nostrils.

The next two obstacles, a ditch and a fence, were easily passed, but Vronsky heard Gladiator's galloping and snorting closer. He urged on his mare and felt with joy that she easily increased her speed, and he heard the sound of Gladiator's hoofs again at the former distance behind.

Vronsky now had the lead, as he had wished and as Cord had advised, and he was confident of success. His excitement and joy, and his tenderness for Frou-Frou, grew stronger and stronger. He wished to glance round but dared not do so, and he tried to keep calm and not to urge his mare, but to let her retain a reserve of strength such as he felt that Gladiator still had.

There remained the most difficult obstacle; if he crossed it ahead of the others, he would come in first. He was galloping up to the Irish bank. He and Frou-Frou both saw the bank while still some way off, and to both of them came a momentary doubt. He noticed the mare's hesitation by her ears and raised his whip, but immediately felt that his doubt was groundless: the mare knew what was wanted, and, as he expected, she increased her speed, took off exactly at the right moment, and gave a leap the force of which carried her far across the ditch. Then without effort and without changing her legs Frou-Frou continued her gallop.

'Bravo, Vronsky!' he heard the voices of a knot of people he knew—friends of his regiment—who were standing by this obstacle. He could not fail to recognize Yashvin's voice, though he did not see him.

'Oh, my beauty!' he thought of Frou-Frou, as he listened to

what was happening behind. 'He is over it!' he thought, as he
heard Gladiator again galloping behind him. There remained one
last water jump, only a yard and a half wide. Vronsky did not even
look at it, but hoping to win by a distance, began working the
reins with a circular movement, raising and dropping the mare's
head in time with her stride. He felt she was using her last reserve
of strength; not only her neck and shoulders were wet, but on her
withers, her head, and her pointed ears the sweat stood in drops,
and she was breathing short and sharp. But he knew that her
reserve of strength was more than enough for the remaining five
hundred yards. It was only by feeling himself nearer to the ground
and by the smoothness of the pace that Vronsky knew how much
the mare had increased her speed. She leapt the ditch as if she did
not notice it, seeming to fly across it like a bird. But at that very
moment Vronsky, to his horror, felt that something terrible had
happened. He himself, without knowing it, had made the unpardonable mistake of dropping back in his saddle and pulling up
her head. Before he could realize this, the white legs of the
gelding flashed close by him and Makhotin passed at a rapid gallop.
Vronsky was touching the ground with one foot. He scarcely had
time to free his leg before Frou-Frou fell on her side, and snorting
heavily and with her delicate damp neck making vain efforts to
rise, began struggling on the ground at his feet, like a wounded,
fluttering bird. Owing to Vronsky's awkward movement she had
dropped her hind legs and broken her back. But he only understood this much later. Now he only saw that Makhotin was quickly
galloping away, while he, reeling, stood alone on the muddy, stationary ground; before him, breathing heavily, lay Frou-Frou, who,
bending her head toward him, gazed at him with her beautiful eyes.
Still not understanding what had happened, Vronsky pulled at
the reins. The mare again began to struggle like a fish, causing the
flaps of the saddle to creak; she got her front legs free, but unable
to lift her hind-quarters, struggled and immediately again fell on
her side.

His face distorted with passion, pale and with quivering jaw,
Vronsky kicked her with his heel in the belly and again pulled at
the reins. But she did not move and, nuzzling the ground, only
looked at her master with eloquent eyes.

'Ah, ah, ah!' groaned Vronsky, seizing his head. 'Ah! what have
I done?' he exclaimed. 'The race is lost! And the fault mine—
shameful and unpardonable. And this dear, unfortunate mare
ruined! Ah! what have I done?'

Onlookers, a doctor, an attendant, and officers of his regiment
ran toward him. To his regret he felt that he was himself sound and
unhurt. The mare had broken her back and it was decided to shoot

her. Vronsky was unable to reply to questions or to speak to anyone. He turned away and, without picking up his cap that had fallen from his head, left the racecourse without knowing where he was going. He felt miserable. For the first time in his life he experienced the worst kind of misfortune—one that was irretrievable, and caused by his own fault.

Yashvin overtook him with his cap and led him home, and in half an hour Vronsky came to himself. But the memory of that steeplechase long remained the most painful and distressing memory of his life.

Chapter XXVI

Externally Karenin's relations with his wife remained the same. The only difference was that he was even more occupied than before. As in former years, at the beginning of the spring he went abroad to recuperate his health, which was upset each year by the winter's work. And as usual he returned in July and at once with increased energy took up his customary work. And as usual his wife had moved to the country house while he remained in Petersburg.

Since their conversation on the night of the Princess Tverskaya's party he had never spoken to Anna of his suspicions and jealousy, and that habitual tone of his which seemed to mock at some one was exactly suited to his present relations with her. He was rather colder toward her. He appeared only to be slightly dissatisfied with her for that first night's talk which she had evaded. In his behaviour to her there was a shade of vexation, but nothing more. 'You did not wish to have an explanation,' he seemed to say to her in imagination,'so much the worse for you. Now you will ask me to explain, and I shall not do so. So much the worse for you,' he thought, like a man who having vainly tried to extinguish a fire should be vexed at his vain exertions and say to it: 'Well, go on and burn, it is your own fault.'

He who was so wise and astute in official affairs did not realize the insanity of such an attitude toward his wife. He did not understand it because it would have been too terrible to realize his real situation, and he had closed, locked, and sealed that compartment of his soul which contained his feelings for his family—that is, his wife and son.

He who had been a considerate father, since the end of that winter had become particularly cold toward his son, and treated him in the same bantering manner as he did his wife. 'Ah, young man!' was the way in which he addressed him.

Karenin thought and said that in no previous year had he had so much official business as this year; but he was not conscious of the fact that this year he invented work for himself, and that this was one of the means of keeping that compartment closed where lay his feelings for and thoughts of his family, which became more terrible the longer they laid there. If anyone had ventured to ask him what he thought of his wife's conduct, the mild and gentle Karenin would not have given any answer, but would have been angry with the man who put such a question. That was why Karenin's face bore a stern, proud expression when anyone asked about his wife's health. He did not wish to think about his wife's conduct and feelings at all, and he really did not think about them.

The country house the Karenins regularly occupied in summer was in Peterhof, and generally the Countess Lydia Ivanovna also lived nearby and was in constant touch with Anna. That year the Countess Lydia Ivanovna refused to live in Peterhof, did not once come to see Anna, and hinted to Karenin the undesirability of Anna's intimacy with Betsy and Vronsky. Karenin stopped her severely, expressing the opinion that his wife was above suspicion, and from that time began to avoid the Countess. He did not wish to see, and did not see, that many people in Society already looked askance at Anna; he did not wish to understand, and did not understand, why his wife particularly insisted on moving to Tsarskoe Selo, where Betsy lived and near which place Vronsky's regiment was stationed. He did not let himself think about this and did not think about it; yet at the bottom of his soul, without admitting it to himself or having any proofs or even suspicions of it, he nevertheless knew certainly that he was a wronged husband, and was therefore profoundly unhappy.

How often during the eight years of happy married life with his wife, when he saw others who were unfaithful wives or deceived husbands, had Karenin said to himself, 'How could they let it come to that? How is it they do not end such a hideous state of things?' But now, when the misfortune had fallen on his own head, he not only did not think of how to end it, but did not wish to recognize it at all—and did not wish to recognize it just because it was too terrible, too unnatural.

Since his return from abroad Karenin had been twice at the country house. Once he dined there, and the other time he spent an evening with some visitors, but he had not once stayed the night, as he used to do in former years.

The day of the races was a very busy one for Karenin; but in the morning when he made his plans for the day he decided that immediately after an early dinner he would go to see his wife at the country house, and from there to the races, at which the whole Court would be present and where he ought to appear. He would call on his wife, because he had decided to do so once a week for the sake of propriety. Besides, he had that day to give her money for her expenses, due according to their custom by the fifteenth of each month.

Having with the mental control habitual to him considered these matters concerning his wife, he did not allow his thoughts to run on further about her.

He had a very busy morning. On the previous day the Countess Lydia Ivanovna had sent him a pamphlet by a celebrated traveller in China, and a letter asking him to receive this traveller, who for various reasons was very interesting and necessary to them. Karenin had not had time to finish the pamphlet the evening before, and did so in the morning. Then he received petitioners, heard reports, gave audiences, assigned posts and ordered dismissals, apportioned rewards, pensions, and salaries, and attended to correspondence— everyday matters, as he called them, which took up so much of his time. After that came personal matters—a visit from his doctor and one from his steward. The latter did not keep him long. He only handed Karenin the money he wanted and gave him a short account of the state of his affairs, which was not quite satisfactory, for it happened that, owing to their having been from home a good deal, more had been spent that year than usual and there was a deficit. But the doctor, a celebrated Petersburg physician who was on friendly terms with Karenin, took up a good deal of time. Karenin had not expected him that day and was surprised to see him, and yet more surprised that the doctor questioned him very particularly about his state of health, sounding his chest and tapping and feeling his liver. Karenin did not know that his friend Lydia Ivanovna, having noticed that he was not in good health that summer, had asked the doctor to go and see his patient. 'Do it for my sake,' the Countess Lydia Ivanovna had said.

'I will do it for the sake of Russia, Countess,' replied the doctor.

'An invaluable man!' the Countess Lydia Ivanovna had exclaimed.

The doctor was very dissatisfied with Karenin's state of health. He found him insufficiently nourished and his liver much enlarged, and that the waters had had no effect at all. He prescribed as much physical exercise and as little mental strain as possible, and above all no worries of any kind—that is, he advised what was for Karenin as impossible as not to breathe, and he went away leaving Karenin with a disagreeable consciousness that something was wrong with him which could not be remedied.

In the porch, after leaving Karenin, the doctor met Slyudin, Karenin's private secretary, whom he knew very well. They had been at the University together, and though they very seldom met, they respected one another and were good friends, and to no one but Slyudin would the doctor have expressed his opinion about his patient.

'I am very glad you have been to see him,' said Slyudin. 'He is not well, and I believe that . . . Well, what is it?'

'It is this,' said the doctor, beckoning over Slyudin's head to his coachman to drive up. 'It's this,' and with his white hands he took a finger of his kid glove and stretched it; 'If you try to break a cord that is slack it is not easy to break it, but strain that cord to its utmost and the weight of a finger will snap it. And he, by his hard work and the conscientious way he does it, is strained to the utmost; and there is a pressure from outside, and a heavy one,' concluded the doctor, raising his eyebrows significantly. 'Will you be at the races?' he added, descending the steps to his brougham.

'Yes, yes, of course it takes a lot of time,' he replied to some remark of Slyudin's which he had not quite caught.

After the doctor, who had taken up so much time, came the famous traveller, and Karenin, thanks to the pamphlet he had just read and to what he knew before, greatly impressed the traveller by the depth of his knowledge of the subject and the breadth of his enlightened outlook.

At the same time as the traveller, a provincial Marshal of the Nobility was announced with whom Karenin had some things to talk over. When he too had left, he had to finish his everyday business with his private secretary and had also to drive to see an important personage on a grave and serious matter. He only managed to get back at five, his dinner-time, and having dined with his private secretary, he invited the latter to drive with him to his country house and go to the races with him.

Without acknowledging it to himself, Karenin now looked out for opportunities of having a third person present at his interviews with his wife.

Chapter XXVII

Anna was upstairs standing in front of a mirror pinning, with Annushka's help, a last bow to her dress, when she heard the wheels of a carriage grating on the gravel at the entrance.

'It is too early for Betsy,' she thought, and glancing out of the window she saw the carriage, and sticking out of it a black hat and Karenin's familiar ears. 'How unfortunate! Can he mean to stay the night?' thought she, and so awful and horrible appeared to her the consequences that might result therefrom that, without a moment's hesitation, she went out to meet him with a bright beaming face; and feeling within herself the presence of the already familiar spirit of lies and deceit, she gave herself up to it at once and began speaking without knowing what she was going to say.

'Ah, how nice this is!' she said, giving her husband her hand and smilingly greeting Slyudin as a member of the household. 'You are staying the night, I hope?' were the first words prompted by the spirit of lies. 'And now we shall go together. Only it is a pity that I promised to go with Betsy. She will be coming for me.'

Karenin made a grimace at the mention of Betsy's name.

'Oh, I will not separate the inseparables,' he said in his usual facetious tone. 'I will go with Slyudin. The doctors have ordered me to walk. I will walk part way and imagine that I am still taking the waters.'

'There is no hurry,' said Anna. 'Would you like some tea?' She rang.

'Tea, please, and tell Serezha that his father is here. Well, how is your health? You have not been here before' she went on, turning to Slyudin; 'See how pretty my verandah is.'

She spoke very simply and naturally, but too much and too fast. She felt this herself, especially as by the inquisitive way Slyudin looked at her she noticed that he seemed to be watching her.

Slyudin immediately went out on to the verandah, and she sat down by her husband.

'You are not looking quite well,' she said.

'No,' he replied, 'the doctor came to see me this morning and robbed me of an hour. I feel that some friend of mine must have sent him: my health is so precious . . .'

'Yes, but what did he say?'

She questioned him about his health and his work, persuading him to take a rest and to move out to her in the country.

She said all this lightly, rapidly, and with peculiarly sparkling eyes; but Karenin did not now attach any importance to this tone of hers. He only heard her words, and gave them only their direct meaning. And he answered simply, though jokingly. In all this conversation nothing particular passed but never afterwards could Anna recall this short scene without being tormented by shame.

Serezha came in, preceded by his governess. Had Karenin allowed himself to observe, he would have noticed the timid, confused look which the child cast first at his father and then at his mother. But he did not want to see, and did not see, anything.

'Ah, young man! He has grown. He is really getting quite a man. How do you do, young man?'

And he held out his hand to the frightened boy.

Serezha, who had always been timid with his father, now that the latter addressed him as 'young man,' and that the question whether Vronsky was a friend or a foe had entered his head, shrank from him. He looked round at his mother, as if asking for protection. Only with his mother he felt at ease. Karenin meanwhile talked to the governess with his hand on his son's shoulder, and Serezha felt so extremely uncomfortable that Anna saw he was about to cry.

Anna, who had blushed when the boy came in, saw how distressed he was, and, rising, lifted Karenin's hand off her son's shoulder, kissed the boy, led him out on to the verandah, and returned at once.

'Well, it's time we were going,' she said, glancing at her watch. 'I wonder Betsy has not come . . .'

'Yes,' said Karenin, and interlacing his hands he cracked his fingers. 'I also came to bring you some money, since "nightingales are not fed on fables,"' he added. 'I expect you want it?'

'No, I don't. . . . Yes, I do,' she replied without looking at him, and blushing to the roots of her hair. 'But I suppose you will call here after the races.'

'Oh, yes!' answered Karenin. 'And here is the ornament of Peterhof, the Princess Tverskaya,' he added, glancing out of the window at an approaching carriage of English build with a small body placed very high. 'What elegance! Charming! Well then, we will start too.'

The Princess Tverskaya did not get out, only her footman in his black hat, cape, and gaiters jumped down at the front door.

'I am going, good-bye!' said Anna, and giving her son a kiss she went up to Karenin and held out her hand to him. 'You were very kind to come.'

Karenin kissed her hand.

'Well then, *au revoir!* You will come back for tea, that is right!' she said, and went out gay and radiant. But as soon as she ceased to see him she became conscious of the place on her hand his lips had touched and she shuddered with repulsion.

Chapter XXVIII

When Karenin appeared at the racecourse Anna was already sitting beside Betsy in the Grand Stand: the stand where all the highest Society was assembled. She saw her husband from afar. Two men—her husband and her lover—were the two centres of her life, and without the aid of her senses she was aware of the presence of either. From afar she already felt the approach of her husband, and involuntarily watched him amid the surging crowd through which he was moving. She saw how he approached the Grand Stand, now condescendingly replying to obsequious bows, now amiably and absent-mindedly greeting his equals, now watchfully waiting to catch the eye of the great ones of this world and raising his large round hat, which pressed on the tips of his ears.

She knew all these ways of his and they were all repulsive to her. 'Nothing, but ambition, nothing but a wish to get on—that is all he has in his soul,' she thought; 'and lofty views, love of enlightenment, and religion, are all only means toward getting on.'

She knew by the way he looked at the Ladies' Stand that he was trying to find her (he looked straight at her, without recognizing her amid the sea of muslin, ribbons, feathers, sunshades, and flowers), but she purposely disregarded him.

'Alexey Alexandrovich!' the Princess Betsy called to him, 'I am sure you don't see your wife; here she is!'

He smiled his usual cold smile.

"There is so much splendour here that my eyes are dazzled,' he replied, and approached the stand. He smiled at Anna as a husband should smile when meeting his wife whom he has seen shortly before, and greeted the Princess and other acquaintances, giving to each what was due—that is to say, joking with the ladies and exchanging greetings with the men. At the foot of the stand stood an adjutant-general respected by Karenin, and noted for his intelligence and education. With him Karenin entered into conversation.

There was an interval between two races, so that nothing hindered the conversation. The adjutant-general disapproved of the races. Karenin replied, defending them. Anna heard his high measured voice and did not miss a single word. Each word seemed to her false and grated painfully on her ear.

When the four-verst steeplechase was beginning she leaned forward, and did not take her eyes off Vronsky while he went up to his horse and mounted it, and at the same time she heard her husband's repulsive, unceasing voice. She was tormented by anxiety for Vronsky, but suffered even more from what seemed to her the incessant flow of her husband's shrill voice with its familiar intonations.

'I am a bad woman, a ruined woman,' she thought, 'but I dislike lies. I cannot stand falsehood, but *his* food is falsehood. He knows everything, sees everything—what then does he feel, if he can talk so calmly? If he were to kill me, and if he were to kill Vronsky, I should respect him. But no, lies and propriety are all he cares about,' said Anna to herself, without considering what she really wanted of her husband or what she would have liked him to be. Nor did she understand that Karenin's peculiar volubility, which so irritated her, was only an expression of the anxiety and unrest within him. As a child that has been hurt skips about, making its muscles move in order to dull its pain, so Karenin needed mental activity to smother those thoughts about his wife which in her presence and in the presence of Vronsky, and amid the continual mention of his name, forced themselves upon him. And as it is natural for the child to skip about, so it was natural for him to speak cleverly and well. He said: 'The danger in military, that is, cavalry, steeplechases is an unavoidable element of the racing. If England can point to the most brilliant cavalry charges in military history, it is entirely due to the fact that she has historically developed this capacity in her men and horses. Sport in my opinion has great value, but we, as usual, see only what is most external.'

'Not external at all,' said the Princess Tverskaya. 'They say one of the officers has broken two ribs.'

Karenin smiled his usual smile, which showed his teeth but expressed nothing.

'Granted, Princess,' said he, 'that that is not external, but internal. But that is not the point,' and he again turned to the General with whom he was talking seriously: 'Do not forget that it is military men who are racing, men who have chosen that career, and one must admit that every calling has a reverse side of its medal. It is directly involved in their military duty. The monstrous sports of prize-fighting, or the Spanish bull-fights, are indications of barbarism, but specialized sport is a sign of progress.'

'No, I shan't come again; it excites me too much,' said the Princess Betsy. 'Don't you think so, Anna?'

'It is exciting, but one cannot tear oneself away,' said another lady. 'If I had been a Roman, I should never have missed a gladiatorial show.'

Anna said nothing, but without putting down her glasses looked steadily at one point.

At that moment a highly-placed general made his way through the stand. Interrupting his speech, Karenin rose hurriedly, but with dignity, and bowed low to this general.

'You are not racing,' said the latter to him jokingly.

'My race is a harder one,' replied Karenin respectfully.

And though the answer did not mean anything, the general made as though he had heard a clever reply from a clever man, and quite appreciated *la pointe de la sauce.* [3]

'There are two sides to it,' continued Karenin, 'that of the performers and that of the spectators. The love of such spectacles is the surest proof of low development in the onlookers, I admit, but . . .'

'Princess, a bet!' came the voice of Oblonsky from below, addressing Betsy. 'Whom are you backing?'

'Anna and I are betting on Kuzovlev,' replied Betsy.

'And I on Vronsky. A pair of gloves?'

'All right.'

3. The flavour of the sauce; the point of his witty remark.

'What a fine scene, is it not?'

Karenin was silent while others were speaking near him, but began again immediately.

'I agree that unmanly sports . . .' he was continuing.

But at that moment the race began and all conversation ceased. Karenin was silent too, as everybody rose and turned their eyes toward the stream. Karenin was not interested in the races and therefore did not watch the riders, but began absent-mindedly looking at the spectators with his weary eyes. His gaze rested on Anna.

Her face was pale and stern. She evidently saw nothing and nobody, with one exception. Her hand convulsively grasped her fan, and she held her breath. He looked at her and hurriedly turned away, scrutinizing other faces.

'Yes that lady—and those others—are very excited too; it is quite natural,' he said to himself. He did not wish to look at her, but his eyes were involuntarily drawn toward her. He again watched her face, trying not to read what was so plainly written on it, but against his will he read in it with horror that which he did not want to know.

The first fall—Kuzovlev's at the stream—excited every one, but Karenin saw clearly by Anna's pale, triumphant face that he whom she was watching had not fallen. When after Makhotin and Vronsky had jumped the big barrier the officer following them fell on his head and swooned, a murmur of horror passed through the whole crowd; but Karenin saw that Anna did not even notice the fall and with difficulty understood what those around her were talking about. He looked at her more and more often, and more intently. Anna, though fully engrossed by the sight of the galloping Vronsky, became aware of the cold eyes of her husband bent upon her from one side.

She glanced for an instant at him with a look of inquiry, and, slightly frowning, turned away again.

'Oh, I don't care,' she seemed to say to him, and then did not once look at him again.

The steeplechase was unlucky: more than half of the seventeen officers were thrown and hurt. By the end of the race every one was disturbed, and this disturbance was increased by the fact that the Emperor was displeased.

Chapter XXIX

Every one was loudly expressing disapproval and repeating the words some one had uttered: 'They will have gladiators and lions next,' and every one was feeling the horror of it, so that when Vronsky fell and Anna gave a loud exclamation, there was nothing

remarkable about it. But afterwards a change came over Anna's
face which was positively unseemly. She quite lost self-control.
She began to flutter like a captive bird, now rising to go, now
addressing Betsy.

'Let us go!' she said.

But Betsy did not hear her. She was leaning over to speak to a
General who was below.

Karenin approached Anna and politely offered her his arm.

'Come, if you like,' he said in French; but Anna listened to
what the General was saying and did not notice her husband.

'He too has broken his leg, they say. It's too bad,' the General
said.

Anna, without replying to her husband, raised her glasses and
looked toward the spot where Vronsky had fallen; but it was so
far off, and so many people had crowded there, that it was impossible to distinguish anything. She put down her glasses and was
about to go; but at that moment an officer galloped up and reported
something to the Emperor. Anna bent forward to listen.

'Stiva! Stiva!' she called to her brother.

But he did not hear her. She was again on the point of going.

'I again offer you my arm if you wish to go,' said her husband,
touching her arm.

With a look of repulsion she drew back, and without looking at
him replied:

'No, no, leave me alone, I shall stay here.'

She now saw an officer running to the Grand Stand from the
place where Vronsky had fallen. Betsy waved her handkerchief to
him. The officer brought the news that the rider was unhurt but
that the horse had broken its back.

On hearing this Anna quickly sat down and hid her face behind
her fan. Karenin saw that she was crying, and that she was unable to
keep back either her tears or the sobs that made her bosom heave.
He stepped forward so as to screen her, giving her time to recover.

'For the third time I offer you my arm,' he said after a while,
turning toward her. Anna looked at him and did not know what to
say. The Princess Betsy came to her aid.

'No, Alexey Alexandrovich,' she put in, 'I brought Anna here
and I have promised to take her back again.'

'Excuse me, Princess,' he said, smiling politely but looking her
firmly in the eyes, 'but I see that Anna is not very well, and I wish
her to come with me.'

Anna looked round with alarm, rose obediently and put her hand
on her husband's arm.

'I will send to him and find out, and will let you know,' Betsy
whispered to her.

On leaving the stand Karenin as usual spoke to people he met, Anna as usual had to reply and make conversation: but she was beside herself and walked as in a dream, holding her husband's arm.

'Is he hurt or not? Is it true? Will he come or not? Shall I see him to-night?' she thought.

In silence she took her place in her husband's carriage, and in silence they drove out of the crowd of vehicles. In spite of all he had seen, Karenin would still not allow himself to think of his wife's real position. He only saw the outward symptoms. He saw that she had behaved with impropriety and he considered it his duty to tell her so. But it was very difficult for him to say that and nothing more. He opened his mouth to say that she had behaved in an unseemly way, but involuntarily said something quite different.

'After all, how inclined we all are to these cruel spectacles,' he said. 'I notice . . .'

'What? I do not understand,' said Anna contemptuously.

He was offended and at once began to say what he had meant to. 'I must tell you . . .' he said.

'It's coming—the explanation!' she thought and felt frightened.

'I must tell you that you behaved improperly to-day,' he said in French.

'How did I behave improperly?' she said aloud, quickly turning her head and looking him straight in the eyes, now without any of the former deceptive gaiety but with a determined air beneath which she had difficulty in hiding the fright she felt.

'Don't forget,' said he to her, pointing at the open window behind the coachman's box; and, slightly rising, he lifted the window.

'What did you consider improper?' she asked again.

'The despair you were unable to conceal when one of the riders fell.'

He expected a rejoinder from her; but she remained silent, looking straight before her.

'I asked you once before to conduct yourself in Society so that evil tongues might be unable to say anything against you. There was a time when I spoke about inner relations; now I do not speak of them. I speak now of external relations. Your conduct was improper and I do not wish it to occur again.'

She did not hear half that he said, but felt afraid of him and wondered whether it was true that Vronsky was not hurt. Was it of him they were speaking when they said that he was not hurt but the horse had broken its back? She only smiled with simulated irony when he had finished; and she did not reply because she had not heard what he said. Karenin had begun to speak boldly, but when he realized clearly what he was talking about, the fear she was experiencing communicated itself to him. He saw her smile and a strange delusion possessed him. 'She smiles at my suspicions. In a moment she will tell me what she told me then: that these suspicions are groundless and ridiculous.'

Now that a complete disclosure was impending, he expected nothing so much as that she would, as before, answer him mockingly that his suspicions were ridiculous and groundless. What he knew was so terrible that he was now prepared to believe anything. But the expression of her frightened and gloomy face did not now even promise deception.

'Perhaps I am mistaken,' said he. 'In that case I beg your pardon.'

'No, you were not mistaken,' she said slowly, looking despairingly into his cold face. 'You were not mistaken. I was, and cannot help being, in despair. I listen to you but I am thinking of him. I love him, I am his mistress, I cannot endure you, I am afraid of you, and I hate you.... Do what you like to me.'

And throwing herself back into the corner of the carriage she burst into sobs, hiding her face in her hands. Karenin did not move, and did not change the direction in which he was looking, but his face suddenly assumed the solemn immobility of the dead, and that expression did not alter till they reached the house. As they were driving up to it, he turned his face to her still with the same expression and said:

'Yes! But I demand that the external conditions of propriety shall be observed till'—his voice trembled—'till I take measures to safeguard my honour and inform you of them.'

He alighted first and helped her out. In the presence of the servants he pressed her hand, re-entered the carriage, and drove off toward Petersburg.

After he had gone the Princess Betsy's footman brought Anna a note.

'I sent to Alexey to inquire about his health. He writes that he is safe and sound, but in despair.'

'Then he will come,' thought she. 'What a good thing it is that I spoke out.'

She looked at the clock. She had three hours still to wait, and memory of the incidents of their last meeting fired her blood. 'Dear me, how light it is! It is dreadful, but I love to see his face, and I love this fantastic light. . . . My husband! Ah yes. . . Well, thank heaven that all is over with him!'

Chapter XXX

As always happens where people congregate, the usual crystallization, if we may so call it, of Society took place in the little

German watering-place to which the Shcherbatskys had come, assigning to each person a definite and fixed position. As definitely and inevitably as a particle of water exposed to the frost assumes the well-known form of a snow crystal, so did each new-comer on his arrival at the watering-place immediately settle into his natural position.

'Fürst Shcherbatsky sammt Gemahlin und Tochter,' [4] by the lodgings they occupied, by their name, and by the people they were acquainted with, at once crystallized into their definite and preordained place.

There was a real German Fürstin [5] at the watering-place that season, and consequently the crystallizing process was accomplished with special energy.

Princess Shcherbatskaya particularly wished to introduce her daughter to the German Royal Princess, and on the second day after their arrival performed that rite.

Kitty made a low and graceful curtsy in her very simple dress— that is to say, very stylish summer gown ordered from Paris. The Royal Princess said: 'I hope the roses will soon return to this pretty little face,' and at once a definite path was firmly established for the Shcherbatskys from which it was impossible to deviate.

They made acquaintance with the family of an English 'Lady,' with a German Countess and her son who had been wounded in the last war, with a Swedish savant, and with a Mr. Canut and his sister. But the people with whom they necessarily associated most were a Moscow lady, Mary Evgenyevna Rtishcheva, and her daughter, whom Kitty found unpleasant because her illness was due to the same cause as Kitty's—a love affair; and a Moscow Colonel, whom Kitty from childhood had seen and known in uniform with epaulettes, and who here—with his small eyes, low collars and coloured necktie—looked indescribably comical, and was also wearisome because it was impossible to get rid of him. When all this had become firmly established, Kitty began to feel very dull, especially as her father had gone to Carlsbad and she was left alone with her mother. She was not interested in the people she knew, for she felt that nothing new would come from them. Her chief private interest at the watering-place consisted in observing those whom she did not know and making conjectures about them. It was a characteristic of Kitty's always to expect to find the most excellent qualities in people, especially in those she did not know. And now, when guessing who and what kind of people the strangers were, and in what relation they stood to one another, Kitty attributed to them extraordinary and splendid characters, and found

4. Prince Shcherbatsky with his wife and daughter.
5. Princess.

confirmation in her observations.

Among these people she was especially interested in a young Russian girl who had come to the watering-place with an invalid Russian Lady, Madame Stahl, as every one called her. Madame Stahl belonged to the highest Society, but she was so ill that she could not walk, and only on fine days occasionally appeared on the promenade in a bath-chair. But—not so much from illness as from pride, as the Princess Shcherbatskaya explained—Madame Stahl was not acquainted with any of the Russians there. The Russian girl looked after Madame Stahl, and also, as Kitty noticed, became intimate with all those who were seriously ill (of whom there were many in the place) and waited on them in the most natural way. This Russian girl, Kitty decided, was not related to Madame Stahl, but neither was she a paid companion. Madame Stahl called her by the diminutive 'Varenka,' and others called her Mademoiselle Varenka. But besides the fact that it interested Kitty to observe the relations of this girl with Madame Stahl and with others, she experienced (as often happens) an inexplicable attraction toward this Mlle Varenka, and felt, when the girl's eyes met hers, that the feeling was mutual.

This Mlle Varenka was not exactly past her early youth, but seemed to be a person destitute of youthfulness: she might be nineteen years old or she might be thirty.

If one examined her features, she was good-looking rather than plain, despite her unhealthy complexion. Her figure would have been good had she not been too thin and her head too large for her medium height; but she was not likely to prove attractive to men. She was like a beautiful flower which though not yet in full bloom is already beginning to fade and has no scent. Another reason why she could not be attractive to men was because she lacked that of which Kitty had too much—a restrained flame of vitality and consciousness of her own attractiveness. She seemed always occupied with something there could be no doubt about, and therefore it seemed that no side issue could interest her. By this contrast to herself Kitty was specially attracted. She felt that in her and in her way of life could be found a model of what she herself was painfully seeking: interest in life, the worth of life—outside the social relations of girls to men, which now seemed disgusting to Kitty, who regarded them as shameful exhibitions of goods awaiting a buyer. The more Kitty observed her unknown friend, the more she was convinced that this girl really was the perfect being she imagined her to be, and the more she wished to make her acquaintance.

The two girls came across one another several times a day, and every time they met Kitty's eyes said: 'Who are you? What are you? Surely you are the delightful creature I imagine you to be?

But for heaven's sake'—her look added—'do not think that I shall force myself on you. I simply admire and love you.' 'I too love you, and you are very, very sweet. I should love you still more if I had the time,' the stranger's look replied. And Kitty saw that the girl really was always occupied: now taking the children of some Russian family home from the Wells, now carrying an invalid's plaid or wrapping it round her, now trying to soothe an irritable patient, now choosing and buying biscuits for some one's coffee.

Soon after the Shcherbatskys' arrival, two new persons who provoked everybody's disapproval began to appear of a morning at the Wells. They were a very tall, round-shouldered man with black eyes, naïve and at the same time dreadful, and enormous hands, who wore an old overcoat too short for him, and a slightly pock-marked, sweet-faced woman, badly and tastelessly dressed. Having recognized them to be Russians, Kitty at once began to make up a beautiful and touching romance about them. But the Princess, having found out from the visitors' list that they were Nicholas Levin and Mary Nikolaevna, explained to Kitty what a bad man this Levin was, and all her dreams about those two people vanished. Not so much because of what her mother had told her, as because the man was Constantine's brother, these two people appeared very disagreeable to Kitty. This Levin, by his habit of jerking his head, now inspired an irrepressible feeling of aversion in her.

It seemed to her that his large, dreadful eyes, which followed her insistently, expressed hatred and irony, and she tried to avoid encountering him.

Chapter XXXI

It was a dull day, it rained the whole morning, and the invalids with their umbrellas crowded the covered gallery.

Kitty was walking with her mother and the Moscow Colonel, who swaggered gaily in his short, German coat, bought ready-made in Frankfurt. They kept to one side of the gallery, trying to avoid Levin, who was walking on the other side. Varenka in her dark dress and a black hat with turned-down brim, was pacing the whole length of the gallery with a blind Frenchwoman, and each time she met Kitty they exchanged a friendly look.

'Mama, may I speak to her?' asked Kitty, following her unknown friend with her eyes and noticing that she was moving toward the Well and that they could meet her there.

'Well, if you want to so much, I will inquire about her first and will speak to her myself,' answered her mother. 'What do you see particular in her? I expect she's a companion. If you like I will make Madame Stahl's acquaintance. I knew her sister-in-law,' added the Princess, raising her head proudly.

Kitty knew that her mother was offended that Madame Stahl seemed to avoid making her acquaintance. Kitty did not insist.

'She is wonderfully sweet!' she said, looking at Varenka, who was handing a tumbler to the Frenchwoman. 'See how naturally and sweetly she does it.'

'How absurd your infatuations are,' said the Princess. 'Come, we'd better turn back,' she added, as she noticed Levin coming toward them with his companion and a German doctor, to whom he was talking loudly and angrily.

They were just turning to go back, when they suddenly heard voices not merely loud, but shouting. Levin had stopped and was shouting, and the doctor was also excited. A crowd collected about them. The Princess and Kitty withdrew hurriedly, but the Colonel joined the crowd to find out what the noise was all about.

In a few minutes he overtook Kitty and her mother.

'What was the matter?' asked the Princess.

'It's shameful and scandalous,' replied the Colonel. 'The one thing to fear is meeting Russians abroad. That tall gentleman has been quarrelling with the doctor and insulting him, because he is dissatisfied with the doctor's treatment. He shook his stick at him! It's simply shameful!'

'Ah, how unpleasant!' said the Princess. 'But how did it all end?'

'Luckily that . . . you know the girl with a hat like a mushroom —she's Russian, I think—intervened,' said the Colonel.

'Mlle Varenka?' asked Kitty in a pleased tone.

'Yes, yes. She knew what to do before anyone else. She took that fellow by the arm and led him away.'

'There, Mama,' said Kitty. 'And you are surprised that I admire her.'

The next day, watching her unknown friend, Kitty noticed that she was already on the same footing with Levin and his young woman as she was with her other protégés. She went up to them, talked to them, and acted as interpreter for the woman, who spoke nothing but Russian.

Kitty begged her mother more than ever to allow her to make Varenka's acquaintance, and, much as the Princess disliked appearing to take the first step toward getting acquainted with Madame Stahl, who allowed herself to be proud of something or other, she made inquiries about Varenka, and, having learnt particulars which allowed her to conclude that though there might be little good there would be no harm in this acquaintance, she herself approached Varenka.

Choosing a moment when her daughter had gone to the Well and Varenka had stopped in front of a baker's shop, the Princess went up to her.

'Allow me to introduce myself,' said the Princess with her dignified smile. 'My daughter has fallen in love with you. Perhaps you don't know me. I . . .'

'It is more than mutual, Princess,' replied Varenka hurriedly.

'What a good action you performed yesterday for our unfortunate fellow-countryman!' said the Princess.

Varenka blushed. 'I don't remember; I don't think I did anything,' said she.

'Oh, yes, you saved that Levin from unpleasantness.'

'Well, you see, his companion called me, and I tried to soothe him; he is very ill and was dissatisfied with his doctor. I am used to looking after invalids of that kind.'

'Oh, yes, I have heard that you live in Mentone with your aunt, I think, Madame Stahl. I knew her sister-in-law.'

'No, she is not my aunt. I call her Mama, but I am not related to her. She adopted me,' answered Varenka, and blushed again.

This was said so simply, and the frank and open expression of her face was so amiable, that the Princess understood what made Kitty so fond of this Varenka.

'Well, and what about that Levin?'

'He is leaving,' answered Varenka.

Just then Kitty, beaming with joy that her mother had made acquaintance with her unknown friend, returned from the Well.

'There, Kitty, your great wish to make acquaintance with Mlle . . .'

'Varenka,' prompted Varenka with a smile, 'everybody calls me so.'

Kitty blushed with joy, long and silently pressing her new friend's hand, which lay passively in hers. But though her hand did not return the pressure, Mlle Varenka's face shone with a soft and pleased, though rather sad, smile, which disclosed her large but splendid teeth.

'I have long wished it myself,' she said.

'But you are so busy . . .'

'Oh, on the contrary, I have no occupation at all,' answered Varenka; but at that very moment she had to leave her new friends because two little Russian girls, the children of one of the invalids, ran up to her.

'Varenka, Mama wants you!' they shouted.

And Varenka went with them.

Chapter XXXII

The particulars the Princess Shcherbatskaya learnt about Varenka's past and about her relations with Madame Stahl, and about Madame Stahl herself, were the following:

Madame Stahl, of whom some people said that she had tormented her husband to death, while others said that, by his immoral conduct, he had tormented her, had always been a sickly and ecstatic woman. When her first baby was born, she being already divorced from her husband, it died at once; and her relations, knowing how susceptible she was and fearing that this news might kill her, changed her dead child for one who had been born that night in the same house in Petersburg, the daughter of a *chef* at the palace. That child was Varenka. Madame Stahl learnt afterwards that Varenka was not her daughter, but continued to bring her up, the more readily because it happened that very soon Varenka had no relations left.

Madame Stahl had lived continuously abroad in the South for more than ten years, hardly ever leaving her bed. Some people said that she had made for herself a position in Society by her pose as a philanthropic and highly religious woman; others said that she really was the highly moral being, living only to do good, that she seemed to be. No one knew what her religion was: Roman Catholic, Protestant, or Greek Orthodox, but one thing was certain, namely, that she was in friendly relations with the most highly-placed personages of all the churches and denominations.

Varenka always lived with her abroad, and all who knew Madame Stahl knew and liked Mlle Varenka, as everybody called her.

Having learnt all these particulars, the Princess saw nothing to object to in a friendship between her daughter and Varenka, especially as Varenka's manners and education were excellent—she spoke French and English admirably, and, above all, she brought Madame Stahl's regrets at having been deprived through illness of the pleasure of making the Princess's acquaintance.

When she had made Varenka's acquaintance Kitty became more and more fascinated by her friend and found new virtues in her every day.

The Princess, having heard that Varenka sang very well, invited her to come and sing to them one evening.

'Kitty plays, and we have a piano,—though not a good one,—and you would give us great pleasure,' said the Princess with her feigned smile, which was especially unpleasant to Kitty now because she noticed that Varenka did not wish to sing. Varenka, however, came in the evening and brought her music. The Princess had also invited Mary Evgenyevna with her daughter and the Colonel.

Varenka did not seem at all abashed by the fact that strangers were present, and she went straight up to the piano. She could not accompany herself but she sang at sight admirably. Kitty, who played well, accompanied her.

'You have an exceptional talent,' said the Princess, after Varenka had sung her first song excellently.

Mary Evgenyevna and her daughter thanked her and praised her singing.

'See,' said the Colonel, looking out of the window, 'what an audience has assembled to hear you.' Underneath the window a considerable crowd really had collected.

'I am very glad it gives you pleasure,' said Varenka simply.

Kitty looked at her friend with pride. She was enraptured by her singing, her voice, her face, and above all by her manner,—by the fact that Varenka evidently attached no importance to her own singing and was quite indifferent to the praise she got; she only seemed to ask: 'Have I to sing again or is it enough?'

'If it were I,' thought Kitty, 'how proud I should feel! How glad I should be to see that crowd under the windows! But she is quite indifferent. She only wished not to refuse, and to give Mama pleasure. What is it in her? What gives her this power to disregard everything and to be so quietly independent? How I should like to know this, and to learn it from her!' thought Kitty, gazing into the calm face. The Princess asked Varenka to sing again, and she sang another song just as truly, clearly, and well, standing straight at the piano, and beating time on it with her thin brown hand.

The next piece in the music book was an Italian song. Kitty played the prelude and looked round at Varenka.

'Let us skip this one,' said Varenka, blushing.

Kitty anxiously and inquiringly fixed her eyes on Varenka's face. 'Well then, another one,' she said, hurriedly turning over the pages, immediately realizing that there was something particular connected with that song.

'No,' answered Varenka, putting her hand on the music and smiling. 'No, let us sing that one.' And she sang the piece just as calmly, coldly, and well as the previous ones.

When she had finished everybody again thanked her and went to drink tea. But Kitty and Varenka went out into the little garden belonging to the house.

'Am I not right, you have some memory attached to that song?' asked Kitty. 'Don't tell me about it,' she added hurriedly, 'only say if I am right!'

'Why not? I will tell you,' said Varenka simply; and without waiting for a reply continued: 'Yes, there is a memory attached to it and it was painful once. I loved a man and used to sing that song to him.'

Kitty, deeply moved, gazed silently with wide-open eyes at Varenka.

'I loved him and he loved me; but his mother would not have it, and he married another. He lives not far from us now, and I see him sometimes. You did not think that I too have had a romance?' she said, and on her handsome face there flickered for an instant a spark of the fire which, Kitty felt, had once lighted up her whole being.

'I—not think it? Why, if I were a man I could not have loved anyone else after knowing you. But I can't understand how, to satisfy his mother, he could forget you and make you unhappy. He must be quite heartless.'

'Oh no. He is a very good man, and I am not unhappy; on the contrary, I am very happy. Well, we shan't sing any more to-day?' she added, and went toward the house.

"How good you are, how good!" exclaimed Kitty, stopping her and kissing her. 'If only I could be a little bit like you!'

'Why should you be like anyone? You're very good as you are,' said Varenka, smiling her gentle, weary smile.

'No, I am not at all good. But tell me . . . Wait a bit, let us sit down again,' said Kitty, making Varenka sit down on a garden seat beside her. 'Tell me, is it possible that you are not offended at the thought that a man despised your love? That he did not wish . . . ?'

'But he did not despise it; I believe that he loved me, but he was an obedient son . . .'

'Yes, but if it had not been his mother's doing, but his own?' said Kitty, feeling that she had given away her secret and that her face, burning with a blush of shame, had already betrayed her.

'Then he would have behaved badly and I should not regret him,' replied Varenka, evidently conscious that they were now speaking not about her but about Kitty.

'But the humiliation?' said Kitty. 'One cannot forget the humiliation, one cannot,' and she remembered the look she gave Vronsky at the ball, when the music stopped.

'Where is the humiliation? You did not do anything wrong?'

'Worse than wrong, shameful.'

Varenka shook her head and put her hand on Kitty's.

'Shameful in what respect?' she said. 'You could not have told a man who was himself indifferent to you that you loved him?'

'Of course not; I never said a single word, but he knew it. No, no; there are such things as looks and ways of behaving. If I live to be a hundred I shall never forget it.'

'What does it matter? I don't understand. The question is, do you love him now or not?' said Varenka, calling everything by its plain name.

'I hate him: and I cannot forgive myself.'

'But what does it matter?'

'The shame, the humiliation . . .'

'Dear me, if every one were as sensitive as you are!' said Varenka. 'There is no girl who has not gone through the same sort of thing. And it is all so unimportant.'

'Then what is important?' asked Kitty, looking into her face with surprised curiosity.

'Ah, many things are important,' replied Varenka, not knowing what to say. But at that moment they heard the Princess's voice from the window:

'Kitty, it is getting chilly! Either take a shawl or come in.'

'Yes, I really must be going!' said Varenka, rising. 'I have to look in at Madame Berthe's; she asked me to.'

Kitty held her hands, and with passionate curiosity and entreaty questioned Varenka with her eyes: 'What—what is most important? What gives you such peace? You know, tell me!' But Varenka did not even understand what Kitty's eyes were asking. She only knew that she had to call on Madame Berthe and get home in time for Mama's midnight tea. She went in, collected her music, and having said good-night to everybody, prepared to go.

'Allow me to see you home,' said the Colonel.

'Yes, how can you go alone at this time of night?' agreed the Princess. 'I will at any rate send Parasha with you.'

Kitty noticed that Varenka had difficulty in suppressing a smile at the idea that she needed anyone to see her home.

'Oh no, I always go out alone and nothing ever happens to me,' she said, taking up her hat. And kissing Kitty again, but without telling her what was most important, she went out with vigorous steps with her music under her arm, and disappeared in the semi-darkness of the summer night, carrying with her the secret of what was important, and to what she owed her enviable tranquillity and dignity.

Chapter XXXIII

Kitty also became acquainted with Madame Stahl, and this acquaintanceship, together with Varenka's friendship, not only had a great influence on Kitty, but comforted her in her sorrow. What comforted her was that a perfectly new world was revealed to her, a world that had nothing in common with her past: an exalted, admirable world, from the heights of which it was possible to regard that past calmly. It was revealed to her that besides that instinctive life she had lived hitherto there was also a spiritual life. That life was revealed by religion, but a religion that had nothing in common with that which Kitty had known since her childhood and which found expression in Mass and vespers at the private chapel of the Widows' Almshouse where one could meet one's friends, and in learning Slavonic texts by heart with the priest. This was a lofty, mystical religion connected with a series of beautiful thoughts and feelings, which it was not only possible to believe because one was told to, but even to love.

Kitty did not learn all this from words. Madame Stahl spoke with her as with a dear child who gives one pleasure by reminding one of one's own past, and only once mentioned that love and faith alone can bring relief in all human sorrows and that no sorrows are too trivial for Christ's compassion. Then she immediately changed the subject. But in Madame Stahl's every movement, every word, every 'heavenly' look (as Kitty called it), and especially in the whole story of her life, which Kitty learnt from Varenka, she discovered what was important and what she had not known before.

But however lofty may have been Madame Stahl's character, however touching her story, and however elevated and tender her words, Kitty could not help noticing some perplexing traits in her. She noticed that Madame Stahl, when inquiring about Kitty's relatives, smiled contemptuously, which did not accord with Christian kindness. And once, when Kitty met a Roman Catholic priest at the house, she observed that Madame Stahl carefully hid her face behind the lampshade and smiled in a peculiar manner. Trifling as these things were, they disturbed Kitty, and she felt doubts about Madame Stahl. But Varenka, lonely, without relatives or friends, with her sad disillusionment, wishing for nothing and regretting nothing, personified that perfection of which Kitty only allowed herself to dream. In Varenka she saw that it was only necessary to forget oneself and to love others in order to be at peace, happy, and good. And such a person Kitty wished to be. Having now clearly understood what was *most important*, Kitty was not content merely to delight in it, but immediately with her whole soul devoted herself to this newly-revealed life. She formed a plan for her future life, based on what Varenka told her about the work of Madame Stahl and of others whom she named. Like Madame Stahl's niece, Aline, of whom Varenka told her a great deal, Kitty determined, wherever she lived, to seek out the unfortunate, help them as much as she could, distribute Gospels, and read the Gospel to the sick, to criminals, and to the dying. The idea of reading the Gospels to criminals, as Aline did, charmed Kitty particularly. But all these were secret dreams, which she did not speak of either to her mother or to Varenka.

However, while waiting for the time when she could put her plans into operation on a larger scale, Kitty, imitating Varenka, here at the watering-place where there were so many sick and unhappy people, easily found opportunities to apply her new rules.

At first the Princess only noticed that Kitty was strongly influenced by her *engoument* [6] as she called it, for Madame Stahl and especially for Varenka. She noticed that Kitty not only imitated Varenka's activities, but involuntarily copied her manner of walking, speaking, and blinking her eyes. But afterwards the Princess also noticed that, apart from this infatuation, a serious spiritual change was taking place in her daughter.

She saw that in the evening Kitty read the Gospels in French (given her by Madame Stahl)—which she had not done before—that she avoided her Society acquaintances and made up to the invalids who were under Varenka's protection, and especially to the family of Petrov, a poor, sick artist. Kitty evidently prided herself on fulfilling the duties of a sister-of-mercy in that family. This was all very well, and the Princess had nothing against it, especially as Petrov's wife was quite a well-bred woman, and the German Princess, having noticed Kitty's activities, praised her, calling her a ministering angel. It would have been quite right had it not been overdone. But the Princess saw that her daughter was going to extremes and spoke to her about it.

'Il ne faut jamais rien outrer,' [7] she said to her one day.

But her daughter did not reply; she only felt in her soul that one could not speak of overdoing Christianity. How was it possible to exaggerate, when following the teaching which bids us turn the other cheek when we are struck, and give our coat when our cloak is taken? But the Princess disliked this excess, and disliked it all the more because she felt that Kitty did not wish to open her whole heart to her. And Kitty really did hide her new views and feelings from her mother. She kept them secret not from want of respect and love, but just because her mother was her mother. She would have revealed them to anyone sooner than to her.

'It seems a long time since Anna Pavlovna was here,' said the Princess once, speaking of Mrs Petrova. 'I invited her and she did not seem pleased.'

'I did not notice anything, Mama,' said Kitty, flushing up.

'Is it long since you went to see them?'

'We are all arranging to go for a drive up the mountains to-morrow,' replied Kitty.

'Well, go if you like,' said the Princess, looking intently into her daughter's confused face and trying to guess the cause of her confusion.

That same day Varenka came to dinner, and said that Anna Pavlovna had changed her mind about going to the mountains to-morrow.

The Princess noticed that Kitty blushed again.

6. Infatuation.
7. You should never overdo anything.

'Kitty, have you not had some unpleasantness with the Petrovs?' the Princess asked when they were again alone together. 'Why has she stopped sending the children here and coming herself?'

Kitty replied that nothing had passed between them and that she did not at all understand why Anna Pavlovna seemed displeased with her. Kitty spoke the truth: she did not know why Anna Pavlovna had changed toward her, but she guessed it. She guessed it to be something that she could not tell her mother and did not even say to herself. It was one of those things which one knows and yet cannot say even to oneself—so dreadful and shameful would it be to make a mistake.

Again and again she went over in memory all the relations she had had with that family. She remembered the naïve pleasure expressed in Anna Pavlovna's round, good-natured face whenever they met; remembered their secret consultations about the patient, and their plots to draw him away from his work which the doctor had forbidden and to take him for walks, and the attachment to her felt by the youngest boy, who called her 'my Kitty,' and did not want to go to bed without her. How good it had all been! Then she recalled Petrov's thin, emaciated figure in his brown coat, with his long neck, his thin, curly hair, his inquiring blue eyes,—which had at first seemed to her terrible,—and his sickly efforts to appear vigorous and animated in her presence. She remembered her first efforts to conquer the repulsion she felt for him, as for all consumptives, and her efforts to find something to say to him. She remembered the timid look, full of emotion, with which he gazed at her, and the strange feeling of compassion and awkwardness, followed by a consciousness of her own benevolence, that she had experienced. How good it had all been! But all that had been at first. Now for some days past all had suddenly been spoilt. Anna Pavlovna now met Kitty with affected amiability and constantly watched her husband and her.

Could his touching pleasure when she drew near be the cause of Anna Pavlovna's coldness?

'Yes,' she remembered, 'there was something unnatural in Anna Pavlovna, quite unlike her usual kindness, when the day before yesterday she said crossly:

' "There, he has been waiting for you and would not drink his coffee without you, though he was growing dreadfully weak."

'Yes, and perhaps my giving him his plaid may also have been unpleasant to her. It was such a simple thing, but he took it so awkwardly, and thanked me so much that I myself felt awkward. And then that portrait of me, which he did so well! And above all

—that look, confused and tender. . . . Yes, yes, it is so!' Kitty said to herself quite horrified; and then, 'No, it is impossible, it must not be! He is so pathetic.'

This doubt poisoned her delight in her new life.

Chapter XXXIV

Quite toward the end of the season Prince Shcherbatsky, who from Carlsbad had gone on to Baden and Kissingen to see some Russian friends and to 'inhale some Russian spirit,' as he expressed it, returned to his family.

The views of the Prince and Princess on life abroad were diametrically opposed. The Princess found everything admirable, and, in spite of her firmly-established position in Russian Society, tried when abroad to appear like a European lady, which she was not—being thoroughly Russian. She therefore became somewhat artificial, which made her feel uncomfortable. The Prince, on the contrary, considered everything foreign detestable and life abroad oppressive, and kept to his Russian habits, purposely trying to appear more unlike a European than he really was.

He returned looking thinner, with the skin on his cheeks hanging loose, but in the brightest of spirits. His spirits were still better when he saw Kitty completely recovered. The news of her friendship with Madame Stahl and Varenka, and the information the Princess gave him of the change she had observed in Kitty, disturbed him and aroused in him his usual feelings of jealousy toward anything that drew his daughter away from him and of fear lest she might escape from his influence into regions inaccessible to him. But these unpleasant rumours were soon drowned in that sea of kind-hearted cheerfulness which was always within him and which was increased by the Carlsbad water.

The day after his arrival the Prince, attired in a long overcoat, and with his Russian wrinkles, and his slightly puffy cheeks supported by a stiff collar, went out in the brightest of spirits to the Springs with his daughter.

The morning was lovely: the bright, tidy houses with their little gardens, the sight of the red-faced, red-armed, beer-saturated German housemaids, and the clear sunshine, cheered the heart; but the nearer one came to the Spring the more often one met sick people, whose appearance seemed yet sadder amid these customary well-ordered conditions of German life. Kitty was no longer struck by this contrast. The bright sunshine, the gay glitter of the green trees, and the sounds of music had become for her the natural framework of all these familiar figures, and of the changes for better or for worse which she watched. But to the Prince the radiance of the

June morning, the sounds of the band playing a fashionable and merry valse, and particularly the appearance of the sturdy maid-servants, seemed improper and monstrous in contrast with all those melancholy living-corpses collected from all parts of Europe.

In spite of the pride and the sense of renewed youth which he experienced while walking arm-in-arm with his favourite daughter, he felt almost awkward and ashamed of his powerful stride and his large healthy limbs. He had almost the feeling that might be caused by appearing in company without clothes.

'Introduce me, introduce me to your new friends,' he said to his daughter, pressing her arm with his elbow 'I have even taken a liking to your nasty Soden because it has done you so much good. But it's sad—this place of yours, very sad. Who is that?'

Kitty told him the names of the acquaintances and others whom they met. Just at the entrance to the gardens they met the blind Madame Berthe with her guide, and the Prince was pleased by the tender look on the old Frenchwoman's face when she heard Kitty's voice. With French exaggeration she at once began talking to him, admiring him for having such a delightful daughter, and in Kitty's presence praised her up to the skies, calling her a treasure, a pearl, and a ministering angel.

'Then she must be angel No. 2,' the Prince remarked with a smile. 'She calls Mlle Varenka angel No. 1.'

'Oh, Mlle Varenka is a real angel, *allez*,' said Madame Berthe.

In the gallery they met Varenka herself. She was walking hurriedly toward them with an elegant little red bag in her hand.

'See! Papa has come!' said Kitty to her.

Simply and naturally, as she did everything, Varenka made a movement between a bow and a curtsy and immediately began talking to the Prince just as she talked to everybody, easily and naturally.

'Of course I know you, I've heard all about you,' the Prince said to her with a smile, by which Kitty saw with joy that her father liked Varenka. 'Where are you off to in such a hurry?'

'Mama is here,' said she, turning to Kitty. 'She did not sleep all night and the doctor advised her to go out. I am taking her her work.'

'So that is angel No. 1!' said the Prince when Varenka had gone. Kitty saw that he would have liked to make fun of Varenka, but was unable to do so because he liked her.

'Well, let us see all your friends,' he added, 'including Madame Stahl, if she will condescend to recognize me.'

'Oh, do you know her, Papa?' asked Kitty, alarmed by an ironical twinkle in the Prince's eyes when he mentioned Madame Stahl.

'I knew her husband and her too, slightly, before she joined the

Pietists.' [8]

'What are Pietists, Papa?' asked Kitty, dismayed by the fact that what she valued so highly in Madame Stahl had a name.

'I don't know very well myself. I only know that she thanks God for everything, including all misfortunes, . . . and thanks God for her husband's death. And it seems funny, for they did not get on well together. . . . Who is that? What a pitiful face,' he said, noticing an invalid of medium height who sat on a bench in a brown coat and white trousers which fell into strange folds over his emaciated legs. The man raised his straw hat above his thin curly hair, uncovering a high forehead with an unhealthy redness where the hat had pressed it.

'It is Petrov, an artist,' Kitty replied, blushing. 'And that is his wife,' she added, indicating Anna Pavlovna, who on their approach went away with apparent intention, following a child who had run along the path.

'Poor man, what a nice face he has!' said the Prince. 'Why did you not go up to him? He looked as if he wished to say something to you.'

'Well, come back then,' said Kitty, turning resolutely. 'How are you to-day?' she asked Petrov.

Petrov rose with the aid of a stick and looked timidly at the Prince.

'This is my daughter,' said the Prince; 'allow me to introduce myself.'

The artist bowed and smiled, exposing his strangely glistening white teeth.

'We were expecting you yesterday, Princess,' he said to Kitty.

He staggered as he said it, and to make it appear as if he had done this intentionally, he repeated the movement.

'I meant to come, but Varenka told me that Anna Pavlovna sent word that you were not going.'

'Not going?' said Petrov, flushing and immediately beginning to cough and looking round for his wife. 'Annetta, Annetta!' he said loudly, and the veins in his white neck protruded like thick cords.

Anna Pavlovna drew near.

'How is it you sent word to the Princess that we were not going?' he said in an irritable whisper, his voice failing him.

8. Pietism was a movement started by Philip Jacob Spener, who in 1675 published his *Pia disedaria*. It advocated an earnest study of the Bible in private meetings and an altered style of preaching, to implant Christianity in the inner man. A disciple of Spener's, August Hermann Francke, founded a famous orphanage at Halle and the movement spread over Middle and Northern Germany. The organization of the Moravian Church in 1727 was an outcome of the movement. It had a considerable following in Russia early in the nineteenth century, and politically was usually connected with reactionary tendencies, as in the case of Magnitsky, one of the ministers in Alexander I's later years.

'Good morning, Princess,' said Anna Pavlovna with a forced smile, quite unlike her former way of greeting Kitty. 'I am very pleased to make your acquaintance,' she went on, turning to the Prince. 'You have long been expected, Prince!'

'How is it you sent to tell the Princess we were not going?' the painter whispered hoarsely and still more angrily, evidently irritated because his voice failed him and he could not give his words the expression he desired.

'Oh, dear me! I thought we were not going,' said his wife with vexation.

'How so? When . . .' he was interrupted by a fit of coughing, and made a hopeless gesture with his hand.

The Prince raised his hat and went away with his daughter.

'Oh, oh!' he sighed deeply. 'What poor things!'

'Yes, Papa,' replied Kitty. 'And you know they have three children, no servants, and hardly any means. He receives something from the Academy,' she explained animatedly, trying to stifle the excitement resulting from the strange alteration in Anna Pavlovna's manner toward her. 'And there's Madame Stahl,' said Kitty, pointing to a bath-chair on which, under a sunshade, lay something supported by pillows, wrapped up in grey and pale-blue. It was Madame Stahl. Behind her was a sullen-looking, robust German workman who pushed her bath-chair. At her side stood a fair-haired Swedish Count, whom Kitty knew by name. Several patients lingered near by, gazing at this lady as at something out of the common.

The Prince approached her, and Kitty immediately noticed in his eyes that ironical spark which so disturbed her. He went up to Madame Stahl, and spoke to her extremely politely and nicely in that excellent French which so very few people speak nowadays.

'I do not know whether you will remember me, but I must recall myself to you in order to thank you for your kindness to my daughter,' he said, raising his hat and not putting it on again.

'Prince Alexander Shcherbatsky,' said Madame Stahl, lifting toward him her heavenly eyes, in which Kitty detected displeasure. 'I am very pleased. I have grown very fond of your daughter.'

'Your health is still not good?'

'No, but I am accustomed to it,' said Madame Stahl, and introduced the Swedish Count to the Prince.

'You are very little changed,' said the Prince. 'I have not had the honour of seeing you for ten or eleven years.'

'Yes, God sends a cross and gives the strength to bear it. It often seems strange to think why this life should drag on. . . . On that side!' she said irritably to Varenka, who was not wrapping the plaid round her feet the right way.

'To do good, probably,' said the Prince, whose eyes were laughing.

'That is not for us to judge,' said Madame Stahl, detecting a something hardly perceptible on the Prince's face. 'Then you will send me that book, dear Count? Thank you very much,' she added, turning to the young Swede.

'Ah!' exclaimed the Prince, seeing the Moscow Colonel standing near by, and with a bow to Madame Stahl he moved away with his daughter and with the Moscow Colonel, who had joined them.

'That is our aristocracy, Prince!' remarked the Colonel, wishing to appear sarcastic. He had a pique against Madame Stahl because she did not wish to be acquainted with him.

'Always the same,' answered the Prince.

'Did you know her before her illness, Prince? I mean before she was laid up?'

'Yes, I knew her when she first became an invalid.'

'I hear she has not been up for ten years.'

'She does not get up, because her legs are too short. She has a very bad figure . . .'

'Papa, impossible!' exclaimed Kitty.

'Evil tongues say so, my love. But your Varenka does get it,' he added. 'Oh, those invalid ladies!'

'Oh no, Papa,' Kitty objected warmly. 'Varenka adores her. And besides, she does so much good! Ask anyone you like! Everybody knows her and Aline Stahl.'

'Perhaps,' he said, pressing her arm with his elbow. 'But it is better to do good so that, ask whom you will, no one knows anything about it.'

Kitty was silent, not because she had nothing to say, but because she did not want to reveal her secret thoughts even to her father. Yet—strange to say—though she had made up her mind not to submit to her father's opinion and not to let him enter her sanctuary, she felt that the divine image of Madame Stahl which she had carried in her bosom for a whole month had irrevocably vanished, as the figure formed by a cast-off garment vanishes when one realizes how the garment is lying. There remained only a short-legged woman who was always lying down because she had a bad figure, and who tormented poor unresisting Varenka for not tucking her plaid the right way. And by no efforts of imagination could the former Madame Stahl be recalled.

Chapter XXXV

The Prince imparted his good spirits to his household, his friends, and even to his German landlord.

On returning from the Spring with Kitty, the Prince, who had invited the Colonel, Mary Evgenyevna, and Varenka to come and take coffee, had a table and chairs brought out into the garden under a chestnut tree and breakfast laid there. The landlord and the servants brightened up under his influence. They knew his generosity, and in a quarter of an hour the sick Hamburg doctor, who lived upstairs, was looking with envy from his window at the merry party of healthy Russians gathered under the chestnut tree. Beneath the trembling shadow-circles of the leaves, at one end of a table covered with a white cloth and set out with coffee-pot, bread, butter, cheese and cold game, sat the Princess in a cap with lilac ribbons, handing out cups of coffee and sandwiches. At the other end sat the Prince, making a substantial meal and talking loudly and merrily. He spread out his purchases before him: carved caskets, spillikins, and paper-knives of all kinds, of which he had bought quantities at all the different watering-places, and he gave them away to everybody, including Lischen, the maid, and the landlord, with whom he joked in his funny broken German, assuring him that not the waters had cured Kitty but his excellent food, especially his plum soup. The Princess laughed at her husband for his Russian ways, but was livelier and brighter than she had ever been during her stay at the watering-place. The Colonel smiled, as he always did at the Prince's jokes; but with regard to Europe (which he thought he had carefully studied) he sided with the Princess. The good-natured Mary Evgenyevna shook with laughter at everything the amusing Prince said, and even Varenka, in a way new to Kitty, succumbed to a feeble but infectious laughter inspired by the Prince's jokes.

All this cheered Kitty up, but she could not help being troubled. She could not solve the problem unconsciously set her by her father's jocular view of her friends and of the life she had begun to love so much. To the problem was added the change in her relations with the Petrovs, which had been so clearly and unpleasantly demonstrated that morning. Everybody was merry, but Kitty could not be merry, and this troubled her still more. She felt almost as she used to feel when, as a child, she was locked up in a room for punishment and heard her sister's merry laughter.

'Now, why have you bought that mass of things?' asked the Princess, smiling and passing her husband a cup of coffee.

'One goes out walking, comes to a shop, and they ask one to buy something. It's "*Erlaucht, Excellenz, Durchlaucht.*" [9] Well, by the time they get to "*Durchlaucht*" I can't resist, and ten thalers are gone.'

'That's all because you are bored,' said the Princess.

'Bored, of course I am! The time hangs so heavy, my dear, that

9. Eminence, Excellence, Serene Highness.

one does not know what to do with oneself.'

'How can you be bored, Prince? There is so much that is interesting in Germany now,' said Mary Evgenyevna.

'But I know all your interesting things: plum-soup and pea-sausages. I know them. I know it all.'

'No, say what you please, Prince, their institutions are interesting,' said the Colonel.

'What is there interesting about them? They are as self-satisfied as brass farthings; they've conquered everybody. Now tell me what am I to be pleased about? I have not conquered anybody, but here I have to take off my own boots and even put them outside the door myself. In the morning I have to get up and dress at once and go down to the dining-room to drink bad tea. Is it like that at home? There one wakes up without any hurry, gets a bit cross about something, grumbles a bit, comes well to one's senses, and thinks everything well over without hurrying.'

'But "time is money," don't forget that,' said the Colonel.

'It all depends on what time! There are times when one would give a whole month for a shilling and there are times when you would not give half an hour at any price. Is not that so Kitty? Why are you so glum?'

'I'm all right.'

'Where are you off to? Stay a little longer,' he said, turning to Varenka.

'I must get home,' said Varenka, rising and bursting into another fit of laughter. When she had recovered, she took leave and went into the house for her hat.

Kitty followed her. Even Varenka seemed different now. She was not worse, but different from what Kitty previously had imagined her to be.

'Oh dear, I have not laughed so much for a long time!' said Varenka, collecting her sunshade and bag. 'What a dear your Papa is!'

Kitty remained silent.

'When shall we meet?' asked Varenka.

'Mama was going to call on the Petrovs. Will you be there?' asked Kitty, trying to sound Varenka.

'I will,' answered Varenka. 'They are preparing to leave, so I have promised to help them pack.'

'Then I'll come too.'

'No, why should you?'

'Why not, why not, why not?' asked Kitty with wide-open eyes, and holding Varenka's sunshade to prevent her going. 'No, wait a bit, and tell me why not.'

'Oh, nothing. Only your Papa has returned, and they don't feel at ease with you.'

'No, no, tell me why you do not wish me to be often at the Petrovs? You don't, do you? Why?'

'I have not said so,' replied Varenka quietly.

'No, please tell me!'

'Shall I tell you everything?' said Varenka.

'Everything, everything!' said Kitty.

'There is nothing special to tell, only Petrov used to want to leave sooner but now does not want to go,' said Varenka smiling.

'Well, go on,' Kitty hurried her, looking at her with a frown.

'Well, I don't know why, but Anna Pavlovna says he does not want to go, because you are here. Of course that was tactless, but they quarrelled about you. And you know how excitable such invalids are.'

Kitty frowned yet more, and remained silent, and only Varenka spoke, trying to soften and soothe Kitty, and foreseeing an approaching explosion of tears or words, she knew not which.

'So it is better for you not to go. . . . And, you understand, don't be hurt . . .'

'It serves me right, it serves me right!' Kitty began hurriedly, snatching Varenka's sunshade out of her hands, and looking past her friend's eyes.

Varenka felt like smiling at her friend's childish anger but feared to offend her.

'Why—serves you right? I don't understand,' she said.

'It serves me right, it serves me right!' Kitty began hurriedly, not heartfelt. 'What business had I with a stranger? So it comes about that I am the cause of a quarrel, and have been doing what nobody asked me to do. Because it is all pretence, pretence and pretence! . . .'

'But what motive had you for pretending?' said Varenka softly.

'Oh, how stupid, how stupid! There was no need at all. . . . It was all pretence!' Kitty said, opening and shutting the sunshade.

'But with what object?'

'To appear better than others to myself and to God—to deceive everybody. No, I shall not give in to that again! Let me be bad, but at any rate not false, not a humbug!'

'But who is a "humbug"?' asked Varenka reproachfully. 'You speak as if . . .'

But Kitty was in one of her fits of passion. She would not let Varenka finish.

'I am not talking about you, not about you at all. You are perfection. Yes, yes, you are all perfection; but how can I help it if I am bad? It would not have happened if I were not bad. So let me be what I am, but not pretend. What is Anna Pavlovna to me? Let them live as they like, and I will live as I like. I cannot be different. . . . And it's all not the thing, not the thing!'

'But what is not the thing?' said Varenka, quite perplexed.

'It's all not the thing. I can't live except by my own heart, but you live by principles. I have loved you quite simply, but you, I expect, only in order to save me, to teach me.'

'You are unjust,' said Varenka.

'But I am not talking about others, only about myself.'

'Kitty!' came her mother's voice, 'come here and show Papa your corals.'

Kitty took from the table a little box which held the corals, and with a proud look, without having made it up with her friend, went to where her mother was.

'What's the matter? Why are you so red?' asked both her mother and father together.

'Nothing,' she said. 'I'll come back in a minute,' and ran away.

'She is still here,' thought Kitty. 'What shall I say to her? Oh dear! What have I done, what have I said? Why have I offended her? What am I to do? What shall I say to her?' thought Kitty and stopped at the door.

Varenka, with her hat on, sat at the table examining the spring of her sunshade, which Kitty had broken. She looked up.

'Varenka, forgive me, forgive me!' whispered Kitty, coming close to her. 'I don't remember what I said. I . . .'

'Really, I did not wish to distress you,' said Varenka with a smile. Peace was made. But with her father's return the world in which she had been living completely changed for Kitty. She did not renounce all she had learnt, but realized that she had deceived herself when thinking that she could be what she wished to be. It was as if she had recovered consciousness; she felt the difficulty of remaining without hypocrisy or boastfulness on the level to which she had wished to rise.

Moreover, she felt the oppressiveness of that world of sorrow, sickness and death in which she was living. The efforts she had been making to love it, now seemed tormenting, and she longed to get away quickly to the fresh air, back to Russia, to Ergushovo, where as she knew from a letter her sister Dolly had moved with the children.

But her affection for Varenka was not weakened. When taking leave of her, Kitty tried to persuade her to come and stay with them in Russia.

'I will come when you are married,' said Varenka.

'I shall never marry.'

'Well, then I shall never come.'

'Then I will marry for that purpose only. Mind now, don't

forget your promise!' said Kitty.

The doctor's prediction was justified. Kitty returned to Russia quite cured! She was not as careless and light-hearted as before, but she was at peace. Her old Moscow sorrows were no more than a memory.

Part III

Chapter I

Sergius Ivanich Koznyshev, wishing to take a rest from mental work, went to stay with his brother in the country instead of going abroad as usual. According to his views country life was preferable to any other, and he had now come to his brother's house to enjoy it. Constantine Levin was very pleased, especially as he no longer expected his brother Nicholas to come that summer. But in spite of his affection and respect for Koznyshev, Constantine did not feel at ease with his step-brother in the country. To Constantine the country was the place where one lived—that is to say, where one rejoiced, suffered, and laboured; but to Koznyshev the country was, on the one hand, a place of rest from work, and, on the other, a useful antidote to depravity, an antidote to which he resorted with pleasure and with a consciousness of its utility. To Constantine the country seemed a good place because it was the scene of unquestionably useful labour; to Koznyshev it seemed good because one could and should do nothing there. Besides this, Koznyshev's attitude toward the peasants jarred on Constantine. Koznyshev was wont to say that he knew and loved the common people: he often conversed with peasants, and was able to do it well, frankly, and without affectation, deducing from every such conversation data in the peasants' favour and proofs of his own knowledge of the people. Constantine regarded the peasants as the chief partners in a common undertaking, and despite his respect and the feeling of a blood-tie—probably, as he said, sucked in with the milk of his peasant nurse—he as partner in their common undertaking, though often filled with admiration for the strength, meekness, and justice of these people, was very often (when the business required other qualities) exasperated with them for their carelessness, untidiness, drunkenness, and untruthfulness. Had Constantine been asked whether he liked the peasants, he would not have known what to answer. He both liked and disliked them, just as he liked and disliked all human beings. With his natural kind heart he of course liked human beings more than he disliked them, and naturally the peasants were included; but he could not like or dislike the people as if they were something apart, because he not only lived among them, his interests closely bound up with theirs, but he considered himself one of the people and could not find in himself any special qualities or defects which placed him in contrast with them. Moreover, though he had long lived in very close relations with the peasants, as their master, mediator, and above all as their adviser (the peasants trusted him, and would often come thirty miles to consult him), he had no definite opinion concerning them. Had he been asked whether he knew the people, he would have been just as much at a loss for a reply as he was for a reply to the question whether he liked them. To say that he knew the peasants was tantamount to saying that he knew human things. He continually observed and learnt to know all sorts of human beings, among them human beings of the peasant class, whom he considered interesting, constantly discovering in them new traits and altering his opinions accordingly. Koznyshev, on the other hand, just as he praised country life as a contrast to the life he disliked, liked the peasants as a contrast to the class he disliked, and regarded them as a contrast to humanity in general. His methodical mind had formed definite views on the life of the people, founded partly on that life itself, but chiefly on its contrast. He never altered his opinions about the people nor his sympathetic attitude toward them. In the disputes which took place between the brothers when discussing the peasants, Koznyshev was always victorious, just because he had definite views about them, their character, attributes, and tastes; while Constantine had no definite and fixed views, and was often guilty of self-contradiction when arguing on that subject.

Koznyshev thought his younger brother a splendid fellow, with his heart in the right place, but with a mind which, though rather quick, was swayed by the impression of the moment and was therefore full of contradictions. With an elder brother's condescension he sometimes explained to him the meaning of things, but could find no pleasure in discussion, because he could gain too easy a victory.

Constantine considered his brother to be a man of great intellect, noble in the highest sense of the word, and gifted with the power of working for the general welfare. But the older he grew and the more intimately he came to know his brother, the oftener the thought occurred to him that the power of working for the general welfare—a power of which he felt himself entirely destitute—was not a virtue but rather a lack of something: not a lack of kindly honesty and noble desires and tastes, but a lack of the power of living, of what is called heart—the aspiration which makes a man choose one out of all the innumerable paths of life that present themselves, and desire that alone. The better he knew his brother, the more he noticed that Koznyshev and many other social workers were not led to this love for the common good by their hearts, but because they had reasoned out in their minds that it was a good thing to do that kind of work, and took to it accordingly. What strengthened this conviction, was noticing that his brother did not take the question of the general welfare, or of the immortality of the soul, any more to heart than a game of chess, or the construction of a new machine.

Another thing which made Constantine Levin feel his brother's presence inconvenient was that in the country, especially during the summer, while Levin was always busy with the farm and the long summer days were too short for doing all that had to be done, Koznyshev was resting. But even though he was resting from mental labours, and was not writing, he was so used to mental activity that he liked expressing his thoughts in an elegant, concise style, and liked having a listener. His most usual and natural listener was his brother; and therefore, despite their friendly relations, Constantine felt uncomfortable at leaving him alone. Koznyshev loved to lie basking in the sunshine, talking lazily.

'You can't imagine what a pleasure this complete laziness is to me: not a thought in my brain—you might send a ball rolling through it.'

But it wearied Constantine to sit listening to him, particularly because he knew that during his absence the manure was being carted into the field, and it was impossible to guess where they would throw it if he were not there to see. The ploughshares too would not be screwed up properly, but taken off; and then he would be told that these ploughs were a silly invention: 'How can they be compared to our old Russian plough?' and so on.

'Haven't you walked about enough in this heat?' said Koznyshev.

'No; I must just look in at the office for a moment,' answered Levin, and off he ran to the fields.

Chapter II

At the beginning of June Levin's old nurse and housekeeper, Agatha Mikhaylovna, happened to slip as she was carrying to the cellar a jar of mushrooms which she had just pickled, and sprained her wrist. A talkative young medical man who had only just qualified and been appointed doctor for the Zemstvo district arrived, examined the hand, said it was not dislocated, and enjoyed a talk with the celebrated Sergius Ivanich Koznyshev. He told him all the gossip of the district to show off his enlightened views and complained of the unsatisfactory conditions prevailing there. Koznyshev listened attentively, asked questions, and, enlivened by the presence of a new listener, became quite chatty, made some pointed and weighty remarks respectfully appreciated by the young doctor, and reached that state of animation his brother so well knew, which generally followed a brilliant and lively conversation. After the doctor's departure Koznyshev felt inclined to go to the river with his fishing-rod. He was fond of angling, and seemed proud of being able to like such a stupid occupation. Constantine, who was obliged to go to the cornfields and meadows, offered to give his brother a lift in his trap.

It was just the time of year, the turning-point of summer, when the result of that year's harvest becomes assured, when the autumn sowings have to be considered, and when the hay harvest is close at hand; when the grey-green rye waves its formed but as yet not swollen ears lightly in the wind; when the green oats, with irregular clumps of yellow grass interspersed, stand unevenly on late-sown fields; when the early buckwheat spreads out and hides the ground; when the fallow land, trodden as hard as a stone by the cattle, is half-ploughed, with here and there long strips omitted as too hard for the plough; when the smell of dried heaps of manure in the fields mingles with the honied perfume of the grasses; and waiting for the scythe, the lowland meadows lie smooth as a lake by the river's banks, showing here and there black heaps of weeded sorrel stalks. It was the time of that short pause before the labour, yearly renewed, of getting in the harvest, which always demands all the peasants' strength for its accomplishment. The promise of the harvest was splendid, the weather clear and hot, and the short night dewy.

The brothers had to pass through the forest on their way to the meadows. Koznyshev was all the while filled with admiration for the beauty of the thickly-leaved forest, and kept pointing out to his brother the old lime trees, looking so dark on the shady side, covered with creamy buds all ready to burst into blossom; of the new shoots, sparkling like emeralds, on the trees. Constantine Levin did not like talking or hearing about the beauty of nature. Words seemed to detract from the beauty of what he was looking at. He assented to what his brother said but could not help thinking of other things. When they emerged from the forest his attention was arrested at the sight of a fallow field and a hillock, here and there yellow with grass or broken up and cut into squares, in some parts speckled with heaps of manure, or even ploughed. A string of carts was moving over the field. Levin counted the carts, and was pleased to see that sufficient manure was being brought. At sight of the meadows his thoughts turned to the hay harvest. The thought of the hay harvest always touched him to the quick. When they reached the meadow Levin stopped. At the roots of the thick grass the morning dew still lingered, and Koznyshev, afraid of wetting his feet, asked his brother to drive him across the meadow to the willow clump near which perch could be caught. Though Constantine was loth to crush his grass, he drove across the meadow. The tall grass twined softly about the wheels and the horse's legs, leaving seeds on the wet spokes and hubs.

Koznyshev sat down by the willows, while Levin led away his horse, and, having tethered it, stepped into the immense grey-green sea of grass, so dense that the wind could not ruffle it. In the meadow, which was flooded every spring, the silky grass, now scattering its seeds, reached almost to his waist. When Constantine Levin had passed right across the meadow and reached the road, he met an old man with a swollen eye carrying bees in a swarm-carrier.

'Have you found one, Fomich?' he asked.

'Found one, indeed, Constantine Dmitrich! I only hope not to lose our own. This is the second time a swarm has got away, and it's only thanks to those lads there that I've got this one back. They were ploughing for you, and unharnessed a horse and galloped after it. . . .'

'Well, Fomich, what do you think? Shall we begin mowing, or wait a little?'

'Oh, well, our custom is to wait till St. Peter's Day, but you always mow earlier. Why not, God willing? The grass is fine; there will be more room for the cattle.'

'And what do you think of the weather?'

'That's God's business—perhaps the weather will keep fine too.'

Levin went back to his brother.

Though he had caught nothing, Koznyshev did not feel bored and seemed in the best of spirits. Levin saw that he had been roused by his conversation with the doctor and wanted to have a talk. Levin, on the contrary, was impatient to get home in order to give orders about hiring the mowers on the morrow, and to decide about the hay harvest, which greatly occupied his mind.

'Well, let's go,' said he.

'Where's the hurry? Let's sit here a little. How wet you are! Though nothing bites, it's pleasant; hunting and similar sports are good because they bring one in touch with nature. . . . How lovely this steel-coloured water is!' said he. 'And these grassy banks always remind me of that riddle—you know—"The grass says to the water, We will shake, we will shake. . . ."'

'I don't know that riddle,' replied Levin in a dull tone.

Chapter III

'Do you know, I've been thinking about you,' said Koznyshev. 'From what the doctor told me—and he is by no means a stupid young fellow—the things going on in your district are simply disgraceful. I have already told you, and I say it again, it is not right to stop away from the Zemstvo meetings, and in general to take no part in its activities! If all the better sort stand aside, of course heaven only knows what will happen. We expend money for salaries, but there are no schools, no medical assistance, no midwives, no chemists, no anything!'

'You know I have tried,' Levin replied slowly and reluctantly, 'but I can't! So what am I to do?'

'Why can't you? I confess I don't understand. I can't admit it to be indifference or inaptitude; is it possible that it is mere laziness?'

'Neither the one nor the other—nor the last. I have tried and seen that I can do nothing,' said Levin.

He did not pay much attention to what his brother was saying. Peering into the distance across the river, he made out something black in the cornfield, and could not see whether it was only a horse or the steward on horseback.

'Why can you do nothing? You have made an attempt, and because according to your judgment it was a failure, you gave it up. Fancy having so little ambition!'

'Ambition?' reiterated Levin, stung by his brother's words. 'I do not understand it. If at college they had told me that others understood the integral calculus and I did not, that would have been a case for ambition; but in these matters the first requisite is a conviction that one has the necessary ability, and above all that it is all very important.'

'Well, and is it not very important?' said Koznyshev, stirred by the perception that his occupations were regarded as unimportant and especially by his brother's evident inattention to what he was saying.

'They don't appear important to me. Do what you will, they don't grip me,' replied Levin, having made out that what he saw was the steward, who was probably dismissing the peasants from their ploughing too soon, for they were turning the ploughs over. 'Is it possible they have finished ploughing?' thought he.

'Come now! After all,' continued the elder brother with a frown on his handsome, intelligent face, 'there are limits to everything! It is all very well to be a crank, to be sincere and dislike hypocrisy—I know that very well—but what you are saying has either no meaning at all or a very bad meaning. How can you consider it unimportant that the people, whom you love, as you maintain . . .'

'I never maintained it,' thought Levin. . . .

'. . . are dying without help? Ignorant midwives murder the babies, and the people remain steeped in ignorance, at the mercy of every village clerk; while you have in your power the means of helping them, and yet are not helping because you do not consider it important!'

And Koznyshev confronted his brother with this dilemma: 'Either you are so undeveloped that you don't see all that you might do, or you don't want to sacrifice your peace of mind or your vanity—I don't know which—in order to do it.' Constantine felt that there was nothing for him but to submit or else to own to a lack of love for the common cause, and he felt wounded and grieved.

'Both the one and the other,' said he resolutely. 'I can't see how it is to be done . . .'

'What? Don't see how medical help can be given, by distributing the money in a proper way . . .'

'Well, it seems impossible to me. . . . To give medical help over the whole three thousand square miles of our district, with our deep snow, impassable when it begins melting, our snowdrifts, and the pressure of work at harvest time, is impossible. Besides, I have no faith in medicine generally . . .'

'Come now! That is unjust. . . . I could cite thousands of cases to you. . . . And how about schools?'

'Schools? What for?'

'What do you mean? Is it possible to doubt the utility of education? If it is good for you, why not for everybody?'

Constantine felt himself morally cornered, and in consequence became excited and involuntarily betrayed the chief cause of his indifference to social questions.

'All this may be very good, but why should I trouble about medical centres which I should never use or schools to which I should never send my children, and to which the peasants would not wish to send theirs either?—and to which I am not fully convinced they ought to send them?' said he.

This unexpected view of the question took Koznyshev by surprise, but he immediately formed a new plan of attack.

He remained silent awhile, lifted his rod and threw the line again, and then turned to his brother with a smile.

'Now let's see. . . . There is need of a medical centre after all. Did we not send for the district doctor for Agatha Mikhaylovna?'

'But I think her hand will remain crooked all the same.'

'That's very questionable. . . . And then a peasant who can read and write is more useful to you and worth more.'

'Oh no! Ask anyone you like,' said Constantine, decidedly. 'A peasant who can read and write is far worse as a labourer. They can't mend the roads, and when they build a bridge they steal.'

'However, all that is not to the point,' said Koznyshev, frowning; he did not like to be contradicted, especially when he was met with arguments that incessantly shifted their ground, introducing new considerations without sequence so that it was difficult to know which of them to answer first. 'Wait a bit. Do you admit that education is a good thing for the people?'

'I do,' replied Levin unguardedly, and at once realized that he had not said what he really thought. He felt that, since he admitted this much, it would be proved to him that he was talking meaningless twaddle. How it would be proved to him he did not know; but he knew that it certainly would be proved logically, and waited for that proof.

The proof turned out to be far simpler than Constantine anticipated.

'If you admit it to be good,' said Koznyshev, 'then, as an honest man, you cannot help loving and sympathizing with such movements and wishing to work for them.'

'But I am not yet prepared to say that such work is desirable,' returned Levin, reddening a little.

'What? Why, you said just now . . .'

'I mean I consider it neither desirable nor possible.'

'You can't tell without having tried it.'

'Well, let's grant it is so,' said Levin, though he did not grant it at all. 'Still, I don't see why I should be bothered with it.'

'What do you mean?'

'No: since we have started on the topic, perhaps you had better explain it to me from a philosophical point of view,' said Levin.

'I don't see what philosophy has to do with it,' replied Koznyshev in a tone that made it seem—at least Levin thought so—that he did not consider his brother had a right to argue on philosophical questions. This irritated Levin.

'This is what it has to do with it,' he said, getting heated. 'I believe that in any case the motive power of all our actions is our personal happiness. At present I, a nobleman, see nothing in our Zemstvo that could conduce to my welfare. The roads are not better and cannot be made better, and my horses do manage to pull me over the bad ones. I don't require doctors and medical centres; I don't need the magistrate; I never apply to him and never will. I not only do not require schools, but they would even do me harm, as I have already told you. To me the Zemstvo means nothing but a tax of eighteen kopecks a desyatina, my having to go to the town, sharing a bed with bugs, and listening to all sorts of nonsense and nastiness; and my personal interests do not prompt me to do it!'

'Come,' smilingly interrupted Koznyshev, 'it was not our personal interest which induced us to work for the emancipation of the serfs, and yet we did it.'

'No, no!' Constantine interrupted, growing more and more heated. 'The emancipation of the serfs was quite a different matter. There was a personal interest in that: we wanted to throw off a yoke that was oppressing us all—all good men. But to be member of a Council, to discuss how many cesspool cleaners are required and how the drains should be laid in a town in which I am not living, to be on the jury and try a peasant who has stolen a ham, to sit for six hours on end listening to all sorts of rubbish jabbered by the counsel and prosecutor, and to the President asking our idiot Aleshka:

' "Prisoner at the bar, do you plead guilty to the indictment of having stolen a ham?"

' "Eh-h-h?" '

Constantine Levin was being carried away, and was personating the judge and the idiot Aleshka; it seemed to him that all this was relevant to the case in point. But Koznyshev shrugged his shoulders.

'Well, what do you want to prove by that?'

'I only want to prove that I will always stand up with all my power for the rights which touch me and my personal interests. When they searched us students, and gendarmes read our letters, I was ready to defend with all my power my right to education and liberty. I understand conscription which touches the fate of my children, of my brothers and myself, and I am ready to discuss what concerns me; but how to dispose of forty thousand roubles of Zemstvo money, or how to try the idiot Aleshka, I neither understand nor can take part in.'

Constantine Levin spoke as if the dam of his flood of words had been broken. Koznyshev smiled.

'And to-morrow you may be going to law. Would you rather be tried in the old Criminal Court?'

'I won't go to law. I am not going to cut anybody's throat, so I shall never be in need of that sort of thing. All those Zemstvo institutions of ours,' he said, again jumping off to a subject that had no bearing on the case in point, 'are like those little birches that are cut down for decorations at Whitsuntide, and we Russians stick them up to imitate the woods that have grown up naturally in Western Europe. I cannot water these birches or believe in them from my soul.'

Koznyshev only shrugged his shoulders to express his wonder at this sudden introduction of little birches into their discussion, though he had at once grasped his brother's meaning.

'Wait a moment! One can't reason that way, you know,' he remarked; but Constantine wishing to justify the failing of which he was aware in himself (his indifference to the general welfare), continued:

'I think that no activity can endure if it is not based on personal interest. That is the common and philosophical truth,' said he, emphasizing the word *philosophical*, as if he wanted to show that he might talk about philosophy as much as anyone else.

Koznyshev smiled again. 'He too has some philosophy or other to serve his inclinations,' he thought.

'You'd better leave philosophy alone,' said he. 'The principal task of philosophy has always, in all ages, been to find the necessary connection existing between personal and general interests. But that is not the point. I need only correct your illustration to get at the point. The birches are not stuck in: some of them are planted, and others are sown and have to be tended carefully. Only those peoples have a future, only those peoples can be called historic, that have a sense of what is important and great in their institutions, and value them.'

And to prove the inaccuracy of Levin's views, Koznyshev carried the conversation into the realm of philosophy and history, which was beyond Constantine's reach.

'As to your not liking it, pardon me, but that only comes of our Russian laziness and seignorial habits, and I am sure that in your case it is a temporary error and will pass.'

Constantine was silent. He felt himself beaten at every point, yet was sure that his brother had not understood what he had been trying to say, only he did not know why this was so: whether it was because he could not express himself clearly, or because his brother either could not or did not wish to understand him. But he did not go deeply into these questions, and without replying to his brother began reflecting on a totally different and personal matter.

Koznyshev wound up his last line, untied the horse, and they started on their homeward way.

Chapter IV

The personal matter that occupied Levin while he was talking with his brother was this. The year before, when visiting a field that was being mown, he had lost his temper with his steward, and to calm himself had used a remedy of his own—he took a scythe from one of the peasants and himself began mowing.

He liked this work so much that he went mowing several times: he mowed all the meadow in front of his house, and when spring came he planned to devote several whole days to mowing with the peasants. Since his brother's arrival, however, he was in doubt whether to go mowing or not. He did not feel comfortable at the thought of leaving his brother alone all day long, and he also feared that Koznyshev might laugh at him. But while walking over the meadow he recalled the impression mowing had made on him, and almost made up his mind to do it. After his irritating conversation with his brother he again remembered his intention.

'I need physical exercise; without it my character gets quite spoilt,' thought he, and determined to go and mow, however uncomfortable his brother and the peasants might make him feel.

In the evening Constantine went to the office and gave orders about the work, sending round to the villages to tell the mowers to come next day to the Kalina meadow, the largest and finest he had.

'And please send my scythe to Titus to be sharpened, and have it taken to the meadow to-morrow: I may go mowing myself,' he said, trying to overcome his confusion.

The steward smiled and said, 'All right, sir.'

That evening, at tea, Levin said to his brother:

'The weather looks settled; to-morrow we begin mowing.'

'I like that work very much,' said Koznyshev.

'I like it awfully too. I have mown with the peasants now and then, and to-morrow I want to mow all day.'

Koznyshev looked up at his brother in surprise.

'How do you mean? All day, just like the peasants?'

'Yes, it is very pleasant,' replied Levin.

'It is splendid physical exercise, but you will hardly be able to hold out,' remarked Koznyshev, without the least sarcasm.

'I have tried it. At first it seems hard, but one gets drawn into it. I don't think I shall lag behind . . .'

'Dear me! But tell me, how do the peasants take it? I expect they laugh at their crank of a master?'

'No, I don't think so; but it is such pleasant work, and at the same time so hard, that one has no time for thinking.'

'But how can you dine with them? It would not be quite the thing to send you claret and roast turkey out there?'

'No; I will just come home at their dinner-time.'

Next morning Constantine got up earlier than usual, but giving instructions about the farming delayed him, and when he came to the meadow each man was already mowing his second swath.

From the hill, as he came to his first swath, he could see, in the shade at his feet, a part of the meadow that was already mown, with the green heaps of grass and dark piles of coats thrown down by the mowers.

As he drew nearer, the peasants—following each other in a long straggling line, some with coats on, some in their shirts, each swinging his scythe in his own manner—gradually came into sight. He counted forty-two of them.

They moved slowly along the uneven bottom of the meadow, where a weir had once been. Levin recognized some of his own men. Old Ermil, wearing a very long white shirt, was swinging his scythe, with his back bent; young Vaska, who had been in Levin's service as coachman, and who at each swing of his scythe cut the grass the whole width of his swath; and Titus, Levin's mowing master, a thin little peasant, who went along without stopping, mowing his wide swath as if in play.

Levin dismounted and, tethering his horse by the roadside, went up to Titus, who fetched another scythe from behind a bush and gave it to Levin.

'It's ready, master! Like a razor, it will mow of itself,' said Titus, taking off his cap and smiling as he handed the scythe.

Levin took it and began to put himself in position. The peasants, perspiring and merry, who had finished their swaths came out onto the road one after another and laughingly exchanged greetings with the master. They all looked at him, but no one made any remark until a tall, shrivelled, beardless old man, wearing a sheepskin jacket, stepped out on to the road and addressed him:

'Mind, master! Having put your hand to the plough, don't look back!'

And Levin heard the sound of repressed laughter among the mowers.

'I will try not to lag behind,' he said, taking his place behind Titus and waiting his turn to fall in.

'Mind!' repeated the old man.

Titus made room for Levin, and Levin followed him. By the roadside the grass was short and tough, and Levin, who had not done any mowing for a long time and was confused by so many eyes upon him, mowed badly for the first ten minutes, though he swung his scythe with much vigour. He heard voices behind him:

'It's not properly adjusted, the grip is not right. See how he has to stoop!' said one.

'Hold the heel lower,' said another.

'Never mind! It's all right: he'll get into it,' said the old man. 'There he goes . . .'

'You are taking too wide a swath, you'll get tired out.' . . . 'He's the master, he must work; he's working for himself!' . . . 'But look how uneven!' . . . 'That's what the likes of us used to get a thump on the back for.'

They came to softer grass, and Levin, who was listening without replying, followed Titus and tried to mow as well as possible. When they had gone some hundred steps Titus was still going on without pausing, showing no signs of fatigue, while Levin was already beginning to fear he would not be able to keep up, he felt so tired.

He swung his scythe, feeling almost at the last gasp, and made up his mind to ask Titus to stop. But just at that moment Titus stopped of his own accord, stooped, took up some grass and wiped his scythe with it. Levin straightened himself, sighed, and looked

back. The peasant behind him was still mowing but was obviously
tired too, for he stopped without coming even with Levin and
began whetting his scythe. Titus whetted his own and Levin's, and
they began mowing again.

The same thing happened at Levin's second attempt. Titus swung
his scythe, swing after swing, without stopping and without getting
tired. Levin followed, trying not to lag behind, but it became
harder and harder until at last the moment came when he felt he
had no strength left, and then Titus again stopped and began
whetting his scythe. So they finished the first row. And this long
row seemed to Levin particularly difficult; but when it was done
and Titus with his scythe over his shoulder turned about and
slowly retraced his steps, placing his feet on the marks left on the
mown surface by the heels of his boots, and Levin went down his
own swath in the same way, then—in spite of the perspiration
that ran down his face in streams and dripped from his nose, and
though his back was as wet as if the shirt had been soaked in
water—he felt very light-hearted. What gave him most pleasure was
the knowledge that he would be able to keep up with the peasants.

The only thing marring his joy was the fact that his swath was
not well mown. 'I must swing the scythe less with my arms and
more with the whole of my body,' he thought, comparing Titus's
swath, cut straight, as if by measure, with his own, on which
the grass lay scattered and uneven.

As Levin was aware, Titus had been mowing his swath with
special rapidity, probably to put his master to the test, and it
chanced to be a very long one. The next swaths were easier, but
still Levin had to work with all his might to keep even with the
peasants. He thought of nothing and desired nothing, except not to
lag behind and to do his work as well as possible. He heard only
the swishing of the scythes and saw only the receding figure of
Titus, the convex half-circle of the mown piece before him, and the
grasses and heads of flowers falling in waves about the blade of his
scythe, and ahead of him the end of the swath where he would rest.

Suddenly he was conscious of a pleasant coolness on his hot
perspiring shoulders, without knowing what it was or whence it
came. He glanced up at the sky whilst whetting his scythe. A dark
cloud was hanging low overhead, and large drops of rain were
falling. Some of the peasants went to put on their coats; others as
well as Levin felt pleasure in the refreshing rain and merely moved
their shoulders up and down.

They came to the end of another swath. They went on mowing
long and short rows, good and poor grass. Levin had lost all count
of time and had really no idea whether it was late or early. His
work was undergoing a change which gave him intense pleasure.

While working he sometimes forgot for some minutes what he was about, and felt quite at ease; then his mowing was nearly as even as that of Titus. But as soon as he began thinking about it and trying to work better, he at once felt how hard the task was and mowed badly.

He finished a swath and was about to start another when Titus paused and went up to the old man, and both looked at the sun.

'What are they talking about, and why don't they start another swath?' thought Levin. It did not occur to him that the peasants, who had been mowing unceasingly for four hours, wanted their breakfast.

'Breakfast-time, master,' said the old man.

'Is it time? Well, then, breakfast!'

Levin handed his scythe to Titus, and with the peasants, who were going to fetch the bread that lay with their coats, went across the swaths of the long mown portion of the meadow, slightly sprinkled with rain. Only then he remembered that he had not been right about the weather and that the rain was wetting the hay.

'The hay will be spoilt,' said he.

'It won't hurt, master. "Mow in the rain, rake when it's fine!"'

Levin untied his horse and rode home to his coffee.

By the time Levin had finished breakfast Koznyshev had only just got up, and Levin went back to the meadow before Koznyshev had come to table.

Chapter V

After breakfast Levin got placed between a humorous old man who invited him to be his neighbour and a young peasant who had only got married last autumn and was now out for his first summer's mowing.

The old man went along holding himself erect, moving with regular, long steps, turning out his toes, and with a precise and even motion that seemed to cost him no more effort than swinging his arms when walking, he laid the grass in a level high ridge, as if in play or as if the sharp scythe of its own accord whizzed through the juicy grass.

Young Mishka went behind Levin. His pleasant young face, with a wisp of grass tied round the forehead over his hair, worked all over with the effort; but whenever anyone glanced at him he smiled. Evidently he would have died rather than confess that the work was trying.

Between these two went Levin. Now, in the hottest part of the day, the work did not seem so hard to him. The perspiration in which he was bathed was cooling, and the sun which burnt his back, his head and his arm—bare to the elbow—added to his strength and perseverance in his task, and those unconscious intervals when it became possible not to think of what he was doing recurred more and more often. The scythe seemed to mow of itself. Those were happy moments. Yet more joyous were the moments when, reaching the river at the lower end of the swaths, the old man would wipe his scythe with the wet grass, rinse its blade in the clear water, and dipping his whetstone-box in the stream, would offer it to Levin.

'A little of my kvas? It's good!' said he, with a wink.

And really Levin thought he had never tasted any nicer drink than this lukewarm water with green stuff floating in it and a flavour of the rusty tin box. And then came the ecstasy of a slow walk, one hand resting on the scythe, when there was leisure to wipe away the streams of perspiration, to breathe deep, to watch the line of mowers, and to see what was going on around in forest and field.

The longer Levin went on mowing, the oftener he experienced those moments of oblivion when his arms no longer seemed to swing the scythe, but the scythe itself his whole body, so conscious and full of life; and as if by magic, regularly and definitely without a thought being given to it, the work accomplished itself of its own accord. These were blessed moments.

It was difficult only at those times when it was necessary to interrupt the movement which had become unconscious, and to think in order to mow around a molehill or a space where the hard sorrel stalks had not been weeded out. The old man accomplished this with ease. When he came to a molehill he would change his action, and with a short jerk of the point and then of the heel of his scythe he would mow all around the molehill. And while doing this he noted everything he came to: now he plucked a sorrel stalk and ate it, or offered it to Levin; now he threw aside a branch with the point of his scythe, or examined a quail's nest from which the hen bird had flown up, almost under the scythe; or he caught a snake, lifting it with the scythe-point as with a fork, and after showing it to Levin, threw it away.

Levin and the young fellow on the other side of him found such changes of action difficult. Both of them, having got into one strained kind of movement, were in the grip of feverish labour and had not the power to change the motion of their bodies and at the same time to observe what lay before them.

Levin did not notice how time passed. Had he been asked how long he had been mowing, he would have answered 'half an hour,' although it was nearly noon. As they were about to begin another swath the old man drew Levin's attention to the little boys and girls approaching from all sides along the road and through the long grass, hardly visible above it, carrying jugs of kvas stoppered with rags, and bundles of bread which strained their little arms.

'Look at the midges crawling along!' he said, pointing to the children and glancing at the sun from under his lifted hand. They completed two more swaths and then the old man stopped.

'Come, master! It's dinner-time,' said he with decision. All the mowers on reaching the river went across the swaths to where their coats lay, and where the children who had brought their dinners sat waiting for them. The men who had driven from a distance gathered in the shadow of their carts; those who lived nearer sheltered under the willow growth, on which they hung grass.

Levin sat down beside them; he did not want to go away.

All the peasants' restraint in the presence of the master had vanished. The men began preparing for dinner. Some had a wash. The young lads bathed in the river; others arranged places for their after-dinner rest, unfastened their bags of bread and unstoppered their jugs of kvas. The old man broke some rye bread into a bowl, mashed it with a spoon handle, poured over it some water from his tin, broke more bread into it and salted it, and then, turning to the East, said grace.

'Come, master, have some of my dinner,' said he, kneeling in front of his bowl.

The bread and water was so nice that Levin gave up all intention of going home to lunch. He shared the old man's meal and got into conversation with him about his domestic affairs, taking a lively interest in them and telling him about his own, giving him all the particulars which would interest the old peasant. When the old man got up and, having said grace, lay down beneath the willows with an armful of grass under his head, Levin did the same, regardless of the flies, importunate and persistent in the sunshine, and of the crawling insects that tickled his perspiring face and body. He at once fell asleep, waking only when the sun touched the opposite side of the willows and reached him. The old man had already been long awake and sat setting the scythes for the young men.

Levin looked round and hardly recognized the place, everything was so altered. A wide expanse of the meadow was already mown, and with its swaths of grass already giving off perfume, shone with a peculiar fresh brilliance in the oblique rays of the descending sun. The bushes by the river where the grass had been cut and the river itself with its curves, previously invisible, were now glittering like steel; and the people getting up and moving about, the steep wall of yet uncut grass, and the hawks soaring over the bare meadow, struck him as something quite new. When he was fully awake Levin began to calculate how much had been done and how much could still be done that day.

An extraordinary amount had been done by the forty-two men. The larger meadow, which in the days of serfdom had taken thirty men two days to mow, was all finished except some short patches at the corners. But Levin wanted to get as much as possible done that day, and it was vexatious to see the sun already declining. He was not feeling at all tired and was only longing to work again and to accomplish as much as he could.

'What do you think—could we manage to get Mashkin Heights mown to-day?' he asked the old man.

'Well, God willing, we might! The sun is not very high though. Perhaps—if the lads could have a little vodka!'

At half-time, when they sat down again and those who smoked were lighting their pipes, the old man informed the young fellows that if they mowed the Mashkin Heights there would be vodka.

'What? Not mow that? Come along, Titus; we'll get it clear in no time!'

'You can eat your fill at night. Let's begin!' shouted different voices, and the mowers took their places, finishing their bread as they went.

'Now then, lads! Keep going!' said Titus, starting off ahead almost at a trot.

'Go on, go on!' said the old man, hurrying after him and easily catching him up. 'Take care, I'll mow you down!'

And young and old vied with each other at mowing. But in spite of their haste they did not spoil the grass, and the swaths fell just as evenly and exactly as before. The small patch that was left in the last corner was mown in five minutes; and whilst the last mowers were finishing their swaths, those in front, carrying their coats over their shoulders, were already crossing the road toward Mashkin Heights.

The sun was already setting toward the trees when, with their tin boxes rattling, they entered the wooded ravine of the Heights.

The grass that in the middle of the ravine reached to their waists was delicate, soft, and broad-bladed, speckled here and there with cow-grass.

After a short consultation as to whether they should mow the ravine across or lengthwise, Prokhor—a gigantic dark man and a famous mower—took the lead. He went in front, mowed a swath, turned around and restarted; following him all the others took their places, going downhill along the creek and back up to the very skirts of the wood. The sun had set behind the wood and now shone only on the mowers at the top of the hill, while in the valley, where the mists were rising, they were in cool, dewy shade. The work proceeded briskly.

The scented grass, cut down with a sound that showed how juicy it was, fell in high ridges. On the short swaths the mowers crowded together, their tin boxes clattering, their scythes ringing whenever they touched, the whetstones whistling upon the blades, and their merry voices resounding as they urged each other on.

Levin was again mowing between the old man and the lad. The old man, who had put on his sheepskin jacket, was still as jolly, witty, and easy in his movements as before. In the wood their scythes continually cut down wood mushrooms, grown plump amid the juicy grass. The old man stooped each time he came upon one, picked it up, and put it inside his jacket, saying, 'Another treat for my old woman.'

It was easy to cut the wet soft grass, but on the other hand it was very difficult to go up and down the steep slopes of the ravine. This, however, did not trouble the old man. Swinging his scythe just as usual, taking short steps with feet shod in large bast-plaited shoes, he slowly climbed the slopes; and though his whole body and his loosely-hanging trousers shook, he did not miss a single mushroom or a curious grass, and continued joking with the other peasants and with Levin. Levin followed, and often thought he would certainly fall when climbing a mound with his scythe in his hand—a mound so steep that it would have been hard to climb even unencumbered. Still, he managed to climb it and to do all that had to be done; and he felt as if some external force were urging him on.

Chapter VI

Mashkin Heights were mown, and the peasants, having completed their last swaths, put on their coats and went home in high spirits. Levin, having regretfully taken leave of them, mounted and rode home. He looked back from the top of the hill. He could not see the men, for the mist rising from the hollow hid them; but he heard their merry rough voices, laughter, and the clanking of the scythes.

Koznyshev had long had his dinner, and was in his room drinking iced water with lemon, while looking over the papers and magazines just arrived by post, when Levin rushed in, his tangled hair clinging to his moist brow, his shirt saturated back and front and dark with perspiration, and cried out joyfully:

'We have finished the whole of the meadow! How delightful it is! wonderful! And how have you got on?' Levin had quite forgotten the unpleasant conversation of the previous day.

'Dear me, what a sight you are!' said Koznyshev, turning to his brother with a momentary look of vexation. 'The door—the door!

Shut it!' he exclaimed. 'You've certainly let in a whole dozen!'

Koznyshev could not bear flies, and opened the windows in his room only at night, keeping the door carefully closed.

'No, not one, I swear. And if I have, I'll catch it! . . . You would not believe what enjoyment it was! And how have you spent the day?'

'Quite well. But have you really been mowing all day? You must be as hungry as a wolf. Kuzma has everything ready for you.'

'No, I don't want to eat; I have had something there. But I'll go and wash.'

'Yes, yes, go; and I will come presently.' Koznyshev shook his head as he looked at his brother. 'Go, go, and be quick!' he added with a smile, as, gathering together his books, he prepared to go too. He also felt suddenly quite cheerful and did not wish to part from his brother. 'And where were you when it rained?'

'What rain was that? Only a few drops. . . . Well, then, I'll come back directly. So you have spent the day all right? That's good.' And Levin went off to dress.

Five minutes later the brothers met again in the dining-room. Though Levin had imagined that he was not hungry, and sat down to table only not to offend Kuzma, yet when he began eating he thought everything delicious. Koznyshev smiled as he looked at him.

'Oh, yes, there's a letter for you,' said he. 'Kuzma, please bring it. It's downstairs. And mind you shut the door.'

The letter was from Oblonsky. Levin read it aloud. Oblonsky wrote from Petersburg: 'I have had a letter from Dolly. She is in Ergushevo, and everything is out of gear there. Please go and see her and help her with your advice—you know all about everything. She will be so glad to see you. She is quite alone, poor thing; my mother-in-law is still abroad.'

'That's splendid! I will certainly go and see her,' said Levin. 'Or shall we both go? She is such a good woman; don't you think so?'

'Is it far from here?'

'A little over twenty-five miles or maybe even thirty, but the road is excellent. We'll have a fine drive.'

'I shall be very glad,' replied Koznyshev, still smiling. The sight of his younger brother had a distinctly cheering influence on him.

'I must say you have an appetite!' he said, glancing at the sun-burnt ruddy face bent over the plate.

'Fine! You would hardly believe what a remedy it is for every kind of folly. I am thinking of enriching Medicine with a new word: *Arbeitskur*[1]!'

'You would hardly require it, I should say.'

1. Work-cure.

'No, but those who suffer from their nerves do.'

'Yes, it ought to be tested. You know, I thought of coming to the meadow to have a look at you, but it was so unbearably hot that I got only as far as the forest! I sat there a little, and then went through the forest to the village, where I met your old wet-nurse and sounded her as to what the peasants think of you. From her I understood that they do not approve of your doing it. She said: "It's not gentlefolk's work." It seems to me that on the whole, in the people's opinion, a very decided demand for what they call "gentlefolk's work" exists, and they don't approve of the gentry going outside the bounds they set for them.'

'Possibly; but it is a pleasure such as I have never in my life experienced before, and there is nothing wrong in it. Don't you think so too?' replied Levin. 'If they don't like it, it can't be helped. Besides, I think it's all right. Eh?'

'I see that on the whole you are well satisfied with your day.'

'Very well indeed! We finished the meadow. And I chummed up with a fine old man! You can't imagine what a charming fellow he is.'

'Well, then, you are satisfied with your day, and so am I. First of all I solved two chess problems—one a very good one, beginning with a pawn move. I'll show it you. And afterwards I thought over our yesterday's conversation.'

'What about yesterday's conversation?' asked Levin, who had finished dinner and sat blissfully blinking and puffing, quite unable to remember what yesterday's conversation had been about.

'I think you are partly right. Our disagreement lies in the fact that you consider personal interests the motive power, while I think every man with a certain degree of education ought to be interested in the general welfare. You may be right in thinking that activity backed by material interest is best; but your nature is altogether *primesautière* [2] as the French say: you want passionate, energetic activity, or nothing at all.'

Levin listened to his brother but understood absolutely nothing and did not wish to understand. He was only afraid his brother might put some question which would elicit the fact that he was not paying attention.

'That's what it is, old chap,' said Koznyshev, patting Constantine's shoulder.

'Yes, of course! But what matter? I don't insist on my view,' replied Levin, with a guilty, childlike smile. 'What can I have been disputing about?' he thought. 'Of course I was right, and he was right too, so it's all right! . . . But I must go round to the office.'

He rose, stretching himself and smiling. Koznyshev smiled too.

2. Impulsive.

'Shall we go for a stroll together?' he said, not wishing to part from his brother, who seemed to be exhaling freshness and vigour. 'Come along! We could call in at the office if you want to.'

'Oh, dear me!' exclaimed Levin, so loudly that he scared Kozny-shev.

'What's the matter?'

'How's Agatha Mikhaylovna's arm?' asked Levin, slapping his head. 'I had forgotten all about it.'

'Much better.'

'Well, I'll run and see her, all the same. You won't have got your hat before I am back.'

And his heels clattered swiftly down the stairs, making a noise like a rattle.

Chapter VII

Oblonsky had gone to Petersburg to fulfil a very necessary duty —which to officials seems most natural and familiar, though to lay-men it is incomprehensible—that of reminding the Ministry of his existence, without the performance of which rite continuance in Government service is impossible. Having taken away with him all the money there was in the house, he contrived while attending to duty to pass his time very pleasantly, going to races and visiting at country houses. Meanwhile, to curtail expenses, Dolly and her children moved to the country. She went to Ergushevo, the estate which had formed part of her dowry, about thirty-five miles distant from Levin's Pokrovsk, and the very place where in spring the for-est had been sold.

The old mansion on the estate had been pulled down long ago, but there was a smaller house which had been enlarged and done up by the Prince. Some twenty years before, when Dolly was still a child, that house had seemed roomy and convenient, though in common with all houses of the kind it stood away from the drive and had not a south aspect. It was old and beginning to decay. In the spring, when Oblonsky went there to sell the forest, Dolly had asked him to look over the house and have all necessary repairs done. Like all guilty husbands Oblonsky was very anxious about his wife's comfort, so he looked over the house himself and gave orders to have everything done that seemed to him necessary. According to him it was necessary to reupholster the furniture with new cretonne, to put up curtains, make the garden tidy, plant flowers and build a bridge by the lake; but he forgot many other things which were essential, and thus caused Dolly a great deal of trouble.

Try as he would to be a considerate husband and father, Oblon-sky never could remember that he had a wife and children. He had the tastes of a bachelor and understood no others. When he returned to Moscow he informed his wife that all was being prepared, that the house would look like a new toy, and advised her to move thither. Her departure for the country suited Oblonsky in every way: it was good for the children, expenses would be cut down, and he would be freer. His wife, on the other hand, considered going to the country for the summer to be absolutely necessary for the children, especially for the little girl who had not recovered her strength after the scarlet fever; and also in order to escape the humiliation of small debts for fuel, fish, boots, and so on, which tormented her. Besides this she liked the idea of going to her house in the country because she intended to get her sister Kitty, who was to return from abroad at midsummer and who had been ordered bathing, to join her there. Kitty wrote from her watering-place that nothing seemed so attractive as spending the summer with Dolly at Ergushevo, which was full of childhood's memories for both of them.

The first days in the country were very trying for Dolly. In her girlhood she had lived there and it had left an impression on her mind as a place of refuge from all the unpleasantness of town; life there, though very plain (Dolly was reconciled to that), was cheap and comfortable; everything was cheap there and easy to get, and it would do the children good. But when she came there as mistress of the house she saw that things were quite different from what she had expected.

The day after her arrival it poured with rain and in the night the rain came through into the passage and nursery, so that the children's beds had to be carried into the drawing-room. There was no scullery-maid. Of the nine cows some, according to the dairymaids, were about to calve, others had calved for the first time, some were too old, and the rest were difficult to milk, so there was no butter and scarcely enough milk even for the children. There were no eggs. It was impossible to get a chicken, and they were obliged to boil and roast tough old purple-coloured roosters. No peasant women could be got to scrub the floors: they were all out planting potatoes. It was impossible to go for a drive because one of the horses was restive and would not run in harness. There was no place for bathing, the river banks being all trampled over by the cattle and exposed to the road; it was not even possible to walk in the garden because the fence was broken and the peasants' cattle could get in, and the herd included a terrible bull that was given to bellowing and would therefore probably toss. There was nowhere to hang dresses, because what few wardrobes there were would not shut, or else opened of themselves when anyone passed by. There were no big pots or pans, no copper in the wash-house, and not even an ironing board in the maids' room.

Dolly, meeting with these difficulties, so terrible from her point of view, instead of finding peace and rest, was at first driven to despair. She bustled about and did her utmost; but feeling the hopelessness of her position, had to fight with the tears that rose every moment to her eyes.

The steward, formerly a non-commissioned officer, to whom Oblonsky had taken a fancy and whom he had promoted from hall porter to steward because of the man's handsome and respectful appearance, took no interest in his mistress's troubles, only saying in a deferential tone, 'Quite impossible, the people are so abominable,' and did nothing to help her.

The position seemed irremediable; but just as in other households, there was here in the Oblonskys' house one inconspicuous yet most important and useful person: Matrena Filimonovna. She consoled her mistress, assuring her that everything would 'shape itself' (this phrase was her own, and Matthew had learnt it from her), and she went to work deliberately and without excitement.

She at once made friends with the steward's wife, and on the very day of the removal drank tea with her and with the steward beneath the laburnums, discussing arrangements. A club was soon established beneath the laburnums, consisting of Matrena Filimonovna, the steward's wife, the village elder, and the office clerk; and by means of this club the troubles began gradually to subside, so that in a week's time everything had really 'shaped itself.' The roof was mended, a scullery-maid—a relative of the elder's—was engaged, hens were bought, the cows gave enough milk, the garden was fenced in, a wringer was made by the carpenter, hooks were put into the wardrobes, which no longer opened at their own sweet will; an ironing board covered with coarse cloth lay across the arm of a chair and a chest of drawers in the maid's room, and the smell of hot irons soon pervaded the room.

'There, you see! And you were quite in despair!' said Matrena Filimonovna, pointing to the board.

Even a bathing-house was constructed out of straw-plaited screens. Lily started bathing, and at least part of Dolly's expectations were fulfilled, if not that of a quiet, at least that of a comfortable, country life. Dolly could not be quiet with six children, of whom one would fall ill, another be in danger of falling ill, a third be in want of something, a fourth show symptoms of something bad in his disposition, etc., etc. Very, very rare were the short intervals of quiet. But these cares and anxieties were the only kind of happiness possible for Dolly. Had it not been for them she would have been left to her thoughts about the husband who did not love her. Besides, painful as were for a mother the fear of illness, and sorrow at the appearance of evil tendencies in her children, those children were already beginning to repay her care by affording her small joys. These joys were so trifling as to be as imperceptible as grains of gold among the sand, and in moments of depression she saw nothing but the sand; yet there were brighter moments when she felt nothing but joy, saw nothing but the gold.

Now in the country solitude she grew more often aware of these joys. Often when watching her children she made great efforts to convince herself that she was mistaken, that being their mother she was not impartial; and yet she could not help telling herself that they were charming children, all the six, each in his or her own way, all of them such as are rarely to be met with; and she was happy in them and proud of them.

Chapter VIII

At the end of May, when the house was more or less in order, Dolly received from her husband an answer to her letter of complaint. He wrote asking her to forgive his not having seen to everything, and saying that he would come as soon as possible. That possibility, however, had not been fulfilled, and up to the beginning of June Dolly was still living without him in the country.

On the Sunday before St Peter's Day Dolly took all her children to Communion. When talking intimately with her mother and sister Dolly often astonished them by her freedom of thought on religious matters. She had a strange religion of her own, firmly believing in the transmigration of souls, and not caring about Church dogmas. But in her family she fulfilled (not merely to set an example, but with her whole heart) all that the Church demanded, and was very uneasy because for about a year the children had not received Communion. So now, with the entire approval of Matrena Filimonovna, she resolved that this ceremony should be performed.

Several days previously she decided how all the children should be dressed. New frocks were made, old ones altered, hems and frills let down, buttons sewn on, and ribbons got ready. One of the frocks, which the English governess had undertaken to alter, was the cause of much bad blood. The governess put the bodice darts in the wrong places, cut out the arm-holes too big, and nearly spoilt the dress. It fitted so tight round Tanya's shoulders that it was painful to see her; but Matrena Filimonovna was inspired to insert wedge-shaped pieces and to make a fichu to cover the defect. The frock was put right, but it very nearly caused a quarrel with the governess. However, in the morning everything was right; and toward nine o'clock—the hour till which the priest had been asked to defer mass—the children, beaming with joy, stood in all their finery by the carriage at the porch, waiting for their mother.

Instead of the restive Raven, the steward's Brownie had been harnessed to the carriage on Matrena Filimonovna's authority, and Dolly, who had been detained by the cares of her own toilet, came out in a white muslin dress and took her seat in the carriage.

Dolly, somewhat excited, had dressed and done her hair with care. At one time she used to dress for her own sake, in order to look well and be attractive; later on as she grew older dressing became less and less agreeable to her, because it made the loss of her good looks more apparent; but now it again gave her pleasure and excited her. She was not dressing for her own sake, not for her own beauty, but in order, as the mother of all those charming children, not to spoil the general effect. She gave her mirror a last glance and was satisfied with herself. She looked well: not in the way she had wished to look when going to a ball, but well for the object she had in view at present.

There was no one in church except peasants, domestics and their womenfolk; but Dolly saw, or thought she saw, the rapture produced in them by her children and herself. The children were not only beautiful in their fine clothes but were also very sweet in their behaviour. It's true Alesha did not stand very well: he kept turning round to see the back of his jacket; but nevertheless he was wonderfully sweet. Tanya stood like a grown-up person and looked after the little ones. Little Lily was charming in her naïve wonder at everything around, and it was difficult to repress a smile when, having swallowed the bread and wine, she said in English, 'More, please!'

On the way home the children were very quiet, feeling that something solemn had taken place.

At home also all went well, only at lunch Grisha began whistling and—what was still worse—would not obey the governess and had to go without his pudding. Dolly would not have sanctioned any punishment on such a day had she been present, but she was obliged to support the governess and so confirmed the sentence that Grisha was not to have pudding. This rather spoilt the general joyfulness.

Grisha cried and said he was being punished although it was Nikolenka that had whistled, and that he was not crying about the pudding (he didn't mind that!) but because of the injustice. This was too sad, and Dolly decided to speak to the governess and get her to forgive Grisha, and went off to find her. But as she was passing through the dancing-room she saw a scene which filled her heart with such joy that tears came to her eyes and she pardoned the little culprit herself.

The little fellow was sitting on the ledge of the corner window of the dancing-room, and beside him stood Tanya with a plate. On

the plea of giving her dolls some dinner she had obtained leave
from the governess to take her plateful of pudding to the nursery,
but had brought it to her brother instead. Still crying over the injustice done him, he ate the pudding, muttering between sobs:
'Eat some yourself . . . let us both eat . . . together!'

Tanya, affected first by pity for Grisha and then by the consciousness of her own virtuous action, also had tears in her eyes, but
did not decline to eat her share of the pudding.

When they saw their mother they were frightened, but glancing
at her face they knew they were acting rightly and, with their
mouths full of pudding, began to laugh and wipe their smiling lips
with their hands, smearing their beaming faces with tears and jam.

'Dear me! Your nice white frock! Tanya! . . . Grisha!' cried
their mother, trying to save the frock, but smiling a blissful, rapturous smile.

The new clothes were taken off, the little girls had their overalls
and the boys their old jackets, and orders were given to harness
(to the steward's chagrin) his Brownie again, to take the whole family mushroom-hunting, and later to the bathing-house. The sound
of rapturous squealing filled the nursery, and did not cease till they
started on their drive.

They gathered a basketful of mushrooms; even Lily found one.
Previously Miss Hull used to find one and point it out to her; but
this time Lily herself found a fine big one and there was a general
shout of delight: 'Lily has found a mushroom!'

After that they drove to the river, left the horses under the birch
trees, and entered the bathing-house. Terenty the coachman tied
to a tree the horses, that were swishing their tails to drive away the
flies, stretched himself full length in the shade, pressing down the
high grass, and smoked his pipe, while from the bathing-house came
the sound of the incessant merry squealing of the children.

Although it was troublesome to look after all the children and
keep them out of mischief, and difficult to remember whose were
all those little stockings and drawers, not to mix up the shoes of all
those different feet, to untie, unbutton, and then fasten up again
all the tapes and buttons, yet Dolly, who had always been fond of
bathing and considered it good for the children, knew no greater
pleasure than bathing them. To hold in her hands all those plump
little legs, to draw on their stockings, to take the naked little bodies
in her arms and dip them in the water, to hear them shrieking now
with fear and now with delight, and to see her cherubs gasping
and splashing, with their frightened yet merry eyes, was a great
joy.

When half the children were dressed again, some smartly-dressed
peasant women who had been gathering herbs came up and halted

shyly by the bathing-house. Matrena Filimonovna called to one of these to ask her to dry a bath-sheet and a chemise that had fallen into the water, and Dolly entered into conversation with them. The peasant women, who had begun by laughing behind their hands without comprehending her questions, soon became bolder and more talkative, and at once captivated Dolly by their frank admiration of her children.

'Just look at the little beauty, as white as sugar!' said one, gazing admiringly at Tanya and stroking her head. 'But she's thin.'

'Yes, she's been ill.'

'Why, you seem to have been bathing that one too!' said the other woman, looking at the baby.

'No, she is only three months old,' Dolly answered proudly.

'Dear me!'

'And have you any children?'

'I had four; two are left, a boy and a girl. I weaned her in the spring.'

'How old is she?'

'In her second year.'

'Why did you nurse her so long?'

'It's our custom—for three fasts . . .'

And the conversation turned upon the topic that interested Dolly more than any other: confinements, children's illnesses, husbands' whereabouts, and whether they came home often.

Dolly did not want to part from the peasant women; their conversation pleased her so much because their interests were exactly similar to hers. What pleased Dolly most was the women's evident admiration for the great number of children she had, and their loveliness.

The women amused her and offended the English governess, who noticed that she was the object of their laughter, which she did not understand. One of the young women was watching the governess, who was dressing after all the others, and seeing her put on a third petticoat could not refrain from remarking:

'Look at her! She's wrapping herself up and wrapping herself up, and hasn't got enough round her yet!' and all the women burst out laughing.

Chapter IX

Surrounded by her children, all freshly bathed and with heads still damp, Dolly with a kerchief tied round her own head was nearing home when the coachman said:

'There's a gentleman coming—I think it's the Pokrovsk squire.'

Dolly leant forward and was pleased to see the familiar figure of Levin, who in a grey hat and coat was walking toward them. She

was always glad to see him, but on this day was more pleased than
ever because he would now see her in all her glory. No one could
understand the dignity of her position better than Levin. On seeing
her he found himself confronted by just such a picture of family
life as his fancy painted.

'You are like a hen with her chickens, Darya Alexandrovna!'
'Oh, I'm so glad!' said she, holding out her hand.
'You're glad, yet you never sent me word. My brother is staying
with me. It was from Stiva I heard, at last, that you were here.'
'From Stiva?' asked Dolly in a surprised tone.
'Yes, he wrote that you had moved here, and he thought I might
be of some use to you,' replied Levin, and having said this grew
confused. Without finishing what he was going to say he continued
walking beside the trap, breaking off twigs from the lime trees and
biting them. He was confused because he imagined that Dolly
might not like to accept the help of a stranger in matters that
ought to be attended to by her husband. She really did not like
the way Oblonsky had of forcing his family affairs upon strangers,
and knew at once that Levin understood this. It was for his quick
perception and delicacy of feeling that Dolly liked him.
'Of course I understood that this only meant you wanted to see
me, and was very pleased. I can well imagine how strange everything here must seem to you, used as you are to managing a town
house; and if you require anything I am quite at your disposal.'
'Oh no!' said Dolly. 'At first it was inconvenient, but now everything is quite comfortable, thanks to my old nurse,' she said, indicating the nurse, who, aware that she was being mentioned, looked
at Levin with a bright and friendly smile. She knew him, knew that
he would be a good match for the young lady, and hoped the affair
would come off.
'Won't you sit down, sir? We'll move closer together,' she said to
Levin.
'No, I will walk. Children, who will race the horses with me?'
Though the children did not know Levin well and did not remember when they had last seen him, they did not feel toward him
any of that strange shyness and antagonism so often felt by children
toward grown-up people who 'pretend,' which causes them to suffer
so painfully. Pretence about anything sometimes deceives the wis-
est and shrewdest man, but, however cunningly it is hidden, a child
of the meanest capacity feels it and is repelled by it.
Whatever Levin's defects may have been, there was not a trace
of pretence about him; therefore the children evinced toward him
the same friendliness that they saw in their mother's face. The two
eldest, responding to his invitation, at once jumped out to him and
ran with him as they would have done with their nurse, Miss Hull,

or their mother. Lily wanted to go too, and her mother handed her to him; he put her on his shoulder and ran on.

'Don't be afraid! Don't be afraid, Darya Alexandrovna! There's no fear of my hurting or dropping her,' said he, smiling brightly at the mother.

And as she looked at his easy, strong, considerate, careful and ultra-cautious movements, the mother lost her fears and looked at them with a smile of approval.

Here in the country among the children, and in the company of Dolly whom he found very congenial, Levin's spirits rose to that childlike merriment Dolly liked so much in him. He ran about with the children, taught them gymnastics, amused Miss Hull by his broken English, and talked to Dolly about his rural occupations.

After dinner, left alone with him on the verandah, Dolly alluded to Kitty.

'Do you know Kitty is coming here to spend the summer with me?'

'Really?' said he, flushing up; and to change the subject he at once added: 'Well, then, shall I send you two cows? If you insist on squaring accounts, pay me five roubles a month, if your conscience allows it.'

'No, thank you. We are getting on all right now.'

'Well, then, I will just have a look at your cows and, with your permission, will give directions about the feeding. Everything depends on the feeding.'

To change the conversation Levin went on to explain to Dolly a theory of dairy farming which maintained that a cow was only a machine for the transformation of fodder into milk, and so on. While saying all that, he was passionately longing and yet dreading to hear every particular concerning Kitty. He feared that the peace of mind he had acquired with so much effort might be destroyed.

'Yes, but all that has to be looked after, and who is going to do it?' remarked Dolly unwillingly.

Having with Matrena Filimonovna's help got her household into working order, she did not care to make any change; besides, she had no confidence in Levin's knowledge of farming. Arguments about cows being milk-producing machines did not commend themselves to her, for she imagined that such arguments were calculated only to interfere with farming. All these matters appeared much simpler to her: all that was necessary, as Matrena Filimonovna said, was to give Spotty and Whiteflake more food and drink, and to see that the cook did not take the kitchen refuse to the laundress for her cow. That was clear. But arguments about cereal and grass feeding were questionable and vague and, above all, she was anxious to talk about Kitty.

Chapter X

'Kitty writes that she wishes for nothing so much as seclusion and quiet,' said Dolly after a pause in the conversation.

'And her health! Is she better?' asked Levin anxiously.

'Yes, thank God! she has quite recovered. I never believed that she had lung trouble.'

'Oh, I am so glad!' said Levin, and Dolly thought she saw something pathetic and helpless in his face as he said it, and then silently looked at her.

'Tell me, Constantine Dmitrich,' said Dolly with her kind though slightly ironical smile, 'why are you angry with Kitty?'

'I? . . . I am not angry,' said Levin.

'Yes, you are. Why did you not call either on us or on them when you were in Moscow?'

'Darya Alexandrovna,' said he, blushing to the roots of his hair, 'I am surprised that one so kind as you are should not feel what the reason was. How is it that you have no pity for me, knowing as you do . . .'

'What do I know?'

'You know I proposed and was rejected,' muttered Levin, and the tenderness he had a moment ago felt for Kitty was changed into a feeling of anger at the insult.

'Why did you think I knew?'

'Because everybody knows it.'

'In that, at any rate, you are mistaken; I did not know it, though I had my suspicions.'

'Well, anyhow you know it now.'

'All I knew was that something had happened that tormented her dreadfully, and she asked me never to speak about it. And since she has not told me, she won't have told anybody. . . . Well, what did happen between you? Tell me.'

'I have told you what happened.'

'When was it?'

'When I last visited you.'

'Do you know,' said Dolly, 'I am terribly, terribly sorry for her! You are suffering only through pride . . .'

'That may be,' said Levin, 'but . . .'

She interrupted him.

'But for her, poor child, I am terribly, terribly sorry. Now I understand everything.'

'Well, Darya Alexandrovna, please excuse me!' he said, rising. 'Good-bye, Darya Alexandrovna; *au revoir!*'

'No, wait a bit,' she answered, holding him by the sleeve. 'Wait a bit. Sit down.'

'Please, please don't let us talk about it!' said he, sitting down again, conscious as he did so that a hope which he had thought dead and buried was waking and stirring within him.

'If I did not care for you,' Dolly went on, the tears rising to her eyes, 'if I did not know you as well as I do . . .'

The feeling that seemed dead was coming to life again, rising and taking possession of Levin's heart.

'Yes, now I understand it all,' continued Dolly. 'You can't understand it, you men who are free and have the choice. You always know for certain whom you love; but a young girl in a state of suspense, with her feminine, maidenly delicacy, a girl who only knows you men from a distance and is obliged to take everything on trust —such a girl may and does sometimes feel that she does not know what to say.'

'Yes, if her heart does not tell her. . . .'

'Oh, no! The heart does tell her; but just imagine, you men, having views on a girl, come to the house, get to know her, observe her and bide your time, and when you are quite certain that you love her you propose . . .'

'Well, it's not quite like that.'

'Never mind! You propose when your love is ripe, or when the balance falls in favour of one of those between whom your choice lies. But a girl is not asked. She is expected to choose for herself, yet she has no choice; she can only say "Yes" or "No." '

'Yes, a choice between me and Vronsky,' thought Levin, and the dead hope that had begun to revive in his soul died again and only weighed painfully on his heart.

'Darya Alexandrovna,' said he, 'in that way one may choose a dress, or . . . purchases . . . anything . . . but not love. The choice is made, and so much the better . . . a repetition is impossible.'

'Oh, that pride, that pride!' said Dolly, speaking as if she despised him for the meanness of his feelings compared to those which only women know. 'When you proposed to Kitty she was just in that state when it was impossible for her to give an answer: she was undecided—undecided between you and Vronsky; she saw him every day, you she had not seen for a long time. I admit that had she been older . . . I, for instance, could not have been undecided in her place. To me he was always repulsive, and so he has proved in the end.'

Levin recalled Kitty's answer. She had said, '*It cannot be.*'

'Darya Alexandrovna,' he replied drily, 'I value your confidence in me, but think you are mistaken. Whether I am right or wrong, that pride which you so despise makes any thought of your sister impossible for me—do you understand me?—perfectly impossible.'

'I will only add just this: you understand that I am speaking about my sister, whom I love as much as my own children. I do not say she loved you; I only wished to tell you that her refusal proves nothing.'

'I don't know!' said Levin, jumping up. 'If you know how you hurt me! It is just as if you had lost a child, and they kept on telling you: "Now he would have been so and so, and might be living and you rejoicing in him, but he is dead, dead, dead . . . !"'

'How funny you are!' said Dolly, regarding Levin's agitation with a sad yet mocking smile. 'Yes, I understand it more and more,' she added meditatively. 'Then you won't come to see us while Kitty is here?'

'No, I won't. Of course I will not avoid her, but whenever I can I will try to save her the unpleasantness of meeting me.'

'You are very, very funny!' Dolly repeated, looking tenderly into his face. 'All right then! Let it be as if nothing had been said about it.'

'What have you come for, Tanya?' said Dolly in French to her little girl, who had just come in.

'Where is my spade, Mama?'

'I am speaking French, and you must answer in French.'

The little girl had forgotten the French for spade, so her mother told her and went on to say, still in French where she would find the spade. All this was disagreeable to Levin. Nothing in Dolly's house or about her children seemed half as charming as before. 'Why does she talk French with the children?' he thought. 'How unnatural and false it is! And the children feel it. Teach them French and deprive them of sincerity,' thought he, not knowing that Dolly had considered the point over and over again and had decided that even to the detriment of their sincerity the children had to be taught French.

'Where are you hurrying to? Stay a little longer.'

So Levin stayed to tea, though his bright spirits had quite vanished and he felt ill at ease.

After tea he went out to tell his coachman to harness, and when he returned he found Dolly excited, a worried look on her face and tears in her eyes.

In Levin's absence an event took place which suddenly put an end to the joy and pride that Dolly had been feeling all day. Grisha and Tanya had a fight about a ball. Dolly, hearing their screams, ran up to the nursery, and found them in a dreadful state. Tanya was holding Grisha by the hair, and he, his face distorted with anger, was hitting her at random with his fists. Dolly's heart sank when

repetitive

she saw this. A shadow seemed to have fallen on her life; she recognized that these children, of whom she had been so proud, were not only quite ordinary but even bad and ill-bred children, with coarse animal inclinations—in fact, vicious children. She could think and speak of nothing else, and yet could not tell Levin her trouble.

Levin saw that she was unhappy, and tried to comfort her by saying that it did not prove that anything was wrong with them, that all children fought; but as he spoke he thought to himself: 'No, I'll not humbug my children and won't speak French with them. But I shan't have children like these. All that is needed is not to spoil or pervert children, and then they will be splendid. No, my children will not be like these!'

He said good-bye and left, and she did not try to detain him any longer.

Chapter XI

In the middle of July the Elder from the village belonging to Levin's sister (which lay fifteen miles from Pokrovsk) came to see Levin and report on business matters and on the hay-harvest. The chief income from his sister's estate was derived from the meadows, which were flooded every spring. In former years the peasants used to buy the grass, paying seven roubles per acre for it. When Levin took over the management of the estate he looked into the matter, and, concluding that the grass was worth more, fixed the price at eight roubles. The peasants would not pay so much, and Levin suspected them of keeping other buyers off. Then he went there himself and arranged to have the harvest gathered in partly by hired labourers and partly by peasants paid in kind. The local men opposed this innovation by all the means in their power, but the plan succeeded, and in the first year the meadows brought in almost double. The next and third years the peasants still held out and the harvest was got in by the same means. But this year the peasants had agreed to get the harvest in and take one-third of all the hay in payment. Now the Elder had come to inform Levin that the hay was all made, and that for fear of rain he had asked the steward to come, and in his presence had apportioned the hay and had already stacked eleven stacks of the landlord's share.

From the Elder's vague replies to Levin's questions as to how much hay the largest meadow had yielded, from his haste to apportion the hay without waiting for permission, and from the general tone of the peasant, Levin knew that there was something not quite square about the apportionment, and decided to go and investigate the matter himself.

Levin arrived at his sister's village at noon and left his horse with a friendly old peasant, the husband of his brother's nurse. Wishing to hear particulars of the hay-harvest from this old man, Levin went to speak to him in his apiary. Parmenich, a loquacious, handsome old man, welcomed Levin joyfully, showed him over his homestead, and told him all about the swarming of his bees that year; but to Levin's questions about the hay-harvest he gave vague and reluctant answers. This still further confirmed Levin's suspicions. He went to inspect the hay, examined the stacks, and saw that there could not be fifty cartloads in each. To put the peasant to the proof Levin ordered the carts on which the hay was being moved to be fetched, and one of the stacks to be carried to the barn. There were only thirty-two loads in the stack. In spite of the Elder's explanations that the hay had been loose, but had settled down in the stacks, and his swearing that all had been done in a 'godly way,' Levin insisted that the hay had been apportioned without his order and that he would not accept the stacks as containing fifty loads each. After lengthy disputes it was settled that the peasants themselves should take those eleven stacks, counting them at fifty loads each, and that the owner's share should be measured afresh. These disputes and the apportioning of the haycocks went on till it was time for the evening meal. When the last of the hay had been apportioned, Levin entrusted the rest of the supervision to the steward and seated himself on a haycock marked with a willow branch, looking with enjoyment at the meadow teeming with busy people.

Before him, within the bend of the river, beyond a marsh, moved a line of gaily-clad women, merrily chattering in their ringing voices, while the scattered hay was quickly forming into grey waving ridges on the light-green meadow. Men with hayforks followed the women, and the ridges grew into tall, wide and light haycocks. To the left, carts rattled along the bare meadow, and one after another the haycocks vanished, picked up in enormous forkfuls, and their places were taken by heavy carts with their huge loads of scented hay overhanging the horses' backs.

'Make hay while the sun shines, and you'll have plenty,' remarked the old beekeeper, sitting down beside Levin. 'It's more like tea than hay! See them picking it up, like ducklings picking up the food you've thrown to them!' he added, pointing to where the hay was being loaded on the carts. 'They've carted a good half since dinner-time. . . . Is that the last?' he shouted to a lad who was driving past, standing on the front of a cart and flicking the ends of his hempen reins.

'The last one, father,' shouted the lad, reining in the horse and smilingly turning to a rosy young woman who, also smiling, sat inside the cart; then he drove on again.

'Who is that? Your son?' asked Levin.

'My youngest,' replied the old man with a smile of affection.

'A fine fellow!'

'Not a bad lad.'

'And already married?'

'Yes, just over two years.'

'Have they any children?'

'Children! All the first year he didn't understand anything; and we chaffed him,' answered the old man. 'Well, this is hay! Regular tea!' said he again, in order to change the subject.

Levin looked more attentively at Vanka Parmenich and his wife. They were loading their cart not far away. Vanka stood inside the cart patting and stamping down evenly in the cart the enormous bales of hay which his young wife first passed to him in armfuls and then pitched up on the fork. The young woman was working with ease, cheerfulness and skill. The fork could not at once penetrate the broad-bladed compressed hay, so she first loosened it with the prongs, then with a quick and springy movement, putting all the weight of her body on the fork, quickly straightened her red-girdled figure and stood erect, her full bosom thrown forward beneath the pinafore and turning the fork dexterously she pitched the hay high up into the cart. Vanka, with evident desire to save her every moment of unnecessary exertion, hurriedly caught the hay in his outspread arms and smoothed it evenly in the cart. When she had lifted the remaining hay to him with a rake, she shook the chaff from her neck, straightened the kerchief that had slipped from her forehead, which showed white where the sun had not reached it, and crawled under the cart to help rope up. Vanka showed her how to do this, and burst out laughing at something she said. Strong, young, newly-awakened love shone in both their faces.

Chapter XII

The hay was roped. Vanka jumped down and taking the bridle led away the good, well-fed horse. His wife threw her rake on top of the load, and swinging her arms went with vigorous steps to join the other women who had gathered in a circle. Having come out upon the road, Vanka took his place in the line of carts. The women, carrying their rakes over their shoulders, followed the carts, their coloured dresses gleaming brightly and their chatter ringing merrily. One of the women with a strange gruff voice started a song and sang it to the end, when fifty powerful voices, some gruff and others shrill, all at once took it up with a will.

The singing women were drawing nearer to Levin and he felt as if a thundercloud of merriment were approaching. The cloud moved past, enveloping him and the haycock upon which he sat, and the other haycocks, the carts, the whole of the meadow, and the distant fields. They all seemed to vibrate and heave with the strains of that wild, madly-merry song, interspersed with screams and whistling. Levin envied them their healthy gaiety and felt a wish to take part in that expression of the joy of living; but he could do nothing except lie and look and listen. When the company and their songs vanished out of sight and hearing, an oppressive feeling of discontent with his own lonely lot, his physical idleness and his hostility to the world overcame Levin. Some of those very peasants who had disputed with him about the hay—whom either he had wronged or who had tried to cheat him—those very peasants had bowed pleasantly to him, evidently not harbouring, and unable to harbour, any ill-will toward him, being not only unrepentant but even forgetful that they had been trying to cheat him. All had been drowned in the sea of their joyful common toil. God had given them the day and the strength, and both the day and the strength had been devoted to labour which had brought its own reward. For whom they had laboured and what the fruits of their labour would be was an extraneous and unimportant affair.

Levin had often admired that kind of life, had often envied the folk who lived it; but that day, especially after what he had seen for the first time of the relations between Vanka Parmenich and his young wife, it struck him that it depended on himself to change his wearisome, idle, and artificial personal life for that pure, delightful life of common toil.

The old man who had been sitting beside him had long since gone home. The peasants who lived near by had also gone home, and those from a distance had gathered together to have supper and spend the night in the meadow. Levin, unnoticed by them, still lay on the haycock, looking, listening, and thinking. The peasants who were staying in the meadow kept awake almost all the short summer night. At first the sounds of merry general talk and shouts of laughter over their supper could be heard, then songs and more laughter. The whole long day of toil had left upon them no trace of anything but merriment.

Just before dawn all became silent. The sounds of night—the ceaseless croaking of frogs, the snorting of horses through the morning mist over the meadow—could alone be heard. Awaking to reality Levin rose from his haycock, and glancing up at the stars realized that the night was nearly over.

'Well, then, what shall I do? How shall I do it?' he asked himself, trying to find expression for what he had been thinking and the feelings he had lived through in that short night. All his ideas and feelings separated themselves into three different lines of thought. The first was how to renounce his old life and discard his quite useless education. This renunciation would afford him pleasure and was quite easy and simple. The second was concerned with his notion of the life he now wished to lead. He was distinctly conscious of the simplicity, purity, and rightness of that life, and was convinced that in it he would find satisfaction, peace, and dignity, the absence of which was so painful to him. But the third thought was the question of how to make the change from his present life to that other one. And here no clear idea presented itself to his mind. Should he have a wife? Should he have work and the necessity to work? Should he leave Pokrovsk, buy land, join a peasant commune, marry a peasant girl? 'How am I to do it?' he again asked himself, and could find no reply. 'However, I have not slept all night and can't render a clear account of myself now,' he thought, 'but I'll clear it up later. One thing is certain: this night has decided my fate. All my former dreams of a family life were nonsense —not the right thing. Everything is much simpler and better than that. . . .

'How beautiful!' he thought, looking up at a strange mother-of-pearl coloured shell formed of fleecy clouds, in the centre of the sky just over his head. 'How lovely everything is, this lovely night! And how did this shell get formed so quickly? A little while ago when I looked at the sky all was clear, but for two white strips. My views of life have changed in just the same unnoticeable way.'

Leaving the meadow, he went down the high road toward the village. A slight breeze was blowing and all looked grey and dull. There is generally a period of gloom just before daybreak and the complete triumph of light over darkness. Shivering with cold Levin walked rapidly with his eyes fixed on the ground.

'What's that? Who can it be coming?' thought he, hearing the tinkling of bells and raising his head. At a distance of forty paces along the road on which he was walking he saw a coach with four horses abreast and luggage on top approaching him. The horses were pressing close together away from the ruts, but the skilful driver, sitting sideways on the box, guided them so that the coach wheels ran smoothly on the road.

That was all Levin noticed, and without wondering who might be inside he glanced in at the window absent-mindedly.

In one corner an elderly woman was dozing; and close to the window sat a young girl who had just wakened and was holding the ribbons of her white nightcap with both hands. Bright and thoughtful, full of that complicated refinement of a life to which Levin was a stranger, she looked across him at the glow of dawn.

At the very moment when this vision was about to disappear, her candid eyes fell on him. She recognized him and joyful surprise lit up her face. He could not be mistaken. There were no other eyes in the world like them. In the whole world there was only one being able to unite in itself the universe and the meaning of life for him. It was Kitty. He guessed that she was on her way from the station to her sister's house at Ergushevo. All that had so disturbed Levin during the sleepless night and all his resolutions vanished suddenly. He recalled with disgust his thoughts of marrying a peasant girl. There alone, inside that coach on the other side of the road, so rapidly receding from him, was the one possible solution of that riddle which had been weighing on him so painfully of late.

She did not look out again. The sound of the wheels could no longer be heard; the tinkling of the bells grew fainter. The barking of dogs proved that the coach was passing through the village, and only the empty fields, the village before him, and he himself walking solitary on the deserted road, were left.

He looked up at the sky, hoping to find there the shell he had been admiring, which had typified for him the reflections and feelings of the night. There in the unfathomable height a mystic change was going on and he could see no sign of anything like a shell; but a large cover of gradually diminishing fleecy cloudlets was spreading over half the sky, which had turned blue and grown brighter. It answered his questioning look with the same tenderness and the same remoteness.

'No,' said he to himself. 'Beautiful as is that life of simplicity and toil, I cannot turn to it. I love *her*!'

Chapter XIII

None but those who knew Karenin most intimately knew that this apparently cold and sober-minded man had one weakness, quite inconsistent with the general trend of his character. Karenin could not with equanimity hear or see a child or a woman weeping. The sight of tears upset him and made him quite incapable of reasoning. The chief of his staff and his secretary knew this and warned women who came with petitions that they should on no account give way to tears if they did not want to spoil their case. 'He will get angry and won't listen to you,' they said; and in such cases the mental perturbation which tears produced in Karenin really found expression in hurried bursts of anger. 'I can do nothing for you. Kindly go away!' he would shout on these occasions.

When Anna on their way home from the races announced to him what her relations with Vronsky were and immediately hid her face in her hands and began crying, Karenin, despite his indignation with her, was as usual overcome by that mental perturbation. Being aware of this and of the fact that any expression he could at that moment find for his feelings would be incompatible with the situation, he tried to conceal all signs of life within himself and neither moved nor looked at her. That was the cause of the strange deathlike look on his face which had so struck Anna. When they reached home he helped her out of the carriage and, mastering himself by an effort, took leave of her with his usual courtesy, uttering non-committal words; he said he would let her know his decision next day.

His wife's words, confirming as they did his worst suspicions, had given Karenin a cruel pain in his heart. This pain was rendered more acute by physical pity for her, evoked by her tears. But when alone in the carriage, to his surprise and joy he felt completely relieved of that pity and of the suspicions and jealousy that had lately so tormented him.

He felt like a man who has just had a tooth drawn which has been hurting him a long time. After terrible pain and a sensation as if something enormous, bigger than his whole head, were being pulled out of his jaw, he feels, scarcely believing in his happiness, that the thing which has so long been poisoning his life and engrossing his attention no longer exists, and that it is possible again to live, think, and be interested in other things. What Karenin experienced was a feeling of this kind: it had been a strange and terrible pain, but it was past, and he felt he could again live, and think of other things beside his wife.

'Without honour, without heart, without religion; a depraved woman! I knew it and could see it all along, though I tried out of pity for her to deceive myself,' thought he. And it really seemed to him that he had always seen it. He recalled all the details of their past life, and details which he had not previously considered wrong now proved to him clearly that she had always been depraved.

'I made a mistake when I bound up my life with hers, but in my mistake there was nothing blameworthy, therefore I ought not to be unhappy. It is not I who am guilty,' he said to himself, 'but it is she. She does not concern me. She does not exist for me.'

What would happen to her and to her son, toward whom his feelings had changed as they had toward her, no longer occupied his mind. The one thing that preoccupied him was the question of how he could best divest himself of the mud with which she in her fall had bespattered him: of how to do it in the way which would be most decent, most convenient for him, and consequently fairest, and how he should continue his active, honest, and useful career. 'I ought not to be unhappy because a despicable woman has committed a crime, but I must find the best way out of this painful situation in which she has placed me. And find it I will,' said he to himself, frowning more and more. 'I'm not the first and shall not be the last'; and without taking into account the historical instances of wives' unfaithfulness, beginning with Menelaus and *La*

Belle Hélène,[3] whose memory had just recently been fresh in everybody's mind, quite a number of cases of the infidelity of modern wives in high society occurred to Karenin.

'Daryalov, Poltavsky, Prince Karibanov, Count Paskudin, Dram . . . Yes, even Dram—that honest, business-like fellow . . . Semenov, Chagin, Sigonin . . .' he passed them in review. 'It's true a kind of unreasonable ridicule falls on these men, but I never could see it in any other light than as a misfortune, and felt nothing but sympathy,' Karenin reflected, though it was not true: he had never felt any sympathy of the kind, and the more cases he had come across of husbands being betrayed by their wives the better the opinion he had had of himself. 'It is a misfortune that may befall anyone and it has befallen me. The only question is, how best to face the situation.' And he began mentally reviewing the courses pursued by other men in similar positions.

'Daryalov fought a duel. . . .'

In his youth Karenin had been particularly attracted by the idea of duelling, just because he was physically a timid man and was quite aware of it. He could not think without horror of a pistol being levelled at him, and had never used any kind of weapon. This horror had in his youth often induced him to take mental measure of his strength, in case he should ever be confronted by a situation in which it would be necessary to face danger. Since, however, he had achieved success and gained a firm position in the world he had long forgotten that feeling; but the old habit now revived and claimed its own, and the fear of being a coward was again so strong that he considered this point a long time and flattered his vanity with the idea of a duel, though he knew beforehand that he would on no account fight one.

'Of course our Society is still so uncivilized—not as in England —that very many' (among the many were those whose opinion Karenin particularly valued) 'would regard a duel as the right thing; but what object would be gained? Supposing I challenged him . . .' continued Karenin; and vividly picturing to himself the night he would spend after the challenge, and the sensation of having a pistol pointed at him, he shuddered and realized that he would never do it.

'Supposing,' he went on, 'they showed me how to do it, placed me, and I pulled the trigger . . .' He closed his eyes . . . 'and it turned out that I had killed him . . .' and he shook his head to drive away the stupid thought. 'What sense is there in killing a man in order to define one's relations with a guilty wife and a son?

3. *La Belle Hélène*, a comic opera, by Offenbach, just then in vogue in Moscow and Petersburg.

Nevertheless, I shall have to decide what to do with her.

'But what is even more likely—and sure to happen—is that I should be killed or wounded. Then I, an innocent man, should be the victim. That would be still more senseless. And this is not all. A challenge from me would not be an honest action. Do I not know beforehand that my friends would never allow me to go so far as to fight a duel, would not allow a statesman whom Russia needs to expose himself to danger? What, then, would happen? This would happen: I, knowing beforehand that matters would never be allowed to reach a dangerous point, should have challenged a man in order to cover myself with false glamour. That would be dishonest, it would be false, it would be deceiving myself as well as others. No! a duel is unthinkable and no one expects it of me. My aim is to safeguard my reputation, which I need for the uninterrupted pursuit of my career.' His official pursuits, which had always appeared essential to Karenin, now assumed even greater importance.

Having considered and rejected the idea of a duel, Karenin turned his thoughts to divorce, the next expedient of which some of the wronged husbands he remembered had availed themselves. Going over all the cases of divorce he knew—there were very many, and in the highest Society, with which he was well acquainted—Karenin could not recall one in which the purpose of the divorce was the one he had in view. In all these cases the husband had ceded or sold the unfaithful wife, and the very person who according to law had no right to re-marry entered into fictitious, pseudo-legal relations with a pretended husband. Karenin saw that in his own case it would be impossible to obtain a legal divorce— that is, a divorce in which the guilty wife would be simply cast off. He knew that in their complex conditions of life it would not be possible to obtain those coarse proofs of a wife's infidelity which the law demanded; he knew that in that life there was a certain convention of refinement which would not allow him to bring forward such proofs, had they existed, because such an action would make him sink even lower than she in public opinion. To attempt a divorce could only lead to a lawsuit and a scandal which would give his enemies great opportunity for calumny, and would lower his high position in Society. The chief object of his life, the settling of conditions with the least possible amount of disturbance, could not be furthered by divorce. Besides, it was evident that as a consequence of divorce the wife would break off relations with her husband and unite with her lover. In Karenin's soul, however, despite the complete and contemptuous indifference he thought he felt for his wife, there was one feeling left with regard to her: an objection to her being in a position to unite unhindered with Vronsky, so making her crime advantageous to her. The very thought of it irritated him to such an extent that he groaned with inner pain, rose, and changed his place in the carriage; and for a long while after that he sat wrapping his fluffy rug round his bony, easily-chilled legs.

'Besides a formal divorce, it would be possible to act as Karibanov, Paskudin, and that good-natured Dram did, and just separate,' he resumed when he had grown calm again; but this measure would have all the inconvenience of a divorce-scandal, and would throw his wife into Vronsky's arms just in the same way. 'No, it is impossible, impossible!' he said aloud, again wrapping the rug round his legs, 'I cannot be unhappy, and she and he must not be happy.'

The jealousy that had tormented him during the period of uncertainty had left him when his wife's words had with great pain drawn that aching tooth. But another feeling had now taken the place of the jealousy: it was a wish that his wife's guilt should meet with retribution. He did not acknowledge it to himself, but in the depths of his soul he wished her to suffer for impairing his peace of mind and his honour. And having reviewed the possibilities of a duel, of divorce, and of separation, and having again rejected them, Karenin came to the conclusion that there was only one course to be followed: to keep her with him, hiding from the world what had happened, and taking all necessary steps to put a stop to her love-affair, and above all (though he did not confess this to himself) to punish her. 'I must inform her of my decision, that after considering the painful situation in which she has placed her family, I think that an external *status quo* would be better for both parties than any other expedient, and that I am prepared to keep to that on the strict understanding on her part that she will obey my will and break off relations with her lover.' In confirmation of this decision, after it had already been reached, another powerful argument occurred to Karenin. 'It is only by this course that I can conform with religion,' said he to himself. 'It is the only way that makes it possible for me not to disown my guilty wife and to give her a chance of repenting, and even, painful as it will be, to devote part of my powers to her redemption.'

Though Karenin knew that he could have no moral influence on his wife, that all his attempts to redeem her would lead to nothing but lies, and although during the painful moments he had lived through he had not once thought of seeking guidance in religion, now that his decision was, as he imagined, in conformity with religion, its sanction afforded him great satisfaction and even some comfort. It was pleasant to think that no one would have a right to say that in such an important crisis in his life he had not acted in accordance with that religion whose banner he had always held aloft amid general coldness and indifference.

Proceeding to consider further details, Karenin could not even see why his relations with his wife should not remain almost the same as before. He could of course never again revive his respect for her; but there was no occasion for him to spoil his own life and to suffer just because she had proved a bad and unfaithful wife.

'Yes, time goes on; and time, which cures everything, will restore the old conditions,' said Karenin to himself. 'That is, it will restore them in so far that I shall not have this worry during the rest of my life. She must be unhappy, but I am not guilty and therefore I cannot suffer.'

Chapter XIV

By the time he reached Petersburg Karenin had not only resolved to keep to his decision, but had mentally composed a letter to his wife. On entering the hall of his house he glanced at the letters and papers which had been sent from the Ministry and ordered them to be brought into his study.

'Tell him to unharness; and no one is to be admitted, he said in answer to the hall-porter's inquiry, accentuating with a certain pleasure the word *admitted*. It was a sign that he was in good spirits.

He paced twice up and down his study and then halted at the gigantic writing-table, on which his valet had already lit six candles. Cracking his fingers, he sat down and arranged his writing materials. With his elbow on the table and his head bent to one side he sat and thought for a minute, and then wrote without an instant's pause. He did not begin by addressing her, and wrote in French, using the plural pronoun *you*, which in French does not sound as cold and distant as it does in Russia.

'During our last conversation I expressed my intention of communicating my decision with reference to the subject of that conversation. Having carefully and fully considered everything, I now write to fulfil my promise. My decision is as follows: Whatever your actions may have been, I do not consider myself justified in severing the bonds with which a Higher Power has united us. A family must not be broken up through the caprice, perversity, or even crime, of one of the married couple, and our life must go on as heretofore. This is unavoidable for my sake, for yours, and for that of our son. I am perfectly convinced that you have repented, and are repenting, of the action which has led to this letter, and will completely co-operate with me to eradicate the cause of our discord and to forget the past. If not, you can yourself foresee what awaits you and your son. I hope to talk all this over with you in more detail at a personal interview. As the summer season is drawing to a close, I would ask you to return to Petersburg as soon as possible, and not later than Tuesday. All necessary preparations shall be made for your return. I beg you to note that I attach importance to this request of mine.

A. KARENIN.

'P.S.—I enclose some money, which you may need for your expenses.'

He read the letter over and was satisfied with it, especially with having remembered to enclose the money; there was not a single cruel word or threat in it, yet it was not yielding in tone. Above all it provided a golden bridge for her to return by. Having folded the letter, smoothed it out with a massive ivory paper-knife, and put it and the money in an envelope—with the pleasure that the use of his well-arranged writing appliances always caused him—he rang.

'Give this to the messenger, and tell him to take it to the country, to Anna Arkadyevna, to-morrow,' he said, and got up.

'Yes, your Excellency! Shall tea be served in the study?'

Karenin assented, and, toying with his paper-knife, went to his arm-chair, beside which a lamp was burning, and a French book about the Eugubine Tables was lying ready.[4] Above the arm-chair hung a beautifully painted portrait of Anna by a celebrated artist. To Karenin the splendidly painted black lace on the head, the black hair, and the beautiful white hand with many rings on the third finger, suggested something intolerably bold and provocative. After looking at the portrait for about a minute he shuddered and his lips trembled and made a sound like 'brr' as he turned away. He sat down hurriedly and opened his book. He tried to read but could not awaken in himself the lively interest he had felt for the Eugubine Tables. His eyes were on the book but he was thinking about something else. He was not thinking of his wife but of a complication that had recently arisen in his official activity and at present constituted the chief interest of his work. He felt that he now saw more deeply than ever into that complication, and that a capital idea (he might say that without flattering himself) had occurred to him, which would disentangle the whole business, raise him in his official career, upset his enemies, and therefore be of the greatest value to the State. As soon as the footman, who had brought in the tea, had left the room, Karenin rose and went to the writing-table. Drawing toward himself the portfolio of current affairs, with a scarcely perceptible smile of self-satisfaction, he took a pencil from the stand and became absorbed in reading some intricate papers he

4. This is an allusion to an article by Michel Bréal on 'Les Tables eugubines' in the *Revue des Deux Mondes* of November 1874. The seven Eugubine tables bore Umbrian inscriptions concerning religious rites. They were discovered in 1444 in the town of Gubbio, anciently Iguvium, but in the Middle Ages Eugubium.

had sent for, relating to the impending complication. The complication was this: Karenin's official peculiarity, his characteristic trait (every successful official has his special trait), which together with his determined ambition, self-restraint, honesty, and self-confidence, had made him successful, consisted in a contempt for red-tape, a curtailment of correspondence, economy, and (as far as possible) a direct relation with real facts. It so happened that the important Committee of June 2nd had had brought before it the question of irrigation in the Zaraysk Province, which belonged to Karenin's Department, and presented a striking example of unproductive expenditure and useless red-tape methods. Karenin knew that this was really so. The field-irrigation of the Zaraysk Province had been started by the predecessor of Karenin's predecessor. A great deal of money had been and was being spent quite unproductively on that business, and it was evident that the scheme would lead to nothing. When Karenin had first taken up his present post he had at once realized this and had wished to stop it; but, till he felt himself firmly seated, he knew that it would not be wise to do so, as too many interests were involved. Afterwards, being occupied with other matters, he had simply forgotten the business. Like all such matters it went on of itself, by inertia. (Many people lived by it, especially one very moral and musical family in which the daughters all played stringed instruments. Karenin was acquainted with that family and gave away one of the daughters at her marriage.) The raising of this question by a hostile Department was, in Karenin's opinion, dishonest, because in every Ministry there were still graver matters which, out of recognized official decency, no one ever questioned. But since the gauntlet had been thrown down, he would take it up boldly and would demand the appointment of a special Committee to investigate and report upon the work of the Committee of Irrigation in the Zaraysk Province, but at the same time he would not yield an inch to those gentlemen who had raised the question. He would demand the appointment of a special Committee to inquire into the case of the subject races in that Province.[5]

5. The question of the 'subject races' that occupied Karénin resembled the celebrated affair of the Bashkír lands in the Ufa and Orenburg provinces. In the middle of the nineteenth century the Bashkírs had about thirty million acres of land in those provinces and many people from elsewhere came to settle there, renting or leasing land from them. The land was not properly surveyed and separate holdings were merely indicated by sign-posts, which led to misunderstandings and disputes. Special regulations were then issued relating to the holding of the settlers, as well as to purchasers of unoccupied State lands in the two provinces. These regulations aimed at increasing the number of Russian settlers, and were scandalously misapplied with the connivance of local authorities for the dishonest appropriation of both State and Bashkír land. Enormous tracts of valuable timber and other land were bought for trifling sums by local officials and their relations and were resold at an exorbitant profit. The defenceless Bashkírs were defrauded of their land and the law was violated.

Reports of this systematic exploitation gradually spread, and at last got into the press and were made use of by the enemies of P. A. Valúev, the Minister of the Imperial Estates.

The case of the subject races had been accidentally raised at the Committee of 2nd June and had been energetically insisted on by Karenin as a matter of urgency in view of their wretched condition. At the Committee this question had caused conflict between several Ministries. The Ministry opposed to Karenin had argued that the condition of the subject races was most flourishing and that the projected rearrangement might destroy their prosperity, while, if there was really anything unsatisfactory, it all resulted from the neglect by Karenin's Department of the measures prescribed by the law. Now Karenin meant to demand, first, that a new Commission should be formed to investigate locally the conditions of the subject races; secondly, should those conditions prove to be such as they appeared to be from the official reports already received, that another scientific Commission should be appointed to study the causes of this deplorable condition of the subject races, in the following aspects: (*a*) Political, (*b*) Administrative, (*c*) Economic, (*d*) Ethnographic, (*e*) Material, and (*f*) Religious; thirdly, that information should be demanded from the hostile Department concerning the measures it had taken during the last ten years to avert the unfavourable conditions to which the subject races were now exposed; and fourthly and finally, that that Department should be required to explain why it had acted in direct contradiction to the meaning of the fundamental and organic law (Vol. —, Article 18, and footnote to Article 36, as appeared from the statements submitted to the Committee and numbered 17015 and 18308, of 5th December 1863 and 7th June 1864. A flush of animation suffused Karenin's face as he rapidly wrote out a summary of these ideas. Having covered a sheet of foolscap he rose, rang, and sent off a note to his Chief Secretary, asking for some necessary references that had to be looked up.

After walking up and down the room he again looked at the portrait, frowned, and smiled contemptuously. He once more took up the book on the Eugubine Tables, and, having reawakened an interest in them, at eleven o'clock went to bed, and when as he lay there he remembered what had occurred with his wife, it no longer appeared to him in such gloomy colours.

Chapter XV

Though Anna had angrily and obstinately contradicted Vronsky when he said that her position was an impossible one, in the depths

---

Valúev, though not personally involved in the abuses, was very dilatory in investigating the affair. Eventually he had to retire, the Governor-General of Orenburg was dismissed, and a Senatorial Revision Committee on the affair was appointed, which resulted in a large number of officials being committed for trial.

of her soul she felt that the situation was a false one and wished with all her heart to put an end to it. On her way back from the races, in a moment of excitement—in spite of the pain it caused her—she had told her husband everything, and she was glad she had done so. After he left her, she told herself that she was glad she had told him, that now everything would be definite—at any rate, the falsehood and deception would no longer exist. She thought it quite certain that her position would be cleared up for good. Her new position might be a bad one but it would be definite, and there would be no vagueness or falsehood. The pain she had inflicted on herself and her husband would now, she thought, be compensated for by the fact that the matter would be settled. She saw Vronsky that same evening, but did not tell him what had passed between her and her husband, though he would have to be told before her position could be settled.

When she woke up in the morning the first thing that came into her mind was what she had said to her husband, and it now appeared so terrible that she could not understand how she had been able to utter such strange and coarse words and could not imagine what result they would have. But the words had been spoken and Karenin had gone away without saying anything.

'I saw Vronsky and did not tell him. Just as he was going away I wished to call him back and tell him, but changed my mind, because my not having done so at first would have appeared strange. Why did I not tell him?'

And in answer to this question a hot blush of shame spread all over her face. She knew what had stopped her, knew she had been ashamed. The situation which the night before had appeared to be clearing up now seemed quite hopeless. She dreaded the disgrace, which she had not considered before.

When she thought of what her husband would do, the most terrible fancies came into her head. She fancied that presently the steward would come and turn her out of the house and that her disgrace would be proclaimed to all the world. She asked herself where she would go when turned out, and found no answer.

When she thought about Vronsky, she imagined that he did not love her, that he was beginning to find her a burden, and that she could not offer herself to him; and in consequence she felt hostile toward him. She felt as if the words she had used to her husband, which she kept repeating in imagination, had been said by her to every one and that every one had heard them.

She had not the courage to look into the eyes of the people she lived with. She could not make up her mind to call her maid, and still less to go down and face her son and his governess.

The maid, who had long been listening at the door, at last came

in of her own accord. Anna looked inquiringly into her eyes and
blushed with alarm. The maid begged pardon and said she thought
she had heard the bell.

She brought a dress and a note. The note was from Betsy, who
reminded her that she (Betsy) was that day expecting Lisa Merkalova and the Baroness Stolz, with their admirers Kaluzhsky and old
Stremov, to a game of croquet.

'Do come, if only to study manners and customs. I expect you,'
she wrote in conclusion.

Anna read the note and sighed deeply.

'I don't want anything, anything at all,' she said to Annushka,
who was moving the bottles and brushes on the dressing-table. 'I
will get dressed and come down at once. I want nothing, nothing
at all.'

Annushka went out, but Anna did not get dressed. She remained
in the same position with head and arms drooping. Every now and
then her whole body shuddered as she tried to make some movement or to say something, and then became rigid again. 'Oh, my
God! My God!' she kept repeating, but neither the word God
or my had any meaning for her. The thought of seeking comfort
in religion, though she had never doubted the truth of the religion
in which she had been brought up, was as foreign to her as asking
Karenin for help would have been. She knew that she could find
no help in religion unless she was prepared to give up that which
alone gave a meaning to her life. She was not only disturbed, but
was beginning to be afraid of a new mental condition such as she
had never before experienced. She felt as if everything was being
doubled in her soul, just as objects appear doubled to weary eyes.
Sometimes she could not tell what she feared and what she desired. Whether she feared and desired what had been, or what
would be, and what it was she desired she did not know.

'Oh, dear! What am I doing!' she said to herself suddenly, feeling pain in both sides of her head. When she came to her senses
she found that she was clutching her hair and pressing her temples
with both hands. She jumped up and began pacing up and down
the room.

'Coffee is ready, and Ma'm'selle and Serezha are waiting,' said
Annushka, coming in again and finding Anna in the same position.

'Serezha? what of Serezha?' Anna asked, reviving suddenly, as for
the first time that morning she remembered the existence of her
son.

'It seems he has got into trouble,' answered Annushka with a
smile.

'Into trouble, how?'

'You had some peaches in the corner room; it seems he has eaten one of them on the quiet.'

The thought of her son at once took Anna out of the hopeless condition she had been in. She remembered that partly sincere but greatly exaggerated rôle of a mother living for her son which she had assumed during the last few years; and felt with joy that in the position in which she found herself she had still one stay, independent of her relations with her husband and Vronsky. That stay was her son. Whatever position she might accept she could not give up her son.

Let her husband disgrace her, let Vronsky grow cold toward her and continue to live his own independent life (again she thought of him with bitterness and reproach), she could not give up her son. She had an aim in life and must act so as to ensure her position toward her son, while they had not yet taken him from her. She must take him away. That was the only thing to do at present. She must be calm and escape from this terrible situation.

The thought of decided action concerned with her son—of going away somewhere with him—made her feel calmer.

She dressed quickly and with determined steps entered the drawing-room, where Serezha and his governess were waiting breakfast for her as usual. Serezha, dressed all in white, was standing by a table under a looking-glass, and arranging some flowers he had brought, with bent head and back, showing that strained attention familiar to her in which he resembled his father.

His governess was looking exceptionally stern. Serezha exclaimed in a piercing voice, as he often did, 'Ah! Mama!' and stopped, hesitating whether to go and bid her good-morning and leave the flowers, or to finish the crown he was making and take it to her.

The governess began to give a long and detailed account of his misconduct, but Anna did not listen to her. She was wondering whether to take her also or not.

'No, I won't,' she decided. 'I will go alone with my son.'

'Yes, that was very wrong,' said Anna, and putting her hand on his shoulder she looked at him not with a severe but with a timid expression which confused and gladdened the boy. She kissed him.

'Leave him to me,' she said to the astonished governess, and still holding his hand she sat down at the breakfast table.

'Mama! I . . . I . . . I . . .' he said, trying to find out from her face what he was to expect for eating the peach.

'Serezha,' she said as soon as the governess had gone away, 'it was wrong, but you won't do it again? . . . You love me?'

She felt the tears coming into her eyes.

'As if I could help loving him,' she said to herself, looking into his frightened and yet happy face. 'And is it possible that he would take sides with his father to torment me?' The tears were already streaming down her cheeks, and in order to hide them she jumped up abruptly and went out on to the verandah.

After the thunderstorms of the last few days the weather had grown clear and cold.

She shivered with cold, and with the terror that seized her with new power out in the open air.

'Go to Mariette,' she said to Serezha, who had come out after her; and she began pacing up and down the straw matting of the verandah.

'Is it possible that they will not forgive me or understand that it could not have been otherwise?' she asked herself.

She stopped and looked at the crown of an aspen trembling in the wind, with its clean-washed leaves glistening brilliantly in the cold sunshine, and she felt that they would not forgive, that everybody would now be as pitiless toward her as the sky and the trees, and again she felt that duality in her soul.

'No, no, I must not think,' she said to herself; 'I must get ready to go. Where? When? Whom shall I take with me?'

'To Moscow? Yes, by the evening train, with Annushka and Serezha, and with only the most necessary things. But first I must write to both of them.'

She quickly went to her sitting-room and wrote to her husband. 'After what has happened I can no longer remain in your house. I am going away and taking my son. I do not know the law and therefore I do not know to which of his parents a son must be left, but I am taking him because I cannot live without him. Be generous and leave him to me!'

Up to that point she wrote quickly and naturally; but the appeal to his generosity, in which she did not believe, and the necessity of finishing the letter with something moving, stopped her. . . .

'I cannot speak of my fault and my repentance, because . . .' She stopped again, unable to connect her thoughts. 'No, I will say nothing,' she thought, tore up the letter, re-wrote it, omitting the reference to his generosity, and sealed it.

The other letter she meant to write was to Vronsky.

'I have informed my husband,' she began, and was unable to write any more. It seemed so coarse and unwomanly. 'Besides, what can I write to him?' she asked herself; and again she blushed with shame. She thought of his calmness, and a feeling of vexation with him made her tear the paper to pieces, with the one sentence written on it.

'There is no need to write anything,' she thought, closed her blotting-book, went upstairs to tell the governess and the servants that she was going to Moscow that evening, and then began packing.

Chapter XVI

In all the rooms of the country house porters, gardeners, and footmen went about carrying out the things. Cupboards and chests of drawers stood open, twice the nearest shop had been sent to for balls of string. The floor was strewn with newspapers. Two trunks, several bags, and some strapped-up rugs had been taken down to the hall. A closed carriage and two *izvozchiks* were waiting at the front porch. Anna, who had forgotten her agitation while she was working, stood at a table in the sitting-room packing her hand-bag when Annushka drew her attention to the noise of approaching carriage wheels. Anna looked out and saw Karenin's messenger in the porch ringing the bell.

'Go and see what it is,' she said, and, calmly prepared for anything, sat down in an easy-chair and folded her hands on her knees. A footman brought her a thick envelope addressed in her husband's handwriting.

'The messenger has been told to wait for an answer,' he said.

'All right,' she replied, and as soon as he had gone she tore open the envelope with trembling fingers.

A packet of new still unfolded notes in a paper band fell out. She unfolded the letter and read the end first: 'All necessary preparations shall be made for your return. I beg you will note that I attach importance to this request of mine,' she read. Having glanced through it, she went back and read it again from the beginning. When she had finished she felt cold, and knew that a more dreadful misfortune had befallen her than she had ever expected.

She had that morning repented of having told her husband and wished it were possible to unsay her words; and here was a letter treating her words as unsaid and giving her what she had desired; but now the letter appeared more terrible than anything she could have imagined.

'He's in the right, he's in the right!' she muttered; 'of course he always is in the right, he is a Christian, he is magnanimous! Yes, a mean, horrid man! And no one but I understands or will understand it, and I cannot explain it. They say he's a religious, moral, honest, and wise man, but they do not see what I have seen. They do not know how for eight years he has been smothering my life, smothering everything that was alive in me, that he never once thought I was a live woman, in need of love. They do not know how at every step he hurt me and remained self-satisfied. Have I not tried, tried with all my might, to find a purpose in my life? Have I not tried to love him, tried to love my son when I could no longer love my husband? But the time came when I understood that I could no longer deceive myself, that I am alive, and cannot be blamed because God made me so, that I want to love and live. And now? If he killed me—if he had killed him,—I would have borne anything, I would have forgiven anything! But no! He . . .

'How was it I did not guess what he would do? He will do what is consistent with his low nature. He will be in the right, but as for me who am already disgraced he will disgrace me more and more!

' "You can yourself forsee what awaits you and your son!" '—she repeated the words of the letter. 'That is a threat that he will take my son from me, and probably their stupid laws will permit it. But don't I know why he said it? He does not believe in my love for my son or he despises it. He always did snigger at it! He despises that feeling of mine, but he knows that I will not give up my son, that I cannot give him up, that without my son I cannot live even with the man I love,—that if I forsook my son I should act like a horrid disreputable woman. He knows that and knows that I have not the power to do it.'

' "Our life must go on as heretofore" '—she recalled another sentence of the letter. 'That life was painful before, lately it has been dreadful. What will it be now? And he knows it all; knows that I cannot repent of breathing, of loving, knows that nothing but lies and deception can come of this arrangement, but he wants to continue to torture me. I know him; I know that he swims and delights in falsehood as a fish does in water. But no! I will not give him that pleasure, come what will. I will break this web of lies in which he wishes to entangle me. Anything is better than lies and deception!

'But how? Oh God! oh God! Was a woman ever as unhappy as I am? . . . No, I shall break it off, break it off!' she exclaimed, jumping up and forcing back her tears. And she went to the table to write him another note, though she knew in the depths of her soul that she would not have the strength to break anything off, nor to escape from her former position, however false and dishonest it might be.

She sat down at her writing-table, but instead of writing she folded her arms on the table and put her head on them, and began to cry, sobbing with her whole bosom heaving, as a child cries.

She wept because the hopes of clearing up and defining her position were destroyed for ever. She knew beforehand that everything would remain as it was and would be even far worse than before. She felt that, insignificant as it had appeared that morning, the position she held in Society was dear to her, and that she would not have the strength to change it for the degraded position of a woman who had forsaken husband and child and formed a union with her lover; that, however much she tried, she could not become stronger than herself. She would never be able to feel the freedom of love, but would always be a guilty woman continually threatened with exposure, deceiving her husband for the sake of a shameful union with a man who was a stranger and independent of her, and with whom she could not live a united life. She knew that it would be so, and yet it was so terrible that she could not even imagine how it would end. And she cried, without restraint, like a punished child.

The approaching step of the footman recalled her to herself, and hiding her face from him she pretended to be writing.

'The messenger is asking for the answer,' he said.

'The answer? Yes, let him wait: I will ring,' said Anna.

'What can I write?' she thought. 'What can I decide alone? What do I know? What do I want? What do I love?' And she felt again a schism in her soul, and again was frightened by the feeling; so she seized the first pretext for action that occurred to her to divert her thoughts from herself. 'I must see Alexey,' as she called Vronsky in her thoughts. 'He alone can tell me what to do. I shall go to Betsy's and perhaps shall meet him there,' quite forgetting that the evening before when she had told him she was not going to the Princess Tverskaya's, he had replied that in that case he would not go either. She wrote to her husband:

'I have received your letter.—A,' rang, and gave the note to the footman.

'We are not going,' she said to Annushka, who had just come in. 'Not going at all?'

'No, but don't unpack till to-morrow, and let the carriage wait. I am going to see the Princess.'

'What dress shall I put out?'

Chapter XVII

The croquet match to which the Princess Tverskaya had invited Anna was to be played by two ladies and their admirers. The two ladies were the chief representatives of a choice new Petersburg circle called, in imitation of an imitation of something, *Les sept merveilles du monde.*[6] These ladies belonged to a circle which, though higher, was entirely hostile to the set Anna frequented. Old Stremov—one of Petersburg's influential men, and Lisa Merkalova's adorer—was also officially hostile to Karenin. These considerations had made Anna reluctant to come, and it was to her refusal that the hints in Princess Tverskaya's note had referred. But now the hope of seeing Vronsky had brought Anna.

She arrived at the Princess Tverskaya's house before the other visitors.

Just as she arrived Vronsky's footman, who with his well-brushed whiskers looked like a Gentleman of the Bedchamber, also came up.

6. The Seven Wonders of the World.

He stopped at the door, took off his cap, and let her pass. Anna saw him, and only then remembered that the evening before Vronsky had said that he was not coming. Probably he had sent a note to say so.

As she was taking off her outdoor things in the hall she heard the footman—who even pronounced his r's like a Gentleman of the Bedchamber—say: 'From the Count to the Princess,' as he delivered the note.

She felt inclined to ask where his master was; she wanted to go home and write to him to come to her house, or to go to him herself. But none of these things could be done. She heard in front of her the bell that announced her arrival, and the Princess Tverskaya's footman was already standing half-turned toward her at an open door, waiting for her to enter the inner rooms.

'The Princess is in the garden; she will be informed immediately. Will you not come into the garden?' said another footman in the next room.

The feelings of irresolution and indefiniteness were just the same as at home, or even worse, because she could do nothing; she could not see Vronsky but had to stay there, in this company of strangers so out of sympathy with her present mood. But she wore a costume that she knew suited her, she was not alone but surrounded by a luxurious setting of idleness, and she felt easier than at home; she had no need to think of what to do. Everything did itself. When she met Betsy coming toward her in a white costume that struck Anna by its elegance, Anna smiled at her as usual. The Princess Tverskaya came accompanied by Tushkevich and a young girl, a relation, who to the great delight of her provincial parents was spending the summer with the fashionable Princess.

There must have been something unusual about Anna's look, for Betsy noticed it at once.

'I have slept badly,' answered Anna, gazing at the footman, who she guessed was bringing Vronsky's note.

'How glad I am that you have come!' said Betsy. 'I am tired, and am going to have a cup of tea before they arrive. Won't you and Masha go and just try the croquet-lawn where the grass is cut?' she said to Tushkevich. 'We can have a heart-to-heart talk over our tea. We'll have a cosy chat, won't we?' she added in English, pressing the hand with which Anna held her sunshade.

'Yes, especially as I cannot stay long. I must go to the old Countess Vrede—I promised to, ages ago,' said Anna, to whom falsehood—so alien to her by nature—had now become so simple and natural in Society that it even gave her pleasure. Why she had said something she had not even thought of a moment before, she could not have explained. Her only reason for saying it was that since Vronsky was not coming she must secure her freedom and try to see him in some other way. But why she had mentioned the old Lady-in-Waiting Vrede, to whom, among many other people, she owed a visit, she could not have explained; and yet as it happened she could have thought of nothing better had she tried to invent the most cunning means of seeing Vronsky.

'No, I won't let you go on any account,' said Betsy, fixing her eyes intently on Anna. 'I should be really hurt, if I were not so fond of you. It's just as if you thought my company might compromise you! Please bring us tea in the little drawing-room,' she said to the footman, screwing up her eyes as she always did when speaking to a footman.

She took the note from him and read it.

'Alexey has failed us,' she said in French. 'He writes that he cannot come.' She spoke in a natural and matter-of-fact tone, as if it never entered her head that Vronsky had any other interest for Anna than as a croquet player.

Anna was aware that Betsy knew everyting, but when she heard her talk about Vronsky she always felt a momentary conviction that Betsy knew nothing about it.

'Ah!' said Anna, in an indifferent tone as if she cared very little about it, and went on with a smile: 'How could your company compromise anyone?' This play with words, this concealment of a secret, had a great charm for Anna, as it has for all women. It was not the necessity for secrecy, not its purpose, but the process itself that was fascinating.

'I cannot be more Catholic than the Pope,' she said. 'Stremov and Lisa Merkalova are the cream of the cream of Society! They are received everywhere, and I'—she put special stress on that I —'never was severe or intolerant: I simply have not the time.'

'No! Perhaps you do not want to meet Stremov? Let him and Alexey Alexandrovich break lances at their Committee Meetings, that has nothing to do with us. In Society he is the most amiable man I know, and a passionate croquet player. You'll see! And in spite of his ridiculous position as Lisa's old admirer, you should see how he carries it off. He is very charming. Sappho Stolz you do not know. She is quite a new type.'

While Betsy was saying this Anna saw by her bright intelligent look that she partly understood Anna's position and was devising something. They were in a small sitting-room.

'But I must write to Alexey;' and Betsy sat down at the table, wrote a few words, and put the paper in an envelope. 'I am writing to ask him to come to dinner; I have one lady too many. See if I have made it pressing enough! Excuse me! I must leave you for a minute; please close the envelope and send it,' she said from the doorway; 'I have some orders to give.'

Without thinking for an instant Anna sat down at the table with Betsy's note, and without reading it added at the bottom: 'I must see you. Come to Vrede's garden. I shall be there at six.' She closed it, and Betsy returning sent it off in her presence.

Over their tea, which was brought them in the cool little drawing-room, the two women really had before the arrival of the visitors the cosy chat the Princess Tverskaya had promised Anna. They passed in review all who were expected to come, and their conversation dwelt at some length on Lisa Merkalova.

'She is very nice and was always attractive to me,' said Anna.

'You must love her: she dotes on you. Yesterday she came to me at the races and was quite in despair that she had missed you. She said that you are a real heroine for a novel, and that were she a man she would have committed a thousand follies for your sake. Stremov tells her she is committing them as it is!'

'Yes, but do tell me! I never can understand,' said Anna after a pause, in a tone that clearly proved she was not putting an idle question and that what she was asking about was more important to her than it ought to be; 'do tell me what are her relations with Prince Kaluzhsky, whom they call Mishka? I have not often met them. . . . What are they?'

Betsy looked at her with smiling eyes. 'It is a new fashion,' she replied. 'They have all adopted that fashion. They have kicked over the traces, but there are different ways of doing it.'

'Yes, but what are her relations with Kaluzhsky?'

Betsy burst into an unexpected, merry and uncontrollable peal of laughter, a thing she rarely did. 'You are encroaching on the Princess Myagkaya's domain! That is a question an *enfant terrible* might put!' and Betsy evidently tried to, but could not, control herself, and again burst out into the infectious kind of laughter peculiar to those who laugh seldom. 'You must ask them!' she uttered, while tears of laughter choked her voice.

'It is all very well for you to laugh,' said Anna, who could not help laughing too, 'but I never was able to understand it. I cannot understand the husband's position.'

'The husband's! Lisa Merkalova's husband carries her rugs after her and is always at her service. But what there is behind it all, no one really cares to know. Don't you know that in good Society no one talks or even thinks about certain details of the toilet? It is just the same in such cases.'

'Will you be at Rolandaki's fête?' asked Anna in order to change the subject.

'I don't think so,' answered Betsy, and without looking at her friend she began filling the little translucent cup with aromatic tea.

She moved one of the cups toward Anna, got out a pachitos,[7] placed it in a silver holder, and lit it.

'You see,' she said, 'I am in a lucky position! I understand you and I understand Lisa. Lisa's is one of those naïve natures who, like children, are unable to understand the difference between right and wrong. At least she did not understand it when she was very young. And now she knows that that rôle of not understanding becomes her. Now perhaps she is purposely ingenuous,' and Betsy smiled pointedly. 'But still it becomes her. You see a thing may be looked at tragically and turned to a torment, or looked at quite simply, and even gaily. Perhaps you are inclined to take things too tragically.'

'How I wish I knew others as I know myself!' said Anna, seriously and thoughtfully. 'Am I worse than others or better? Worse, I think.'

'Enfant terrible! enfant terrible!' Betsy repeated. 'But here they come!'

Chapter XVIII

Sounds of footsteps and a man's voice, then that of a woman followed by laughter, reached them, and the expected visitors entered the room, Sappho Stolz and a young man, shining with a superabundance of health, known as Vaska. It was evident that he flourished on underdone beef, truffles, and Burgundy. Vaska bowed to the ladies, only glancing at them for a second. He came into the drawing-room behind Sappho and followed her across the room as if he were tied to her, with his glittering eye fixed on her as if he were ready to eat her. Sappho Stolz had fair hair and black eyes. She entered with a short, brisk step, in shoes with high French heels, and shook hands with the ladies with a firm grip like a man.

Anna had never met this celebrity before, and was struck by her beauty, by the extravagant fashion of her costume, and by the boldness of her manners. On her head the delicate golden hair (her own and others') was built up into such an erection that her head was as large as her shapely, well-developed and much-exposed bust. At each strenuous step as she advanced, the shape of her knees and thighs was distinctly visible under her dress, and one involuntarily wondered just where, behind, under her heaped and swaying bustle, the real, graceful little body ended which was so exposed at the top and so hidden at the back and below.

Betsy hastened to introduce her to Anna.

'Just fancy! We nearly ran over two soldiers,' she began at once, winking and smiling as she threw back her train which she had

7. A straw-covered cigarette.

jerked too much to one side. 'I was with Vaska. . . . Oh, but you are not acquainted!' and she introduced the young man by his sur-name and burst into ringing laughter at her mistake in speaking of him as *Vaska* to a stranger. Vaska again bowed to Anna, but said nothing. He turned to Sappho: 'You have lost the bet: we have ar-rived first. Pay up!' he said smiling.

Sappho laughed still more merrily.

'Surely not now!' she said.

'Never mind, I will have it later.'

'All right! All right! Oh yes!' she suddenly said, addressing her hostess. 'I'm a nice one. I quite forgot . . . I have brought you a visitor! Here he is.'

The unexpected young visitor Sappho had brought with her and forgotten was nevertheless so important a personage that, in spite of his youth, both ladies rose to greet him.

He was Sappho's new admirer, and followed at her heels just like Vaska.

Then the Prince Kaluzhsky arrived, and Lisa Merkalova with Stremov. Lisa Merkalova was a slight brunette with a lazy Oriental type of face and beautiful (everybody said unfathomable) eyes. The character of her dark costume, as Anna at once noticed and appreci-ated, was perfectly suited to her style of beauty.

Just to the same extent as Sappho was compact and spruce Lisa was limp and pliant.

But to Anna Lisa was by far the more attractive.

When Betsy had spoken to Anna about her, she had said that Lisa was playing the rôle of an ingenuous child; but when Anna saw her she knew that this was untrue. She was really ingenuous, and a perverted but a sweet and irresponsible woman. It is true she had adopted the same tone as Sappho, and, as in Sappho's case, two ad-mirers followed her as if tied to her and devoured her with their eyes; one a young and the other an old man; but in her there was something superior to her surroundings,—she had the radiance of a real diamond among false stones. This radiance shone out of her beautiful and really unfathomable eyes. The weary yet passionate look of those eyes, with the dark circles beneath them, was striking in its perfect sincerity.

Looking into those eyes every one felt as if they knew her per-fectly, and knowing her could not help loving her. At the sight of Anna her whole face lit up with a joyful smile.

'Oh! I *am* pleased to see you!' she said, walking up to Anna. 'Yesterday at the races I was just trying to get near you when you went away. I was so anxious to see you, yesterday especially. Was it not dreadful?' and she gave Anna a look that seemed to reveal her whole soul.

'Yes, I never thought it would be so exciting,' replied Anna, blushing.

The company rose to go into the garden.

'I won't go,' said Lisa, smiling and sitting down beside Anna. 'You won't go either? Who wants to play croquet?'

'I like it,' said Anna.

'Tell me, how do you manage not to feel bored? It cheers me to look at you. You are full of life, but I am bored.'

'You bored? Why, yours is the gayest set in Petersburg,' said Anna.

'It may be that those who are not in our set are still more bored, but we—I at any rate—do not feel merry, but terribly, terribly bored.'

Sappho lit a cigarette and went out into the garden with the two young men. Betsy and Stremov stayed at the tea-table.

'Bored!' said Betsy. 'Sappho said that they had a very jolly time at your house yesterday.'

'Oh dear! It was so dull!' said Lisa Merkalova. 'We went back to my place after the races. Always the same people, the very same! Always the same goings on, the very same! We spent the whole evening lolling about on sofas. What was there jolly about it? Do tell me how you manage not to get bored?' said she again to Anna. 'One has only to look at you to see that you are a woman who may be happy or unhappy, but who is not dull. Teach me how you do it!'

'I do not do anything,' said Anna, blushing at these insistent questions.

'That is the best way,' Stremov joined in. Stremov was a man of about fifty, getting grey, but still fresh-looking, with a very plain though intelligent face full of character. Lisa Merkalova was his wife's niece and he spent all his spare time with her. On meeting Anna Karenina he, like a clever man of the world, being Karenin's enemy in the service, tried to be specially amiable to her, the wife of his foe.

'Don't do anything!' he repeated with a smile. 'That is the best way. I have always told you,' he went on, turning to Lisa Merkalova, 'that if one wishes not to be bored one must not expect to be bored, just as one must not be afraid of not falling asleep if one wishes to avoid sleeplessness. That is what Anna Arkadyevna says.'

'I should have been pleased to have said it, for it is not only wise, but true,' said Anna, smiling.

'No, but tell me why one cannot fall asleep and cannot help being bored?'

'To fall asleep one must have worked, and also to amuse oneself one must have worked.'

'Why should I work when no one wants my work? And I can't

and won't do it just for a pretence.'

'You are incorrigible,' said Stremov without looking at her, and again turned to Anna.

As he rarely met Anna he could not say anything to her except trivialities, but he said these trivialities, about her return from the country to Petersburg and of how fond the Countess Lydia Ivanovna was of her, in a way that expressed his whole-hearted desire to be agreeable to her, and to show her his respect and even more.

Tushkevich came in to say that everybody was waiting for the croquet players.

'No, please don't go!' begged Lisa Merkalova when she heard that Anna was leaving. Stremov joined her in the entreaty.

'The contrast will be too great,' he remarked, 'if you go to see the old Countess Vrede after leaving this company here. Besides, your visit will give her an opportunity to backbite, while here, on the contrary, you arouse the best feelings, quite opposed to backbiting.'

Anna hesitated for a moment. The flattering words of this clever man, the naïve, childish sympathy which Lisa Merkalova expressed to her, all these familiar Society surroundings made her feel so tranquil, while what was lying in wait for her was so hard, that for a moment she doubted whether to remain and put off the dread moment of explanation. But recalling what awaited her when alone at home if she took no decision, and remembering her action (the recollection of which was terrible) when she took hold of her hair with both hands, she took her leave and went away.

Chapter XIX

In spite of his apparently reckless existence, Vronsky was a man who hated disorder. While quite young and still in the Cadet Corps he had experienced the humiliation of a refusal when, having got into debt, he had tried to borrow money, and since then he had never again allowed himself to get into such a position.

To keep things straight he was in the habit, some five or six times a year according to circumstances, of secluding himself and clearing up all his affairs. He called it having a clean up, or *faire la lessive*.[8] The morning after the races he woke late, and without having a bath or shaving he put on a linen tunic and, spreading out before him his money, his accounts, and his bills and letters, he set to work.

When Petritsky—who knew that on such occasions Vronsky was often cross—on waking saw his friend at his writing-table, he dressed quietly and went out without disturbing him.

Every one, knowing intimately all the complexities of his own

8. Doing the wash.

circumstances, involuntarily assumes that these complexities and the difficulty of clearing them up are peculiar to his own personal condition, and never thinks that others are surrounded by similar complexities. And so thought Vronsky. And not without some inward pride, nor without some justification, he reflected that any other man would long ago have got embroiled and been obliged to act badly if placed in a situation as difficult as his. But Vronsky felt that it was necessary for him to investigate his affairs just at that time in order to keep out of trouble.

He began by first attacking his money problems, as the easiest to deal with. Having noted down in his small handwriting on a piece of notepaper all he owed, he made up the account and found that it came to seventeen thousand and a few hundred roubles. Having struck out the odd hundreds in order to have a round sum, counted his money and looked over his bank-book, he found that he had 1800 roubles, and there was no prospect of receiving any more before the New Year. After reading over the list of his debts, he divided them into three classes, each of which he noted down separately. Under the first head came the debts that had to be paid at once, or the money for which had at any rate to be kept ready, so that they could be paid on demand without any delay. These debts came to about 4000 roubles: 1500 for a horse and 2500 he had incurred by standing security for his young comrade Venevsky, who in Vronsky's presence had lost that sum to a card-sharper. Vronsky had wished to pay at the time—he had the money with him—but Venevsky and Yashvin insisted that they would pay, and would not permit Vronsky, who had not even been playing, to do so. This was all very fine, but Vronsky knew that in this dirty business, his share in which was simply a verbal guarantee for Venevsky, he must have the 2500 roubles ready to throw to the sharper, and then have no more to do with him. So that for the first part of his debt he must have 4000 roubles ready. Eight thousand roubles under the second heading were less important: they were owing chiefly for the use of the racecourse stables, to the oats and hay-dealer, to the Englishman, to the saddler and others. In respect of these debts it was necessary to pay out 2000 roubles, in order to be quite secure.

The remaining debts were owing to shops, hotels, and to his tailor, and there was no need to trouble about them. So he needed 6000 roubles for immediate use, and had only 1800 roubles ready money. To a man with an income of 100,000 roubles a year, as everybody said Vronsky had, it would seem that such debts could not cause any difficulty, but the fact was that he was far from having the 100,000 roubles. His father's immense fortune, which alone brought in 200,000 a year, had not been divided between the brothers. When the elder brother, having a number of debts, married the Princess Varya Chirkova, the daughter of a penniless Decembrist,[9] Alexey gave up to his brother the income from his father's fortune, stipulating for only 25,000 roubles a year for himself. At that time Alexey told his brother that this would suffice for him till he married, which in all probability he never would do. And his brother, commanding one of the most expensive regiments, and newly married, could not refuse this gift. Their mother, who had her own private fortune, allowed Alexey about 20,000 roubles a year in addition to the 25,000 agreed upon, and Alexey spent it all. Latterly his mother, having quarrelled with him about his connection with Anna and his departure from Moscow, had stopped his allowance. Consequently Vronsky, who was in the habit of spending 45,000 roubles a year, having this year received only 25,000, found himself in difficulties. He could not ask his mother to help him out of them. Her last letter in particular had irritated him, for it contained hints that she was willing to help him to gain success in Society and in the service, but not to help him live in a manner that scandalized all good Society. His mother's wish to bribe him offended him to the bottom of his soul and increased his coldness toward her. Yet he could not go back on his generous promise, although, dimly foreseeing some eventualities of his connection with Anna, he felt that it had been too lightly given and that, even though unmarried, he might need the whole hundred thousand a year. But it was impossible to go back on it. He had only to remember his brother's wife and how that dear, excellent Varya at every opportunity showed him that she remembered his generosity and appreciated it, to realize the impossibility of withdrawing what he had given. It was as impossible as to beat a woman, to steal, or to tell a lie. There was only one possible and necessary way out of it, on which Vronsky decided without a moment's hesitation: to borrow ten thousand roubles from a money-lender, which he could easily do, to cut down his expenses, and to sell his racehorses. Having decided on this, he at once wrote a note to Rolandaki, who had more than once offered to buy his horses. Then he sent for the money-lender and the Englishman, and allotted what money he had among the different bills. Having finished this business he wrote a cold and abrupt reply to his mother. Then taking from his pocket-book three notes from Anna he re-read them, burnt them, and recalling a conversation he had had with her the evening before, fell into a reverie.

9. The Decembrists were those officers and others who in December 1825 conspired to secure a Constitution for Russia on the accession of Nicholas I. Some of them were executed, others were exiled to Siberia and their estates confiscated.

Chapter XX

Vronsky was particularly fortunate in that he had a code of rules which clearly defined what should and should not be done. This code covered a very small circle of conditions, but it was unquestionable, and Vronsky, never going beyond that circle, never for a moment hesitated to do what had to be done. The code categorically determined that though the card-sharper must be paid, the tailor need not be; that one may not lie to a man, but might to a woman; that one must not deceive anyone, except a husband; that one must not forgive an insult but may insult others, and so on. These rules might be irrational and bad but they were absolute, and in complying with them Vronsky felt at ease and could carry his head high. Only quite lately, in reference to his relations to Anna, had he begun to feel that his code did not quite meet all circumstances, and that the future presented doubts and difficulties for which he had no guiding principle.

His present relations to her and her husband were clear and simple to him. They were very clearly and exactly defined in the code of rules by which he was guided.

She was a respectable woman who had given him her love, and he loved her; therefore she was for him a woman worthy of as much or even more respect than a legitimate wife. He would have let his hand be cut off before he would have allowed himself by word or hint to insult her, or fail to show her all the respect that a woman can possibly desire.

His relations toward Society were also clear. Every one might know or suspect, but no one must dare to speak about the matter, or he was prepared to silence the speaker and make him respect the non-existent honour of the woman he loved.

His relations to her husband were simplest of all. From the moment that Anna gave him her love he considered his own right to her indefeasible. Her husband was only a superfluous person and a hindrance. No doubt he was in a pitiable position, but what was to be done? The only right the husband had was, weapon in hand, to demand satisfaction, and that Vronsky from the first was prepared to give him.

But latterly new inner relations had sprung up between himself and her, which frightened him by their indefiniteness. Only yesterday she had told him that she was pregnant, and he felt that this news and what she expected of him called for something that was not fully defined by his code of rules. He was taken by surprise, and at the moment when she told him of her condition his heart had suggested his proposal to her to leave her husband. He had made this proposal, but now, thinking it over, he saw clearly that it would be better to avoid that plan, and yet, while he told himself so, he feared that this might be wrong.

'When I told her to leave her husband, that meant that she should unite herself with me. Am I ready for that? How can I take her away now that I have no money? No doubt I could arrange that . . . but how could I go away with her while I am in the army? Having proposed it, I must be ready to carry it out—that is to say I must find the money and leave the army.'

He pondered. The question of whether to leave or not to leave the army led him to another private matter—almost the chief, though the secret, interest of his life.

Ambition was the old motive of his childhood and youth, one which he did not acknowledge even to himself, but which was so strong a passion that it now struggled against his love. His first steps in Society and in the service had been successful, but two years ago he had made a bad blunder. Wishing to show his independence and to get promotion, he had refused a post that was offered him, hoping that this refusal would enhance his value, but it turned out that he had been too bold and he was passed over. Having then perforce to assume the rôle of an independent character, he played it very adroitly and cleverly, as though he had no grudge against anyone, did not feel himself at all offended, and only wished to be left in peace to enjoy himself. In reality he had begun to feel dissatisfied about the time that he went to Moscow the year before.

He felt that the rôle of the independent man, who could have anything but wanted nothing, was beginning to pall, and that many people were beginning to think he could never do anything more than be an honest, good-natured fellow. His intrigue with Anna Karenina, which had caused such a sensation and attracted so much notice in Society, by investing him with fresh glamour had for a while quieted the worm of ambition that gnawed him, but a week ago that worm had reawakened with fresh vigour.

A playmate of his childhood, and his fellow-pupil at the Cadet Corps, Serpukhovskoy, who belonged to the same social circle, and who had finished the same year as himself and had been his rival in the classroom, at gymnastics, in mischief, and in ambitious dreams, had just returned from Central Asia, where he had gained two steps in official rank and had won a distinction rarely awarded to so young a General.[1]

As soon as he reached Petersburg people began to talk about him as a rising star of the first magnitude. Of the same age as Vronsky, and his messmate, Serpukhovskoy was already a General expecting an appointment that might have an influence on State affairs; while Vronsky, though independent and brilliant and beloved by

1. In 1873 the Central Asian khanate of Khiva was annexed by Russia by General Kaufman's conquest.

an enchanting woman, remained only a Cavalry Captain and was allowed to be as independent as he pleased. 'Of course I am not jealous and could not be jealous of Serpukhovskoy, but his promotion shows me that if one bides one's time the career of such a man as myself may be very quickly made. Three years ago he and I were in the same position. If I retire I burn my boats. By remaining in the service I lose nothing. She herself said that she did not want to change her position; and I, having her love, cannot envy Serpukhovskoy.' And slowly twisting his moustache he rose from the table and walked across the room. His eyes shone with peculiar brightness and he felt that firm, calm, and joyful mood which always came when he had cleared up the situation. Everything was clear and distinct, as after his former periodical stocktakings. He shaved, had a cold bath, dressed, and went out.

Chapter XXI

'I have come for you; your washing has taken a long time!' said Petritsky. 'Well, is it done?'

'Yes, it's done,' said Vronsky, smiling with his eyes and twirling the ends of his moustache as carefully as if, after the order he had established in his affairs, any too vigorous or rapid movement might upset it.

'After it, you always look as if you had come out of a Russian bath,' said Petritsky, 'and I have come straight from Gritska' (the name by which they called their Commanding Officer). 'They're expecting you.'

Vronsky looked at his comrade without answering, thinking about something else.

'Is that where the music is?' he said, listening to the familiar strains, now audible, of brass instruments playing polkas and waltzes. 'What's up?'

'Serpukhovskoy has arrived.'

'Ah! I did not know,' exclaimed Vronsky.

His smiling eyes shone still more brightly.

Having made up his mind that he was happy in his love, and having sacrificed his ambitions to it, or at any rate assumed that rôle, Vronsky could no longer feel envious of Serpukhovskoy nor vexed with him for not coming straight to see him on reaching the regiment. Serpukhovskoy was a good friend and he was glad that he would see him.

'I am very glad.'

Colonel Dëmin occupied a large country house, and the whole party were gathered together on the roomy verandah. In the grounds, what first met Vronsky's eyes were the soldier-singers in their white linen uniforms, standing beside a cask of vodka, then the jolly, healthy figure of the C.O. surrounded by his officers. Having come out on the top step of the verandah, he was gesticulating and above the noise of the band (which was playing a quadrille of Offenbach's) was loudly giving orders to some soldiers who were standing somewhat apart. A group of soldiers, a sergeant-major and some other non-commissioned officers, came up to the verandah at the same time as Vronsky. After returning to the table, the Commander again came forward with a glass of champagne in his hand and announced a toast: 'To the health of our late comrade, the gallant General, Prince Serpukhovskoy! Hurrah!'

Following the Commander, champagne glass in hand, Serpukhovskoy came down smiling:

'You are growing younger every day, Bondarenko!" he remarked to the ruddy-faced, smart-looking sergeant-major, serving for a second term, who stood just in front of him.

Vronsky had not seen Serpukhovskoy for three years. He had matured and had grown whiskers, but still had just as good a figure, and was just as striking—not so much for his good looks as for the delicacy and nobility of his face and bearing. One change Vronsky noticed in him was that quiet and permanent radiance which comes upon the faces of people who have succeeded and feel assured that everybody recognizes their success. Vronsky knew that kind of radiance, and noticed it at once on Serpukhovskoy's face.

As he was descending the steps Serpukhovskoy noticed Vronsky. A smile of joy lit up his face. He jerked his head backwards and raised his glass, welcoming Vronsky, and showing by this gesture that he must first go to the sergeant-major, who was already stretching himself and puckering his lips for a kiss.

'Ah, here he is!' exclaimed the Commander, 'and Yashvin told me that you were in one of your dismal moods.'

Serpukhovskoy kissed the smart-looking sergeant-major on his moist fresh lips and, wiping his mouth on his handkerchief, stepped up to Vronsky.

'Well, I am glad!' he said, taking him apart and pressing his hand.

'You look after him,' shouted the Commander to Yashvin, and went out to the soldiers.

'Why were you not at the races yesterday? I thought I should see you there,' asked Vronsky, examining Serpukhovskoy.

'I did come, but late. Excuse me!' he added, and turned to his adjutant. 'Please give orders to distribute this money equally among the men.'

He hurriedly took three one-hundred-rouble notes out of his pocket-book and blushed.

'Vronsky, will you eat something, or have a drink?' said Yashvin.

'Hey! Bring the Count something to eat! Here, drink this!'

The carousing at the colonel's house continued long.

They drank a great deal. Serpukhovskoy was lifted and tossed by
the officers. Then the C.O. was tossed. Then the C.O. danced with
Petritsky in front of the singers. After that, feeling rather weak, he
sat down on a bench in the yard and began demonstrating to
Yashvin Russia's superiority to Prussia, especially in cavalry charges,
and the carousal quieted down for a moment. Serpukhovskoy went
to the dressing-room to wash his hands, and found Vronsky there.
Vronsky had taken off his coat and was washing his hairy red neck
under the washstand tap, rubbing it and his head with his hands.
When he had finished his ablutions Vronsky sat down beside
Serpukhovskoy on a little sofa in the dressing-room and began a
conversation of great interest to both of them.

'I used to hear all about you from my wife,' said Serpukhovskoy.
'I am glad you saw a good deal of her.'

'She is friends with Varya, and they are the only women in
Petersburg whom it is a pleasure for me to meet,' said Vronsky
with a smile. He smiled because he foresaw the turn their conversation would take and was pleased.

'The only ones?' asked Serpukhovskoy, smiling.

'Yes, and I used to hear about you, but not only from your
wife,' said Vronsky, checking the hint by a serious look. 'I am very
glad of your success but not at all surprised. I expected even more.'

Serpukhovskoy smiled. Vronsky's opinion of him evidently gave
him pleasure and he saw no reason to hide it.

'I, on the contrary—I must frankly admit—expected less. But I
am pleased, very pleased; I am ambitious, it is my weakness, and
I acknowledge it.'

'Perhaps you would not if you were not successful,' said Vronsky.

'I do not think so,' and Serpukhovskoy smiled again. 'I do not
mean to say I could not live without it, but it would be a bore. Of
course I may be making a mistake, but I believe I have some capacity for the career I have adopted, and that in my hands power of
any kind, if I ever possess it, will be used in a better way than in
the hands of many whom I know,' said he with the radiant consciousness of success. 'Therefore the nearer I am to getting it the
more pleased I am.'

'It may be so for you, but not for every one. I used to think
the same, yet here I am living and find that it is not worth while
living for that alone,' said Vronsky.

'There you are! There you are!' said Serpukhovskoy, laughing. 'I
had begun by saying that I used to hear about you, about your
refusal. . . . Of course I approved of it. But there is a way of
doing a thing, and I think that, though your action was good

in itself, you did not do it in the right way.'

'What is done is done, and you know that I never go back on what I have done. Besides, I am quite all right.'

'All right for a time! But you will not remain satisfied for long. I should not say that to your brother. He is a dear child, just like this host of ours: hear him!' he added, listening to the cries of 'Hurrah!' 'And he is happy, but that would not satisfy you.'

'I do not say that it would.'

'And that is not all: men like you are wanted.'

'By whom?'

'By whom? By Society; by Russia. Russia is in need of men, needs a Party—without it everything is going and will go to the dogs.'

'What do you mean? Bertenev's Party, in opposition to the Russian Communists?'

'No,' said Serpukhovskoy, frowning with vexation at being suspected of such nonsense. '*Tout ça est une blague.*[2] It always has existed and always will. There are no Communists whatever. But scheming people always have invented and always will invent some harmful and dangerous Party. That's an old trick. What is wanted is an influential Party of independent men like you and me.'

'But why—' Vronsky named several influential men, 'why are not they independent men?'

'Only because they have not, or had not by birth, an independent position—had no name, were not born as near the sun as we were. They can be bought by money or by affability, and must invent a theory to keep their positions. And they bring forward some idea, some theory (in which they themselves do not believe and which does harm) merely as a means of procuring government quarters and a salary. *Cela n'est pas plus fin que ça* [3] if you happen to see their cards. Maybe I am worse and more foolish than they, though I do not see why I am worse than they. Anyhow you and I have one great advantage: we cannot be bought so easily. And such men are more needed than ever.'

Vronsky listened attentively, but it was not so much the meaning of Serpukhovskoy's words that interested him as his outlook on these questions, for Serpukhovskoy was already dreaming of a struggle with the powers-that-be and already had sympathies and antipathies in that sphere, whereas Vronsky's interest in the service was limited to his own squadron. Vronsky realized, too, how powerful Serpukhovskoy might become by his undoubted capacity for reflection and comprehension, and by his intellect and gift of speech, so seldom met with in the Society in which he lived. And, ashamed as he was of the fact, he felt jealous.

2. All that is humbug.
3. That's all there is in it.

'All the same I lack the most necessary thing,' he replied. 'I lack the wish for power. I had it once, but it is gone.'

'Pardon me, that is not true,' said Serpukhovskoy with a smile.

'Yes, it is, it is true . . . at present—to be quite frank,' added Vronsky.

'Yes, it is true at present—that is another matter, but the present will not last for ever.'

'Perhaps,' said Vronsky.

'You say "perhaps," ' continued Serpukhovskoy as if he had guessed Vronsky's thoughts; 'but I say, *certainly*. That is why I wanted to see you. You acted rightly: I quite understand it. But you must not persevere in it. I only ask you to give me *carte blanche*. I am not patronizing you. . . . Though why should I not patronize you? You have so often patronized me! I hope our friendship is above that sort of thing! Yes,' he said with a smile tender as a woman's, 'Give me *carte blanche*, leave the regiment, and I will draw you on imperceptibly.'

'But try to understand that I do want nothing except that everything should remain as it is,' said Vronsky.

Serpukhovskoy rose and said, as he stood before Vronsky, 'You say, "that all should remain as it is"! I know what you mean, but hear me! We are both of the same age; it may be that in number you have known more women than I have,' the smile of Serpukhovskoy's face and his gesture showed that Vronsky need have no fear, and that he would touch the tender spot gently and carefully. 'But I am married, and believe me, that "knowing only your wife, whom you love"—as somebody once said—"you can understand all women better than if you knew thousands." '

'We will come in a minute,' Vronsky shouted to an officer who looked in, having been sent by the C.O. to call them.

Vronsky was anxious now to hear the rest of what Serpukhovskoy had to say.

'Here is my opinion. Women are the chief stumbling-block in a man's career. It is difficult to love a woman and do anything else. To achieve it and to love in comfort and unhampered, the only way is to marry! How am I to put to you what I think?' and Serpukhovskoy, who was fond of similes, went on: 'Wait a bit! Wait a bit! . . . Yes, if you had to carry a load and use your hands at the same time, it would be possible only if the load were strapped on your back: and that is marriage. I found that out when I married. I suddenly had my hands free. But if you drag that load without marriage, your hands are so full that you can do nothing else. Look at Mazankov, at Krupov! They have ruined their careers because of women.'

'But what women!' said Vronsky, recalling the Frenchwoman

and the actress with whom these men were entangled.

'So much the worse! The more assured the position of the woman in the world, the worse it is! That is not like merely dragging a load with one's hands, it is like wrenching it from some one else.'

'You have never loved,' said Vronsky softly, with his eyes looking straight before him and with Anna in his thoughts.

'Perhaps not! But another point: women are always more materialistic than men. Men make of love something enormous, but women are always *terre-à-terre*.' [4]

'Coming, coming!' he said, turning to a footman who had entered. But the footman had not come to call them, as Serpukhovskoy thought. He brought Vronsky a note.

'Your man brought this from the Princess Tverskaya.'

Vronsky opened the note and his face flushed. 'My head has begun aching,' he said. 'I shall go home.'

'Well, then, good-bye! Do you give me *carte blanche*?'

'We'll talk it over another time. I will look you up in Petersburg.'

Chapter XXII

It was already past five, and in order not to be late and not to use his own horses, which were known to everybody, Vronsky took Yashvin's hired carriage and told the coachman to drive as fast as possible. The old four-seated hired vehicle was very roomy; he sat down in a corner, put his legs on the opposite seat, and began to think. A vague sense of the accomplished cleaning up of his affairs, a vague memory of Serpukhovskoy's friendship for him, and the flattering thought that the latter considered him a necessary man, and above all the anticipation of the coming meeting, merged into one general feeling of joyful vitality. This feeling was so strong that he could not help smiling. He put down his legs, threw one of them over the other, and placing his arm across it felt its firm calf, where he had hurt it in the fall the day before, and then, throwing himself back, sighed deeply several times.

'Delightful! O delightful!' he thought. He had often before been joyfully conscious of his body, but had never loved himself, his own body, as he did now. It gave him pleasure to feel the slight pain in his strong leg, to be conscious of the muscles of his chest moving as he breathed. That clear, cool August day which made Anna feel so hopeless seemed exhilarating and invigorating to him and refreshed his face and neck, which were glowing after their washing and rubbing. The scent of brilliantine given off by his moustache seemed peculiarly pleasant in the fresh air. All that he saw from the carriage window through the cold pure air in the pale

4. Matter-of-fact; down to earth.

light of the evening sky seemed as fresh, bright and vigorous as
he was himself. The roofs of the houses glittered in the evening
sun; the sharp outlines of the fences and corners of buildings, the
figures of people and vehicles they occasionally met, the motionless
verdure of the grass and trees, the fields of potatoes with their
clear-cut ridges, the slanting shadows of the houses and trees,
the bushes and even the potato ridges—it was all pleasant and like
a landscape newly painted and varnished.

'Get on, get on!' he shouted to the coachman, thrusting himself
out of the window; and taking a three-rouble note from his pocket
he put it into the man's hand as the latter turned round. The
coachman felt something in his hand, the whip cracked, and the
carriage rolled quickly along the smooth macadamized high road.

'I want nothing, nothing but that happiness,' he thought, staring
at the ivory knob of the bell between the front windows of the
carriage, his mind full of Anna as he had last seen her.

'And the longer it continues the more I love her! And here is the
garden of Vrede's country house. Where is she? Where? Why?
Why has she given me an appointment here, in a letter from
Betsy?' he thought; but there was no longer any time for thinking.
Before reaching the avenue he ordered the coachman to stop,
opened the carriage door, jumped out while the carriage was still
moving, and went up the avenue leading to the house. There was
no one in the avenue, but turning to the right he saw her. Her
face was veiled, but his joyous glance took in that special manner of
walking peculiar to her alone: the droop of her shoulders, the poise
of her head; and immediately a thrill passed like an electric current
through his body, and with renewed force he became conscious of
himself from the elastic movement of his firm legs to the motion of
his lungs as he breathed, and of something tickling his lips. On
reaching him she clasped his hand firmly.

'You are not angry that I told you to come? It was absolutely
necessary for me to see you,' she said; and at sight of the serious
and severe expression of her mouth under her veil his mood
changed at once.

'I angry? But how did you get here?'

'Never mind!' she said, putting her hand on his arm. 'Come, I
must speak to you.'

He felt that something had happened, and that this interview
would not be a happy one. In her presence he had no will of his
own: without knowing the cause of her agitation he became infected by it.

'What is it? What?' he asked, pressing her hand against his side
with his elbow and trying to read her face.

She took a few steps in silence to gather courage, and then suddenly stopped.

'I did not tell you last night,' she began, breathing quickly and heavily, 'that on my way back with Alexey Alexandrovich I told him everything . . . said I could not be his wife, and . . . I told him all.'

He listened, involuntarily leaning forward with his whole body as if trying so to ease her burden. But as soon as she had spoken he straightened himself and his face assumed a proud and stern expression.

'Yes, yes, that is better! A thousand times better! I understand how hard it must have been for you,' he said, but she was not listening to his words—only trying to read his thoughts from his face. She could not guess that it expressed the first idea that had entered Vronsky's mind: the thought of an inevitable duel; therefore she explained that momentary look of severity in another way. After reading her husband's letter she knew in the depths of her heart that all would remain as it was, that she would not have the courage to disregard her position and give up her son in order to be united with her lover. The afternoon spent at the Princess Tverskaya's house had confirmed that thought. Yet this interview was still of extreme importance to her. She hoped that the meeting might bring about a change in her position and save her. If at this news he would firmly, passionately, and without a moment's hesitation say to her: 'Give up everything and fly with me!' she would abandon her son and go with him. But the news had not the effect on him that she had desired: he only looked as if he had been offended by something. 'It was not at all hard for me—it all came about of itself,' she said, irritably. 'And here . . .' she pulled her husband's note from under her glove.

'I understand, I understand,' he interrupted, taking the note but not reading it, and trying to soothe her. 'I only want one thing, I only ask for one thing: to destroy this situation in order to devote my life to your happiness.'

'Why do you tell me this?' she said. 'Do you think I could doubt it? If I doubted it . . .'

'Who's that coming?' said Vronsky, pointing to two ladies who were coming toward them. 'They may know us!' and he moved quickly in the direction of a sidewalk, drawing her along with him. 'Oh, I don't care!' she said. Her lips trembled and her eyes seemed to him to be looking at him with strange malevolence from under the veil. 'As I was saying, that's not the point! I cannot doubt that, but see what he writes to me. Read—' she stopped again.

Again, as at the first moment when he heard the news of her having spoken to her husband, Vronsky yielded to the natural feeling produced by the thoughts of his relation to the injured husband. Now that he held his letter he could not help imagining to himself the challenge that he would no doubt find waiting for him that evening or next day, and the duel, when he would be standing with the same cold proud look as his face bore that moment, and having fired into the air would be awaiting the shot from the injured husband. And at that instant the thoughts of what Serpukhovskoy had just been saying to him and of what had occurred to him that morning (that it was better not to bind himself) flashed through his mind, and he knew that he could not pass on the thought to her.

After he had read the letter he looked up at her, but his look was not firm. She understood at once that he had already considered this by himself, knew that whatever he might say he would not tell her all that he was thinking, and knew that her last hopes had been deceived. This was not what she had expected.

'You see what a man he is!' she said in a trembling voice. 'He . . .'

'Forgive me, but I am glad of it!' Vronsky interrupted. 'For God's sake hear me out!' he added, with an air of entreaty that she would let him explain his words. 'I am glad because I know that it is impossible, quite impossible for things to remain as they are, as he imagines.'

'Why impossible?' said Anna, forcing back her tears and clearly no longer attaching any importance to what he would say. She felt that her fate was decided.

Vronsky wanted to say that after what he considered to be the inevitable duel it could not continue; but he said something else.

'It cannot continue. I hope that you will now leave him. I hope . . .' he became confused and blushed, 'that you will allow me to arrange and to think out a life for ourselves. To-morrow . . .' he began, but she did not let him finish.

'And my son?' she exclaimed. 'You see what he writes? I must leave him, and I cannot do that and do not want to.'

'But for heaven's sake, which is better? To leave your son, or to continue in this degrading situation?'

'Degrading for whom?'

'For everybody, and especially for you.'

'You call it degrading! do not call it that; such words have no meaning for me,' she replied tremulously. She did not wish him to tell untruths now. She had only his love left, and she wanted to love him. 'Try to understand that since I loved you everything has changed for me. There is only one single thing in the world for me: your love! If I have it, I feel so high and firm that nothing can be degrading for me. I am proud of my position because . . . proud of . . . proud . . .' she could not say what she was proud

of. Tears of shame and despair choked her. She stopped and burst
into sobs. He also felt something rising in his throat, and for the
first time in his life he felt ready to cry. He could not explain what
it was that had so moved him; he was sorry for her and felt that
he could not help her, because he knew that he was the cause of
her trouble, that he had done wrong.

'Would divorce be impossible?' he asked weakly. She silently
shook her head. 'Would it not be possible to take your son away
with you and go away all the same?'

'Yes, but all that depends on him. Now I go back to him,' she
said dryly. Her foreboding that everything would remain as it was
had not deceived her.

'On Tuesday I shall go back to Petersburg and everything will
be decided. Yes,' she said, 'but don't let us talk about it.'

Anna's carriage, which she had sent away and ordered to return
to the gate of the Vrede Garden, drove up. Anna took leave of
Vronsky and went home.

Chapter XXIII

On Monday the usual meeting of the Committee of the Second
of July took place. Karenin entered the Council room, greeted the
members and the president as usual, and took his seat, his hand
lying ready on the papers before him. Among these papers were
the statistics that he needed and a draft of the statement he was
going to make. But he did not really require the figures. He remembered them all and did not even consider it necessary to go
over in his mind what he was going to say. He knew that when
the time came, and he saw his opponent before him vainly trying
to look indifferent, his speech would naturally be far more fluent
and better than if he prepared it beforehand. He felt that the contents of his speech would be so important that every word would
be significant. Yet as he listened to the general reports his face
wore a most innocent and artless look. Looking at his white hands
with the thick veins and the delicate long fingers toying with the
two edges of a white sheet of paper before him, and at his head
wearily bent to one side, no one would have expected that words
would flow from his lips which would raise a terrible storm and
make the members shout each other down, forcing the president to
call them to order. When the Reports had been heard, Karenin in
his quiet thin voice informed the meeting that he wished to bring
to their notice some considerations of his own on the question of
the settlement of the native races, and the attention of the meeting turned to him. Karenin cleared his throat, and, as was his
wont when making a speech, without looking at his opponent he
fixed his eyes on the first man opposite him—a quiet little old man

who never had any views in connection with the Special Committee—and began to explain his considerations. When he came to the Fundamental and Organic Law his opponent jumped up and began to raise objections. Stremov (who was also on the Special Committee), stung to the quick, began justifying himself, and the meeting became quite a stormy one. But Karenin triumphed and his motion was carried; three new Special Committees were formed, and the next day nothing was talked about in a certain Petersburg set but that meeting. Karenin's success was even greater than he had expected.

When he woke on the Tuesday morning he recalled with pleasure his victory of the previous day, and could not help smiling, even while wishing to appear indifferent, when the secretary, with a desire to flatter him, reported the rumours that had reached him concerning what had happened at the meeting.

Busy with the secretary, Karenin quite forgot that it was Tuesday, the day fixed for Anna's return, and was surprised and unpleasantly startled when the footman came in to inform him of her arrival.

Anna returned to Petersburg early in the morning, and as she had wired that the carriage should be sent for her he might have expected her. But he did not come out to meet her when she arrived. She was told that he had not yet come out of his study, where he was busy with his secretary. She sent word to her husband that she had arrived and went to her boudoir, where she set to work sorting her things, expecting that he would come in to see her. But an hour passed and he did not come. She went down into the dining-room on a plea of giving orders and purposely spoke in a loud voice, thinking that he would come; but although she heard him go to his study door to take leave of the secretary, he did not come to her. She knew that according to his habit he would soon go away to his work and she wished to see him first, that their relations might be defined.

She passed through the ballroom to his study and resolutely went in. When she entered he was sitting in his official uniform evidently ready to start, with his elbows on a little table, looking wearily in front of him. She saw him before he saw her and knew that he was thinking about her.

When he saw her he was about to rise, but changed his mind as his face flushed—a thing Anna had never seen it do before. However, he quickly rose and came toward her, looking not at her eyes but at her forehead and hair. He came up, took her hand, and asked her to sit down.

'I am very glad you have come,' he said, sitting down beside her. He evidently wished to say something, but faltered. Several times he tried to speak, but stopped. Although while preparing for this interview she had been teaching herself to despise and blame him, she did not know what to say, and pitied him. There was silence for some time.

'Is Serezha well?' he asked; and without waiting for a reply he added, 'I am not dining at home to-day and must be going at once.'

'I meant to go away to Moscow,' she said.

'Oh no, you were quite right to come,' he replied, and again became silent. Seeing that he had not the strength to begin, she began for him.

'Alexey Alexandrovich!' she said, studying his face and without dropping her eyes under his gaze fixed on her hair, 'I am a guilty woman and a bad one, but I am what I was before, as I then told you. I have come to tell you now I cannot make any change.'

'I am not questioning you about it,' he replied suddenly in a firm tone and looking with hatred straight into her eyes. 'I had expected it.' Under the influence of anger he had evidently regained perfect self-possession. 'But I repeat again what I then told you and subsequently wrote,' he went on in a shrill thin voice, 'I again repeat that I will not know it; I ignore it as long as it is not known to the rest of the world, as long as my name is not dishonoured. Therefore I warn you that our relations must remain what they have been, and that if you let yourself be *compromised* I shall be obliged to take measures to safeguard my honour.'

'But our relations cannot be what they were before,' Anna began in a timid voice, looking at him with frightened eyes.

When she saw his quiet gestures, heard his shrill, childish, and sarcastic voice, her repulsion toward him destroyed the pity she had felt for him, and she now experienced nothing but fear and anxiety to clear up the situation at any cost.

'I cannot be your wife, since I . . .' she began.

He laughed in a cruel, cold manner. 'I suppose the kind of life you have chosen has affected your principles. I respect or despise both so much—I respect your past and despise your present—that the interpretation you give to my words was far from my thoughts!'

Anna sighed and hung her head.

'I cannot understand, however, that with your independent mind,' he went on, getting heated, 'informing your husband of your infidelity and appearing to see nothing unseemly in it, you should consider it unseemly to continue to fulfil a wife's duties to your husband!'

'Alexey Alexandrovich, what do you want of me?'

'What I want, is not to meet that person here, and for you to behave in such a way that neither Society nor the servants shall be able to accuse you,—for you not to see that man. I think that is not much to ask! And in return you will enjoy all the advantages of a wife without fulfilling her duties. That is all I have to say! Now I must be going. . . . And I shan't be back to dinner.' He rose and went toward the door. Anna too rose. He bowed silently and let her pass first.

Chapter XXIV

The night Levin had spent on the haycock had not passed without leaving its mark: he became disgusted with the agricultural pursuits on which he was engaged and lost all interest in them. In spite of the splendid harvest he had never, or thought he had never, encountered so many failures, or so much hostility from the peasants, as that year; and the cause of those failures and that hostility were now quite plain to him. The delight he had felt in the labour itself, occasioned by his having drawn nearer to the peasants, his jealousy of them, his envy of their life, his desire to adopt that kind of life (which had not been a mere desire that night but a real intention, the details of which he had considered), all these things together had so changed his outlook on the working of his estate that he could no longer feel his former interest in the work, or help noticing the unpleasant relation to the labourer on which it was all based. Herds of cattle of an improved breed like Pava, the tilled land ploughed with good ploughs, the nine fields surrounded with willows, the hundreds of acres of deeply manured land, the seed drills and all such things, were splendid if they could be worked by himself alone or with the help of friends and people in sympathy with him. But now he clearly saw (the book on agriculture which he was writing, in which the labourer was the chief factor in farming, helped much in this direction) that the agricultural work he was carrying on was founded on a bitter and obstinate struggle between himself and his labourers, in which on the one side—his —there was a continual and strenuous attempt to bring everything into accord with what were considered the best models, while on the other side there was the natural order of things. And he saw that in his struggle, in spite of extreme efforts on his part, and without any effort or even intention on the part of others, the only results achieved were that neither side was the winner, and that fine tools and splendid cattle and soil were quite uselessly damaged. But the chief point was that not only was the energy expended on the work wasted, but he could not help feeling now, when he saw the meaning of his pursuit laid bare before him, that the aim of his efforts was a most unworthy one. What was the essential cause of that hostility? He struggled to get every penny he could, and had to do so or he would not have been able to pay his labourers their wages, and they struggled to be allowed to work quietly, pleasantly, and just as they were used to work. It was to his interest that every labourer should get through as much work as possible and at the same time give his mind to it, not injuring the winnowing machine, the horse-rake, or the threshing machine, but working intelligently. The labourer wished to work in the pleasantest way possible, with intervals of rest, and especially to think unconcernedly about other things without having to reason. During that summer Levin noticed this continually.

He gave orders to mow the clover for hay, choosing the inferior fields overgrown with grass and hemlock and not fit for seed; and they cut down all the best seed clover, defended themselves by saying that the foreman ordered them to do it, and comforted him with the assurance that he would get splendid hay; while he knew that they had done it simply because that clover was easiest to mow. He sent out the horse-rake to turn the hay and it got broken while tossing the first few rows, because the peasant found it dull to sit in the seat under the rotating wings; and Levin was told: 'Don't worry, sir! The women will toss it all in no time!'

The English ploughs turned out useless, because it never entered the peasant's head to lift the ploughshares as he turned, and forcing them through at the turning he spoiled the ground and strained the horses; and Levin was told not to worry! The horses were allowed to stray into the wheat-field because not one of the peasants wanted to be watchman, and in spite of its having been forbidden the labourers took turns to watch the horses at night; so Vanka, who had been at work all day, fell asleep, and confessed his guilt, saying, 'I am in your hands, sir!'

Three of the best calves had been overfed by being turned into the meadow where the clover had been cut, without any water to drink; and the peasants would on no account admit that the clover had injured them. To comfort Levin he was told that his neighbour had lost a hundred and twelve head of cattle in three days. All this happened not because anyone wished to harm Levin or his farming; on the contrary he well knew that they liked him and considered him a plain gentleman—high praise from a peasant. It was done simply because the labourers wished to work merrily and without care, while his interests were not only foreign and incomprehensible to them but flatly opposed to their own just interests. Levin had long felt dissatisfied with his relation to the work on his estate. He had seen that the boat was leaking but had not found or looked for the leak, and perhaps had purposely deceived himself, for had he been disillusioned in that work, he would have had nothing left. But now he could deceive himself no longer.

His agricultural pursuits had not only ceased to interest him but had become repulsive, and he could no longer give his mind to them.

Added to this there was Kitty Shcherbatskaya not more than twenty miles away, and he wanted to meet her, yet could not. When he called on Dolly, she had asked him to come again and come with the object of once more proposing to her sister, letting him feel that her sister would now accept him. Levin himself having seen Kitty Shcherbatskaya knew that he had not ceased to love her, yet he could not go to the Oblonskys' house while she was there. That he had proposed and she had refused him had put an insuperable barrier between them.

'I cannot ask her to be my wife just because she cannot be the wife of the man she wanted,' he said to himself, and this thought rendered him cold and hostile toward her.

'I shall not have the strength to speak to her without reproach or to look at her without ill will, and she will only hate me all the more—as it is only right she should! Besides, how can I go there now after what Darya Alexandrovna told me? Can I help betraying what she told me? And I should come magnanimously to forgive her, to have pity on her! I—stand before her in the rôle of one who forgives her and honours her with his love! Why did Darya Alexandrovna tell me this? I might have met her accidentally and then all would have come naturally, but now it is impossible!'

Dolly sent to him to ask for a side-saddle for Kitty.

'I have been told,' she wrote, 'that you have a side-saddle. I hope you will bring it yourself.'

That was more than he could stand. 'How can an intelligent woman with any delicacy so humiliate a sister?' He wrote ten notes and tore them all up, sending the saddle at last without any reply. To say that he would come was impossible, because he could not come; to say that something prevented him from coming, or that he was leaving home, was still worse. He sent the saddle without an answer, conscious of doing something shameful; and next day, putting the disagreeable management of the estate into the hands of the steward, he went away to a distant district to visit his friend Sviyazhsky, who had splendid shooting and had long been asking him to come and stay with him.

The snipe marshes in the Surovsky district had for a long time appeared tempting to Levin, but he had put off his visit because of his farm-work. But now he was glad to go away from the proximity of Kitty and from his farm, and especially to go shooting, an occupation which served him as the best solace in all his troubles.

Chapter XXV

There was no railway or stage-coach to the Surovsky district, and Levin went in his own *tarantas*.

Half-way he stopped to feed his horses at a well-to-do peasant's house. The bald-headed, fresh-faced old man, with a red beard which was growing grey round the cheeks, opened the gates and pressed close to the post to let the three-horsed vehicle enter. After showing the coachman to a place in a lean-to, in a large, clean, tidy, newly-constructed yard where stood some charred wooden ploughs, the old man invited Levin to enter the house. A cleanly-dressed young woman with goloshes on her stockingless feet was washing the floor in the passage. The dog that followed Levin frightened her, but when she was told that it would not hurt her she at once began to laugh at her own alarm. After pointing to the door with her bare arm she again stooped, hiding her handsome face, and went on scrubbing.

'Want a samovar?' she asked.

'Yes, please.'

The room Levin entered was a large one with a tiled stove and a partition. Under the shelf with the icons stood a table decorated with a painted pattern, a bench, and two chairs. By the door stood a little cupboard with crockery. The shutters were closed and there were not many flies in the room, which was so clean that Levin took care to keep Laska (who had been bathing in the puddles on the way) from trampling on the floor, telling her to lie down in a corner by the door. Having looked round the room, he went out into the back-yard. The good-looking woman in goloshes, with two empty pails swinging from a wooden yoke, ran down before him to fetch water from the well.

'Look alive!' the old man called merrily after her, and approached Levin. 'Is it to Nicholas Ivanich Sviyazhsky you are going, sir? He too stops at our place,' he began garrulously, leaning on the banisters of the porch. In the midst of his conversation about his acquaintanceship with Sviyazhsky the gates creaked again, and the labourers returning from the fields came into the yard with their ploughs and harrows. The horses harnessed to the ploughs and harrows were big and well-fed. The labourers evidently belonged to the household. Two young fellows wore print shirts and peaked caps, two others were hired men and wore homespun shirts; one of these was old and the other young.

The old master of the house left the porch and went to unharness the horses.

'What have they been ploughing?' asked Levin.

'Between the potatoes. We too rent a little land. Don't let the gelding out, Fedof, lead him to the trough. We'll harness another.'

'I say, father! have those ploughshares I ordered been brought?' asked a tall, robust young fellow, evidently the old man's son.

'There in the passage,' answered the old man, winding the reins into a ring and throwing them on the ground. 'Fix them on before we finish dinner.'

The good-looking woman returned, her shoulders pressed down by the weight of the full pails, and went into the house. Other women, young and handsome, middle-aged, old and plain, some with children, others without, appeared from somewhere.

The chimney of the samovar began to hum. The labourers and the family, having attended to the horses, went in to dinner.

Levin took his provisions out of the *tarantas* and invited the old man to have tea with him.

'Why, I don't know! We have had tea once to-day,' said he, evidently pleased to accept the invitation. 'Well, just for company!'

Over their tea Levin heard the whole history of the old man's farm. Ten years previously he had rented about four hundred acres from the landowner, and the year before he had bought them outright and rented another nine hundred from a neighbouring proprietor. A small part of the land—the worst—he let, and with the aid of his family and two hired men cultivated about a hundred and twenty acres. The old man complained that his affairs were in a bad way. But Levin knew that he only did so for propriety's sake and that in reality his farm was flourishing. Had his affairs been in a bad way he would not have bought land at thirty-five roubles an acre, would not have married three of his sons and a nephew, and would not have twice rebuilt his homestead after fires, nor rebuilt it better each time. In spite of the old peasant's grumbling one could see that he was justly proud of his property, of his sons, his nephew, his daughters-in-law, his horses, his cows, and especially of the fact that his whole household and farm held together. From their conversation Levin gathered that he was not against new methods either. He had planted many potatoes which had already flowered and were forming fruit, as Levin had noticed when passing the fields on the way, while Levin's own potatoes were just beginning to flower. He ploughed the land for the potatoes with an English plough, which he had borrowed from a landowner. He also sowed wheat. Levin was struck especially by one little detail. The old peasant used the thinnings of the rye as fodder for the horses. Many a time when Levin had seen this valuable food wasted he had wanted to have it gathered up, but had found this impossible. On this peasant's fields this was being done, and he could not find words enough to praise this fodder.

'What is there for the young women to do? They carry the heaps out on to the road and a cart comes and fetches them.'

'There now! We landlords don't get on well because of the labourers,' said Levin, handing him a tumbler of tea.

'Thank you,' said the old man as he took the tea, but he refused sugar, pointing to a bit he still had left.⁵ 'How can one rely on work with hired labourers?' he said, 'it is ruination! Take Sviyazhsky now. We know what sort of soil his is, black as poppy-seed, but he cannot boast of his harvests either. It's want of attention.'

'And yet you too use hired labour on your farm?'

'Ours is peasant's business; we look after everything ourselves. If a labourer is no good, let him go! We can manage for ourselves.'

'Father, Finogen wants some tar fetched,' said the woman with the goloshes, coming in.

'That's how it is, sir,' said the old man, rising; and after crossing himself several times he thanked Levin and went out. When Levin went into the back room to call his coachman he found the whole peasant family at dinner. The women served standing. The vigorous young son with his mouth full of buckwheat porridge was saying something funny, and everybody laughed heartily—the woman with the goloshes laughing more merrily than anyone as she refilled the bowl with cabbage soup.

The handsome face of this woman with the goloshes might very well have had something to do with the impression of welfare that this peasant household produced on Levin; that impression was anyhow so strong that he never lost it. And all the rest of the way to Sviyazhsky's he every now and then recalled that household, as if the impression it had left on him demanded special attention.

Chapter XXVI

Sviyazhsky was Marshal of the Nobility in his district. He was five years older than Levin and had long been married. His young sister-in-law, whom Levin thought very pleasant, lived with them. He knew that both Sviyazhsky and his wife wanted to see her married to him, Levin. He knew this as certainly as all so-called eligible young men know these things, though he could never have said so to anyone; and he also knew that although he wanted to marry, and although this girl, to all appearance very fascinating, ought to make a splendid wife, he could as soon fly as marry her, even had he not been in love with Kitty. And this knowledge spoilt the pleasure which he hoped his visit to Sviyazhsky would give him.

Levin had thought of this when he received Sviyazhsky's invitation, but in spite of it he made up his mind that this idea of Sviyazhsky's intentions was only an unfounded conjecture of his and that he would go. Besides, at the bottom of his heart he wanted to put himself to the test and again to estimate his feelings for the girl. Sviyazhsky's home life was extremely pleasant, and Sviyazhsky himself was the best type of public-spirited landlord that Levin had

---

5. Russian peasants, for the sake of economy, seldom put sugar to dissolve in their tea, but take a lump and nibble it between their drinks of tea.

ever known, and Levin always found him very interesting.

Sviyazhsky was one of those people—they invariably amazed Levin—whose judgment was very logical though never original and was kept quite apart from their conduct, while their manner of life was very definite and stable, its tendency being quite independent of their judgment, and even clashing with it. Sviyazhsky was an extreme Liberal. He despised the gentry and considered the majority of noblemen to be secretly in favour of serfdom, and only prevented by cowardice from expressing their views. He considered Russia to be a doomed country like Turkey, and the Russian government so bad that he did not think it worth while seriously to criticize its actions; yet he had an official position, was a model Marshal of the Nobility, and when he travelled always wore a cockade and a red band to his cap. He imagined that to live as a human being was possible only in foreign countries, where he went to stay at every opportunity; yet he carried on very complicated and perfected agricultural pursuits in Russia and carefully followed and knew what was being done there. He considered the Russian peasant to be one degree higher than the ape in development, yet at district elections no one shook hands with the peasants and listened to their opinions more willingly than he. He believed in neither God nor Devil, yet he was much concerned by the question of improving the condition of the clergy and limiting parishes, and was at the same time particularly active in seeing that the church should be retained in his village.

On the Woman's Question he sided with the extreme advocates of woman's freedom and especially the right to work; yet he lived with his wife in such a way that it gave everybody pleasure to see the friendly relationship in which they passed their childless life, and had so arranged that his wife did nothing and could do nothing except share her husband's efforts to spend their time as pleasantly and merrily as possible.

Had Levin not possessed the faculty of giving the best interpretation to people's characters, Sviyazhsky's character would have presented no difficulty or problem to him; he would only have called him a fool or a good-for-nothing, and everything would have been clear. But he could not call him a fool, because Sviyazhsky was not only very intelligent but also a very well-educated man, who carried his education with extreme modesty. There was no subject with which he was not acquainted, but he only exhibited his knowledge when forced to do so. Still less could Levin call him a good-for-nothing, because Sviyazhsky was certainly an honest, kind-hearted, and clever man, always joyfully and actively engaged on work highly prized by all around, and certainly a man who could never consciously do anything bad.

Levin tried but could not understand him, and regarded him and his life as a living enigma.

The Sviyazhskys were friendly with Levin, and therefore he allowed himself to sound Sviyazhsky and try to get to the very foundation of his philosophy of life; but it was all in vain. Each time that Levin tried to penetrate deeper than the reception rooms of the other's mind, which were always open to anybody, he noticed Sviyazhsky seemed a little confused. A just perceptible look of fear appeared on his face, as if he were afraid that he would be understood by Levin, whom he met with good-natured, jocose resistance.

Now, after his disillusion with the work on his estate, Levin was especially pleased to stay a while with Sviyazhsky. Not to mention the fact that the sight of the happy doves in their well-ordered nest, so content with themselves and everybody else, had a cheering effect on him, he now wanted, dissatisfied with life as he was, to get at the secret which gave Sviyazhsky such clearness, definiteness, and cheerfulness.

Levin also knew that he would meet neighbouring landowners at the Sviyazhskys'; and it would be very interesting to talk and hear about farming, the harvest, the hire of labour, and all those questions which, though considered very low, seemed to him most important.

'These matters might not have been so important in the time of serfdom and may be unimportant in England. In these cases the conditions were or are settled; but with us everything has only just been changed, and is only beginning to settle down. The question of how things will settle down is the only important question in the whole of Russia,' thought Levin.

The shooting did not prove as good as he had expected. The marsh had dried up and there were hardly any snipe. He went about all day and only brought back three, but on the other hand he brought back, as he always did after a day's shooting, a splendid appetite, good spirits, and the stimulated mental condition which in his case always accompanied physical exertion. And when out shooting, while he did not seem to be thinking at all, he again and again thought about the old peasant and his family, and felt as if the impression made on him called not only for his attention, but for the solution of some problem related thereto.

In the evening at tea a very interesting conversation sprang up, just as Levin had expected, in the company of two landlords who had come about some guardianship business.

Levin sat beside the hostess at the tea-table, and was obliged to converse with her and her sister, who was sitting opposite him. The hostess was a short, fair, round-faced woman, beaming with smiles and dimples. Levin tried to find out through her the answer to the riddle, so important to him, presented by her husband; but he had not full freedom of thought because he felt painfully uncomfortable. This painful discomfort was due to the fact that her sister sat opposite to him in a dress that seemed to him to have been put on especially for his benefit, with a particularly low, square-cut decolletage showing her white bosom. Though her bosom was so white, or perhaps because it was so white, this squarecut deprived Levin of his freedom of thought. He imagined, probably quite mistakenly, that the bodice was cut like that on his account; he felt that he had no right to look at it and tried not to do so, but felt guilty because it was cut so. Levin felt as if he were deceiving some one, as if he ought to offer some explanation which was impossible, and therefore he kept blushing and was restless and uncomfortable. His discomfort communicated itself to the pretty sister, but the hostess did not seem to notice anything and purposely drew her sister into the conversation.

'You say,' the hostess continued, 'that my husband cannot feel an interest in anything Russian? On the contrary, though he is happy abroad, he is never so happy there as here. He feels in his own sphere. He is so busy, and he has a gift for taking an interest in everything. Oh! you have not been to see our school!'

'I saw it. . . . It is a little ivy-covered house?'

'Yes, that is Nastya's business,' she said, pointing to her sister.

'You yourself teach?' asked Levin, trying to look beyond the bodice, but conscious that if he looked in her direction he must see it.

'Yes, I have been and am still teaching, but we have a splendid mistress. And we have started gymnastics.'

'No thanks! No more tea,' said Levin, and unable to continue the conversation, though he knew he was behaving rudely, he got up blushing. 'I hear a very interesting conversation there,' he added, and went to the other end of the table where his host and the two landlords were sitting. Sviyazhsky sat sideways, leaning his elbow on the table and turning his cup round with one hand, while with the other he gathered his beard together, lifted it to his nose as if smelling it, and let it go again. He looked with his glittering black eyes straight at an excited landowner, with a grey moustache, whose words evidently amused him. The landowner was complaining about the peasants. Levin saw clearly that Sviyazhsky could have answered the landowner's complaint so that the meaning of the latter's words would have been destroyed at once, but owing to his position he could not give that answer, and listened not without pleasure to the landowner's funny speech.

This landowner with the grey moustache was evidently an inveterate believer in serfdom, and a passionate farmer who had lived long in the country.

Levin saw signs of this in the way the man was dressed—he wore an old-fashioned shiny coat which he was evidently not used to—and in his intelligent, dismal eyes, his well-turned Russian, his authoritative tone, evidently acquired by long practice, and in the firm movement of his fine large sunburnt hands, the right one having an old engagement-ring on the fourth finger.

Chapter XXVII

'If it were not a pity to give up what has been set going . . . after spending so much toil . . . I would throw it all up, sell out and, like Nicholas Ivanich, go away . . . to hear *La belle Hélène*,' said the landowner, a pleasant smile lighting up his wise old face.

'But we see you don't give it up,' said Nicholas Ivanich Sviyazhsky, 'so it seems it has its advantages.'

'Just one advantage: I live in my own house, which is neither bought nor hired. And there is always the hope that the people will come to their senses. You would hardly believe what drunkenness and debauchery there is! The families have all separated; they have not a horse nor a cow left. They are starving, yet if you hire one of them as a labourer, he'll spoil and break things, and will even lodge complaints with the magistrate.'

'On the other hand you, too, complain to the magistrate.'

'I complain? Never! Nothing could induce me to! It would cause such gossip that one would be sorry one tried it. At the works now they took money in advance, and went off. And what did the magistrate do? Why, acquitted them! Things are only kept going by the village tribunal and the village elder. He thrashes them in the old style. If it were not for that, one had better give up everything and flee to the ends of the earth.' The landowner evidently meant to tease Sviyazhsky, but the latter did not take offence; on the contrary, he evidently enjoyed it.

'Well, you see, we carry on our work without such measures, I and Levin and he,' Sviyazhsky said smiling, and pointing to the other landowner.

'Yes, Michael Petrovich gets on, but ask him how? Is his what you would call "rational" farming?' said the landowner, ostentatiously using the word 'rational.'

'My farming is very simple, thank heaven!' said Michael Petrovich. 'My farming is to have money ready for the autumn taxes. The peasants come along, and say, "Be a father to us! Help us!" Well, of course they are all our own people, our neighbours: one pities them, and lends them what they want, enough to pay the one-third then due, but one says, "Remember, lads! I help you, and you must help me when necessary—at the oat-sowing or hay-making or harvest time." And one agrees for so much work from each family. But it is true there are some dishonest ones among them.'

Levin, who had long been acquainted with these patriarchal methods, exchanged a glance with Sviyazhsky, and, interrupting Michael Petrovich, addressed the landowner with the grey moustache.

'How then, in your opinion, should one carry on at present?'

'Why, carry on the way Michael Petrovich does: either pay the peasants in kind, or rent it to them! That is quite possible but the wealth of the community as a whole is ruined by such methods. Where my land used to yield ninefold under serfdom with good management, it only now yields threefold when the labourers are paid in kind. Russia has been ruined by the emancipation of the peasants.'

Sviyazhsky looked at Levin with smiling eyes, and even made a just perceptible sarcastic sign to him ridiculing the old man, but Levin did not consider the landowner's words ridiculous, he understood him better than he did Sviyazhsky. Much of what the landowner said subsequently, to prove that Russia was ruined by the Emancipation, even appeared to him to be very true, new, and undeniable. The landowner was evidently expressing his own thoughts —which people rarely do—thoughts to which he had been led not by a desire to find some occupation for an idle mind, but by the conditions of his life: thoughts which he had hatched in his rural solitude and considered from every side.

'The fact of the matter is, you see, that progress can only be achieved by authority,' he said, evidently wishing to show that education was not foreign to him. 'Take, for instance, the reforms of Peter the Great, Catherine, and Alexander. Take European history. In the realm of agriculture it is still more so. To name only potatoes, they even had to be introduced by force into this country. Our primitive ploughs you know have not been always used. They must have been introduced at the time of the Rurik Princes, and doubtless by force. Now in our case we landlords under serfdom applied improved methods of agriculture: we introduced the winnowing machines and all sorts of tools, organized the carting of manure—all by our authority, and the peasants at first resisted and afterwards copied us. Now that serfdom has been abolished and the power taken out of our hands, our agriculture where it has been brought to a high level must descend to a savage and primitive condition. That is how I look at the matter.'

'But why? If your farming is rational you can carry it on with hired labour,' said Sviyazhsky.

'I have no power. By means of whose labour am I to carry it on?'

'Here we have it! The labour-power is the chief element of agriculture,' thought Levin.

'Hired labourers,' replied Sviyazhsky.

'Hired labourers don't want to work well with good tools. Our labourers understand one thing only: to get drunk like swine, and when drunk to spoil everything you put into their hands. They'll water the horses at the wrong time, tear good harness, change a wheel with an iron tire for one without, or drop a bolt into the threshing machine in order to break it. They hate to see anything that is beyond them. That is why the level of agriculture has gone down. The land is neglected, overgrown with wormwood or given to the peasants, and where a million bushels used to be produced they now only produce a hundred thousand. The wealth of the nation has decreased. If the same step had been taken with due consideration. . . .'

And he began to develop his plan of emancipation, which might have prevented this dislocation.

But it did not interest Levin, and, as soon as the landlord had finished, Levin returned to the first proposition, and, trying to get Sviyazhsky to express his views seriously, said to him:

'The fact that our agriculture is sinking, that it is impossible, our relation to the peasants being what it is, to carry on our rational farming profitably, is quite true.'

'I don't think so,' said Sviyazhsky, now quite serious. 'All I see is that we do not know how to farm, and that our farming in the days of serfdom was not at too high but on the contrary at too low a level. We have no machines, no good horses, no proper management and we do not know how to keep accounts. Ask any farmer; he cannot tell you what is profitable for you and what is not.'

'Italian bookkeeping!' said the landowner scornfully. 'Keep your accounts as you will—if they spoil everything you have got, you won't have a profit!'

'Why spoil everything? They will break your inferior Russian threshers, but they cannot break my steam threshing-machine. The poor Russian hack, what d'you call it? . . . of the breed that you have to drag along by the tail, can be spoiled; but if you keep Flemish drays or good Russo-Danish horses, they won't spoil them. And it's by such means that we must raise agriculture to a higher level.'

'Yes, if one can afford it, Nicholas Ivanich! It is all very well for you, but I have a son at the university to keep, and to pay for the little ones' education at the secondary school, so that I cannot buy Flemish drays.'

'We have got banks for such cases.'

'Yes, and finish by being sold up by auction! . . . No, thank you!'

'I do not believe that it is either advisable or possible to raise the level of agriculture,' said Levin. 'I go in for it, and have means, but I never could do anything. I do not know to whom banks are useful. I at any rate never spent money on improvements without loss. Expensive cattle bring me a loss, and machinery too.'

'Yes, that is quite true,' said the landowner with the grey moustache, and he even laughed with satisfaction.

'And I am not the only one,' continued Levin. 'I can refer you to many farmers who carry on rational farming, and with rare exceptions they all make a loss on it. You just tell us, is your farming profitable?' said Levin, and at once noticed a momentary expression of fright which he had observed before on Sviyazhsky's face when he tried to penetrate beyond the reception rooms of his mind. Besides, this question was not quite honest. His hostess had told him at tea that they had engaged that summer a German from Moscow, an expert bookkeeper, and paid him five hundred roubles to audit their accounts; and he found that they lost three thousand roubles odd a year on their farming. She did not remember the exact figure, though the German had calculated it down to a quarter of a kopeck.

The landowner smiled when the profits of Sviyazhsky's farming were mentioned, evidently aware of the sort of profits that his neighbour the Marshal of the Nobility was able to make.

'It may be unprofitable,' answered Sviyazhsky, 'but that only shows that I am either a bad farmer or that I spend capital to raise the rent.'

'Oh dear! The rent!' exclaimed Levin, quite horrified. 'There may be such a thing as rent in Europe, where the land has been improved by the labour put into it, but with us the land gets poorer by the labour put into it, that is, by being worked out. Therefore there can be no such thing as rent.'

'No rent? Rent is a natural law.'

'Then we are outside that law: rent does not explain anything in our case, but on the contrary only causes confusion. But you had better tell us how the theory of rent can be . . .'

'Would you like some curds and whey? Mary, send us some curds and whey or some raspberries here,' said Sviyazhsky to his wife. 'This year the raspberries are lasting an extraordinarily long time,' and Sviyazhsky got up cheerfully and moved away, evidently regarding the conversation as finished at the very point where to Levin it seemed to be just beginning.

Having lost his interlocutor Levin continued the conversation with the landowner, trying to prove to him that all our difficulties arise from the fact that we do not wish to understand the characteristics and habits of our labourers; but the landowner, like every-body who thinks individually and in solitude, was obtuse to other thoughts and tenacious of his own.

He insisted that the Russian peasant was a pig and loved piggish-ness, and that, to lead him out of the pigsty, authority was needed, but there was no such authority. A stick was necessary, but we had exchanged the thousand-year-old stick for some kind of lawyers and prisons, in which the good-for-nothing stinking peasants were fed with good soup and provided with a given number of cubic feet of air.

'Why do you think,' asked Levin, trying to bring him back to the question, 'that we could not establish some relation with labour which would make it remunerative?'

'It will never be done with Russians! We have no authority!' answered the landowner.

'What new conditions could be discovered?' said Sviyazhsky who, having eaten his curds and whey and lit a cigarette, now returned to the disputants. 'Every possible relation to the power of labour has been defined and investigated,' he said. 'The remnant of bar-barism, the primitive commune with its mutual guarantees, falls to pieces of itself, serfdom has been abolished, and there is nothing left but free labour; its forms are defined and ready and we must accept them. The labourer, the hired man, the farmer, you cannot get away from them.'

'But the rest of Europe is not satisfied with that system.'

'No, it is dissatisfied and it is seeking new methods. It will prob-ably find them.'

'All I wish to say is,' said Levin, 'why should we not seek them for ourselves?'

'Because it would be just the same as inventing new methods of building a railway. They are invented and ready.'

'But if they don't suit us? If they are stupid?' said Levin.

And again he noticed a look of fear in the eyes of Sviyazhsky.

'Oh yes, it is all child's play for us: we have discovered what Europe is looking for! I know all that, but excuse me, do you know what has been accomplished in Europe with regard to the labour question?'

'Not much.'

'The question is at present occupying the best brains in Europe. There is the Schulze-Delitzsch movement. . . . Then there is a whole gigantic literature on the labour question, with the most Liberal Lassalle tendency. . . . The Mulhausen system—that is already a fact. I expect you know about it.'

'I have some idea about it, but very vague.'

'Oh, you only say so, I am sure you know about it just as well as

I do! I am, of course, not a professor of Sociology, but it interests
me, and really if it interests you, you had better study the matter.'

'But what have they arrived at?'

'Excuse me . . .'

The landowners had risen, and Sviyazhsky, having again checked
Levin in his disagreeable habit of prying beyond the reception
rooms of his mind, went to see his visitor off.

Chapter XXVIII

Levin felt intolerably bored by the ladies that evening. He was
more than ever excited by the thought that the dissatisfaction with
work on the land which he now experienced was not an exceptional
state of mind, but the result of the condition of agriculture in
Russia generally, and that some arrangement that would make the
labourers work as they did for the peasant at the halfway-house was
not an idle dream but a problem it was necessary to solve. And he
felt that it could be solved, and that he must try to do it.

Having said good-night to the ladies and promised to stay a
whole day longer in order to ride with them and see an interesting
landslide in the State forest, Levin before going to bed went to his
host's study to borrow the books on the labour question which
Sviayazhsky had offered him. Sviyazhsky's study was an enormous
room lined with book-cases. There were two tables in it, one massive writing-table, the other a round one on which lay a number
of newspapers and journals in different languages, arranged like the
rays of a star round the lamp in the centre. Beside the writing-table
was a stand with gold-labelled drawers containing various business
papers.

Sviyazhsky got down the books and settled himself in a rocking-
chair.

'What is it you are looking at?' he asked Levin, who, having
stopped at the round table, was looking at one of the journals.

'Oh, there is a very interesting article there,' he added, referring
to the journal Levin held in his hand. 'It turns out that the chief
agent in the Partition of Poland was not Frederick at all,' he added
with gleeful animation. 'It turns out . . .'

And with characteristic clearness he briefly recounted these new
and very important and interesting discoveries. Though at present
Levin was more interested in agriculture than in anything else, he
asked himself while listening to his host, 'What is there inside
him? And why, why does the Partition of Poland interest him?' And
when Sviyazhsky had finished he could not help asking him, 'Well,
and what of it?' But Sviyazhsky had no answer to give. It was interesting that 'it turns out,' and he did not consider it necessary to explain *why* it interested him.

'Yes, and I was greatly interested by that cross old landowner,' said Levin with a sigh. 'He is intelligent and said much that is true.'

'Oh, pooh! He is secretly a rooted partisan of serfdom, like all of them!' said Sviyazhsky.

'Whose Marshal you are . . .'

'Yes, but I marshal them in the opposite direction,' said Sviyazhsky, laughing.

'What interests me very much is this,' said Levin: 'he is right when he says that our rational farming is not a success and that only money-lending methods, like that quiet fellow's, or very elementary methods, pay, . . . Whose fault is it?'

'Our own, of course! but it is not true that it does not pay. Vasilchikov makes it pay.'

'A factory. . . .'

'I still cannot understand what you are surprised at. The people are on so low a level both of material and moral development that they are certain to oppose what is good for them. In Europe rational farming answers because the people are educated; therefore we must educate our people—that's all.'

'But how is one to educate them?'

'To educate the people three things are necessary: schools, schools, schools!'

'But you yourself just said that the people are on a low level of material development: how will schools help that?'

'Do you know, you remind me of the story of the advice given to a sick man: "You should try a laxative."—"I have, and it made me worse." "Try leeches."—"I have, and they made me worse." "Well, then, you had better pray to God."—"I have, and that made me worse!" It is just the same with us. I mention political economy; you say it makes things worse. I mention Socialism; you say, "still worse." Education? "Worse and worse."'

'But how will schools help?'

'By giving people other wants.'

'Now that I never could understand,' replied Levin, hotly. 'How will schools help the peasants to improve their material conditions? You say that schools and education will give them new wants. So much the worse, for they won't be able to satisfy them. And in what way knowing how to add and subtract and to say the catechism will help them to improve their material condition, I never could understand! The other evening I met a woman with an infant in her arms and asked her where she was going. She replied that she had been to see the "wise woman" because her boy had convulsions, and she took him to be cured. I asked her what cure the wise woman had for convulsions. "She puts the baby on a perch among the fowls and says something." '

'Well, there is your answer! Education will stop them from carrying their children to the roosts to cure them of convulsions,' said Sviyazhsky with a merry smile.

'Oh, not at all!' said Levin, crossly. 'That treatment seems to me just a parallel to treating the peasants by means of schools. The people are poor and ignorant, this we know as surely as the woman knows that the child has convulsions because it screams. But why schools should cure the ills of poverty and ignorance is just as incomprehensible as why hens on their perches should cure convulsions. What needs to be cured is their poverty.'

'Well, in this at least you agree with Spencer, whom you dislike so much; he too says that education may result from increased well-being and comfort—from frequent ablutions, as he expresses it—but not from the ability to read and reckon . . .'

'Well, I am very glad, or rather very sorry, that I coincide with Spencer; but it is a thing I have long known. Schools are no remedy, but the remedy would be an economic organization under which the people would be better off and have more leisure. Then schools would come.'

'Yet all over Europe education is now compulsory.'

'And how do you agree with Spencer yourself in this matter?'

A frightened look flashed up in Sviyazhsky's eyes and he said with a smile:

'Yes, that cure for convulsions is splendid! Did you really hear it yourself?'

Levin saw that he would not succeed in finding a connection between this man's life and his thoughts. It was evidently all the same to him what conclusions his reasoning led to: he only needed the process itself, and he did not like it when the process of reasoning led him up a blind alley. That he disliked and evaded by turning the conversation to something pleasantly jocular.

All the impressions of that day, beginning with the impression of the peasant at the halfway-house which seemed to serve as a foundation for all the other impressions and ideas, agitated Levin greatly. There was this amiable Sviyazhsky, who kept his opinions only for social use, and evidently had some other bases of life which Levin could not discern, while with that crowd, whose name is legion, he directed public opinion by means of thoughts foreign to himself; and that embittered landowner with perfectly sound views he had wrung painfully from life, but wrong in his bitterness toward a whole class, and that the best class in Russia; and Levin's own discontent with his own activity, and his vague hope of finding a remedy for all these things—all this merged into a feeling of restlessness and expectation of a speedy solution.

Left alone in the room assigned to him, and lying on a spring mattress which bounced unexpectedly whenever he moved a leg or an arm, it was long before Levin could sleep. Not one of the talks he had with Sviyazhsky, though much that was clever had been said by the latter, interested him; but the landowner's arguments required consideration. Levin involuntarily remembered all that the man had said, and corrected in imagination the answers he himself had given.

'I ought to have said to him: "You say that our farming is not a success because the peasants hate all improvements and that these should be introduced by force; and if farming did not pay at all without these improvements, you would be right. But it succeeds where and only where (as in the case of the man at the halfway-house) the labourers act in conformity with their habits. Your and our common dissatisfaction with farming shows that we, and not the peasants, are at fault. We have long pushed on in our own way—the European way—without considering the nature of the labour force available. Let us consider the labourer not as an abstract labour force but as a Russian peasant with his own instincts, and let us arrange our farming accordingly. Imagine!" I ought to have said to him,"that your farming is conducted like that old man's: that you have found means to interest the labourers in the results of their work, and have found improvements which they must recognize as such—then, without impoverishing the soil, you will get double and treble the crops you get now. Divide equally and give half the produce to labour, and the share left for you will be larger, and the labour force will receive more. And to do this we must lower the level of cultivation and give the peasants an interest in its success. How this can be done is a question of details, but it is certainly possible." '

This thought strongly excited Levin. He lay awake half the night considering the details necessary for carrying his thought into effect. He had not meant to leave next day, but now decided to go away early in the morning. Moreover there was the sister-in-law with the square-cut bodice, who occasioned in him a feeling akin to shame and repentance caused by the commission of a bad action. Above all he had to get away immediately to propose his new plan to the peasants before the winter corn was sown, so that that work might be done on the new conditions. He decided completely to reverse his former methods of farming.

Chapter XXIX

The carrying out of Levin's plans presented many difficulties, but he struggled with all his might and attained if not all he desired, at any rate a possibility of believing without self-deception that the

thing was worth doing. One of the chief difficulties was that the
farming was actually going on and it was impossible to stop it all
and start afresh; so that the machine had to be altered while it
was working.

When, on the evening of his return, he informed the steward of
his intentions, the steward with evident pleasure agreed with that
part of the plan which showed that all that had been done up to
then was foolish and unprofitable. He remarked that he had always
said so but had not been listened to. But to Levin's proposal that
he, like the peasants, should participate as a shareholder would in
the farming, the steward only put on a look of great depression and
expressed no definite opinion, but at once began to speak of the
necessity of carting the last sheaves of rye next day and of starting
the second ploughing; so that Levin felt that it was not the time
for his plans to be considered.

When speaking of the matter to the peasants and offering
them land on the new conditions. Levin again met with the same
difficulty; they too were so fully occupied with the labour of the
day that they had no time to consider the advantages and dis-
advantages of the venture.

The naïve peasant, the cowman Ivan, quite understood Levin's
offer of letting him and his family have a share in the profits of
the dairy farm, and quite sympathized with this undertaking: but
when Levin impressed upon him the benefit that would accrue to
him in the future, a look of anxiety and regret that he could not
stop to listen to it all appeared on Ivan's face, and he hurriedly
remembered some task that could not be put off, seized a hay-fork
to remove the hay from the enclosure, fetched water, or cleared
away the manure.

Another stumbling-block was the peasant's invincible mistrust of
the possibility of a landlord having any other aim than that of
robbing them as much as possible. They were firmly convinced
that his real aim (whatever he might say) would always be hidden
in what he did not tell them. And they themselves, when they
talked, said much, but never said what they really wanted. Besides
all this (Levin felt that the splenetic landowner was right), the
peasants put as the first and unalterable condition in any agreement,
that they should not be obliged to use any new methods or new
kinds of tools for their work. They agreed that a Western plough
ploughed better, that a cultivator worked quicker, but they found a
thousand reasons why they could not use either the one or the
other; and, though he was convinced that it would be necessary to
lower his standards of farming, he disliked having to give up
improvements the benefit of which was so clear. Yet in spite of all
these difficulties he got his way and by autumn the scheme began

to work, or at any rate it seemed so to him.

At first Levin thought of letting the whole of his farm as it stood to the peasants, to the labourers, and to his steward, on the new co-partnership lines, but he very soon saw that this was impossible and decided to divide up the different parts. The cattle-yard, the fruit and vegetable gardens, the meadows and the corn-fields, divided into several parts, should come under different sections. The naïve Ivan, who, it seemed to Levin, best understood the plan, formed an *artel* [6] consisting chiefly of his own family, and became partner in the dairy section. The far field that had lain fallow for eight years was, with the aid of the intelligent carpenter Theodore Rezunov, taken up by six peasants' families on the new co-operative lines, and the peasant Shuraev rented the vegetable gardens on similar terms. The rest remained as before; but these three sections were the beginning of a new order, and fully occupied Levin.

It is true that the dairy farm did not as yet go on any better than before, and Ivan strongly opposed heating the cowsheds and making butter from fresh cream, maintaining that cows required less food when kept in the cold and that butter made from sour cream went further; and that he expected his wages to be paid as before, not being at all interested to know that they were not wages but an advance on account of profits.

It was true that Theodore Rezunov's group did not plough the corn land twice with the English plough as they had agreed to do, pleading lack of time. It was true that the peasants of that group, though they had agreed to farm the land on the new conditions, did not speak of it as co-operatively held land, but as land held for payment in kind; and that the members of that group and Rezunov himself said to Levin: 'If you would only accept money for the land it would be less trouble for you, and we should feel freer.' Moreover, these peasants, on all sorts of pretexts, kept putting off the building of the cattle-sheds and granary they had agreed to put up on this land, and dragged the matter on till winter.

It was true that Shuraev had taken steps to sublet the kitchen garden in small lots to the other peasants; he evidently quite misunderstood, and apparently intentionally misunderstood, the conditions on which the land was let to him.

It was true that often when talking to the peasants, and explaining to them the advantages of the plan, Levin felt that they were only listening to the sound of his voice and were quite determined, whatever he might say, not to let themselves be taken in. He felt this especially when talking to the most intelligent

---

6. An *artel* was a workman's profit-sharing association with mutual responsibility, then common in Russia.

of them, Rezunov, and noticing the play in his eyes, which clearly indicated his derision of Levin and a firm resolve that if anyone was taken in it should not be Rezunov.

But in spite of this, Levin thought matters were getting on, and that by keeping strict accounts and insisting on having his way he would eventually be able to prove to the peasants the advantage of these new arrangements, and that things would then go on of themselves.

These affairs added to the rest of the farming which remained on his hands, and the indoor work on his book, so filled Levin's whole summer that he hardly ever made time to go out shooting. At the end of August he heard from a servant who brought back the side-saddle that the Oblonskys had gone back to Moscow. He felt that by not having answered Dolly Oblonskaya's letter (a rudeness he could not remember without blushing) he had burned his boats and could never visit there again. He had treated the Sviyazh-skys just as badly, having left their house without saying good-bye. But neither would he ever visit them again. That made no difference to him now. The rearrangement of his farming interested him more than anything had ever done in his life. He read through the books lent him by Sviyazhsky, and, having ordered various others that he required, he read books on political economy and socialistic books on the same subject, but, as he had expected, he found nothing in them related to his undertaking. In the works on political economy—in Mill for instance, which he studied first and with great ardour, hoping every moment to find a solution of the questions that occupied him—he found various laws deduced as governing the state of agriculture in Europe, but he could not see why these laws, inapplicable to Russia, should be considered universal! It was the same with the socialistic books: they were either beautiful but inapplicable fancies which had carried him away when he was still at the university, or they were improvements and patchings-up of the order existing in Europe, with which agricultural affairs in Russia have nothing in common. Political economy maintained that the laws by which the wealth of Europe had developed and is developing are universal and unquestionable laws. The socialistic teaching declared that development on those lines leads to ruin. But neither the one set of books nor the other so much as hinted at explaining what Levin, and all the Russian peasants and landowners with their millions of hands and acres, should do to make them as productive as possible for the general welfare.

Having taken up this question he conscientiously read everything relating to it; and he purposed going abroad in the autumn to study the question further there, so that what had often happened to him with other questions should not be repeated. Often, just as he was beginning to understand the idea in his interlocutor's mind and to explain his own, he would suddenly be asked: And what about Kauffmann and Jones, and Dubois and Michelli? Have you not read them? You should do so: they have elucidated the question!

He now clearly saw that Kauffmann and Michelli had nothing to tell him. He knew what he wanted. He saw that Russia had splendid soil and splendid labourers, and that in some cases (such as that of the peasant at the halfway house) the labourers and land produced much: but that in the majority of cases, when capital was expended in the European way, they produced little, and that this happened simply because the labourers are only willing to work and work well, in the way natural to them, and that their opposition was not accidental but permanent, being rooted in the spirit of the people. He thought that the Russian people whose mission it is to occupy and cultivate enormous unoc-cupied tracts of land, deliberately, as long as any land remains unoccupied, kept to the methods necessary for that purpose and that those methods are not at all as bad as is generally thought. This he wanted to prove theoretically in his book and practically by his farming.

Chapter XXX

By the end of September the timber for the cattle-yard to be fenced in on the land let to the peasant-group was carted, the butter was all sold and the profits divided. Everything on the estate was going well practically, at least Levin thought so. To elucidate matters theoretically and to finish his book, which, ac-cording to his dreams, would not only revolutionize political econ-omy but completely abolish that science and lay the foundation of a new science (that of the relation of the people to the land) it was only necessary to go abroad and there study what had been done on the subject and find convincing proofs that what had been done there was not what was needed. Levin was only waiting for the wheat to be delivered and to get paid for it, before leaving for abroad. But rain set in, making it impossible to get in what re-mained of the corn and potatoes, stopped all the work, and even prevented the delivery of the wheat. The mud made the roads impassable: two mills had been carried away by floods, and the weather was getting worse and worse.

On the thirtieth of September the sun showed itself in the morning, and, in hopes of fine weather, Levin began seriously preparing for his departure. He gave orders that the grain was to be got ready for carting and sent the steward to the merchant to collect the money for the wheat, while he himself went round to give final instructions before leaving.

Having got through all his business, soaked by the streams of water that had run in at the neck of his leather coat and at the top of his high boots, but in the most buoyant and animated spirits, he returned home in the evening. The weather grew still worse toward evening, and the frozen sleet beat the whole body of his drenched horse so painfully that it shook its head and ears and went sideways. But Levin under his hood felt comfortable; he looked cheerfully round, now at the turbid streams that ran down the ruts, now at the drops that hung from every bare twig, now at the white spots of unthawed sleet that lay on the planks of the bridge or on the heaps of still juicy willow leaves lying in a thick layer round a denuded tree. Notwithstanding the gloomy aspect of nature around him he felt peculiarly elated. His conversation with the peasants of the outlying village showed that they were beginning to get used to the new conditions. An old inn-keeper, into whose house he had gone to dry himself, evidently approved of Levin's plan and had offered to join a group to buy cattle.

'I need only push on steadily toward my aim and I shall achieve it,' he thought, 'and it is worth working and striving for. It is not a personal affair of my own but one of public welfare. The whole system of farming, and above all the position of the people, must be completely altered: instead of poverty—wealth and satisfaction for all; instead of hostility—concord and a bond of common interest. In a word—a revolution bloodless but immense; first in our own small district, then throughout the province, throughout Russia, and the whole world—for a good thought must be fruitful. Yes, it is an aim worth working for! The fact that the author of it is myself Constantine Levin, who once went to a ball in a black tie, whom Kitty Shcherbatskaya refused, and who seems so pitiful and insignificant to himself, proves nothing. I feel sure that Franklin [7] felt just as insignificant and distrusted himself just as I do when he remembered his past. All that does not matter. He too probably had an Agatha Mikhaylovna to whom he confided his secrets.'

With such thoughts Levin reached home when it was already dark.

The steward, having been to the merchant, had returned bringing an instalment of the money for the wheat. An arrangement had been made with the innkeeper, and the steward, while away, had learnt that the corn had nowhere been got in, so that Levin's hundred and sixty stacks still in the fields were a trifle compared to what others were losing.

Having dined, Levin as usual sat down in his easy-chair with a

7. Tolstoy admired Benjamin Franklin and recommended that his works be published in a mass edition in Russia.

book, and while reading continued to think about his impending journey in connection with the book he was writing. To-day the importance of his work presented itself to him with especial clearness, and whole paragraphs of their own accord shaped themselves in his mind, expressing the gist of his thoughts. 'I must write that down,' thought he. 'That must form a short preface, such as I formerly considered unnecessary.' He rose to go to his writing-table, and Laska, who was lying at his feet, stretched herself, also got up, and looked round at him as if asking where she was to go to. But he had no time to write his thoughts down, for the peasants' foremen had come, and Levin went into the hall to speak to them.

After arranging about the next day's work by seeing the peasants who had come on business, Levin went to his study and sat down to his work. Laska lay down under the table, and Agatha Mikhaylovna with her knitting sat down in her usual place.

Having written for some time, Levin suddenly with particular vividness remembered Kitty, her refusal, and their last meeting. He rose and began to pace up and down the room.

'What is the use of fretting?' said Agatha Mikhaylovna. 'Why do you always sit at home? You should go to a watering-place now that you have got ready.'

'So I shall: I am going the day after to-morrow, Agatha Mikhaylovna, only I must finish my business.'

'Eh, what is your business? Have you not done enough for the peasants as it is! Why, they are saying, "Your master will get a reward from the Tsar for it!" And it is strange: why should you bother about the peasants?'

'I am not bothering about them: I am doing it for myself.'

Agatha Mikhaylovna knew all the details of Levin's farming plans. He often laid bare his thoughts before her in all their details, and frequently argued with her and disagreed with her explanations. But this time she quite misunderstood what he said.

'Of course one must think of one's soul before everything else,' she remarked with a sigh. 'There was Parfen Denisich, who was no scholar at all, but may God grant everyone to die as he did!' she said, referring to a servant who had died recently: 'he received Holy Communion and Extreme Unction.'

'I am not speaking about that,' he said. 'I mean that I am doing it for my own profit. My gains are bigger when the peasants work better.'

'But whatever you do, an idler will always bungle. If he has a conscience he will work, if not, you can do nothing with him.'

'But you yourself say that Ivan looks after the cattle better now.'

'I only say,' answered Agatha Mikhaylovna, evidently not speaking at random but with strict sequence of thought, 'you must marry, that is all!'

Her mention of the very thing he was just thinking about grieved and hurt him. He frowned, and without replying again sat down to his work, repeating to himself all that he had been thinking about its importance. Only occasionally, in the stillness, he listened to the clicking of her needles and, remembering what he did not wish to remember, made a wry face.

At nine o'clock he heard the sound of a bell and the heavy lurching of a carriage through the mud.

'There now! Visitors have come to you,' said Agatha Mikhaylovna, rising and going toward the door. 'Now you won't feel dull.' But Levin overtook her. His work was not getting on now and he was glad of a visitor, whoever it might be.

Chapter XXXI

Halfway to the front door Levin heard a familiar sound of coughing in the hall, but the noise of his own footsteps prevented his hearing it clearly and he hoped he was mistaken. Then he saw the whole of his brother's long, bony, familiar figure, and it seemed that there could be no mistake, but he still hoped he was mistaken and that this tall man, who was taking off his overcoat and coughing, was not his brother Nicholas.

Levin was fond of his brother but to be with him was always a torment. Under the sway of the thoughts that had come to him and of Agatha Mikhaylovna's reminders, he was in an unsettled and confused state of mind and the forthcoming meeting with his brother seemed particularly distressing. Instead of a cheerful, healthy stranger who, he hoped, would have diverted him from his mental perplexity, he had to meet his brother, who knew him through and through and would disturb his innermost thoughts and force him to make a clean breast of everything. And that was what he did not desire.

Angry with himself for this bad feeling Levin ran into the hall; and as soon as he had a near view of his brother his feeling of disappointment vanished and was replaced by pity. Dreadful as his emaciation and illness had previously made Nicholas, he was now still thinner and weaker than ever. He was a mere skeleton covered with skin.

He stood in the hall jerking his long, thin neck, drawing a scarf from it, and smiling in a strangely piteous manner. When he saw this meek, submissive smile, Levin felt his throat contract convulsively.

'There! I *have* come to see you,' said Nicholas in a hollow voice, without taking his eyes for an instant from his brother's face. 'I have long wanted to, but did not feel well. Now I am much better,' and he wiped his beard with the thin palms of his hands.

'Yes, yes!' answered Levin. He was still more terrified, when, kissing his brother's face, his lips felt the dryness of the skin and he saw his large strangely brilliant eyes close at hand.

Some weeks before this Constantine Levin had written to tell his brother that, after the sale of a few things which till then had remained undivided, Nicholas was entitled to his share, which came to about 2000 roubles.

Nicholas said that he had now come to fetch that money, but chiefly to visit his own nest and touch his native soil, in order like the heroes of old to gather strength from it for the work that lay before him. In spite of the fact that he was more round-shouldered than ever and that, being so tall, his leanness was startling, his movements were quick and sudden as formerly. Levin took him to his room.

Nicholas changed his clothes, a thing he never used to do, brushed his thin, straight hair and went smiling upstairs.

He was in a most affectionate and cheerful mood, such as Levin remembered his often being in as a child: and he even mentioned Sergius Ivanich without irritation. When he met Agatha Mikhaylovna he joked with her and questioned her about the other old servants. The news of Parfen Denisich's death affected him strangely. A look of fear appeared on his face but he immediately recovered himself.

'After all, he was old,' he remarked and changed the subject. 'Well, I will spend a month or two with you and then I will go to Moscow. D'you know, Myagkov has promised me a post and I am entering the Civil Service. I will now arrange my life quite differently,' he continued. 'You know, I have got rid of that woman?'

'Mary Nikolaevna? Why, what for?'

'Oh, she was a horrid woman! She has caused me a lot of unpleasantness,' but he did not say in what the unpleasantness consisted. He could not explain that he had turned Mary Nikolaevna away because she made his tea too weak, and chiefly because she waited on him as on an invalid.

'Besides, I want to alter my life completely. Of course, like everybody else, I have done stupid things, but property is the least consideration and I don't regret mine. Health is the great thing, and my health, thank God, has improved.'

Levin listened, trying but unable to think of what to say. Nicholas probably felt the same; he began questioning his brother about his affairs, and Levin was glad to talk about himself because he could do so without any pretence. He told Nicholas of his plans and activities.

Nicholas listened but evidently was not interested.

These two men were so near akin and so intimate with one an-

other, that between them the least movement or intonation expressed more than could be said in words.

At present the same thought filled both their minds and dominated all else: Nicholas's illness and approaching death. But neither
of them dared speak of it, and not having expressed the one
thing that occupied their thoughts, whatever they said rang false.
Never before had Levin felt so glad when an evening was over and
it was time to go to bed. Never had he been so unnatural and
artificial, even with an outsider or when making a formal call, as
he was that day. And his consciousness of this artificiality and
the remorse he felt for it made him more unnatural. He wished to
weep over his dear, dying brother, but had to listen and keep up a
conversation about how Nicholas was going to live.

The house being damp, and only his bedroom heated, Levin put
his brother to sleep behind a partition in that room.

Nicholas went to bed but, whether he slept or not, kept tossing
and coughing like a sick man and, when unable to clear his throat,
muttering some complaint. Sometimes he sighed deeply and said,
'Oh, my God!' Sometimes, when the phlegm choked him, he
muttered angrily, 'Oh, the devil!' Levin long lay awake listening
to him. His thoughts were very various, but they all led up to
death.

Death, the inevitable end of everything, confronted him for
the first time with irresistible force. And that Death which was
present in his dear brother (who, waking up, moaned and by habit
called indiscriminately on God and on the devil) was not so far
away as it had hitherto seemed to be. It was within himself too—
he felt it. If not to-day, then to-morrow or thirty years hence,
was it not all the same? But what that inevitable Death was, he
not only did not know, not only had never considered, but could
not and dared not consider.

'I am working, I want to do something, and I had forgotten
that it will all end in Death!'

He sat on his bed in the dark, doubled his arms round his
knees and thought, scarcely breathing from the mental strain. But
the more mental effort he made the clearer he saw that it was
undoubtedly so: that he had really forgotten and overlooked one
little circumstance in life—that Death would come and end everything, so that it was useless to begin anything, and that there was
no help for it. Yes, it was terrible, but true.

'But I am still alive: what am I to do now? What am I to do?'
he said despairingly. He lit a candle, got up carefully, went to the
looking-glass, and began examining his face and hair. Yes! There
were grey hairs on his temples. He opened his mouth: his back
teeth were beginning to decay. He bared his muscular arms. Yes, he

was very strong. But Nicholas, who was breathing there with the remains of his lungs, had once had a healthy body too; and he suddenly remembered how as children they used to go to bed together and only waited till Theodore Bogdanich had left the room to throw pillows at one another and to laugh and laugh so irrepressibly that even the fear of Theodore Bogdanich could not stop that overflowing bubbling consciousness of the joy of living. 'And now that sunk and hollow chest. . . . And I, who do not know what will happen to me, or why . . .'

'Kha, kha! Oh, the devil! What are you fidgeting for! Why don't you sleep?' his brother's voice called to him.

'Oh, I don't know, just sleeplessness.'

'And I have slept well; I don't perspire now. See, feel my shirt, it's not damp!'

Levin felt it, returned behind the partition, and put out the candle, but was long unable to sleep. Just when the question of how to live had become a little clearer to him, a new insoluble problem presented itself—Death.

'Well, he is dying, he will die before spring. How can he be helped? What can I say to him? What do I know about it? I had forgotten there was such a thing!'

Chapter XXXII

Levin had long ago noticed that after people have made one uncomfortable by their pliancy and submissiveness they soon become unbearably exacting and aggressive. He felt that this would happen with his brother. And really Nicholas's meekness did not last long. The very next morning he grew irritable and cavilled at everything his brother said, touching his most sensitive spots.

Levin felt guilty but could do nothing. He felt that if they both spoke without dissimulation and straight from the heart, they would only look into one another's eyes and Constantine would say nothing but, 'You will die! You will die!' and Nicholas would only say in reply: 'I know I shall die and I am afraid, afraid, afraid!' That was all they would say if only they spoke straight from the heart. But that would make life impossible; therefore Constantine tried to do what all his life he had tried and never known how to do (although he had often observed that many people were able to do it well), something without which life was impossible: he tried to say something different from what he thought; and he felt all the time that it sounded false and that his brother detected him and grew irritable.

On the third day of his stay Nicholas challenged his brother to explain his plans to him once more, and not only found fault with them but purposely confused them with communism.

'You have only taken an idea from others, and distorted it, and you wish to apply it where it is inapplicable.'

'But I tell you that the two things have nothing in common! Communists deny the justice of property, capital, or inheritance, while I do not deny that main stimulus' (it was repulsive to Levin to find himself using such words, but since he had been engrossed in his work he had involuntarily begun using more and more foreign words), 'but want only to regulate labour.'

'That is it. You have taken other people's idea, dropped all that gave it force, and wish to make one believe that it is something new,' said Nicholas, angrily jerking his neck.

'But my idea has nothing in common . . .'

'That idea,' said Nicholas Levin with a sarcastic smile and angrily glistening eyes, 'that idea at any rate, if one may say so, has a geometric charm of definiteness and certainty. It may be utopian; but granting the possibility of making a *tabula rasa* [8] of the past—and abolishing private property and families—then labour comes by its own. But you have nothing . . .'

'Why do you muddle it? I was never a communist.'

'But I have been, and now I think it is premature but reasonable, and that it has a future as Christianity had in the first centuries.'

'I only think that the force of labour must be dealt with in a scientifically experimental manner. It must be studied and its characteristics . . .'

'But that is quite unnecessary! That force finds its own form of activity in accord with its degree of development. There used to be slaves everywhere, then *metayers*;[9] and we have labour paid in kind, and renters, and hired labour: so what are you looking for?'

At these words Levin suddenly grew warm, for at the bottom of his heart he felt that it was true—true that he wished to balance between communism and the existing forms of life, and that this was hardly possible.

'I am seeking for a way of making labour profitable for me and for the labourers,' he answered hotly. 'I want to establish . . .'

'You do not want to establish anything. You simply want to be original, as you always have done, and to show that you are not just exploiting the peasants, but have ideas!'

'You think so? Well, then, leave me alone!' said Levin, and he felt that a muscle was uncontrollably quivering in his left cheek.

'You have no convictions and never had any; you only want to flatter your self-esteem.'

'Well, all right! But leave me alone.'

'I will, and high time too! You can go to the devil! And I am sorry I came!'

8. Clean slate.
9. Farmers who have use of land on condition they give half of the produce to the owner.

However much Levin tried afterwards to pacify his brother, Nicholas would not listen to it, but said that it was much better for them to part. And Levin saw that life had become simply intolerable for his brother.

Nicholas had quite made up his mind to go. Constantine came to him again and in an unnatural manner asked his forgiveness if he had offended him in any way.

'Ah, this is magnanimity!' said Nicholas, and smiled. 'If you wish to be in the right, I can let you have that pleasure. You are in the right: but all the same I shall go away.'

Only just before he left, Nicholas kissed Constantine, and suddenly said with a strange and serious look at his brother, 'Do not think too badly of me, Kostya!' and his voice trembled.

These were the only sincere words that had passed between them. Levin understood that they were meant to say, 'You see that I am in a bad way, and perhaps we shall not meet again.' He understood this, and tears trembled in his eyes. He again kissed his brother, but he did not know what to answer.

Three days after his brother's departure Levin left for abroad. He surprised young Shcherbatsky, Kitty's cousin, whom he happened to meet at a railway station, by his moroseness.

'What is the matter with you?' asked Shcherbatsky.

'Nothing much, but there is little to be happy about in this world.'

'Little? You'd better come to Paris with me instead of going to some Mulhausen or other. You'll see how jolly it will be!'

'No, I have done with that; it is time for me to die.'

'That is a fine thing!' said Shcherbatsky, laughing. 'I am only preparing to begin to live.'

'Yes, I thought so too till lately; but now I know that I shall soon die.'

Levin was saying what of late he had really been thinking. He saw death and the approach of death in everything; but the work he had begun interested him all the more. After all, he had to live his life somehow, till death came. Everything for him was wrapped in darkness; but just because of the darkness, feeling his work to be the only thread to guide him through that darkness, he seized upon it and clung to it with all his might.

Part IV

Chapter I

The Karenins, husband and wife, continued to live in the same house and to meet daily, but they were wholly estranged. Karenin made it a rule to see his wife every day, so as not to give the servants any grounds for making conjectures, but he avoided dining at home. Vronsky never came to the Karenins' house, but Anna met him elsewhere and her husband knew it.

The situation was a torment to all three, and not one of them could have stood it for a single day but for the hope that it would change and that the whole matter was only a temporary, though painful trial. Karenin expected the passion to pass, as everything passes; all would be forgotten and his name not dishonoured. Anna, who was responsible for the situation, and for whom among the three it was most painful, bore it because she not only expected, but felt sure, that very soon everything would be settled and cleared up. She had not the least idea what would settle it, but was quite certain that it would not come very soon. Involuntarily submitting to her judgment, Vronsky too expected something, not dependent on him, to clear up all these difficulties.

In the middle of the winter he spent a very dull week. He had been chosen to act as guide to a foreign Prince, and was obliged to show him the sights of Petersburg. Vronsky had a distinguished appearance, possessed the art of carrying himself with respectful dignity, and was in the habit of associating with people of that class. That was why he was chosen to attend the Prince; but the task seemed a hard one to him. The Prince did not want to miss seeing anything about which he might be questioned at home and he also wanted to enjoy as many Russian amusements as possible; and Vronsky was obliged to accompany him in both cases. In the mornings they went sight-seeing, and in the evenings took part in the national amusements. The Prince enjoyed unusually good health even for a Prince, and by means of gymnastics and care of his body had developed his strength to such a degree that, in spite of the excess he indulged in when amusing himself, he looked as fresh as a big green shining cucumber. He had travelled a great deal, and considered that one of the chief advantages of the present convenient ways of communication was the easy access they afforded to national amusements. He had been to Spain, where he arranged serenades and became intimate with a Spanish woman who played the mandoline. In Switzerland he had shot a chamois, in England he had jumped hedges in a pink coat and shot two hundred pheasants for a bet. He had been in a harem in Turkey, ridden an elephant in India, and now in Russia he wanted a taste of distinctive Russian amusements.

Vronsky, who was, so to say, the Prince's chief master of ceremonies, had great difficulty in organizing all the Russian amusements offered to the Prince by various people: trotting-races, pancakes, bear-hunting, and drives in three-horse sledges, gypsies, and Russian sprees with smashing of crockery. And the Prince imbibed the Russian spirit with the greatest ease, smashed trays full of crockery, made gypsy girls sit on his lap, and yet seemed to be always asking: 'What next? Is this the whole of the Russian spirit?'

But, on the whole, of all the Russian amusements the Prince liked the French actresses, a ballet girl, and white-seal champagne best. Vronsky was used to Princes, but whether it was that he himself had lately changed, or whether his intimacy with this Prince was too close, that week at any rate appeared very wearisome to him. All that week he felt like a man attending a lunatic and afraid for his own reason too. He was obliged to be on his guard the whole time not to deviate from the path of severe official respect, for fear of being insulted. The Prince's manner toward the very people who, to Vronsky's astonishment, were ready to go through fire and water to provide Russian amusements for him, was contemptuous. His opinion of Russian women, whom he wanted to study, more than once made Vronsky flush with indignation.

But the chief reason why the Prince's presence oppressed Vronsky was that he saw himself reflected in the Prince, and what he saw in that mirror was not flattering to his vanity. The Prince was a very stupid, very healthy and very cleanly man—and nothing more. He was a gentleman, it is true, and Vronsky could not deny it. He was quiet and not cringing with those above him, free and simple with his equals, and contemptuously good-natured with his inferiors. Vronsky was the same, and considered it very meritorious to be so, but in his relations with the Prince he was the inferior and felt indignant with that condescendingly good-natured treatment.

'Stupid ox! Can I really be like that myself?' he thought.

However this may have been, he parted from the Prince (who went on to Moscow) and received his thanks. Vronsky was very pleased to be rid of the embarrassing situation and the unpleasant mirror. He took leave of him at the railway station on the seventh day, on returning home from a bear-hunt, after which there had been demonstrations of Russian 'prowess' all night.

Chapter II

On returning home Vronsky found a note from Anna awaiting him. She wrote, 'I am ill and unhappy. I cannot go out, neither can I go on any longer without seeing you. Come this evening; Alexey Alexandrovich is going to the Council at seven and will remain there till ten.' After wondering for a moment at the strangeness of her asking him straight out to come to her house in spite of her husband's injunctions, he decided to go.

He had that winter been promoted to the rank of colonel, had left the regiment, and was living alone. Immediately after lunch he lay down on the sofa. Five minutes later the memory of the disreputable scenes at which he had been present during the last few days became jumbled and connected with pictures of Anna and a peasant who had played an important part as a beater at the bear-hunting; and Vronsky fell asleep. He woke up in the dark trembling with fear, and hurriedly lit a candle. 'What has happened? What horrors I dreamt! Yes, yes, the peasant, the beater—I think he was small and dirty with a tangled beard—was stooping down and doing something or other, and suddenly began to say strange words in French. That is all there was in that dream,' he thought. 'But why did it seem so terrible?' He vividly recalled the peasant and the incomprehensible words that the man had uttered, and a shudder of terror ran down his back. 'What nonsense!' he thought, glancing at his watch. It was already half-past eight.

He rang for his valet, dressed hurriedly, and went out into the porch, having quite forgotten his dream and feeling worried only by the fact that he was late. As he drove up to the Karenins' porch he again glanced at his watch and saw that it was ten minutes to nine. A high narrow brougham with a pair of grey horses stood before the front door. 'She was coming to me,' thought Vronsky; that would have been better. It is unpleasant for me to enter this house. But no matter! I cannot hide,' he thought; and with the manner, habitual to him since childhood, of one who has nothing to be ashamed of, Vronsky got out of his sledge and went to the door. The door opened and the hall porter with a rug over his arm called to the coachman. Vronsky, though not in the habit of noticing details, noticed the look of surprise on the man's face. In the doorway he nearly knocked up against Karenin. The gas-light lit up Karenin's worn, bloodless face beneath the black hat, and his white tie showing from beneath the beaver collar of his overcoat. His dull, expressionless eyes were fixed on Vronsky's face. Vronsky bowed, and Karenin silently moved his lips, lifted his hand to his hat, and went out. Vronsky saw him get into the carriage without looking round, take the rug and a pair of opera-glasses through the carriage window; then he disappeared in the darkness. Vronsky entered the hall. His brows were knit and his eyes shone with a proud, angry light.

'That is a nice position!' he thought. 'If he struggled, if he defended his honour, I could act and could express my feelings; but this weakness or meanness. . . . He puts me in the position of an imposter—which I did not and do not mean to be.'

Since the explanation with Anna in the Vrede Gardens Vronsky's ideas had changed. Involuntarily submitting to Anna's weakness, who, ready in advance to accept anything, gave herself up to him entirely and expected him to decide her fate, he had long ceased to imagine that their union could end in the way he had then expected. His ambitious plans had receded to the background, and feeling that he had come out of the range of activity in which everything was definite, he completely gave himself up to his passion, and that passion bound him closer and closer to her.

While still in the hall he heard her retreating footsteps, and knew that she had been waiting and listening for him, but had now gone back to the drawing-room.

'No!' she cried when she saw him, and at the first sound of her voice tears filled her eyes. 'No! If things go on like this for long, it will happen much, much sooner!'

'What, my dear?'

'What! I wait in torment, one hour, two hours. . . . No, no! I won't! . . . I cannot quarrel with you. I expect you could not help it. No, I won't!'

She put both her hands on his shoulders and gazed at him long, with a deep look of ecstasy and yet searchingly. She scrutinized his face to make up for the time she had not seen him. She compared, as she did at every interview with him, the image her fancy painted of him (incomparably finer than, and impossible in, actual existence) with his real self.

Chapter III

'You met him?' she asked when they sat down at a table under the lamp. 'This is your punishment for being late.'

'Yes, but how did it happen? He had to be at the Council!'

'He had been and had come back, and afterwards went somewhere else. But never mind: don't speak about it. Where have you been? With the Prince all this time?'

She knew all the details of his life. He wished to say that he had been up all night and had fallen asleep, but seeing her excited and happy face he felt ashamed. So he said that he had to go and report the Prince's departure.

'But now that is all over? He has gone?'

'Yes, thank heaven! That is all over. You would hardly believe how intolerable it was.'

'Why? Is it not the kind of life all you young men lead?' she said, frowning; and taking up her crochet-work from the table began disentangling the hook without looking at Vronsky.

'I have long since abandoned that kind of life,' he said, wondering at the change in her face and trying to penetrate its meaning. 'And I must own,' he went on, smiling and showing his compact row of teeth, 'that I seem to have been looking in a

mirror the whole of this week while watching that kind of life, and
it was very unpleasant.' She held her work in her hands, without
crocheting, gazing at him with a strange, glittering, unfriendly
look.

'Lisa called on me this morning; they still visit me in spite of
the Countess Lydia Ivanovna,' she said, 'and she told me about
your Athenian party. How disgusting!'

'I was only going to say that . . .'

She interrupted him.

'It was Thérèse, whom you knew before?'

'I was going to say . . .'

'How horrid you men are! How is it that you can forget that a
woman cannot forget these things?' she said, getting more and
more heated and thereby betraying the cause of her irritation.
'Especially a woman who cannot know your life. What do I know?
What did I know? Only what you tell me. And what proof have I
that you tell me the truth?'

'Anna, you hurt me. Don't you believe me? Have I not told
you that I have not a thought that I would hide from you?'

'Yes, yes!' she said, evidently trying to drive away her jealous
thoughts. 'But if you only knew how hard it is for me! I believe
you, I do believe you. . . . Well, what were you going to say?'

But he could not at once remember what he had wished to say.
These fits of jealousy which had lately begun to repeat themselves
more and more frequently, horrified him and, however much he
tried to hide the fact, they made him feel colder toward her, although he knew that the jealousy was caused by love for him.
How often he had told himself that to be loved by her was happiness! and now that she loved him as only a woman can for whom
love outweighs all else that is good in life, he was much further
from happiness than when he had followed her from Moscow.
Then he thought himself unhappy, but happiness was all in the
future; now he felt that the best happiness was already in the past.
She was not at all such as he had first seen her. Both morally
and physically she had changed for the worse. She had broadened
out, and as she spoke of the actress there was a malevolent look on
her face which distorted its expression. He looked at her as a man
might look at a faded flower he had plucked, in which it was
difficult for him to trace the beauty that had made him pick and so
destroy it. Yet in spite of this he felt that though at first while his
love was strong he would have been able, had he earnestly desired
it, to pull that love out of his heart—yet now when he imagined,
as he did at that moment, that he felt no love for her, he knew
that the bond between them could not be broken.

'Well, what were you going to tell me about the Prince? I have driven away the demon,' she added. They spoke of jealousy as 'the demon.' 'Yes, what had you begun telling me about the Prince? What was it you found so hard to bear?'

'Oh, it was intolerable!' he said, trying to pick up the lost thread of what he had in his mind. 'He does not improve on nearer acquaintance. If I am to describe him, he is a finely-bred animal like those that get prizes at cattle-shows, and nothing more,' he concluded in a tone of vexation, which awoke her interest.

'Oh, but in what way?' she rejoined. 'Anyhow he must have seen much, and is well educated. . . .'

'It is quite a different kind of education—that education of theirs. One can see that he has been educated only to have the right to despise education, as they despise everything except animal pleasures.'

'But don't all of you like those animal pleasures?' she remarked, and he again noticed on her face that dismal look which evaded his.

'Why do you take his part so?' he said, smiling.

'I don't take his part, and it is a matter of complete indifference to me, but I should say that as you did not like these pleasures you might have declined to go. But it gives you pleasure to see Thérèse dressed as Eve . . .'

'Again! Again the demon!' said Vronsky, taking the hand which she had put on the table, and kissing it.

'Yes, but I can't help it! You don't know how I have suffered while waiting for you! I don't think I have a jealous nature. I am not jealous; I trust you when you are here near me; but when you are away, living your life, which I don't understand . . .'

She turned away from him and, managing at last to disentangle her hook, with the aid of her forefinger, began to draw the stitches of white wool, shining in the lamplight, through each other, the delicate wrist moving rapidly and nervously within her embroidered cuff.

'Well, and what happened? Where did you meet Alexey Alexandrovich?' she suddenly asked, her voice ringing unnaturally.

'I knocked up against him in the doorway.'

'And he bowed like this to you?' She drew up her face, half closed her eyes and quickly changed the expression of her face, folding her hands; and Vronsky saw at once upon her beautiful face the very look with which Karenin had bowed to him. He smiled, and she laughed merrily, with that delightful laughter from the chest which was one of her special charms.

'I can't at all understand him,' said Vronsky. 'Had he after your explanation in the country broken with you, had he challenged me, yes! But this sort of thing I do not understand. How can he put up with such a position? He suffers, that is evident.'

inability to communicate as downfall?

'He?' she said, sarcastically. 'He is perfectly contented.'

'Why are we all tormenting each other when everything might be so comfortable?'

'But not he! As if I did not know him, and the falsehood with which he is saturated! . . . As if it were possible for a man with any feeling to live as he is living with me! He understands and feels nothing. Could a man of any feeling live in the same house with his guilty wife? Could he talk to her and call her by her Christian name?' And without meaning to, she again mimicked him: 'Ma chère Anna; my dear!'

'He is not a man, not a human being. He is . . . a doll! No one else knows it, but I do. Oh, if I were he, I should long since have killed, have torn in pieces, a wife such as I, and not have called her "Ma chère Anna." He is not a man but an official machine. He does not understand that I am your wife, that he is a stranger, a superfluous . . . But don't let us talk about him.'

'You are unjust, unjust my dear,' said Vronsky, trying to pacify her. 'But still, don't let us talk about him. Tell me what you have been doing? What is the matter with you? What is that illness of yours? What does the doctor say?'

She looked at him with quizzical joy. She had evidently remembered other comical and unpleasant sides of her husband's character and waited for an opportunity to mention them.

He continued:

'I expect it is not illness at all, but only your condition. When is it to be?'

The mocking light in her eyes faded, but a smile of a different kind—the knowledge of something unknown to him, and gentle sadness—replaced the former expression on her face.

'Soon, soon. You were saying that our position was full of torment and should be put to an end. If you only knew how hard it is on me! What would I not give to be able to love you freely and boldly! I should not be tortured, I would not torment you with my jealousy. . . . It will happen soon, but not in the way we think.' And at the thought of how it was going to happen she felt so sorry for herself that the tears came into her eyes and she could not continue. She laid her hand, sparkling with rings and the whiteness of the skin, on his sleeve.

'It will not happen as we think. I did not want to tell you, but you make me do it. Soon, very soon, everything will get disentangled and we shall be able to rest and not torment each other any more.'

'I do not understand,' he said, though he did understand.

'You were asking when? Soon, and I shall not survive it. Don't interrupt,' she said hurriedly. 'I know it, and know it for certain.

I shall die, and I am very glad that I shall die: I shall find deliver-ance and deliver you.'

The tears ran down her cheeks; he stooped over her hand and began kissing it, trying to hide the emotion which he knew to be groundless, but could not master.

'That is right, that is better,' she said, firmly pressing his hand. 'This is all, all that remains to us.'

He recovered and lifted his head.

'What rubbish, what senseless rubbish you are talking!'

'No, it is not! It is true.'

'What is true?'

'That I am going to die; I have had a dream.'

'A dream?' Vronsky instantly remembered the peasant of his dream.

'Yes, a dream,' she said. 'I dreamed it a long time ago. I thought I had run into my bedroom, that I had to fetch or find out something there: you know how it happens in dreams,' and her eyes dilated with horror. 'And in the bedroom there was some-thing standing in the corner.'

'Oh, what nonsense! How can one believe? . . .'

But she would not allow him to stop her. What she was saying was of too much importance to her.

'And that something turned round, and I saw it was a peasant with a rough beard, small and dreadful. I wanted to run away, but he stooped over a sack and was fumbling about in it. . . .'

She showed how he fumbled in the sack. Her face was full of horror. And Vronsky, remembering his dream, felt the same horror filling his soul.

'He fumbles about and mutters French words, so quickly, so quickly, and with a burr, you know: "*Il faut le battre, le fer: le broyer, le pétrir.* . . ."[1] And in my horror I tried to wake, but I woke still in a dream and began asking myself what it could mean; and Korney says to me: "You will die in childbed, in childbed, ma'am. . . ." Then I woke.'

'What nonsense, what nonsense!' said Vronsky, but he felt that there was no conviction in his voice.

'Well, don't let us talk about it. Ring the bell, I will order tea. But wait, it won't be long and I . . .'

But suddenly she stopped. The expression of her face changed instantaneously. The horror and agitation were replaced by an expression of quiet, serious, and blissful attention. He could not understand the meaning of this change. She had felt a new life quickening within her.

---

1. It must be beaten, the iron: pound it, knead it.

Chapter IV

Karenin after meeting Vronsky in his own porch went on as had been his intention to the Italian Opera. He sat through the first two acts and saw everybody that it was necessary for him to see. On his return home he carefully looked at the coat-stand, and noticing that no military coat hung there he went to his study as usual; contrary to his habit, however, he did not go to bed but walked up and down the room till three in the morning. The feeling of anger with his wife, who would not observe the rules of propriety and fulfil the only condition he had insisted on, that is, that she should not see her lover in his house, gave him no rest. She had not fulfilled his condition and he was obliged to punish her and carry out his threat: to divorce her and take away her son. He knew the difficulties connected with such a step: but he had said he would do it and now was obliged to do it. The Countess Lydia Ivanovna had hinted to him that that was the best way to get out of the situation, and he knew that of late the practice of divorce had been brought to such a state of perfection that he saw a possibility of overcoming the formal difficulties. Besides, misfortunes never come singly, and the affair of the subject races and the irrigation of the Zaraysk Province had caused Karenin so much unpleasantness in his official capacity that he had of late felt extremely irritable.

He did not sleep at all, and his wrath, increasing in a kind of gigantic progression, had reached its utmost limits by the morning. He dressed in haste, and as if he were carrying a cup brimful of wrath and were afraid of spilling any and of losing with his anger the energy he needed for an explanation with his wife, he went to her room as soon as he knew that she was up.

Anna, who thought that she knew her husband so well, was struck by his appearance when he entered. His brow was knit, and his eyes, gloomily fixed before him, avoided looking at her; his lips were firmly and contemptuously closed. In his step, his movements, and the sound of his voice was such determination and firmness as his wife had never known in him. He entered her boudoir and without saying 'Good morning!' went straight to her writing-table, took up her keys, and opened the drawer.

'What do you want?' she exclaimed.

'Your lover's letters.'

'They are not there,' she said, closing the drawer; but this action proved to him that he had guessed rightly, and rudely pushing away her hand he quickly drew out a letter-case in which he knew that she kept her most important papers. She wished to snatch away the letter-case, but he thrust her aside.

'Sit down: I must speak to you,' he said, taking the letter-case under his arm and pressing it so tight with his elbow that his shoulder went up. Astonished and abashed, she silently looked at him.

'I told you that I would not allow you to see your lover here.'

'I wanted to see him in order . . .'

She paused, unable to invent a reason.

'I do not go into particulars of why a woman wants to see her lover.'

'I wanted, I only wanted . . .' she said, flushing. His coarseness irritated her and gave her boldness. 'Is it possible you do not feel how easy it is for you to insult me?' she said.

'It is possible to insult an honest man or an honest woman, but to tell a thief that he is a thief is only *la constatation d'un fait*.[2] I have not seen this new trait of cruelty in you before.'

'You call it cruelty when a husband gives his wife complete freedom while he affords her honourable shelter, on the one condition that she should observe the laws of propriety. Is that cruelty?'

'It is worse than cruelty, it is—baseness, if you want to know!' Anna exclaimed in a burst of anger, and rose to go.

'No!' he shouted in his squeaky voice, which now rose to a higher note than usual; and seizing her so tightly by the wrists with his large fingers that the bracelet he pressed left red marks, he forced her back into her seat.

'Baseness? Since you wish to use that word—it is baseness to abandon a husband and a son for a lover and to go on eating the husband's bread!'

Her head dropped. She did not say what she had said to her lover the day before, that Vronsky was her real husband and that he (Karenin) was superfluous, she did not even think it. She felt all the justice of his words and only said softly:

'You cannot describe my position as being worse than I know it to be; but why do you tell me all this?'

'Why do I tell you? Why!' he went on just as angrily, 'that you should know that as you have not fulfilled my wish that propriety should be observed, I shall take steps to put an end to this situation.'

'Soon, very soon, it will come to an end of itself!' she muttered, and at the thought of the nearness of death, which she now desired, tears again filled her eyes.

'It will end sooner than you and your lover imagine! You want to satisfy animal passions . . .'

'Alexey Alexandrovich! This is not only ungenerous, but not even gentlemanly—to hit one who is down.'

'That's all very well, but you think only of yourself! The suf-

2. The statement of a fact.

ferings of the man who was your husband do not interest you. What do you care that his whole life is wrecked and how much he has suf . . . suf . . . suffled!'

Karenin was speaking so rapidly that he blundered and could not pronounce the word, and at last said *suffled*.

That struck her as funny; but immediately after she felt ashamed that anything could seem funny to her at such a moment. And for the first time she felt for him and put herself for an instant in his place, and was sorry for him. But what could she say or do? She bowed her head in silence. He too was silent for a while and then again began in a less squeaky voice, coldly emphasizing certain chance words that had no special importance.

'I came to tell you . . .' said he.

She looked up at him. 'No, it was an illusion,' she thought, calling to mind the expression of his face when he blundered over the word *suffled*. 'No! As if a man with those dull eyes and that self-satisfied immobility could feel!'

'I cannot change anything,' she whispered.

'I have come to tell you that I am going to Moscow to-morrow and shall not return to this house again, and that you will hear my decision through the lawyer whom I shall employ in the divorce suit. My son will stay with my cousin, said Karenin, making an effort to remember what he had wanted to say about his son.

'You want Serezha in order to hurt me,' she said, looking at him from under her brows. 'You do not care for him. . . . Leave me Serezha!'

'Yes, I have even lost my affection for my son, because he is connected with my repulsion for you. But all the same I shall take him away. Good-bye!'

And he was about to go, but now she stopped him.

'Alexey Alexandrovich! Leave me Serezha!' she whispered again. 'That is all I have to say: leave me Serezha till my . . . I shall soon be confined, leave him!'

Karenin flushed, and pulling away his hand left the room without a word.

Chapter V

The famous Petersburg lawyer's waiting-room was full when Karenin entered it. Three women: an old lady, a young lady, and a tradesman's wife; and three gentlemen: one a German banker with a ring on his finger, another a bearded merchant, and the third an irate official in uniform with an order hanging from his neck, had evidently long been waiting. Two clerks sat at their tables writing, and the sound of their pens was audible. The writing-table accessories (of which Karenin was a connoisseur) were unusually good, as he could not help noticing. One of the clerks, without rising from his chair, screwed up his eyes and addressed Karenin ill-humouredly.

'What do you want?'

'I want to see the lawyer on business.'

'The lawyer is engaged,' replied the assistant sternly, and indicated with his pen the persons who were waiting.

'Can he not find time to see me?' said Karenin.

'He has no spare time, he is always busy. Be so kind as to wait.'

'Then I will trouble you to give him my card,' said Karenin with dignity, seeing the impossibility of preserving his incognito.

The assistant took the card and, though he evidently did not approve of what he read on it, went out of the room.

Karenin approved in theory of public trial, but for certain high official reasons he did not quite sympathize with some aspects of its application in Russia, and he condemned these applications as far as he could condemn anything that had been confirmed by the Emperor. His whole life had been spent in administrative activity, and therefore when he disapproved of anything his disapproval was mitigated by a recognition of the inevitability of mistakes and the possibility of improvement in everything. In the new legal institutions he disapproved of the position occupied by lawyers. But till now he had never had to deal with a lawyer and so had disapproved only in theory; now his disapproval was strengthened by the unpleasant impression he received in the lawyer's waiting-room.

'He will be here in a moment,' said the assistant, and in fact, a minute or two later, in the doorway appeared the long figure of an elderly jurisconsult who had been conferring with the lawyer, followed by the lawyer himself.

The lawyer was a short, thick-set, bald-headed man, with a black beard tinged with red, long light-coloured eyebrows, and a bulging forehead. He was as spruce as a bridegroom, from his white necktie and double watchchain to his patent leather boots. His face was intelligent and peasant-like, but his dress was dandified and in bad taste.

'Come in, please!' said the lawyer to Karenin, and gloomily ushering his client in before him, he closed the door.

'Won't you take a seat?' He pointed to a chair beside a writing-table covered with papers, and himself took the principal seat, rubbing his little hands with their short fingers covered with white hair and bending his head to one side. But hardly had he settled down when a moth flew across the table. The lawyer, with a rapidity one could not have expected of him, separated his hands, caught the moth, and resumed his former position.

'Before I begin speaking of my case,' said Karenin, who had followed the lawyer's movements with astonishment, 'I must mention that the business about which I have to speak to you must be strictly private.'

A scarcely perceptible smile moved the lawyer's drooping reddish moustache.

'I should not be a lawyer if I could not keep the secrets entrusted to me! But if you would like a confirmation . . .'

Karenin glanced at him and saw that his intelligent grey eyes were laughing, as if he knew everything in advance.

'You know my name?' continued Karenin.

'I know you and, like every Russian, I know—' here he again caught a moth—'your useful activity,' said the lawyer bowing.

Karenin sighed, collecting his courage, but having once made up his mind he went on in his squeaky voice without timidity or hesitation, emphasizing a word here and there.

'I have the misfortune,' began Karenin, 'to be a deceived husband, and I wish legally to break off relations with my wife—that is, to be divorced, but in such a way that my son should not remain with his mother.'

The lawyer's grey eyes tried not to laugh but they danced with irrepressible glee, and Karenin saw that it was not only the glee of a man getting profitable business; there was triumph and delight, and a gleam resembling the evil-boding gleam he had seen in his wife's eyes.

'You want my assistance to obtain a divorce?'

'Just so! But I must warn you that there is a risk that I may be wasting your time. I have come only for a preliminary consultation. I wish for a divorce, but the form in which it can be obtained is of importance to me. It is quite possible that if the forms do not coincide with my requirements I shall forgo my legitimate desire.'

'Oh, that is always so,' said the lawyer, 'that is always open to you.'

The laywer looked down at Karenin's feet, feeling that the sight of his irrepressible joy might offend his client. He glanced at a moth that flew past his nose and his hand moved, but did not catch it, out of respect for Karenin's situation.

'Although the general outline of our laws relating to this matter is known to me,' continued Karenin, 'I should like to know the forms in which such cases are conducted in practice.'

'You wish me to state,' the lawyer said, still not raising his eyes and adopting, with a certain pleasure, his client's manner of speech, 'the various methods by which your desire can be carried out?'

And on Karenin's nodding affirmatively the lawyer continued, only occasionally casting a glance at Karenin's face, which had grown red in patches.

'Divorce, under our laws,' he said, with a slight shade of disapproval of the laws, 'as you are aware, may be granted in the following cases. . . . You must wait!' he exclaimed, addressing his assistant who had looked in at the door; but he rose all the same, spoke a few words to his assistant, and sat down again. 'In the following cases: physical defect in husband or wife; five years' absence without news'—and he bent one of his short hairy fingers—'and in cases of adultery,' he uttered the word with evident pleasure. 'These are subdivided as follows,' and he went on bending down his thick fingers, though the cases and the subdivisions evidently could not be classed together, 'physical defects in husband or in wife, and adultery of husband or of wife.' As all his fingers had been used he straightened them all out and continued:

'That is the theoretical view; but I suppose you have done me the honour of applying to me in order to learn the practical application of the law. Therefore, guided by the precedents, I have to inform you that cases of divorce all come to the following:—there is, I suppose, no physical defect or absence without news? . . .'

Karenin nodded affirmatively.

'—come to the following: adultery of husband or wife and the detection of the guilty party by mutual consent, or involuntary detection without such consent. I must add that the latter case is seldom met with in practice,' and with a momentary glance at Karenin the lawyer became suddenly silent, like a man who when selling pistols has described the advantages of the different kinds, and waits for his customer's decision. But Karenin remained silent, and so he began again: 'The most usual, simple, and reasonable way I consider to be adultery by mutual consent. I should not venture so to express myself were I talking to a man of undeveloped mind,' said the lawyer, 'but I expect it is comprehensible to you.'

Karenin was, however, so much upset that he did not at once understand the reasonableness of adultery by mutual consent and his perplexity was expressed in his looks; but the lawyer immediately helped him.

'Two people can no longer live together—there is the fact. And if both agree about that, the details and formalities become unimportant, and at the same time it is the simplest and surest method.'

Karenin quite understood now. But he had religious requirements which hindered his acceptance of this method.

'It is out of the question in the present case,' said he. 'Only one measure is possible: involuntary detection confirmed by letters which I have.'

At the mention of letters the lawyer pressed his lips together and gave vent to a high-pitched sound of pity and contempt.

'Please remember that cases of this kind, as you know, are decided by the Ecclesiastical Department, and the reverend Fathers in such cases are keenly interested in the minutest details,' he said, with a smile that showed his fellow-feeling with the reverend Fathers' taste. 'Letters may certainly serve as a partial confirmation, but direct evidence from witnesses must be produced. In general, if you do me the honour to entrust the case to me, leave me to choose the means which should be used. He who desires a result accepts the means of obtaining it.'

'If it is so . . .' Karenin began, growing suddenly pale; but at that moment the other suddenly rose and went to the door to speak to his assistant, who had again come to interrupt him.

'Tell her we have not got a cheap sale on here!' he said and came back again.

As he was returning he furtively caught another moth. 'A fine state my furniture will be in when summer comes!' he thought, and frowned.

'Yes, you were saying . . .' he began.

'I will write and let you know what I decide,' said Karenin, rising and holding on by the table. After a short pause he said, 'I may conclude from your words that a divorce could be obtained. I would also ask you to let me know your terms?'

'It is quite possible, if you allow me full liberty of action,' said the lawyer, without taking any notice of the last question. 'When may I expect to hear from you?' he added, moving toward the door, his eyes and patent-leather boots shining.

'In a week's time. And you will be so good as to let me know whether you are willing to undertake the case, and on what terms.'

'Very well.'

The lawyer bowed deferentially, let his client pass out, and being left alone abandoned himself to his happy mood. He felt so cheerful that, contrary to his custom, he allowed a reduction to the bargaining lady and gave up catching moths, having made up his mind to have his furniture re-covered next winter with velvet, like Sigonin's.

Chapter VI

Karenin had gained a brilliant victory at the Committee Meeting of the seventeenth of August; but the consequence of that victory undermined his power. The new committee for investigating the conditions of the subject-races from every point of view had been formed and sent to its field of action with unusual promptitude and energy, stirred up by Karenin. Three months later the committee sent in its report. The subject-races' conditions had been

investigated from the political, administrative, economic, ethno-
graphical, material, and religious points of view. All the questions
had received splendidly-drafted answers: answers not open to doubt,
since they were not the result of human thoughts (always liable
to error), but were the outcome of official labours. All the answers
were based on official data: Reports from Governors and Bishops,
based on Reports from district authorities and ecclesiastical superin-
tendents, based in their turn on Reports from rural administrative
officers and parish priests; therefore these answers could not admit
to any doubt. All the questions as to why they had bad harvests,
for instance, or why the natives kept to their own creeds and so on,
questions which without the convenience of the official machine
don't get solved and can't get solved for centuries, had received
clear and certain solutions. And the solutions arrived at were in
accord with Karenin's opinions. But Stremov, who had been
touched to the quick at the last meeting, made use of tactics for
which Karenin was not prepared. Stremov suddenly changed over
to Karenin's side, bringing several other members in his train, and
not only warmly supported the measures advocated by Karenin, but
proposed other more extreme measures of the same nature. These
measures, going beyond Karenin's original idea, were accepted, and
then Stremov's tactics became manifest. The measures, carried to
extremes, proved so stupid that persons in office, public opinion,
intellectual women, and the Press, all at the same moment fell
upon them, expressing indignation at the measures themselves,
and at Karenin, their acknowledged originator. Stremov stood
aside, pretending to have blindly followed Karenin's plans and to
be himself indignant now at what had been done, thus under-
mining Karenin. But, in spite of failing health and family troubles,
Karenin did not give in. There was a split in the Committee. Some
of the members, with Stremov at their head, excused their mistake by maintaining that they had put their faith in the report
presented by the Revisory Committee directed by Karenin; and
said that that Committee's report was nonsense and nothing but
waste paper. Karenin and a number of others saw danger in so
revolutionary an attitude toward official documents and continued
to support the data presented by the Committee. In consequence,
the higher circles and even Society became quite confused and,
though everybody was deeply interested in the question, no one
could make out whether the subject-races were really suffering and
perishing or were flourishing. Karenin's position, partly in consequence of this and partly from the contempt that fell on him as a
result of his wife's infidelity, became very shaky. In these circumstances he took an important resolution. He announced, to the
surprise of the Committee, that he would ask to be allowed to go

and investigate the matter himself, and having received permission
he started for the distant Provinces.

Karenin's departure was much talked about, especially because
just before starting he formally returned the post-fare sufficient to
pay for twelve horses all the way to his destination, which had
been advanced to him.

'I consider it very fine of him,' the Princess Betsy said, referring
to it in a conversation with Princess Myagkaya. 'Why should they
pay for post-horses when everybody knows that we now have railways everywhere?'

But the Princess Myagkaya did not agree, and was even irritated
by Princess Tverskaya's views.

'It is all very well for you to talk who possess I don't know how
many millions,' she said. 'But I am very glad when my husband
goes on inspection-tours in summer. It is very good for his health,
and pleasant for him; and we have an arrangement by which this
allowance goes for the hire of a carriage and coachman for me.'

On his way to the distant Provinces Karenin stopped three
days in Moscow. On the day after his arrival he went to call on
the Governor-General. At the crossing of Gazetny Street, where
there is always a crowd of carriages, and *izvozchiks*, he suddenly
heard some one calling out his name in such a loud and cheerful
voice that he could not help looking around. On the pavement at
the corner of the street, in a short fashionable overcoat and a
small fashionable hat, his teeth gleaming between his smiling red
lips, young, gay, and beaming, stood Oblonsky, determinedly and
insistently shouting and demanding that Karenin should stop. He
was holding with one hand the window of a carriage (from which
the head of a lady in a velvet bonnet and two little children's
heads were leaning out) and was smilingly beckoning with his
other hand to his brother-in-law. The lady too with a kind smile
waved her hand to Karenin. The lady with the children was
Dolly.

Karenin did not wish to see anyone in Moscow, and certainly not
his wife's brother. He raised his hat and was going on, but Oblonsky
told the coachman to stop and ran across the snow.

'What a shame not to have sent word! Been here long? And I
went into Dusseaux's hotel yesterday and saw "Karenin" on the
board, and it never entered my head that it could be you!' said
Oblonsky, thrusting his head in at the carriage window, 'else I
should have looked you up. I am so glad to see you!' and he kicked
his feet together to knock off the snow. 'What a shame not to
send word!'

'I could not find time: I am very busy,' Karenin answered drily.

'Come and speak to my wife; she is so anxious to see you.'

Karenin unfolded the rug he had wrapped round his legs, which were so sensitive to the cold, got out of the carriage, and making his way through the snow approached Dolly.

'What is the matter, Alexey Alexandrovich? Why do you avoid us in this way?' Dolly smilingly asked.

'I was exceedingly busy! Very pleased to see you,' he said in a tone that expressed clearly that he was very sorry. 'How are you?'

'And how is my dear Anna?'

Karenin muttered something and was about to go, when Oblonsky stopped him.

'D'you know what we'll do to-morrow? Dolly, ask him to come and dine with us! We shall invite Koznyshev and Pestsov, so as to let him taste the Moscow intellectuals.'

'Yes, do come!' said Dolly. 'We shall expect you at five or six, just as you like. But how is my dear Anna? It is so long . . .'

'She is well,' replied Karenin frowning. 'I shall be very pleased,' and he went back to his carriage.

'Then you will come?' cried Dolly.

Karenin muttered something which Dolly could not catch amid the noise of passing vehicles.

'I shall call to-morrow!' shouted Oblonsky to him.

Karenin got into his carriage and sat far back, so as neither to see nor to be seen.

'Queer chap!' said Oblonsky to his wife, and after glancing at his watch waved his hand in front of his face as a sign of endearment to his wife and children, and walked jauntily away along the pavement.

'Stiva, Stiva!' Dolly called, and blushed.

He turned round.

'You know that I must buy coats for Grisha and Tanya. Give me some money.'

'Never mind! Tell them I will pay!' and nodding his head to an acquaintance who was driving past he disappeared round the corner.

Chapter VII

The next day was Sunday. Oblonsky went to the rehearsal of a ballet at the Imperial Theatre and gave to Masha Chibisova—a pretty dancer, who through his patronage had just obtained an engagement—a coral necklace he had promised her the evening before; and behind the scene, in the midday darkness of the theatre, contrived to kiss her pretty face, which was brightened by his present. Besides giving her the necklace he wished to make an appointment to meet her after the ballet. Having explained that he could not be there at the beginning of the performance, he promised to come for the last act, and take her to supper. From the theatre Oblonsky went to the market, and himself selected the fish and asparagus for dinner; and at noon he was already at Dusseaux's Hotel, where he had to call on three people who, fortunately for him, had all put up at the same place. These were: Levin, who had only just returned from abroad; the newly-appointed head of his department who was making a tour of inspection in Moscow; and Karenin, his brother-in-law, whom he wanted to secure for dinner.

Oblonsky liked a good dinner, but liked still more giving a dinner-party: not a big affair, but one select in food, drink, and guests. With the programme for that day's dinner he was very satisfied; there would be perch (brought alive to the kitchen) and asparagus, the *pièce de résistance* [3] was to consist of a splendid but quite plain joint of roast beef, and the wines would be well chosen: so much for the food and drink. As for the guests there would be Kitty and Levin, and, in order that they should not be too conspicuous, a girl cousin and young Shcherbatsky; here the *pièce de résistance* was to consist of Sergius Ivanich Koznyshev and Alexey Alexandrovich Karenin: Sergius Ivanich, a Muscovite and a philosopher, and Alexey Alexandrovich, a Petersburger and a practical politician. Besides these he meant to ask the well-known crank and enthusiast Pestsov, a Liberal and a great talker, a musician and historian, and the dearest of fifty-year-old boys, who would serve as sauce or condiment to Koznyshev and Karenin; and would stir them all up and set them by the ears.

The second instalment of the forest money had been paid and was not yet all spent. Dolly had been very nice and kind of late, and the thought of his dinner-party pleased Oblonsky in every respect. He was in very high spirits. Just two circumstances were not quite satisfactory, but they were drowned in the ocean of kind-hearted joviality which overflowed his heart. These two circumstances were as follows: From the fact that when he had met Karenin in the street the previous day the latter had treated him with cold stiffness, and had not called or even informed them of his arrival—from this, added to the rumour about Anna and Vronsky that had reached him, Oblonsky concluded that all was not as it should be between the husband and wife.

This was one of the unpleasant things, while the other was the fact that his new superior, like all new superiors, had the reputation of being a dreadful man who got up at six in the morning, worked like a horse, and expected his subordinates to do the same. This superior also had the reputation of having the manners of a bear, and he was reported to hold views diametrically opposed to those of his predecessor and, till now, of Oblonsky also. On the

3. The main dish, the main course.

previous day Oblonsky had appeared on Service business in uniform; the new superior was very pleasant and chatted with him as with an old acquaintance; therefore Oblonsky now considered it his duty to call on him in a morning coat. The thought that the new superior might not take this in good part was the second unpleasant circumstance, but Oblonsky felt instinctively that everything would 'turn out' splendidly. 'After all, they're all human beings, all men, just like us poor sinners,' he thought, as he entered the hotel. 'What is there to be angry and quarrel about?'

Walking down the corridor with his hat tilted on one side, he said, 'How do you do, Vassily?' to a servant he knew. 'You've grown whiskers! Levin—number seven, eh? Will you show me the way? And please find out whether Count Anichkin' (the new superior) 'will receive me.'

'Yes sir,' replied Vassily with a smile. 'It's a long time since you've been here.'

'I was here yesterday, but came by the other entrance. Is this number seven?'

Levin was standing in the middle of the room beside a peasant from Tver, measuring a fresh bearskin with a yard measure, when Oblonsky entered.

'Ah! Killed it?' cried Oblonsky. 'Fine thing! A she-bear? How d'you do, Arkhip?'

He shook hands with the peasant and sat down without taking off his overcoat or hat.

'Do take your things off and stay,' said Levin, removing the hat.

'No, I have no time. I've only come in for a moment,' replied Oblonsky, throwing open his coat. Later on he took it off and stayed for an hour, talking to Levin about bear-hunting and also about personal matters.

'Now please tell me what you did abroad, and where you have been,' said Oblonsky, when the peasant had left.

'Well, I stayed in Germany, in Prussia, in France, and in England—not in the capitals but in manufacturing centres. I've seen many new things and am glad I went.'

'Yes, I know your idea of settling the working-class problem.'

'Not at all! In Russia there cannot be a working-class problem. In Russia the question turns on the relation between the labourers and the land. They have the same problems there, but with them it is a case of patching up what has already been spoilt—while here . . .'

Oblonsky listened to Levin with attention.

'Yes, yes,' he said, 'very likely you are right. But I am glad you are in good spirits and go bear-hunting, and work, and are full of enthusiasms, because Shcherbatsky told me he met you and you were down in the mouth, and kept talking about death. . . .'

'Well, what of that? I never stop thinking of death,' said Levin. 'It really is time for me to die. All those things are mere nonsense. I will tell you frankly: I value my idea and my work immensely, but really . . . Just think! This whole world of ours is only a speck of mildew sprung up on a tiny planet; yet we think we can have something great—thoughts, actions! They are all but grains of sand!'

'But, my dear fellow, all that is as old as the hills.'

'It is old. . . . But, do you know, when you have once grasped it clearly, everything becomes so insignificant! If you once realize that to-morrow, if not to-day, you will die and nothing will be left of you, everything becomes insignificant! I consider my ideas very important, yet they too turn out to be insignificant—and would be, even if it were as possible to carry them out as it was to surround this bear. And so one passes one's life finding distraction in hunting or in work, merely not to think of death.'

Oblonsky listened to Levin with an affectionate and subtle smile.

'Well, of course! So now you have come round to my notion. Do you remember how you used to fly at me for seeking enjoyment in life? Do not be so severe, O moralist! . . .'

'But of course the good in life is . . .' Levin became confused. 'Oh, I don't know. All I know is, that we shall all die soon.'

'Why soon?'

'And do you know, life has less charm when one thinks of death, but it is more peaceful.'

'On the contrary, it is even brighter toward the end! However, I must be going,' returned Oblonsky, rising for the tenth time.

'Don't go yet!' said Levin, trying to detain him. 'When shall we meet again? I am leaving to-morrow.'

'Well, I'm a good one! Why, I came on purpose . . . You must come and dine with us to-day. Your brother is coming, and my brother-in-law, Karenin.'

'Is he here?' asked Levin, and was going to inquire about Kitty. He had heard that she went to Petersburg at the beginning of the winter to visit her sister, who had married a diplomatist. He did not know whether she had returned, but changed his mind and thought: 'Whether she comes or not will make no difference.'

'Then you will come?'

'Yes, of course.'

'Well, then, at five, and in morning dress!' And Oblonsky got up and went downstairs to call on his new superior. His instinct had not deceived him; the dreadful new superior turned out to be a most affable man. Oblonsky had lunch with him and sat talking so long that it was going on for four when he arrived at Karenin's.

Chapter VIII

Karenin, after returning from church, spent the rest of the morning in the hotel. That day he had two matters to see to: to interview a deputation from a subject-race, which was in Moscow at that time, and give them instructions, and to write to the lawyer as he had promised. The interview, though the deputation had been summoned on his initiative, was an affair that presented many difficulties and even dangers, and Karenin was very glad that it chanced to be in Moscow when he was there. The members of the deputation had not the least comprehension of their rôle or of their duties. They were naïvely convinced that their business consisted in explaining their needs and the existing state of affairs, and of asking for help from the Government. They could decidedly not understand that some of their statements and demands would play into the hands of the hostile party, and thereby ruin their case. Karenin had a prolonged tussle with them, and wrote out for them a programme which they were not to overstep, and having dismissed them he wrote two letters to Petersburg. One of them contained instructions regarding this deputation. In this matter his chief helper was the Countess Lydia Ivanovna, who was a specialist in deputations. No one else could so well pilot a deputation or give it a good start.

When he had finished with the deputation Karenin wrote to the lawyer, without the least hesitation giving him permission to act at his own discretion, and enclosing three notes from Vronsky to Anna which he had found in the writing-case he had taken possession of.

Having left his home with the intention of never returning to his family, and having seen the lawyer and communicated— though only to that one person—this intention, and particularly after converting this matter of life into an affair of ink and paper, Karenin had grown more and more used to the notion; so that carrying it into effect now seemed to him possible. He was just closing his letter to the lawyer when he heard Oblonsky's voice.

Oblonsky was disputing with Karenin's servant, and insisting that he should be announced.

'No matter!' thought Karenin. 'It is even better so. I will tell him about my position with regard to his sister at once, and will explain why I cannot dine at his house.'

'Ask the gentleman in!' he said in a loud voice, collecting his papers and placing them inside a blotter.

'There, you see, you were lying to me! He is at home!' came the voice of Oblonsky in answer to the man who had been trying to stop him, as he entered the room, taking off his overcoat as he came. 'I'm awfully glad I have found you in! Well, I hope . . .' began Oblonsky, cheerfully.

'I can't come,' Karenin, who was standing, said coldly, without offering his visitor a seat.

Karenin had expected to enter at once upon the cool relation in which he would henceforth stand toward the brother of the wife against whom he was beginning divorce proceedings; but he had not counted upon the flood of kindliness which overflowed the banks of Oblonsky's soul.

Oblonsky opened his clear and shining eyes wide.

'Why can't you? What do you mean?' he demanded in French, quite taken aback. 'Oh no, you have promised and we are reckoning on you.'

'I must tell you that I can't come because the family connection hitherto subsisting between us must now be severed.'

'What? I mean, how? Why?' said Oblonsky, smiling.

'Because I am about to take proceedings to divorce your sister, my wife. I was obliged to. . . .'

But before Karenin could finish what he was about to say, Oblonsky did something quite unexpected. He uttered an exclamation of dismay and sat down in an easy-chair.

'Dear me, Alexey Alexandrovich! What are you talking about?' he cried, a look of pain appearing on his face.

'It is true.'

'Forgive me, but I can't—I can't believe it . . .'

Karenin sat down, conscious that his words had not the effect he had anticipated, that he would be obliged to give an explanation, and that whatever that explanation might be, it would not alter his relation to his brother-in-law.

'Yes, I am under the painful necessity of applying for a divorce,' he continued.

'I will tell you just one thing, Alexey Alexandrovich! I know you to be a first-rate and a just man; I know Anna to be—excuse me! I cannot change my opinion of her—a fine, a splendid woman; and therefore forgive me, but I cannot believe this. There must be some misunderstanding!' said Oblonsky.

'Ah, if it were only a misunderstanding! . . .'

'Wait a moment—I understand,' Oblonsky interrupted him. 'But of course . . . Only this: one should not be in a hurry. No! One shouldn't, shouldn't be in a hurry.'

'I was not in a hurry,' replied Karenin coldly. 'In a case like this it was impossible to consult anyone. I have quite made up my mind.'

'But it is awful!' said Oblonsky, sighing deeply. 'One thing I would do, Alexey Alexandrovich, if I were you—I entreat you to do it! You have not yet commenced proceedings, as I understand? Well, before doing so, see my wife and talk it over with her! She cares for Anna as for a sister, she is fond of you, and she is a wonderful woman. For heaven's sake, talk it over with her! Do me this favour, I entreat you!' *mirrors beginning of book*

Karenin considered, and for a while Oblonsky gazed at him, full of sympathy, without breaking the silence. 'You will come and see her?'

'I hardly know. The reason I did not call on you is that I think our relationship must be altered.'

'Why? I don't see it. Allow me to believe that beside our family relationship, you share at least to some extent the friendly feeling I have always had for you . . . and sincere respect,' added Oblonsky, pressing the other's hand. 'Even if your worst suspicions proved correct, I never took upon myself, and never will, to judge either side; and I see no reason why our relations should change. But do, now do come and see my wife!'

'Ah, we look at the matter differently,' said Karenin, coldly. 'However, don't let us talk about it.'

'But why won't you come? Supposing you came to dinner to-day? My wife expects you. Do come, and above all, do talk it over with her. She is a wonderful woman. For heaven's sake—I implore you on my bended knees!'

'If you wish it so much, I will come,' said Karenin with a sigh, and anxious to change the subject he inquired about a matter interesting to them both—Oblonsky's new superior, a man who, though still young, had suddenly been given so important a post.

Karenin had never liked Count Anichkin, their opinions had always been at variance, and now he could not repress a feeling of spite, quite comprehensible to anyone in an official position, toward a more successful man.

'Well, and have you seen him?' said Karenin with a venomous smile.

'Oh yes, he came to the Council yesterday. He seems to know his business perfectly and is very active.'

'Yes, but in what direction?' asked Karenin. 'Toward getting things done, or toward changing what has been done already? The curse of our State is its red-tape administration, of which he is a worthy representative.'

'I really don't know what his tendencies are, but I do know that he is a first-rate fellow,' replied Oblonsky. 'I have just been to see him, and he really is a first-rate chap. We had lunch, and I showed him how to make that stuff—you know—wine with oranges. It is very refreshing, and it is amazing that he did not know of it. He liked it very much. Yes, he certainly is a first-rate chap.'

Oblonsky looked at his watch.

'Dear me, it is getting on for five and I have still to call on Dolgovushin! . . . Well, then, do please come to dinner! You have no idea how grieved I and my wife will be if you don't.'

Karenin parted from his brother-in-law in a very different manner to that in which he had met him.

'I have promised, and I will come,' he answered in a dejected tone.

'Believe me, I appreciate it and hope that you will not regret it,' Oblonsky replied, smiling. As he put on his overcoat while walking away his arm touched the servant's head. He laughed and went out. 'Five o'clock, and morning dress, if you please!' he sang out, returning to the door.

Chapter IX

It was past five, and some of the visitors had already arrived, when the master of the house came home. He entered together with Sergius Ivanich Koznyshev and Pestsov, who had met on the doorstep. Those two were the chief representatives of the Moscow intellectuals, as Oblonsky called them. Both were men respected for their characters and abilities. They respected one another, but in almost everything they were completely and hopelessly at variance, not because they belonged to different schools of thought but just because they belonged to one camp (their enemies confused them one with the other), and in that camp each of them had his own shade. And as there is nothing less amenable to agreement than disagreement on semi-abstract themes, they not only disagreed in their opinions but had long been accustomed without anger to ridicule each other's incorrigible delusions.

They were entering when Oblonsky overtook them, and were talking about the weather. Prince Alexander Dmitrich Shcherbatsky, and young Shcherbatsky, Turovtsyn, Kitty, and Karenin were already in the drawing-room.

Oblonsky noticed at once that, without him, things were going badly in the drawing-room. His wife in her gala dress, a grey silk, evidently worried both about the children who would have to dine alone in the nursery, and about her husband who had not returned, had not managed in his absence to mix the guests properly. They all sat like 'a parish priest's wife visiting' (as the old Prince Shcherbatsky expressed it), evidently puzzled as to why there were all assembled there, and forcing out words in order not to remain silent. The good-natured Turovtsyn clearly felt quite out of it, and the smile on his thick lips, with which he met Oblonsky, said as clearly as words, 'Well, my friend, you *have* planted me among the clever ones! To have a drink at the Château des Fleurs would be more in my line.' [4] The old Prince sat silent, his shining eyes looking askance at Karenin, and Oblonsky saw that he had already prepared some remark wherewith to polish off that dignitary of State, whom people were invited to as to a dish of sturgeon. Kitty kept looking toward the door, gathering courage not to blush when Constantine Levin should enter. Young Shcherbatsky, who had not been introduced to Karenin, tried to look as if this did not make him feel at all awkward. Karenin himself, as the Petersburg way is when one dines with ladies, was in evening dress with a white tie, and Oblonsky saw by his face that he had come only to keep his promise, and by being in that company was fulfilling an unpleasant duty. He was the chief cause of the iciness which had frozen all the visitors till Oblonsky's arrival.

On entering the drawing-room Oblonsky made his excuses, explaining that he had been kept by the particular Prince who was his usual scapegoat whenever he was late or absent, and in a moment he had reintroduced everybody, and having brought Karenin and Koznyshev together, he started them off on the subject of the Russification of Poland, and they immediately caught on, Pestsov joining them. Having patted Turovtsyn on the shoulder, he whispered something funny in his ear, and got him to sit down next to Dolly and the old Prince. Then he told Kitty that she was looking very nice, and introduced young Shcherbatsky to Karenin. In a moment he had kneaded all that Society dough in such a way that the drawing-room was in first-rate form, and was filled with animated voices. Only Constantine Levin had not arrived. However, that was all for the best, for Oblonsky, on looking in at the dining-room, saw to his horror that the port-wine and sherry were from Depret and not from Levé, and having given orders to send the coachman as quickly as possible to Levé he turned to go back to the drawing-room. [5]

But he met Levin at the door.

'I am not late?'

'As if you ever could help being late!' said Oblonsky taking his hand.

'Are there many people here? Whom have you got?' asked Levin with a blush, knocking the snow off his cap with his glove.

'All our own people. Kitty is here. Come, I will introduce you to Karenin.'

4. The 'Château des Fleurs' was a place of amusement in Moscow of a Parisian *café chantant* type.
5. Depret and Levé were well-known wine merchants in Moscow who dealt in French wines of their own vintages.

Oblonsky, in spite of being a Liberal, knew that to be acquainted with Karenin could not but be an honour, and therefore treated his best friends to that honour. But at that moment Constantine Levin was not in a state fully to appreciate the pleasure of such an acquaintance. He had not seen Kitty since the memorable evening when he had met Vronsky, excepting for that one moment when he had caught sight of her on the high road. In the depths of his soul he had felt sure that he should meet her that evening, but to maintain his freedom of thought he had tried to assure himself that he did not know it. Now, when he heard that she was here, he was suddenly filled with such joy and at the same time with such fear, that it took away his breath and he could not utter what he wished to say.

'What was she like? The same as before, or as she was that morning in the carriage? What if Darya Alexandrovna had spoken the truth? Why should it not be true?' he thought.

'Oh, do introduce me to Karenin!' he brought out with difficulty, and with despairing determination he entered the drawing-room and saw her.

She was not as she had been before, nor as he had seen her in the carriage. She was quite different.

She was frightened, shy, shamefaced, and therefore even more charming. She saw him as soon as he entered. She had been waiting for him. She was filled with joy, and that joy made her feel so confused that for a moment when, as he was approaching the hostess, he again glanced at her, Kitty herself, he, and Dolly all thought she would not be able to control herself but would burst into tears. She blushed, grew pale, then blushed again, and quite rigid, with only her lips quivering slightly, sat waiting for him. He came up, bowed, and silently held out his hand. Had it not been for the light quivering of her lips and the moisture that made her eyes brighter, her smile would have appeared almost calm when she said:

'What a long time it is since we saw one another!' while with a desperate resolve her cold hand pressed his.

'You have not seen me but I saw you,' said Levin with a beaming smile of joy. 'I saw you on your way to Ergushovo from the station.'

'When?' she asked him with surprise.

'You were driving to Ergushovo,' said Levin, feeling that the happiness with which his heart was overflowing was taking his breath away. 'How did I dare to connect anything that was not innocent with this pathetic being! Yes, what Darya Alexandrovna told me seems to be true,' he thought.

Oblonsky took his arm and led him up to Karenin.

'Let me introduce you,' and he gave their names.

'Very pleased to meet you again,' said Karenin coldly, as he shook hands with Levin.

'Are you acquainted?' said Oblonsky with surprise.

'We spent three hours together in a railway carriage,' said Levin with a smile, 'but we parted filled with curiosity, as people do after a masquerade, at any rate I did.'

'Dear me! If you please,' said Oblonsky, motioning them toward the dining-room.

The men went to the side-table in the dining-room, on which stood bottles with six kinds of vodka and plates with as many sorts of cheese with and without silver cheese-knives, caviar, herrings, different kinds of tinned delicacies, and slices of French rolls.

They stood round the scented vodka and the delicacies, and the conversation about the Russification of Poland between Koznyshev, Karenin, and Pestsov gradually slackened in the expectation of dinner.

Koznyshev, who knew better than anyone how at the end of a most abstract and serious dispute unexpectedly to administer a grain of Attic salt and thereby to change his interlocutor's frame of mind, did so now.

Karenin was arguing that the Russification of Poland could only be accomplished by high principles which the Russian Administration must introduce.

Pestsov insisted that one nation can assimilate another only when the former is more densely populated.

Koznyshev agreed with both, but with limitations. When they had left the drawing-room Koznyshev, to finish the conversation, remarked with a smile:

'Consequently for the Russification of the alien nationalities, there is but one means: to breed as many children as possible. . . . So my brother and I are acting worst of all, and you married gentlemen, and especially Stephen Arkadyevich, are acting most patriotically. How many have you got?' he asked, turning to the host with a kindly smile and holding out a tiny wine-glass to be filled.

Everybody laughed, and Oblonsky most merrily of all.

'Yes, that is the very best way,' he said, chewing some cheese and filling the glass with a special kind of vodka. And the conversation was really ended by the joke.

'This cheese is not bad. May I help you to some?' asked the host.

'Have you really been doing gymnastics again?' he went on turning to Levin, and with his left hand he felt Levin's muscle. Levin smiled, tightening his arm, and under Oblonsky's fingers a lump like a Dutch cheese and hard as steel bulged out beneath the fine cloth of Levin's coat.

'Here's a biceps! A real Samson!'

'I expect great strength is needed for bear-hunting,' said Karenin, who had the vaguest notions about sport, as he helped himself to cheese and broke his slice of bread, cut as fine as a cobweb.

Levin smiled.

'None at all. On the contrary a child can kill a bear,' he said, making room, with a slight bow, for the ladies who were coming up to the side-table with the hostess.

'You have killed a bear, I hear?' said Kitty, vainly trying to catch a wayward slippery pickled mushroom with her fork, and so shaking the lace of her sleeve through which her arm gleamed white. 'Have you any bears near your estate?' she added, turning her lovely little head toward him and smiling.

There was, it would seem, nothing unusual in what she had said, but for him what a meaning there was, inexpressible in words, in every sound and every movement of her lips, her eyes, and her hands as she said it! There was a prayer for forgiveness, and trust in him, and a caress—a tender, timid caress, and a promise, and hope, and love for him in which he could not but believe and which suffocated him with joy. *contrast w/ V & A who cannot communicate*

'No, we went to the Tver Province. On my return journey I met your brother-in-law, or rather your brother-in-law's brother-in-law, on the train,' he said smiling. 'It was a funny meeting.'

And gaily and amusingly he told how after not sleeping all night he, in his sheep-skin coat, had rushed into Karenin's compartment.

'The guard (regardless of the proverb[6]) judged me by my clothes and wished to turn me out, but I began to use long words and . . . you too,' he went on turning to Karenin (whose Christian name and patronymic he had forgotten), 'judging me by my peasant coat were going to turn me out, but afterwards you took my part, for which I am very grateful.'

'The rights of passengers to a choice of seats are very ill-defined,' said Karenin, wiping the tips of his fingers on his handkerchief.

'I noticed that you were not quite sure what to make of me,' said Levin with a good-natured smile, 'so I hastened to start an intellectual conversation, to expiate my sheep-skin.'

Koznyshev, while continuing his conversation with the hostess, listened with one ear to his brother, turning his eyes toward him, and thought, 'What has happened to him to-day? He behaves

---

6. The proverb is:
   'At meeting you're judged by your clothes,
   At parting you're judged by your wits.'

like a conqueror.' He did not know that Levin felt as if he had grown a pair of wings. Levin knew that she was listening to his words and liked hearing him, and that was the only thing he cared about. Not only in that room but in the whole world there existed for him nothing but Kitty and himself; and he had now acquired a great significance and importance. He felt himself at a height that made him giddy, and there, somewhere far below, were all these good excellent Karenins, Oblonskys, and the rest of the world.

Quite casually, without looking at them and just as if there was no other place to put them, Oblonsky placed Levin and Kitty side by side.

'Well, you might sit here,' he said to Levin.

The dinner was as good as the dinner service, a thing of which Oblonsky was a connoisseur. The soup, Marie Louise, had succeeded to perfection, the tiny pasties melted in one's mouth and were flawless. Two footmen and Matthew, wearing white ties, manipulated the food and the wines unostentatiously, quietly, and quickly. The dinner was a success on the material side, and no less so on the non-material side. The conversation, sometimes general and sometimes tête-à-tête, never ceased, and toward the end became so animated that the men left the table without ceasing to talk, and even Karenin was infected.

Chapter X

Pestsov liked to bring his discussions to a finish, and had not been satisfied with Koznyshev's remark, especially as he felt the fallacy of his own opinion.

'I did not mean,' he began over his soup, addressing Karenin, 'the density of population alone, but in conjunction with fundamentals and not principles.'

'It seems to me,' replied Karenin deliberately and languidly, 'that it is one and the same thing. In my opinion only that nation which is more highly developed can influence another, only that . . . .'

'But the question is,' interrupted Pestsov in his deep voice—he was always in a hurry to speak and always seemed to stake his whole soul on what he was talking about—'what does "higher development" consist of? The English, the French, or the Germans, which of them is more highly developed? Which will nationalize the other? We see that the Rhine has become Frenchified, yet the Germans do not stand on a lower level!' he shouted. 'There is some other law!'

'I think that the influence will always be on the side of the truly educated,' said Karenin slightly raising his eyebrows.

'But what should we consider to be the signs of "true education"?' said Pestsov.

'I fancy that those signs are well known,' replied Karenin.

'Are they fully known?' intervened Koznyshev with a subtle smile. 'At present a purely classical education is regarded as the only real education, but we hear lively discussions from both sides and cannot deny that the opposite view has many arguments in its favour.'

'You are a classic, Sergius Ivanich! Have a glass of claret?' said Oblonsky.

'I am not expressing my opinion of either kind of education,' replied Koznyshev, smiling at him condescendingly as at a child and holding out his glass. "All I say is that both sides have weighty arguments in their favour,' he continued, addressing himself to Karenin. 'I have had a classical education, but can personally find no place in that controversy. I see no clear proofs that a classical education should be preferred to a modern education.'

'Natural science has just as great an educational and mind-developing influence,' Pestsov joined in. 'Take astronomy, take botany, or zoology with its system of general laws!'

'I can't quite agree with you,' answered Karenin. 'It seems to me that we must admit that the process of studying the forms of a language has in itself a beneficial effect on mental development. Besides it is impossible to deny that the influence of the classics is in the highest degree a moral one, whereas unfortunately with instruction in natural science are connected those dangerous and false teachings which are the bane of the present times.'

Koznyshev was going to say something but Pestsov's deep bass interrupted him. He began with great warmth to prove the false-ness of this opinion. Koznyshev quietly waited to put in his word, evidently ready with a triumphant retort.

'But one cannot help admitting,' he said with his subtle smile, turning to Karenin, 'one cannot help admitting that it is difficult to weigh exactly all the pros and cons of the different studies, and that the question, which kind of education should be preferred, would not have been so easily decided had there not been on the side of classical education that advantage which you have just mentioned: the moral advantage, *disons le mot* [7] —the anti-nihilistic influence.'

'Exactly.'

'Were it not for the advantage of this anti-nihilistic influence on the side of classical education we should have considered the question longer, and should have weighed the arguments on both sides,' said Koznyshev, subtly smiling. 'We should have given a

---

7. Let us come right out and say it.

free field to both systems. But now we know that those classical education-pills contain the salutary virtue of anti-nihilism and we offer them boldly to our patients. . . . But supposing it has not that salutary virtue after all?' he concluded, adding the grain of Attic salt.

Everybody laughed at Koznyshev's 'pills,' and Turovtsyn, who had at last heard the something funny for which he had been waiting as he listened to the conversation, laughed particularly loudly and merrily.

Oblonsky had made no mistake in inviting Pestsov. With Pestsov there, intellectual conversation could not stop for a moment. Hardly had Koznyshev with his joke put an end to the discussion of one question before Pestsov immediately raised another.

'One cannot even admit that the Government had that aim in view,' he said. 'The Government is evidently guided by general considerations and is indifferent to the influence its measures may have. For instance, it ought to consider the education of women injurious, yet it established courses of lectures and universities for women.'

And the conversation at once veered to a new subject—the education of women.

Karenin expressed the view that the higher education of women is generally confounded with the question of women's emancipation, and that was the only reason for considering it injurious.

'I, on the contrary, think that these two questions are firmly bound together,' said Pestsov. 'It is a vicious circle. Women are deprived of rights because of their lack of education, and their lack of education results from their lack of rights. We must not forget that the subjection of women is so widespread and so old that we often refuse to recognize the abyss that separates them from us.'

'You said "rights",' remarked Koznyshev, who had been waiting for Pestsov to stop, 'the right of serving on a jury, on Town Councils, of being Presidents of local Government Boards, Civil Servants, Members of Parliament . . . ?'

'Undoubtedly.'

'But if women, in some rare exceptional cases, can fill these posts, it seems to me that you should not speak of "rights." It would be more correct to say "duties." Everybody will agree that when we fill the office of juryman, town councillor, or telegraph clerk, we feel that we are fulfilling a duty. So it would be more correct to say that women are seeking for duties, and quite rightly. And we must sympathize with this desire of others to help in man's work for the community.'

'You are quite right,' said Karenin. 'I think the only question is whether they are capable of fulfilling these duties.'

'In all probability they will be extremely capable,' interjected Oblonsky, 'when education is more widely diffused among them. We see this. . . .'

'And how about the old proverb?' remarked the old Prince, who had long been listening to the conversation with a humorous twinkle in his small glittering eyes. 'My daughters won't mind my mentioning it. Women's hair is long, but their wits. . . .' [8]

'They thought the same of the Negroes before their emancipation,' said Pestsov angrily.

'The thing that seems strange to me is that women should look for new duties,' said Koznyshev, 'while, as we see, men unfortunately generally avoid theirs.'

'Duties are connected with rights, power, money, honours: that is what women are seeking,' said Pestsov.

'It is just as if I were to strive for the right of being a wet nurse, and were offended because they pay women for it and won't pay me,' said the old Prince.

Turovtsyn burst into loud laughter, and Koznyshev felt sorry he had not made that remark himself. Even Karenin smiled.

'Yes, but a man can't be a wet nurse,' said Pestsov, 'while a woman . . .'

'Oh yes, an Englishman on board ship did once nurse his baby,' said the old Prince, allowing himself this indelicacy in his daughter's presence.

'There will be about as many women officials as there are of such Englishmen,' said Koznyshev.

'Yes, but what is a girl to do if she has no home?' said Oblonsky, agreeing with Pestsov and supporting him, and thinking of the dancer Chibisova, whom he had in his mind all the time.

'If you looked carefully into that girl's story, you would find that she had left her family or a sister's family, where she might have done woman's work,' said Dolly, irritably and unexpectedly intervening in the conversation. She probably guessed what girl her husband had in his mind.

'But we are defending a principle, an idea!' said Pestsov in his sonorous bass. 'Women wish to have the right to be independent and educated. They are hampered and oppressed by the consciousness that this is impossible for them.'

'And I am hampered and oppressed by the knowledge that they won't take me as a wet-nurse in the Foundlings' Hospital,' repeated the old Prince, to the great joy of Turovtsyn, who laughed till he dropped the thick end of a piece of asparagus into the sauce.

---

8. The Russian proverb runs: 'Woman's hair is long, but her wits are short.'

Chapter XI

Everybody took part in the general conversation except Kitty and Levin. At first when the influence of one nation or another was being talked about, thoughts of what he had to say on the subject involuntarily came into Levin's mind; but these thoughts, formerly so important to him, now only flickered through his mind as in a dream and were not of the slightest interest. It even struck him as strange that they should care to talk about things that could make no difference to anyone. In the same way what was being said about the rights of the education of women should have interested Kitty. How often she had thought about that question when she remembered her friend abroad and the irksome state of dependence in which Varenka lived, how often she had wondered what would be her own fate if she did not get married, and how many times she had argued about it with her sister. But now it did not interest her at all. She and Levin were carrying on their own separate conversation, and it was not even a conversation but a kind of mystic intercourse, which every moment bound them closer and closer and created in both a feeling of joyful fear before the unknown upon which they were entering.

They began by Levin's telling Kitty in answer to her question of how he could have seen her in the carriage in the summer, how he was going back from the hay fields along the high road and met her.

'It was early in the morning. I expect you had only just woke up. Your mother was asleep in her corner. It was a lovely morning. I was going along and wondering who that could be in a four-horsed coach, a splendid team with bells, and for an instant you appeared and I saw you at the window sitting like this, holding the strings of your cap with both hands and thinking very deeply about something,' he said and smiled. 'How I wish I knew what you were thinking about! Something important?'

'Was I not very untidy?' she thought, but seeing the rapturous smile which the recollection of these details evoked she felt that the impression she had produced was a very pleasing one. She blushed and laughed joyously. 'I really don't remember.'

'How pleasantly Turovtsyn laughs!' said Levin, looking with pleasure at his moist eyes and shaking body.

'Have you known him long?' asked Kitty.

'Who does not know him?'

'I see you think he is a bad man.'

'Not bad, but a mere cipher.'

'He is not. Change your opinion quickly,' said Kitty. 'I too did not think much of him, but he is . . . he is a dear fellow and wonderfully kind-hearted. He has a heart of gold.'

'How did you manage to find out his heart?'

'He and I are great friends. I know him very well. Last winter soon after . . . soon after you came to us,' she said with a penitent and at the same time a trustful smile, 'Dolly's children all had scarlet fever and he happened to call. And fancy!' she went on in a whisper, 'he was so sorry for her that he stopped and helped her to nurse the children. Really, he stayed three weeks in the house and looked after the children like a nurse.'

'I am telling Constantine Dmitrich about Turovtsyn and the scarlet fever,' she said, leaning over toward her sister.

'Yes? it was wonderful! he is splendid!' said Dolly, looking toward Turovtsyn who felt that he was being talked about, and giving him a gentle smile.

Levin looked at Turovtsyn again and wondered how it was he had failed to realize what a charming man he was.

'I am sorry, very sorry. I shall never again think ill of anyone!' he said merrily; expressing what he sincerely felt at the moment.

Chapter XII

In the conversation which had been begun on the rights of women there were raised some questions not freely to be discussed in the presence of ladies concerning the inequalities of marriage relations. Pestsov more than once during dinner-time flew at these questions, but Koznyshev and Oblonsky carefully diverted him from them.

When they rose from table and the ladies had left the room, Pestsov did not follow them but turned to Karenin and began to state the chief cause of inequality. The inequality between husband and wife, in his opinion, lay in the fact that the infidelity of a wife and that of a husband were unequally punished both by law and by public opinion.

Oblonsky hurriedly offered Karenin a cigar.

'No, I don't smoke,' quietly replied Karenin, and, as if wishing to show that he was not afraid of the conversation, he turned with a cold smile to Pestsov.

'I imagine that the cause of the prevailing opinion lies in the very nature of things,' he said, and was about to go to the drawing-room, but Turovtsyn quite unexpectedly addressed him.

'Have you heard about Pryachnikov?' said Turovtsyn, animated by the champagne he had drunk, and impatient to break his silence, which had long oppressed him. And with a kindly smile on his moist and rosy lips, he went on addressing himself chiefly to Karenin, the principal guest.

'Vasya Pryachnikov, as I was told to-day, has fought a duel with

Kvitsky and killed him.'

As one always seems to knock a sore place, so that day Oblonsky felt that unfortunately the conversation kept striking Karenin's sore place. He again made an attempt to draw his brother-in-law away, but Karenin himself asked with interest:

'What did Pryachnikov fight about?'

'His wife. He behaved like a brick! Challenged the other and killed him!'

'Oh!' said Karenin indifferently, and raising his eyebrows he went to the drawing-room.

'I am so glad you came,' said Dolly with a frightened smile, as she met him in the sitting-room through which he had to pass: 'I must speak with you. Let us sit down here.'

Karenin, with the same look of indifference, produced by his raised eyebrows, sat down beside her and feigned a smile.

'Yes,' he said, 'especially as I wished to ask you to excuse me for having to go away at once. I am leaving Moscow to-morrow.'

Dolly was firmly convinced of Anna's innocence, and felt herself growing pale and her lips trembling from anger with this cold, unfeeling man who so calmly intended to ruin her innocent friend.

'Alexis Alexandrovich,' she said, looking into his eyes with desperate determination. 'I asked you about Anna and you did not give me an answer. How is she?'

'I think she is well, Darya Alexandrovna,' replied Karenin without looking at her.

'Alexis Alexandrovich, forgive me, I have no right to . . . but I love Anna like a sister, and respect her; and I beg, I implore you to tell me what has happened between you; what do you accuse her of?'

Alexey Alexandrovich winced, and almost closing his eyes bowed his head.

'I expect your husband has told you the reasons which make me consider it necessary to change my former relations with Anna Arkadyevna,' he said without looking in her eyes, discontentedly eyeing Shcherbatsky who was passing through the sitting-room.

'I don't, I don't believe it, I cannot believe it!' Dolly said, clasping her bony hands with an energetic movement. She rose quickly, put her hand on Karenin's sleeve and said, 'We shall be disturbed here, come this way, please.'

Dolly's excitement affected Karenin. He rose and obediently followed her into the schoolroom. They sat down at the table covered with leather cloth all cut about with penknives.

'I don't believe it, I don't!' she uttered, trying to catch his eyes, which avoided hers.

'One can't disbelieve facts, Darya Alexandrovna,' said he, emphasizing the word *facts*.

'But what has she done?' asked Darya Alexandrovna. 'What is it she has done?'

'She has despised her duties and betrayed her husband. That is what she has done,' he said.

'No, no, it can't be! No, for God's sake! . . . you are mistaken,' said Dolly, raising her hands to her temples and closing her eyes.

Karenin smiled coldly with his lips only, wishing to prove to her and to himself the firmness of his conviction; but this passionate defence, though it did not shake him, lacerated his wound. He began speaking with more animation.

'It is difficult to make a mistake when a wife herself announces to her husband that eight years of married life and a son have all been an error, and that she wants to begin life from the beginning again,' he said crossly, sniffing.

'Anna and—vice. . . . I cannot combine them, I cannot believe it!'

'Darya Alexandrovna,' he said, now looking straight at Dolly's kind, excited face and feeling his tongue involuntarily loosened. 'I would give much for the possibility of doubting. While I was in doubt it was hard, but not so hard as it is now. While I doubted, I had hope; but now there is no hope left and all the same I doubt everything. I doubt everything so much that I hate my son, and sometimes believe he is not my son. I am very unhappy.'

There was no need for him to say this. Dolly had understood it as soon as he looked her in the face. She felt sorry for him, and her faith in her friend's innocence was shaken.

'Oh, it is terrible, terrible! But can it be true that you have decided on a divorce?'

'I have decided to take the final step. There is nothing else for me to do.'

'Nothing to do, nothing to do!' she muttered with tears in her eyes. 'No, there is something else to do,' she said.

'That is just what is so terrible in this kind of grief, that you can't do as in all other troubles—losses or deaths—just bear your cross, but here you must act,' he said, as if guessing her thoughts. 'You must come out of the degrading position in which you are placed; it is impossible to live three together.'

'I understand, I understand very well,' said Dolly and her head dropped. She was silent, thinking of herself and her own sorrow, and then suddenly and energetically she raised her head and folded her hands as in prayer. 'But wait! You are a Christian. Think of her! What will become of her if you throw her off?'

'I have thought, Darya Alexandrovna, and have thought deeply,' said Karenin. His face flushed in blotches and his dim eyes looked straight at her. Dolly now pitied him with all her heart. 'I did that very thing when she herself informed me of my shame; I let everything go on as before. I gave her a chance to turn over a new leaf, and I tried to save her. With what result? She disregarded my very easy demand—that she should observe the proprieties,' he went on, getting heated. 'One may save a person who does not wish to perish; but if a nature is so spoilt and depraved that it regards ruin as salvation, what can one do?'

'Anything but divorce!' answered Dolly.

'But what is "anything"?'

'No, this is too awful. She will be nobody's wife, she will be ruined.'

'What can I do?' said Karenin, shrugging his shoulders and raising his eyebrows. The recollection of his wife's last delinquency irritated him so much that he again became as cold as he had been at the beginning of the conversation. 'I am very grateful for your sympathy, but it is time for me to go,' he said rising.

'No, wait a bit! You should not ruin her. Wait a bit. I will tell you about myself. I married, and my husband deceived me; in my anger and jealousy I wished to abandon everything, I myself wished . . . But I was brought to my senses, and by whom? Anna saved me. And here I am living; my children growing, my husband returns to the family and feels his error, grows purer and better, and I live . . . I have forgiven, and you must forgive.'

Karenin listened, but her words no longer affected him. All the bitterness of the day when he decided on a divorce rose again in his soul. He gave himself a shake and begin to speak in a loud and piercing voice.

'I cannot forgive; I don't wish to and don't think it would be right. I have done everything for that woman, and she has trampled everything in the mud which is natural to her. I am not a cruel man, I have never hated anyone, but I hate her with the whole strength of my soul and I cannot even forgive her, because I hate her so much for all the wrong she has done me!' he said with tears of anger choking him.

'Love those that hate you,' whispered Dolly shamefacedly.

Karenin smiled contemptuously. He had long known all that, but it could not apply to his case.

'Love them that hate you, but you can't love them whom you hate. Forgive me for having upset you. Every one has trouble enough of his own!' And having got himself under control, Karenin quietly rose, said good-bye and went away.

Chapter XIII

When everybody was leaving the table Levin wanted to follow
Kitty into the drawing-room but was afraid she would not like it
because it would make his attentions to her too obvious. So he
stopped with the group of men, taking part in their conversation.
But without looking through the open door at Kitty he was
conscious of her movements, her looks, and the place in the drawing-
room where she sat.

He began at once, and without the slightest effort, to fulfil the
promise he had made her, of thinking well of and always liking
everybody. The conversation had turned to the question of village
communes, in which Pestsov saw some special principle which he
called the 'choral principle.' Levin did not agree either with
Pestsov or with his brother Sergius, who, in a way of his own, both
admitted and did not admit the importance of the Russian Communal System. But he talked to them only with the idea of getting
them to agree and softening their controversy. He was not at all
interested in what he himself said, still less in what they were
saying, and only desired one thing—that everybody should feel
contented and pleased. He now knew the one thing that was
important. And that one thing was at first there in the drawing-
room, but afterwards began moving and paused in the doorway.
Without looking round he felt a pair of eyes and a smile directed
toward him, and he could not help turning. She stood in the doorway with Shcherbatsky and was looking at him.

'I thought you were going to the piano,' he said, moving toward
her. 'That is what I miss in the country—music.'

'No, we were only coming to call you away. Thank you for
coming,' she said, rewarding him with a smile as with a gift.
'What is the use of arguing? No one ever convinces another.'

'Yes, you are quite right,' said Levin, 'for the most part, people
argue so warmly only because they cannot make out what it is
that their opponent wants to prove.'

Levin had often noticed in arguments among the most intelligent
people that after expending enormous efforts, and an immense
number of logical subtleties and words, the disputants at last
became conscious of the fact that the thing they had been at such
pains to prove to one another had long ago, from the very beginning
of the controversy, been known to them but that they liked
different things and were disinclined to mention what they liked
lest it should be attacked. He had experienced the fact that
sometimes in the middle of a discussion one understands what it
is that one's opponent likes, and suddenly likes it oneself, and
immediately agrees with him, when all proofs become superfluous

and unnecessary. Sometimes the reverse happens; one at last mentions the thing one likes, for the sake of which one has been devising arguments, and if this is said well and sincerely, one's opponent suddenly agrees and ceases to dispute. This was what he wanted to express.

She wrinkled her forehead, trying to understand. But as soon as he began to explain she understood.

'I see: one must find out what one's opponent is contending for, what he likes, and then one can . . .'

She had completely grasped and found the right expression for his badly-expressed thought. Levin smiled joyfully: he was so struck by the change from the confused wordy dispute with his brother and Pestsov to this laconic, clear, and almost wordless communication of a very complex idea.

Shcherbatsky left them, and Kitty went up to a table prepared for cards, sat down, took a piece of chalk, and began drawing concentric circles on the new green cloth of the table.

They went back to the conversation at dinner about women's rights and occupations. Levin agreed with Dolly, that a girl who does not get married can find woman's work in the family. He supported this view by saying that no family can dispense with a help, and that in every family, rich or poor, there are and must be nurses, either paid or belonging to the family.

'No,' said Kitty, blushing, but looking all the more boldly at him with her truthful eyes: 'A girl may be so placed that she cannot enter into a family without humiliation, while she herself. . . .'

He understood the allusion.

'Oh yes!' he said, 'yes, yes, yes, you are right, you are right!'

And he understood all that Pestsov at dinner had been trying to prove about the freedom of women, simply because he saw in Kitty's heart fear of the humiliation of being an old maid, and, loving her, he too felt that fear and humiliation, and at once gave up his contention.

There was a pause. She still continued drawing on the table with the chalk. Her eyes shone with a soft light. Submitting to her mood, he felt in his whole being an ever-increasing stress of joy.

'Oh, I have scribbled over the whole table!' she said, and putting down the chalk moved as if to get up.

'How can I remain here alone, without her?' he thought horror-struck, and took up the chalk. 'Don't go,' he said, and sat down at the table.

'I have long wished to ask you something!'

He looked straight into her kind though frightened eyes.

'Please do.'

'There,' he said, and wrote the following letters,—W, y, a: i, c, n, b; d, y, m t, o, n? These letters stood for: When you answered: it can not be; did you mean then, or never? It was quite unlikely that she would be able to make out this complicated sentence; but he looked at her with an expression as if his life depended on her understanding what those letters meant.

She glanced seriously at him and then, leaning her puckered forehead on her hand, began reading. Occasionally she looked up at him, her look asking him: 'Is it what I think?'

'I have understood,' she said with a blush.

'What word is this?' he asked pointing to the 'n' which stood for never.

'The word is never,' she said, 'but that's not true.'

He quickly rubbed out what he had written, handed her the chalk and rose.

She wrote: T, I, c, n, a, o.

Dolly's sorrow, caused by her talk with Karenin, was quite dispelled when she saw those two figures: Kitty with the chalk in her hand, looking up at Levin with a timid, happy smile, and his fine figure bending over the table, with his burning eyes fixed now on the table, now on her. Suddenly his face beamed; he had understood. The letters meant 'Then I could not answer otherwise.'

He looked at her questioningly, and timidly.

'Only *then*?'

'Yes,' answered her smile.

'And n. . . . And now?' he said.

'Well, then, read this. I will tell you what I wish, what I very much wish!' and she wrote these initial letters: T, y, m, f, a, f, w, h. This meant, 'that you might forgive and forget what happened.'

He seized the chalk with nervous, trembling fingers, broke it, and wrote the initial letters of the following: 'I have nothing to forget or forgive, I never ceased to love you.'

She looked at him with an assured smile that did not waver. 'I understand,' she whispered.

He sat down and wrote out a long sentence. She understood it all, and without asking if she was right, took the chalk, and wrote the answer at once.

For a long time he could not make out what she meant and he often looked up in her eyes. He was dazed with happiness. He could not find the words she meant at all; but in her beautiful eyes, radiant with joy, he saw all that he wanted to know. And he wrote down three letters. But before he had finished writing she read it under his hand, finished the sentence herself, and wrote the answer: 'Yes.'

'Playing "secretary"?' said the old Prince approaching them.
'Come now, we must be going, if you mean to come to the
theatre.'

Levin rose and accompanied Kitty to the door.

Everything had been said in that conversation. She had said
that she loved him, and would tell her father and mother, and he
had said that he would call in the morning.

Chapter XIV

When Kitty had left and Levin remained alone he felt so restless without her and so impatient to live more and more quickly
through the hours till morning when he would see her again and
be plighted to her for ever, that he dreaded like death the fourteen
hours he would have to spend without her. In order not to be alone
and to deceive time, he needed to be with and to talk to somebody.
Oblonsky would have been the pleasantest companion for him
now, but he was going to an evening party as he said (really to the
ballet). Levin only had time to tell him he was happy and fond
of him and would never, never forget what he had done for him.
Oblonsky's look and smile showed Levin that he understood him
rightly.

'Then it's not time to die yet?' asked Oblonsky with feeling,
pressing Levin's hand.

'N-n-n-oo!' said Levin.

Dolly too, when saying good-bye to him, spoke as if congratu-
lating him, saying: 'I am so glad you and Kitty have met again.
We must value old friendship.' Levin did not like her remark.
She did not understand how high and unattainable for her all this
was, and she should not have dared to refer to it. Levin took leave
of them but, not to remain alone, he fastened on to his brother.

'Where are you going?'

'To a Town Council meeting.'

'Well, I'll come with you. May I?'

'Why not? Let us go,' answered Koznyshev, smiling. 'What has
happened to you to-day?'

'To me? Happiness is with me,' said Levin, letting down the
window of the carriage in which they were driving. 'You don't
mind? It is so stuffy here. Happiness is with me. Why have you
never got married?'

Koznyshev smiled.

'I am very glad, she seems a fine gi . . .' he began.

'Don't, don't, don't speak!' exclaimed Levin, seizing the collar of
his brother's fur-coat and lapping it over his face. 'She is a fine
girl' were words so ordinary, so insignificant, so inappropriate to
his feelings.

Koznyshev laughed merrily, a thing he rarely did.

'Anyhow I may say I am very glad.'

'You may say that to-morrow, to-morrow, but nothing more! Nothing, nothing, silence . . .'[9] said Levin, and again wrapping the collar round his brother's face he added: 'I am very fond of you! Will they really let me in to the meeting.'

'Of course you can come.'

'What are you speaking on to-night?' asked Levin not ceasing to smile.

They arrived at the Council, and Levin listened to the secretary haltingly reading an official report which he evidently did not understand himself, but from his face Levin saw what a nice, kind, and splendid fellow he was. That was plain from the confused and embarrassed manner in which he read the report. Then followed the discussion. They were debating the grant of some money and the laying of some pipes, and Koznyshev spoke about something for a long time in a triumphant tone and stung two of the members; another member, having noted something on a bit of paper, started timidly, but went on to answer him very venomously and neatly. And then Sviyazhsky (he too was there) also said something very finely and nobly. Levin listened to them and clearly saw that neither the sums of money nor the pipes had any real existence, there was nothing of the kind, and he saw also that they were not at all angry but were all very kind and estimable fellows, and that it was all very good and pleasant. They were doing no one any harm, and everybody was pleased. What seemed remarkable to Levin was that they were all perfectly transparent to him that day, and that by means of little signs which he had never noticed before he recognized the soul of each and clearly saw that they were all kind and, in particular, were all extremely fond of him. That was quite evident from the way they spoke to him, and the tenderness and affection with which they all, even strangers, looked at him.

'Well, are you contented?' asked Koznyshev.

'Quite. I never thought it would be so interesting. Fine! splendid!'

Sviyazhsky came up and asked Levin to come home with him and have some tea. Levin could not at all think or remember why he had ever felt dissatisfied with Sviyazhsky or what he had thought lacking in him. He was an intelligent and remarkably kind fellow.

'I shall be very pleased,' said Levin, and asked about Sviyazhsky's wife and sister-in-law. And by a strange connection of ideas, as that sister-in-law was connected in his fancy with the idea of

---

9. 'Nothing, nothing, silence . . .' is a quotation repeatedly made use of from Gógol's *Memoirs of a Madman.*

marriage, it appeared to him that he could not tell anybody of his happiness so appropriately as Sviyazhsky's wife and sister-in-law, and he was very glad to go and see them.

Sviyazhsky questioned him about his affairs in the country, as usual disbelieving in the possibility of devising anything that had not already been discovered in Western Europe: but now Levin did not consider this at all unpleasant. On the contrary he felt that Sviyazhsky was right, and that the whole business was insignificant, and he noticed the wonderful gentleness and delicacy with which Sviyazhsky avoided saying that he was right. The ladies were especially nice; it seemed to Levin that they already knew all about it and sympathized with him but did not mention it out of delicacy. He remained at the house two or three hours, talking about different matters, but thinking only of the one thing that filled his soul and not noticing that they were dreadfully weary of him and ought long ago to have been in bed. Sviyazhsky, yawning, showed him to the hall and wondered at the strange state his friend was in. It was past one. Levin returned to the hotel and the thought of how with his impatience he would spend the remaining ten hours frightened him. The attendant on duty lighted his candle and was going away, but Levin stopped him. Egor, the attendant, of whom Levin had taken no notice heretofore, turned out to be a very intelligent, good, and above all very kind man.

'I say, Egor, don't you find it difficult to keep awake?'

'What's one to do? Our work is of that sort. It is easier in a gentleman's house, but one earns more here.'

It turned out that Egor had a family, three boys and a girl who was a seamstress and whom he wanted to marry to an assistant in a harness business.

Levin took this opportunity to express to Egor his opinion that in marriage the chief thing is—love, and that when there is love there will always be happiness, because happiness lies always within oneself.

Egor listened very attentively and evidently quite understood Levin, but in confirmation of it remarked, quite unexpectedly to Levin, that when he was in the service of nice people he was always satisfied with his masters and that he was satisfied with his present master although he was a Frenchman.

'A wonderfully kind man!' thought Levin.

'And you, Egor, when you married, did you love your wife?'

'How can one help it?' answered Egor.

And Levin saw that Egor too was in an exultant state and wished to tell him all his most intimate feelings.

'My life too was very curious. From a child I . . .' he began with shining eyes, evidently infected by Levin's exultation as men get infected by others' yawning.

But at that moment a bell rang; Egor went away and Levin remained alone. He had scarcely eaten anything at dinner and had refused both tea and supper at Sviyazhsky's, but could not think of eating. He had not slept the night before but could not think of sleep either. The room was cool, but he felt suffocated with heat. He opened the little window [1] and sat down on a table in front of it. Beyond a snow-covered roof he could see a gilt fretwork cross adorned with chains on the dome of a church and above it the three-cornered constellation of the Charioteer with the bright yellow star Capella. He looked now at the cross, now at the star, and inhaled the fresh frosty air which flowed with a regular current into the room, following, as in a dream, the images and memories that arose in his fancy. Towards four o'clock he heard steps in the corridor and looked out. It was the gambler Myaskin whom he knew, returning from the club. He passed dejectedly, frowning and coughing. 'Poor, unfortunate fellow!' thought Levin, and tears of affection and pity for the man filled his eyes. He wished to speak to him and comfort him, but recollecting that he had nothing over his shirt he changed his mind and again sat down in front of the little window to bathe in the cold air and to gaze at that beautifully-shaped silent cross, full of meaning for him, and at the ascending bright yellow star. When it was past six o'clock he began to hear the floor-polishers, and the church bell ringing for service, and he felt he was beginning to grow cold. He shut the little window, washed, dressed, and went out into the street.

Chapter XV

The streets were still empty. Levin went to the Shcherbatskys' house. The front door was locked, everybody was still sleeping. He went back to his room in the hotel and ordered coffee. The day-waiter, not Egor this time, brought it to him. Levin wished to have a talk with him, but the bell rang and the waiter went away. Levin tried to drink a little coffee, and put a piece of roll into his mouth, but his mouth could do nothing with it. He took the piece out of his mouth, put on his overcoat and went out to walk about again. It was past nine when he reached the Shcher-batskys' porch a second time. The inmates of the house were only just up, and the cook was going out to buy provisions. It would be necessary to live through another two hours at least.

All that night and morning Levin had lived quite unconsciously, and felt quite outside the conditions of material existence. He had not eaten for a whole day, had not slept for two nights, had spent

1. The *fortochka* or small inset window customary in Russia, which allows of fresh air being let into the room in winter without cooling it too much.

several hours half-dressed and exposed to the frost, yet he felt not only fresher and better than ever before, but quite independent of his body: he moved without his muscles making any effort, and felt capable of anything. He was sure that he could fly upwards or knock down the corner of a house, were it necessary. He spent the rest of the time walking about the streets, looking at his watch, and gazing around.

And what he then saw he never saw again. Two children going to school, some pigeons that flew down from the roof, and a few loaves put outside a baker's window by an invisible hand touched him particularly. These loaves, the pigeons, and the two boys seemed creatures not of this earth. It all happened at the same time; one of the boys ran after a pigeon and looked smilingly up at Levin; the pigeon flapped its wings and fluttered up, glittering in the sunshine amid the snow-dust that trembled in the air; from the window came the scent of fresh-baked bread and the loaves were put out. All these things were so unusually beautiful that Levin laughed and cried with joy. After a long round, through the Gazetny Street and the Kislovka, he returned to the hotel, put his watch in front of him, and sat down waiting till it should be twelve. In the next room they were saying something about machines and fraud, and coughing as people do of a morning. They did not realize that the watch hand was drawing nearer to twelve. The hand reached twelve. Levin went out into the porch. The *izvoshchiks* evidently knew all about it. With joyful faces they surrounded Levin, disputing among themselves, and offering him their services. Trying not to offend the others, and promising to let them too drive him later on, he hired one and told him to drive to the Shcherbatskys'. The *izvozchik* was charming with the white band of his shirt showing from under his coat and clinging closely to his full, red, sturdy neck. That *izvozchik's* sledge was high and comfortable and never after did Levin drive in one like it, and the horse was a good one too and tried its best to trot fast, but did not move from the place. The *izvozchik* knew the Shcherbatskys' house, and rounding his elbows in a manner specially respectful to his fare, called 'Whoa!' and stopped at the porch. The Shcherbatskys' hall-porter certainly knew everything. That was evident from the smile in his eyes and the tone in which he said:

'It's long since you were here last, Constantine Dmitrich!'

Not only did he know everything, but he evidently rejoiced and made efforts to hide his joy. Glancing into his kind old eyes, Levin felt something new even in his own happiness.

'Are they up?'

'Come in, sir! Won't you leave it here?' he said, when Levin turned back for his cap. That meant something.

'Whom shall I announce you to?' asked the footman.

The footman was young, of the new-fashioned kind and a dandy, but a very kind and good fellow, and he too understood it all.

'The Prince . . . The Princess . . . The young lady . . .' said Levin.

The first person he met was Mlle Linon. She was passing through the dancing-hall and her curls and her face shone. He had scarcely begun to speak to her when he heard the rustle of a dress outside the door, his eyes no longer saw Mlle Linon, and the joyful terror of the nearness of his happiness seized him. Mlle Linon hurriedly left him and went toward the other door. As soon as she had gone out he heard the sound of very, very rapid light steps on the parquet floor, and his joy, his life, his own self, the best in himself, that which he had sought and yearned for so long, advanced very, very rapidly towards him. She did not walk but was borne toward him by some invisible force.

He saw nothing but her clear, true eyes, frightened by the same joy of love which filled his own heart. Those eyes beamed nearer and nearer to him, dazzling him with their glow of love. She stopped so close that she touched him. Her arms rose and her hands dropped on his shoulders.

She had done everything she could—she had run up to him and given herself entirely, shyly, and joyfully. He put his arms round her and pressed his lips to her mouth that was waiting for his kiss.

She too had not slept all night and had waited for him the whole morning.

Her mother and father had definitely given their consent and were happy in her happiness. She had waited for him. She had wished to be the first to announce to him his and her joy. She had prepared herself to meet him alone, and had rejoiced at the idea, yet had felt timid and bashful and had not known what she would do. She had heard his step and his voice and had waited behind the door for Mlle Linon to go. Mlle Linon had gone away. Without thinking or asking herself what next, she had come to him and acted as she had.

'Come to Mama!' she said, taking him by the hand. For some time he could not say anything, not so much because he feared that words might spoil the loftiness of his feelings, as because every time he wished to speak he felt that, instead of words, tears of joy would come. He took her hand and kissed it.

'Can it be true?' he said at last in a smothered voice. 'Dear, I cannot believe that you love me.'

She smiled at the word 'dear,' and at the timid look he gave her.

'Yes!' she said significantly and slowly. 'I am so happy!'

Without letting go of his hand, she entered the drawing-room. The Princess, on seeing them, breathed quickly and immediately burst into tears, then she at once laughed and ran up to them with energy such as Levin never expected from her, and putting her arms round his head kissed him and wetted his cheeks with her tears.

'Then it's all finished! I am so glad. Love her. I am so glad . . . Kitty!'

'Well, you've settled it quickly!' said the old Prince, trying to be indifferent; but Levin noticed that his eyes were moist when he addressed him. 'I have long, I have always wished it!' said the old Prince, taking Levin's hand and drawing him nearer. 'Even at the time when this scatterbrain intended . . .'

'Papa!' exclaimed Kitty and closed his mouth with her hands.

'Well, well, I won't!' he said. 'I am very, very . . . plea . . . Oh, how stupid I am!'

He embraced Kitty, kissed her face, her hand, then her face again, and made the sign of the cross over her.

And Levin was seized with a new feeling of affection for this man who had been strange to him before, when he saw how Kitty long and tenderly kissed his fleshy hand.

Chapter XVI

The Princess sat in her armchair silently smiling, and the Prince seated himself beside her. Kitty stood close to her father's chair, still holding his hand. No one spoke.

The Princess was the first to break the silence and bring all their thoughts and feelings back to the practical side of life, and for the first moments this seemed strange and even painful to them all.

'When is it to be? There is the betrothal, and cards must be sent out. And when is the wedding to be? What do you think, Alexander?'

'Here he is,' said the old Prince, pointing to Levin. 'He is the principal person concerned.'

'When?' said Levin, blushing. 'To-morrow! If you ask me—the betrothal to-day and the wedding to-morrow!'

'Oh, don't, *mon cher!* What nonsense!'

'Well then, next week.'

'He seems quite mad.'

'Why not?'

'What an idea!' said the mother with a pleased smile at his haste. 'And the trousseau?'

'Is it possible that there must be a trousseau and all that sort of thing?' Levin thought, horror-struck. 'However. . . . As if a trousseau and a betrothal ceremony and all that could spoil my happiness! Nothing can spoil it!' He looked up at Kitty and noticed that the thought of a trousseau did not in the least upset her; so he thought, 'It is necessary, evidently.'

'Well, you see, I don't know at all; I only expressed my wish,' he said, to excuse himself.

'Then we will decide. We can have the betrothal, and send out the cards at once. That will be all right.'

The Princess went up to her husband, kissed him and was about to go away, but he stopped her, embraced her, and tenderly, like a young lover, kissed her several times, with a smile. The old couple seemed to have become confused for the moment, and not to know whether it was they who were again in love or only their daughter. When they had gone Levin came up to his betrothed and took her hand. He had now mastered himself and was able to speak, and there was much he had to say to her; but what he said was not at all what he had intended.

'How well I knew it would happen! I never dared hope, yet in my soul I was always certain,' said he. 'I believe it was predestined.'

'And I,' she said. 'Even when . . .' she stopped, and again went on, her truthful eyes looking into his face resolutely, 'even when I drove my happiness from me I always loved you only, but I was carried away. I must ask you: can you forget it?'

'Perhaps it was all for the best. You have much to forgive me. I must tell you. . . .'

He referred to one of the things he had decided to tell her. He meant to confess, from the first, about two matters: that he was not as pure as she, and that he was an agnostic. It was painful but he thought he ought to tell her both these things.

'No, not now, later!' he said.

'All right, later; but certainly tell me! I am afraid of nothing. I must know everything. Now it's settled. . . .'

He finished the sentence. 'It is settled that you will have me, whatever I may be. . . . You will not reject me. . . . Yes?'

'Yes, yes!'

Their conversation was interrupted by Mlle Linon, who with a feigned yet affectionate smile came to congratulate her favourite pupil. Before she had gone out, the servants entered with their congratulations. Afterwards relatives arrived, and that beatific tumult began which did not cease until the day after the wedding. All that time Levin felt uncomfortable and bored, but the stress of his joy went on increasing. All that time he felt that many things he did not know were expected of him, but he did all he was told, and it all gave him joy. He had thought that his courtship would be quite unlike any other, that the ordinary conditions of courtship would spoil his peculiar happiness; but he ended by doing what others do, and his happiness was thereby only increased, becoming more and more peculiar to him, unlike anyone else's was or is.

'Now we shall eat some sweets,' said Mlle Linon, and off went Levin to buy sweets. 'I am very pleased indeed,' said Sviyazhsky, 'I advise you to go to Fomin's for the flowers.'—'Are they necessary?' and off he went to Fomin's. His brother told him he ought to borrow some money because he would have a lot of expense: there would be presents. . . . 'Are presents required?' and off he rushed to Fulda, the jeweller's.

At the confectioner's, florist's, and jeweller's, he noticed that they were expecting him, that they were pleased to see him, and triumphed in his happiness just like everyone else with whom he had anything to do at that time. It was extraordinary that not only was everybody fond of him, but all the hitherto unsympathetic, cold, or indifferent persons were delighted with him, gave way to him in everything, treated his feelings with delicate consideration, and shared his own opinion that he was the happiest man on earth because his betrothed was the height of perfection. Kitty felt just the same. When the Countess Nordston took the liberty of hinting that she had hoped for something better, Kitty got so heated and proved so convincingly that no one on earth could be better than Levin, that the Countess had to admit it, and thereafter never encountered Levin in Kitty's presence without a smile of delight.

The confession he had promised her was the one painful episode of that time. He consulted the old Prince, and with his permission gave Kitty his diary, which contained the facts that were tormenting him. He had written the diary with the intention of showing it to his future bride-elect. The confession of his agnosticism passed without a remark. She was religious and had never doubted the truth of her religion, but the lack of external religion in him did not affect her at all. She knew, through her love, his whole soul, and saw in it what she desired, and the fact that that spiritual condition is called agnosticism was quite indifferent to her. The other confession made her weep bitterly.

Levin had not handed her the diary without an inward struggle. He knew that between him and her there could and should be nothing secret, and therefore he decided that it was his duty; but he had not considered how the confession might affect her: he had not put himself in her place. Only when he came that evening, before going to the theatre, and entered her room to see in her tear-stained face the misery caused by the irremediable sorrow he had brought about, did he realize from that sweet, pathetic face what an abysm separated his tainted past from her dovelike purity, and he was horror-struck at what he had done.

'Take, take those dreadful books back!' she cried, pushing away the note-books that lay on the table before her. 'Why did you give me them? . . . But no—it was best after all,' she added, pitying the despair on his face. 'But it is dreadful, dreadful!'

His head drooped and he remained silent, unable to speak.

'You will not forgive me?' he whispered.

'Yes, I have forgiven you, but it is dreadful!'

However, his happiness was so great that this confession did not impair it, but only gave it a new tinge. She forgave him, but after that he felt yet more unworthy of her, morally bowed still lower before her, and valued still more highly his undeserved happiness.

Chapter XVII

Involuntarily reviewing the impressions left on his mind by the conversations at dinner and after, Karenin returned to his solitary room. What Dolly had said about forgiveness had merely vexed him. Whether or not to apply the Christian principle to his own case was too difficult a question to be lightly discussed, and Karenin had long since answered it in the negative. Of all that had been said the words of the silly good-natured Turovtsyn had sunk deepest into his mind—'*He acted like a brick, challenged the other man, and killed him.*' Evidently everybody had agreed with that, though they were too polite to say so. 'However, that point is settled and not worth thinking about,' said Karenin to himself; and with nothing in his mind but his impending journey and his work of inspection, he went to his room and asked the doorkeeper, who followed him, where his valet was. The man replied that the valet had just gone out. Karenin ordered tea, sat down at a table, took up Froom,[2] and began planning his journey. journey.

'Two telegrams,' said the valet, entering. 'Excuse me, your Excellency—I had only just gone out.'

Karenin took the telegrams and opened them. The first contained the news that Stremov had obtained the very appointment Karenin had been hoping for. He threw down the telegram and flushed. Rising, he began to pace the room. '*Quos vult perdere dementat,*'[3] he thought, *quos* being those who had had a hand in making the appointment. He was vexed, not so much at having missed that post himself and at having been obviously passed over, as at the incomprehensible and surprising impact that they did not realize how much less suitable than anyone else was that

---

2. *Froom's Railway Guide for Russia and the Continent of Europe* (1870).
3. When God wants to destroy someone, he first makes him mad.

voluble windbag, Stremov. How was it they did not see that by giving him that post they were ruining themselves and their own prestige?

'Something else of the same kind,' he thought bitterly, as he opened the second telegram. It was from his wife, and *Anna*, written in blue pencil, was the first word he saw. '*I am dying, I beg and entreat you, come! I shall die easier for your forgiveness*,' he read. Smiling contemptuously, he threw down the telegram. His first thought was that beyond doubt it was only falsehood and cunning.

'She would not hesitate at any deception. She was going to be confined; perhaps that is the illness. But what can they be aiming at? To legitimize the child, compromise me, and prevent divorce?' he reflected. 'But there is something about dying. . . .' He re-read the telegram, and was suddenly struck by the direct meaning of the words. 'Supposing it is true?' he said to himself. 'If it is true, and at the moment of suffering and approach to death she is sincerely repentant, and I, believing it to be false, refuse to come? It would not only be cruel and everybody would condemn me, but it would be stupid on my part.

'Peter, keep the carriage! I am returning to Petersburg,' he told the valet.

He decided to go back to Petersburg and see his wife.

If the news of her illness were false, he would go away again saying nothing; but if she were really ill and dying, and wished to see him before her death, he would, should he find her still living, forgive her; and should he arrive too late he would perform his last duty to her.

While on his way he did not again think about what he should do.

With the sense of fatigue and want of cleanliness resulting from a night spent in a railway carriage, Karenin drove through the fog of a Petersburg morning, along the deserted Nevsky, looking straight before him and not thinking of what awaited him. He dared not think of it, because when he imagined what would happen he could not drive from his mind the thought that her death would at once resolve all the difficulties of the situation. Bakers, the closed shops, night *izvozchiks* and men sweeping the pavements passed before his eyes, and watching all this he tried to stifle the thought of what lay before him and of what he dared not desire and yet could not help desiring. The carriage stopped at the porch. A carriage with a coachman asleep on the box and an *izvozchik* were standing at the entrance. As he entered the hall Karenin dragged forth his resolve as it were from a remote corner of his brain, and conned it over. It said: 'If it is all a fraud, then calm contempt and leave again; if true, do what is proper.'

The door was opened by the hall-porter before Karenin had
time to ring. The porter, Petrov, otherwise Kapitonich, looked
strange in an old coat without a tie, and in slippers.

'How is your mistress?'

'Safely delivered yesterday.'

Karenin halted and turned pale. Now he clearly realized how
much he had desired her death.

'And her health?'

Korney, wearing his morning apron, came running downstairs.
'Very bad,' he said. 'There was a consultation yesterday and
the doctor is here now.'

'Take my things,' said Karenin; and somewhat relieved by the
news that there was still some hope of her dying, he entered the
ante-room. On the hall-stand was hanging a military coat, and he
noticed it.

'Who is here?'

'The doctor, the midwife, and Count Vronsky.'

Karenin passed on to the inner apartments.

There was no one in the drawing-room, but the midwife, with
lilac ribbons in her cap, came out of Anna's boudoir. She approached Karenin, and with a familiarity bred by death's approach
took him by the hand and led him toward the bedroom.

'Thank God you have come! She talks only about you and
nothing but you,' said she.

'Be quick and bring the ice!' came the authoritative sound of
the doctor's voice from the bedroom.

Karenin entered the boudoir. Beside the table, sitting with his
side toward the back of a low chair, was Vronsky, his hands covering his face, weeping. At the sound of the doctor's voice he jumped
up, uncovered his face, and saw Karenin. But at sight of her husband he was filled with such confusion that he again sat down,
drawing his head down between his shoulders as if trying to become invisible. Then, making an effort, he rose and said:

'She is dying. The doctors say there is no hope. I am entirely in
your hands . . . but allow me to remain here, please! . . . However, I am in your hands. I . . .'

The sight of Vronsky's tears made Karenin aware of the approach of that mental perturbation which other people's visible
sufferings always aroused in him, and turning away his head he
went toward the door without heeding what Vronsky was saying.
Anna's voice, talking about something, came from the bedroom.
It sounded cheerful and animated, and its articulation was extremely distinct. Karenin entered and went up to the bed. She lay
with her face toward him. Her cheeks were rosy red, her eyes
glittered, and her little white hands, from which the cuffs of her

dressing-jacket had been pushed back, toyed with the corner of the blanket, twisting it.

She appeared not only fresh and well but in the best of spirits. She spoke rapidly, in a ringing voice with extraordinarily accurate intonations, full of feeling.

'Because Alexey . . . I am speaking of Alexey Alexandrovich—how strange and terrible that they are both called Alexey, is it not?—Alexey would not have refused me. I should have forgotten and he would have forgiven. . . . But why does he not come? He is kind, he himself does not know how kind he is. Oh God! What weariness! Give me some water, quick! Oh, but it will be bad for her, for my little girl! Well, all right—well, let her have a nurse. Well, I agree, it will be better so. He will come back and it will pain him to see her. Take her away!'

'Anna Arkadyevna, he has come! Here he is,' said the midwife, trying to draw Anna's attention to Alexey Alexandrovich.

'Oh, what nonsense!' Anna went on, taking no notice of her husband. 'But let me have her, let me have my little girl! He has not come yet. You say he won't forgive me, because you don't know him. No one knew him, only I, and even for me it has become hard. One must know his eyes. Serezha's are just the same—that's why I can't bear to see them. Have they given Serezha his dinner? Don't I know that everybody will forget? He would not forget. Serezha must be moved into the corner room, and Mariette must be asked to sleep with him.'

Suddenly she recoiled, became silent and frightened, and put her arms before her face as if in expectation of a blow; she had seen her husband.

'No, no!' she began again. 'I am not afraid of him. I am afraid of death. Alexey, come here! I am in a hurry, because I have no time. I have not long to live, I shall soon become feverish and then I shall no longer understand anything. Now I understand, understand everything and see everything!'

Over Karenin's drawn face came a look of suffering; he took her hand and was about to say something, but could not speak. His lower jaw trembled; he struggled with his agitation, every now and then glancing at her. And every time he did so he saw her eyes looking at him with such tender and ecstatic emotion as he had never before seen in them.

'Wait a bit—you don't know . . . Wait, wait! . . .' she paused as if to collect her thoughts. 'Yes,' she continued, 'yes, yes, yes! This is what I wished to say. Don't be surprised at me; I am still the same. . . . But there is another in me as well, and I am afraid of her. She fell in love with that other one, and I wished to hate you but could not forget her who was before. That other is not I. Now

I am the real one, all of me. I am dying now, I know I am; ask him. Even now I feel it. Here they are, my hands and feet and fingers, whole hundredweights are on them. My fingers, see how enormous they are! But all this will soon end. . . . I only want one thing: forgive me, forgive me completely! I am dreadfully bad, but the nurse told about the holy martyr—what was her name?—she was worse. And I shall go to Rome, there is a wilderness there and then I shall be in nobody's way. I shall only take Serezha and the little girl. . . . No, you cannot forgive me! I know that it cannot be forgiven. No, no, go! You are too good!' With one hot hand she held his, while with the other she pushed him away.

The perturbation in Karenin's soul went on increasing and reached a point where he gave up struggling against it. Suddenly he felt that what he had taken for perturbation was on the contrary a blissful state of his soul, bringing him joy such as he had never before known. He was not thinking that the law of Christ, which all his life he had wished to fulfil, told him to forgive and love his enemies, but a joyous feeling of forgiveness and love for his enemies filled his soul. He knelt with his head resting on her bent arm which burnt through its sleeve like fire, and sobbed like a child. She put her arm round his bald head, moved closer to him, and looked up with an expression of proud exaltation.

'Here he is; I knew! Now good-bye to all, good-bye! . . . They have come again, why don't they go away? . . . Oh, take these furs off me!'

The doctor moved her arms and carefully drew the bedclothes over her shoulders. She meekly lay down on her back and gazed with radiant eyes straight before her.

'Remember that the only thing I want is your forgiveness, I wish for nothing else. . . . Why does *he* not come in?' she cried, calling to Vronsky on the other side of the door. 'Come, come! Give him your hand.'

Vronsky came to her bedside and, on seeing Anna, again hid his face in his hands.

'Uncover your face! Look at him! He is a saint,' said she. 'Uncover, yes, uncover your face!' she went on angrily. 'Alexey Alexandrovich, uncover his face! I want to see him.'

Karenin took Vronsky's hands and moved them away from his face, terrible with its look of suffering and shame.

'Give him your hand. Forgive him. . . . '

Karenin held out his hand, without restraining the tears that were falling.

'Thank God, thank God!' she cried. 'Now everything is ready. Only to stretch my legs a little. That's right—now it's splendid. How badly those flowers are drawn, not a bit like violets,' and she

pointed to the wallpaper. 'Oh, my God, my God! When will it all
come to an end? Doctor, give me some morphia! Give me morphia!
Oh, my God, my God!' And she began to toss in her bed.

The doctor and his colleagues said it was puerperal fever, which
in ninety-nine cases out of a hundred ended fatally. All day she was
feverish, delirious, and unconscious. At midnight she lay insensible,
with hardly any pulse.

The end was expected every moment.

Vronsky went away, but came again in the morning to inquire.
Karenin met him in the ante-room and said: 'Remain here: she
may ask for you,' and himself showed him into Anna's boudoir.
Toward morning she had become excited and animated, and her
thoughts and words flowed rapidly; but again this state lapsed into
unconsciousness. On the third day she was just the same, and the
doctors gave some hope. That day Karenin went out into the boudoir where Vronsky sat, and having closed the door took a seat
opposite him.

'Alexey Alexandrovich,' said Vronsky, feeling that an explanation was coming. 'I am unable to think, unable to understand.
Spare me! However painful it may be to you, believe me it is still
more terrible for me.'

He was about to rise, but Karenin took him by the hand and
said:

'I beg you to hear me; it is necessary. I must explain to you my
feelings, those that have guided me and will guide me in future,
so that you may not misunderstand me. You know that I resolved
on a divorce and had even taken steps toward obtaining it. I will
not conceal from you that when I took action I was in a state of
indecision; I suffered, and I confess that I was haunted by a desire
for vengeance. On receiving the telegram I came here with the
same feeling—more than that, I wished for her death. But . . .'
He stopped and reflected whether he should reveal his feelings or
not. 'But I saw her and forgave her. And the joy of forgiving has
revealed my duty to me. I have wholly forgiven—I want to turn
the other cheek—I want to give my cloak because my coat has
been taken. I only pray God that the joy of forgiving may not be
taken from me.'

Tears filled his eyes, and their clear calm expression struck
Vronsky.

'That is my position. You may trample me in the mud, make
me the laughing-stock of the world,—I will not forsake her and
will never utter a word of reproach to you,' continued Karenin. 'My
duty is clearly defined: I must and will remain with her. If she
wishes to see you I will let you know; but now I think it will be

best for you to leave.'

He rose, and sobs broke his voice. Vronsky got up at once, and stooping before him looked up into his face without unbending his back. He could not understand Karenin, but felt that here was something high, and inaccessible to one with his outlook on life.

Chapter XVIII

After his conversation with Karenin Vronsky went out on to the Karenins' porch and then stopped, recalling with difficulty where he was and where he ought to go. He felt ashamed, humiliated, guilty, and deprived of the possibility of cleansing himself from his degradation. He felt himself knocked quite out of the rut along which he had hitherto trodden so proudly and so lightly. All the apparently solid habits and rules of his life suddenly seemed false and inapplicable. The deceived husband—who up till now had appeared a pitiful creature, an accidental and rather ridiculous obstacle to his happiness—suddenly recalled by her and raised to a pedestal that inspired the utmost respect, that husband in his lofty elevation turned out to be, not only not cruel, false, or absurd, but kind, simple, and dignified. Vronsky could not help being conscious of this. They had suddenly exchanged rôles. Vronsky felt Karenin's greatness and his own humiliation. Karenin's rightness and his own wrongdoing. He felt that the husband in his sorrow was magnanimous, while he himself was mean and trivial in his deceptions. But the consciousness of his degradation toward the man whom he had unjustly despised accounted for but a small portion of his grief. He was unspeakably miserable because his passion for Anna, which he imagined had of late begun to cool, had become even stronger now that he knew her to be lost to him for ever. During her illness he had learnt to know her thoroughly, had seen into her very soul; and it seemed to him that he had never loved her before. And just now, when he knew her and loved her in the right way, he had been humiliated before her and had lost her for ever, leaving her nothing but a shameful memory of himself. But most terrible of all was the ridiculous, shameful figure he had cut when Karenin was pulling his hands from before his shame-suffused face. He stood on the porch of the Karenins' house as one in a maze, and did not know what to do next.

'Shall I call an *izvozchik*?' inquired the hall-porter.

'Yes, an *izvozchik*.'

Returning home after the three sleepless nights, Vronsky did not undress but lay down prone on a sofa, with his head on his folded arms. His head was heavy. Fancies, memories, and most strange thoughts followed one another with extreme rapidity and

clearness: now he saw himself pouring out medicine for the patient and overfilling the spoon, then he saw the midwife's white
hands, or Karenin's curious pose as he knelt on the floor by her
bedside.

'To sleep, to forget!' he said to himself with the calm certainty
of a healthy man that being tired and in want of sleep he would
at once fall asleep. And in fact in a moment his thoughts grew
confused and he began to fall into the abyss of forgetfulness. The
waves of the sea of unconscious life were beginning to close over
his head when all at once he felt as if he had received a violent
electric shock. He started so violently that his whole body was
thrown upwards on the springs of the sofa, and leaning on his
hands he rose to his knees in fear. His eyes were wide open as
if he had not slept at all. The heaviness of his head and the languor
of his limbs, of which he had been aware a moment previously,
had suddenly vanished.

'You may trample me in the mud,' he seemed to hear Karenin
saying; and he saw Anna's feverish face and brilliant eyes gazing
with tenderness and love, not at him but at Karenin; he saw his
own stupid and ridiculous figure when Karenin was drawing his
hands away from his face. He stretched out his legs and again threw
himself upon the sofa, in the same position as before and shut his
eyes.

'Sleep, sleep,' he kept repeating to himself. But with his eyes
closed he could see yet more distinctly Anna's face as he had seen it
on that memorable evening before the race. 'All that is ended
and never will be again, and she wishes to efface it from her memory. I can't live without it. Then how can we be reconciled—how
can we be reconciled?' said he aloud, and went on unconsciously
repeating those words. This reiteration prevented other images and
memories which were thronging his brain from arising. But the
repetition of those words did not long hinder his imagination from
working. Again, following each other with great rapidity, his happiest moments rose in his fancy; and with them his recent humiliation. 'Take away his hands,' Anna's voice is saying. Karenin pulls
away his hands and he is conscious of the shame-suffused and
stupid expression of his own face.

He still lay trying to fall asleep, though he had lost all hope of
succeeding, and kept repeating in a whisper random words connected with disjointed thoughts, in order to prevent other images
from rising. He listened and heard repeated in a strange mad whisper the words, 'Unable to value, unable to avail myself; unable to
value, unable to avail myself.'

'What is this? Am I going mad?' he asked himself. 'Perhaps!
What else makes people go mad? What makes them shoot them-

selves?' he replied to his own thought; and opening his eyes he was surprised to see, close to his head, an embroidered cushion worked by Varya, his brother's wife. Fingering a tassel of the cushion, he tried to think of Varya as he had last seen her. But to think of anything extraneous was painful, 'No, I must sleep!' He moved the cushion and pressed his head against it, but his eyes would not remain closed without effort. He jumped up and sat down. 'That's at an end for me,' he thought, 'I must think over what I must do, what is left me.' His thoughts glided quickly over his life unconnected with his passion for Anna.

'Ambition? Serpukhovskoy? Society? The Court?' he could not dwell on any of these things. He rose from the sofa, took off his coat, loosened his belt, and, baring his shaggy chest to breathe more freely, walked across the room. 'That's how one goes mad,' he said again, 'and how one shoots oneself so as not to be ashamed,' he concluded slowly. Going up to a door he closed it, then with fixed gaze and tightly clenched teeth, approached the table, took up his revolver, examined it, turned it to a loaded chamber, and pondered. For a minute or two he stood motionless with bowed head, a strained expression of effort on his face, holding the revolver in his hand. 'Of course!' he said to himself, as if led to a definite conclusion by a logical, continued, and clear line of reasoning. In reality that convinced 'Of course!' was merely the outcome of the repetition of a round of fancies and recollections similar to those he had already gone over dozens of times in the last hour. They were the same memories of happiness lost for ever, the same thoughts of the senselessness of all that life had in store for him, and the same consciousness of his humiliation. And they followed in the same sequence. 'Of course!' he said again when thought returned a third time to that point in the enchanted circle of memories and ideas; and placing the revolver against the left side of his chest, with a strong movement of his whole hand as if to clench the fist, he pulled the trigger. He did not hear the sound of a shot, but a powerful blow on the chest knocked him off his feet. He wished to steady himself by the table, dropped the revolver, reeled, and sat down on the floor, looking about him in astonishment. He did not recognize his room as he looked up at the curved legs of the table, and at the waste-paper basket and the tiger-skin rug. The quick step of his servant, coming through the drawing-room, brought him to his senses. He made an effort and understood that he was on the floor, and, seeing blood on the tiger-skin and on his hand, realized that he had tried to shoot himself.

'Stupid! . . . Missed,' he muttered, feeling with his hand for the revolver. It was close to him but he sought it further away. Continuing his search he leaned over to the other side, and unable to keep his balance, fell over bleeding.

The elegant servant with the whiskers, who often complained to his friends about the weakness of his nerves, was so upset when he saw his master lying on the floor, that he left him to bleed to death, and ran away to get help. In an hour's time Varya arrived, and with the assistance of three doctors whom she had summoned from every quarter, and who all arrived at the same time, she got the wounded man to bed, and then stayed in the house to nurse him.

Chapter XIX

The mistake Karenin had made when, preparing to see his wife, he had not considered the possibility either of her repentance being real or of her recovery, faced him in all its significance two months after his return from Moscow. But this mistake was not entirely caused by his omitting to consider that contingency, but also by the fact that, up to the day when he was face to face with his dying wife, he had not known his own heart. By his sick wife's bedside he had for the first time in his life given rein to that feeling of tender sympathy which the suffering of others evoked in him and which he had till then been ashamed of, as of a weakness; and his pity for her, remorse at having wished for her death, and above all the joy of forgiving, in itself gave him not only relief from suffering but inward peace such as he had never before experienced. Suddenly he felt that the very thing that had been a source of suffering to him had become a spiritual joy, and that what had seemed insoluble as long as he indulged in censure, recriminations, and hatred, had become simple and clear when he forgave and loved.

He forgave his wife and pitied her for her sufferings and remorse. He forgave Vronsky and pitied him, especially when reports of Vronsky's desperate action reached him. He pitied his son too, more than he had done before, and reproached himself for not having paid more attention to him. But for the newborn little girl he had a peculiar sentiment, not of pity alone but even of tenderness. At first commiseration alone drew his attention to the delicate infant, not his daughter, who had been neglected during her mother's illness and would certainly have died then had it not been for his solicitude; and he himself hardly knew how he grew fond of her. Several times a day he went to the nursery, and remained there so long that the nurses, who had been shy in his presence, became quite used to him. Sometimes he would sit for half an hour gazing at the saffron and red downy, wrinkled little face of the sleeping infant, watching the movements of the frowning little forehead and the plump little hands with the bent fingers and palms that rubbed the tiny eyes and nose. At such moments especially Karenin felt quite calm and at peace with himself, seeing nothing exceptional in his position and nothing that ought to be altered.

But as time went on he saw more and more clearly that, however natural his position might appear to him at the time, he would not be allowed to remain in it. He was conscious that, beside the good spiritual force which governed his soul, there existed a coarse power, as potent if not more so; and that this power would not grant him the humble peace he desired. He felt that everybody looked at him with questioning surprise without understanding him, expecting something from him; and especially he was aware of the insecurity and artificiality of his relation to his wife.

When her softened mood caused by the nearness of death had passed, Karenin began to notice that Anna feared him, was oppressed by his presence, and avoided looking him straight in the eyes. It was as if she wished, yet could not make up her mind, to say something, and foreseeing that their present relation could not continue, expected something from him too.

At the end of February Anna's newborn daughter, also named Anna, happened to fall ill. Karenin had been in the nursery that morning, and having given orders to send for the doctor, had gone to the Department. Toward four o'clock, having finished his work, he returned home. On entering the ante-room he saw there a handsome footman in gold-braided livery with a bearskin cape, holding a cloak lined with white fur.

'Who is here?' asked Karenin.

'Princess Elisabeth Federovna Tverskaya,' answered the footman with a smile,—as it seemed to Karenin. All through that difficult time Karenin noticed that all his social acquaintances, especially the women, displayed a particularly lively interest in him and his wife. He noticed in all these acquaintances a kind of joy, which they suppressed with difficulty, like the joy he had noticed in the lawyer's eyes and again just now in the footman's. Everybody seemed elated, as if they were giving some one in marriage. When they met him they inquired with scarcely hidden pleasure about Anna's health.

The presence of Princess Tverskaya and the memories associated with her, coupled with the fact that he had never liked her, was unpleasant to Karenin, and he went straight to the nursery. In the front nursery Serezha, lying with his chest on the table and his legs on a chair, was drawing something and chattering merrily. An English nursery governess, who since Anna's illness had replaced the French governess with the boy, sat doing some crochet-work. She hurriedly rose, curtseyed, and nudged Serzha.

Karenin passed his hand over his son's hair, answered the governess's inquiry about Anna's health, and asked what the doctor had said about baby.

'The doctor says there is no danger and has ordered baths, sir.'

'But she is still suffering,' remarked Karenin, listening to the crying child in the next room.

'I think the nurse is unsuitable, sir,' said the Englishwoman with decision.

'Why do you think so?' he asked, stopping short.

'The same thing happened in Countess Paul's case. The baby was medically treated and then it turned out to be merely hungry and nothing more. The nurse had no milk, sir.'

Karenin reflected a moment and then entered the other room. The little girl lay with her head thrown back, wriggling in the wet-nurse's arms, and would neither take the breast nor cease screaming, despite the hushing of two nurses who were bending over her.

'Still no better?' asked Karenin.

'Very restless,' said the head-nurse in a whisper.

'Miss Edwards says that perhaps the nurse has no milk,' he said.

'I think so too, Alexey Alexandrovich.'

'Then why did you not say so?'

'Whom could I speak to? Anna Arkadyevna is still ill . . .' said the old nurse in a dissatisfied tone.

The nurse was an old family servant, and in her simple words Karenin thought he noticed a hint at his position.

The baby screamed louder, catching her breath and growing hoarse. The old nurse with a gesture of vexation came up and took her from the wet-nurse, and began pacing up and down, rocking the baby in her arms.

'The doctor must be asked to examine the nurse,' said Karenin.

The healthy-looking wet-nurse in her finery, evidently afraid of being dismissed, muttered something to herself as she covered her well-developed breast, and smiled contemptuously at the idea of her not having sufficient milk. In that smile also Karenin thought he saw himself and his position ridiculed.

'Unfortunate child!' said the nurse, hushing the baby and continuing to walk up and down with it. Karenin sat down on a chair and with a look full of suffering and despondency watched the nurse as she paced the room. When the child was pacified and laid in her deep cot, and the nurse after smoothing the little pillow went away. Karenin rose, and stepping with difficulty on tiptoe approached the infant. For a moment he stood silent, regarding the child with the same despondent expression; but suddenly a smile, wrinkling the skin on his forehead and making his hair move, came out on his face, and he quietly left the room.

He rang the bell in the dining-room and told the servant to send for the doctor once more. He was vexed with his wife for not troubling about the charming baby, felt disinclined to go in and see her while in that frame of mind, and also disinclined to meet the Princess Betsy; but his wife might think it strange if he did not come in as usual, and so he mastered himself and went to her bedroom. Stepping on the soft carpet, as he approached the door he involuntarily overheard a conversation which he had no wish to hear.

'If he had not been going away I should understand your refusal and his too. But your husband must be above that,' Betsy was saying.

'It is not for my husband's sake but for my own that I don't wish it. Don't talk about it,' answered Anna in an excited voice.

'Yes, but you can't but wish to say good-bye to a man who tried to shoot himself for your sake. . . .'

'It's just for that reason that I don't wish it.'

Karenin, with a frightened and guilty face, stopped short and thought of returning unnoticed; but coming to the conclusion that this would be undignified he turned, coughed, and went toward the bedroom door. The voices became silent and he entered.

Anna, in a grey dressing-gown, with her black hair cropped short but already growing again like a thick brush over her round head, sat on a couch. As usual when she saw her husband all her animation vanished from her face; she bowed her head and glanced uneasily at Betsy. Betsy, dressed in the very latest fashion, her hat soaring high above her head like a shade over a lamp, in a dove-coloured dress with very pronounced diagonal stripes going one way on the bodice and the other way on the skirt, was sitting beside Anna, her flat tall figure very erect and her head bent. She met Karenin with an ironical smile.

'Ah!' she exclaimed, as if in surprise, 'I am so glad you are at home. I have not seen you since Anna's illness. I have heard everything . . . all about your attentiveness. Yes, you are a wonderful husband!' she said with a significant and affable expression, as if she were conferring on him an Order of Highmindedness for his conduct toward his wife.

Karenin bowed coldly, and kissing his wife's hand asked about her health.

'I think I am better,' she said, avoiding his eyes.

'But your face looks feverish,' said he, emphasizing the word *feverish*.

'We have been talking too much,' said Betsy. 'I know it was selfish of me and I am going.'

She rose, but Anna, suddenly blushing, quickly seized her hand.

'No, please stay! I must tell you . . . you, I mean,' and she turned toward her husband, the colour spreading over her neck and forehead. 'I don't wish to hide anything from you.'

Karenin cracked his fingers and bowed his head.

'Betsy says Count Vronsky wanted to come and say good-bye before leaving for Tashkend.' She was not looking at her husband, and evidently was in a hurry to get through what she meant to say at any cost. 'I said I could not receive him.'

'You said, my love, that it would depend on Alexey Alexandrovich.' Betsy corrected her.

'Oh no! I can't receive him, and it would lead . . .' She stopped suddenly and glanced inquiringly at her husband, who was not looking at her. 'In a word, I don't wish . . .'

Karenin drew nearer and was going to take her hand.

Her first impulse was to draw away her hand from his moist one with the thick swelling veins, that was seeking hers; but with evident effort she pressed it.

'I am very grateful for your confidence, but . . .' he began in confusion, feeling with vexation that what he could so clearly decide within himself he was unable to discuss in the presence of the Princess Tverskaya, who appeared to him the personification of that coarse power which would rule his life in the eye of the world, and which prevented him from yielding to his feelings of love and forgiveness. He stopped and looked at the Princess.

'Well, good-bye, my precious!' said Betsy, rising again. She kissed Anna and went out. Karenin followed her.

'Alexey Alexandrovich! I know you to be a really high-minded man,' said Betsy, stopping short in the little sitting-room and once again pressing his hand with peculiar warmth. 'I am only an outsider, but am so fond of her and respect you so much that I will take the liberty of advising you. Receive him! Alexey Vronsky is honour personified, and besides he is leaving for Tashkend.'

'Thanks for your sympathy and advice, Princess! But the question whom my wife will and whom she will not receive she will decide for herself.'

He said this from force of habit, with a dignified raising of his eyebrows, but immediately remembered that whatever he might say there would be no question of dignity in his position, and saw the confirmation of this in the suppressed cruel and ironical smile with which Betsy glanced at him when he had spoken.

Chapter XX

Karenin took leave of Betsy when they reached the dining-room and returned to his wife. She was lying down, but on hearing his step she quickly sat up in her former place and glanced at him with apprehension. He saw that she had been crying.

'I am very grateful to you for your confidence,' he repeated in Russian what he had said in French in Betsy's presence. When speaking Russian to her he called her 'thou,'[4] and that always irritated her. 'And I am very grateful for your decision. I too think that, as he is going away, there is no need whatever for Count Vronsky to come here. However . . .'

'But I have already said so! Then why repeat it?' Anna suddenly interrupted him, with an irritation she could not repress. 'No need whatever,' she thought, 'for a man to come and take leave of a woman he loves, for whose sake he wanted to die and has ruined himself, a woman who cannot live without him! No need whatever!' And she pressed her lips together and lowered her glistening eyes, looking at his hands with their swollen veins, which he was slowly rubbing together.

'Let us say no more about it,' she added more calmly.

'I left it to you to decide the matter, and am very glad to see . . .' began Karenin.

'That my wish coincides with yours,' she rapidly completed his sentence, exasperated by the slowness with which he spoke, and knowing beforehand what he would say.

He assented. 'Yes, and Princess Tverskaya's intrusion into this most difficult family matter is entirely out of place. . . . Especially as she . . .'

'I don't believe anything they say about her,' Anna put in quickly. 'I know that she is sincerely fond of me.'

Karenin sighed and paused. She was agitatedly toying with the tassels of her dressing-gown, glancing at him with that tormenting feeling of physical repulsion for which she blamed herself, but which she could not overcome. The one thing she was longing for was to get rid of his obnoxious presence.

'I have just sent for the doctor,' said he.

'I am quite well—why should I need the doctor?'

'Yes, but the little one keeps screaming, and they say the nurse has not enough milk.'

'Then why would you not let me nurse her, when I entreated you to? She is a child anyhow' (he understood what she meant by that *anyhow*) 'and they will kill her.' She rang, and ordered the baby to be brought. 'I asked to be allowed to nurse her, and I wasn't; and now I am blamed.'

'I don't blame . . .'

'Yes, you are blaming me! Oh God, why did I not die?' and she began to sob. 'Forgive me, I am upset! I am unjust,' she went on, controlling herself. 'But go . . .'

---

4. In Russian as in French and other languages the second person singular is used in conversation between intimates and also in speaking to inferiors.

'No, it can't go on like that,' he told himself with conviction after leaving his wife.

Never before had his impossible situation (as the world thought it)—his wife's hatred, and the strength of that coarse power which, in direct opposition to his inward mood, dominated his life and demanded fulfilment of its decrees and a change in his relation to his wife—never before had the impossibility of his position appeared so evident. He saw clearly that the world and also his wife were demanding something from him, but exactly what this something was he did not comprehend. All this was arousing a feeling of animosity in his soul, spoiling his peace of mind and depriving his achievement of all value. He considered it better for Anna to break off her relations with Vronsky; but if everyone thought this impossible, he was even ready to allow those relations to be renewed, so long as no slur was thereby cast on the children, he was not deprived of them, and his position was not altered. Bad as this would be, it would be preferable to a complete rupture, which would place her in a hopeless and shameful position, and deprive him of all he loved. But he felt powerless; he was aware in advance that everybody would be against him and that he would not be allowed to do what now seemed so natural and good, that he would be obliged to do what was wrong but what seemed to them proper.

Chapter XXI

Before Betsy had passed out of the dining-room Oblonsky, who had just come from Eliseyev's, where newly-arrived oysters were to be had, met her in the doorway.

'Ah, Princess! What a pleasure to meet you,' he began. 'And I have been at your house.'

'We meet only for a moment, as I am just going,' said Betsy, smiling and putting on her glove.

'Wait a little, Princess, before putting on your glove! Let me kiss your hand! There is nothing for which I am more thankful than for the revival of the old custom of hand-kissing,' and he kissed Betsy's hand. 'When shall I see you again?'

'You don't deserve it,' said Betsy, smiling.

'Yes, I well deserve it, because I have become the most serious of men. I not only settle my own, but other people's family affairs,' said he with a significant glance.

'Oh, I am very glad!' said Betsy, at once understanding that he referred to Anna. She returned to the dining-room with him and they stood together in a corner. 'He will kill her,' said Betsy in a significant whisper. 'This is impossible, impossible. . . .'

'I am very glad you think so,' returned Oblonsky, shaking his head with an expression of grave, woebegone commiseration. 'That is why I have come to Petersburg.'

'The whole town is talking of it,' she said. 'It is an impossible situation. She is fading away, fading away! He does not understand that she is one of those women who cannot play with their feelings. One of two things must happen: either he must take her away, acting energetically—or he must divorce her. But all this is stifling her.'

'Yes, yes . . . exactly!' said Oblonsky, sighing. 'I have come because of that—I mean, not entirely because of it. . . . I have been made a Chamberlain, and had to tender my thanks. But the chief thing is to get this affair settled.'

'Well then, may God help you,' said Betsy.

Having seen her down to the hall and again kissed her hand, a little above the glove just where the pulse beats, and having told her some rubbish so daring that she did not know whether to be angry or to laugh, Oblonsky went to his sister's room. He found her in tears.

Though he was overflowing with high spirits Oblonsky immediately fell into a sympathetic and romantic mood suited to hers, inquired after her health and asked how she had spent the morning.

'Very, very badly. This afternoon and morning and all other days, past and future,' she replied.

'I think you give way to melancholy. You should rouse yourself, and look life straight in the face. I know it is hard, but . . .'

'I have heard it said that women love men for their very faults,' Anna began suddenly, 'but I hate him for his virtues. I cannot live with him. Try and realize it: even his looks have a physical effect on me and drive me beside myself. I cannot live with him! What am I to do? I was unhappy and thought it impossible to be more so; but I could never have imagined such a terrible position as I am now in. Will you believe it? Knowing that he is a kind and generous man—that I am not worth his little finger—nevertheless I hate him! I hate him for his generosity. And there is nothing left for me but . . .'

She was going to say 'death,' but he did not let her finish.

'You are ill and excited,' said he. 'Believe me, you are greatly exaggerating the case. There is nothing so very terrible about it.'

Oblonsky smiled. No one else in his place, having to deal with such despair, would have permitted himself to smile, for a smile would have appeared callous. But in his smile there was so much kindness and almost feminine tenderness that it was not offensive, but soothing and pacifying. His soft comforting words and smiles had as soothing and calming an effect as almond oil, and Anna soon felt this.

'No, Stiva,' said she. 'I am lost, quite lost! And even worse than lost. I am not lost yet; I cannot say "all is finished"; on the contrary, I feel that all is not yet finished. I am like a tightly-strung cord which must snap. But all is not yet finished . . . and it will end in some dreadful manner.'

'Oh no! One can loosen the string gently. There is no situation from which there is no escape.'

'I have been thinking and thinking. Only one . . .'

Again he understood from her frightened face that she considered death to be the only escape, and did not let her finish.

'Not at all!' he replied. 'Listen. You can't see your position as I can. Let me tell you my frank opinion.' Again he smiled his almond-oil smile. 'I will begin at the beginning: you married a man twenty years older than yourself. You married without love and without knowing what love is. That was a mistake, I grant.'

'A dreadful mistake!' said Anna.

'But again I say that is an accomplished fact. Next, let us admit that you had the misfortune to fall in love, not with your husband. That is a misfortune, but that too is an accomplished fact. Your husband has accepted that and forgiven you.' He paused between each sentence, expecting her to make objections; but she made no answer. 'That is so? Now comes the question: Can you go on living with your husband? Do you wish it? Does he wish it?'

'I don't know at all.'

'But you yourself say you cannot endure him?'

'No, I did not say so. I take back those words. I know nothing, I understand nothing.'

'Yes, but let me . . .'

'You can't understand. I feel that I am flying headlong over some precipice but must not even try to save myself. And I can't.'

'Never mind, we'll spread out something to catch you. I understand that you cannot take it upon yourself to express your wishes and feelings.'

'I have no wishes at all . . . except that everything were at an end.'

'And he sees that, and knows it. Do you think it weighs on him less than on you? You suffer and he suffers; what can come of that? While a divorce would solve the whole problem,' said Oblonsky not without difficulty expressing his main idea, and looking at her significantly.

She replied only by shaking her cropped head; but by the expression of her face, suddenly illuminated with its old beauty, he saw that the only reason she did not wish for this solution was because it seemed to her an impossible happiness.

'I am dreadfully sorry for you both! How happy I should be if I could arrange it,' continued Oblonsky, now smiling more boldly. 'Don't, don't say a word! If only God helps me to say what I feel! I shall go to him.'

Anna looked at him with dreamy, shining eyes, but said nothing.

Chapter XXII

Oblonsky, with the same rather solemn expression with which he was wont to take the chair at Council meetings, entered Karenin's study. Karenin, with his arms crossed behind him, was pacing up and down, meditating on the very subject that his wife and Oblonsky had been discussing.

'I am not disturbing you?' asked Oblonsky, experiencing at the sight of his brother-in-law a feeling of embarrassment quite unusual with him. To hide that embarrassment he took out a cigarette-case with a new kind of fastening which he had only just bought, smelt the leather of which it was made, and took out a cigarette.

'No. Do you want anything?' Karenin answered reluctantly.

'Yes. I wished . . . I must have . . . I must have a talk with you,' said Oblonsky, surprised at his own unaccustomed timidity.

That timidity was so unexpected and strange that Oblonsky could not believe it was his conscience telling him that what he was about to do was wrong. He made an effort and conquered it.

'I hope you believe in my affection for my sister and my sincere attachments and respect for yourself,' said he, flushing.

Karenin stopped. He made no reply, but the expression of submissive self-sacrifice on his face struck Oblonsky.

'I intended to talk to you about my sister and your mutual position,' said Oblonsky, still struggling with his unwonted timidity.

Karenin smiled sadly, looked at his brother-in-law, and without replying went to the table and took from it an unfinished letter which he handed to him.

'I think about that subject incessantly, and this is what I have begun to write, as I think I can put it better in writing, and my presence is distasteful to her,' he said, holding out the letter.

Oblonsky took the letter, looked with perplexed amazement at the dull eyes fixed on him, and began reading:

'I see that my presence is distasteful to you. Hard as it was for me to assure myself of this, I see that it is so, and there is no help for it. I do not blame you, and God is my witness that when I saw you ill, I resolved with my whole soul to forget everything that had come between us and to begin a new life. I do not regret and never shall regret what I did, as my only desire was for your welfare, the welfare of your soul; but now I see that I have not succeeded. Tell me yourself what would give you real happiness and peace of mind! I submit myself entirely to your wishes and sense of justice.'

Oblonsky returned the letter and went on looking at his brother-in-law with the same amazement, not knowing what to say. That silence was so disconcerting to both, that Oblonsky's lips twitched painfully as he silently and fixedly gazed at Karenin's face.

'That is what I wanted to tell her,' said Karenin as he turned away.

'Yes, yes!' said Oblonsky, tears choking him and preventing his reply. 'Yes, yes I understand you,' he brought out at last.

'I must know what she wants,' said Karenin.

'I am afraid she does not understand her position herself. She is no judge of it,' replied Oblonsky, growing more composed. 'She is crushed, literally crushed by your generosity. If she reads this letter she will not have the strength to say anything—she will only hang her head lower than ever.'

'Yes, but under these circumstances how is an explanation to be arrived at? . . . How am I to find out what she wishes?'

'If you will permit me to express my opinion, I think it is for you to say what you think should be done in order to put an end to this state of affairs.'

'Then you think that an end should be put to it?' Karenin interrupted him. 'But how?' he added, moving his hands before his eyes in a manner unusual with him. 'I don't see any possible way out.'

'There is a way out of every situation,' said Oblonsky, rising and growing excited. 'There was a time when you wished to break with her. . . . Should you be now convinced that you cannot make each other mutually happy . . .'

'Happiness can be defined so differently! However, I am ready to agree to anything—I want nothing at all. What way out is there, in our case?'

'If you wish to know my opinion,' said Oblonsky with the same soothing, almondy-tender smile with which he had addressed Anna —a kindly smile so convincing that Karenin, conscious of his own weakness and yielding to it, was involuntarily ready to believe anything Oblonsky should say,—'she would never say so, but there is one way out, one thing she might wish! It would be, to terminate your relations and everything that reminds her of them. As I look at it, in your case it is necessary to clear up your newly-arisen relation to one another. And this new relation can only be established when both are free.'

'Divorce!' Karenin interrupted with disgust.

'Yes, divorce, I think. Yes, divorce,' Oblonsky answered, reddening. 'That would be the most reasonable way, from every point of view, for a couple placed as you are. What is to be done if they find out that life together has become impossible, as might happen anywhere?'

Karenin sighed heavily and closed his eyes.

'There is only one thing to consider: does either party wish to remarry? If not, it is very simple,' went on Oblonsky, gradually overcoming his embarrassment.

Karenin, his face drawn with distress, muttered something to himself and made no reply. He had considered a thousand times all this which appeared so simple to Oblonsky, and it seemed to him not only far from simple but altogether impossible. An action for divorce, with the details of which he was now acquainted, seemed impossible, because a feeling of self-respect and his regard for religion would not allow him to plead guilty to a fictitious act of adultery, and still less to allow the wife he had forgiven and whom he loved to be detected in the act and disgraced. For other and yet more important reasons also, divorce seemed out of the question.

In case of a divorce, what would become of his son? To leave him with his mother was not possible; the divorced mother would have another, an illegitimate family, in which the position and education of a stepson would in all probability be a bad one. Should he keep him himself? He knew that would be revengeful and he did not wish for revenge. But besides all this, what made divorce seem to Karenin more impossible than any other course was that by consenting to it he would by that very act ruin Anna. What Dolly had said in Moscow, to the effect that in considering a divorce he was thinking of himself and not of Anna, who would then be irretrievably lost, had sunk into his heart. And having connected these words with his forgiveness and with his attachment to the children, he now understood them in his own way. To agree to a divorce—to give her her freedom—would mean, as he looked at it, to deprive himself of the only thing that bound him to life, the children he loved; and to deprive her of the last support on the path of virtue and cast her to perdition. As a divorced wife she would form a union with Vronsky which would be both illegal and sinful, because according to the law of the Church a wife may not remarry as long as her husband is living. 'She will form a union with him and within a year or two he will either abandon her or she will unite with someone else,' thought Karenin; 'and I, by consenting to an illegal divorce, shall be the cause of her ruin.' Hundreds of times he had thought it over and had come to the conclusion that a divorce was not merely less simple than his brother-in-law considered it, but quite out of the question. He did not believe a word of what Oblonsky was saying, and for all his arguments had scores of refutations ready; yet he listened, feeling that those words expressed that coarse and mighty power which overruled his life and to which he would have to submit.

'The only question is, on what conditions you will agree to a divorce. She does not want anything, does not ask for anything, but leaves all to your generosity.'

'Oh God, O God! How have I deserved this?' thought Karenin, recalling the particulars of a divorce-suit in which the husband took all the blame on himself; and with the same ashamed gesture with which Vronsky had covered his face, he hid his own in his hands.

'You are upset. I quite understand. But if you consider . . .'

'Whosoever shall smite thee on thy right cheek, turn to him the other also . . . and if any man will take away thy coat, let him have thy cloak also,' thought Karenin.

'Yes, yes!' he cried in a shrill voice. 'I will take the disgrace, and even give up my son . . . but . . . but had we not better let it alone? However, do as you like!' and turning away so that his brother-in-law should not see his face, he sat down on a chair by the window. It was very bitter, and he felt ashamed; yet mixed with the bitterness and the shame he felt a sense of joy and emotion at the greatness of his own humility.

Oblonsky was touched. He remained silent for a while.

'Alexey Alexandrovich! Believe me, she will esteem your generosity,' said he. 'But evidently it was God's will,' he added, and having said it felt how silly it was, and could hardly help smiling at his own stupidity.

Karenin would have answered, but could not for his tears.

'It is a fatal disaster and has to be faced. I regard this disaster as an accomplished fact and am trying to help both you and her,' Oblonsky went on.

When he left his brother-in-law's room Oblonsky was touched, but this feeling did not spoil his contentment at having successfully arranged the matter, for he was certain that Alexey Alexandrovich would not go back on his word. To his contentment was added an idea that had just occurred to him. When the affair was all settled he would ask his wife and intimate friends a riddle: 'What is the difference between me and a chemist?' Answer: 'A chemist makes solutions which do not make anyone happy, but I have made a dissolution and made three people happy!' Or, 'Why am I like a chemist? . . . When . . . However, I will improve on it later,' he said to himself with a smile.

Chapter XXIII

Although Vronsky's wound had missed the heart it was dangerous, and for several days he lay between life and death. When he was first able to talk again his brother's wife Varya was alone with him.

'Varya!' he said looking sternly at her, 'I shot myself accidentally! Never speak of it, please, and tell everybody else that. Or else it would be too stupid.'

Without saying a word Varya bent over him and looked in his face with a joyful smile. His eyes were clear and no longer feverish, but their expression was stern.

'Well, thank God!' she exclaimed. 'You are not in pain?'

'A little, here,' and he pointed to his chest.

'Then let me change the bandage.'

He looked at her silently, his broad jaws set, while she bandaged him. When she had finished he said:

'I am not delirious. . . . Please manage so that no one shall say that I shot myself on purpose.'

'But no one does say so. Only I hope you will not go shooting accidentally any more,' she said with an inquiring smile.

'I expect I shan't, but it would have been better . . .' and he smiled gloomily.

Despite these words and that smile, which greatly perturbed Varya, when the inflammation left him and he became convalescent he felt that he had rid himself entirely of one part of his grief. By his action he seemed to have washed off the shame and degradation he had previously felt. Now he could think quietly about Karenin, fully realizing his generosity without being humiliated thereby. Besides that, he got into his old rut again. He found he could look people in the face once more, and he was able to live in accord with his former habits. The one thing he could not tear out of his heart, although he continually struggled against it, was a regret bordering on despair at having lost Anna for ever. That now, having atoned for his guilt toward her husband, he would be obliged to give her up and never place himself between her with her remorse and her husband, was clear to his mind; but he could not eradicate from his heart a regret for the loss of her love—could not efface from his memory the moments of happiness he had known with her, moments he had valued so lightly, but the image of which with all their charm pursued him still.

Serpukhovskoy thought out a post for him in Tashkend and Vronsky accepted the proposition without the least hesitation. But the nearer the hour for his departure approached the harder seemed the sacrifice he was making to what he considered his duty. His wound was quite healed and he went about making preparations for his journey to Tashkend. 'Only to see her once more, and then to bury myself, to die!' he thought, as he was making a round of farewell calls, and he expressed this thought to Betsy. It was with this message that Betsy went to Anna, and she brought him an answer in the negative.

'So much the better,' thought Vronsky when he heard it. 'It would have been a weakness—would have taken away all the strength I have left.'

Next day Betsy herself came and announced that she had received, through Oblonsky, the definite news that Karenin consented to a divorce and that therefore Vronsky might see Anna. Without so much as taking the trouble of seeing Betsy to the door, or of asking when he could see Anna and where her husband was, Vronsky, in spite of all his resolutions, at once went to the Karenins'. Without seeing anyone or anything he ran up the stairs and entered her room with hurried steps—almost at a run. Without thinking, or considering whether they were alone or not, he embraced her and covered her face, hands, and neck with kisses.

Anna had prepared herself for this meeting and had thought about what she would say to him; but she had no time to say any of it, seized by his passion. She wished to calm him and herself, but it was too late. His passion communicated itself to her. Her lip trembled so that for a long time she could not speak.

'Yes, you have taken possession of me and I am yours,' she brought out at last, pressing his hands to her bosom.

'It had to be!' said he. 'As long as we live it will have to be. Now I am sure of it.'

'It is true,' she said, growing paler and paler, putting her arms about his head. 'Still, there is something terrible in this after what has been.'

'It will pass, it will all pass, and we shall be so happy. If our love could be stronger, there being something terrible in it would make it so,' he said, raising his head with a smile that showed his fine teeth.

She could not help smiling in answer, not to his words but to his enamoured eyes. She took his hand and stroked with it her cold cheek and cropped hair.

'I don't know you with this short hair! You have improved so, you little boy!—But how pale you are!'

'Yes, I feel very weak,' she said with a smile, and her lip trembled again.

'We will go to Italy and you will soon get well,' said he.

'Is it possible that we shall be like husband and wife, alone, a family, you and I?' she said, looking closely into his eyes.

'I am only surprised that it could ever have been otherwise.'

'Stiva says *he* will agree to anything, but I cannot accept *his* generosity,' she said dreamily, gazing past Vronsky's face. 'I don't want a divorce. Nothing matters to me now. Only I don't know what he will decide about Serezha.'

He was quite unable to understand how she could, at the moment of their first reunion, think about her son and divorce. As if all that were not immaterial!

'Don't talk and don't think about it,' he said, playing with her hand and trying to draw her attention to himself; but she continued to gaze past him.

'Oh, why did I not die? It would have been best!' she said, the tears streaming noiselessly down her cheeks; but unwilling to pain him, she tried to smile.

To refuse the flattering offer of a post at Tashkend, which was a dangerous one, would have seemed disgraceful and impossible according to Vronsky's former views. But now without a moment's hesitation he did refuse it and, observing that his superiors frowned upon his action, at once resigned his commission. A month later Karenin and his son were left alone in the house, and Anna went abroad with Vronsky—not only without getting a divorce but having resolutely refused it.

BOOK II

Part V

Chapter I

The Princess Shcherbatskaya at first considered it out of the question to have the wedding before Lent, to which there remained but five weeks, but could not help agreeing with Levin that to put it off until after Lent might involve waiting too long, for Prince Shcherbatsky's old aunt was very ill and likely to die soon, and then the family would be in mourning and the wedding would have to be considerably deferred. Consequently, having decided to divide her daughter's trousseau into two parts, a lesser and a larger, the Princess eventually consented to have the wedding before Lent. She decided that she would have the smaller part of the trousseau got ready at once, and would send on the larger part later; and she was very cross with Levin because he could not give her a serious answer to her question whether he agreed with this arrangement or not. This plan would be all the more convenient because the young couple intended immediately after the wedding to go to the country, where the larger part of the trousseau would not be required.

Levin continued in the same condition of delirium as before, imagining that he and his joy were the chief or only purpose of all existence, and that he need not now think or bother about anything, as other people would see to everything for him. He had not even any plans or aims for the future, but left these to others to decide, quite sure that everything would turn out splendidly. His brother Sergius Ivanich, Oblonsky, and the Princess directed his actions. He quite agreed to every proposal. His brother borrowed money for him, the Princess advised him to return to the country after the wedding, and Oblonsky suggested going abroad. He agreed to everything. 'Do whatever you like, whatever pleases you! I am happy, and my happiness cannot be made or marred by anything you do,' he thought. When he told Kitty of Oblonsky's advice that they should go abroad, he was quite surprised at her opposition to it and to find that she had definite ideas of her own about their future life. She knew that in the country Levin had work of which he was fond. As he saw, she not only did not understand that work but did not wish to understand it. This, however, did not prevent her considering it very important, and besides, she knew their home would be in the country, and she wanted to go— not abroad, where they were not going to live—but to where her home would be. This decided expression of her wish surprised Levin, but as it was quite immaterial to him, he at once begged Oblonsky to go to the house in the country, just as if it were Oblonsky's duty to go, and arrange everything there according to his own good taste.

'I say,' Oblonsky asked Levin one day after his return from the country, where he had made all preparations for the young couple, 'have you got a certificate to show that you have received communion?'

'No. Why?'

'They won't marry you without it.'

'But I think it is nine years since I went to communion!' exclaimed Levin. 'I haven't thought about it.'

'You are a good one!' remarked Oblonsky, laughing. 'And you call *me* a Nihilist! But it won't do, you know; you must confess and receive the sacrament.'

'When? There are only four days left.'

But Oblonsky arranged that too. And Levin began to fast. But as an unbeliever who yet respected the beliefs of others, it was very oppressive for him to be present and take part in any Church ceremonies. And in his present softened state of mind the necessity of pretending not only oppressed him but seemed to him quite impossible. To be obliged to lie or blaspheme now—at the very height of his glory, when his life was just bursting into flower! He felt incapable of doing either the one or the other. But however much he questioned Oblonsky as to the possibility of obtaining a certificate without actually taking communion, the latter declared it to be impossible.

'Besides, what does it amount to—two days! And the priest is such a nice old man. He will draw that tooth for you so that you will scarcely feel it.'

Standing in church during the first service he attended, Levin tried to revive the memories of his youth and the strong religious feeling with which at the age of sixteen or seventeen he had been imbued. But he immediately became convinced that it was out of his power to do so. He then tried to regard it all as a meaningless, empty custom, like making a round of calls, but felt equally unable to do that. In matters of religion Levin, like most of his contemporaries, had very indefinite views. He could not believe in it, and yet was not firmly convinced that it was all false. Therefore, unable either to believe in the importance of what he was doing or to regard it with indifference as an empty formality, all the time he was preparing for the sacrament he felt awkward and ashamed, for an inner voice told him it was false and wrong to do what was to him incomprehensible.

During the service he would sometimes listen to the prayers, trying to see in them a meaning which would not clash with his opinions, or, finding that he could not understand and had to disapprove of them, he would try not to listen but to occupy his mind with observation of what was going on or with recollections which passed with extraordinary clearness through his brain as he stood idly in the church. He stood through the mass and vespers and evensong, and the next day, having got up earlier than usual, he went to church before breakfast to hear morning prayers and to confess.

No one else was in the church except a soldier-beggar, two old women, and the clergy.

The young deacon, the two halves of his long back clearly distinguishable through his thin under-cassock, met him, and going at once to a small table beside the wall, began reading the prayers. While he was reading, and especially during the frequent and rapid repetitions of 'Lord, have mercy upon us!'—which sounded like 'Lordvmercypons!'—Levin felt as if his mind were closed and sealed up, and that, if he did make it stir now, nothing but confusion would result; therefore as he stood behind the deacon he continued his own train of thought, without listening or trying to comprehend what was being read. 'How wonderfully expressive her hand is!' he thought, recalling how they had sat at the corner table the day before. As was nearly always the case just then, they had nothing to say to each other, and she had put her hand on the table and kept opening and closing it until she herself began to laugh at its motions. He remembered how he had kissed the hand and afterwards examined the converging lines on the rosy palm. Again 'Lordvmercypons!' thought he, crossing himself, bowing, and watching the movements of the bowing deacon's flexible back. 'Then she took my hand and examined the lines and said, "You have a splendid hand!" ' and he glanced at the deacon's stumpy hand and at his own. 'Well, it will soon be over now,' he thought. 'No—I believe it is all going to begin again,' and he listened to the prayer. 'Yes, it *is* coming to an end. There he is, bowing down to the ground. That always happens just before the end.' Having stealthily received a three-rouble note into his hand under its velvet cuff, the deacon said he would put down Levin's name, and went briskly into the chancel, his new boots clattering over the paved floor of the empty church. A minute later he put his head out and beckoned to Levin. The sealed-up thoughts began stirring in Levin's head, but he hastened to drive them away. 'It will get settled somehow,' he thought, and went to the ambo. On going up the steps and turning to the right he saw the priest. The latter, an old man with a thin grizzled beard and kind, weary eyes, stood beside the lectern turning over the leaves of a missal. Bowing slightly to Levin he began at once in his stereotyped tone to read the prayers. At the end he bowed to the ground and turned to Levin.

'Christ, though unseen, is here present to receive your confession,' he said, pointing to a crucifix. 'Do you believe in the teachings of the Holy Apostolic Church?' continued the priest, turning his eyes away and folding his hands beneath his stole.

'I have doubted, and still doubt, everything,' replied Levin in a voice unpleasant to himself, and stopped.

The priest paused a few seconds to see whether Levin would say anything more, and then closing his eyes said rapidly, with a strong provincial accent:

'Doubts are natural to human weakness, but we must pray that our merciful Lord will strengthen us. What are your particular sins?' he continued without the slightest pause, as if anxious not to waste time.

'My chief sin is doubt. I doubt everything and am in doubt nearly all the time.'

'Doubt is natural to human weakness,' repeated the priest. 'What do you doubt in particular?'

'Everything. Sometimes I even doubt the existence of God,' said Levin involuntarily, and was horrified at the impropriety of his words. But they seemed to have no effect on the priest.

'What doubt can there be of the existence of God?' he asked with a faint smile.

Levin was silent.

'What doubt can you have of the Creator when you see His creation?' continued the priest in his rapid, stereotyped voice. 'Who has adorned the vault of Heaven with luminaries? Who has decked the earth with beauty? How could it all be, without a Creator?' he asked, with an inquiring glance at Levin.

Levin felt that it would not be proper to enter into a philosophic discussion with a priest, and therefore merely replied to the direct questions, 'I don't know.'

'You don't know? Then how can you doubt that God created everything?' said the priest in puzzled amazement.

'I don't understand it at all,' said Levin, blushing, and feeling that his words were silly and that they could not but be silly.

'Pray to God and entreat Him! Even the holy Fathers doubted and prayed God to strengthen their faith. The devil is very powerful and we must resist him. Pray to God,' he repeated hurriedly.

The priest paused awhile as if in thought.

'I hear you are about to enter into holy matrimony with the daughter of my parishioner and spiritual son, Prince Shcherbatsky?'

he added with a smile. 'A splendid young woman!'

'Yes,' answered Levin, with a blush for the priest. 'Why need he ask me that at confession?' he thought.

And as if in answer to the thought, the priest said:

'You are about to enter into matrimony and God may give you children, is it not so? Then what sort of education can you give your little ones if you do not conquer in yourself the temptations of the devil, who is leading you into unbelief?' he asked in mild rebuke. 'If you love your offspring, then you, as a kind father, will desire not only riches, luxury, and honours for your child, but will desire his salvation, his spiritual advancement by the light of truth. Is that not so? And when your innocent little one asks, "Papa, who has created everything that pleases me in this world— earth, water, sun, flowers, grass?" what will you say? Will you really say to him, "I don't know"? You cannot help knowing, since God in His great mercy has revealed it to you. Or your child may ask you, "What awaits me beyond the tomb?" What will you tell him if you yourself know nothing? How will you answer him? Will you leave him to the temptations of the world and the devil? That is wrong!' The priest ceased and, with his head on one side, regarded Levin with mild kindly eyes.

This time Levin did not reply, not because he did not wish to enter upon a discussion with a priest, but because no one had ever yet put such questions to him; and also because, before his little one could begin asking such questions, there would be plenty of time to consider what the answers should be.

'You are entering upon a time of life,' the priest went on, 'when you must choose your path and keep to it, so pray that God in His goodness may help you and have mercy on you!' he concluded. 'May the Lord our God Jesus Christ, in the goodness and bounty of His love for mankind, pardon thee . . .'; and having pronounced the absolution, the priest blessed him and let him go.

When he got home that day Levin felt relieved at having done with an unpleasant episode in such a way that he had not been obliged to tell lies. Besides, he was left with a vague feeling that what the nice kind old man had said to him was not as stupid as it had seemed at first, and that there was something in it that ought to be elucidated. 'Of course, not now,' thought he, 'but later on.' He felt more than ever before that there was a kind of vagueness in his soul, a want of clearness, and that with regard to religion he was in the same position that he saw so distinctly and disliked in others, and for which he found fault with his friend Sviyazhsky.

He spent that evening with his betrothed at the Oblonskys' and was in particularly high spirits. Explaining to Oblonsky the state of elation he was in, he said he felt as pleased as a dog that was being taught to jump through a hoop, and which, having accomplished what was demanded of it, barks and wags its tail and jumps for joy upon the tables and window-sills.

Chapter II

On his wedding-day Levin, according to custom—the Princess and Dolly insisted on his strictly conforming to custom—did not see his bride, and dined at his hotel with three bachelors who happened to drop in. Sergius Ivanich, Katavasov, an old fellow-student at the university and now a professor of Natural Science, whom Levin had chanced to meet in the street and induced to come, and Chirikov, his best man, a Moscow magistrate and a bear-hunting comrade of Levin's. The dinner was a very merry one. Sergius Ivanich was in the best of spirits and was tickled by Katavasov's originality. Katavasov, feeling that his originality was observed and appreciated, showed it off. Chirikov gaily and good-naturedly backed up every one else.

'There now!' said Katavasov with a drawl, a habit he had fallen into when lecturing. 'What a talented fellow our friend Constantine Dmitrich used to be! I am speaking of one who is not with us, because he is no more. In those days he loved science. When he left the university he had human interests; but now half his talents are bent on self-deception and the other half toward justification of that deception.'

'I have never come across a more decided foe of marriage than yourself,' remarked Sergius Ivanich.

'No. I am no foe of marriage, but I believe in division of labour! Those who can do nothing else must beget offspring, and the others must help them to culture and happiness. That is how I look at it. There are hosts of aspirants who aim at mixing those two professions, but I am not one of them!'

'How delighted I shall be when I hear of your falling in love!' said Levin. 'Pray invite me to your wedding!'

'I am in love already.'

'Yes, with a mollusk! Do you know,' said Levin, turning to his brother, 'Katavasov is writing a work on nutriment and . . .'

'Oh, don't confuse matters! What does it matter what I write about? The fact is, I really do love mollusks.'

'But they would not prevent you loving a wife!'

'They would not, but the wife would.'

'Why?'

'Oh, you'll soon find out! Now you like farming, sport. . . . Well, you just wait and see!'

'You know, Arkhip came to-day to say that in Prudno there are lots of elk and two bears,' said Chirikov.

'Well, you'll have to get them without me.'

'There you are!' said Sergius Ivanich. 'Good-bye to bear-hunting in future! Your wife won't allow it.'

Levin smiled. The idea that his wife would not allow it seemed so agreeable that he was prepared to forgo the pleasure of ever setting eyes on a bear again.

'All the same, it's a pity that those two bears will be killed without you. Do you remember that time in Hapilovka? What fine sport we had!' said Chirikov.

Levin did not wish to deprive him of the illusion that somewhere there could be something good without her, therefore he said nothing.

'This custom of taking leave of celibacy is not without its reason,' said Sergius Ivanich. 'However happy you may be, you can't help regretting your freedom.'

'Now confess that you feel like the bridegroom in Gogol's play who jumped out of the window?' teased Chirikov.

'Of course he feels so, but won't own up,' said Katavasov, and burst out laughing.

'Well, the window is open. . . . Let us be off to Tver. One is a she-bear. We can go straight for her lair. Yes, let's catch the five o'clock train! And leave them to do as they please here,' said Chirikov, smiling.

'I am ready to swear I can't find in my soul a trace of regret for my freedom,' said Levin, with a smile.

'Ah, but your soul is in such chaos at the present moment that you are unable to find anything there! Wait till you've settled down a bit, then you'll find it,' said Katavasov.

'No, I should even now have some consciousness that despite my feelings' (he did not wish in Katavasov's presence to use the word *love*) 'and my happiness I was yet sorry to lose my freedom. But quite on the contrary, it is precisely of this loss of freedom that I am glad!'

'Very bad! A hopeless case!' said Katavasov. 'Well, let us drink to his recovery, or let us wish that at least a hundredth part of his dreams come true. Even that will be such joy as was never seen on earth!'

Soon after dinner the visitors left to get ready for the wedding.

When he was alone, Levin, thinking over the remarks of the three bachelors, once more asked himself whether there was in his soul any of that regret for his freedom that they had been speaking about. The question made him smile. 'Freedom? What is the good of freedom? Happiness consists only in loving and desiring: in wishing her wishes and in thinking her thoughts, which means having no freedom whatever; that is happiness!'

'But do I know her thoughts, wishes, or feelings?' a voice suddenly whispered. The smile faded from his face and he pondered. And all at once a strange sensation came over him. He was possessed by fear and doubt, doubt of everything.

'Supposing she does not love me? Supposing she is only marrying me just to get married? Supposing she does not herself know what she is doing?' he asked himself. 'She might bethink herself and only when she is already married find out that she does not and never could love me. . . .' And strange and most evil thoughts about her came into his mind. He became jealous of Vronsky just as he had been the year before, as if it had been but yesterday that he saw her with him. He suspected that she had not told him the whole truth. Suddenly he jumped up. 'No, this won't do!' he said to himself despairingly. 'I will go to her and tell her for the last time that we are now free, and that perhaps we had better keep so! Anything would be better than continual shame, misery, infidelity!' With his heart full of despair and bitterness toward every one, toward himself and her, he left the hotel and went to her.

He found her in one of the back rooms. She was sitting on a trunk and making some arrangements with one of the maids, sorting a pile of differently coloured dresses that hung over the backs of chairs or lay on the floor.

'Oh!' she cried when she saw him, and her face lit up with joy. 'Why have you . . . ? Well, I . . . this is a surprise! And I am sorting my old dresses to give them away. . . .'

'Ah, that is very nice,' he said gloomily, with a glance at the maid.

'You may go, Dunyasha. I will call you,' said Kitty. 'What is the matter with you?' she asked as soon as the maid was gone. She had noticed his strange expression, at once excited and gloomy, and was seized with alarm.

'Kitty, I am in torture! I cannot bear it alone,' he cried in a despairing tone, standing before her and looking imploringly into her eyes. Already in her loving, truthful face he could read that what he was going to tell her would lead to nothing, but he felt that he still wanted to hear her disavowal.

'I have come to say that there is still time . . . All this business can still be put a stop to!'

'What? I don't understand in the least. What is the matter with you?'

'What I have said a thousand times and cannot help thinking —that I am not worthy of you! It cannot be that you have agreed to marry me. Think it over . . . you have made a mistake. Think it well over! You cannot love me? . . . I . . . you'd better tell me . . .' he went on without looking at her. 'I shall be unhappy, of course. Let them all say what they like: anything is better than the misfortune . . . Anyhow, it would be better now while there is still time!'

'I don't understand,' she said, thoroughly frightened. 'Do you mean you refuse . . . Why stop . . . ?'

'Yes, if you don't love me.'

'Are you mad?' she exclaimed, flushing with vexation; but his face was so piteous that she suppressed her vexation, and throwing the dresses on a chair sat down closer to him. 'What are you thinking about? Tell me everything.'

'I think you cannot love me. What could you love me for?'

'O God, what can I do? . . .' she cried, and began to weep.

'Oh, what have I done!' he exclaimed, and kneeling before her he began kissing her hands. When the Princess came in five minutes later she found them quite reconciled. Kitty had not only assured him that she loved him, but had even given him, in answer to his question, the reasons why. She told him she loved him because she completely understood him, because she knew that it was necessary for him to love, and that all that he loved was good. This seemed quite clear to him. When the Princess entered they were sitting side by side on the trunk, sorting the dresses and disputing because Kitty wanted to give Dunyasha the brown dress she had worn when Levin proposed to her, while he insisted that that dress should not be given to anyone and that she should give Dunyasha a blue one instead.

'How is it you don't understand? She is dark and it won't suit her. . . . I have considered it all.'

When the Princess heard why he had come, she grew angry half in fun and half in earnest, and told him to go home and dress and not to delay Kitty, whose hair had to be done by the hairdresser, due to arrive immediately.

'She has scarcely eaten anything all these days and has grown quite plain; and here you come and upset her with your nonsense!' said she. 'Be off, be off, my dear!'

Guilty and ashamed, but comforted, Levin returned to his hotel. His brother, Dolly, and Oblonsky, all in evening dress, were waiting to bless him with the icon. Dolly had to return home to fetch her son, who, his hair oiled and curled, was to drive in the bride's carriage and hold an icon. Then a carriage had to be sent to fetch the groomsman, and another was to take Sergius Ivanich and return again. Altogether there were many complicated arrangements to consider. One thing was certain: there was no time to be lost, for it was already half-past six.

The Blessing was not a success. Oblonsky, standing in a comically-solemn attitude beside his wife, took the icon and told Levin to bow to the ground; then he blessed him, smiling a kindly amused smile, and kissed him three times. Dolly did the same, then she hurried away and again became confused about the arrangements for the carriages.

'Then this is what we must do: you go and fetch him in our carriage, and Sergius Ivanich, if he will be so kind, will go first and will send the carriage back.'

'Of course, I shall be very pleased!'

'And we will follow immediately with him. . . . Have your trunks been sent off?' inquired Oblonsky.

'Yes, they have,' replied Levin, and told Kuzma to get his things out that he might dress.

Chapter III

A crowd of people, mostly women, had assembled outside the church, which was brightly lit up for the wedding. Those who had arrived too late to get into the middle of the throng pressed round the windows, pushing and disputing and trying to peer in between the bars.

More than twenty carriages had already been ranged along the street by the mounted police. A police-officer, unmindful of the frost, stood at the entrance looking brilliant in his blue uniform. More carriages kept driving up, and now ladies with flowers in their hair got out, holding up their trains; or men appeared who doffed their military caps or black hats as they entered the church. Inside the building the candles in both chandeliers were already lit, as well as all the candles in front of the icons. The golden glitter on the crimson background of the iconostasis, the gilt ornaments of the icons, the silver of the chandeliers and candlesticks, the flag-stones of the floor, the mats, the banners above the choir, the steps of the ambo, the ancient books black with age, the cassocks and sur-plices, were all inundated with light. On the right of the well-heated church a staid though animated conversation was going on amidst the swallow-tail coats, white ties, uniforms, brocades, velvets and satins, hair, flowers, bare shoulders and arms and long gloves—the sound of which re-echoed strangely from the high dome above. Every time the door creaked every one turned round, expecting to see the bride and bridegroom enter. But the door had opened more than ten times and each time it turned out to be a guest who had been detained and now joined the crowd on the right, or a spectator who had managed to deceive or soften the heart of the police officer and who joined the throng of strangers on the left; and both relatives and spectators had passed through every phase of antici-pation.

At first they expected the bride and bridegroom to enter at any moment, and attached no importance to the delay. Then they turned more and more often toward the door, wondering whether anything had happened. At length the delay became awkward, and the friends and relatives tried to look as if they were not thinking about the bride and bridegroom but were absorbed in their conversations.

The archdeacon, as if to draw attention to the value of his time, coughed impatiently, making the windows vibrate. From the choir, growing weary of waiting, came the sound of voices being tried and the blowing of noses. The priest continually sent a chanter or deacon to see whether the bridegroom had arrived, and he himself, in his purple surplice with the embroidered girdle, went with increasing frequency to the side door in expectation of the bridegroom. At last one of the ladies looked at her watch and said, 'Well, this is strange!' and then all the guests became restless and expressed their surprise and dissatisfaction aloud. The best man went to find out what had occurred.

All this while Kitty, long since ready in her white dress, long veil, and crown of orange blossoms, stood with an old lady who was to accompany her and her sister, the Princess Lvova, at a window of the ballroom at the Shcherbatskys', for the last half hour vainly expecting her best man to come and announce that the bridegroom had reached the church.

Levin meanwhile, in trousers but without coat or waistcoat, was pacing up and down his room, perpetually putting his head out at the door and glancing up the corridor. But in the corridor there was nobody, and in despair he returned and addressed Oblonsky, who was quietly smoking.

'Was ever a man in such a terribly idiotic position?' he demanded.

'Yes, it is stupid,' Oblonsky concurred with a soothing smile. 'But don't worry, it will be here in a minute.'

'Oh, how can I help it?' said Levin with suppressed fury. 'And these idiotic open waistcoats—it's impossible!' He glanced at his crumpled shirt-front. 'And suppose the things have already gone to the station!' he exclaimed in despair.

'Then you'll have to wear mine.'

'I ought to have done that long ago.'

'It is better not to look ridiculous. Wait! It will all "shape itself"!'

The fact of the matter was that when Levin told his old servant Kuzma to get his things ready, Kuzma had duly brought his dress coat, waistcoat and what else he considered necessary.

'But the shirt?' Levin exclaimed.

'You've got it on,' Kuzma replied with a quiet smile.

He had not thought of leaving out a clean shirt, and having been told to pack everything and send it to the Shcherbatskys', whence they were to start that evening, he had done so and had left out only the dress suit. The shirt Levin had been wearing since the morning was crumpled and quite unfit to wear with the fashionable low-cut waistcoat. It was too far to send to the Shcherbatskys', so they sent out to buy one; but as it was Sunday all the shops had closed early. They sent for one of Oblonsky's, but it was much too wide and too short. They were obliged to send to the Shcherbatskys' after all, and the things had to be unpacked. Meantime in the church every one was waiting for the bridegroom; while he was pacing up and down like a caged beast, looking despairingly along the corridor, remembering all he had said to Kitty and wondering what she must be thinking now.

At last the guilty Kuzma, quite out of breath, rushed in with the shirt.

'Only just in time—they were hoisting the trunk into the cart,' he gasped.

Three minutes later Levin, not looking at the clock to avoid upsetting himself still more, ran as fast as he could down the corridor.

'That won't help matters,' remarked Oblonsky, smiling, and following without haste. 'It will all "shape itself," all "shape itself" . . . I assure you!'

Chapter IV

'Here they are! There he is! Which one? Is it the younger one? And look at her, poor dear! More dead than alive!' people in the crowd were saying as Levin met his bride at the door and entered the church with her.

Oblonsky told his wife the reason of the delay, and the guests smiled and whispered to one another. Levin saw no one and nothing; he did not take his eyes off his bride.

Every one said she had grown plainer during the last few days, and in her bridal dress was nothing like so pretty as usual; but Levin thought otherwise. He looked at her hair dressed high beneath the long veil and white flowers, at the high frill that covered her long neck at the sides and showed it in front in a particularly maidenly way, and at her strikingly slender waist. He thought she was prettier than ever: not that those flowers, the veil, or the dress ordered from Paris enhanced her beauty in any way, but because, despite all the carefully planned richness of her attire, the look on her sweet face and lips was still that look of innocent truthfulness.

'I thought you meant to run away,' she said, smiling at him.

'It was such a stupid thing that happened! I am ashamed to tell it,' he said with a blush, and was obliged to turn round to the approaching Sergius Ivanich.

'Nice story that, about your shirt!' said Sergius Ivanich with a smile and shake of the head.

'Yes, yes!' answered Levin, unable to understand what was being said.

'Now then, Kostya!' said Oblonsky, feigning consternation. 'You've got to decide an important point, and you're in exactly the right frame of mind to appreciate its importance. I have been asked whether you will have new candles or used ones to hold? The difference is ten roubles,' he added, puckering his lips into a smile. 'I have settled it, but perhaps you will not be satisfied.'

Though he knew it was a joke, Levin could not smile.

'Well then, is it to be fresh candles or used ones? That is the question!'

'Yes, yes! Fresh ones.'

'Well, I'm very glad that question is settled,' said Oblonsky with a smile. 'How stupid people do become under these circumstances!' he went on, turning to Chirikov, when Levin with an absent-minded glance at him moved off toward his bride.

'Kitty, mind you step first upon the mat!' said Countess Nordston, coming up to them. 'You are a fine fellow!' she added, addressing Levin.

'Aren't you frightened?' asked Kitty's old aunt Mary Dmitrievna.

'Are you cold? You look pale. Wait a moment, put your head down,' said Kitty's sister, Princess Lvova, and raising her plump, beautiful arms she adjusted the flowers on Kitty's head.

Dolly advanced and was about to say something, but could not speak and began crying and laughing in an unnatural manner. Kitty gazed at everybody with a look as absent-minded as Levin's.

Meanwhile the clergy put on their vestments and the priest and deacon came forward to the lectern that stood near the entrance doors. The priest turned to Levin and said something that Levin did not hear.

'Take the bride's hand and lead her,' said the best man.

For a long time Levin could not be made to understand what he had to do, and they were a long while trying to set him right. Just as they were going to give it up because he would either use the wrong hand or else take her by the wrong one, he at last understood that with his right hand, without changing his position, he must take her by her right hand. When at last he had taken her hand properly, the priest went a few steps in front of them and halted at the lectern. The crowd of friends and relatives, their voices buzzing and the ladies' trains rustling, moved after them.

Some one stooped down to arrange the bride's train. The church became so quiet that the drops of wax were heard falling from the candles.

The old priest, with his sacerdotal headgear and his locks of grey hair, glistening like silver, combed back behind his ears, drew his small old hands out from beneath his vestments of heavy silver cloth with a large gold cross on the back, and began turning over some pages on the lectern.

Oblonsky stepped up cautiously, whispered something to him, made a sign to Levin, and stepped back again.

The priest lit two wax candles decorated with bowers, and holding them askew in his left hand so that the wax kept slowly dripping, turned to the young couple. It was the same priest who had heard Levin's confession. He looked wearily and sadly at the bride and bridegroom, sighed, and disengaging his right hand from the vestments, held it up in blessing over the bridegroom, and then over the bride; only in his manner when he placed his fingers on Kitty's bowed head there was a shade of tenderness. Then he gave them the candles, took the censer, and slowly stepped away from them.

'Is it really true?' thought Levin, and glanced round at his bride. He could see her profile slightly from above, and by the just perceptible movements of her lips and eyelashes he knew she was aware of his look. She did not turn, but her high frilled collar moved, rising to her pink little ear. He saw that a sigh had been suppressed within her breast and that the little hand in its long glove holding the candle trembled. All the worry about his shirt, his lateness, the conversation of their relatives, their displeasure and his ridiculous mishap, suddenly vanished from his mind and he felt happy though scared.

The handsome, tall senior deacon in a silver cloth alb, his curled hair parted down the middle, came briskly forward lifting his stole with a practised movement of two fingers, and stopped opposite the priest.

'Bless us, Lord!' slowly succeeding one another, and vibratingly resonant, came the solemn tones.

'Blessed be our God, now and hereafter, for ever and ever!' replied the old priest meekly, in a sing-song voice, continuing to turn something over on the lectern. Then, harmoniously filling the whole church from windows to vaulted roof, a full chord sung by the invisible choir rose, swelled, hung for a moment, and softly died away.

There were prayers as usual for peace and salvation from above, for the Synod, for the Emperor and also for the servants of God betrothed that day, Constantine and Catherine.

'Let us pray to the Lord that He may send them perfect love, peace, and help!' the whole church seemed to breathe with the senior deacon's voice.

Levin listened to the words and was struck by them. 'How did they find out that it is help, exactly help that I need?' he wondered, remembering his late fears and doubts. 'What do I know? What can I do in this awful matter without help? Help is exactly what I need now!'

When the deacon had finished the prayer for the Imperial family, the priest holding a book turned to the bride and bridegroom.

'Eternal God who joinest them that were separate,' he read in his mild sing-song voice, 'and hast ordained for them an indissoluble union in love; Thou who didst bless Isaac and Rebecca and hast kept Thy promise to their heirs, bless these Thy servants, Constantine and Catherine, and lead them on the path of righteousness! Most merciful God, Lover of man, we praise Thee! Glory be to the Father, and to the Son, and to the Holy Ghost, now and hereafter and for ever and ever!'

'Amen!' from the invisible choir, again floated through the air.

' "Joined them that were separate"—what a depth of meaning is in those words, and how well they fit in with what I am feeling at this moment!' thought Levin. 'Does she feel the same?'

Looking round he met her eyes. From the expression in them he concluded that she understood them as he did; but this was not so. She understood hardly anything of the service and was not even listening to the words of the ceremony. She could neither listen nor understand, so deep was the one feeling that filled her soul and became ever stronger and stronger. It was a feeling of joy at the fruition of what had been for the last month and a half going on in her soul, of that which for those six weeks had gladdened and tortured her. On the day when, in the ballroom of the house in Arbat Street, she in her brown dress had gone up to him and silently plighted herself to him, on that day and in that hour a complete rupture seemed to have taken place within her soul between her former life and this other new and entirely unknown life—although in fact the old life still went on. Those six weeks had been the most blissful and at the same time the most trying of her life. The whole of her life, all her desires and hopes, were concentrated on this one man, still incomprehensible to her, to whom she was bound by a feeling—even more incomprehensible than the man himself—which now attracted and now repelled her. Meantime she went on living under the conditions of her old life and was horrified at herself: at her utter and unconquerable indifference to all her past, the things, habits, and people who had loved and still loved her, to her mother who was hurt by her

indifference, to her dear, affectionate father whom she had previously loved more than anyone else on earth. At one moment she
was horrified at this indifference, and the next moment rejoiced at
that which caused her indifference. She could not think of or desire
anything but life with this man; but, as that life had not yet
begun, she could not even clearly picture it to herself. There was
only anticipation, fear, and joy at something new and unknown; and
now at any moment the anticipation and uncertainty, and the remorse at repudiating her former life, would all come to an end
and something new would begin. This new life could not help
being terrible in consequence of its incertitude, but terrible or not
it was already an accomplished fact within her soul six weeks ago,
and was now only being sanctified.

Again turning to the reading-desk the priest with some difficulty
picked up Kitty's little ring, and asking Levin for his hand put the
ring on the tip of his finger. 'The servant of God, Constantine, is
betrothed to the servant of God, Catherine,' and having put a big
ring on Kitty's slender, rosy finger, pathetic in its weakness, the priest
repeated the same words.

Several times the couple tried to guess what was expected of
them, and blundered each time, the priest prompting them in
whispers. When what was necessary had at length been complied
with, he made the sign of the cross over them with the rings and
again gave the larger one to Kitty and the little one to Levin, and
again they blundered and passed the rings twice backwards and forwards without doing what was necessary.

Dolly, Chirikov, and Oblonsky came forward to help them. The
result was some confusion, whispering, and smiles, but the expression of solemn emotion on the young couple's faces did not
change; on the contrary, while they fumbled with their hands they
looked even more solemn and serious than before, and the smile
with which Oblonsky whispered to them to put on their rings involuntarily died on his lips. He felt that any kind of smile would
hurt their feelings.

'Thou hast from the beginning created them male and female,'
read the priest when they had exchanged rings. 'Through Thee the
wife is knit to the husband for a helpmeet and to procreate the
human race. Therefore, O God our Lord, who sentest down Thy
truth upon Thy heritage, and gavest Thy promises to our fathers from generation to generation of Thy chosen people, look
down upon thy servant Constantine and Thy servant Catherine and
strengthen them in their union with faith and concord in truth
and love. . . .'

Levin felt more and more that his ideas of marriage and his
dreams of how he would arrange his life had been but childishness,

and that this was something he had never understood and was now still further from understanding, although it was happening to him; and in his breast a tremor rose higher and higher, and the unruly tears came to his eyes.

Chapter V

All Moscow, including both relatives and friends, had congregated in the church. During the marriage ceremony, in the brilliantly illuminated building, among the crowd of elegantly dressed women and girls and men in evening dress with white ties, or in uniform, conversation in the low tones required by propriety never flagged. It was usually started by the men, for the women were absorbed in watching every detail of the service, which always fascinates them.

In the circle nearest the bride were her two sisters, Dolly the elder and the calm and beautiful Princess Lvova, who had come from abroad.

'Why is Marie in lilac? It's almost as unsuitable at a wedding as black,' remarked Mrs. Korsunskaya.

'With her complexion it's her only salvation,' replied Princess Drubetskaya. 'I wonder they are having the wedding in the evening, like tradespeople.'

'It is prettier. I was married in the evening too,' answered Mrs. Korsunskaya, and sighed as she remembered how sweet she had looked that day, how absurdly enamoured her husband then was, and how different things were now.

'They say that one who has been best man more than ten times never marries, and I wanted to be one for the tenth time to make myself safe, but was too late,' Count Sinyavin was saying to the pretty young Princess Charskaya, who had designs on him.

She answered only with a smile. She was looking at Kitty and thinking of the time when she would be standing there beside Count Sinyavin, just as Kitty now stood, and how she would then remind him of his joke.

Young Shcherbatsky told the old Maid of Honour Nikolayeva that he intended to put the crown on Kitty's chignon, for luck.[1]

'One ought not to wear a chignon,' replied the Maid of Honour, who had long ago made up her mind that if the old widower for whom she was angling ever married her, their wedding should be of the simplest.

Koznyshev was talking to Dolly, jokingly assuring her that the custom of going away after the wedding was spreading because newly-married couples always felt rather uncomfortable.

---

1. The best man and the groomsman hold heavy metal crowns above the heads of bride and bridegroom at a certain part of the service, and it is considered specially lucky if the crowns are actually put on.

'Your brother has a right to feel proud. She is wonderfully sweet. You must be feeling envious.'

'I am past all that, Darya Alexandrovna,' he answered, and his face became unexpectedly sad and serious.

Oblonsky was telling his sister-in-law the pun he had made about 'dissolving marriages.'

'I must put her wreath straight,' she replied, without listening.

'What a pity she has grown so much plainer!' remarked Countess Nordston to the Princess Lvova. 'All the same he is not worth her little finger. Don't you agree?'

'No, I like him very much, and not just because he will be my brother-in-law,' answered the Princess. 'How well he behaves! And it is so difficult to behave well under these circumstances, and not be ridiculous—and he is not ridiculous or stiff, and is evidently touched.'

'I suppose you quite expected this?'

'Almost. She always liked him.'

'Well, let us see which of them will step first on the mat!² I have given Kitty my advice.'

'It does not matter,' replied Princess Lvova. 'We are all submissive wives, it is in our nature.'

'Well, I stepped on the mat before Vasily! And you, Dolly?'

Dolly, who was standing near, heard, but did not reply. Her eyes were moist and she could not have spoken without bursting into tears. She rejoiced at the sight of Kitty and Levin, but going back to the past she thought of her own wedding, kept glancing at the beaming Oblonsky, and, forgetting the present, remembered nothing but her own young and innocent love. She remembered not herself only, but all the women with whom she was intimate or acquainted: thought of them as they had been at that most solemn moment of their lives, when, like Kitty, they had stood beneath the nuptial crown with love, hope and fear in their hearts, renouncing the past and entering upon the mystic future. Among the brides that came to her mind was her dear Anna, about whose impending divorce she had recently heard. She too had once stood with veiled head, pure and crowned with orange blossom. 'And now? How strange!' she murmured.

All the details of the ceremony were followed not only by the two sisters, the friends and relatives, but also by women onlookers who were quite strangers, and who—breathless with excitement and afraid of missing anything, even a single movement or expression of the bride's or bridegroom's face, and annoyed by the indifference of the men—did not answer and indeed often did not

---

2. During part of the service the couple stand upon a small mat. The one who first steps upon it is supposed to become the predominant partner.

hear the latter when they jested or made irrelevant remarks.

'Why is her face so tear-stained? Is she being married against her will?'

'Against her will, indeed, to such a fine fellow! Is he a Prince?'

'And is that her sister in white satin again? . . . Now hear how the deacon will roar, "Wives, obey your husbands"!'

'Is it the Chudovsky Choir?'

'No, the Synod's.'

'I asked the footman. It seems he will take her to his estate straight off.'

'He's dreadfully rich, they say. That's why they have given her to him.'

'Oh no, they are a very nice couple.'

'There now, Mary Vasilyevna! You were maintaining that crinolines were being worn fuller at the back! Just look at that one in the puce dress—an ambassador's wife, they say. See how it's draped: this way, and back again.'

'What a darling the bride is, like a lamb decked for the slaughter! But whatever you may say, one does feel sorry for a girl.'

So chattered the crowd of women who had managed to get inside the church.

Chapter VI

When the first part of the ceremony was over, a verger spread out a piece of pink silk cloth in front of the lectern. The choir began singing a psalm to some elaborate and complicated melody in which the bass and tenor continually repeated each other; and the priest, turning round, motioned the couple to the piece of pink silk. Often as they had heard the saying that the one who stepped first on the mat would be head of the household, neither Levin nor Kitty could think of that as they took those few steps, nor did they hear the loud remarks and disputes of those who maintained that he was first, and of others who said that they did it both together.

After the usual questions of whether they wished to be married and whether they had promised themselves to others, and their answers, which sounded strange to themselves, the second part of the service began. Kitty listened to the words of the prayer, trying to comprehend their meaning but unable to do so. Triumph and radiant joy filled her heart more and more as the ceremony proceeded, and made it impossible for her to be attentive.

They prayed: 'That they may live in chastity for the good of the fruits of the womb, and find joy in their sons and daughters.' It was declared that God had created woman from Adam's rib, and that 'For this cause shall a man leave his father and mother and

cleave unto his wife, and they twain shall be one flesh'; and that
'This is a great mystery.' They prayed that God should make them
fruitful and bless them as he blessed Isaac and Rebecca, Joseph,
Moses and Zipporah, and that they should see their children's
children. 'It is all very beautiful,' thought Kitty as she heard these
words, 'and could not be different.' And a smile of joy, which
involuntarily communicated itself to all who regarded her, shone
on her radiant face.

'Put it quite on!' came the words of advice when the priest had
put crowns on their heads and Shcherbatsky, his hand in its
three-buttoned glove trembling, held the crown high above Kitty's
head.

'Put it on,' she whispered, smiling.

Levin glanced round at her, was struck by the joyous radiance of
her face, and was involuntarily infected by her feeling. He felt
bright and joyous as she did.

With light hearts they heard the Epistle read and the roll of
the senior deacon's voice in the last verse, for which the outsiders
present had been waiting impatiently. With light hearts they drank
the warm wine and water from the shallow cup, and their spirits
rose still higher when the priest, throwing back his vestments,
took their hands in his and led them round the lectern while a
bass voice sang, *Rejoice, O Isaiah!* Young Shcherbatsky and Chirikov, who were supporting the crowns and getting entangled in the
bride's train, smiled too and were pleased without knowing why,
when they chanced to lag behind or jostle the young couple if
the priest happened to stop. The spark of joy that was glowing in
Kitty's heart seemed to have spread to every one in the church.
Levin fancied that the priest and deacon wanted to smile just as he
did.

Having lifted the crowns from their heads, the priest read the
last prayer and congratulated the married couple. Levin glanced at
Kitty and thought he had never seen her like that before, so enchanting with the new light of happiness irradiating her face. He
wished to speak to her, but did not know whether it was all over
yet. The priest helped him out of the difficulty, saying softly, with
a smile on his kindly mouth, 'Kiss your wife; and you, kiss your
husband!' He took the candles from their hands.

Levin kissed her carefully on her smiling lips, offered his arm,
and with a feeling of strange nearness led her out of the church.
He could not believe it was all true, and only realized it when
their surprised and timid glances met and he felt that they were
already one.

After supper that same night the young couple left for the
country.

Chapter VII

Vronsky and Anna had already been travelling together in Europe for three months. They had visited Venice, Rome, and Naples, and had only just reached a small Italian town where they meant to make a longer stay.

A handsome head-waiter, his thick hair greased with pomatum and parted from the nape upward, dressed in a swallow-tail coat, with a wide lawn shirt-front and a bundle of charms dangling on his rotund stomach, with his hands in his pockets, his eyes screwed up contemptuously, was answering a bystander's questions in a severe tone. Hearing steps ascending the stairs at the other side of the entrance, the waiter turned and recognized the Russian Count who occupied the best rooms in the hotel. He respectfully took his hands out of his pockets, bowed, and said that the courier had been, and that the business of renting the palazzo was settled. The steward was ready to sign the contract.

'Ah, I am very glad,' said Vronsky. 'And is the lady in?'

'The lady has been for a walk, but has now returned,' replied the waiter.

Vronsky took off his soft, broad-brimmed hat and wiped his perspiring forehead and his hair, which he had allowed to grow half-way down his ears and wore brushed back so as to hide his bald patch. After an absent-minded glance at the man who was still standing there watching him, he was about to go in.

'This gentleman is a Russian and was asking about you,' said the head-waiter.

With a mixture of vexation at the impossibility of evading his acquaintances anywhere and of desire to find something to distract the monotony of his life, Vronsky looked round again at the man, who had first moved away and then halted; and at the same moment the eyes of both brightened.

'Golenishchev!'

'Vronsky!'

It was really Golenishchev, his fellow-student in the Corps des Pages. In the Corps Golenishchev had been a Liberal, had left the Corps a civilian, and had never served. On leaving the Corps the two friends had separated and had met but once since then.

On that occasion Vronsky found that Golenishchev had chosen some high-flown Liberal activity and therefore felt he must despise Vronsky's profession and activities. Consequently Vronsky had then treated him with the cold, proud aloofness of which he was master, which meant: 'You may like or dislike my way of life. It is a matter of absolute indifference to me, but if you wish to know me you must respect me.' And Golenishchev had remained contemptuously indifferent to Vronsky's attitude, so that this meeting ought to have separated them still further. Yet now they brightened up and exclaimed with pleasure at recognizing one another. Vronsky would never have thought he could be so pleased to see Golenishchev, but probably he was himself unaware how bored he was. He forgot the unpleasant impression left by their last encounter, and with an open and joyful countenance held out his hand to his old schoolfellow. A similar expression of pleasure replaced the former anxious look on Golenishchev's face.

'How pleased I am to see you!' said Vronsky, a friendly smile disclosing his fine white teeth.

'I heard the name of Vronsky but I did not know which Vronsky. I am very, very pleased.'

'Come in! Well, and what are you doing?'

'Oh, I have been here over a year. I am working.'

'Ah!' said Vronsky in an interested tone. 'Well, come in.'

And according to the usual way with Russians, instead of saying what he wanted to hide from the servants in Russian, he began speaking French.

'You know Madame Karenina? We are travelling together. I am now going to her,' he said in French, attentively watching Golenishchev's expression.

'Ah? I did not know,' Golenishchev replied in a tone of indifference, though he was quite aware of it. 'Been here long?' he added.

'I? . . . Three days,' answered Vronsky, still attentively scrutinizing his friend's face. 'Yes, he is a decent fellow and looks at the matter in the right way,' said Vronsky to himself, understanding the meaning of the other's look and the change of subject. 'I can introduce him to Anna, as he sees the matter rightly.'

During the three months he had spent abroad with Anna, Vronsky when coming across new people had always asked himself how the new person would be likely to regard his relations with Anna, and in most cases he had found that the men he met understood it in the 'right' way. But had he, and those who understood the matter in the 'right' way, been asked what this understanding amounted to, they would have been much puzzled how to reply.

At bottom, those who in Vronsky's opinion understood it the 'right' way did not understand it in any special way, but behaved in general as well-bred persons do with regard to all the complicated and unanswerable problems which surround life on every side: they conducted themselves properly, avoiding insinuations and inconvenient questions. They pretended to understand completely the significance and meaning of the situation, to countenance and even approve of it, but to consider it out of place and unnecessary to explain all this.

Vronsky at once guessed that Golenishchev was one of that sort, and was therefore doubly pleased to have met him; and Golenishchev behaved to Anna, when he had been introduced, as well as Vronsky could have wished. Evidently he avoided, without the least effort, everything in conversation that might have sounded awkward.

He had never met Anna before and was struck by her beauty, and still more by the simplicity with which she accepted her position. She blushed when Vronsky showed Golenishchev in, and the childlike flush that suffused her open and handsome face pleased him exceedingly. But what pleased him most was that at once, and apparently intentionally to prevent any possibility of misapprehension in the stranger's mind, she called Vronsky simply Alexey, and said that they were about to move into a house of their own, called a palazzo, which they had just taken. This straightforward and simple attitude toward her own position pleased Golenishchev. Noticing Anna's good-natured, bright, and energetic manner, he thought that, knowing both Karenin and Vronsky as he did, he quite understood her. He thought he understood what she herself was quite unable to understand: how, though she was the cause of her husband's unhappiness and had abandoned him and her son and lost her own good name, she could feel energetic, cheerful and happy.

'It is mentioned in the guide-book,' said Golenishchev, referring to the palazzo Vronsky was taking. 'There is a fine Tintoretto there . . . one of his later period.'

'I say, the weather is glorious: let us go and have another look at it,' said Vronsky to Anna.

'I should like to very much. I'll just go and put on my hat. You say it's hot?' she asked, stopping at the door and looking inquiringly at Vronsky, while a bright flush again suffused her face.

From her look Vronsky understood that she did not yet know what attitude he wished to adopt toward Golenishchev, and was afraid she might not have behaved suitably.

He answered with a long and tender look. 'No, not very hot,' he said.

She thought she had understood him completely and above all that he was satisfied with her. She gave him a smile and went out with rapid steps.

The two friends looked at each other, and in both faces appeared an embarrassed expression, as if Golenishchev—who obviously admired her—tried but failed to hit on the right thing to say about her; and as if Vronsky both feared and wished that he should succeed.

'Well, and so you have settled down here?' said Vronsky in order to begin a conversation. 'You are still busy at the same thing?' he went on, recollecting that he had heard the other was writing something.

'Yes, I am writing the second part of *Two Principles*,' said Golenishchev, flushing with pleasure at the question. 'To be quite exact, I mean, I am not yet writing, but am collecting the materials. The book will be much fuller and will deal with almost all the questions. We in Russia are slow to realize that we are the inheritors of Byzantium,' and he began a long and heated explanation.

At first Vronsky felt uncomfortable because he did not know even the first part of *Two Principles*, which the author mentioned as if it were well known. But later on, when Golenishchev began expounding his view, and Vronsky was able to follow him, even though he was ignorant of *Two Principles* he listened with interest, for the man talked well. Yet Vronsky was surprised at, and sorry to see, the irritable excitement with which Golenishchev spoke on the subject that interested him. The longer he talked the more his eyes flashed, the more hastily he retorted on imaginary opponents, and the more agitated and offended became his face. Remembering him as a thin, active, good-natured, and noble boy, always at the head of his class, Vronsky could not understand the cause of the agitation, nor approve of it. What most displeased him was that Golenishchev, a man belonging to good Society, should put himself on the same level with certain scribblers who irritated him and made him angry. Was it worth while? He did not like this, but nevertheless he felt that Golenishchev was not happy and he was sorry for him. Signs of distress, of insanity almost, were apparent in his mobile and rather good-natured face as, without even observing that Anna had re-entered the room, he continued expressing his views with haste and warmth.

When Anna returned with her hat and mantle on, and stood beside him toying with her sunshade with quick motions of her beautiful hand, Vronsky with a feeling of relief turned from Golenishclev's eyes which were fixed on him plaintively. With renewed love he glanced at his charming companion, so full of vitality and joy. With an effort Golenishchev recollected himself, but he was at first dejected and morose. Anna, however, who at that time was amiably disposed to every one, soon revived him by her simple and cheerful manner. After trying several topics of conversation she led him on to the subject of art, about which he talked very well, and listened to him with attention. They walked to the house they had taken and looked over it.

'I am very pleased about one thing,' said Anna to Golenishchev when they had returned to the hotel. 'Alexey will have a nice studio. You must certainly have that room, Alexey,' she added, having understood that Golenishchev was to be on an intimate footing with them and that there was no need to pretend in his presence.

'Do you paint?' inquired Golenishchev, turning quickly to Vronsky.

'Yes, I went in for it long ago, and now have begun a little,' answered Vronsky with a blush.

'He is very talented,' said Anna with a pleased smile. 'Of course I am no judge, but people who do know say so.'

Chapter VIII

During this, the first period of her freedom and rapid recovery, Anna felt unpardonably happy and full of the joy of life. The memory of her husband's grief did not poison her happiness. On the one hand this memory was too terrible to dwell upon, and on the other hand her husband's misfortune had meant for her too great a joy for repentance to be possible. The recollection of all that had happened to her since her illness; her reconcilation with her husband, the rupture, the news of Vronsky's wound, his reappearance in her husband's house, the preparations for divorce, the parting from her home and son—all now seemed a delirious dream from which she had wakened abroad and alone with Vronsky. The memory of the evil done to her husband aroused in her a feeling akin to repulsion, such as a man might feel who when in danger of drowning had shaken off another who clung to him. That other was drowned; of course it was wrong, but it had been the only way of escape and it was better not to recall such terrible details.

One comforting reflection about her conduct had come to her in the first moment of the rupture, and when she now remembered the past she also recalled that reflection. 'I was the inevitable cause of unhappiness to him,' she thought, 'but I don't wish to profit by his calamity. I too am suffering and must suffer: I am losing what I most cherished—my good name and my son. I have done wrong, and therefore do not ask for happiness and do not want a divorce. I must go on suffering from the shame and from the separation from my son.' But sincerely as Anna desired to suffer, she was not suffering. She was not conscious of degradation. With the tact they both possessed, and by avoiding Russian ladies abroad, the two never placed themselves in a false position and always met people who pretended to understand their mutual relations much better than they themselves understood them. The parting from her son whom she loved, did not trouble her at first either. The little girl, *his* child, was so sweet, and Anna had grown so attached to her since she was the only child left to her, that she rarely thought of her son.

The desire to live, enhanced by her recovery, was so powerful, and the conditions of her life were so novel and pleasant, that Anna felt unpardonably happy. The better she knew Vronsky the more she loved him. She loved him both for his own sake and for his love of her. To possess him entirely was a continual joy to her. His nearness was always pleasant. All the traits of character, with which she became better and better acquainted, seemed inexpressibly delightful. His appearance, altered by civilian dress, was as attractive to her as to a girl in love. In all he said, thought, or did, she saw something peculiarly noble and exalted. She herself was frightened at the rapture with which he inspired her; she sought, but could not find, anything in him that was not beautiful. She dared not let him see her consciousness of her own inferiority. To her it seemed that if he knew of it he would the sooner cease to love her, and there was nothing she now feared more— though she had no reason to do so—than the loss of his love. But she could not help being grateful to him for his treatment of her, and showing him how much she valued it. He, who in her opinion had such a decided vocation for statesmanship, in which he ought to have played a conspicuous part, had sacrificed his ambitions for her and never showed the least regret. He was even more lovingly respectful to her than before, and the thought that she must never be allowed to feel the awkwardness of her situation never left his mind for a moment. He, so virile a man, not only never contradicted her, but where she was concerned seemed to have no will of his own and to be only occupied in anticipating her every wish. She could not help appreciating this, although his strained attentiveness, the atmosphere of solicitude with which he surrounded her, became burdensome at times.

Vronsky meanwhile, in spite of the complete fulfilment of what he had so long desired, was not completely happy. He soon felt that the realization of his longing gave him only one grain of the mountain of bliss he had anticipated. That realization showed him the eternal error men make by imagining that happiness consists in the gratification of their wishes. When first he united his life with hers and donned civilian clothes, he felt the delight of freedom in general, such as he had not before known, and also the freedom of love—he was contented then, but not for long. Soon he felt rising in his soul a desire for desires—boredom. Involuntarily he began to snatch at every passing caprice, mistaking it for a desire and a purpose. Sixteen hours daily had to be filled somehow, living abroad as they did completely at liberty, quite cut off from the round of social life that had filled his time in Petersburg. The pleasures of a bachelor's life, enjoyed by him on his previous

travels abroad, were not to be thought of now, for one attempt of
that kind had produced in Anna an unexpected fit of depression
quite disproportionate to the offence of a late supper with some
acquaintances. Intercourse with local Society or with the Russians
was, in consequence of the indefiniteness of their relation, likewise
impossible. Sight-seeing, apart from the fact that he had already
seen everything, had for him—a Russian and an intelligent man—
none of that inexplicable importance the English manage to attach
to it.

As a hungry animal seizes every object it meets, hoping to find
food in it, so Vronsky unconsciously seized now on politics, now
on new books, now on pictures.

As in his youth he had shown aptitude for art, and not knowing
how to spend his money had begun to collect engravings, he now
settled down to painting and began to work at it, putting into it
the surplus stock of desire which demanded satisfaction.

He had a talent for understanding art and for imitating it with
accuracy and good taste, and he imagined that he possessed the
real power an artist needs. After wavering for some time between
various kinds of art—religious, historical, genre or realistic—he
began to paint. He understood all the different kinds and was able
to draw inspiration from all, but he could not imagine that it is
possible to be quite ignorant of the different kinds of art and to be
inspired directly by what is in one's own soul, regardless of whether
what one paints belongs to any particular school. As he did not
know this, and was not inspired directly by life but indirectly by
life already embodied in art, he found inspiration very readily and
easily, and equally readily and easily produced paintings very similar to the school of art he wished to imitate.

He liked the graceful and effective French School of painting
best, and in that style began painting a portrait of Anna dressed as
an Italian, and he, as well as every one else who saw it, considered
the portrait a great success.

Chapter IX

The neglected old palazzo with its high stucco ceilings, its wall
frescoes and mosaic floors, with heavy yellow damask hangings at
the big windows, vases standing on brackets and mantelshelves,
carved doors, and sombre halls filled with pictures,—that palazzo, when they had moved into it, by its very appearance kept
alive in Vronsky the pleasant delusion that he was not so much a
Russian landowner and Master of the Hunt without duties as an
enlightened connoisseur and art patron, and withal a modest artist
himself, who had renounced the world, his connections and ambitions, for the sake of the woman he loved.

The rôle Vronsky had chosen, with their removal to the palazzo, was quite successful; and having through Golenishchev made the acquaintance of several interesting persons, he felt tranquil for a time. He painted studies from nature under the direction of an Italian professor, and studied Italian life in the Middle Ages. Medieval Italian life had at that time become so fascinating to him that he even began to wear his hat and throw his cloak across his shoulder in a medieval manner which was very becoming to him.

'Here we live and know nothing,' said Vronsky one morning to Golenishchev, who had come to see him. 'Have you seen Mikhaylov's picture?' and he passed his visitor a Russian newspaper that had just arrived, and pointed to an article on a Russian artist who was living in that town, and had just finished a picture long talked of and bought before completion. The article reproached the Government and the Academy for leaving a remarkable artist without encouragement or help.

'I have,' answered Golenishchev. 'Of course he is not without talent, but his tendency is quite a false one. He has that Ivanov-Strauss-Renan attitude toward Christ and religious art.'[3]

'What is the subject of his picture?' asked Anna.

'Christ before Pilate. Christ is pictured as a Jew with all the realism of the New School.'

Led on by this question about the subject of the picture to one of his favourite topics, he began to explain.

'I can't understand how one can make so gross an error! In the art of the old masters Christ was given a definite embodiment: therefore, if they want to depict not God but a revolutionary or a sage, let them choose some historic character—Socrates, Franklin, Charlotte Corday—but certainly not Christ! They choose the one person who must not be chosen as a subject for art, and then . . .'

'And is it true that this Mikhaylov is so poor?' inquired Vronsky, thinking that he, as a Russian Maecenas, ought to help this artist regardless of whether his picture was good or bad.

'Hardly. He is a wonderful portrait-painter. Have you seen his portrait of Vasilchikova? But it seems he does not want to paint any more portraits, so it is possible he may be in want. I say that . . .'

'Couldn't one ask him to paint Anna Arkadyevna's portrait?' said Vronsky.

'Why mine?' said Anna. 'After the one you painted I want no other. Better have one of Annie' (as she called her little girl). 'There she is!' she added, looking from the window at the hand-

---

3. In 1858 the painter A. A. Ivanov exhibited in St. Petersburg his huge painting "Christ's Apparition before the People." The German scholar David Strauss (1808–1874), the French Ernest Renan (1823–1892) and others also took the direction of interpreting Jesus Christ as a more human and historical, and less traditionally religious figure. Tolstoy was skeptical toward the new school of thought and art.

some Italian nurse who had taken the baby into the garden, and then immediately glancing round at Vronsky. The handsome nurse, whose head Vronsky was painting for his picture, was the only and secret sorrow of Anna's life. Vronsky painted her, admired her beauty and her 'medievalism,' and Anna dared not confess to herself that she was afraid of being jealous of the nurse; so she treated the woman with special kindness and spoilt her and her little son.

Vronsky too looked out of the window and into Anna's eyes, and at once turned to Golenishchev saying:

'Do you know this Mikhaylov?'

'I have met him. But he is a crank and quite uneducated. You know, he is one of those wild modern folk one so often meets nowadays; you know! One of those freethinkers who have been brought up from the beginning in disbelief, negation, and materialism. Formerly,' Golenishchev went on, either not noticing or not wishing to notice that both Anna and Vronsky wanted to speak, 'formerly a freethinker was a man brought up with ideas of religion, law, and morality, who himself, through struggle and pain, had attained freedom of thought; but now a new type of born freethinkers has appeared. These grow up without so much as hearing that there used to be laws of morality and religion, and that there was once authority in these things; they grow up simply with the idea of negation—that is, as heathens. He is one of these. He is the son of a head footman, I think, and has had no education. When he entered the Academy and won a reputation for himself he, not being stupid, wanted to get some education. So he resorted to what seemed to him to be the wellspring of education—the magazines. You see, formerly a man who wished to get an education—a Frenchman, let us say—would have commenced studying all the classics, theologians, dramatists, historians, and philosophers, and with what mental labour he would have been confronted! But among us at the present day he tumbled straight into the literature of negation and rapidly assimilated the essence of the negative teaching, and there he was! And that is not all. Twenty years ago he would have found in that kind of literature signs of the struggle with authority and of an outlook centuries old, and from that struggle would have deduced that something else had existed; but as it is, he stumbles on a kind of literature that does not even deign to dispute the old point of view, saying straight off, "There is nothing but evolution, selection, the struggle for existence, and nothing more"! In my article I . . .'

'Do you know what we'll do?' cried Anna, who for some time had been furtively exchanging looks with Vronsky and knew that the latter was not at all interested in the education of the artist but was only concerned to help him by giving him a commission for a portrait. 'Do you know what we'll do?' she resolutely interrupted Golenishchev, who was in the full flow of his speech.

'Let us go and see him.'

Golenishchev pulled himself up and unwillingly agreed, but as the artist lived in a distant part of the town they decided to hire a carriage.

An hour later Anna, seated beside Golenishchev with Vronsky facing them, drove to a new ugly house in a distant quarter of the town. Having learnt from the house-porter's wife who came out to meet them that Mikhaylov allowed visitors into his studio, but was at that moment at his lodgings a few steps away, they sent her with their cards to beg permission to see his pictures.

Chapter X

Mikhaylov, the artist, was at work as usual when Vronsky's and Golenishchev's cards were brought him. Every morning he worked in the studio at his big picture.

On returning home he had been angry with his wife because she had not managed to pacify the landlady, who clamoured for the rent.

'Have I not told you scores of times not to enter upon discussions? At best you are only a fool, and when you begin arguing in Italian you become a treble fool!' he said at the end of a long dispute.

'Then you shouldn't get into arrears! It's not my fault! If I had any money . . .'

'Shut up, for heaven's sake!' cried Mikhaylov with tears in his voice, stopping his ears with his hands as he went into his work-room behind a partition and locked the door behind him.

'What an idiot!' he muttered to himself as he seated himself at the table, and having opened a portfolio he at once set to work with particular ardour at an unfinished drawing.

He never worked with such ardour or so successfully as when things were going badly with him, and especially after a quarrel with his wife. 'Oh lord! If only I could escape somewhere!' he thought as he worked. He was sketching the figure of a man in a fit of anger. He had sketched him before, but had been dissatisfied with the result. 'No, the other one was better. . . . Where is it?' He went back to his wife, and frowning, without looking at her, asked his eldest little girl where the paper was that he had given them. The paper with the drawing that he had thrown away was found, but it was dirty now and spotted with candle grease. Nevertheless, he took it, put it on his table, and, stepping backward and screwing up his eyes, began examining it. Suddenly he smiled and flung up his arms joyfully.

'That's it! That's it!' he said, and taking up his pencil he began drawing rapidly. A grease spot had given the figure a new pose.

He copied that new pose, and, suddenly remembering the energetic pose and prominent chin of a shopman from whom he had
bought cigars, he gave the figure that man's face and chin. He
laughed with joy, for the inanimate, artificial figure had come to
life, and was just the thing. The figure was alive, clear, and well-
defined. It was possible to correct the drawing to accord with the
requirements of the pose; it was possible and even necessary to
place the feet further apart, to alter the position of the left arm,
and to throw back the hair. But while making these corrections he
did not alter the pose but only removed what interfered with its
character. He removed, if one may say so, the coverings which
partially obscured the figure, every fresh stroke making its energy
and power more apparent and more as it had been suddenly revealed to him by the effects of the grease spot. He was carefully
finishing the drawing when the cards were brought to him.

'Directly! Directly!'

He went out to his wife. 'Come, Sasha, don't be angry,' he said,
smiling timidly and tenderly. 'You were wrong and so was I. I'll
settle it all!'

Having made it up with his wife he put on an olive-green overcoat with a velvet collar, and a hat, and went to the studio. His
successful drawing was already forgotten. Now he was pleased and
excited by the visit to his studio of these grand Russians who had
come in a carriage.

About his picture—the one at present on the easel—he had
at the bottom of his heart a firm opinion: that no one had ever
painted anything like it. He did not consider his picture better
than all Raphael's, but he knew that what he wanted to express
in that picture had never yet been expressed by anyone. Of that
he was firmly convinced, and had long been so—ever since he had
begun painting it; yet the opinion of others, whoever they might
be, seemed to him of great importance, and disturbed him to the
depths of his soul. Every remark, even the most trivial, which
showed that those who judged it saw even but a small part of what
he himself saw in it, moved him deeply. He always attributed to
those judges a better understanding than his own, and always expected to hear from them something he had himself not noticed in
his work, often fancying that in their criticisms he had really found
that something.

With rapid steps he approached the door of his studio, and in
spite of his excitement was struck by the soft light on Anna's
figure as she stood in the shadow of the porch listening to something Golenishchev was vehemently saying, and at the same time
evidently wishing to look at the approaching artist. He was himself
unconscious that as he approached them he seized and absorbed

this impression, just as he had retained the tobacconist's chin and hidden it away where he could find it when it was wanted. The visitors, already disenchanted by Golenishchev's account of the artist, were still further disillusioned by his appearance. Of medium height, thick-set and with a loose gait, Mikhaylov in his brown hat, olive-green overcoat and narrow trousers (at a time when wide ones had long since come into fashion), and especially his commonplace broad face, expressing a combination of timidity and a desire to be dignified, created an unpleasant impression.

'Come in, please!' he said, trying to put on an air of indifference, as he entered the hall and took a key from his pocket to unlock the door.

Chapter XI

On entering his studio the artist again cast a glance at his visitors and took note of Vronsky's face, especially his jaw. Although his artistic perceptions never slept, and although he was growing more and more excited as the moment approached when his picture was to be criticized, he quickly and shrewdly, from imperceptible data, formed his opinion of these three persons. Of Golenishchev he thought, 'That one is a Russian who lives here.' Mikhaylov did not remember his name or where he had seen him or what they had talked about; he remembered only his face, as he remembered every face he had ever seen; but he also remembered that it was one of the faces he had mentally put aside with the enormous class of falsely important faces, faces lacking expression. A mass of hair and a very open forehead gave a superficial significance to that face, which had an insignificant, childish, restless expression concentrated in the narrow bridge of the nose. Vronsky and Anna, according to Mikhaylov's conception, were in all probability distinguished wealthy Russians, who like all these wealthy Russians comprehended nothing of art but pretended to be amateurs and critics. 'Probably they've seen all the antiquities, and are now going the round of the modern painters, the German quack and the stupid English pre-Raphaelite, and to complete the series have come to see me too,' he thought. Well, he knew the dilettantes' way of examining the studios of modern artists (the cleverer they were the worse they were) with the one purpose of being able to say afterwards that art had deteriorated and that the more modern art one sees the more evident it becomes that the old masters were inimitable. He expected all this, saw it in their faces, in the careless indifference with which they talked among themselves, looked at the lay figures and busts, and unconcernedly walked about while waiting for him to uncover his picture. But in spite of all this, as he turned over his studies, pulled up the blinds,

and withdrew the sheet from his picture, he felt very excited—all
the more so because, though he regarded distinguished and wealthy
Russians as mostly beasts and fools, Vronsky and especially Anna
pleased him.

'There!' he said, stepping aside with his loose gait, and pointing
to the picture. 'This is *Pilate's Admonition*—Matthew, chapter
xxvii,' he went on, conscious that his lips were beginning to tremble
with excitement; and he stepped behind the visitors.

During the few moments that they were silently gazing at it,
Mikhaylov also regarded it with the indifferent eye of a stranger. In
those few moments he believed in advance that the highest and
justest of criticisms was going to be pronounced by these very
visitors whom he had so despised a moment before. He forgot all
that he had thought of his picture during the three years that he
had worked at it, forgot all its merits, which he had not doubted,
and saw it from the fresh point of view of an indifferent stranger,
and he saw nothing good in it. He saw in the foreground Pilate's
vexed face and Christ's calm one, and behind them the faces of
Pilate's servants and of John, watching what was taking place. Each
of those faces that with so much searching, so many faults and
corrections, he had evolved with its own character, each representing so much pain and pleasure, and all of them so often placed
and replaced to obtain harmony; all the shades of colour and tone
elaborated with such effort—all these, regarded as a whole from
those others' point of view, now seemed trivialities a thousand times
repeated. The face that was most dear to him, that of Christ, the
centre of the picture, which had so enraptured him when he first
discovered it, now, regarded from the others' standpoint, seemed
quite worthless. He saw a well-painted—and not even that, for he
detected a multitude of errors—repetition of those innumerable
Christs: Titian's, Raphael's, Rubens's, with the same soldiers and
the same Pilates. It was trivial, poor, stale, and even badly painted,
weak and lacking harmony. They would be in the right when they
began to say falsely-polite things in the presence of the artist, and
to pity and laugh at him behind his back.

The silence grew too unbearable, though it had not lasted more
than a minute. To break it and to appear calm, he made an effort
and addressed Golenishchev.

'I think I have had the pleasure of meeting you?' he said, glancing uneasily now at Anna and now at Vronsky, in order not to lose
any detail of their expressions.

'Of course! We first met at Rossi's. Don't you remember that evening when the Italian lady recited—the new Rachel?' began
Golenishchev glibly, turning away from the picture to the artist
without the slightest regret. Noticing, however, that Mikhaylov was

waiting to hear his criticism of the picture, he said:

'Your picture has progressed very much since I last saw it, and now, as then, I am specially struck by the figure of Pilate. One can so well understand that man, a kind, first-rate fellow, but an official to his very backbone, who does not know what he is doing. But it seems to me . . .'

The whole of Mikhaylov's mobile face suddenly lighted up. His eyes brightened. He wanted to speak but was too agitated, and pretended to cough instead. Little as he valued Golenishchev's capacity to understand art, unimportant as was his remark about the truth of Pilate's official expression while what was important remained unmentioned, and offensive as this trivial (it might have seemed to him) remark before anything had been said about what was most important, Mikhaylov was delighted with it. His opinion of that figure was the same. The fact that this opinion was but one of a million of other opinions which—as Mikhaylov well knew—would all have been just, did not for him detract from the importance of Golenishchev's remark. He took a liking for Golenishchev because of that remark, and his depression changed suddenly into delight. In an instant his whole picture became alive before his eyes, with the inexpressible complexity of everything that lives. He wished to say that it was just so that he understood Pilate, but his trembling lips would not obey him and he was unable to speak. Vronsky and Anna were talking in the hushed voice in which—partly not to offend the artist, and partly not to utter aloud a stupid remark such as is so easily made when speaking about art—people generally talk at picture exhibitions. Mikhaylov thought that on them too the picture had created an impression, and went up to them.

'How wonderful Christ's expression is!' said Anna. That expression pleased her more than all else she saw, and she felt that it was the centre of the picture, and that therefore praise of it would be agreeable to the artist. 'One sees he is sorry for Pilate.'

This too was one of a million just remarks which might have been made with reference to his picture and the figure of Christ. She said he was sorry for Pilate. In Christ's expression there should be pity because there was love in it, a peace not of this world, a readiness for death, and a knowledge of the vanity of words. Of course there was an official expression in Pilate's face and pity in Christ's, for the former was the embodiment of carnal and the latter of spiritual life. All this and much more floated through Mikhaylov's mind; and again his face shone with ecstasy.

'Yes, and how well that figure is done, and what an atmosphere there is! One could walk round it,' said Golenishchev, showing evidently by this remark that he did not approve of the content and idea of the figure.

'Yes, its mastery is wonderful! How those figures in the background stand out! This is technique,' said Vronsky, addressing Golenishchev and alluding to a conversation they had had about Vronsky's despair of attaining technical mastery.

'Yes, yes, wonderful!' chimed in Golenishchev and Anna. In spite of his elation, this remark about technique grated painfully on Mikhaylov's heart, and, glancing angrily at Vronsky, he suddenly frowned. He often heard the word *technique* mentioned, and did not at all understand what was meant by it. He knew it meant a mechanical capacity to paint and draw, quite independent of the subject-matter. He had often noticed—as now when his picture was being praised—that technique was contrasted with inner quality, as if it were possible to paint well something that was bad. He knew that much attention and care were needed not to injure one's work when removing the wrappings that obscure the idea, and that all wrappings must be removed, but as to the art of painting, the technique, it did not exist. If the things he saw had been revealed to a little child, or to his cook, they would have been able to remove the outer shell from their idea. And the most experienced and technical painter could never paint anything by means of mechanical skill alone, if the outline of the subject-matter did not first reveal itself to his mind. Moreover, he saw that if technique were spoken of, then he could not be praised for it. In all he painted and ever had painted he saw defects that were an eyesore to him, the results of carelessness in removing the shell of the idea, which he could not now remedy without spoiling the work as a whole. And in almost all the figures and faces he saw traces of wrappings that had not been entirely removed and that spoilt the picture.

'One thing might be said, if you will allow me to make the remark,' began Golenishchev.

'Oh, I shall be very pleased: pray do!' said Mikhaylov with a feigned smile.

'It is, that you have made Him a man-God, and not a God-man. However, I know that you wished to do so.'

'I could not paint a Christ whom I had not in my soul,' Mikhaylov rejoined gloomily.

'Yes, but in that case, if I may say what I think . . . Your picture is so good that a remark of mine cannot do it any harm, besides which it's only my personal opinion . . . yours is different, the idea itself is different. But let us take Ivanov, for example. I consider that if Christ is to be brought down to the level of an historic figure, it would be better to choose another historic theme, a fresh one as yet untouched.'

'But if this is the highest theme open to art?'

'Other themes can be found if one looks for them. But the fact is, art won't stand discussion and argument. Yet Ivanov's picture suggests both to a believer and an unbeliever the question: Is this a God or not a God? And the unity of impression is destroyed.'

'Why so? To me it seems that for educated people such questions can no longer exist,' said Mikhaylov.

Golenishchev did not agree with this, and keeping to his first contention that unity of impression is indispensable in art, he confuted Mikhaylov.

The artist was perturbed, but could find nothing to say in defence of his opinion.

Chapter XII

Anna and Vronsky had long been exchanging glances, regretting their friend's clever loquacity, and at last Vronsky without waiting for his host crossed the room to look at another and smaller picture.

'Oh, how charming! How charming! Wonderful! Charming!' he and Anna began both at once.

'What is it they like so much?' wondered Mikhaylov. He had forgotten all about that picture, painted three years before. He had forgotten all the sufferings and raptures he had gone through on account of that work, when it alone had occupied him unremittingly day and night for three months. He had forgotten it, as he forgot all his finished pictures. He did not even like looking at it, and had only brought it out because he was expecting an Englishman who wished to buy it.

'That's nothing—only an old study,' he said.

'How good!' remarked Golenishchev, evidently sincerely impressed by the charm of the picture.

It represented two boys angling in the shade of a willow. The elder had just thrown the line and, quite absorbed in his occupation, was carefully drawing the float from behind a bush; the younger one lay in the grass, leaning on his elbows with his fair tousled head in his hands, and with dreamy blue eyes gazing at the water. What was he thinking about?

Their delight in his picture aroused in Mikhaylov his former excitement, but he feared and disliked their idle interest in his past work, and therefore, though their praises gave him pleasure, he tried to draw his visitors' attention to a third picture.

But Vronsky inquired whether this picture was for sale. To Mikhaylov, in his excitement over their visit, this mention of money matters was very disagreeable.

'It is put out for sale,' he replied, frowning darkly.

When the visitors had left, Mikhaylov sat down before his pic
ture of Pilate and Christ and mentally reviewed all that had been
said, and even what was not said but only hinted by the visitors.
Strange to say, what had had weight with him while they were
there and he looked at things from their point of view suddenly
lost all significance now. He looked at his picture with his artistic
perception fully alert, and reached that assurance of the perfection,
and consequent importance, of his picture which he needed to attain the intensity of effort—excluding all other interests—without
which he could not work.

The foreshortening of Christ's foot was, however, not right. He
took his palette and commenced working. While correcting the foot
he kept glancing at the figure of John in the background, which
the visitors had not even remarked, but which he knew to be the
height of perfection. When he had completed the foot he was
about to do something to that figure, but felt that he was too agitated. He could work neither when he was too indifferent nor
when he was too highly roused and saw everything too distinctly.
There was only one stage between calmness and inspiration, at
which work was possible, and to-day he was too excited. He was
about to cover his picture, but paused, and holding up the sheet
stood a long time with a rapturous smile gazing at the figure of
John. At length, tearing himself away from it regretfully, he let the
sheet fall over the picture and went home, tired but happy.

Vronsky, Anna, and Golenishchev were particularly animated and
high-spirited on their way back. They talked about Mikhaylov and
his pictures. The word *talent*, which they understood to mean an
innate and almost physical capacity, independent of mind and
heart, and which was their term for everything an artist lives
through, occurred very often in their conversation, since they required it as a name for something which they did not at all understand, but about which they wanted to talk. They said that it was
impossible to deny his talent, but that his talent could not develop
because of his lack of education—the common misfortune of our
Russian artists. But the picture of the boys had gripped their
memories and they kept coming back to it.

'How charming! How well he has hit it off, and how simply! He
does not even understand how good it is. Yes, we must not miss the
opportunity of purchasing it,' Vronsky declared.

Chapter XIII

Mikhaylov sold Vronsky the picture and consented to paint
Anna's portrait. On the appointed day he came and began working.

After the fifth sitting the portrait struck every one not only by its
likeness but also by its beauty. It was strange that Mikhaylov had

been able to discover that special beauty. 'One needed to know and love her as I love her, to find just that sweetest spiritual expression of hers,' thought Vronsky, though he himself had only learnt to know that 'sweetest spiritual expression' through the portrait. But the expression was so true that it seemed both to him and to others that they had always known it.

'How long have I been struggling without accomplishing anything?' he said, referring to the portrait he was painting; 'and he just looked, and painted this! That is where technique comes in.'

'That will come in good time,' said Golenishchev, consolingly. In his opinion Vronsky had talent, and especially the education that gives a lofty outlook on art. Golenishchev's conviction that Vronsky possessed talent was supported by the fact that he required Vronsky's sympathy and praise for his articles and ideas, and felt that praise and encouragement should be mutual.

In another man's house, and particularly in Vronsky's palazzo, Mikhaylov was quite a different man from what he was in his studio. He was unpleasantly deferential, as if fearful of intimacy with persons whom he did not respect. He addressed Vronsky as 'Your Excellency,' and never stayed to dinner, though Anna and Vronsky both invited him, and he never came except for a sitting. Anna was even kinder to him than to others, and was grateful for her portrait. Vronsky was more than polite to him, and was evidently interested in the artist's opinion of his (Vronsky's) picture. Golenishchev never missed an opportunity to instil into Mikhaylov a true understanding of art. But the latter remained equally cold toward them all. Anna felt by his look that he liked looking at her, but he avoided conversation with her. When Vronsky talked about his art Mikhaylov remained stubbornly silent, and as stubbornly silent when they showed him Vronsky's picture; and he was evidently oppressed by Golenishchev's discourses, to which he made no rejoinder.

Altogether, his reserved, disagreeable, and apparently hostile attitude when they came to know him better much displeased them, and they were glad when the sittings were over, the beautiful portrait was theirs, and his visits ceased.

Golenishchev was the first to express the thought that was in all their minds, namely, that Mikhaylov was simply jealous of Vronsky.

'We won't say "jealous" because he has talent, but he is vexed that a man of the Court, a rich man, and a Count into the bargain (men like him hate all that), should, without any particular difficulty, do as well or even better than he, who has devoted his whole life to the work. Especially, there is the education which he lacks.'

Vronsky took Mikhaylov's part, but in the depth of his heart he believed what Golenishchev said, for he considered that a man of that other and lower world must envy him.

Anna's portrait, the same subject painted from nature by both of them, should have shown him the difference between Mikhaylov and himself; but Vronsky did not see it. He merely left off painting Anna, deciding that it would be superfluous now. He went on, however, with his mediæval picture. And he, as well as Golenishchev, and especially Anna, thought it very good because it resembled famous pictures much more than Mikhaylov's did.

Meanwhile Mikhaylov, though Anna's portrait had much engrossed him, was even better pleased than they when the sittings were over and he was no longer obliged to listen to Golenishchev's disquisitions on art and was able to forget Vronsky's paintings. He knew it was not possible to forbid Vronsky to trifle with art, knew that he and all the dilettanti had a perfect right to paint what they liked—but to him it was unpleasant. One cannot forbid a man's making a big wax doll and kissing it. But if the man came and sat down with his doll in front of a lover, and began to caress it as the lover caresses his beloved, it would displease the lover. It was this kind of unpleasantness that Mikhaylov experienced when he saw Vronsky's pictures: he was amused, vexed, sorry, and hurt.

Vronsky's interest in art and the Middle Ages did not last long. He had sufficient taste for art to be unable to finish his picture. He ceased painting it because he was dimly conscious that its defects, little noticeable at first, would become striking if he went on. The same thing happened to him as to Golenishchev, who, feeling that he had nothing to express, continually deceived himself by saying that his thought had not yet ripened and that he was bringing it to maturity and preparing materials. But Golenishchev was embittered and tormented by it, while Vronsky could not deceive and torment himself, and above all could not become embittered. With characteristic firmness he left off painting, without any explanations or excuses.

But without that occupation his life and Anna's—who was surprised at his disenchantment—appeared very dull in the Italian town. All of a sudden the palazzo became so obviously old and dirty, so disagreeably familiar were the stains on the curtains, the cracks in the floor, the cracked stuccoes of the cornices, and so wearisome became Golenishchev, the Italian professor, and the German traveller, who were also always the same, that a change was necessary. So they decided to return to Russia and live in the country. In Petersburg Vronsky planned to separate his property from his brother's, and Anna to see her son. The summer they intended to spend on Vronsky's large family estate.

Chapter XIV

Levin had been married three months. He was happy, but in quite a different way from what he had expected. At every step he met disillusionments in his old fancies and new and unexpected enchantments. He was happy, but having embarked on family life he saw at every step that it was not at all what he had anticipated. At every step he took he felt as a man would feel who, after admiring the smooth happy motion of a little boat upon the water, had himself got into the boat. He found that besides sitting quietly without rocking he had to keep a lookout, not for a moment forget where he was going, or that there was water under his feet, and that he had to row, although it hurt his unaccustomed hands; in short, that it only looked easy, but to do it, though very delightful, was very difficult.

As a bachelor seeing the married life of others—their petty cares, their disputes, their jealousies—he used mentally to smile contemptuously. In his future married life he was sure he would have nothing of this kind, and even the external forms of his married life would be quite unlike other people's. And now, behold! his life with his wife had not shaped itself differently, but was all made up of those petty trifles which he had formerly so despised, but which now, against his will, assumed a strange and incontestable importance. Levin saw that the arrangement of all those trifles was not at all so easy as he had formerly supposed. Though he had imagined his ideas about family life to be most exact, he, like all men, had involuntarily pictured it to himself as merely the enjoyment of love—which nothing should be allowed to hinder and from which one should not be distracted by petty cares. He should, he thought, do his work, and rest from it in the joys of love. She should be loved—and that was all. But, like all men, he forgot that she too must work; and was surprised how she, the poetic, charming Kitty, could, during the very first weeks and even in the first days of married life, think, remember, and fuss about tablecloths, furniture, spare-room mattresses, a tray, the cook, the dinner, and so forth. During their engagement he had been struck by the definiteness with which she declined a trip abroad and decided to go to the country, as if she knew of something that was necessary, and could think of something besides their love. He had been pained by it then, and now was repeatedly pained by her petty cares. But he saw that this was necessary to her, and, loving her, though he could not understand what this was all about, and laughed at her worries, he could not help admiring it. He laughed at the way she placed the furniture that had been brought from Moscow, and rearranged his and her own rooms, hung up curtains, decided about rooms for future visitors and for Dolly, arranged the room for her new maid, gave orders about dinner to the old cook, and entered into discussions with Agatha Mikhaylovna, taking the commissariat into her own hands. He saw the old cook smile admiringly and listen to her inexperienced and impossible orders; saw that Agatha Mikhaylovna shook her head thoughtfully and kindly at her young mistress's arrangements in the storeroom; saw that Kitty was peculiarly charming when she came, half laughing and half crying, to report that her maid, Masha, was used to considering her merely as a young lady in her mother's house, and that therefore no one would obey her. It struck him as very charming, but strange, and he thought it would have been better without all that.

He did not realize the feeling of change that she was experiencing after her life at home. There she had sometimes wished for cabbage with kvas, or sweets, and could not have them; but now she might order whatever she pleased, and could if she liked buy heaps of sweets, spend any amount of money, and order all the puddings she pleased.

She looked forward joyfully to Dolly's coming with the children, especially because she meant to give each of them their favourite puddings, and because Dolly would appreciate her new arrangements. Without herself knowing why or wherefore, the management of the house attracted her irresistibly. Instinctively feeling the approach of spring, and knowing that there would be wet weather, she built her nest as she could, hastening to build it while yet learning how to do it.

Kitty's absorption in these trifles, quite contrary to Levin's early ideal of lofty happiness, was one of his disappointments; yet that sweet absorption, the meaning of which he could not understand but which he could not help liking, was also one of his new enchantments. Another disenchantment and new enchantment was afforded by their quarrels. Levin had never thought it possible that between him and his wife there could ever be any but tender, respectful, and loving relations; and yet from the very beginning they had quarrelled: she had said he did not love her, but only loved himself, and began to cry and wave her arms. This first quarrel arose because Levin had ridden over to see his new farm and returned half an hour late, having attempted a short cut home and lost his way. He rode home thinking only of her, of her love and of his happiness, and the nearer he came the warmer grew his tenderness for her. He ran into the room with the same feelings as, and even stronger ones than, those with which he had gone to the Shcherbatskys' house to propose—and to his astonishment was met with such a dismal look as he had never seen on her face before. He tried to kiss her but she pushed him away.

'What's the matter?'

'You seem merry . . .' she began, wishing to say something calmly stinging.

But directly she opened her mouth, words of reproach, senseless jealousy, and everything else that had been torturing her during the half-hour she had sat motionless waiting at the window, burst from her. Then it was that he first clearly understood what he did not realize when leading her out of church after the wedding: that she was not only very close to him but that he could not now tell where she ended and he began. He understood this by a tormenting sensation of cleavage which he experienced at that moment. For an instant he was offended, but immediately knew he could not be offended with her because she was himself. For a moment he felt like a man who, receiving a blow from behind, angrily and revengefully turns round to find his assailant and realizes that he has accidentally knocked himself, that there is no one to be angry with and that he must endure and try to still the pain.

Never again did he feel this so strongly as this first time, and for a long time he could not recover his balance. His natural feelings prompted him to justify himself and prove that she was in the wrong; but to prove her in the wrong would mean irritating her still more, and widening the breach which was the cause of all the trouble. One impulse, an habitual one, drew him to shift the blame from himself and lay it upon her; but another, and more powerful one, drew him to smooth over the breach as quickly as possible and not allow it to widen. To remain under so unjust an accusation was painful, but to justify himself and hurt her would be still worse. Like a man half-asleep and oppressed with pain, he wanted to tear off the aching part and cast it from him, but found on waking that the aching part was—himself. All he could do was to try to soothe the ache and endure it, and this he did.

They made it up. Having realized that she was in the wrong, though she did not acknowledge it, she became more tender to him, and they enjoyed a new and doubled happiness in their love. But this did not prevent such collisions recurring quite frequently, and on very unexpected and trivial provocation. These collisions were often caused by each not realizing what was important to the other, and also by the fact that in those early days they were often in low spirits. When one of them was in good spirits and the other was not, peace was not broken; but if both chanced to be out of sorts, collisions resulted from causes so trifling as to be incomprehensible. Often afterwards they could not remember what they had quarrelled about. However, when both were in good spirits their happiness was doubled—and yet the early days of their married life were very trying.

All that time they were conscious of peculiar strain, as if the chain that bound them were being pulled first one way and then the other. Altogether, the honeymoon—the first month of their marriage, from which Levin had expected so much—was not delightful, but remained in both their recollections as the most oppressive and humiliating time of their lives. They both tried in after life to efface from their memories all the ugly shameful circumstances of this unhealthy time, during which they were rarely in a normal state and rarely themselves. Only in the third month of their married life, after returning from Moscow where they had spent a month, did their life begin to run more smoothly.

Chapter XV

They had just returned from Moscow and were glad of the solitude. He was in his study and sat at the table writing. She, in the dark lilac dress she had worn during the first days of her marriage and which was specially memorable and dear to him, sat with her embroidery on that same old leather-covered sofa which had stood in the study through his father's and grandfather's times. As he sat thinking and writing he was all the while blissfully conscious of her presence. He had not abandoned his work on the estate, or on the book in which the foundations of a new farming system were to be explained; but as those thoughts and that work formerly appeared to him trivial and insignificant in comparison with the gloom that overshadowed all existence, so now they appeared trivial and insignificant in comparison with his future prospects all bathed in the bright sunshine of happiness.

He went on with his work with a feeling that the centre of gravity of his attention had shifted, and that he consequently saw the matter differently and with greater clearness. Formerly this work had been his salvation from life. He used to feel that without it life would be too dismal, and now he needed it in order that his life should not be too monotonously bright.

Having set to work again on his manuscript and read over what he had written, he was glad to find that the work seemed worth doing. Many of his former thoughts now appeared superfluous and extreme, but many omissions became clear to him when he went over the matter afresh. He was writing a fresh chapter on why agriculture was not profitable in Russia. He argued that Russia's poverty was caused not only by a wrong distribution of landed property and a false policy, but that of late years those evils had been fostered by a foreign civilization artificially grafted upon Russia, especially as to ways of communication—viz., the railways, which had conduced to a centralization in the cities, a growth of luxury, and consequently to a development of factories at the expense of agriculture, and, attendant upon this, to credit operations and speculation. It seemed to him that when the growth of a nation's wealth is normal these things follow only after a considerable amount of labour has been devoted to agriculture, and after the latter has been placed in its rightful—or at any rate in a definite—position: that a nation's wealth ought to grow proportionately at the same rate in all its branches, and especially in such a way that the other branches should not outdistance agriculture; that means of communication should conform to the agricultural conditions, and that with our wrong methods of using the land, the railways—called into existence not by economic but political necessity—had come prematurely, and instead of promoting agriculture as had been expected, had interfered with it and hindered it by stimulating the development of manufactures and credit. Therefore, as the one-sided and premature development of a single organ in an animal would injure its general development, so credit, railways, and the forced growth of manufactures—though undoubtedly necessary in Europe, where the time is ripe for them—had in Russia only harmed the general development of wealth by thrusting aside the most important current question, namely, the organization of agriculture.

While he was writing his thoughts, she was thinking about his unnatural attention to young Prince Charsky, who had been very tactlessly paying court to her on the day before their departure from Moscow. 'Why, he's jealous!' she thought. 'Oh dear! How sweet and silly he is, jealous of me! If he only knew that all the rest of them are no more than Peter the cook to me!' and she glanced with a feeling of proprietorship, strange to herself, at the nape of his red neck. 'Though it's a pity to interrupt him at his work (but he'll have time enough) I must see his face. Will he feel that I am looking at him! I want him to turn . . . I will it! Well!' and she opened her eyes wider, trying thereby to increase the force of her look.

'Yes, they divert all the sap, they produce a false glamour,' he muttered, pausing, and feeling that she was looking at him he turned round smiling.

'Well?' he asked with a smile, and rose.

'He has turned!' she thought. 'Nothing, I only wanted to make you turn round,' said she, gazing at him and trying to discover whether he was vexed at the interruption.

'I say, how delightful it is for us to be alone together! For me, I mean . . .' he said, coming toward her with a beaming smile of happiness.

'It is delightful for me too! I shan't go anywhere, especially not to Moscow.'

'And what were you thinking about?'

'I? . . . I was thinking. . . . No, no! Go and write, don't let

me distract you,' she said, puckering her lips. 'And I must cut out
these little holes, you see!'

Taking up her scissors she began cutting.

'Come, tell me what it was,' he said, sitting down beside her and
watching the circular movement of her tiny scissors.

'Oh, what was I thinking about? About Moscow, and about the
nape of your neck.'

'Why should such happiness come just to me? It's not natural. It
is too beautiful!' he said, kissing her hand.

'To me the more beautiful it is the more natural it seems.'

'Your hair comes to a point behind,' he said, carefully turning
her head round.

'A point? Yes, so it does. There! But enough! We are engaged on
serious matters!'

But their serious matters did not get on, and they jumped apart
guiltily when Kuzma came to say that tea was served.

'And have they returned from town?' Levin inquired of Kuzma.

'They've just come and are unpacking.'

'Be quick and come,' she said as she left the study, 'or else I shall
read all the letters without you. And after that let's have a duet.'

Left alone, having put away his papers in the new portfolio she
had bought, he washed his hands at the new washstand with the
new and elegant utensils that had also appeared through her agency.
He smiled at his thought and shook his head disapprovingly at it. A
feeling resembling repentance tormented him. There was something contemptible, effeminate, Capuan, [4] as he called it, in his
present life. 'It is not right to live so,' he thought. 'Soon it will be
three months since I did anything worth mentioning. This is almost
the first day that I have really set to work seriously, and what has
come of it? Scarcely had I begun when I stopped. Even my usual
duties—all almost abandoned! The farm work—why, I hardly even
go and see about that! Sometimes I am sorry to part from her, sometimes I can see she is dull. And I used to think that up to the time
of my marriage life would go on just so-so, anyhow, and not count
for much; but that after marriage real life was going to begin. And
now that is nearly three months ago, and I have never spent my
days more idly or uselessly! No, this can't go on. I must make a beginning. Of course it is not her fault; there is nothing to reproach
her with. I ought to have been firmer and upheld my independence
as a man. This way I shall get into bad habits and teach them to her
too. . . . Of course it is not her fault,' he said to himself.

But it is difficult for a dissatisfied man not to reproach some one

4. From Capua, a town near Naples, Italy. According to Livy, in the Second Punic War,
Hannibal's troops spent a winter in Capua, were softened by the luxuries of the town, and
defeated by Roman armies. Tolstoy in his diaries applied the neologism "Capuan" to periods
of laziness and relaxation.

else, namely, the person most closely connected with the subject of his dissatisfaction. And Levin dimly felt that though she was not herself in fault—she never could be in fault—it was the fault of her bringing up, which was too superficial and frivolous. 'That fool Charsky! I know she wanted to stop him but did not know how,' he thought. 'Yes, except for the interest she takes in the housekeeping, —that interest she certainly has,—her clothes, and her embroidery, she has no real interests. She takes no interest in our work, in the farm, in the peasants, or in music, though she is quite good at that, or in books. She does nothing and is quite content.' In his heart he blamed her, but he did not understand that she was preparing herself for a period of activity which was inevitably coming, when at one and the same time she would be her husband's wife, the mistress of the house, and a bearer, nurturer, and educator of her children. He did not understand that, but she knew it instinctively; and while getting ready for her gigantic task she did not reproach herself for the moments of careless and happy love that she now enjoyed while building her nest for the future.

Chapter XVI

When Levin came upstairs his wife was sitting beside the new silver samovar with a new tea-service before her, reading a letter from Dolly, with whom she kept up a regular and active correspondence. She had made old Agatha Mikhaylovna sit at a little table with a cup of tea she had poured out for her.

'You see, your lady has made me sit with her,' said Agatha Mikhaylovna, glancing with a friendly smile at Kitty.

In these words of Agatha Mikhaylovna's Levin read the conclusion of the drama which had lately been enacted between Agatha Mikhaylovna and Kitty. He perceived that despite Agatha Mikhaylovna's grief at the advent of the new mistress who had taken the reins of management into her own hands, Kitty had conquered and had made the old woman love her.

'There! I've opened your letter,' said Kitty, handing him a badly-written letter. 'It is from that woman, I think—your brother's . . . No, I have not read it. . . . These are from home, and from Dolly. Fancy! Dolly took Grisha and Tanya to a children's party at the Sarmatskys'! Tanya went as a marquise.'

But Levin did not listen. He blushed as he took Mary Nikolaevna's letter. This was the second letter he had received from the woman who had been his brother's mistress. In the first she wrote that his brother had sent her away for no fault of hers, adding with touching naïveté that though she was again in want she did not ask or desire anything, but wrote because she was crushed by the thought that Nicholas Dmitrich would perish without her, his health being so bad. She begged Levin to keep watch over his brother. This time she wrote differently: she had found Nicholas Dmitrich, had joined him in Moscow, and had gone with him to a provincial town where he had obtained a post in the Civil Service. But he had quarrelled with his chief, and they had started again for Moscow when he fell so ill on the way that it was hardly likely he would ever get up again. She wrote: 'He keeps on speaking of you; besides, there is no money left.'

'Read it. . . . Dolly writes about you,' Kitty began with a smile, but paused suddenly, noticing the changed expression on her husband's face. 'What's the matter? What is it?'

'She writes that my brother Nicholas is on his deathbed. I am going.'

Kitty's look changed at once. Thoughts of Tanya as a marquise and of Dolly had quite vanished.

'When are you going?' she asked.

'To-morrow.'

'I shall go too, may I?'

'Kitty! What do you mean?' he said reproachfully.

'What, indeed?' she replied, offended that he seemed opposed to and vexed at her offer. 'Why should I not go? I shan't be in your way. I . . .'

'I am going because my brother is dying,' said Levin, 'but why should you . . . ?'

'Why? For the same reason as you.'

'At such an important time, she thinks only of how dull it will be for her alone here,' he thought; and this motive in connection with something so important vexed him.

'It is impossible,' he replied sternly.

Agatha Mikhaylovna, seeing that a quarrel was imminent, softly put down her cup and went out. Kitty did not even notice her. The tone in which her husband had said these words hurt her, especially as he evidently disbelieved what she had said.

'And I say that if you go I shall go with you. I will certainly go!' she said hastily and angrily. 'Why is it impossible? Why do you say it is impossible?'

'Because it means going goodness knows where, and by what roads! to what inns! You would be in my way,' said Levin, endeavouring to keep cool.

'Not at all! I shan't want anything, and where you can go I can.'

'Well, if only because that woman is there, with whom you cannot associate . . .'

'I don't know and don't want to know anything about who and what is there. I know that my husband's brother is dying, that my husband is going to him, and that I am going with my husband in order . . .'

'Kitty, don't be angry! But just think, this matter is so important —it hurts me to think that you are mixing up with it your weakness, your dislike of remaining alone. Well, if you feel dull alone—well, go to Moscow!'

'There, you see! You *always* attribute bad and vile motives to me,' she began, with tears of anger and resentment. 'I am all right, not weak, nor anything. . . . I feel that it's my duty to be with my husband when he is in trouble, but you wish to hurt me on purpose, you purposely don't want to understand me!'

'No, this is awful . . . being a sort of slave!' exclaimed Levin, unable to restrain his annoyance any longer, but immediately conscious that he had dealt a blow to himself.

'Then why did you marry? You might have been free! Why, since you are repenting?' she said, and jumped up and ran into the drawing-room.

When he came in after her, she was sobbing. He began speaking, trying to find words not so much to dissuade as to pacify her. But she did not listen and did not agree to anything he said. He stooped and took her resisting hand; he kissed her hand, her hair, and again her hand, but she remained silent. But when he took her face in his hands and said 'Kitty!' she suddenly recovered, cried a little, and then they made it up.

It was settled that they would start together the next day. Levin told his wife he believed she only wanted to go that she might be of use, and agreed that Mary Nikolaevna's presence at his brother's would not make it at all improper; but he was going, dissatisfied in the depths of his heart with both himself and her. He was dissatisfied with her because she could not face letting him go when it was necessary (and how strange it was to think that he, who such a short time ago dared not believe in the happiness of her loving him, now felt unhappy because she loved him too much!), and dissatisfied with himself because he had not maintained his authority. Still less could he with conviction agree that the woman who was with his brother did not matter, and he thought with terror of all the encounters that might take place. The single fact that his wife, his Kitty, would be in the same room with a girl off the streets made him shudder with repulsion and horror.

Chapter XVII

The hotel in the provincial town where Nicholas Levin was lying ill was one of those provincial hotels arranged after new and improved models, with the best intentions of cleanliness, comfort and even elegance, but which, owing to the people who use them, very soon degenerate into mere dirty pothouses with pretensions to

modern improvements, these very pretensions making them worse
than the old-fashioned inns which were simply dirty. This hotel had
already reached this stage: everything—the soldier in a dirty uniform smoking a cigarette at the front door, acting as a hall-porter,
the dismal and unpleasant ornamental cast-iron staircase, the free
and easy waiter in a dirty dress coat, the general room with a dusty
bouquet of wax flowers decorating the table, the dust and slovenli-
ness everywhere, mingled with a kind of modern, self-satisfied rail-
way-induced state of bustle. All this caused a feeling of depression
in the Levins after their fresh home life; especially as the air of artificiality about this hotel was quite irreconcilable with what was
awaiting them.

As usual, after the inquiry as to what priced rooms they desired,
it turned out that there was not a single good room vacant: one
good room was occupied by a railway inspector, another by a lawyer
from Moscow, a third by the Princess Astafyeva from the country.
There was just one dirty room to be had, but they were promised
that an adjoining one would be free by the evening. Vexed with his
wife because his expectations were being realized—namely, that, at
the moment of arrival when his heart was seized with agitation at
the thought of his brother's condition, he was obliged to look after
her instead of running to him at once—Levin led her into their
room.

'Go, go!' she said with a timid, guilty look at him. He went out
silently, and at the very door came upon Mary Nikolaevna, who had
heard of his arrival but had not dared to enter. She was just the
same as he had seen her in Moscow—the same stuff dress without
collar or cuffs, and the same kindly, dull, pock-marked face, only
somewhat stouter.

'Well? How is he? What is it?'

'Very bad! Does not get up. He was expecting you all the time.
He . . . you . . . are with your wife?'

For a moment he did not understand the cause of her confusion,
but she immediately explained it.

'I will go . . . I will go to the kitchen,' she brought out. 'He will
be pleased. He heard, and he knows and remembers her abroad.'

Levin understood that she referred to his wife, and did not know
what to say.

'Come along, come!' he said.

But he had hardly moved when the door opened and Kitty
looked out. Levin blushed with shame and vexation at his wife for
having placed herself and him in this awkward position; but Mary
Nikolaevna blushed still more. She shrank together, flushed till tears
filled her eyes, and seizing the ends of her shawl began twisting
them in her red fingers not knowing what to say or do.

At the first glance Levin saw an expression of eager curiosity in the look with which Kitty gazed at this incomprehensible and terrible woman, but it lasted only an instant.

'Well, how is he? How is he?' she said, addressing first her husband and then the woman.

'But we can't talk in the corridor!' said Levin, looking crossly at a man who was just passing along with jerky steps, ostensibly on business of his own.

'Well, then, come in,' said Kitty to Mary Nikolaevna, who had regained her self-control; but, having noticed her husband's frightened face, she added: 'or go on and send for me,' and she turned back and entered her room. Levin went to his brother.

He had not expected what he saw and felt when he reached his brother's side. He had expected to find him in that state of self-deception which, he had heard, was frequent in consumptive cases and which had so struck him at the time of his brother's visit to him in the autumn. He had expected to find the physical signs of approaching death more definite: greater weakness, greater emaciation, but still the same sort of condition generally. He had expected to feel the same sorrow at the loss of a loved brother and the same horror of death he had then experienced, but to a greater degree, and had prepared himself for all this; but what he found was quite different.

In the dirty little room, its dado filthy with spittle, its partition too thin to exclude the sound of voices, and its air impregnated by the stifling smell of impurities, on a bed drawn away from the wall lay a body covered with a blanket. One arm of that body lay outside the blanket, and the enormous hand, like a rake, seemed to be attached in some incomprehensible way to a long thin spindle that was quite straight from the end to the middle. The head lay on its side on the pillow. Levin could see the moist thin hair on the temples and the drawn transparent-looking forehead.

'Impossible that this terrible body can be my brother Nicholas,' he thought. But he drew nearer, saw the face, and doubt was no longer possible. In spite of the dreadful change on the face, Levin had only to glance at those living eyes raised toward him, to notice the slight movement of the mouth beneath the clammy moustache, in order to understand the dreadful truth that this dead body was his living brother.

The glittering eyes glanced severely and reproachfully at the brother who was entering, and this glance immediately established living relations between living people. Levin at once felt the reproach in the look fixed on him, and a sense of repentance because of his own happiness.

When Constantine took him by the hand, Nicholas smiled. The

smile was very faint, hardly perceptible, and in spite of it the stern expression of the eyes did not change.

'You did not expect to find me like this?' he said, speaking with difficulty.

'Yes . . . no . . .' said Levin, confusing his words. 'How is it you did not let me know sooner, I mean at the time of my marriage? I inquired for you everywhere.'

He was impelled to speak in order not to remain silent, but did not know what to say, especially as his brother made no reply but only gazed fixedly at him, evidently trying to fathom the meaning of every word. Levin told his brother that his wife had come with him. Nicholas seemed pleased at this, but said he was afraid the condition he was in might frighten her. A silence followed. Suddenly Nicholas moved and began to talk. From his expression Levin expected him to say something specially significant and important, but Nicholas only talked about his health. He found fault with the doctor, and regretted that he could not have a celebrated Moscow doctor; so Levin understood that he was still hoping.

Taking advantage of the first moment of silence, Levin got up, wishing to free himself if only for a few minutes from his painful sensations, and said he would fetch his wife.

'All right, and I will have the place cleaned up a bit. It is dirty here, and it smells, I should think. Masha! Tidy up,' said the invalid with an effort. 'And when you have finished, go away,' he added, with a questioning look at his brother.

Levin did not reply. He went out and stopped in the corridor. He had said he would bring his wife, but now, analysing the impressions he was experiencing, he made up his mind that he would on the contrary try to dissuade her from entering the sick-room. 'Why should she too be tortured as I am?' he reflected.

'Well, how is he?' Kitty asked with a frightened look.

'Oh, it's awful! Awful! Why did you come?' said Levin.

Kitty was silent a moment, looking timidly and pitifully at her husband; then she approached and took hold of his elbow with both hands.

'Kostya, take me to him! It will be easier for us to bear it together! Just take me there and then go away,' she began. 'Try and realize that for me to see you and not to see him is much more painful. There I can perhaps be of use to him and you. Please let me!' she entreated as if her happiness depended on it.

He was obliged to yield, and having recovered, and quite forgotten Mary Nikolaevna, he returned with Kitty to his brother.

Stepping lightly and glancing repeatedly at her husband, showing him a brave face full of sympathy, she entered the sick-room, and, turning without haste, noiselessly closed the door. With noiseless steps she advanced toward the bedside, went round so that he need not turn his head, and at once grasping his enormous skeleton hand with her fresh young one, pressed it, and with that sympathetic, quiet animation which gives no offence and is natural only to women, she began to talk to him.

'It was in Soden we met, but we were not acquainted,' she said. 'You little thought I should one day be your sister?'

'You would not have known me again?' he asked, with a smile that had lit up his face at her entrance.

'Oh yes, I should! What a good thing it is that you did send us word! Not a day passed without Kostya's thinking and being anxious about you.'

The sick man's animation did not last long. She had not finished speaking before that stern reproachful look of envy, felt by the dying for the living, settled on his face.

'I'm afraid you are not quite comfortable here,' she said, turning away from his penetrating glance and looking round the room. 'We shall have to ask the landlord for another room, and see that we are nearer to each other,' she said to her husband.

Chapter XVIII

Levin could not look at his brother calmly and could not be either natural or tranquil in his presence. When he entered the sick-room his eyes and his attention became clouded without his being conscious of it, and he did not see or distinguish the various details of his brother's condition. He smelt the terribly foul air, saw the dirt and disorder, the agonizing posture of the body, and heard the groans; but he felt there was no help for it. It never entered his head to consider all these details and imagine how that body was lying under the blanket, how the emaciated, doubled-up shins, loins, and back were placed, and whether it would not be possible to place them more comfortably or do something, if not to make him comfortable, at least to make his condition a little more tolerable. A cold shudder crept down his back when he began to think of those details. He was convinced beyond doubt that nothing could be done to prolong that life or to alleviate those sufferings, and the sick man was conscious of his brother's conviction that there was no help for him, and this irritated him. This made Levin's position still harder. To be in the sick-room was torture to Levin, but to be absent from it was still worse. He went out continually on all sorts of pretexts, coming back and going out again, incapable of remaining alone. But Kitty felt and acted quite differently. When she saw the invalid she pitied him, and that pity produced in her woman's soul not the horror and repulsion which it evoked in her husband but a need for action, for finding out all the particulars of his condition, and a desire to help him. Those very details, the thought of which alone filled her husband with horror, at once arrested her attention. She sent for the doctor, sent to the chemist's, made the maid she had brought with her help Mary Nikolaevna sweep, dust, and wash; and herself washed and scrubbed some articles and spread something under the blanket. At her command things were brought in and taken out of the sick-room. She herself went several times to their own room and, without paying any attention to the people she met, brought back with her sheets, pillowcases, towels, and shirts.

The waiter, who was serving a meal to some engineers in the drawing-room, came up several times at her summons with a cross look on his face, but could not help fulfilling her orders; she gave them with such gracious insistence that it was impossible to disobey her. Levin disapproved of all this, not believing that any good could come of it to the invalid. Above all he was afraid that his brother might get angry about it. But the sick man, though apparently indifferent to it all, was not angry but only ashamed, and on the whole appeared rather interested in what she was doing for him. When Levin opened the door, on his return from the doctor's whither Kitty had sent him, he saw the invalid at the moment when at Kitty's command Mary Nikolaevna and the waiter were putting a clean shirt on him. The long white skeleton back with the enormous shoulder-blades and protruding ribs and vertebrae was bare, and Mary Nikolaevna with the waiter's help somehow got one of the shirt-sleeves twisted and could not guide the long limp arm into it. Kitty, having hurriedly shut the door behind Levin, was not looking that way; but the invalid moaned and she came toward him.

'Be quick!' she said.

'Don't come here,' muttered the sick man angrily. 'I can myself . . .'

'What do you say?' asked Mary Nikolaevna. But Kitty had heard, and understood that he felt embarrassed and uncomfortable at being stripped in her presence.

'I'm not looking,' she said, helping the arm in. 'Mary Nikolaevna, you go round to the other side and put it right,' she added.

'There is a little bottle in my handbag,' she went on, turning to her husband. 'You know, in the side pocket! Please go and get it, and meanwhile everything will be put straight here.'

When Levin returned with the bottle he found the invalid arranged in bed and everything around him quite altered. Instead of the foul smell there was an odour of vinegar and of scent, which Kitty—pouting her lips and puffing out her rosy cheeks—was blowing through a little glass tube. There was no trace of dust left about; there was a mat beside the bed; on the table medicine bottles and a bottle of water were neatly placed, also a pile of folded linen which would be required later, and Kitty's embroidery. On another table by the bedside were a glass of some refreshing drink and some powders. The invalid himself, washed and with his hair brushed, lay between clean sheets in a clean shirt, its white collar round his abnormally thin neck, gazing with a new look of hope at Kitty and not taking his eyes off her.

The doctor whom Levin had fetched, and whom he had found at a club, was not the one who had hitherto attended Nicholas, with whom the patient was dissatisfied. The new doctor took out a stethoscope and sounded him, shook his head, prescribed some medicine and gave extremely precise instructions about giving the medicine and about diet. He ordered raw or very lightly boiled eggs, and seltzer water with new milk at a certain temperature. When the doctor had gone the patient said something to his brother of which Levin caught only the last words: 'your Kate'; but by the look he gave her Levin saw that his brother was praising her. He asked 'Kate,' as he called her, to come nearer.

'I feel much better,' he said. 'Had I been with you I should have recovered long ago. How pleasant!'

He took her hand and drew it toward his lips, but as if fearful that this might be disagreeable to her he changed his mind, let her hand drop, and merely stroked it. Kitty took his hand in both of hers and pressed it.

'Now turn me over on the left side and go to bed,' he murmured.

No one heard what he said, but Kitty understood him. She understood because her mind incessantly watched for his needs.

'On the other side,' she said to her husband, 'he always sleeps on that side. Turn him over. It is unpleasant to call the servants, and I cannot do it. Can you?' she said, addressing Mary Nikolaevna.

'I am afraid to,' answered Mary Nikolaevna.

Dreadful as it seemed to Levin to put his arms round that terrible body, to grasp those parts under the blanket which he did not wish to remember, yet submitting to his wife, he thrust his arms under the blanket, with that determined expression which she knew, and despite his great strength was struck by the strange heaviness of those emaciated limbs. While he was turning him, with the enormous lean arm about his neck, Kitty quickly and unostentatiously turned and beat the pillow, and arranged the invalid's head and the hair that again clung to the temples. The patient retained his brother's hand in his. Levin felt that he wished to do something with his hand and was pulling at it, and yielded with a sinking heart. Yes, his brother drew the hand to his lips and kissed it. Levin, trembling, choking with sobs and unable to utter a word, left the room.

Chapter XIX

'Thou hast hid these things from the wise and prudent, and hast revealed them unto babes,' thought Levin while talking with his wife that night.

He thought of the Gospel text not because he considered himself wise—he did not—but because he could not help knowing that he was more intelligent than his wife and Agatha Mikhaylovna; he could not help knowing that when he thought about death he thought with all the powers of his soul. He knew too that many great and virile minds, whose thoughts on that subject he had read, had pondered it, and yet did not know a hundredth part of what his wife and Agatha Mikhaylovna knew on the subject. Different as were those two women, Agatha Mikhaylovna and Kitty—or 'Kate' as Nicholas called her, and as Levin was also fond of calling her now—in that respect they were exactly alike. Both knew with certainty what Life was and what Death was, and though they would have been quite unable not only to answer but even to understand the questions which confronted Levin, neither doubted the importance of those phenomena, and they both had exactly the same outlook upon them—an outlook shared not only by them but by millions of others. The proof that they knew surely what death was, lay in the fact that they knew without a minute's hesitation how to behave with the dying and did not fear them. But Levin and others, though they were able to say a great deal about death, evidently did not know anything, for they feared it and had no notion what to do when people were dying. Had Levin now been alone with his brother Nicholas, he would have looked at him with horror, and would have waited about in still greater horror not knowing what to do next.

More than that, he did not know what to say, how to look, or how to step. To talk of indifferent things seemed an affront, and he could not do it; to talk of death and dismal things was likewise impossible, and it was equally impossible to keep silent. 'I fear that if I look at him he will think I am watching. If I don't look, he will imagine I am thinking of something else. If I walk on tiptoe he will be displeased, and yet I am ashamed to tread on the whole of my foot.' But Kitty evidently did not think and had no time to think of herself. She, prompted by some inner conviction, thought of him, and everything came out right. She talked to him about herself and about her wedding, smiled, sympathized, caressed him, mentioned cases of recovery, and it was all successful, so she evidently knew what she was about. The proof that her and Agatha Mikhaylovna's behaviour was not instinctive, animal, and unreasoning lay in the fact that they both demanded for the dying man something of greater importance than mere physical care, something that had nothing in common with physical conditions. Agatha Mikhaylovna, speaking of the old man who had died, had said: 'Well, God be thanked! He received Communion and Extreme Unction; God grant everybody to die so!' Just in the same way Kitty, besides all her cares about linen, bedsores, and cooling drinks, had managed on the very first day to persuade the invalid of the necessity of receiving Communion and Extreme Unction.

When Levin returned to their two rooms for the night he sat with hanging head not knowing what to do. Not only could he not think of supper, of getting ready for the night, of considering what they were to do; he could not even talk to his wife: he was ashamed to. Kitty, on the contrary, was more active than usual and even more animated. She ordered supper to be brought, unpacked their things herself, helped to make the beds, and did not forget to sprinkle insect powder on them. She was in that highly-wrought state when the reasoning powers act with great rapidity: the state a man is in before a battle or a struggle, in danger, and at the decisive moments of life—those moments when a man shows once and for all what he is worth, that his past was not lived in vain but was a preparation for these moments.

All she did was well done, and before midnight everything was sorted, clean, and neat, so that their apartments showed a resemblance to her own rooms at home: beds made, combs, brushes and looking-glasses laid out, and covers spread.

It seemed to Levin that it would be inexcusable to eat, sleep, or even to talk, and he felt that his every movement was improper. She, however, sorted combs and brushes, and did it all in such a way that there was nothing offensive about it .

However, they could not eat anything, nor sleep for a long time, and even did not go to bed till very late.

'I am very glad I have persuaded him to receive Extreme Unction to-morrow,' she said as she sat in her dressing-jacket before her folding-glass and combed her soft fragrant hair with a small comb. 'I have never been present, but Mama told me that there are prayers for the restoration of health . . .'

'Do you really think he can recover?' he asked, looking at the back of her round little head, at the narrow parting which closed every time she drew the comb forward.

'I asked the doctor. He says he can't live more than three days. But how can they know? Still, I am very glad I persuaded him,' she said, turning her eyes toward her husband from behind her hair. 'Everything is possible,' she added with the peculiar and rather cunning expression which always appeared on her face when she spoke of religious matters.

Since their talk about religion during their engagement neither he nor she had ever started a conversation on that subject; but she continued to observe the rites, went to church, and prayed, always with the same quiet conviction that it was necessary to do so. In spite of his assurances to the contrary she was persuaded that he was a Christian, like, and even better than, herself, and that all he said about it was one of his funny male whims, like his sayings about her embroidery: that good people darn holes, while she cut holes on purpose . . . and so on.

'Yes, you see that woman Mary Nikolaevna could not arrange all that,' said Levin. 'I . . . I must confess I am very, very glad you came. You are purity itself, and . . .' He took her hand and did not kiss it (to do so with death so near seemed to him unbecoming), but only pressed it, looking guiltily into her brightening eyes.

'It would have been so painful for you alone,' she said, and raising her arms high so that they hid her cheeks, now flushed with pleasure, she twisted her braided hair and pinned it up at the back of her head.

'No,' she continued, 'she did not know how to . . . Luckily I learnt a good deal in Soden.'

'Can there have been such sick people there?'

'Oh, worse.'

'It is so terrible to me that I cannot help seeing him as he was when young. . . . You would not believe what a charming lad he was, and I did not understand him then.'

'I quite believe it, quite. I feel that we *should have been* friends, he and I . . .' she said, and, frightened at her own words, she glanced at her husband, and tears filled her eyes.

'Yes, *would have been*,' he said sadly. 'He is really one of those of whom it is said, they are not for this world.'

'However, we have hard days before us—let us go to bed,' said Kitty with a glance at her tiny watch.

Chapter XX

DEATH

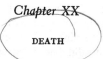

Next day the patient received Communion and Extreme Unction. During the ceremony he prayed fervently. In his large eyes, fixed upon an icon which had been placed on a little table covered with a coloured cloth, was a look of such passionate entreaty and hope that Levin was frightened at seeing it. He knew that this passionate entreaty and hope would only make the parting from the life he so loved more difficult. Levin knew his brother and the direction of his thoughts, knew that he had become a sceptic not because it was easier for him to live without faith, but because step by step modern scientific explanations of the phenomena of the universe had driven out his faith; he knew therefore that this return to the old faith was not legitimate, not a similar result of thought, but was only a temporary, selfish and irrational hope of recovery. Levin knew too that Kitty had strengthened that hope by tales of extraordinary recoveries of which she had heard. Knowing all this, Levin suffered much as he saw that look full of entreaty and hope, that emaciated hand lifted with effort, in making the sign of the cross, to touch the drawn skin of the forehead, the protruding shoulder-blades and the hollow hoarse chest which could no longer contain that life for which the invalid was praying. During the sacrament Levin did that which, agnostic though he was, he had done a thousand times before. He said, addressing himself to God, 'If Thou dost exist, heal this man (such things have often happened), and Thou wilt save both him and me!'

After receiving Extreme Unction the invalid suddenly felt better. He did not cough once for a whole hour, smiled, kissed Kitty's hand, thanking her with tears in his eyes, and said he felt well, had no pain, but had an appetite and felt stronger. He even sat up when they brought him some soup, and asked for a cutlet too. Hopeless as his case was, obvious as it was that he could not recover, Levin and Kitty were for that hour both in the same state of excitement, happy yet timid and fearful of being mistaken.

'Better?—Yes, much better.—Wonderful!—It is not at all wonderful.—Still, he's better!' they said in whispers, smiling at one another. But this illusion did not last long. The invalid fell quietly asleep, but awoke half an hour later with a fit of coughing, and immediately every hope fled from those around him and from himself. The reality of his sufferings destroyed it, leaving no trace nor even any recollection of the former hopes, in Levin, Kitty, or the patient himself.

Not referring to what he had believed half an hour previously, as though he were ashamed to remember it, Nicholas told them to give him a bottle of iodine covered with perforated paper for inhaling. Levin handed it to him, and at once the look of passionate hope with which the invalid had received Extreme Unction was fixed on his brother, demanding from him a confirmation of the doctor's words to the effect that inhaling iodine worked miracles.

'Kitty is not here?' he asked hoarsely, glancing round when Levin reluctantly confirmed the doctor's statement.

'No? Then I can tell you . . . It's for her sake I went through that comedy—she is such a dear! But you and I cannot deceive ourselves like that! Now, in this I do believe,' he said, clutching the bottle with his bony hand and beginning to inhale from it.

Between seven and eight o'clock that evening Levin and his wife were drinking tea in their room when Mary Nikolaevna rushed in breathless.

'He is dying!' she whispered. 'I'm afraid he'll die immediately.'

Both ran to his room. He was sitting up with his long back bent, leaning his elbows on the bed and hanging his head.

'What do you feel?' asked Levin in a whisper, after a pause.

'I feel I am departing,' uttered Nicholas with an effort, but very distinctly, as if he were pressing the words out of his body. He did not lift his head but only turned up his eyes, failing to reach his brother's face. 'Kate, go away,' he added.

Levin jumped up and in a commanding whisper told her to leave the room.

'Departing!' Nicholas repeated.

'Why do you think that?' asked Levin, in order to say something.

'Because I am departing,' he repeated, as if that word pleased him. 'It's the end.'

Mary Nikolaevna approached.

'You had better lie down, you would feel easier,' she said.

'I'll soon be lying,' he said softly. 'Dead!' he added cynically and angrily. 'Well, lay me down if you like.'

Levin laid his brother on his back, sat down beside him, and holding his breath gazed at his face. The dying man lay with closed eyes, but at intervals the muscles of his forehead worked as if he were thinking deeply and intently. Levin involuntarily meditated upon what was taking place within his brother at that moment, but, in spite of all the efforts of his mind to follow, he saw by the expression of that calm stern face and the play of the muscle above one eyebrow that something was becoming clear to the dying man which for Levin remained as dark as ever.

'Yes, yes! That's so!' Slowly pausing between the words, the dying man murmured, 'Wait a bit.' He was silent again. 'That's so!' he drawled in a tone of relief, as if he had found a solution. 'Oh God!' he muttered with a heavy sigh.

Mary Nikolaevna felt his feet. 'Growing cold,' she whispered.

For a long, a very long, time as it seemed to Levin the invalid lay motionless, but he still lived and at long intervals sighed. Levin was already wearied by the mental strain. He felt that despite all his mental efforts he could not understand what was 'so' and was already lagging far behind his dying brother. He was no longer able to reflect on the actual problem of death, and could not hinder thoughts about what he would soon have to do: to close his brother's eyes, dress him, order a coffin. And strange to say he felt quite cold, and experienced neither joy nor grief nor a sense of loss, still less of pity, for his brother. If he had any feeling left for him it was more like envy of that knowledge which the dying man now possessed and which he might not share.

For a long time he sat leaning over Nicholas, waiting for the end. But the end did not come. The door opened and Kitty appeared. Levin rose to stop her, but at that moment he heard the dying man move.

'Don't go,' said Nicholas, and stretched out his hand. Levin gave him his hand, signing angrily with the other to his wife.

With his brother's hand in his, Levin sat half an hour, then an hour, and yet another hour. He now no longer thought about death at all. He was wondering what Kitty was doing, who lived in the next room, and whether the doctor had a house of his own. He wished to eat and sleep. Carefully disengaging his hand he felt his brother's feet. They were cold, but he was still breathing. Levin tried to go out on tiptoe, but the invalid moved again and said, 'Don't go. . . .'

Day began to dawn, but the sick man's condition remained the same. Levin gently disengaged his hand, and without looking at his brother went to his own room and fell asleep. When he woke, instead of the news he expected, that his brother was dead, he heard that his former condition had returned. He again sat up, coughed, ate and talked, no longer of death, expressed hopes of recovery, and was even more irritable and depressed than before. No one, neither his brother nor Kitty, could comfort him. He was angry with every one, said disagreeable things, blamed everybody for his sufferings, and demanded that they should fetch a celebrated doctor from Moscow. To all questions of how he felt, he gave the same answer, with an angry and reproachful look: 'I am suffering terribly, intolerably!'

The sick man suffered more and more, especially from bedsores which would no longer heal, and he grew more and more irritable with those about him, particularly because they did not bring the doctor from Moscow. Kitty tried to help him and comfort him in every possible way, but it was all in vain, and Levin saw that she herself was worn out physically and mentally, though she would not admit it. That consciousness of death which had been evoked in them all by his farewell to life on the night he had sent for his brother was destroyed. Every one knew he would soon and inevitably die, that he was already half dead. Every one wished that he would die quickly, and they all, concealing that feeling, brought him bottles of medicine, went to fetch medicines and doctors, and deceived him and themselves and one another. It was all a lie: a repulsive, insulting, blasphemous lie; and as a result of his character, and because he loved the dying man more than the others did, Levin felt that lie most painfully.

Levin, who had long wished to reconcile his brothers, even if only at the moment of death, had written to Sergius Ivanich, and having received his answer read it to Nicholas. Sergius Ivanich wrote that he could not come personally, but, in touching words, asked his brother's pardon. The invalid made no comment.

'What am I to write to him?' asked Levin. 'I hope you are not angry with him?'

'No, not at all,' answered Nicholas, vexed at the question. 'Tell him to send me a doctor.'

Another three days of torture went by. The sick man was still in the same condition. Every one who saw him now desired his death: the waiters in the hotel, the proprietor, all the other visitors there, the doctor, Mary Nikolaevna, Levin, and Kitty. Only the invalid himself did not show that desire, but on the contrary was angry because the doctor had not been fetched, and he continued taking medicine and talking of life. Only at rare moments, when opium made him forget his incessant sufferings for a moment, did he sometimes when half asleep express what was stronger in his soul than in any of the others': 'Oh, if only it were over!' or 'When will this end!'

His sufferings, regularly increasing, did their work of preparing him for death. There was no position that did not cause him pain; no moments of forgetfulness; no part of his body that did not hurt and torment him. Even the memories, impressions, and thoughts within his body now aroused in him the same sort of repulsion as the body itself. The sight of other persons, their words, his own recollections, gave him nothing but pain. Those about him felt this, and unconsciously did not permit themselves either to move freely, talk, or express their own wishes in his presence. His life was quite swallowed up in a consciousness of suffering and a desire to be released from it.

It was clear the change was taking place within him which would bring him to regard death as a fulfilment of his desires, as happiness. Formerly every separate desire caused by suffering or privation, such as hunger or thirst, was relieved by some bodily action which brought enjoyment; but now privation and suffering were not followed by relief, but the attempt to obtain relief occasioned fresh suffering. Therefore all his desires were merged into one: a desire to be released from all this pain and from its source—his body. He had no words to express his desire for this liberation, and therefore did not speak of it; but went on from habit demanding satisfaction of those wishes that could be fulfilled. 'Turn me on the other side,' he said, and immediately afterwards asked to be put back as he had been. 'Give me some beef tea . . . take it away. . . . Tell me something! Why don't you speak?' Then as soon as they began to talk he shut his eyes and expressed weariness, indifference, and disgust.

On the tenth day after their arrival in that town Kitty fell ill. She had a headache, was sick, and could not leave her bed all the morning.

The doctor explained her illness as the result of fatigue and agitation, and ordered mental tranquillity.

After dinner, however, Kitty got up and went as usual to the sick man, taking her embroidery. Nicholas looked at her sternly when she entered, and smiled contemptuously when she said she had been ill. That day he continually blew his nose and moaned piteously.

'How do you feel?' she asked him.

'Worse,' he answered with an effort. 'It hurts!'

'Where does it hurt?'

'Everywhere.'

'To-day it will end, you'll see,' said Mary Nikolaevna in a whisper, but so that the invalid, whose senses were very acute, was, as Levin saw, sure to hear her. Levin said 'Hush!' and turned to look at his brother. Nicholas had heard, but the words had no effect on him; his look remained reproachful and strained.

'Why do you think so?' Levin asked, when she had followed him into the corridor.

'He has begun to clutch at himself,' replied Mary Nikolaevna.

'Clutch? How?'

'Like this,' she said, pulling at the folds of her stuff dress. And Levin noticed that all day long the sick man really kept catching at himself as if wishing to pull something off.

Mary Nikolaevna's prophecy was fulfilled. Toward night the patient could no longer raise his hands, and only gazed straight before him without changing the attentive concentrated expression of his eyes. Even when his brother or Kitty bent over him so that he could see them, he did not look at them. Kitty sent for the priest to read the prayers for the dying. While the priest read, the dying man showed no sign of life: his eyes were closed. Levin, Kitty, and Mary Nikolaevna stood by the bedside. The prayers were not yet ended when the dying man stretched himself, sighed and opened his eyes. Having finished the prayer, the priest touched the cold forehead with his cross which he then wrapped in his stole, and after standing in silence another two minutes, touched the enormous bloodless hand, which was growing cold.

'He is passed away,' said the priest and turned to go; but suddenly the clammy moustache of the dying man moved and from the depth of his chest through the stillness came his voice, sharp and distinct:

'Not quite! . . . Soon.'

A moment later his face brightened, a smile appeared under the moustache, and the women who had gathered round him began zealously to lay out the body.

The sight of his brother and the proximity of death renewed in Levin's soul that feeling of horror at the inscrutability, nearness, and inevitability of death which had seized him on that autumn evening when his brother had arrived in the country. That feeling was now stronger even than before; he felt even less able than before to understand the meaning of death, and its inevitability appeared yet more terrible to him; but now, thanks to his wife's presence, that feeling did not drive him to despair; in spite of death, he felt the necessity of living and loving. He felt that love had saved him from despair, and that that love under the menace of despair grew still stronger and purer.

Scarcely had the unexplained mystery of death been enacted before his eyes when another mystery just as inexplicable presented itself, calling to love and life.

The doctor confirmed their supposition about Kitty. Her illness was pregnancy.

Chapter XXI

From the moment that Karenin understood from his conversations with Betsy and Oblonsky that all that was asked of him was that he should leave his wife in peace and not trouble her with his presence and that his wife herself wished this, he felt so lost that he could decide nothing for himself, did not know what he now wanted, and having placed himself in the hands of those who with so much pleasure busied themselves with his affairs, he consented to everything. Only after Anna had left his house, and the English governess sent to ask him whether she was to dine with him or alone, did he for the first time clearly understand his position, and he was horror-struck at it.

What was most painful in his situation was his inability to reconcile his past life with the present state of things. It was not the past when he lived happily with his wife that perplexed him, the transition from that past to the consciousness of his wife's infidelity he had already painfully passed through; that had been trying, but it was comprehensible. Had his wife then, after confessing her infidelity, left him, he would have been grieved and unhappy, but he would not have felt himself to be in such an unintelligible impasse as now. He could not at all reconcile his recent forgiveness, his emotion and love for his sick wife and for another man's baby, with the present position: with the fact that, as if in reward for all that, he was now left alone, disgraced, ridiculed, not wanted by anyone and despised by all.

The first two days after his wife's departure Karenin received petitioners, and his private secretary, attended Committee Meetings, and went to the dining-room to dinner as usual. Without rendering account to himself why he did it, during those two days he tried with all his might to appear calm and even indifferent. When answering questions as to what should be done with Anna's room and belongings, he made the greatest efforts to seem like a man by whom what had taken place had not been unforeseen, and who did not consider it extraordinary. In this he succeeded: no one could have observed in him any signs of despair. But on the third day, when Korney brought him a bill from a firm of milliners which Anna had forgotten to pay, and informed him that the shopman had come in person, he had him brought in.

'Excuse me, your Excellency, for taking the liberty of troubling you! But if you wish us to address ourselves to her Excellency, please be so good as to let us have her address!'

Karenin appeared to be considering, when suddenly he turned round and sat down at the table. Dropping his head on his hands he sat thus for a long time, tried several times to speak, but stopped short.

Comprehending his master's emotion, Korney asked the assistant to come again another time. Karenin, left alone, realized that he could not any longer maintain an appearance of firmness and calm. He ordered the carriage that was waiting to be unharnessed, said that he would receive no one, and did not appear at dinner.

He felt that he could not bear the general pressure of contempt and harshness which he had clearly seen in the faces of that shop-assistant and of Korney, and of every one without exception whom he had met during those two days. He felt that he could not divert from himself people's hatred, because that hatred was caused not by his badness (had it been so he might have tried to be better) but by his disgraceful and repulsive misery. He knew that for that reason—because his heart was rent in pieces—they would be pitiless toward him. He felt that people would destroy him, as dogs kill a tortured dog that is whining with pain. He knew that the only way of escape from men was to hide his wounds from them. He had unconsciously tried to do so for two days, and now felt himself unable to continue the unequal struggle.

His despair was heightened by the consciousness that he was quite alone in his sorrow. Not only was there not a soul in Petersburg to whom he could express what he felt, who would pity him, not as a high official, not as a member of a society, but simply as a suffering human being—but nowhere at all had he any such friend.

Karenin had been left an orphan. There were two of them: he

had a brother. They could not remember their father, and their mother died when Alexey Alexandrovich was ten years old. They had small means. Their uncle, Karenin, a high official and at one time a favourite with the late Emperor, brought them up.

Having taken a medal on finishing, both at school and at the university, Karenin, by his uncle's help, started at once on a conspicuous path in the Civil Service, and from that time devoted himself entirely to official ambition. Neither at school nor at the university, nor afterwards in the Service, did he enter into friendly relations with anyone. His brother was nearest to his heart, but he served under the Ministry of Foreign Affairs and always lived abroad, where he died soon after Alexey Alexandrovich's marriage.

At the time when he was Governor of a Province, Anna's aunt, a rich provincial lady, introduced him, who though not a young man was a young Governor, to her niece, and contrived to put him in such a position that he was obliged either to propose or leave the town. Karenin hesitated long. At that time there were as many reasons for the step as against it, but there was no such decisive reason as to make him neglect his rule of refraining when in doubt. But Anna's aunt intimated to him, through an acquaintance, that he had already compromised the girl, and that he was in honour bound to propose to her. He proposed, and devoted to his betrothed and to his wife all the feeling of which he was capable.

His attachment to Anna excluded from his soul any need he had felt for affectionate relations with other persons; and now, among all his acquaintances, he had no intimate friend. He was connected with many people, but had friendly relations with none. He knew many persons whom he could invite to dinner, could ask to take part in anything he was interested in or to use their influence for some petitioner, and with whom he could frankly discuss the actions of other men and of the Government; but his relations with these persons were confined to a sphere strictly limited by custom and habit from which it was impossible to escape. There was a fellow-student at the university with whom he had subsequently become friendly, and to whom he might have spoken of his grief; but that fellow-student was now curator in a distant educational district. Of the Petersburg people the most intimate and most likely were the doctor, and Michael Vasilich Slyudin, his private secretary.

Slyudin was an unaffected, intelligent, kindly and moral man, who, Karenin felt, had a personal liking for himself; but their five years' official activity together had built a barrier in the way of any intimate talk between them.

Once Karenin, having finished signing documents, remained silent a long time, glancing now and then at Michael Vasilich, and tried several times but was unable to begin speaking. He had prepared a phrase: 'You have heard of my misfortune?' but it ended by his saying merely the usual, 'Then you will get this ready for me?' and letting him go.

The other person, the doctor, was also well-inclined toward Karenin, but they had long ago come to a tacit understanding that they were both overwhelmed with work and had no time to spare.

Of his women friends, including the principal one among them, the Countess Lydia Ivanovna, Karenin did not think at all. All women, as such, appeared to him dreadful and repulsive.

Chapter XXII

Karenin had forgotten the Countess Lydia Ivanovna, but she had not forgotten him. At that most painful time of lonely despair she came to his house and entered his study unannounced. She found him in the posture in which he had long sat, resting his head on his hands.

'*J'ai forcé la consigne!*' [5] she said as she entered with hurried steps, breathing heavily from her rapid movement and from excitement. 'I have heard everything. Alexey Alexandrovich, my dear friend!' she continued firmly clasping his hand in both hers and gazing with her beautiful dreamy eyes into his.

Karenin rose frowning, and disengaging his hand moved a chair toward her.

'If you please, Countess!—I do not receive because I am ill,' he said, and his lips trembled.

'My dear friend!' repeated the Countess with her eyes fixed on him; and suddenly the inner corners of her eyebrows rose, forming a triangle on her forehead, and her plain yellow face grew still plainer; but Karenin felt that she was sorry for him and ready to cry. He was moved, and seizing her plump hand began kissing it.

'My dear friend!' she repeated in a voice broken by emotion, 'you must not give way to sorrow. Your sorrow is great, but you will find consolation.'

'I am broken, I am stricken! I am no longer a man!' said Karenin, releasing her hand but continuing to gaze into her tearful eyes. 'My position is terrible because I cannot find support anywhere, cannot find it even in myself.'

'You will find support; do not seek it in me, though I want you to believe in my friendship,' she replied with a sigh. 'Love is the only support, that love which He has bequeathed us! His yoke is easy,' she went on with that ecstatic look he knew so well. 'He will support you and help you!'

Though it was evident that she was touched by her own lofty sentiments, and though her words proceeded from that new, ec-

5. 'I've forced my way in.'

static, mystic influence which had lately spread through Petersburg and which Karenin had considered superfluous, it was pleasant to him to hear them now.

'I am weak—I am done for! I did not foresee it, and don't understand it now!'

'My dear friend!' Lydia Ivanovna said once more.

'It is not the loss of what no longer exists, it is not that,' continued Karenin. 'I don't regret that, but I cannot help feeling ashamed before others of the position I am in. That is wrong, but I can't help it, I can't.'

'It is not you who have performed that great act of forgiveness which fills me and everybody else with rapture, but He that dwells within your heart,' said the Countess Lydia Ivanovna, turning up her eyes ecstatically, 'and therefore you must not be ashamed of your action.'

Karenin frowned, and bending his hands backward began cracking his fingers.

'One must know all the details,' he said in a high-pitched voice. 'Human strength has its limits, Countess, and I have reached the limits of mine. All day long I have had to take domestic decisions resulting from' (he emphasized the word 'resulting') 'my new solitary position. The servants, the governess, the bills . . . These petty flames have burnt me, and I was unable to bear it. At dinner . . . yesterday, I very nearly left the table. I could not bear the way my son looked at me. He did not ask me the meaning of it all, but he wanted to ask, and I could not endure his look. He was afraid of looking at me. But this is not all. . . .'

Karenin was going to mention the bill that had been brought him, but his voice shook and he paused. He could not think of that bill, made out on blue paper, for a bonnet and ribbons, without pitying himself.

'I understand, dear friend,' said the Countess Lydia Ivanovna. 'I understand it all. Not in me will you find help and consolation, though I have come to help you if I can. If I could take all those trivial humiliating cares off your shoulders? . . . I see that a woman's word, a woman's direction, is wanted. Will you entrust it to me?'

Karenin silently and gratefully pressed her hand.

'We will look after Serezha together. I am not good in practical matters, still I will undertake it—I will be your housekeeper. Do not thank me. I am not doing it of myself. . . .'

'I cannot help thanking you!'

'But, my dear friend, do not give way to that feeling you were speaking about—of being ashamed of that which is the utmost height of Christianity! "He that humbleth himself shall be exalted," and you must not thank me! You must thank Him, and ask Him for help. In Him alone you will find peace, comfort, salvation, and love!' And raising her eyes to Heaven she began to pray, as Karenin understood from her silence.

Karenin listened to her now, and those very expressions, which formerly had seemed to him if not disagreeable at least superfluous, now seemed natural and comforting. He did not like that new ecstatic influence. He was a believer, interested in religion chiefly from a political point of view, and this new teaching which allowed itself some novel interpretation, just because it paved the way for disputes and analyses, was repugnant to him on principle. He had formerly regarded the new teaching with coldness and even hostility, and had never discussed it with the Countess Lydia Ivanovna (who was carried away by it), but had carefully and silently evaded her challenges. Now for the first time he listened to her words with pleasure and without mental rejoinder.

'I am very, very grateful to you, both for your actions and your words,' said he when she had finished praying.

The Countess Lydia Ivanovna once more pressed both the hands of her friend.

'Now I am going to act,' she said, smiling and wiping the traces of tears from her face. 'I am going to see Serezha. Only in extreme cases will I apply to you,' and she rose and went out.

The Countess went to Serezha's part of the house and there, watering the frightened boy's cheeks with her tears, told him that his father was a saint and that his mother was dead.

The Countess kept her word. She really took upon herself the care of arranging and managing Karenin's household, but she had not exaggerated when she said she was not good at practical matters. None of her directions could be carried out without alteration, and the alterations were made by Karenin's valet, Korney, who now imperceptibly directed the whole household. Quietly and tactfully, while helping his master dress, he would inform him of anything that was necessary. But nevertheless Lydia Ivanovna's help was in the highest degree effective, for it gave Karenin the moral support of the consciousness of her affection and respect, and especially of the fact that she had nearly converted him to Christianity (as it consoled her to believe); that is to say, she had changed him from an apathetic, indolent believer into a fervent and firm adherent of that new interpretation of the Christian teaching which had lately spread in Petersburg. For Karenin it was easy to accept that interpretation. Like Lydia Ivanovna and others who shared these views, Karenin was quite devoid of that deep imaginative faculty of the soul by which ideas aroused by the imagination become so vivid that they must be brought into conformity with other ideas and with reality. He saw nothing impossible or incongruous in the notion that death which exists for the unbeliever did not exist for him, and that as he possessed complete faith—of the measure of which he himself was the judge—there was no longer any sin in his soul, and he already experienced complete salvation here on earth.

It is true that the frivolity and falseness of this view of his faith were vaguely felt by Karenin. He knew that when, without thinking that his forgiveness was the act of a Higher Power, he had surrendered to his faith, he had experienced more joy than when, as now, he was perpetually thinking that Christ lived in his soul, and that while signing documents he was fulfilling His will. But it was absolutely necessary for Karenin to think thus; it was so necessary for him in his humiliation to possess at least this imaginary exaltation, from the height of which he, the despised of all, was able to despise others, that he clung to his mock salvation as if it were the real thing.

Chapter XXIII

The Countess Lydia Ivanovna when quite a young and ecstatic girl was married to a rich, aristocratic, very good-natured, and most jovial profligate. About two months after their marriage her husband left her, and only answered her ecstatic assurances of tenderness with ridicule and even with animosity—which those who knew the Count's good-nature, and who saw no fault in the ecstatic Lydia, were quite unable to explain. Since then, though not divorced, they lived apart; and when the husband did meet his wife he always treated her with an unchanging venomous irony which seemed inexplicable.

The Countess Lydia had long ago ceased to be in love with her husband, but since then had never ceased to be in love with somebody else. She was in love with several persons at once, both men and women; she had been in love with almost every one who was specially notable. She was in love with all the new Princes and Princesses who became connected with the Imperial family, she was in love with a Metropolitan, a vicar, and a priest. She had been in love with a journalist, three Slavs, Komisarov,[6] one of the Ministers, a doctor, an English missionary, and now with Karenin. All these passions, ever waxing or waning, did not interfere with her carrying on very widespread and complicated relations with the Count and Society. But from the time she took Karenin under her special protection after his misfortune—from the time she exerted herself in his house, labouring for his welfare—she felt that all her other passions were unreal, and that she now truly loved only Karenin. The feeling she now had for him seemed to her stronger

---

6. A man who saved the life of Alexander II by knocking the pistol from the hand of a would-be assassin.

than any of her former sentiments. Analysing that feeling, and comparing it with her previous loves, she saw clearly that she would not have been in love with Komisarov had he not saved the Tsar's life, nor with Ristich-Kudzhitsky[7] but for the Slavonic question; but that she loved Karenin for himself, for his lofty, misunderstood soul, for the high-pitched tone of his voice with the long-drawn inflections which she thought charming, for his weary eyes, for his character, and for his soft hands with their swollen veins. She was not only glad to meet him, but searched his face for signs of the impression she created on him. She wished to please him not merely by words, but by her whole self. For his sake she now paid more attention to her dress than ever before. She caught herself meditating on what might have been had she not married and had he been free. She blushed with excitement when he entered the room, and could not repress a smile of delight when he said something agreeable to her.

For some days the Countess Lydia Ivanovna had been greatly excited. She had heard that Anna and Vronsky were in Petersburg. It was necessary to save Karenin from meeting her, necessary even to save him from the painful knowledge that that dreadful woman was in the same town with him, and that he might come across her at any moment.

Lydia Ivanovna found out through acquaintances what 'those disgusting people,' as she called Anna and Vronsky, intended to do, and tried so to direct her friend's steps during those days that he should not meet them. A young adjutant, a comrade of Vronsky's, through whom she had her information, who hoped through her influence to obtain a concession, told her that they had finished their affairs and were leaving Petersburg next day. Lydia Ivanovna was beginning to breathe freely again, when next morning she received a note and with horror recognized the handwriting. It was Anna Karenina's. The envelope was as thick as parchment; there was a large monogram on the narrow yellow sheet, and the letter had a delicious perfume.

'Who brought it?'

'A commissionaire from the hotel.'

It was some time before the Countess Lydia Ivanovna could sit down to read the letter. Her agitation brought on a fit of asthma, to which she was subject. When she grew calmer, she read the following, written in French:

'MADAME LA COMTESSE!—The Christian feelings which fill your heart encourage me to what I feel to be the unpardonable boldness of writing to you. I am unhappy at being parted from my son. I entreat you to permit me to see him once before my departure. For-

---

7. Jovan Ristich-Kudzhitsky (1831–1899) was a Serb statesman, regent of Prince Milan Obrenovich, and an opponent of Turkish and Austrian influence in Serbia. He was very widely known in Russia.

give me for reminding you of myself. I address myself to you, instead of to Alexey Alexandrovich, only because I do not wish to give pain to that high-minded man by reminding him of myself. Knowing your friendship for him, I feel that you will understand me. Will you send Serezha to me, or shall I come to the house at an appointed time, or will you let me know when and where I can meet him away from home? I do not anticipate a refusal, knowing the magnanimity of the person on whom the decision depends. You cannot imagine the yearning I have to see him, and therefore cannot imagine the gratitude which your help will awaken in me.—ANNA.'

Everything in that letter irritated the Countess Lydia Ivanovna: its matter, the hint contained in the word 'magnanimity,' and especially what seemed to her its free and easy tone.

'Say there will be no answer,' said the Countess Lydia Ivanovna, and at once opened her blotter and wrote to Karenin that she hoped to meet him about one o'clock at the Palace, at the Birthday Reception.

'I must talk over an important and sad matter with you, and we can arrange where. Best of all at my house, where I will have your special tea ready. It is necessary. He sends a cross, but He also sends strength to bear it,' she added, to prepare him somewhat.

The Countess Lydia Ivanovna generally wrote two or three notes a day to Karenin. She liked that way of communicating with him, which had an elegance and secrecy absent in their personal interviews.

Chapter XXIV

The congratulations at the Palace were over. Meeting as they were going out, acquaintances chatted about the latest news, the newly awarded honours, and the changes among the highest officials.

'How would it do to appoint Countess Mary Borisovna, Minister of War? and Princess Vatkovskaya, Chief of the Staff?' said a grey-haired old man in a gold-embroidered uniform to a tall and beautiful Maid of Honour, in answer to her question about the promotions.

'And me, aide-de-camp,' replied the Maid of Honour with a smile.

'Your post is already assigned to you: in the Ecclesiastical department with Karenin as your assistant.'

'How do you do, Prince?' added the old man, shaking hands with some one who had just come up.

'What were you saying about Karenin?' inquired the Prince.

'He and Putyatov have received the Order of Alexander Nevsky.'

'I thought he had it already.'

'No. Just look at him,' said the old man, pointing with his gold-trimmed hat to Karenin who, in Court uniform, with a new red ribbon round his shoulder, stood in the doorway with an important member of the State Council. 'As happy and contented as a brass farthing,' he added, pausing to shake hands with an athletic, handsome chamberlain.

'No, he has aged,' said the chamberlain.

'From hard work. He is always writing projects now. He will not release that unfortunate fellow until he has expounded everything, point by point.'

'Aged indeed! *Il fait des passions!* [8] I think that now the Countess Lydia Ivanovna is jealous of his wife.'

'Oh, come! Please don't say anything bad about the Countess.'

'But is it bad that she is in love with Karenin?'

'And is it true that his wife is here?'

'Of course not here in the Palace, but she is in Petersburg. I met her and Alexey Vronsky walking arm in arm on the Morskaya.'

'*C'est un homme qui n'a pas* [9] . . .' began the chamberlain, but stopped short to make way for and to bow to a member of the Imperial family who passed by.

In this way they chattered unceasingly about Karenin, blaming him and laughing at him, while he, barring the way to the member of the State Council whom he had buttonholed, and not pausing for a moment for fear he might slip away, expounded point by point some financial project of his.

Almost at the same time that his wife had left Karenin, the most painful thing that can befall an official—the cessation of his ascent in the Service—had befallen him. That cessation was an accomplished fact, clearly visible to every one, though Karenin himself had not yet realized that his career was at an end. Whether it was his conflict with Stremov or the misfortune with his wife, or simply that he had reached his predestined limit—at any rate it had that year become obvious to every one that his career was over. He still held an important post, was member of many Commissions and Committees, but he was finished, and from him nothing further was to be looked for. Whatever he might say, whatever he might propose, was listened to as if all he was proposing had long been known and was what no one wanted. But Karenin was not sensible of this: on the contrary, being now outside Government work, he saw more clearly than ever the defects and mistakes made by others, and considered it his duty to point out how those mistakes might be rectified. Soon after the parting with his wife he began writing a pamphlet on the new legal procedure—the first of

8. Women are crazy about him.
9. That's a man who does not have . . .

an innumerable series of unwanted pamphlets on every administrative department which it was his fate to write.

But Karenin, far from noticing the hopelessness of his position in officialdom and being troubled by it, was more satisfied with his work than ever.

'He that is married careth for the things that are of the world, how he may please his wife . . . but he that is unmarried careth for the things that belong to the Lord and how to please the Lord,' says the Apostle Paul; and Karenin, who was now guided in all his actions by the Scriptures, often recalled that text. He thought that since he had been without a wife he had served the Lord by means of these very projects more than before.

The evident impatience of the Member of the Council did not trouble Karenin, who left off expounding his project only when the Councillor, profiting by a royal personage's passing, slipped away.

Left alone, Karenin bowed his head, collecting his thoughts, and then turned absent-mindedly toward the door where he hoped to meet the Countess Lydia Ivanovna. 'How strong and healthy they all are physically,' he thought, glancing at the powerfully-built chamberlain with his well-brushed and perfumed whiskers, and at the red neck of a Prince in a tightly-fitting uniform, whom he had to pass on his way. 'It is truly said that everything in the world is sin,' he thought, again glancing out of the corners of his eyes at the chamberlain's calves.

Moving his feet deliberately, Karenin, with his usual air of weariness and dignity, bowed to those gentlemen who were talking about him, and his eyes searched through the doorway for the Countess.

'Ah, Alexey Alexandrovich!' cried the old man with a malevolent gleam in his eyes as Karenin passed him bowing coldly. 'I have not yet congratulated you,' he went on, pointing to Karenin's newly-awarded ribbon.

'Thank you,' replied Karenin. 'What a *beautiful* day it is,' he added, laying, as was his wont, peculiar stress on the word 'beautiful.'

He knew that they were laughing at him, but he no longer looked for anything except hostility from them; he was already accustomed to it.

Having caught sight, just as she entered, of the Countess Lydia Ivanovna's yellow shoulders emerging from her corset, and of her beautiful dreamy eyes summoning him, Karenin smiled, revealing his white impeccable teeth, and went up to her.

Lydia Ivanovna's dress had cost her a great deal of trouble, as was the case with all her attire of late. Her purpose in dressing was now quite the reverse of what she had had in view thirty years ago. Then she had wished to adorn herself somehow, the more the better; now, on the contrary, she was obliged to be adorned so unsuitably to her age and figure, that she was only concerned that the incongruity between these adornments and her own appearance should not be too dreadful. As far as Karenin was concerned she attained her object, and to him she seemed attractive. In his eyes she was the only islet, not of kindly feeling only but of affection, in the ocean of hostility and ridicule which surrounded him.

As he now ran the gauntlet of those mocking eyes he was drawn toward her enamoured look as naturally as a plant is drawn toward the sun.

'I congratulate you,' she said, indicating the ribbon by a look.

Repressing a smile of pleasure, he shrugged his shoulders and closed his eyes, as if to say that it could not give him pleasure. The Countess Lydia Ivanovna knew very well that it was one of his greatest pleasures, though he would never confess it.

'How is our angel?' asked she, meaning Serezha.

'I can't say I am quite satisfied with him,' replied Karenin, raising his eyebrows and opening his eyes. 'And Sitnikov too is dissatisfied with him.' Sitnikov was the tutor to whom Serezha's secular education was entrusted. 'As I told you, he shows a certain coldness toward those most important questions which should stir the soul of every man and child,' he went on, speaking on the only subject which interested him outside the Service—the education of his son.

When with Lydia Ivanovna's help he had returned to life and activity, he had felt it his duty to take his son's education in hand. Never having occupied himself with educational matters before, he devoted some time to studying the matter theoretically. After reading several books on anthropology, pedagogics, and didactics, he formed a plan of education, and having engaged the best Petersburg educationalist for supervision, he set to work. And this undertaking occupied him continually.

'Yes, but his heart! I see in him his father's heart, and with such a heart a child can't be bad!' said Lydia Ivanovna, enthusiastically.

'Perhaps. Well, as far as I am concerned I do my duty, which is all I can do.'

'Will you come and see me?' said the Countess after a pause. 'We must talk over something painful to you. I would have given anything to save you from certain memories, but other people think differently. I had a letter from her. She is here in Petersburg.'

Karenin started at the reference to his wife, but immediately his face assumed a death-like immobility which showed utter helplessness in the matter.

'I expected it,' he said.

The Countess Lydia Ivanovna looked at him ecstatically, and her eyes filled with tears of rapturous admiration at the loftiness of his soul.

Chapter XXV

When Karenin entered the Countess Lydia Ivanovna's snug little boudoir, which was full of old china and had its walls covered with portraits, the hostess was not yet there.

She was changing her dress.

Upon a round table covered with a cloth stood a Chinese tea service and a silver kettle over a spirit lamp. Karenin glanced absent-mindedly at the numberless familiar portraits decorating the boudoir, and sitting down by the table opened a New Testament that was on it. The rustle of the Countess's silk dress roused him.

'Well, now we can sit down quietly,' said she with an agitated smile, as she squeezed herself in between the table and sofa, 'and have a chat over our tea.'

After a few words of preparation the Countess, breathing heavily and blushing, handed him the letter she had received.

When he had read the letter Karenin was silent for a long time.

'I don't consider that I have a right to refuse,' he said timidly, raising his eyes.

'My dear friend, you see no evil in anyone!'

'On the contrary, I see that everything is evil. But is it right . . .'

His face expressed uncertainty and a desire for advice, support, and guidance in a matter he did not understand.

'No,' she interrupted him, 'there are limits to everything! I understand immorality,' she said, not quite sincerely, for she never could have understood that which leads women to immorality, 'but I do not understand cruelty . . . and to whom? To you! How can she stay in the town you are in? But it's quite true, "Live and learn"! And I am learning to understand your loftiness and her baseness.'

'But who will throw the stone?' said he, evidently pleased with his rôle. 'I have quite forgiven her, and therefore cannot refuse her what her love for her son demands.'

'But is it love, dear friend? Is it sincere? Granted that you have forgiven her, and do forgive her; but have we the right to act thus toward the soul of that angel? He thinks she is dead. He prays for her and asks God to forgive her her sins, and it is better so. But this . . . what will he think?'

'I had not thought of that,' said Karenin, evidently agreeing with her.

The Countess covered her face with her hands and remained

silent. She was praying.

'If you ask my advice,' she said, when her prayer was ended and she uncovered her face, 'I do not advise you to do it! Do I not see how you are suffering, how this has reopened all your wounds! Of course as usual you are not thinking of yourself. But what can it lead to? Renewed pain for yourself, and pain for the child! If there is anything human left in her, she herself should not desire it. No, I advise you unhesitatingly not to allow it, and with your permission I will write to her.'

Karenin agreed, and the Countess Lydia Ivanovna wrote in French as follows:

'MADAME!—To remind your son of you might lead to his asking questions which it would be impossible to answer without implanting in his soul a spirit of condemnation for what should be holy to him, and therefore I beg you to take your husband's refusal in the spirit of Christian love. I pray the Almighty to be merciful to you.—COUNTESS LYDIA.'

This letter achieved the secret purpose which the Countess Lydia Ivanovna hid even from herself. It wounded Anna to the depths of her soul.

Karenin too, on returning home from Lydia Ivanovna's, could not give his attention to his usual occupations nor find that spiritual peace of a believer who has found salvation, which he had felt before.

The memory of his wife who was so guilty toward him, and toward whom he was so saintly, as the Countess Lydia Ivanovna had justly told him, should not have upset him; but he was not at ease: he could not understand the book he was reading, could not drive away tormenting memories of his relations with her, and of the mistakes which, as it now appeared to him, he had committed in regard to her. The memory of the manner in which, when returning from the races, he had received her confession of unfaithfulness (especially the fact that he had demanded of her only external propriety and had not challenged Vronsky) tormented him with remorse. The memory of the letter he had written to her also tormented him; above all his forgiveness, which no one wanted, and his care for another man's child, burned his heart with shame and regret.

He now felt a similar sense of shame and remorse when thinking of his whole past with her, and recalling the awkward words in which, after much hesitation, he had proposed to her.

'But wherein am I to blame?' he asked himself, and as usual that question suggested another: Did those others—those Vronskys and

Oblonskys and those fat-calved chamberlains—feel differently, love differently, marry differently? And there rose before his mind's eye a whole row of those vigorous, strong, self-assured men, who had always involuntarily attracted his curiosity and attention. He drove these thoughts from him, and tried to convince himself that he was not living for the present temporal life but for eternal life, and that his soul was full of peace and love. But the fact that in this temporary insignificant life he had committed, as it seemed to him, some trivial errors, tormented him as much as if the eternal salvation in which he believed did not exist. But this temptation did not last long, and soon that tranquil elevation, thanks to which he could forget the things he did not wish to remember, was re-established in his soul.

Chapter XXVI

'Well, Kapitonich?' said Serezha, as on the day before his birthday he returned rosy and bright from a walk, and gave his overcoat to the tall old hall-porter, who looked smilingly down from his height at the little fellow. 'Well, has the bandaged official been to-day? Has Papa seen him?'

'He has seen him. As soon as the secretary left, I announced him,' answered the hall-porter with a wink. 'Let me take it off for you.'

'Serezha!' said his tutor, a Slav, stopping in the doorway that led to the inner rooms, 'take it off yourself.' But Serezha, though he heard his tutor's weak voice, paid no heed to it. He stood holding on by the porter's shoulder-strap and looking into his face.

'Well, and has Papa done what he wanted?'

The hall-porter nodded affirmatively.

The bandaged official, who had called seven times to petition Karenin about something, interested both Serezha and the hall-porter. Serezha had met him in the hall, and had heard him piteously begging the porter to announce him to Karenin, and saying that he and his children were face to face with death.

Since then, having again met the official in the hall, Serezha had become interested in him.

'And was he very glad?' he asked.

'How could he help being glad? He nearly jumped for joy as he went away.'

'And has anything been brought?' inquired Serezha, after a pause.

'Well, sir,' said the porter, shaking his head and whispering, 'there is something from the Countess.'

Serezha knew at once that the hall-porter was speaking of a birthday present for him from the Countess Lydia Ivanovna.

'You don't say so? Where is it?'

'Korney has taken it in to your Papa. I should think it's a fine thing.'

'What size? About so big?'

'Not quite, but a fine thing.'

'A book?'

'No, just a thing. Go, go! Vasily Lukich is calling you,' said the hall-porter, hearing the approaching step of the tutor, and gently disengaging the little hand in the half-drawn-off glove which held him by his shoulder-strap, as he nodded and winked toward the tutor.

'Vasily Lukich, one moment!' said Serezha with that bright and affectionate smile which always overcame the conscientious Vasily Lukich.

Serezha was in too high spirits, too happy not to share with his friend the hall-porter another family joy about which he had heard from Lydia Ivanovna's niece, whom he met walking in the Summer Gardens. This joy appeared to him particularly important because it coincided with the satisfaction of the official, and his own happiness that a present had been brought. To Serezha it seemed that this day was one on which everybody ought to be happy and gay.

'Do you know, Papa has received the Order of Alexander Nevsky?'

'Of course I do! People have already been calling to congratulate him.'

'Well, and is he pleased?'

'How can he help being pleased at the Tsar's favour? It shows he's deserved it,' replied the hall-porter sternly and seriously.

Serezha grew thoughtful as he peered into the hall-porter's face, which he had studied in minute detail—especially the chin which hung beneath the grey whiskers and which no one saw but Serezha, who always looked up at him.

'And your daughter, has she been here lately?'

The hall-porter's daughter was a ballet-dancer.

'How can she come on week-days? They have to learn too, and so must you, sir! Go along!'

On entering the schoolroom, instead of sitting down to his lessons, Serezha told his tutor of his guess that the parcel that had been brought must be a railway train.

'What do you think?' he asked.

But Vasily Lukich only thought that Serezha must prepare his grammar lesson, as his teacher was coming at two.

'Oh, but just tell me, Vasily Lukich!' said Serezha, suddenly, after sitting down at the table with a book in his hand. 'What is higher than the Alexander Nevsky? You know Papa has received the Order of Alexander Nevsky?'

Vasily Lukich replied that the Order of Vladimir was higher. 'And higher still?'

'The highest is the St. Andrew.'

'And higher still?'

'I don't know.'

'Even you don't know!' And Serezha, leaning his elbows on the table, began to reflect.

His reflections were most complex and varied. He imagined his father suddenly receiving the Orders of Vladimir and Saint Andrew, and how much kinder in consequence he would be to-day at lesson-time, and how he himself when he grew up would receive all the Orders, and that they would invent one higher than the Saint Andrew. As soon as it was invented he would gain it. A yet higher one would be invented, and he would immediately get that one too.

In these reflections time passed until the teacher arrived. The lesson on the attributes of Time, Place, and Manner of Action had not been learnt. The teacher was not only dissatisfied but also saddened. His sadness touched Serezha. He did not feel guilty for not having learned his lesson, for try as he would he positively could not do it. While the teacher was explaining, he believed him and seemed to understand, but as soon as he was left alone he positively could not remember or understand how so short and simple a word as *suddenly* could be an *attribute of the manner of action*; but all the same he was sorry he had grieved his teacher.

He chose a moment when the teacher was looking silently into the book:

'Michael Ivanovich, when is your birthday?' he suddenly asked.

'You would do better to think of your work. Birthdays do not signify anything to reasonable beings. It is just a day like any other, on which we must work.'

Serezha looked attentively at his teacher, at his thin little beard and his spectacles which had slipped down the bridge of his nose, and became so engrossed in thought that he no longer heard what his teacher was explaining. He was aware that the teacher himself did not believe what he was saying; he felt that by the tone in which the words were uttered. 'But why have they all agreed to speak in the same way about the dullest and most useless things? Why does he repulse me? Why does he not love me?' he asked himself sadly, and could find no answer.

Chapter XXVII

After the teacher's lesson Serezha had a lesson from his father. Before his father came Serezha sat at the table playing with a pocket-knife and thinking. Among his favourite occupations was keeping a look out for his mother when he went out walking. He did not believe in death in general, and especially not in *her* death, despite what Lydia Ivanovna had told him and his father had confirmed, and therefore even after he had been told she was dead, he went on looking for her when on his walks. He imagined that every well-developed and graceful woman with dark hair was his mother. At the sight of any such woman a feeling of such tenderness awoke in his heart that he grew breathless and tears came to his eyes. He expected that at any moment she would approach and lift her veil. Then he would see her whole face, she would smile, embrace him, and he would smell her peculiar scent, feel the tenderness of her touch, and cry with joy as he had done one evening when he lay at her feet and she tickled him, while he shook with laughter and bit her white hand with the rings on the fingers. Later on, when he accidently heard from his nurse that she was not dead, and his father and Lydia Ivanovna explained that to him she was dead because she was bad (which he could not at all believe, for he loved her), he continued to look out for and wait for her. There had been a lady with a purple veil in the Summer Garden to-day whom he had watched with a sinking heart as she came toward him along the path. The lady did not come up to them and disappeared somewhere. To-day Serezha was more than ever conscious of a flow of love for his mother in his heart, and now as he sat lost in thought, waiting for his father, he notched the whole edge of the table with his knife, looking before him with shining eyes and thinking about her.

Vasily Lukich roused him. 'Your Papa is coming!'

Serezha jumped up, approached his father, kissed his hand, and looked at him attentively, trying to find some sign of his joy at receiving the Order of Alexander Nevsky.

'Have you had a nice walk?' asked Karenin, as he sat down in his arm-chair, drew toward him an Old Testament and opened it. Although Karenin had more than once told Serezha that every Christian ought to be well acquainted with Bible history, he often in Old Testament history had to consult the book, and Serezha noticed this.

'Yes, Papa, it was very amusing,' answered Serezha, sitting down sideways on his chair and beginning to rock it, which was forbidden. 'I met Nadenka' (Nadenka was Lydia Ivanovna's niece, who was being educated at her aunt's house). 'She told me you had received another Order, a new one. Are you glad, Papa?'

'First of all, don't rock your chair,' said Karenin. 'Secondly, it's not the reward but the work that is precious. I wish you understood that. You see, if you take pains and learn in order to get a reward, the work will seem hard; but when you work' (Karenin said this remembering how he had sustained himself that morning by a sense of duty in the dull task of signing a hundred and eighteen papers)—'if you love your work, you will find your reward in that.'

Serezha's eyes, that had been shining with affection and joy, grew dull and drooped under his father's gaze. It was the same long-familiar tone in which his father always addressed him, and to which Serezha had already learnt to adapt himself. His father always talked to him, Serezha felt, as if he were some imaginary boy out of a book, quite unlike Serezha; and with his father he always tried to pretend to be that boy out of a book.

'You understand me, I hope,' said the father.

'Yes, Papa,' answered the boy, pretending to be that imaginary boy.

The lesson consisted in learning by heart some verses from the Gospels and repeating the beginning of the Old Testament. Serezha knew the Gospel verses pretty well, but whilst saying them he became so absorbed in the contemplation of a bone in his father's forehead, which turned very sharply above the temple, that he became confused and put the end of one verse where the same word occurred after the beginning of another. It was evident to Karenin that the boy did not understand what he was saying, and this irritated him.

He frowned and began an explanation that Serezha had heard many times already, and could never remember because he understood it too clearly; just as he could not remember that the word *suddenly* was an *attribute of the manner of action*. Serezha looked at his father with scared eyes, and could only think of whether his father would make him repeat what he had just said, as he sometimes did. This thought frightened him so much that he no longer understood anything at all. However, his father did not make him repeat it, but went on to the lesson from the Old Testament. Serezha related the events themselves quite well, but when he had to answer questions as to what some of the events symbolized, he knew nothing about it, though he had been punished before for not knowing this lesson. The part, however, about which he could not say anything at all but only floundered, cut the table, and rocked his chair, was that about the antediluvian patriarchs. He did not know any of them except Enoch, who was taken up to Heaven alive. Previously he had remembered the others' names, but now he had quite forgotten them, chiefly because Enoch was his favourite in the whole Old Testament, and attached to Enoch's being taken up to Heaven there was a long string of thought in his head, which now occupied his mind while he looked fixedly at his father's watch-chain and at a half-unfastened button of his waistcoat.

He did not in the least believe in death, which was so often mentioned to him. He did not believe that people he loved could die, nor above all that he himself would die. That seemed to him quite impossible and incomprehensible. But he was told that everybody would die; he had even asked people whom he trusted and they all confirmed it; his nurse too said so, though reluctantly. But Enoch had not died, so not everybody died, 'and why should not anybody deserve the same in God's sight, and be taken up to Heaven alive?' thought Serezha. Bad people, that is to say those he did not like, might die; but the good ones might all be like Enoch.

'Well, who were the patriarchs?'

'Enoch, Enos . . .'

'But you have already mentioned them. This is bad, Serezha, very bad! If you do not take pains to know what is most necessary for a Christian, then what can interest you? I am displeased with you, and Peter Ignatych'—this was the chief educationalist—'is also displeased with you. . . . I shall have to punish you.'

His father and the educationalist were both displeased with Serezha, and he really learnt badly. Yet it could not at all be said that he was an incapable boy. On the contrary he was far more capable than the boys whom the educationalist set before him as models. His father from his point of view considered that the boy did not try to learn what he was being taught. As a matter of fact, he could not learn it. He could not, because there were more urgent demands on his soul than those put forward by his father and the educationalist. The two kinds of demands were opposed, and he was in direct conflict with his instructors. He was nine years old and quite a child, but he knew his soul, it was dear to him, and he guarded it as the eyelid guards the eye, and never let anyone enter his heart without the key of love. His instructors complained that he would not learn, yet his soul was overflowing with longing for knowledge. So he learnt, from Kapitonich, from his nurse, from Nadenka, and from Vasily Lukich, but not from his teachers. The water which his father and the educationalists expected would turn their mill-wheels had long since leaked out and was working somewhere else.

His father punished Serezha by not letting him go to see Lydia Ivanovna's niece Nadenka, but this punishment turned out luckily for Serezha. Vasily Lukich was in good spirits and showed him how to make windmills. He spent all the evening working, and dreaming how a windmill could be made on which one could ride, either by seizing one of the sails or by tying oneself to it and spinning round. He did not think about his mother all the evening; but when in bed he suddenly remembered her, and prayed in his own words that to-morrow, on his birthday, she should stop hiding herself and should come to him.

'Vasily Lukich! Do you know for what I have been praying extra?'

'To learn better?'

'No.'

'For toys?'

'No. You will never guess! It's lovely, but a secret! When it comes true, I will tell you. You have not guessed.'

'No, I can't guess. You'd better tell me,' said Vasily Lukich, smiling, which he rarely did. 'Well, lie down, and I'll put out the candle.'

'But I can see better without a candle what I have been praying for! There, I nearly told you the secret!' said Serezha with a merry laugh.

When the candle had been taken away he heard and felt his mother. She stood above him and caressed him with a loving look. But then windmills appeared, and a knife, and all became confused, and he fell asleep.

Chapter XXVIII

When Vronsky and Anna reached Petersburg they put up at one of the best hotels: Vronsky separately on the first floor, and Anna with the baby, the nurse, and a maid, upstairs in a large suite consisting of four rooms.

On the day they arrived Vronsky went to see his brother. There he met his mother, who had come from Moscow on business. His mother and his sister-in-law received him just as usual, asked him about his trip abroad and spoke of mutual acquaintances, but did not say a single word about his union with Anna. His brother, however, having come to see him next morning, asked about her, and Alexey Vronsky told him frankly that he regarded his union with her as a marriage, that he hoped to arrange a divorce for her, and would then marry her, and that meanwhile he considered her his wife, just like any other wife, and he asked his brother to say so to their mother and to his own wife.

'If the world does not approve of it, I don't care,' said Vronsky, 'but if my relatives wish to treat me as a relation, they must adopt a similar attitude toward my wife.'

The elder brother, who had always respected his younger brother's opinions, was not sure whether he was right or wrong, until the world had decided the point; but for his own part he had nothing against it and went up with Alexey to see Anna.

In his brother's presence Vronsky spoke to Anna merely as to a close acquaintance, as he always did in the presence of a third party; but it was assumed that his brother knew of their relations, and they spoke of Anna's going to Vronsky's estate.

Despite all his experience of the world, Vronsky, in the new position in which he found himself, was making a terrible mistake. He might have been expected to understand that Society was closed to him and Anna; but some sort of vague notion got into his head that though it used to be so in olden times, yet now, when there was so much progress (without noticing it, he had become an advocate of every kind of progress), public opinion had changed and it was possible that they would be received in Society. 'Of course they will not receive her at Court, but intimate friends can and should see things the right way,' he thought.

It is possible to sit for some hours with one's legs doubled up without changing one's position if one knows there is nothing to prevent one's doing so, but if a man knows that he must sit with his legs doubled up he will get cramp, and his legs will begin to jerk and strain in the direction in which he would like to stretch them. This was what Vronsky experienced with regard to Society. Though in the depths of his soul he knew that Society was closed to them, he tried whether it would not change and whether it would not receive them. But he very soon noticed that though the great world was open to him personally, it was closed to Anna. As in the game of cat and mouse, the arms that were raised to allow him to get inside the circle were at once lowered to prevent Anna from entering.

One of the first Petersburg Society ladies he met was his cousin Betsy.

'At last!' she exclaimed joyfully when they met. 'And Anna? I am so glad! Where are you staying? I can imagine how dreadful our Petersburg must appear to you after your delightful journey; I can picture to myself your honeymoon in Rome. And the divorce? Is it all arranged?'

He noticed that Betsy's delight cooled down when she learnt that Anna had not yet been divorced.

'They will throw stones at me, I know,' she said, 'but I shall come and see Anna. Yes, I will certainly come. You are not staying here long?'

And really she came to see Anna that same day; but her manner was very different from what it had formerly been. She was evidently proud of her boldness and wished Anna to appreciate the fidelity of her friendship. She did not stay more than ten minutes, chattering Society gossip, and as she was leaving said:

'You have not told me when you will be divorced? Of course I have kicked over the traces, but others, straight-laced people, will give you the cold shoulder until you get married. And it is so simple nowadays! *Ça se fait.*[1] So you are leaving on Friday? I am sorry we shan't see one another again!'

From Betsy's tone Vronsky might have realized what he had to

---

1. It is a thing that is done.

expect from Society, but he made another attempt with his relations. Of his mother he had no hopes. He knew that his mother, who had been so delighted with Anna when she first made her acquaintance, was now merciless toward her for having caused the ruin of her son's career. But he placed great hopes on Varya, his brother's wife. She, he thought, would cast no stones, but would simply and resolutely go and see Anna and receive her at her own house.

The day after his arrival Vronsky called on her, and having found her alone, expressed his wish.

'You know how fond I am of you, Alexey,' she replied when she had heard him out, 'and how ready I am to do anything for you; but I have kept silent because I knew I could be of no use to you and Anna Arkadyevna.' She pronounced the formal 'Anna Arkadyevna' with peculiar precision. 'Please don't think I am condemning you. Not at all! Perhaps in her place I should have done the same. I do not and cannot enter into details,' she added, looking timidly into his gloomy face. 'But we must call things by their real names. You wish me to go and see her and to receive her, and so rehabilitate her in Society; but please understand that I *cannot* do it! I have daughters growing up, and I must move in Society, for my husband's sake. Suppose I go to see Anna Arkadyevna; she will understand that I cannot ask her to my house, or must do it in such a way that she does not meet those who see things differently. That would offend her. I am not able to raise her . . .'

'But I don't consider that she has fallen lower than hundreds of people whom you do receive!' said Vronsky still more gloomily, and rose in silence, having understood that his sister-in-law's determination was final.

'Alexey, don't be angry with me! Please understand that it is not my fault,' said Varya, looking at him with a timid smile.

'I am not angry with you,' he said just as gloomily, 'but I am doubly pained. I am pained too because this breaks our friendship. No, not breaks it, but weakens it. You understand that for me too there can be no other course!'

With those words he left her.

Vronsky understood that it was vain to make any further attempts and that they would have to spend those few days in Petersburg as in a strange town, avoiding contact with their former world in order not to lay themselves open to unpleasantnesses and insults which were so painful to him. One of the most disagreeable features of his position in Petersburg was that Karenin seemed to be everywhere and his name in every mouth. It was impossible to start any conversation without its turning upon Karenin, impossible to go anywhere without meeting him. So at least it seemed to

Vronsky, as a man with a sore finger feels that he is continually knocking that finger against everything as if on purpose.

The stay in Petersburg seemed to him still more trying because he noticed all the time in Anna a new and to him incomprehensible mood. At one moment she appeared to be in love with him, and at the next would turn cold, irritable, and impenetrable. Something tormented her and she hid it from him, appearing not to notice the insults that were poisoning his life, and which should have been still more painful to her with her acuteness of perception.

Chapter XXIX

One of Anna's reasons for returning to Russia was to see her son. From the day she left Italy the thought of that meeting did not cease to agitate her. The nearer they came to Petersburg the greater its joy and importance appeared. She did not ask herself how she should contrive it. It seemed to her natural and simple that she should see her son when she was in the same town with him. But on reaching Petersburg her present social position presented itself clearly to her, and she realized that it would be difficult to arrange the meeting.

She had been in Petersburg two days. The thought of her son did not leave her for an instant, but she had not yet seen him. She felt she had not the right to go straight to the house where she might encounter Karenin. Possibly they might even not admit her.

It was painful to her even to think of writing to and coming into contact with her husband: she could be calm only when she did not think of him. To meet her son when he was out for a walk, after finding out when and where he went, was not enough: she had been preparing herself so for that meeting, had so much to say to him, and so much wanted to embrace and kiss him! Serezha's old nurse might have helped and advised her, but she was no longer in Karenin's household. In this uncertainty, and in searching for the old nurse, two days had gone by.

Having heard about Karenin's intimate friendship with the Countess Lydia Ivanovna, Anna on the third day resolved to write her a letter, which cost her much effort, and in which she intentionally mentioned that permission to see her son must depend on her husband's magnanimity. She knew that if that letter were shown to him, he, continuing his magnanimous rôle, would not refuse her request.

The commissionaire who delivered her letter brought back the most cruel and unexpected reply: that there would be no answer! Never had she felt so humiliated as when, having called in the commissionaire, she heard from him the full account of how he had waited and had then been told that there would be no answer.

Anna felt herself humiliated and wounded, but she saw that the Countess Lydia Ivanovna was right from her own point of view. Her grief was the more poignant because she had to bear it alone. She could not share it with Vronsky and did not wish to. She knew that, though he was the chief cause of her misery, the question of her seeing her son would seem to him quite unimportant. She knew he would never be able to appreciate the depth of her anguish, and that his coldness if the matter were mentioned would make her hate him. And she feared that, more than anything else in the world, and therefore hid from him everything concerning her son.

Having spent all that day at the hotel considering how she might see her son, she resolved to write to her husband. She had already composed the letter when she received Lydia Ivanovna's reply. The Countess's silence had made her feel humble, but the letter and what she read between its lines so irritated her, its malevolence seemed so revolting when compared with her passionate and legitimate love for her son, that she became indignant with others and ceased to blame herself.

'That coldness, that pretence of feeling!' she said to herself. 'They want to wound me and torture the child, and shall I submit to them? Not on any account! She is worse than I. Anyhow, I don't lie!' And there and then she resolved that next day, Serezha's birthday, she would go straight to her husband's house, and would bribe the servants or deceive them, but would at any cost see her son and destroy that monstrous falsehood with which they surrounded the unfortunate child.

She drove to a toyshop, purchased a lot of toys, and devised a plan of action. She would go early in the morning, at about eight, when Karenin would certainly not be up. She would have ready in her hand some money to give to the hall-porter and the footman, in order that they should let her in. Without raising her veil she would say she had been sent by Serezha's god-father to wish him many happy returns of the day and that she was to put the toys by his bedside. The only thing she did not prepare was what she would say to her son. Much as she thought about that she could not prepare the words.

Next morning Anna went alone, and at eight o'clock got out of the hired carriage and rang the bell at the front door of the house which used to be her home.

'Go and see what it is. It's some lady,' said Kapitonich, who was not yet dressed, and in overcoat and goloshes peeped from the window at the veiled lady standing close to the door. His assistant, a lad whom Anna did not know, had hardly opened the door when she entered, and taking a three-rouble note from her muff hastily thrust it into his hand.

'Serezha . . . Sergey Alexeyich!' she said, and walked on. After examining the note the porter's assistant stopped her at the inner glass door.

'Whom do you want?' he asked.

Noticing the stranger's confusion, Kapitonich himself came out, admitted her, and inquired what she wanted.

'I come from Prince Skorodumov to see Sergey Alexeyich,' said she.

'He is not up yet,' said the hall-porter, carefully scrutinizing her face.

Anna had not foreseen at all that the totally unaltered appearance of the hall of the house where she had lived for nine years would so deeply affect her. One memory after another, both joyful and painful, rose in her mind, and for a moment she forgot why she had come.

'Would you like to wait?' said Kapitonich, helping her off with her cloak.

Having done so he glanced again at her face and, recognizing her, silently bowed low.

'Come in, Your Excellency,' he said.

She wished to speak, but her voice refused to utter a sound; with a look of guilty entreaty at the old man she went with light steps up the stairs. Bending forward and catching the steps with his goloshes, Kapitonich ran after her, trying to overtake her.

"The tutor may be there and not yet dressed. I will announce you.'

Anna continued to ascend the familiar steps without understanding what the old man was saying.

'This way, please! To the left! Please excuse its not being quite clean. He has been moved to the old sitting-room now,' said the hall-porter, panting. 'Allow me! Please wait a little, Your Excellency. I'll just look in,' he said, having overtaken her. He opened a big door and vanished behind it. Anna paused and waited. 'He's only just woke up,' said the porter when he came out again.

Just as he spoke Anna heard the sounds of a child yawning; she recognized her son by the sound of the yawn and pictured him vividly before her.

'Let me in, let me in!' she cried, and entered at the big door. To the right of the door stood a bed on which sat the boy, his night-shirt unbuttoned, bending his little body backward, stretching himself and finishing his yawn. At the moment when his lips were closing they extended into a blissful sleepy smile, and with that smile he again fell slowly and sweetly backwards.

'Serezha!' she whispered, drawing nearer with inaudible steps.

During the time they had been parted and under the influence of that gush of love which she had felt for him of late she had always imagined him as a little fellow of four, the age when she had loved him best. Now he was not even as she had left him; he was still further removed from the four-year-old child; he had grown still more and had got thinner. What did it mean? How thin his face was! How short his hair! How long his arms! How changed since she had left him! But still it was he: the slope of the head was his, the lips were his, the soft neck and the broad shoulders.

'Serezha!' she repeated, just above the child's ear.

He raised himself again on his elbow, moved his tousled head from side to side as if seeking for something, and opened his eyes. Silently and questioningly he gazed for a few moments at his mother, who stood motionless before him; then suddenly smiling blissfully, he closed his heavy eyelids and fell once more, not backwards, but forwards into her arms.

'Serezha, my dear little boy!' she uttered, catching her breath and embracing his plump little body.

'Mama!' he muttered, wriggling about in her arms so as to touch them with different parts of his body.

Sleepily smiling with closed eyes, he moved his plump hands from the back of his bed to her shoulders, leaning against her and enveloping her in that sweet scent of sleepiness and warmth which only children possess, and began rubbing himself against her neck and shoulder.

'I knew!' he said, opening his eyes. 'To-day is my birthday. I knew you would come! I'll get up directly . . .'

While saying this he was again falling asleep.

Anna watched him with greedy eyes. She noticed how he had grown and changed during her absence. She recognized and yet did not quite recognize his bare legs, now so big, which he had freed from the blanket, and his cheeks, now grown thinner, and the short locks of hair at the back of his head, where she had so often kissed him. She touched it all, and could not speak: tears were choking her.

'What are you crying about, Mama?' he asked, now quite awake. 'Mama, what are you crying about?' he exclaimed in a fretful voice.

'I won't cry . . . I am crying for joy! It is so long since I saw you. I won't, I won't,' she said, swallowing her tears and turning away. 'But it's time for you to get dressed,' she said after a pause when she had recovered; and without releasing his hands she sat down by his bed on a chair on which his clothes were lying ready.

'How do you dress without me? How do you . . .' She tried to speak simply and cheerfully, but could not, and turned away again.

'I don't wash with cold water. Papa says I mustn't. You have not seen Vasily Lukich? He will come presently. And you are sitting on my clothes!'

And Serezha burst out laughing. She looked at him and smiled.

'Mama! Dearest, darling!' he shouted, again throwing himself upon her, and embracing her, as if he only now, having seen her smile, clearly realized what had happened.

'You don't want that,' he said, taking off her bonnet; and on seeing her without it, he began kissing her again as though he had only just seen her.

'Well, and what did you think about me? You did not think I was dead?'

'I never believed it!'

'You didn't believe it, my darling?'

'I knew! I knew!' he cried, repeating his favourite phrase, and seizing her hand, which was caressing his hair, he pressed her palm to his mouth, covering it with kisses.

Chapter XXX

Meanwhile Vasily Lukich, who had not at first understood who the lady was, having realized from what he heard that she was the mother who had left her husband and whom he, having come to the house only after she had left it, had never seen, hesitated whether to go in or not, or whether to tell Karenin. Having at last concluded that his duty was to get Serezha up at the appointed time, and that therefore he need not consider who was sitting there—the boy's mother or anyone else—but that he must do his duty, he dressed, went up to the door, and opened it.

But the caresses of the mother and son, the sound of their voices and what they were saying, made him change his mind.

He shook his head, sighed, and closed the door again. 'I will wait another ten minutes,' he said to himself, coughing and wiping away his tears.

Meanwhile among the servants there was great commotion. They all knew that the mistress had come, that Kapitonich had admitted her, and that she was now in the nursery. But the master always went to the nursery before nine, and they all understood that a meeting between him and his wife was inconceivable and must be prevented. Korney, the valet, went down into the hall-porter's room to inquire who had let her in, and hearing that it was Kapitonich who had done so, he reprimanded the old man. The hall-porter remained obstinately silent; but when the valet said he 'ought to get the sack,' Kapitonich rushed at Korney and, flourishing his hands about before Korney's face, began to speak out:

'Yes, I daresay you would not have let her in! I've been in service here ten years, and have had nothing but kindness: you had better go up and tell her, "You be off, please!" You're an artful one, you are! You'd better look after yourself and how to fleece the master of fur coats!'

'Soldier!' said Korney, contemptuously, and turned to the nurse who had just entered. 'Now, judge for yourself, Mary Efimovna,' he said to her. 'He's let her in without telling anybody; and Alexey Alexandrovich will be ready in a minute and will go to the nursery.'

'Dear! Dear! What a business!' said the nurse. 'You must detain him somehow, Korney Vasilich—the master, I mean! And I'll run and get her out of the way. What a business!'

When the nurse entered, Serezha was just telling his mother how he and Nadenka fell down together when ice-hilling, and turned three somersaults. She was listening to the sound of his voice, saw his face and the play of his features, felt his hands, but did not understand what he was saying. She must go away, must leave him— that was all she thought and felt. She heard Vasily Lukich's step as he came to the door and coughed, and then the steps of the nurse as she entered; but she sat as if turned to stone, powerless to speak or rise.

'Madam, dear!' the nurse began, coming up to Anna and kissing her hands and shoulders. 'What joy God has sent our little one on his birthday! And you have not changed at all.'

'Oh, nurse dear, I did not know you were in the house,' said Anna, rousing herself for a moment.

'I don't live here; I live with my daughter, and have only come to wish him many happy returns, Anna Arkadyevna, dear!'

Suddenly the nurse burst into tears and again began to kiss Anna's hand.

Serezha, with bright eyes and beaming smile, holding his mother with one hand and his nurse with the other, jumped with his plump bare feet on to the carpet. The tenderness of his beloved nurse for his mother sent him into raptures.

'Mama! She often comes to see me, and when she comes . . .' he began, but stopped, noticing that his nurse was whispering something in his mother's ear, and that a look of fear and of something like shame, that did not at all suit her face, appeared there.

She came up to him and said, 'My darling!'

She could not say good-bye, but the expression of her face said it and he understood. 'Darling, darling Kutik!' she said, calling him by the pet name she used when he was quite little, 'you won't forget me? You . . .' but she could say no more.

How many things she thought of later that she might have said! But now she did not know what to say and could not speak. But Serezha understood all she wanted to tell him. He understood that she was unhappy and that she loved him. He had even understood what the nurse had said in a whisper. He had caught the words 'always before nine o'clock,' and he understood that they referred to his father and that his mother and father must not meet. This he had grasped, but he could not make out why that look of fear and shame appeared on her face. . . . She could not have done wrong, and yet seemed afraid and ashamed of something. He wanted to ask a question which would clear up his doubts, but dared not; he saw that she suffered and he was sorry for her. He pressed against her in silence, and then whispered:

'Don't go—he is not coming yet!'

His mother moved him away from her, to see whether he really believed what he was saying; and in the frightened look on his face she saw not only that he was speaking about his father, but that he was, as it were, asking her what he ought to think of him.

"Serezha, my darling!' she said, 'love him! He is better and kinder than I am, and I am to blame toward him. When you are grown up you will be able to judge.'

'There is nobody better than you! . . .' he cried out in desperation through his tears, and seizing her by her shoulders he hugged her with all his might, his arms trembling with the effort.

'Darling little one!' said Anna, and began to cry in the same weak and childlike way as he.

At that moment the door opened and Vasily Lukich entered.

Steps were heard approaching the other door, and the nurse said in a frightened whisper, 'Coming! . . .' and handed Anna her bonnet.

Serezha sank down on his bed and began to sob, hiding his face in his hands. Anna moved the hands away, kissed him again on his wet face, and went rapidly out. Karenin was advancing toward her. When he saw her, he stopped and bowed his head.

Despite what she had just said,—that he was better and kinder than she was—after casting at him a rapid glance which took in his whole figure to the minutest detail, she was seized by a feeling of loathing and anger toward him and of jealousy for her son. She swiftly let down her veil and with quickened steps almost ran out of the room.

She had not had time even to unwrap the toys she had chosen with so much love and sadness the day before, and she took them back with her.

Chapter XXXI

Greatly as Anna had desired to see her son, and long as she had thought of and prepared herself for the interview, she had not at all expected that it would affect her so powerfully. On returning to her lonely suite in the hotel she could not for a long time understand why she was there. 'Yes, it is all ended and I am alone again,' she said to herself; and without taking off her bonnet she sat down in an easy-chair by the fireplace. With her eyes fixed on a bronze clock, standing on a table between the windows, she began pondering.

The French maid, whom she had brought from abroad, came and asked whether she would not dress. She looked at her in astonishment and replied, 'Later.' A waiter offered her coffee. 'Later,' she said.

The Italian nurse, having smartened up the baby girl, came in and held her out to Anna. The plump, well-nourished baby, as usual when she saw her mother, turned her little hands—so fat that they looked as if the wrists had threads tied tightly round them —palms downward and, smiling with her toothless mouth, began waving them as a fish moves its fins, making the starched folds of her embroidered frock rustle. It was impossible not to smile, not to kiss the little thing; impossible not to hold out a finger to her, which she caught, screaming and wriggling the whole surface of her little body; impossible not to approach one's lips to her mouth and let her draw them in, her way of kissing. And Anna did all these things. She took her in her arms, dandled her, and kissed her fresh cheek and bare elbows; but, at the sight of this child, she realized still more clearly that what she felt for her could not even be called love in comparison with her feeling for Serezha. Everything about this baby was sweet, but for some reason she did not grip the heart. Upon the first child, though by an unloved man, all Anna's unsatisfied capacity for loving was lavished; but the girl was born under most trying conditions and had not received a hundredth part of the care given to the first child. Besides, everything about the baby was still prospective, while Serezha was already an individual and a beloved one; thoughts and feelings were already struggling in his mind; he understood and loved and judged her, she thought, recalling his words and looks. And from him she was for ever sundered, not only physically but spiritually, and there was no remedy for it.

She returned the baby to its nurse, sent them away, and opened a locket with Serezha's portrait as a baby about the same age as the little girl. Rising, she removed her bonnet and took from the table an album in which were photographs of her son at different ages. She wanted to compare these likenesses and began drawing them out of the album. She took them all out but one, the last and best of the photographs. He was there in a white shirt, astride a chair, his brows frowning while his mouth smiled. This was his most characteristic and best expression. She caught hold of a corner of this photo several times with her deft little hand, the slender white fingers of which moved with special strenuousness that day, but each time they slipped and she could not get the picture out. There was no knife on the table, and she drew out the photo next to it (one, taken in Rome, of Vronsky with long hair and wearing a round hat), and with it pushed out her son's photo. 'Yes, there he is!' she said with a glance at Vronsky's likeness, and suddenly remembered that he was the cause of her present grief. She had not called him to mind all that morning; but now, having caught sight of that manly, noble face, so familiar and dear to her, she felt an unexpected flow of love toward him.

'But where is he? How can he leave me alone in my anguish?' she suddenly thought with a sense of reproach, forgetting that she herself had hidden from him all that concerned her son. She sent to ask him to come up to her at once. She awaited him, thinking with a sinking heart of the words in which she would tell him everything and of the expressions of his love which would comfort her. The servant returned with the reply that he had a visitor, but would come up at once, and wished to know whether he might bring with him Prince Yashvin, who had just arrived in Petersburg. 'So he won't come alone,' she thought, 'he won't come so that I can tell him everything, but will bring Yashvin. . . .' And suddenly a strange idea crossed her mind: what if he had ceased to love her? Going over in her mind the events of the last few days, she thought she perceived in everything a confirmation of that dreadful thought: in the fact that he had not dined at home the day before, and that he had insisted on having separate apartments while in Petersburg, and that even now he was not coming alone, perhaps to avoid a *tête-à-tête* with her.

'But he must tell me. I must know it! If I know it, then I know what I shall do,' she told herself, powerless to imagine the position she would find herself in when she was convinced of his indifference. She imagined that he had ceased to love her, and she was almost in despair: which roused in her a feeling of peculiar excitement. She rang for her maid, and going into the dressing-room paid more attention to her toilet than she had done all these days, as if, having ceased to love her, his love might be recalled by her wearing the dress and having her hair done in the style most becoming to her.

She heard the bell before she was ready. When she entered the drawing-room not his eyes but Yashvin's met hers. Vronsky was examining her son's photos, which she had forgotten on the table, and did not hurry to look at her.

'We are acquainted,' she said, placing her little hand in the enormous hand of the embarrassed Yashvin, whose confusion did not seem to accord with his huge figure and rough face. 'We have been acquainted since last year's races. . . . Let me have them,' she added, with a rapid movement taking from Vronsky the photos he was looking at, and glancing at him impressively with glistening eyes. 'Were the races good this year? I saw the races on the Corso in Rome instead! But of course you don't care for life abroad,' she went on with a pleasant smile. 'I know you and know all your tastes, though we have met so seldom.'

'I am very sorry to hear it, for my tastes are mostly bad,' said Yashvin, biting the left side of his moustache.

After a short talk, noticing that Vronsky looked at the clock, Yashvin asked her whether she would be staying long in Petersburg, and straightening his immense body picked up his cap.

'Not long, I think,' she replied with embarrassment, glancing at Vronsky.

'Then we shall not meet again?' said Yashvin, rising; and then turning to Vronsky he asked, 'Where are you dining?'

'Come and dine with me,' said Anna resolutely, as if vexed with herself for her embarrassment, yet blushing as she always did when she revealed her position to a fresh person. 'The dinners here are not good, but at any rate you will see one another. Of all his regimental friends Alexey liked you best.'

'I shall be very pleased,' said Yashvin, with a smile which showed Vronsky that he liked Anna very much.

Yashvin bowed and went out. Vronsky remained behind.

'You are going too?' she asked.

'I am late as it is,' he answered. 'Go on! I shall catch you up in a minute!' he shouted to Yashvin.

She took his hand and looked fixedly at him, trying to think of something to say to prevent his leaving her.

'Wait—I have something to tell you,' she said, and raising his short hand she pressed it to her neck. 'Was it wrong of me to ask him to dinner?'

'You have done very well,' he replied, showing his compact row of teeth in a calm smile, and kissing her hand.

'Alexey, you have not changed toward me?' she asked, squeezing his hand in both hers. 'Alexey, I am in torment here! When are we going?'

'Soon, very soon! You would hardly believe how trying our life here is to me too,' he said, drawing away his hand.

'Well, then go! Go!' she said in an offended tone, and quickly left him.

Chapter XXXII

When Vronsky returned Anna had not yet come home. He was told that, soon after he left, a lady came to see her and they went away together. Her departure without mentioning where she was going, her prolonged absence, and the fact that she had been away somewhere in the morning without telling him about it, added to her strangely excited look that morning, and the animosity with which in Yashvin's presence she had almost snatched her son's photographs out of his hands, made Vronsky reflect. He decided that it was necessary to have an explanation with her, and he waited for her in the drawing-room. But Anna did not return alone; she brought with her her old maiden aunt, Princess Oblonskaya. She it was who had been to see Anna that morning, and they had been shopping together. Anna seemed not to notice the worried look of inquiry on Vronsky's face, but chattered gaily about what she had been buying. He saw that something unusual was taking place within her: her eyes glittered with an expression of strained attention when her look rested on him, and in her speech and motions there was that nervous quickness and grace which, during the first period of their intimacy, had so captivated him, but which now troubled and alarmed him.

The table was laid for four. They were all assembled and about to enter the little dining-room, when Tushkevich arrived with a message for Anna from the Princess Betsy. The Princess asked to be excused for not coming to say good-bye; she was not well, but asked Anna to come and see her between half-past six and nine. Vronsky glanced at Anna when that definite time was mentioned, which showed that care had been taken to prevent her meeting anyone there; but Anna did not seem to observe it.

'I'm sorry that between half-past six and nine is just the time when I cannot come,' she replied with a faint smile.

'The Princess will be very sorry.'

'And I too.'

'I expect you are going to hear Patti?' asked Tushkevich.

'Patti? That's an idea! I would go if I could get a box.'

'I could get you one,' said Tushkevich.

'I should be very, very grateful if you would!' replied Anna. 'But won't you stay and dine with us?'

Vronsky slightly shrugged his shoulders. He could not in the least understand what Anna was after. Why had she brought the old Princess, why had she asked Tushkevich to stay to dinner, and, strangest of all, why was she sending him to get her a box for the opera? Was it conceivable that, in her position, she was going to the opera when Patti was to sing, and when all the subscribers, her Society acquaintances, would be present? He looked seriously at her, but she answered him with the same provocative glance of high spirits or desperation, the meaning of which he could not make out. At dinner Anna was aggressively merry, seeming to flirt with both Tushkevich and Yashvin. After dinner Tushkevich went to get a box and Yashvin to have a smoke. Vronsky went with Yashvin down to his own rooms, but after sitting with him a while, ran upstairs again. Anna was already dressed in a light silk dress cut low in front and trimmed with velvet—a dress she had had made in Paris; and on her head she wore some rich, white lace, which outlined her face and set off her brilliant beauty to great advantage.

'You are really going to the theatre?' said he, trying not to look at her.

'Why do you ask in such a frightened way?' she said, again offended because he did not look at her. 'Why should I not go?'

She appeared not to grasp the meaning of her words.

'Of course there is no reason whatever,' he replied with a frown.

'That's just what I say,' she answered, purposely ignoring the sarcasm of his tone and calmly pulling up her long perfumed glove.

'Anna! For heaven's sake, what has come to you?' he said, trying to recall her to her senses, as her husband once used to do.

'I don't understand your question.'

'You know it is out of the question for you to go.'

'Why? I am not going alone! The Princess Barbara has gone to dress, and is coming with me.'

He shrugged his shoulders with a bewildered and despairing look.

'But don't you know . . .?' he began.

'I don't want to know!' she almost screamed. 'I don't! Do I repent of what I have done? No! No! No! If it had to begin again from the beginning I should do just the same. For us, for you and me, only one thing is important: whether we love each other. No other considerations exist. Why do we live here, separated and not seeing one another? Why can't I go? I love you, and it's all the same to me,' she said, changing from French into Russian, while her eyes as she looked at him glittered with a light he could not understand, 'so long as you have not changed toward me! Why don't you look at me?'

He looked at her. He saw all the beauty of her face and of her dress, which suited her as her dresses always did. But now it was just this beauty and elegance that irritated him.

'My feelings cannot change, you know that; but I beg you not to go! I entreat you!' he said, again speaking French with tender entreaty in his voice but with a cold look in his eyes.

She did not hear his words, but saw the coldness of his look, and replied irritably:

'And I beg you will explain why I should not go.'

'Because it might cause you . . .' He became confused.

'I don't understand you at all! Yashvin *n'est pas compromet-tant*,[2] and Princess Barbara is no worse than other people. Ah, here she is!'

Chapter XXXIII

Vronsky for the first time felt vexed and almost angry with Anna for her unwillingness to realize her position. This feeling was strengthened by the fact that he could not tell her the reason of his vexation. Had he told her frankly what he thought he could have said:

'To appear dressed as you are at the theatre, accompanied by the Princess, whom everybody knows, means not only to acknowledge your position as a fallen woman, but to throw down a challenge to Society—which means, to renounce it for ever.'

But he could not say this to her. 'But how can she fail to understand it? And what is happening to her?' he asked himself. He felt that his regard for her had diminished and his consciousness of her beauty increased simultaneously.

He went down frowning to his rooms, and taking a seat beside Yashvin, who sat with his long legs stretched out on a chair drinking brandy and seltzer, ordered the same for himself.

'You were talking about Lankovsky's Powerful. He is a good horse, and I advise you to buy him,' said Yashvin, glancing at his comrade's gloomy countenance. 'It's true he has a goose rump, but his legs and head leave nothing to be desired.'

'I think I'll take him,' replied Vronsky.

This conversation about horses interested him, but he never forgot Anna, and involuntarily listened to the steps in the corridor and glanced at the clock on the mantelpiece.

'Anna Arkadyevna sent me to say that she has gone to the theatre,' said a servant.

Yashvin emptied another glass of brandy into the sparkling water, drank it, and then rose, buttoning his coat.

'Well, let us go,' he said, smiling slightly under cover of his big moustache, and showing by that smile that he understood the cause of Vronsky's depression, but did not attach importance to it.

'I'm not going,' said Vronsky dismally.

'Well, I have got to, I promised. Then *au revoir!* But why not come to the stalls? Take Krasinsky's place,' Yashvin added as he went out.

'No, I have something to do.'

'With a wife one has trouble, but with one who is not a wife it's worse,' thought Yashvin as he left the hotel.

Left alone, Vronsky got up and began pacing the room.

2. Yashvin's company is not compromising.

'What is on to-day? The fourth *abonnement.* . . . Alexander will be there with his wife, and probably Mother also. That's to say, all Petersburg will be there. . . . Now she has gone in, taken off her cloak and come forward into the light. Tushkevich, Yashvin, the Princess Barbara . . .' he pictured them to himself. 'And what of me? Am I afraid, or have I put her under Tushkevich's protection? Whichever way one looks at it, it's a stupid position. . . . Why does she put me in such a position?' he said with a wave of his arm.

As he made this gesture he struck the little table on which the seltzer and a decanter of brandy were standing and almost knocked it over. In trying to save it from falling he overturned it, and in his vexation kicked it and rang the bell.

'If you wish to remain in my service,' he said to the valet when the latter came in, 'remember your duties. There must be none of this sort of thing. You must clear it away.'

The valet, conscious that he was not to blame, but, glancing at his master, saw by his face that there was nothing for it but to keep silence; so, stooping quickly, he knelt on the carpet and began sorting out the whole and broken glasses and bottles.

'That's not your business! Send a waiter to clear it up, and get out my dress suit!'

Vronsky entered the theatre at half-past eight. The performance was in full swing. The attendant, an old man, helped him off with his overcoat, recognized him, and, addressing him as 'Your Excellency,' suggested that he need not take a ticket for his coat, but should merely call for 'Theodore' when he wanted it. There was nobody in the brightly illuminated corridor except the attendant and two footmen, who, with their masters' coats over their arms, stood listening outside a door. Through a door slightly ajar came the sounds of a muffled staccato accompaniment by the orchestra and of a female voice rendering a musical phrase with precision. The door was closed immediately and he did not hear the end of the phrase nor the trill after it, but knew from the thunder of applause behind the door that the trill was finished. When he entered the auditorium, brilliantly illuminated by chandeliers and bronze gas brackets, the noise still continued. On the stage the singer, in a glitter of bare shoulders and diamonds, was bowing low and smiling as she picked up with the help of the tenor—who held her hand—bouquets that had been clumsily flung across the footlights; she went up to a gentleman, with hair shiny with pomatum and parted in the middle, who was stretching his long arms across the footlights to hand her something—and the whole audience in the stalls and in the boxes stirred, leaned forward, shouted and applauded. The conductor from his raised seat helped to pass the bouquets, and rearranged his white tie. Vronsky went to the middle of the floor, then stopped and looked around him. To-day he paid less attention than ever to the familiar surroundings: the stage, the noise, and all that well-known, uninteresting, motley herd of audience in the packed theatre.

In the boxes sat the same kind of ladies with the same kind of officers behind them as usual; the same kind of people, heaven only knew who; the same gaily-dressed women, uniforms, frock coats; the same dirty crowd in the gallery; and in the whole of that throng, in the boxes and front seats, some forty *real* men and women. To these oases Vronsky at once turned his attention and immediately got into touch with them.

The act had just finished when he came in, so before going to his brother's box he went up to the front row and paused beside Serpukhovskoy, who was standing with his knee bent, tapping the wall of the orchestra with his heel. He had noticed Vronsky afar off and welcomed him with a smile.

Vronsky had not yet seen Anna, he intentionally avoided looking her way; but from the direction in which people were looking he knew where she was. He glanced around unobtrusively, but did not look at her: prepared for the worst, he looked for Karenin. Luckily for him, Karenin was not in the theatre that evening.

'How little of the military man is left in you!' remarked Serpukhovskoy. 'You might be a diplomatist, an artist, or anything of that kind.'

'Yes, as soon as I returned home I put on a black coat,' Vronsky replied with a smile, slowly taking out his opera-glasses.

'Now in that, I confess, I envy you! I, when I come back from abroad and put this on again, regret my freedom,' he said, touching his shoulder-knot.

Serpukhovskoy had long ago ceased to trouble himself about Vronsky's career, but was as fond of him as ever and was particularly amiable to him now.

'A pity you were late for the first act!'

Vronsky, listening with one ear, levelled his glasses first at the lower tier and then at the boxes in the dress circle, taking them all in review. Next to a lady wearing a turban, and a bald old man who blinked angrily just as Vronsky's moving glass reached him, he suddenly saw Anna's proud head, strikingly beautiful, and smiling in its frame of lace. She was in the fifth box in the lower tier, some twenty paces from him. She sat in the front of the box and, slightly turning back, was saying something to Yashvin. The poise of her head on her fine broad shoulders, and the gleam of restrained excitement in her eyes and her whole face, reminded him precisely of how he had seen her at the ball in Moscow. But her beauty affected him very differently now. There was no longer anything mysterious in his feelings for her, and therefore though her beauty attracted him even more strongly, it also offended him. She was not looking his way, but he felt that she had already seen him.

When Vronsky directed his glasses that way again he noticed that the Princess Barbara was very red, and that she was laughing unnaturally and looking round incessantly at the next box, while Anna, tapping with her closed fan the red-velvet edge of the box, was gazing fixedly somewhere else, not seeing, and evidently not wishing to see, what was taking place in the next box. Yashvin's face wore the expression it had when he was losing at cards. He was frowning and drawing the left side of his moustache further and further into his mouth, looking askance at the adjoining box.

In that box to the left were the Kartasovs. Vronsky knew them and knew that Anna had been acquainted with them. The wife, a thin little woman, was standing up in her box with her back to Anna, putting on an opera-cloak which her husband was holding for her. Her face looked pale and angry and she was speaking excitedly. Kartasov, a stout bald-headed man, kept glancing round at Anna while trying to pacify his wife. When the wife left the box the husband loitered behind, trying to catch Anna's eye and evidently wishing to bow to her. But Anna, with obvious intention, took no notice of him and, turning round, was saying something to Yashvin, whose cropped head was bent toward her. Kartasov went out without bowing and the box remained empty.

Vronsky could not make out what had taken place between the Kartasovs and Anna, but he saw that it was something humiliating for Anna. He realized that from what he had seen, and especially from Anna's face, who, he knew, was summoning her utmost strength to sustain the rôle she had undertaken. She fully succeeded in playing that rôle—of external tranquillity. Those who did not know her and her set, and heard none of the expressions of pity, indignation, or surprise uttered by the women because she had allowed herself to appear in public and to show herself so ostentatiously in her lace headdress and in all her beauty, admired the composure and loveliness of the woman, and did not suspect that she felt as though pilloried.

Knowing that something had happened, but not knowing just what, Vronsky felt painfully agitated, and, hoping to find out something, set out for his brother's box. Intentionally leaving the auditorium at the opposite side to where Anna was, he encountered the Commander of his old regiment, who stood talking to two acquaintances. Vronsky heard them mention the name of Karenin, and noticed how the Commander hastened to call him loudly by name, with a significant glance at the others.

'Ah, Vronsky! When are you coming to see us at the regiment? We can't let you go away without a feast. You are one of our very own!' said the Commander.

'I shall not have time . . . I'm very sorry! Some other time,' said Vronsky, and ran up the stairs to his brother's box.

In the box was Vronsky's mother, the old Countess, with her iron-grey curls. Varya and the Princess Sorokina he met in the corridor outside.

Having conducted the Princess Sorokina back to Vronsky's mother, Varya held out her hand to her brother-in-law and at once began to talk of the matter that interested him. He had rarely seen her so excited.

'I consider it mean and disgusting, and Madame Kartasova had no right to do it! Madame Karenina . . .' she began.

'But what is it? I don't know.'

'Haven't you heard?'

'You know I shall be the last to hear of it!'

'Is there a creature more venomous than that Kartasova?'

'But what has she done?'

'My husband told me. . . . She insulted Madame Karenina. Her husband began conversing with her from his box, and Kartasova flew at him! It seems she said something insulting out loud, and then went out.'

'Count, your *maman* wants you,' said the Princess Sorokina, looking out of the box door.

'I have been expecting you all the time,' said his mother with a sarcastic smile. 'I never see anything of you.'

Her son saw that she could not repress a smile of satisfaction.

'Good evening, *maman*! I was coming to you,' he replied coldly.

'Why don't you go *faire la cour à* [3] *Madame Karenine?*' she added, when the Princess Sorokina had stepped aside. '*Elle fait sensation. On oublie la Patti pour elle!* [4]

'*Maman*! I asked you not to speak to me about that subject,' he answered frowning.

'I am saying what every one says.'

Vronsky did not reply, and after a few words addressed to the Princess Sorokina he left the box. In the doorway he met his brother.

'Ah, Alexey!' said his brother. 'What a shame! That woman is a fool, that's all. . . . I was just going to see her! Let's go together.'

Vronsky did not listen to him. He hurried downstairs feeling that

---

3. To court.
4. She is making a sensation. They are forgetting Patti because of her.

he must do something, he knew not what. He was disturbed both by vexation with Anna for placing herself and him in this false position, and by pity for her sufferings. He descended to the stalls and went straight to Anna's box, in front of which stood Stremov talking to her.

'There are no more tenors. *Le moule en est brisé!* [5]

Vronsky bowed to her and stopped to shake hands with Stremov.

'I think you got here late and missed the finest *aria*,' said Anna to him, with a mocking glance as it seemed to him.

'I am a poor judge,' he replied, looking severely at her.

'Like Prince Yashvin, who considers that Patti sings too loud,' she returned with a smile.

'Thank you!' she said, taking with her small gloved hand a programme Vronsky had picked up for her; and suddenly at that instant her beautiful face quivered. She rose and went to the back of the box.

Noticing that during the next act her box remained empty, Vronsky left the theatre amid cries of 'hush' from the audience, which had become quiet to listen to the *cavatina*. He went to his hotel.

Anna had already returned. When Vronsky entered she was still dressed as she had been at the theatre. She was sitting in the first arm-chair by the wall, fixedly gazing before her. She glanced at him and immediately resumed her former posture.

'Anna!' he said.

'It's all your fault! Your fault!' she exclaimed with tears of despair and spite in her voice, and rose.

'But I asked, I entreated you not to go!—I knew it would be unpleasant for you!'

'Unpleasant!' she cried. 'It was awful! However long I may live I shall never forget it! She said it was a disgrace to sit near me.'

'The words of a stupid woman,' he said. 'But why risk it? Why provoke . . .'

'I hate your calmness! You should not have driven me to it. If you loved me . . .'

'Anna! Is it a question of my love? . . .'

'Yes! If you loved me as I love you, if you suffered the anguish I do . . .' she replied with a frightened glance at him.

He was sorry for her and yet vexed with her. He assured her of his love, because he saw that that alone could pacify her now, and did not reproach her with words, though he reproached her in his heart.

And those assurances of love, which to him appeared so trivial that he felt ashamed to utter them, she drank in, and gradually became calm. Next day, fully reconciled, they left for the country.

5. The mould for them is smashed.

Part VI

Chapter I

Dolly and her children were spending the summer with her sister Kitty at Pokrovsk. The house on her own estate was quite dilapidated, so Levin and his wife persuaded her to spend the summer with them. Oblonsky quite approved of this arrangement. He said he greatly regretted that his duties prevented his spending the summer with his family in the country, which would have given him the greatest pleasure; and he remained in Moscow, visiting the country occasionally for a day or two at a time. Besides the Oblonskys with all their children and their governess, the Levins had other visitors—the old Princess, who considered it her duty to watch over her inexperienced daughter *in that condition*; and also Varenka, Kitty's friend from abroad, who was keeping her promise to visit her friend now that she was married. All these were relations and friends of Kitty's, and, though Levin liked them, he regretted his own—the Levin—world and order of things, which was being submerged by this influx of 'the Shcherbatsky element,' as he put it to himself. Only one of his relatives, Sergius Ivanich, visited him that summer—and he was a man of the Koznyshev type and not a Levin, so that the Levin spirit was quite overwhelmed.

In the Levin house, so long empty, there were now so many people that nearly every room was occupied, and the old Princess was obliged almost daily to count those present before sitting down to a meal. If there chanced to be thirteen, she would make a grandchild sit at the side-table. And Kitty, who conducted her household with great assiduity, had no little trouble to procure all the chickens, turkeys, and ducks, of which, with the visitors' and the children's summer appetites, very many were required.

The whole family was assembled at dinner. Dolly's children, their governess, and Varenka were planning where they should hunt for mushrooms; Koznyshev, who by his intellect and learning commanded a respect almost amounting to veneration from all the visitors, surprised every one by joining in the conversation about mushrooms.

'You must take me too! I am very fond of looking for mushrooms,' he said with a glance at Varenka. 'I consider it a very good occupation.'

'Why, certainly! We shall be very pleased,' replied Varenka with a blush. Kitty and Dolly exchanged significant looks. The intellectual and learned Koznyshev's offer to go and gather mushrooms with Varenka confirmed a suspicion that had greatly occupied Kitty's mind of late. She hastened to say something to her mother so that her glance should pass unnoticed.

After dinner Koznyshev sat down by the drawing-room window, continuing his conversation with his brother over a cup of coffee and glancing now and then at the door through which the children, who were preparing to set out on the mushroom hunt, would enter. Levin sat down on the window-sill beside his brother.

Kitty stood near her husband, evidently waiting for the end of the conversation—which did not interest her—before speaking to him.

'In many ways you have changed since your marriage, and for the better,' said Koznyshev, smiling at Kitty and apparently not much interested in his conversation with his brother; 'but you have remained true to your passion for defending the most paradoxical views.'

'Kate, it is not good for you to be standing,' said her husband, with a meaning look, moving a chair toward her.

'Ah, well! there's no time now,' added Koznyshev as the children came running in.

In advance of them all, at a sideways gallop, came Tanya in tightly pulled-up stockings, running toward Koznyshev, flourishing a basket and his hat. Having boldly approached him, her beautiful eyes beaming (eyes so like her father's), she gave him his hat and made a movement as if to put it on him, her shy and gentle smile softening the boldness of the action.

'Varenka is waiting,' she said, carefully placing his hat on his head when she saw from his smile that she had permission to do so.

Varenka, who was wearing a yellow print dress and a white kerchief on her head, stood in the doorway.

'I'm coming, Mlle Varenka,' said Koznyshev, drinking up his coffee and pocketing his handkerchief and cigar-case.

'What a darling my Varenka is, isn't she?' Kitty said to her husband as soon as Koznyshev had risen. She said it so that the latter could hear, with an evident desire that he should do so. 'And how handsome, how nobly handsome! . . . Varenka!' she exclaimed. 'You will be in the wood by the mill? We will drive there.'

'You quite forget your condition, Kitty,' said the old Princess, hurrying in. 'You should not shout so.'

Varenka, hearing Kitty's voice and her mother reprimanding her, came up with her light step. The quickness of Varenka's movements, the colour suffusing her animated face, all showed that something unusual was taking place within her. Kitty knew what that unusual thing was, and watched her attentively. She had now called Varenka only to give her a silent blessing for the important event which, according to Kitty, was to happen in the woods that day after dinner.

'Varenka, I shall be very happy if a certain thing comes to pass,' she whispered, kissing her.

'And are you coming with us?' Varenka, quite confused, asked Levin, pretending not to have heard what had been said to her.

'I will come, but only as far as the threshing-floor. I shall stay there.'

'Oh, why should you?' said Kitty.

'I must look at the new waggons, and count them,' said Levin. 'And where will you be?'

'On the balcony.'

Chapter II

All the women of the household were assembled on the balcony. They always liked to sit there after dinner, but to-day they had special business there. Besides the sewing of little shirts and the knitting of swaddling bands, on which they were all engaged, to-day jam was being made there in a way new to Agatha Mikhaylovna: without the addition of water to the fruit. Kitty was introducing this new way, which had been employed in her old home; but Agatha Mikhaylovna, to whom this work had formerly been entrusted, and who considered that nothing that used to be done in the Levin house could be wrong, had, despite her directions, put water to the strawberry and the wild strawberry jam, declaring it to be indispensable. She had been detected doing this, and now the raspberry jam was being made in every one's presence, as Agatha Mikhaylovna had to be convinced that without water the jam could turn out well.

Agatha Mikhaylovna, with a flushed face and aggrieved expression, her hair ruffled and her thin arms bared to the elbow, was shaking the preserving pan over the brazier with a circular movement, looking dismally at the raspberries and hoping with all her heart that they would harden and not get cooked through. The old Princess, conscious that against her, as chief adviser in the matter of jam boiling, Agatha Mikhaylovna's wrath should be directed, tried to look as if she were thinking of other things and was not interested in the raspberries. She talked of other matters, but watched the brazier out of the corner of her eye.

'I always buy dress materials for the maids myself, at the sales,' the Princess said, continuing the conversation. 'Is it not time to take the scum off, my dear?' she added, turning to Agatha Mikhaylovna. 'It is not at all necessary for you to do it yourself, besides it's hot,' she said, stopping Kitty.

'I will do it,' said Dolly, and she got up and began carefully sliding the spoon over the surface of the bubbling syrup, and now and then, to remove what had stuck to the spoon, she tapped it against a plate already covered with the yellowish pink scum, with blood-red streaks of syrup showing beneath it. 'How they'll lick it up at tea-time!' she thought of the children, remembering how she herself, when a child, used to marvel that the grown-ups did not eat the scum—the nicest part.

'Stiva says it's better to give them money,' Dolly remarked, returning to the interesting topic of what presents it was best to give to servants, 'but . . .'

'How can one give them money!' said the Princess and Kitty with one voice. 'They value presents so!'

'Well, I for instance got our Matrena Semenovna not exactly poplin, but something of that kind, last year,' said the Princess.

'Yes, I remember she wore it on your Name day.'

'The pattern is charming—so simple and refined. I would have had one made like it myself if she hadn't had it. It is something like Varenka's, and so pretty and cheap.'

'Well, I think it is ready now,' said Dolly, dripping syrup from the spoon. 'When it begins to string, it is ready. Boil it up a little longer, Agatha Mikhaylovna.'

'Oh, these flies!' cried Agatha Mikhaylovna crossly. 'It will come out just the same.'

'Oh, how sweet he is—don't frighten him!' exclaimed Kitty unexpectedly, looking at a sparrow that had settled on the railing, turned a raspberry stalk over, and was pecking at it.

'Yes, but keep away from the brazier,' said her mother.

'A propos de Varenka,' said Kitty in French, which they had been talking all the time so that Agatha Mikhaylovna should not understand them. 'Do you know, Mama, I am somehow expecting it to be settled to-day! You understand what I mean. How nice it would be!'

'Dear me! What a skilful matchmaker!' teased Dolly. 'How carefully and adroitly she brings them together!'

'Come, Mama! Tell me what you think about it?'

'What am I to think? He,' he meant Koznyshev, 'could have made the best match in Russia any time; now he is no longer so young, but all the same I am sure many would marry him even now. . . . She is very good-natured, but he might . . .'

'Oh, but, Mama, try and understand why nothing better could be imagined either for him or for her. First of all, she is simply charming!' expostulated Kitty, crooking one finger.

'He certainly likes her very much,' Dolly chimed in.

'Secondly, his position in the world is such that neither property nor the social position of his wife matters to him at all. He only needs a good, sweet, quiet wife.'

'Yes, one certainly can trust her,' again chimed in Dolly.

'Thirdly, she must love him; and that too is . . . In a word, it would be splendid! I expect when they come back from the wood it will all be settled. I shall see it at once by their eyes. I should be so glad! What do you think, Dolly?'

'But don't get excited; there is no need at all for you to get excited,' admonished her mother.

'But I am not excited, Mama! I think he will propose to-day.'

'Ah, how strange it is when and how a man proposes. . . . There is a sort of barrier, and suddenly down it goes,' said Dolly with a dreamy smile, recalling her past with Oblonsky.

'Mama, how did Papa propose to you?' Kitty suddenly inquired.

'There was nothing special about it—it was quite simple,' answered the Princess, but her face brightened at the memory.

'No, but how . . . ? You really loved him before you were allowed to talk to one another?'

Kitty felt a particular charm in being able now to talk with her mother as an equal about those chief events in a woman's life.

'Of course he loved me; he used to visit us in the country.'

'But how was it decided, Mama?'

'I suppose you think you discovered something new? It was just the same—it was decided by the eyes, by smiles . . .'

'How well you put it, Mama! By the eyes and by smiles, that's just it!' chimed in Dolly.

'But what were the words he said?'

'What words did Constantine say to you?'

'He wrote with chalk. It was wonderful. . . . How long ago it seems!' she replied.

And the three women meditated silently on the same subject. Kitty was the first to break the silence. She recalled the whole of the winter preceding her marriage, and her infatuation with Vronsky.

'There's one thing . . . that old love-affair of Varenka's,' she said, following the natural sequence of her thoughts. 'I wished to tell Koznyshev somehow, to prepare him. Men, all of them, are terribly jealous of our pasts.'

'Not all,' said Dolly. 'You judge by your own husband. He is still tormented by the memory of Vronsky, isn't he? Am I not right?'

'You are,' answered Kitty, her eyes smiling dreamily.

'But I do not know,' interposed the Princess, defending her maternal watchfulness over her daughter, 'what there is in your past to trouble him! That Vronsky courted you? Such things happen to every girl.'

'Oh, but we are not talking about that,' said Kitty, blushing.

'No, excuse me!' her mother continued. 'And then you yourself would not let me talk it over with Vronsky. Don't you remember?'

'Oh Mama!' said Kitty, looking pained.

'Nowadays one can't hold you girls in. . . . Your relations with him could not have gone beyond what was proper, else I should have spoken to him myself! However, my love, it won't do for you to get agitated. Please remember that and keep calm.'

'I am quite calm, Mama.'

'How happily it turned out for Kitty that Anna came,' said Dolly, 'and how unhappily for her! The exact reverse,' she added, struck by her thought. 'Then Anna was so happy and Kitty considered herself miserable. Now it's the exact reverse! I often think of her.'

'She's not worth thinking about! A horrid, disgusting woman without a heart,' said their mother, unable to forget that Kitty had not married Vronsky but Levin.

'What is the use of talking about that?' expostulated Kitty with vexation. 'I don't think about it, and don't want to,' she said, listening to her husband coming up the balcony steps. 'I don't want to think about it.'

'About what don't you want to think?' he asked as he came up.

No one answered and he did not repeat the question.

'I am sorry I have intruded into your women's domain,' he said, glancing round at them all with a dissatisfied air, and realizing that they had been talking of something they would not have talked of in his presence.

For an instant he felt that he shared Agatha Mikhaylovna's dissatisfaction that the jam was boiled without water, and with the alien Shcherbatsky influence in general. He smiled, however, and went up to Kitty.

'Well?' he asked, looking at her with the expression with which every one addressed her nowadays.

'Quite all right,' replied Kitty with a smile. 'And your affairs?'

'The waggons'll hold three times as much as peasant carts. Shall we go and fetch the children? I have ordered the trap.'

'What? Are you going to take Kitty in the trap?' said her mother reproachfully.

'Only at a walking pace, Princess.'

Levin never called the Princess *Maman*, as sons-in-law usually do, and this displeased the Princess. But though he liked and respected her very much, Levin could not address her so without violating his feeling for his dead mother.

'Come with us, Mama,' said Kitty.

'I don't wish to see such unreasonable doings.'

'Well, then I'll go on foot! Walking is good for me,' and Kitty rose, went to her husband and took his arm.

'It's good for you in moderation,' said the Princess.

'Well, Agatha Mikhaylovna, is the jam done?' asked Levin, smiling at her and wishing to cheer her up. 'Has it turned out well the new way?'

'I suppose so. We'd have thought it overdone.'

'It's better so, Agatha Mikhaylovna: it won't ferment, and we have no ice left in the cellar and nowhere to keep it cool,' said Kitty, immediately seeing her husband's intention and addressing the old woman in the same spirit. 'On the other hand, your pickling is such that Mama says she never tasted anything like it!' she added, smiling and putting the old woman's kerchief straight.

Agatha Mikhaylovna looked crossly at Kitty.

'You need not comfort me, ma'am! I just look at you and *him*, and then I feel happy,' she said, and that disrespectful way of speaking of her master as *him* seemed touching to Kitty.

'Come with us and get mushrooms! You will show us the right places.'

Agatha Mikhaylovna smiled and shook her head, as much as to say: 'Though I should like to be cross with you, I can't do it.'

'Please follow my advice,' said the old Princess, 'cover the jam with paper soaked in rum, and then it will not get mouldy, even without ice.'

Chapter III

Kitty was particularly glad of the opportunity of being alone with her husband, for she had noticed the shadow of pain that flitted over his face, which so vividly reflected all his emotions, when he came on the balcony, asked what they were talking about and received no reply.

When they started on their walk in advance of the others and had passed out of sight of the house on to the hard, dusty road, strewn with rye-ears and grain, she leaned more heavily on his arm and pressed it. He had already forgotten that momentarily unpleasant impression, and being alone with her experienced, now that the thought of her pregnancy never left him, a feeling still novel and joyful to him of pleasure, entirely free from sensuality, at the nearness of a beloved woman. They had nothing to say to one another, but he wanted to hear the sound of her voice, which like her look had been changed by pregnancy. In her voice as in her look there was now a certain softness and seriousness, as of a person continually intent on one beloved task.

'You're sure you won't be tired? Lean more on me,' he said.

'No. I am so glad of a chance to be alone with you; and I own that, nice as it is to have them all, I regret our winter evenings alone together.'

'They were pleasant, but this is still better. . . . Both are better,' he said, pressing her hand.

'Do you know what we were talking about when you came in?'

'About the jam?'

'Yes, about jam, and then . . . about how people propose.'

'Ah!' said Levin, listening more to the sound of her voice than to her words, thinking all the while about the road, which now led through the wood, and avoiding places where she might take a false step.

'And about Sergius and Varenka. Did you notice? . . . I want it so much,' she went on. 'What do you think about it?' and she looked into his face.

'I don't know what to think,' Levin replied with a smile. 'Sergius seems very strange to me in that regard. I told you . . .'

'Yes—that he was in love with that girl who died. . . .'

'It happened when I was still a child; I only knew of it from what I was told. I remember him at that time. He was wonderfully charming. But since then I have observed him with women: he is amiable, and some of them please him, but I feel that for him they are simply human beings, not women.'

'Yes, but now with Varenka? . . . There seems to be something . . .'

'Perhaps there is. . . . But one must know him. He is a peculiar, a wonderful man. He lives only a spiritual life. He is a man of too pure and lofty a nature.'

'What! Would that lower him?'

'No, but he is so used to living a purely spiritual life that he cannot reconcile himself to realities, and, after all, Varenka is a reality!'

Levin had by this time become accustomed to express his thoughts boldly, without troubling to put them into precise phraseology; he knew that at such loving moments as the present his wife would understand what he meant from a mere hint, and she did understand him.

'Yes, but in her there is not so much of that reality as there is in me; I know he would never have loved me. She is all spirit.'

'Oh no! He is very fond of you, and it is always such a pleasure to me when my people are fond of you.'

'Yes, he is kind to me, but . . .'

'But it's not like poor Nicholas. . . . You would have loved one another,' said Levin, finishing her sentence for her. 'Why not speak of him?' he added. 'Sometimes I blame myself for not doing so; it will end by my forgetting him. Oh, what a dreadful, what a charming man he was! . . . Yes, what were we talking about?' he concluded after a pause.

'You think he can't fall in love, then?' said Kitty, putting his thoughts into her own words.

'Not exactly that he can't fall in love,' Levin answered with a smile, 'but he has none of that weakness which is necessary . . . I always envied him, and even now, when I am so happy, I still envy him.'

'You envy him because he can't fall in love?'

'I envy him because he is better than I am,' replied he, smiling. 'He does not live for himself. His whole life is subordinated to duty. And so he can be calm and contented.'

'And you?' said Kitty with a mocking smile of loving amusement.

She could not have expressed the sequence of thoughts that made her smile; but the last deduction was that her husband, in extolling his brother and depreciating himself, was not quite sincere. But she knew that this insincerity was the outcome of his affection for his brother, of a sense of shame at his own excessive happiness, and especially of that desire to improve which never left him; she loved this in him, and therefore smiled.

'And you? What are you dissatisfied with?' she said with the same smile.

Her disbelief in his dissatisfaction with himself was pleasant, and unconsciously he challenged her to give reasons for her disbelief.

'I am happy, but dissatisfied with myself . . .' he answered.

'How can you be dissatisfied if you are happy?'

'I mean . . . How shall I put it? . . . In my heart I wish for nothing more, except that you shouldn't stumble. Oh dear! How can you jump so!' he said, interrupting the conversation to rebuke her for making too quick a movement while stepping over a branch that lay across the path. 'But when I examine myself and compare myself with others, especially with my brother, I feel how bad I am.'

'In what way?' asked she, still smiling. 'Don't you do anything for others? What about your small holdings, your farming, and your book?'

'No. I feel it now more than ever—and it is your fault,' he answered, pressing her arm, 'that it's not the right thing. I do it, but it is superficial. If I could love all that work as I love you . . . but of late I have been doing it like a task set me. . . .'

'Well then, what do you say to Papa?' asked Kitty. 'Is he bad too, because he does nothing for the common good?'

'He? Oh no! But one must have your father's simplicity, clearness, and kindness, and have I got all that? I don't act and I worry. It's you who have done it. Before you were there, and *that*,' he said with a glance at her figure, which she understood, 'I put all my strength into my work; but now I can't and I feel ashamed. I do it just like a task that has been set me. I pretend . . .'

'Then would you now like to change places with Sergius Ivanich?' asked Kitty. 'Would you prefer to do that public work, and love that given task as he does, and nothing more?'

'Of course not!' replied Levin. 'However, I am so happy that I don't understand anything. . . . So you think he will propose to-day?' he added after a pause.

'I do, and I don't. But I want him to, awfully! Wait, we'll see.' She stooped and picked an ox-eye daisy by the roadside. 'There, begin! He will propose, he won't . . .' and she handed him the flower.

'He will, he won't,' said Levin, pulling off the veined white petals.

'No, no!' exclaimed she, watching his fingers excitedly, as she seized his hand to stop him. 'You've pulled off two at once.'

'Well then, we won't count this tiny one,' said he, picking off a short ill-formed petal. 'And here's the trap overtaking us.'

'Aren't you tired, Kitty?' the Princess called out.

'Not at all.'

'If so you'd better get in, if the horses are quiet and go at a walking pace.'

But it was not worth while to drive as they had nearly reached the place, and so they all went on foot.

Chapter IV

Varenka with the white kerchief over her black hair, surrounded by the children and good-naturedly and cheerfully busy with them, and evidently excited by the possibility of an offer of marriage from a man she liked, looked very attractive. Koznyshev walked by her side and did not cease admiring her. Looking at her he remembered all the charming things he had heard her say, and all he knew of her that was good, and he grew more and more conscious that what he felt for her was something rare, something he had felt but once before, a long, long time ago, when he was very young. His sense of pleasure at her nearness went on increasing until it reached a point where, when placing in her basket an enormous wood mushroom with a thin stem and up-curling top, he looked into her eyes and, noting the flush of joyful and frightened agitation that suffused her face, he himself became embarrassed and gave her a smile that said too much.

'If it is so, I must think it over and come to a decision, and not let myself be carried away like a boy by the impulse of the moment,' he told himself.

'Now I will go and gather mushrooms quite on my own account, or else my harvest will not be noticeable,' said he, and went away from the skirts of the wood, where they were walking about on the short silky grass under sparsely growing old birches, and penetrated deeper into the wood, where among the white birch trunks grew grey-stemmed aspens and dark hazel bushes. When he had gone some forty paces he stepped behind a spindle bush with pink and red earring-shaped blossoms, and paused, knowing that he could no longer be seen. Around him everything was quiet. Only the hum of flies, like that of a swarm of bees, sounded continually high up in the birch trees beneath which he stood, and occasionally the children's voices reached him. Suddenly, from the skirts of the wood not far off, he heard Varenka's contralto voice calling to Grisha, and a smile of pleasure lit up his face. Conscious of that smile, Koznyshev shook his head disapprovingly at his own state and taking out a cigar began to light it. He was long unable to strike a match against the bark of a birch. The delicate white outer bark adhered to the phosphorus, and the light went out. At last one match did burn up, and the scented smoke of the cigar, like a broad swaying sheet definitely outlined, moved forwards and upwards over the bush under the overhanging branches of the birch-tree. Watching the sheet of smoke, he went on slowly, meditating on his condition of mind.

'Why not?' he thought. 'If it were just a sudden impulse or passion—if I only felt this attraction, this mutual attraction (it is mutual), but felt that it was contrary to the whole tenor of my life, and that by giving way to it I should be false to my vocation and duty . . . But it is nothing of the kind. The one thing I can find against it is that when I lost Marie I told myself that I would remain true to her memory. That is the only thing I can say against my feeling . . . That is important,' thought Koznyshev, conscious nevertheless that this consideration could not have any importance for him personally, although in the eyes of others it might spoil his poetic rôle. 'But, apart from that, however much I searched I could find nothing to say against my feeling. If I had chosen by reason alone, I could find nothing better!'

He recalled the women and girls he had known, but try as he would he could not recall one who united in herself to such a degree all, literally all, the qualities which he, thinking the matter over in cold blood, would desire in a wife. She had all the charm and freshness of youth but was no longer a child, and if she loved him, loved him consciously as a woman ought to love. That was one favourable consideration. The second one was: she was not only far from worldly, but evidently felt a repulsion from the world, yet she knew the world and had all the ways of a woman of good Society, without which a life-companion would be unthinkable for him. The third was: she was religious, not irresponsibly religious and kindhearted like a child—like Kitty for instance—but her life was based on religious convictions. Even down to small details Koznyshev found in her all that he desired in a wife: she was poor and solitary, so that she would not bring into her husband's house a crowd of relations and their influence, as he saw Kitty doing. She would be indebted to her husband for everything, which was a thing he had always desired in his future family life. And this girl, uniting all these qualities, loved him. He was modest, but could not help being aware of this. And he loved her. One of the opposite arguments was his age. But he came of a long-lived race, he had not a single grey hair, no one thought he was forty, and he remembered that Varenka had said it was only in Russia that men of fifty considered themselves old, and that in France a man of fifty considered himself *dans la force de l'âge*,[1] while one of forty was *un jeune homme*.[2] And what was the use of counting by years, when he felt as young at heart as he had been twenty years ago? Was it not youth that he was experiencing now, when coming out again on the other side of the wood he saw, in the bright slanting sunbeams, the graceful form of Varenka in her yellow dress and with a basket on her arm, stepping lightly past the trunk of an old birch, and when the impression of Varenka merged into one with the view that had so struck him with its beauty: the view of the field of ripening oats bathed in the slanting sunbeams and the old forest beyond, flecked with yellow, fading away into the bluish distance. His heart leapt with joy. His feelings carried him away. He felt that the matter was decided. Varenka, who had bent to pick a mushroom, rose buoyantly and glanced round. Throwing away his cigar Koznyshev went toward her with resolute steps.

Chapter V

'Mlle Varenka! When very young I formed my ideal of the woman I should love and whom I should be happy to call my wife. I have lived many years, and now in you for the first time I have met what I was in search of. I love you, and offer you my hand.'

This was what Koznyshev said to himself when he was already within ten steps of Varenka. Kneeling and with outstretched arms defending some mushrooms from Grisha, she was calling little Masha.

'Come along, little ones! There are a lot here,' she cried in her delightful mellow voice.

On seeing Koznyshev approaching she did not move; yet everything told him that she felt his approach and was glad of it.

'Well, have you found anything?' she asked from beneath her white kerchief, turning her handsome face toward him, with a gentle smile.

'Not one,' said Koznyshev. 'And you?'

She did not reply, being busy with the children who surrounded her.

'There's another, near the branch,' she said, pointing to a small

1. In the prime of life.
2. A young man.

mushroom cut across its firm pinkish crown by a dry blade of grass from beneath which it had sprung up. Varenka rose when Masha had picked the mushroom, breaking it into two white pieces. 'It reminds me of my childhood,' she added, moving away from the children with Koznyshev.

They went a few paces in silence. Varenka saw that he wanted to speak, and guessing the subject she grew faint with joy and fear. They had gone far enough not to be overheard, but he still had not begun. It would have been better for Varenka to remain silent. It would have been easier after a silence to say what they wished to say than after talking about mushrooms; yet against her will, and as if by accident, she said:

'So you have not found anything? But of course deep in the wood there are always fewer.'

Koznyshev sighed and did not speak. He was vexed that she had spoken about mushrooms. He wished to bring her back to her first remark about her childhood, but without wishing to, after a pause, he replied to her last words:

'I have only heard that the white boleti grow chiefly on the outskirts, but I can't even tell which are the white ones.'

A few more minutes passed; they had gone still further from the children and were quite alone. Varenka's heart beat so that she seemed to hear it, and she felt herself growing red and then pale and red again.

To be the wife of a man like Koznyshev after her difficult life with Madame Stahl seemed to her the height of bliss. Besides, she was almost sure she loved him, and now in a moment it must be decided. She was frightened: frightened of what he might or might not say.

'He must make his declaration now or never'; Koznyshev also felt this. Everything—Varenka's look, her blush, her downcast eyes—betrayed painful expectation. He saw it and was sorry for her. He even felt that to say nothing now would be to offend her. His mind went rapidly over all the arguments in favour of his decision. He repeated to himself the words with which he had intended to propose; but instead of those words some unexpected thought caused him to say:

'What difference is there between the white boleti and the birch-tree variety?'

Varenka's lips trembled with emotion when she replied:

'There is hardly any difference in the tops, but only in the stems.'

And as soon as those words were spoken, both he and she understood that all was over, and that what ought to have been said would not be said, and their excitement, having reached its climax, began to subside.

'The stem of the birch-tree boletus reminds one of a dark man's beard two days old,' remarked Koznyshev calmly.

'Yes, that's true,' answered Varenka with a smile, and involuntarily the direction of their stroll changed. They began to return to the children. Varenka felt pained and ashamed, but at the same time she experienced a sense of relief.

Koznyshev when he got home and went again over all his reasons, came to the conclusion that at first he had judged wrongly. He could not be unfaithful to Marie's memory.

'Gently, gently, children!' shouted Levin almost angrily, stepping in front of his wife to shield her, when the crowd of children came rushing at them with shrieks of delight.

Behind the children Koznyshev and Varenka came out of the wood. Kitty had no need to question Varenka: from the calm and rather shamefaced look on both faces she knew that her plan had not been realized.

'Well?' inquired her husband on their way home.

'Won't bite,' answered Kitty with a smile and manner of speaking like her father, which Levin often observed in her with pleasure.

'Won't bite? How do you mean?'

'Like this,' she said, taking her husband's hand, raising it to her mouth, and slightly touching it with her closed lips. 'As one kisses the bishop's hand.'

'Who won't bite?' said he, laughing.

'Neither! And it should have been like this . . .'

'Mind, here are some peasants coming . . .'

'They didn't see!'

Chapter VI

During the children's tea the grown-ups sat on the balcony and talked as if nothing had happened, though they all, especially Koznyshev and Varenka, knew very well that something had happened which though negative was highly important. They both experienced what is felt by a pupil who has failed in an examination and has to remain in the same class or be finally expelled from the school. Every one talked with peculiar animation about extraneous topics. Levin and Kitty felt particularly happy and in love with one another that evening. Their happiness in their love involved an unpleasant reflection on those who desired, but had failed, to secure the same happiness, and made them feel ashamed.

'Take my word for it, Alexander won't come,' said the old Princess.

They were expecting Oblonsky by the evening train, and the old Prince had written that he would perhaps accompany him.

'And I know why,' continued the Princess. 'He says young married folk should be left to themselves for a while.'

'Yes, Papa has really abandoned us,' said Kitty. 'We have not seen him . . . And are we young married folk? . . . Why, we are such old ones now!'

'Only if he doesn't come I too shall say good-bye to you children,' said the Princess with a sorrowful sigh.

'Oh, what an idea, mama!' rejoined both her daughters.

'Just consider him! Why, at present . . .'

And suddenly the old Princess's voice unexpectedly quavered. Her daughters said no more and glanced at one another. 'Mama always finds something sad,' this glance seemed to say. They did not know that pleasant as it was for her to stay with her daughter and necessary as she felt herself to be there, she suffered keenly, both on her own and on her husband's account, since they gave their last and favourite daughter in marriage and the family nest was left empty.

'What is it, Agatha Mikhaylovna?' Kitty asked suddenly when the old woman stopped in front of her with a look of mystery and importance.

'How about supper?'

'Oh, that's just right,' said Dolly. 'You go and give your orders, and I will hear Grisha his lesson. He hasn't done anything to-day.'

'That's a rebuke for me! No, Dolly! I will go,' said Levin, jumping up.

Grisha, who had entered a High School, had some home-work to prepare during the summer holidays. While still in Moscow Dolly had begun learning Latin with him, and on coming to the Levins made it a rule to go over with him, at least once a day, the most difficult lessons—Latin and arithmetic. Levin offered to replace her, but having once heard Levin giving the lesson and noticing that he was not doing it the same way as the master who had coached the boy in Moscow, she—though embarrassed and anxious not to offend Levin—told him resolutely that the text-book must be followed in the master's way and that she would rather give the lessons herself. Levin was vexed with Oblonsky for carelessly leaving it to the boy's mother to look after his lessons which she did not understand, instead of doing it himself, and he was vexed with the masters also for teaching the children so badly; but he promised his sister-in-law to give the lessons in the way she wished. So he went on teaching Grisha not in his own way but according to the book, and therefore did it half-heartedly and often missed a lesson. So it had happened that day.

'No, I will go, Dolly! You stay here,' he said. 'We shall do it all properly by the book. Only when Stiva comes we shall go shooting and then I shall miss the lessons.'

And Levin went off to find Grisha.

Varenka spoke in the same way to Kitty. Even in the Levins' well-ordered household she found ways to be of use.

'I will see about supper,' she said, 'and you stay here'; and she rose to accompany Agatha Mikhaylovna.

'Yes, do. I expect they could not get any chickens, but there are our own . . .' answered Kitty.

'Agatha Mikhaylovna and I will arrange it,' and Varenka went out with the old woman.

'What a nice girl!' said the Princess.

'Not *nice*, Mama, but so charming that there is no one else like her!'

'So you are expecting Stephen Arkadyevich to-night?' asked Koznyshev, evidently disinclined to join in a conversation about Varenka. 'It would be hard to find two brothers-in-law more unlike,' he went on with his subtle smile; 'the one always on the move, living always in Society like a fish in water; the other, our Constantine here, lively, quick, sensitive to everything, but as soon as he appears in Society either shutting up altogether or floundering about absurdly like a fish on dry land!'

'Yes, he is very thoughtless,' said the Princess to Koznyshev. 'I was just going to ask you to tell him that it is impossible for her'— she indicated Kitty—'to remain here, and that she must certainly come to Moscow. He says, "Get a doctor to come out here" . . .'

'Mama, he will do all that's necessary and will agree to everything,' interpolated Kitty, annoyed with her mother for asking Koznyshev's opinion on such a matter.

In the midst of their conversation they heard the snorting of horses and the scraping of wheels on the gravel of the avenue.

Dolly had not had time to rise to go to meet her husband, before Levin had jumped out of the window of the room below, where he had been teaching Grisha, and had lifted the boy out too.

'It's Stiva!' shouted Levin from under the balcony. 'We have finished, Dolly, don't worry!' he added, running like a boy to meet the carriage.

'*Is, ea, id; ejus, ejus, ejus,*' [3] shouted Grisha, hopping down the avenue.

'And some one with him. It must be Papa!' shouted Levin, who had stopped at the bend of the avenue. 'Kitty, don't come down those steep steps, go round!'

But Levin was mistaken in supposing that one of the men in the *calèche* was the old Prince. When he came nearer he saw, sitting beside Oblonsky, a stout handsome young man wearing a Scotch bonnet with long ribbons streaming behind. It was Vasenka Veslovsky, a second cousin of the Shcherbatskys, a brilliant Petersburg-

3. He, she, it, his, hers, its.

Moscow young man. 'A most splendid fellow and a passionate sportsman,' as Oblonsky said when he introduced him.

Not at all dismayed by the disappointment he caused by appearing instead of the old Prince, Veslovsky gaily greeted Levin, reminding him that they had met before, and lifting Grisha he caught him up into the vehicle over the pointer Oblonsky had brought with him.

Levin did not get in, but followed the *calèche*. He was rather vexed that the old Prince, whom he liked more and more the better he knew him, had not come, and vexed because this Vasenka Veslovsky, a quite superfluous stranger, had come. Veslovsky seemed to him still more alien and superfluous when they arrived at the porch—at which the whole animated group of grown-ups and children had gathered—and he saw Vasenka Veslovsky kissing Kitty's hand with a particularly tender and gallant air.

'We, your wife and I, are cousins and old acquaintances,' said Vasenka Veslovsky, once again giving Levin's hand a very, very hard squeeze.

'Well, is there any game?' asked Oblonsky of Levin, scarcely giving himself time to say a word of greeting to everybody. 'He and I have the cruellest intentions. . . . Why, mama! They have not been in Moscow since then. . . . Here, Tanya! That's for you! . . . Please get it out of the *calèche*, behind there . . .' he was saying to those about him. 'How much refreshed you are looking, Dolly, dear!' he went on, kissing his wife's hand again and holding it in his own while he patted it with the other hand.

Levin, who but a few moments before had been in the brightest of spirits, was now looking dismally at every one, dissatisfied with everything.

'Whom was he kissing yesterday with those same lips?' he thought as he looked at Oblonsky caressing his wife. He looked at Dolly, and was not pleased with her either.

'Of course she does not believe in his love. Then why is she so pleased? Disgusting!' thought he.

He looked at the Princess, who a few moments before had seemed so nice, and did not like the way she welcomed that beribboned Vasenka, as if to her own house.

Even Koznyshev, who had also come out of the porch, displeased Levin by the feigned friendliness with which he greeted Oblonsky, whom, as Levin knew, he neither liked nor respected.

And Varenka too seemed disgusting because of the manner in which she with her *saint nitouche* [4] air made that gentleman's acquaintance, while all her thought was how to get married.

But most repugnant of all was Kitty, for the way she fell in with

4. Holy unapproachable.

the gay tone of that gentleman, who appeared to consider his arrival in the country a regular festival for everybody, and particularly objectionable was the smile with which she responded to his smiles.

Talking noisily, they all went into the house, but as soon as all were seated Levin turned and left the room.

Kitty noticed that something was wrong with her husband. She tried to seize an opportune moment to speak to him alone; but he hurried away from her, saying that he must go to the office. It was long since the farm work had seemed so important to him as it did that evening. 'For them it is always a holiday,' he thought, 'yet here we have work that is no holiday task, which cannot be put off, and without which life is impossible.'

Chapter VII

Levin did not return until they called him to supper. On the stairs stood Kitty and Agatha Mikhaylovna, deliberating what wines to serve.

'But why all this fuss? Serve the same as usual.'

'No; Stiva does not drink it. . . . Kostya! Wait a moment—what's the matter with you?' said Kitty, hurrying after him, but, without waiting for her, he went away pitilessly with big strides to the dining-room, where he immediately joined in the general animated conversation which was kept going by Vasenka Veslovsky and Oblonsky.

'Well then, shall we go shooting to-morrow?' Oblonsky inquired.

'Yes! Do let's go!' cried Veslovsky, changing from one chair to another and sitting sideways with one of his fat legs doubled under him.

'I shall be very pleased! Let's go. And have you had any shooting this year?' Levin asked, gazing intently at this leg but with that pretended politeness of his which Kitty knew so well, and which suited him so ill. 'I don't know whether we shall get any snipe, but there are plenty of woodcock, only one must go early. Will it tire you? Aren't you tired, Stiva?'

'I! Tired? I've never been tired yet. Let's not go to bed at all! Let's go for a walk.'

'Yes, really! Don't let us go to bed! Delightful!' chimed in Veslovsky.

'Oh, we are quite convinced that you can do without sleep and deprive others of theirs,' said Dolly with that scarcely perceptible irony with which she now generally addressed her husband. 'I think it's already time . . . I'm going: I don't take supper.'

'Oh no, stay here, Dolly dear!' said Oblonsky, stepping across to her side of the long supper-table. 'I have much more to tell you.'

'I don't expect you have any news.'

'Do you know, Veslovsky has been to see Anna? And he is going there again. You know it's only some seventy versts off. I shall certainly go over. Veslovsky, come here!'

Vasenka came over to the ladies, and took a seat beside Kitty.

'Oh, do tell me! You have been to see her? How is she?' asked Dolly.

Levin remained at the other end of the table, and while not ceasing to talk with the Princess and Varenka, saw that Oblonsky, Dolly, Kitty, and Veslovsky were carrying on an animated and mysterious conversation. Moreover, he saw his wife had an expression of serious feeling as she gazed attentively at Vasenka's handsome face while he was vivaciously narrating something.

'It's very nice at their place,' Vasenka was saying, talking of Vronsky and Anna. 'Of course I do not take it upon myself to judge, but in their house one feels oneself to be in the family.'

'What do they mean to do?'

'I believe they mean to go to Moscow for the winter.'

'How nice it would be for us to meet there! When are you going, Stephen Arkadyevich?' asked Vasenka.

'I shall spend July with them.'

'And will you go?' Oblonsky asked his wife.

'I have long wanted to go and certainly shall go,' replied Dolly. 'I know her, and am sorry for her. She is a splendid woman. I shall go alone when you are away, and won't inconvenience anyone. It will even be better without you.'

'That's all right,' replied he; 'and you, Kitty?'

'I? Why should I go?' said Kitty, flushing deeply and glancing round at her husband.

'Are you acquainted with Anna Arkadyevna?' Veslovsky asked her. 'She is very attractive.'

'Yes,' said Kitty, with a still deeper blush, and she rose and went to her husband.

'So you are off shooting to-morrow?' she asked.

Levin's jealousy during those few minutes had gone far, especially after the blush that had suffused her face when speaking to Veslovsky. Now as he listened to her question he interpreted it in his own way. Strange as it seemed to him when he remembered it later, it now appeared clear to him that she asked whether he was going shooting, only because she wanted to know whether he would give that pleasure to Vasenka Veslovsky, with whom he fancied she was already in love.

'Yes, I am going,' he answered in an unnatural voice that was disagreeable to himself.

'No—wait a day, because Dolly has seen nothing of her husband. You could go the day after to-morrow,' said she.

Levin now interpreted her words thus: 'Do not part me from *him*. Your going does not matter to me, but do let me enjoy the society of this charming young man!'

'Oh, if you wish it we will stay at home to-morrow,' replied Levin with particular amiability.

Meanwhile Vasenka, without the least suspicion of the sufferings his presence was causing, rose from the table after Kitty and followed her, smiling pleasantly.

Levin saw that smile. He grew pale and for a moment could hardly breathe. 'How dare he look like that at my wife!' he thought, boiling with rage.

'To-morrow then? Please let's go!' said Vasenka, sitting down and once more doubling his leg under him, as his habit was.

Levin's jealousy rose still higher. Already he fancied himself a deceived husband, necessary to his wife and her lover only to provide them with the comforts of life and with pleasures. . . . But nevertheless he asked Vasenka in an amiable and hospitable manner about his shooting, his gun, his boots—and agreed to go shooting next day.

Happily for Levin the old Princess put a stop to his sufferings by herself getting up and advising Kitty to go to bed. But he did not escape a fresh pang. Taking leave of his hostess, Vasenka again wanted to kiss her hand; but Kitty, blushing, drew away her hand, and said with naïve rudeness, for which she was afterwards reprimanded by her mother:

'That's not customary in our house.'

In Levin's eyes Kitty was to blame for having laid herself open to such behaviour, and still more to blame for so awkwardly showing that it displeased her.

'What's the good of going to sleep, eh?' said Oblonsky, who after the few glasses he had drunk at supper was in his pleasantest and most poetic mood. 'Look, Kitty!' he went on, pointing to the moon rising behind the lime-trees. 'How lovely! Veslovsky, now's the time for a serenade! Do you know he has a fine voice? We have been rehearsing on the way. He has brought some beautiful songs—two new ones. He ought to sing them with Mlle Varenka.'

After the rest had separated for the night Oblonsky long walked in the avenue with Veslovsky, and their voices could be heard practising a new song.

Levin sat listening to them and frowning, in an easy-chair in his wife's bedroom, meeting her inquiries as to what was the matter with stubborn silence. But when at length she asked with a timid smile: 'Aren't you displeased about something connected with Veslovsky?' he gave vent to his feelings and told her everything. He himself was offended by what he was saying, and this still further irritated him.

He stood before her, his eyes glittering terribly under his frowning brows, and pressed his powerful arms to his breast, as if trying with all his might to restrain himself. The expression of his face would have been hard and even cruel, but for a look of suffering which touched her. His jaw trembled and his voice faltered.

'Understand that I am not jealous: that is a vile word! I cannot be jealous nor believe that . . . I cannot say what I feel, but it is dreadful. . . . I am not jealous, but I am offended and humiliated that anyone dares imagine—dares look at you with such eyes . . .'

'What eyes?' said Kitty, trying to remember as honestly as she could all the words and gestures of the evening and all their shades of meaning.

In the depth of her soul she was conscious that there had been something just at the moment when Veslovsky had followed her to the other end of the table, but she dared not own this even to herself, much less make up her mind to tell him and so increase his pain.

'And what attraction can there be about me as I am . . .'

'Ah!' he exclaimed, seizing his head in his hands. 'You had better not say anything! . . . So, if you were attractive . . .'

'Oh no, Kostya! Wait—listen!' she implored with a look of pained commiseration. 'What can you be thinking of, since men do not exist for me? They don't! They don't! . . . Well then, would you like me not to see anybody?'

For the first moment his jealousy had offended her: she was annoyed that the least relaxation, even the most innocent, was forbidden her; but now she would gladly have sacrificed not merely trifles like that, but anything, to free him from the torments he was suffering.

'Try and understand the horror and absurdity of my position,' he continued in a despairing whisper. 'He is in my house, and strictly speaking he has done nothing improper except by his free and easy manner and doubling up his legs! He considers it to be in the best form, and therefore I have to be polite to him!'

'Come, Kostya, you are exaggerating!' remonstrated Kitty, at the bottom of her heart pleased by the force of love for her which was now expressing itself in his jealousy.

'The worst of it all is that you—are as you always are, and now when you are my holy of holies and we are so happy—so specially happy—suddenly this good-for-nothing comes along . . . No, not good-for-nothing. . . . Why am I abusing him? He does not concern me. But our happiness, mine and yours . . . why . . . ?'

'Do you know, I see how it happened . . .' Kitty began.

'How? How?'

'I noticed your look while we were talking at supper.'

'Yes, yes!' said he in a frightened tone.

She told him what they had been talking about, and while she spoke she was breathless with excitement. Levin paused, and then after scrutinizing her pale, frightened features, suddenly clapped his hands to his head.

'Kate, I have been tormenting you! My darling, forgive me! It was madness! Kate, it is all my fault. How could I torture myself like that about such nonsense?'

'Oh no! I am sorry for you.'

'For me? Me? Because I am a madman! But why should I make you wretched? It is dreadful to think that a mere stranger can destroy our bliss!'

'Of course, and that is what offends me . . .'

'Well then, I will keep him here all the summer on purpose. I will lavish attentions on him,' said Levin, kissing her hands. 'You'll see! To-morrow . . . Oh, but we are going out to-morrow.'

Chapter VIII

Next day, before the ladies were up, the vehicles—a cart and a small trap—stood at the porch waiting for the sportsmen; and Laska, having long ago made out that they were going shooting, after yelping and jumping about to her heart's content, was sitting in the cart beside the coachman, regarding the doorway whence the sportsmen had not yet emerged, with excitement and with disapproval of the delay. The first to appear was Vasenka Veslovsky in new boots reaching half-way up his fat thighs, his green blouse girdled with a new cartridge-belt smelling of leather, and on his head the Scotch bonnet with the ribbons. He carried a new English gun without a sling. Laska jumped down to him and greeted him by leaping about. In her own way she asked him how soon the others would come out, but, receiving no reply, she returned to her post of expectancy and again sat motionless with her head turned sideways and one ear pricked up. At length the door opened noisily and out bounded, spinning round and round in the air, Krak, Oblonsky's yellow spotted pointer, followed by Oblonsky himself with a gun in his hand and a cigar in his mouth.

'Quiet, quiet, Krak!' he said affectionately to the dog, which was throwing its paws up against his stomach and chest and getting them entangled in his game-bag. Oblonsky was wearing raw hide shoes, bands of linen wound round his feet instead of socks, a pair of tattered trousers and a short coat. On his head were the ruins of some sort of hat; but his gun was of a new type, as neat as a toy, and his game-bag and cartridge-belt, though much worn, were of the best quality.

Vasenka had been ignorant that the stylishness of a real sports-man consists in being dressed in rags but having one's shooting implements of the very best quality. He realized it now that he saw Oblonsky in his rags, yet shining with his elegant, well-nurtured, cheerful and gentlemanly figure, and resolved to follow his example next time.

'Well, and where is our host?' he inquired.

'He has a young wife,' answered Oblonsky, with a smile.

'Yes, and such a charming one.'

'He was ready-dressed. I expect he has run back to her.'

Oblonsky was right in this surmise. Levin had run back to ask his wife once more whether she had forgiven him his foolishness of the previous day, and also to entreat her 'for heaven's sake' to take care of herself; and especially to keep further away from the chil-dren who at any moment might collide with her. Then he had to obtain a repeated assurance that she was not angry with him for going away for two days, and also to beg her to be sure next day to send a man on horseback with a note—only a word or two—that he might know that all was well with her.

It was always painful for Kitty to part from her husband for two days; but seeing his animated figure, which seemed particularly large and powerful in high shooting-boots and white blouse, and the radiant exhilaration of the sportsman in him, incomprehensible to her, she forgot her own pain in his gladness and parted from him cheerfully.

'Sorry, gentlemen!' he said, running out on to the porch. 'Is the lunch put in? Why is the roan on the right? Well, never mind! Laska, be quiet! Go and lie down!'

'Let them out with the flock,' he said, turning to the herdsman who was waiting for orders about some young sheep. 'Sorry! There's another rascal coming.'

Levin jumped down from the cart where he had already seated himself, to meet the carpenter who was approaching with a sazhen measure in his hand.

'There, you see! You did not come to the office last night, and now you are detaining me. Well, what is it?'

'Won't you have one more turning made? Three more steps will be enough, then we'll get it exact. It will be much more comfort-able.'

'You should have obeyed me,' said Levin with vexation. 'I told you to set up the string-boards first, and then to make the grooves. You can't alter it now. Do as I tell you and make a new one.'

The facts of the matter were that in the new wing that was being built the carpenter had spoilt the staircase, having made it without calculating the elevation, so that when it was put in position all the steps sloped. Now he wanted to use that staircase, adding three steps to it.

'It will be much better so.'

'But where will it reach to with three additional steps?'

'Excuse me, sir!' said the carpenter, smiling contemptuously. 'It will reach to the exact spot. It will just stretch from the bottom, you see,' he went on with a persuasive gesture, 'and go up and up till it gets there.'

'Why, but three steps will add to its length as well. . . . Where will it get to?'

'It will go up from the bottom, I mean, and reach to the top,' the carpenter repeated obstinately and persuasively.

'It will reach up to the wall and half-way to the ceiling!'

'Oh no, excuse me! You see it will start from the bottom and go up and up and just reach.'

Levin pulled out his ramrod and drew the staircase in the dust.

'There! You see?'

'As you please,' said the carpenter, his eyes suddenly brightening; evidently he had at last understood. 'It seems we'll have to make another.'

'Well then, do as I told you,' Levin shouted as he climbed into the cart. 'Drive on! Hold the dogs, Philip!'

Having left the cares of home and estate behind him, Levin experienced such a strong sense of the joy of life and anticipation, that he felt disinclined to talk. Besides, he experiencd that feeling of concentrated excitement which every sportsman knows when approaching the scene of action. If his mind was occupied with anything now, it was only with questions, whether they would find anything in the Kolpensky marsh, how Laska would compare with Krak, and how he would shoot to-day. 'If only I don't disgrace myself before that stranger! If only Oblonsky's shooting does not beat mine!' was his thought.

Oblonsky shared these feelings and was likewise not talkative. Vasenka Veslovsky alone chattered incessantly and merrily. Now, as he listened to him, Levin felt ashamed of his injustice toward him the day before. Vasenka was really a good sort, simple, kind-hearted, and very jolly. Had Levin come across him when still a bachelor, they would have become intimate. Levin did not quite like his holiday outlook on life and a sort of free and easy stylishness about him. He seemed to lay claim to lofty and unquestionable importance because he had long nails, a Scotch bonnet, and everything else in keeping; but one could forgive him this for the sake of his good-nature and breeding. He attracted Levin by his good education, his splendid accent in French and English, and by the fact that he belonged to Levin's own class.

Vasenka greatly admired the Don Steppe horse attached on the left.[5] He went into raptures over it. 'How delightful it must be to gallop across the Steppes on a Steppe horse, eh? Don't you think so?' he said. He seemed to picture a gallop on a Steppe horse as something wild and poetical; nothing came of it, but his naïveté, in connection with his good looks, sweet smile, and graceful movements, was very attractive. Whether it was that Veslovsky's nature was congenial to him, or that, to expiate his sin of yesterday, he tried to see only what was good in him, Levin liked Veslovsky's company.

When they had gone about three versts, Veslovsky suddenly missed his cigars and pocket-book, and did not know whether he had lost them or left them on his table. He had three hundred and seventy roubles in the pocket-book, and therefore the matter could not be ignored.

'Do you know, Levin, I will gallop home on this Don side-horse! That will be grand, eh?' he said, preparing to get out.

'No, why?' replied Levin, conjecturing that Veslovsky must weigh not less than fifteen stone. 'I will send the coachman.'

So the coachman rode back on the side-horse and Levin drove the other two himself.

Chapter IX

'Well, where are we going? Tell us all about it,' said Oblonsky.

'The plan is this. We are now going as far as Gvozdevo. On this side of Gvozdevo there is a good marsh for snipe, and beyond it are splendid snipe marshes, and there are some double-snipe there too. It's too hot now, but we shall get there toward evening (it's twenty versts), and will shoot there in the evening; we'll spend the night there, and then to-morrow we shall go to the big marshes.'

'And is there nothing by the way?'

'There is, but it would delay us; and besides, it's hot! There are two nice little places, but we should hardly find anything there.'

Levin himself felt inclined to stop at those little places, but, as they were near home, they were always within his reach and they were small, so that there was not room enough for three persons to shoot there. So he stretched a point and said they would hardly find anything there. When they came to a small marsh he wished to drive past it, but Oblonsky, with the practised eye of a sportsman, noticed the marshy place from the road.

'Oughtn't we to go there?' he asked, pointing to the marsh.

'Levin, do let us! How delightful!' begged Vasenka Veslovsky, and

---

5. One (and often two) of the three horses was loosely harnessed and ran at the side.

Levin could not but agree.

Scarcely had they stopped before the dogs flew toward the marsh, racing one another.

'Krak! . . . Laska!'

The dogs returned.

'There is not room for three: I'll wait here,' said Levin, hoping they would find nothing but the peewits, which the dogs had raised, and which, swaying as they flew, cried plaintively above the marsh.

'No! Come along, Levin, let's go together,' said Veslovsky.

'Really, there's not room! Back, Laska! . . . Laska! . . . You don't want two dogs?'

Levin remained with the trap and looked enviously at the sportsmen. They went over the whole marsh, but there was nothing there except waterfowl and some peewits, one of which Veslovsky killed.

'There, you see I was not grudging you the marsh!' said Levin. 'It only meant losing time.'

'No, it was enjoyable all the same. You saw?' said Vasenka Veslovsky, climbing awkwardly into the cart with his gun and the peewit. 'How well I got this one! Didn't I? Well, shall we soon get to the real place?'

Suddenly the horses started, Levin knocked his head against the barrel of some one's gun, and there was a report. Actually the report came first, but to Levin it seemed the other way about. What had happened was, that Vasenka Veslovsky when uncocking his gun had pulled one trigger while uncocking the other side. The charge went into the ground without hurting anyone. Oblonsky shook his head and laughed reproachfully at Veslovsky. But Levin had no heart to admonish him: for one thing because any reproach from him would appear to be provoked by the danger he had escaped and by the bump which had risen on his head; and also because Veslovsky was at first so naïvely grieved, and then laughed so good-naturedly and contagiously at their general perturbation, that Levin could not help joining in the laugh.

When they reached the second marsh, which was of considerable size and would take a good deal of time Levin tried to dissuade them from getting out. But again Veslovsky persuaded him, and again, the marsh being a narrow one, Levin as a hospitable host remained with the vehicles.

Krak immediately went toward the hummocks. Vasenka Veslovsky was the first to follow the dog. Before Oblonsky had time to approach, a snipe rose. Veslovsky missed it, and it flew over to an unmown meadow. The bird was left to Veslovsky. Krak found it again and pointed. Veslovsky killed the bird and went back to the vehicles.

'Now you go, and I will remain with the horses,' he said.

A sportsman's jealousy was beginning to torment Levin. He handed the reins to Veslovsky and went into the marsh.

Laska, who had long been whining plaintively, as if complaining of the injustice, rushed straight forward to a likely spot covered with hummocks and known to Levin, where Krak had not yet been.

'Why don't you stop her?' shouted Oblonsky.

'She won't disturb them,' answered Levin, pleased with his dog and hurrying after her.

Laska became more and more intent on her pursuit, the nearer she got to the hummocks. A small marsh bird only diverted her attention for an instant. She described a circle in front of the hummocks, and began another, but suddenly shuddered and stopped dead.

'Come along, Stiva!' Levin shouted, feeling his heart beat more rapidly, and suddenly, as if some bar had been withdrawn from his strained sense of hearing, he lost the faculty of measuring distance, and was struck by sounds which reached him clearly but without any order. He heard Oblonsky's steps and took them for the distant tramp of horses; he heard the crumbling of a bit of hummock on which he stepped and which broke off, pulling out the grass by the roots, and he took it for the noise of a snipe on the wing; behind him he heard too a sound of splashing for which he could not account.

Picking his way, he approached the dog.

'Seize it!'

It was not a double-snipe but a snipe that rose before the dog. Levin raised his gun, but just as he was taking aim the splashing sounded louder and nearer, mingled with Veslovsky's voice shouting strangely and loudly. Levin knew he was aiming behind the snipe, but fired, nevertheless.

After making sure he had missed, he turned and saw that the trap and horses were no longer on the road but in the marsh.

Veslovsky, wishing to watch the shooting, had driven into the marsh, where the horses had stuck fast.

'What the devil brings him here?' muttered Levin to himself, turning back to the vehicle. 'Why did you leave the road?' he asked drily, and calling the coachman, set to work to get the horses out.

Levin was vexed that he had been put off his shot, and that his horses had been led into the bog, and especially that neither Oblonsky nor Veslovsky (neither of whom knew anything about harness) helped him and the coachman to unharness the horses and get them out of the bog. Without a word of reply to Vasenka, who was assuring him that it was quite dry there, Levin worked silently with the coachman to disengage the horses. But when heated with the work, and seeing Veslovsky pulling at the splashboard so strenuously and zealously that he actually wrenched it off, Levin reproached himself with being influenced by his sentiments of the previous day and with treating Veslovsky too coldly, and he tried to efface his unfriendliness by particular courtesy. When everything was in order and the vehicles had been brought back to the road, Levin gave orders for lunch to be served.

'Bon appétit! Bonne conscience! Ce poulet va tomber jusqu'au fond de mes bottes,' [6] remarked Vasenka, who had brightened up again, repeating a French saying while he finished a second chicken. 'Now our misfortunes are ended and all will be well. But for my sin I must sit on the box. Don't you think so, eh? No, no! I am Automedon—wait and see how I will drive you!' he said, keeping hold of the reins, in reply to Levin who wanted him to let the coachman drive. 'No, I must expiate my sin, and besides, it's delightful on the box,' and he was off.

Levin was rather afraid Veslovsky would tire out the horses, especially the roan on the left, whom he did not know how to hold in; but he could not resist Veslovsky's high spirits, the songs he sang all the way while sitting on the box, the stories he told, and his representation of the English way of driving four-in-hand; and after lunch they were all in the best of spirits when they reached the Gvozdevo marsh.

Chapter X

Veslovsky drove so fast that they arrived at the marsh too soon, while it was still hot.

When they got to the real marsh, the object of their journey, Levin involuntarily wished to rid himself of Vasenka and go about unhindered. Oblonsky evidently wanted the same thing, and on his face Levin noticed the preoccupation which every true sportsman feels before the shooting begins, and also a little good-natured cunning, characteristic of him.

'Well, what shall we do . . . ? It's a splendid marsh, and I see there are hawks too,' said Oblonsky, pointing at two large birds circling above the sedges. 'Where there are hawks, there is sure to be game.'

'Well then, gentlemen,' said Levin with a somewhat gloomy expression, pulling up his boots and examining his percussion caps, 'you see that sedge?' He pointed to a dark-green little island in an enormous half-mown wet meadow stretching along the right bank of the river. 'The marsh begins here, just in front of us: you can see, where it is greener? From there it goes to the right, where those

6. A good appetite! a good conscience! This chicken will go down to the bottom of my boots.

horses are; there are hummocks, and double-snipe; and it goes round that sedge to the alder grove and down to the mill. Look! Just there, by that little bay. That's the best place. I once shot seventeen grouse there. . . . We will separate, going different ways with the two dogs, and will meet again by the mill.'

'Well then, who goes to the left and who to the right?' asked Oblonsky. 'The space on the right is broader, so you two go there together, and I will keep to the left,' he added with affected indifference.

'Good! We'll make the best bag,' chimed in Vasenka.

Levin could not avoid agreeing, and they separated.

They had hardly entered the marsh when both dogs began searching together and started off toward a rusty-looking spot in the marsh. Levin knew Laska's method of search—careful and dubious; he knew it, and expected to see a flight of snipe.

'Veslovsky, walk beside me—beside me!' he whispered with bated breath to his comrade, who was splashing in the water behind him, and the direction of whose gun, after the accidental shot by the Kolpensky marsh, involuntarily interested Levin.

'No, I don't want to hamper you. Don't trouble about me.'

But Levin recollected Kitty's parting words: 'Mind, and don't shoot one another!' Nearer and nearer came the dogs, keeping out of each other's way and each following its scent. The expectation of finding snipe was so strong that the smacking sound of his heel as he drew it out of the rusty mud sounded to Levin like the cry of a bird, and he grasped the butt end of his gun firmly.

'Bang! Bang!' he heard just above his ear. Vasenka had fired into a flight of ducks that were circling above the marsh far out of range and were at that moment flying straight toward the sportsmen. Levin had barely time to turn, before he heard the cry of a snipe, then another, and a third, and about eight more rose one after the other.

Oblonsky got one just as it was preparing to begin its zigzag flight, and the bird fell like a small lump into the bog. Oblonsky quietly aimed at another which was flying low toward the sedges, and at the moment of the report that one too fell, and it could be seen jumping up among the cut sedges, fluttering with one white-edged uninjured wing.

Levin was not so lucky: he fired at the first snipe too near, and missed; he followed it with his gun when it had already risen, but at that instant another rose just at his feet and diverted his attention, and he missed again.

While they were reloading another bird rose, and Veslovsky, who had finished reloading, fired two charges of small shot over the water. Oblonsky picked up his two snipe and looked with sparkling eyes at Levin.

'Well, now let's part,' he said, and limping with his left foot, and holding his gun ready, he whistled to his dog and went off in one direction. Levin and Veslovsky went in the other.

Levin, if his first shots were unsuccessful, always became excited and annoyed, and shot badly all the rest of the day. So it was this time. There were a great many snipe. They kept rising before the dogs and at the very feet of the sportsmen, and Levin might have recovered himself; but the oftener he fired the more he disgraced himself before Veslovsky, who was puffing away merrily, in and out of range, never killing anything, but not in the least abashed thereby. Levin hurried, grew impatient, and became more and more flurried, until at last he fired almost without hope of killing anything. Even Laska seemed to feel this. Her search became more and more indolent, and she looked round at the sportsmen as if in perplexity and with reproach. Shot followed shot. Powder smoke enveloped the sportsmen, but in the large roomy net of the game-bag were only three light little birds, and even of these one had been shot by Veslovsky, and another belonged to them both. Meanwhile from the opposite side of the marsh came not frequent but, as it seemed to Levin, significant reports from Oblonsky's gun, followed almost every time by a cry to the dog, 'Krak! Krak! Fetch it!'

That excited Levin still more. The snipe unceasingly circled above the sedges. The cry near the ground and sound in the air came incessantly from every side. The snipe that had risen previously and had been flying about descended in front of the sportsmen. Not two but dozens of hawks now soared above the marsh.

Having traversed more than half the marsh, Levin and Veslovsky came to a spot where the peasants' meadow land was divided into long strips, the ends abutting on the sedge and separated by narrow lines where the grass had been trodden down or cut. Half of those strips were already mown.

Though there was little hope of finding as many birds in the unmown strips as on the mown part, Levin, having promised Oblonsky to meet him, went with his companion farther on over the mown and unmown strips.

'Hullo, you sportsmen!' shouted one of several peasants who were sitting beside a cart from which the horses had been taken out. 'Come and have something with us! A drink of vodka!'

Levin turned round.

'Come along! Never mind!' shouted a merry, bearded, red-faced peasant, showing a row of white teeth and holding aloft a greenish vodka bottle that glittered in the sunshine.

'*Qu'est ce qu'ils disent?*' [7] asked Veslovsky.

'They are calling us to drink vodka. I expect they have been dividing the meadow. I should go and have a drink,' said Levin, not quite disinterestedly, hoping that the vodka would tempt Veslovsky and lure him away.

'Why are they offering it?'

'Oh, they are only making merry. Really, you should go to them. It will interest you.'

'*Allons! C'est curieux!*' [8]

'Go along! Go, you'll find the way to the mill!' cried Levin, and on looking round was pleased to see Veslovsky making his way out of the marsh toward the peasants, stooping and stumbling with his weary feet and holding his gun at arm's length.

'You come too!' shouted a peasant to Levin. 'Come! Have a bite of pie!'

Levin badly wanted a drink of vodka and a bit of bread. He felt faint and could hardly drag his staggering legs out of the bog, and for an instant he was in doubt. But the dog pointed. His weariness vanished, at once he went easily through the marsh toward the dog. Just at his feet rose a snipe; he fired and killed it. The dog continued pointing. 'Fetch it!' Another bird rose before the dog. Levin fired, but that day he had no luck: he missed, and when he went to look for the bird he had killed, he could not find it. He tramped all over the sedge, but Laska was incredulous of his having killed anything, and when he sent her to look for it, she only made a pretence and did not really search.

Even without Vasenka, whom he had blamed for his ill-luck, things went no better. Here, too, were plenty of birds, but Levin missed one after another.

The slanting rays of the sun were still hot; his clothes were wet through with perspiration and stuck to his body; his left boot, full of water, was heavy and made a smacking sound; down his face, grimy with powder, ran drops of sweat; a bitter taste was in his mouth, the smell of powder and rust was in his nose, and the perpetual cry of the snipe was in his ears; he could not touch the barrels of his gun, they were so hot; his heart thumped with short, quick beats; his hands trembled with excitement and his tired feet stumbled as he dragged them over the hummocks and through the bog; but still he went on and shot. At last, after a disgraceful miss, he threw his gun and hat on the ground.

'No! I must pull myself together.' he thought, picked up his gun and hat, called Laska to heel, and got out of the marsh. When he reached a dry place he sat down on a hummock, took off his boot

7. What are they saying?
8. Come! It is interesting.

and emptied it, then went back to the marsh, drank a little of the rusty water, wetted the heated barrels and bathed his face and hands. Feeling refreshed, he returned to the spot where a snipe had settled, firmly resolved not to get flurried.

He tried to keep calm, but the same thing happened again. His finger pulled the trigger before he had taken aim. Things went from bad to worse.

He had only five birds in his bag when he came out of the marsh by the alder grove where he was to meet Oblonsky.

Before he saw him, he saw his dog. Krak, quite black with fetid marsh slime, sprang out from beneath the upturned root of an alder with the air of a conqueror and sniffed at Laska. Behind Krak, in the shade of the alders, appeared Oblonsky's stately figure. He came toward Levin red and perspiring, with his shirt unbuttoned, still limping as before.

'Well? You have been firing a good deal!' he said with a merry smile.

'And you?' asked Levin. But there was no need to ask, for he already saw the full bag.

'Oh, not bad!'

He had fourteen birds.

'A famous marsh! I expect Veslovsky was in your way. One dog for two people is inconvenient,' said Oblonsky, to soften his triumph.

Chapter XI

When Levin and Oblonsky reached the peasant's hut where Levin used to put up, Veslovsky was there before them. He sat in the middle of the room, holding with both hands to a bench, from which a soldier—a brother of the mistress of the house—was tugging him by his slime-covered boots, and he was laughing with his infectiously merry laugh.

'I have only just got here. *Ils ont été charmants!* [9] Fancy! They fed me and gave me drink. What bread—wonderful! *Délicieux!* And the vodka . . . I never tasted better! And they positively would not take any money, and kept on saying, "No offence!" or something of that sort.'

'Why should they take money? They were entertaining you, you see! Do they keep vodka for sale?' said the soldier who had at last succeeded in dragging off one wet boot together with a blackened stocking.

Despite the dirtiness of the hut, soiled by the sportsmen's boots, the dirty dogs that were licking themselves there, and despite the smell of bog and of powder and the absence of knives and

9. They were charming.

forks, the sportsmen drank tea and ate supper with a relish known only when one is out shooting. Washed and clean they betook them-selves to a hay-barn that had been swept out and where the coach-man had made up beds for the gentlemen.

Though it was already dusk, none of the sportsmen wanted to sleep.

After fluctuating between recollections and stories of the shoot-ing, of dogs, and of other shooting parties, the talk reached a theme that interested all three. A *propos* of Vasenka's repeated expres-sions of delight at the charm of the arrangements for the night, of the scent of hay, and of a broken cart (which he thought was broken because its fore wheels had been removed), of the good-nature of the peasants who had treated him to vodka, and of the dogs which lay each at its master's feet, Oblonsky told them about the delights of a shooting party with Malthus at which he had been last summer. Malthus was a well-known railway magnate. Oblonsky spoke of the marshes which Malthus had leased in the Province of Tver, of how they were preserved, of the vehicles—dog-carts—in which the sportsmen were driven thither, and of the marquee that was set up for lunch beside the marsh.

'I don't understand you,' said Levin, rising on his heap of hay. 'How is it that those people don't disgust you? I understand that lunch with good claret is very nice, but is it possible that that very luxury does not disgust you? All those people, like the holders of our drink-monopolies formerly, get their money in ways that earn contempt—they disregard that contempt—and afterwards, by means of what they have dishonestly earned, they buy off that con-tempt.'

'Perfectly true!' chimed in Vasenka Veslovsky 'Perfectly true! Of course Oblonsky does it out of *bonhomie*,[1] and then others say, "Well, if Oblonsky goes there . . ." '

'Not at all!' Levin could hear that Oblonsky said this with a smile; 'I simply don't consider him more dishonest than any of the rich merchants or noblemen. They have all alike made money by work and intelligence.'

'Yes, but what work? Is it work to get a concession and resell it?'

'Of course it is work! Work in this sense, that if it were not for him and others like him, there would be no railways.'

'But it is not work such as that of a peasant or a savant.'

'Granted! But it is work in the sense that his activity yields re-sults: railways. But then you consider railways useless!'

'That's quite another question. I am prepared to admit that they are useful. But every acquisition out of proportion to the toil con-tributed is dishonourable.'

1. Good-nature.

'But who is to decide the proportion?'

'What is dishonourable is the acquisition by wrong means: by cunning,' said Levin, conscious that he could not clearly define the boundary between honesty and dishonesty; 'such as the profits made by banks—the acquisition of enormous wealth without work, just as in the days of the drink-monopolists,—only the form has changed. *Le roi est mort, vive le roi!* [2] Hardly were the monopolies stopped before railways and banks appeared: other means of acquiring wealth without work.'

'Well, all you say may be quite correct and ingenious. . . . Down, Krak!' exclaimed Oblonsky to the dog that was scratching itself and turning round in the hay. He was obviously convinced of the truth of his own view and was therefore calm and deliberate. 'But you have not defined the boundary between honest and dishonest work. I receive a bigger salary than my head clerk, though he knows the work better than I do; is that dishonest?'

'I don't know!'

'Well, then, I'll tell you. That you receive for your work on the estate a profit, let's say of five thousand roubles, while our peasant host, work as he may, cannot get more than fifty, is just as dishonest as my receiving more than my head-clerk, or Malthus getting more than a railway mechanic. In fact I notice a quite unjustifiable hostility on the part of the public toward these men, and it seems to me that it is envy . . .'

'Oh, no! That's not fair,' said Veslovsky. 'It can't be envy, and there is something not clean in their business.'

'No, allow me!' Levin broke in. 'You say it is unjust for me to receive five thousand while the peasant gets only fifty roubles; that's true. It is an injustice and I feel it, but . . .'

'Yes, indeed. Why do we eat and drink, go shooting and do no work, while he is always, always working?' said Vasenka Veslovsky, evidently for the first time in his life thinking of this, and therefore speaking quite genuinely.

'Yes, you feel it, but you won't give him your estate,' said Oblonsky, purposely provoking Levin.

A covert hostility had sprung up between the two brothers-in-law of late, as if being married to two sisters had evoked a sense of rivalry as to which of them would make the best of his life, and now this hostility found expression in the personal tone the discussion was assuming.

'I don't give it away because nobody demands that of me, and if I wanted to I could not do it,' replied Levin; 'besides, there is no one to give it to.'

'Give it to this peasant; he won't refuse.'

2. The king is dead, long live the king!

'Yes, but how should I set about it? Should I go with him and execute a conveyance?'

'I don't know; but if you are convinced that you have no right . . .'

'I'm not at all convinced. On the contrary, I feel that I have no right to give it away, that I have duties toward the land and toward my family.'

'No, allow me—if you consider such inequality unjust, why don't you act accordingly?'

'But I do act so, only in a negative sense, in the sense that I will not seek to increase the inequality that exists between my position and theirs.'

'Pardon me! That is a paradox.'

'Yes, that is a sophistical explanation,' put in Veslovsky. 'Oh, our host!' he said, addressing a peasant who had opened the creaking barn doors and was entering. 'So you are not asleep yet?'

'No, how can I sleep? I thought you gentlemen were asleep, but then I heard you chatting. I want to get a crook here. She won't bite?' he asked, cautiously stepping with bare feet.

'And where are you going to sleep?'

'We are going to pasture the horses to-night.'

'Oh, what a night!' cried Veslovsky, gazing at the corner of the hut and the carts, visible in the faint afterglow through the now open barn-doors as in a frame. 'Just listen! It's women's voices singing, and not at all badly. Who is that singing, mine host?'

'Why, the maid-servants close by.'

'Come, let's go for a walk! We shan't sleep, you know. Oblonsky, come along!'

'If only one could . . . go without getting up!' said Oblonsky, stretching himself. 'It's delightful to lie still.'

'Well, then I'll go alone,' said Veslovsky, rising quickly and putting on his boots. 'Good-bye, gentlemen! If it's jolly I will call you. You have treated me to game, and I won't forget you!'

'Isn't he a fine fellow?' said Oblonsky when Veslovsky had gone out and the peasant had shut the doors after him.

'Yes, fine,' answered Levin, continuing to think of the question they had been discussing. It seemed to him that he had expressed his thoughts and feelings as clearly as he could, yet both the others —sincere and not stupid men—had agreed that he was comforting himself with sophistry. This perturbed him.

'That's what it is, my friend! One of two things: either you confess that the existing order of Society is just, and then uphold your rights; or else own that you are enjoying unfair privileges, as I do, and take them with pleasure.'

'No! If it were unjust, you could not use such advantages with

pleasure; at any rate I could not. The chief thing for me is, not to
feel guilty.'

'I say, hadn't we really better go?' put in Oblonsky, evidently
weary of the mental strain. 'We can't go to sleep, you know. Come
on, let's go!'

Levin did not reply. The words he had used when he said he
was acting justly in a negative sense occupied his mind. 'Is it possible that one can act justly only in a negative sense?' he asked
himself.

'Hasn't the fresh hay a strong scent!' remarked Oblonsky, sitting
up. 'Nothing will make me sleep. Vasenka is up to something out
there. Don't you hear the laughter and his voice? Shan't we go too?
Let's!'

'No, I am not going,' answered Levin.

'Maybe you are stopping here on principle?' said Oblonsky,
smiling, as he searched in the dark for his cap.

'No, not on principle, but why should I go?'

'D'you know, you will bring trouble on yourself,' said Oblonsky,
having found his cap and getting up.

'Why?'

'Don't I see how you have placed yourself with your wife? I heard
you discussing as a question of first-rate importance, whether you
should go away shooting for two days or not! That's all very well
for an idyll, but it can't last a lifetime. A man should be independent—he has his own masculine interests. A man must be manly,'
said Oblonsky, opening the door.

'Is that to say, he should court the maid-servants?' asked Levin.

'Why not, if it's amusing? *Ça ne tire pas à conséquence!* [3] My
wife won't be the worse for it, and I shall have a spree. The important part is to guard the sanctity of the home! Nothing of that kind
at home; but you needn't tie your hands.'

'Perhaps!' said Levin drily, and turned on his side. 'To-morrow
one should start early, and I shall wake no one but shall start at
daybreak.'

'*Messieurs! Venez vite!*' [4] came the voice of Veslovsky, who had
come back. '*Charmante!* It's my discovery. *Charmante!* A perfect
Gretchen, and I have already made her acquaintance. Really, very
pretty!' he said in such an approving way, as if she had been made
pretty specially for him, and he was satisfied with the maker.

Levin pretended to be asleep, but Oblonsky, having put on his
slippers and lit a cigar, left the barn, and their voices soon died
away.

Levin could not fall asleep for a long time. He heard his horses
chewing hay; then how the master and his eldest son got ready and

3. It leads to no consequences.
4. Gentlemen, come quickly.

rode away for the night to pasture their horses; then how the soldier settled down to sleep on the other side of the barn with his nephew, their host's little son; he heard the boy in his treble voice imparting to his uncle his impressions of the dogs, which seemed to him terrible and enormous; then how the boy asked what those dogs were going to catch, and he heard how the soldier replied in a hoarse and sleepy voice that the sportsmen would go next day to the marshes and fire guns, adding, to stop the questioning: 'Sleep, Vaska, sleep, or else look out!' Soon the soldier himself began to snore, and all was still, except for the neighing of the horses and the cry of snipe. 'Can it only be done in a negative sense?' Levin repeated to himself. 'Well, what then? It's not my fault.' And he began to think of the coming day.

'To-morrow I will start early in the morning, and make up my mind not to get excited. There are quantities of snipe and double-snipe too. And when I come back, there will be a note from Kitty. Well, perhaps Stiva is right! I am not manly with her, I have grown effeminate. . . . Well, what's to be done! Again, the negative answer.'

Through his sleep he heard laughter and Veslovsky's and Oblonsky's merry talk. He opened his eyes for an instant: they were standing chatting in the open doorway, brightly lit up by the moon which had now risen. Oblonsky was saying something about the freshness of a girl, comparing her to a fresh kernel just taken from its shell; and Veslovsky was laughing his merry infectious laugh, and repeating something that had probably been told him by a peasant: 'You'd better strive for a wife of your own!'

'Gentlemen! To-morrow at dawn!' Levin mumbled drowsily, and fell asleep.

Chapter XII

Waking at early dawn Levin tried to rouse his companions. Vasenka, lying prone with one stockinged leg outstretched, was sleeping so soundly that it was impossible to get any answer out of him. Oblonsky, half asleep, refused to budge so early. Even Laska, sleeping curled into a ring on a corner of the hay heap, got up reluctantly, and lazily stretched and adjusted first one hind leg and then the other. Having put on his boots, taken his gun, and carefully opened the creaking barn doors, Levin went out into the street. The coachmen were asleep beside the vehicles, the horses were drowsing. Only one of them was lazily eating oats, scattering them over the edge of the trough. The outside world was still grey.

'Why have you risen so early, my dear?' said his aged hostess, who came out of her hut, addressing him cordially as a good old acquaintance.

'Why, I am off shooting, Granny! Can I get to the marsh this way?'

'Straight along at the back of the huts, past our threshing floors, my dear; and then through the hemp-field. There's a path.'

Carefully stepping with her bare sunburnt feet the old woman showed him the way and lifted for him one of the bars enclosing the threshing-floor.

'Go straight on, and you'll step right into the marsh. Our lads took the horses that way last night.'

Laska ran ahead gaily along the footpath, and Levin followed at a brisk pace, continually glancing at the sky. He did not wish the sun to rise before he reached the marsh. But the sun did not tarry. The moon, which was still giving light when first he went out, now shone only like quicksilver; the morning star, previously so noticeable, now had to be looked for; what had been vague spots on the distant field were now clearly visible. They were shocks of rye. As Levin walked through the tall scented hemp, which had already shed its pollen, the dew, invisible till the sun had risen, wetted him to above the waist. In the translucent stillness of the morning the slightest sounds were audible. A bee flew past his ear, whistling like a bullet. He looked close and saw another and a third. They all came from behind the wattle fence of an apiary, and flying across the hemp-field disappeared in the direction of the marsh. The path led him straight to the marsh, which was recognizable by the mist rising from it, thicker at one spot and thinner at another, so that the sedge and willow bushes looked like islets swaying in the mist. At the edge of the marsh the peasant boys and men who had pastured their horses in the night lay, covered with their coats, having fallen asleep at daybreak. Not far from them, three hobbled horses were moving about. One of them clattered its shackles. Laska walked beside her master, seeking permission to run forward and looking around. When he had passed the sleeping peasants and reached the first wet place, Levin examined his percussion caps and allowed Laska to go. One of the horses, a well-fed three-year-old chestnut, on seeing the dog, started, lifted his tail, and snorted. The other horses, also alarmed, splashed through the water with their hobbled feet, making a sound of slapping as they drew their hoofs out of the thick clayey mud, and began floundering their way out of the marsh. Laska paused with a mocking look at the horses and a questioning one at Levin. He stroked her, and whistled as a sign that she might now set off.

Joyful and preoccupied, Laska started running across the bog, which swayed beneath her feet.

On entering the marsh Laska at once perceived, mingled with the various familiar smells of roots, marsh, grass, and rust, and with the unfamiliar smell of horse dung, the scent of the birds—those strong-smelling birds that excited her most—spreading all over the place. Here and there among the marsh mosses and docks, that smell was very strong; but it was impossible to decide in which direction it grew stronger or weaker. To find this out it was necessary to go further away in the direction of the wind. Hardly aware of her legs under her, Laska ran at a strained gallop, which she could cut short at a bound should occasion arise, to the right, away from the morning breeze which blew from the east, and then turned to windward. After inhaling the air with distended nostrils she knew at once that not their scent only but they themselves were there, before her, not one only but many of them. She slackened speed. They were there, but she could not yet determine exactly where. To decide this she began working round in a circle, when her master's voice disturbed her. 'Laska! Here!' he said, pointing to the other side. She stood still, as if asking him whether it would not be better to continue as she had begun; but he repeated his command in a stern voice, pointing to a group of hummocks covered with water where there could not be anything. She obeyed, pretending to search in order to please him, went over the whole place and then returned to the first spot and immediately scented them once more. Now that he was not hindering her, she knew what to do, and without looking where she was stepping, stumbling over hummocks and getting into the water, but surmounting the obstacles with her flexible strong legs, she began the circle which was to make everything clear. *Their* scent came to her more and more pungently, more and more distinctly, and all at once it became quite clear to her that one of them was here behind a hummock, five steps in front. She stopped and her whole body grew rigid. The shortness of her legs prevented her seeing anything before her, but from the scent she could tell that it was not five paces off. She stood, more and more conscious of its presence and enjoying the anticipation. Her rigid tail was outstretched, only its very tip twitching. Her mouth was slightly open and her ears erect. One of her ears had turned back while she ran, she breathed heavily but cautiously, and yet more cautiously looked toward her master, turning her eyes rather than her head. He, with his familiar face but ever terrible eyes, came stumbling over the hummocks, but unusually slowly, she thought. So it seemed to her, though in reality he was running.

Noticing Laska's peculiar manner of searching, as lowering her body almost to the ground she appeared to be dragging her broad hind paws, he knew that she was pointing at snipe, and while running up to her he prayed inwardly for success, especially with the first bird. Having come close up to her he looked beyond, and from his height saw with his eyes what she had found with her nose. In the space between the hummocks, at a distance of about a sazhen, he could see a snipe. It sat with turned head, listening. Then, just spreading its wings slightly and folding them again, it vanished round a corner with an awkward backward jerk.

'Seize it! Seize it!' shouted Levin, pushing Laska from behind.

'But I can't go,' thought she. 'Where should I go to? From here I scent them, but if I go forward, I shall not know what I am doing, nor where they are, nor who they are.' But now he pushed her with his knee, saying in an excited whisper, 'Seize it, Laska! Seize it!'

'Well, if he wishes it, I will, but I can no longer answer for anything,' thought Laska, and rushed forward at full tilt between the hummocks. She now scented nothing more, but only saw and heard without understanding anything.

With lusty cries and a sound of the beating of concave wings so peculiar to the double-snipe, a bird rose; and, following the report of the gun, it fell heavily on its white breast ten paces from the first spot into the wet bog. Another rose behind Levin without waiting to be disturbed by the dog. By the time Levin had turned toward it, it had already gone far: but his shot reached it. After flying some twenty feet, the second snipe rose at an acute angle, and then, turning round and round like a ball, fell heavily on a dry spot.

'Now, things will go right,' thought Levin, putting the warm fat snipe into his bag. 'Eh, Laska dear, will things go right?'

When, having reloaded, Levin went on again, the sun, though still invisible because of the clouds, had already risen. The moon had lost all her brilliancy and gleamed like a little cloud in the sky. Not a single star was any longer visible. The marsh grass that had glittered like silver in the dew was now golden. The rusty patches were like amber. The bluish grasses had turned yellowish green. Marsh birds were busy in the dew-bespangled bushes that cast long shadows beside the brook. A hawk had woke up and was sitting on a haycock, turning its head from side to side and looking discontentedly at the marsh. Crows were flying to the fields, and a barefooted boy was already driving the horses toward an old man, who had got up from beneath his coat and sat scratching himself. The powder-smoke spread like milk over the green grass.

A boy ran up to Levin.

'Uncle, there were ducks here yesterday!' he shouted, following Levin from afar.

And Levin felt increased pleasure in killing three snipe one after another within sight of this little boy, who expressed his approval.

Chapter XIII

The sportsman's saying, that if you don't miss your first beast or first bird your day will be successful was justified.

Tired, hungry, and happy, Levin returned to his lodging toward ten o'clock, having tramped some thirty versts and bringing nineteen red-fleshed birds, besides a duck tied to his girdle, as there was no room for it in his bag. His comrades had wakened long before and had had time to get hungry and have their breakfast.

'Wait a bit—wait a bit! I know there are nineteen,' said Levin, for a second time counting his snipe and double-snipe, which no longer had the important appearance they bore when on the wing, but were twisted, dried up, smeared with congealed blood, and had heads bent to one side.

The tale was correct, and Oblonsky's envy gratified Levin. He was also pleased that on his return he found a messenger had already arrived from Kitty with a note.

'I am quite well and happy. If you were uneasy about me, you may be quite at ease now. I have a new bodyguard—Mary Vlasyevna,' this was the midwife, a new and important personage in the Levins' family life. 'She has come to see me and finds me perfectly well, and we have got her to stay till your return. All are cheerful and well, so don't hurry and even stay another day if your sport is good.'

These two joys, his successful shooting and the news from his wife, were so great that two small unpleasantnesses which occurred after the shooting were easy to disregard. One was that the chestnut side-horse, having evidently been overworked the previous day, was off its feed and seemed dull. The coachman said it had been strained.

'It was overdriven yesterday, Constantine Dmitrich,' he said. 'Why, it was driven hard for ten versts!'

The other unpleasantness, which for a moment upset his good-humour, but about which he afterwards laughed heartily, was that of all the provisions that Kitty had provided so lavishly that it had appeared impossible to eat them up in a week, nothing was left! Returning tired and hungry from his sport, Levin so vividly anticipated the pies that on approaching his lodging he seemed to smell and taste them—just as Laska scented game—and he immediately ordered Philip to serve them. It turned out that there were no pies, nor even any chicken left!

'He *has* an appetite!' said Oblonsky, laughing and pointing to Vasenka Veslovsky. 'I don't suffer from lack of appetite, but he's quite surprising . . .'

'*Mais c'est delicieux,*' Veslovsky praised the beef he had eaten.

'Well, it can't be helped!' said Levin, looking morosely at

Veslovsky. 'Well then, bring me some beef, Philip!'

'The beef has been eaten, and the bone was given to the dogs,' answered Philip.

Levin was so annoyed that he said crossly: 'Something might have been left for me!' and he felt inclined to cry. 'Well then, draw the birds and stuff them with nettles,' said he in a trembling voice to Philip, trying not to look at Veslovsky; 'and ask at least for some milk for me.'

Later on, when he had satisfied his hunger with the milk, he felt ashamed of having shown annoyance to a stranger, and he began laughing at his hungry irritation.

In the evening they again went out shooting, when Veslovsky also killed some birds, and late at night they set off home.

The drive back was as merry as the drive out had been. Veslovsky now sang, now recalled with relish his adventures with the peasants who entertained him with vodka and said 'No offence!'; and now his night exploits, the games and the maid-servant, and the peasant who asked him whether he was married, and learning that he was not said: 'Don't hanker after other men's wives, but above all things strive to get one of your own!' These words particularly amused Veslovsky.

'Altogether I am awfully pleased with our outing . . . And you, Levin?'

'I am very pleased with it too,' said Levin sincerely. He was glad not only to feel no hostility such as he had felt at home toward Vasenka Veslovsky, but on the contrary to feel quite friendly toward him.

Chapter XIV

Next morning at ten o'clock Levin, having made the round of his farm, knocked at the door of Vasenka's room.

'*Entrez!*' shouted Veslovsky. 'Excuse me—I have only just finished my ablutions,' he said smiling, as he stood before Levin in his underclothes.

'Please don't mind me,' and Levin sat down by the window. 'Have you slept well?'

'Like the dead! What a day it is for shooting!'

'What do you drink, tea or coffee?'

'Neither. Nothing before lunch. I am really quite ashamed. I expect the ladies are already up? It would be fine to go for a walk now. You must show me your horses.'

When they had walked round the garden, visited the stables, and even done some gymnastics together on the parallel bars, Levin returned to the house with his guest and entered the drawing-room with him.

'We had fine sport, and so many new impressions!' said Veslovsky, approaching Kitty, who sat at the samovar. 'What a pity ladies are deprived of that pleasure.'

'Well, what of it? He must say something to the mistress of the house,' Levin told himself. He again thought he noticed something in the smile and conquering air with which the visitor addressed Kitty. . . .

The Princess, who sat at the other end of the table with Mary Vlasyevna and Oblonsky, called Levin and began a conversation about moving to Moscow for Kitty's confinement and taking a house there. Just as all the preparations for the wedding had been disagreeable to him, since they detracted by their insignificance from the majesty of what was taking place, so now the preparations for the coming birth, the time of which they were reckoning on their fingers, appeared to him yet more offensive. He always tried not to hear those conversations about the best way of swaddling the future infant, tried to turn away and not see those mysterious endless knitted binders and three-cornered pieces of linen, to which Dolly attached special importance,—and all the rest. The birth of a son (he was certain it would be a son) which they promised him, but in which he still could not believe, so extraordinary did it seem, appeared to him on the one hand such an immense and therefore impossible happiness, and on the other such a mysterious event, that this pretended knowledge of what was going to happen and consequent preparations as for something ordinary, something produced by human beings, seemed to him an indignity and a degradation.

But the Princess did not understand his feelings and attributed his unwillingness to think and speak about it to thoughtlessness and indifference, and therefore gave him no peace. She was now commissioning Oblonsky to see about a house, and called Levin to her.

'I don't know at all, Princess. Do as you think best,' he said.

'You must decide when you will move.'

'I really don't know. I know that millions of children are born without Moscow and without doctors; then why . . .'

'Well, if that's . . .'

'Oh no! Just as Kitty likes.'

'But one can't talk to Kitty about it! Why, do you want me to frighten her? You know, only this spring Nataly Golitsin died because she had a bad doctor.'

'I will do whatever you tell me to,' he replied morosely.

The Princess began telling him, but he did not listen to her. Though this talk with the Princess upset him, it was not that but what he saw by the samovar which made him morose.

'No, this is impossible,' he thought, glancing occasionally at Vasenka, who was leaning toward Kitty and saying something, with his handsome smile, and at Kitty, blushing and agitated.

There was something impure in Vasenka's attitude, his look and his smile. Levin even saw something impure in Kitty's pose and smile; and again the light faded from his eyes. Again, as on the previous occasion, he suddenly, without the least interval, felt thrown from the height of happiness, peace, and dignity into an abyss of despair, malevolence, and degradation. Again everyone and everything became revolting to him.

'Well then, Princess, let it be just as you think best,' he said, turning away.

' "Heavy is the Autocrat's crown!" ' [5] said Oblonsky banteringly, evidently alluding not only to the Princess's conversation, but also to the cause of Levin's agitation, which he had observed. 'How late you are to-day, Dolly!'

They all rose to greet Dolly. Vasenka only rose for a moment, and with the absence of politeness to women which is characteristic of modern young men, barely bowed and again continued his conversation, laughing at something.

'Masha has worn me out. She slept badly and is terribly capricious this morning,' said Dolly.

The conversation with Kitty begun by Vasenka again dealt with Anna and with the question whether love can rise above social conditions. This conversation was unpleasant to Kitty and upset her, both by the subject itself and by the tone in which it was carried on, but especially because she already knew the effect it would have on her husband. But she was too simple and innocent to know how to stop it, or even how to conceal the superficial pleasure which this young man's evident attentions caused her. She wished to put an end to the conversation, but did not know how. Whatever she did, she knew, would be noticed by her husband and would all be construed into something wrong. And really when she asked Dolly what was the matter with Masha, and Vasenka—waiting for this uninteresting conversation to finish—gazed indifferently at Dolly, her question seemed to Levin a piece of unnatural and disgusting cunning.

'Well, shall we go to pick mushrooms to-day?' said Dolly.

'Yes, please, and I will go too,' said Kitty, and blushed. She had been going, out of politeness, to ask Vasenka whether he would go with them, but refrained. 'Where are you going, Kostya?' she asked her husband with a guilty look as he passed by with resolute steps. This guilty look confirmed all his suspicions.

'The mechanic arrived during my absence and I have not yet

seen him,' he answered, without looking at her.

He went downstairs, but had not had time to leave his study before he heard his wife's familiar footsteps following him with imprudent rapidity.

'What is it?' he asked drily. 'We are busy.'

'Excuse me,' she said addressing the German mechanic, 'I have a few words to say to my husband.'

The German was about to go out, but Levin said to him:

'Don't trouble!'

'The train is at three?' asked the German, 'I must not miss it.' Levin did not answer him but went out with his wife.

'Well, what have you to say to me?' he asked in French.

He did not look her in the face and did not notice that she (in her condition) stood with her whole face twitching, and had a pitiful, crushed appearance.

'I . . . I want to tell you that it's impossible to live like this— it's torture!' she muttered.

'The servants are there, in the pantry,' he said angrily; 'don't make a scene.'

'Well then, come here!'

They were in a passage, and Kitty wished to enter the next room; but the English governess was there, giving Tanya a lesson.

'Well, come into the garden!'

In the garden they came upon a man weeding a path, and without any longer considering that the man saw her tear-stained eyes and his excited face, or that they looked like people running away from some calamity, they went on with rapid feet, feeling that they must speak out and convince each other, must be alone together, and thereby both escape from the torment both were experiencing.

'One can't live like this! It is torture! I suffer and you suffer. Why?' she asked, when they had at last reached a secluded seat at the corner of the limetree avenue.

'Only tell me this: was there something improper, impure, degradingly horrid in his tone?' he said, standing in front of her in the same attitude as on that night, with fists pressing his chest.

'There was,' she said in a trembling voice. 'But, Kostya, do you really not see that I am not to blame? From the time I came down I wanted to adopt a tone . . . but these people . . . Why did he come? How happy we were!' she said, choking with sobs that shook the whole of her expanded body.

The gardener saw with surprise that, though nothing had been pursuing them and there had been nothing to run away from, and they could not have found anything very blissful on that seat, they passed him on their way back to the house with quieted and beaming faces.

Chapter XV

After seeing his wife upstairs, Levin went to Dolly's part of the house. She too was in great trouble that day. She was walking up and down the room and speaking angrily to a little girl who stood howling in a corner:

'You'll stand in that corner all day, and will have your dinner alone, and you will not see a single doll, and I won't have a new frock made for you!' she was saying, unable to think of any more punishments for the child.

'Oh, she is a horrid child!' she cried, addressing Levin. 'Where do these vile tendencies in her come from?'

'But what has she done?' asked Levin rather indifferently. He wanted to consult her about his own affairs, and was annoyed at having come at an inopportune moment.

'She and Grisha went away among the raspberry canes and there . . . I can't even tell what she did. One regrets Miss Elliot a thousand times—this one does not look after the children; she's only a machine. . . . *Figurez vous que la petite* . . .'[6]

Dolly told Masha's crime.

'That proves nothing; it is not a bad tendency, but just mischievousness,' Levin comforted her.

'But you are upset about something? Why have you come?' asked Dolly. 'What's happening there?'

And by the tone of her question Levin knew that it would be easy for him to tell her what he meant to say.

'I was not there, but have been in the garden alone with Kitty. We have quarrelled for the second time since . . . Stiva's arrival.'

Dolly gazed at him with wise, comprehending eyes.

'Well, tell me, hand on heart—was there . . . not on Kitty's side, but on that gentleman's . . . a tone which might be unpleasant . . . not unpleasant but terrible and offensive to a husband?

'That is to say . . . how am I to put it? . . . Stop! Stop in the corner!' she said turning to Masha, who noticing a scarcely perceptible smile on her mother's face was turning round. 'The world would say he has behaved as all young men behave. *Il fait la cour à une jeune et jolie femme*,[7] and a Society husband should be merely flattered by it.'

'Yes, yes,' answered Levin gloomily, 'but you noticed it?'

'Not I only, but Stiva too. He told me frankly after tea: "*Je crois que Veslovsky fait un petit brin de cour à Kitty!*" '[8]

6. Fancy! the child . . .
7. He pays court to a young and pretty woman.
8. I believe Veslovsky is courting Kitty a wee bit.

'Well, all right, now I am tranquil. I will turn him out,' said Levin.

'What do you mean? Have you gone mad?' exclaimed Dolly, terrified. 'What do you mean, Kostya? Consider!' she went on, laughing. 'You can go to Fanny now,' she said to Masha. 'No, if you like I will tell Stiva and he will take him away. One can say you are expecting visitors. Certainly, he does not suit your household . . .'

'No, no; I'll do it myself.'

'But you will quarrel?'

'Not at all! It will be a pleasure for me, a real pleasure,' said Levin with sparkling eyes. 'Come, forgive her, Dolly! She won't do it again,' he pleaded, referring to the small culprit, who had not gone to Fanny, but stood hesitatingly before her mother, looking up from under her brows, expecting and trying to catch her eye.

Dolly looked at her. The little girl burst into sobs and buried her face in her mother's lap, and Dolly placed her thin tender hand on the child's head.

'What is there in common between us and him?' thought Levin, as he went in search of Veslovsky.

Passing through the hall he ordered the *calèche* to be harnessed to drive to the station.

'One of the springs broke yesterday,' replied the footman.

'Well, then, the *tarantas*, but make haste! Where is the visitor?'

'He has gone to his room.'

Levin found Vasenka, who had unpacked his portmanteau and spread out his new songs, trying on a pair of leggings and preparing for a ride.

Whether there was something unusual in Levin's face, or whether Vasenka himself felt that *'le petit brin de cour'* which he had started was out of place in this family, he was embarrassed (as far as is permissible to a man in Society) by Levin's entry.

'You wear leggings for riding?'

'Yes, it's much cleaner,' said Vasenka, placing his fat foot on a chair, fastening the bottom hook, and smiling good-naturedly.

He was certainly a good-natured fellow, and Levin felt sorry for him and ashamed of himself as a host, when he noticed the shyness of Vasenka's look. On the table lay a piece of stick which when doing gymnastics that morning they had broken, trying to raise the warped parallel bars. Levin took the broken stick and began pulling off the splintered bits at the end, not knowing how to begin.

'I wished . . .' He stopped, but suddenly remembering Kitty and all that had happened, he said, looking Veslovsky firmly in the eyes: 'I have ordered the horses to be harnessed for you.'

'What do you mean?' Vasenka began with surprise. 'To drive where?'

'For you, to the station,' answered Levin gloomily, pulling splinters.

'Why, are you going away, or has anything happened?'

'It happens that I am expecting visitors,' replied Levin more rapidly, breaking off the splintered bits of the stick with his strong fingers. 'Or no, I am not expecting visitors and nothing has happened, yet I request you to leave. You may explain my impoliteness as you please.'

Vasenka drew himself up.

'I ask *you* for an explanation,' he said with dignity, having at last understood.

'I can't give you an explanation,' said Levin softly and slowly, trying to control the trembling of his jaw, 'and it is better for you not to ask.'

As the splinters were now all broken off, Levin grasped the thick ends in his fingers and split the stick, carefully catching a piece as it fell.

Probably the sight of those strained arms, those muscles he had felt that morning when doing gymnastics, and the gleaming eyes, low voice and trembling jaws, convinced Vasenka more than the words. He shrugged his shoulders, smiled contemptuously, and bowed.

'Can I not see Oblonsky?'

The shrug and smile did not irritate Levin. 'What else is there for him to do?' he thought.

'I will send him to you at once.'

'What is this nonsense?' said Oblonsky, when he had heard from his friend that he was being driven out of the house, and had found Levin in the garden, where he was walking while awaiting the departure of his visitor. '*Mais c'est ridicule!* What fly has stung you? *Mais c'est du dernier ridicule!*[9] Why, do you imagine that if a young man . . .'

But the place where the fly had stung Levin was evidently still sore, for he again grew pale when Oblonsky wished to refer to his reason, and hastily interrupted him.

'Please don't explain my reasons! I can't do otherwise! I feel ashamed before you and before him. But I don't think it will grieve him much to go away, and his presence is unpleasant to me and to my wife.'

'But he feels insulted! *Et puis, c'est ridicule!*'[1]

'And I feel insulted and tortured! And I have done nothing wrong and don't deserve to suffer.'

'Well, I never expected this of you! *On peut être jaloux, mais*

9. But it's ridiculous. . . . But it's the height of absurdity.
1. And besides, it's absurd!

à ce point c'est du dernier ridicule!' [2]

Levin turned away from him quickly and went far down one of the avenues, where he continued walking up and down alone. Soon he heard the rattle of the *tarantas*, and through the trees saw Vasenka, seated on hay (unluckily the *tarantas* had no seat), with the Scotch bonnet on his head, jolting over the ruts as he was driven down the other avenue.

'What does that mean?' wondered Levin when the footman ran out of the house and stopped the vehicle. It was on account of the mechanic, whom Levin had quite forgotten. He bowed and said something to Veslovsky, then climbed into the *tarantas*, and they drove away together.

Oblonsky and the Princess were indignant at Levin's conduct. He himself felt not only that he was in the highest degree ridiculous, but quite guilty and disgraced; but recalling what he and his wife had suffered, and asking himself how he would act another time, he answered that he would do just the same again.

In spite of all this, by the end of the day every one, except the Princess, who could not forgive Levin's conduct, became unusually animated and merry, like children after a punishment or adults after an oppressive official reception; so that in the Princess's absence they talked about Vasenka's expulsion as of an historic event. Dolly, who had inherited her father's gift of putting things humorously, made Varenka collapse with laughter when she related for the third or fourth time, with ever fresh humorous additions, how she was just putting on some new ribbons in the visitor's honour, and was about to go into the drawing-room, when suddenly she heard the clatter of the old cart. 'And who was inside the cart? Who but Vasenka, with his Scotch bonnet and his songs and his leggings, sitting on the hay!'

'At least you might have let him have the brougham! . . . And then I hear: "Stop!" "Well," think I, "they've relented." I look again and they had popped a fat German in with him and were driving them both off . . . ! And so my ribbons were all in vain. . . .'

Chapter XVI

Dolly carried out her intention of going to see Anna. She was very sorry to grieve her sister and to do anything that was unpleasant to Levin: she felt that they were right in not wishing to have anything to do with Vronsky, but felt it her duty to visit Anna and show her that the altered circumstances could not change her own feelings toward her.

Not to depend on the Levins for that journey, Dolly sent to the

2. One may be jealous, but to such a point it is the height of absurdity!

village to hire horses; but Levin hearing of it came and reproached her.

'Why do you think your going would be unpleasant to me? Even if it were unpleasant it would be still more unpleasant for me if you did not use my horses,' he said. 'You never told me definitely that you were going. And that you should hire horses in the village is, in the first place, unpleasant to me, and besides that, they will undertake the job but won't get you there. I have horses, and if you don't wish to grieve me, you will take them.'

Dolly had to agree, and on the appointed day Levin had four horses ready for his sister-in-law, as well as a relay—having made it up of farm and riding horses—not at all a handsome team, but one able to get her to her destination in a day. As horses were also required for the Princess, who was leaving, and for the midwife, it was inconvenient to Levin; but he could not be so inhospitable as to allow Dolly to hire horses while staying with him. Besides, he knew that the twenty roubles she would have had to pay for the journey were of importance to her, and he felt her distressing financial embarrassments as if they had been his own.

Acting on Levin's advice, Dolly started before daybreak. The road was good, the *calèche* comfortable, the horses ran merrily, and on the box beside the coachman instead of a footman sat an office clerk whom Levin sent with her for safety. Dolly dozed, and only woke up when approaching the inn where the horses were to be changed.

After drinking tea at the prosperous peasant's house where Levin had stopped when on his way to Sviyazhsky's, and conversing with the women about their children and with the old man about Count Vronsky, of whom he spoke very highly, Dolly continued her journey at ten o'clock. At home her care of the children never gave her leisure to think, but now, during this four hours' drive, all the thoughts she had repressed crowded suddenly into her mind, and she reviewed her whole life from all sides as she had never done before. Her thoughts seemed strange to her. At first she thought of the children, about whom, though the Princess and especially Kitty (she had greater faith in Kitty) had promised to look after them, she still felt anxious. 'If only Masha does not get into mischief again, or a horse does not kick Grisha, and if only Lily's digestion does not get more upset.' But then questions of the present began to be replaced by those of the immediate future. She began thinking that she would have to move into another house in Moscow for the winter, have the drawing-room furniture re-covered, and a new winter coat made for the eldest girl. Then came problems of a more remote future: how she should start her children in the world. 'With the girls it will be comparatively easy,' she thought, 'but how about the boys?

'At present I am teaching Grisha, but that is only because I am free now and not having a baby. Of course Stiva is not to be counted on, but with the help of kind people I shall start them somehow. . . . But in case of another child . . .' And it occurred to her how inaccurate it is to say that woman's curse is the bringing forth of children. 'Travail, that's nothing—but pregnancy is torture,' she thought, with her last pregnancy and the death of her infant in mind. And she recalled a talk she had had with a young woman at the halting-place. In answer to the question whether she had any children, the good-looking young peasant wife had cheerfully replied:

'I had one girl, but God released me. I buried her in Lent.'

'And are you very sorry?' asked Dolly.

'What's there to be sorry about? The old man has plenty of grandchildren as it is. They're nothing but worry. You can't work or anything. They're nothing but a tie . . .'

This answer had seemed horrible to Dolly, despite the good-natured sweetness of the young woman's looks, but now she could not help recalling it. In those cynical words there was some truth. 'Altogether,' she thought, looking back at the whole of her life during those fifteen years of wedlock, 'pregnancy, sickness, dullness of mind, indifference to everything, and above all disfigurement. Even Kitty—young, pretty Kitty—how much plainer she has become! And I when I am pregnant become hideous, I know. Travail, suffering, monstrous suffering, and that final moment . . . then nursing, sleepless nights, and that awful pain!'

Dolly shuddered at the mere thought of the pain she had endured from sore nipples, from which she had suffered with almost every baby. 'Then the children's illnesses, that continued anxiety; then their education, nasty tendencies,' (she recalled little Masha's delinquency among the raspberry canes), 'lessons, Latin. . . . It is all so incomprehensible and difficult. And above all, the death of these children . . .' And once more the cruel memory rose that always weighed on her mother-heart: the death of her last baby, a boy who died of croup; his funeral, the general indifference shown to the little pink coffin, and her own heartrending, lonely grief at the sight of that pale little forehead with the curly locks on the temples, and of the open, surprised little mouth visible in the coffin at the instant before they covered it with the pink lid ornamented with a gold lace cross.

'And what is it all for? What will come of it all? I myself, without having a moment's peace, now pregnant, now nursing, always cross and grumbling, tormenting myself and others, repulsive to my husband—I shall live my life, and produce unfortunate, badly brought-up and beggared children. Even now, if we had not spent this summer with Kostya and Kitty, I don't know how we should have managed. Of course Kostya and Kitty are so considerate that we don't feel it; but it can't go on so. They will have children of their own and won't be able to help us; as it is, they are put to inconvenience. Is Papa, who has kept scarcely anything for himself, to help us? . . . So I can't even give the children a start myself, unless it's with other people's help and with humiliation. Well, supposing the best: that none of the other children die, and that I somehow suceed in bringing them up; at the very best they will only escape being ne'er-do-wells. That is all I can hope for. And for this, so much suffering and trouble. . . . My whole life ruined!' Again she remembered what the young woman had said. Again the recollection was repulsive to her, but she could not help admitting that there was a measure of crude truth in the words.

'Is it much further, Michael?' she asked the clerk, to dispel the thoughts that frightened her.

'They say it's seven versts from this village.'

The *calèche* was descending the village street to a small bridge. A crowd of merry peasant women, with ready-twisted sheaf-binders hanging from their shoulders, were crossing the bridge, chattering loudly and merrily. The women stopped on the bridge, inquisitively scrutinizing the *calèche*. All the faces turned toward her seemed to Dolly to be healthy and bright, mocking her with their joy in life. 'Everybody lives, everybody enjoys living,' Dolly continued her reflections when, after passing the peasant women and having reached the top of the incline, they were going at a trot, the old *calèche* comfortably swaying on its soft springs, 'and I, released as from a prison, from the world that is killing me with its worries, have only now collected my thoughts for a moment. Everybody lives: these women, and my sister Nataly, and Varenka, and Anna to whom I am going,—only not I!

'And they are all down on Anna! What for? Am I better than she? I at least have a husband whom I love. Not as I wished to love, but still I do love him; but Anna did not love hers. In what is she to blame? She wishes to live. God has implanted that need in our souls. It is quite possible I might have done the same. I don't even know whether I did well to listen to her at that terrible time when she came to me in Moscow. I ought then to have left my husband and begun life anew. I might have loved and been loved, the real way. And is it better now? I don't respect him. I need him,' she thought of her husband, 'and I put up with him. Is that any better? I was still attractive then, still had my good looks,' she went on, feeling that she wanted to see herself in a glass. She had a small traveling looking-glass in her bag, and felt inclined to take it out;

but glancing at the backs of the coachman and the clerk who sat swaying beside him, she knew she would feel ashamed if one of them chanced to look round, and she did not take it out.

Yet even without looking in the glass she thought it might not be too late even now. She remembered Koznyshev, who was particularly amiable to her; Stiva's friend the good-natured Turovtsin, who had helped her nurse her children when they had scarlet fever and who was in love with her; and then there was a very young man who considered—so her husband told her as a joke—that she was the handsomest of the three sisters. And the most passionate and impossible romances occurred to Dolly's fancy. 'Anna has acted excellently, and I at any rate shall not reproach her at all. She is happy, she is making another happy and is not dragged down as I am, but she is no doubt as fresh, clever, and frank as ever,' she thought; and a roguish smile puckered her lips, chiefly because while thinking of Anna's romance she invented an almost similar romance for herself with an imaginary, composite man who was in love with her. Like Anna, she confessed everything to her husband, and Oblonsky's surprise and embarrassment at the announcement made her smile.

Wrapped in such dreams she reached the turning from the high road, which led to Vozdvizhensk.

Chapter XVII

The coachman stopped the horses and looked round toward a field of rye on the right, where some peasants sat beside a cart. The clerk wished to get down, but then, changing his mind, shouted authoritatively and beckoned to a peasant. The breeze, which they had felt while driving, died down when they stopped; and horse-flies settled on the sweating horses, which angrily tried to brush them off. The metallic sound of a scythe being hammered beside the cart ceased, and one of the peasants rose and came toward the calèche.

'Look at him, stuck fast!' shouted the clerk angrily at the peasant, who was slowly stepping with bare feet over the ruts of the dry, hard-trodden road. 'Be quick!'

The curly-headed old man, with a piece of bast tied round his head, his rounded back dark with perspiration, increased his speed, approached the calèche and put his sunburnt arm on the mud-guard.

'Vozdvizhensk? The squire's house? To the Count's?' he repeated. 'There! When you have passed that bend turn to the left, and go right down the drive and you'll knock up straight against it. But whom do you want? The squire?'

'Are they at home, my good man?' said Dolly vaguely, not knowing how to speak of Anna even to a peasant.

'I expect so,' said the peasant, shifting from one bare foot to the other, leaving in the dust a clear imprint of it with its five toes. 'I expect so,' he repeated, evidently desiring a talk. 'More visitors arrived yesterday. Visitors! Just awful. . . . What do you want?' He turned toward a lad beside the cart who was shouting something. 'Quite right—a while ago they passed by here on horseback, to see the reaper. Now they must be at home again. And who may you be?'

'We have come a long way,' replied the coachman, climbing back on to the box. 'And you say it's not far?'

'I tell you it's just there, where you come out,' and he went on rubbing his hand along the mud-guard of the *calèche*.

A young, healthy-looking, thick-set lad also came up.

'Could I get a job, harvesting?' he asked.

'I don't know, my lad.'

'There, you see, when you've turned to the left you'll knock straight up against it,' said the peasant, evidently unwilling to let them go, and wishing to talk.

The coachman started, but hardly had they gone round the corner when the peasants called out to them.

'Stop, friend! Stop!' shouted two voices.

The coachman pulled up.

'They are coming! Here they are themselves!' cried the man, pointing to four persons on horseback and two in a char-a-banc coming along the road.

It was Vronsky with his jockey, Veslovsky and Anna on horseback, and Princess Barbara with Sviyazhsky in the char-a-banc. They had been for a ride and to see some newly-arrived reaping machines in operation.

When the *calèche* pulled up, the riders advanced at a foot pace. Anna rode in front beside Veslovsky. She rode quietly, on a small sturdy English cob with a close-cropped mane and short tail. Dolly was struck by the beauty of her head with locks of black hair which had escaped from under her top hat, her full shoulders and fine waist in the black riding-habit, and her whole quiet graceful bearing.

For a moment she thought it unsuitable for Anna to be riding on horseback. In Dolly's mind the idea of horse-riding for women was connected with youthful coquetry, which in her opinion was unsuitable to a woman in Anna's position; but when she saw her closer she at once became reconciled to Anna's riding. Despite her elegance, everything about Anna—her bearing, clothes and movements—was so simple, quiet, and dignified, that nothing could seem more natural.

At Anna's side, on a heated bay cavalry horse, stretching out his fat legs and evidently admiring himself, rode Vasenka Veslovsky, wearing the Scotch bonnet with waving ribbons, and Dolly could not repress a merry smile on recognizing him. Behind them rode Vronsky. He was on a thoroughbred dark bay, which was obviously heated by galloping, and he was using the reins to hold it in.

Behind him rode a short man dressed as a jockey. Sviyazhsky and the Princess Barbara in a new char-a-banc, to which was harnessed a tall trotter, were overtaking the riders.

Anna's face immediately brightened into a joyful smile when she recognized Dolly in the little figure pressed back in a corner of the old *calèche*. She gave an exclamation, started in her saddle and touched her horse into a gallop. Riding up to the *calèche* she jumped unaided from the horse and, holding up her habit, ran toward Dolly.

'It's what I thought, but dared not expect! What a pleasure! You cannot imagine how delighted I am!' she cried, now pressing her face to Dolly's and kissing her, now leaning back to gaze smilingly at her.

'What joy, Alexey!' she said, turning to Vronsky, who had dismounted and was walking toward them.

Vronsky, taking off his grey top hat, approached Dolly.

'You can have no idea how pleased we are that you have come,' he said, putting peculiar emphasis into his words, while a smile exposed his strong white teeth.

Vasenka Veslovsky, without dismounting, raised his cap and welcomed the visitor, joyously waving his ribbons above his head.

'That is the Princess Barbara,' Anna said, in answer to Dolly's glance of inquiry when the char-a-banc came nearer.

'Oh!' said Dolly, and her face involuntarily expressed displeasure.

The Princess Barbara was her husband's aunt, she had long known her and did not respect her. She knew that the Princess Barbara had all her life been a hanger-on to various rich relatives; but that she—a relation of Dolly's husband—should now be living in the house of Vronsky, a perfect stranger to her, offended Dolly. Anna noticed Dolly's expression, became confused, blushed, let her habit slip out of her hands, and stumbled over it.

Dolly walked up to the char-a-banc and coldly greeted Princess Barbara. She was acquainted with Sviyazhsky too. He asked how his friend the crank was getting on with his young wife, and having glanced at the ill-matched horses and the patched mud-guard of the *calèche*, offered the ladies seats in the char-a-banc.

'I will go in that vehicle,' he said. 'My horse is a quiet one, and the Princess drives splendidly.'

'No, stay as you are,' said Anna, who had also come up, 'and we two will go in the *calèche*,' and giving Dolly her arm she led her away.

Dolly was dazzled by the elegant equipage of a kind she had never seen, by the beautiful horses and the elegant, brilliant persons about her. But what struck her most was the change that had taken place in Anna, whom she knew and loved. Another woman less observant, who had not known Anna before, especially one who had not thought the thoughts that were in Dolly's mind on the way, would not have noticed anything peculiar in Anna. But now Dolly was struck by that temporary beauty which only comes to women in moments of love, and which she now found in Anna's face. Everything in that face: the definiteness of the dimples on cheeks and chin, the curve of her lips, the smile that seemed to flutter around her face, the light in her eyes, the grace and swift-ness of her movements, the fulness of her voice, even the manner in which she replied—half-crossly, half-kindly—to Veslovsky, who asked permission to ride her cob that he might teach it to lead with the right leg when galloping—everything about her was peculiarly attractive, and she seemed to know it and to be glad of it.

When the two women took their seats in the *calèche*, both were seized with shyness. Anna was abashed by the attentively inquiring look Dolly bent upon her; Dolly, after Sviyazhsky's remark about the 'vehicle,' felt involuntarily ashamed of the ramshackle old *calèche*, in which Anna had taken a seat beside her. Philip the coachman and the clerk shared that feeling. The clerk, to hide his embarrassment, bustled about, helping the ladies in, but Philip be-came morose and made up his mind not to be imposed upon by this external superiority. He smiled ironically as he glanced at the raven trotter of the char-a-banc, deciding that that horse was good for nothing but a promenade, and could not do its forty versts on a hot day at one go.

The peasants beside the cart all got up and looked with merry curiosity at the visitor, making their own comments.

'Glad they are: have not met for a long time!' said the curly-haired old man with the piece of bast tied round his head.

'There now, Uncle Gerasim! That raven gelding would cart the sheaves in no time.'

'Just look! Is that a woman in breeches?' cried one, pointing to Vasenka Veslovsky, who was getting into the side-saddle.

'No, it's a man. See how easily he jumped up!'

'I say, lads! It seems we are not to have a sleep!'

'What chance of a sleep to-day?' said the old man, blinking at the sun. 'It's too late! Take your scythes and let's get to work.'

Chapter XVIII

Anna was looking at Dolly's thin wan face with its dust-filled wrinkles, and wishing to tell her just what she thought: that Dolly looked thinner and worse. But remembering that her own looks had improved and that Dolly's eyes had told her so, she sighed and began talking about herself.

'You are looking at me,' she said, 'and wondering whether I can be happy, placed as I am? Well, what do you think? I am ashamed to confess it, but I . . . I am unforgivably happy! Something magical has happened to me: like a dream when one feels frightened and creepy, and suddenly wakes up to the knowledge that no such terrors exist. I have wakened up! I have lived through sufferings and terrors, but for a long time past—especially since we came here—I have been happy! . . .' she said, looking at Dolly timidly and with a questioning smile.

'I am so glad!' answered Dolly, smiling, but in a colder tone than she intended. 'I am very glad for your sake. Why did you not write to me?'

'Why? . . . Because I did not dare . . . you forget my position.'

'To me? You dared not? If only you knew how I . . . I consider . . .'

Dolly wanted to tell Anna what she had been thinking that morning; but for some reason it now seemed out of place. 'However, we will talk about all that later. What is this? What are all those buildings? Quite a town!' she asked, to change the subject, pointing to the red and green roofs visible above a living green wall of acacias and lilacs.

But Anna did not answer her.

'No, no! What view do you take of my position? What do you think? What?' she asked.

'I imagine . . .' Dolly began; but at that moment Vasenka Veslovsky, who had got the cob to lead with the right foot, galloped past in his short jacket, bumping heavily on the leathers of the side-saddle. 'It goes all right, Anna Arkadyevna!' he shouted. Anna did not even glance at him; but it still seemed to Dolly out of place to begin to discuss this big subject in the *calèche*, so she briefly replied:

'I don't take any view. I always loved you, and if one loves, one loves the whole person as he or she is, and not as one might wish them to be.'

Anna, turning her eyes away from her friend and screwing them up (this was a new habit of hers and unfamiliar to Dolly), grew thoughtful, trying thoroughly to grasp the meaning of the remark. Having evidently understood it in the sense she wished, she glanced at Dolly.

'If you had any sins,' she said, 'they would all be forgiven you for coming here and for those words!'

And Dolly noticed that tears had started to her eyes. She silently pressed Anna's hand.

'But what are those buildings? What a lot of them there are!' said she after a moment's silence, repeating her question.

'They are the employees' houses, the stud farm, and the stables,' answered Anna. 'And here the park begins. Everything had been neglected, but Alexey has had it all renovated. He is very fond of this estate, and—a thing I never expected of him—he is quite enthusiastic in managing the place. But of course his is such a talented nature! Whatever he takes up, he does splendidly! He is not only not bored, but passionately engrossed in his occupations. He has grown into a first-rate, prudent landlord, as I recognize; in farming matters he is even stingy, but only in farming. Where it is a question of thousands he does not count them,' she said, with that joyous sly smile with which women often speak of the secret characteristics, discovered by them alone, of the man they love. 'Do you see that big building? It is the new hospital. I think it will cost more than a hundred thousand roubles. That is his hobby just now. And do you know why he started it? The peasants asked him to let them some meadows at a reduced rent, I think, and he refused, and I reproached him with being stingy. Of course it was not that alone, but one thing with another caused him to start that hospital, to show, you know, that he is not stingy. *C'est une petitesse* [3] if you like, but I love him the better for it! And now you will see the house in a moment. It was his grandfather's, and it has not been altered at all on the outside.'

'How fine!' said Dolly, looking with involuntary surprise at a handsome house with a row of columns standing out among the variously tinted foliage of the old trees in the garden.

'It is fine, is it not? And from upstairs the view is wonderful.'

They drove into a gravelled courtyard surrounded by flowers, where two men were making a border of rough porous stones round a well-forked flower-bed, and stopped beneath a roofed portico.

'Ah, they've already arrived,' said Anna, looking at the horses that were being led away from the front door. 'Don't you think that one is a beautiful horse? It is a cob, my favourite. . . . Bring it here, and get me some sugar. Where is the Count?' she asked the two elegant footmen who had rushed out. 'Ah, there he is!' she went on, seeing Vronsky and Veslovsky coming out to meet her.

'In which room are you putting the Princess?' Vronsky asked in French, addressing Anna, and without waiting for her answer he once more welcomed Dolly, and this time he kissed her hand. 'The large room with the balcony, I should think.'

'Oh no! That's too far off! The corner room will be better, we shall see more of one another there. Well, let's go in,' said Anna,

3. It is a small thing.

who had given her favourite horse the sugar the footman had brought.

'*Et vous oubliez votre devoir*,'[4] said she to Veslovsky, who was also standing in the portico.

'*Pardon! J'en ai tout plein les poches*,'[5] he answered with a smile, plunging his fingers into his waistcoat pocket.

'*Mais vous venez trop tard*,'[6] she said, wiping with her handkerchief the hand which the horse had wetted as it took the sugar.

Anna turned to Dolly. 'How long can you stay? Only a day! That's impossible.'

'I have promised . . . and the children,' answered Dolly, feeling embarrassed because she had to get her bag out of the *calèche* and because she knew her face was covered with dust.

'No, Dolly darling! . . . Well, we will see. Come! Come along!' and Anna led the way to Dolly's room.

It was not the grand room that Vronsky had suggested, but one for which Anna apologized to Dolly. And this room needing an apology was full of luxuries, such as Dolly had never lived among, which reminded her of the best hotels abroad.

'Well, dearest! How happy I am!' said Anna, who in her riding-habit had sat down for a moment beside Dolly. 'Tell me about yourselves. I meet Stiva in passing, but he can't tell me about the children. How is my pet, Tanya? Grown a big girl, I suppose?'

'Yes, quite big,' answered Dolly shortly, and was herself surprised that she could talk so coldly about her children. 'We are very comfortable at the Levins',' she added.

'There now! Had I only known that you don't despise me . . .' said Anna, 'you should all have come to us. You know Stiva and Alexey are old and great friends,' she added and suddenly blushed.

'Yes, but we are so comfortable . . .' answered Dolly with embarrassment.

'However, my joy makes me talk nonsense! But really, dear, I am so glad to see you,' said Anna, kissing her again. 'You have not yet told me how and what you think about me, and I want to know everything. But I am glad that you will see me just as I am. Above all, I don't want you to think that I wish to prove anything. I don't want to prove anything: simply I wish to live, not hurting anyone but myself. I have a right to do that, have I not? However, that needs a long talk, and we will talk it all well over later. Now I will go and dress and will send you the maid.'

Chapter XIX

Left alone, Dolly surveyed the room with a housewife's eye. All she saw when driving up to the house and passing through it, and

4. And you forget your duty.
5. Pardon me, my pockets are full of it.
6. But you have come too late.

now in her room, gave her the impression of abundance and elegance and of that novel European luxury which she had read about in English novels, but had never yet seen in Russia in the country. Everything was new, from the new French wall-papers to the carpet which covered the whole floor. The bed had a spring and an overlay mattress, with a specially shaped bolster and small pillows with silk slips. The marble washstand, the dressing-table, the couch, the tables, the bronze clock on the mantelpiece, the curtains and door-hangings were all costly and new. The smart lady's maid with hair stylishly done, and wearing a dress more fashionable than Dolly's, who came to offer her services, was as new and expensive as everything else in the room. Dolly found her politeness, tidiness, and attention pleasant, but did not feel at ease with her; she was ashamed to let her see the patched dressing-jacket, which as ill-luck would have it she had brought by mistake. She was ashamed of the very patches and darns on which she at home prided herself. At home it was clear that six jackets required twenty-four *arshins* of nainsook at sixty-five kopeks, which comes to more than fifteen roubles, besides the trimmings and the work; and she had saved all that. But before the maid she felt not exactly ashamed but uncomfortable.

Dolly felt much relieved when Annushka, whom she had known a long time, came into the room. The smart maid had to go to her mistress, and Annushka remained with Dolly.

Annushka was evidently very pleased that the lady had come, and chattered incessantly. Dolly noticed that she wanted to express her opinion of her mistress's position, and especially of the Count's love of and devotion to Anna, but Dolly carefully stopped her whenever she began to speak about that subject.

'I grew up with Anna Arkadyevna; she is dearer to me than anything. Is it for us to judge? And how he seems to love . . .'

'Kindly have this washed if possible,' interrupted Dolly.

'Yes, ma'am! We have two women always specially kept for washing small things, and the clothes are all done with a machine. The Count goes into everything himself. What a husband . . .'

Dolly was glad when Anna came in and thereby put an end to Annushka's chatter.

Anna had changed into a very simple lawn dress. Dolly looked carefully at this simple dress. She knew what such simplicity meant and cost.

'An old acquaintance,' said Anna, pointing to Annushka.

Anna was now no longer embarrassed. She was free and at her ease. Dolly saw that she had quite got over the impression produced by her arrival, and had adopted a superficial tone of equanimity which seemed to close the door that led to the compartment where her feelings and intimate thoughts were kept.

'Well, and how is your little girl, Anna?' asked Dolly.

'Annie?' (so she called her daughter Anna). 'Quite well. Greatly improved. Would you like to see her? Come, I'll show her to you . . . . I've had such trouble with the nurses,' she began. 'We had an Italian wet nurse for her. Good, but so stupid! We wanted to send her back, but the child is so used to her that we are still keeping her.'

'Well, and how have you arranged . . . ?' Dolly began, meaning to ask what name the little girl would bear; but seeing a sudden frown on Anna's face she changed the question and said: 'How have you arranged? Have you already weaned her?'

But Anna had understood.

'That is not what you were going to ask? . . . You wished to ask about her name? Am I not right? It troubles Alexey. She has no name. That is, her name is Karenina,' said Anna, screwing up her eyes till only the meeting lashes could be seen. 'However, we will talk about all that later,' said she, suddenly brightening. 'Come! I will show her to you. *Elle est très gentille*,[7] and can crawl already.'

In the nursery the luxury noticeable in the rest of the house struck Dolly still more strongly. Here were perambulators ordered from England, an apparatus to teach a baby to walk, a specially constructed piece of furniture like a billiard-table for the baby to crawl on, swings, and baths of a new special kind. All these were English, strongly made, of good quality, and evidently very expensive. The room was large, very lofty and light.

When they entered the little girl was sitting in her smock in a little arm-chair at a table, having her dinner of broth which she was spilling all over her little chest. A Russian nursemaid was feeding the child and evidently herself eating also. Neither the wet nurse nor the head nurse were to be seen: they were in the next room, where one could hear them talking in a peculiar French, the only tongue in which they could converse.

On hearing Anna's voice a smart tall Englishwoman with an unpleasant face and a dissolute look came into the room, rapidly shaking her fair curls, and at once began excusing herself, though Anna had not accused her of anything. To each word of Anna's the Englishwoman quickly repeated, 'Yes, my lady!' several times.

The dark-browed, dark-haired, rosy little girl, with her firm ruddy little body covered with gooseflesh, pleased Dolly very much, despite the severe expression with which she regarded the new visitor; she even felt a little envious of the child's healthy appearance. The way the little girl crawled also greatly pleased Dolly. Not one of her children had crawled like that. The baby looked wonderfully sweet when she was put down on the carpet, with her little

7. She is very sweet.

frock tucked up behind. Glancing round at the grown-up people
with her large radiant black eyes, like a little animal, evidently
pleased that she was being admired, she smiled, and turning out
her feet, energetically supported herself on her hands, drew her
lower limbs forward, and then again advanced her hands.

But Dolly did not at all like the general atmosphere of that
nursery, especially the English nurse. Only by the fact that a nice
woman would not have accepted a post in such an irregular household as Anna's could Dolly explain to herself how Anna, with her
knowledge of people, could have engaged for her little girl such an
unpleasant and disreputable Englishwoman. Besides that, from a
few words she heard, Dolly at once understood that Anna, the wet
nurse, the head nurse, and the baby were not in touch with one
another, and that the mother's appearance was not a usual occurrence. Anna wished to get the baby her toy and could not find it.
But the most astonishing thing was that when asked how many
teeth the baby had, Anna made a mistake and knew nothing of the
two latest teeth.

'I feel it hard sometimes that I am as it were superfluous here,'
said Anna on leaving the nursery, lifting her train to avoid the toys
that lay beside the door. 'It was quite different with the first one.'

'I thought—on the contrary,' said Dolly timidly.

'Oh no! You know I have seen him, Serezha,' said Anna, screwing
up her eyes as if peering at something far off. 'However, we will
talk about that afterwards. Would you believe it, I am just like a
starving woman to whom a full meal has been served, and who does
not know what to begin on first? The full meal is you and the talks
I am going to have with you, and which I could not have with anyone else, and I don't know on what to begin first! *Mais je ne vous
ferai grâce de rien!* [8] I must speak out about everything. Yes, I
must give you a sketch of the people you will meet here,' she began. 'I will begin with the woman: Princess Barbara. You know
her, and I know your and Stiva's opinion of her. Stiva says the one
aim of her life is to prove her superiority to Aunt Catherine Pavlovna. That is quite true; but she is kind, and I am very grateful to
her. There was a moment in Petersburg when I needed a chaperon.
Just then she turned up. Really she is kind. She made my position
much easier. I see you do not realize all the difficulty of my position
. . . there in Petersburg,' she added. 'Here I am quite tranquil and
happy; but about that later on. I must continue the list. Then
there's Sviyazhsky: he is a Marshal of Nobility and a very decent
fellow, but he wants something from Alexey. You see, with his
means, now that we have settled in the country, Alexey can have
great influence. Then there is Tushkevich: you have met him, he was

8. But I shall not let you off anything!

always with Betsy. Now he has been deposed and has come to us. As Alexey says he is one of those men who are very agreeable if one takes them for what they wish to appear, *et puis, il est comme il faut*,[9] as the Princess Barbara says. Then there's Veslovsky . . . you know him. He is a nice boy,' she said, and a roguish smile puckered her lips. 'What outrageous affair was that with Levin? Veslovsky told Alexey, and we simply can't believe it. *Il est très gentil et naïf*,'[1] she added with the same smile. 'Men need distraction, and Alexey needs an audience; so I value all this company. Things must be lively and amusing here, so that Alexey shall not wish for anything new! Then you will also see our steward. He is a German, very good, and knows his business. Alexey thinks highly of him. Then there's the doctor, a young man, not exactly a Nihilist, but —you know, eats with his knife . . . but a very good doctor. Then there's the architect . . . *une petite cour!*'[2]

Chapter XX

'Well, here's Dolly for you, Princess! You wanted so much to see her,' said Anna as she and Dolly came out onto the large stone verandah where in the shade, before an embroidery frame, the Princess Barbara sat embroidering a cover for an easy-chair for Count Vronsky. 'She says she won't have anything before dinner, but will you order lunch? I'll go and find Alexey and bring them all here.'

The Princess Barbara received Dolly affectionately but rather patronizingly, and at once began explaining that she was staying with Anna because she had always loved her more than did her sister Catherine Pavlovna, who had brought Anna up; and that now, when everyone had thrown Anna over, she considered it her duty to help Anna through this transitional and most trying period.

'Her husband will give her a divorce, and then I shall go back to my solitude; but at present I can be of use and I fulfil my duty, however hard it may be, not like others. . . . And how kind you are, and how well you have done to come! They live like the best of married couples. It is for God to judge them, not for us. Think of Biryuzovsky and Avenyeva. . . . And even Nikandrov! And how about Vasilyev with Mamonova, and Lisa Neptunova . . . ? No one said anything against them? And in the end they were all received again. . . . And then *c'est un intérieur si joli, si comme il faut. Tout-à-fait à l'anglaise. On se réunit le matin au breakfast et puis on se sépare.*[3] Every one does what he likes till dinner. Dinner is at seven. Stiva did very well to send you. He must keep

---

9. And then, he is good form.
1. He is very nice and naïve.
2. A little court!
3. It is such a pretty, such a refined home. Quite in the English style. We assemble for breakfast, and then we separate.

in with them. You know, through his mother and brother he can do anything. And then they do much good. Has he not told you about his hospital? *Ce sera admirable.*[4] Everything comes from Paris.'

Their conversation was interrupted by Anna, who had found the men in the billiard-room and brought them back with her to the verandah. As there was still plenty of time before dinner, and the weather was beautiful, several different ways of passing the next two hours were proposed. There were a great many ways of spending time at Vozdvizhensk, all differing from those at Pokrovsk.

'*Une partie de*[5] lawn tennis,' suggested Veslovsky with his pleasing smile. 'We will be partners again, Anna Arkadyevna!'

'No, it's too hot: better let's walk through the garden and go for a row, to let Darya Alexandrovna see the banks,' suggested Vronsky.

'I will agree to anything,' said Sviyazhsky.

'I think Dolly will find a walk the pleasantest, won't you? And then we can go in the boat,' said Anna.

All agreed to this. Veslovsky and Tushkevich went to the bathing-house, promising to get the boat ready there and to wait for the others.

Two couples—Anna with Sviyazhsky and Dolly with Vronsky—walked down a garden path. Dolly was somewhat embarrassed and troubled by the quite novel circle she found herself in. In the abstract, theoretically, she not only excused but even approved of Anna's action. As is frequently the case with irreproachably moral women who become tired of the monotony of a moral life, she from a distance not only excused a guilty love but even envied it. Besides, she loved Anna from her heart. But actually seeing her among these people so alien to herself, with their fashionable tone which was quite new to her, Dolly felt ill at ease. In particular it was disagreeable to her to see the Princess Barbara, who forgave them everything for the sake of the comforts she enjoyed there.

In general, in the abstract Dolly approved the step Anna had taken, but it was unpleasant to her to see the man for whose sake the step had been taken. Besides, she had never liked Vronsky. She considered him very proud, and saw nothing in him to justify that pride, except his wealth. But involuntarily he, here in his own house, imposed on her more than ever, and she could not feel at ease with him. She experienced the same kind of shyness in his presence that she had felt when the lady's maid saw her jacket. As with the maid she felt not exactly ashamed but uncomfortable about the patches, so with him she felt not exactly ashamed but ill at ease about herself.

Feeling embarrassed, she tried to think of something to talk

4. It will be admirable.
5. A game of.

about. Though she thought that, being so proud, he would not be pleased to hear his house and garden admired, yet not finding any other subject for conversation, she said she liked his house very much.

'Yes, it is a very handsome building and in a good old style,' he said.

'I like the courtyard in front of the portico very much. Was it like that before?'

'Oh no!' he replied, and his face lit up with pleasure. 'If you had only seen that courtyard in spring!'

And he began, at first with reserve but more and more carried away by his subject, to draw her attention to various details of the adornment of the house and garden. One could see that, having devoted great pains to the improvement and decoration of his place, Vronsky felt compelled to boast of them to a fresh person, and was heartily pleased by Dolly's praises.

'If you care to see the hospital and are not too tired—it is not far. Shall we go?' he suggested, glancing at her face to assure himself that she really was not bored.

'Will you come, Anna?' he said, turning to her.

'We'll come. Shall we?' she asked Sviyazhsky. '*Mais il ne faut pas laisser le pauvre Veslovsky et Tushkevich se morfondre là dans le bateau!*' [6] We must send to let them know. Yes, it is a monument he is erecting here,' said Anna to Dolly, with the same sly knowing smile with which she had previously spoken about the hospital.

'Oh, it's a great undertaking!' said Sviyazhsky. But, not to seem to be making up to Vronsky, he immediately added a slightly condemnatory remark. 'But I am surprised, Count, that you, who are doing so much for the people from a sanitary point of view, should be so indifferent to the schools!'

'*C'est devenu tellement commun, les écoles,*' [7] answered Vronsky. 'Of course that's not the reason, but I . . . I have been carried away. This is the way to the hospital,' he said, turning to Dolly and pointing to a turning that led out of the avenue.

The ladies opened their sunshades and entered the sidewalk. After several turnings they passed through a gate, and Dolly saw on the high ground before her a large, red, nearly completed building of a fanciful shape. The still unpainted iron roof shone dazzlingly in the sunshine. Beside the finished building another as yet surrounded by scaffolding was being built. Workmen wearing aprons stood on the scaffolding laying bricks, pouring water from wooden pails, or smoothing the mortar.

'How quickly your work gets on!' said Sviyazhsky. 'When I was

---

6. But we must not let poor Veslovsky and Tushkevich to be bored waiting in the boat.

7. Schools have become so common.

last here there was no roof.'

'It will be finished by autumn. The interior is nearly completed,' said Anna.

'And what is this new building?'

'That will be the doctor's quarters and the dispensary,' replied Vronsky; and seeing the architect in his short jacket coming toward them, he apologized to the ladies and went to meet him.

Avoiding the pit from which the men were taking mortar, he stopped and began heatedly discussing something with the architect.

'The pediment is still too low,' he answered Anna's question as to what it was all about.

'I said the foundations ought to be raised,' said Anna.

'Yes, of course that would have been better, Anna Arkadyevna,' replied the architect, 'but it's done now.'

'Yes, I am very much interested in it,' said Anna to Sviyazhsky, who expressed surprise at her knowledge of architecture. 'The new building ought to be in line with the hospital, but it was an after-thought and was begun without a plan.'

Having finished talking with the architect Vronsky rejoined the ladies and led them to the hospital.

Although they were still working at the cornices outside and painting inside on the ground floor, the upper story was nearly fin-ished. Ascending the broad cast-iron staircase to the landing, they entered the first large room. The walls were plastered with imita-tion marble, and the enormous plate-glass windows were already in place; only the parquet floor was not finished, and the carpenters who were planing a square of the parquet left their work, and re-moving the tapes that kept their hair out of the way, bowed to the gentlefolk.

'This is the waiting-room,' said Vronsky. 'There will be a desk, a table and a cupboard here: nothing more.'

'This way! We will pass here. Don't go near the window!' said Anna, feeling whether the paint was dry. 'Alexey, the paint is dry already,' she added.

From the waiting-room they passed into the corridor. Here Vron-sky showed them the new system of ventilation which had been installed. Then he showed the marble baths and the beds with peculiar spring mattresses. Then he took them to one ward after an-other: to the store-room, the linen-room; showed the stoves built on a new plan, then some silent trollies to convey necessary articles, and much besides. Sviyazhsky appreciated everything like one who is acquainted with all the newest improvements. Dolly was simply surprised at what she had never before seen, and wishing to under-stand it all, asked for information about every detail, which evidently gratified Vronsky.

'Yes, I think this will be the only quite correctly planned hospital in Russia,' said Sviyazhsky.

'And will you have a maternity ward?' inquired Dolly. 'That is so much wanted in the country. I often . . .'

Despite his courtesy, Vronsky interrupted her.

'This is not a maternity home but a hospital, and is intended for all illnesses, except infectious ones,' he said. 'But have a look at this . . .' and he moved a chair for convalescents, just arrived from abroad, toward Dolly. 'Just look!' He sat down in the chair and began moving it. 'A patient is unable to walk—still too weak, or has something the matter with his feet; but he wants fresh air, so he goes out, takes a ride . . .'

Everything interested Dolly and everything pleased her, especially Vronsky himself with his natural and naïve enthusiasm. 'Yes, he is a very nice, good fellow,' she thought again and again, not listening to him but looking at him, understanding his expression, and mentally putting herself in Anna's place. In this animated state she liked him so much that she understood Anna's being able to fall in love with him.

Chapter XXI

'No, I think the Princess Darya Alexandrovna is tired and horses do not interest her,' said Vronsky to Anna, who was suggesting that they should go to the stud farm where Sviyazhsky wanted to look at a new stallion. 'You go, and I will see the Princess back to the house and will have a talk with her—if you do not mind?' he added, turning to Dolly.

'I don't understand anything about horses, and shall be very pleased to,' answered Dolly, taken rather by surprise.

She saw by Vronsky's face that he wanted something of her. She was not mistaken. As soon as they had passed through the gate back into the garden, he glanced in the direction Anna had taken, and having assured himself that she could not hear or see them, he began.

'You have guessed that I want to talk to you,' he said, looking at her with laughter in his eyes. 'I know that you are a friend of Anna's.' He took off his hat, and with his handkerchief mopped his head, which was getting bald.

Dolly did not reply and only looked at him with alarm. Alone with him she suddenly felt frightened: his laughing eyes and stern expression scared her.

Many diverse suppositions as to what he was about to say flitted through her brain. 'He will ask me to come and stay with them and bring the children, and I shall have to refuse; or to get together a

circle for Anna in Moscow. . . . Or maybe it's about Vasenka
Veslovsky and his relations with Anna? Or possibly about Kitty,
and that he feels guilty toward her?' Everything she surmised was
unpleasant, but she did not hit on what he actually wished to speak
about.

'You have so much influence over Anna and she is so fond of you,'
he said. 'Help me!'

Dolly looked with timid inquiry at his energetic face, which was
now wholly and now partly in the sunlight that fell between the
lime trees, and then was again darkened by their shadow. She
waited for what more he would say; but he walked by her side in
silence, prodding the gravel with his stick as he went.

'As you have come to see us—and you are the only one of Anna's
former friends who has (I do not count the Princess Barbara)—I feel
you have done so not because you consider our position normal, but
because, realizing all the hardship of that position, you love her as
before and wish to help her. Have I understood you rightly?' he
asked, turning toward her.

'Oh, yes!' answered Dolly, closing her sunshade, 'but . . .'

'No,' he interrupted; and forgetting that he was placing his companion in an awkward position, he stopped, so that she was obliged
to stop also. 'No one feels all the hardship of Anna's position more
than I do; and that is naturally so, if you do me the honour of regarding me as a man with a heart. I am the cause of that position
and therefore I feel it.'

'I understand,' said Dolly, involuntarily admiring him for the
frank and firm way in which he said it. 'But just because you feel
you have caused it, I'm afraid you exaggerate it,' she said. 'I understand that her position in Society is a hard one.'

'In Society it is hell!' he said quickly with a dark frown. 'It is impossible to imagine greater moral torments than those she endured
for two weeks in Petersburg . . . I beg you to believe me!'

'Yes, but here, so long as neither Anna nor you . . . feel that you
need Society . . .'

'Society!' he exclaimed with contempt. 'What need can I have of
Society?'

'Till then, and that may be always, you are happy and tranquil. I
see that Anna is happy, quite happy, she has already told me so,'
said Dolly smiling; and involuntarily while saying it she doubted
whether Anna was really happy.

But Vronsky, it seemed, did not doubt it.

'Yes, yes,' he said. 'I know that she has revived after all her suffering; she is happy; she is happy in the present. But I? . . . I am
afraid of what is before us. . . . I beg your pardon! You want to
move on?'

'No, I don't mind.'

'Well then, let us sit down here.'

Dolly sat down on a seat at the turn of the avenue. He stood before her.

'I see she is happy,' he repeated, and the doubt as to whether Anna was really happy struck Dolly yet more strongly. 'But can it continue? Whether we acted rightly or wrongly is another question; the die is cast,' he said, changing from Russian into French, 'and we are bound together for life. We are united by what are for us the holiest bonds of love. We have a child, we may have other children. Yet the law and the circumstances of our position are such that thousands of complications appear which at present, while resting after all her sufferings and trials, she neither sees nor wishes to see. That is natural. But I cannot help seeing them. My daughter is not mine by law, but Karenin's. I hate this falsehood!' he said with an energetic gesture of denial, and looked at Dolly with a gloomily questioning expression.

She made no answer, but only looked at him. He continued:

'Some day a son may be born, my son, and he will by law be a Karenin, and not heir either to my name or my property, and however happy we may be in our family life, and whatever children we may have, there will be no legal bond between them and me. They will be—Karenin's! Imagine the hardship and horror of this situation! I have tried to speak to Anna about it, but it irritates her. She does not understand and I cannot speak out about it to *her*. Now look at the other side of it. I am happy, happy in her love, but I need an occupation. I have found one. I am proud of it, and consider it more honourable than the occupations of my former comrades at Court or in the Service. I certainly would not exchange my work for theirs. I am working here, remaining on the spot, and I am happy and contented, and we need nothing more for our happiness. I like my activities. *Cela n'est pas un pis-aller,*[8] on the contrary . . .'

Dolly observed that at this point his explanation was confused, and she could not quite understand why he had wandered from the point, but she felt that having once begun to speak of his intimate affairs, of which he could not speak to Anna, he was not telling her everything, and that the question of his work in the country belonged to the same category of intimate thoughts as the question of his relations with Anna.

'Well, to continue!' he said, recovering himself. 'The principal thing is that when working I want the assurance that the work will not die with me, that I shall have heirs; and that I have not got. Imagine the situation of a man who knows in advance that children

8. It's not that there is no better alternative.

born of him and of the woman he loves will not be his, but some one else's—some one who will hate them and will have nothing to do with them! You know it is dreadful!'

He paused, evidently greatly excited.

'Yes, of course, I quite understand. But what can Anna do?' asked Dolly.

'Well, this brings me to the point of my talk,' he went on, calming himself with an effort. 'Anna can do it; it depends on her. . . . Even to be able to petition the Emperor for permission to adopt the child, a divorce will be necessary, and that depends on Anna. Her husband was willing to have a divorce—your husband had almost arranged it—and I know he would not refuse now. It is only necessary to write to him. He then replied definitely that if she expressed the wish, he would not refuse. Of course,' he said gloomily, 'that is one of those Pharasaic cruelties of which only heartless people are capable. He knows what torture every recollection of him causes her, and knowing her he still demands a letter from her. I understand that it is painful for her, but the reasons are so important that one must *passer par-dessus toutes ces finesses de sentiment. Il y va du bonheur et de l'existence d'Anne et de ses enfants!* [9] I do not speak of myself, though it's very hard on me, very hard,' he said with a look as if he were menacing some one for making it so hard on him. 'And so, Princess, I shamelessly cling to you as the anchor of salvation! Help me to persuade her to write to him and demand a divorce!'

'Yes, certainly,' said Dolly thoughtfully, vividly remembering her last conversation with Karenin. 'Yes, certainly,' she repeated resolutely, remembering Anna.

'Use your influence with her, get her to write, I don't wish and am almost unable to speak to her about it.'

'Very well, I will speak to her. But how is it she herself does not think of it?' asked Dolly, suddenly remembering that strange new habit Anna had of screwing up her eyes. And she remembered that it was just when the intimate side of life was in question that Anna screwed up her eyes. 'As if she were blinking at her life so as not to see it all,' thought Dolly. 'Certainly I will speak to her, for my own sake and for hers,' she said in reply to his expression of gratitude.

They got up and went back to the house.

Chapter XXII

Finding Dolly already returned, Anna looked attentively into her eyes as if asking about the talk she had had with Vronsky, but she did not ask in words.

9. One must get over all these refinements of sentiment. The happiness and existence of Anna and her children depend on it.

'I think it's nearly dinner-time,' she said. 'We have not yet seen anything of one another. . . . I am counting on this evening. Now I must go and dress, and you too, I suppose. We have dirtied ourselves on the buildings.'

Dolly went to her room, feeling amused. She had nothing to change into as she was already wearing her best dress; but to give some sign that she had prepared for dinner, she asked the maid to brush her dress, and she put on clean cuffs, pinned a fresh bow to her dress and placed some lace in her hair.

'This is all I was able to do,' she smilingly said to Anna, who came to her in a third dress, again extremely simple.

'Yes, we are very formal here,' Anna remarked, as if excusing her own smartness. 'Alexey is seldom so pleased about anything as he is at your having come. He is decidedly in love with you,' she added. 'But aren't you tired?'

There was no time to discuss anything before dinner. When they entered the drawing-room the Princess Barbara and the men were already there. The men wore frock coats, except the architect, who was in a dress suit. Vronsky introduced the doctor and the steward to his visitor; the architect had already been presented at the hospital.

The fat butler—his round, clean-shaven face and starched white tie shining—announced dinner. The ladies rose; Vronsky asked Sviyazhsky to take in Anna, and himself went up to Dolly. Veslovsky offered his arm to the Princess Barbara before Tushkevich could do so, so that the latter, the steward, and the doctor went in by themselves.

The dinner, the dining-room, the dinner-service, the servants and the wine and the food were not merely in keeping with the general tone of modern luxury in the house, but seemed even more luxurious and more modern than the rest. Dolly observed all this luxury, which was new to her, and, as a housewife herself controlling a household, she could not help noting the details (though she had no hope of putting what she observed to practical use in her own home, so far was such luxury above her way of life) and asking herself how it was all done and by whom. Vasenka Veslovsky, her husband, and even Sviyazhsky and many others whom she knew, never thought about these things, and readily believed, what every decent host wishes his guests to feel, that all that is so well arranged at his house has cost him no trouble but has come about of itself. Dolly, however, knew that not even a milk pudding for the children's lunch comes of itself, and that therefore so complicated and splendid an organization must have needed some one's careful attention; and from the way Vronsky surveyed the table, gave a sign with his head to the butler, and asked her whether she would take cold or hot soup, she concluded that it had all been done by, and depended

on, the master's care. It was evident that it depended no more on
Anna than on Veslovsky. Anna, Sviyazhsky, the Princess, and Veslovsky were all equally guests, gaily making use of what was provided for them.

Anna was the hostess only in what concerned the conversation.
And that difficult task for the mistress of a house with a small circle
which included such people as the steward and the architect—people of quite a different world, who tried not to be abashed by the
unfamiliar luxury and were unable to take any sustained part in the
general conversation—Anna managed with her usual tact, naturally
and even with pleasure, as Dolly observed.

Reference was made to Tushkevich and Veslovsky having been
for a row by themselves, and Tushkevich began to tell about the
last boat races at the Petersburg Yacht Club. But at the first pause
Anna turned to the architect, to draw him into the conversation.

'Nicholas Ivanich,' she said (referring to Sviyazhsky), 'was struck
by the way the new building had grown since his last visit; even I,
who go there every day, am always surprised how quickly it gets on.'

'It is pleasant to work with his Excellency,' answered the architect with a smile. He was a dignified, respectful and quiet man. 'It is
not like having to do with the Local Authorities,' said he. 'Where
they would scribble over a whole ream of paper, I merely report to
the Count; we talk it over, and three words settle the matter.'

'American methods!' said Sviyazhsky with a smile.

'Yes. There they erect buildings rationally . . .'

The conversation passed on to the abuses in the government of
the United States, but Anna quickly turned it to another theme so
as to draw the steward out of his silence.

'Have you ever seen a reaping machine?' she asked Dolly. 'We
had been to look at them when we met you. I saw them myself for
the first time.'

'How do they act?' asked Dolly.

'Just like scissors. It's a board and a lot of little scissors. Like
this . . .'

Anna took a knife and a fork in her beautiful white hands, sparkling with rings, and began to demonstrate. She was obviously aware
that her explanation would not be understood, but as she knew that
she spoke pleasantly and that her hands were beautiful, she went on
explaining.

'Rather like penknives!' said Veslovsky playfully, never taking his
eyes from her.

Anna smiled slightly, but did not answer him. 'Is it not true, Karl
Fedorich, that it is like scissors?' she asked, turning to the steward.

'Oh, ja!' answered the German. 'Es ist ein ganz einfaches Ding.' [1]
and he began to explain the construction of the machine.

1. Oh yes! It is quite a simple thing.

'It's a pity it does not bind the sheaves. I saw one at the Vienna Exhibition that bound the sheaves with wire,' remarked Sviyazhsky. 'That kind would be more profitable,'

'*Es kommt darauf an. . . . Der Preis vom Draht muss ausgerechnet werden,*' [2] and the German, drawn from his silence, turned to Vronsky. '*Das lässt sich ausrechnen, Erlaucht!*' [3] The German was already putting his hand to the pocket where he kept a notebook with a pencil in which he made all his calculations, but remembering that he was at dinner, and noticing Vronsky's cold look, he desisted. '*Zu complicirt, macht zu viel Klopot,*' [4] he concluded.

'*Wünscht man Dokhots, so hat man auch Klopots,*' [5] said Vasenka Veslovsky, making fun of the German. '*J'adore l'allemand!*' [6] said he, turning to Anna with the same smile as before.

'*Cessez!*' [7] said she with mock severity.

'And we thought we should find you on the field, Vasily Semenich! Were you there?' she said to the doctor, a sickly-looking man.

'I had been there, but had evaporated,' said the doctor, with dismal jocularity.

'Then you have had some good exercise?'

'Magnificent!'

'And how is the old woman? I hope it is not typhus?'

'No, it's not exactly typhus, but she's not in a good state.'

'What a pity!' said Anna, and having thus paid a tribute of politeness to the retainers, she turned to her friends.

'All the same, it would be difficult to construct a reaper from your description, Anna Arkadyevna,' Sviyazhsky chaffed her.

'Oh, why not?' said Anna, with a smile which said that she knew there had been something engaging in her way of describing the reaper and that Sviyazhsky had noticed it. This new trait of youthful coquetry jarred on Dolly.

'But then, Anna Arkadyevna's knowledge of architecture is wonderful,' remarked Tushkevich.

'Oh, yes! Yesterday I heard Anna Arkadyevna mention damp courses and plinths,' said Veslovsky. 'Am I saying it right?'

'There's nothing to be surprised at, considering how much I hear and see of it,' said Anna. 'And you, I'm sure, don't even know what houses are made of!'

Dolly noticed that Anna did not like the playful tone that had arisen between herself and Veslovsky, yet could not help falling in with it.

2. It all depends. . . . The price of the wire must be allowed for.
3. It can be calculated, Excellency!
4. Too complicated, too much trouble.
5. If one wants income one must also have trouble. (The Russian word for income is *dokhod*. Veslovsky mispronounces it, and introduces it into a German sentence for fun.)
6. I adore German.
7. Leave off!

Vronsky behaved in this matter quite unlike Levin. He evidently did not attach any importance to Veslovsky's chatter, and even encouraged it.

'Come, Veslovsky! Tell us what keeps the bricks together!'

'Cement, of course!'

'Bravo! And what is cement?'

'Well . . . it's something like paste . . . no, putty!' replied Veslovsky, rousing general laughter.

The conversation among the diners—except the doctor, the architect and the steward, who sat in gloomy silence—was incessant, now gliding smoothly, now catching on something and touching one or other of them to the quick. Once Dolly was stung to the quick, and so aroused that she even flushed up, and afterwards wondered whether she had said anything superfluous and disagreeable. Sviyazhsky began talking about Levin, and mentioned his peculiar view that machines only did harm in Russian agriculture.

'I have not the pleasure of knowing the gentleman,' said Vronsky with a smile, 'but probably he has never seen the machines which he condemns; or if he has seen and tried them, has done it just anyhow, and not with a foreign-made but with a Russian machine. And what opinions are possible on so plain a matter?'

'Turkish opinions,' said Veslovsky, turning to Anna with a smile.

'I cannot defend his opinions,' said Dolly, flaring up 'but I can say that he is a very well-informed man, and if he were here he would be able to answer you, although I cannot.'

'I am very fond of him, and we are great friends,' said Sviyazhsky with a good-natured smile. '*Mais pardon, il est un petit peu toqué!* [8] For instance, he maintains that the Zemstvos and Magistrates are quite unnecessary, and he won't have anything to do with them.'

'That is our Russian indifference,' said Vronsky, pouring water from an iced decanter into a very thin glass with a stem: 'not to realize the duties our rights impose on us, and therefore to deny those duties.'

'I know no one who fulfils his duties more strictly,' said Dolly, irritated by Vronsky's superior tone.

'I, on the contrary,' continued Vronsky, who was evidently for some reason touched to the quick by this conversation, 'I, on the contrary, such as I am, feel very grateful for the honour they have done me, thanks to Nicholas Ivanich'—he indicated Sviyazhsky—'by electing me Justice of the Peace. I consider that the duty of going to the meetings, and considering a peasant's case about a horse, is as important as anything else I can do. I shall consider it an honour if they elect me to the Zemstvo. It is only so that I can make

8. But, excuse me, he is a little cracked.

a return for the advantages I enjoy as a landowner. Unfortunately people do not understand the importance the large landowners should have in the State.' To Dolly it sounded strange to hear how assured he was of being in the right, here at his own table. She remembered how Levin, who held the opposite opinion, was equally positive in his opinions at his own table. But she was fond of Levin, and therefore sided with him.

'Then we may expect to see you at the next Session, Count?' asked Sviyazhsky. 'But you must come in good time, so as to be there on the eighth. If you would only do me the honour of stopping with me . . .'

'And I rather agree with your brother-in-law,' said Anna, 'though I do not go to his lengths,' she added with a smile. 'I'm afraid we have too many of these public obligations nowadays. Formerly we used to have so many officials that there had to be an official for everything that was done, and now we have public workers for everything! Alexey has not been here six months, and I think he is already a Member of five or six different institutions: Guardian of the Poor, Justice of the Peace, a Member of a Council, a juryman, and Member of some Commission on Horses. . . . *Du train que cela va,*[9] all his time will be taken up that way. And I fear that with the multiplication of these positions they become a mere form. Of how many institutions are you a member, Nicholas Ivanich?' she asked, addressing Sviyazhsky; 'more than twenty, isn't it?'

Although Anna spoke playfully, irritation was perceptible in her tone. Dolly, who was attentively watching her and Vronsky, noticed it at once. She also saw that at this conversation Vronsky's face immediately assumed a serious and obstinate expression. Noticing these things, and that the Princess Barbara hastened to change the subject by speaking of their Petersburg acquaintances, and remembering that in the garden Vronsky had spoken about his activities inopportunely, she understood that with this question of public work some private difference between Anna and Vronsky was connected.

The dinner, the wine, the service were all very good, but they were all such as Dolly—though she had become unused to them—had seen before at dinner-parties and balls, and like those functions they bore a character of impersonality and strain; therefore on an everyday occasion and in a small gathering they produced an unpleasant impression on her.

After dinner they sat awhile on the verandah. Then they played lawn-tennis. The players, having chosen their partners, took their places on the carefully levelled and rolled croquet lawn, on the two sides of a net stretched between two small gilded pillars. Dolly

9. At the rate at which it is going.

tried to play, but was long unable to understand the game, and by the time she did understand it she was so tired that she sat down beside the Princess Barbara to watch the others. Her partner Tuskevich also gave it up; but the rest played for a long time. Sviyazhsky and Vronsky both played very well and seriously. They intently followed the ball sent to them, neither hurrying nor hesitating, ran toward it with agility, waited for it to bounce, and then striking it with the racket sent it back across the net with good aim and precision. Veslovsky played worse than the others. He was too eager, but to make up for that his gaiety inspired his companions. His laughter and shouts never ceased. He, as well as the other men, had with the ladies' permission taken off his coat, and his large handsome figure in white shirt-sleeves, his ruddy perspiring face and impetuous movements, stamped themselves on the memories of the onlookers.

As soon as Dolly that night had gone to bed and closed her eyes, she saw Vasenka Veslovsky rushing hither and thither on the croquet lawn.

While they were playing Dolly was not feeling happy. She did not like the bantering tone between Anna and Veslovsky that continued during the game, nor the unnaturalness of grown-up people when they play childish games in the absence of children. But not to disturb the others and to while away the time, after resting she rejoined the players and pretended to like it. All that day she felt as if she were acting in a theatre with better actors than herself, and that her bad performance was spoiling the whole affair.

She had come with the intention of staying two days if she could adapt herself to the life. But that evening during the game she resolved to leave next day. Those painful maternal worries, which she had so hated on her journey, now after a day spent without them appeared in quite a different light and drew her back to them.

When, after evening tea and a row in the boat at night-time, Dolly entered her bedroom alone, took off her dress and sat down to do up her thin hair for the night, she felt great relief.

Even the thought that Anna would come in a moment was disagreeable to her. She wished to be alone with her thoughts.

Chapter XXIII

Dolly was ready to get into bed when Anna in her night-gown came into the room.

Several times during the day Anna had begun to talk about intimate matters, but after a few words she had always paused, saying: 'Later on when we are alone we will talk it all over. I have so much to say to you!'

Now they were alone, but Anna did not know what to speak

about. She sat by the window, looking at Dolly and mentally reviewing all those stores of intimate topics that had seemed inexhaustible, and could find nothing to say. It seemed to her at that moment as if everything had already been said.

'Well, and how's Kitty?' she asked with a deep sigh and a guilty glance at Dolly. 'Tell me the truth, Dolly: is she not angry with me?'

'Angry? No!' replied Dolly with a smile.

'But she hates and despises me?'

'Oh no! But you know one does not forgive those things!'

'No, no,' said Anna, turning away and looking out of the open window. 'But it was not my fault, and whose fault was it? What does being in fault mean? Could things have been different? Now, what do you think? Could it have happened to you not to be Stiva's wife?'

'I really don't know. But I want you to tell me this . . .'

'Yes, yes, but we have not finished about Kitty. Is she happy? They say he's a fine fellow.'

'It is not enough to say he's a fine fellow; I do not know a better man.'

'Oh, I am so glad! I am very glad! It is not enough to say he's a fine fellow,' she repeated.

Dolly smiled.

'But tell me about yourself. I have much to talk to you about and I have been talking with . . .' Dolly did not know what to call him. She did not like to call him either 'the Count' or 'Alexey Kirilich.'

'With Alexey?' said Anna. 'I know you have. But I want to ask you frankly, what do you think of me and of my life?'

'How can I tell you all at once? I really don't know.'

'Oh, but all the same, tell me! . . . You see what my life is. But don't forget that you see us in summer, when you have come and we are not alone. . . . But we came here in early spring and lived quite alone, and we shall live alone again. I don't wish for anything better. But imagine me living alone, without him, *alone*, and that will happen . . . everything shows that it will often happen,— that he will spend half his time from home,' she said, rising and taking a seat nearer to Dolly. 'Of course,' she went on, interrupting Dolly, who was about to reply, 'of course I won't keep him against his will! I don't keep him. One day there are races and his horses are running; he goes. I am very glad. But think of me, imagine my position. . . . But why talk of it!' She smiled. 'Well then, what did he talk about to you?'

'He talked about what I myself wanted to ask you, so it is easy for me to be his advocate: about whether it isn't possible . . . whether it can't . . .' Dolly hesitated, 'how to remedy, to improve your position . . . you know my opinions. . . . But all the same, if it is possible you should get married.'

'That is, get a divorce?' said Anna. 'Do you know, the only woman who called on me in Petersburg was Betsy Tverskaya? You know her, of course? *Au fond c'est la femme la plus dépravée qui existe.*[1] She had a liaison with Tushkevich, deceiving her husband in the worst way, and she told me that she did not wish to know me as long as my position was irregular . . . ! Don't think I am making any comparison . . . I know you, my darling. . . . But I could not help remembering. . . . Well then, what did he say to you?' she repeated.

'He said that he suffers on your account and on his own. Perhaps you will say it is egotism, but what legitimate and noble egotism! He wants, first of all, to legitimatize his daughter and to be your husband and have a right to you.'

'What wife, what slave could be such a slave as I am in my position?' Anna sullenly interrupted her.

'But the chief thing he wants is that you should not suffer.'

'That is impossible! Well?'

'And his most legitimate wish is that your children should not be nameless.'

'What children?' said Anna, screwing up her eyes and not looking at Dolly.

'Annie, and those that will come . . .'

'He may be at ease about that: I shall not have any more children.'

'How do you know you won't?'

'I shan't, because I don't want them.'

And in spite of her agitation Anna smiled on noticing the naïve expression of curiosity, surprise and terror on Dolly's face.

'After my illness the doctor told me . . .'

. . . .

'Impossible!' said Dolly, with wide-open eyes. To her this was one of those discoveries which leads to consequences and deductions so enormous that at the first moment one only feels that it is impossible to take it all in, but that one will have to think over it again and again.

This discovery, which suddenly explained to her those hitherto incomprehensible families where there were only one or two children, awoke in her so many thoughts, reflections and contradictory feelings that she could say nothing, and only stared at Anna with wide-open eyes full of astonishment. It was the very thing she had dreamt of, but now on learning that it was possible, she was horrified. She felt that it was too simple a solution of too complex a

---

1. At bottom, she's the most depraved woman in existence.

question.

'*N'est-ce pas immoral?*' [2] was all she said after a pause.

'Why? Remember I have to choose between two things: either to become pregnant, that is ill, or to be the friend and comrade of my husband—for he is my husband all the same,' said Anna, in a tone of intentional levity.

'Well, yes, of course,' said Dolly, listening to the very arguments which she had put to herself but not finding them so convincing as before.

'For you and for others,' said Anna, as if guessing her thoughts, 'there may still be some doubt, but for me . . . Remember, I am not a wife; he loves me as long as his love lasts! Well, how am I to keep his love? In this way?'

She curved her white arms in front of her stomach.

With unusual rapidity, as happens at times of great agitation, thoughts and recollections crowded into Dolly's mind. 'I could not attract Stiva,' she thought; 'he left me for others, and the first one for whom he betrayed me did not hold him, though she was always pretty and bright! He threw her over and took another. Is it possible that Anna will attract and keep Count Vronsky in this way? If he looks for that sort of thing, he will find women whose dresses and manners are still brighter and more attractive. And however white and shapely her bare arms may be, however beautiful her full figure and her flushed face surrounded by that black hair—he will find others still more beautiful, as my horrid, pitiable and dear husband looks for and finds them!'

Dolly made no answer and only sighed. Anna noticed the sigh, which expressed dissent, and continued. She had other arguments in store, and such powerful ones that they could not be answered.

'You say it is not right? But you must consider,' she went on. 'You forget my position. How can I desire children? I am not talking of the suffering: I am not afraid of that. But think who my children would be! Unfortunate beings, who would have to bear a stranger's name! By the very fact of their birth they would have to be ashamed of their mother, their father, their birth!'

'But that's just why a divorce is necessary!'

Anna did not listen. She wanted to reproduce the arguments with which she had so often convinced herself.

'What was my reason given me for, if I am not to use it to avoid bringing unfortunate beings into the world?'

She glanced at Dolly, but not pausing for a reply continued:

'I should always feel guilty toward those unhappy children,' said she. 'If they don't exist at any rate they are not unhappy, but if they are unhappy I alone shall be to blame.'

2. Isn't it immoral?

These were the very arguments Dolly had put to herself; but now she listened without understanding them. 'How can one be guilty toward beings who don't exist?' thought she. And suddenly the question came into her mind, whether it could be better in any case for her favourite Grisha if he had never existed? This appeared to her so monstrous and strange that she shook her head to dispel the confusion of insane thoughts that whirled in her brain.

'Well, I don't know; but it is not right,' she said with a look of disgust.

'Yes, but don't forget what you are and what I am.' . . . And besides,' added Anna, in spite of the abundance of her arguments and the poverty of Dolly's, apparently agreeing that it was not right,— 'don't forget the chief thing: that I am not in the same position as you! The question for you is, whether you desire not to have any more children; for me it is, whether I desire to have them. And that is a great difference. Don't you see that, situated as I am, I cannot desire them?'

Dolly did not reply. She suddenly felt that she was so far away from Anna that there were questions on which they could never meet, and about which it was best not to talk.

Chapter XXIV

'Then there is all the more need to regularize your position if possible,' said Dolly.

'Yes, if possible,' Anna said, in what had suddenly become quite a different—a quiet and sad—voice.

'Is a divorce not possible? I was told your husband had agreed . . .'

'Dolly, I don't want to speak about it!'

'Well then, we won't,' Dolly hastened to say, noticing the look of pain on Anna's face. 'But I see that you look at things too dismally.'

'I? Not at all! I am very cheerful and satisfied. You saw that *je fais des passions* [3] . . . Veslovsky.'

'Yes, to tell you the truth, I don't like Veslovsky's manner,' said Dolly, wishing to change the subject.

'Oh, not at all! It tickles Alexey, and that's all; he is only a boy and entirely in my hands; you know, I manage him just as I please. He is just the same to me as your Grisha . . . Dolly!' she said suddenly, changing her tone, 'you say I look at things too dismally! You cannot understand. It is too dreadful. I try not to look at them at all!'

'But I think you ought to. You must do all that is possible.'

'But what is possible? Nothing! You say I must marry Alexey, and that I don't consider that. I not consider that!' she repeated,

3. I make conquests.

and flushed. She rose, drew herself up, sighed deeply, and with her light steps began pacing up and down the room, pausing occasionally. 'I not consider it? Not a day, not an hour passes without my thinking about it and blaming myself for what I think . . . because those thoughts are enough to drive one mad! To drive one mad!' she repeated. 'When I think of it I cannot fall asleep without morphia. Well, all right. Let us discuss it quietly. They speak of divorce. For one thing, *he* would not agree now. *He* is now under the Countess Lydia Ivanovna's influence.'

Dolly, sitting upright in her chair, with a pained expression of sympathy turned her head to follow Anna's movements.

'One must try,' she said gently.

'Let's grant that. But what would it mean?' said Anna, evidently expressing a thought she had considered a thousand times and knew by heart. 'It means that I, who hate him but yet acknowledge myself to blame toward him—and I do think him magnanimous—I must humiliate myself by writing to him . . . ! Well, supposing I make that effort and do it: I shall receive either an insulting answer or his consent. Supposing I get his consent . . .' Anna at that instant had reached the other end of the room and stopped there, doing something to the window curtain. 'I receive his consent, and my so . . . son? They will not give him to me. He will grow up despising me, in the house of his father whom I have left. Understand that I love equally, I think, and both more than myself—two beings: Serezha and Alexey.'

She came back to the middle of the room and, pressing her chest with her arms, paused before Dolly, in her white dressing-gown her figure appeared peculiarly tall and broad. She bent her head and, trembling all over with emotion, looked from under her brows with moist, glittering eyes at the thin, piteous-looking little Dolly in her patched dressing-jacket and nightcap.

'I love those two beings only, and the one excludes the other! I cannot unite them, yet that is the one thing I desire. And if I can't have that, nothing matters—nothing, nothing! It will end somehow, therefore I can't—I don't like speaking about it. So don't reproach me, don't condemn me for anything! You in your purity cannot understand all I suffer!'

She came and sat down beside Dolly, peering into her face with a guilty look, and took her by the hand.

'What are you thinking? What are you thinking of me? Don't despise me! I don't deserve contempt. I am simply unhappy. If anyone is unhappy, it is I!' she murmured, and, turning away, she wept.

Left alone, Dolly said her prayers and got into bed. She had pitied Anna from the bottom of her heart while they were talking; but now she could not make herself think about her. Recollections of home and of her children rose in her imagination with a new and peculiar charm. That world of her own now seemed so precious and dear that she did not wish on any account to spend another day away from it, and she decided certainly to go home on the morrow.

Meanwhile Anna, returning to her boudoir, took a wineglass and put into it some drops of medicine, the chief ingredient of which was morphia. Having drunk it and sat still for a few moments, she entered her bedroom cheerfully and gaily.

When she came in Vronsky regarded her attentively. He tried to find some trace of the conversation which he knew, by her having remained so long in Dolly's room, must have taken place. But in her expression of restrained excitement, which concealed something, he detected nothing except that beauty which, though familiar, still captivated him, her consciousness of this, and her desire that it should act on him. He did not wish to ask her what they had been talking about, but hoped that she would tell him of her own accord. However, she only said:

'I am glad you like Dolly. You do?'

'But I have known her a long time. I think she is very kind, *mais excessivement terre-à-terre*.[4] But all the same I was very glad she came.'

He took Anna's hand and looked inquiringly into her eyes.

She, misunderstanding that look, smiled at him.

Next morning, in spite of her hosts' entreaties, Dolly prepared to go home. Levin's coachman in his by no means new coat, and a hat something like a post-boy's, with his horses that did not match and the old *calèche* with mended mud-guards, drove up gloomily but resolutely to the covered, sand-strewn portico.

Taking leave of the Princess Barbara and of the men was unpleasant to Dolly. After spending a day together both she and her hosts felt distinctly that they did not suit one another and that it was better for them not to associate. Only Anna felt sad. She knew that when Dolly was gone no one would call up in her soul the feelings which had been aroused by their meeting. To have those feelings awakened was painful, but still she knew that they were the best part of her soul, and that that part of her was rapidly being choked by the life she was leading.

When they had driven into the fields Dolly experienced a pleasant feeling of relief, and she was about to ask the men how they had liked the Vronskys' place, when suddenly Philip the coachman himself remarked:

'They're rich, that they are, but yet they gave us only two bushels

4. Excessively matter-of-fact; prosaic.

of oats. The horses had eaten every grain before cock-crow! What's two bushels? Only a bite. Nowadays oats are forty-five kopeks at the inns. When anyone comes to our place, no fear, we give their horses as much as they'll eat.'

'A stingy gentleman . . .' confirmed the clerk.

'Well, and did you like their horses?' asked Dolly.

'The horses? Fine's the only word for them! And the food is good too. But it did seem so dull to me, Darya Alexandrovna! I don't know how you found it,' he added, turning his handsome, kindly face toward her.

'I felt the same. Well, shall we get back by evening?'

'We ought to.'

On returning home and finding every one safe and extremely nice, Dolly gave a very animated account of her visit, of how well she had been received, of the luxury and good taste at the Vronskys', and of their amusements, and would not let anyone say a word against them.

'One must know Anna and Vronsky—I have got to know him better now—in order to understand how kind and pathetic they are,' said she with entire sincerity, forgetting the indefinite feelings of dissatisfaction and embarrassment she had experienced there.

Chapter XXV

Vronsky and Anna went on living in the country in the same way, still taking no steps to obtain a divorce, all the summer and part of the autumn. They had agreed not to go away anywhere; but the longer they lived alone the more they both felt—especially in autumn when there were no visitors—that they would not be able to hold out and that a change was inevitable.

Their life seemed one that could not be improved upon: they had ample means, good health, a child, and both had occupations of their own. In the absence of visitors Anna still continued to devote attention to her person, and read a great deal—both novels and such serious books as were in fashion. She ordered all the books that were praised in the foreign newspapers and magazines they received, and read them with the attention one gives only to what one reads in solitude. She studied also from books and from technical papers all the subjects with which Vronsky was occupied, so that he often came straight to her with questions about agriculture, architecture, and sometimes even horse-breeding or sport. He was astounded at her knowledge and memory, and at first used to doubt her information and want it confirmed. She would then find what he wanted in books and show it him.

The arrangement of the hospital also interested her. There she not only helped, but arranged and planned many things herself.

Nevertheless, her chief preoccupation was still herself—herself in so far as Vronsky held her dear and in so far as she could compensate him for all he had given up. Vronsky appreciated this, which had become the sole aim of her life—a desire not only to please him but also to serve him; but at the same time he was troubled by these love-meshes in which she tried to entangle him. As time went on, the oftener he felt himself caught in these meshes the more he desired, not exactly to escape from them but to try whether they really interfered with his freedom. Had it not been for this ever-increasing desire for freedom—not to have a scene each time he had to go to town to a meeting or to the races—Vronsky would have been quite content with his life. The rôle he had chosen, that of a rich landowner—one of those who should constitute the kernel of the Russian aristocracy—was not only quite to his taste but, now that he had lived so for half a year, gave him ever-increasing pleasure. His affairs, which occupied and absorbed him more and more, progressed excellently. In spite of the tremendous sums the hospital, the machinery, the cows which he imported from Switzerland, and many other things were costing him, he was sure that he was not wasting his substance but increasing it. Where it was a question of income—the sale of forest land, of corn or wool, or the leasing of land—Vronsky was as hard as flint and could hold out for his price. In all operations on a large scale, both on this and on his other estates, he kept to the simplest and safest methods, and was extremely economical and careful in his expenditure on small details. Despite all the cunning and artfulness of the German steward, who tried to lead him into expenditure and presented all estimates in such a way that it at first appeared as if much would be required, though on consideration the thing could be done more cheaply and an immediate profit obtained, Vronsky did not submit to him. He listened to what the steward had to say and questioned him, but only consented when the things to be ordered or built were the latest, as yet unknown in Russia, and likely to astonish people. Besides, he decided on a big outlay only when he had money to spare, and when spending he went into every detail and insisted on getting the very best for his money. So that from the way he managed his business it was clear that he was not wasting but increasing his property.

In October there were the Nobility elections in the Kashin Province, in which Vronsky's, Sviyazhsky's, Koznyshev's, Oblonsky's, and also a small part of Levin's estates were situated.

Various circumstances, as well as the men who took part in them, caused these elections to attract public attention. They were much discussed and preparations were made for them. People living in Moscow and Petersburg as well as others from abroad, who had never come to any elections, assembled at these.

Vronsky had long ago promised Sviyazhsky to be present.

Before the elections, Sviyazhsky, who often visited at Vozdvizhensk, called for Vronsky.

The day before, Vronsky and Anna had almost quarrelled about his proposed journey. It was autumn, the dullest and most depressing time of year in the country, and so Vronsky, bracing himself for a struggle, announced his departure in a sterner and colder way than he had ever before used to Anna. But, to his surprise, Anna took the news very quietly and only asked when he would return. He looked at her attentively, not understanding this calm manner. She answered his look with a smile. He knew her capacity for withdrawing into herself, and knew that she only did it when she had come to some resolution in her own mind without telling him of her plans. He feared this; but he so wished to avoid a scene that he pretended to believe, and to some extent sincerely believed, in what he wished to believe, namely, in her reasonableness.

'I hope you won't be bored?'

'I hope not,' replied Anna. 'I received a box of books from Gautier's [5] yesterday. No, I won't be bored.'

'She means to adopt this tone—well, so much the better!' thought he, 'or else it would be the usual thing again.'

And so, without challenging her to a frank explanation, he left for the elections. It was the first time since their union that he had parted from her without a full explanation. On the one hand this fact disturbed him, but on the other hand it seemed the best way. 'At first there will be, as now, something uncertain, something concealed; but afterwards she will get used to it. In any case I can give her everything else, but not my independence as a man,' he reflected.

Chapter XXVI

In September Levin moved to Moscow for Kitty's confinement. He had already been living there a whole month without occupation, when Sergius Ivanich Koznyshev, who had an estate in the Kashin Province and took a great interest in the forthcoming elections, prepared to attend them. He asked his brother, who had a vote for the Seleznev district, to accompany him. Levin had also some very important business to attend to in Kashin for his sister who lived abroad. It was in connection with a wardship and the receiving of money due to her for land transferred to the peasants.

Levin was still wavering, but Kitty, who had noticed that he was dull in Moscow and had advised him to go, without saying anything to him ordered for him the uniform necessary for the occasion,

5. Gautier had a well-known French bookshop in Moscow, founded in 1799.

which cost eighty roubles. And it was these eighty roubles paid for
the uniform which chiefly decided him. So he went to Kashin.

Levin had been five days in Kashin, going daily to meetings and
taking a great deal of trouble over his sister's business, which he
was still unable to arrange. The Marshals of the Nobility were all
busy with the elections, and he could not get even the simple matter in connection with the wardship settled. The other business,
that of getting the money paid, also met with obstacles. After long
efforts to get an injunction removed the money was all ready to be
paid out; but the notary—a very obliging man—could not give the
warrant because it needed the President's signature, and the President was engaged at the Session and had not appointed a substitute.
All those worries, the going from place to place, conversations with
very kind good people who quite understood the unpleasantness of
the petitioner's position but were unable to help him, and all these
efforts which yielded no results, produced in Levin a painful feeling
akin to the vexatious helplessness one experiences when trying to
employ physical force in a dream. He felt this frequently when talking to his very good-natured legal adviser. This legal adviser seemed
to do all that was possible and to strain every nerve to get Levin out
of his difficulties. 'Look here!' he would say, 'just try this—go to
so-and-so, and to so-and-so.' And the adviser would make an elaborate plan to circumvent the fatal difficulty which was at the root of
all this trouble. But he would immediately add: 'All the same you
will be put off; however, have a try!' And Levin tried, and went
again and again. Everybody was kind and amiable, but still it turned
out that what he wanted to circumvent started up again in another
place and impeded him once more. It was specially annoying to
Levin to be quite unable to understand with whom he was contending, and whom the delay in his business could profit. No one, not
even his lawyer, seemed to know this. If Levin could have understood it, as he understood the reason for having to stand in a queue
at a booking-office, he would not have felt hurt or vexed; but no
one could explain to him the reason for the obstacles he encountered in these business transactions.

However, Levin had changed considerably since his marriage; he
had become patient, and if he did not understand why things were
arranged thus, he told himself that, not knowing everything, he
could not judge, and that probably things had to be so; and he
tried not to be indignant.

And now, being present at the elections and taking part in them,
he also tried not to condemn, not to dispute, but as far as possible
to understand the matter—on which good and honest men, whom
he respected, were engaged with so much seriousness and enthusiasm. Since his marriage so many new and serious aspects of life

had been revealed to him, which owing to his superficial acquaintance with them had formerly seemed unimportant, that he
anticipated and looked for a serious meaning in this election business also.

Koznyshev explained to him the meaning and importance of the
changes anticipated as a result of the elections. The Marshal of the
Nobility for the Province—in whose hands the law placed so much
important public business: wardships (such as the one about which
Levin was now in trouble), the care of enormous sums of money
belonging to the nobility, public schools for boys and girls, military
schools, elementary education according to the new Law, and finally
the Zemstvo—the Marshal of the Province, Snetkov, was one of
the old type of nobles. He had run through an enormous fortune,
was a kind man, honest in his way but quite unable to understand
present-day requirements. He always sided with the Nobility in
everything, openly opposed the spread of popular education, and
gave a class character to the Zemstvo, which should have such
enormous importance. It was necessary to put in his place a new,
up-to-date, practical, and quite modern man, and to manage matters
so as to extract from the rights granted to the Nobility (not as
nobles, but as an element of the Zemstvo) all the advantages of self-
government which could be obtained from them. In the wealthy
Province of Kashin, always ahead of all others, such forces were now
assembled that, if matters were here managed as they should be, it
might serve as an example to other Provinces and to the whole of
Russia. The affair was therefore of great importance. To replace
Snetkov as Marshal, Sviyazhsky was proposed, or, better still,
Nevedovsky, an ex-professor, a remarkably intelligent man, and a
great friend of Koznyshev's.

The Session was opened by the Governor of the Province, who in
his speech to the nobles told them that in choosing occupants for
posts they should show no partiality, but should choose according
to merit and for the welfare of the country, and that he hoped the
honourable Nobility of Kashin would strictly fulfil its duty as it had
done in previous elections, and would justify their sovereign's high
confidence in them.

Having finished his speech the Governor left the hall, and the
noblemen, noisily, vivaciously, some of them even rapturously, followed him out with enthusiasm, and stood around him as he was
putting on his fur coat and talking in a friendly way with the Marshal of the Province. Levin, wishing to enter fully into everything
and not to miss anything, stood there too in the crowd, and heard
the Governor say: 'Please tell Mary Ivanovna that my wife is very
sorry she has to go to the Orphanage.' Then the noblemen gaily
scrambled for their overcoats and all drove to the cathedral.

In the cathedral Levin, with the others, raised his hand, repeating the words of the priest, and swore by the most awful oaths to fulfil all the things the Governor had hoped for. Church services always touched Levin, and when he was uttering the words, 'I kiss the cross,' and looked round at the crowd of men, young and old, who were repeating the same words, he felt moved.

On the second and third days matters were dealt with concerning the funds of the Nobility and the Girls' High Schools, which, Koznyshev explained, were quite unimportant; so Levin, busy going from place to place on the business he had in hand, did not trouble about them. On the fourth day the audit of the Provincial Funds was undertaken, and now for the first time there was a conflict between the new and old parties. The Commission entrusted with the task of auditing reported to the Assembly that the sums were all correct. The Marshal of the Nobility rose and with tears in his eyes thanked the Nobility for their confidence. The nobles loudly applauded him and pressed his hand. But at that moment one of the nobles of Koznyshev's party said he had heard that the Commission had not audited the Funds, considering that a verification would be an insult to the Marshal of the Province. A member of the Commission imprudently confirmed this. Then a small, very young-looking, but very venomous man began saying that probably the Marshal of the Province would be pleased to account for the Funds, and that the excessive politeness of the members of the Commission was depriving him of that moral satisfaction. Thereupon the members of the Commission withdrew their report and Koznyshev began very logically to prove that they must admit either that they had audited the accounts or that they had not done so, and to elaborate this dilemma. A speaker of the opposite party replied to Koznyshev. Then Sviyazhsky spoke, and then the venomous gentleman once more. The debate continued for a long time and did not come to any conclusion. Levin was surprised that they disputed about it so long, especially as, when he asked Koznyshev whether he thought that money had been misappropriated, he received the reply:

'Oh no! He is an honest fellow, but this old-fashioned patriarchal and family management of the Nobility's affairs must be put a stop to!'

On the fifth day the election of the District Marshals took place. For some of the districts the election was stormy enough; but for the Selezensk district Sviyazhsky was elected without opposition, and he gave a dinner-party at his house that evening.

Chapter XXVII

On the sixth day the Provincial elections were to be held. The large and small halls were full of noblemen in various uniforms. Many had come for that day only. Men who had long not met—

some from the Crimea, some from Petersburg, and some from abroad—came together in those halls. At the Marshal's table, beneath the portrait of the Emperor, discussions were in full swing.

Both in the large and small halls the noblemen were grouped together in their parties, and from the hostility and suspicion of their glances, from the cessation of their conversations when a stranger approached, and from the fact that some of them even went whispering into the farther corridor, it was evident that each party had secrets it kept from the other. By their external appearance the nobles were sharply divided into two sorts: the old and the young. The old, for the most part, either wore old-fashioned buttoned-up uniforms of their class and carried swords and hats, or wore the naval, cavalry, or infantry uniforms to which each was individually entitled. The uniforms of the old noblemen were cut in the old-fashioned way, with puffs at the shoulders, and were clearly too small for them, being short-waisted and narrow as if their wearers had grown out of them. The young men wore long-waisted loose uniforms wide across the shoulders with white waistcoats, or else were in uniforms with black collars embroidered with laurel leaves—the emblem of the Ministry of Justice. To the young party also belonged the Court uniforms, which here and there ornamented the crowd.

But the division into young and old did not coincide with the separation into parties. Some of the young ones, as Levin observed, belonged to the old party, and on the other hand some very aged noblemen conversed in whispers with Sviyazhsky and evidently were warm partisans of the new party.

Levin stood with his own group in the Small Hall, which was used as a refreshment and smoking room, listening to what was being said and vainly straining his mental powers to understand it all. Koznyshev was the centre around whom the rest were grouped. He was now listening to Sviyazhsky and Hlyustov, the Marshal of another district, who also belonged to their party. Hlyustov was unwilling to go with the members for his district to invite Snetkov to stand again for election. Sviyazhsky was persuading him to do so and Koznyshev approved of this. Levin did not see why his party should ask the Marshal to stand, when they wished to defeat him.

Oblonsky, who had just had something to eat and drink, came toward them in his Chamberlain's uniform, wiping his mouth with his scented and bordered lawn handkerchief.

'We are holding the position, Sergius Ivanich!' said he, smoothing back his whiskers. And after listening to the conversation he backed Sviyazhsky's opinion.

'One district is sufficient, and Sviyazhsky evidently belongs to the Opposition,' he said, and every one but Levin understood him.

'Well, Kostya! You too seem to have got a taste for it?' he said, turning to Levin and taking him by the arm. Levin would have been glad to get a taste for it but could not understand what the point was, and, stepping aside from the group, he told Oblonsky of his perplexity as to why the Marshal of the Province should be asked to stand again.

'O *sancta simplicitas!*'[6] said Oblonsky, and briefly and clearly explained the matter to Levin.

'If, as in former elections, all the districts nominated the Provincial Marshal, he would be elected, receiving white balls from every one. This we do not want. Now eight districts are willing to invite him to stand again; if two districts refuse to do so, Snetkov may decline to stand and then the old party might choose another of their members, and then all calculations would be upset. But if only Sviyazhsky's district does not invite him, Snetkov will stand. He will even get a good number of votes, so that the Opposition will be misled, and when a candidate of ours stands they will give him some votes.' Levin understood, but not fully, and wished to put some further questions when suddenly every one began talking at once, and moving noisily toward the Large Hall.

'What is it? What? Who? An authorization? To whom? What? Rejected! No authorization! Flerov is not admitted! What if he is being prosecuted? In that way they can exclude anybody! It's mean! The law!' Levin heard shouted from various sides, and he went toward the Large Hall with all the others, who were hastening on apparently afraid of missing something or other. Hemmed in by a crowd of noblemen, he approached the Provincial table, at which the Provincial Marshal, Sviyazhsky, and the other leaders were having a heated dispute.

Chapter XXVIII

Levin was standing some way off. He could not hear distinctly because of the stertorous and hoarse breathing of one nobleman near him and the creaking of the stout shoes of another. He could hear only the distant soft voice of the Marshal, then the shrill voice of the venomous nobleman, and then Sviyazhsky's voice. They were disputing, as far as he could make out, about a paragraph of the law and the meaning of the words: 'against whom legal proceedings are pending.'

The crowd separated to make way for Koznyshev to approach the table. He waited for the venomous nobleman to conclude, and then said he considered the proper course would be to consult the wording of the Act and requested the Secretary to look it up. The Act provided that in case of a difference of opinion the question should be balloted upon.

6. Oh saintly simplicity!

Koznyshev read the Act aloud, and began to explain its meaning, but a tall, thick-set, round-shouldered landowner with a dyed moustache, wearing a tight uniform, the high collar of which squeezed up his neck at the back, interrupted him. Advancing to the table he struck his ring against it, shouting in a loud voice:

'Vote! Put it to the ballot! Enough talking! Vote!'

At this several voices were heard, and the tall landowner with the ring, growing more and more spiteful, shouted louder and louder: but it was impossible to make out what he was saying.

He was demanding the very thing Koznyshev was proposing; but he evidently hated Koznyshev and his party, and this hatred communicated itself to all those on his side, and in turn evoked a similar, though more decently expressed, feeling of conflicting anger from the opposing party. Shouts arose, and for a moment there was such confusion that the Marshal had to call for order.

'Vote! Vote! Every one who is a nobleman will understand. . . . We shed our blood. . . . The Emperor's confidence. . . . Don't audit the Marshal; he's not a shop assistant! . . . But that's not the point! . . . Kindly ballot! . . . Abominable!' was heard shouted by spiteful furious voices from every side. The looks and expressions on the faces were yet more spiteful and furious than the words. They expressed implacable hatred. Levin could not at all understand what was the matter, and was astounded at the ardour with which they discussed the question whether Flerov's case should be put to the ballot or not. He forgot, as Koznyshev afterwards explained to him, the syllogism that for the common welfare it was necessary to displace the Marshal of the Province; but to defeat the Marshal it was necessary to have a majority of votes; to obtain that majority it was necessary to secure for Flerov the right to vote; and to secure Flerov's eligibility it was necessary to explain the meaning of the Law.

'A single vote may decide the whole matter, and one must be serious and consistent if one wishes to be of public service,' Koznyshev had said in conclusion. But Levin had forgotten that, and it pained him to see these good men, whom he respected, in such an unpleasant, malevolent state of excitement. To free himself from this feeling he went, without waiting to hear the end of the discussion, into the refreshment-room, where there was no one except the waiters at the buffet. When he saw the waiters busily wiping crockery and arranging plates and wine-glasses, and saw their calm yet animated faces, he experienced an unexpected feeling of relief, as if he had come out of a close room into fresh air. He began pacing up and down the room, watching the waiters with pleasure. He was particularly pleased by one old man with grey whiskers, who while evincing contempt for the young men who were making fun of him was teaching them how to fold napkins. Levin was just preparing to start a conversation with the old waiter when the Secretary of the Court of Nobility, an old man whose specialty it was to know all the nobles of the Province by name and patronymic, diverted his attention.

'Please come, Constantine Dmitrich!' said he. Your brother is looking for you. The vote is being taken.'

Levin entered the Hall, was given a white ball, and, following his brother, Sergius Ivanich, approached the table at which Sviyazhsky stood with an ironical and impressive look on his face, gathering his beard into his fist and smelling at it. Koznyshev inserted his hand in the ballot-box and placed his ball somewhere, and, making way for Levin paused beside him. Levin came up, but having entirely forgotten how the matter stood and being confused he turned to Koznyshev with the inquiry, 'Where am I to put it?' He spoke in a low voice at a time when people near by were talking, so he hoped his question would not be heard. But the talk stopped and his improper question was heard. Koznyshev frowned.

'That depends on each man's convictions,' he said severely.

Several persons smiled. Levin blushed, hastily thrust his hand under the cloth that covered the box, and, as the ball was in his right hand, dropped it on the right side. When he had done so he recollected that he ought to have put in his left hand also, and thrust it in, but it was too late; and feeling still more confused he hurried away to the very back of the room.

'One hund'ed and twenty-six fo'! Ninety-eight against!' came the Secretary's voice, dropping his r's. Then followed a sound of laughter; a button and two nuts had been found in the ballot box. Flerov was qualified and the new party had scored. But the old party did not consider itself defeated. Levin heard Snetkov being asked to stand; and he saw that a crowd of nobles surrounded the Marshal, who was speaking. Levin drew near. Replying to the nobles, Snetkov spoke of the confidence and affection of the Nobility, of which he was not worthy, his merit consisting only in his loyalty to the Nobility, to whom he had devoted twelve years of service. Several times he repeated the words: *have served to the extent of my power— faithfully and truly—I appreciate and thank . . .'* Then suddenly, choked by tears, he stopped, and left the room. Whether those tears resulted from a consciousness of injustice done him, or from love for the Nobility, or from the strained situation in which he found himself, surrounded by enemies, at any rate his emotion communicated itself. The majority of the nobles were touched and Levin felt a tenderness for Snetkov.

In the doorway the Marshal came into collision with Levin.

'Sorry! Please excuse me!' he said, speaking as to a stranger; but, recognizing Levin, he smiled timidly. It seemed to Levin that Snetkov wished to say something, but could not speak from agitation. The expression of his face and his whole figure, in uniform with crosses and white trousers trimmed with gold braid, as he went hurriedly along, reminded Levin of a hunted animal conscious that things are going badly with him. This expression on the Marshal's face touched Levin, particularly because, just the day before, he had been to his house about the wardship and had there seen him in all the dignity of a kind-hearted family man. The large house with the old family furniture; the old footmen by no means smart, rather shabby, but respectful—evidently former serfs who had remained with their master; the stout, good-natured wife, in a lace cap and Turkish shawl, caressing her pretty grand-daughter (a daughter's daughter), the manly young son in the sixth form of the High School, who had just come home and who kissed his father's large hand in greeting; the impressive kindly words and gestures of the host—all this had yesterday awakened Levin's involuntary respect and sympathy. Now the old man seemed touching and pathetic to Levin and he wished to say something pleasant to him.

'So you are to be our Marshal again,' said he.

'Hardly!' replied the Marshal, looking round with a frightened expression. 'I am tired and old. There are others worthier and younger than I, let them serve.'

And the Marshal disappeared through a side-door.

The most solemn moment had arrived. The elections were about to begin. The leaders of both parties were making estimates and calculating on their fingers the white and black balls they could reckon on.

The debate about Flerov had given the new party not merely his vote but also a gain in time, so that they had had a chance to bring up three more nobles who, by the machinations of the old party, were to be prevented from taking part in the election. Two of these noblemen, who had a weakness for wine, had been made drunk by Snetkov's agents, and the uniform of the third had been carried off.

The new party, having heard of this, had had time while Flerov's case was being discussed to send two of their men in a carriage to supply that nobleman with a uniform and to bring one of the tipsy ones to the Assembly.

'I have brought one. I soused him,' said the landowner who had been to fetch him, approaching Sviyazhsky. 'He'll do.'

'He's not very drunk—he won't fall down?' asked Sviyazhsky, swaying his head.

'No, he's fine. If only they don't give him anything here. . . . I told the man at the bar on no account to let him have anything!'

Chapter XXIX

The narrow room in which they were eating and smoking was full of noblemen. The excitement was ever increasing and anxiety was noticeable on all the faces. Especially excited were the leaders, who knew all the details and the estimates of votes. They were directors of the impending battle. The others, like the rank and file before a battle, though preparing for the fight, sought distraction meanwhile. Some of them ate, standing or hastily sitting down at the table; others smoked cigarettes, pacing up and down the long room, and talked to friends they had not seen for a long time.

Levin did not want to eat and did not smoke; he did not wish to join his own set—Koznyshev, Oblonsky, Sviyazhsky and the others —because among them, in animated conversion, stood Vronsky, wearing his uniform as an equerry. Levin had noticed him at the elections the day before and had carefully avoided meeting him. He went to the window and sat down, looking at the different groups and listening to what was being said around him. He felt sad, chiefly because he saw that every one else was animated, preoccupied, and busy, while only he and a mumbling, toothless, quite old man in naval uniform who had sat down beside him were uninterested and inactive.

'He is such a rascal! I told him not to! Really! In three years he could not collect it'—a short, round-shouldered landowner with pomaded hair that hung down on the embroidered collar of his uniform was saying energetically, stamping loudly with the heels of the new boots he had evidently put on specially for this occasion. And casting a discontented glance at Levin, he suddenly turned away.

'Yes, it's a dirty business, say what you will' remarked an undersized man with a feeble voice.

Following those two a whole crowd of landowners, surrounding a stout General, hastily approached Levin. Obviously they were seeking a place where they could talk without being overheard.

'How dare he say I gave orders to steal his trousers? I expect he drank them. I snap my fingers at him and his princely title! He has no right to say it: it's mean!'

'But excuse me! They rely on the statute,' some one in another group was saying. 'The wife ought to be registered as belonging to the Nobility.'

'What the devil do I care about the statute? I speak frankly. That's what the Nobility are for. One must have confidence.'

'Come, your Excellency! A glass of *fine champagne!*' [7]

Another group followed close on the heels of a nobleman who

7. Cognac.

was shouting loudly. He was one of those who had been made drunk.

'I always advised Mary Semenovna to let her estate, because she will never make it pay,' said a pleasant-voiced landowner with a grey moustache, wearing the uniform of Colonel of the former General Staff. It was the landowner Levin had met at Sviyazhsky's house. He knew him at once. The landowner also recognized Levin and they shook hands.

'Very pleased to see you! Of course I remember you very well. Last year, at Sviyazhsky the Marshal's house.'

'Well, how is your husbandry getting on?' Levin inquired.

'Oh, still the same—with a loss,' replied the landowner as he stopped beside Levin, with a resigned smile and a look of calm conviction that it must be so. 'And how do you come to be in our Province?' he asked. 'Have you come to take part in our *coup d'état?*' he went on, pronouncing the French words firmly but badly.

'All Russia has assembled here: Chamberlains and almost Ministers.' He pointed to the portly figure of Oblonsky in his Chamberlain's uniform with white trousers, walking beside a General.

'I must confess to you that I only imperfectly understand the meaning of these Nobility elections,' said Levin.

The landowner looked at him.

'But what is there to understand? It has no meaning whatever. The Nobility is an obsolete institution, which continues to act through inertia. Look at the uniforms! They tell the tale: this is an assembly of Justices of the Peace, permanent officials, and so on, but not of nobles!'

'Then why do you come?' asked Levin.

'From habit, for one thing. Then one must keep up one's connections. It's a sort of moral obligation. And then, to tell the truth, I have a private reason. My son-in-law wishes to stand for a permanent membership: they are not well off and I want him to get it. But why do such gentlemen come?' he went on, indicating the venomous gentleman who had spoken at the Provincial table.

'He is one of the new Nobility.'

'New if you like, but not the Nobility. They are landowners; we are country squires. They, as noblemen, are committing suicide.'

'But you say it is an obsolete institution!'

'It is obsolete certainly; but all the same one should treat it more respectfully. Take Snetkov. . . . Whether we are good or bad, we have been growing for a thousand years. You know, if we had to make a garden in front of our house, we should plan it out; and if a century-old tree is growing on that spot—though it may be rugged and old, yet you won't cut it down for the sake of a flower-bed, but will plan your beds so as to make use of the old tree! It can't be grown in a year,' he remarked cautiously, immediately changing the subject. 'Well, and how is your husbandry getting on?'

'Oh, not well. I get about five per cent.'

'Yes, but you don't reckon your own work. You know you too are worth something! Now, take me. Before I took to farming I was getting three thousand roubles a year in the Service. Now I work harder than I did in the Service, and like yourself I clear about five per cent., and that only with luck. And my own labour goes for nothing.'

'Then why do you go on with it, if it is a clear loss?'

'Well, you see . . . one goes on! What would you have? It's a habit, and one knows that it's necessary! I will tell you, moreover,' and leaning his elbow on the window and having started talking, the landowner went on: 'My son has no taste at all for husbandry. It is clear he will be a scholar, so that there will be no one to continue my work, and yet I go on! Just now, you know, I have planted an orchard.'

'Yes, yes,' said Levin, 'that is quite so! I always feel that I am getting no real profit out of my estate and yet I go on. . . . One feels a sort of duty toward the land.'

'I'll tell you something,' continued the landowner. 'My neighbour, a merchant, called on me, and we went over the farm and garden together. He said, "Everything is going as it should, only your garden is neglected," though my garden is quite in order. "If I were you, I should cut down those limes, but it must be done when the sap rises. You must have a thousand limes here, and each one of them would yield a good lot of linden timber, which now fetches a good price, and serves for making bath-house frames." '

'Yes, and with that money he would buy cattle, or a piece of land for a mere song, and would lease it to the peasants,' added Levin with a smile, having evidently more than once come across such calculations. 'And he will make a fortune, while you and I must be thankful if we can keep what we have and leave it to our children.'

'You are married, I hear?' said the landowner.

'Yes,' replied Levin with proud satisfaction. 'Yes, it is curious,' he continued. 'We live without gaining anything, as if we were appointed, like the vestals of old, to guard some fire or other.'

The landowner smiled under his grey moustache.

'There are those among us too . . . for example our friend Sviyazhsky, or Count Vronsky, who has now settled here, who want to turn agriculture into an industry; but as yet that leads only to loss of capital.'

'But why don't we do like the merchant? Why don't we cut down our limes for bast?' said Levin, returning to the thought that had struck him.

'Why, as you have said, we guard the fire! The other is not work for the Nobility. Our work is not done here, at the elections, but at our homes. We have a class instinct as to what should not be done. I see it in the peasants too sometimes: a proper peasant always tries to get hold of as much land as possible. However bad the land, still he ploughs it. It brings him also no profit, but pure loss.'

'Just like us,' said Levin. 'Very, very glad to have met you,' he added, seeing Sviyazhsky approaching.

'We two have met for the first time since we were at your house,' said the landowner, 'and have indulged in a chat.'

'Yes, and have you been abusing the new order?' asked Sviyazhsky with a smile.

'We won't deny it.'

'Unburdening our souls!'

Chapter XXX

Sviyazhsky took Levin's arm and led him back to his own group.

This time it was impossible to avoid Vronsky. He was standing with Oblonsky and Koznyshev, and looked straight at Levin as he came up.

'Very pleased! I think I had the pleasure of meeting you . . . at the Princess Shcherbatsky's?' said he, holding out his hand to Levin.

'Yes, I well remember our meeting,' said Levin, and blushing scarlet immediately turned and spoke to his brother.

Smiling slightly, Vronsky continued his conversation with Sviyazhsky, evidently having no desire to start a conversation with Levin; but Levin, while talking to his brother, kept looking round at Vronsky, trying to think of something to say to him, in order to mitigate his rudeness.

'What is delaying matters now?' asked Levin, glancing at Sviyazhsky and Vronsky.

'Snetkov. He must either decline or accept,' replied Sviyazhsky.

'Well, and has he agreed or not?'

'That's just it: neither the one nor the other,' answered Vronsky.

'And if he should refuse, who will stand?' asked Levin, looking at Vronsky.

'Whoever likes,' replied Sviyazhsky.

'Will you?' asked Levin.

'Certainly not I,' said Sviyazhsky, becoming embarrassed and casting an alarmed glance at the venomous gentleman, who was standing beside Koznyshev.

'Who then? Nevedovsky?' said Levin, feeling that he had put his foot in it somehow.

But this was still worse. Nevedovsky and Sviyazhsky were the two prospective candidates.

'Not I, not on any account!' said the venomous gentleman.

So this was Nevedovsky! Sviyazhsky introduced him to Levin.

'Well, has it touched you to the quick too?' said Oblonsky, winking at Vronsky. 'It's like the races. It makes one inclined to bet on the result.'

'Yes, it does touch one to the quick,' replied Vronsky, 'and having once taken the matter up, one wants to carry it through. It's a struggle!' he said frowning, and closed his powerful jaw.

'What a capable man Sviyazhsky is! How clearly he puts everything!'

'Oh yes,' replied Vronsky absent-mindedly.

There was a pause, during which Vronsky, since he had to look at something, looked at Levin: at his feet, his uniform, and then his face, and noticing the sombre eyes fixed upon him he remarked, just to say something:

'And how is it that you, living constantly in the country, are not a Justice of the Peace? You are not in the uniform of a Justice?'

'Because I consider that the Magistracy is an idiotic institution,' morosely replied Levin, who had all the time been looking for an opportunity of speaking to Vronsky, to atone for his rudeness at their first encounter.

'I don't think so; on the contrary . . .' said Vronsky with calm surprise.

'It's a game,' Levin interrupted. 'We don't need any Justices of the Peace. I have not had a single case in eight years, and when I did have one it was decided wrongly. The Justice's Court is forty versts from my house. To settle a matter worth two roubles I should have to send an attorney who costs me fifteen.'

And he related how a peasant stole some flour from a miller, and how when the miller spoke to him about it the peasant sued him for libel. All this was untimely and foolish, and Levin himself was conscious of it even while he spoke.

'Oh, he is such a crank!' said Oblonsky with his smoothest and oiliest smile. 'But come! I think the ballot has begun . . .'

And they separated.

'I don't understand,' said Koznyshev, who had observed his brother's awkward sally, 'I don't understand how one can be so entirely devoid of political tact! That is what we Russians lack. The Marshal of the Province is our opponent and you are *ami cochon* with him [8] and ask him to stand. But Count Vronsky . . . I do not make a friend of him; he invited me to dinner and I shan't go; but he is one of our party, so why make an enemy of him? Then you ask Nevedovsky whether he will stand. That kind of thing is not done!'

8. You are quite thick with him.

'Oh, I understand nothing about it! It is all trifling,' said Levin, gloomily.

'There, you say it's all trifling, but when you begin on it you make a mess of everything.'

Levin remained silent and they entered the Large Hall together.

The Marshal of the Province, though he felt in the air that there was a plot prepared against him, and though he had not been unanimously asked to stand, had still decided to do so. There was silence in the hall, and the Secretary loudly announced that Michael Stepanich Snetkov, Captain of the Guards, was nominated for the post of Provincial Marshal, and that the ballot would now be taken.

The District Marshals carried little plates filled with ballot balls from their own tables to the Provincial table, and the election began.

'Put it on the right,' whispered Oblonsky to Levin as the latter, with his brother, followed the Marshal to the table. But Levin had forgotten the plan which had been explained to him, and was afraid that Oblonsky was making a mistake when he said 'right.' Surely Snetkov was their opponent! While approaching the box he had the ball in his right hand, but, thinking it was a mistake, he shifted it to his left hand just as he reached the box, and evidently placed it to the left. An expert standing beside the box, who by the mere motion of an elbow could tell where every ball was put, made a wry face. There was nothing for him to exercise his penetration upon this time.

All became silent again, and one heard the balls being counted. Then a solitary voice proclaimed the number for and against. The Marshal had received a considerable majority. A clamour arose and every one rushed to the door. Snetkov entered and the noblemen thronged around him with congratulations.

'Well, is it over now?' Levin asked his brother.

'It's only beginning!' Sviyazhsky smilingly answered for Koznyshev. 'The other candidate may get still more votes.'

Levin had again forgotten about that. He only now remembered that there was some subtlety in it, but he was too bored to recollect what it was. He was overcome by depression and wanted to get out of that crowd.

As no one was paying any attention to him, and he apparently was not wanted by anybody, he went quietly to the small refreshment-room and again felt great relief when he saw the waiters. The old waiter offered him something to eat and Levin accepted. Having eaten a cutlet and beans, and talked with the old man about his former masters, Levin, not wishing to return to the hall where he had felt so out of his element, went up into the gallery.

The gallery was crowded with smartly-dressed women who leaned over the balustrade and tried not to miss a single word of what was being said below. Beside the women sat or stood elegant lawyers, spectacled High School teachers, and officers. Every one was talking about the elections and how tired out the Marshal was and how interesting the debates had been. In one group Levin heard them praising his brother. A lady was saying to a lawyer:

'How glad I am to have heard Koznyshev! It was worth while going a little hungry. Delightful! So clear and audible! There now, no one speaks like that in your Court—except perhaps Maydel, and even he is far less eloquent!'

Having found a vacant place at the balustrade, Levin leant over and began to look and listen.

The noblemen were sitting behind partitions, arranged according to their districts. In the centre of the room stood a man in uniform, who announced in a loud shrill voice:

'As candidate for the post of Provincial Marshal, Captain Eugene Ivanich Apukhtin will now be balloted for.' Then followed a dead silence, and a feeble voice was heard saying:

'Declines!'

'Court Councillor Peter Petrovich Bol will now be balloted for,' cried the voice of the man in uniform.

'Declines,' shouted a youthful squeaky voice.

A similar announcement was made, and again followed by 'Declines.' So it went on for about an hour. Levin, leaning over the balustrade, looked on and listened. At first he was surprised and wanted to understand what it meant; then, coming to the conclusion that he could not understand it, he grew bored. Then, remembering the agitation and anger he had witnessed on all faces, he felt sad, and with the intention of leaving the place went downstairs. As he was passing through the corridor behind the gallery he came across a dispirited High School pupil with bloodshot eyes pacing up and down. On the stairs he met a couple: a lady running up swiftly in her high-heeled shoes, and the Assistant Public Prosecutor.

'I said you would be in time,' the Assistant said, as Levin stepped aside to let the lady pass.

Levin was already descending the stairs to the exit and getting out his cloakroom ticket when the Secretary caught him. 'Please come, Constantine Dmitrich! They are voting!'

The candidate who was standing was Nevedovsky, who had so decidedly declined.

Levin went up to the door of the hall: it was locked. The Secretary knocked, the door opened and two landowners with flushed faces plunged out past Levin.

'I can't stand it!' cried one of the red-faced landowners. Then the head of the Provincial Marshal was thrust out at the doorway. His face was dreadful from its expression of exhaustion and fear.

'I told you to let no one out!' he shouted to the doorkeeper.

'I was letting people in, Your Excellency!'

'Oh, Lord!' said the Marshal of the Province with a deep sigh; and with his weary legs in the white trousers dragging, and hanging his head, he went down the middle of the hall to the chief table.

Nevedovsky had a majority as they had expected and he was now Marshal of the Province. Many were cheerful, many contented and happy, many were in ecstasy, and many dissatisfied and miserable. The old Marshal was in despair and could not hide it. When Nevedovsky left the hall the crowd surrounded him and followed him enthusiastically as it had followed the Governor of the Province on the first day, when he opened the meeting, and as it had followed Snetkov when he was successful.

Chapter XXXI

The newly-elected Marshal of the Province and many of the victorious new party dined that evening at Vronsky's.

Vronsky had come to the elections because he felt dull in the country, in order to proclaim to Anna his right to freedom, to repay Sviyazhsky by supporting him at these elections for all the trouble he had taken for Vronsky at the Zemstvo elections, and most of all to perform strictly all the duties of the position he had taken up as nobleman and landowner. But he had not at all expected that the election business would interest him so much and so touch him to the quick, or that he could do it so well. He was quite a new man in this circle of noble landowners, but he evidently was a success; and he was not mistaken in thinking that he had already gained influence among them. This influence was promoted by his wealth, by his title, by the splendid house in the town which had been lent him by his old acquaintance Shirkov, a financier who had founded a flourishing bank in Kashin; by the excellent *chef* whom he had brought from his estate; by his friendship with the Governor, who had been a former comrade and one whom Vronsky had even protected; but above all by his simple behaviour in treating every one alike, which had quickly induced most of the noblemen to change their opinion as to his supposed pride. He himself felt that, except that crazy fellow married to Kitty Shcherbatsky, who, *à propos de bottes,*[9] had with rabid virulence told him a lot of pointless nonsense, every nobleman whose acquaintance he had made had become his partisan. He saw clearly, and others

9. Quite irrelevantly.

acknowledged, that he had contributed very much to Nevedovsky's success. Now, at his own table, celebrating Nevedovsky's election, Vronsky experienced a pleasant feeling of triumph. The elections themselves interested him so much that he began to think that if he were married by the next triennial election he would himself put up, just as, when a jockey had won him a prize, he had wished to ride a race himself.

They were now celebrating the jockey's victory. Vronsky sat at the head of the table; on his right was the young Governor, a General of the Emperor's suite. For everybody else the General was the master of the Province, who had solemnly opened the sessions and made a speech, and, as Vronsky saw, aroused both respect and servility in many present, but for Vronsky he was 'Maslov Katka'— the nickname he had had in the *Corps des Pages*—who felt embarrassed in his presence and whom Vronsky tried to *mettre à son aise.*[1] On Vronsky's left sat Nevedovsky with his youthful, dogged, and venomous look. Toward him Vronsky was simple and courteous.

Sviyazhsky bore his failure cheerfully. It was not even a failure for him; as he himself said to Nevedovsky, champagne glass in hand, no better representative of the new course which the Nobility ought to follow could have been found. And therefore all that was honest, as he remarked, was on the side of to-day's success and triumphed in it.

Oblonsky too was pleased that he had spent his time merrily and that every one was satisfied. At the excellent dinner the episodes of the elections were discussed. Sviyazhsky comically mimicked the old Marshal's tearful speech and, turning to Nevedovsky, remarked that His Excellency would have to adopt a different and more complex method of auditing the funds than tears! Another witty nobleman narrated how footmen with knee-breeches and stockings had been imported to wait at the ball which the Marshal of the Province had intended to give and that they would now have to be sent back, unless the new Marshal would give a ball with stockinged footmen.

During the dinner they continually spoke of Nevedovsky as 'Our Provincial Marshal' and addressed him as 'Your Excellency.'

This was uttered with the same pleasure with which a newly-married woman is addressed as Madame and called by her husband's name. Nevedovsky pretended not merely to be indifferent to but to despise this title; but it was evident that he felt happy and exercised self-control to avoid betraying a delight ill-suited to the new Liberal circle in which they found themselves.

During the dinner several telegrams were sent to persons interested in the elections. Oblonsky, who was feeling very jolly, sent

1. To put at his ease.

one to Dolly which ran as follows: 'Nevedovsky elected by majority of twenty. Congratulations. Tell news.' He dictated it aloud, saying, 'I must cheer them up!' But Dolly, on receiving the telegram, only sighed over the rouble it had cost, and understood that it had been sent toward the end of a dinner. She knew that Stiva had a weakness at the end of a dinner-party *faire jouer le télégraphe*. [2]

Everything, including the splendid dinner and the wines—which did not come from Russian merchants, but were imported ready-bottled from abroad—was very distinguished, simple, and gay. The company of twenty men had been selected by Sviyazhsky from adherents of the new movement and from Liberals, men who were also witty and respectable. Healths were drunk, also half in jest, to the new Provincial Marshal, to the Governor, to the Bank Director, and to 'our amiable host.'

Vronsky was satisfied. He had not at all expected to find such a pleasant tone in the provinces.

When dinner was over things became still merrier. The Governor asked Vronsky to accompany him to a concert in aid of 'our Servian brothers,' which was being arranged by his wife, who wished to make Vronsky's acquaintance.

'There will be a ball afterwards and you will see our Society beauty! Really, she is quite remarkable.'

'Not in my line,' answered Vronsky, who was fond of that English expression, but he smiled and promised to come.

When they had already quitted the table and had all begun smoking, Vronsky's valet came up to him with a letter on a salver.

'From Vozdvizhensk, by express messenger,' he said with a significant glance.

'It is extraordinary how much he resembles the Public Prosecutor Sventitsky,' remarked one of the guests in French of the valet, while Vronsky, frowning, read his letter.

The letter was from Anna. Even before he read it he knew its contents. Expecting the elections to end in five days, he had promised to return on the Friday. It was now Saturday, and he knew that the letter contained reproaches for his not having returned punctually. The letter he had sent off the evening before had probably not yet reached her.

The contents of the letter were just what he expected, but its form was unexpected and particularly unpleasant to him. 'Annie is very ill. The doctor says it may be inflammation. I lose my head when alone. The Princess Barbara is not a help but a hindrance. I expected you the day before yesterday, and yesterday, and am now sending to find out where you are and what the matter is. I wished to come myself, but changed my mind knowing that you would not

2. To set the telegraph going.

like it. Give me some reply that I may know what to do."

Baby was ill, and she wished to come herself! Their child ill, and this hostile tone!

The innocent mirth of the elections and this dismal burdensome love to which he must return struck Vronsky by their contrast. But he had to go, and he took the first train that night for his home.

Chapter XXXII

Before Vronsky went to the elections Anna, having considered that the scenes which took place between them every time he went away could only tend to estrange them instead of binding them closer, resolved to make every possible effort to bear the separation calmly. But the cold, stern look on his face when he came to tell her he was going offended her, and even before he had gone her composure was upset.

Later on, meditating in solitude on that look—which expressed his right to freedom—she, as usual, came only to a consciousness of her own humiliation. 'He has the right to go when and where he pleases. Not only to go away, but to leave me. He has every right and I have none at all. But, knowing this, he ought not to do it! But really what has he done? . . . He has looked at me coldly and severely. Of course it is indefinable, intangible, but it was not so formerly, and that look means much,' she thought. 'That look shows that he is beginning to grow cold.'

Though she was convinced that this was the case, she could not do anything, could not in any way change her relation to him. Just as heretofore, she could hold him only by means of her love and attractiveness; and just as heretofore, only by occupations by day and morphia by night could she stifle the terrible thought of what would happen if he ceased to love her. True, there was one means, not of holding him—for that purpose she wished for nothing except his love—but of putting herself in such a position that he could not abandon her. That means was divorce and marriage. She began to wish for this, and decided to agree the first time he or Stiva should mention it to her.

With these thoughts in her mind she spent five days, the days she expected him to be away.

Walks, talks with the Princess Barbara, visits to the hospital, and above all reading, reading one book after another, filled her time. But on the sixth day, when the coachman returned from the station without him, she felt that she was no longer able to stifle the thought of him and of what he was doing. Just then her little girl fell ill. Anna nursed her, but this did not divert her thoughts, especially as the illness was not dangerous. Try as she might she could not love that child and she could not make a pretence of love. Toward the evening of that day, being alone, Anna felt such terror on Vronsky's account that she decided to go to town, but after careful consideration she wrote that contradictory letter which Vronsky received, and without reading it over she sent it by express messenger. Next morning she received his letter and regretted her own. She anticipated with horror a repetition of that stern look he had thrown at her when leaving, especially when he should learn that the little girl was not dangerously ill. But still she was glad she had written. Anna now acknowledged to herself that he was weary of her and would regret giving up his freedom to return to her; yet in spite of this she was glad that he would come. Let him feel weary, but let him be here with her so that she might see him and know his every movement.

She was sitting in the drawing-room, reading by lamp-light a new book by Taine, listening to the wind outside,[3] and expecting every moment the arrival of the carriage. Several times she had thought she heard the sound of wheels but had been mistaken; at last she heard not only the wheels but also the coachman's voice and a dull rumbling in the portico. Even the Princess Barbara, who was playing patience, confirmed this, and Anna, flushing, rose, but instead of going downstairs, as she had already done twice, she stood still. She suddenly felt ashamed of having deceived him and still more afraid of how he might treat her. The feeling of injury had already passed, and she only feared the expression of his displeasure. She remembered that the child had been quite well since yesterday. She was even vexed with her for having recovered as soon as the letter had been sent. Then she recollected that he was here, all of him, his hands, his eyes. She heard his voice, and forgetting everything else ran joyfully to meet him.

'Well, how is Annie?' he asked timidly, looking up at Anna as she ran down to him.

He was sitting on a chair, and the footman was pulling off his warm boots.

'Oh, it's nothing! She's better.'

'And you?' he asked, giving himself a shake.

She took his hand in both hers and drew it to her waist, not taking her eyes off him.

'Well, I'm very glad,' he said, coldly surveying her coiffure and the dress which, he knew, she had put on for him.

All this pleased him, but it had already pleased him so often! And the stern and stony look, which she so dreaded, settled on his face.

'Well, I am very glad. And you are well?' said he, wiping his wet

3. *On Reason*, a book by the French critic and philosopher Hippolyte Taine (1828–1893) was published in 1870. In Part 7, ch. 31, a woman sitting next to Anna in the railroad car and Anna herself pronounce the sentence, "Perhaps reason is given to us in order to be rid of what troubles us," the former in French, the latter in Russian. In Tolstoy's drafts for the novel, Anna is shown as a reader of de Tocqueville, Carlyle, and Taine.

beard with his handkerchief, and kissing her hand.

'No matter,' she thought, 'if only he is here. When he is here he can't and daren't fail to love me!'

The evening passed happily and cheerfully in the company of the Princess Barbara, who complained to him that in his absence Anna had been taking morphia.

'What am I to do? I could not sleep. . . . My thoughts kept me awake. When he is here I never take it, or hardly ever.'

He told her about the elections, and Anna knew how by questions to lead him on to just what pleased him—his success. She told him about everything that interested him at home, and all her news was most cheerful.

But late at night, when they were alone, Anna, seeing that she had regained full mastery of him, wanted to efface the depressing impression of the look he gave her apropos of the letter, and said:

'But confess that you were vexed to get my letter, and did not believe me?'

As soon as she had said this she knew that, however lovingly disposed he might be to her, he had not forgiven her for that letter.

'Yes,' he answered. 'It was such a strange letter. Annie was ill, yet you wished to come yourself!'

'That was all true.'

'I don't doubt it.'

'Yes, you do doubt it! I see you are displeased.'

'Not for a moment. I am only displeased, really, that you seem not to wish to admit that there are duties . . .'

'Duties to go to a concert . . .'

'Don't let us talk about it,' he said.

'Why should we not talk about it?' she replied.

'I only wished to say that one may have unavoidable business. Now, for instance, I shall have to go to Moscow about the house. . . . Oh, Anna, why are you so irritable? Don't you know that I can't live without you?'

'If that is so,' replied Anna in a suddenly changed voice, 'it must be that you are weary of this life. . . . Yes, you will come for a day and go away again, as men do . . .'

'Anna, that is cruel. I am ready to give my whole life . . .'

But she did not listen to him.

'If you go to Moscow, I shall go too! I will not stop here. Either we must separate or live together.'

'You know that that is my desire! But for that . . .'

'A divorce is necessary? I will write to him! I see I cannot live like this. . . . But I will go to Moscow with you.'

'You speak as if you were threatening me! Why, I don't wish for anything so much as not to be separated from you,' said Vronsky, smilingly.

But not a cold look only but the angry look of a hunted and exasperated man flashed in his eyes as he spoke those tender words.

She saw that look and rightly guessed its meaning.

The look said, 'If so, this is a misfortune!' It was a momentary impression, but she never forgot it.

Anna wrote to her husband asking him for a divorce; and at the end of November, having parted from the Princess Barbara, who had to go to Petersburg, she moved to Moscow with Vronsky. Daily expecting Karenin's reply, to be followed by a divorce, they now established themselves like a married couple.

Part VII

Chapter I

The Levins had been more than two months in Moscow. The date on which, according to the most exact calculations of persons experienced in such matters, Kitty should have been confined had long passed; but she had not yet been delivered, nor were there any signs that the time was nearer now than it had been two months previously. The doctor, the midwife, Dolly, her mother, and especially Levin (who could not think without horror of what was coming), began to experience impatience and anxiety; Kitty alone was perfectly calm and happy.

She now distinctly realized the awakening of a new sense of tenderness for the coming (and for her to some extent already existing) child, and she yielded with pleasure to that feeling. It was no longer entirely part of herself, but now and then lived its own independent life. Sometimes this occasioned her pain, but at the same time she wanted to laugh because of this strange new joy.

All whom she loved were with her, and all were so kind to her and so attentive, and everything was presented to her in so pleasant an aspect, that had she not known it must soon come to an end she could not have desired a better or pleasanter life. The only thing that marred the charm of this life was that her husband was not as she loved him best, not as he used to be in the country.

She loved his quiet, kindly and hospitable manner on his estate. In town he always seemed restless and on his guard, as if afraid lest some one should insult him or, worse still, her. There, on his estate, feeling that he was in his right place, he was never in a hurry to go anywhere and was always occupied. Here in town he was always in a hurry, as if fearing to miss something, and yet he had nothing to do. She was sorry for him. She knew that to others he did not appear to need pity. On the contrary, when Kitty watched him in company—as one sometimes watches a person one loves, trying to see him from a stranger's point of view, so as to realize the impression he makes on others—she saw, even with some jealous fear, that far from needing pity he was very attractive, by his good breeding, his rather old-fashioned and timid politeness to women, his powerful figure, and, as she thought, his uncommonly expressive face. But she understood him not from without but from within, and saw that in town he was not himself; she could not otherwise define his condition. Sometimes in her heart she reproached him for not knowing how to live in town; at other times she confessed that it was really hard for him to arrange his life here satisfactorily.

Indeed, what could he do? He did not care for cards. He did not go to the club. She knew now what consorting with merry people of Oblonsky's sort meant—it meant drinking and then driving somewhere. . . . She could not think without horror of where men drove to in such cases. Go into Society? But she knew that to do so he would have to find pleasure in being with young women, and she could not wish that. Stay at home with her and her mother and sisters? But, agreeable and amusing as the same oft-repeated conversations might be to her—talks about 'Alines and Nadines,' as the old Prince called those talks between the sisters—she knew they must bore him. Then what was left for him to do? Continue to write his book? He did try to do it, and began by going to a public library to take notes and look up references he required; but, as he explained to her, the less he did the less time he seemed to have. And he also complained that he had talked too much about his book here, so that all his ideas had become confused and he had lost interest in them.

The one advantage of this town-life was that here they never quarrelled. Whether it was that the conditions of town-life were different, or that they had both grown more careful and reasonable in this respect—at any rate, in Moscow they never had quarrels resulting from jealousy such as they had feared when they moved to town.

An event even occurred of great importance to them both in this respect, namely, Kitty's meeting with Vronsky.

The old Princess, Mary Borisovna, Kitty's godmother, who had always been very fond of her, particularly wished to see her. Though Kitty was not going out anywhere because of her condition, yet she went with her father to see the venerable old lady, and there met Vronsky.

The only thing Kitty could reproach herself with when that visit was over was that for an instant, on recognizing Vronsky's once so familiar figure in his civilian clothes, she grew breathless, the blood rushed to her heart, and she felt a deep flush suffusing her face. But this lasted only a few seconds. Her father, purposely addressing Vronsky in a loud voice, had not finished what he was saying before she was quite ready to face Vronsky, and if need be to converse with him just as she conversed with the Princess Mary Borisovna; especially so that everything down to the lightest intonation and smile might be approved by her husband, whose unseen presence she seemed to feel above her at that moment.

She exchanged a few words with Vronsky, and even smiled at a joke he made about the elections, to which he alluded as 'our parliament.' (She had to smile to show that she understood the joke.) But she at once turned to the Princess Mary Borisovna and did not once look round at Vronsky till he rose to go. Then she looked at him, but evidently only because it is impolite not to look at a man when he is bowing to you.

She was grateful to her father for not saying anything to her about this encounter with Vronsky; but, by his peculiar tenderness to her during their daily walk after the visit, she saw that he was pleased with her. She was pleased with herself. She had not at all expected to find strength to shut down somewhere deep in her heart all memories of her former feelings for this man, and not merely to appear but really to be quite tranquil and calm in his presence.

Levin blushed much more than she had done when she told him she had met Vronsky at the Princess Mary Borisovna's. It was very difficult for her to tell him this, and still more difficult to go on giving him details of the meeting, as he did not ask anything, but only frowned and looked at her.

'I am very sorry you were not there,' she said; 'I don't mean present in the room. . . . I should not have behaved so naturally with you there. . . . I am now blushing much more—much, much more,' she added blushing to tears, 'but I am sorry you could not look in through a crack.'

Her truthful eyes told Levin that she was satisfied with herself, and in spite of her blushes he grew calm at once, and began questioning her, which was just what she wanted. When he had heard all, down to the fact that just for the first second she could not help blushing, but that afterwards she had felt as natural and easy as with anyone she might happen to meet, he became quite happy, and said he was very glad it had happened and in future he would not behave as stupidly as he had done at the election, but would try to be as friendly as possible with Vronsky next time he met him.

'It is so painful to think that there is a man who is almost my enemy,—whom I dislike to meet,' said Levin. 'I am very, very glad!'

Chapter II

'Well then, please call on the Bols,' said Kitty to her husband when, at about eleven o'clock in the morning, he came to her room before going out. 'I know you are dining at the club. Papa put your name down. But what are you going to do this morning?'

'Only going to see Katavasov,' answered Levin.

'Why so early?'

'He promised to introduce me to Metrov. I want to have a talk with him about my work. He is a celebrated Petersburg scholar,' replied Levin.

'Oh yes! It was his article you praised so? Well, and then?' inquired Kitty.

'Then I may call round at the Courts about my sister's case.'

'And the concert?'

'Oh, what's the good of my going alone?'

'Oh yes, do go! They are giving those new pieces. . . . It used to interest you so. I should certainly go.'

'Well, in any case I will come back before dinner,' he said, glancing at his watch.

'But put on a morning coat, so that you can call on the Countess Bol on the way.'

'Is it absolutely necessary then?'

'Yes, absolutely! He called on us. Why, where is the difficulty? You'll call on your way, you'll sit down, talk about the weather for five minutes, and then get up and go away.'

'Well, will you believe it? I have got so out of the habit that it makes me feel ashamed. A stranger arrives, sits down, remains a while doing nothing, disturbs them, upsets himself, and goes away again.'

Kitty laughed.

'But as a bachelor you used to pay calls?' she said.

'I did, but I always felt ashamed, and now I am so out of the habit of it that, seriously, I would rather go without dinner for two days than pay that call! It is so embarrassing! I feel the whole time that they will be offended and will say, "Why have you come when you have no business here?"'

'No, they won't be offended. I will vouch for that!' said Kitty, looking laughingly into his face. She took his hand. 'Well, good-bye! . . . Please call on them!'

He was about to go after kissing her hand, when she stopped him.

'Kostya, do you know I have only fifty roubles left?'

'Well, what of that? I'll call at the bank and get some. . . . How much?' he asked, with a dissatisfied look familiar to her.

'No, wait a moment.' She held him by the hand. 'Let's talk it over, it bothers me. I don't think I spend on anything superfluous, and yet the money simply flies away! There is something we don't do right.'

'Not at all,' he said, coughing and looking at her from under his brows.

She knew that cough. With him it was a sign of great displeasure, not with her but with himself. He was really dissatisfied, not because they had spent so much, but because he had been reminded of a matter which, well knowing that something was wrong, he wished to forget.

'I have told Sokolov to sell the wheat and draw the money for the mill in advance. We shall have money in any case.'

'Yes, but I'm afraid that in general too much . . .'

'Not at all, not at all!' he repeated. 'Well, good-bye, darling!'

'But, really, sometimes I am sorry I listened to Mama! How nice it would have been in the country! As it is I have worn you all out, and we are wasting money . . .'

'Not at all, not at all! Not once since our marriage have I said to myself that things might have been better than they are. . . .'

'Is that true?' she said, looking into his eyes.

He had said it without thinking, to comfort her. But when he looked and saw those dear, truthful eyes questioningly fixed on him, he repeated the words from the bottom of his heart. 'Decidedly I am forgetting her,' he thought, remembering what was so soon awaiting them.

'Will it be soon? How do you feel?' he whispered, taking both her hands in his.

'I have so often thought so, that now I have given up thinking.'

'And you are not afraid?'

She smiled contemptuously.

'Not an atom!' she answered.

'Well, should there be anything—I shall be at Katavasov's.'

'No, there won't be anything: don't imagine it. I shall go for a walk on the boulevard with Papa. We will call at Dolly's. I'll expect you before dinner . . . Oh, yes! Do you know, Dolly's situation is becoming quite impossible! She is deep in debt, and has no money. Mama and I were talking about it with Arseney' (so she called her sister's, the Princess Lvova's, husband), 'and we decided to set you and him at Stiva. It is quite impossible. We can't speak to Papa about it. . . . But if you and he . . .'

'But what can we do?' said Levin.

'Well, anyhow, you will see Arseney. Have a talk with him, and he will tell you what we decided.'

'I'm ready to agree with Arseney beforehand. Well, I'll call on him then. . . . By the way, if I go to the concert, I'll go with

Nataly. Well, good-bye!'

At the porch Kuzma, an old servant of his bachelor days, who was now managing the household in town, stopped Levin.

'Krasavchik' (one of the pair of carriage horses brought from the country) 'has been re-shod but still goes lame,' said he. 'What are your orders?'

On first coming to Moscow Levin had taken an interest in the horses they brought from the country. He wanted to arrange the matter as well and as cheaply as possible; but it turned out that their own horses cost them more than hired ones would have done, and they hired horses as well.

'Send for the vet, maybe it's a bruise.'

'Yes, and what will Catherine Alexandrovna do?' asked Kuzma.

Levin no longer thought it strange, as he had done when he first came to Moscow, that to go from the Vozdvizhenka Street to Sivtsev-Vrazhek it was necessary to harness a pair of strong horses to a heavy carriage to drive through the snowy slush a quarter of a verst, to keep the carriage waiting there for four hours, and to pay five roubles for it. Now all this seemed quite natural.

'Hire a pair of horses, to be harnessed to our carriage.'

'Yes, sir!'

And, thanks to the conditions of town life, having thus simply and easily solved a difficulty which in the country would have required much exertion and personal attention, Levin went out, called an *izvoshchik*, and drove to the Nikitskaya. On his way he thought no more about money, but considered how he could make the acquaintance of the Petersburg scholar, who was studying sociology, and how he would talk to him about his book.

Only during the very first days in Moscow had the unproductive but inevitable expenditure, so strange to country folk, yet demanded on all sides, startled Levin. Now he was used to it. In this respect the thing had happened to him which is said to happen to drunkards. 'The first glass you drive in like a stake, the second flies like a crake, and after the third they fly like wee little birds.' When he had changed the first hundred-rouble note to buy liveries for the footman and hall porter, he had involuntarily calculated that those useless liveries—which, however, were absolutely necessary, judging by the surprise of the old Princess and Kitty at his hint that one could do without liveries—would cost as much as the hire of two labourers for the summer months, that is, of one for about three hundred working days between Easter and Advent—and each a day of heavy labour from early morning till late in the evening. He parted with that hundred-rouble note not without a struggle. The next such note he changed to buy provisions for a family dinner, costing twenty-eight roubles; and though he remembered that twenty-eight roubles was the price of nine chetverts of oats mown, bound into sheaves, threshed, winnowed, sifted, and shovelled with sweat and groans, nevertheless it went more easily than the first. The notes he now changed no longer evoked such calculations, but flew away like wee birds. Whether the pleasure afforded by what it purchased corresponded to the labour expended in acquiring the money was a consideration long since lost sight of. His farming calculations that there is a price below which certain grain must not be sold were forgotten too. The rye—after he had so long held out for a certain price—was sold fifty kopeks a chetvert cheaper than had been offered him a month ago. Even the calculation that it would be impossible to live for a year at that rate of expenditure without running into debt—even that calculation had lost its meaning. The one thing needful was to have money in the bank, without asking whence it came, so as to be always sure of the wherewithal to get to-morrow's beef. Till now he had always observed that rule; he had always had money in the bank. But now he had no money remaining there, and did not quite know where to get any. It was this that had upset him for a moment when Kitty reminded him about money; however, he had no time to think about it. While driving he thought of Katavasov and of making Metrov's acquaintance.

Chapter III

During his stay in Moscow Levin had renewed his intimacy with his fellow-student of university days, now Professor Katavasov, whom he had not seen since his marriage. He liked Katavasov because of his clear and simple outlook on life. Levin thought Katavasov's clear outlook resulted from the poverty of his nature, and Katavasov thought Levin's inconsequential opinions resulted from a lack of mental discipline; but Katavasov's clarity pleased Levin, and the abundance of Levin's undisciplined thoughts pleased Katavasov, so they liked to meet and argue.

Levin had read some parts of his book to Katavasov, who liked it. Happening to meet Levin at a public lecture the previous day, Katavasov had told him that the celebrated Metrov, whose article had so pleased Levin, was in Moscow and was much interested in what Katavasov had told him of Levin's work, that he would be at his house next day about eleven in the morning and would be very pleased to make Levin's acquaintance.

'Decidedly you are improving—quite a pleasure to see it,' said Katavasov as he welcomed Levin in the little drawing-room. 'I heard the bell and thought "It's impossible he can have come punctually." . . . Well, what d'you think of the Montenegrins? They are born warriors!' [1]

'What's happened?' asked Levin.

Katavasov in a few words told him the latest news, and, taking him into the study, introduced Levin to a tall, sturdy, and very agreeable-looking man. It was Metrov. The conversation rested for a time on politics and on how the highest circles in Petersburg regarded the latest events. Metrov quoted words on the subject attributed to the Emperor and one of the Ministers, which he had from a reliable source. Katavasov, however, had heard with equal definiteness that the Emperor said something quite different. Levin tried to imagine a situation in which both utterances might have been made, and the subject was dropped.

'He has written almost a book on the natural condition of the labourer in relation to the land,' said Katavasov. 'I am not a specialist, but as a naturalist I liked his not taking humanity as something outside zoological laws, but on the contrary regarding it as dependent on its surroundings, and searching in this dependence for the laws of its development.'

'That is very interesting,' said Metrov.

'I really began to write a book on agriculture, but being occupied with the chief instrument in agriculture, the labourer,' said Levin with a blush, 'I involuntarily arrived at quite unexpected results.'

And Levin began carefully, as if feeling his way, to expound his views. He knew that Metrov had written an article running counter to the generally accepted teachings of political economy, but how far he could hope for his sympathy with his own novel views Levin did not know, and could not gather from the expression of the Professor's quiet and intelligent face.

'But in what do you perceive the peculiar quality of the Russian worker?' asked Metrov. 'In his zoological qualities, so to say, or in the conditions in which he is placed?'

Levin detected in this very question a thought with which he did not agree; but he continued to expound his view, which was that the Russian labourer's view of the land is quite different from that of other nations. To illustrate this theory he hastened to add that, in his opinion, this attitude of the Russian people was due to their consciousness of a mission to people the vast unoccupied tracts in the East.

'It is easy to be led astray when drawing conclusions as to the general vocation of a people,' said Metrov, interrupting Levin. 'The condition of the labourer will always depend on his relation to land and capital.'

---

1. The subject referred to is the Balkan rising (see notes on p. 698).

And without letting Levin finish explaining his idea, Metrov began expounding to him the peculiarity of his own teaching.

What that peculiarity consisted in Levin did not understand, because he did not even try to do so. He saw that Metrov, like the others, despite the article in which he refused the teachings of the economists, still regarded the position of the Russian labourer merely from the standpoint of capital, wages, and rent. Though he had to admit that in the Eastern and greater part of Russia rents were still *nil*, that wages—for nine-tenths of the eighty millions of the Russian population—represented only sustenance for themselves, and that capital did not yet exist except in the form of most primitive tools, yet he regarded every labourer merely from that one point of view, though on many points he disagreed with the economists and had his own theory of wages, which he explained to Levin.

Levin listened reluctantly and at first made objections. He wanted to interrupt Metrov and to state his own idea, which he considered would render a further statement of Metrov's view superfluous. But afterwards, having convinced himself that they looked at the question so differently that they would never understand one another, he ceased making objections and merely listened. Though what Metrov was saying now no longer interested him at all, he felt some pleasure all the same in hearing him. His vanity was flattered by the fact that so learned a man should explain his opinions to him so willingly, so carefully, and with such faith in Levin's knowledge of the subject that he sometimes by a mere hint indicated a whole aspect of the matter. Levin attributed this to his own worth, not knowing that Metrov, who had exhausted the matter with all his intimates, was particularly pleased to speak about it to any fresh person, and, in general, willingly spoke to everybody about the subject with which he was occupied and which was not yet clear to himself.

'I'm afraid we shall be late,' said Katavasov, glancing at the clock as soon as Metrov had finished his disquisition.

'Yes, there is a meeting of the Society of Amateurs in honour of Svintich's jubilee,' Katavasov went on, in answer to Levin's inquiry. 'Peter Ivanovich' (Metrov) 'and I have arranged to go. I have promised to read a paper on his work on Zoology. Come with us, it will be very interesting.'

'Yes! It is quite time,' remarked Metrov. 'Come with us, and then, if you care to, come home with me. I should very much like to hear your work.'

'Oh no, it is still so unfinished! But I shall be pleased to go to the meeting.'

'And have you heard? I handed in a separate report,' Katavasov called out from the next room, where he was changing his coat.

They began a conversation about a controversy in the university, which was one of the most important events in Moscow that winter. Three old professors on the Council had not accepted the opinion of the younger ones; the younger ones presented a separate resolution. This resolution was, in the opinion of some people, a dreadful one, while according to others it was very simple and just. The professors were divided into two camps.

The side to which Katavasov belonged accused their opponents of mean treachery and deception; while the others imputed— youthfulness and disrespect for authority. Levin, though he did not belong to the university, had since his arrival in Moscow more than once heard and conversed about this affair, and had formed his own opinion on the subject; and he took part in the conversation which was continued in the street until they all three arrived at the old university buildings.

The meeting had already begun. At the table covered with a cloth at which Katavasov and Metrov took their seats six men were sitting, and one of them, with his head bent close over a manuscript, was reading something. Levin took one of the vacant chairs which were standing round the table, and in a whisper asked a student who was sitting there what was being read. With a displeased look at Levin the student replied: 'The biography!'

Though the biography of the scientist did not interest Levin, he listened involuntarily and learned a few interesting facts about the celebrated man's life.

When the reader had finished, the chairman thanked him and read aloud some verses for the jubilee sent by the poet Ment, adding a few words of thanks to the poet. Then Katavasov, in his loud strident voice, read his paper on the scientific work of the man whose jubilee it was.

When Katavasov had finished, Levin looked at his watch, saw that it was getting on for two, and thought that there would be no time to read his manuscript to Metrov before the concert, and besides, he no longer felt inclined to do so. During the readings he had also been thinking about the talk they had had. It was now clear to him that though Metrov's views might perhaps be of importance, his own ideas were of importance too, and these views could be formulated and lead to results only if each of them worked separately along the lines he had selected, but communicating them to one another could not lead to any result. Making up his mind to decline Metrov's invitation, therefore, Levin approached him as soon as the meeting ended. Metrov introduced him to the chairman, with whom he was discussing the political news. In this connection Metrov told the chairman the same thing that he had already told Levin, and Levin made the same remarks as he had made in the morning, but for the sake of diversity expressed also a new view of his own—which had but just entered his head. After that they began talking about the university question. As Levin had already heard all that, he hastened to tell Metrov that he regretted he was unable to accept his invitation, shook hands, and drove off to the Lvovs'.

Chapter IV

Lvov, who was married to Kitty's sister Nataly, had passed all his life in the capitals and abroad, where he had been educated and where he had been in the diplomatic service.

The year before, he had quit the diplomatic service, not because of any unpleasantness (he never had unpleasantness with anyone), but moved to the Moscow Court Ministry in order to be able to give his boys the best education.

Despite very acute differences in their habits and opinions, and the fact that Lvov was older than Levin, they became very intimate and attached to one another that winter.

Levin found Lvov at home, and entered unannounced.

Wearing an indoor jacket with a belt, morocco leather shoes, and with a *pince-nez* of blue glass on his nose, Lvov sat in an easy-chair reading a book lying on a lectern before him, and carefully held at a distance in his shapely hand a cigar half turned to ashes.

His handsome, refined, and still young-looking face, to which the curly, glossy, silver hair gave a still more well-bred appearance, lit up with a smile when he saw Levin.

'Good! And I was just going to send to you. Well, and how is Kitty? Take this chair, it's more comfortable.' He rose and pushed forward a rocking-chair. 'Have you read the last circular in the *Journal de St Pétersbourg?* I think it splendid,' said he with a slightly French accent.[2]

Levin told him what he had heard from Katavasov of what was said in Petersburg, and, after some talk on politics, Levin recounted how he had made Metrov's acquaintance and had gone to the meeting. This interested Lvov very much.

'There now! I envy you for having the entrance to that interesting scientific world,' he said, and having started talking he changed, as he usually did, into French, which he spoke more easily. 'It's true I have no time to spare, my work and occupation with the children deprive me of that; besides, I am not ashamed to confess that my education was far too insufficient.'

2. The *Journal de St. Pétersbourg* was a privately owned Petersburg daily paper, founded in 1842 and published in French. It received a subsidy from the Treasury and was practically the organ of the Russian Foreign Office.

'I don't think so,' said Levin with a smile, feeling, as usual,
touched by the other's low opinion of himself, which was not in the
least affected from desire to appear, or even to be, modest, but was
quite sincere.

'Oh, yes! I now feel how little educated I am! Even for the
children's lessons I often have to refresh my memory, or even
simply to learn things. For it is not enough to have masters, one
must have a supervisor as well, just as you have both labourers and
an overseer on your estate. I was just reading,' and he showed Levin
Buslaev's Grammar which lay on the lectern. 'They expect Misha to
know this, and it is so difficult. . . . Will you explain this to
me? He says here . . .'[3]

Levin tried to explain that it is impossible to understand it and
that it must just be learnt by heart; but Lvov did not agree with
him.

'Yes! You laugh at it!'

'On the contrary! You have no idea how, when I see you, I am
always learning what awaits me—the education of my children.'

'Oh, come! You've nothing to learn from me!' said Lvov.

'All I know is that I never saw better brought up children than
yours,' said Levin, 'and do not wish for better children.'

Lvov evidently tried to restrain the expression of his delight, but
a radiant smile lit up his face.

'If only they turn out better than I! That is all I desire. You do
not yet know all the difficulties one has with boys who, like mine,
have been neglected through our life abroad,' said he.

'They'll catch it all up. They are such gifted children! The chief
thing is the moral training. That is what I learn by watching your
children.'

'You talk of moral training! You can't imagine how difficult that
is! You have hardly mastered one fault when another crops up and
there is a fresh struggle. One must have the support of religion—
you remember our talk about that? . . . No father relying on his
own strength, without that support, could educate a child.'

This conversation, on a topic that always interested Levin, was
cut short by the entrance of the beautiful Nataly Alexandrovna,
who came in dressed to go out.

'Oh, I didn't know you were here,' she said, evidently not at all
sorry but rather pleased at having interrupted a conversation which
she had heard long ago, and of which she was weary. 'And how is
Kitty? I am dining with you to-day. Look here, Arseney,' she said,
turning to her husband, 'you will take the carriage . . .'

3. Professor F. I. Busláev of Moscow University was a member of the Academy of Science and
author of several erudite works. The one here in question was no doubt his *Textbook of Russian
Grammar compared with Church Slavonic.*

And husband and wife began discussing what they would do that day. As the husband had to go and meet some one officially, and the wife was going to the concert and then to a public meeting of the South-Eastern Committee, there was much to decide and arrange. Levin, as one of the family, had to take part in the deliberations. It was settled that Levin would drive with Nataly to the concert and to the public meeting, and from there they would send the carriage to the office to fetch Arseney, who would call for his wife and take her on to Kitty's, or if he was detained by business he would send the carriage back, and Levin would accompany her.

'He spoils me, you know,' said Lvov to his wife, indicating Levin. 'He assures me that our children are splendid, though I see so much that is bad in them.'

'Arseney goes to extremes, as I always tell him,' said his wife. 'If you look for perfection, you will never be satisfied. What Papa says is perfectly true; when we were brought up they went to one extreme, and kept us children in the attics while our parents lived on the first floor; but now it's just the reverse—the lumber room for the parents and the first floor for the children! Nowadays parents are hardly allowed to live, and everything is for the children.'

'Why not, if that is pleasanter?' said Lvov with his handsome smile, touching her hand. 'Those who don't know you would think you were not a mother but a stepmother!'

'No, extremes are not right in any case,' said Nataly quietly, putting his paper-knife in its right place on the table.

'Ah! Come here, you perfect children!' said Lvov to two handsome boys, who, after bowing to Levin, approached their father, evidently wishing to ask him something.

Levin wanted to talk to them and hear what they would say to their father, but Nataly spoke to him, and then Makhotin, a fellow official of Lvov's, came in Court uniform to fetch Lvov to meet some one; and an unending conversation began about Herzegovina, the Princess Korzinskaya, the Duma, and the Countess Apraxina's sudden death.

Levin had forgotten the commission he had been charged with and only remembered it when on his way to the ante-room.

'Oh, Kitty wished me to have a talk with you about Oblonsky,' he said, when Lvov paused on the stairs as he was seeing his wife and Levin down.

'Yes, yes. *Maman* wishes us, *les beaux-frères*,[4] to come down on him,' said Lvov, blushing. 'But why should I?'

'Well then, I will be down on him!' said his wife smiling, as she stood in her white fur-lined cloak waiting for them to finish their talk. 'Come, let us go!'

---

4. The brothers-in-law.

Chapter V

At the Matinée Concert there were two very interesting items.[5]
One was *King Lear on the Heath*, a fantasia, and the other was
a quartet dedicated to the memory of Bach. Both pieces were new
and in the new style, and Levin wished to form an opinion on them.
When he had conducted his sister-in-law to her seat, he took his
station behind a pillar, resolved to listen as attentively and as conscientiously as possible. He tried not to let his mind wander nor to
let his impression of the music be marred by looking at the white-
tied conductor's arm-waving, which always so unpleasantly distracts
one's attention from the music; nor by the ladies with their bon-
nets, the ribbons of which were so carefully tied over their ears for
the concert; nor by all those other persons who were either not interested in anything or were interested in all sorts of things other
than music. He carefully avoided the musical experts and great
talkers, and stood with lowered eyes gazing straight before him,
listening.

But the longer he listened to the *King Lear* fantasia, the further
he felt from the possibility of forming any definite opinion. The
musical expression of some emotion seemed perpetually on the
point of beginning, when it suddenly broke into fragments of the
expression of other emotions or even into unrelated sounds which,
elaborate though they were, were only connected by the whim of
the composer. Even these fragments of musical expression, though
some of them were good, were unpleasing because they were quite
unexpected and unprepared for. Mirth, sadness, despair, tenderness, triumph, came forth without any cause, like the thoughts of
a madman. And, as in the mind of a madman, these emotions vanished just as unexpectedly.

Throughout the performance Levin felt like a deaf person watching a dance. He was quite perplexed when the music stopped and
felt very tired as a result of strained attention quite unrewarded.
From all sides came loud applause. Every one rose, began to walk
about, and to talk. Wishing to clear up his own perplexity by
hearing other people's impressions, Levin went to look for the
experts, and was pleased to find a celebrated one chatting with his
own acquaintance, Pestsov.

'Wonderful!' Pestsov was saying in his deep bass. 'How do you do,
Constantine Dmitrich? . . . Especially shapely, plastic, and rich
in colour, if one may say so, is the passage where you feel the approach of Cordelia, the woman, *das ewige Weibliche*,[6] and she enters upon a struggle with fate.'

5. In M. A. Balákirev's musical suite *King Lear* (written about 1860 in the 'new style') there is
   an episode representing Lear and the Fool on the heath during the storm, as well as the theme
   of Cordelia.
6. The eternal feminine.

'Why, what has Cordelia to do with it?' Levin asked timidly, having quite forgotten that the fantasia presented King Lear on the heath.

'Cordelia appears . . . here!' said Pestsov, tapping with his fingers the glossy programme he was holding, and handing it to Levin.

Only then did Levin recollect the title of the fantasia, and hastened to read the Russian translation of a passage from Shakespeare, which was printed on the back.

'You can't follow without it,' said Pestsov turning to Levin, as the man he had been talking to had gone away and he had no one else to talk to.

During the interval Levin and Pestsov began a discussion on the merits and defects of the Wagnerian tendency in music. Levin maintained that the mistake of Wagner and of all his followers lay in trying to make music enter the domain of another art, and that poetry commits the same error when it depicts the features of a face, which should be done by painting, and, as an example of this kind of error, he mentioned a sculptor who carved in marble certain poetic phantasms arising round the pedestal of his statue of a poet. 'The sculptor's phantasms so little resembled phantasms that they even clung to a ladder,' said Levin. He liked this phrase, but could not remember whether he had not used it before, and to Pestsov himself, and after saying it he grew embarrassed.[7]

Pestsov argued that art was all one, and that it can only reach its highest manifestations by uniting all the different kinds of art.

Levin could not listen to the second part of the concert, for Pestsov, who stood beside him, talked all the while and found fault with the piece because of its unnecessary and sickly affectation of simplicity, comparing it with the simplicities of the pre-Raphaelite school of painting. On going out Levin met several other acquaintances, with whom he talked about politics, music, and mutual friends; among others he met Count Bol. He had quite forgotten his intended visit to him.

'Well then, go at once,' said the Princess Lvova, to whom he mentioned the matter. 'Perhaps they won't receive you, and then call for me at the meeting. You have time enough.'

Chapter VI

'Perhaps they don't receive to-day?' said Levin as he entered the hall of Countess Bol's house.

7. Tolstóy had in mind a work Antokólsky submitted to the Academy of Art in 1875 in anticipation of the Púshkin celebration held in Moscow in 1880. He represented Púshkin sitting on a stone bench on a rock, and on ledges of the rock as on a ladder, fenced in by railings, figures of characters from Púshkin's works—Boris Godunóv, the Miserly Knight, Tatiána, Mazeppa, Pugachëv, and so on—are ascending, some of them actually holding on to the railings.

'They do; please walk in,' said the hall-porter, determinedly helping him off with his overcoat.

'What a nuisance!' thought Levin with a sigh, as he pulled off one
glove and smoothed his hat. 'What is the good of my going in?
And what on earth am I to say to them?'

As he entered the first drawing-room he met in the doorway the
Countess Bol, who with an anxious and stern expression was giving
orders to a servant. When she saw Levin she smiled and asked him
into the next room, a smaller drawing-room, whence came the
sound of voices. In that room, seated in arm-chairs, were the Countess's two daughters and a Moscow Colonel with whom Levin was
acquainted. Levin went up to them, said 'How-do-you-do,' and sat
down on a chair beside the sofa, holding his hat in his hand.

'How is your wife? Have you been to the concert? We could not
go. Mama had to attend the funeral.'

'Yes, I have heard. . . . How sudden it was!' said Levin.

The Countess came in and sat down on the sofa, and she too inquired about his wife and about the concert.

Levin answered, and repeated his remark about the suddenness
of the Countess Apraxina's death.

'But she always was delicate.'

'Were you at the opera last night?'

'Yes, I was.'

'Wasn't Lucca splendid?' [8]

'Yes, splendid,' he replied, and as he was quite indifferent to
what they might think of him, he repeated what they had heard
hundreds of times about the peculiarities of that singer's talent.
The Countess Bol pretended to be listening. When he had said
enough and paused, the Colonel, who till then had kept silent, began also to talk about the opera and about the lighting of the opera-
house. At length, having mentioned the *folle journée* [9] that was
being got up at Tyurin's, he laughed, rose noisily, and went away.
Levin rose too, but saw by the Countess's face that it was not yet
time for him to leave. He had to endure another minute or two, so
he sat down again.

As, however, he kept on thinking how silly it was, he found
nothing to speak about and remained silent.

'You are not going to the public meeting? They say it will be
very interesting,' began the Countess.

'No, but I promised my sister-in-law to call for her there,' said
Levin.

There was a pause, and the mother exchanged glances with her

8. Pauline Lucca (1841–1908), born in Vienna of Italian parents, was a famous soprano singer
   and highly talented actress. Engaged as Court singer in Berlin she resigned her position, and
   sang with great success in Italian opera in London, the United States, all over Europe, and
   —particularly in the seventies—in Russia.
9. Mad fête.

daughter.

'Well, I expect it's time now,' thought Levin, and rose. The ladies shook hands with him and asked him to tell his wife *mille choses* [1] from them.

The hall-porter as he helped him on with his overcoat asked where he was staying, and at once entered his address in a large well-bound book.

'Of course it's all the same to me, but still it makes one ashamed, and it's awfully stupid,' thought Levin, comforting himself with the reflection that everybody does it; and he went on to the meeting of the committee, where he had to meet his sister-in-law in order to accompany her to his own home.

At the meeting of the committee there were a great many people and almost the whole of Society. Levin was in time to hear a summary which everybody said was very interesting. When that had been read the Society folk gathered into a group, and Levin met Sviyazhsky, who asked him to be sure and come that evening to a meeting of the Agricultural Society where an important report was to be read. He also met Oblonsky, who had just come from the races, and many other persons he knew. Levin again expressed, and heard, various opinions about the meeting, the new fantasia, and a trial. But probably as a result of the mental fatigue he was beginning to feel, he made a slip when talking of the trial, and he afterwards remembered that slip with vexation several times. Speaking of the punishment awaiting a foreigner, who was being tried in Russia, and of how unjust it would be to banish him from the country, Levin repeated what he had heard said the day before by a man he knew.[2]

'It seems to me that to send him abroad would be like punishing a pike by throwing it into the water,' said Levin; and only afterwards remembered that that thought, apparently given out as his own, and which he had heard from his acquaintance, was taken from one of Krylov's fables, and that his acquaintance had repeated it from a feuilleton.

Having conducted his sister-in-law to his house, where he found Kitty cheerful and quite all right, Levin went off to the club.

---

1. To give his wife their love.
2. The foreigner referred to was Strausberg. He had started as a newspaper reporter and insurance agent in London, and early in the 'fifties was sent to Germany and Austria with proposals to build railways. He rapidly acquired a large fortune, and became known as *der Schienenkönig*. He acquired factories and mines as well as the Berlin city slaughter-houses and the influential Vienna newspaper *Die Post*. He built a railway in Russia and was connected with several banks. Extending his operations to Roumania, he incurred immense losses, his credit collapsed, and so did his undertakings generally. In 1875 he was arrested in Moscow, and tried in connexion with the failure of the Moscow Commercial Bank in which he was intimately concerned. He was sentenced to be banished to Siberia, but being a foreign subject was, in fact, merely expelled from Russia. A few years later he died in abject poverty.

Chapter VII

Levin arrived at the club in good time. Members and visitors were driving up as he got there. He had long not been there—not since the days when after leaving the university he had lived in Moscow and gone out into Society. He remembered the club and the external details of its rooms, but had quite forgotten the impression it then made upon him. But as soon as he entered the semicircular courtyard, got out of his sledge and entered the porch, where he was met by a hall-porter with a shoulder-belt who noiselessly opened the door and bowed to him; as soon as he saw in the hall the coats and goloshes of those of the members who realized that it was easier to take off their goloshes downstairs than to go up in them; and as soon as he heard the mysterious ring of the bell that announced his ascent; and while mounting the shallow steps of the carpeted stairs perceived the statue on the landing, and saw upstairs the third hall-porter in club livery—whom he recognized, though the man had aged—who opened the door for him without haste or delay, gazing at the new arrival—directly he saw all this, Levin was enveloped in the old familiar atmosphere of the place, an atmosphere of repose, ease, and propriety.

'Let me have your hat, sir,' said the porter to Levin, who had forgotten the club rule that hats must be left at the entrance. 'It's a long time since you were here! The Prince entered your name yesterday. Prince Oblonsky is not here yet.'

This hall-porter not only knew Levin but knew all his connections and relatives as well, and at once mentioned some of his intimate friends.

Passing first through a room in which were several screens, and then a room on the right in which was a partition and a fruit-stall, Levin, having overtaken and passed an old man who was walking slowly, entered the noisy and crowded dining-room.

He passed among the tables, which were nearly all occupied, surveying the guests. Here and there he came across all sorts of people he knew: old and young, some whom he only just knew and some with whom he was intimate. There was not one angry or anxious face among them. All seemed to have left their cares and anxieties behind them in the hall with their hats, and to be preparing to enjoy the material blessings of life at their leisure. Sviyazhsky and Shcherbatsky, Nevedovsky and the old Prince, Vronsky and Koznyshev, all were there.

'Why are you so late?' asked the old Prince with a smile, holding out his hand over his shoulder. 'How is Kitty?' he added, smoothing the table-napkin, which he had tucked in behind a button of his waistcoat.

'She's all right: they are all three dining together.'

'Ah! Alines-Nadines! Well, there's no room at our table. Go to that table, and be quick and secure a seat,' said the old Prince, and turning away he carefully took a plate of fish soup that was handed to him.

'Levin! Here!' shouted some one a little farther off, in a kindly voice. It was Turovtsin. He sat beside a young military man, and two chairs were tilted against their table. Levin joined them with pleasure. He always liked that good-natured spendthrift Turovtsin; with him was associated the memory of his proposal to Kitty; but to-day, after all those strained intellectual conversations, Turovtsin's good-natured face was particularly welcome.

'These are for you and Oblonsky. He will be here in a minute.'

The military man, with merry, ever-laughing eyes, who held himself very erect, was Gagin, from Petersburg. Turovtsin introduced him.

'Oblonsky is always late.'

'Ah, here he is!'

'Have you just come?' asked Oblonsky, hastening toward them. 'How do you do? Had any vodka? Well then, come!'

Levin rose and went with him to a large table on which stood various kinds of vodka and a very varied assortment of *hors d' œuvres*. It might have been thought that from a score of different *hors d'œuvres* it would be possible to select one to any taste, but Oblonsky ordered something special, and one of the liveried footmen brought it at once. They drank a glass of vodka each and returned to their table.

While they were still at their soup Gagin ordered a bottle of champagne and had four glasses filled. Levin did not refuse the proffered wine, and ordered another bottle. He was hungry, and ate and drank with great pleasure, and with still greater pleasure took part in the simple merry talk of his companions. Gagin, lowering his voice, related a new Petersburg anecdote which, though it was indecent and stupid, was so funny that Levin burst into loud laughter and people turned to look at him.

'That's in the style of the story, "That's just what I can't bear"; do you know it?' asked Oblonsky. 'Oh, it's delightful! Bring another bottle! . . .' he called to the waiter, and immediately began telling the story.

'With Peter Ilyich Vinovsky's compliments,' interrupted an old waiter, bringing two delicate glasses of still sparkling champagne on a tray, and addressing Oblonsky and Levin. Oblonsky took a glass, and exchanging a look with a bald, red-haired man with a moustache who sat at the other end of their table, smilingly nodded to him.

'Who is that?' inquired Levin.

'You once met him at my house, do you remember? A nice fellow!'

Levin followed Oblonsky's example and took the glass.

Oblonsky's anecdote was very amusing too. Then Levin told one, which also was appreciated. Then they talked about horses, about that day's races, and how gallantly Vronsky's Atlasny had won the first prize. Levin hardly noticed how the dinner passed.

'Ah, here they are!' said Oblonsky, just as they were finishing, leaning back in his chair and stretching out his hand to Vronsky, who was approaching with a tall Colonel of the Guards. Vronsky's face too was lit up by the general pleasant good-humor of the club. Gaily leaning his arm on Oblonsky's shoulder, he whispered something to him, and with the same merry smile held out a hand to Levin.

'Very glad to meet you,' he said. 'I looked for you that day at the elections, but was told you had already left.'

'Yes, I left that same day. We were just speaking about your horse. I congratulate you!' said Levin.

'That was good going!'

'Oh yes; you keep racehorses too?'

'No; my father did, and I remember them and know something about them.'

'Where did you dine?' asked Oblonsky.

'At the second table, behind the pillars.'

'He has been congratulated!' remarked the Colonel. 'It's the second time he's won the Imperial prize. If only I had the luck at cards that he has with horses! . . . But why waste the golden moments? I'm off to the "infernal regions,",'[3] added he, and walked away.

'That's Yashvin,' said Vronsky in reply to Turovtsin's question, as he took a vacant chair beside them. He drank a glass of champagne they offered him, and ordered another bottle. Whether influenced by the club or by the wine he had drunk, Levin chatted with Vronsky about the best breeds of cattle, and was very pleased to find that he had not the least animosity toward the man. He even told Vronsky among other things that he had heard from his wife that she had met him at the Princess Mary Borisovna's.

'Oh, the Princess Mary Borisovna! Isn't she charming?' cried Oblonsky, and related an anecdote about her which made them all laugh. Vronsky especially burst into such good-natured laughter that Levin felt quite reconciled to him.

'Well, have you finished?' asked Oblonsky, rising and smiling. 'Let's go!'

---

3. The name of a gambling room in the English Club.

Chapter VIII

On leaving the table Levin, feeling that as he went his arms swung with unusual regularity and ease, passed with Gagin through the lofty apartments to the billiard-room. When they had traversed the Large Hall he met his father-in-law.

'Well, and how do you like our Temple of Idleness?' said the Prince, giving him his arm. 'Come, let's walk about a little.'

'Yes, a walk is just what I want, and to have a- look around. It interests me.'

'Yes, it interests you, but my interest is different to yours. You look at those old men,' said the Prince, indicating a round-shouldered member with a hanging nether lip, hardly able to shuffle along in his soft boots, who met and passed them, 'and you imagine they were born *shlyupiks*?'

'*Shlyupiks!* What's that?'

'You see, you don't even know the word! It is a club term. You know the game of egg-rolling? Well, an egg that has been rolled very often becomes a *shlyupik*.[4] And so it is with ourselves: we keep coming and coming to the club until we turn into *shlyupiks*. There! Now you're laughing, but we are already thinking of how we shall become *shlyupiks* . . . ! You know Prince Chechensky?' asked the Prince, and Levin saw by his face that he was going to say something droll.

'No, I don't.'

'You don't? What, the well-known Prince Chechensky? Well, never mind! He is always playing billiards, you know. Three years ago he was not yet among the *shlyupiks* and he showed a bold front, calling others *shlyupiks*. Well, one day he arrives, and our hall-porter . . . You know Vasily? . . . Oh yes, that fat one; he is a great wit. Well, Prince Chechensky asks him: "I say, Vasily, who is here? Any of the *shlyupiks*?" And Vasily replies: "Well, yes: you're the third one!" Yes, my lad! That's how it is!'

Chatting and exchanging greetings with acquaintances they chanced to meet, Levin and the Prince passed through all the rooms: the large one, in which card-tables were already arranged and habitual partners were playing for small stakes; the sofa-room, where they were playing chess and where Koznyshev sat talking to some one; the billiard-room, where by a sofa in a recess a merry party, which included Gagin, were drinking champagne. They looked in at the 'infernal regions' too, where round a table, at which Yashvin had already taken his seat, crowded a number of backers. Taking care not to make a noise they entered the dim reading-

4. A hard-boiled egg that has been repeatedly cracked till it has become soft and useless for the game.

room, where, under shaded lamps, a young man with an angry countenance sat turning over one newspaper after another, and a bald General was engrossed in what he was reading. They also went into the room which the Prince termed 'the wise room.' There three gentlemen were arguing about the latest political news.

'Will you come, Prince? Everything is ready,' said one of his habitual partners, finding him there, and the Prince went away. Levin sat down for a while and listened, but remembering all the conversations he had that day heard, he suddenly felt terribly bored. He rose hastily and went to look for Oblonsky and Turovtsin, with whom he had felt merry.

Turovtsin, with a tankard of something to drink, was sitting on the high sofa in the billiard-room, and Oblonsky was talking to Vronsky by the door in the far corner.

'She is not exactly dull, but that indefinite, unsettled position . . .' Levin overheard, and was hastening away when Oblonsky called him.

'Levin!' said he; and Levin noticed that though in Oblonsky's eyes there were not actually tears, they were moist, as they always were when he had been drinking or when he felt touched. To-day it was both.

'Levin, don't go,' he said, holding him tightly by the elbow, evidently not wishing to let him go on any account.

'This is my true, almost my best friend,' he said to Vronsky. 'You too are even more near and dear to me; and I want you to be friends, and I know that you will be friendly and intimate because you are both good fellows.'

'Well, then there's nothing for it but to kiss and be friends!' said Vronsky, good-naturedly jesting and holding out his hand.

He quickly grasped Levin's outstretched hand and pressed it.

'I am very, very glad,' said Levin, pressing Vronsky's hand.

'Waiter! Bring a bottle of champagne,' said Oblonsky.

'And I am glad too,' said Vronsky.

But in spite of Oblonsky's wish and theirs they had nothing to say to one another, and both knew it.

'You know, he is not acquainted with Anna,' said Oblonsky to Vronsky. 'And I particularly wish to take him to see her. Let's go, Levin.'

'Really?' said Vronsky. 'She will be very glad. I would go home at once, but I am anxious about Yashvin and want to stay here till he has finished.'

'Oh, is he in a bad way?'

'He keeps on losing and I alone can restrain him.'

'Then what do you say to pyramids? Levin, will you play? Oh, capital,' said Oblonsky. 'Place the balls for pyramids,' he added, turning to the billiard-marker.

'They have been ready a long time,' replied the marker, who had already placed the balls in a triangle and was rolling the red ball about to pass the time.

'Well, come along!'

After the game Vronsky and Levin joined Gagin at his table, and at Oblonsky's invitation Levin began betting on aces. Vronsky sat beside the table, surrounded by friends who were continually coming to him, or else went to the 'infernal regions' to see what Yashvin was up to. Levin experienced an agreeable sense of relief from the mental weariness of the morning. He was glad the hostility between Vronsky and himself was ended, and the impression of tranquillity, decorum, and pleasure did not leave him.

When they had finished their play Oblonsky took Levin's arm. 'Well then, let us go to Anna's. Now, at once! She will be at home. I promised her long ago to bring you. Where were you going to-night?'

'Nowhere in particular. I had promised Sviyazhsky to go to the Agricultural Society's meeting, but I'll come with you if you like,' replied Levin.

'Capital! Let's go! . . . Find out whether my carriage has come,' said Oblonsky to a footman.

Levin went to the table, paid the forty roubles he had lost betting on the aces, paid the club bill to an old footman who stood by the door and who seemed in some miraculous way to know what it came to, and, swinging his arms in a peculiar way, passed through the whole suite of rooms to the exit.

Chapter IX

'The Oblonsky carriage!' shouted the hall-porter in a stern bass. The carriage drove up and they got in. Only for the first few moments, while they were leaving the courtyard of the club, did Levin retain that sense of club calm, pleasure, and undoubted decorum in his surroundings; but as soon as the carriage had passed out into the street and he felt it jolting on the uneven road, heard the angry shouts of an *izvoshchik* they met, saw in the ill-lit street the red signboards of a vodka dealer and of a small shop, that sense was dissipated, and he began to consider his actions and to ask himself whether he was doing right in going to see Anna. 'What would Kitty say?' But Oblonsky would not let him reflect, and as if guessing his doubts tried to dispel them.

'How glad I am that you will make her acquaintance,' said he. 'Do you know, Dolly has long wished it: and Lvov called on her and goes to see her. Though she is my sister,' Oblonsky continued. 'I may safely say that she is a remarkable woman. Well, you'll see! Her position is a very trying one, especially just now.'

'Why especially just now?'

'We are negotiating with her husband about a divorce. He agrees; but there are difficulties about their son, and the affair, which should have been ended long ago, has already been dragging on for three months. As soon as she gets the divorce she will marry Vronsky. How stupid that old ceremony is, walking round and round singing, "Rejoice, Israel!"—a ceremony in which nobody believes and which stands in the way of people's happiness!' interpolated Oblonsky. 'Well, and then their position will be as regular as mine or yours.'

'What is the difficulty?' asked Levin.

'Oh, that is a long and tiresome story! Everything is so indefinite in this country. But the point is that she has been living for several weeks in Moscow, where everybody knows her and him, awaiting the divorce, without going out anywhere or seeing any woman except Dolly, because, you understand, she does not want people to come and see her as a charity. Even that fool Princess Barbara has left her, considering it improper! Well, you see, any other woman in her position might fail to find resources in herself. But she . . . you'll see how she has arranged her life, how quiet and dignified she is! . . . To the left, in the side street opposite the church!' shouted Oblonsky, leaning out of the carriage window. 'Faugh! How hot!' he said, throwing his already unfastened overcoat still wider open in spite of 12 degrees of frost.[5]

'But she has a child; I suppose she is occupied with her?' said Levin.

'I think you see in every woman only a female, *une couveuse!*[6] necessarily occupied with children if at all!' said Oblonsky. 'No! I believe Anna is bringing her up splendidly, but one does not hear about her. Her occupations are, firstly, writing. I can see you smiling sarcastically, but you are wrong! She is writing a children's book and does not speak of it to anyone, but she read it to me and I showed the manuscript to Vorkuyev. . . . You know, the publisher . . . he writes himself, I think. He is an expert, and says it is a remarkable work. But you think she is a woman author? Not at all! She is first of all a woman with a heart, you'll see! She now has a little English girl, and a whole family she is interested in.'

'Why, is it a philanthropic undertaking?'

'There you are! At once looking out for something bad! It's not philanthropy, it's kind-heartedness. They had—I mean Vronsky

5. In Russia the Reaumur thermometer was used: 12°R. of frost = 5° Fahrenheit (27°F. of frost).
6. A breeder hen.

had—an English trainer, a master in his own line, but a drunkard. He took completely to drink, got delirium tremens, and has deserted his family. She saw them, helped them, and became interested in them, and now the whole family is on her hands—and she doesn't do it patronizingly, just with money, but she herself coaches the boys in Russian for the High School, and she has taken the girl into the house. But you'll see her.'

The carriage drove into the courtyard, and Oblonsky rang loudly at the front door, before which a sledge was standing.

Without asking the porter who opened the door whether Anna was in, Oblonsky entered the hall. Levin followed, more and more in doubt as to whether he was acting well or badly.

Glancing in the mirror, Levin saw that he was red in the face, but he was sure he was not tipsy, and he followed Oblonsky up the carpeted stairs. On the top landing a footman bowed to Oblonsky as to some one he knew well, and Oblonsky, asking who was with Anna Arkadyevna, received the answer that it was Mr. Vorkuyev.

'Where are they?'

'In the study.'

Passing through a small dining-room, panelled in dark wood, Oblonsky and Levin entered the study across the soft carpet. It was lit by a lamp with a large dark shade. Another reflector-lamp fixed to the wall illuminated a large full-length portrait of a woman, which attracted Levin's involuntary attention. It was Anna's portrait painted in Italy by Mikhaylov. While Oblonsky passed behind a screen of trellis-work—and the man's voice that had been speaking became silent—Levin looked at the portrait, which in the bright illumination seemed to step out of its frame, and he could not tear himself away from it. He forgot where he was, and without listening to what was being said gazed fixedly at the wonderful portrait. It was not a picture, but a living and charming woman with curly black hair, bare shoulders and arms, and a dreamy half-smile on lips covered with elegant down, looking at him victoriously and tenderly with eyes that troubled him. The only thing that showed she was not alive was that she was more beautiful than a living woman could be.

'I am so glad,' he heard a voice saying near by, evidently addressing him, the voice of the very woman whom he had admired in the portrait. Anna had come out from behind the screen to meet him, and Levin saw in the dim light of the study the woman of the portrait, in a dark dress of different shades of blue, not in the same attitude, not with the same expression, but on the same height of beauty as that on which the artist had caught her in the portrait. In reality she was less brilliant, but there was something about her new and attractive which was not in the portrait.

Chapter X

She had risen to greet him, not concealing her pleasure at seeing him.

The tranquillity with which she extended to him her energetic little hand, introduced him to Vorkuyev, and, indicating a pretty red-haired child who sat in the same room doing needlework, spoke of her as her ward, showed the manners (familiar and pleasant to Levin) of a woman of good society, always self-possessed and natural. 'I am very, very pleased,' she repeated, and from her lips these simple words seemed to Levin to possess a peculiar meaning. 'I have long known and liked you, both for your friendship to Stiva and for your wife's sake. . . . I only knew her for a very short time, but she left on me the impression of a lovely flower . . . just a flower! And she will soon be a mother!'

She spoke easily and without haste, occasionally turning her eyes from Levin to her brother. Levin felt that the impression he was creating was a good one and immediately became at ease and as natural and comfortable with her as if he had known her from childhood.

'We came into Alexey's room to have a smoke,' she said in reply to Oblonsky's question whether he might smoke; and glancing at Levin, instead of asking him whether he smoked, she drew a tortoise-shell cigar-case nearer and took from it a straw cigarette.

'How are you to-day?' asked her brother.

'Pretty well. Nerves as usual!'

'Isn't it wonderfully good?' said Oblonsky, noticing that Levin kept looking at the portrait.

'I have never seen a better portrait.'

'And it's a wonderful likeness, isn't it?' asked Vorkuyev.

Levin glanced from the portrait to the original. A special brightness lit up Anna's face when she felt his eyes on her. Levin flushed, and to hide his confusion was about to ask her if it was long since she had seen Dolly, but at that instant Anna herself began to speak.

'We were just talking with Ivan Petrovich [7] about Vashchenko's last pictures. Have you seen them?'

'Yes, I have,' replied Levin.

'But excuse me, I interrupted you? You were going to say . . .'

Levin asked whether she had seen Dolly lately.

'She was here yesterday. She is very angry with the High School because of Grisha. The Latin master, it seems, has been unjust to him.'

'Yes, I have seen the pictures and did not like them very much,' Levin said, returning to the subject she had started.

7. Vorkuyev.

Levin did not now speak at all in the matter-of-fact way in which he had talked that morning. Every word of his conversation with her assumed a special importance. It was pleasant to speak to her and yet more pleasant to listen to her.

Anna not only talked naturally and cleverly, but cleverly and carelessly, not attributing any value to her own ideas, but attributing great value to those of her interlocutor.

The conversation touched on the new direction taken by art and the new illustrations of the Bible by a French artist.[8] Vorkuyev accused the artist of realism pushed to coarseness. Levin said the French had carried conventionality in art further than anyone else, and therefore saw special merit in a return to realism. In their ceasing to lie they saw poetry.

Never had any clever thought uttered by Levin given him so much satisfaction as this. Anna's face brightened all over when she suddenly appreciated the remark. She laughed.

'I am laughing as one laughs on seeing a very striking likeness! What you have said quite characterizes present-day French art, painting and even literature: Zola, Daudet. But perhaps it is always like that—they form their conceptions from imaginary conventional figures, and when they have made every possible combination of these, they tire of the conventional figures and begin to devise more natural and correct ones.'[9]

'Yes, that's it exactly,' said Vorkuyev.

'So you have been to the club?' she said, addressing her brother.

'What a woman!' thought Levin, and, quite forgetting himself, he gazed fixedly at her beautiful mobile face, which had now suddenly quite changed. Levin did not hear what she was speaking about while she leaned toward her brother but was struck by the change in her expression. After being so lovely in its tranquillity, her face suddenly expressed a strange curiosity, anger, and pride. But this lasted only a moment. She screwed up her eyes, as if she were remembering something.

'However, that won't interest anyone,' she said; and turning to the little English girl, she added in English, 'Please order tea in the drawing-room.'

The child rose and went out.

'Well, has she passed her examination,' inquired Oblonsky.

'Splendidly! She is a very capable girl, and has a sweet nature.'

'You'll finish by being fonder of her than of your own.'

8. Gustave Doré's illustrations to the Bible were published in 1865. He also painted religious and historical pictures and was a successful sculptor.
9. Neither Zola nor Daudet has then (in the seventies) attained the fame and prominence they achieved later, but even in their early works a striving for a strictly realistic presentation of actualities was apparent in which Tolstóy saw a natural reaction from the conventionality that had long dominated French art and literature.

'How like a man! There is no more or less in love. I love my child with one kind of love and her with another.'

'I was just saying to Anna Arkadyevna,' remarked Vorkuyev, 'that if she were to devote to the general business of educating Russian children a hundredth part of the energy she bestows on this English child, she would be doing a great and useful work.'

'Yes, but, say what you like, I can't do it. Count Alexey urged me very much.' As she spoke the words 'Count Alexey' she turned a timidly petitioning glance toward Levin and he involuntarily replied with a respectful and confirmatory glance. 'He urged me to take an interest in the village school. I went several times. They are very nice children, but I could not attach myself to the work. You mention energy. . . . Energy is based on love; and where is one to get the love? One can't order it! I've become fond of this girl, you see, without knowing why.'

Again she glanced at Levin. And her smile and glance told him that she was speaking for him alone, valuing his opinion and knowing in advance that they would understand one another.

'Yes, I quite understand,' Levin replied. 'It is impossible to put one's heart into a school or an institution of that kind, and I think that is just why philanthropic establishments always give such poor results.'

After a pause she smiled and said, 'Yes, yes, I never could do it. *Je n'ai pas le cœur assez large* [1] to love a whole orphanage-full of unpleasant little girls. *Cela ne m'a jamais réussi!* [2] There are so many women who have created for themselves a social position in that way. And now especially,' she went on with a sad, confiding expression, as though addressing her brother but evidently speaking to Levin, 'now when I so need some occupation, I can't do it!' And with a sudden frown (Levin understood that she was frowning at herself for having spoken about herself) she changed the subject. 'I have heard it said of you,' said she to Levin, 'that you are a bad citizen, and I have defended you as best I could.'

'How did you defend me?'

'That varied with the attacks. However, won't you come and have some tea?' She rose and took up a book bound in morocco-leather.

'Let me have it, Anna Arkadyevna,' said Vorkuyev, pointing to the book. 'It is well worth it.'

'Oh no, it is so unfinished!'

'I have told him about it,' remarked Oblonsky to his sister, indicating Levin.

'You should not have done so. My writings are something like those little baskets and carvings made in prisons, which Lisa Merka-

1. My heart is not big enough.
2. I never could succeed with that.

lova used to sell to me. She used to preside over the prison department of a Society,' she added, turning to Levin. 'And those unfortunate people achieved miracles of patience.'

And Levin perceived yet another feature in this woman whom he
already liked so much. In addition to her intelligence, grace, and
beauty, she also possessed sincerity. She did not wish to hide from
him the hardships of her position. When she had finished speaking
she sighed, and all at once her face assumed a stern expression and
became rigid. With that expression her face seemed even more
beautiful than before; but it was a novel look; it was outside the
circle of expressions, radiating happiness and creating happiness,
which the artist had caught when painting her portrait. Levin again
looked at the portrait and at her figure as, arm-in-arm with her
brother, she passed through the lofty doorway, and he felt a tenderness and pity for her which surprised him.

She asked Levin and Vorkuyev to pass on into the drawing-room,
and herself remained behind to speak to her brother. 'About the
divorce? About Vronsky? About what he was doing at the club?
About me?' Levin wondered; and he was so excited about what she
might be saying to Oblonsky that he hardly listened to what Vorkuyev was telling him about the merits of Anna's story for children.

Over their tea they continued the same kind of pleasant and interesting talk. There was not a single moment when it was necessary
to seek for a subject of conversation; on the contrary one felt that
there was not time enough to say what one wanted to say, but willingly refrained in order to hear what she was saying. It seemed to
Levin that all that was said, not only by her, but also by Vorkuyev
and Oblonsky, assumed a special importance owing to her attention
and remarks.

While following this interesting conversation Levin all the time
continued to admire her: her beauty, her cleverness, her good education, together with her simplicity and sincerity. He listened and
talked, and all the time thought of her, of her inner life, trying to
guess her feelings. And he, who had formerly judged her so severely,
now by some strange process of reasoning justified her and at the
same time pitied her and feared that Vronsky did not fully understand her. Toward eleven, when Oblonsky rose to leave (Vorkuyev
had already gone), Levin felt as if he had only just arrived. He got
up regretfully.

'Good-bye!' she said, retaining his hand and gazing at him with a
look that drew him to her. 'I am very pleased *que la glace est
rompue.*' [3] She let go his hand and screwed up her eyes.

'Tell your wife that I am just as fond of her as ever, and that if
she cannot forgive me my situation, I wish her never to forgive me.

3. That the ice is broken.

To forgive, she would have to live through what I have lived through, and may God preserve her from that!'

'Certainly, yes, I will tell her . . .' said Levin, blushing.

Chapter XI

'What a wonderful, sweet, pathetic woman!' he thought as he and Oblonsky went out into the frosty air.

'Well? Didn't I tell you?' said Oblonsky, who saw that Levin had been entirely vanquished.

'Yes,' responded Levin pensively, 'an extraordinary woman! Not on account of her intellect, but her wonderful sincerity. . . . I am dreadfully sorry for her.'

'God willing, everything will now soon be settled! Well, another time, don't judge in advance,' said Oblonsky, opening the door of his carriage. 'Good-bye! We are not going the same way.'

Without ceasing to think of Anna and of all the words—simple in the extreme—which they had interchanged, recalling every detail of the expressions of her face, entering more and more into her situation and feeling more and more sorry for her, Levin reached home.

At home he heard from Kuzma that Kitty was well and that her sisters had not long been gone, and he was given two letters. These he read in the ante-room, so as not to let them divert his attention later on. One was from his steward, Sokolov, who wrote that the wheat could not be sold, because only five-and-a-half roubles a chetvert was bid, and added that there was no other source from which to get money. The other letter was from his sister, who reproached him for not having settled her business yet.

'Well, we'll sell it at five-and-a-half, if they won't give more.' Levin promptly settled the first matter with great ease, though it had previously appeared to him so difficult. 'It's surprising how all one's time gets taken up here,' he thought with reference to the second letter. He felt himself to blame because he had not yet done what his sister asked of him. 'To-day again I did not go to the Court, but to-day I really had no time.' And resolving that he would attend to it next day without fail, he went to his wife. On his way he ran over in his mind the whole of the past day. All the events had consisted of conversations: conversations to which he listened or in which he had taken part. All these conversations were about matters he would never have occupied himself with had he been in the country, but here they were very interesting. All of them had been good, and only two things were not quite pleasant. One was what he had said about the pike, and the other was that there was something not quite right about his tender pity for Anna.

Levin found his wife sad and depressed. The three sisters' dinner-party would have gone off very well, but he had not come in as they expected and they had all become bored. Then the sisters left, and she remained alone.

'Well, and what have you been doing?' she asked, looking him in the eyes, which had a suspicious glitter in them. But, not to hinder his relating everything, she masked her observation and listened with an appreciative smile while he told her how he had spent the evening.

'I was very pleased to meet Vronsky. I felt quite at ease and quite natural with him. You see, I shall now try to avoid meeting him again, but the constraint will no longer exist . . .' said he, and remembering that whilst 'trying to avoid meeting him again' he had gone straight to Anna's, he blushed. 'There now! We say the people drink, but I don't know who drinks most—the common people or our own class! The common people drink on holidays, but . . .'

But Kitty was not interested in the question of how the people drink; she had seen his blush and wanted to know the reason.

'Well, and where did you go then?'

'Stiva particularly begged me to call on Anna Arkadyevna.'

On saying this Levin blushed still more, and his doubts as to whether he had done right or wrong in going to see Anna were finally solved. He now knew that he should not have gone there.

Kitty's eyes opened in a peculiar manner and flashed at the mention of Anna's name, but making an effort she hid her agitation and so deceived him.

'Ah!' was all she said.

'I am sure you won't be angry with me for going. Stiva asked me to, and Dolly wished it, continued Levin.

'Oh no!' she said, but he saw by her eyes the effort she made to control herself, and it boded him no good.

'She is very charming, very, very much to be pitied, and a good woman,' he said, telling her about Anna and her occupations and the message she had sent.

'Yes, of course she is much to be pitied,' said Kitty when he had finished. 'From whom were your letters?'

He told her, and misled by her quiet manner went to undress.

When he returned he found Kitty still sitting in the chair where he had left her. When he drew near she looked at him and burst into sobs.

'What is it? What is it?' he asked, well aware what it was.

'You have fallen in love with that horrid woman! She has bewitched you! I saw it in your eyes. Yes, yes! What can come of it? You were at the club drinking and drinking, and gambling, and then you went . . . to whom? No, let's go away . . . I will leave to-morrow!'

It was long before Levin could pacify his wife. At last he managed it, but only by acknowledging that a sense of pity, after the wine he had drunk, had misled him, that he had yielded to Anna's artful influence, and that he would avoid her in future. One thing that he sincerely confessed was that, living so long in Moscow with nothing but talk and food and drink, he was going silly. They talked till three in the morning, and only then were they sufficiently reconciled to fall asleep.

Chapter XII

When her visitors had taken their leave Anna did not sit down, but began pacing up and down the room. Though she had involuntarily done all in her power to awaken love in Levin (as at that time she always did to all the young men she met), and though she knew she had succeeded in as far as was possible with an honourable married man in one evening, and though she had liked him very much (despite the marked difference between Vronsky and Levin from a man's point of view, she, as a woman, saw in them that common trait which had caused Kitty to fall in love with them both), yet as soon as he had left the room she ceased to think about him.

One thought, and one only, pursued her remorselessly in different forms. 'If I produce such an effect on others, on this married man who loves his wife, why is *he* so cold toward me? . . . And it's not coldness, for I know he loves me, but something fresh now divides us. Why has he been away all the evening? He sent word by Stiva that he could not leave Yashvin, but must keep an eye on his play. Is Yashvin such a child? But admitting that it's true—he never lies—then behind that truth there is something else. He is glad of a chance to show me that he has other obligations. I know he has, I agree to that. But why prove it to me? He wishes to give me proofs that his love of me must not interfere with his freedom. But I don't need proofs; I need love! He ought to understand the hardship of my life here in Moscow. Is it life? I do not live, but only wait for a solution which is deferred and still deferred. Again no answer! And Stiva says he can't go to see Alexey Alexandrovich; and I can't write again. I can't do anything, begin anything, change anything! I restrain myself, wait, invent occupations for myself,—the English family, writing, reading, but all that is only deception, it is all a kind of morphia. He ought to pity me,' said she, feeling tears of self-pity rising to her eyes.

She heard Vronsky's vehement ring at the front door and quickly dried her eyes. She even sat down near the lamp and opened a book, pretending to be tranquil. She must let him see that she was displeased that he had not returned when he had promised—displeased, that should be all; she would on no account show him her grief, and still less her self-pity. She might pity herself, but he must not pity her. She did not want strife and blamed him for wanting to fight, but yet she involuntarily took up a fighting attitude.

'Well, you've not been bored?' he asked cheerfully and with animation, coming up to her. 'What a terrible passion gambling is!'

'No, I have not been bored, I have long ago learnt not to feel dull. Stiva and Levin were here.'

'Yes, I knew they were coming to see you. And how did you like Levin?' he asked, taking a seat beside her.

'Very much. They only left a short while ago. What did Yashvin do?'

'He was lucky and won seventeen thousand. I called him away and very nearly got him to come. But he went back and now has lost more than he had won.'

'Then what was the good of your staying with him?' she said, suddenly raising her eyes to his face. Her look was cold and hostile. 'You told Stiva you were staying to bring Yashvin away, but you have left him.'

A similar expression of cold readiness to fight appeared on his face.

'For one thing, I did not give him any message for you; and for another I never say what is not true. But chiefly, I wanted to stay, so I stayed,' he replied with a frown. 'Anna! Why? Why? . . .' he asked after a short pause, bending toward her and opening his hand, hoping that she would place hers in it.

She was pleased by this appeal to tenderness. But some strange evil power prevented her from yielding to her impulse, as if the conditions of the struggle did not allow her to submit.

'Of course you wished to stay, and stayed. You always do what you wish. But why tell me? Why?' she said, becoming more and more agitated. 'Does anyone dispute your right? But you want to be in the right, so in the right you must be!'

His hand closed, he leaned back, and his face assumed a still more stubborn look.

'For you it's a matter of obstinacy,' she said, after gazing intently at him and suddenly finding a name for that look that irritated her so. 'Just obstinacy! For you it is a question whether you will conquer me, and for me . . .' Again she felt sorry for herself and nearly burst into tears. 'If you only knew what it means to me! When I feel as I do now, that you are hostile toward me—hostile is the right word—if you only knew what that means to me! If you knew how near I am to a catastrophe at such moments . . . how afraid I am! Afraid of myself!' And she turned away to hide her sobs.

'But what is it all about?' he said, horrified at her expression of despair, and again leaning toward her he took her hand and kissed it. 'What have I done? Do I seek amusement outside our home? Do I not avoid the society of women?'

'I should hope so!' she said.

'Well then, tell me what I should do to make you easy? I am ready to do anything to make you happy,' he went on, touched by her despair. 'What would I not do to spare you such grief as this, about I know not what! Anna! . . .'

'Nothing, nothing!' she replied. 'I don't know myself whether it is this lonely life, or nerves. . . . But don't let's talk about it! What about the races? You haven't told me about them,' and she tried to hide her triumph at her victory, for the victory was hers after all.

He asked for supper, and began telling her about the races; but by his tone and by his looks, which grew colder and colder, she saw that he had not forgiven her her victory, and that the obstinacy, against which she had fought, had again taken possession of him. He was colder to her than before, as if he repented of having submitted; and remembering the words which had given her victory—'I am near a catastrophe and afraid of myself'—she realized that they were a dangerous weapon and must not be used a second time. She felt that side by side with the love that united them there had grown up some evil spirit of strife, which she could not cast out of his heart and still less out of her own.

Chapter XIII

There are no conditions of life to which a man cannot accustom himself, especially if he sees that every one around him lives in the same way. Three months previously Levin would not have believed that he could quietly fall asleep under the circumstances in which he now found himself: that while leading an aimless, senseless life, one moreover that was above his means; after tippling (he could call what had happened in the club by no other name), after showing unsuitable friendship to the man with whom his wife had once been in love, and after a still more unsuitable visit to a woman who could only be called a fallen woman, and after being allured by her and having grieved his wife—that in such circumstances he could quietly fall asleep. But under the influence of weariness, a sleepless night, and the wine he had drunk, he slept soundly and peacefully.

At five in the morning the creak of an opening door awoke him. He jumped up and looked round. Kitty was not in the bed beside him. But on the other side of the partition a light was moving, and he heard her step.

'What is it? What is it? . . .' he muttered, not yet quite awake. 'Kitty, what is it?'

'Nothing,' said she, coming candle in hand from beyond the partition. 'I only felt a little unwell,' she added with a peculiarly sweet and significant smile.

'What? Has it begun? Has it?' he asked in a frightened voice. 'We must send . . .' And he began to dress hurriedly.

'No, no,' she said smiling, holding him back with her hand. 'I'm sure it's nothing. I only felt slightly unwell; but it is over now.'

She came back to her bed, put out the candle, lay down, and remained quiet. Though that quietness, as if she were holding her breath, and especially the peculiar tenderness and animation with which, returning from the other side of the partition, she had said: 'It's nothing!' seemed to him suspicious, yet he was so sleepy that he fell asleep at once. Only afterwards he remembered that bated breath, and realized all that had passed in her dear sweet soul while she lay motionless by his side, awaiting the greatest event of a woman's life.

At seven o'clock he was awakened by her touch on his shoulder and a soft whisper. She seemed to hesitate between regret at waking him and a desire to speak to him.

'Kostya, don't be frightened. It's nothing, but I think . . . We must send for Mary Vlasevna.'

The candle was burning again. She was sitting on the bed holding in her hands some knitting she had lately been doing.

'Please don't be frightened! It's nothing. I'm not a bit afraid,' she said on seeing his alarmed face, and she pressed his hand to her breast and then to her lips.

He jumped up hastily, hardly aware of himself, and without taking his eyes off her put on his dressing-gown and stood still, gazing at her. It was necessary for him to go, but he could not tear himself away from the sight of her. He had loved that face and known all its expressions and looks, but he had never seen her as she was now. How vile and despicable he appeared to himself before her as she now was, when he recollected the grief he had caused her yesterday! Her flushed face surrounded with soft hair that had escaped from beneath her nightcap shone with joy and resolution.

Little as there was of affectation and conventionality in Kitty's general character, yet Levin was astonished at what was revealed to him now that every veil had fallen and the very kernel of her soul shone through her eyes. And in this simplicity, this nakedness of soul, she whom he loved was more apparent than ever. She looked at him smilingly, but suddenly her eyebrows twitched, she raised her head, and coming quickly to him she took hold of his hand and clinging close she enveloped him in her hot breath. She was suffering, and seemed to be complaining to him of her pain. And for a moment from force of habit he felt as if he were in fault. But her look expressed a tenderness which told him that she not only did not blame him, but loved him because of those sufferings. 'If I am not to blame for it, who is?' he thought, involuntarily seeking a culprit to punish for these sufferings; but there was no culprit. She suffered, complained, triumphed in her sufferings, rejoiced in them and loved them. He saw that something beautiful was taking place in her soul, but what it was he could not understand. It was above his comprehension.

'I have sent for Mama. And you, go quickly and fetch Mary Vlasevna. . . . Kostya! . . . No, it's nothing. It's past.'

She moved away from him and rang.

'Well, go now. Pasha is coming. I am all right.'

And Levin saw with amazement that she again took up the knitting which she had fetched in the night, and recommenced work.

As Levin went out at one door he heard the maid enter at the other. He stopped at the door and heard Kitty give detailed instructions to the maid, and with her help herself move the bed.

He dressed, and while the horse was being harnessed—for it was early, and no *izvozchiks* were about yet—he ran back to the bedroom not on tiptoe but, as it seemed to him, on wings. Two maids were busy moving something in the bedroom. Kitty was walking up and down and knitting, rapidly throwing the thread over the needle and giving orders.

'I am going straight to the doctor's. They have already gone for Mary Vlasevna, but I will call there too. Is anything else wanted? Oh yes, to Dolly!'

She looked at him, evidently not listening to what he was saying.

'Yes, yes! Go,' she said rapidly, frowning and motioning him away with her hand.

He was already on his way through the drawing-room when suddenly a piteous moan, that lasted only a moment, reached him from the bedroom. He stopped and for a moment could not understand it.

'Yes, it was she,' he said and, clasping his head with his hands, he ran downstairs.

'Lord have mercy! Pardon and help us!' he repeated the words that suddenly and unexpectedly sprang to his lips. And he, an unbeliever, repeated those words not with his lips only. At that instant he knew that neither his doubts nor the impossibility of believing with his reason—of which he was conscious—at all prevented his appealing to God. It all flew off like dust. To whom should he appeal, if not to Him in whose hands he felt himself, his soul, and his love, to be?

The horse was not yet ready, but feeling particularly energetic, physically strong and alert to meet what lay before him, so as not to lose a moment he did not wait for it but started off on foot, telling Kuzma to catch him up.

At the corner he encountered a night *izvozchik* hurrying along. In the little sledge sat Mary Vlasevna in a velvet cloak with a shawl over her head. 'Thank God!' he muttered, recognizing with delight her little blonde face, which now wore a particularly serious and even severe expression. Without stopping the *izvozchik* he ran back beside her.

'So it began about two hours ago, not more?' she asked. 'You will find the doctor, but don't hurry him. And get some opium at the chemist's.'

'So you think it may go all right? God have mercy and help us!' said Levin as he saw his horse coming out of the gateway. Jumping into the sledge beside Kuzma, he ordered him to drive to the doctor's.

Chapter XIV

The doctor was not yet up, and his footman said he had gone to bed late and given orders that he was not to be called, but the footman added that he would be up soon. The man was cleaning lamp-glasses and seemed quite absorbed in his task. This attention to his glasses and indifference to what was taking place at the Levins' astonished Levin at first, but he immediately recollected himself and realized that no one knew or was bound to know his feelings, and that it was therefore all the more necessary to act calmly, deliberately, and firmly in order to break through this wall of indifference and to attain his aim. 'Do not hurry and do not omit anything,' he said to himself, conscious of an increasing uplift of his physical powers and of his attention to all that lay before him.

Having learnt that the doctor was not up yet, Levin, out of the many plans that occurred to him, decided on the following: Kuzma should go with a note to another doctor, while he himself would go to the chemist for the opium; and if the doctor was not up when he returned he would bribe the footman—or if that was impossible, he would enter by force and wake the doctor at all costs.

At the chemist's a skinny dispenser, with the same indifference with which the footman had cleaned his lamp-glasses, closed with a wafer a packet of powders for which a coachman was waiting, and refused to let Levin have any opium. Trying not to hurry and not to get excited, Levin gave the names of the doctor and of the midwife, explained why the opium was wanted, and tried to persuade the dispenser to let him have it. The dispenser asked in German whether he might sell it; and receiving permission from some one behind a screen, took out a bottle and a funnel, slowly poured it from a large bottle into a small one, stuck on a label, and, in spite of Levin's request that he should not do so, sealed up the bottle, and was about to wrap it up. This was more than Levin could stand; he resolutely snatched the bottle out of the man's hands and rushed out at the big glass door. The doctor was not up yet, and the footman, now busy putting down a carpet, refused to wake him. Levin deliberately took out a ten-rouble note, and speaking slowly but without losing time, handed him the note and explained that Dr Peter Dmitrich (how great and important this Peter Dmitrich, formerly so insignificant, now appeared to Levin!) had promised to come at any time, and that he would certainly not be angry and must therefore be called at once.

The footman consented and went upstairs, asking Levin to step into the waiting-room.

Levin could hear the doctor at the other side of the door coughing, walking about, washing, and speaking. Some three minutes elapsed; to Levin they seemed more than an hour. He could not wait any longer.

'Peter Dmitrich! Peter Dmitrich!' he called out in a tone of entreaty through the open door. 'For heaven's sake forgive me! . . . Receive me as you are! It's over two hours . . .'

'Immediately! Immediately!' answered a voice, and Levin was astounded to detect that the doctor was smiling as he said it.

'Just for one moment!'

'Immediately!'

Two minutes more passed while the doctor put on his boots and two more while he put on his clothes and brushed his hair.

'Peter Dmitrich!' Levin again began in a piteous voice, but at that instant the doctor came out, dressed and with his hair brushed. 'These people have no conscience,' thought Levin. 'Brushing their hair while we are perishing!'

'Good morning!' said the doctor, holding out his hand and, as it seemed to Levin, teasing him by his calm manner. 'Don't hurry! Well?'

Trying to be as exact as possible, Levin began recounting every unnecessary detail of his wife's position, continually interrupting himself to beg the doctor to accompany him at once.

'Don't be in such a hurry. You see you are inexperienced, I am sure I shall not be needed, but I promised, and if you like I will come. But there is no hurry. Please sit down. Won't you have a cup of coffee?'

Levin gave the doctor a look which asked whether he was not laughing at him. But the doctor had no idea of laughing.

'I know, I know,' he said with a smile. 'I am a family man myself. We husbands are the most miserable of creatures at these times. I have a patient whose husband always runs away into the stable on such occasions!'

'But what is your opinion, Peter Dmitrich? Do you think it may go all right?'

'All the symptoms are favourable.'

'Then you will come at once?' said Levin, looking angrily at the servant who brought in the coffee.

'In an hour's time.'

'No, for heaven's sake . . . !'

'Well, only let me finish my coffee.'

The doctor began on his coffee. Both kept silence.

'Well, the Turks are being seriously beaten! Did you read yesterday's telegram?' asked the doctor, chewing a piece of roll.

'No, I can't stand it!' said Levin, jumping up. 'So you will come in a quarter of an hour?'

'In half an hour.'

'On your honour?'

Levin got home just as the Princess arrived, and they met at the bedroom door. There were tears in the Princess's eyes and her hands shook. When she saw Levin she embraced him and began to cry.

'Well, Mary Vlasevna, darling?' she asked, seizing the hand of the midwife who came toward them with a beaming but preoccupied expression.

'It's going to be all right,' she said. 'Persuade her to lie down; it will be easier for her.'

From the moment when he woke up and understood what was the matter Levin had braced himself to endure what might await him, without reasoning and without anticipating anything—firmly suppressing all his thoughts and feelings, determined not to upset his wife but on the contrary to calm and support her. Not allowing himself even to think of what was about to happen and how it would end, judging by inquiries he had made as to the time such affairs usually lasted, Levin mentally prepared himself to endure and to keep his heart under restraint for something like five hours, which seemed to him within his power. But when he returned from the doctor's and again saw her sufferings, he began repeating more and more often: 'God pardon and help us!' sighing and lifting his head, afraid lest he should not be able to bear the strain and should either burst into tears or run away, so tormenting was it for him. And only one hour had passed!

But after that hour another passed, a second, a third, and all the five hours that he had set himself as the longest term of possible endurance, and still the situation was unchanged; and he went on enduring, for there was nothing else to do but to endure—thinking every moment that he had reached the utmost limit of endurance and that in a moment his heart would burst with pity.

But the minutes went by, and the hours, and other hours, and his suffering and terror and strain grew tenser.

The ordinary conditions of life, without which nothing can be imagined, no longer existed for Levin. He lost the sense of time. Sometimes minutes—those minutes when she called him to her and he held her moist hand, now pressing his with extraordinary strength and now pushing him away—seemed to him like hours; and then again hours seemed but minutes. He was surprised when Mary Vlasevna asked him to light a candle behind the partition, and he learnt that it was already five o'clock in the evening. Had he been told it was ten in the morning he would not have been more astonished. He had just as little idea of where he was at that time as he had of when it all took place. He saw her burning face, now bewildered and full of suffering, and now smiling and soothing him. He saw the Princess red, overwrought, her grey hair out of curl, and with tears which she energetically swallowed, biting her lips. He saw Dolly, he saw the doctor smoking thick cigarettes, and Mary Vlasevna with a firm, resolute, and tranquillizing look on her face, and the old Prince pacing up and down the ballroom and frowning. But he did not know how they came and went, nor where they were. The Princess was one moment in the bedroom with the doctor, and the next in the study, where a table laid for a meal had made its appearance; and next it was not the Princess, but Dolly. Afterwards Levin remembered being sent somewhere. Once he was told to fetch a table and a sofa. He did it with zeal, believing that it was necessary for her sake, and only later discovered that he had been preparing a sleeping-place for himself. Then he was sent to the study to ask the doctor about something. The doctor answered him, and then began talking about the scenes in the city Duma. Then he was sent to fetch an icon with silver-gilt mounts from the Princess's bedroom, and he and the Princess's old lady's maid climbed on a cupboard to get down the icon, and he broke the little lamp that burned before it, and the old servant tried to comfort him about his wife and about the lamp. He brought the icon back with him, and put it at the head of Kitty's bed, carefully pushing it in behind the pillows. But where, when, and why all this was done he did not know. Nor did he understand why the Princess took his hand, and looking pitifully at him, entreated him to be calm; nor why Dolly tried to persuade him to eat something and led him out of the room; nor why even the doctor looked seriously and sympathizingly at him, offering him some drops.

He only knew and felt that what was happening was similar to what had happened the year before in the hotel of the provincial town on the deathbed of his brother Nicholas. Only that was sorrow and this was joy. But that sorrow and this joy were equally beyond the usual conditions of life: they were like openings in that usual life through which something higher became visible. And, as in that case, what was not being accomplished came harshly, painfully, incomprehensibly; and while watching it the soul soared, as then, to heights it had never known before, at which reason could not keep up with it.

'Lord, pardon and help us!' he kept repeating incessantly to himself, appealing to God, in spite of a long period of apparently complete estrangement, just as trustingly and simply as in the days of childhood and early youth.

During the whole of that time he was alternately in two different moods. One day when not in her presence: when with the doctor, who smoked one thick cigarette after another and extinguished them against the rim of the overflowing ashpan; when with Dolly and the Prince, where they talked about dinner, politics, or Mary Petrovna's illness, and when Levin suddenly quite forgot for an instant what was happening and felt just as if he was waking up; and the other was in her presence, by her pillow, where his heart was ready to burst with pity and yet did not burst, and there he prayed unceasingly to God. And every time when the screams that came from the bedroom roused him from momentary forgetfulness he succumbed to the same strange error that had possessed him in the first moments: every time, on hearing the scream, he jumped up and ran to justify himself, but recollected on the way that he was not to blame and that he longed to protect and help her. But when, looking at her, he again saw that to help was impossible, he was seized with horror and said, 'Lord, pardon and help us!' And the longer it lasted the stronger grew both his moods: out of her presence he became calmer, quite forgetting her, and at the same time both her sufferings and his feeling of the impossibility of helping her became more and more poignant. He would jump up, wishing to run away somewhere, but ran to her instead.

Sometimes when she had called him again and again, he was half-inclined to blame her. But seeing her meek smiling face and hearing her say, 'I have worn you out,' he blamed God; but the thought of God made him at once pray for forgiveness and mercy.

Chapter XV

He did not know whether it was late or early. The candles were all burning low. Dolly had just entered the study and suggested that the doctor should lie down. Levin sat listening to the doctor's stories of a quack magnetizer and staring at the ash of the doctor's cigarette. It was an interval of rest and oblivion. He had quite forgotten what was going on. He listened to the doctor's tale and understood it. Suddenly there was a scream unlike anything he had ever heard. The scream was so terrible that Levin did not even jump up, but looked breathlessly with a frightened and inquiring glance at the doctor, who bent his head on one side to listen and smiled approvingly. Everything was so out of the ordinary that nothing any longer surprised Levin. 'Probably it had to be so,' thought he and remained sitting still. 'But who was it screaming?' He jumped up and rushed into the bedroom on tiptoe, past Mary Vlasevna and the Princess, and stopped at his place at the head of the bed. The screaming had ceased, but there was a change; what it was he could not make out or understand, nor did he want to understand it; but he read it in Mary Vlasevna's face. She looked pale and stern, and as resolute as before, though her jaw trembled a little and her eyes were fixed intently on Kitty. Kitty's burning face, worn with suffering, with a lock of hair clinging to her clammy forehead, was turned toward him trying to catch his eye. Her raised hands asked for his. Seizing his cold hands in her perspiring ones she pressed them to her face.

'Don't go! Don't go! I am not afraid, I am not afraid!' she said rapidly. 'Mama! Take off my earrings, they are in the way! You are not afraid? Soon, Mary Vlasevna, soon . . . !'

She spoke very rapidly and tried to smile, but all at once her face became distorted and she pushed him away.

'No, this is awful! I shall die . . . die! . . . Go! Go!' she cried, and again he heard that scream unlike any other cry.

Levin clasped his head in his hands and ran out of the room.

'It's all right, it's all right! All goes well!' Dolly called after him.

But say what they might, he knew that now all was lost. Leaning his head against the door-post he stood in the next room, and heard some one shrieking and moaning in a way he had never heard till then, and he knew that these sounds were produced by what once was Kitty. He had long ceased wishing for a child, and now he hated that child. He did not now even wish her to live, but only longed that these terrible sufferings should end.

'Doctor, what is it? What is it? Oh, my God!' he cried, grasping the hand of the doctor who had just entered.

'It's coming to an end,' said the doctor, with a face so serious that Levin thought that *end* meant death.

Quite beside himself, he rushed into her room. The first thing he saw was Mary Vlasevna's face. It was still more frowning and stern. Kitty's face was not there. In its place was something terrible, both because of its strained expression and because of the sounds which proceeded from it. He let his head drop upon the wood of the bedstead, feeling that his heart was breaking. The terrible screaming did not cease, but grew yet more awful until, as if it had reached the utmost limit of horror, it suddenly ceased. Levin could scarcely believe his ears, but there was no room for doubt. The screaming had ceased, and he heard a sound of movement, of rustling, of accelerated breathing, and her voice, faltering, living, tender, and happy, as it said 'It's over.'

He raised his head. With her arms helplessly outstretched upon the quilt, unusually beautiful and calm she lay, gazing silently at him, trying unsuccessfully to smile.

And suddenly, out of the mysterious, terrible, and unearthly world in which he had been living for the last twenty-two hours, Levin felt himself instantaneously transported back to the old every-day world, but now radiant with the light of such new joy that it was insupportable. The taut strings snapped, and sobs and tears of joy that he had not in the least anticipated arose within him, with such force that they shook his whole body and long prevented his speaking.

Falling on his knees by her bedside he held his wife's hand to his lips, kissing it, and that hand, by a feeble movement of the fingers, replied to the kisses. And meanwhile at the foot of the bed, like the flame of a lamp, flickered in Mary Vlasevna's skilful hands the life of a human being who had never before existed: a human being who, with the same right and the same importance to himself, would live and would procreate others like himself.

'Alive! Alive! And a boy! Don't be anxious,' Levin heard Mary Vlasevna say, as she slapped the baby's back with a shaking hand.

'Mama, is it true?' asked Kitty.

The Princess could only sob in reply.

And amid the silence, as a positive answer to the mother's question, a voice quite unlike all the restrained voices that had been speaking in the room made itself heard. It was a bold, clamorous voice that had no consideration for anything, it was the cry of the human being who had so incomprehensibly appeared from some unknown realm.

Before that, if Levin had been told that Kitty was dead, and that he had died with her, that they had angel children, and that God was there present with them—he would not have been astonished. But now, having returned to the world of actuality, he had to make great efforts to understand that she was alive and well, and that the creature that was yelling so desperately was his son. Kitty was alive, her sufferings were over; and he was full of unspeakable bliss. This he comprehended, and it rendered him entirely happy. But the child? Whence and why had he come? Who was he? . . . He could not at all accustom himself to the idea. It seemed something superfluous, something overflowing, and for a long time he was un-able to get used to it.

Chapter XVI

Toward ten o'clock the old Prince, Koznyshev, and Oblonsky were with Levin, and having talked about the young mother they had begun discussing other matters. Levin listened to them and at the same time involuntarily thought of the past and of what had been going on before that morning, remembering himself as he had been yesterday before this event. A hundred years seemed to have elapsed since then. He felt as if he were on some unattainable height, from which he painstakingly descended in order not to hurt the feelings of those with whom he was conversing. He talked, but never ceased thinking of his wife, of the details of her present condition, and of his son—to the idea of whose existence he painstakingly tried to accustom himself. That feminine world which since his marriage had received a new and unsuspected significance for him, now rose so high in his estimation that his imagination could not grasp it. He heard a conversation about yesterday's dinner at the club and thought, 'What is happening to her now? Is she asleep? How is she? What is she thinking about? Is our son, Dmitry, crying?' And in the middle of the conversation, in the middle of a phrase, he suddenly jumped up and left the room.

'Send and let me know whether I may see her,' said the old Prince.

'All right, directly!' answered Levin, and, without pausing, went to her room.

She was not asleep, but was talking quietly with her mother, making plans for the christening.

Made neat, her hair brushed, a smart cap trimmed with something blue on her head, she lay on her back with her arms outside the quilt, and met his look with a look which drew him toward her. That look, already bright, grew still brighter as he approached. On her face was the same change from the earthly to that which was beyond earth, as is seen on the faces of the dead; but in their case it is a farewell, in hers it was a welcome. Again an agitation, similar to that which he had felt at the moment of the birth, gripped his heart. She took his hand and asked whether he had slept. He could not answer and, conscious of his weakness, turned away.

'And I have been dozing, Kostya!' she said. 'And now I feel so comfortable.'

She was gazing at him, but suddenly her face changed.

'Let me have him, Mary Vlasevna, and he will see him too!'

'Well then, we'll let Papa have a look,' said Mary Vlasevna, lifting something red, strange, and quivering, and bringing it nearer. 'But wait a bit, let's first get dressed,' and Mary Vlasevna put the quiver-

ing red object on the bed, and began unwrapping it and then
swaddling it again, raising and turning it with one finger, and
powdering it with something.

Levin, gazing at this tiny piteous being, vainly searched his soul
for some indications of paternal feeling. He felt nothing for it but
repulsion. But when it was stripped and he caught a glimpse of
thin, thin little arms and legs saffron-coloured, but with fingers
and toes, and even with thumbs distinguishable from the rest; and
when he saw how, as though they were soft springs, Mary Vlasevna
bent those little arms which stuck up, and encased them in linen
garments, he was so filled with pity for that being, and so alarmed
lest she should hurt it, that he tried to restrain her hand.

Mary Vlasevna laughed.

'Don't be afraid, don't be afraid!'

When the baby had been swaddled and made into a firm doll,
Mary Vlasevna turned it over as if proud of her work, and stepped
aside that Levin might see his son in all his beauty.

Kitty turned her eyes and gazed fixedly in the same direction.
'Let me have him, let me have him!' she said, and was even going to
raise herself.

'What are you doing, Catherine Alexandrovna? You must not
move like that! Wait a moment, I'll give him to you. Let's show
Papa what a fine fellow we are!'

And Mary Vlasevna held out to Levin on one hand (the other
merely supporting the nape of the shaky head) this strange, limp,
red creature, that hid its head in its swaddling clothes. But there
was also a nose, blinking eyes, and smacking lips.

'A beautiful baby!' said Mary Vlasevna.

Levin sighed bitterly. This beautiful baby only inspired him with
a sense of repulsion and pity. These were not at all the feelings he
had expected.

He turned away while Mary Vlasevna laid the child to the unaccustomed breast.

Suddenly a laugh made him lift his head. It was Kitty laughing.
The baby had taken the breast.

'Well, that's enough! That's enough!' said Mary Vlasevna; but
Kitty would not part with the baby. He fell asleep in her arms.

'Now look at him,' said Kitty, turning him so that Levin could
see him. The old-looking little face wrinkled up still more and the
baby sneezed.

Smiling, and hardly able to keep back tears of tenderness, Levin
kissed his wife and quitted the darkened room.

What he felt toward this little creature was not at all what he had
anticipated. There was nothing merry or joyful in it; on the contrary, there was a new and distressing sense of fear. It was the con-

sciousness of another vulnerable region. And this consciousness was at first so painful, the fear lest that helpless being should suffer was so strong, that it quite hid the strange feeling of unreasoning joy and even pride which he experienced when the baby sneezed.

Chapter XVII

Oblonsky's affairs were in a bad state.

Two-thirds of the money for the forest had already been spent, and by allowing a discount of ten percent. he had obtained from the merchant almost the whole of the last third. But the latter would not advance any more of the money, especially as Dolly, who had that winter for the first time plainly claimed a right to her own property, had refused to endorse the contract with a receipt for the last third of the payment. Oblonsky's whole salary went for household expenses and the liquidation of small pressing bills. He had no money at all.

This was unpleasant, inconvenient, and, in Oblonsky's opinion, ought not to continue. The cause, as he understood it, was that he received too small a salary. The position had certainly been a very good one a few years ago, but it was so no longer. Petrov, the Bank director, got Rs. 12,000. Sventitsky, Director of a Company, got Rs. 17,000; and Mitin, having founded a bank, got Rs. 50,000. 'Evidently I have been asleep and have been forgotten!' thought Oblonsky. And he began pricking up his ears and looking around, and by the end of the winter he had discovered a very good post and begun an attack on it, first from Moscow through aunts, uncles, and friends; and then in spring, when the matter had ripened, he himself went to Petersburg. This post was one of those, now far more numerous than formerly, carrying salaries from one thousand to fifty thousand roubles a year: soft profitable jobs. It was a Membership of the Committee of the Joint Agency of the Mutual Credit Balance of Southern Railways and Banking Houses. Like all such posts it required such immense knowledge and activity as could hardly be united in one man. And as there was no one found who united those qualities, it was at any rate better for the post to be filled by an honest rather than a dishonest man. Oblonsky was not only an honest man—placing no special emphasis on the word— but he was an honest man with an emphasis, in the special sense attaching to the word in Moscow, where they say: 'An honest worker, an honest writer, an honest journalist, an honest institution, an honest tendency,' meaning not only that the man or the institution are not dishonest, but also that they are capable, on occasion, of being objectionable to the Government. Oblonsky moved in those Moscow circles where the word was used, and was there considered an honest man, so that he had a better claim to the post than other people.

The post carried a salary of from seven to ten thousand roubles a year, and Oblonsky could hold it without resigning his official position. It depended on two Ministers, one lady, and two Jews; and though they had already been prepared it was necessary for Oblonsky to see all these people in Petersburg. Moreover, he had promised his sister Anna to obtain a decisive answer about the divorce from Karenin. So, having got fifty roubles from Dolly, he went to Petersburg.

Sitting in Karenin's study and listening to his article on 'The Causes of the Bad State of Russian Finance,' Oblonsky only waited for him to conclude to speak about his own affairs and about Anna.

'Yes, it is very true,' Oblonsky agreed when Karenin, taking off the *pince-nez* without which he could no longer read, looked up inquiringly at his former brother-in-law. 'It is very true in detail, but all the same the principle of to-day is Freedom.'

'Yes, but I bring forward another principle which embraces the principle of freedom,' said Karenin, accentuating the word 'embraces,' and putting his *pince-nez* on again to re-read the part where this was said.

Turning over the beautifully written, very broad-margined manuscript, Karenin re-read the convincing passage:

'I do not want protection for the benefit of private individuals, but for the common good—for the lowest and for the highest classes equally,' he said, looking at Oblonsky over his *pince-nez.* 'But *they* cannot understand this, *they* are concerned only with their private interests and are carried away by phrases.'

Oblonsky knew that when Karenin began talking about what *they* did and thought—*they* being those who did not wish to accept his projects, and were the cause of all the evil in Russia—the end of the subject was near at hand, and he therefore willingly abandoned the principle of Freedom and agreed entirely. Karenin was silent, thoughtfully turning over the leaves of his manuscript.

'Oh, by the way!' said Oblonsky, 'I wanted to ask you to take an opportunity, when you see Pomorsky, to put in a word for me, and to tell him that I should very much like to get the vacant post of Member of the Committee of the Joint Agency of the Mutual Credit Balance of Southern Railways.' The name of the post that was so near his heart was already familiar to Oblonsky and he pronounced it rapidly without any blunder.

Karenin inquired what was the work of this new Committee, and pondered. He was considering whether in the activity of this Committee there was not something at variance with his own projects. But as the work of the new institution was very complicated and his project covered a very extensive domain, he could not decide this immediately, and taking off his *pince-nez* said:

'Certainly I could speak to him; but, really, why do you want the post?'

'The salary is good, up to nine thousand, and my means . . .'

'Nine thousand,' repeated Karenin, and frowned.

The large figure of the salary reminded him that, in that respect, the post Oblonsky was aspiring to was opposed to the main idea of his projects, which always tended toward economy.

'I consider, and I have written an article on the point, that the enormous salaries paid nowadays are a symptom of the false economic position of our administration.'

'Yes, but what would you have?' said Oblonsky. 'Let's say a bank director gets ten thousand,—he's worth it, you know! Or an engineer gets twenty thousand. It's a live business, anyway.'

'I consider that a salary is payment for value received and should be subject to the law of supply and demand. If that law is ignored when fixing a salary, as for instance when I see that, of two engineers who have passed through the same Institute and are equally well instructed and capable, one receives forty thousand and the other is satisfied with two thousand; or when lawyers or hussars who have no special knowledge are appointed Directors of banks or companies and receive gigantic salaries, I conclude that these salaries are not fixed by the law of supply and demand but by personal influence. This is an abuse important in itself, which has a bad effect on the State service. I consider . . .'

Oblonsky hastened to interrupt his brother-in-law.

'Yes,' said he, 'but you will agree that a new and unquestionably useful institution is being started. Anyway, it is a live business! It is particularly desired that the work should be managed honestly,' concluded Oblonsky, with an emphasis on the word.

But the Moscow meaning of 'honest' was unintelligible to Karenin.

'Honesty is only a negative quality,' said he.

'But you would greatly oblige me, all the same, if you would put in a word—when you happen to see Pomorsky,' said Oblonsky.

'But it depends chiefly on Bolgarinov, I think,' said Karenin.

'Bolgarinov quite agrees, as far as he is concerned,' returned Oblonsky with a blush.

He blushed at the mention of Bolgarinov, because he had that morning been to see the Jew and the visit had left an unpleasant impression on his mind.

Oblonsky was firmly convinced that the business he wished to serve was new, alive, and honest; but that morning when Bolgarinov, with obvious intention, made him wait two hours in his waiting-room with other petitioners, he had suddenly felt uncomfortable.

Whether it was that he, Prince Oblonsky, a descendant of Rurik, was waiting two hours in a Jew's waiting-room, or that, for the first time in his life he was departing from the example set by his ancestors of serving the State only and was entering on a new field, at any rate he felt uncomfortable. During those two hours in Bolgarinov's waiting-room he had walked about boldly, smoothing his whiskers, entering into conversation with other applicants, inventing a joke to tell, of how he had waited at the Jew's, carefully concealing his feelings from others and even from himself.

But all the time he felt uncomfortable and vexed without knowing why. Was it that nothing would come of his pun 'I had business with a Jew, but could not get at him even to say *ajew* (adieu),' or was it something else? And when Bolgarinov at length received him with extreme politeness, evidently triumphing on his humiliation, and very nearly refused his request, Oblonsky hastened to forget it as quickly as he could; and only now on recollecting it blushed.

Chapter XVIII

'Now there's another matter; you know what it is . . . about Anna,' said Oblonsky after a short pause, when he had shaken off the unpleasant recollection.

As soon as Oblonsky mentioned Anna's name Karenin's face entirely changed. Instead of its former animation it expressed weariness and lifelessness.

'What is it you wish of me?' Karenin said, turning round in his chair and folding his *pince-nez*.

'A decision, some decision, Alexey Alexandrovich! I address myself to you not as . . .' He was going to say, 'as an offended husband,' but, afraid of injuring his case thereby, he changed the expression to 'not as a statesman' (this sounded inappropriate) 'but simply as a man, a kind man and a Christian! You should have pity on her.'

'What do you mean exactly?' asked Karenin in a low tone.

'Why, pity her! If you had seen her as I have, who have spent the whole winter with her, you would pity her. Her position is awful! Literally awful!'

'It seems to me,' returned Karenin in a more high-pitched, almost squeaky voice, 'that Anna Arkadyevna has everything she herself desired.'

'Oh, Alexey Alexandrovich! For God's sake don't let us have any recriminations! What is past is past! You know what she wants and is waiting for: the divorce.'

'But I understood that Anna Arkadyevna declined a divorce if I insisted on keeping my son. I answered in that sense and thought the matter was closed. I consider it closed,' shrieked Karenin.

'For heaven's sake don't excite yourself,' said Oblonsky, touching his brother-in-law's knee. 'The matter is not closed. If you will let me recapitulate, this is how matters stood: When you parted, you were great, as magnanimous as a man can possibly be; you consented to everything: her freedom and even a divorce. She appreciated that. Yes, don't think otherwise! She really appreciated it! She appreciated it to such a degree that, at the moment, feeling herself to blame toward you, she did not consider and could not consider everything. She renounced everything. But facts and time have shown that her situation is tormenting and impossible.'

'Anna Arkadyevna's life cannot interest me,' interposed Karenin, lifting his brows.

'Allow me not to believe that,' Oblonsky rejoined gently. 'Her situation is tormenting to her and does not benefit anyone. "She has deserved it," you may say. She knows that and does not ask you for anything. She says plainly that she dare not ask anything. But I, and all her relatives, who all love her, beg and implore you! Why should she be so tormented? Who gains by it?'

'Excuse me! You seem to be placing me in the position of defendant,' Karenin remonstrated.

'Oh, no, no! Not at all! Understand me!' said Oblonsky, now touching Karenin's hand, as if he were sure that the contact would soften his brother-in-law. 'All I say is that her position is tormenting, and could be made easier by you, without any detriment to yourself. I would arrange everything for you so that you would not be bothered. You see, you promised!'

'The promise was given before, and I thought the question about my son had settled the matter. . . . Besides, I hoped that Anna Arkadyevna would have generosity enough . . .' uttered Karenin with difficulty, his lips trembling and his face turning pale.

'She leaves everything to your generosity! She asks, she pleads for one thing only: help her out of the intolerable position she is in! She no longer asks for her son . . . Alexey Alexandrovich! You are a good man. Enter for a moment into her situation. The question of a divorce is for her—in her position—one of life and death. If you had not promised before, she would have grown reconciled to her position and have gone on living in the country. But as you had promised, she wrote to you and moved to Moscow. And now in Moscow where every time she meets anyone it is like a knife in her heart, she has been living for six months every day expecting your decision. Why, it's like keeping a man condemned to death with the halter round his neck for months, promising him either death or a reprieve! Have pity on her, and I undertake to arrange . . . Your scruples . . .'

'I am not speaking of that . . . of that . . .' Karenin interrupted him in a disgusted tone. 'But perhaps I promised something I had no right to promise.'

'Then you refuse what you promised?'

'I have never refused to do what is possible, but I want time to consider in how far what was promised is possible.'

'No, Alexey Alexandrovich!' said Oblonsky, jumping to his feet. 'I will not believe that! She is as wretched as a woman can be, and you cannot refuse such a . . .'

'As far as what I promised is possible. *Vous professez d'être un libre penseur;* [4] but I, as a believer, in so important a matter cannot act contrary to the Christian law.'

'But in Christian communities, and in ours too as far as I know, divorce is permitted,' said Oblonsky. 'Divorce is also permitted by our Church. And we see . . .'

'It is permitted, but not in that sense.'

'Alexey Alexandrovich, I don't recognize you!' said Oblonsky after a pause. 'Was it not you (and did we not appreciate it?) who forgave everything, and, moved just by Christian feeling, were ready to sacrifice everything? You yourself said: "Give your coat when they would take your cloak . . ."! And now . . .'

'I beg,' began Karenin in a shrill voice, suddenly rising to his feet, pale and with trembling jaw, 'I beg you to stop . . . stop . . . this conversation!'

'Oh, no! Well then, forgive me! forgive me if I have pained you,' said Oblonsky with an embarrassed smile, holding out his hand. 'I only delivered my message as an envoy.'

Karenin gave him his hand, reflected, and then said:

'I must think it over and seek for guidance. The day after tomorrow I will give you a final answer,' he added, after consideration.

Chapter XIX

Oblonsky was just leaving when Korney entered and announced: 'Sergey Alexeyich!'

'Who is Sergey Alexeyich?' Oblonsky was about to ask, but immediately recollected.

'Oh, Serezha!' he said. 'Sergey Alexeyich! Why, I thought it was the Director of the Department!' and he remembered that Anna had asked him to see the boy.

He recalled the timid pathetic look with which Anna at parting from him had said: 'Anyhow, you will see him. Find out everything: where he is, who is with him. And, Stiva . . . if it is possible . . . Isn't it possible?' He had understood what 'If it is possible' meant. It meant, if it is possible to arrange the divorce so that

4. You profess to be a free thinker.

she should have her son. . . . But now Oblonsky saw that it was useless even to think of that; he was, however, glad to see his nephew.

Karenin reminded his brother-in-law that they never mentioned his mother to the boy, and asked him not to say a word about her. 'He was very ill after that unexpected interview with his mother,' remarked Karenin. 'We even feared for his life. But sensible treatment and sea-bathing in the summer have restored his health, and now, on the doctor's advice, I send him to school. The influence of his schoolfellows has really had a good effect on him, and he is quite well and learns well.'

'Hullo! What a fine fellow! True enough, it's not little Serezha now, but a complete Sergey Alexeyich!' said Oblonsky, smiling as he looked at a handsome boy in a blue jacket and long trousers who entered the room boldly and confidently. The lad looked healthy and bright. He bowed to his uncle as to a stranger, but recognizing him he blushed and turned away from him quickly as if offended and angry about something. The boy came up to his father and handed him his school report.

'Well, that's pretty good,' said his father. 'You may go now.'

'He has grown thin and tall, and is no longer a child but a regular boy,' said Oblonsky. 'I like it. Do you remember me?'

The boy glanced swiftly at his father.

'I do, *mon oncle*,' he answered, looking at his uncle and then again lowering his eyes.

His uncle called him nearer and took his hand.

'Well, how are things?' said he, wishing to start a conversation, but not knowing what to say.

The boy, blushing and not answering, gently withdrew his hand from his uncle's grasp. As soon as Oblonsky released it, after a questioning glance at his father, he hastily left the room like a bird let out of its cage.

A year had passed since Serezha last saw his mother. Since then he had not heard any more of her. During this year he had been sent to school, and had learned to know his schoolmates and to like them. The dreams and memories of his mother which, after their interview, had made him ill, no longer occupied him. When they rose in his memory he took pains to drive them away, considering them shameful and fit only for girls, but not for a boy and a chum. He knew that his father and mother had had a quarrel which separated them; knew that it was his fate to remain with his father, and he tried to accustom himself to that thought.

He felt uncomfortable at meeting his uncle, who resembled his mother, because it awakened those very memories which he considered shameful. It was the more disagreeable because from some words he had overheard while waiting outside the study door, and especially from his father's and uncle's faces, he guessed that they had been talking about his mother. And in order not to blame the father with whom he lived and upon whom he depended, and above all not to give way to the sensibility which he considered so degrading, Serezha tried not to look at that uncle, who had come to upset his peace of mind, and not to think of what was called to mind by the sight of him.

But when Oblonsky, who had come out after him, saw him on the stairs, and called him and asked how he spent his time between lessons at school, Serezha, in his father's absence, got into conversation with him.

'We play at railways now,' he said, answering the question. 'You see, it's this way: two sit down on a bench; they are passengers. One stands on the same bench. The others all harness themselves to it —they may do it with their hands or their belts—and then off they go through all the rooms. The doors are opened beforehand. . . . It's not easy to be the guard!'

'That's the one who stands up?' asked Oblonsky with a smile.

'Yes. It needs courage and quickness, especially if they stop suddenly, or if somebody falls down.'

'Yes, that's no joke,' said Oblonsky, looking sadly into those animated eyes so like the mother's—an infant's eyes no longer, and no longer altogether innocent. And, in spite of his promise to Karenin, he could not refrain from speaking of Anna.

'Do you remember your mother?' he suddenly asked.

'No, I don't!' hurriedly replied Serezha, and blushing scarlet he hung down his head. His uncle could get nothing more out of him.

Half an hour later the Slav tutor found his pupil on the stairs, and for a long while could not make out whether he was in a temper or was simply crying.

'I expect you hurt yourself when you fell down?' said the tutor. 'I told you it was a dangerous game. I shall have to tell your head master about it.'

'If I had hurt myself no one would have known it, that is quite certain!'

'Well then, what is it?'

'Leave me alone! If I do remember, or if I don't . . . what business is it of his? Why should I remember? Leave me alone!' he said, now addressing not his tutor but the world in general.

Chapter XX

As was his wont, Oblonsky did not spend his time idly while in Petersburg. Besides business—his sister's divorce and his post—it was as usual necessary for him, as he said, to refresh himself in

Petersburg after the mustiness of Moscow.

Moscow, despite its *cafés chantants* and its omnibuses, was still a stagnant pool. Oblonsky always felt this. After living in Moscow, especially in the bosom of his family, Oblonsky always felt his spirits flag. When he had spent a long time in Moscow without a break, he reached a state in which he began to be upset by his wife's ill-humour and reproaches, by the health and education of the children, and the petty details of his work; even the fact that he was in debt worried him then. But he only needed to spend some time in Petersburg among the set in which he moved, where people lived, really *lived*, instead of vegetating as in Moscow, and at once all these cares vanished and melted away like wax before a fire.

His wife? . . . Only that day he had been talking to Prince Chechensky. He had a wife and family with grown-up sons who were pages at Court; and another family, an illegitimate one, in which there were other children. Though the first family was all right, Prince Chechensky felt happier with the second family. He took his eldest son to visit the second family, and told Oblonsky that he considered it developed his son and was good for him. What would they say to that in Moscow?

Children? In Petersburg children did not hinder their fathers' living. Children were brought up in educational establishments, and there were none of those barbaric views that were becoming so prevalent in Moscow—Lvov's was a case in point—that the children should have every luxury and the parents nothing but work and worry. Here people understood that a man must live his own life like a civilized being.

The Service! . . . Service too was not here that strained, hopeless drudgery that it was in Moscow; here there was an interest in the Service. Meeting the right person, a service rendered, a felicitous remark, the ability to perform certain tricks, made a man's career in a moment, as was the case with Bryantsov, whom Oblonsky had met the day before, and who was now a great dignitary. Service of that kind had an interest.

But it was the Petersburg outlook on money matters that had a particularly soothing effect on Oblonsky. Bartnyansky, who spent at least fifty thousand roubles a year at the rate he was living, had the day before made a notable remark to him on the point.

As they were having a chat before dinner, Oblonsky had said to Bartnyansky:

'You are, I think, intimate with Mordvinsky? You could do me a good turn if you would put in a word for me. There is a post I should like to get . . . Member of the Agency . . .'

'Never mind the name, I shouldn't remember it! . . . But why do you want to mix in those railway concerns, with Jews? . . .

Look at it how you like, it's horrid!'

Oblonsky did not tell him that it was a 'live' business. Bartnyansky would not have understood that.

'I am hard up; having nothing to live on.'

'But you do live.'

'Yes, but in debt.'

'Really? Is it much?' asked Bartnyansky sympathetically.

'A great deal: about twenty thousand roubles.'

Bartnyansky burst into merry laughter.

'Oh, you lucky fellow!' he cried. 'My debts amount to a million and a half, and I have nothing! But, as you see, I still find it possible to live!'

Oblonsky knew this to be true, not only from hearsay but from actual fact. Zhivakhov, whose debts amounted to three hundred thousand roubles, didn't possess a penny and yet he lived, and how he lived! Count Krivtsov, whose case had long been considered hopeless, still kept two mistresses. Petrovsky had run through five millions, continued living in just the same style, and even directed the Finance Department and received a salary of twenty thousand.

But, apart from that, Petersburg acted pleasantly on Oblonsky physically. It made him younger. In Moscow he sometimes noticed some grey hairs; fell asleep after dinner; stretched himself; walked slowly upstairs, breathing heavily; felt dull among young women, and did not dance at balls. In Petersburg he always felt that he had shaken off ten years.

In Petersburg he felt what the sixty-year-old Prince Peter Oblonsky, who had just returned from abroad, had described to him only the day before.

'Here we don't know how to live,' Peter Oblonsky had said. 'Would you believe it? I spent the summer in Baden and really felt quite like a young man. I see a young woman, and my fancy . . . I dine, drink a little, and feel strong and full of spirits. I returned to Russia and had to be with my wife, and in the country besides, and in a fortnight I took to a dressing-gown and gave up dressing for dinner! And as to thinking about young women! . . . Why, I had turned into quite an old man! There was nothing left for me but to think of saving my soul. . . . Then I went to Paris, and again recovered.'

Stephen experienced just the same difference as Peter Oblonsky. In Moscow he let himself go to such an extent that, had he continued to live there long, he might even have come to the soul-saving stage; but in Petersburg he again felt quite a smart fellow.

Between the Princess Betsy Tverskaya and Oblonsky there existed long-established and very peculiar relations. Oblonsky in fun always paid court to her, and told her the most indecent things also in fun, knowing that she liked that more than anything. The day after his interview with Karenin, Oblonsky, calling on her, felt so youthful that he went accidentally to such lengths in this bantering courtship and humbug that he did not know how to get out of it, for unfortunately she was not merely unattractive but actually repulsive to him. This tone had sprung up between them because he was very attractive to her. So he had been very pleased when the Princess Myagkaya turned up, and put an end to their *tête-à-tête*.

'Ah, so you are here!' she said on seeing him. 'Well, how is your poor sister? Don't look at me like that,' she added. 'Since every one has been attacking her—all those who are a hundred thousand times worse than she—I have thought she has acted splendidly. I can't forgive Vronsky for not letting me know when she was in Petersburg. I would have gone to her and gone with her everywhere. Please give her my love. . . . Well, tell me about her.'

'Yes, her situation is a hard one . . .' Oblonsky began, in the simplicity of his heart taking the Princess Myagkaya's words for genuine coin when she said 'Tell me about her.' But the Princess Myagkaya immediately interrupted him, as was her habit, and commenced telling her own tale.

'She has done what everybody, except myself, does secretly, and she would not deceive, and has acted splendidly. And the best thing she did was to leave that half-witted brother-in-law of yours! Excuse me. Every one used to say, "He is so clever, so clever." I alone said that he was stupid. Now that he has got so chummy with Lydia Ivanovna and Landau, every one says he is half-witted; and I should be glad not to agree with everybody, but this time I can't help it.'

'But do explain to me what it means!' said Oblonsky. 'Yesterday I called on him about my sister's affair and asked him for a definite answer. He did not give me an answer, but said he must think it over; and this morning instead of an answer I have received an invitation for this evening to go to the Countess Lydia Ivanovna's.'

'Ah, that's it, that's it!' Princess Myagkaya began joyfully. 'They will ask Landau and see what he says.'

'Ask Landau? Why? Who is Landau?'

'What? You don't know Jules Landau, *le fameux Jules Landau, le clairvoyant?* [5] He also is half-witted, but your sister's fate depends on him. See what comes of living in the provinces: you know nothing! Landau, you see, was a *commis* [6] in Paris and went to see a doctor. He fell asleep in the doctor's waiting-room, and while asleep began giving advice to all the patients, and very strange advice too. Afterwards, the wife of Yury Meledinsky—the invalid, you know—

5. The famous Jules Landau, the clairvoyant.
6. Shop-assistant.

heard of that Landau, and took him to see her husband. He is treating her husband. No good has been done in my opinion, for he is still just as weak, but they believe in him and take him about with them. So they brought him to Russia. Here every one rushed at him, and he began treating everybody. He cured the Countess Bezzubova, and she took such a fancy to him that she adopted him.'

'Adopted! How?'

'Simply adopted him! He is now no longer Landau, but Count Bezzubov. However, that's not to the point; but Lydia—I am very fond of her, but her head is not screwed on right—naturally has rushed at this Landau, and now nothing is settled either by her or by Karenin without him, so your sister's fate is now in the hands of this Landau, *alias* Count Bezzubov.'

Chapter XXI

After an excellent dinner and a large quantity of cognac at Bartnyansky's, Oblonsky, only a little after the appointed time, entered the Countess Lydia Ivanovna's house.

'Who is with the Countess? The Frenchman?' Oblonsky asked the hall-porter, noticing on the hall-stand Karenin's overcoat, which he recognized, and a strange, absurd-looking paletot with clasps.

'Alexey Alexandrovich Karenin and Count Bezzubov,' the hall-porter replied severely.

'The Princess Myagkaya guessed correctly,' thought Oblonsky as he ascended the stairs. 'Strange! But it would be just as well to make friends with her. She has tremendous influence. If she would say a word to Pomorsky, the job is done.'

It was still quite light out of doors, but in the Countess Lydia Ivanovna's small drawing-room the blinds were down and the lamp alight.

At the round table beneath a lamp sat the countess and Karenin, conversing in low tones. A short lean man, with hips like a woman's knock-kneed, very pale, handsome, with beautiful shining eyes and long hair that hung over the collar of his frock-coat, stood at the opposite end of the room, looking at the portraits on the wall. After greeting the hostess and Karenin, Oblonsky involuntarily glanced at the stranger once more.

'Monsieur Landau!' The Countess addressed him with a softness and caution that struck Oblonsky. And she introduced them.[7]

---

7. Tolstóy had seen D. D. Home, the famous medium, in Paris in 1857 and has made use of his impression of him in his description of Landau. Robert Browning depicted him as Sludge the Medium. In 1857 Home had appeared in Paris, attracted the attention of Napoleon III and the Empress Eugénie, and had at once become a popular person in French aristocratic salons. That same year he became a Roman Catholic, but was expelled from Rome as a sorcerer in 1864. In 1866 a Mrs. Lyon adopted him as her son and assigned to him £60,000, which sum she subsequently compelled him to restore.

Landau hurriedly looked round, approached smilingly, laid upon Oblonsky's outstretched hand his own moist and motionless one, went back, and continued looking at the portraits. The Countess and Karenin glanced at each other significantly.

'I am very pleased to see you, especially to-day,' said the Countess Lydia Ivanovna, pointing to a seat beside Karenin.

'I introduced him to you as *Landau*,' she said softly, glancing at the Frenchman and then back at Oblonsky, 'but really he is Count Bezzubov, as you probably know. But he does not like that title.'

'Yes, I have heard,' replied Oblonsky. 'They say he has completely cured the Countess Bezzubova.'

'She called on me to-day, and was so pathetic,' said the Countess, turning to Karenin. 'This separation is dreadful for her. It is such a blow to her!'

'Is he going definitely?' inquired Karenin.

'Yes, he is going to Paris. He heard a voice yesterday,' said the Countess, with a look at Oblonsky.

'Ah, a voice!' Oblonsky remarked, feeling that he must be as careful as possible in this company, where something peculiar occurred, or was supposed to occur, to which he as yet lacked a clue.

After a momentary pause the Countess Lydia Ivanovna, as if coming to the important point, turned with a subtle smile to Oblonsky.

'I have known you a long time, and am very pleased to know you more intimately. *Les amis de nos amis sont nos amis.*[8] But to be a friend, one must enter into the state of the friend's soul, and I fear you will not do so in relation to Alexey Alexandrovich. You understand what I am speaking about?' she said, lifting her beautiful dreamy eyes.

'To some extent, Countess! I understand that Alexey Alexandrovich's position . . .' said Oblonsky, not quite grasping what it was all about, and therefore wishing to keep to generalities.

'The change is not in his external position,' Lydia Ivanovna said severely as her enamoured eyes followed Karenin, who had risen and joined Landau. 'His heart is changed; he has been given a new heart, and I fear that you may not have realized fully that change which has been accomplished within him.'

'Well, broadly speaking, I can picture to myself the change. We

In 1859 Home had arrived in Russia with the wealthy Count G. A. Kushelëv-Bezboródko whom he had met in Florence.

In Russia, as a Russian journalist then remarked, 'he performed his best trick, before abandoning further performances'—and married a relation of Count Kushelëv-Bezboródko receiving with her a considerable sum of money.

The similarity of Bezboródko with the name Bezzúbov employed in the novel, suggests that Tolstóy had that occurrence in mind when he transformed Landau into Count Bezzúbov.

8. The friends of our friends are our friends.

have always been friendly, and now . . .' Oblonsky said, answering her look with a tender gaze, while he considered with which of two Ministers she was the more closely connected—so as to judge which of them he should ask her to influence on his behalf.

'The change that has taken place in him cannot weaken his love for his neighbour; on the contrary, that change must strengthen his love. But I fear you don't understand me. Won't you have some tea?' she said, indicating with her eyes the footman who was handing tea round on a tray.

'Not quite, Countess. Of course his misfortune . . .'

'Yes, a misfortune which has turned into a great blessing, because his heart became new and is filled with Him,' she said, glancing at Oblonsky with love-sick eyes.

'I think I might ask her to mention me to both,' thought he.

'Oh, certainly, Countess!' he said. 'But I think such changes are so very intimate that nobody, not even the closest friend, cares to speak about them.'

'On the contrary! We must speak, and so help one another.'

'Yes, of course, but there are such differences of conviction, and besides . . .' said Oblonsky with a gentle smile.

'There cannot be any differences in what concerns the holy Truth!'

'Oh no, of course not! But . . .' and, becoming embarrassed, Oblonsky stopped short. He realized that it was a question of religion.

'It seems to me he will fall asleep directly,' said Karenin in a significant whisper, approaching Lydia Ivanovna.

Oblonsky turned. Landau was sitting by the window, leaning against the arm and back of an easy-chair, with his head hanging down. Noticing the looks directed toward him, he smiled a childishly naïve smile.

'Take no notice of him,' said Lydia Ivanovna, and with an agile movement she pushed forward a chair for Karenin. 'I have noticed . . .' she began, when a footman entered with a note. Lydia Ivanovna rapidly read the note and, excusing herself, with extreme rapidity wrote and despatched the answer and returned to the table. 'I have noticed,' she continued her interrupted sentence, 'that Muscovites, men especially, are most indifferent to religion.'

'Oh no, Countess! I think Muscovites have the reputation of being the most steadfast believers,' replied Oblonsky.

'But, as far as I know, you unfortunately are one of the indifferent?' Karenin remarked to him, with a weary smile.

'How can one be indifferent?' said Lydia Ivanova.

'I am in this respect not precisely indifferent, but rather expectant,' said Oblonsky with his most mollifying smile. 'I do not think that for me the time for those questions has yet come.'

Karenin and Lydia Ivanovna exchanged looks.

'We never know whether our time has come or not,' Karenin said sternly. 'We should not consider whether we are ready or not; grace is not influenced by human calculations. Sometimes it does not descend on those who seek it, but descends on the unprepared, as on Saul.'

'No, not yet, I think,' said Lydia Ivanovna who was watching the Frenchman's movements. Landau rose and came up to them.

'You will allow me to listen?' he asked.

'Oh yes! I did not wish to disturb you,' said Lydia, looking tenderly at him. 'Sit down beside us.'

'Only one must not shut one's eyes, so as to deprive oneself of light,' Karenin continued.

'Oh, if you only knew the happiness we experience, feeling His continual presence in our souls!' cried the Countess Lydia Ivanovna with a beatific smile.

'But one may sometimes feel incapable of ascending to such heights,' remarked Oblonsky, conscious that he was not quite honest in acknowledging the existence of religious heights, yet not venturing to confess his scepticism in the presence of one who, by a single word to Pomorsky, might secure him the desired post.

'You mean to say, he is prevented by sin?' said Lydia Ivanovna. 'But that is a false view. Sin does not exist for a believer; sin has already been atoned for. . . . Excuse me!' she added, glancing at the footman who entered with another note. She read it, and answered by word of mouth: 'Tell him, "To-morrow at the Grand Duchess's." . . . For those who believe, there is no sin,' she went on.

'Yes, but faith without works is dead,' said Oblonsky, recalling that sentence from the catechism, and only by a smile maintaining his independence.

'There it is, from the Epistle of St James,' said Karenin, addressing Lydia Ivanovna in a somewhat reproachful tone. Evidently this was a point they had discussed more than once. 'How much harm has been done by a false interpretation of that passage! Nothing turns so many from the faith as that interpretation, "I have no works, and therefore cannot have faith." Yet it is not so said anywhere; just the contrary is said.'

'To labour for God with works; to save one's soul by fasting,' said the Countess Lydia Ivanovna with fastidious disdain, 'those are the barbarous opinions of our monks. . . . Yet it is not so said anywhere. It is much simpler and easier,' she added, looking at Oblonsky with the same encouraging smile with which at Court she encouraged young Maids of Honour who were confused by their new surroundings.

'We are saved by Christ, who suffered for us. We are saved by faith,' Karenin chimed in, showing his approval of her remark by a look.

'Vous comprenez l'anglais?'[9] asked Lydia Ivanovna, and having received an affirmative answer she rose and began looking among the books on a shelf. 'I want to read Safe and Happy, or, Under the Wing,'[1] she said with a questioning look at Karenin. And having found the book and sat down again, she opened it. 'It is quite short. It describes the way to acquire faith, and the joy, higher than anything else on earth, with which it fills the soul. A believer cannot be unhappy, because he is not alone. But you will see . . .' She was about to begin reading when the footman came in again. 'Borozdina? Say "To-morrow at two." . . . Yes,' she went on, keeping her finger in the book to mark the place, and sighed, looking with her beautiful dreamy eyes straight before her. 'This is how true faith acts. You know Mary Sanina? You have heard of her misfortune? She lost her only child. She was in despair. Well, and what happened? She found this Friend, and now she thanks God for her child's death. That is the happiness faith gives!'

'Oh yes, it is very . . .' began Oblonsky, glad that she was going to read and give him time to get his ideas together. 'No, evidently it will be better not to ask for anything to-night,' he reflected; 'only let me get away from here without making a mess of things!'

'It will be dull for you,' said the Countess Lydia Ivanovna, turning to Landau, 'as you don't understand English; but it is quite short.'

'Oh, I shall understand,' replied Landau with the same smile, and closed his eyes.

Karenin and Lydia Ivanovna exchanged significant looks, and the reading began.

Chapter XXII

Oblonsky felt completely puzzled by the strange and novel conversations he was listening to. Generally the complications of Petersburg life had an exhilarating effect on him, lifting him out of the Moscow stagnation. But he liked and understood complications in spheres congenial and familiar to him; in these strange surroundings he felt puzzled and dazed and could not take it all in. Listening to the Countess Lydia Ivanovna and feeling the fine eyes, naïve or cunning—he did not know which—of Landau fixed upon him, Oblonsky began to be conscious of a peculiar sort of heaviness in his head.

The most varied ideas were mixed up in his mind. 'Mary Sanina

9. You understand English?
1. The titles of evangelical tracts connected with the visit to St. Petersburg in 1874 of Lord Granville Redstock (1831–1913), who preached salvation through faith in the salons of high society.

is glad that her child is dead. . . . I should like to have a smoke.
. . . To be saved one need only have faith; the monks don't know
how to do it, but the Countess Lydia Ivanovna knows. . . . And
what is so heavy in my head? Is it the brandy, or is it because all
this is so very strange? All the same, I think I have not done anything to shock them up till now. But still it won't do to ask her
help now. I have heard that they make one pray. Supposing they
make me pray! That would be too stupid! And what nonsense she
is reading, but her enunciation is good. . . . Landau Bezzubov.
. . . Why is he Bezzubov?' Suddenly Oblonsky felt his nether
jaw dropping irresistibly for a yawn. He smoothed his whiskers to
hide the yawn, and gave himself a shake. But then he felt himself
falling asleep, and nearly snored. He roused himself, just when the
Countess Lydia Ivanovna uttered the words: 'He is asleep.'

Oblonsky awoke in a fright, feeling guilty and detected. But he
was immediately comforted by noticing that the words 'He is
asleep' did not apply to him but to Landau. The Frenchman had
fallen asleep just as Oblonsky had done. But whereas Oblonsky's
sleep would, he imagined, have offended them—he did not really
even think this, for everything seemed so strange—Landau's sleep
delighted them extremely, especially Lydia Ivanovna.

'Mon ami,' said she, carefully holding the folds of her silk dress to
prevent its rustling, and in her excitement calling Karenin not
'Alexey Alexandrovich' but 'mon ami,' 'donnez-lui la main. Vous
voyez?' [2] . . . Hush!' she said to the footman, who came in again.
'I am not receiving.'

The Frenchman slept or pretended to sleep, leaning his head
against the back of the chair, and his moist hand lying on his knee
moved feebly, as if catching something. Karenin rose, and though
he tried to be cautious he caught against the table. He went up to
the Frenchman and placed his hand in his. Oblonsky also rose and,
opening his eyes wide to wake himself up in case he was asleep,
looked first at one and then at the other. It was all quite real, and
Oblonsky felt his head getting worse and worse.

'Que la personne qui est arrivée la dernière, celle qui demande,
qu'elle sorte! Qu'elle sorte!' [3] the Frenchman said, without opening
his eyes.

'Vous m'excuserez, mais vous voyez. . . . Revenez vers dix
heures, encore mieux demain.' [4]

'Qu'elle sorte!' repeated the Frenchman impatiently.

'C'est moi, n'est-ce pas?' [5] And having received an answer in the
affirmative, Oblonsky—forgetting the request he had wanted to

---

2. My friend, give him your hand. You see?
3. Let the person who arrived last, the one who questions, go out! Let him go out!
4. You must excuse me, but you see . . . Come back at about ten, or better still, to-morrow.
5. It's I, is it not?

make to Lydia Ivanovna, forgetting his sister's affairs, and with the one desire to get away from there as quickly as possible—went out on tiptoe, and ran out into the street as from an infected house. After which he talked and joked for a long time with an *izvoshchik*, trying to regain his senses as soon as possible.

At the French Theatre, where he arrived in time for the last act, and afterwards at the Tartar Restaurant, where he had some champagne, Oblonsky was able to some extent to breathe again in an atmosphere congenial to him, but nevertheless he was not at all himself that evening.

When he returned to Peter Oblonsky's house, where he was staying, he found a note from Betsy. She wrote that she greatly wished to finish the conversation they had begun, and asked him to call next day. Scarcely had he finished reading the note and made a wry face over it, when he heard downstairs the heavy steps of men carrying something heavy.

He went down to see what it was. It was Peter Oblonsky rejuvenated again. He was so drunk that he could not get up the stairs, but on seeing Oblonsky he ordered the men to put him on his feet and, clinging to Stephen, he went with him to his room, began relating how he had spent the evening, and fell asleep there.

Oblonsky was in low spirits, a thing that rarely happened to him, and could not fall asleep for a long time. Everything he recalled was nauseous, but most repulsive of all, like something shameful, was the memory of the evening at Lydia Ivanovna's.

Next day he received from Karenin a definite refusal to divorce Anna, and understood that this decision was based on what the Frenchman had said the evening before, in his real or pretended sleep.

Chapter XXIII

Before any definite step can be taken in a household, there must be either complete division or loving accord between husband and wife. When their relations are indefinite it is impossible for them to make any move.

Many families continue for years in their old ruts, hated by both husband and wife, merely because there is neither complete discord nor harmony.

Both for Vronsky and for Anna life in Moscow in the heat and dust, when the sun no longer shone as in spring but burned as in summer, when all the trees on the boulevards had long been in leaf and the leaves were already covered with dust, was intolerable; nevertheless they did not move to Vozdvizhensk, as they had long ago decided to do, but stayed in Moscow, which had become obnoxious to them both, because of late there had not been harmony between them.

The irritation which divided them had no tangible cause, and all attempts at an explanation not only failed to clear it away but increased it. It was an inner irritation, caused on her side by a diminution of his love for her, and on his by regret that for her sake he had placed himself in a distressing situation, which she, instead of trying to alleviate, made still harder. Neither of them spoke of the cause of their irritation, but each thought the other in the wrong, and at every opportunity tried to prove that this was so.

For her he, with all his habits, thoughts, wishes, mental and physical faculties—the whole of his nature—consisted of one thing only: love for women, and this love she felt ought to be wholly concentrated on her alone. This love was diminishing; therefore, in her judgment, part of his love must have been transferred to other women, or to one other woman. She was jealous, not of any one woman, but of the diminution of his love. Not having as yet an object for her jealousy, she sought one. At the slightest hint she transferred her jealousy from one object to another. Now she was jealous of the coarse women with whom, through his bachelor connections, he might so easily come into contact; now of the Society women whom he might meet; now of some imaginary girl whom he might marry after repudiating her. This last jealousy tormented her more than anything else, especially since in an expansive moment he had carelessly told her that his mother understood him so little that she had tried to persuade him to marry the young Princess Sorokina.

And being jealous, Anna was indignant with him and constantly sought reasons to justify her indignation. She blamed him for everything that was hard in her situation. The torture of expectation, living betwixt heaven and earth, which she endured there in Moscow, Karenin's dilatoriness and indecision, her loneliness—she attributed all to him. If he loved her he would fully understand the difficulty of her situation, and would deliver her from it. That they were living in Moscow, instead of in the country, was also his fault. He could not live buried in the country as she desired. He needed society, and so he had placed her in this terrible position, the misery of which he would not understand. And it was likewise his fault that she was for ever parted from her son.

Even the rare moments of tenderness which occurred between them did not pacify her; in his tenderness she now saw a tinge of calm assurance which had not been there before and irritated her.

It was growing dusk. Anna, all alone, awaiting his return from a bachelor dinner-party, paced up and down his study (which was the room in which the street noises were least audible), recalling in detail every word of their yesterday's quarrel. Passing ever backwards from the memorably offensive words of the quarrel to their cause, she at last got back to the beginning of their conversation. For a long time she could not believe that the dispute had begun from a perfectly inoffensive conversation about a matter that did not touch the heart of either. Yet it was so. It had all begun by his laughing at High Schools for girls, which he considered unnecessary and she defended. He spoke disrespectfully of the education of women in general, and said that Hannah, her little English *protegée*, did not at all need to know physics.

This provoked Anna. She saw in it a contemptuous allusion to her own knowledge; and she invented and uttered a phrase in retaliation which should revenge the pain he had caused her.

'I don't expect you to understand me and my feelings, as an affectionate man would; but I did expect ordinary delicacy,' she said.

And he really had flushed with vexation and had said something disagreeable. She did not remember her reply to it, but remembered that in answer he had said with obvious intent to hurt her too:

'I can take no interest in your partiality for that little girl, because I can see that it is unnatural.'

The cruelty with which he annihilated the world which she had so painfully constructed for herself to be able to endure her hard life, the injustice of his accusation that she was dissembling and unnatural, roused her indignation.

'I am very sorry that only what is coarse and material is comprehensible and natural to you,' she retorted and left the room.

When he came to her in the evening they did not refer to the quarrel, but both felt that it was only smoothed over, not settled. To-day he had been away from home all day, and she had felt so lonely, and it was so painful to feel herself at discord with him, that she wished to forget it all, to forgive and make it up with him. Wishing even to blame herself and to justify him, she said to herself:

'I am to blame; I am irritable and unreasonably jealous. I will make it up with him and we will go back to the country. There I shall be calmer.'

'Unnatural!' She suddenly remembered the word that had hurt her most, though it was not so much the word as his intention to pain her. 'I know what he wanted to say: he wanted to say that it is unnatural not to love one's own daughter and yet to love another's child. What does he know of love for children,—of my love for Serezha whom I have given up for his sake? And that desire to hurt me! No, he must be in love with some other woman; it can't be anything else.'

Then, realizing that in her attempt to quiet herself she had again completed the circle she had already gone round so often, and had returned to her former cause of irritation, she was horror-struck at herself 'Is it possible that I can't . . . ? Is it possible that I can't take it on myself?' she wondered, and began again from the beginning. 'He is truthful, he is honest. He loves me. I love him. In a few days I shall get my divorce. What more do I need? I need calm and confidence; and I will take the blame on myself. Yes, now, as soon as he comes back, I will tell him I was to blame, though in fact I was not, and we will go away!'

And not to continue thinking, and not to yield to irritation, she rang and ordered her trunks to be brought, to pack their things for the country.

At ten o'clock Vronsky returned.

Chapter XXIV

'Well, have you had a good time?' she asked, coming out to meet him with a meek and repentant look on her face.

'Just as usual,' he answered, perceiving at a glance that she was in one of her pleasant moods. He was already accustomed to these transitions, and to-day was specially glad, because he himself was in the best of spirits.

'What do I see? Ah, that's right!' he said, pointing to the trunks in the ante-room.

'Yes, we must go away. I went for a drive, and it was so lovely that I longed to be in the country. There isn't anything to keep you, is there?'

'It is my only wish. I'll come in a moment and we'll have a talk. I will only go and change. Order tea.'

And he went to his room.

There was something offensive in his saying: 'Ah, that's right!'— as one speaks to a child when it stops being capricious—and still more offensive was the contrast between her guilty tone and his self-confident one. For a moment she felt a desire to fight rising within her, but with an effort she mastered it and met him with her former cheerfulness.

When he returned she told him, partly repeating words she had prepared, how she had spent the day and her plans for the move to the country.

'Do you know, it came to me almost like an inspiration?' said she. 'Why must we wait here for the divorce? Won't it do just as well in the country? I can't wait any longer. I don't want to hope, I don't want to hear anything about the divorce. I have made up my mind that it shall not influence my life any more. Do you agree?'

'Oh yes!' he answered, looking uneasily at her excited face.

'Well, and what have you been doing? Who was there?' she asked after a pause.

Vronsky named the guests. 'The dinner was capital, the boat-races and everything quite nice, but in Moscow they can't get on without doing something ridiculous. . . . Some sort of a lady turned up—the Queen of Sweden's swimming instructress—and displayed her art.'

'What? She swam?' asked Anna, with a frown.

'Yes, in some sort of red *costume de natation* [6]—a hideous old creature! Well then, when are we to be off?'

'What an absurd fancy! And did she swim in some particular way?' asked Anna, without answering his question.

'Nothing particular at all. I said it was awfully absurd. . . . Well, when do you think of going?'

Anna shook her head, as though driving away an unpleasant thought.

'When are we going? Why, the sooner the better. We can't get ready by to-morrow; but the day after?'

'Yes. . . . No! Wait a bit! The day after to-morrow is Sunday, and I must go and see *maman*,' said Vronsky, and became confused, because as soon as he had mentioned his mother he felt an intent and suspicious gaze fixed upon him. His embarrassment confirmed her suspicions. She flushed and moved away from him. It was no longer the Queen of Sweden's instructress, but the Princess Sorokina who lived in the country near Moscow with the Countess Vronskaya who presented herself to Anna's imagination.

'You could go there to-morrow!' she said.

'No, I tell you! The power of attorney and money for the affair I am going there about will not have arrived by to-morrow,' he replied.

'If that's so, then we won't go at all!'

'But why not?'

'I won't go any later! Monday, or not at all.'

'Why's that?' said Vronsky, as if in surprise. 'There's no sense in that.'

'You see no sense in it because you don't care at all about me. You don't want to understand what my life is. The one person I was interested in here was Hannah—you say that is all pretence! You said yesterday that I don't love my daughter but pretend to love that English girl, and that it is unnatural! I should like to know what sort of life can be natural for me here!'

For a moment she recollected herself and was horrified at having broken her resolution. Yet though she knew she was ruining her cause, she could not restrain herself, could not forbear point-

6. Swimming costume.

ing out to him how wrong he was, and could not submit to him.

'I never said that; I only said that I do not sympathize with that sudden affection.'

'Why do you, who boast your truthfulness, not speak the truth?'

'I never boast and never tell untruths,' he said softly, restraining his rising anger. 'It is a great pity if you don't respect . . .'

'Respect was invented to fill the empty place where love ought to be! But if you no longer love me, it would be better and more honourable to say so!'

'Oh really! This is becoming unbearable!' exclaimed Vronsky, rising from his chair. And standing before her he slowly brought out: 'Why are you testing my patience?' He looked as if he could have said much more, but restained himself. 'It has its limits!'

'What do you mean by that?' she cried, glancing with terror at the definite expression of hatred on his whole face, and especially in the cruel, menacing eyes.

'I mean to say . . .' he began, but stopped. 'I must ask what you want of me!'

'What can I want? I can only want you not to abandon me, as you are thinking of doing,' she said, having understood all that he had left unsaid. 'But I don't want that, that is secondary. What I want is love, and it is lacking. Therefore all is finished!'

She moved toward the door.

'Stop! St-o-op!' said Vronsky, his brow still knit, but holding her back by the hand. 'What is the matter? I said we must put off our departure for three days, and you replied that I lie and am not an honourable man.'

'Yes! And I repeat that a man who reproaches me because he has given up everything for my sake,' said she, recalling the words of a still earlier quarrel, 'is worse than a dishonourable man! He is a heartless man!'

'No! There are limits to one's endurance,' he exclaimed, and quickly let go her hand.

'He hates me, that is clear,' thought she, and silently, without looking round and with faltering steps, she left the room. 'He loves another woman, that is clearer still,' she said to herself as she entered her own room. 'I want love, and it is lacking. So everything is finished!' she repeated her own words, 'and it must be finished.'

'But how?' she asked herself, and sat down in the arm-chair before the looking-glass.

Thoughts of where she would now go: to the aunt who had brought her up, to Dolly, or simply abroad by herself; of what *he* was now doing, alone in the study; of whether this quarrel was final or whether a reconciliation was still possible; of what all her former Petersburg acquaintances would say of her now; how Karenin would regard it; and many other thoughts about what would happen now after the rupture, passed through her mind, but she did not give herself up entirely to these thoughts. In her soul there was another vague idea, which alone interested her, but of which she could not get hold. Again remembering Karenin, she also remembered her illness after her confinement, and the feeling that never left her at that time. She remembered her words, 'Why did I not die?' and her feelings then. And suddenly she understood what was in her soul. Yes, that was the thought which would solve everything. 'Yes, to die! Alexey Alexandrovich's shame and disgrace, and Serezha's, and my own terrible shame—all will be saved by my death. If I die he too will repent, will pity me, will love me and will suffer on my account!' With a fixed smile of self-pity on her lips she sat in the chair, taking off and putting on the rings on her left hand, and vividly picturing to herself from various points of view his feelings after she was dead.

Sounds of approaching steps, his steps, distracted her thoughts. Pretending to be putting away her rings, she did not even turn round.

He came up to her, and taking her hand said softly:

'Anna, let us go the day after to-morrow, if you wish it. I will agree to anything.'

She remained silent.

'What is it?' he asked.

'You know yourself!' said she, and at the same moment, unable to restrain herself any longer, she burst into tears.

'Abandon me! Abandon me!' she murmured between her sobs. 'I will go away to-morrow. I will do more. . . . What am I? A depraved woman. A stone round your neck! I don't wish to torment you, I don't! I will set you free. You don't love me, you love some one else!'

Vronsky implored her to be calm, and assured her that there was not an atom of foundation for her jealousy, that he never had ceased, and never would cease, to love her, that he loved her more than ever.

'Anna, why torture yourself and me like this?' he said, kissing her hands. His face now wore a tender expression, and she thought she detected in his voice the sound of tears, and their moisture on her hand. And instantly her despairing jealousy changed into desperate, passionate tenderness. She embraced him, and covered his head, his neck, and his hands with kisses.

Chapter XXV

Feeling that they were entirely reconciled, next morning Anna began actively to make preparations for their move. Though it was not settled whether they would go on the Monday or on the Tuesday, as each the night before had yielded to the other's wish, Anna made all ready for their start, feeling now quite indifferent whether they went a day sooner or later. She stood in her room before an open trunk, sorting clothes, when he came in earlier than usual and ready-dressed.

'I will go to *maman* at once. She can send me the money through Egorov and I shall be ready to go to-morrow,' said he.

Good as the mood she was in might be, the reference to the move to the country pricked her.

'Oh no, I shall not be ready myself,' she said, and immediately thought: 'So it was possible to arrange things as I wished!—No, do as you wished to. Go to the dining-room, I will come directly. I will only sort out these things that are not wanted,' she said, placing some more articles on the heap of old clothes already piled up on Annushka's arms.

Vronsky was eating his beefsteak when she entered the dining-room.

'You would hardly believe how disgusting these rooms have become to me!' she said, sitting down to her coffee beside him. 'There is nothing worse than these furnished apartments! They are expressionless and soulless. This clock, the curtains, and, above all, the wall-papers are a nightmare! I think of Vozdvizhensk as of a Promised Land. You are not sending off the horses yet?'

'No, they will follow us. Are you driving out anywhere?'

'I wanted to go to the Wilsons, to take her a dress. So it is decided that we go to-morrow?' she said in a cheerful voice; but suddenly her face changed.

Vronsky's valet came in to fetch a receipt for a telegram from Petersburg. There was nothing odd in his receiving a telegram, but, as if wishing to hide something from her, he told the man that the receipt was in his study and hastily turned to her, saying:

'I shall certainly get everything ready to-morrow.'

'From whom was the telegram?' she asked, not listening to him.

'From Stiva,' he replied reluctantly.

'Why didn't you show it me? What secret can Stiva have from me?'

Vronsky called back the valet and told him to bring the telegram.

'I did not wish to show it you, because Stiva has a passion for telegraphing. What is the use of telegraphing when nothing has been settled?'

'About the divorce?'

'Yes, but he wires: "Could get no answer. Promises a decisive answer soon." But read it yourself.'

Anna took the telegram with trembling hands and saw exactly what Vronsky had said, but at the end were added the words:

'Little hope, but I'll do everything possible and impossible.'

'I said yesterday that it is all the same to me when I get the divorce, or even whether I get it at all,' she said, flushing. 'There was no need at all to conceal it from me.' And she thought: 'In the same way he may hide and is hiding from me his correspondence with women.'

'Oh, Yashvin wanted to come this morning with Voytov,' said Vronsky. 'It seems he has won from Pevtsov all and even more than Pevtsov can pay—about sixty thousand roubles.'

'But why do you imagine,' said she, irritated at his intimating to her so obviously, by this change of subject, that he saw she was losing her temper, 'that this news interests me so much that it is necessary to conceal it? I said that I don't want to think about it, and I wish that you were as little interested in it as I am.'

'It interests me because I like definiteness,' he replied.

'Definiteness depends not on forms, but on love,' said she, growing more and more irritated not at his words but at the tone of cool tranquillity with which he spoke. 'Why do you want it?'

'Oh God! Again about love!' he thought with a wry face.

'Don't you know why? For your own sake and for that of the children we may have!' said he.

'We shan't have any.'

'That's a great pity,' he said.

'You want it for the children, but you don't think of me,' she pursued, quite forgetting or not hearing that he said: 'for *your own* sake and for the children.'

The possibility of having children had long been a subject of dispute, and it irritated her. She explained his desire to have children as showing that he did not value her beauty.

'Oh, I said *for your sake*! Most of all for your sake,' he repeated, his face contorted as with pain, 'because I am convinced that a great deal of your irritability is due to our indefinite position.'

'Yes, there it is! Now he has stopped pretending, and all his cold hatred for me is apparent,' she thought, not listening to his words, but gazing with horror at the cold and cruel judge who looked out of his eyes provokingly.

'That is not the reason,' she said, 'and I can't even understand how what you call my "irritability" can be caused by that; I am entirely in your power. What indefiniteness of position is there? Quite the contrary!'

'I am very sorry you don't wish to understand me,' he interrupted, stubbornly intent on expressing his thought. 'The indefiniteness consists in your imagining that I am free.'

'You may be perfectly at rest on that matter!' she rejoined, and turning away she began to drink her coffee.

She took her cup, sticking out her little finger, and raised it to her mouth. After a few sips she glanced at him, and from the expression of his face clearly realized that her hand, her movement, and the sound made by her lips were repulsive to him.

'It is perfectly indifferent to me what your mother thinks and whom she wishes to marry you to,' she went on, putting down her cup with a trembling hand.

'But we are not talking about that.'

'Yes, about that very thing! And believe me, a heartless woman, be she old or young, your mother or a stranger, does not interest me and I don't want to have anything to do with her.'

'Anna, I beg you not to speak disrespectfully of my mother.'

'A woman whose heart has not divined wherein her son's happiness and honour lies has no heart!'

'I repeat my request that you should not speak disrespectfully of my mother, whom I respect!' said he, raising his voice and looking sternly at her.

She did not reply. Looking intently at his face and hands, she remembered their reconciliation the day before and his passionate caresses in all their details. 'Just such caresses he has lavished, and wants to lavish, on other women,' she thought.

'You don't love your mother! It's all words, words, words!' she said, looking at him with hatred.

'If that's so, we must . . .'

'Decide . . . and I have decided,' sne said and was about to go away, but just then Yashvin entered. Anna said 'Good morning,' and stopped.

Why, when a storm was raging within her and she felt that she was at a turning-point which might lead to terrible consequences —why she need, at that moment, dissemble before a stranger who sooner or later would know all about it, she did not know: but immediately calming the storm within her, she sat down again and began talking to the visitor.

'Well? How are your affairs? Has the money been paid?' she asked Yashvin.

'Oh, I don't know. I don't think I shall get it all, and on Wednesday I must go. And you?' asked Yashvin, looking at Vronsky with half-closed eyes and evidently divining that there had been a quarrel.

'The day after to-morrow, I believe,' replied Vronsky.

'But you have been meaning to go for a long time past?'

'Yes, but now it's decided,' said Anna, looking straight into Vronsky's eyes with an expression that told him he must not think of the possibility of a reconciliation.

'Is it possible you are not sorry for that unfortunate Pevtsov?'

she said, continuing her conversation with Yashvin.

'I never asked myself, Anna Arkadyevna whether, I am sorry or not. You see, my whole fortune is here,' and he pointed to a side pocket, 'and now I am a rich man but I shall go to the club to-night and shall perhaps leave it a beggar. You see, he who sits down to play against me, wishes to leave me without a shirt, and I treat him the same! So we struggle, and therein lies the pleasure!'

'But supposing you were married? How would your wife feel about it?' asked Anna.

Yashvin laughed.

'I expect that's why I never married, and never meant to.'

'How about Helsingfors?' said Vronsky, joining in the conversation, and he glanced at Anna who had smiled. Meeting his look, her face suddenly assumed a coldly severe expression, as if to say: 'It is not forgotten. It is still the same!'

'Is it possible you were ever in love?' she asked Yashvin.

'Oh heavens! How many times! But, you see, some men find it possible to sit down to cards and yet to be able always to leave when the time comes for an assignation! Now I can engage in love-making, but always so as not to be late for cards in the evening. That's how I manage.'

'No, I am not asking about that, but about the real thing.' She was going to say *Helsingfors*, but did not want to repeat the word Vronsky had used.

Voytov, who was buying a horse from Vronsky, arrived, and Anna rose and left the room.

Before leaving the house Vronsky came to her room. She wished to pretend to be looking for something on the table, but feeling ashamed of the pretence, looked straight into his face with a cold expression.

'What do you want?' she asked in French.

'Gambetta's certificate; I have sold him,' he replied in a tone which said more clearly than words: 'I have no time for explanations, and they would lead to nothing.'

'I am not at all in the wrong toward her,' he thought. 'If she wants to punish herself, *tant pis pour elle!*' [7] But, as he was going out, he thought she said something, and suddenly his heart ached with pity for her.

'What, Anna?'

'Nothing,' she answered, in the same cold quiet manner.

'If it's nothing, then *tant pis!*' he thought, again chilled. Turning away, he went out. As he was going out he caught sight in a looking-glass of her pale face and trembling lips. He even wished to stop and say a comforting word to her, but his legs carried him out of

7. So much the worse for her.

the room before he had thought of anything to say. All that day he spent away from home, and when he returned late at night the maid told him that Anna Arkadyevna had a headache and asked him not to go to her room.

Chapter XXVI

Never before had they been at enmity for a whole day. This was the first time it had been so, and this was not even a quarrel. It was an evident acknowledgment of complete estrangement. How could he look at her as he had looked when he came into the room for the certificate? Look at her, see that her heart was torn by despair, and go out in silence with that calmly indifferent look? Not only had he cooled toward her, but he hated her because he loved another woman—that was clear.

And recalling all the cruel words he had uttered, Anna invented other words which he evidently had wished to say and could have said to her, and she grew more and more exasperated.

'I do not hold you,' he might have said. 'You may go where you please. You probably did not wish to be divorced from your husband so that you could go back to him. Go back! If you need money, I will give you some. How many roubles do you want?' All the cruellest words that a coarse man could say, he, in her imagination, said to her, and she did not forgive him for them any more than if he had really said them.

'And was it not last night that he, an honourable and truthful man, swore he loved me? Have I not often before despaired needlessly?' she said to herself immediately after.

All that day, except when she went to the Wilsons—which took her about two hours—Anna passed in doubting whether all was over or whether there was still hope of a reconciliation, and whether she ought to leave at once or to see him again. She waited for him all day, and in the evening when she went to her room, having left word for him that she had a headache, she thought: 'If he comes in spite of the maid's message, it means that he still loves me. If not, it means that all is over, and then I will decide what I am to do . . . !'

At night she heard his carriage stop, heard him ring, heard his steps, and his voice talking to the maid. He believed what he was told, did not want to learn more, and went to his room! So all was over!

And death, as the sole means of reviving love for herself in his heart, of punishing him, and of gaining the victory in that contest which an evil spirit in her heart was waging against him, presented itself clearly and vividly to her.

Now it was all the same whether they went to Vozdvizhensk or not, whether she got a divorce or not—it was all useless. All she wanted was to punish him.

When she poured out her usual dose of opium and thought that she need only drink the whole phial in order to die, it seemed to her so easy and simple that she again began thinking with pleasure of how he would suffer, repent, and love her memory when it was too late. She lay in bed with open eyes, looking at the stucco cornice under the ceiling by the light of a single burnt-down candle, and at the shadow of the screen which fell on it, and she vividly imagined what he would feel when she was no more, when she was for him nothing but a memory. 'How could I say those cruel words to her?' he would say. 'How could I leave the room without saying anything? But now she is no more! She has gone from us for ever! She is there . . .' Suddenly the shadow of the screen began to move and spread over the whole of the cornice, the whole ceiling. Other shadows rushed toward it from another side; for an instant they rushed together, but then again they spread with renewed swiftness, flickered, and all was darkness. 'Death!' she thought. And such terror came upon her that it was long before she could realize where she was and with trembling hand could find the matches to light another candle in the place of the one that had burnt down and gone out. 'No—anything, only to live! Why, I love him! And he loves me! All this has been, but will pass,' she said, feeling that tears of joy at this return to life were running down her cheeks. And to escape from her fears, she hastily went to him in his study.

He was sleeping in the study and was sound asleep. She came up, and holding the light above him looked at him long. Now, when he was asleep, she loved him so that she could not restrain tears of tenderness while looking at him; but she knew that if he were to wake he would look at her with a cold expression, conscious of his own integrity, and that before telling him of her love she must prove to him that he was to blame toward her. Without waking him she returned to her room, and after a second dose of opium toward morning she fell into a heavy but troubled sleep, without ever ceasing to be conscious of herself.

In the morning a terrible nightmare, which had come to her several times even before her union with Vronsky, repeated itself and woke her. An old man with a tangled beard was leaning over some iron and doing something, while muttering senseless words in French; and as always in that nightmare (this was what made it terrible) she felt this peasant was paying no attention to her but was doing something dreadful to her with the iron. And she awoke in a cold perspiration.

When she got up, the previous day appeared in her memory as in a fog.

There had been a quarrel. It was what had happened several times before. 'I said I had a headache, and he did not come to see me. To-morrow we shall leave. I must see him and get ready for the move,' she thought. And hearing that he was in the study she went to him. As she passed through the drawing-room she heard a vehicle stop at the front door, and, looking out of the window, she saw a young girl in a lilac hat leaning out of the carriage window and giving an order to the footman who was ringing at the front door. After some talking in the hall, some one came upstairs and she heard Vronsky's step outside the drawing-room. He was going quickly downstairs. Again Anna went to the window. There he was on the steps, without a hat, going down to the carriage. The young girl in the lilac hat handed him a parcel. Vronsky said something to her and smiled. The carriage rolled away; he ran rapidly upstairs again.

The fog that had obscured everything within her was suddenly dissipated. Yesterday's feelings wrung her aching heart with fresh pain. She could not now understand how she could have humiliated herself so as to remain a whole day with him in his house. She went to his study to announce to him her decision.

'It was the Princess Sorokina with her daughter who came to bring me the money and documents from *maman*. I could not get them yesterday. How is your head—better?' he said quietly, not wishing to see or understand the gloomy and solemn look on her face.

She stood silent in the middle of the room, looking at him intently. He glanced at her, frowned for an instant, and continued to read a letter. She turned, and slowly moved from the room. He could still call her back, but she reached the door and he remained silent, and only the rustle of the paper as he turned a page was heard.

'Oh, by the way—' he said when she was already in the doorway—'we are definitely going to-morrow, aren't we?'

'You, but not I,' she said, turning round toward him.

'Anna, it is impossible to live like this . . .'

'You, but not I,' she repeated.

'This is becoming intolerable!'

'You . . . you will repent of this!' she said, and left him.

Alarmed by the despairing look with which she had said these words, he jumped up, intending to run after her, but, recollecting himself, he sat down again, tightly clenching his teeth and frowning. This—as it seemed to him—unbecoming and indefinite threat irritated him. 'I have tried everything,' he thought, 'the only thing left is to pay no attention,' and he began getting ready to drive to town, and to go again to his mother's to obtain her signature to a power of attorney.

She heard the sound of his steps in the study and dining-room. He paused at the drawing-room door. But he did not return to her; he only gave an order that they should let Voytov have the horse in his absence. Then she heard the carriage drive up and the door open, and he went out again. But now he re-entered the hall, and some one ran upstairs. It was his valet, who had come for the gloves his master had forgotten. She went back to the window and saw him take the gloves without looking, and, having touched the coachman's back with his hand, say something to him. Then, without turning to look up at the window, he sat down in the carriage in his usual posture, crossing one leg over the other, and, putting on a glove, disappeared round the corner.

Chapter XXVII

'Gone! Is it finished?' said Anna to herself as she stood by the window; and in answer to that question, the impressions left by the darkness when her candle went out and by the terrible dream, merging into one, filled her heart with icy horror.

'No, it is impossible!' she exclaimed and, crossing the room, she rang loudly. She was so terrified at being alone that she did not wait for the servant but went out to meet him.

'Find out where the Count has gone,' she said.

The man replied that the Count had gone to the stables.

'The Count told me to let you know that, in case you should wish to go out, the carriage will return very soon.'

'Very well. Wait a moment. I will just write a note. Send Michael with it to the stables at once. Quickly!'

She sat down and wrote:

'I was to blame. Come home. We must talk it over. For God's sake come; I am frightened.'

She stuck it down and gave it to the man.

Then, afraid to remain alone now, she followed him out of the room and went to the nursery.

'How is this? That's not it—this is not he! Where are his blue eyes and his sweet timid smile?' was her first thought on seeing her plump, rosy little girl with curly black hair, instead of Serezha, whom, in the disorder of her mind, she had expected to find in the nursery. The little girl, sitting at the table, persistently and firmly hammered on it with the stopper of a bottle, gazing blankly at her mother with her two black-currants of eyes. Having, in answer to the questions of the English nurse, said that she was quite well and that they were going to the country next day, Anna sat down beside the child and began twirling the stopper round in front of her. But the child's loud ringing laughter and a movement of her eyebrows reminded Anna so vividly of Vronsky, that, repressing her sobs, she rose hurriedly and left the room. 'Is it really all over? No, it cannot be,' she thought. 'He will come back. But how will he explain to me that smile, and his animation after he had spoken to her? But even if he does not explain it, I will believe him all the same. If I don't believe him, there is only one way left for me . . . and I don't want that.'

She looked at the clock. Twelve minutes had passed. 'Now he has received my note and is on his way back. It won't be long; another ten minutes. . . . But supposing he does not come? No, that's impossible! He must not find me with red eyes. I'll go and wash them. Oh! And did I brush my hair or not?' she asked herself; but could not remember. She felt her head with her hand. 'Yes, my hair was done, but I don't in the least remember when.' She did not even trust her hand, and went up to the mirror to see whether her hair really was done or not. It was, but she could not remember doing it. 'Who is that?' she thought, gazing in the mirror at the feverish, frightened face with the strangely brilliant eyes looking at her. 'Yes, that is I!' she suddenly realized, and looking at her whole figure she suddenly felt his kisses, shuddered, and moved her shoulders. Then she raised her hand to her lips and kissed it.

'What is it? Am I going mad?' and she went to her bedroom, where Annushka was tidying up.

'Annushka!' she said, stopping before the maid and looking at her, without knowing what she would say to her.

'You wished to go to see the Princess Oblonskaya,' said the maid, apparently understanding her.

'Darya Alexandrovna? Yes, I will go.'

'A quarter of an hour there, a quarter of an hour back; he is already on the way, he will be here in a minute.' She looked at her watch. 'But how could he go away leaving me in this condition? How can he go on living, without having made it up with me?' She went to the window and looked out into the street. He might have got back by this time; but her calculations might be incorrect, and again she began trying to remember when he had left, and reckoning the minutes.

Just as she was going to compare her watch with the large clock some one drove up. Glancing out of the window she saw his *calèche*. But no one came upstairs, and she heard voices below. Her messenger had returned in the carriage. She went down to him.

'I did not find the Count. He had gone to the Nizhny railway station,' he said.

'What do you want? What is this?' she asked the rosy, jolly-looking Michael, as he handed her back her note.

'Oh of course! He did not receive it,' she remembered.

'Go with this note to the Countess Vronskya's country house; do you know it? And bring back an answer at once,' she told the man.

'But what shall I do myself?' she thought. 'Yes, I will go to Dolly's, of course, or else I shall go out of my mind! And I can telegraph as well!' And she wrote out a telegram.

'*I must speak to you, come at once.*'

Having sent off the telegram, she went to dress. Ready-dressed and with her bonnet on, she again looked at Annushka's placid and now still rounder face. Evident compassion showed plainly in those kindly little grey eyes.

'Annushka, my dear! What am I to do?' muttered Anna sobbing, as she sank helplessly into an arm-chair.

'Why take it so to heart, Anna Arkadyevna? Such things will happen. Go out and get it off your mind,' advised the maid.

'Yes, I will go,' said Anna, recovering and rousing herself; 'and if a telegram comes during my absence, send it to Darya Alexandrovna's. . . . No, I'll come back myself.'

'But I must not think, I must do something, go away, get out of this house at any rate,' she said to herself, listening with horror to the terrible beating of her heart, and she hurriedly went out and got into the *calèche*.

'Where to, ma'am?' asked Peter, before getting onto the box.

'To the Oblonskys', on the Znamenka.'

Chapter XXVIII

The weather was bright. All the morning there had been a fine drizzling rain, but it had now just cleared up. The iron roofs, the pavement flag-stones, the cobbles of the road, the wheels, the leather, brass, and tin of the carriages—all shone brightly in the May sunshine. It was three o'clock, the busiest time in the streets.

Sitting in the corner of the comfortable *calèche*, which rocked gently on its elastic springs to the rapid trot of the pair of greys, Anna—amid the incessant rattle of wheels and the rapidly changing impressions in the open air—again going over the events of the last days, saw her position quite differently from what it had seemed at home. Now the idea of death no longer seemed so terrible and clear, and death itself no longer seemed inevitable. She reproached herself now with the humiliation to which she had descended. 'I entreated him to forgive me. I have surrendered to him. I have confessed that I am to blame. Why? Can I not live without him?' She began reading the signboards. ' "Office and Stores. . . . Dental surgeon. . . ." Yes, I will tell Dolly everything. She is not fond of Vronsky. It will be humiliating and painful, but I will tell her everything. She is fond of me and I will follow her advice. I won't submit to him; I won't let him educate me. . . . "Filippov, Bakery. . . ." It is said that they send dough to Petersburg. The Moscow water is so good. Oh, and the wells in Mytishchi, and the pancakes! . . .' And she remembered how, long, long ago, when she was only seventeen, she visited the Troitsa Monastery with her aunt. "We drove with horses, for there was then no railway. Can it really have been I, that girl with the red hands? How many things that then seemed to me excellent and unattainable have since become insignificant, and things that then existed are now for ever unattainable! Should I then have believed that I should descend to such humiliation? How proud and satisfied he will be to get my note! But I will show him . . . How nasty that paint smells! Why are they always painting and building? "Dress-making and Millinery," ' she read. A man bowed to her. It was Annushka's husband. 'Our parasite,' she remembered how Vronsky had said the words. 'Our? Why "our"? It is dreadful that one cannot tear out the past by the roots. We cannot tear it out, but we can hide the memory of it. And I will hide it!' At this point she recollected her past with Karenin and how she had effaced the memory of him. 'Dolly will think I am leaving a second husband and that I am therefore certainly unjustifiable. Do I want to be justified? I can't!' she said to herself, and wished to cry. But she immediately began to wonder what those two young girls could be smiling at. 'Love, probably! They don't know how far from joyous it is, how low . . . The boulevard and children. Three boys running about playing at horses. Serezha! And I shall lose everything and shan't get him back. Yes, I shall lose everything if he does not return. He may have missed the train and be back already. Wanting to humiliate yourself again!' she said to herself. 'No! I shall go to Dolly's, and will tell her frankly: "I am unhappy, I deserve it; I am guilty, but all the same I am unhappy. Help me!" . . . These horses, this carriage, how horrid it is of me to be in this carriage—they are all his, but I shall not see them any more.'

'Is anyone here?' she asked in the ante-room.

'Catherine Alexandrovna Levina,' answered the footman.

'Kitty! That same Kitty with whom Vronsky was in love,' thought Anna. 'She whom he remembered affectionately. He regrets not having married her. And of me he thinks with hate and regrets having joined himself to me!'

When Anna arrived the two sisters were consulting about feeding the baby. Dolly went out alone to meet the visitor who at that moment had come to interrupt their talk.

'So you have not left yet? I was myself coming to see you,' said Dolly. 'I had a letter from Stiva to-day.'

'We also had a telegram from him,' replied Anna, looking round for Kitty.

'He writes that he cannot understand what Alexey Alexandrovich really wants, but that he won't leave without getting an answer.'

'I thought you had a visitor. May I see the letter?'

'Yes, Kitty,' answered Dolly with embarrassment. 'She is in the nursery. She has been very ill.'

'I heard about it. May I see the letter?'

'I will fetch it at once. But he has not refused; on the contrary, Stiva is hopeful,' added Dolly, pausing at the door.

'I have no hope, and don't even desire it,' said Anna.

'What does it mean? Kitty considers it humiliating to meet me!' thought Anna when she was left alone. 'Maybe she is right. But it is not for her, who was in love with Vronsky—it is not for her to let me feel it, even if it is true! I know that no respectable woman can receive me in my position. I knew that from the first moment I sacrificed everything for him. And this is the reward! Oh, how I hate him! And why have I come here? It is still worse for me; it is harder than ever!' She heard the voices of the sisters conferring together in the next room. 'And what am I going to tell Dolly now? Console Kitty by letting her see that I am unhappy and letting her patronize me? No, and even Dolly would not understand. It is no use speaking to her. But it would be interesting to see Kitty and show her how I despise everybody and everything: how indifferent everything is to me.'

Dolly came back with the letter. Anna read and silently returned it.

'I knew it all,' she said, 'and it does not interest me in the least.'

'But why? I, on the contrary, am hopeful,' said Dolly, looking at Anna with curiosity. She had never seen her in such a strange and irritable mood. 'When are you leaving?' she asked.

Anna, screwing up her eyes, gazed straight before her without answering.

'Is Kitty hiding from me then?' she asked, looking toward the door and blushing.

'Oh, what nonsense! She is nursing her baby and has difficulty with it, and I was advising her. . . . She is very pleased. She will come directly,' Dolly said awkwardly, not knowing how to tell an untruth. 'Oh, here she is!'

When she heard that Anna had come Kitty did not wish to appear; but Dolly persuaded her. Having mustered up her courage, Kitty came in and, blushing, went up to Anna and held out her hand.

'I am very pleased—' she began in a trembling voice.

Kitty was confused by the struggle within her between hostility toward this bad woman and a desire to be tolerant to her; but as soon as she saw Anna's lovely and attractive face, all the hostility vanished at once.

'I should not have been surprised if you had not wanted to see me. I have got used to everything. You have been ill? Yes, you are changed!' said Anna.

Kitty felt that Anna looked at her with animosity. She attributed that animosity to the awkward position Anna, who had formerly patronized her, now felt herself to be in, and she was sorry for her.

They talked about Kitty's illness, about the baby, and about Stiva; but evidently nothing interested Anna.

'I came to say good-bye to you,' she said, rising.

'When are you leaving?'

But Anna again, without replying, turned to Kitty.

'Yes, I am very glad to have seen you,' she said with a smile. 'I have heard so much about you from everybody, and even from your husband. He called on me and I liked him very much,' she added, with obvious ill intent. 'Where is he?'

'He has gone to the country,' answered Kitty, blushing.

'Remember me to him; be sure you do!'

'I will be sure to,' repeated Kitty naïvely, looking compassionately into her eyes.

'Well then, good-bye, Dolly!' And kissing Dolly and pressing Kitty's hand, Anna hurried away.

'She is still the same and as attractive as ever. Charming!' said Kitty when she was once more alone with her sister. 'But there is something pathetic about her, terribly pathetic!'

'Yes, but to-day there is something peculiar about her,' said Dolly. 'When I was seeing her out, there in the ante-room, I thought she was going to cry.'

Chapter XXIX

Anna reseated herself in the *calèche* in a state of mind even worse than when she left home. To her former torments was now added a feeling of being affronted and repudiated, of which she had been clearly sensible during the meeting with Kitty.

'Where to, ma'am? Home?' asked Peter.

'Yes, home,' she said, now not even thinking of where she was going.

'How they looked at me, as at something dreadful, incomprehensible, and strange! . . . What can he be telling that other man so warmly?' she thought, glancing at two pedestrians. 'How is it possible to tell another what one feels? I meant to tell Dolly, but it's a good thing I didn't. How glad she would have been at my misfortune! She would have concealed it; but her chief feeling would have been joy that I am punished for the pleasures she has envied me. Kitty would have been still more pleased. How well I can read her! She knows I was more than usually amiable to her husband. She is jealous of me and hates me, and she also despises me. In her eyes I am an immoral woman. If I were immoral I could make her husband fall in love with me . . . if I wanted to. And I did want to. There is some one satisfied with himself!' she thought, seeing a fat ruddy man who was driving past in the opposite direction, and who, taking her for an acquaintance, lifted his shiny hat above his bald and shiny head, but then discovered that he was mistaken. 'He thought he knew me. But he knows me as little as does anyone else in the world. I don't even know myself! "I know my appetites," as the French say. Those boys want some of that dirty ice-cream; they know that for a certainty,' she thought, as she saw two boys stopping an ice-cream vendor, who lifted down a tub from his head and wiped his perspiring face with the end of the cloth. 'We all want something sweet and tasty; if we can get no bon-bons, then dirty ice-creams! And Kitty is just the same: if not Vronsky, then Levin. And she envies and hates me. And we all hate one another: Kitty me, and I Kitty! Now that is true. "*Tyutkin Coiffeur.*" . . . *Je me fais coiffer par Tyutkin.*[8] . . . I shall tell him that when he comes back,' she thought and smiled. But just then she recollected that now she had no one to tell anything funny to. 'Besides, there is nothing amusing or merry. Everything is nasty. They are ringing for vespers, and how carefully that tradesman is crossing himself, as if he were afraid of dropping something! What are those churches, that ringing, and these lies for? Only to conceal the fact that we all hate each other, like those cabmen who are so angrily swearing at one another. Yashvin says: "He wants to leave me without a shirt, and I him." Now that's true!'

With these thoughts, which occupied her so that she even forgot to think of her troubles, she arrived at the porch of their house. Only when she saw the hall-porter coming out to meet her did she remember that she had sent the note and the telegram.

'Is there an answer?' she asked.

'I will look,' he replied, and glancing at his desk he took up and handed her the thin square envelope of a telegram. 'I cannot return before ten—Vronsky,' she read.

'And the man has not yet returned?'

'No, ma'am,' answered the hall-porter.

'Well, in that case I know what I must do,' said she to herself, and conscious of a vague sense of wrath and a desire for vengeance rising within her, she ran upstairs. 'I shall go to him myself. Before quitting him for ever, I will tell him everything. I never hated anyone as I hate that man!' thought she. Seeing his hat on the hat-rail,

8. Hairdresser. I have my hair dressed by Tyutkin.

she shuddered with aversion. She did not realize that his telegram was in answer to hers and that he had not yet received her note. She imagined him now calmly conversing with his mother and the Princess Sorokina, and rejoicing at her sufferings. 'Yes, I must go at once,' she thought, not yet sure where to go to. She wished to get away as soon as possible from the feelings she experienced in that terrible house. The servants, the walls, the things in the house, all repelled and angered her, and oppressed her like a weight.

'Yes, I must go to the railway station, and if I don't find him, I must go *there* and expose him.' She looked at the time-table published in the daily paper. The train left at 8.20 p.m. 'I shall have time.' She gave the order to harness another pair of horses, and busied herself packing her handbag with things necessary for a few days. She knew she would not return. She vaguely resolved on one of the plans that passed through her mind. After what would occur at the railway station or at the Countess's estate she would go on by the Nizhni railway to the first town and remain there.

Dinner was served. She went to the table, smelt the bread and cheese and as the smell of everything eatable revolted her, she sent for the carriage and went out. The house already threw a shadow right across the street; the evening was bright, and the sun still warm. Annushka, who came out with Anna's things, and Peter, who put them into the carriage, and the coachman, who was evidently dissatisfied, were all objectionable to her and irritated her by their words and movements.

'I shan't need you, Peter.'

'But how about your ticket?'

'Well, as you like, I don't care,' she replied with annoyance.

Peter jumped up on the box, and with his arm akimbo told the coachman to drive to the station.

Chapter XXX

'There, again it is that girl! Again I understand it all,' Anna said to herself as soon as the carriage started and, rocking slightly, rattled over the stones; and again different impressions succeeded one another in her brain.

'What was the last thing I thought of that was so good?' She tried to remember it. ' "Tyutkin, Coiffeur"? No, not that. Oh yes! What Yashvin said: the struggle for existence and hatred are the only things that unite people. No, you are going in vain,' she mentally addressed a company of people in a *calèche* with four horses, who were evidently going out of town on a spree. 'And the dog you have with you won't help you! You can't escape from yourselves.' Glancing in the direction in which Peter was looking, she saw a workman, nearly dead-drunk, with his head swaying about, who was being led off somewhere by a policeman. 'That one is more likely to,' she thought. 'Count Vronsky and I have also been unable to find that pleasure from which we expected so much.' And now for the first time Anna turned the bright light in which she saw everything upon her relations with him, about which she had always avoided thinking. 'What did he look for in me? Not so much love as the satisfaction of his vanity.' She remembered his words, the expression of his face, suggestive of a faithful setter's, in the early days of their union. Everything now confirmed her view. 'Yes, there was in him the triumph of successful vanity. Of course there was love too; but the greater part was pride in his success. He boasted of me. Now that is past. There is nothing to be proud of. Not to be proud but to be ashamed! He has taken from me all he could, and now he does not need me. He is weary of me and is trying not to act dishonourably toward me. Yesterday he betrayed himself—he wants the divorce and a marriage in order to burn his boats. He loves me, but how? *The zest is gone!*' she said to herself in English. 'That man wants to astonish everybody and is very well satisfied with himself,' she thought, glancing at a rosy-faced shop-assistant who was riding a hired horse. 'No, I have no longer the right flavour for him. If I go away he will, at the bottom of his heart, be pleased.'

That was not a surmise. She saw it clearly in the piercing light which now revealed to her the meaning of life and of human relations.

'My love grows more and more passionate and egotistic, and his dwindles and dwindles, and that is why we are separating,' she went on thinking. 'And there is no remedy. For me everything centres in him, and I demand that he should give himself up to me more and more completely. But he wants more and more to get away from me. Before we were united we really drew together, but now we are irresistibly drifting apart; and it cannot be altered. He tells me I am unreasonably jealous, and I have told myself that I am unreasonably jealous; but it is not true. I am not jealous, but dissatisfied. But . . .' She opened her mouth and changed her place in the carriage from agitation produced by a sudden thought. 'If I could be anything but his mistress, passionately loving nothing but his caresses—but I cannot and do not want to be anything else. And this desire awakens disgust in him, and that arouses anger in me, and it cannot be otherwise. Don't I know that he would not deceive me, that he has no designs on that Sorokina, that he is not in love with Kitty, and will not be unfaithful to me? I know all that, but that does not make it easier for me. If, without loving me, he is kind and tender to me from a sense of duty, but what I desire is lacking—that would be a thousand times worse than anger! It would be hell! And that is just how it is. He has long ceased to love

me. And where love ceases, there hate begins. . . . I don't know
these streets at all. Here is a hill, and houses and houses. . . .
And in the houses are people, and more people. . . . There is no
end to them, and they all hate one another. Well, supposing I picture to myself what I want in order to be happy? Well, I get divorced, and Alexey Alexandrovich gives me Serezha, and I marry
Vronsky!' Remembering Karenin, she pictured him to herself with
extraordinary vividness as if he stood before her, with his mild, dull,
lifeless eyes, the blue veins of his white hands, his intonations, his
cracking fingers, and remembering the feeling that had once existed
between them and which had also been called love, she shuddered
with revulsion. 'Well, I get divorced and become Vronsky's wife!
What then? Will Kitty cease looking at me as she did this afternoon? No. Will Serezha stop asking and wondering about my two
husbands? And between Vronsky and myself what new feeling can
I invent? Is any kind—not of happiness even but of freedom from
torture—possible? No! No!' she now answered herself without the
least hesitation. 'It is impossible! Life is sundering us, and I am
the cause of his unhappiness and he of mine, and neither he nor I
can be made different. Every effort has been made, but the screws
do not act. . . . A beggar woman with a baby. She thinks I pity
her. Are we not all flung into the world only to hate each other, and
therefore to torment ourselves and others? There go schoolboys—
they are laughing. Serezha?' she remembered. 'I thought I loved
him, too, and was touched at my own tenderness for him. Yet I live
without him and exchanged his love for another's, and did not complain of the change as long as the other love satisfied me.' And she
thought with disgust of what she called 'the other love.' The clearness with which she now saw her own and every one else's life
pleased her. 'It's the same with me, and Peter and Theodore the
coachman, and with that tradesman, and with all the people that
live away there by the Volga where those advertisements invite one
to go, and everywhere and always,' she thought as she drove up to
the low building of the Nizhny station, where the porters ran out
to meet her.

'Shall I take a ticket to Obiralovka?' asked Peter.

She had quite forgotten where and why she was going, and only
understood the question by a great effort.

'Yes,' she said, giving him her purse; and hanging her little red
handbag on her arm, she descended from the carriage.

As she moved among the crowd toward the first-class waiting-
room she gradually recalled all the details of her position and the
resolutions between which she vacillated. And again hope and despair, alternately chafing the old sores, lacerated the wounds of her
tortured and violently fluttering heart. Sitting on the star-shaped

couch, waiting for her train, she looked with repulsion at those who passed in and out. They were all objectionable to her. She thought now of how she would reach the station and would write him a note, and of what she would write, and of how he was now (without understanding her sufferings) complaining of his position to his mother, and of how she would enter the room and what she would say to him. And then she thought how happy life might still be, and how tormentingly she loved and hated him and how dreadfully her heart was beating.

Chapter XXXI

The bell rang. [9] Some young men, ugly and bold-faced, passed by hurriedly and yet attentive to the impression they created. Peter, in his livery and gaiters, with his dull animal face, also crossed the room, and came to her to see her into the train. Two noisy men became quiet as she passed them on the platform, and one of them whispered to the other something about her: something nasty, of course. She mounted the high step of the railway carriage and seated herself in an empty compartment on the dirty—though once white—cover of the spring seat. Peter with a stupid smile raised his gold-braided hat to take leave of her; an insolent guard slammed the door to and drew the latch. A misshapen lady with a bustle (Anna mentally stripped that woman and was horrified at her deformity) and a girl, laughing affectedly, ran past outside.

'Catherine Andreevna has everything, *ma tante!*' cried the little girl.

'Quite a child, and yet already affected and pulling faces,' thought Anna. In order not to see anyone, she rose quickly and sat down by the opposite window of the empty compartment. A grimy, misshaped peasant in a cap from under which his tousled hair stuck out, passed that window, stooping over the carriage wheels. 'There is something familiar about that misshaped peasant,' she thought. And remembering her dream she went to the opposite door, trembling with fright. The guard opened it to let in a husband and wife.

'Do you wish to get out?'

Anna did not answer. Neither the guard nor those entering noticed the horror on her face beneath the veil. She went back to her corner and sat down. The couple sat down opposite her, attentively but stealthily examining her dress. Both the husband and the wife seemed to Anna disgusting. The husband asked if she would allow him to smoke, evidently not because he wanted to, but to enter into conversation with her. Having received her permission, he began speaking to his wife in French, about things he wanted to speak about still less than he wanted to smoke. They talked nonsense in-

9. At the departure of Russian trains, a bell was rung three times, at set intervals, to give passengers an idea of how imminent the departure was.

sincerely, only in order that she should hear them. Anna saw distinctly how weary they were of one another and how they hated each other. And it was impossible not to hate such ugly wretches.

She heard the second bell ring, and then a moving of luggage, noise, shouting and laughter. It was so clear to Anna that no one had any cause for joy that this laughter jarred on her painfully, and she wished to stop her ears, not to hear it. At last the third bell rang, the engine whistled and creaked, the coupling chains gave a jerk, and the husband crossed himself. 'It would be interesting to ask him what he means by it,' thought Anna, regarding him spitefully. She looked out of the window, past the lady, at the people on the platform who had been seeing the train off, and who appeared to be gliding backward. With rhythmic jerks over the joints of the rails, the carriage in which Anna sat rattled past the platform and a brick wall, past the signals and some other carriages; the sound of wheels slightly ringing against the rails became more rhythmical and smooth; the bright evening sunshine shone through the window, and a breeze moved the blind. Anna forgot her fellow-travellers; softly rocked by the motion of the carriage and inhaling the fresh air, she again began to think:

'Where did I leave off? At the point that I cannot imagine a situation in which life would not be a torment; that we all have been created in order to suffer, and that we all know this and try to invent means of deceiving ourselves. But when you see the truth, what are you to do?'

'Reason has been given to man to enable him to escape from his troubles,' said the lady, in French, evidently pleased with her phrase and mincing with her tongue.

These words seemed to answer Anna's thought.

'To escape from his troubles,' Anna mentally repeated. And glancing at the red-cheeked husband and his thin wife, she saw that the sickly wife considered herself misunderstood, and that the husband deceived her and encouraged her in her opinion of herself. Directing her searchlight upon them, Anna thought she saw their story and all the hidden recesses of their souls. But there was nothing of interest there, and she continued her reflections.

'Yes, it troubles me very much, and reason was given us to enable us to escape; therefore I must escape! Why not put out the candle, if there is nothing more to look at? If everything is repulsive to look at? But how? Why did that guard run past holding the handrail? Why are those young men in the next carriage shouting? Why are they talking and laughing? It's all untrue, all lies, all deception, all evil! . .'

When the train stopped at the station, Anna got out with the crowd of passengers, and shunning them as if they were lepers, stopped on the platform trying to remember why she had come there and what she had intended to do. Everything that had appeared possible before was now so difficult to grasp, especially in this noisy crowd of odious people who would not leave her in peace. Porters rushed up, offering their services. Young men passed along the platform, clattering their heels on the planks, talking loudly and gazing at her; and people she met tried to get out of her way on the wrong side. Recollecting that she meant to go on if there was no reply, she stopped a porter and asked him whether there was not a coachman bringing a note from Count Vronsky there.

'Count Vronsky? Some one from there was here just now, to meet the Princess Sorokina and her daughter. What is the coachman like?'

While she was talking to the porter, Michael the coachman, rosy and cheerful, came up in his smart blue coat with a watch-chain, evidently proud of having carried out his errand so well, and handed her a note. She opened it, and her heart sank even before she read it.

'Very sorry the note did not catch me. I shall be back at ten,' Vronsky wrote in a careless hand.

'Yes, I expected it!' she said to herself with a malicious smile.

'All right, you may go home,' she said softly to Michael. She spoke softly, because the rapid beating of her heart impeded her breathing. 'No, I will not let you torture me,' she thought, addressing her threat not to him nor to herself but to that which forced her to suffer, and she walked along the platform, past the station buildings.

Two maid-servants, strolling about on the platform, turned their heads to look at her, and made some audible remarks about her dress. 'It's real,' they said of the lace she was wearing. The young men did not leave her in peace. Gazing into her face and laughing and shouting unnaturally they again passed by. The station-master asked her in passing whether she was going on. A boy selling kvas fixed his eyes on her. 'O God! where am I to go?' she thought, walking further and further along the platform. She stopped at the end of it. Some ladies and children, who had come to meet a spectacled gentleman and were laughing and talking noisily, became silent and gazed at her as she passed them. She walked faster away from them to the very end of the platform. A goods train was approaching. The platform shook, and it seemed to her as if she were again in the train.

Suddenly remembering the man who had been run over the day she first met Vronsky, she realized what she had to do. Quickly and lightly descending the steps that led from the water-tank to the rails, she stopped close to the passing train. She looked at the bottom of the trucks, at the bolts and chains and large iron wheels of the slowly-moving front truck, and tried to estimate the middle point between the front and back wheels, and the moment when that point would be opposite her.

'There!' she said to herself, looking at the shadow of the car on the mingled sand and coal dust which covered the sleepers. 'There, into the very middle, and I shall punish him and escape from everybody and from myself!'

She wanted to fall half-way between the wheels of the front car, which was drawing level with her, but the little red handbag which she began to take off her arm delayed her, and then it was too late. The middle had passed her. She was obliged to wait for the next truck. A feeling seized her like that she had experienced when preparing to enter the water in bathing, and she crossed herself. The familiar gesture of making the sign of the cross called up a whole series of girlish and childish memories, and suddenly the darkness, that obscured everything for her, broke, and life showed itself to her for an instant with all its bright past joys. But she did not take her eyes off the wheels of the approaching second car, and at the very moment when the midway point between the wheels drew level, she threw away her red bag, and drawing her head down between her shoulders threw herself forward on her hands under the car, and with a light movement as if preparing to rise again, immediately dropped on her knees. And at the same moment she was horror-struck at what she was doing. 'Where am I? What am I doing? Why?' She wished to rise, to throw herself back, but something huge and relentless struck her on the head and dragged her down. 'God forgive me everything!' she said, feeling the impossibility of struggling. . . . A little peasant muttering something was working at the rails. The candle, by the light of which she had been reading that book filled with anxieties, deceptions, grief, and evil, flared up with a brighter light than before, lit up for her all that had before been dark, flickered, began to grow dim, and went out for ever.

Part VIII

Chapter I

Nearly two months had gone by. It was already the middle of the hot summer, but Sergius Ivanich Koznyshev was only now preparing to leave Moscow.

In Koznyshev's life during that time events of importance for him had taken place. His book, the result of six years' labour, entitled, *An Attempt to Review the Foundations and Forms of Government of Europe and Russia,* had been finished a year ago. Some parts of it and the introduction had appeared in periodicals, and other parts had been read by Koznyshev to people of his set, so that the ideas of the work could not be very novel to the public; but all the same Koznyshev expected that the publication of the book would create a serious impression on Society, and if not a revolution in science, at any rate a strong agitation in the scientific world.

The book had been issued last year after careful revision, and had been sent out to the booksellers.

Not asking anyone about it, reluctantly and with feigned indifference replying to his friends' inquiries as to how it was going, and not even asking the book-sellers how it was selling, Koznyshev watched keenly and with strained attention for the first impression his book would produce in Society and in literature.

But a week passed, and another, and a third, and no impression was noticeable in Society. His friends, the specialists and the scholars, sometimes—from politeness—mentioned it; his other acquaintances, not interested in learned works, did not mention it to him at all. In Society, now particularly occupied with something else, absolute indifference reigned. In the periodicals also, for a whole month, there had not been any mention of the book.

Koznyshev had calculated exactly the time necessary for a review to be written; but a month passed, and another, and the silence continued.

Only in the *Northern Beetle*, in a facetious feuilleton about the singer Drabanti who had lost his voice, were a few contemptuous remarks interpolated about Koznyshev's book, indicating that it had long ago been condemned by everybody and consigned to general ridicule.

At last, in the third month, a criticism appeared in a serious magazine. Koznyshev knew the author of the article. He had met him once at Golubkov's.

The author was a very young and sickly journalist; very bold as a writer, but extremely uneducated, and shy in personal intercourse.

Despite his entire contempt for this man, Koznyshev began reading the review most respectfully. The article was horrible.

The critic had evidently understood the book in an impossible way. But he had so adroitly selected his quotations that to those who had not read the book (and evidently hardly anyone had read it) it would appear quite clear that the whole book was nothing but a collection of high-sounding words, not even used appropriately (as was indicated by notes of interrogation), and that its author was a totally ignorant man. All this was put with so much wit that Koznyshev himself would not have been averse to wielding it; and that was what was dreadful.

Notwithstanding the thorough conscientiousness with which Koznyshev verified the correctness of the critic's arguments, he did not dwell for a moment on the deficiencies and mistakes which were ridiculed, but at once involuntarily began to recall his meeting and conversation with the author of the review, down to the minutest details.

'Did not I offend him in some way?' he asked himself.

And remembering how when he met him he had corrected the young man's use of a word that betrayed ignorance, Koznyshev found an explanation of the article.

That review was followed by dead silence both in print and in conversation concerning the book, and Koznyshev saw that his six years' work, carried out with so much devotion and labour, was entirely thrown away.

His position was the more painful because, having finished his book, he no longer had any literary work such as had previously occupied the greater part of his time.

He was intelligent, well-educated, healthy and active, but did not know how to employ his energy. Discussions in drawing-rooms, at meetings, at assemblies, in committees, and everywhere where one could speak, took up part of his time; but being an habitual town-dweller he did not allow himself to be entirely absorbed by discussions as his inexperienced brother did when he was in Moscow; so he had much superfluous leisure and mental energy.

Fortunately for him, at this most trying time after the failure of his book, in place of the questions of Schism, [1] our American friends, [2] the Samara Famine, [3] the Exhibitions, and Spiritualism, the Slavonic

---

1. 'Schism.' This refers to the Uniats of a Polish province, whose conversion to the Orthodox Russian Church was celebrated in 1875. It turned out that this conversion had been arranged by the local civil and ecclesiastical authorities under whose influence the necessary resolutions had been passed in the parishes. But the population ignored these resolutions and availed themselves of the services of migratory Uniat priests for their baptisms, marriages, and burials. This led to many prosecutions for apostasy being undertaken by the Orthodox Church, which in turn occasioned much discussion.

2. 'Our American friends.' A special mission arrived in Russia from the United States in July 1866 to congratulate Alexander II on his escape from Karakózov's attempts on his life, and to express gratitude for the moral support afforded by Russia to the Federal Government. (Russia had sent a squadron to America in 1863 during the Civil War, as a friendly gesture.) Captain Fox, the head of the mission, was received by Alexander II on July 27th in a triumphal audience, and in general the American delegates received an extremely warm welcome both from the government and from public organizations. The cordial relations between Russia and the United States continued to be a subjet of general interest for the next ten or twelve years.

3. 'The Samára Famine.' In June 1873 Tolstóy and his family visited a new estate he had bought in the Buzulúk district of Samára province. Interesting himself as he always did in the condition of the peasantry, he was appalled by the evidence he encountered of an approaching calamity. There had been a failure of crops for two years running, which had undermined the peasants' prosperity and exhausted all their reserves of grain stored up in former years. A drought that year destroyed the harvest, and the population, having no resources, was faced with famine. The local administration took no steps to meet the situation, and the country in general and

question[4]—which had previously only smouldered in Society—came to the front, and Koznyshev who had previously been one of the promoters of that cause devoted himself to it entirely.

Among the people to whom he belonged, nothing was written or talked about at that time except the Serbian war. Everything that the idle crowd usually does to kill time, it now did for the benefit of the Slavs: balls, concerts, dinners, speeches, ladies' dresses, beer, restaurants—all bore witness to our sympathy with the Slavs.

With much that was spoken and written on the subject Koznyshev did not agree in detail. He saw that the Slav question had become one of those fashionable diversions which, ever succeeding one another, serve to occupy Society; he saw that too many people took up the question from interested motives. He admitted that the papers published much that was unnecessary and exaggerated with the sole aim of drawing attention to themselves, each outcrying the other. He saw that amid this general elation in Society those who were unsuccessful or discontented leapt to the front and shouted louder than anyone else: Commanders-in-Chief without armies, Ministers without portfolios, journalists without papers, and party leaders without followers. He saw there was much that was frivolous and ridiculous; but he also saw and admitted the unquestionable and ever-growing enthusiasm which was uniting all classes of Society, and with which one could not help sympathizing. The massacre of our co-religionists and brother Slavs evoked sympathy for the sufferers and indignation against their oppressors. And the heroism of the Serbs and Montenegrins, fighting for a great cause, aroused in the whole nation a desire to help their brothers not only with words but by deeds.

Also there was an accompanying fact that pleased Koznyshev. It was the manifestation of public opinion. The nation had definitely

---

the central government did not even know anything about the threatened disaster, so utterly cut off was that outlying province of Samára. Tolstóy personally investigated the affairs of every tenth household in the village nearest to his estate and rode over the neighbouring districts for fifty miles round collecting detailed information. He then wrote a long letter vividly and convincingly depicting the disastrous situation. This was published in the *Moscow Védomosti*, and produced a great sensation, compelling the government to take action, besides attracting private contributions amounting to some two million roubles. The people were thus enabled to last out through that year, which was followed by two years of abundant harvests which fully set them on their feet again.

These events naturally supplied a topic of conversation even after the danger was over.

4. 'The Slavonic question.' The movement on behalf of the Slav nationalities which began at the time of the rising of Bosnia and Herzegovina against the Turks in 1875, and increased in 1876 with the revolt of the Bulgarians (suppressed by the 'Bulgarian atrocities') and with the outbreak of the Serbo-Turkish war, was acute at that time.

The movement was energetically promoted by the Panslav circles (J. S. Aksákov, Yuri Samárin, etc.) and its reactions were apparent in Russian society, producing among other things the 'volunteer movement'. Hundreds of Russians of all classes went to enlist in the Serbian Army, though being undisciplined they proved of little use on encountering trained Turkish troops. The movement as a whole induced the Russian Government to declare war on Turkey in 1877.

expressed its wishes. As Koznyshev put it, 'the soul of the nation had become articulate.' The more he went into this question, the clearer it seemed to him that it was a matter which would attain enormous proportions and become epoch-making.

He devoted himself completely to the service of that great movement and forgot to think about his book.

His whole time was now so taken up that he was unable to answer all the letters and demands addressed to him.

After working all through the spring and part of the summer, it was not till July that he prepared to go to his brother's in the country.

He went, both to enjoy a fortnight's rest, and—in that holy of holies of the people, the very heart of the country—to enjoy the sight of that uplift of the national spirit, of which he and all the town-dwellers were fully convinced. Katavasov, who had promised Levin to visit him, and had long been meaning to keep that promise, accompanied Koznyshev.

Chapter II

Hardly had Koznyshev and Katavasov reached the station, got out of their carriage, and looked for the footman who had followed with their luggage, before some Volunteers [5] drove up with four *izvozchiks*. The Volunteers were met by ladies who brought them nosegays and who, with the crowd that rushed after them, accompanied them into the station.

One of the ladies who had met the Volunteers spoke to Koznyshev at the exit from the waiting-room.

'You too have come to see them off?' she asked in French.

'No, Princess, I am going to my brother's for a rest. And do you always come to see them off?' he asked with a slight smile.

'How can one help it?' replied the Princess. 'Is it true that eight hundred have already gone from here? Malvinsky would not believe me.'

'More than eight hundred: counting those who did not go from Moscow direct, more than a thousand,' said Koznyshev.

'There now! I said so!' the lady said joyfully. 'And isn't it true that about a million roubles have been collected?'

'More than that, Princess.'

'And what a telegram there is to-day! They have beaten the Turks again!'

'Yes, I read it,' he answered. They were talking of the latest tele-

---

5. The period referred to is July 1876, when, after the Bulgarian atrocities, Serbia and Montenegro and Herzegovina were rising against Turkey. Many Russian Volunteers joined the insurgents, and eventually, in April 1877, Russia declared war to obtain autonomy or independence for the Christian provinces of Turkey.

gram, confirming the report that for three consecutive days the Turks had been beaten at all points and were in flight, and that a decisive battle was expected next day.

'Oh, I say! There is a splendid young man who wants to go. I don't know why they are making difficulties. I wished to speak to you about him. I know him, please write a note for him! He was sent by the Countess Lydia Ivanovna.'

Having obtained such details as the Princess could give about the young petitioner, Koznyshev went into the first-class waiting-room, wrote a note to the person on whom the decision depended, and gave it to the Princess.

'Do you know that the notorious Count Vronsky is going by this train?' remarked the Princess with a triumphant and significant smile, when Koznyshev had found her again and given her the note.

'I heard he was going, but did not know when. Going by this train?'

'I have seen him. He is here. Only his mother is seeing him off. After all, it is the best thing he could do.'

'Oh yes, certainly.'

While they were speaking the crowd rushed past them toward the dining-table. They too moved on, and heard the loud voice of a man who, with a glass in his hand, was making a speech to the Volunteers: 'To serve the Faith, humanity, and our brothers!' said the gentleman, raising his voice more and more. 'Mother Moscow blesses you in the great undertaking! *Zhivio!* [6] he concluded in a loud and tearful voice.

Every one shouted '*Zhivio!*' and a fresh crowd surged into the refreshment-room, nearly knocking the Princess off her feet.

'Ah, Princess! What do you think of that!' said Oblonsky, beaming with a joyous smile, as he suddenly appeared in the midst of the crowd. 'Wasn't it finely and cordially expressed! Bravo! . . . And Sergius Ivanich! Now, you should say something, so that . . . just a few words, you know, of encouragement; you do it so well,' he added with an affectionate, respectful and solicitous smile, gently pushing Koznyshev forward by the arm.

'No, I am just going.'

'Where to?'

'To my brother's in the country,' answered Koznyshev.

'Then you'll see my wife; I have written to her, but you'll see her sooner. Please tell her you have seen me and it's *all right!* She will understand. However, tell her, if you'll be so kind, that I am appointed Member of the Committee of the Joint . . . But she will understand! You know, *les petites misères de la vie humaine,* [7] he

6. Serbian: Hail!
7. The little miseries of human life.

said to the Princess, as if to excuse himself. 'And the Princess My-agkaya, not Lisa but Bibish, is really sending a thousand rifles and twelve nurses! Did I tell you?'

'Yes, I have heard,' replied Koznyshev reluctantly.

'What a pity you are going away,' said Oblonsky. 'To-morrow we are giving a dinner to two of those who are going to the war: Dmitry Bartnyansky from Petersburg and our Veslovsky—Vasenka. They are both going. Veslovsky married recently. A fine fellow! Isn't he, Princess?' he added, turning to the lady.

The Princess without replying glanced at Koznyshev. But the fact that Koznyshev and the Princess seemed to wish to get rid of him did not abash Oblonsky in the least. He looked smilingly now at the feather on the Princess's bonnet and now about him, as if trying to remember something. Noticing a lady with a collecting-box he beckoned to her and put in a five-rouble note.

'I can't look calmly at those collecting-boxes while I have any money,' he remarked. 'And what a telegram that was to-day! Fine fellows, those Montenegrins!'

'You don't say so!' he exclaimed, when the Princess told him that Vronsky was going by that train. For a moment Oblonsky's face looked sad, but a minute later when, with a slight spring in his step and smoothing his whiskers, he entered the waiting-room where Vronsky was, Oblonsky had quite forgotten how he had sobbed with despair over his sister's corpse, and he saw in Vronsky only a hero and an old friend.

'With all his faults one must do him justice,' the Princess said to Koznyshev as soon as Oblonsky had left them. 'His is a thoroughly Russian, Slavonic nature! Only I'm afraid it will be painful for Vronsky to see him. Say what you will, that man's fate touches me. Have a talk with him on the journey,' said the Princess.

'Yes, I might if opportunity offers.'

'I never liked him. But this atones for much. Not only is he going himself, but he is taking a whole squadron at his own expense.'

'So I heard.'

The bell rang. Everybody thronged toward the door.

'There he is!' said the Princess, pointing to Vronsky who, in a long overcoat and a black broad-brimmed hat, was passing with his mother on his arm. Oblonsky walked beside him, talking with ani-mation.

Vronsky was frowning and looking straight before him, as if not hearing what Oblonsky was saying.

Probably at Oblonsky's indication, he looked round to where Koznyshev and the Princess were standing and silently raised his hat. His face, which was aged and full of suffering, seemed petrified.

Coming up to the train, Vronsky, letting his mother pass before him, silently disappeared into one of the compartments.

On the platform 'God save the Tsar' was struck up, followed by 'hurrah' and '*zhivio*'! One of the Volunteers, a tall, hollow-chested, very young man, was bowing in a specially noticeable way, waving over his head a felt hat and a bouquet. From behind him two officers and an elderly man with a large beard and a greasy cap thrust their heads out, and also bowed.

Chapter III

Having taken leave of the Princess, Koznyshev with Katavasov, who had joined him, entered the very crowded carriage, and the train started.

At the Tsaritsyno station the train was met by a melodious choir of young people singing *Slavsya*.[8] Again the Volunteers bowed and thrust their heads out, but Koznyshev did not pay attention to them: he had had so much to do with Volunteers that he was already familiar with their general type and it did not interest him. Katavasov, however, whose scientific occupations had offered him no opportunities of studying the Volunteers, was much interested in them and questioned Koznyshev about them.

Koznyshev advised him to go into the second-class carriage and have a talk with some of them. At the next station Katavasov followed this advice.

As soon as the train stopped he changed carriages and made acquaintance with the Volunteers. They were sitting in a corner talking loudly, evidently aware that the attention of their fellow-passengers and of Katavasov, who had just entered, was directed toward them. The tall, hollow-chested young man talked louder than any of them. He was evidently drunk, and was speaking of something that had happened at his school. Opposite him sat an officer, no longer young, wearing a military jacket of the Austrian Guards. He listened smilingly to the young man and tried to stop him. The third Volunteer, wearing an artillery uniform, sat beside them on a trunk. A fourth one was asleep.

Getting into conversation with the young man, Katavasov learnt that he had been a rich Moscow merchant but had run through a large fortune before he was twenty-two. Katavasov did not like him because he was effeminate, spoilt, and delicate; he was evidently sure, especially now that he was tipsy, that he was performing an heroic deed, and he bragged most unpleasantly.

The second, the retired officer, also made an unpleasant impression on Katavasov. He was, apparently, a man who had tried everything. He had had a post on the railway, been a steward, and had started factories, and he talked about it all quite needlessly, using

8. A patriotic song.

inappropriate technical terms.

But Katavasov liked the third, an artilleryman, very much. He was a modest, quiet man, who evidently deferred to the knowledge of the retired Guardsman and to the heroic self-sacrifice of the merchant and did not talk at all about himself. When Katavasov asked him what prompted him to go to Serbia, he modestly replied:

'Well, everybody is going. One must help the Serbs. One's sorry for them.'

'Yes, it's particularly artillerymen they are short of,' said Katavasov.

'But I have not served long in the artillery: perhaps they will put me in the infantry or cavalry.'

'Why into the infantry, when they need artillerymen most of all?' said Katavasov, concluding from the artilleryman's age that he must have risen to a considerable rank.

'I did not serve in the artillery long. I am a retired Cadet,' he said, and began to explain why he had not passed the examination for a commission.

All this put together produced on Katavasov a disagreeable impression, and when the Volunteers got out at a station to have a drink he wished to verify this unfavourable impression by a talk with somebody. One of the passengers, an old man in a military overcoat, had been listening all the time to Katavasov's conversation with the Volunteers. When they were left alone together Katavasov addressed him.

'What a variety there is in the positions of all these men who are going there!' Katavasov remarked vaguely, wishing to express his own opinion but at the same time to draw the old man.

The old soldier had been through two campaigns. He knew what a military man ought to be, and by the appearance and talk of those men, and by the swagger with which they applied themselves to their flasks on the way, he considered them bad soldiers. Besides that, he lived in a provincial town and wanted to speak of a discharged soldier of his town who had volunteered, a drunkard and thief whom no one would employ any longer. But, knowing by experience that in the present state of public feeling it was dangerous to express any opinion contrary to the prevailing one, and especially dangerous to censure the Volunteers, he also watched Katavasov.

'Well, men are wanted there,' he said, with laughing eyes. And they began talking about the latest war news, each concealing from the other his perplexity as to whom to-morrow's battle was to be with, since the Turks, according to the latest intelligence, had been beaten at all points. And so they parted without either of them having expressed his opinion.

Katavasov returning to his carriage involuntarily prevaricated; and in telling Koznyshev his observations of the Volunteers, let it appear that they were excellent fellows.

At the station of a big town the Volunteers were again greeted with songs and cheers; again women and men turned up with collecting-boxes, the provincial ladies presented nosegays and accompanied the Volunteers to the refreshment-bar; but all this was far feebler and weaker than in Moscow.

Chapter IV

When the train stopped at the Provincial capital, Koznyshev, instead of going to the refreshment-room, walked up and down the platform.

The first time he passed the Vronskys' compartment he noticed that the blind was down. But the next time he passed he saw the old Countess at the window. She beckoned to him.

'You see I am going with him as far as Kursk,' said she.

'Yes, so I heard,' replied Koznyshev, stopping by her window and glancing inside. 'What a fine action this is of his!' he added, noticing that Vronsky was not there.

'Yes, but after his misfortune what could he do?'

'What a dreadful occurrence!' remarked Koznyshev.

'Oh, what I have endured! But come in. . . . Oh, what I have endured!' she repeated when Koznyshev had entered and taken a seat beside her. 'You cannot imagine it! For six weeks he spoke to no one and ate only when I implored him to. One could not leave him a moment alone. We took away everything that he could kill himself with. We lived on the ground floor, but one could not tell what he might do. You know he had once before shot himself on her account?' she said, and the old woman's brows knit at the recollection. 'Yes, she ended as such a woman deserved to end. Even the death she chose was mean and vulgar.'

'It is not for us to judge, Countess,' Koznyshev remarked with a sigh, 'but I understand how distressing it was for you.'

'Oh, don't speak of it! I was living on my estate and he was with me. A note was brought. He wrote an answer and sent it off. We had no idea that she was herself there at the station. In the evening I had only just gone to my room when my Mary told me that at the station a lady had thrown herself under a train. I felt as if I had received a blow!—I knew it was she! The first thing I said was: "Don't tell him!" But he had already been told. His coachman had been there and saw it all. When I ran to his room he was beside himself—it was terrible to see him. He did not say a word, but off he galloped to the station. I don't know what happened there, but they brought him back like a corpse. I should not have known him. *"Prostration complète,"* the doctor said. Then came raving mad-

ness, almost! . . . Ah, one can't speak of it!' exclaimed the Countess with a gesture of her arm. 'A terrible time! No, say what you
will, she was a bad woman. Such desperate passions! Only to prove
something unusual. Well, she proved it! She ruined herself and two
splendid men—her husband and my unfortunate son.'

'And how about her husband?' inquired Koznyshev.

'He took her little girl. Alexey at first agreed to everything. But
now he is greatly distressed at having given up his daughter to a
stranger. But he can't go back on his word. Karenin came to the
funeral; but we tried to arrange so that he and Alexey should not
meet. For him, the husband, it is better. She has set him free. But
my poor son had given himself up to her entirely. He had thrown
up everything—his career, me; and then she did not even pity him,
but deliberately dealt him a deathblow. No, say what you will, her
death itself was the death of a base woman, without religion. God
forgive me! I cannot help hating her memory when I see my son's
ruin!'

'But how is he now?'

'It is a God-sent help for us, this Serbian war! I am an old woman
and understand nothing about it, but for him it is a godsend. Of
course I, as his mother, fear for him; and above all I hear that
ce n'est pas très bien vu à Pétersburg.[9] But it can't be helped! It was
the only thing that could rouse him. His friend, Yashvin, had lost
everything at cards and was going to Serbia. He came to see him and
persuaded him to go. Now it interests him. Please have a talk with
him. I want him to have some distraction. He is so sad. Unluckily,
too, his teeth have started aching. But he will be very glad to see
you. Please have a talk with him. He is walking about on the other
side.'

Koznyshev said he would be very pleased, and crossed over to the
other platform.

Chapter V

In the slanting shadow of a pile of sacks heaped up on the platform, Vronsky, in a long overcoat, his hat pulled down low and his
hands in his pockets, was walking up and down like an animal in a
cage, turning sharply every twenty paces. To Koznyshev as he approached it seemed that Vronsky saw but pretended not to see him.
But Koznyshev did not care. He was above any personal considerations with Vronsky.

In his eyes Vronsky at that moment seemed an important worker
in a great cause, and Koznyshev considered it his duty to encourage
and cheer him. He went up to him.

Vronsky paused, looked at Koznyshev, recognized him, and ad-

9. It is not very favourably regarded in Petersburg.

vancing a few steps to meet him, pressed his hand very very hard.

'Perhaps you did not wish to see me,' said Koznyshev, 'but can I not be of some use to you?'

'There is no one whom it would be less unpleasant for me to meet than yourself,' returned Vronsky. 'Excuse me. There is nothing that is pleasant in life for me.'

'I understand, and I wanted to offer you my services,' said Koznyshev, gazing into Vronsky's face, which bore evident signs of suffering. 'Do you not want a letter to Ristich [1] or to Milan [2] ?'

'Oh no!' replied Vronsky, as if it cost him an effort to understand. 'If you don't mind, let us walk up and down. It is so stuffy in the carriage. A letter? No, thank you. No introductions are needed to enable one to die! Unless indeed to the Turks! . . . ' he added, smiling with his lips only. His eyes retained their expression of angry suffering.

'Yes, but it may be easier for you to establish connections (which will be necessary anyway) with some one who has been prepared. However, as you please. I was very glad to hear of your decision. The Volunteers are being very much attacked and a man like yourself will raise them in public opinion.'

'As a man I have this quality, that I do not value my life at all and that I have physical energy enough to hack my way into a square and slay or fall—that I am sure of. I am glad that there is something for which I can lay down the life which I not only do not want, but of which I am sick! It will be of use to somebody,' and he moved his jaw impatiently because of the incessant gnawing pain in his tooth, which even prevented him from speaking with the expression he desired.

'You will recover, I prophesy it,' said Koznyshev, feeling touched. 'To free one's brothers from oppression is an aim worth both dying and living for. God grant you outward success and inward peace,' he added, holding out his hand.

Vronsky grasped the hand warmly.

'Yes, as a tool I may be of some use. But as a man I—am a ruin!' said he, pausing between the words.

The acute pain in the strong tooth, filling his mouth with saliva, hindered his speaking. He remained silent, gazing at the wheels of the approaching tender, which was slowly and smoothly gliding over the rails.

Suddenly a quite different feeling, not of pain but of tormenting inward discomfort, made him for a moment forget his toothache.

---

1. Jovan Rístich, a prominent Serbian statesman. At the time of the Serbo-Turkish war in 1876 he was Minister of Foreign Affairs and directed Serbian politics in a Russophil direction.
2. Though the proposed proclamation of Milan Obrenovič as King of Serbia was already spoken of at that time, it did not actually take place till 1882. In 1889 he had to resign the crown and leave the country.

At the sight of the tender and the rails, and under the influence of conversation with some one he had not met since the catastrophe, he suddenly remembered *her*; that is, remembered what was left of her when, like a madman, he ran into the railway shed where on a table, stretched out shamelessly before the eyes of strangers, lay the mangled body still warm with recent life. The head, left intact, with its heavy plaits and the curls round the temples, was thrown back; and on the lovely face with its half-open red lips was frozen an expression—pitiful on the lips and horrible in the fixed open eyes—an expression which repeated, as if in words, the terrible phrase about his repenting it—which she had uttered during their quarrel.

He tried to remember her as she was when he had met her the first time—also at a railway station—mysterious, charming, loving, seeking and giving joy, and not cruelly vindictive as he remembered her at the last. He tried to recall his best moments with her, but they were for ever poisoned. He could think of her only as triumphant, having carried out the threat of inflicting on him totally useless but irrevocable remorse. He ceased to feel the pain in his tooth, and sobs distorted his face.

Having twice walked past the sacks and mastered himself, he turned calmly to Koznyshev:

'You have not seen any telegram later than yesterday's? Yes, they have been beaten a third time, but a decisive battle is expected tomorrow.'

And having spoken about the proposed proclamation of Milan as King and of the immense results this might have, they returned to their respective carriages after the second bell had already sounded.

Chapter VI

As he had not known when he would be able to leave Moscow, Koznyshev had not sent a telegram to his brother asking to be met at the station, and Levin was not at home when, toward noon, Katavasov and Koznyshev, dark as Arabs with the dust in the little *tarantas* they had hired at the station, drew up at the porch of the Pokrovsk house. Kitty, who was sitting on the balcony with her father and sister, recognized her brother-in-law and ran down to meet him.

'Aren't you ashamed of yourself for not letting us know?' she said, holding out her hand to him and offering her forehead for a kiss.

'We got here first-rate without troubling you,' replied Koznyshev. 'I am so dusty that I dare not touch you. I was so busy that I did not know when I could tear myself away. And you, as usual,' said he, smiling, 'are enjoying tranquil happiness beyond the current in your peaceful backwater. And here is our friend, Theodore Vasilyevich, who has come at last.'

'But I am not a Negro! When I have had a wash I shall look like a human being!' Katavasov said in his usual jesting way, holding out his hand and smiling, his teeth looking particularly bright in contrast with his black face.

'Kostya will be so pleased! He has gone to the farm. It is time he was back.'

'Always busy with his husbandry! "In the backwater" hits it exactly,' remarked Katavasov. 'And we in town can see nothing but the Serbian war! Well, and what does my friend think of it? Surely not the same as other people?'

'Oh, nothing in particular—the same as everybody,' Kitty answered, rather embarrassed and glancing round at Koznyshev. 'Well, I'll send for him. Papa is staying with us. He has not long returned from abroad.'

And having arranged that Levin should be sent for and that the dusty visitors should be shown where to wash—one of them in Levin's study and the other in Dolly's former room—and about lunch for them, Kitty, exercising the right of moving quickly of which she had been deprived during pregnancy, ran up the balcony stairs.

'It's Sergius Ivanich and Katavasov, the Professor,' said she.

'Oh, how trying in this heat!' said the Prince.

'No, Papa, he is very nice, and Kostya is very fond of him,' Kitty replied with a smile as of entreaty, having noticed a sarcastic expression on her father's face.

'I don't mind.'

'You go and entertain them, dear,' Kitty said to her sister. 'They met Stiva at the station, he is quite well. And I will run to Mitya. As ill-luck will have it I have not fed him since breakfast. He will be awake now and is certainly screaming.' And feeling the flow of milk, she went with rapid steps to the nursery.

It was not a mere guess—the bond between herself and the baby had not yet been severed—and she knew surely by the flow of milk within herself that he was wanting food.

She knew he was screaming before she reached the nursery. And so he was. She heard his voice and increased her speed. But the faster she went the louder he screamed. It was a fine healthy voice, only hungry and impatient.

'Has he been screaming long, Nurse? Long?' she asked hurriedly, sitting down and preparing to nurse the baby. 'Be quick and give him to me! Oh, Nurse! How tiresome you are; come, you can tie up his cap afterwards!'

The baby was convulsed with hungry yells.

'But one must, you know, ma'am,' said Agatha Mikhaylovna, who was almost always in the nursery. 'He must be properly tidied up! Goo! Goo!' she cooed to him, paying no attention to the mother.

The nurse brought the baby to his mother, and Agatha Mikhaylovna followed behind, her face softened with tenderness.

'He knows me, he does! It's God's truth, Catherine Alexandrovna, dear, he knows me!' cried Agatha Mikhaylovna, raising her voice above the baby's.

But Kitty did not listen. Her impatience was increasing with the baby's.

As a result of their impatience matters were long in getting settled. The baby got hold in the wrong place and was angry.

At last, after desperate screaming and choking, matters went smoothly, and both mother and child felt calmed and were silent.

'But he too, poor mite, is all in a perspiration,' whispered Kitty, feeling him with her hand. 'Why do you think he knows you?' she added, moving her eyes so as to see the baby's. They looked roguishly at her, she thought, from beneath his cap, which had slipped forward, and she watched the rhythmical rise and fall of his cheeks and the little hand with the rosy palm making circular movements.

'It's impossible! If he knew anyone it would be me,' Kitty replied to Agatha Mikhaylovna's statement, and smiled.

She smiled because, though she said it was impossible for him to know, she was sure in her heart that he not only knew Agatha Mikhaylovna, but that he knew and understood everything, even many things that no one else knew, and which she, his mother, had learnt to know and understand through him. For Agatha Mikhaylovna, for the nurse, for his grandfather and even for his father, Mitya was a living being requiring only material care; but for his mother he had already long been a moral being, with whom she had already had a long series of spiritual relations.

'Well, wait till he wakes up and you will see for yourself. When I do like that, he quite brightens up, the dear! He brightens up like a sunny morning,' said Agatha Mikhaylovna.

'Well, all right, all right! We shall see,' Kitty whispered. 'But now go away, he is falling asleep.'

Chapter VII

Agatha Mikhaylovna went out on tiptoe; the nurse pulled down the blind, drove away the flies from under the muslin curtain of the cot and also a bumble-bee that was buzzing against the window-pane, and sat down, waving a birch branch above the mother and child.

'Oh, the heat! the heat! . . . If God would only send a little rain!' she said.

'Yes, yes! Hush! . . .' was all Kitty answered as she sat softly rocking herself and tenderly pressing the little plump arm, which looked as if a thread had been tied round the wrist, and was still feebly waving while Mitya kept shutting and opening his eyes. This hand disturbed Kitty; she wanted to kiss it, but was afraid to do so lest she would wake her baby. At last the arm ceased waving and the eyes closed. Only now and then the baby, continuing his business, lifted his long curved lashes and looked at his mother with moist eyes that seemed black in the dim light. The nurse stopped waving the branch and began to doze. From upstairs was heard the roll of the Prince's voice and of Katavasov's laughter.

'I expect they've got into conversation in my absence,' thought Kitty, 'but all the same it's provoking that Kostya is away. I expect he has gone to the apiary again. Though I am sorry that he goes there so often, yet I am also glad of it. It is a distraction for him. He is more cheerful now than he was in spring. Then he was so gloomy, and suffered so much, that I was becoming alarmed about him. And how funny he is!' she whispered with a smile.

She knew what was tormenting her husband. It was his want of faith. Although had she been asked whether she thought that if he did not believe in the future life he would perish, she would have had to acknowledge that he would, yet his lack of faith did not make her unhappy; and she, who accepted the doctrine that salvation was impossible for an unbeliever, while loving her husband's soul more than anything in the world, smiled when she thought of his disbelief and called him funny.

'Why has he been reading those philosophies for a whole year?' she thought. 'If it's all written in those books, he can understand it. If what they say is untrue, why read them? He says himself that he would like to believe. Then why does he not believe? It must be because he thinks too much. And he thinks too much because of his solitude. He is always alone, alone. He can't talk to us about everything. I think he will be glad of these visitors, especially of Katavasov. He likes arguing with them,' she reflected, and then turned her mind to the problem of where she had better arrange for Katavasov to sleep—in a separate room or with Koznyshev? And here a thought suddenly struck her which made her start with excitement and even disturb Mitya, who gave her a severe look in consequence. 'I don't think the laundress has brought the things back and the spare sheets are all in use. If I don't see to it, Agatha Mikhaylovna will give Sergius Ivanich used bed-linen!' and the very thought of this sent the blood into Kitty's face.

'Yes, I must see about it,' she decided, and returning to her former train of thought she remembered that there was something important, something spiritual, that she had not yet thought out and tried to recollect what it was. 'Oh yes! Kostya is an unbeliever,' she thought again with a smile.

'Well, he is an unbeliever! Better let him be that, than be like Madame Stahl, or like what I wanted to be when I was abroad. No, he will never pretend.'

Then a recent proof of his kindness came vividly to her mind. Two weeks before, Dolly had received a penitent letter from her husband. He implored her to save his honour and to sell her estate to pay his debts. Dolly was in despair; she hated her husband, despised him, pitied him, made up her mind to divorce him and to refuse; but ended by consenting to sell part of her estate. With an involuntary smile of emotion, Kitty remembered her own husband's shamefacedness after that, and his repeated awkward attempts to approach the subject he had on his mind, and how at length, having discovered the only way of helping Dolly without offending her, he suggested to Kitty that she should give her sister her own part of the estate, a device that had not occurred to her.

'How can he be an unbeliever with such a heart? And his dread of hurting anybody's feelings, even a child's! Everything for others, nothing for himself! Sergius Ivanich quite regards it as Kostya's duty to act as his steward, and so does his sister. And now Dolly and her children are his wards! And then there are all those peasants who come to him every day as if it were his business to help them.

'Yes, only be like your father, only be like him!' she whispered, giving Mitya to the nurse, and touching his cheek with her lips.

Chapter VIII

Since the moment when, at the sight of his beloved and dying brother, Levin for the first time looked at the questions of life and death in the light of the new convictions, as he called them, which between the ages of twenty and thirty-four had imperceptibly replaced the beliefs of his childhood and youth, he had been less horrified by death than by life without the least knowledge of whence it came, what it is for, why, and what it is. Organisms, their destruction, the indestructibility of matter, the law of the conservation of energy, development—the terms that had superseded these beliefs—were very useful for mental purposes; but they gave no guidance for life, and Levin suddenly felt like a person who has exchanged a thick fur coat for a muslin garment and who, being out in the frost for the first time, becomes clearly convinced, not by arguments, but with the whole of his being, that he is as good as naked and that he must inevitably perish miserably.

From that moment, without thinking about it and though he continued living as he had done heretofore, Levin never ceased to feel afraid of his ignorance.

Moreover, he was vaguely conscious that what he had called his convictions were really ignorance and, more than that, were a state of mind which rendered knowledge of what he needed impossible.

At the commencement of his married life the new joys and new duties he experienced completely stifled these thoughts; but lately, since his wife's confinement, while living in Moscow without any occupation, the problem demanding solution had presented itself more and more insistently to him.

For him the problem was this: 'If I don't accept the replies offered by Christianity to the questions my life presents, what solutions do I accept?' And he not only failed to find in the whole arsenal of his convictions any kind of answer, but he could not even find anything resembling an answer.

He was in the position of a man seeking for food in a toyshop or at a gunsmith's.

Involuntarily and unconsciously, in every book, in every conversation, and in every person he met, he now sought for their relation to those questions and for a solution to them.

What astounded and upset him most in this connection, was that the majority of those in his set and of his age, having like himself replaced their former beliefs by new convictions like his own, did not see anything to be distressed about, and were quite contented and tranquil. So that, besides the principal question, Levin was tormented by other questions: Were these people sincere? Were they not pretending? Or did they understand, possibly in some different and clearer way than he, the answers science gives to the questions he was concerned with? And he studied painstakingly both the opinions of those people and the books which contained their answers.

One thing he had discovered since these questions had begun to occupy him, namely, that he had been mistaken in imagining from his recollections of his youthful university circle, that religion had outlived its day and no longer existed. All those near to him who lived good lives were people who believed: the old Prince, Lvov, of whom he had grown so fond, his brother, Koznyshev, and all the womenfolk. His wife believed as he had done in early childhood, and ninety-nine out of a hundred of the Russian people, the whole of the people whose lives he most respected, also believed. Another thing was that, having read a great many books, he became convinced that those who shared his outlook understood only what he had understood, explaining nothing and merely ignoring those problems without a solution to which he felt he could not live,— but trying to solve quite other problems which could not interest him, such as, for instance, the development of organisms, a mechanical explanation of the soul, and so on.

Besides, during the time of his wife's confinement an extraordinary thing had happened to him. He, an unbeliever, began to pray, and while praying believed. But that moment had passed, and he could not allot any place in his life to the state of mind he had then experienced.

He could not admit that he had then known the truth and was now making a mistake; because, as soon as he reflected calmly about it, it all fell to pieces; nor could he acknowledge that he had then been mistaken, for he prized the state his soul had then been in, and by acknowledging it to be a result of weakness he would have defiled those moments. He was painfully out of harmony with himself and strained all his spiritual powers to escape from this condition.

Chapter IX

These thoughts oppressed and tormented him, now more and now less strongly, but never left him. He read and thought, and the more he read and thought the further he felt from his goal.

Latterly in Moscow and in the country, having convinced himself that he could get no answer from the materialists, he read through and re-read Plato, Spinoza, Kant, Schelling, Hegel, and Schopenhauer, those philosophers who explained life otherwise than materialistically.

Their thoughts seemed to him fruitful when he read, or was himself devising refutations of other teachings, the materialistic in particular; but as soon as he began reading, or himself devised, solutions to life's problems, the same thing occurred every time. Following long definitions of vague words such as *spirit, will, freedom, substance,* and deliberately entering the verbal trap set for him by the philosophers, or by himself, he seemed to begin to understand something. But he had only to forget that artificial line of thought, and to return direct from real life to what had appeared satisfactory so long as he kept to the given line of thought—and suddenly the whole artificial edifice tumbled down like a house of cards, and it was evident that the edifice had been constructed of those same words differently arranged, and without regard for something in life more important than reason.

At one time, while reading Schopenhauer, he replaced the word *will* by the word *love,* and this new philosophy comforted him for a day or two, as long as he did not stand aside from it; but it, too, collapsed when he viewed it in relation to real life, and it turned out to be a muslin garment without warmth.

His brother Koznyshev advised him to read Homyakov's theological writings. Levin read the second volume of them, and, in spite of its polemical, polished, and witty style, which at first repelled him, he was struck by its teaching about the Church. He was struck by the thought that it is not given to isolated man to attain divine truth, but that it is given to a community united by love—the Church. He was pleased by the thought that it was easier to believe in an existing living Church which embraces all the beliefs of men and has God at its head and is therefore holy and infallible, and from it to accept belief in God, a distant, mysterious God, the Creation, and so on. But afterwards on reading the history of the Church, first by a Roman Catholic and then by a Greek-Orthodox writer, and finding that each essentially infallible Church repudiated the other, he became disenchanted with Homyakov's teaching about the Church; and that edifice crumbled to dust just as the philosophical structures had done.

All that spring he was not himself and experienced terrible moments.

'Without knowing what I am, and why I am here, it is impossible to live. Yet I cannot know that, and therefore I can't live,' he said to himself.

'In an infinity of time, matter, and space, a bubble organism separates itself, maintains itself awhile, and then bursts, and that bubble is—I!'

This was a distressing falsehood, but it was the sole and last result of centuries, and the age-long labour of human thought in that direction.

It was the ultimate belief, on which, in almost all branches, all the systems of human thought were based. It was the ruling conviction, and of all other explanations Levin, without knowing when or how, had involuntarily chosen it as being at any rate the clearest.

But it was not only false, it was the cruel mockery of some evil power: a wicked and disgusting power and one to which it was impossible to submit.

It was necessary to free oneself from that power. The means of escape were in the hands of every man. An end had to be put to that dependence on an evil power; and there was one means—death.

And though he was a happy and healthy family man, Levin was several times so near to suicide that he hid a cord he had lest he should hang himself, and he feared to carry a gun lest he should shoot himself.

But he did not hang or shoot himself and went on living.

Chapter X

When Levin thought about what he was and why he lived, he could find no answer and was driven to despair; but when he left off asking himself those questions, he seemed to know what he was and why he lived, for he acted and lived unfalteringly and definitely—recently even more unfalteringly than before.

When he returned to the country in June, he went back to his ordinary occupations—husbandry, intercourse with the peasants and with his neighbours, management of his house and of his sister's and brother's affairs, which were entrusted to him, relations with his wife and relatives, cares about his baby, and a new hobby—beekeeping, which he took up with enthusiasm that spring—occupied all his time.

These matters interested him, not because he justified them to himself by any general theories as he had done previously; on the contrary, being now on the one hand disenchanted by the ill-success of his former occupations for the general welfare, and on the other hand too much occupied with his own thoughts and by the mass of affairs that overwhelmed him from all sides, he quite abandoned all calculation of public utility, and these matters interested him only because it seemed to him that he had to do what he was doing, and could not act otherwise.

Formerly (it had been so almost from childhood and increasingly so till his complete maturity) when he tried to do anything for the good of everybody, for humanity, for Russia, for the whole village, he had noticed that the thoughts of it were agreeable, but the activity itself was always unsatisfactory; there was no full assurance that the work was really necessary, and the activity itself, which at first seemed so great, ever lessened and lessened till it vanished. But now since his marriage, when he began to confine himself more and more to living for himself, though he no longer felt any joy at the thought of his activity, he felt confident that his work was necessary, saw that it progressed far better than formerly, and that it was always growing more and more.

Now, as if involuntarily, he cut ever deeper and deeper into the earth, so that he, like a ploughshare, could not get out without turning the sod.

For the family to live as their grandfathers and fathers had been accustomed to live, that is at the same educational level, and so to bring up their children, was undoubtedly necessary. It was just as necessary as to dine when hungry; and therefore just as it was necessary to prepare dinner, so it was necessary to arrange the husbandry at Pokrovsk in such a way as to derive an income from it. As surely as one must pay one's debts, so surely was it necessary to keep the patrimony in such a state that when his son inherited it, he would thank his father, as Levin thanked his grandfather, for all that he had built and planted. To do this he must not lease the land, but must farm it himself, keep cattle, manure the fields, and plant woods.

It was as impossible not to look after his brother's and sister's affairs, and those of all the peasants who came for advice and were accustomed to do so, as it is impossible to abandon a baby you are already holding in your arms.

It was necessary to look after the comforts of his sister-in-law and her children, who had been invited, and of his wife and child, and it was impossible not to pass at least a small portion of each day with them.

All this, with game-shooting, and his new hobby of beekeeping, filled up the whole of that life of his which seemed to him, when he thought about it, to have no meaning.

But besides knowing definitely what he had to do, Levin also knew how to do it all, and which affair was the more important of any two.

He knew that he must hire labourers as cheaply as possible; but that he must not take them in bondage for less than they were worth by advancing them money, though this would be very profitable. He might sell straw to the peasants in a time of shortage, though he felt sorry for them; but an inn or a public-house, although it brought in a revenue, must be done away with. Felling trees must be punished as severely as possible, but if peasants let their cattle stray he must not exact fines from them; and though it grieved the watchmen and weakened discipline, the strayed cattle must not be detained.

He must lend money to Peter to liberate him from the usurers to whom he was paying ten per cent. a month; but he must neither reduce or postpone the payments of rent by the peasants who were in default. The steward must not be excused when the small meadow was not mown and the grass was wasted; but grass must not be mown on the eighty desyatinas which had been planted with young trees. He must not pardon a labourer who went home at a busy time because his father had died—sorry as he might be for the man—part of his pay had to be deducted for the precious months during which he had been absent; but he could not neglect giving a monthly allowance to old domestic serfs who were of no use at all to him.

Levin knew, too, that on returning home the first thing he must do was to go to his wife, who was unwell, and that the peasants who had been waiting for three hours to see him could wait a little longer; and he knew that in spite of all the pleasure of hiving a swarm, he must forgo that pleasure, let the old beekeeper hive the swarm without him, and go to talk to the peasants who had found him at the apiary.

Whether he was acting well or ill he did not know, and far from laying down the law about it, he now avoided talking or thinking about it.

Thinking about it led him into doubts and prevented him from seeing what he should and should not do. But when he did not think, but just lived, he unceasingly felt in his soul the presence of an infallible judge deciding which of two possible actions was the better and which the worse; and as soon as he did what he should not have done, he immediately felt this.

In this way he lived, not knowing or seeing any possibility of knowing what he was or why he lived in the world, and he suffered so much from that ignorance that he was afraid he might commit suicide, while at the same time he was firmly cutting his own particular definite path through life.

Chapter XI

The day when Koznyshev arrived at Pokrovsk was one of Levin's most distressing days.

It was the most pressingly busy season of the year, when an extraordinary tension of self-sacrificing labour manifests itself among all the peasants, such as is never shown in any other condition of life, and such as would be highly esteemed if the people who exhibit this quality esteemed it themselves, if it were not repeated every year, and if the results of that tension were not so simple.

To mow or reap the rye and oats, and cart them, to finish mowing the meadows, to re-plough the fallow land, to thresh the seed corn and sow the winter rye—all this seems simple and ordinary; yet to get it all done, it is necessary that all the peasants, from the oldest to the youngest, should work unceasingly those three or four weeks, three times as hard as usual, living on kvas, onions, and black bread, threshing and carting the sheaves by night and sleeping not more than two or three hours out of the twenty-four. And this is done every year, all over Russia.

Having lived most of his life in the country and in close contact with the peasants, Levin always felt, at this busy time, that this general stimulation of the peasants communicated itself to him.

Early in the morning he rode to where the first rye was being sown, then to see the oats carted and stacked, and returning home when his wife and sister-in-law were getting up he drank coffee with them, and then walked to the farm where the new threshing machine was to be started to thresh the seed corn.

All that day, when talking to the steward and the peasants and at home with his wife, Dolly, her children, and his father-in-law, Levin's thoughts were busy with the one and only subject, outside his farming, that interested him at this time, and in everything he sought its relation to his questions: 'What am I? Where am I? And why am I here?'

Standing in the cool shade of the newly-thatched barn, with its wattle walls of hazel, which had not yet shed its scented leaves, pressed against the freshly stripped aspens of the roof-tree under the thatch, he looked now through the open doorway into which the dry and bitter chaff-dust rushed and whirled, at the grass round the threshing-floor lit up by the hot sunshine and at the fresh straw that had just been brought out of the barn, now at the bright-headed and white-breasted swallows that flew in chirping beneath the roof and, flapping their wings, paused in the light of the doorway, and now at the people who bustled about in the dark and dusty barn; and he thought strange thoughts:

'Why is all this being done?' he wondered. 'Why am I standing here, obliging them to work? Why do they all make such efforts and try to show me their zeal? Why is my old friend Matrena toiling so (I doctored her after the fire, when she was struck by a girder)?' he thought, looking at a thin peasant woman who pushed the grain along with a rake, her dark sunburnt bare feet stepping with effort on the hard uneven barn floor. 'She recovered then, but to-day or to-morrow, or in ten years' time, they will bury her and nothing will be left of her, nor of that smart girl with the red skirt, who with such dexterous and delicate movements is beating the chaff from the ears. She too will be buried, and that piebald gelding too—and that one very soon,' he reflected, looking at a horse breathing quickly with falling and rising belly and inflated nostrils, as it trod on the slanting wheel that moved under it. 'They will bury her, and so they will Theodore, who is feeding the machine, his curly beard full of chaff and his shirt torn on his white shoulder. Yet he loosens the sheaves and gives directions, shouts at the women, and quickly puts right the strap on the fly-wheel. And, moreover, not they only but I too shall be buried and nothing will be left. What is it all for?'

He thought this, and at the same time looked at his watch to calculate how much they could thresh in an hour. He had to know this in order to set them their day's task accordingly.

'They've been nearly an hour, and have only just started on the third heap,' thought he, approached the man who was feeding the machine, and shouting above its din, told him to put in less at a time.

'You put in too much at a time, Theodore! Don't you see, it gets jammed and that's why it does not go well! Feed it in evenly!'

Theodore, black with the dust that stuck to his perspiring face, shouted something in reply, but still did not do as Levin wished.

Levin went up to the roller, motioned Theodore aside, and himself began feeding the machine.

Having worked till the peasants' dinner-hour, which soon came, he left the barn together with Theodore and began chatting, standing beside the neat yellow freshly-reaped stack of seed-rye on the threshing-floor.

Theodore came from the farther village, the one where Levin had formerly let the land to be worked co-operatively. At present it was let to the innkeeper.

Levin got into conversation with Theodore about that land, and asked whether Plato, a well-to-do and worthy peasant of that village, would not rent that land next year.

'The rent is too high, Constantine Dmitrich,' answered Theodore, picking out the ears of rye from the front of his damp shirt.

'But how does Kirilov make it pay?'

'Why shouldn't Mityuka' (as he contemptuously called the innkeeper) 'make it pay, Constantine Dmitrich? That fellow will press hard, but he'll get his own! He will have no pity on a Christian! But as if Daddy Plato would ever skin a man! He'll lend, and sometimes he'll let a man off, and so run short himself. It all depends on the sort of man.'

'But why should he let anyone off?'

'Oh well, you see, people differ! One man lives only for his own needs: take Mityuka, who only stuffs his own belly, but Plato is an upright old man. He lives for his soul and remembers God.'

'How does he remember God? How does he live for the soul?' Levin almost cried out.

'You know how: rightly, in a godly way. You know, people differ! Take you, for instance, you won't injure anyone either . . .'

'Yes, yes! Good-bye!' uttered Levin, gasping with excitement, and turning away, he took his stick and walked quickly away toward home. At the peasant's words about Plato living for his soul, rightly, in a godly way, dim but important thoughts crowded into his mind, as if breaking loose from some place where they had been locked up, and all rushing toward one goal, whirled in his head, dazzling him with their light.

Chapter XII

Levin went along the high-road with long strides, attending not so much to his thoughts—he could not yet disentangle them—as to a condition of his soul he had never before experienced.

The words the peasant had spoken produced in his soul the effect of an electric spark, suddenly transforming and welding into one a whole group of disjointed impotent separate ideas which had always interested him. These ideas, though he had been unconscious of them, had been in his mind when he was talking about letting the land.

He felt something new in his soul and probed this something with pleasure, not yet knowing what it was.

'To live not for one's needs but for God! For what God? What could be more senseless than what he said? He said we must not live for our needs—that is, we must not live for what we understand and what attracts us, what we wish for, but must live for something incomprehensible, for God whom nobody can understand or define. Well? And did I not understand those senseless words of Theodore's? And having understood them, did I doubt their justice? Did I find them stupid, vague, or inexact?

'No, I understood them just as he understands them: understood completely and more clearly than I understand anything in life; and I have never in my life doubted it, and cannot doubt it. And not I alone but every one—the whole world—only understands that completely. Nobody is free from doubt about other things, but nobody ever doubts this one thing, everybody always agrees with it.

'And I sought for miracles, regretted not to see a miracle that might convince me! A physical miracle would have tempted me. But here is a miracle, the one possible, everlasting miracle, all around me, and I did not notice it!

'Theodore says that Kirilov, the innkeeper, lives for his belly. That is intelligible and reasonable. We all, as reasoning creatures, cannot live otherwise. And then that same Theodore says that it is wrong to live for one's belly, and that we must live for Truth, for God, and at the first hint I understand him! I and millions of men who lived centuries ago and those who are living now: peasants, the poor in spirit, and sages, who have thought and written about it, saying the same thing in their obscure words—we all agree on that one thing: what we should live for, and what is good. I, and all other men, know only one thing firmly, clearly, and certainly, and this knowledge cannot be explained by reason: it is outside reason, has no cause and can have no consequences.

'If goodness has a cause, it is no longer goodness; if it has a consequence—a reward, it is also not goodness. Therefore goodness is beyond the chain of cause and effect.

'It is exactly *this* that I know and that we all know.

'What greater miracle could there be than that?

'Can I possibly have found the solution of everything? Have my sufferings really come to an end?' thought Levin as he strode along the dusty road, oblivious of the heat, of his fatigue, and filled with a sense of relief from long-continued suffering. That feeling was so joyous that it seemed questionable to him. He was breathless with excitement and, incapable of going further, he turned from the road into the wood and sat down on the uncut grass in the shade of the aspens. Taking the hat from his perspiring head, he lay down, leaning his elbow upon the juicy, broad-bladed forest grass.

'Yes, I must clear it up and understand it,' he thought, gazing intently at the untrodden grass before him, and following the movements of a green insect that was crawling up a stalk of couch grass and was hindered in its ascent by a leaf of goutwort. 'What have I discovered?' he asked himself, turning back the leaf that it should not hinder the insect and bending another blade for the creature to pass on to. 'What gladdens me? What have I discovered?

'I have discovered nothing. I have only perceived what it is that I know. I have understood the Power that not only gave me life in the past but is giving me life now. I have freed myself from deception and learnt to know my Master.

'I used to say that in my body, in this grass, in this insect . . . (There! It did not want to get on to that grass, but has spread its wings and flown away) there takes place, according to physical, chemical, and physiological laws, a change of matter. And in all of us, including the aspens and the clouds and nebulæ, evolution is proceeding. Evolution from what, into what? Unending evolution and struggle. . . . As if there could be any direction and struggle in infinity! And I was surprised that, in spite of the greatest effort of thought on that path, the meaning of life, the meaning of my impulses and my aspirations, was not revealed to me. But now I say that I know the meaning of my life: it is to live for God, for the soul. And that meaning, in spite of its clearness, is mystic and wonderful. And such is the meaning of all existence. Ah yes! Pride!' he said to himself, turning over face downwards and beginning to tie blades of grass into knots, trying not to break them.

'And not only mental pride but mental stupidity. And chiefly dishonesty of mind, simply dishonesty. Just mind-swindling,' he repeated.

He briefly reviewed the whole course of his thoughts during the last two years, beginning with the clear and obvious thought of death at the sight of his beloved brother hopelessly ill.

Having then for the first time clearly understood that before every man, and before himself, there lay only suffering, death, and eternal oblivion, he had concluded that to live under such conditions was impossible; that one must either explain life to oneself so that it does not seem to be an evil mockery by some sort of devil, or one must shoot oneself.

But he had done neither the one nor the other, yet he continued to live, think, and feel, had even at that very time got married, experienced many joys, and been happy whenever he was not thinking of the meaning of his life.

What did that show? It showed that he had lived well, but thought badly.

He had lived (without being conscious of it) by those spiritual
truths which he had imbibed with his mother's milk; but in
thought he had not only not acknowledged those truths, but had
studiously evaded them.

Now it was clear to him that he was only able to live, thanks to
the beliefs in which he had been brought up.

'What should I have been and how should I have lived my life, if
I had not had those beliefs, and had not known that one must live
for God, and not for one's own needs? I should have robbed, lied,
and murdered. Nothing of that which constitutes the chief joys of
my life would have existed for me.' And although he made the
greatest efforts of imagination, he could not picture to himself the
bestial creature he would have been, had he not known what he
was living for.

'I looked for an answer to my question. But reason could not give
me an answer—reason is incommensurable with the question. Life
itself has given me the answer, in my knowledge of what is good and
what is bad. And that knowledge I did not acquire in any way; it
was given to me as to everybody, *given* because I could not take it
from anywhere.

'Where did I get it from? Was it by reason that I attained to the
knowledge that I must love my neighbour and not throttle him?
They told me so when I was a child, and I gladly believed it, because they told me what was already in my soul. But who discovered
it? Not reason! Reason has discovered the struggle for existence and
the law that I must throttle all those who hinder the satisfaction
of my desires. That is the deduction reason makes. But the law of
loving others could not be discovered by reason, because it is unreasonable.'

Chapter XIII

Levin remembered a recent scene between Dolly and her children. Left by themselves, the children had started cooking raspberries over a candle, and pouring jets of milk into their mouths.
When their mother caught them at this pursuit, she began in
Levin's presence to impress on them how much trouble what they
were wasting had cost grown-up people, that that trouble had been
taken for them, that if they broke cups they would not have anything to drink tea out of, and if they spilt milk they would not
have anything to eat and would die of hunger.

And Levin was struck by the quiet dull disbelief with which the
children listened to these remarks from their mother. They were
only grieved that their amusing game had been ended, and they did
not believe a word of what she was saying. And they could not believe it, because they could not imagine the whole volume of all

they consumed, and therefore could not conceive that what they were destroying was the very thing they lived on.

'That's quite a different matter,' they thought. 'And not in the least interesting or important, because those things always have been and always will be. It is always the same thing over and over again. There is no need for us to think about that, it's all ready for us; but we want to think out something of our own invention and new. Now we've thought of putting raspberries in a cup and cooking them over a candle, and of pouring milk into each other's mouths like fountains. That is amusing and new, and not at all worse than drinking out of cups.'

'Don't we, and didn't I, do just the same, when intellectually I sought for the meaning of the forces of nature and the purpose of human life?' he went on thinking.

'And don't all the philosophic theories do the same, when by ways of thought strange and unnatural to man they lead him to a knowledge of what he knew long ago, and knows so surely that without it he could not live? Is it not evident in the development of every philosopher's theory that he knows in advance, as indubitably as the peasant Theodore and not a whit more clearly than he, the chief meaning of life, and only wishes, by a questionable intellectual process, to return to what every one knows?

'Supposing now that the children were left alone to procure or make cups for themselves and to milk the cows and so on. Would they play tricks? No, they would die of hunger! Suppose we, with our passions and thoughts, were left without the conception of God, a Creator, and without a conception of what is good, and without an explanation of moral evil!

'Try to build up anything without these conceptions!

'We destroy because we have our fill spiritually. We are children indeed!

'Whence comes the joyful knowledge I have in common with the peasant, and which alone gives me peace of mind? Where did I get it?

'I, educated in the conception of God, as a Christian, having filled my life with the spiritual blessings Christianity gave me, brimful of these blessings and living by them, I, like a child, not understanding them, destroy them—that is, I wish to destroy that by which I live. But as soon as an important moment of life comes, like children when they are cold and hungry, I go to Him, and even less than the children whose mother scolds them for their childish mischief do I feel that my childish attempts to kick because I am filled should be reckoned against me.

'Yes, what I know, I know not by my reason but because it has been given to me, revealed to me, and I know it in my heart by faith in the chief thing which the Church proclaims.

'The Church? The Church?' Levin repeated to himself. He turned over, and leaning on his elbows began looking at a herd of cattle in the distance approaching the river on the other side.

'But can I believe in all that the Church professes?' he asked himself, testing himself by everything which might destroy his present peace of mind. He purposely thought of those teachings of the Church which always seemed most strange to him, and that tried him. 'The Creation.—But how do I account for existence? By existence! By nothing!—The devil and sin?—And how do I explain evil? . . . A Saviour? . . .

'But I know nothing, nothing! And can know nothing but what is told to me and to everybody.'

And it now seemed to him that there was not one of the dogmas of the Church which could disturb the principal thing—faith in God, in goodness, as the sole vocation of man.

Each of the Church's doctrines might be represented by faith in serving truth rather than serving one's personal needs. And each of them not only did not infringe that belief but was necessary for the fulfillment of the chief miracle ever recurring on earth: the possibility of every one, millions of most diverse people, sages and idiots, children and old men, peasants, Lvov, Kitty, beggars and kings, indubitably understanding one and the same thing, and forming that life of the spirit which alone is worth living for and which alone we prize.

Lying on his back he was now gazing at the high cloudless sky. 'Don't I know that that is infinite space, and not a rounded vault? But however I may screw my eyes and strain my sight, I cannot help seeing it round and limited, and despite my knowledge of it as limitless space I am indubitably right when I see a firm blue vault, and more right than when I strain to see beyond it.'

Levin ceased to think, and only as it were hearkened to mystic voices that seemed to be joyously and earnestly discussing something.

'Can this really be faith?' he wondered, afraid to believe in his happiness. 'My God, I thank Thee!' he uttered, repressing his rising sobs, and wiping away with both hands the tears that filled his eyes.

Chapter XIV

Levin looked straight before him, and saw the herd of cattle and then his trap and his horse Raven and the coachman who, having driven up to the cattle, was speaking to the herdsman; after that, close by, he heard the sound of wheels and the snorting of a well-fed horse; but he was so engrossed in his thoughts that he did not wonder why the coachman was coming for him.

That occurred to him only when the coachman drove up and called to him.

'The mistress has sent me! Your brother and another gentleman have come!'

Levin got into the trap and took the reins.

As if just awakened from a dream, it was long before he could collect his thoughts. He looked at the well-fed horse, lathered between its legs and on its neck where the reins chafed it—looked at Ivan the coachman sitting beside him, and remembered that he had been expecting his brother, that his wife was probably disturbed at his long absence, and he tried to guess who the visitor that had come with his brother might be. His brother, his wife, and the unknown visitor appeared in a different light to him now. It seemed to him that his relations with every one would now be changed. 'There will be no disputes; with Kitty never any quarrels again; with the visitor, whoever he may be, I shall be amiable and kind; and with the servants, with Ivan, everything will be different.'

Tightly holding in the good horse, who snorted impatiently and pulled at the reins, Levin kept turning to glance at Ivan, who sat beside him not knowing what to do with his unoccupied hands and continually pushing down his shirt as the wind blew it out. Levin tried to think of some pretext for beginning a conversation with him. He wanted to say that it was a pity Ivan had pulled the saddle-girth so tight, but that would have sounded like a reproof, and Levin desired an amicable conversation. But he could think of nothing else to say.

'Bear to the right, sir, there's a stump there,' said the coachman, taking hold of the rein.

'Please leave it alone and don't teach me!' said Levin, annoyed at the coachman's interference. Just as it always did, interference vexed him, and he immediately felt how wrong had been his conclusion that his spiritual condition could at once alter his manner when confronted with reality.

When they were still a quarter of a verst from the house, Levin saw Grisha and Tanya running toward him.

'Uncle Kostya! Mama is coming and Grandpapa and Sergius Ivanich, and some one else!' they cried, clambering into the trap.

'Who else?'

'An awfully dreadful man! And he goes like that with his hands,' said Tanya, standing up in the trap and mimicking Katavasov.

'Young or old?' asked Levin with a laugh, as Tanya's gestures reminded him of some one.

'Oh, if only it is not some one disagreeable!' he thought.

As soon as he had turned the corner of the road and saw those who were approaching he at once recognized Katavasov in a straw hat, waving his arms just as Tanya had represented.

Katavasov was very fond of talking about philosophy, having a conception of it which he had acquired from naturalists who had never studied it, and in Moscow Levin had latterly had many disputes with him.

One of those disputes, in which Katavasov evidently thought he had been the victor, was the first thing Levin remembered when he recognized him.

'But I will not now on any account dispute or express my opinions lightly,' he thought.

After alighting from the trap and welcoming his brother and Katavasov, Levin asked where Kitty was.

'She has taken Mitya to Kolok,' which was a wood not far from the house. 'She wanted to let him sleep there; it's so hot in the house,' said Dolly. Levin always advised his wife not to take the child into the wood, considering it dangerous, and this news was disagreeable to him.

'She wanders about with him from place to place,' said the old Prince with a smile. 'I advised her to try taking him to the ice-cellar!'

'She meant to come to the apiary. She thought you were there. We are going there,' said Dolly.

'Well, and what are you doing?' asked Koznyshev, lagging behind with his brother.

'Oh, nothing particular. Busy with the estate as usual,' answered Levin. 'Have you come for a good stay? We expected you long ago.'

'For about a fortnight. I had a lot to do in Moscow.'

At these words the brothers' eyes met, and Levin—in spite of the desire he always felt, and now more than ever, for friendly and especially for simple relations with his brother—felt ill at ease while looking at him. He dropped his own eyes, not knowing what to say.

Mentally reviewing the subjects that might interest Koznyshev and divert him from the Serbian war and the Slavonic Question, at which he had hinted when mentioning his work in Moscow, Levin asked about Koznyshev's book.

'Have any reviews of your book appeared?' he asked.

Koznyshev smiled at the obvious intent of the question.

'No one concerns himself with it, and I least of all,' he replied. 'Look there, Darya Alexandrovna! It's going to rain,' he added, pointing with his umbrella to some white clouds that had appeared above the aspen trees.

And those words were enough to re-establish between the brothers the not exactly hostile, but cold, relations which Levin so wished to avoid.

Levin joined Katavasov.

'How right you were to come!' he said.

'I have long been meaning to! Now we'll have some talks, and we'll see! Have you read Spencer?'

'No, I have not finished him,' replied Levin. 'However, I don't need him now.'

'How's that? That's interesting! Why not?'

'Well, I have finally convinced myself that I shan't find solutions of the questions I am concerned about in him, or in people of his kind. Now . . .'

But he was suddenly struck by the calm and cheerful expression of Katavasov's face, and felt so sorry to lose the spiritual condition which he was evidently spoiling by his conversation, that recollecting his resolution he ceased speaking.

'However, we'll have a talk later on,' he said. 'If we are going to the apiary, it's this way, along this path,' he added, addressing the whole party.

When by the narrow footpath they had reached the unmown glade covered on one side by a thick growth of bright John-and-Maries, with tall spreading bushes of dark green sneezewort between them, Levin asked his guests to sit down in the deep cool shade of the young aspens—upon a bench and some tree stumps specially arranged for visitors to the apiary who might be afraid of bees—while he went to the hut to fetch bread, cucumbers, and fresh honey for the grown-up people as well as for the children.

Trying to make as few brusque movements as possible and listening to the bees that flew past him more and more often, he went along the path to the hut. At the very entrance a bee became entangled in his beard and began buzzing, but he carefully liberated it. He went into the shady lobby and from a peg in the wall took down his veil, put it on, and with his hands deep in his pockets entered the fenced-in apiary where—standing in regular rows and tied with bast to stakes—in the middle of a space where the grass had been mown, stood the old beehives,[3] every one familiar to him, and each with a history of its own, while along the wattle fence stood the new hives with the swarms hived that year. In front of the hives, flickering before his eyes and circling and fluttering over the same spot, played bees and drones, and between them flew the working bees always to or from the wood with the blossoming lime trees, fetching and bringing back their loads.

In his ears rang incessantly a variety of sounds: now of a busy working bee flying swiftly past, now of a buzzing idle drone, then of the excited bee sentinels guarding their treasure from a foe and prepared to sting. On the other side of the fence an old man was

---

3. Hollowed-out stumps of trees placed upright.

making a hoop and did not notice Levin, who stopped in the middle of the apiary without calling him.

He was glad of this opportunity to be alone and recover from reality, which had already so lowered his spiritual condition.

He remembered that he had already got angry with Ivan, treated his brother coldly, and spoken heedlessly to Katavasov.

'Can it possibly have been but a momentary mood that will pass without leaving a trace?' he wondered.

But at that instant returning into that mood, he felt with joy that something new and important had occurred within him. Reality had temporarily veiled the spiritual tranquillity he had found, but it remained with him.

Just as the bees, now circling round him, threatening him and distracting his attention, deprived him of complete physical calm and forced him to shrink to avoid them, so the cares that had beset him from the moment he got into the trap had deprived him of spiritual freedom; but that continued only so long as they surrounded him. And as, in spite of the bees, his physical powers remained intact, so his newly realized spiritual powers were intact also.

Chapter XV

'Kostya! Do you know with whom Sergius Ivanich travelled coming here?' said Dolly, after she had distributed cucumbers and honey among the children. 'With Vronsky! He is on his way to Serbia.'

'Yes, and not alone, but is taking a squadron at his own expense!' said Katavasov.

'That is like him,' said Levin. 'But are Volunteers really still going?' he added with a glance at Koznyshev.

Koznyshev did not reply, but with the blunt side of a knife carefully extracted from a bowl in which lay a wedge of white honeycomb a live bee that had stuck in the running honey.

'Yes, I should think so! You should have seen what went on at the station yesterday!' said Katavasov, audibly biting into a cucumber.

'Well, how is one to understand it? In heaven's name, Sergius Ivanich, explain to me where all these Volunteers are going and whom they are fighting,' said the old Prince, evidently continuing a conversation that had been started during Levin's absence.

'The Turks!' answered Koznyshev quietly smiling, having extracted the bee which, black with honey, moved its legs helplessly as he shifted it from the knife to a firm aspen leaf.

'But who has declared war on Turkey? Ivan Ivanich Ragozov and the Countess Lydia Ivanovna, assisted by Madame Stahl?'

'No one has declared war, but people sympathize with their suffering neighbours and wish to help them,' replied Koznyshev.

'But the Prince is not talking of help,' interposed Levin, taking his father-in-law's side, 'but of war! He says that private people cannot take part in war without the consent of the Government.'

'Kostya, look! Here's a bee! Really, we shall get stung!' cried Dolly, waving away a wasp.

'But that's not a bee, it's a wasp,' said Levin.

'Well, and what is your theory?' asked Katavasov with a smile, evidently challenging Levin to a discussion. 'Why have private individuals no right?'

'My theory is this: On the one hand war is such a bestial, cruel and terrible affair, that no single man—not to speak of a Christian —can take on himself personally the responsibility for beginning a war. It can only be done by a Government, which is summoned to it and is brought to it inevitably. On the other hand, by law and by common sense, in the affairs of State, and especially in the matter of war, citizens renounce their personal will.'

Koznyshev and Katavasov, ready with their rejoinders began speaking both together.

'That's just the point, my dear fellow, that cases may arise when the Government does not fulfil the will of its citizens and then Society announces its own will,' said Katavasov.

But Koznyshev evidently did not approve of this reply. He frowned at Katavasov's words and said something different.

'It is a pity you put the question that way. There is no declaration of war in this case, but simply an expression of human, Christian feeling. Our brothers by blood and religion are being killed. Well, say they were not even our brothers or co-religionists, but simply children, women, and old people; one's feelings are outraged, and Russians hasten to help to stop those horrors. Imagine that you were going along a street and saw a tipsy man beating a woman or a child; I think you would not stop to ask whether war had or had not been declared against that man, but you would rush at him and defend the victim!'

'But I would not kill the man,' replied Levin.

'Yes, you would.'

'I don't know. If I saw such a thing, I might yield to my instinctive feeling; I can't say beforehand. But there is no such instinctive feeling about the oppression of the Slavs, nor can there be.'

'Perhaps you have none, but others have,' said Koznyshev with a dissatisfied frown. 'Among the people there live traditions of Orthodox Christians suffering under the yoke of the "Infidel Mussulman." The people have heard of their brothers' sufferings, and have spoken out.'

'Perhaps,' said Levin evasively, 'but I don't see it. I myself am one of the people, and I don't feel it.'

'Nor do I,' said the Prince. 'I was living abroad and read the papers, and must own that I could not at all understand why, even before the Bulgarian atrocities, all Russians suddenly grew so fond of their Slavonic brothers, while I don't feel any love for them. I was much grieved and thought I was a monster or that the Karlsbad waters had that effect on me! But on getting back I was relieved, for I see that there are others besides me who are only interested in Russia and not in their brother-Slavs. Constantine is one.'

'Personal opinions don't count in this matter,' said Koznyshev. 'It is not an affair of personal opinions, when all Russia—the people— has expressed its will.'

'But, forgive me, I don't see it. The people know nothing about it,' said the Prince.

'Oh, Papa! Don't they? And on Sunday, in church?' remarked Dolly, who had been following the conversation. 'Please bring a towel,' she said to the old man, who was looking smilingly at the children. 'It's impossible that all . . .'

'But what was there in church on Sunday? The priest was ordered to read it. He did so. The people understood nothing, but they sighed as they always do during a sermon,' continued the Prince. 'They were told that there would be a collection in the church for a soul-saving object, so they each took out a kopek and gave it, but what it was for—they did not know!'

'The people can't help knowing. A consciousness of their destiny always exists in the people, and at moments like the present it becomes clear to them,' said Koznyshev positively, glancing at the old beekeeper.

The handsome old man, with a black beard turning grey in places and thick silvery hair, stood motionless with a bowl of honey in his hand, gazing kindly and calmly down from his height at the gentlefolk, clearly neither understanding them nor wishing to understand.

'Yes, that is so,' he said to Koznyshev, and moved his head significantly.

'Yes, you'd better ask him! He neither knows nor thinks about it,' said Levin. 'Have you heard about the war, Mikhaylich?' he asked, addressing the old man. 'What they read in the church? What do you think? Ought we to fight for the Christians?'

'Why should we think? Alexander Nikolayevich, the Emperor, has thought for us, and will think for us on all matters. He can see better. . . . Shall I bring some more bread and give the laddie a bit?' he asked Dolly, pointing to Grisha, who was finishing his crust.

'I have no need to ask,' said Koznyshev. 'We have seen, and still see, hundreds and hundreds of men who give up everything to serve the righteous cause, and who come from all ends of Russia and openly and clearly express their thoughts and aims. They bring their mites, or go themselves, and say straight out why they do it. What does that mean?'

'It means, it seems to me,' said Levin, beginning to get excited, 'that in a nation of eighty millions there can always be found not hundreds, as is now the case, but tens of thousands of men who have lost their social position, happy-go-lucky people who are always ready to go . . . into Pugachev's robber band [4] or to Khiva, or to Serbia . . .'

'I tell you it's not hundreds, and not the happy-go-lucky people, but the best representatives of the people!' said Konznyshev, as irritably as if he were defending the last of his possessions. 'And the donations? There at any rate the whole people directly expresses its will.'

'That word *people* is so indefinite,' said Levin. 'Clerks in district offices, schoolmasters, and one out of a thousand peasants, may know what it is all about. The rest of the eighty millions, like Mikhaylich, not only don't express their will, but have not the least idea what it is they have to express it about! What right have we then to say it is the will of the people?'

Chapter XVI

Koznyshev, an experienced dialectician, did not rejoin but immediately turned the conversation into another region.

'Well, if you want to gauge the national spirit arithmetically, of course that is very difficult to do! Voting has not been introduced in our country, and cannot be because it does not express the people's will, but there are other means. It is felt in the air, it is felt by the heart. Not to mention the undercurrents that have stirred in the motionless sea of the nation and which are evident to every unprejudiced person, look at Society in the narrower sense! The most divergent parties in the intellectual world, previously so hostile to one another, have all merged into one. All differences are at an end, and all the social organs say one and the same thing, all have felt an elemental force that has seized them and carries them all in one direction.'

'Yes, all the papers say the same thing,' said the Prince, 'that's true. So much the same that they are just like frogs before a storm! They prevent our hearing anything else!'

'Frogs or no frogs . . . I don't publish a newspaper and don't

---

4. Pugachev was the leader of a very serious rebellion in the reign of Catherine the Great.

want to defend them, but I am speaking of the unanimity of the intelligent world,' said Koznyshev, turning to his brother. Levin was going to reply, but the old Prince interrupted him.

'About that unanimity, something else can be said,' rejoined the Prince. 'There's my son-in-law, Stephen Arkadyevich, you know him. He has now got the post of Member of the Committee of a Commission of something or other—I don't remember. Anyhow, there is nothing to do there. Well, Dolly, it's no secret! and the salary is eight thousand. You just ask him if his work will be any use, and he will prove to you that it is most necessary! And he is a truthful man, but one can't help believing in the usefulness of eight thousand roubles.'

'Yes, he asked me to tell Darya Alexandrovna that he has got the post,' said Koznyshev discontentedly, considering that what the Prince was saying was not to the point.

'So it is with the unanimity of the Press. It has been explained to me: as soon as there is a war their revenue is doubled. How can they help considering that the fate of the people and the Slavs—and all the rest of it?'

'There are many papers I don't like, but that is unfair,' said Koznyshev.

'I would make only one stipulation,' continued the Prince. 'Alphonse [5] Karr put it very well, before the war with Prussia. "You think war unavoidable? Very well! He who preaches war—off with him in a special legion to the assault, to the attack, in front of everybody else!"'

'The editors would be fine!' remarked Katavasov, laughing loudly, and picturing to himself the editors of his acquaintance in that chosen legion.

'Oh, but they'd run away,' said Dolly, 'and only be a hindrance.'

'And if they run, put grapeshot behind them, or Cossacks with whips!' said the Prince.

'That is a joke, and excuse me, Prince, not a good joke,' said Koznyshev.

'I don't see that it is a joke, that . . .' began Levin, but Koznyshev interrupted him.

'Every member of Society is called upon to do his proper task,' he said. 'And men of thought perform theirs by expressing public opinion. The unanimous and complete expression of public opinion is a service rendered by the Press, and is also a gratifying phenomenon. Twenty years ago we should have been silent, but now we hear the voice of the Russian people, who are ready to arise as one man and to sacrifice themselves for their oppressed brethren. That is a great step and a sign of power!'

---

5. Alphonse Karr (1808–1890) was a French satirist and journalist whom Tolstóy cited in one of his earliest tales, *Childhood*, and also in one of the last, *After the Ball*.

'But it's not a question of sacrificing themselves only, but of killing Turks,' remarked Levin timidly. 'The people sacrifice and are ready to sacrifice for the good of their souls, but not for murder,' he added, involuntarily connecting the conversation with the thoughts that so engrossed him.

'What is that: "for their souls"? You know that expression is a puzzling one for a naturalist. What is a soul?' Katavasov inquired with a smile.

'Oh, you know!'

'No, I swear I have not the slightest idea!' said Katavasov, laughing loudly.

' "I come not to bring peace, but a sword," said Christ,' rejoined Koznyshev, from his own standpoint, quoting quite simply, as if it were quite comprehensible, the very passage from the Gospels that always perplexed Levin more than any other.

'Yes, that is so!' repeated the old man, who was standing near by, answering a glance that was accidentally thrown at him.

'No, my dear sir! You are beaten! Completely beaten!' shouted Katavasov merrily.

Levin flushed with annoyance, not at being beaten, but because he had not refrained from the dispute.

'No, I must not dispute with them,' he thought. 'They are clad in impenetrable armour, and I am naked.'

He saw that it was not possible to convince his brother and Katavasov, and still less did he see any possibility of himself agreeing with them. What they advocated was that same pride of intellect that had nearly ruined him. He could not agree that some dozen of men, among whom was his brother, had the right to assert, on the strength of what they were told by some hundreds of grandiloquent Volunteers who came to the city, that they and the newspapers expressed the will and the opinion of the people: an opinion, moreover, which found expression in vengeance and murder. He could not agree with this, because he neither saw the expression of those thoughts in the people among whom he lived, nor did he find any such thoughts in himself (and he could not consider himself as other than one of those who constituted the Russian people). Above all, he could not agree because he, together with the people, did not know and could not know wherein lay the general welfare, but knew definitely that the attainment of this welfare was only possible by a strict fulfilment of the law of goodness which is revealed to every man, and therefore could not desire or preach war for any kind of general aims. He said the same as Mikhaylich and the people who expressed their thought in the legend of the invitation to the Varyags [6]: 'Come and rule over us!

6. The Norse chiefs who, at the dawn of Russian history, were invited by the Slav tribes of Russia to come and rule over them and establish order.

We joyfully promise complete obedience. All labours, all humilia-
tions, all sacrifices we take upon ourselves; but we will not judge
or decide!' But the people now, according to his brother, were renouncing that exemption they had purchased at so high a price.

He wanted to ask why, if public opinion is an infallible judge, is
a Revolution and a Commune not as lawful as the movement in
favour of the Slavs? But all these were thoughts that could not decide anything. One thing could be seen indubitably, namely, that
this dispute was irritating his brother at the moment, and that
therefore it was wrong to continue it, so Levin ceased to argue, and
drew his visitors' attention to the clouds that were gathering and to
the fact that they had better get home before the rain began.

Chapter XVII

The Prince and Koznyshev got into the trap and drove off; the
rest of the party, hastening their steps, went home on foot.

But the cloud, now whiter now blacker, approached so rapidly
that it was necessary to hurry still more to reach home before the
rain came. The fore part of the cloud, low and black like sooty
smoke, rushed with unusual swiftness across the sky. When they
were still about two hundred paces from the house the wind had
already risen, so that at any moment a downpour might be expected.

The children, with frightened and joyful yells, ran on in front.
Dolly, struggling with difficulty with the skirts that clung to her
legs, no longer walked but ran, her eyes fixed on the children. The
men, holding their hats, went on with long strides. They were just
reaching the porch when a large drop broke against the edge of the
iron gutter. The children, followed by the grown-ups, ran, talking
merrily, under the shelter of the roof.

'And Catherine Alexandrovna [7]?' Levin asked Agatha Mikhaylovna, who, carrying shawls and plaids, met them in the hall.

'We thought she was with you,' she answered.

'And Mitya?'

'In Kolok, I expect, and Nurse is with them.'

Levin snatched up the plaids and rushed to the Kolok.

In that short time the centre of the cloud had already so moved
over the sun that it was as dark as during an eclipse. The wind obstinately, as if insisting on having its way, pushed Levin back and,
tearing the leaves and blossoms off the lime trees and rudely and
strangely uncovering the white branches of birches, bent everything
in one direction: the acacias, the flowers, the dock leaves, the grass,
and the crests of the trees. The girls who had been working in the
garden rushed screeching under the roof of the servants' quarters.
A white curtain of pouring rain was already descending over the

7. Speaking to the servant Levin gives Kitty her full name.

distant wood and half the neighbouring field, and was advancing rapidly toward the Kolok. The moisture of the rain, shattered into minute drops, filled the air.

Lowering his head and fighting against the wind which was tearing the plaids out of his hands, Levin had almost reached the Kolok and could see something gleaming white behind an oak, when suddenly everything burst into flame, the earth seemed on fire, and just overhead the vault of heaven seemed to crack.

When he opened his dazzled eyes the first thing Levin saw with horror through the dense curtain of rain that now separated him from the Kolok was the strangely altered position of the green crown of a familiar oak in the middle of the wood. 'Has it been struck?' he had barely time to think when, with quicker and quicker motion, the crown of the oak disappeared behind the other trees, and he heard the crash of a big tree falling on to other trees.

The flash of lightning, the sound of thunder, and the sudden cold sensation of his body that was being drenched, merged for Levin into one feeling of horror.

'Oh God! Oh God! only not on them!' he said.

And though it occurred to him at once how senseless was his prayer that they should not be killed by the oak that had already fallen, he repeated it, knowing that he could do nothing better than utter that senseless prayer.

Having run to the spot where they generally went, he did not find them there.

They were at the other end of the wood, under an old lime tree, and were calling him. Two figures in dark dresses (they had been light-coloured before) stood bending over something. They were Kitty and the nurse. The rain was already passing and it was growing lighter when Levin reached them. The bottom of the nurse's dress was dry, but Kitty's dress was wet through and clung close to her. Though the rain had stopped, they were still standing in the same postures that they had adopted when the storm began: they stood leaning over a perambulator with a green hood.

'Alive? Safe? Thank God!' he muttered, running up to them and splashing through the puddles with one shoe half off and full of water.

Kitty's wet and rosy face was turned to him, timidly smiling beneath her bedraggled hat.

'Well, aren't you ashamed of yourself? I don't understand how one can be so imprudent!' he reproached his wife in his vexation.

'Really, it was not my fault. I was just wishing to go when he became restless. We had to change his things. We had hardly . . .' Kitty began excusing herself.

Mitya was safe and dry and slept undisturbed.

'Well, thank God! I don't know what I am saying!'

They collected the wet baby-things, and the nurse took the baby in her arms and carried him. Levin walked beside his wife, feeling guilty at having been vexed, and stealthily, so that the nurse should not see, pressing Kitty's hand.

Chapter XVIII

Throughout the whole day, amid most varied conversations in which he took part only with what one may call the external side of his mind, Levin, despite his disillusionment with the change that should have taken place in him, did not cease to be joyfully aware of the fullness of his heart.

After the rain it was too wet to go out walking, besides which the thunder-clouds had not cleared from the horizon, and, now here now there, passed thundering and darkening along the borders of the sky. So the whole company spent the rest of the day at home.

No more disputes arose; on the contrary, after dinner every one was in the best of spirits.

First Katavasov amused the ladies with his original jokes, which on first acquaintance with him always pleased people, and afterwards, encouraged by Koznyshev, he recounted his very interesting observations on the differences in character, and even in physiognomy, between male and female house-flies and on their life. Koznyshev too was in good spirits and at tea, led on by his brother, expounded his views of the future of the Eastern question, and did it so simply and well that every one listened attentively.

Only Kitty could not hear him to the end, she was called away to bath Mitya.

A few minutes after she had gone, Levin too was called to her in the nursery.

Leaving his tea and regretting the interruption in the interesting conversation, yet uneasy as to why he was sent for, as this only happened on important occasions, Levin went to the nursery.

Though Koznyshev's plan, which Levin had not heard to the end —of how a liberated Slavonic world, forty millions strong, should, together with Russia, commence a new epoch in history—interested him very much as something quite new to him, and though he was disturbed by curiosity and anxiety as to why he had been summoned, yet as soon as he had left the drawing-room and was alone, he immediately recollected his thoughts of the morning. And all these considerations of the importance of the Slavonic element in universal history seemed to him so insignificant in comparison with what was going on in his soul, that he immediately forgot them all and returned to the frame of mind he had been in that morning.

He did not now recall, as he had done before, the whole course of his thoughts (he did not now need to). He at once returned to the feeling that directed him, which was related to those thoughts, and he found that feeling in his soul yet more powerful and definite than before. Now it was not as it used to be with him when he had invented ways of tranquillizing himself and had been obliged to recapitulate the whole train of reflections in order to arrive at the feeling. Now, on the contrary, the feelings of joy and tranquillity were more vivid than before and his thoughts could not keep pace with them.

He went through the verandah and looked at two stars that had appeared on the already darkening sky, and suddenly he remembered: 'Yes, as I looked at the sky I thought that the vault I see is not a delusion, but then there was something I did not think out, something I hid from myself,' he thought. 'But whatever it was, it cannot have been a refutation. I need only think it over, and all will become clear.'

Just as he was entering the nursery he remembered what it was he had hidden from himself. It was that if the principal proof of the existence of a Deity is His revelation of what is good, why is that revelation confined to the Christian Church alone? What relation to that revelation have the Buddhist and the Mahomedan faiths, which also teach and do good?

It seemed to him that he had a reply to that question; but he had no time to express it to himself before he entered the nursery.

Kitty was standing, with her sleeves rolled up, beside the bath in which the baby was splashing about, and hearing her husband's step she turned her face toward him, beckoning him with a smile. With one hand supporting the head of the plump kicking baby who floated on his back, with the other she squeezed the water from a sponge over him, regularly exerting the muscles of her arm.

'There, come and look! Look!' she said when her husband came up. 'Agatha Mikhaylovna was right. He does recognize!'

The point was that Mitya had that day obviously and undoubtedly begun to recognize his own people.

Directly Levin approached the bath he was shown an experiment which succeeded perfectly. The cook, who had been called specially for the purpose, bent over him. He frowned and moved his head from side to side in a protesting way. Kitty bent over him, and his face lit up with a smile, he pressed his hand into the sponge and bubbled with his lips, producing such a contented and peculiar sound that not only Kitty and the nurse, but Levin too, went into unexpected raptures.

The nurse lifted the baby out of the bath with one hand and poured fresh water over him, then he was wrapped up and dried, and after a penetrating yell he was given to his mother.

'Well, I am glad you are beginning to be fond of him,' said Kitty to her husband, when with the child at her breast she had sat down in her usual place. 'I am very glad, for I was beginning to be grieved about it. You said you felt nothing for him.'

'No, did I say I felt nothing? I only said I was disillusioned.'

'What! Disillusioned with him?'

'Not so much with him as with my own feeling; I had expected more. I had expected that, like a surprise, a new, pleasant feeling would awaken in me. And then, instead of that, nothing but repulsion and pity . . .'

She listened attentively, replacing on her slender fingers, across the baby, the rings she had taken off to bath Mitya.

'And above all, the anxiety and pity were far greater than the pleasure. But to-day, after that fright during the storm, I have realized how much I love him.'

Kitty brightened up with a smile.

'Were you very frightened?' she asked. 'I was too, but to me it appears more dreadful now that it is past. I shall go and look at that oak. But how nice Katavasov is! And in general the whole day has been so pleasant? And you are so nice to your brother when you like. . . . Well, go to them. It is always hot and steamy here after the bath.'

Chapter XIX

When on leaving the nursery Levin was alone, he at once remembered the thought that had not seemed quite clear.

Instead of going back to the drawing-room, whence came the sound of voices, he stopped on the verandah and leaning on the balustrade gazed at the sky.

It had grown quite dark, and to the south, where he was looking, the sky was clear. The clouds were in the opposite direction. There lightning flashed and distant thunder rolled. Levin listened to the rhythmical dripping of raindrops from the lime trees in the garden, and looked at a familiar triangular constellation and at the Milky Way which with its branches intersected it. At every flash of lightning not only the Milky Way but even the bright stars vanished; but immediately afterwards they reappeared in the same places, as if thrown there by some unerring hand.

'Well, what is perplexing me?' Levin asked himself, feeling in advance that the solution of his doubts, though as yet unknown to him, was already in his soul.

'Yes, the one evident, indubitable manifestation of the Deity is the law of goodness disclosed to men by revelation, which I feel within myself and in the confession of which I do not so much unite myself as I am united, whether I will or not, with other people in one community of believers which is called the Church. But the Jews, Mahomedans, Confucians, Buddhists—what of them?' he questioned, putting to himself the query that seemed to him dangerous. 'Is it possible that those hundreds of millions of people are deprived of that highest blessing, without which life has no meaning?' he pondered, but he immediately corrected himself. 'But what am I asking about?' he said to himself. 'I am asking about the relation to the Deity of all the different beliefs of mankind. I am asking about the general revelation of God to the whole universe with all those cloudy nebulæ. What am I doing? To me personally, to my heart, has been indubitably revealed a knowledge unattainable by reasoning, and I obstinately wish to express that knowledge by reason and in words.

'Do I not know that it is not the stars that are moving?' he asked himself, looking at a bright planet that had already shifted its position by the top branch of a birch tree. 'But I, watching the movement of the stars, cannot picture to myself the rotation of the earth and I am right in saying that the stars move.

'And could the astronomers understand and calculate anything if they took into their calculation the whole of the complicated and varied motions of the earth? All their wonderful conclusions as to the distances, weight, movements, and disturbances of the heavenly bodies are based on their visible movement round a stationary earth—on this very movement that is now before me, and which has been the same to millions of people during the centuries, and that has been and will be the same and can always be verified. And just as astronomers' conclusions would be idle and uncertain were they not based on observations of the visible sky in relation to one meridian and one horizon, so would my conclusions be idle and uncertain were they not founded on that understanding of goodness which was and will be the same always and for every one, and which has been revealed to me by Christianity and can always be verified in my soul. The question of other creeds and their relation to the Deity I have not the right or possibility of deciding.'

'Oh, you've not gone?' suddenly asked Kitty, who was passing that way to the drawing-room. 'Nothing has upset you, has it?' she inquired, peering attentively into his face by the starlight.

But she would not have been able to discern its expression had not a flash of lightning that effaced the stars lit it up. By the light of that flash she saw the whole of his face and, noticing that he was calm and happy, she smiled at him.

'She understands,' thought he, 'she knows what I am thinking about. Shall I tell her or not? Yes, I will. . . .' But just as he was going to speak, she began:

'Oh, Kostya! Be good and go to the corner room and see how they have arranged things for Sergius Ivanich! I can't very well do it myself. Have they put in the new washstand?'

'Yes, certainly I will,' said Levin, standing upright and kissing her.

'No, I had better not tell her,' he thought when she had passed out before him. 'It is a secret, necessary and important for me alone, and inexpressible in words.

'This new feeling has not changed me, has not rendered me happy, nor suddenly illuminated me as I dreamt it would, but is just like my feeling for my son. It has not been a surprise either. But be it faith or not—I do not know what it is—this feeling has also entered imperceptibly through suffering and is firmly rooted in my soul.

'I shall still get angry with Ivan the coachman in the same way, shall dispute in the same way, shall inopportunely express my thoughts; there will still be a wall between my soul's holy of holies and other people; even my wife I shall still blame for my own fears and shall repent of it. My reason will still not understand why I pray, but I shall still pray, and my life, my whole life, independently of anything that may happen to me, is every moment of it no longer meaningless as it was before, but has an unquestionable meaning of goodness with which I have the power to invest it.' [8]

---

8. This novel was published in a monthly magazine edited by M. N. Katkóv, an influential publicist who also edited a Moscow daily paper.

Part of it appeared in that magazine during the first months of 1875, and it was continued in the first months of 1876, and again in June 1877. Then trouble arose between Katkóv and Tolstóy and its publication was stopped.

Katkóv was a warm supporter of the Slavophil movement and advocated the war with Turkey; whereas, as appears in Part 8 of the novel, Tolstóy regarded the agitation for war as factitious and harmful.

Katkóv wished him to suppress that part or to alter its tone, but Tolstóy would not do so, preferring to risk being denounced as unpatriotic and to face also the editor's refusal to continue publication.

Eventually Katkóv cut out Part 8 and returned it to Tolstóy, publishing only a brief summary of it written by someone else, under the heading 'What happened after the death of Anna Karénina'.

BACKGROUNDS AND SOURCES

Publication History of *Anna Karenina*

In 1870, after having written *War and Peace*, Tolstoy compiled and wrote his *Azbuka* (a primer for elementary school instruction and reading), and then spent the years 1872 and 1873 trying to write a novel about the age of Peter the Great. He then turned to *Anna Karenina*, and worked on it between 1873 and 1877. It was published in the monthly magazine *Russky Vestnik*, between 1875 and 1877, with the exception of the epilogue (Part VIII), which was printed separately. The novel came out in three volumes, in book form, in January 1878, with some stylistic changes from the magazine version.

Extracts from Letters, Dairies, and Newspapers†

[*Letter to A. A. Fet—August 30, 1869*]

Do you know what this summer was for me? Unceasing delight with Schopenhauer and a number of spiritual enjoyments such as I never had experienced. I took notes on all his works and read him and continue to read him (I also read Kant), and no student in the course of his studies probably learned so much and came to know so much as I this summer.

I do not know if I shall change my opinion, but at present I am convinced that Schopenhauer is the greatest genius of all mankind.

You said that somewhere he wrote certain things about philosophical topics just for himself. How and what things? This is a whole world improbably clearly and beautifully reflected. I began to translate him. Won't you too translate him? We would publish him together. When I read him, I can't understand how his name can have remained unknown. There is only one explanation, that which he repeats so often—that except for idiots there is almost nobody else in the world.[1]

[*Diary of Tolstoy's wife (S. A. Tolstoy)—February 14, 1870*]

All last summer he[2] read and studied philosophy. He was enthusiastic over Schopenhauer; he considered Hegel a pile of empty phrases. He himself thought a great deal, and he thought tormentedly. He often said

---

† This section aims at presenting passages from the letters of Tolstoy and his correspondents and other materials, such as his wife's diaries, so as to give a documentary or source account of the process of the novelist's work in writing *Anna Karenina*. The translations are by George Gibian.

1. Leo Tolstoy, *Polnoe sobranie sochinenii*, Jubilee Edition, Vol. 61 (Moscow, 1953), p. 219. A. A. Fet (1820–1892) was a poet and a friend of Tolstoy.

2. "He" refers to her husband, Leo Tolstoy, during the summer of 1869.

that his brain was aching, that some awful business was going on in him, that everything was finished for him, time for him to die.[3]

[Diary of Tolstoy's wife—March 19, 1873]

Last night L. suddenly said to me: "I have written a sheet and a half, and I believe it is good." I didn't take much notice of these words, thinking they referred to still another attempt to describe the age of Peter the Great. But later I found that he had begun to write a modern novel about family life. It is strange he should have started it so suddenly.

Seriozha [Tolstoy's son] was urging me to give him something to read out loud to the old aunt. I gave him Pushkin's *Tales of Belkin*, but the aunt had fallen asleep. Being too lazy to go downstairs and take the book to the library, I put it on the window in the living room. The next morning at coffee time, L. took this book and started reading it, and was enthusiastic about it.

At first, in this part of Annenkov's edition, he found some critical notes and said, "I am learning a lot from Pushkin. He is my father, and one must learn from him." Then he read out loud to me about how in the old days the landlords lived and traveled on highways, and the manner of life of the aristocrats in the age of Peter the Great became clear to him, which gave him particular pain, but in the evening he read various extracts and, under Pushkin's influence, he started writing.[4]

[Diary of Tolstoy's wife—February 14, 1870]

Fairy tales and folk poems brought him into rapture. The poem (*bylina*) about Danil Lovchanin gave him the idea of writing a play about that theme. Fairy tales and types such as Ilya of Murom, Alyosha Popovich,[5] and many others gave him the idea of writing a novel and of using the characters of Russian folk heroes for that novel. He particularly liked Ilya of Murom. In his novel he wanted to describe him as an educated and very intelligent young man, a peasant by origin, who studied in a university.[6]

[News item in Tulskie Gubernskie Vedomosti (Tula Province News)—1872]

On the 4th of January, at 7 o'clock at night, an unknown young woman, very well dressed, having arrived at the station Yasenki of the

---

3. N. N. Gusev, *Letopis' zhizni i tvorchestva L. N. Tolstogo, 1828–1890* (Moscow, 1958), p. 363. Page references after all passages in this section, unless otherwise stated, are to Gusev's compilation of biographical materials about Tolstoy.
4. B. I. Bursov, *L. N. Tolstoy: Seminarii* (Leningrad, 1963), p. 115.
5. Heroes of Russian folk oral epic poems.
6. Tolstoy at the time was planning to compile four books of children's readings for different age groups, starting with a primer, Gusev, p. 365.

Moscow–Kursk railway, in Krapivensk Uyezd, went up to the rails, and, when freight train no. 7 was passing, she made the sign of the cross and threw herself on the rails under the train, which cut her in two. An inquiry is being conducted into the incident.[7]

[Letter to N. N. Strakhov—March 22, 1872]

This is a model of those techniques and of the language in which I am writing and shall write for adults. * * * I have hardly started writing and probably will not begin before the winter [a novel about the age of Peter the Great]. All my time and energy are taken up by the primer.[8]

[Diary of Tolstoy's wife—March 18–19, 1873]

[Tolstoy writes the first sketch of *Anna Karenina* and] is content with his work.[9]

[Tolstoy's wife's letter to T. A. Kuzminskaya—March 19, 1873]

Yesterday Lyovochka suddenly unexpectedly began to write a novel about contemporary life. The subject of the novel is an unfaithful wife and the whole drama which grew out of it.[1]

[Letter to N. N. Strakhov—March 25, 1873]

Almost all my working hours of this winter I devoted to Peter—that is, I was calling back the spirits of that age—and suddenly a week ago, my wife brought up to me from downstairs the *Tales of Belkin*. Somehow after having worked, I picked up this volume of Pushkin, and, it seems to me for the seventh time, I read all of it, as always. I didn't have the strength to tear myself away, and I read it as though for the first time. But that is not all; he as it were solved all my doubts. Not only had I never been so delighted by Pushkin before, but it seems to me that I was never so delighted by anything. *The Shot, The Egyptian Nights, The Captain's Daughter!* And there is a fragment—"The guests gather together in the summer house." Unwittingly, unexpectedly, without myself knowing why and how it will come out, I invented people and events. I went on and continued, and then of course I began changing the story; suddenly it jelled so beautifully and strongly that it turned into

7. The woman, whose name was Anna Stepanovna Pirogova, was the common-law wife of Tolstoy's neighboring landlord, A. N. Bibikov. Tolstoy had known her. He went to see the autopsy carried out in the barracks at Yasenki. Tolstoy's wife said that the suicide gave Tolstoy the idea for the ending of the novel, as well as for the name of the heroine, Anna. Gusev, p. 384.
8. Tolstoy is referring to his reading of Pushkin's story *The Prisoner of the Caucasus*. Strakhov was a critic and friend of Tolstoy. See his article later in this volume. Gusev, p. 388.
9. Gusev, p. 403.
1. Tatiana A. Kuzminskaya, née Bers, was Tolstoy's wife's younger sister, who had married her cousin Kuzminsky. "Lyovochka" is an affectionate diminutive for "Lev" (Leo). Gusev, p. 403.

a novel of which I have now finished a rough draft. It is a novel that is very much alive, fiery, and completed. I am very pleased with it and if God grants me health, it will be ready in two weeks. It has nothing in common with all the things I was struggling with all year.[2]

[Letter to N. N. Strakhov—May 11, 1873]

I am writing a novel which has nothing to do with Peter I. I have been writing it for more than a month and I have finished a rough draft. This is the first novel in my life which has really taken hold of my heart. I am all carried away by it. Despite that, philosophical questions interest me very much this spring. In a letter which I did not send you, I wrote you about that novel and how the idea came into my head without my wishing it, thanks to divine Pushkin, whom by chance I picked up and whom I read all the way through with new enthusiasm.[3]

[Letter to N. N. Strakhov—August 24, 1873]

You write that now you expect something from me in a more severe style, similar to my attempts at a primer. To my shame I have to confess that now I am reworking and putting finishing touches on that novel about which I wrote you and which is written in the lightest possible, unsevere style. I wanted to kick up my heels with this novel and now I can't finish it. I am afraid it will come out badly; that is, you won't like it.[4]

[Letter to N. N. Strakhov—February 13, 1874]

I am very busy and work a lot. I am very glad that long ago when I wrote you, I didn't start publishing the novel. I am not capable of drawing a circle in any other way than by completing it and then correcting the mistakes in its beginning. Only now am I finishing my circle and I am correcting and correcting. Never before had it happened to me that I wrote so much without reading any of it to anybody and without even telling any of it to anybody, and I feel terribly like reading it to somebody * * * I am tired of working, of rewriting, of polishing final drafts, and I wish that somebody would praise me and that it were possible not to work any more. I don't know if it will be good. I seldom see things in such a light that I like everything. But I have already written and polished so much, and the circle is almost completed, and I have already become

2. Unmailed letter to Strakhov. Tolstoy decided it was premature to inform Strakhov about his work on the new novel. Strakhov received the letter from Tolstoy later. (Ten drafts of different beginnings of *Anna Karenina* have been preserved and printed in Soviet editions.) Gusev, pp. 403–404.
3. Bursov, *Seminarii*, pp. 115–16.
4. Bursov, p. 116.

so weary of rewriting that two weeks from now I want to go to Moscow and give it to Katkov's printer.[5]

[Letter to M. N. Katkov—middle of February 1875]

In the last chapter I cannot touch anything. "Vivid realism," as you put it, is my sole tool because I cannot use either pathos or reflections. And this is one of the places on which the whole novel rests. If it is false, then everything is false.[6]

[Letter from N. N. Strakhov—March 21, 1875]

[N. N. Strakhov writes to Tolstoy that the "excitement" created by *Anna Karenina* "is not dying down" and that "the second installment" has still greater success than the first.]

There are such varied comments that I can't report all of them. They reproach you for being cynical in the examination of Kitty and the scene of the seduction; but the ones who are more intelligent, for example N. Ya. Danilevsky, are enthusiastic, really enthusiastic about your modesty. All the details of the seduction are left out and the story begins only with the moment when shame and repentance have begun to be felt. * * * Tonight I heard a very intelligent remark: Your objectivity is so great that your moral judgment over characters terrifies one. In this regard *War and Peace* is easier to understand and simpler. That is, of course, true.[7]

[Letter to N. N. Strakhov—around March 31, 1875]

[He was pleased by Danilevsky's approval of *Anna Karenina*.]

Samarin said to me: "There, where you have two lines of asterisks, I guessed two chapters were supposed to be, and it is a pity that they are not there." I answered him: "A pity that all filth was left out? Even if I were to rewrite everything from the start a hundred times, in this place I wouldn't change anything." I thought that was only my own opinion, and you won't believe how glad I was to discover that there are people like Danilevsky who understand purity.[8]

---

5. Bursov, p. 116.
6. Tolstoy sent M.N. Katkov, the editor of *The Russian Messenger*, the galley proofs for the second issue of the magazine and objected to Katkov's letter about Chapter 11 of the novel. Gusev, p. 434.
7. Gusev, p. 440.
8. A reply to Strakhov's letter of March 21. Yuri F. Samarin (1819–1876) was a friend of Tolstoy, a Slavophile, and author of political and social works. Grigori P. Danilevsky (1829–1890) was a historical novelist. Gusev, pp. 440–441.

*[Tolstoy's conversation with the painter Kramskoy
during a walk they took together]*

Kramskoy: What do you respect?

Tolstoy: The Samara wilderness, with its farmers, the Bashkirs, about whom Herodotus could have written. Homer ought to have done it and I don't know how. I'm studying. I've even learned Greek to read Homer. He sings and shouts and it's all about the truth. Peace comes in the steppe.

K: But how's your novel, Lev Nikolayevich?

T: I don't know. One thing's certain. Anna's going to die—vengeance will be wreaked on her. She wanted to rethink life in her own way.

K: How should one think?

T: One must try to live by the faith which one has sucked in with one's mother's milk and without arrogance of the mind.

K: You mean, believe in the church?

T: Look, the sky's cleared. It is pale blue. One has to believe that the pale blue up there is a solid vault. Otherwise one would believe in revolution. . . .[9]

[I. S. Turgenev's letter to Y. P. Polonsky—May 13, 1875]

I don't like *Anna Karenina*, although one finds some truly magnificent pages (the race, the mowing, the hunt), but it is all sour; it smells of Moscow, of incense, of old maidishness, of Slavophilism, aristocratism, and so on.[1]

[Letter to N. N. Strakhov—March 6, 1874]

Yesterday I gave the printer part of the manuscript, about seven printer's sheets. Altogether there will be forty printer's sheets.[2] I hope to have everything published by May. In Moscow for the first time I read a few chapters to Tiutchev's daughter and to Y. Samarin. I chose them both as very cold, intelligent, and sensitive people, and it seemed to me that the reading made very little impression. I didn't like it any the less for it, but threw myself to finishing and rewriting still more eagerly. I think it will be good, but people won't like it and it will not be successful, because it is very simple.[3]

9. Quoted in *Tolstoy: A Biography* by A. N. Wilson, p. 278 (New York: W. W. Norton & Company, Inc., 1988). Reprinted by permission. Tolstoy was then in the middle of writing *Anna Karenina*, around 1875.
1. The letter reflects Turgenev's Westernizing leanings. Gusev, p. 443.
2. A printer's sheet (equivalent to our "signature") is sixteen pages.
3. Fyodor Tiutchev (1803–1873) was a great lyrical poet. For Samarin, see footnote 8 above. Bursov, pp. 116–117.

[*Letter to N. N. Strakhov—July 27, 1874*]

Even before I got your letter, I followed your advice; that is, I worked on my novel. But I so dislike what has been set in type that I made a definite decision to destroy the printed sheets and do over the whole beginning concerning Levin and Vronsky. They will be the same, but they will be better. I hope to take up this work in the fall and to finish it.[4]

[*Letter to P. D. Golokhvastov—July 29, 1874*]

Strakhov was here the other day. He wanted to inspire me with passion for my novel, but I took it and threw it aside. It is terribly repulsive and disgusting.[5]

[*Letter to N. N. Strakhov—August 30, 1874*]

My novel is not progressing, but thanks to you I believe that it is worth finishing and I hope to do it this year.[6]

[*Letter from A. A. Fet to Tolstoy—undated,*
middle of February, 1875]

How can I thank you for *Karenina*? * * * What can I say about the artistic mastery of the whole novel, about the simple craftsmanship? What art of introducing new characters! What charming description of the ball! What a magnificent plot![7]

[*Letter to N. N. Strakhov—undated letter,*
probably February 23, 1875]

If you have time and feel like it, please let me know what you hear or read about these chapters, that is, if it makes sense. There are many weak places. I will name them to you: the arrival of Anna at home and her stay at home, Chapters 22 and 23 of Part I; the conversation in the Shcherbatsky family after the doctor's visit up to the discussion among the sisters, Chapters 1 and 2 of Part II; the salon in Petersburg, Chapter 6 of Part II. If there are any condemnations of those places, please let me know.[8]

4. Bursov, p. 117.
5. Pavel D. Golokhvastov (1838–1892) was a historical writer particularly interested in Russian folk poetry. Bursov, p. 117.
6. Bursov, p. 117.
7. Bursov, p. 117.
8. Bursov, p. 117.

[Letter from A. A. Fet to Tolstoy—March 26, 1876]

Even in *Karenina* there are dullish chapters. People will say to me: they are necessary for the cohesion of the whole. But I shall say: that is not my business.

But I do know that the whole and the details are high carat gold. In some operas there is a trio without accompanying music. Each of the three voices (in *Robert*) sings its own melody and the result makes one's soul want to fly to the heavens. Such a trio is sung by Anna Karenina, her husband, and Vronsky at the bedside of the sick woman. What content! What power! I am convinced that you yourself reach such height only in moments of clear inspiration. Everybody feels that this novel is a stern, honest judgment passed on our entire way of life, from the peasant to the beef-like prince. People feel that an eye watches them from above which is equipped differently than their blind-since-birth little peepers. What they consider indubitable, honorable, good, desirable, excellent, enviable is shown to be dull, gross, senseless, ridiculous.[9]

[Letter from Tolstoy to N. N. Strakhov—around April 23, 1876]

If I wanted to say in words all that I had in mind to express by my novel, I should have to write the same novel which I wrote all over again. If nearsighed critics think that I wanted to describe only what I like, how Oblonsky dines and what shoulders Anna has, they are mistaken.

In everything, in almost everything that I have written, I was guided by the need to bring together ideas linked among themselves, in order to achieve self-expression. But every idea expressed by itself in words loses its meaning, becomes terribly debased when it is taken alone, out of the linking in which it is found. This linking is based not on an idea, I think, but on something else, and to express the essence of that linking in any way directly by words is impossible, but it is possible indirectly, with words describing images, actions, situations. One of the most obvious proofs of this for me was Vronsky's suicide attempt, which you liked. It was never so clear to me before. The chapter about how Vronsky accepted his role after meeting the husband had been written for a long time. I started correcting it and completely unexpectedly for me, but quite certainly, Vronsky started to shoot himself. Now it turns out that for what follows, it was organically necessary.[1]

9. Gusev, p. 454.
1. Gusev, pp. 456–457.

[Diary of Tolstoy's wife—November 20, 1876]

L. N. was just now saying to me how the ideas for his novel came to him: "I was sitting downstairs in my study and observing a very beautiful silk line on the sleeve of my robe. I was thinking about how people get the idea in their head to invent all those patterns and ornaments of embroidery, and that there exists a whole world of woman's work, fashions, ideas, by which women live. All that must be very cheerful, and I understood that women could love this and occupy themselves with it. And, of course, at once my ideas moved to Anna and suddenly that line of thought gave me a whole chapter. Anna is deprived of all these joys of occupying herself with the woman's side of life, because she is alone. All women have turned away from her, and she has nobody to talk to about all that which composes the everyday, purely feminine occupations."[2]

[Diary of Tolstoy's wife—March 2, 1877]

L. N. went to his desk yesterday and, pointing at the manuscript, said: "Oh, to finish this novel (*Anna Karenina*) as fast as possible and to start something new! Now my idea is clear to me. In order for a work to be good, one must love its main basic idea, as in *Anna Karenina* I love the idea of a family. In *War and Peace* I loved the idea of the people, because of the war of 1812; and now it is so clear to me that in my new work I shall love the idea of the Russian people in the sense of a ruling force."[3]

[Letter from A. A. Fet to Tolstoy—April 12, 1877]

I am not speaking about the art of the details. * * * But what artistic boldness in the description of childbirth! Nobody since the creation of the world had done that nor will anybody. Fools will be shouting about Flaubertian realism, but here everything is ideal. I jumped up when I reached the place about the two holes into the world of spirit, into nirvana. Those are two visible and eternally mysterious windows, birth and death.[4]

---

2. Tolstoy was referring to Chapter 28, Part 5. Gusev, p. 462.
3. Gusev, p. 468.
4. Fet was writing to Tolstoy about his impressions of those chapters of *Anna Karenina* which were published in the March issue of *The Russian Messenger*. Gusev, p. 471.

[Draft of telegram to M. N. Katkov—May 22, 1877]

I beg you to return the original of the epilogue. From now on I do not wish to have any dealings with the *Russian Messenger*.[5]

[Memoirs of N. N. Strakhov—summer, 1877]

In the summer of 1877, I was Count Leo Tolstoy's guest in Yasnaya Polyana during June and July, and I suggested to him going through *Anna Karenina* in order to prepare it for a separate edition. I began to read it first, to correct punctuation and obvious errors, and to point out to Leo places which for some reason seemed to me to be in need of improvement—for the most part, even perhaps exclusively, errors in the language and unclear places. Thus first I read it and made my corrections, and after me Leo. So the work went until the middle of the novel, but then Leo Nikolaevich, getting more and more carried away by his work, overtook me, and I corrected after him and mainly went over his corrections in order to make sure that I understood them and made them out correctly, because ahead of me was the reading of the proofs.

In the morning after having talked our fill over coffee (they served it at noon on the terrace), we separated and each of us went to work. It was agreed that an hour or half an hour before dinner (at five o'clock) we would go for a walk in order to refresh ourselves and work up an appetite. Pleasant as the work was for me, still, because of my typical punctuality. I usually did not miss the appointed hour, and having made myself ready for the walk, I would call Leo Nikolaevich. He was almost always late, and sometimes it was hard to tear him away from his work. In such cases, traces of tension could very clearly be seen in him. One could note a slight flushing. Leo Nikolaevich was absent-minded and ate very little for dinner. We worked in this manner every day for over a month. This strenuous labor was fruitful. Much as I loved the novel in its original form, I fairly quickly convinced myself that Leo Nikolaevich's corrections were always made with amazing skill, that they clarified and deepened that which had seemed clear even without it, and they were always strictly in keeping with the spirit of the whole. As far as my corrections went, which concerned only language, I noticed one peculiarity which, although it wasn't unexpected to me, nevertheless was very pronounced. Leo Nikolaevich firmly defended every last word he had written and did not agree even to what seemed to be the most innocent changes. From his explanations, I became convinced that he values his language to an unusual degree, in spite of the apparent non-

5. M. N. Katkov, the editor of *The Russian Messenger*, refused to print the last part of *Anna Karenina*. Katkov disagreed with Tolstoy's opposition to the volunteer movement of Russians to aid the Serbs against Turkey. In June, *The Russian Messenger*, instead of publishing the last part of *Anna Karenina*, printed a note titled "From the Editor," summing up the content of the last part in a few lines. Gusev, p. 474.

chalance and unevenness of his style. He thinks about every single word, every single turn of phrase no less than the most punctilious poet.[6]

[Letter to N. N. Strakhov—undated, probably May 21 or 22, 1877]

It seems that Katkov does not share my views. It could not have been otherwise because I condemn precisely people like him. Respectfully humming and hawing, begging me to tone this down, to leave that out, he has made me feel fed up with him. I already let them know that if they don't print it in the way that I want, then I will not publish with them at all, and that's what I'm going to do.[7]

[Letter to the editor of New Time—June 10, 1877]

The editors showed their sense of obligation to the subscribers by refusing to print the ending of the novel and then in their care for the satisfaction of the curiosity of their readers by retelling for them the content of the unprinted part. They tried to convince them that the novel itself was finished, that nothing important followed. * * *

But there is one deficiency in this note. It fails to say that the last part of the novel had already been set in type and was being prepared for the May issue, but was not printed for the sole reason that the author did not agree to leave out of it some of the places which the editors wanted left out. The editors on their part did not agree to print it without the omissions, although the author proposed to the editors to make all the explanations which they might find necessary.

These last chapters of *Anna Karenina* are now being printed in a separate edition.[8]

[Letter from S. A. Rachinsky to Tolstoy—January 6, 1878]

Two words about *Anna Karenina*—this is indubitably your best work. The past part diminished the impact, not because it is weaker than the others (on the contrary, it is full of depth and subtlety), but because of a basic deficiency in the construction of the whole novel. The book lacks architectonics. Two themes not connected in any way develop in the novel side by side, and they develop magnificently. How I enjoyed the acquaintance of Levin with Anna Karenina. You must agree that this is one of the best episodes of the novel. Here the opportunity presented itself to tie together all the threads of the story and to provide

---

6. Quotation from Strakhov's recollections of September 18, 1880, of his collaboration with Tolstoy in preparing the text of *Anna Karenina* for publication in book form. Yasnaya Polyana was Tolstoy's country estate. Gusev, pp. 475–76.

7. Bursov, *Seminarii*, p. 119.

8. *New Time (Novoe vremya)* was a newspaper. Tolstoy's letter was never sent by him. Its text was preserved in three drafts as well as its final version. Bursov, p. 119.

a unified conclusion. But you did not want this. God be with you. *Anna Karenina* will nevertheless remain the best contemporary novel and you the first contemporary writer.[9]

[Letter to S. A. Rachinsky—January 27, 1878]

Your opinion about *Anna Karenina* seems wrong to me. On the contrary, I take pride in the architectonics. The vaults are thrown up in such a way that one cannot notice where the link is. That is what I tried to do more than anything else. The unity in the structure is created not by action and not by relationships between the characters, but by an inner continuity.[1]

9. S. A. Rachinsky (1833–1902) was a botany professor at Moscow University who resigned in 1868 and devoted his life to teaching peasant children in a country school on his brother's estate.
1. Bursov, p. 119.

CRITICISM

FYODOR M. DOSTOEVSKY

[The Russian View of Human Guilt and Crime]†

* * * It was precisely at that time, *i.e.*, last spring, one evening, that I happened to meet in the street one of our writers most beloved to me. We meet very rarely, once in several months, and always accidentally, mostly in the street. He is one of the most eminent members of that group of five or six of our belles-lettrists whom in their conjunction, for some reason, people are used to call "the Pleiad." At least, critics, after the public, have specially segregated them from the rest of the belles-lettrists; this has been in effect for some time—the same group of five, and "the Pleiad" does not increase in number.

I like to meet this kind romancer of whom I am so fond, and it give some pleasure to prove to him, among other things, that I flatly refuse to believe he has grown antiquated—as he maintains—and that he is not going to write anything else. From my brief conversation with him I always carry away some fine, perspicacious word.

That time there were plenty of topics for conversation: the war had already begun. But at once and directly he turned to *Anna Karenina*. I had just then finished reading the seventh part, with which the novel came to a close in *The Russian Messenger*. In his appearance, my interlocutor is not an enthusiastic man. But on that occasion he impressed me with his firmness and ardent insistence upon his opinion of *Anna Karenina*.

"This is an unheard-of, outstanding thing. Who among our writers can match him? And in Europe, who can exhibit at least anything equal to his? Has there been in their literature, in recent years, and long before, a work which would be comparable to his?"

In this verdict—which I fully shared—I was chiefly impressed with the fact that this reference to Europe precisely fitted in with the questions and perplexities which, at that time, arose of their own accord in the minds of so many people. The book in my opinion directly assumed the proportions of a fact capable of giving Europe an answer on our behalf, of that long-sought fact which we could point out to Europe. Of course, people will start vociferating scoffingly that this is only lit-

† Reprinted with the permission of Charles Scribner's Sons, an imprint of Macmillan Publishing Company from *The Diary of a Writer*. Translated and annotated by Boris Brasol. Copyright 1949 Charles Scribner's Sons; copyright renewed © 1976 Maxwell Fassett, Executor of Estate of Boris Brasol.

Dostoevsky's comments were published by him in the July–August 1877 (pp. 186–190) issue of his magazine, A Writer's Diary, which he wrote, edited, and published singlehandedly. Supplied with an informative, lengthy introduction by Gary Saul Morson, A Writer's Diary is available in a complete translation by Kenneth Lantz, in two volumes (Evanston, IL; Northwestern University Press, 1993 and 1994).

erature, a novel of some kind; that it is ridiculous to exaggerate so greatly and appear in Europe with nothing but a novel. I know that people will vociferate and laugh, but this doesn't trouble me: I am not exaggerating and I am looking at things soberly. I know myself that, as yet, this is but a novel; that this is but a drop of what is needed; however, to my way of thinking the principal thing is that this drop already exists, it is given, it is here in reality and in truth. Therefore, if it exists; if Russian genius has proved capable of generating this *fact*, it is not doomed to impotence; it can create; it can give something which is its *own*; it can originate its *own* and finish uttering it when the times and the seasons come to pass.

Besides, this is far from being only a drop. Here, too, I am not exaggerating: I am fully aware of the fact that not only in some individual member of the Pleiad, but in the Pleiad as a whole, strictly speaking, you will not find that which is called ingenious, creative force. In all our literature there have been but three unquestioned men of genius with an unquestioned "new word"—Lomonosov, Pushkin and partly Gogol. And this whole Pleiad (including the author of *Anna Karenina*) emerged directly from Pushkin, one of Russia's greatest men, who, however, is still far from being understood and explained.

In Pushkin there are two principal, or guiding, ideas, and both comprise the symbol of the whole future character, of the whole future mission of Russia, and, therefore,—of our whole future destiny. The first idea is the *universality* of Russia, her responsiveness and actual, unquestioned and most profound kinship with the geniuses of all ages and nations of the world. This thought was expressed by Pushkin not as a mere suggestion, doctrine or theory; not as a dream or prophecy, but it was *actually* fulfilled by him, embodied forever in his ingenious creations and proved by the latter. He was a man of the ancient world; he was a German; he was an Englishman, profoundly cognizant of his genius, of the anguish of his aspirations (*Feast During the Plague*), and he was also the poet of the East. He said and proclaimed to all these peoples that Russian genius knew them, understood them,—was contiguous with them, that, as a kinsman, it could fully *reincarnate* itself in them; that universality was given only to the Russian spirit—the future mission to comprehend and to unite all the different nationalities, eliminating all their contradictions.

Pushkin's second idea is his turn toward the people, his sole reliance upon their strength; his covenant that in the people, and only in them, we shall fully discover our Russian genius and the cognizance of its destiny. And again, not only did Pushkin point this out, but he was the first actually to achieve it. It was with him that in Russia began the conscious turn toward the people, which was unthinkable before him, ever since the time of Peter's reform. All our present-day Pleiad has been laboring pursuant to his dictates, and after Pushkin it had uttered nothing *new*. All embryos were in him, and were indicated by Pushkin. As against this, they elaborated that which they did with such opulence of power, with such depth and precision that Pushkin, of course, would have recognized them.

It stands to reason that *Anna Karenina*, in its idea, is not a new or unheard-of thing in Russia. On the contrary we could directly point out to Europe that its source is Pushkin, himself the brightest, firmest and most undeniable proof of the independence of Russian genius and its right to the greatest, most universal, pan-human and all-assimilating significance in the future. (Alas, no matter how much we might point out, our writers would not be read in Europe for a long time to come; and even should the Europeans start reading them, they would not understand and prize them. In fact, they are altogether unable to prize them, not because of the paucity of their intellectual faculties, but because we constitute to them a wholly different world, as if we had descended from the moon, so that it is even difficult for them to admit our very existence. All this I know, and I speak of "pointing out to Europe" only as my own conviction of our right to our independence in the face of Europe.)

Nevertheless *Anna Karenina*, as an artistic production, is perfect. It has appeared at an opportune moment, and in our epoch no work in European belles-lettres can compare with it. Secondly, by its idea, the novel is something inherently ours, our *own*, specifically something constituting our Russian peculiarity as distinguished from the European world, our national "new word," or, at least, its beginning—precisely such a word as one doesn't hear in Europe, which, however, she needs so badly, despite all her haughtiness.

I am unable to embark here upon literary criticism, and will merely say a few words.

In *Anna Karenina* is expressed a view of human guilt and criminality. People are portrayed in abnormal circumstances. Evil existed before them. Caught in the whirl of deceit, people commit crime and fatally perish. It will be perceived that this is a thought dealing with the most beloved and antiquated European themes. However, how is this problem solved in Europe? Everywhere in Europe it is solved in a twofold manner. First solution: The law has been laid down, framed, formulated and conceived during millennia. Evil and good are defined, weighed, measured, and their degrees have been historically ascertained by the sages of mankind by means of uninterrupted training of the human soul and highly scientific elaboration of the extent of the cohesive force of human intercourse. It is ordered to abide blindly by this enacted code. He who fails to abide by it, he who violates it, pays for it with his freedom, his property, his life, pays literally and inhumanly. "I know"—says their own civilization—"that this is blind, cruel, impossible, since a final formula of behavior cannot be elaborated while mankind is still in the middle of the road; however, since there is no other solution, one has to abide by the written code,—abide literally and inhumanly; without this it would be worse. At the same time, despite all the abnormality and absurdity of the organization which we call the great European civilization, let the forces of the human spirit be healthy and intact; let it not dare to think that the ideal of the beautiful and the lofty has been dimmed; that the conceptions of good and evil are being distorted and twisted; that normality is continually replaced by conventionality; that simplicity and naturalness are perishing, being continually suppressed by accumulating deceit!"

The second solution is the reverse: "Inasmuch as society is abnormally organized, it is impossible to make the human entity responsible for its consequences. Therefore, the criminal is irresponsible, and at present crime does not exist. To overcome crime and human guilt, it is necessary to overcome the abnormality of society and its structure. Since it takes long to cure the existing order of things, and besides, inasmuch as no medicine has been discovered, it is necessary to destroy society *in toto* and to sweep away the old order, as it were with a broom. After that everything has to be started anew, upon different foundations, which are still unknown, but which nevertheless cannot be worse than the existing order and which, contrariwise, comprise many chances for success. The main hope is in science."

Such, then, is the second solution: people are looking forward to the future ant-hill, and meanwhile the world will be stained with blood. No other solutions of guilt and human delinquency are being offered by the Western European world.

However, in the Russian author's approach to culpability and human delinquency it is clearly revealed that no ant-hill, no triumph of "the fourth estate," no elimination of poverty, no organization of labor will save mankind from abnormality, and therefore,—from guilt and criminality. This is expressed in an immense psychological analysis of the human soul, with tremendous depth and potency, with a realism of artistic portrayal hitherto unknown in Russia. It is clear and intelligible to the point of obviousness that evil in mankind is concealed deeper than the physician-socialists suppose; that in no organization of society can evil be eliminated; that the human soul will remain identical; that abnormality and sin emanate from the soul itself, and finally, that the laws of the human spirit are so unknown to science, so obscure, so indeterminate and mysterious, that, as yet, there can neither be physicians nor *final* judges, but that there is only He who saith: "Vengeance belongeth unto me; I will recompense." He alone knows the *whole* mystery of the world and man's ultimate destiny. And man, as yet, with the pride of infallibility, should not venture to solve anything—the times and the seasons have not yet come. The human judge himself must know that he *is* not the final judge; that he himself is a sinner; that in his hands—scales and measures will be an absurdity, *if* holding the scales and the measures he fails to submit to the law of the still insoluble mystery and to resort to the only solution—to Mercy and Love. And that man should not perish in despair of the ignorance of his paths and destinies, of the conviction of the mysterious and fatal inevitability of evil, he has been given a solution. It is cleverly traced by the poet in the ingenious scene of the penultimate part of the novel,—in the scene of the mortal illness of the heroine, when criminals and enemies are suddenly transformed into superior beings, into brothers, who have forgiven each other everything; beings who by mutual all-forgiveness, have removed from themselves deceit, guilt and crime, and thereby at once acquitted themselves with full cognizance of the fact that they have become entitled to acquittal.

But later, at the end of the novel, in a dark and dreadful picture of the degradation of the human spirit, traced step by step, in the delineation of that fatal condition when evil, having taken possession of man binds his every move, paralyzes every desire of resistance, every thought, every wish to combat darkness, invading the soul, which deliberately, with delight, with a passion for vengeance, is conceived by the soul as light,—in that picture there is so much edification for the human judge, for him who holds the scales and the measures that, of course, he will exclaim with fear and perplexity: "Nay, it is not always that vengeance belongeth unto me, and not always I who shall recompense." And he will not cruelly accuse the gloomily fallen criminal of having neglected the light of the solution,—always pointed out to him—and of having *deliberately* rejected it. At least, the human judge will not cling to the letter of the law.

If we possess literary works of such power of thought and execution, why couldn't we *later* have our own science, our economic and social solutions? Why does Europe deny us independence, *our own* word?—These questions arise of their own accord. Indeed, one cannot presume the ridiculous thought that nature has bestowed upon us merely literary gifts. All the rest is a matter of history, of circumstances and of conditions of time. Thus, at least, our Europeans should be reasoning in anticipation of the judgment of the European Europeans.

NIKOLAI N. STRAKHOV

[Levin and Social Chaos]†

Anna Karenina is a work which is not free of artistic imperfections, but which represents a high artistic achivement. In the first palce, its subject is so simple and general that for a long time many people were not able to find it interesting and did not imagine that contemporaneity and instructiveness could be found in a novel. The story falls into two parts, or two layers, only loosely connected in their outer form, but having a close inner connection. The first concerns the urban, metropolitan life, and tells how Anna fell in love with Vronsky, formed a relationship with him and left her husband for him, but after living with Vronsky became so weary of passion that she threw herself beneath a railroad car. The second plane, which is more general and has greater basic significance, is the story of the country dweller Levin: it tells how he made a declaration of love, proposed, fasted and prepared himself for his wedding, married, how a son was born to him and at last started to recognize his parents.

The great originality of the author is displayed in the striking signif-icance and interest which these everyday events acquire because of the depth and clarity with which he presents them. The general idea of the novel, although not always conceived with equal force, appears very clearly: the reader cannot escape from its inexpressibly grave impression, in spite of the absence of any gloomy characteres and events, and in spite of the abundance of absolutely idyllic scenes. Not only does Anna come to suicide without any striking outward reasons or sufferings, but Levin, who is blessed in everything and who leads such a normal life, also feels the inclination towards suicide at the end, and saves himself from it only with the religious thoughts suddenly awakened in him when a muzhik[1] tells him that it is necessary to remember God and to live for one's soul. This is the moral of the novel, on which Tolstoy bases the introduction to the story "What Men Live By."

Karenina lives by her passion. Prior to this passion she was spiritually deprived. This worldly, court life, in which there is no nourishment for the soul, in which concerns are artificial and illusory, is portrayed for us with amazing acuity and clarity. Anna and Vronsky are just about the best people of this milieu, because their natural feelings have risen

† From N. N. Strakhov, *Kriticheskie stat'i ob I. S. Turgeneve i L. N. Tolstom* (1862–1885) (*Critical Articles about Turgenev and Tolstoy*), (St. Petersburg, 1895), pp. 447–451. Translated by Zoreslava Kushner. N. N. Strakhov (1828–1896) was a close friend and correspondent of Tolstoy, as well as of Dostoevsky. He was the author of many book reviews and critical literary articles. He warned against excessive imitation of the West and stressed the distinctive aspects of Russian historical developments.
1. A Russian peasant.

above all the artificial preoccupations which make up the joys and griefs of their circle. They give themselves over to their love completely: to the end this love remains Anna's sole life, which is why she loses it. *Anna Karenina* belongs to the number of extraordinarily rare works in which the passion of love is realistically portrayed. In spite of the fact that love and sensuality are the usual themes of stories and novels, authors are generally satisfied with leading the young couple on stage and, while telling of all kinds of meetings and conversations, leave it up to the imagination of the reader to suggest what feelings and sensations surround these meetings and conversations. By contrast, in *Anna Karenina* the spiritual process itself of passion is described exactly—a thing so new and unusual that many critics and readers could not even understand it and expressed their bewilderment in print. Passion arises here from the first glance, without preliminary conversations about tastes and convictions. According to traditional novels, this is the way it should be, but we have for some reason almost forgotten these old stories. Thereafter passion grows, and the author describes its every phase as clearly and forcibly as at that first glance of the lovers. The feeling reveals itself ever more fully; Anna becomes jealous, for, as is said in *Ruslan*:[2]

> Whoever loves, entertains jealousy involuntarily.

The essence of jealousy, the inner battle of Anna and Vronsky is told so convincingly and distinctly that is terrifying to see the inescapable consequences. The unhappy Anna, who puts her whole soul into her passion, inevitably has to burn up in this flame. When she senses that her sole happiness is betraying her, she calls upon death. She does not manage to wait out the cooling of ardor or the unfaithfulness of Vronsky. She dies not from insult or unhappiness, but from her love. The story is moving and cruel, and if the author were not so merciless toward his main characters, if he could betray his own inescapable truthfulness, he would be able to make us cry bitterly over this unhappy woman who is destroyed by her irrevocable devotion to passion. But the author has taken it further. He has sketched for us in detail the *unwholesomeness* of this passion, which does not submit to any higher principle nor is made spiritual by obedience to anything else. But more than this. In the moments of upheaval and illness, conscious glimmerings of a purely spiritual origin occur for Anna and her husband (recall Anna's illness after childbirth and Karenin's forgiveness of Vronsky), glimmerings which are quickly overcome by the shadows of other feelings and thoughts hostile to them. Only Vronsky remains thoroughly carnal from beginning to end.

In this way, with frightening truth, this world of total blindness and total gloom is shown to us. In contrast to it stands the apparently more radiant world of Levin, a sincere and simple man, with many faults but

---

2. From the long narrative poem *Ruslan and Lyudmila* (1820), by Alexander Pushkin.

with a pure heart. Karenin and Vronsky are bureaucratic and military types; Levin is a landowner type. He is one of three brothers: the eldest, Koznyshev, of a different father, is a Slavophile; the second, Nikolai Levin, is a nihilist; the third, Konstantin Levin, the hero of the novel, is a representative of the simple Russian man without any ready-made theories. This juxtaposition is extremely instructive; it gives us sketches of the main intellectual attitudes in our society, a page from our intellectual discontent. The best representative of this discontent, who has all the sympathies of the author on his side, is Konstantin Levin, a man who always philosophizes about the most abstract problems and who will not accept popular solutions. Naturally, this tendency toward philosophizing is a strictly Russian feature, and all our contemporary literature unanimously testifies that this philosophizing was never more prevalent than it is today.

The novel, however, portrays for us not the philosophizing, but the life of Levin, to its highest fruition, and the author wanted to show us precisely how Levin's thoughts arise from the events of his life, from the irresistible feelings of his heart. To all outward appearances, his is a highly prosperous life. Levin is a fine man, young and strong; he does everything with enthusiasm and is very devoted to his farming; he marries the woman he loves and becomes a happy family man. The picture of all this satisfaction and happiness is among the best and truly amazing pages of the book. We can then ask, from where could these gloomy thoughts come, and even thoughts of suicide? If we look closely, we can feel the emptiness of his life and we can understand the spiritual hunger of Levin. The author leads Levin to clash with the most diverse spheres of people and events, and shows with marvelous lucidity how Levin cannot attach himself to any of these spheres. He is terribly solitary, and solitary in proportion to his sensitivity, genuineness, and sincerity, which do not allow any compromises and turn away from all falsehood. Thus the best of the people introduced in the novel is least of all capable of merging with the surrounding life. He rejects it, and this rejection is even stronger because it is done without commotion and involuntarily; Levin does not accuse anyone, he does not attack anything—he simply walks away from what is contrary to him.

At the end of the novel the wave of general agitation, rippling through at the time of the Serbian war, is portrayed. Levin also separates himself at this point, moving away from that wave towards those deep popular social classes, which remained untouched, although they had fully submitted to the wave in the general course of their own lives. At the time this episode created much commotion, and even the journal which published *Anna Karenina* refused to print it. But actually the novel contains many other episodes which are much more dismal. In spite of the extreme gentleness of the moral, hardly ever has a more gloomy picture of the whole Russian existence been presented. Only the world of the peasants, which lies in the furthest background and appears only infrequently, shines with a peaceful bright light, and it is only with this world that Levin does occasionally merge. He feels, nevertheless, that he cannot do this altogether.

What remains for Levin? What remains for a man who succumbs to such a cruel estrangement from the surrounding life? Only he himself and his private life remain to him. But private life is always the plaything of chance. When his brother Nikolai falls gravely ill, when his wife suffers in childbirth, when lightning strikes the tree under which his infant son is sleeping, and in a thousand other, more petty events, in his own joys and successes, Levin feels that he is in the hands of fate, that the very thread of his life can break instantaneously, as easily as a slender spider's web. This is the source of his despair. "If *my* life and joy are the single goal of life, then this goal is so insignificant, so fragile, so obviously unattainable, that only despair can fill a man and can only choke him but not animate him. Here Levin begins to turn toward religious thoughts.

Such is the obvious meaning of *Anna Karenina*. The problem explored deeply is the eternal problem of human life, and not just of a contemporary type of man or a contemporary problem. If the author did not waste so much realism and so much acuteness on Levin, he could have made of him not just a simple, mortal, awkward and vacillating man, teeming with faults, but some new Hamlet, tortured by his thoughts, not as a consequence of grief or crimes which oppress him, but on the contrary, in the midst of complete external well-being. For this novel actually portrays the waking dream of our day. To our sorrow (or perhaps, to our joy), eternal questions trouble our ordinary people under ordinary circumstances. With us some kind of a shift within the human conscience is going on, infecting whole crowds of all kinds of people, of course from the educated classes. The government clerk who does not believe in his right to rule the earth; the bureaucrat who does not believe in his work and assumes that his effort cannot be worth the pay he receives; the educated and well-off man who envies the muzhik; the father who renounces his own life for the sake of his children; the man in the prime of life amidst his family who finds no purpose in life and is persecuted by thoughts of suicide—these and similar phenomena testify that in this existence, all firm foundations have disappeared, and that the earth trembles under the feet of these people.

Levin finds salvation in religious thoughts, but Anna, who belongs to the artificial, upper strata of society, in spite of all her suffering, does not for one minute come to her senses and does not even know where to turn for salvation. This absence of all serious concepts in the so-called educated people, the absence of all that is called moral, is portrayed with great mastery in the picture of higher society. The whole novel is a representation of the general spiritual chaos reigning in all layers of society, except the very lowest.

MATTHEW ARNOLD

[*Anna Karenina* as Life, Not Literature]†

* * * The famous English novelists have passed away, and have left no successors of like fame. It is not the English novel, therefore, which has inherited the vogue lost by the French novel. It is the novel of a country new to literature, or at any rate unregarded, till lately, by the general public of readers: it is the novel of Russia. The Russian novel has now the vogue, and deserves to have it. If fresh literary productions maintain this vogue and enhance it, we shall all be learning Russian.

The Slav nature, or at any rate the Russian nature, the Russian nature as it shows itself in the Russian novels, seems marked by an extreme sensitiveness, a consciousness most quick and acute both for what the man's self is experiencing, and also for what others in contact with him are thinking and feeling. In a nation full of life, but young, and newly in contact with an old and powerful civilisation, this sensitiveness and self-consciousness are prompt to appear. In the Americans, as well as in the Russiasn, we see them active in a high degree. They are somewhat agitating and disquieting agents to their possessor, but they have, if they get fair play, great powers for evoking and enriching a literature. * * *

* * * I believe many readers prefer to *Anna Karénine* Count Tolstoi's other great novel, *La Guerre et la Paix*. But in the novel one prefers, I think, to have the novelist dealing with the life which he knows from having lived it, rather than with the life which he knows from books or hearsay. If one has to choose a representative work of Thackeray, it is *Vanity Fair* which one would take rather than *The Virginians*. In like manner I take *Anna Karénine* as the novel best representing Count Tolstoi.

* * * We are not to take *Anna Karénine* as a work of art; we are to take it as a piece of life. A piece of life it is. The author has not invented and combined it, he has seen it; it has all happened before his inward eye, and it was in this wise that it happened. Levine's shirts were packed up, and he was late for his wedding in consequence; Warinka and Serge Ivanitch met at Levine's countryhouse and went out walking together; Serge was very near proposing, but did not. The author saw it all happening so—saw it, and therefore relates it; and what his novel in this way loses in art it gains in reality.

For this is the result which, by his extraordinary fineness of perception, and by his sincere fidelity to it, the author achieves; he works in us a sense of the absolute reality of his personages and their doings. Anna's

† Extracts from his essay "Count Leo Tolstoy," which was first published in the *Fortnightly Review*, December 1887, are reprinted from Matthew Arnold's *Essays in Criticism: Second Series* (London, 1898), pp. 254–255, 258, 260–261, 269–271, 274–276.

shoulders, and masses of hair, and half-shut eyes; Alexis Karénine's updrawn eyebrows, and tired smile, and cracking finger-joints; Stiva's eyes suffused with facile moisture—these are as real to us as any of those outward peculiarities which in our own circle of acquaintance we are noticing daily, while the inner man of our own circle of acquaintance, happily or unhappily, lies a great deal less clearly revealed to us than that of Count Tolstoi's creations. * * *

I remember M. Nisard saying to me many years ago at the École Normale in Paris, that he respected the English because they are *une nation qui sait se géner*[1]—people who can put constraint on themselves and go through what is disagreeable. Perhaps in the Slav nature this valuable faculty is somewhat wanting; a very strong impulse is too much regarded as irresistible, too little as what can be resisted and ought to be resisted, however difficult and disagreeable the resistance may be. In our high society with its pleasure and dissipation, laxer notions may to some extent prevail; but in general an English mind will be startled by Anna's suffering herself to be so overwhelmed and irretrievably carried away by her passion, by her almost at once regarding it, apparently, as something which it was hopeless to fight against. And this I say irrespectively of the worth of her lover. Wronsky's gifts and graces hardly qualify him, one might think, to be the object of so instantaneous and mighty a passion on the part of a woman like Anna. But that is not the question. Let us allow that these passions are incalculable; let us allow that one of the male sex scarcely does justice, perhaps, to the powerful and handsome guardsman and his attractions. But if Wronsky had been even such a lover as Alcibiades or the Master of Ravenswood, still that Anna, being what she is and her circumstances being what they are, should show not a hope, hardly a thought, of conquering her passion, of escaping from its fatal power, is to our notions strange and a little bewildering.

I state the objection; let me add that it is the triumph of Anna's charm that it remains paramount for us nevertheless; that throughout her course, with its failures, errors, and miseries, still the impression of her large, fresh, rich, generous, delightful nature, never leaves us—keeps our sympathy, keeps even, I had almost said, our respect * * *

We have been in a world which misconducts itself nearly as much as the world of a French novel all palpitating with 'modernity.' But there are two things in which the Russian novel—Count Tolstoi's novel at any rate—is very advantageously distinguished from the type of novel now so much in request in France. In the first place, there is no fine sentiment, at once tiresome and false. We are not told to believe, for example, that Anna is wonderfully exalted and ennobled by her passion for Wronsky. The English reader is thus saved from many a groan of

---

1. A nation which knows how to restrain and control itself.

impatience. The other thing is yet more important. Our Russian novelist deals abundantly with criminal passion and with adultery, but he does not seem to feel himself owing any service to the goddess Lubricity, or bound to put in touches at this goddess's dictation. Much in *Anna Karénine* is painful, much is unpleasant, but nothing is of a nature to trouble the senses, or to please those who wish their senses troubled. This taint is wholly absent. In the French novels where it is so abundantly present its baneful effects do not end with itself. Burns long ago remarked with deep truth that it *petrifies feeling.* Let us revert for a moment to the powerful novel of which I spoke at the outset, *Madame Bovary.* Undoubtedly the taint in question is present in *Madame Bovary*, although to a much less degree than in more recent French novels, which will be in every one's mind. But *Madame Bovary*, with this taint, is a work of *petrified feeling*; over it hangs an atmosphere of bitterness, irony, impotence; not a personage in the book to rejoice or console us; the springs of freshness and feeling are not there to create such personages. Emma Bovary follows a course in some respects like that of Anna, but where, in Emma Bovary, is Anna's charm? The treasures of compassion, tenderness, insight, which alone, amid such guilt and misery, can enable charm to subsist and to emerge, are wanting to Flaubert. He is cruel, with the cruelty of petrified feeling, to his poor heroine; he pursues her without pity or pause, as with malignity; he is harder upon her himself than any reader even, I think, will be inclined to be.

M. S. GROMEKA

[The Epigraph and the Meaning of the Novel]†

* * * That confused and futile faith in the virtue and strength of a capricious rotation of human passions, which people call an application of the principle of freedom to the area of feeling and love, this quasi-liberal faith receives a mortal blow in the novel *Anna Karenina.* The author has proved to us that in this area, unconditional freedom does not exist; laws exist there. It is up to man's will to agree with them and to be happy, or to transgress against them and to be unhappy.

Here there is no freedom for man's reason, which in our age is nearsightedly and prematurely celebrating its false victory, believing that it can change the laws of man's spirit (ignoring their strength) and transform them according to its abstract conceptions. It is impossible to destroy a family without bringing about its unhappiness, and it is im-

† From the article "The Last Works of Count L. M. Tolstoy," *Russkaia Mysl* (1883), No. 2–4. Translated by George Gibian.

possible to build new happiness on this old unhappiness. It is impossible to ignore public opinion altogether, because even if it is false, nevertheless, it is an irremovable condition of calm and freedom, and open warfare against it poisons, wounds, and cools the most ardent feeling.

Marriage is still the only form of love in which calm, natural and unobstructed feeling builds firm links between people and society, preserving freedom for action, giving strength and stimulus, creating a pure world for children, and creating the soil, the source, and the tool for life. But this pure family principle can be built only on a firm basis of genuine feeling. It cannot be constructed on an external calculation. A subsequent infatuation with passion, like the natural consequence of an old lie, will destroy the passion, improving nothing, and bring about final destruction, because "Mine is the vengeance, and I shall repay."[1]

* * *

D. S. MEREZHKOVSKY

[Tolstoy's Physical Descriptions]†

From the impression made on Vronsky when he sees Anna Karenina for the first time, we learn that from her appearance one can see instantly that she belongs to the upper class, that she is very beautiful, that she has rosy lips, shining eyes which appear dark because of her thick eyelashes, and that an "excess of something so filled her being, that against her will it manifested itself now in the sparkle of her eyes, now in her smile." And again, as the story progresses, gradually, unnoticeably, feature by feature, trait by trait is added on: When she gives her hand to Vronsky, he takes pleasure in "this somehow special, vigorous clasp with which she strongly and boldly shakes his hand." During the conversation with her sister-in-law Dolly, Anna takes her hand in her own "vigorous little hand." The wrist of that hand is "slender, fragile"; we even see the form of the fingers. Oblonsky's daughter Tania, while playing, "pulls off the ring which slips off easily" from the white, *slenderly-tapered* fingers.

In the hands of Anna Karenina, as in the hands of the other characters (perhaps because hands are the single, unconsciously animal part of the

---

1. In a conversation in 1883, Tolstoy called this article excellent: "He explained what I unconsciously put into the work. It is a most beautiful article. I am delighted by it. Finally *Anna Karenina* has been explained." Quoted from Boris Eikhenbaum, *Lev Tolstoy: Semidesyatye gody* (Leningrad, 1960), p. 191.

† From D. S. Merezhkovsky, *L. Tolstoy i Dostoevsky: zhizn', tvorchestvo, i religiia* (*L. Tolstoy and Dostoevsky: Life, Work, Religion*) (St. Petersburg—Moscow, 1912), M. O. Volf Edition of Merezhkovsky's *Collected Works*, Vol. VII, pp. 154–157 and 193–201. Translated by Zoreslava Kushner.

body, always exposed and close to elemental nature), there is even greater expressiveness than in her face: in the hands of Anna lies the charm of her whole being—a union of strength and delicacy. We learn, when she stands in the crowd at the ball, that she "always holds herself exceptionally erect"; when she gets out of a carriage or walks through a room, that she has a "brisk, determined step, carrying her rather full body with strange ease"; when she dances, that she has a "distinct grace, sureness and lightness of movement"; when she arrives for her visit with Dolly and takes off her hat, that her black tresses, which always catch on something, "are constantly curling"; and another time, that "the unruly short tendrils of her curly hair kept escaping on her nape and temples." In those unruly curls of a casually-arranged hairdo, there is such tension, "the sign of something" ever-ready for passion, as there is in the extremely bright glitter of her eyes, in the smile, playing involuntarily, "fluctuating between her eyes and lips." And finally, when she drives out to the ball, we see the nakedness of her body: "a black, low-cut velvet dress revealed her full shoulders and breasts, finely chiseled like old ivory, and her *rounded* arms." This fine chiseling, strength, and *roundness* of her body, as with Platon Karataev, are for Tolstoy a very important and profoundly mysterious feature—of embodiment of Russian beauty.

All these scattered, separate characteristics so complement each other, so correspond to each other, as in a beautiful sculpture, that the form of one member always complements the form of another. For example, the slenderly-tapered fingers and the neck, finely chiseled like old ivory, the uncontrollable sparkle of the eyes, the controlled lightness of movement, and the unruly tendrils constantly curling, the always-escaping hair—all these minute, separate characteristics so agree, that naturally and unwillingly they form one complete, living, unique, special, individual and unforgettable picture in the imagination of the reader, so that, when we finish the book, it seems to us that we have seen Anna Karenina with our own eyes and would know her instantly if we saw her.

This gift, which only Tolstoy possesses to such a degree, which one could call *insight into the flesh*, sometimes—though it is true, rather rarely—draws Tolstoy into excess.

It is so easy and pleasant for him to describe living bodies, the movement of bodies, that at times, as though he were playing, he abuses his facility. We do not complain of him because he describes precisely how a horse begins to move, when spurred: "Zharkov touched the horse with his spurs, which in excitement shuffled its feet three times, not knowing which one to start with, then righted itself and leaped"; or because from the beginning of *Anna Karenina* he hastens to inform us that Stepan Arkadevich Oblonsky, about whom we know nothing so far, has a "full, well-groomed body," and with anatomical precision describes how he "draws in plenty of air into his broad rib cage," and how he walks "with his customary, hearty step, turning out his feet which carry his full body so lightly." This last feature is significant, because in it is noted the familial likeness between brother and sister, between Stepan Arkadevich and Anna Arkadevna, who has the same hearty gait, "carrying her full body with strange ease." If all this seems lush, surely lushness in art is not always extravagance: it is often the most necessary thing. But here is a minor character, one of three who barely appear before they vanish—a nameless regimental commander in *War and Peace*. He has barely managed to appear before us, when we see that he is "broader from his chest to his spine, than from one shoulder to the other," and that he ambles along the front, "his gait shaking at every step, his spine slightly bent." The description of this shaky gait is repeated four times in five pages. Perhaps the observation is true and picturesque, but it is unnecessary and excessive. It is satisfying and important for us to know that Anna Karenina has "slenderly-tapered fingers," but we would not lose much, if he did not inform us that the Tatar footman who serves dinner to Levin and Oblonsky is broad-hipped. It would not be worthwhile to talk about this deficiency of Tolstoy, if sometimes the most individual of all, the special gift which an artist has, were not displayed, not in what he possesses in proper proportion, but precisely in what he has in excess.

The language of body gestures, while it may be less variable, is nevertheless more unmediated and expressive, endowed with a greater force of *suggestion* than the language of words. It is easier to lie with words than with body gestures and facial expressions. They betray the essential hidden nature of a man sooner than words. One glance, one frown, one quiver of a facial muscle, one movement of the body can express that which cannot be expressed with words. Successive series of these unconscious, involuntary movements imprinting themselves, depositing themselves on the face and on the whole external appearance, make up what we call the expression of the face, and what could also be called the expression of the body, because not only the face, but the whole body has its own expression, its spiritual transparency. Certain feelings arouse in us corresponding movements, and vice versa; certain habitual movements bring us closer to corresponding internal states. A man praying folds his hands and bends his knees; but the folding of the hands and the bending of his knees bring him closer to a meditative frame of mind. In this way, there exists an unbreakable current not only from the internal to the external, but also from the external to the internal.

L. Tolstoy uses this "reversible connection of the internal and external" with inimitable artistry. According to the law of universal, mechanical sympathy, which makes a stationary, stretched chord vibrate in answer to the neighboring ringing chord; according to the law of unconscious imitation, which induces in us a desire to laugh or cry at the sight of a crying or laughing man, we experience in the muscles and nerves directing the expressive gestures of our own bodies, upon reading similar descriptions, the beginning of those movements which the artist describes in the external appearance of his characters. And, by means of this sympathetic experience involuntarily going on in our own bodies, that is, by means of the most realistic and shortest path, we enter into their internal world. We begin to live with them and in them.

*   *   *

From the first appearance of Vronsky, almost from the first silent glance at him, and to her last breath, Anna loves and only loves. We scarcely know what she felt and thought, how she lived—it seems that she did not exist before love: one cannot imagine an Anna who does not love. She is entirely love, as if her whole being, body and soul, were fashioned out of love, like the body of Salamander out of fire, and of Ondine out of water.

Between her and Vronsky, unlike Natasha and Pierre, and Kitty and Levin, there is no conscious or spiritual connection. There is only a dark and powerful, physical-spiritual bond—"the bond of the soul with the body." She never speaks with him about anything except love. And even their love speeches are insignificant.

> ". . . I danced more at your one ball in Moscow than I have danced all winter in Petersburg. I have to rest before my journey."
> "And you are determined to leave tomorrow?" asked Vronsky.
> "Yes, I think so," said Anna, as if wondering at the boldness of his question; but as she said this, an uncontrollable quivering sparkle in her eyes and lips inflamed him.

In this social chit-chat, nothing is said in words; but the wordless "quivering sparkle of eyes and smile" completes the unsaid—and this is the decisive moment of passion.

When Vronsky confesses his love to Anna, the words again are insignificant.

> "Don't you know that you are all my life to me? . . . You and I are one to me—and I do not see before us the possibility of peace either for me or for you. I see the possibility of despair, misfortune . . . or I see the possibility of happiness, what happiness! Is it impossible?" . . . he added with his lips only, but she heard.
> She exerted all the powers of her mind to say what she ought; *but instead she fixed on him her eyes filled with love and did not answer at all.*[1]

If we were to compare this helpless, tongue-tied babble of Vronsky, common to the point of pettiness, with the "solemn hymns of love" of

---

1. Part II, Chapter VII.

Sakuntala, of Solomon and Sulamita, of Romeo and Juliet—how poor it would seem! But Anna and Vronsky speak not with words, but only with "the flash of glances and smiles," with the tone of their voices, their expressions, and the movements of their bodies, like animals in love. And how much deeper than all human words is this elemental and animal, wordless language of love!

It is necessary, however, to note that, in general, in Tolstoy's creations the artistic center of gravity, the force of portrayal lies not in the dramatic but in the narrative part, not in the dialogues of the characters, not in what they say, but only in what is said about them. Their speech is frivolous or senseless, but, instead, their silence is profoundly deep and wise. "She was one of those animals," notes Tolstoy about the conduct of Frou-Frou, Vronsky's horse, "who do not speak, it seems, only because the physical structure of their mouth does not allow them this." It can be said about some of Tolstoy's characters, about Vronsky and Nikolai Rostov, for example, that they speak only because the physical structure of their mouth allows them this.

Like Natasha, who speaks in her husband's words, and like Platon Karataev, who speaks in the words of the people, in maxims and proverbs, Anna "has no words of her own." How many unforgettable, personal and characteristic feelings and sensations of Anna Karenina are preserved in our memory—but not one thought, not one personal, peculiar word exclusively her own, not even about love. Yet she does not appear stupid; on the contrary, we gather that she is mentally more complex and superior to Dolly, Kitty, Vronsky, and perhaps even to Levin, who talks so much, alas, too much. But her position in the action of the novel, her complete absorption in passion, is such that she shields us precisely from intelligence, consciousness, higher selflessness and the unsensual aspect of the soul. Who or what is she beyond love? We know only that she is a St. Petersburg woman of high society. But apart from her rank, what historical existence, what culture has she come from? Where do the roots of her being penetrate into Russian soil? Surely she is sufficiently deep and primitive for these roots to exist. What does she think not only of her own, but of love in general and of the family in general; about children, people, duty, nature, art, life, death, God? We know nothing of this, or almost nothing. Instead we know precisely how her hair curls and escapes onto her nape and temples, how her slender fingers taper at the tips, and what a rounded, strong, literally chiseled neck she has: we know every expression of her face, every movement of her body. Her body and, partly, the elemental-animal side of her soul—the "night soul" as Tiutchev calls it—we see with penetrating clarity. Yet surely it is possible that we see the body and soul, even the "personality" of Frou-Frou with no less clarity, for Vronsky's horse also has her own *night soul*," her elemental-animal *face*—and this face is one of the characters of the tragedy. If it is true, as someone affirms, that Vronsky seems like a stallion in an aide-de-camp's uniform, then his horse seems like a charming woman. And, not without purpose, there emerges an elusive, mysteriously ominous fusion of the "eternally feminine" in the charm of Frou-Frou and Anna Karenina, which later deepens more and more.

"Frou-Frou was not without imperfections," but it is precisely these unique, seemingly irregular "personal" traits which captivate Vronsky. With his first glance he is struck by Anna's appearance—by her "breeding" and "blood." And in Frou-Frou, "to a high degree there was a quality which made one forget all her defects": this quality was "blood" and "breeding"; that is, the aristocratism of the body. Both the horse and the woman have an identical *defining expression* of the body, in which power and delicacy, slenderness and strength are united. Anna has a little hand "with slenderly-tapered fingers," *"vigorous"* and *"delicate."* The bones of Frou-Frou's legs "below the knee seemed no thicker than a finger from the front, but were nevertheless unusually broad from the side." The muscles, which stood out under the network of veins and which were covered by the *thin*, mobile hide, smooth as satin, seemed *as strong as bone* . . . In her whole figure and the peculiarity of her head, there was a *defining, vigorous,* and altogether *delicate* expression." They both have an identical, swift lightness and truth; a wingedness of movement, along with an overly passionate, tense, threatening, elemental surplus of life. "The clean-cut head of Frou-Frou, with its prominent, flashing, gay eyes [Anna also has "flashing and gay" eyes], broadened out at the open nostrils, which showed the red blood in the cartilage within." Like Anna, she understands her master "without words." "To Vronsky, at any rate, it seemed that she understood everything which he felt while looking at her." Between them there is a strange, not only physical, animal bond, but also a "spiritual" one. She knows and loves his love, desires and fears his love. "As soon as Vronsky approached her, she drew in a deep breath and rolling back her prominent eye until the white looked bloodshot, she glanced at the passers-by, from the opposite side, shaking her muzzle, and nimbly shifted from one leg to another" (Anna also has this "nimble gait").

"There, dearest, there," said Vronsky, walking up to the horse and soothing her.

But the closer he came, the more excited she grew. Only when he reached her head, she suddenly quieted down and her muscles quiverd under her *thin*, delicate hide. Vronsky petted her *strong* neck, fixed the mane which had fallen to the other side over her pointed withers, and brought his face close to her distorted nostrils, as *slender* as the wings of a bat. She inhaled and exhaled sharply through her distended nostrils, started, pricked up her sharp ear, and extended her *strong* black lip toward Vronsky, as if wanting to grab his sleeve. But remembering the muzzle, she shook it and began to shuffle her *slender* legs.

The words "chiseled," "slender," and "strong" reappear equally in the descriptions of Frou-Frou and Anna.

Vronsky loves the horse not like an animal, but almost like an intelligent creature, like a woman—as if he were in love with her.

" 'Quiet, darling, quiet,' he said, still stroking her with his hand . . . The excitement of the horse communicated itself to Vronsky: He felt that the blood rushed to his heart, and that he, like the horse, wanted to move, to bite; it was both frightening and gay."[2] In the charm of Anna, in which there is something "demonic" and "cruel," there is also something "both frightening and gay." After the meeting with Frou-Frou, he sets out for his meeting with Anna. And that same predatory, threatening, primitive surplus of animal life, which he just felt in himself and in the animal—that beautiful "creature of God"—united him with another, equally beautiful, creature of God—Anna.

Frou-Frou, like the woman, loves the power of her master, and, like Anna, will be submissive to that fearful and sensual power—even unto death, to her last breath, to her last glance. And through both, the inescapable crime of love, the eternal tragedy, the childish play of the death-bearing Eros will be fulfilled.

During the race, when Vronsky has already passed everyone and is on the verge of the goal, gathering her last strength, Frou-Frou flies beneath him like a bird—"Oh, my perfection"—thinks he with infinite kindness and tenderness. She anticipates every movement, every thought, every feeling of her rider; they share one will, one body, one soul—"the bond of soul and body"; they are one. The man and the animal are fused in the ecstasy of some supernatural lightness, in the sensual fulfillment of flight . . . Perhaps, in that one moment, he loves Frou-Frou more than Anna, more than his wondrous and mysterious love.

But then—one clumsy movement,

> shameful and unforgivable: not keeping up with the pace of the horse, he let himself down into the saddle, and all at once his position shifted and he realized that something terrible had happened . . . Vronsky was touching the ground with one foot, and his horse was sinking on that foot. He barely managed to free his foot, when she fell on her side, snorting harshly, and, making vain efforts to rise with her slender sweating neck, she fluttered on the ground at his feet like a wounded bird. The clumsy movement which Vronsky had made had broken her back. But he realized this much later . . . And now he stood swaying on the dusty, unmoving ground; before him, panting deeply, lay Frou-Frou, and, bending her head back, she looked at him with her charming eyes. Not yet understanding what had happened, Vronsky tugged at the

2. Part II, Chapter XXI.

horse by the reins. She fluttered again like a fish, shaking the flaps of the saddle, and straightened out her front legs, but having no strength to pick up the rear, at once tangled herself up and again fell on her side. With a pale face disfigured by passion and with his lower jaw trembling, Vronsky kicked her in the stomach with his heel and again started tugging at the reins. She did not stir, but burying her nose in the ground, only stared at her master with her expressive eyes.

"Aaa!" groaned Vronsky, clutching his head, "Ah, what have I done," he cried. "The race is lost! And it's my own fault, shameful, unforgivable! And this poor, dear, ruined horse! . . . What have I done?"

For the first time in his life he experienced the most extreme misery, an irredeemable misery, and one for which he was himself responsible.[3]

Yes, he read and understood the terrible reproach in the last "expressive" human glance of the animal; he understood that he had committed a truly unrectifiable crime, offering as a sacrifice to his vain whim, in a cruel game, a live, beautiful creature of God, whom he loved.

And who knows, did fate not send him a warning in the death of Frou-Frou? Will he not destroy Anna in a cruel game in the same way? And here, as there, "one clumsy movement, shameful, unforgivable," —though to be sure, unpremeditated, inadvertent—and her overstrained being will break under the overly-heavy burden, will fall, "fluttering at his feet like a wounded bird."

This merciless law of the blind infant god Eros, who plays with death and destruction, this cruelty in sensuality, which makes love similar to hate and physical possession similar to murder, reveals itself even in the most passionate caresses of lovers.

When he looked at Anna, Vronsky

felt what a murderer must feel, when he sees the body which he has deprived of life. . . . There was something horrifying and repulsive in that memory about that, which had been paid for with the terrible price of shame. Shame at her spiritual nakedness choked her and communicated itself to him. But, disregarding his whole horror before the dead body, a murderer must cut into pieces and hide this body, must take advantage of what he has acquired with his murder. And with fury, as if with passion, the murderer throws himself on the *body*, and drags it and hacks at it; thus *he* covered her face and shoulders with kisses.[4]

After Anna's suicide, he sees this same *body*

---

3. Part II, Chapter XXVI.
4. Part II, Chapter XI.

on the barrack table, shamelessly exposed to strangers, bloody, yet still full of the life that had scarcely left her; the untouched head, thrown back, with its heavy plaits and hairs curling at the temples, and on the charming face, with its half-open rosy mouth, a frozen strange pitiful expression on the lips, and a terrible look in the fixed, open eyes, as if expressing in words that terrible thought—"that he would repent of it"—which she had said to him during their quarrel.[5]

In that "expressive glance" of the dead eyes can he not read the same reproach as in the "human" glance of the animal he killed, and can he not understand again, as before, that there had occurred in his life "the most extreme misery, an irredeemable misery, and one for which he was himself responsible"?

In the death of the woman, as in the death of the animal, a tragedy has been accomplished—the eternal violation of the strong against the weak, the crime of a sensual Eros against another, spiritual one—against Him, who said, "Be ye as one, as Thou, Father, art in Me and I in Thee, so may they be one in us."

Probing in the human down to the depth of the animal, in the animal to the human, in the innermost recess of both, Tolstoy finds the first principle, the universal, unifying, symbolic.

But before he digs his way into these underground depths, what thicknesses of rock, what abyss of flesh and blood must he pass through! From Anna Karenina, full of the primitive, always involuntary, innocent surplus of life (is not her whole guilt in that she is too beautiful.

> And glows and loves because
> Not to love is impossible)[6]

to that "shamelessly spread-out bloody body on the barrack table"— what a fearful journey!

Does it not seem that in Tolstoy this last stripping of man of everything human, this reduction of the likeness and image of God to the image of the bestial and cattle-like—in sensuality, in sickness, in childbirth, in death—verges sometimes on purposeless and bitter cruelty? He is not satisfied with the horrible; to the end he seeks the denuded and cynical, the ridiculous and dreadful together, which appear in Dante in the merriment of the devils and in the despair of the sinners.

---

5. Part VIII, Chapter V.
6. Merezhkovsky is quoting freely from Pushkin's poem "On the Hills of Georgia."

BORIS EIKHENBAUM

[*Anna Karenina* and the Literary Tradition]†

Anna Karenina is the only work of nineteenth-century world literature which unites so many seemingly ununitable things as the internal history of passion, topical questions of social life, landlordism, science, philosophy, and art. That is not all: the union of all this manifold and varied material is carried out without the help of any kind of deliberate compositional device. The novel is built on a very open and simple parallelism of two plots. If at times certain connections or junctures are effected between these two plots (Kitty and Vronsky, Anna and Levin), these are light points of contact without any significance. The novel is held together not by the linking of events themselves, but by the linking of themes and images and by the unity of attitude towards them. Tolstoy himself wrote in answer to the critical remarks of S. A. Rachinsky:

> Your opinion about *Anna Karenina* does not seem correct to me. On the contrary, I take pride in the architectonics. The vaults are done in such a way that one cannot even notice the place where they are linked. I took more care in that than in anything else. The unification of the structure is rendered not by action and not by the relationships of characters, but by an inner connection. Believe me, this is not the lack of willingness to accept criticism, especially not from you whose opinion was always excessively generous, but I am afraid that reading through the novel, you did not notice its inner content.[1]

In principle, the novel seems patterned after the European model. It is somewhat like a combination of the traditions of the English family novel and the French adultery novel. In French criticism one could sometimes even come across the view that *Anna Karenina* is a typical French novel: "Generally speaking, this is a novel similar to many in French literature. One must not forget that Tolstoy was under the influence of our nation and had friendly relations with our writers. That is why *Anna Karenina* in a certain sense forces us to recall *Madame*

---

† Boris Eikhenbaum (1886–1959) was the author of hundreds of excellent literary studies. After Marxist and sociologically oriented literary criticism became mandatory in Soviet Russia in the 1930's, his earlier works were criticized as excessively "formalistic" (directed towards issues of artistic form and technique), and he thereafter wrote in a more historical vein. His chief studies of Tolstoy are contained in four books, *Molodoy Tolstoy* (*Young Tolstoy*) (1922), and the trilogy *Lev Tolstoy: Kniga pervaya, 50ye gody* (*Tolstoy: Book I, The Fifties*) (Leningrad, 1928); *Lev Tolstoy: Kniga Vtoraya, 60ye gody* (*Tolstoy: Book II, The Sixties*) (Leningrad, 1931); and *Lev Tolstoy: Semidesyatye gody* (*Tolstoy: The Seventies*) (Leningrad, 1960). The passages in this edition are all taken from the last of these; pp. 151–152, 177–189, and 195–204. Translated by George Gibian.

1. *Russkie propilei* (Moscow, 1916), Vol. II, p. 267.

Bovary."[2] In that regard the French critics are correct when they see in *Anna Karenina* traces of Tolstoy's study of French literature, Stendhal and Flaubert, but, carried away by patriotism, they do not see the main thing—that *Anna Karenina*, not to speak about Russian traditions which go back to Pushkin, as we shall see, does not follow European traditions as much as it brings them to a head and goes beyond them. That did not happen immediately. The history of the composition of *Anna Karenina* is the history of a tense battle with the tradition of the love novel and of attempts at coming out of it into the broad area of human relations. The novel conceals in itself a great inner dynamism. It is not a simple unity, but a dialectical unity, the result of complicated intellectual processes, which the author himself experienced.

[The Composition of *Anna Karenina*: Its Russian and Western Antecedents]

It is not without foundation that Strakhov wrote to Tolstoy: "Vronsky is for you most difficult of all, Oblonsky easiest of all." Indeed, in depicting Vronsky and his relations with Anna, Tolstoy could be guided least of all by personal experience or even by his observations, and therefore had to use literary material. In these parts [dealing with Vronsky's relations with Anna] Tolstoy's novel clearly goes back to the traditions of the European love novel and the Russian "society story." The very name, Vronsky, chosen by Tolstoy after many unsuccesful tries (Gagin, Balashov), sounds like conscious stylization. It is as if Tolstoy intentionally underlines the connection of this character with literary heroes of the 30's (Pronsky, Minsky and others). It is curious that this name is also to be found in Pushkin's rough draft of the unfinished fragment "At the corner of a little square" ("married, it seems, to Vronsky").

Criticism long ago paid attention to the similarity between Tolstoy's novel and Russian family and love novels of the 30's and 40's. In answer to the criticism that Anna is an excessively ordinary woman not characteristic of the times, V. Avseenko wrote, "What does it mean, an ordinary, in other words vulgar, woman? Every new generation answers the question differently. Is Pushkin's Tatyana an ordinary woman? Is Vera in *Hero of Our Time*, with whom Anna Karenina has the closest similarity, an ordinary woman? Is Zinaida Volskaya, whom Pushkin barely sketched in the unfinished draft beginning with the words, 'The guests were gathering at the summer house,' an ordinary woman? The critic in *Molva* speaks with indignation about 'the old-fashionedness' of the chapters about society in Tolstoy's novel: 'It is as if you were reading

2. S. de Pirrelee, "Leon Tolstoi," *Mademoiselle* (1911), No. 19.

a story of the 40's with the artificial ways of high society.' " Tolstoy's novel, indeed, when viewed against contemporary fiction and nonfiction, looked like a return to the old themes of aristocratic literature. In this sense, Tolstoy's return to Pushkin is very remarkable.

*   *   *

*   *   * Tolstoy's art was basically inspired by disharmony—by the contradictions of social and individual consciousness, while the basis of Pushkin's works, despite the tragic contradictions of life, was the full integrity of historical consciousness. Here is the difference between the extreme points, the beginning and the end, of the historical process which produced Russian aristocratic culture of the 19th century. Tolstoy himself pointed out the characteristic difference between his artistic method and Pushkin's method, but left room for the possibility of their having started from common principles. According to S. A. Bers, Tolstoy saw the main difference in the fact that "Pushkin in describing an artistic detail does so lightly and does not worry whether it will be noticed and understood by the reader. He, as it were, comes to the reader with his artistic detail and insists on it before he has clearly explained it." This distinction applies also to his artistic method as a whole: Tolstoy needs special stresses, accents, he needs special, somewhat particular and therefore often paradoxical coloring of states of mind and actions.

*   *   *

During the period of planning *Anna Karenina*, Tolstoy came closest of all to the aesthetics of Pushkin. In its themes and plot, the new novel developed Pushkin's intention inherent in the unfinished works referred to above.[3]

*   *   *

From a historical perspective, Tolstoy's novel, particularly in its first version of 1873–1874, looks like a continuation of Pushkin's *Eugene Onegin*. The same problem is again being solved. The biography of Pushkin's Tatyana ends with the words:

> But I belong to another man.
> And I shall be faithful to him forever.

Tolstoy's Anna is a special kind of reincarnation of Tatyana, sketched by Pushkin himself in unfinished parts of a planned novel.[4] One critic wrote about the enthusiasm of the public for *Anna Karenina*: "Even

---

3. Eikhenbaum refers to *Dubrovsky*, *Captain's Daughter*, *Arab of Peter the Great*, and to certain unfinished fragments of works by Pushkin.
4. Eikhenbaum is referring to a fragmentary draft composition by Pushkin, unpublished in Tolstoy's life, entitled "At the Corner of a Small Square," in which Eikhenbaum believes Pushkin intended to give a new version of Tatyana (the heroine of Pushkin's narrative poem *Eugene Onegin*).

now one meets readers who criticize A. S. Pushkin for having left the public perplexed about the final fate of Onegin and Tatyana." V. Botkin in 1842 wrote to Belinsky,

> I cannot overlook the fact that no matter how high I place *Onegin*, no matter how true and deep and real the ending seems to me, still, I cannot accept Tatyana's position of voluntarily condemning herself to prostitution with her old general. Of course, every artistic work is a special world, and if we enter into it, we oblige ourselves to live by its laws, breathe its air, but what are we to do when we are possessed by other ideas and principles, when that which formerly was considered morality, high sacrifice, bravery, now seems to be immorality, preciosity, and weakness? Poetic works which stand on the universal, historical watersheds of antagonistic world attitudes are themselves in a tragic position.

Belinsky agreed with Botkin and found his last remark particularly deep and just.

This watershed was, of course, felt far more strongly in the 70's, and Tolstoy put his Anna into the new tragic situation into which Pushkin did not want to place his Tatyana.

But Tolstoy's turning towards Pushkin expressed itself not only in thematic and plot similarities. Those are merely the surfaces of that process about which Tolstoy wrote to Strakhov in 1872, the first expression of which was the *Prisoner of the Caucasus*. In Pushkin's prose he saw an example of that same narrative purity and subtlety over which he was so enthusiastic when he read Greek authors. Tolstoy's letters to P. D. Golokhvastov of 1873 show this clearly: "You will not believe," he wrote on March 30th, "that I recently read the *Tales of Belkin* for the seventh time in my life with an enthusiasm which I had not experienced for a long time. A writer must not cease to study this treasure. This new examination affected me strongly."

It is interesting that Tolstoy spoke particularly about "study." He viewed Pushkin's prose as a model, a norm. In a letter of April 9th, he drew a remarkable conclusion from this study:

> Whereby is study important? The area of poetry is infinite like life; but all objects of poetry are eternally grouped according to a known hierarchy, and the mixture of the low with the high or the mistaking of the lower for the higher is one of the main stumbling blocks. In great poets, in Pushkin, the harmonious rightness in the grouping of objects is carried out to perfection. I know that it is impossible to analyze this, but one feels it and one comes to understand it. The reading of talented but disharmonious writers (the same in music and painting) irritates one and seems to stimulate one to work and to broaden one's scope, but this is erroneous. The reading

of Homer and Pushkin narrows one's scope and if it incites one to work, the work is right.

In a letter to Strakhov, Tolstoy underlined "the accidental nature" of the closeness of his future manner with folk art. The point was indeed not in folklore but in new artistic principles. In giving up the naturalistic deviation and "descriptionism" in the last passage quoted, Tolstoy essentially affirmed the necessity for a special poetic of realism, which holds art on the high level of an artistic system. The common principle of realism ("the area of poetry is infinite, like life") does not solve the questions basic to art: selection of material, its valuation and illumination, the principles of style and narration. Reading the *Tales of Belkin*, Tolstoy felt especially the systematic quality of Pushkin, his artistic principles in dealing with material, its articulation, and treatment. Tolstoy dreamed about high art which not only would "reflect" life but would be able to look at it from stage-like elevation, which could speak great and important truths. Hence his thoughts about artistic "hierarchy" and "harmoniously correct division" of objects into high and low groups. Tolstoy called harmonious those writers who have a system of selection and division. Every system of course narrows down its field, but it gives it an inner stability, system and convincingness. This idea had already been stated by Pushkin, only more concretely: "True taste consists not in unreasoned rejection of this word, that phrase, but in a feeling of proportion." Tolstoy also fought against such unreasoning in the selection of material. The basic point of contact between Tolstoy and Pushkin which emerged in this initial period of work on *Anna Karenina* is the demand for a strict artistic system based on the principle of high realism.

* * *

[The Puzzle of the Epigraph, N. Schopenhauer]

Anna Karenina differs from *War and Peace* in its incomparably greater objectivity both of tone and illumination. The whole novel, with the exception of a few places, is written with an attentive but cold tone (to the point of cruelty, Strakhov wrote) like that of observing from outside. Tolstoy does not intrude his judgments and estimations. He watches life from on high and only rarely makes a remark similar to a scientific generalization: "All happy families are like each other, every unhappy family is unhappy in its own way."

A. D. Obolensky,[5] who visited Yasnaya Polyana in the middle 70's, said that Tolstoy turned to him with a question: "Did you read the confession of Levin in *Anna Karenina*?" And after a positive answer

5. A. D. Obolensky was then a student; he was the son of Prince D. A. Obolensky, who was an important official and owned an estate near the monastery of Optina, which Tolstoy visited. Tolstoy talked to A. D. Obolensky in July 1877; A. D. Obolensky gave an account of the conversations.

Tolstoy asked, "Tell me, whose side was I myself on, in your opinion, on the side of Levin or the priest?" Obolensky wrote: "I answered that it is written so truly and so well that from the story itself it is absolutely impossible to tell which side the author himself was on. 'In any event,' I added, 'you could hardly be altogether on the side of the priest.' " [Tolstoy answered:]

> Well, you think I'm on the side of Levin, and today Father Ambrose told me that somebody had been to see him to ask to be accepted into the monastery. This man said that my account of the confession had made a very strong impression on him. Father Ambrose, of course, himself has not read *Anna Karenina* and asked me where it was I had written so well about confession. I really think that I wrote it well. I am myself, of course, on the side of the priest and not at all on the side of Levin, but I rewrote that story four times and still it seemed to me that it was noticeable whose side I was on. And I have noticed that any story makes an impression only when one cannot make out with whom the author sympathizes. I had to write everything in such a way that this would not be noticeable.

The point here essentially is not in the "objectivity" itself, but in the effort to render the higher truth of life which rises above separate phenomena. * * * Here is the essence of Tolstoy's "objectivity," which he sustained particularly clearly and systematically in *Anna Karenina*. Here doubtlessly we see the effects of his studying Pushkin's prose which is also "objective" in this sense and for that reason was partly rejected by the period of the 1860's and 1870's. Tolstoy's leaning toward Pushkin was to some degree an expression of his disagreement with the dominant literature and criticism of his time. *Anna Karenina* was a polemical work directed against the spirit of contemporary literature and public controversy, against the views held about the purpose of art, against ruling forms of realism, against the "woman question," against the "worker question," against the *zemstvos*,[6] against the system of popular education, and against materialistic philosophy. Critics who saw in *Anna Karenina* a demonstration against contemporary progressive thought and who included Tolstoy among the "splendid" authors ("salon art") had some basis for it, just as on the other hand, Dostoevsky had some basis to affirm that one could detect in Tolstoy's novel a clear disagreement with the opinions of the leftist intelligentsia about the nature of social evil and about the causes of guilt and crime. The objective historical significance of the novel (partly as a consequence of Tolstoy's artistic "objectivity") may have proved quite different; but when it appeared, the novel certainly seemed a statement directed against the times.

Tolstoy's recoiling from current literature, his disagreement with it,

6. Regional committees of noblemen; a form of partial local self-government.

prepared the way for his study of Pushkin's prose. * * * It is clear that
Tolstoy studied Pushkin only in regard to artistic problems, those new
"techniques" about which he wrote to Strakhov in 1872.

The closest immediate stimulus to start writing a love novel was
evidently Dumas' book *Man–Woman*, but the germ for it had existed
even earlier. Dumas' book "struck" Tolstoy particularly because he often
thought about this theme and found in Dumas many like ideas and
conclusions. However, Dumas' concluding thesis about a woman who
deceives her husband and leaves him and her child ("kill her!") contradicted Tolstoy's views and necessarily aroused his objections. The biblical
epigraph, "Vengeance is mine, I shall repay," which appeared in the
earliest versions of the novel, is an answer to Dumas' thesis. It is not
necessary to kill her, because the guilty woman will perish, not by the
hand of man, but by that of God. The plot of the novel and the images
changed, becoming more complicated and freeing themselves from connection with Dumas' tract. But the epigraph remained and became
somewhat puzzling. Anna changed from the "repulsive woman," the
"Cain-like female destroying life and the activity of her husband," into
another unhappy, suffering woman, "who lost herself." How could the
epigraph remain and what does it signify?

* * *

One of the attempts to find an honorable way out of the difficulty is
contained in V. Veresaev's[7] reminiscences. Veresaev wrote:

> In the spring of 1907 I was returning from abroad, and from Warsaw
> I traveled in one compartment with a man who turned out to be
> Michael S. Sukhotin, Tolstoy's son-in-law (the husband of his
> daughter Tatyana). Naturally we spoke a great deal about Tolstoy.
> At that time I was writing my book about Dostoevsky and Tolstoy
> called *Living Life*. Among other things I told Sukhotin how I
> understood the significance of the epigraph to *Anna Karenina*,
> "Vengeance is mine, I shall repay." In the novel we see a reflection
> of the deepest spiritual essence of Tolstoy, his unshakable faith that
> life is essentially bright and joyful, that it leads man firmly towards
> happiness and harmony, and that man himself is guilty if he does
> not follow the call of life. In her marriage with Karenin, Anna was
> only a mother, not a wife. Without love, she gave to Karenin that
> which can be bright and joyful only with love. Without love,
> everything turns into mud, lies, and shame. Life does not tolerate
> that. Anna herself feels that a force as though independent of her
> tears her out of her monstrous life and throws her towards a new
> love. If Anna had given herself purely and honorably to that force,

---

7. Vikentii V. Veresaev (1867–1945) was a writer who began as a physician. His many works
include novels, stories, the autobiographical *Notebooks of a Doctor*, and biographical and
critical studies of Dostoevsky, Tolstoy, and Pushkin.

a new life of integrity would have opened before her. But Anna became afraid of human condemnation, of losing her social position. The deep, clear feeling became soiled by lies. It turned into forbidden indulgence; it became petty and confused. Anna took refuge only in love; she became a mistress, as earlier she had been only a mother. In vain was she trying to live with her unnatural, sterile love. Life cannot tolerate that. Slandered, torn asunder, Anna's soul was mercilessly killed by life. Here we can bend our head in silence before the justice of the highest court. If man does not follow the mysterious, joyful call in his soul, if he goes shyly past the greatest joys which life prepares for him, who is to blame if he perishes in darkness and in suffering? A human being went thoughtlessly against her own feeling, and a great law, resplendent in its cruelty, speaks: "Vengeance is mine, I shall repay." Sukhotin's eyes flamed: "That is original. It would be interesting to tell this to Leo Nikolaevich, to see how he would react to such an explanation." "Michael Sergeevich, I take you at your word," I answered. "I beg you to tell him and then write me. Of course I don't doubt that Tolstoy himself sees the epigraph differently, but it would be terribly interesting to know his opinion."

Sukhotin became confused and said that Leo Nikolaevich did not like to talk about his works, but in the end promised to talk to him and to write to me. A month later I really received a letter from him:

Yasnaya Polyana, May 23, 1907

Dear Vikenti Vikentevich:

Don't think I forgot to ask L. N. about the epigraph to *Anna Karenina*. I simply did not find occasion to ask him, since as I told you, L. N. does not like to talk about his belletristic works. Only a few days ago I chose a suitable moment and asked him about "Vengeance is mine, I shall repay." Unfortunately, from his answer it seems that I was right, and not you. I say unfortunately because I like your understanding of the epigraph much better than L. N.'s. I think even L. N. likes your explanation better than his own. At least when I explained to him why I wanted to know how he interpreted the epigraph, he said, "Yes, that is clever, very clever, but I must repeat that I chose that epigraph simply, as I already said, in order to explain the idea that the bad things man does have as their consequence all the bitter things, which come not from people, but from God, and that is what Anna Karenina herself experienced. Yes, I remember that was exactly what I meant to express."[8]

With these simple words, Tolstoy brings some clarity to a complicated question. Essentially he rejects not only the point of view of Veresaev, but interpretations by all the critics who look on the epigraph as the

8. Quoted by Eikhenbaum from V. Veresaev, *Vospominania* (Moscow, 1936), pp. 440–441.

expression of the idea of the novel. According to Tolstoy (particularly at the period when he wrote *Anna Karenina*) no single separate idea can express the whole meaning of a work of art[9] * * * Answering Sukhotin's question, Tolstoy explained not the meaning of the novel, but only the meaning of the epigraph. * * * Above all, the *relationship* between the epigraph and the novel needs to be explained. * * * In answering Sukhotin, Tolstoy did not speak either about Anna's "crime" nor about her suicide as a "punishment." . . . Tolstoy restored a correct understanding of the biblical saying: the stress falls on the words "mine" and "I," not on "vengeance" and "shall repay."

Tolstoy's idea expressed in this epigraph is that the unavoidable consequences of "the bad" are not vengeance by people, but one's own sufferings, which come "not from people." Anna's suicide is only a natural conclusion resulting from all the "bitter things" which Anna experienced. The point is not in her suicide itself (nor in Vronsky's attempt at suicide), but precisely in the fact that passion led her to suffering.

*   *   *

In an early version (1873) the epigraph read, "Vengeance belongs to me."[1] This is evidently an abbreviated, rough note made by Tolstoy for himself. Where could this version have come from, different as it is from the Old Testament or the Gospel—or from Church Slavic and Russian? In the fourth book of Schopenhauer's *The World as Will and Idea*, there is a chapter which deals with juridical concepts—injustice, force, laws, state, and so on. Here he speaks also about the concepts of punishment and revenge. Schopenhauer asserts that "outside the state, the right to punish does not exist." Punishment differs from vengeance by being directed to the future and seeming predestined, whereas vengeance is directed only to the past and is motivated by what has happened. " * * * No man is entitled to act in the role of a purely moral judge and retributor and to punish the actions of another man by the pain which he causes him; consequently, to mete out penance to him for it. That would be extremely excessive self-confidence. Hence the biblical, 'Vengeance is mine, I shall repay.' "

Tolstoy doubtlessly read these pages. We must conclude that he took the epigraph from here and not directly from the Gospel. He read Schopenhauer in the original (there was no Russian translation at that time; Fet's translation appeared in 1881), and in German the statement reads "Meine ist die Rache, spricht der Herr, und ich will vergelten." Without looking it up in the Gospel and not recalling the Russian text

9. Here Eikhenbaum goes on to quote Tolstoy's letter to Strakhov inveighing against trying to abstract one single idea from his novel. See the passage quoted from that letter above, p. 750.
1. In the original Russian, "Otmshchenie moe."

by heart, Tolstoy simply translated the beginning of the saying from the German as "Vengeance belongs to me."

In the early version of *Anna Karenina*, Tolstoy, with the help of Schopenhauer's ethics, argued against Dumas' thesis. Taking as his starting point not only Dumas, but also Schopenhauer, he at first made woman the embodiment of evil and sin. But the novel moved beyond its original narrow confines and grew more complicated. Tolstoy clearly hesitated in his solution to the problem of evil and sin. Theories moved to the background under the pressure of artistic material, and Anna ceased to be guilty in the sense in which she was in the 1873 version. "Your Anna Katenina will arouse endless pity, and still, every lady will see clearly that she is guilty," Strakhov wrote in 1875. The nearer the novel came to completion, the less clear Anna's guilt grew, and the epigraph left over from the earlier version became more and more puzzling. From a transgressor, Anna turned into a victim, and the natural question arose—how did "Vengeance is mine, and I shall repay" apply here?

From Tolstoy's point of view, however, which was based on Schopenhauer's ethics, Anna and Vronsky nevertheless are guilty, not before society or social opinion (as Gromeka[2] asserted), but before life, before "eternal justice." Both of them live a life which is not real because they are guided only by a narrow concept of "will" as desire. They do not, as Levin does, think deeply about the meaning of life. In that sense they are not real people, but slaves of their passion, and egoism. Their love, therefore, transforms itself into suffering—boredom, hate, jealousy. Anna begins to suffer because she makes "the eternal error men make by imagining that happiness consists in the gratification of their wishes."[3] Tolstoy writes about Vronsky: "Soon he felt rising in his soul a desire for desires—Involuntarily he began to snatch at every passing caprice, mistaking it for a desire and a purpose." Anna begins to suffer from jealousy which then grows into the desire for revenge and punishment: "Death stood before her imagination clearly and vividly as the sole means to regenerate love for her in his heart, to punish him, and to win victory in that struggle which the evil spirit that had moved into her heart carried on with him. Now everything was all the same: to go to Vozdvizhenskoe or not, to receive a divorce from her husband or not, everything was unnecessary. Only one thing was necessary—to punish him."[4] Critics have not paid attention to this passage, but it is very important. Here it is emphasized that Anna suffers and perishes not from external causes —not because society condemned her and her husband will not give her a divorce, but from passion itself, from the "evil spirit" which moved

2. See pp. 768–69 above.
3. *Anna Karenina*, Part V, Chapter 8.
4. *Anna Karenina*, Part VII, Chapter 26.

into her. Passion turns into a struggle, a "fateful duel,"[5] in Tiutchev's words. This passion is that "bad thing" about which Tolstoy spoke to Sukhotin, and Anna's and Vronsky's sufferings are "that bitter thing which comes not from people but from God." The Gospel saying which Tolstoy understood in the context of Schopenhauerian ethics kept its general meaning even after the shift of the original plot, without of course covering the entire meaning of the novel.

Thus the epigraph refers to Anna's and Vronsky's fate. "And what about Betsy Tverskaya and Stepan Oblonsky?" the reader who has read M. Aldanov's[6] book will ask. Why do they continue to live cheerfully? This is the question of a man who judges Tolstoy's novel from a legal point of view, not by its essence. Tolstoy was not a lawyer and he did not write his novel for legal study. Here there is no "criminal material"—neither prosecutors nor defense attorneys have anything to do with it. Here is a problem of higher ethics. Betsy Tverskaya and Stepan Oblonsky, like all worldly society, live outside all ethics or morality and therefore stand outside of this problem. Anna and Vronsky became subject to moral judgment ("eternal justice") only because, in the grip of genuine passion, they rose above this world of utter hypocrisy, lying, and emptiness, and entered into the world of human feelings. In the world in which Levin, Anna, and Vronsky live, there Tolstoy and his God have nothing to do with Betsy and other "professional sinners": they exist in the novel as real social evil, which is subject to the verdict of history. Tolstoy, as a genuine realist, was not writing a moralistic novel on the theme of "higher justice," but something else. His epigraph cannot be understood either as a sermon preaching bourgeois morality or as a speech of a confused lawyer who began by accusing and ended by defending.

The characters in *Anna Karenina* (partly as the characters in *War and Peace*) are distributed on a kind of moral ladder. Stiva Oblonsky and Betsy Tverskaya and the like stand near the bottom of society, the inhabitants of which know no moral laws; Anna and Vronsky are higher, but they are slaves of a blind, egoistic passion and, for that very reason, subject to moral judgment; Levin, who also stands on the edge of the precipice, is saved, because he lives in all the fullness of life and aims towards the realization of the moral law. Such is Tolstoy's verdict on his age.

5. A reference to a poem by the poet Fyodor Tiutchev (1803–1873) entitled "Definition of Love."
6. Mark Aldanov, *Tolstoy i Rolland* (Petersburg, 1915). Aldanov's book draws numerous parallels between the works of Tolstoy and those of Romain Rolland and emphasizes the moral aspect of Anna's and Vronsky's relationship.

HENRY GIFFORD AND RAYMOND WILLIAMS

[D. H. Lawrence and Tolstoy: A Critical Debate]†

Henry Gifford: *Anna, Lawrence, and "The Law"*

Lawrence came to self-realisation, I think, in some part through wrestling with Tolstoy, whose 'marvellous sensuous understanding' he rated highly, but whose 'metaphysic' he thought ignoble. The struggle centres on *Anna Karenina*, a book that had engrossed him in student days, and that later bore closely upon his own situation when he married Frieda. Tolstoy betrayed Anna, in Lawrence's view. He denied thereby his 'instinct for life' which should transcend any mere 'theory of right and wrong.' The doctrine of *Anna Karenina* Lawrence held to be blasphemous: and perhaps his final effort at rectification was made in *Lady Chatterley's Lover*.

What is meant by the 'instinct of life,' and how does it show in the novel? One episode defines it excellently: Anna has returned to St. Petersburg and is appalled at the sight of her husband:

> 'Oh heavens, why has he such ears?' she thought, looking at his cold and imposing figure, and particularly with amazement at the fleshy parts of his ears, as they propped up the rim of his round hat. On seeing her he came forward to meet her, forming his lips into his habitual mocking smile and gazing straight at her with his large weary eyes. A certain unpleasant feeling caught at her heart, when she encountered his fixed and weary gaze, as though she had expected to find him different. What struck her particularly was the feeling of dissatisfaction with herself which she experienced on meeting him. The feeling was an old and familiar one akin to a sense of hypocrisy, which she experienced in her relations with her husband; but before she had not noticed this feeling, now she clearly and painfully recognized it.

Similar to her feeling is that of her newly declared lover Vronsky, who looks on Karenin as a dog, sheep or pig fouling the spring where he longs to slake his own thirst. Their reaction belongs to 'the body's life'—the body that 'feels real hunger, real thirst, real joy in the sun or the snow, real pleasure in the smell of roses or the look of a lilac bush,' and real emotions. Karenin's aspect—the fleshy ears, the tired eyes and

† First published in *Critical Quarterly*, 1959, Vol. I, No. 3, and 1960, Vol. II, Nos. 1 and 2. Reprinted by permission of The Critical Quarterly. D. H. Lawrence in his youth had been a great admirer of Tolstoy and considered *Anna Karenina* the greatest novel ever written. Later he rejected Tolstoy's views and attempted to supply a correction in his own novels *Women in Love* and *The Rainbow*. His "misprision" of *Anna Karenina* is a striking example of what Harold Bloom has called a significant mode of literary influence. See abstract of Ph.D. thesis on this topic, *Tolstoy Journal* 1, no. 54.

bantering voice—are signs of his damnation. He is a 'social being'—
one who fails to possess himself, but who, after forgiving Anna and
Vronsky, is soon parted from his fine intentions by the 'brute force' of
social opinion. Anna confesses to her brother 'I can't live with him.
Understand, the sight of him affects me physically. . . .' This response
is the truer, Lawrence would claim, for being involuntary, like the
response of Miss Louisa to the withered clergyman in his own story
Daughters of the Vicar. Such instinctive judgments, as Leavis observes,
'express a moral sense that speaks out of the fulness of life.'

We can distinguish between the 'goodness' of Stiva (which enrages
Dolly in the opening scene) and the 'virtue' of Karenin. Stiva, for all
his moral insouciance, has no truck with falsehood; Karenin, the self-
consciously upright man, lives with it comfortably enough. Anna is like
her brother in radiating this quality of 'goodness.' She has the same
effortless charm, and she appeals by her candour. 'Apart from intelligence, grace, beauty,' Levin reflected on first meeting her, 'she had
truthfulness.' Under necessity, of course, she may abuse this instinct for
truth, living with Karenin while she is expecting Vronsky's child; but
ultimately she cannot disguise from herself the truth. As Lawrence said
in the *Fantasia*, 'let it be a great passion and death, rather than a false
or faked purpose.'

It is possible to see Anna's conduct as a challenge to a false and faking
society (which she braves at the theatre in Moscow), or as an affront to
the family and traditional pieties. Tolstoy does indeed show up the
triviality and insincerity of the 'great world' by Anna's example of passionate and serious loving. As Berdyaev says, we are given 'the truth
and rightness of the love between Anna Karenina and Vronsky as against
the falsehood of Karenin's legalism and pharisaism.' 'By their own souls,'
Lawrence insisted, 'they were right.' Yet Tolstoy could not admit that
'truth and rightness' belong to this love. Anna—a consideration that
hardly occurs to Lawrence—had broken her home, and worse, abandoned the child of her marriage to Karenin. Tolstoy judges her in the
cherished name of the family, the idea which possessed him at the time
of writing this novel. The supreme test is Dolly's visit to Anna in her
second home—a visit that contrasts tellingly with Anna's mission to her
in the opening scenes of unhappiness. Dolly is prepared to forgive, even
to side, with Anna. But she at once divines that the whole establishment
is false, to the extent of Anna's not knowing how many teeth the baby
has. Dolly returns from illusory happiness of the lovers, to the solid
content of her own home. She has been weary on her drive to Anna;
but this is wholly unlike the weariness of Anna's own last drive to
destruction. Her soul is tired rather than sick; and she owes salvation to
the family. She has that inward 'peace of mind' so deeply desired by
many characters in the book.

The ideal of the family is honoured by the Shcherbatskys and by Levin whose old home represents for him 'a whole world'—the world that had been the life and death of his parents. It is the world of Moscow tradition, rather than of Petersburg novelty, and these two cities are here, as elsewhere in Russian literature, used to symbolise the conflict between old pieties and modern pressures. Tolstoy shocked Turgenev by the tenacity of his prejudice. *Anna Karenina* no less than *War and Peace*, combines a wonderful candour with a highly tendentious design. 'When the novelist puts his thumb in the scale,' warned Lawrence, 'to pull down the balance to his own predilections, that is immorality.' About Tolstoy's predilections there can be no doubt. The strategy of the novel is directed against Anna. Has Tolstoy tampered then with his natural feelings?

'Vengeance is mine,' runs the epigraph, 'and I will repay.' The text can be taken variously. It shames the judgment of man (the judgment of the theatre audience who feel insulted by Anna's sitting among them). It may hint at the mercy of God. Yet as the story develops, this promise of vengeance rings ever more terribly in the reader's ears. Anna is doomed to the train wheels, which, as we are reminded by too many hints, have been waiting for her from the start of her infidelity—even since that first shriek of the engine whistle in the blizzard when Vronsky declared his love for her. This is the logic of guilty passion, which breeds in turn frenzy, bitterness, shame and mutual hatred; finally a cynical despair, the moral nihilism of the rake Yashvin, whose words seem so true to Anna.

Levin's wife Kitty is allowed to describe her as 'a vile woman'—and the judgment goes uncontradicted. A few hours before, Levin had been completely won over to Anna, by the spell of 'her beauty and intelligence, her culture, and with these her straightforwardness and sincerity.' Anna was indeed aiming to captivate him; yet the reader, despite Tolstoy's implication that something is subtly wrong, responds to her in the same way as Levin does. Therefore Kitty's outburst—the resentment of a pregnant wife who fears that her husband is being deluded—comes as a shock to us. Lawrence complained (in his essay on *Cavalleria Rusticana*) that Tolstoy deliberately seeks to humiliate Vronsky, that he 'has a perverse pleasure in making the later Vronsky abject and pitiable.' The same might be said of his attitude towards Anna, at this point.

Lawrence's own case makes him a far from unimpeachable witness. Still, a close reading of the book raises certain doubts in our minds: we ask the question that Tolstoy himself asked about one of Maupassant's heroines: 'Why was this beautiful being destroyed? Must it really be so?' Anna, the delinquent, yet captures our allegiance. 'It is the triumph of Anna's charm that remains paramount,' wrote Arnold, '. . . the impression of her large, fresh, rich, generous, delightful nature never leaves us . . . keeps our sympathy, keeps even, I had almost said, our respect.' To have done this, she must have appealed more strongly to her creator than the moralist in him would allow. When he set in motion that iron wheel of retribution, the 'something enormous and inexorable' that crushed Anna, he shrank from her total destruction. As Arnold noted, 'the graceful head is untouched.'

Tolstoy seems to have isolated in Anna, and to some extent in her brother, the pride of the individual life, the 'quickness' that Lawrence so deeply cared for. Dolly, and Kitty, too, are good women, mainstays of the family, but they lack the compelling charm of Anna. Indeed, Dolly is ground down by family cares, so that nothing of the bride remains in her, she becomes wholly the anxious mother. And Tolstoy pits her, shabby and timorous, against the invincible beauty of Anna. He does not shrink from presenting the contrast in its most truthful terms. That is to be expected from Tolstoy's honesty. But in a deeper sense he is not honest; or rather he cannot face the issue, which will not work out for him in accordance with his moral beliefs. Anna must be destroyed. She has been forced into a hideous marriage with Karenin, and there is no way out except through her own destruction. Lawrence was perfectly right in sensing that Tolstoy is already waging war on the flesh. After all, Anna's final reflections on sexual love, disordered though her mind is shown to be, quite simply anticipate Tolstoy's own later views. There is something like a self-mutilation in his punishment of Anna. Lawrence says that he 'denied the Father, and propagated a great system of his recusancy, elaborating his own weakness, blaspheming his strength.' Certainly the Tolstoy of subsequent years—the old man, for instance, whom Gorky knew at Yalta—was often perverse, seldom found peace in himself, clung obstinately to his system, 'a man for whom all questions were settled.'

'The real tragedy of Anna, and of certain characters in Hardy's novels who perished like her,' said Lawrence, 'is that they are unfaithful to the greater unwritten morality,' which he also called 'the Law.' 'All the while,' he contends, 'by their own souls they were right.' Two views of life were at issue in Tolstoy's mind, one of them later to be expressed by Lawrence ('Any creature that attains to its own fulness of being, its own *living* self, becomes unique, a non-pareil') and the other by Eliot ('Those who glitter in the glory of the humming bird, meaning Death'). He affirms them both; and his torment as to which he should follow constitutes perhaps 'the real tragedy' of *Anna Karenina*.

Raymond Williams: *Lawrence and Tolstoy*

Certainly Tolstoy's influence on Lawrence is important. Once we are given the beginning of the thread, we are surprised how far it leads us: especially from *Anna Karenina* to *The Rainbow*, *St. Mawr* and *Lady Chatterley's Lover*. Lawrence's attack on Tolstoy's working-out of *Anna Karenina* is only one clear and conscious incident in a long, complicated and partly unprocess, but it is useful to isolate it, for the time being, because of its exceptional interest. Yet let us leave out the possibility that in attacking *Anna Karenina* Lawrence was defending his own life with Frieda, and the similar interpretation of Tolstoy's own attack on *King Lear*. The novel and the criticism are general facts, and everything that needs to be said can be said in their terms.

We have to consider first a formulation by Lawrence that has become very popular: 'when the novelist puts his thumb in the scale to pull down the balance to his own predilections that is immorality.' The metaphor is vivid, and we all like repeating it, but the issue it raises is very difficult. It seems to be often assumed that the scale in question is some general model, which if we like we can call reality, and hence that we can all take readings on it and watch when the thumb is applied. Obviously we have to work on some such general sense of reality, and some consequent criterion of probability. But if we take the question of *Anna Karenina* as it has been usually posed—the morality of a woman leaving an unsympathetic husband for a man who really awakens her love—we must surely see that there is no simple general-purpose scale. We know from evidence, in actual cases, that this can lead to a creative relationship, or to new forms of frustration and inadequacy, or to disaster. If somebody got out the statistics, we should still have no useful scale for any particular reading. Since we know that in any actual case the outcome will depend on the qualities of the people concerned, and on their actual circumstances, the most we can ask, in literature, is that the event corresponds to the given balance: that the internal logic of the voluntarily created situation should be obeyed. There are cases, undoubtedly, in which we can see this logic being broken, for external reasons such as compatibility to a public or a formula: think, in particular, of the routine 'happy ending,' though the routine 'unhappy ending' and the routine ending of isolation and indecision are also relevant. But this is something different from the author's 'own predilections,' where we are saying either that the author is too weak or stupid to revise his general views in the light of the particular experience he is exploring, or (more insidiously) that we find his general views unacceptable. In the case of Tolstoy, we are surely bound to say that the charge of distorting *Anna Karenina* can only be sustained if we find evidence, from the constituent characters and circumstances of the book, that either for external reasons, or through weakness or stupidity, the given logic of the situation was falsified. But this is very different from any such metaphor as 'the scale.'

Two facts about the general reading of *Anna Karenina* are very noticeable. First, there is the common isolation of characters from their context, as if the tragedy of Anna could be considered apart from the actual relationships with Karenin and Vronsky, and without reference to the society in which these are lived out. The tone of many critics in their comments on Anna, is suspiciously rhapsodical: for to see the novel as a mere framework for the story of a beautiful woman sacrificed to convention is as narrow and sentimental as a similar reading of the *Antigone*. Secondly, there is the extraordinary isolation of the Anna-Vronsky-Karenin story from the novel as a whole, in which it occupies rather less than half the actual narrative. The exclusion of Levin, and of the Levin-Kitty and Stiva-Dolly marriages, is tacit but inadmissible. It is sometimes rationalised by the argument that Anna-Vronsky is the real story, and that the story of Levin (though of course occupying a great deal of space) is simply the result of Tolstoy's incurable autobiographical itch: he had to record his discursive observations on work and faith even though the real story was about the lovers. Actually, this tells us more about the sensibility from which Tolstoy has been read—a sensibility which sustains most modern English fiction and criticism—than it helps in any way with the actual novel. Even in its less obvious form—the tacit exclusion of the Levin story, and of its relevance to the story of Anna and Vronsky—the narrowness is still evident. This is, really, the fashionable 'personal relationships' dogma, in which certain kinds of relationship are abstracted from their context of society, work and belief, in obedience to strong and obscure pressures from our own kind of society. It is worth repeating a fact fairly obvious in reading the novel: that it is a whole structure in which all the elements are closely related and that the complexity of this structure is Tolstoy's actual scale—his basic reading of experience at this time. Readers and critics who isolate the Anna-Vronsky story should consider as just one example of this structure, the sequence of chapters in Part Five, where the marriage of Levin and Kitty is followed by the Italian 'honeymoon' of Anna and Vronsky and then by Levin and Kitty setting up house and living through the first difficulties of their marriage, to the crucial death of Nikolay and the discovery that Kitty is with child. This is not the interweaving of plot and sub-plot, or of two separate stories, but the enactment of a single design.

The strength of Lawrence's case is his recognition of the quickening of life in Anna, after her meeting with Vronsky, but from this point on the actual elements of the novel are distorted, not by Tolstoy, but by his critic. The rejection of Karenin is certainly part of Anna's new 'instinct for life,' but it is much too crudely realised if Karenin is seen as simply damned (the crudeness of the physical disablement of Sir Clifford Chatterley is relevant here). Tolstoy created in Karenin, a memorable figure of the avoidance of love, but he was concerned to analyse rather than simply to damn. All his adult life, Karenin has been afraid of open emotion, of any kind, because of a characteristic fear that in exposing himself he will be hurt. This fear is once, and once only, overcome, in the great stress of the expectation of Anna's death after bearing Vronsky's child, and her powerful appeal to Karenin, accompanied by a temporary rejection of Vronsky:

> There is another woman in me, I'm afraid of her: she loved that man, and I tried to hate you, and could not forget about her that used to be. I'm not that woman. Now I'm my real self, all myself.

To this declaration, Karenin responds, for once breaking his habit and his fear, only to be told by Anna, after her recovery, that she has gone back to her previous position. Thus the pattern of Karenin's whole character has been confirmed: he has 'given way' to emotion, and he has been deeply hurt. His subsequent deterioration is then hardly surprising. The point here is, not that Anna's 'instinct for life' is disproved, but that Tolstoy, quite evidently, is not dealing with cardboard figures of the 'quick' and the 'dead,' but with actual processes of relationship in which love and hate are confirmed or denied. By letting us see this situation from each point of view in turn, rather than predicating the 'quick' and the 'dead'—the 'quick' to be forgiven their weaknesses, the 'dead' to be ritually damned—Tolstoy shows an absence of 'predilections' that is characteristic of his extraordinary maturity as an artist.

The next crucial element is the character of Vronsky. It is true to say that he awakens Anna, but it is one thing to wake somebody, another to live through the day. Lawrence tells us that Tolstoy has a 'perverse pleasure' in humiliating Vronsky, but the question that has to be asked is whether the Vronsky created by Tolstoy (and no other is admissible) is in fact capable of meeting the demands of the love which he has started in Anna. It is worth remembering that our introduction to Vronsky is, in the abortive relationship with Kitty, an introduction if not to a trifler at least to a man unprepared for a relationship of any permanence. Anna's own comment, just before her death, seems in retrospect an accurate account of a relationship with such a man:

> We walked to meet each other up to the time of our love, and since then we have been irresistibly drifting in different directions. And there's no altering that. He tells me I'm insanely jealous, but it's not true. I'm not jealous, but I'm unsatisfied.

Vronsky's qualities are obvious, but it becomes clear, as the relationship with Anna develops, that he lives in a single and limited dimension, in which there is no real place for enduring passion. We can be misled, as Lawrence was often misled, by too simple an idea of 'masculinity.' Tolstoy raises the point in the novel, in Vronsky's reflections on the character of the foreign prince (is being a man something more than being a piece of healthy beef?) More fully, it is raised throughout the novel, by the comparison between Vronsky and Levin, which is surely one of Tolstoy's major themes, and from which Levin emerges as undoubtedly the stronger man. It is quite easy, in a highly civilised society, to be carried away by phrases like 'animal vigour,' but this, as Lawrence sometimes told it, is frankly a cock-and-bull story. A man's strength has to include the tenderness of protection and the warmth of continuing care which are biologically necessary in the human condition. Without these, vigour can be merely destructive, as Tolstoy shows on a small scale in the killing of a mare, and on a larger scale in Vronsky's contribution to the destruction of Anna. When she is isolated, in the country and in Moscow, he repeatedly leaves her alone, to play at politics or to watch Yashvin's gambling. The cold regularity of his reply to her desperate appeals, on the day of her death, is just another 'moment of carelessness,' but it is characteristic of his limited and powerful determination (which, ironically, had first enabled him to break through to Anna). It is significant that Lawrence, reworking this situation in *Lady Chatterley's Lover*, created in Mellors not a Vronsky, but a Levin. Mellors is strong and live, but he is also capable of deep tenderness, and interestingly, has that quality which Tolstoy saw as the means of health in Levin—an intimate and deeply respecting contact with the world of natural growth. Lawrence the critic was, after all, put right by Lawrence the artist, and we can leave it at that.

And yet, in spite of everything, did Tolstoy kill Anna, as a kind of renunciation of love? It is certainly true that Tolstoy insisted, much more than Lawrence, on the social consequences of primary relationships, but then, unlike Larwence, he set all his fiction in real societies, and could hardly avoid what they were showing him: a network of actual and continuing relationships which could not be simply dismissed as puritanism and the grey North. The convention invoked against Anna is indeed shallow and hypocritical, but take a society in which there is no difficulty of divorce, in which an Anna would not be pointed at and avoided, and the human difficulty in substance remains. The child is there, in any society. Frustration and hatred are there, under any laws, if the real relationships are wrong. The tragedy of Anna is affected by her society, but the roots of the tragedy lie much deeper, in a specific relationship (just as, in modern societies in which the old sexual laws and conventions have been practically abandoned, men and women still kill themselves in despair of love.) The action of Anna's tragedy is that she leaves one inadequate man for another but the inadequacy of Karenin lay with an unawakened woman, the inadequacy of Vronsky with a woman grown to passion and demanding it as the continuing centre of her life. The characteristic of Anna, at the highest point of her growth, is that she must live her feelings right through. Living on a limited commitment has been possible once, but it was from this that she broke out. Of course, not as a mature woman: the maturity seemed to be there, when she lived by her limited commitment to Karenin, but it is not there once her full energy is released. One of the few things we do not know enough about in the novel is her original attitude to the marriage to Karenin (this is usually left out of romantic and anti-romantic stories alike). But it is at least clear that she has become a wife and mother without ever having been a girl in love, but now in a situation where much more is needed. The rush of feeling is awakened by and attached to Vronsky, but this is not the whole story; there is also evidence, in her attitude to Vronsky, of the familiar adolescent condition in which overwhelming feeling as it were collides with an object rather than grows towards it. This can be disastrous, even for a girl, if the object is inadequate or irrelevant to the real force of the feeling. But Anna is not a girl; she is still in part the guilty wife and mother, and the combination is terrifying. The ordinary married woman's affair, as with her friends in Petersburg, is a characteristically limited commitment. We see this again in her brother Stiva, in many ways so like her, but unhurt because always essentially uncommitted. Anna shames the half-life of this society, but half-life is often a protection for the weak and the immature. Stiva slips away from difficulty, from any real demand on himself, with his 'almond-oil smile.' Anna, in her delayed rush of feeling, must give herself wholly, without regard for safety, and whether she then survives depends on the quality of the man she is giving herself to. Nothing less is thinkable; the demand is quite absolute. Even her death is a revengeful move to make Vronsky love her more, and this tragic error (common enough in certain kinds of suicide) combines the wholeness and the immaturity which, falling on weak hands, unite to destroy her.

   Tolstoy's logic, given the elements he has created, is sound. But of course Lawrence is right to imply that in choosing these elements Tolstoy was revealing himself. Yet it is no simple question of 'being' and 'social being.' Tolstoy was torn by very deep tensions, and in touch with his own errors, which he did not simply move on from. Aksinia, the serf-girl he had loved, scrubbed floors in his wife's house, and his son by her lived nearby. It is not, as it is sometimes put, a case of a young rake turned old Puritan. It is a man watching his own life, in terms of a society which divided people and exacerbated their necessary difficulties. I agree with Edmund Wilson that there were elements in this complex that he failed to recognize completely, and that there is a consequent dark area in his work, both in its shaping and in its omissions. But we must notice that in *Anna Karenina*, in relation to the tragedy of Anna, there is in the story of Levin an account of the fulfilment of a man who gives himself and commits himself completely. Significantly, this is a slow growth, learned as much from the death of his brother as from the love of Kitty, learned also in work and in the effort towards right working relations with other men. The density of this life of Levin's makes an obvious contrast with the single dimension in which, in their different ways, Vronsky and Karenin and Stiva live (in each of these men the attitude to work, and thence to other men, is seen as related to the differing yet inadequate attitudes to love). Levin translating a hundred-rouble note, lightly spent in Moscow, into the work of men in the fields, is involved with values in a sense equally opposed to the conventions of fashionable society and the mere flouting of them. In learning a reverence towards all that lives, Levin is learning something deeper than either respectability or personal honour. His ability to love Kitty as a wife, and then to love their child, grows from this whole attachment, which is more mature than anything Anna is allowed to live. Vronsky, in the end, wants marriage and a stake in the country, but in these terms the offer is both too much and too little for Anna: she does not want marriage and Vronsky's children, but she needs passion, which on Vronsky's side has gone. A meaningful society, and therefore a meaningful place in it, is for different reasons, beyond both of them. Here is the moving field of all Tolstoy's greatest writing, and there are few writers who can live with him in it. The irony is that Lawrence addressed himself to just these problems, though with less strength and in any case with less time (he died in the year of life in which *Anna Karenina* was begun). It is vitally important that we do not scale Tolstoy down to the limited sensibility (the separation of work from life, and of personal meanings from social meanings) which has recently governed our own culture. We can see the sense of Lawrence's protest, though he had to rework the book to sustain it (first in a critical error, second in a creative transformation). But while Lawrence's strength is of Tolstoy's kind, his weakness is that of our own majority culture, and must be analysed rather than merely repeated. (How dare Mr. Gifford, for example, write such a stale salon sentence as 'Dolly, and Kitty too, are good women, mainstays of the family, but they lack the compelling charm of Anna'? Consider that contrast between 'mainstay' and 'charm.' Does Mr. Gifford really live in that world, or if he does, does he want to?) 'Fulness of being' is when we live as ourselves with others and in our world, and no writer more than Tolstoy, no book more than *Anna Karenina*, illuminates its substance, its consequences, and its demands. As in all tragedy, it is not the fate of characters we rest on, but the living patterns of experience that can help us to live.

Henry Gifford: *Further Notes on* Anna Karenina

There is a sense of outrage in Mr. Williams' reply to my article, *Anna, Lawrence and 'The Law,'* with which one must sympathise. Lawrence's views are too often repeated by admirers who never stop to inspect them; great and complicated novels like *Anna Karenina* do not get the responsible reading, the full view, they deserve; personal relationships too often, in our culture, try to escape from the necessities of communal living. We must agree with Mr. Williams that the Levin side of Tolstoy's novel bears directly upon the predicament of Anna: the home, the family, rural ways, the realities of work stand over against the insecure relationships of the St. Petersburg salon, the world of railway trains and 'escape from it all' to Italy. He is right too in stressing Anna's immaturity, and the fulfillment in Levin's experience, which is denied to her. A just reading of the book will recognize all these values. Why, then, invoke Lawrence and his accusations of blasphemy?

In the twentieth volume of the Russian 'Jubilee' edition of Tolstoy, one may study the suppressed earlier drafts from which, after five years of intermittent toil, *Anna Karenina* as we know it emerged. A novel should be judged by its final form; but Lawrence's sense of a certain unresolved conflict in the work (shared surely by many readers) finds a good deal of support in the evidence of these earlier drafts. Fortunately there is to hand an extremely careful study by Vladimir A. Zhdanov, published in Moscow three years ago, the title of which may be translated as *The Making of Anna Karenina*. From its analyses one may see, perhaps, what is meant by the novelist putting his thumb in the scale. Tolstoy, as George Steiner reminds us in his recent book, nearly always wrote with a 'palpable design.' He distrusted art, and could never fend off the didactic impulse for long. *Anna Karenina* bears the ravages of that ceaseless civil war in its author, though, as Steiner points out, the double plot structure allows Tolstoy to release most of his didactic energies in the Levin story, and to treat Anna more freely and generously than he had intended.

Anna was always, of course, at the book's centre. (Note that even when, subsequently, Levin's story was added, Tolstoy chose to name the book still after her, and contrast this with the thematic titles of his other great works: *War and Peace, The Power of Darkness, Resurrection*.) Her story was to be that of an adulteress, who is first seen in a drawing room behaving not only indiscreetly but shamelessly with her lover. The husband decides that she is possessed by the devil. And this notion appears in more than one of the earlier attempts. An unrepentant Anna (then called Tatyana) returns to her husband after the race-meeting 'with a diabolical flitter in her eyes.' And the husband, in another variant which still keeps the diabolical motive, tells her: 'Our life has been united, and united not by men but by God. . . . In our opinion there is a mystery, and you and I, we feel it . . . I shall do nothing, I cannot and indeed I do not wish to punish. Vengeance is God's.' There can be little doubt that it was Tolstoy, the rigid moralist who planned this story. It might have issued as a crude tract against adultery. The annals of adultery are almost without exception squalid; but there is always 'the possible other case.' Tolstoy by prejudging the matter has suppressed that possibility; and this is what I call putting a thumb in the balance.

But the balance rose against his thumb, all the same. Gradually Karenin (who wasn't so called at first) underwent a change. At the beginning he was a gentle, easily put out, weak and almost unworldly figure, with a kind smile and kind blue eyes. Slowly he turned into the

official; the 'goodness' was taken away from him; his eyes and his bearing
became *cold*; he is Karenin, after, it seems, the Greek word *karenon*,
the head. And so we get the evasive but imposing figure who meets
Anna at the station. Karenin lives like Casaubon in a paper world, and
I would suggest that the author has far less sympathy for him than George
Eliot shows for Casaubon. He is ranged with Levin's half-brother, who
also prepared cut-and-dried formulations to meet the unexpected in life.
True, there is once for Karenin 'the awful daring of a moment's surrender,' when he forgives Anna on her supposed death bed, and Vronsky
too. But very soon after he recognises in the Princess Betsy's tone and
smile that force of social opinion to which he has always bowed. Karenin
is a 'social being': he cares more for appearances than the truth. In that
scene to which Mr. Williams has alluded, when Anna speaks of that
other woman who has possessed her, and Karenin melts in forgiveness,
I believe that didactic impulse has taken control. It seems to me a
contrived moment (like the manifestation of Platon Karataev in *War
and Peace*) but Tolstoy was too honest not to go back on it. Basically I
am sure he was hostile to Karenin, who lives by the head, and is an
emanation of Petersburg.

The counterbalance to Petersburg is Levin's world, Muscovite and
rural. Mr. Williams has every reason for saying that here Tolstoy gets
down to his real values: marriage, the family, the daily order of work in
the fields. Anna, as we know, is condemned to live in a false society;
and it is doubly tragic for her that the lover whom she chooses, in her
denial of that society, should himself be infected deeply with its prej-
udices: he shows indeed what George Eliot called 'spots of commonness.'
Anna, in fact, cannot enter the responsible world of Levin: we know—
and Dolly's visit reveals this—how glossily unreal is the establishment
that she and Vronsky set up in the country, when Vronsky needs occupation. Nobody can dispute the logic of Anna's case: she is necessarily
excluded from some of the richest experiences in human life. When,
therefore, critics like Arnold speak of her 'charm that remains paramount,' are they forgetting the full context? Perhaps—and yet surely it
is not romantic to insist that Anna (even though she has deserted her
child, and virtually destroyed both husband and lover) somehow evades
human judgment? 'Vengeance is mine, saith the Lord.' Anna has done
wrong; nonetheless she stands for qualities of truthfulness and generous
feeling, even of dedication, that are found nowhere else in her milieu.
Anna's protest against the Karenin set, its limited risks and saving hy-
pocrisies, surely wins assent from the reader. But I believe in a more
profound sense Tolstoy felt an involvement with Anna. We may recall
that Levin originally fell in love with the Shcherbatsky family as a whole,
and it is scarcely an exaggeration to say that he married Kitty on grounds
of principle: he thought first of children and the married state, then of
the woman who could provide these. Now Anna has an endowment of

life—call it, as I perhaps unwisely did, a 'compelling charm'—a spontaneity, which obviously attracted Tolstoy. Anna and Levin are the two most complete beings in the novel, and whereas Levin sometimes wearies the reader with his irritable probings after certainty, Anna disarms our prejudice against her: Tolstoy gave her, in spite of himself, an undeniable presence—she is no common creature. Tolstoy, as Pasternak has said in the *Essay in Autobiography*, though, 'a moralist, a leveller, a preacher of a system of justice applicable to every human being without exception, and in equal measure,' yet was in himself startingly original. An egalitarian, yes, but he always saw himself as *primus inter pares*.[1] We know of the crisis that followed *Anna Karenina*: the long years ensuing which were marked by what Lawrence has termed 'recusancy.' Tolstoy never achieved the balance of Shakespeare after *King Lear*. We must not allow our knowledge of his later extremes to read overmuch into *Anna Karenina*. Was he lacerating himself when he drove Anna to her destruction? It is difficult to prove. Certainly he has pursued relentlessly the logic of her situation: one might contend (especially in the light of his earlier drafts) that he argues the case against Anna. His logical victory is complete; but why did he need to embark on such an argument? What led him to conceive Anna, to endow her so lavishly, and then to force her into an ugly marriage and a career of shame ending in a bloody death? There is an agony of spirit here which is never quite subdued by all the affirmations of virtue and responsibility in Levin's world.

GEORGE STEINER

[The Beginning of *Anna Karenina*]†

The very first page of *Anna Karenina* transports our emotions into a world remote from that of Flaubert. The Pauline epigraph—"Vengeance is mine; I will repay"—has a tragic and ambiguous resonance. Tolstoy viewed his heroine with what Mathew Arnold called "treasures of compassion"; he condemned the society which hounds her to destruction. But at the same time he invoked the inexorable retributions of moral law. Equally striking is the fact that a Biblical citation should have been used at all in epigraph to a novel. Passages from Scripture are rarely inwoven into the fabric of nineteenth century European fiction; they tend to destroy the substance of the surrounding prose by their sheer radiance and force of association. Henry James manages to carry it off

1. Latin for "the first among equals."
† From George Steiner, *Tolstoy or Dostoevsky: An Essay in the Old Criticism*. (New York: Alfred A. Knopf, Inc.), pp. 58–71 and 102–105. Copyright © 1959 by George Steiner. Reprinted by permission of Georges Borchardt, Inc., for the author.

in such moments as Lambert Strether's "Verily, verily . . ." at the climax of *The Ambassadors* or in those extraordinary evocations of Babylon in *The Golden Bowl*. But in *Madame Bovary* a Biblical text would ring false and might bring the whole deliberately prosaic structure tumbling down. With Tolstoy (and with Dostoevsky) matters are altogether different. Long citations from the Gospels are woven into *Resurrection*, for example, and into *The Possessed*. We are dealing now with a religious conception of art and a final order of seriousness. So much is at stake beyond the virtues of technical performance that the language of the Apostle seems wonderfully in place and heralds the work like a dark clarion.

Then comes the celebrated opening: "Everything was in confusion in the Oblonskys' house." Traditionally, it had been thought that Tolstoy had derived the idea for it from Pushkin's *Tales of Belkin*. The actual drafts, however, and a letter to Strakhov (published only in 1949) cast some doubt on this. In his definitive version, moreover, Tolstoy prefaced this sentence with a brief maxim: "Happy families are all alike; every unhappy family is unhappy in its own way." Whatever the exact details of composition, the broad rushing power of the beginning is unmistakable and Thomas Mann may well have been right in feeling that no other novel sets out so bravely.

As classical poetics would have it, we plunge in *medias res*[1]—the trivial and yet harrowing infidelity of Stepan Arkadyevich Oblonsky (Stiva). In recounting Oblonsky's miniature adultery, Tolstoy sets forth in a minor key the dominant themes of the novel. Stepan Arkadyevich looks for help to his sister, Anna Karenina. She is on her way to restore peace in his distraught home. That Anna should first appear as a mender of broken marriages is a touch of thrilling irony, of the kind of Shakespearean irony which is so close to compassion. The interview between Stiva and Dolly, his outraged wife, prefigures, despite its comic brilliance, the tragic confrontations between Anna and Alexey Alexandrovich Karenin. But the Oblonsky episode is more than a prelude in which the principal motifs are stated with consummate artistry; it is the wheel which sets the multitudinous wheels of the narrative in effortless motion. For the havoc wrought in Stiva's domestic affairs leads to the encounter of Anna and Vronsky.

Oblonsky goes to his office—he owes his appointment to his formidable brother-in-law—and the true hero of the novel, Konstantin Dimitrievich Levin, "a gymnast who lifts thirteen stone [182 pounds] with one hand," joins him there. And he enters in an immensely characteristic mood. He reveals that he no longer participates in the activities of the rural *zemstvo*, he derides the sterile bureaucracy symbolized by Oblonsky's official sinecure and confesses that he has come to Moscow

1. Latin for "into the middle of things."

out of love for Oblonsky's sister-in-law, Kitty Shtcherbatsky. There we have, gathered into his first entrance, the commanding impulses of Levin's life: his quest for his agronomic and rural reform, his rejection of urban culture, and his passionate love for Kitty.

There follow several episodes in which the personage of Levin is further defined. He meets with his half-brother, the well-known publicist Sergey Ivanovich Koznishev, makes inquiries about his elder brother Nicolas, and then resumes contact with Kitty. It is a profoundly Tolstoyan scene: "The old curly birches of the gardens, all their twigs laden with snow, looked as though freshly decked in sacred vestments." Kitty and Levin skate together and all about them is suffused with a fresh and brilliant light. From the point of view of strict narrative economy, Levin's conversation with Koznishev could be criticized as a digression. But I shall return to this problem, for within the structure of a Tolstoyan novel such digressions play a special role.

Levin rejoins Oblonsky and they lunch together at the Hôtel d'Angleterre. Levin is irritated by its brazen elegance and declares sourly that he would prefer "cabbage soup and porridge" to all the gastronomic spendours which the Tatar waiter lavishes before him. Though enraptured with his meal, Stiva comes back to his afflictions and asks for Levin's opinion on sexual infidelity. The brief dialogue is a masterpiece of narrative poise. Levin cannot comprehend that a man would "go straight to a baker's shop and steal a roll" when he has just dined of his own plenty. His convictions are fiercely monogamous, and when Oblonsky alludes to Mary Magdalen, Levin says bitterly that Christ would never have uttered those words "if He had known how they would be abused. . . . I have a loathing for fallen women." Yet, much later in the novel no man will approach Anna with more compassionate insight. Levin goes on to develop his conception of the uniqueness of love and refers to Plato's *Symposion*. But suddenly he breaks off; there are things in his own life out of tune with his convictions. Much of *Anna Karenina* is concentrated into this moment—the clash between monogamy and sexual freedom, the inconsistencies between personal ideals and personal behaviour, the attempt to interpret experience philosophically at first and thereafter in the image of Christ.

The setting changes to Kitty's home and we meet the fourth principal in the quadrille of love, Count Vronsky. He enters the novel as Kitty's admirer and pursuer. This is more than an example of Tolstoy's technical virtuosity, of his pleasure in refuting the conventional responses of his readers even as life refutes them. It is an expression of the "realism" and "deep-breathing economy" of great art. Vronsky's flirtation with Kitty has the same structural and psychological values as Romeo's infatuation with Rosaline. For the all-transforming impact of Romeo's adoration for Juliet and of Vronsky's passion for Anna can be poetically realized and made sensible only in contrast to a previous love. It is their discovery of the difference between this previous love and the dæmonic totality of a mature passion which impels both men into unreason and disaster. Kitty's girlish infatuation with Vronsky (like Natasha's love of Bolkonsky in *War and Peace*) is similarly a prelude to self-knowledge. It is by virtue of comparison that she will recognize the authenticity of her feelings for Levin. The disenchantment which Vronsky brings about will enable Kitty to relinquish the glitter of Moscow and to follow Levin onto his estates. How subtly and yet how naturally Tolstoy winds his skein.

Kitty's mother, the Princess Shtcherbatsky, reflects on her daughter's future in one of those rambling inner monologues through which Tolstoy conveys family histories. It was all so much simpler in older times, and once again we are confronted with the primary theme of *Anna Karenina*—the problem of marriage in a modern society. Levin appears at the Shtcherbatskys' to propose to Kitty:

> She was breathing heavily, not looking at him. She was feeling ecstasy. Her soul was flooded with happiness. She had never anticipated that the utterance of love would produce such a powerful effect on her. But it lasted only an instant. She remembered Vronsky. She lifted her clear, truthful eyes, and seeing his desperate face, she answered hastily:
> "That cannot be . . . forgive me."
> A moment ago, and how close she had been to him, of what importance in his life! And how aloof and remote from him she had become now!
> "It was bound to be so," he said, not looking at her.
> He bowed, and was meaning to retreat.

In its uncanny rightness this is the kind of passage which defies analysis. It is penetrated with tact and an inviolate grace. Yet, the vision is unswerving in its honesty and nearly in its harshness about the ways of the soul. Kitty does not really know why Levin's offer has flooded her with happiness. But the mere fact mitigates the pathos of the occasion and holds out its obscure promise for the future. In its tension and veracity the episode has something of the finest of D. H. Lawrence.

In the following chapter (XIV) Tolstoy confronts the two rivals and deepens the theme of Kitty's indiscriminate love. The ripeness and persuasion of his art are everywhere apparent. When the Countess Nordston, a loquacious busybody, goads Levin, Kitty is drawn half consciously to the latter's defence—and this despite the presence of Vronsky, to whom she looks with unfeigned joy. Vronsky is shown in the most favourable light. Levin has no difficulty in perceiving what is good and attractive in his fortunate rival. The motifs here are as delicate and ramified as in a scene in Jane Austen; a wrong touch or a misjudgment in the *tempo* would precipitate the mood towards the tragic or the artificial. But beneath the subtleties there is always the steadying vision, the Homeric sense for the reality of things. Kitty's eyes canot help saying to Levin "I am so happy," and his cannot but answer "I hate them all, and you, and myself." But because it is conveyed without sentimentality or elaboration, his bitterness itself is humane.

The soirée ends in one of those family "interiors" which make the Rostovs and the Shtcherbatskys so incomparably "real." Kitty's father prefers Levin and instinctively feels that the Vronsky match may not come off. Listening to her husband, the Princess is no longer confident:

> And returning to her own room, in terror before the unknown future, she, too, like Kitty, repeated several times in her heart, "Lord, have pity; Lord, have pity; Lord, have pity."

It is a sudden and sombre note and marks, very aptly, the transition to the main plot.

Vronsky goes to the railway station to await his mother's arrival from St. Petersburg. He meets Oblonsky, for Anna Karenina is coming on the same train. The tragedy begins, as it will end, on a railway platform (an essay could be written on the role of such platforms in the lives and novels of Tolstoy and Dostsoevsky). Vronsky's mother and the charming Madame Karenina have travelled together, and as Anna is introduced to the Count she tells him "Yes, the countess and I have been talking all the time, I of my son and she of hers." This remark is one of the saddest and most perceptive touches in the entire novel. It is the comment of an older woman to the son of a friend, to a younger man not really of her own generation. Therein lies the catastrophe of the Anna-Vronsky relationship and its essential duplicity. The subsequent tragedy is contracted into a single phrase, and in his genius for bringing this about Tolstoy is of a measure with Homer and Shakespeare.

As the Vronskys and Anna and Stiva move towards the exit, there is an accident: "A guard, either drunk or too much muffled up in the bitter frost, had not heard the train moving back, and had been crushed." (The quiet statement of the two alternatives is characteristically Tolstoyan.) Oblonsky reports on the terrible appearance of the man, and voices are heard debating whether or not he suffered much pain. Half surreptitiously, Vronsky gives two hundred rubles to help the widow. But his gesture is not altogether pure; it is made in the probably ill-defined hope of impressing Madame Karenina. Though it is quickly forgotten, the accident darkens the air. It acts somewhat like the death motif in the overture to *Carmen*, which seems to reverberate softly long after the curtain has risen. It is instructive to compare Tolstoy's handling of this thematic device with Flaubert's allusions to arsenic in the early stages of *Madame Bovary*. The Tolstoyan version is less subtle but more authoritative.

Anna arrives at the Oblonskys' and we are plunged into the warm, comical whirl of Dolly's indignation and growing forgiveness. Anyone doubting that Tolstoy has a sense of humor should watch Anna as she sends her repentant but embarrassed brother to his wife: " 'Stiva,' she said to him, winking gaily, crossing him, and glancing toward the door, 'go, and God help you.' " Anna and Kitty are left together and they speak of Vronsky. Anna praises him in the tone of an older woman encouraging a young girl in love: "But she did not tell Kitty about the two hundred rubles. For some reason it was disagreeable to her to think of it. She felt that there was something that had to do with her in it, and something that ought not have been." Of course, she is right.

Throughout these preliminary chapters two kinds of material are treated with equal mastery. The nuances and shadings of individual psychology are rendered with great precision. The treatment is close and not radically dissimilar from the psychological mosaic-work which we associate with Henry James and Proust. But at the same time the pulse of physical energy and gesture beats loud. The physicality of experience is strongly conveyed and it surrounds, and somehow humanizes, the life of the mind. This can best be shown in the final moments of Chapter XX. The intricate and tightly meshed conversation between Anna and Kitty is trailing off on a vague note of malaise. Kitty fancies that Anna Karenina is "displeased with something." In that instant the room is invaded:

> "No, I'm first! No, I!" screamed the children, who had finished tea, running up to their Aunt Anna.
> "All together," said Anna, and she ran laughing to meet them, and embraced and swung around all the throng of swarming children, shrieking with delight.

The motifs here are evident; Tolstoy once again focuses attention on Anna's relative age and mature status, as well as on her radiant charm. But one marvels at the ease of transition between the rich, inward play of the preceding dialogue and the bright leap of physical action.

Vronsky passes by, but declines to join the family circle. Kitty believes that he has come for her sake but would not show himself "because he thought it late, and Anna's here." She is vaguely troubled, as is Anna herself. On this minor and oblique note begins the tragedy of deceit in which Anna is destined to become enmeshed and which will, at the last, destroy her.

Chapter XXII takes us to the ball, where Kitty, like another Natasha, expects Count Vronsky to declare his love. The affair is wonderfully described and makes the dance at La Vaubyessard, in *Madame Bovary*, seem rather ponderous. This is not because Kitty is gifted with a greater wealth of consciousness than Emma; at this stage in the novel she is a very ordinary young woman indeed. The difference lies altogether in the perspective of the two writers. Flaubert steps back from his canvas and paints at arm's length with cool malignity. Even in translation we can sense that he is striving after special effects of lighting and cadence:

> the chink of gold pieces came clearly from the gaming tables in the next room; then everything was in full swing again; the cornet blared, once again feet tramped in rhythm, skirts ballooned and brushed together, hands joined and separated; eyes lowered one moment looked intently into yours the next.

The ironic distance is preserved, but the vision as a whole is impoverished and made artificial. In *Anna Karenina*, with its omniscient narrator, there is no single point of view. The ball is seen through Kitty's sudden grief, through Anna's dazed enchantment, in the light of Vronsky's nascent passion, and from the point of view of Korsunsky, "the first star in the hierarchy of the ballroom." Setting and personages are indivisible; each detail—and this is where Tolstoy differs trenchantly from Flaubert—is given not for its own sake or for atmosphere but as dramatically pertinent. Through Kitty's anguished observation we watch Vronsky falling under Madame Karenina's spell. It is the young Princess, in her bewilderment and shame, who conveys to us the full quality of Anna's fascination. During the mazurka the latter looks at Kitty with "drooping eyelids." It is a minute touch, but it concentrates, with utter precision, the sense of Anna's cunning and of her potential cruelty. A lesser artist would have shown Anna through Vronsky's eyes. But Tolstoy does what Homer did when he let a chorus of old men catalogue and exalt the splendours of Helen. In both instances we are persuaded through indirection.

The ensuing chapters deepen the portrayal of Levin and we catch a brief glimpse of him on his estate, in his proper element, amid the dark fields, the birch thickets, the problems in agronomy, and the brooding quiet of the land. The contrast with the ball is intended and points to the foremost thematic duality in the novel: Anna, Vronsky, and the social life of the city; Levin, Kitty, and the natural universe. Subsequently these two *leitmotifs* will harmonize and develop in complex patterns. But the prelude as such is completed, and in the last five chapters of Book I the actual conflict—the tragic *agon*—is begun.

Anna prepares to rejoin her husband in St. Petersburg. She settles down in her compartment and reads an English novel, identifying herself wistfully with its heroine. This, together with a famous episode in the following chapter, seems to derive directly from Tolstoy's remembrance of *Madame Bovary*. The train stops at a station in the middle of a snowstorm, and Anna, who is already in a state of exalted tension, steps out into "the frozen, snowy air." Vronsky has followed her and confesses his passion: "All the awfulness of the storm seemed to her more splendid now. He had said what her soul longed to hear, though she feared it with her reason." How simply and even archaically Tolstoy divides the human spirit into soul and reason. Flaubert would not have written that sentence; but in his sophistication lay his narrowness.

The train pulls into St. Petersburg; Anna at once catches the sight of Alexey Alexandrovich Karenin: " 'Oh, mercy! why do his ears look like that?' she thought, looking at his frigid and imposing figure, and especially the ears that struck her at the moment as propping up the rim of his round hat." Is this not Tolstoy's version of Emma Bovary's discovery that Charles makes uncouth noises while eating? When Anna comes home she finds that her little son is less entrancing than she had anticipated. Already her capacities for discrimination and the habits of her moral life are being distorted by a passion of which she is, as yet, only partially aware. To sharpen the dissociation between Anna and the *milieu* to which she has returned, Tolstoy introduces the Countess Lidia, one of Karenin's unctuous and bigoted friends. But at the very moment when we expect Anna to reveal herself, to awaken to her new life, the fever subsides. She grows calm and wonders why her emotions have run riot over so banal and trivial a matter as a momentary flirtation with an elegant young officer.

In the quiet of the evening the Karenins are together. Alexey admits, with his brutal honesty, that he finds Oblonsky's escapade unpardonable. His words are like a flash of lightning on the horizon, but Anna accepts them and rejoices in his candour. At midnight Karenin bids Anna come to bed. The small touches, the slippers, the book under his arm, the precision of the hour tell us that there is in the physical relations of the Karenins a central monotony. As Anna enters the bedroom "the fire seemed quenched in her, hidden somewhere far away." The image acquires, from the given moment, an extraordinary force; but even when bearing most steadfastly on a sexual theme, Tolstoy's genius was chaste. As Gorky observed, the grossest and most concrete erotic language assumed, in Tolstoy's mouth, a natural purity. The sense of erotic incompletion in Anna's marriage is fully realized; but there is nothing here of the corset string which "hissed" around Emma Bovary's hips "like a gliding snake." This is a point of some importance, for it was in his luminous treatment of physical passion that Tolstoy was, at least until his later years, closest to the Homeric mood.

Book I of the novel concludes on a buoyant note. Vronsky returns to his quarters and plunges into the life of revelry and ambition of a young officer in imperial St. Petersburg. It is a life which Tolstoy utterly repudiates, but he is too fine an artist not to show how admirably it suits Vronsky. Only the very last sentences carry us back to the tragic theme. The Count plans to "go into that society where he might meet Madame Karenina. As he always did in Petersburg, he left home not meaning to return till late at night." That seemingly casual remark has a prophetic exactitude. For what lies ahead is darkness.

Much more could be said about the first part of *Anna Karenina*. But even a cursory examination of how the dominant themes are stated and developed should make untenable the myth that the novels of Flaubert or Henry James are works of art whereas the novels of Tolstoy are pieces of life transmuted into masterpieces by some daemonic and artless necromancy. R. P. Blackmur points out that *War and Peace* "does have every quality" which James prescribed when he called for the "deep-breathing economy of an organic form."[2] This is even true of *Anna Karenina*, in which the integrity of Tolstoy's poetic gift was less imperilled by the demands of his philosophy.

When pursuing this notion of the organic in the initial sections of *Anna Karenina*, one is led time and again to a sense of musical analogy. There are effects of counterpoint and harmony in the development of the two principal plots out of the "Oblonsky prelude." There is the use of motifs which will recur with increasing amplitude at later stages in the novel (the accident at the railway station, the bantering discussion on divorce between Vronsky and Baroness Shilton, the "dazzle of red fire" before Anna's eyes). Above all, there is the impression of a multiplicity of themes subordinated to the forward impulse of a grand design. Tolstoy's method is polyphonic; but the major harmonies unfold with tremendous directness and breadth. Musical and linguistic techniques cannot be compared with any degree of precision. But how else is one to elucidate the feeling that the novels of Tolstoy grow out of some inward principle of order and vitality whereas those of lesser writers are stitched together?

But because a novel such as *Anna Karenina* is so massive in its dimensions and because it exercises an immediate control over our emotions, the deliberateness and sophistication of the individual detail tend to escape us. In epic poetry and verse drama the metrical form particularizes our attention and focuses it on the given passage, on the single line or recurrent metaphor. When reading an extended piece of prose (particularly in translation) we submit to the total effect. Hence the belief that the Russian novelists can be grasped in their generality and that little is to be gained from the kind of close study we apply to Conrad, say, or to Proust.

As is shown by his drafts and revisions, Tolstoy laboured over particular problems of narration and presentment with minute attention. But he never forgot that beyond technical virtuosity, beyond "doing the thing beautifully," there lay the thing to be done. He condemned *l'art pour l'art* for being the aesthetics of frivolity. And it is precisely because there is such a large and central world view in Tolstoyan fiction, such a complex humanity and so clear an assumption that great art touches on experience philosophically and religiously, that it is difficult to single

---

2. R. P. Blackmur: "The Loose and Baggy Monsters of Henry James" (*The Lion and the Honeycomb*, New York, 1955).

out the particular element, the specific *tableau* or metaphor and say "here is Tolstoy the technician."

There are set pieces in Tolstoy: the famous mowing scene in *Anna Karenina*, the wolf-hunt in *War and Peace*, the church service in *Resurrection*. There are similes and tropes as carefully wrought as any that we find in Flaubert. Consider, for example, the antinomy of light and darkness which inspired the titles of Tolstoy's two principal dramas and which pervades *Anna Karenina*. In the last sentence of Book VII, Anna's death is communicated through the image of a light kindled into momentary radiance and then quenched for ever; the final sentence of Chapter XI in Book VIII portrays Levin blinded with light as he recognizes the way of God. The echo is deliberate; it resolves the ambiguity latent in the Pauline epigraph and brings towards reconciliation the two major plots. As always in Tolstoy, the technical device is the conveyor of a philosophy. All the great sum of invention in *Anna Karenina* points towards the moral which Levin receives from an old peasant: "We must live not for ourselves but for God."

Without seeking to give a precise definition, Matthew Arnold spoke of the "high seriousness" which distinguishes a small number of works from the greater mass of literary achievement. He found this quality in Dante, for instance, rather than in Chaucer. Perhaps that is as near as we can come to contrasting *Madame Bovary* with *Anna Karenina*. *Madame Bovary* is a great novel indeed; it persuades us through its miraculous skill and through the manner in which it exhausts all the potentialities of its theme. But the theme itself and our identification with it remain, at the last, "too small an affair." In *Anna Karenina* we pass beyond technical mastery to the sense of life itself. The work belongs (in a way in which *Madame Bovary* does not) with the Homeric epics, the plays of Shakespeare, and the novels of Dostoevsky.

[The Ending of *Anna Karenina*]

The vitality of a Tolstoyan novel is achieved not only by the dense interweaving of various plots but also by a disregard of architectural finish and neatness. The major novels of Tolstoy do not "end" as *Pride and Prejudice*, *Bleak House*, or *Madame Bovary* can be said to end. They must be compared not to a skein which is unravelled and rewound, but to a river, incessantly in motion and flowing beyond our sight. Tolstoy is the Heraclitus among novelists.

The problem of how he would conclude *Anna Karenina* intrigued his contemporaries. The earliest outlines and drafts show that Anna's suicide was to be followed by some kind of epilogue. But it was only the outbreak of the Russo-Turkish War, in April 1877, when Tolstoy had already completed Book VII, that inspired him to write the last section of the novel as we now have it. As he first drafted it, Book VIII was a strident denunciation of Russia's attitude towards the war, of the false sentiments lavished on the Serbs and Montenegrins, of the lies spread by an autocratic regime in order to whip up martial enthusiasm, and of the false Christianity of the rich who raised money to buy bullets or cheerily sent men off to slaughter other men in a trumped-up cause. Into this tract for the times (to which Dostoevsky took bitter exception) Tolstoy wove the strands of his novel.

Once again we encounter Vronsky on a railway platform; but this time he is bound for the wars. On his estate, at Pokrovskoie, Levin is feeling his tormented way towards a *vita nuova*, a new understanding of life. The polemic and the psychological motifs are brought into collision; Levin, Koznishev, and Katavasov argue about the events of the day. Levin expounds the Tolstoyan thesis that the war is a fraud imposed by an autocratic clique on an ignorant populace. On the level of debate he is bested by his brother's oratorical skill. This merely convinces him that he must find his own moral code and pursue his pilgrimage without regard to the ridicule which he may incur at the hands of the intelligentsia and of fashionable society. Levin and his guests hasten towards the house under gathering storm clouds. As the tempest bursts, Levin discovers that Kitty and his son are out on the estate ("Chance," said Balzac, "is the world's greatest novelist.") He rushes out and finds them unharmed in the shelter of the lime trees. Fear and relief wrench him away from the world of sophistic arguments and restore him to that of nature and family love. The novel ends in a pastoral mood and on a dawning of revelation. But it is only a dawning, for the questions which Levin asks himself as he stares into the serene depths of the night are precisely those to which neither he nor, at that time, Tolstoy knew an adequate answer. Here, as at the close of Goethe's *Faust*, salvation lies all in the striving.

The eighth Book of *Anna Karenina* impressed contemporaries most forcibly through its polemic against the war. Although Tolstoy softened his tone in two successive versions, Katkov refused to publish either in *The Russian Messenger*, where the rest of the novel had been serialized. Instead, he printed a brief editorial note summarizing the story.

As an expression of Tolstoyan pacifism and a relatively early version of his critique of the czarist regime, the account of the "gentlemen volunteers" and the debate at Pokrovskoie retain considerable interest. More fascinating, however, is the light which these final chapters throw on the structure of the novel as a whole. The injection of a massive political theme into a network of private lives—what Stendhal referred to as "the pistol shot during the concert"—is not restricted to *Anna Karenina*; one need think only of the close of *Nana* or of the epilogue to *The Magic Mountain* in which we find Hans Castrop on the western front. What is remarkable is the fact that Tolstoy should have founded the concluding portion of his novel on events which took place when seven eighths of the work had already been composed and published. Some critics have seen in this a definite failing and believe that the last Book of *Anna Karenina* marks the triumph of the reformer and pamphleteer over the artist.

I think not. The most stringent test of the aliveness of an imagined character—of its mysterious acquisition of a life of its own outside the book or play in which it has been created and far exceeding the mortality of its creator—is whether or not it can grow with time and preserve its coherent individuality in an altered setting. Place Odysseus in Dante's *Inferno* or in Joyce's Dublin and he is Odysseus still, though barnacled from his long voyage through those imaginings and remembrances of civilization which we call myths. How a writer imparts this germ of life to his personages is a mystery; but it is clear that Vronsky and Levin possess it. They live with the times and beyond them.

Vronsky's departure is a gesture of some heroism and abnegation; but Tolstoy's view of the Russo-Turkish War is such that Vronsky's action strikes us as yet another surrender to impulses which are, at bottom, frivolous. This surrender underscores the principal tragedy in the novel. To Levin the war is one of those irritants which exasperate his mind to self-scrutiny. It compels him to make articulate his rejection of prevailing moral codes and prepares him for Tolstoyan Christianity.

Thus, Book VIII of *Anna Karenina*, with its unpremeditated polemic and its tractarian intent, is not an accretion adhering clumsily to the main structure of the novel. It expands and clarifies that structure. The characters respond to the new atmosphere as they would to a change of circumstances in "real life." There are many mansions in a Tolstoyan edifice and in them the novelist and the preacher are equally present. This is possible solely because Tolstoy builds in sovereign disregard of the more formal canons of design. He does not aim at the kind of radical symmetry which we find wonderfully carried through in James's *Ambassadors* or at the self-enclosedness of *Madame Bovary*, in which either addition or retrenchment would be a mutilation. There could well be a Book IX in *Anna Karenina*, recounting Vronsky's search for martial expiation or the beginnings of Levin's new life. Indeed, *A Confession*, on which Tolstoy began work in the fall of 1878, takes up precisely where *Anna Karenina* ends. Or would it be more accurate to say, where it breaks off?

GEORGE GIBIAN

Two Kinds of Human Understanding and the Narrator's Voice in *Anna Karenina*†

Several apparently inconsistent or even contradictory features in *Anna Karenina* strike our attention. On one hand, there are many manifestations of what we might group as activities of reason and will. Tolstoj uses many expressions indicating logical relationships. Conjunctions expressive of causal connections and listings are common. There are abundant references to characters who "understand" something. They also often exert their wills; they plan, they intend. Anna toward the end watches experience by a "bright light", a traditional image for understanding; in a related strand of images, her life is compared to a candle.

On the other hand, however, there is an abundance of passages pointing in the opposite direction: characters who rely, fruitfully, on intuitive or instinctual perceptions; human beings unable to exert their wills; actions done involuntarily or even counter to characters' plans. The truest, most significant actions are sometimes arrived at irrationally. Turning points hinge on the sudden, immediate, unexpected, not on the rational or the willed.

It is the thesis of this article that the presence of these two groups of elements in *Anna Karenina* is connected with Tolstoj's central concern in the novel—his preoccupation with the relationship between reason and unreason; that the interplay between these two principles and his attitude towards them constitute the keys to an understanding of Tolstoj's view of the human condition in general and Anna's and Vronskij's predicament in particular; and that by an examination of the ways in which Tolstoj presented the antitheses of clarity vs. non-clarity, and the verbal and logical versus the non-intellectual and intuitive roads towards understanding, we may come to grips with Tolstoj's basic categories in the book.

Some of the features which will engage our attention are not unique to *Anna Karenina*. Rather they are typical of Tolstoj's outlook and manner of writing in general. Others, however, are either more pronounced in *Anna Karenina* than in his other works, or present only in this work. We shall not examine all of them equally thoroughly, wishing merely to note, not explore, some of them. This essay chiefly proposes to look for a connection between them and in brief, to try to examine one of those "linkings" (*sceplenie*) of which Tolstoj himself spoke and to which he wanted his critics to pay attention:

† Reprinted from Dietrich Gerhardt, ed., *Orbis Scriptus: Dmitrij Tschizewskij zum 70. Geburtstag* (Munich: Wilhelm Fink Verlag, 1966), pp. 315–22 by permission of the author.

In everything, almost everything, that I have written, I was guided
by the need to gather together interrelated thoughts in order to
express myself; but every thought expressed separately by words loses
its meaning and is terribly degraded by being taken out by itself
from that linking in which it is found. The linking itself is brought
about not by thought (I think), but by something else, and to express
the basis of that linking immediately in words is in no way possible;
it can only be done indirectly by describing with words, images,
acts, situations . . .

. . . We need people who would show the senselessness of seeking
out separate ideas in a work of art and would continually guide
readers in that endless labyrinth of linkings which the essence of
art consists of, and to the laws which serve as basis for that linking.

We shall not, then, be exploring the important topics which for the
most part have preoccupied critics and scholars writing about Tolstoj—
such subjects as Tolstoj's manner of interweaving the two main plots of
the novel, of Vronskij-Anna and of Levin-Kitty; the problem of his
attitude towards Anna's destruction and the relevance of the epigraph
"Vengeance is mine, I shall repay"; the divisions of the carefully elaborated and defined social worlds of the book, the country-city sphere,
the various levels of social life in the two capital cities; the tragic course
of the development of Anna and of her and Vronskij's love. Instead, we
shall develop our topic by considering seven features of *Anna Karenina*
which may be related to a basic and hitherto insufficiently recognized
quality of Tolstoj's artistic procedure.

1. The language of *Anna Karenina* is rich in syntactical structures
suggesting that human experience can be arranged clearly and precisely,
sorted out, and neatly ordered, like a classical French garden. There
are many conjunctions of causal connection. *Potomu čto* is especially
common. We find various series—lists of one, two, three; divisions into
sub-categories. The readers of Tolstoj are often struck by what is usually
referred to as the clarity of his style. Comments have been made on the
directness, plainness of his narrative style, which we may call transparent. The world of *Anna Karenina* is not really one of order and causality;
but now we must note the intensity of the appearance of order and
intelligibility which the novel gives, at least superficially, and observe
one group of causes for this impression: the profusion of conjunctions,
series, signposts—*nesmotrja na čto, xotja, tak kak, ne potomu—no
potomu, poètomu.*

2. Related to the first point is the appearance of the word "understand"
(ponjat') which is not merely frequent but emphatic: "Vronskij, understanding that she is in one of her good moods" . . . or "Vronskij
understood that Goleniščev chose some kind of a liberal high-minded
activity, and therefore *(poètomu)* . . . resisted . . ." (In the two or three
pages following, "understood" appears several more times.) This frequent

cropping up of the word "understand" may seem to go still further towards giving the impression of a clear, graspable world, of life as an experience which people can master, divide, analyze, arrange. However, we must be careful. Here we also encounter evidence directly contrary to our argument thus far. *Ponjat'* appears often in the negative form—*ne ponjal*. Thus it also works in a manner contrary to what we have described thus far. The many places where the novel says of someone he or she "did not understand", "could not understand", build an impression of human ignorance, of the world's being beyond man's easy grasp.

3. The theme of understanding and not understanding life is connected by Tolstoj with the image of the "bright light". Anna is being driven in a light carriage, on the last day of her life, in her mad, agonized race. She finds fault with everyone she sees. We might say she projects her mood onto her surroundings. Looking at strangers, she thinks: "Count Vronskij and I also did not find that joy (*udovol'stvie*), although we expected much from it", and then "for the first time she turned that bright light, by which she saw everything, on her relations with him, which she had until then avoided thinking about."

A few lines later Tolstoj repeats his allusion to the light. "That [her thoughts] was no supposition; she saw it clearly, by that penetrating light which now revealed the meaning of life and human relations to her."

To speak of intellectual understanding in terms of a light is one of the oldest, traditional similes. Yet Tolstoj is not using the image in this manner. Anna's bright light does not stand for clear understanding— far from it. If we allowed a stock response to the image, derived from its usage in other contexts in our past reading, to steer us towards applying it to Anna, we should be in serious error. Anna's bright light is the light of her disappointment, resentment, desire to avenge herself, to make Vronskij pay for imagined slights, to make him feel sorry for Anna and to repent. It is the same *distorting* light by which she now judges everyone whom she encounters to be hateful, repulsive, unhappy. Its dazzling brightness blinds instead of revealing. Its clarity is one of special selection, distortion. It is intense but misleading and keeps out the pleasant, positive sides of life. This is made further clear through a second, related image which Tolstoj uses. About to drop on her knees on the rails, Anna experiences a feeling similar to the sensation familiar to her from having prepared herself to walk into water. "She crossed herself. The customary gesture of the sign of the cross called forth in her a whole series of girlish, childish recollections, and suddenly the darkness which was covering everything for her tore apart, and life stood before her for a moment in all its past, bright joys." It is *now* that *true* light illuminates her life for her. Tolstoj continues in the next sentence: "*But* she did not take her eyes off the wheels of the next car which was approaching." Anna commits suicide despite her momentary lucid vision; her deed follows out of the earlier, negative light.

Even when Tolstoj's characters feel they are seeing exceptionally clearly, Anna's illusory (and destructive) light shows, they may be deluded. For as our next category illustrates, more frequently than the opposite, Tolstoj's characters suffer self-deception and frustration of will.

4. Tolstoj's characters often do things which they did not want to do—as if they were doing them against their will. They plan and "intend", but then the reader finds them (and they find themselves) doing or saying or feeling something quite different from what they meant to. Or they say and do things unconsciously. As a result, frequently they are surprised by themselves, by what others do, by what life does. They are shown as not being in control. What they feel, even when it is happiness, may be "not at all what he [Levin] had expected". Levin, visiting his dying brother Nikolaj, "expected" many things, "but he found something quiet different". Some of the central events in the novel are of this kind. Vronskij is going to accept a post in Taškent after his suicide attempt; all between him and Anna is finished, if one is to trust what his mind tells him. Tolstoj describes his decision and plans in detail. But then, in a passage narrated by Tolstoj concisely, and hence all the more strikingly (through the breakneck speed with which it takes place as well as the speed with which it is reported by the novel's narrator, it acquires a sharp cutting power of unexpectedness), it is sufficient for Vronskij to visit Anna—ostensibly to say goodby, for him to change his mind. The two lovers throw everything over and leave together for Europe. Sudden impulse (based on passion) easily, immediately conquers a rational decision of long standing.

A very characteristic passage illustrates our point both in Kitty's inability to live up to her plan of being "coldly-venomous", as well as in the very characteristic, beautifully (and most clearly) analyzed mental turmoil in Levin's mind:

> 'You are having a gay time . . .' she started, wishing to be calmly-venomous. But hardly had she opened her mouth when words of reproach of a senseless jealousy, of all that had tormented her in those half hours, which she had spent motionlessly sitting in the window, burst out of her. Only now, for the first time, did he clearly understand that which he had not understood, when, after the wedding, he had led her out of the church. He understood that she was not only close to him, but that he did not know where she ended and where he began. He understood *(ponjal)* it through that tormenting feeling of doubling *(razdvoenija)* which he felt in that moment. In the first moment he was hurt, but at the same moment he felt that he cannot be hurt by her, that she is himself. He experienced in the first moment a feeling similar to that which a man experiences when, having received a sudden, strong blow from the back, he turns around with indignation and the wish for revenge to find the guilty person, and discovers that it was he himself who

had unwittingly hurt himself, that there is no one at whom to be angry, and that he must endure and calm his pain.

In the turning point of the book, ch. 25 of Part II, we watch the life of Anna and Vronskij together at the moment when they begin to veer away from the hitherto increasing passion, away from the ascending line of movement of the two lovers towards ever greater love, and begin to move downwards, in a descending line. It is the beginning of Anna's personal deterioration: her dissatisfaction, restlessness, growing jealousy, then frenzy, and ultimately death. It is the defeat of "what ought to have happened", if one calculated from a rational consideration of factors involved and from personal emotions—a defeat by "things-as-they-are", by the irrational.

Still another example of the crossing of purposes had been realized by Anna somewhat earlier:

> 'I unavoidably caused the unhappiness of that man [Karenin]', she thought, 'but I do not want to take advantage of that unhappiness. I also suffer and shall suffer. I am doing without that which I cherished more than anything else, I am giving up my honest name and my son. I acted badly and therefore *(potomu)* do not want happiness. I do not want a divorce and I shall suffer shame and separation from my son'. But no matter how sincerely Anna wanted to suffer, she did not suffer. There was no shame . . . Even the separation from her son, whom she loved, did not torment her during the first period.

There are examples of characters beginning to do one thing, and then doing another instead:

"Instead of going into the drawing room, in which he could hear voices, he stopped on the terrace, leaning on the railing, and looked up at the sky."

Or: "He [Vronskij] wanted to say that he had not slept all night and that he feel asleep, but looking at her [Anna's] excited and happy face, he felt ashamed. So he told her that he had had to go to make a report about the departure of the prince."

Extraordinarily often, characters do something unconsciously *(bessoznatel'no)*. In her meeting with Levin, against her better judgment, Anna *bessoznatel'no* tries to stir up his love for her. The passage describing this is particularly important in illustrating Tolstoj's manner. It begins with an extraordinarily clearly structured sentence. There are three concessive phrases beginning with *xotja*. The very distinct articulation gives the impression of experience mastered, ordered. But this rational chain of links in fact states something contrary to man's rational control. It underscores the power over man of his non-rational side. *Despite* the three reasons to the contrary, "Anna stopped thinking about him as soon as he left the room".

5. Sometimes Tolstoj does present his characters performing rational acts, or exerting their wills and succeeding in these efforts, but in such a way as to suggest that this amounts to hypocrisy or self-deception. He depicts them thus only to condemn the characters and to show their sterility. Karenin, for instance, has the ability to make himself forget what he wants to forget, to feel what he wants to feel, but this is presented by Tolstoj as evil, as a lie, as the unfeeling hypocrisy of a cold fish.

Sergej Ivanyč, who has devoted all his life to duty, "is not so much unable to fall in love, as rather lacking in that weakness which is needed to fall in love". This "lack of a weakness" is a serious flaw. It reveals the inability to pass the limits of the confinement by the rational. Sergej Ivanyč is not complete. (But let us not forget, also, that Anna, on the other hand, has too much of the ability to fall in love—and ends destroyed.)

To lack some weak spot, like Sergej Ivanyč; to stress too much control by one's will and reason—like Karenin; to extrapolate confidently and arrogantly an assured expectation of the future from one's ideas of past events—all these are shown by Tolstoj to be snares and weaknesses.

6. *Anna Karenina* is unusually full of passages in which one character looks at another and can "tell" (usually Tolstoj uses the word for "read") the mood and intention of that person, merely from the look, from the expression. It is a rapid, immediate grasp of something from the total Gestalt of the person listened to and looked at. The novel says explicitly at times that the person doing the "reading" did not listen to the words, but "read" what he did in something else. People thus often communicate through "looking at each other"—*peregljadyvajutsja*. This is presented by Tolstoj as a subtle communication superior to the intellectual. It is an intuitive, non-verbal, non-analytic process. Kitty's mother referred to it when Kitty asked her how her father had proposed. The mother replied:

"You think you invented something new? It is always done in the same way—it was settled by the eyes, by smiles."

"But what words did he say?"

"What words did Kostja say to you?" her mother answered.

(Kostja, we know, had written in chalk the initial letters of the words in a long sentence which Kitty was able to decipher with almost supernatural intuitive clairvoyance.)

In particular the children in Tolstoj's works have the sensitivity to read a great deal from one glance. Serjoža looks at his teacher and does not hear what he is saying, yet knows the teacher is saying something that he does not really think.

Anna, in her turn, during her clandestine visit to her son, understands Serjoža's unspoken words with extraordinary acuity: she knows that when Serjoža says "He will not come soon", he is really asking her what he ought to think of his father. Kitty and Levin, as one would expect, enjoy almost perfect non-verbal communication. Kitty understands complex attitudes in Levin, and Levin "unconsciously" invites her to tell the causes for her distrust. In many places in Part VI, ch. 3, only a small part of what is being said is expressed in words spoken by the characters.

It appears, then, from what we have looked at thus far that the novel stresses on one hand the clarity and rationality; and on the other, the mysteries of life and the importance of the non-rational.

What is the relationship between the various ways in which Tolstoj conveys to us his characters' failures in the rational sphere and their great sensitivities in intuitive perceptions and also creates a sense of simplicity and order?

The key to an answer is in the need to distinguish carefully between the characters' experiences and the voice of the narrator. Life is a mystery to the *characters*. It is they who try to understand and fail, who exert their wills inefficaciously, vainly, and who, also, on the other hand, perceive without verbalization, who expect to be happy because all indicates they ought to be—yet find they are not happy, who want to suffer and do not, who fail to fall in love, or who fall in love disastrously and perish. Life is dark to *them*. The best they can do is to understand life intuitively, in the particular as well as in the unity of existence— to cut through complexities with flashes of immediate insight. At worst, they are inhuman: rigid, emotionally and morally crippled. They move on a darkling plain, equipped with the uncertain, delusive light of reason, as well as with the second light—more trustworthy, but intermittent and sometimes even destructive—of immediate feeling and intuition. The latter can lead to excessive passion and then becomes "terrible", fraught with fright and awe, because of the trembling depths which it touches. (Tolstoj emphasizes the terror and awe which Anne feels in the first stages of her love for Vronskij. Anne's central quality, her excess of vivacity *(pereoživlennost')*, here comes into play.)

Whence the sense of clarity and order in the novel, then? They are the narrator's. He is the only one exempt from the blind man's buff played by the characters. The characters do not comprehend what they are doing; he does. He understands both the realms of reason and non-reason. It is he who constructs triple concessive constructions; he tells us the rich complexities of what one glance signified to another character. Experiences too complex for the intellect of the character are simple to the author. The veil of confusion is lifted for him.

The following passage illustrates the subtle modulation from the characters' vision to the narrator's at the phrase "the meaning of which was: *(i smysl kotorogo byl takov)*":

> At this meeting, Vronskij grasped *(ponjal)* that Goleniščev chose some kind of high minded liberal activity and as a result wanted to despise the activity and position of Vronskij. Therefore *(poètomu)*

> Vronskij in his meeting with Goleniščev gave him that cold and proud resistance which he knew how to give to people and the meaning of which was: You may like or you may not like my way of life, but it is all the same to me. You must respect me if you want to be acquainted with me. Goleniščev was contemptuously indifferent to Vronskij's tone. This meeting, it would have seemed, should have split them still more. But now they brightened and exclaimed with joy upon recognizing each other. Vronskij did not at all expect that he would be so glad to see Goleniščev, but probably he did not himself realize *(ne znal)* how bored he had been. He forgot his unpleasant impression at his last meeting and with an open, joyful face reached out his hand to his former colleague.

What is complex and dark is written about by Tolstoj's narrator as if it were neatly laid out, easy, under a glass. He, the narrator, sees clearly, directly; his is the transparent style. He is not on level with his own characters, but like a God, high up, watching from a superior vantage point. It is Tolstoj's basic structural device of the contrast between the *narrator's* perception and manner of speaking and the *characters'* which is responsible for the doubleness of effect of the novel—its rational-clear, and non-rational, intuitive elements. It underscores them, and it unifies and links them.

The distinctions between these two poles, the narrator's and the characters' perceptions, and the rational and non-rational, furthermore tie in with two other features of the novel: the contrast between scenes of routine life and scenes of emergency, and with what is usually called *Tolstoj's "technique of estrangement"*.

7. Another basic element of the structure of Anna Karenina is the alternation of scenes of normal, everyday, routine life (such ordinary scenes, for instance, as the meeting of Vronskij and Goleniščev in Italy) in contrast with extraordinary events, "emergency situations". Tolstoj envisages human beings as living at their most intense in the latter scenes of emergency, when experience is violent, when they do not understand, but rather live in a mental state of turmoil. The "scenes of emergency" in which he places them fall into two categories: some might be called agonies, others ecstasies. Unusual, puzzled, disturbed, tensely involved states of mind and perception, when characters do not quite know what is going on, and feel everything has become strange and new, are present in both types of "emergency situations".

In the normal, everyday scenes, experience is familiar, even regular. In exceptional scenes, which we have called scenes of emergency, the character becomes excited. His reactions to everything are as to something strange. He is in a state of intensive response to his environment. He sees it as surprising, new to him. Examples of such emergency situations, which stand out like peaks jutting above the general level, are: Levin before his wedding; Levin during the birth of his child; the ice skating scene, where Levin sees Kitty; the steeplechase; Vronskij's suicide attempt; Anna before her suicide; Anna and Vronskij during Anna's delivery of her child.

A paragraph which illustrates Tolstoj's handling of such emergency situations is this account of Levin while Kitty was giving birth to a baby:

> Suddenly Levin felt himself transported out of that mysterious, terrible, not of this world world, in which he had lived these twenty-two hours, into the former, ordinary world, which, however, now glittered with such new light of happiness that he could not endure it. The taut strings broke. Sobs and tears of joy, which he had completely failed to expect, broke out of him with such force, shaking his whole body, that for a long time they prevented him from talking.
>
> Previously, if someone had told Levin that Kitty had died and that he had died together with her, and that their children were angels, and that God is there in front of them, he would not have been surprised by anything. But now, having returned to the world of reality, he made great mental efforts to understand that she is alive, healthy, and that the creature so desperately screeching is his son. Kitty was alive; her sufferings had ended. He was unspeakably happy. He understood that and was fully happy because of it. But the child? From where and why had he come? He could in no way understand; he could not accustom himself to that idea. It seemed something excessive, superfluous, to him, to which he would not be able to become accustomed for a long time.

Even within scenes of everyday, ordinary life, Tolstoj shows his characters, we have seen above, as stumbling, making errors, preys of involuntary, unconscious actions and impulses. Ever since the Russian formalists called attention to it, it has been customary to speak of his *technique of "estrangement"* or "making it strange". This is usually taken to be an artistic device intended to avoid stereotyped responses on the reader's part and to give a fresh view of reality, by treating experience as if seen in a new light. Such is indeed much of Tolstoj's writing; but the technique goes deeper than that. It is an outgrowth of Tolstoj's view of the human condition—of what we have been examining throughout this essay; his stress on the difference between "normal", routine, everyday life, and exceptional scenes, moments or periods of unusual tension; and his basic antithesis of the rational and the intuitive. The technique of "making it strange" is derived from and connected with Tolstoj's emphasis on the non-intellectualist side of life. It is a basic structural principle of the book—its artistic root as well as the main spring of what Tolstoj is saying about how people live. In various ways, the novel presents the opinion that the highest values are the irrational, instinctive, spontaneous ones; and that the negative factors in life are the intellectual and rational. Tolstoj disapproves of self-consciousness (dramatized by Varen'ka, whose charity is flawed by being *willed* and whose love for Sergej Ivanyč is stillborn because she lacks heart and passion.) He is suggesting that no simple code, whether Vronskij's or Karenin's, can withstand the impact of actual, intense life. Reason and codes are rigid and inadequate. The proper way of living is to participate in life organically, naturally, instinctively. To Tolstoj the highest moments of life are the states of happy, unintellectual flowing along with the stream of existence, exemplified by Levin's happiness in the bodily exertion of mowing or Levin's and Kitty's "laconic, clear, almost wordless communication" and interpretation of each other's gestures and expressions "without logical subtleties and words."

Anna Karenina is a novel the central effects of which are achieved through an artistic as well as epistemological contrasting of the rational-logical and instinctive-irrational sides of human life. This has been conveyed to almost every reader of the novel; but what is most striking is how this antithesis pervades all areas of the novel, and how the nature of the narrator complicates and sometimes obscures in our minds this antithesis. The narrator himself is not subject to the limitations of the characters; he is never in the dark.

Anna Karenina is a study of human understanding: its limits, its various kinds, its potentialities. (In his *Confession*, a short time later, Tolstoj wrote: "The world is something infinite and unintelligible. Man's life is an ungraspable part of the ungraspable 'all'.") It presents the tragedy of human ignorance—the tragedy of human beings who live under given conditions, over which they enjoy only limited powers of rational analysis, comprehension, and control, and with which they may come to satisfactory terms best of all by using non-rational, intuitive means of approach.

LYDIA GINZBURG

Causal Conditionality†

Tolstoi not only refined conditionality and made it more detailed; he also created an extremely intense variety of it—something like a magnetic field within which his characters move. Tolstoi could leave nothing as

† From Lydia Ginzburg, *On Psychological Prose*, trans. and ed. Judson Rosengrant (Princeton: Princeton University Press, 1991), pp. 259–63. © 1991 by Princeton University Press. Reprinted by permission of Princeton University Press. (The original Russian version, *O psikhologicheskoy proze*, was published in Leningrad in 1971.) Lydia Ginzburg (1902–1990) was the author of many important literary studies. Edward J. Brown called her "one of the most distinguished and original minds to have worked on the nature of verbal art, its processes, and its position within a particular culture."

it appeared to be, could permit nothing to remain untouched (which particularly irritated Turgenev). Everything was continually passed through the creative mechanism of his art, which transformed, explained, and verified it. Because of the intensity of this process, the novel itself was turned into something different, something quite unlike anything that had existed before.

Unlike the writings of Dostoevskii, those of Tolstoi belong to the explanatory and conditioning branch of nineteenth-century psychologism. But conditionality in Tolstoi's hands is extraordinarily particularized, concentrated, and multivalent. The combining of contradictory elements is as a result the basic principle of connection in the Tolstoian artistic structure. Rousseau was aware in the *Confessions* of the multilayered and simultaneous nature of spiritual experience, but that awareness was the consequence of brilliant intuition and of conjectures that were far in advance of their time. For nineteenth-century realism, that simultaneity had already become a necessary result of the multiform conditionality of the individual by means of a myriad of concurrently operative causes.

What had been merely a tendency in the pre-Tolstoian novel became a conscious principle in Tolstoi's writing, another hypostasis of Tolstoian fluidity. Fluidity presupposes process—a conditioned alternation of psychic states. Tolstoi proceeded logically from alternation to combination. He showed that it is possible for a person to be both vainly egocentric and selfless, or to be both overcome with grief and worried about the impression he is making (as is the case with Nikolen'ka Irten'ev at his mother's coffin). He showed how Nikolai Rostov both loved Dolokhov and hated him, how Natasha both loved Prince Andrei (whom she in fact never stopped loving) and felt an irresistible attraction for Anatole,[1] and how Aleksei Aleksandrovich Karenin both knew about his misfortune and did not want to know about it, how he wished to crush Anna with his contempt and was at the same time afraid of her, since he feared the pain she was capable of inflicting on him. External and internal stimuli distributed among the various levels of spiritual life and originating in the different realms of human experience operate simultaneously. Elements that are mutually exclusive from a logical point of view are shown to be compatible from a psychological one. If the personality is conceived as a soul that is always equivalent to itself alone, its contradictions can only be regarded as irrational or puzzling. Such was the romantic enigma, disturbing yet requiring no solution. But if consciousness is movement, if the individual human being is a dynamic entity that contains everything in itself—from physiological irritants to the loftiest spiritual activity—and an entity, moreover, that is capable of responding to every conceivable kind of stimulus, then

---

1. Irtenev is the hero of Tolstoy's trilogy *Youth;* the others are characters in his *War and Peace.*

contradictions in it are not only inevitable; they may also be explained.

Yet individual consciousness for Tolstoi was not merely a chaos of equivalent and contradictory impulses. Without the organization of inner experience, without a hierarchical disposition of the levels of spiritual life, there could be no such thing as *behavior*, let alone the stereotyping of that behavior in the categories of personality or character that were so important to him.

According to the momentary situation he is faced with, the individual selects and activates certain elements of his consciousness, setting those elements into motion and repressing others. Some of the latter are thrust completely into the subconscious, while others coexist in the conscious mind in varying degrees of distinctness and realization. Tolstoi (and even his contemporaries noted this) scrutinized those states located on the borderline between consciousness and the unconscious. Such are his famous depictions of dreams, deliriums, half-awake states, and so on. But it was a much more difficult thing to grasp the mechanics of completely sober, daytime consciousness with its different levels coexisting simultaneously and its combining of logically incompatible contents. Tolstoi investigated, for example, the mechanism by means of which someone may go on living as if he did not know what he in fact does know. In depicting phenomena of this kind, Tolstoi came near in his artistic practice to something like the modern psychological theory of "set" or "attitude"—the special readiness or predisposition with which an individual responds to a given situation.

Tolstoi willingly portrayed those defensive gambits to which the conscious mind resorts in order to avoid destructive impressions. Such gambits are particularly successful in people who lead artificial lives—Aleksei Karenin, for instance.

> It would have been too terrible for him to admit his true situation, and he had closed, locked, and sealed the drawer in his soul that contained his feelings for his family. . . . Aleksei Aleksandrovich did not want to think anything about his wife's conduct and feelings, and he really did not think anything about them. . . . He did not want to understand, and he did not understand why his wife particularly insisted on moving to Tsarskoe Selo, where Betsy lived and where Vronskii's regiment was stationed nearby. . . . Yet deep down in his soul, without ever betraying it to himself, or having for it not merely evidence but even a suspicion, he knew without any doubt that he was a deceived husband, and that he was for that reason profoundly unhappy. (pt. 2, chap. 26)

Karenin does not think, does not see, does not betray to himself, and so on—all phrases that would appear to suggest that the subject here is the thrusting of the contents of spiritual life into the unconscious. But then it turns out that Karenin "knew without any doubt that he was a deceived husband." Tolstoi uses the metaphor of the "sealed drawer" and the everyday phrase "deep down in his soul," but what he really has in mind are the different levels of consciousness, with their differently conditioned but simultaneously operative processes. In regard to Karenin, some of those processes are conditioned by the brutal obviousness of what is taking place, while others are conditioned by his inextinguishable desire to hold on to the habitual external forms of existence and internal sense of himself that he has established. Thus, although he is aware that he is a wronged husband and a contemptible and ridiculous creature in the eyes of society, Karenin tries to his utmost (until Anna's confession) to retain in his life those forms of trust and dignity that are so essential to him.

A man knows what he does not wish to know, but he leaves that knowledge outside the boundaries of those images, those internal models, by which he organizes his personality and behavior. That knowledge exists in the same way that a more direct meaning may exist alongside a euphemism that is used to suppress the significance of an unattractive phenomenon. A handsome man knows that he has a physical defect, but he ignores the fact in order to regard himself as handsome; a decent man knows that he has done something dishonest, but both externally and internally he continues to live as a decent man, as if what happened did not in fact happen. But the situation may change at any moment, bringing about a shift in mental attitude and a rearrangement of its components. And then what a person did not wish to face may suddenly become painfully active.

EDUARD BABAEV

The Tale of Three Portraits†

"Any creation is a work of art only if it reveals a new side of life," Tolstoy said. Therefore a spectator, reader, or listener not only perceives the result, the artist's discovery, but also joins with him in the search for something new.

As Tolstoy saw it, the artist wishing to affect others must himself be a seeker, so that his work will be a search: "If he has found everything and knows everything and teaches or deliberately consoles others, he does not produce an effect." This statement explains a great deal not only in Tolstoy's aesthetics but in art in general.

The novel *Anna Karenina* contains a tale of three portraits which

---

† Eduard Babaev, a Russian scholar, is the author of three books on Tolstoy. This section is taken from his book *Ocherki estetiki i tvorchestva L. N. Tolstogo* (*Essays on Tolstoy's Aesthetics and Literary Works*), trans. George Gibian (Moscow, 1981), pp. 181–86.

embodies an entire theory of art. In many ways it anticipates later statements by Tolstoy. Its aesthetic meaning is developed in the treatise *What is Art?*

In matters of art, Karenin, a rational and deliberate person, holds severe, settled, and definite opinions. He could not commission Anna's portrait from some unacknowledged genius. He turned to the services of a "famous artist" to acquire an expensive salon object.

A portrait by a famous artist, who does not even have a name, simply "a famous painter," adorned Karenin's study. Its cold exquisiteness made even Karenin feel strange. The portrait in its oval, gilt frame hung above an armchair. This was a "portrait of Anna, done beautifully by a famous painter."

Karenin looked at it during the "last evening of their show-down . . . the black lace on her head, done beautifully by the painter, the black hair, and the beautiful white hand with a finger covered by rings" struck him as "unbearably arrogant and provocative."

Karenin could not help making a gesture of extreme estrangement. "Karenin looked at the portrait for a minute, and he trembled so much that his lips shook and made the sound brrr, and he turned away." Karenin himself at that moment was not disposed to understand another person's heart, and the work of art which was hanging in his study said nothing to him.

Tolstoy evidently thought that the likeness of the portrait, no matter how the details are worked out, to the point of illusion of full identity with nature, means nothing if "the kernel has not been extracted, if there is no organic link between the inner world of a person and the shape of his external appearance." As an artist he himself wanted "to make the hidden visible."

A true artist "takes the covers off nature" but the dilettante plays with the old covers, casting them over the model. The difference between Mikhaylov and Vronsky lies in their relation to art. Tolstoy creates an ironic comparative characterization of the master and the amateur.

Mikhaylov works because he cannot not work. He seeks and finds a teacher in nature itself. "He did not betray nature, but only cast off that which hid nature." He so to speak "took off the covers behind which it had not been wholly visible. Each new trait showed the figure in its energetic strength."

The master works cautiously, as if afraid of frightening or wounding nature. It has in it something of Pygmalion, as Baratynsky[1] understood him:

> The carver from the hidden goddess
> Takes off skin after skin.

---

1. Evgeny Baratynsky (1800–1844), a Russian Romantic poet [*Editor*].

Tolstoy discovered this secret of creation ("the taking off of covers") in the great artists, and also in folk masters. They worked according to identical laws: "Great works of art are outside of time. One only needs to set them free, to take away what is superfluous," as Michelangelo said.

Tolstoy pointed to the origin of his metaphor—"the taking off of covers." And he found confirmation everywhere. How his peasant rejoiced when he cut a little figure out of wood and explained it this way: " . . . it is in there . . . I only take stuff off of it."[2] At that moment he too was similar to Michelangelo.

The painter Mikhaylov worked in the same way. In everything that he painted, he saw "defects which strike your eyes, and which he could no longer correct without spoiling his work." In almost all figures and faces, he saw remnants of not fully taken-off covers, which spoiled the painting.

Speaking of Michelangelo, of the folk artist, or the painter Mikhaylov, Tolstoy was actually commenting on his own vision of the world and on his own understanding of the laws of art. "Life is a taking off of covers," Tolstoy argued. In his diary he noted, "Everything became fully clear, life is an illumination, a taking off of covers from that which exists."

In this respect, Mikhaylov is similar to Tolstoy as an artist and as a human being. As far as Vronsky is concerned, he knew nothing of any of these concerns. He followed in the footsteps of the "famous painter." More than anything he wanted to "strengthen his technique," which, Tolstoy believed, is something that all dilettantes pursue.

As early as the 1840's, in the period of the flourishing of the Natural School,[3] the dilettante had become an ironic hero in Russian art. People applied the term "amateurish" and "dilettantish" not only to paintings which were dilettantish in the narrow sense of the word, but also to fully professional works which imitated famous models.

Rome still attracted the attention of Russian painters with its great eternal studies after the ancient manner, although the feeling of antiquity had been lost. Turgenev mocked Shubin in his novel *On the Eve*. "Could there be anything more fake than window dressing of the antique kind!" Stasov exclaimed in one of his notes. The antique seemed window dressing for the reason that another, "real" epoch was starting.

Stasov argued, "We don't need such nonsensical, empty art." As the ideologist of the "Itinerants" (*peredvizhniki*)[4] he could only speak like

2. A. B. Goldenveizer, *Vblizi Tolstogo* [Near Tolstoy], Moscow, 1959, p. 191.
3. A group of writers, led by Nekrasov and Grigorovich, which described characters from low social classes, with attention to a "scientific" accuracy [Editor].
4. A group of Russian artists advocating realistic painting of contemporary subjects from Russian life. Led by the painter Kramskoy (see p. 829), they left official Academy of Arts exhibitions in 1863 [Editor].

that and not in any other way. "Let it [nonsensical and empty art] flourish with ignorant amateurs with pockets filled in Paris and Rome."[5]

The favorite themes of the amateurs were "Romans and Roman women, orgies and bacchanals, wreaths and pipes, marble benches, mother of pearl and Greek tunics."

This showy spectacular kind of painting, represented by numerous models, particularly attracted Vronsky. Since his youth he had the ability to draw, "and since, not knowing how to spend his money, he began to collect engravings, he chose to take up painting." Thus Tolstoy defines the motives which made Vronsky take up the brush.

Vronsky "had the ability to understand art and to imitate art faithfully and tastefully, and he thought that he had exactly that which is needed in a painter." The merciless ridicule with which Tolstoy attacks Vronsky's artistic manner shows that salon amateurishness always irritated him.

An amateur understands all types of paintings very well, but he does not understand that it is possible not to know at all what kinds of painting there are and still to be a true artist. Vronsky has some knowledge, but he lacks a genuine vocation.

In the Eternal City, under the guidance of a Roman professor of painting, Vronsky did sketches from nature and studied medieval Italian painting. Why medieval? Because after the Pre-Raphaelites, English painters who had studied Italian painting of the period before Raphael, it had become fashionable. When Mikhaylov saw Vronsky, he thought to himself that Vronsky had probably already been in the studio of an English Pre-Raphaelite and had come to him in order to complete his survey of the contemporary Roman art world.

Tolstoy also noted that Vronsky had gone to see Tintorettos. That too was fashionable. Tintoretto had been discovered later than other Italian painters. Hippolite Taine had written about him in his *Travels in Italy* (1864). One could not miss this new (although old) name.

In Rome, as a result of his artistic enthusiasms, Vronsky himself also changed. Medieval Italian painting had lately "so captivated Vronsky that he even started wearing a hat and a plaid over this shoulder after the medieval fashion, and it became him very much."

He wanted to see Anna changed, also. He painted her portrait in a most pretentious style: ". . . more than all other kinds he liked the French style, gracious, spectacular, and he began painting Anna's portrait in that style, in an Italian costume, and this portrait seemed very successful to him and all those who saw it."

Vronsky knows very well that his portrait will "resemble famous paintings much more than Mikhaylov's painting did." In his amateur's logic he considers this to be a great virtue. Therefore he regards Mikhaylov

5. V. V. Stasov, *Stat'i i zametki* [Articles and Notes], Moscow, 1952, p. 206.

with a certain amount of pity, both for his poverty and for his lack of skill.

Mikhaylov, on his part, "knew that one cannot forbid Vronsky to take up painting as a hobby; he knew that he and all dilettantes had a complete right to paint what they wanted, but it was unpleasant to him . . ." In this he was like Kramskoy[6] and also like Tolstoy himself. He later applied the term "hobby" not only to amateurs' works but to all art works altogether in which "empty content" predominated.

For Mikhaylov, it was unpleasant to see Vronsky's paintings. He felt something like jealousy when he looked at his works. It was not only disagreeable but insulting to see and to know that he loved the same thing as Vronsky. His feeling of love which is the essence of creativity felt offended.

At the same time, Mikhaylov understood that "one cannot forbid someone to make himself a large doll of wax and to kiss it." "But if this person came with this doll in front of someone who was in love, and began to caress this doll, the way someone in love caresses the woman whom he loves, this would be unpleasant to the person who was in love."

All of Tolstoy's aesthetics is built on this feeling. "A work of art is the fruit of love. But love without any works is dead," Tolstoy said. "Work with love, and we shall love that which you love." For that reason in his Mikhaylov there is intolerance. And jealousy. "Mikhaylov felt this feeling when we saw Vronsky's painting. It was ridiculous and annoying and pitiful and offensive."

He felt annoyed and ridiculous because in Vronsky's painting he did not find genuine art. Since it could be directed at a wax doll—a simulacrum of life, Vronsky's painting did not infect anybody, it could not captivate anybody. It was only a simulacrum of art.

In his book *What is Art?* Tolstoy develops the same theme. "No matter how poetic, how similar to genuine art, spectacular, or interesting an object may be, it is not an object of art if it does not call forth in a human being a feeling of being spiritually united with another person (the author) or with others (listeners or spectators) who perceive that same work of art, a feeling quite distinct from all other joyful feelings."

Vronsky's paintings were all similar to genuine ones, but they yielded no joy. He began his paintings spectacularly, but in no way could he bring them to completion. The dilettante is not able to achieve the closure of a work of art. Vronsky did the best thing that he could do under the circumstances: he gave up painting. It is also very characteristic

6. Ivan Kramskoy (1837–1887) was a famous portraitist who painted a portrait of Tolstoy. In 1863 he resigned from the Academy of Arts and joined the "Thirteen Contestants" who disputed the academy's authority [*Editor*].

that Vronsky is more severe towards Mikhaylov than Mikhaylov is towards Vronsky.

The artist and master felt only ridicule and displeasure at the sight of
the work of a dilettante, but for the dilettante to see the work of a master
was unbearable. Vronsky, leaving Mikhaylov's studio, said to his friend
Golenishchev that "art is not enough . . ." Now he could throw his
coat over his shoulders in the medieval manner, at peace with himself,
and could continue to play at art.

As Levin listened to Anna, the thought came to him that Vronsky
did not understand her and maybe did not even love her. Mikhaylov
felt something similar when he looked at the portrait of Anna in an
Italian dress, done in the spectacular French style. The second portrait,
painted by Vronsky, in some sense was like the first, which remained
behind in Karenin's study. The third portrait of Anna was done by
Mikhaylov. "The portrait impressed everybody from the fifth sitting on,
especially Vronsky, not only by its likeness, but particularly by its special
beauty." Special beauty—that is the opposite of showy. To Vronsky it
even seemed strange: "How could Mikhaylov find that special beauty."

And Vronsky thought to himself:' "One had to love her the way I
loved her in order to find that dearest of all of her spiritual expressions."
Art, as Tolstoy understood it, was the highest way of knowing human
beings. In this way Mikhaylov understood in Anna's character something
that even Vronsky had not understood in her.

Vronsky was mistaken when he thought that he had known something
that he had not known. "Only from this portrait did he come to know
that dearest spiritual expression of hers." "But that expression was so
true," Tolstoy adds, "that it seemed to him and to others that they had
known it for a long time."

A fusion of the artist and the viewer in one feeling which captivated
both of them had taken place. The main characteristic of that feeling
was that "the one who is perceiving merges to such a degree with the
artist that it seems to him that the object which he perceives was made
not by someone else, but by himself, and . . . that he had wanted to
express it for a long time." This statement in Tolstoy's treatise *What is
Art?* can be taken to be the author's commentary on the tale of the three
portraits in *Anna Karenina*. And the meaning of that theory had already
been revealed in the best possible manner in the novel, in those scenes,
for instance, where painting is discussed.

The first portrait of Anna was painted by a famous painter, the second
by an amateur. But both works failed to become works of art because
they left the viewer either indifferent or evoked in him a feeling of
alienation and annoyance. They could not infect him with feelings
which were absent in the mind of their creators, or which the painters
had not been able to transfer to the canvas.

Nothing reveals so clearly the true relationship of Vronsky to Anna as his portrait. In this sense the Italian episode is an important part of the development of the plot of the novel. Vronsky's medieval enthusiasms reveal the "abyss" which was to swallow up both Anna's life and her brief happiness.

Vronsky knew Anna, but he was astonished by the portrait painted by Mikhaylov. Levin did not know Anna, but looking at this portrait, he reflected that Vronsky did not know her and did not understand her. We conclude that only the painter Mikhaylov understood her, and he understood her so well that when Levin saw Mikhaylov's depiction of her, he could no longer condemn her. What an important thought!

"He listened and he talked, but all the time he was thinking about her," Tolstoy writes, "about her inner life, trying to guess her feelings. He who previously had condemned her so severely, now, through some strange train of thought, came to justify and at the same time pity her, and he was afraid that Vronsky did not fully understand her." Such is the effect of true art.

If we think of Tolstoy's novel as a whole, then Tolstoy's art has the same effect on the readers as the portrait painted by Mikhaylov. Of course, Anna's character is more complicated than what the painter expressed when he enclosed her in a "shining circle of happiness," but that Anna, too, is present in the novel.

The ability to infect—that form of understanding exists in life and in art. Among Tolstoy's heroes, Mikhaylov is perhaps not a very outstanding character, but many of Tolstoy's ideas about art are connected with him. From conversations and arguments with Kramskoy, Tolstoy moved on to a great artistic generalization, creating the image of a Russian painter in whom there was also a particle of his own mind.

GARY SAUL MORSON

Anna Karenina's Omens†

Aperture

Instead of either closure or anti-closure, Tolstoy created what I prefer to call *aperture*—that is, a work that does not require an ending and can in principle continue indefinitely. He exploited serialized publication to do so. At the end of each installment, we may of course create a relative closure, subject to revision by future events, much as we sometimes pause in life to look back; we may calculate a subtotal. In

† From Elizabeth Allen and Gary Saul Morson, eds., *Freedom and Responsibility: Essays in Honor of Robert Louis Jackson* (New Haven: Yale University Press, 1994), pp. 71–81. Reprinted by permission of Yale University Press.

most novels, we are also given a grand total, a moment of final closure; but in *War and Peace* and *Anna Karenina*, we are not. As in life, a sequence of relative closures *is all we ever get.*

Dickens and Trollope used the resting points at the end of chapters or installments as parts of a total structure, the completion of which coincides with the last installment. The last installment therefore differs qualitatively from the others, because it allows for no subsequent installment: it completes not just itself, but the whole work. By contrast, the author of *War and Peace* warned in advance that his last installment would be no different from the others, and would complete nothing beyond itself. What we call the ending of the work is in fact nothing more than the last installment we happen to be given. No matter how many installments were to be added, the work would remain open, would maintain its principled aperture.

In his drafts for an introduction to *War and Peace*, and in the essay on the book published while it was being serialized, Tolstoy announces this strategy explicitly: "In printing the beginning of my proposed work, I promise neither a continuation nor a conclusion for it. . . . and this proposed work . . . can least of all be called a novel—with a plot that has growing complexity, and a happy or unhappy denouement, with which interest in the narration ends." On the contrary,

> If I execute [my plan] as I wish, I am convinced, and intend, that the interest in my narrative will not cease when the description of a given epoch is achieved. It seems to me that if my work has any interest, then this interest will continue, as well as be satisfied by each part of this work; as a result of this special characteristic, it cannot be called a novel.

Tolstoy tells us that he has deliberately chosen a "plan"—to guide his characters from 1805 to 1856—that he cannot possibly fulfill. He thereby insures that there cannot be an ending, and so "I strove only so that each part of the work would have an independent interest, *which would consist not in the development of events but in development [itself]*."

We may see this orientation to "development itself" in *Anna Karenina* as well. Most obviously, I have in mind Tolstoy's notorious addition of Part Eight to a novel that many readers had assumed was over with the suicide of its heroine at the end of Part Seven. But time, and *Anna Karenina*, go on. Choices continue, and will continue to continue. George Steiner precisely catches the sense of this device when he asks: and why not Parts Nine and Ten?

Somewhat less obviously for modern readers, Part Eight contains a shocking temporal device to illustrate the work's basis in "development itself." This section involves its characters in the Eastern [Balkan] War, which Levin and Koznyshev discuss and which Vronsky goes off to fight. The point here is that the Eastern War had not begun when the novel began to be serialized, and so (unless we assume that Tolstoy could foresee the historical future), the events of Part Eight *could not* have been part of any original plan. Real contingency plays a role in the creation of the novel as much as it does in the lives of its characters. This is possible, as it would not be in highly structured works, because the work's narration already presumes contingency and the impossibility of structure. Or we might say: the work is open to the real world because the temporalities of the two are so similar. They are both shaped by contingency, and both consist of endless development.

If one believes strongly enough in historical laws, as many members of the intelligentsia did, then it is also possible to make historical statements about the future, and see the present moment's meaning as determined by events to which it is sure to lead. Certain Marxists explain social phenomena as preparations for other social phenomena prescribed to follow, as somehow caused by the utopian future ahead of us. The moment through which we are passing comes to resemble the scene in a movie we happen to be watching. The future may also cast back its shadow if, like numerous characters in *Anna Karenina* and many Russians at the time, one believes in spiritualism or omens. For what is an omen but an instance of foreshadowing visible from *within* the historical or biographical process? One reads the entrails of time.

Anna Karenina contains numerous discussions of such beliefs, much as *War and Peace* explicitly enunciates its author's rejection of historical laws. *Anna Karenina* is, among other things, a book about time, and it rejects, not only in its shape but also in its content, all attempts to understand the present in terms of a future that has not yet happened. Tolstoyan time is asymmetrical. It is one thing to see events conditioned by prior events, quite another to read them as occasioned by events to come. In one remarkable passage, Tolstoy indicates that interpretation of the present in terms of the future leads to a desiccation of each present moment. It will be recalled that part of Seryozha's education consists of learning to understand how events in the Old Testament *prefigure* events in the New Testament. Prefiguration is Divine foreshadowing. Seryozha senses deeply the power of Old Testament narratives, but in his childish wisdom he cannot apply the required and deadening prefigural interpretation:

> Seryozha recounted the events themselves well enough, but when he had to answer questions as to what certain events prefigured, he knew nothing, though he had already been punished over this lesson. The passage at which he was utterly unable to say anything, and began fidgeting and cutting the table and swinging his chair, was the one about the patriarchs before the Flood. He did not know one of them except Enoch, who had been taken up alive to heaven . . . chiefly because Enoch was the character he liked best in the

whole of the Old Testament, and Enoch's being taken to heaven was connected in his mind with the whole long train of thought, in which he became absorbed now while he gazed with fascinated eyes at his father's watch chain and a half-unbuttoned button on his vest.

Enoch's ascent to heaven provides Seryozha with evidence that death does not have to be real and therefore also suggests that his mother has not died, as he has been told. In his childish way, Seryozha responds directly to the story, whereas his father's questions demand that he dispense with any immediate experience of it and take it as occasioned by another, later story. In the name of foreshadowing, Karenin denies the integrity of events.

One may object to my description of Tolstoyan time that *Anna Karenina* itself relies on foreshadowing. After all, from the moment in which Anna sees the trainman run over, the sense of a similar death for her hovers over events. My answer to this objection, which I regard as a significant one, depends on the issue I raised in my title and first paragraph: agency. Just who is it who relies on foreshadowing to provide meaning? It would be helpful to examine first Anna's relation to stories.

[*Narcissism and Stories*]

Tolstoy's *Anna Karenina* offers a psychologically complex exploration of belief in omens. To explore these complexities, let us consider this novel in some detail.

Anna Karenina believes in omens and indulges in fatalism. From the time she meets Vronsky and proclaims the death of the trainman "an evil omen," we see her thinking repeatedly in terms of living out stories that are already told, prepared in advance, and governed by an attractive if implacable fate. Her stories lead to catastrophe but ensure significance.

As her friend Liza Merzlakova observes, Anna imagines that she is "a real heroine out of a [romantic] novel." For Anna, everything seems to fit a melodramatic plot centering on a grand passion; there are neither accidents nor choices. That is why she so often seems to resemble Greta Garbo *playing* Anna Karenina. She lives a story whose shape is already given and for which not just anyone could have been destined. The Garbo film, in fact, captures quite well the story of Anna *as she tells it to herself*. But Tolstoy has told a different story—not of a fated heroine, but of a woman who imagines that she is one.

Fatalism plays a complex role in Anna's thinking. In part, it turns all obstacles into aggravations of passion, as Vronsky, who learns this story from her, correctly observes:

"So it had to be," he said. "So long as we live, it must be so. I know it now."

"That's true," she said. . . . "Still, there is something terrible in it after all that has happened."

"It will all pass, it will all pass; we shall soon be happy. Our love, if it *could* be stronger, will be strengthened because there is something terrible in it."

Tolstoy means us to understand this as a particular and false view of love, by no means the only way in which love can be understood or valued. It is, in fact, an ideology, according to which true life is lived when it is most intense, when it is most heavily plotted, when it most resembles a romance, and when it is farthest of all from ordinary happiness or daily routine.

Tolstoy's view is the precise opposite: real life is lived in the small and ordinary moments. It is both prosaic and undramatic and is lived best when there is no story to tell. The reason that all happy families resemble each other whereas each unhappy family is unhappy in its own way is that unhappy families, like unhappy lives, are dramatic; they have a story and each story is different. But happy families and happy lives, filled with undramatic incidents, do not make a good story; and it is in this sense that they all resemble each other. In his notebooks and letters of the period, Tolstoy at least twice quotes a French proverb farthest of all from Anna's romantic ethos: "Happy people have no history." Plot, especially when known in advance, is an index of error.

Tolstoy would have largely agreed with the central point of Denis de Rougement's analysis of this plot and of the terrible role fate plays in it:

> Love and death, a fatal love—in these phrases is summed up, if not the whole of poetry, at least whatever is popular, whatever is universally moving in European literature. . . . Happy love has no history. Romance only comes into existence where love is fatal, frowned upon, and doomed by life itself. What stirs lyrical poets to their finest flights is neither the delight of the senses nor the fruitful contentment of the settled couple; not the satisfaction of love, but its *passion*.

Tolstoy therefore gives us a double plot in which one love is based on passion (Anna and Vronsky) and the other on prosaics (Levin and Kitty).

Each love has its orientation toward temporality. Prosaic love thrives on the everyday and is therefore shown in moments that have almost no plot significance, for example, the jam-making scene, Kitty's embroidering, or Dolly's little dramas with her children. The ability to live in this prosaic way forms a special temporal zone of happiness that is called "the Shcherbatsky element" because it constitutes the essence of that family's way of living. Levin, who began by loving this family as a whole before he came to love Kitty in particular, tries to learn its largely unarticulated but powerfully felt wisdom.

Levin and Kitty enjoy the small cares of daily life, the work that is, as Levin says, "incontestably necessary." Their focus is on the immediate and the present. By contrast, we find Anna dreaming of other times and other kinds of time. She displays, as romantic love does by its nature, a refusal or an "inability to enjoy the present without imagining it absent." Not presence, but absence; the fatal events to come structure life.

That Anna can at times even take pleasure at the loss of her son, for it fits the tragic plot. Abroad, she tells herself that she is suffering from her separation from her son, and she finds in these reflections comfort and self-justification. They are nonetheless false. "But, however sincerely Anna had meant to suffer, she was not suffering," Tolstoy drily notes.

Readers often wonder why Anna so idealizes Seryozha, who is Karenin's child, and neglects the daughter of the man she loves, though one might expect the opposite. Tolstoy suggests a number of reasons but one of the most important is the romantic tendency to cultivate obstacles and idealize what is absent. Before she has run off with Vronsky, she idealizes him so much when he is absent that she is shocked by the contrast when he is present, because her imaginary picture is "infinitely superior, impossible in reality." When she does live with Vronsky, she can never adjust to daily routine without high drama, and so she is always manufacturing scenes, fabricating crises, sending urgent telegrams, and indulging in jealous fits in which she herself does not believe. In much the same way, Anna loves the child she cannot have and neglects her present child, whose needs are prosaic and unromantic.

Romantic destiny, the sense that one has been chosen for a special and tragic story, feeds narcissism. This is another reason that the Garbo film, precisely because it leaves out all the Levin scenes that have nothing to do with Anna, is so eerily true to Anna's *Anna*. Her sense of a fatal plot governing her life places her in the center of all the stories around her, which is one reason that, almost as soon as she meets Vronsky, she becomes such a poor parent. We sense, as she occasionally realizes, that her love for Seryozha is a role; and we recognize that his importance to her derives almost entirely from what he and his loss mean *to her*. He figures in her thoughts as the one person who would not condemn her. We do not see her worrying about him in respects that have nothing to do with her.

As if to illustrate the moral problems with such a self-image, Tolstoy has the young Kitty briefly indulge it. Kitty imagines that the day on which she hopes that Vronsky will propose (and on which Levin does propose) is somehow fated to be a turning point: she knows this "for certain." These men are part of her story. But when Levin, in all his painful self-doubt and sincere love, awkwardly proposes, she suddenly places herself in his position. Knowing that she will refuse him, she forgets her role and sees the world through his eyes. This scene is one of many in which Tolstoy indicates what is wrong with placing oneself at the center of stories. As Kitty learns, first here and then when helping people at the spa, morality involves the opposite, including the ability to make oneself *the minor character in someone else's story*. Moreover, the day that Kitty regards as fated to decide everything does no such thing, Levin will propose again and be accepted.

Anna: Who Is to Blame?

For Anna, fatalism also serves to relieve her guilt. When Dolly comes to visit her, Anna repeats a speech she has evidently often made to herself.

> "Yes, yes," said Anna, turning out of the open window. "But I was not to blame. And who is to blame? What's the meaning of being to blame? Could it have been otherwise? What do you think? Could it possibly have happened that you didn't become the wife of Stiva?"
>
> "Really, I don't know. . . ."

If everything is fated, no one is responsible, she reasons.

But this way of thinking exacts a price. Focusing on fate, she neglects causes; she foregoes decisions and trusts in inevitability. Alternative, prosaic ameliorations, which do not fit the shape of the story she condemns herself to live, seem pointless to her. So do major choices. Vronsky finds it almost impossible to get her to think practically about her situation, and she does not allow herself to think about it. Before leaving Karenin, "she had not the least idea what would settle the situation, but she firmly believed that something would turn up." Contrast this view with Levin's: faced with daily farm work, he assumes that problems left alone usually get worse, and therefore he continually improvises.

As the story develops, Anna's refusal to examine causes and make appropriate decisions—to take responsibility—grows. Vronsky asks Dolly to get her to face reality and seek a divorce, but Anna refuses. Dolly notices her new habit of averting her eyes when important questions are raised. "Just as though she half shut her eyes to her own life, so as not to see everything," Dolly thinks.

Anna has once refused a divorce when she could have had one, and now she refuses to consider it or any other practical step. "You say I take too gloomy a view of things," she tells Dolly. "I try not to take any view at all. . . . You tell me to marry Alexey, and say I don't think about it. I don't think about it!" She sees only two conceivable endings to her story, one utopian and the other catastrophic, and the utopian one is impossible:

"It is only these two beings [Vronsky and Seryozha] that I love, and one excludes the other. I can't have them together, and that's the only thing I want. And since I can't have that, I don't care about the rest. I don't care about anything, anything. And it will end one way or another, and so I can't. I don't like to talk of it. So don't blame me, don't judge me for anything."

Anna's stories are told from the ending, and nothing else, nothing middle or present, matters. As so often happens, she seems to forget here that she has a daughter. When Tolstoy gives us the lengthy stream of thoughts that leads to Anna's suicide, we may remark that one thing she never thinks of is Annie, who has no role to play in this tragic plot.

Anna: Omens and Their Causes

Anna is not just uttering a phrase when she refers to the trainman's death as an omen. She is in fact as superstitious as she is fatalistic. Indeed, the two qualities often go together, inasmuch as they both construct explanations that elude causality and foreclose choice. Anna believes in prophetic dreams as well.

In one remarkable passage, Anna has her recurrent nightmare about a strange peasant with a sack who says in French that one must beat the iron; and she wakes from that dream into another. In that second dream, she asks the meaning of the first and is told it indicates that she will die in childbirth. The outer dream frames the inner one and gives its meanings; the two dreams together become a self-interpreting omen, and
. when Anna wakes, she believes in her fated death from childbirth. This belief shapes her behavior. Told that the present state of affairs cannot continue, she thinks not of alternatives but of the omen. " 'Soon, very soon, it will end anyway,' she said; and again, at the thought of death near at hand and now desired, tears came into her eye." In the childbirth scene, her feverish thoughts, suffused with the sense of certain death, shape her reactions to both Vronsky and Karenin and so the belief in destiny exerts considerable causal force.

But of course the omen proves false; she survives the birth. This disconfirmation seems to escape her notice, however, and does not affect her acceptance of omens or prophetic dreams. But it does indicate to the reader that the temporality of the novel (and the real world) is not what she imagines. The reader may recall that Levin has explicitly rejected a whole range of superstitions, from omens to the faddish spiritualism of the upper classes.

Anna sees a world in which plots are already written from the future and in which responsibility has no meaning; Tolstoy describes the causes that lead to these beliefs and the real alternatives they disable. In the *Oedipus*, as we have seen, identification with the hero involves a sense of choice, but contemplation of the structure reveals the inevitable outcome shaping all prior events. *Anna Karenina* works in the opposite way: when Tolstoy allows us to identify with the heroine, readers see her as she sees herself, as a foredoomed tragic heroine. But the novel subjects that self-image to scrutiny and discovers in fatalism a self-indulgent and self-destructive choice.

Tolstoy allows us to see why, to a person inclined to tragic plots, the dream might well appear to be an omen. It has all the characteristic marks of a sign from the future: its sense of mystery, the strange images that seem to demand interpretation, its frequent recurrence, the terror it inspires, and, at one point, the fact that Vronsky has a quite similar dream. But Tolstoy also suggests causal explanations for these apparent marks of futurity. For Tolstoy, it is what we have done and what we do that shape both the future and our various anticipations of it. But our attention does not always focus on those shaping events, and so, in the inability to detect causes, we ascribe destinies.

Each element of Anna's dream has occurred either during the scene when Vronsky first meets and flirts with her or during her subsequent train ride home, when the flirtation has progressed quite far. But Anna has not necessarily noticed them. Let us take just one example, the strange peasant. The train for which Vronsky and Stiva have been waiting and on which Anna has been traveling with Vronsky's mother arrives at the station and the passengers disembark:

> The engine rolled up, with the lever of the middle wheel rhythmically moving up and down, and the stooped, muffled figure of the engine driver covered with frost. Behind the tender, setting the platform more and more slowly swaying, came the luggage van with a dog whining in it. At last the passenger cars rolled in, jolting as they came to a standstill.
>
> A dashing guard jumped out, giving a whistle, and after him one by one the impatient passengers began to get down: an officer of the guards, holding himself erect and looking severely about him; a nimble little merchant with a satchel, smiling gaily; a peasant with a sack over his shoulder.
>
> Vronsky, standing beside Oblonsky, watched the carriages and the passengers, totally oblivious of his mother. What he had just heard about Kitty excited and delighted him.

Tolstoy gives no special emphasis to the peasant with a sack, perhaps no more than any observer on the scene would give. After all, peasants and people with sacks were common sights at Russian train stations. Throughout the novel, Tolstoy often describes how people stare at things without taking conscious note they are seeing them, and that is evidently what is happening here. Vronsky is thinking of Kitty, and Anna, most likely, of meeting Vronsky, about whom she has just heard so much. Re-readers of the novel may or may not notice this peasant, but its original readers, and current ones who do not know its story in detail, will likely miss him. The image will register, as it presumably registers with Vronsky and Anna, at the periphery of attention.

So will numerous other elements of this scene and of Anna's train ride home with Vronsky in pursuit. When dreamed, the peasant, like the engine driver, appears muffled and stooped. Dozing off and thinking of Vronsky, Anna half perceives and half transforms into dream material a thin peasant who "seemed to be gnawing at something on the wall," "a fearful shrieking and banging, as though someone was being torn to pieces," and "the voice of a man muffled up." When the train stops, she goes onto the platform, hears "sounds of a hammer on iron," and encounters Vronsky following her. "At that moment the wind, as if surmounting all obstacles, sent the snow flying from the carriage roofs, and clanked some sheet of iron it had torn off. . . . All the awfulness of the storm seemed to her more splendid now. He said what her soul longed to hear, though she feared it with her reason." The emotional charge of these two scenes, the initial thrill and the guilt that grows over time, fuses its barely perceived images into a dream, where they seem arbitrary and therefore prophetic. Anna imagines fate and tragedy where Tolstoy gives us causes and conditions largely outside her notice.

Anna: Loose Ends

By definition, no one can focus on what happens at the periphery of one's attention. Tolstoy uses his essential surplus to describe key facts about his characters that they themselves could not know. Anna imagines that life is structured like a novel, but this novelist's essential surplus indicates that she is mistaken. In this case, authorial omniscience is used to discover those aspects of experience—undetectable from within experience itself—that make it utterly *un*like art.

Life as Tolstoy imagines it does not fit a pattern, as art does. Our lives tend to no goal; neither are they destined to be shaped into a story. They are filled with chance events that nevertheless have lasting effects and are shaped by incidental causes that need not have happened. Events filled with promise lead nowhere. Everything that the essential surplus provides in art—structure, closure, the assurance of significance—is usually absent from life. But people sometimes imagine that life is more or less like novels in this respect. Tolstoy's paradoxical method is to use the essential surplus to make us aware of its pure artifice.

The plot of *Anna Karenina* is exemplary in this respect. In those last moments leading to her suicide, Anna's various false and novelistic beliefs about time and about her life interact. Her growing narcissism and paranoia lead her to eliminate contingency from her world. "In that new glaring light in which she was seeing everything," nothing is accidental and everything has a meaning. She discovers significance in every chance word of every passerby; "Tiutkin, coiffeur" and every other shop sign. All is hateful or false: a man crosses himself, and, looking at him angrily, Anna thinks, "It would be interesting to ask him what meaning he attaches to that."

And in this frame of mind the common images of train stations have been accumulating. While she is still in the carriage, "a deformed peasant covered with dirt, in a cap from which his tousled hair stuck out, passed by that window, stooping down to the carriage wheels. 'There's something familiar about that hideous peasant,' thought Anna. And remembering her dream, she moved away to the opposite door, shaking with terror." Shortly after, standing on the platform, she feels it sway, as it did when she first arrived in Moscow,

> and she imagined that she was in the train again.
> All at once she thought of the man crushed by the train the day she first met Vronsky, and she understood what she had to do. With a rapid, light step she went down the steps that led from the water tank to the rails and stopped close to the approaching train.

"She understood"—she grasped the solution to a riddle—"what she had to do" (*chto ei nado delat'*). Anna identifies the path marked out for her, how the omen will be fulfilled. As her love began with death by a train, so it must end. To her the repeating images are signals of a completed pattern. Time is symmetrical.

It is important to notice here that these are Anna's beliefs, not the author's. Tolstoy has not created a world in which omens are fulfilled; rather, Anna has chosen to fulfill what she takes to be an omen.

In what is perhaps the cruelest passage of the book, Tolstoy indicates what is wrong with her closed temporality. As Anna is preparing to jump, "a feeling such as she had known when about to take the first plunge in bathing came upon her, and she crossed herself"; she performs the very gesture that she has just declared meaningless. But it now suggests a great deal that her system of interpretation has left out: "That familiar gesture brought back into her soul a whole series of memories of her childhood and girlhood, and suddenly the darkness that had covered everything for her was torn apart, and life rose up before her for an instant with all its bright past joys. But she did not take her eyes from the wheels of the second car."

These memories evoke what her story—the tragic story that leads to suicide—has omitted. They begin long before that story, long before she has met Vronsky or even Karenin; and they offer the image of *other possibilities*, other sources of meaning that she has experienced but not brought to mind. They challenge her story's closure, which is her death, with the possibility of alternative plots that have been and might still be. They are, in spite of everything, the loose ends the story does not resolve; they are the signs of her failed authorship of her life, grounds for hope that make one despair. They come just too late, even though she has not jumped yet: for the momentum of her decision carries her forward. Anna does not focus on her childhood memories, which remain at the periphery of her attention, but concentrates instead on the difficult task of timing her jump.

But after Anna has jumped, while she is lying on the tracks and there is nothing more to do, her attention does shift to the other line of thought: and she suddenly recognizes the mistake, now beyond repair, of obsessively neglected other possibilities. Her recognition of these possibilities creates the true terror of her final seconds, as "the light of the candle by which she had read the book filled with troubles, falsehood, sorrow, and evil flared up more brightly than ever before, lighted up for her all that had been shrouded in darkness, flickered, began to grown dim, and was quenched for ever." In this context, what would otherwise be the hackneyed image of a book creates a deep if understated irony because it bespeaks the danger of living as if one's life were already written.

The Surplus against Itself

Tolstoy deeply distrusted not only conventional plots but also plotting per se because they both impose closure and structure on a world that is fundamentally innocent of both. And yet he also was aware that novels must have some structure and something like a coherent plot if they are to be readable at all.

Therefore, he gives the structuring impulse to his character. In so doing, Tolstoy has it both ways: the story gains a structure that the author rejects. The novel relies on a temporality it negates. Tolstoy's fundamental solution to the problem of escaping plot and the lie of the essential surplus was to develop various forms of negative narration.

And yet, it is not clear that this solution entirely succeeds. More often than not, readers have interpreted *Anna Karenina* as if it, and not its heroine, relied on omens and foreshadowing. They have displaced the locus of structuring to the wrong agent.

Why should this have happened? For one thing, readers have so identified with Anna that they have usually adopted her point of view. Because Tolstoy describes Anna's psychology not only convincingly but also from within her perspective, readers assume that he approves of it. The readers join her story and accept her perspective even when counterevidence is readily available.

One often hears versions of the following scenario: Tolstoy might at first have meant to write a novel condemning Anna's values and behavior, but in the course of writing and in the process of giving her a realistic psychology he necessarily came to sympathize with her unawares; and so his moralistic tract was transformed into a great novel essentially against his will. To understand is to forgive.

There is some plausibility to this argument because, as Tolstoy himself noted, the process of writing often does reshape the product, and intentions thereby evolve and shift. The problems with this argument lie elsewhere. For one thing, it is by no means the case that the act of describing someone from within necessarily leads to sympathy, much less to exoneration. One does not have to be Dostoevsky to recognize that very often the better one knows someone, the more one *dis*likes him, as divorce rates and Balkan history attest. When one investigates the circumstances leading to a morally reprehensible act, one often sees that the mentality leading to it could, under different circumstances, lead to much *worse*. The notion that understanding is forgiveness, like the related notion of knowledge as sure antidote to intolerance, would seem to be a sentimentality.

To understand is not necessarily to forgive, and why should it be? What people usually have in mind is that once one appreciates all the circumstances that led to behavior of a given kind, one will recognize that no other choices could have been made. As knowledge increases, alternatives decrease and disappear until they are revealed as only apparent; and one does not blame where there are no real alternatives. There is, in short, a concealed determinism in the argument which, if accepted, would make all moral judgments a mere function of ignorance. Tolstoy and this novel endorse neither determinism nor an ineluctable moral neutrality.

Readers may also read the novel in terms of foreshadowing because that plot is so conventional. Or they may be sympathetic with Anna's ideology of romantic love, which they may take to be not an ideology but what love truly is. Such readers tend to be especially hostile to Karenin and neglectful of Dolly. A novel unsympathetic to Anna would conflict with our culture's fundamental mythology, including our assumption that truly great writers necessarily challenge, not reaffirm, such bourgeois norms as marriage and the family. Readers' expectations are shaped by both thematic and formal presuppositions, and it is extremely difficult to overturn them, especially in the direction opposite to avant-garde beliefs.

Tolstoy tried to retain the essential surplus while turning it against its tacit implications, but it seems that the essential surplus resists negative use.

CARYL EMERSON

[Is Tolstoy Monologic?]†

[A comparison of Dostoevsky's and Tolstoy's heroes] raises some interesting questions about Bakhtin's[1] famous, and far too facile, categorization of Dostoevsky as a "polyphonic" thinker and of Tolstoy as a "monologic" one. Both, it is clear, exhibit a genius for multiplicity. But each writer has a different way of connecting multiplicity with language and with the formation of a self. For Dostoevsky, multiplicity is spatial, coexistent, and—for want of a better word—immortal. Voices are refracted, juxtaposed, but never assimilated or eliminated. Death can be an act in this world, but conflict cannot be resolved through it. Once death occurs, the word that had been embodied returns to the pool of ideas out of which selves are born. The Kingdom of God is located not within you but among you.

For Tolstoy, multiplicity is located elsewhere. It is more linear and temporal than spatial and coexistent. Life is a manner not of seeking external confrontation with other equally and eternally valid ideas, but of processing an idea or a situation at the proper time to guarantee the survival of the organism. For all his robust fullness of setting, Tolstoy is a master at mapping the ways in which people are *not* free. The choices a person can make depend on a very specific and restricted immediate context. Thus Tolstoy's obsession with timing: Vronsky breaking the back of his mare, Varenka and Koznyshev out mushroom picking, the awful last-minute sense of accident in Anna's death, and the horrible casualness with which Petya Rostov is killed in battle. Bakhtin is right, Tolstoy *is* a poet of death—but not because of any special morbidity on Tolstoy's part. This emphasis is, rather, the natural result of a fictive world in which ideological systems exist to serve individual personality, and not the other way around. When the personality is cut off by death, there is an absolute cutoff of one person's unique, unrepeatable accumulation of ideas and interactions. No one but the author is left to step in and fill the gap, with his absolute language and extrapersonal perspective.

The Bakhtinian model, in sum, does not really allow for any investigation of the Tolstoyan sense of self. Bakhtin to the contrary, that self is not consummated through the activity of an unfairly privileged author, sitting above and apart from his characters and completing them from

---

† From Caryl Emerson, "The Tolstoy Connection in Bakhtin," in Gary Saul Morson and Caryl Emerson, eds., *Rethinking Bakhtin* (Evanston, IL: Northwestern University Press, 1989), pp. 168–69. Reprinted by permission of Northwestern University Press.
1. Mikhail Bakhtin (1895–1975) is one of the most influential Russian literary scholars of the twentieth century.

within rather than from without. The Tolstoyan self is simply consummated in another way. Not even the other has power to complete it. Because the self has no single internal point of crystallization, no ideational center, the best it can do is focus, for a while only and at considerable mental effort, on a select sequence of events. These events do not penetrate a given mind "logically." They must confront a highly individualized, contradictory complex of habits, reflexes, and accumulated experience—a complex that is, at the same time, enormously vulnerable to the accidents of the outside world. Just as history, in Tolstoy's construct, has no ultimate coherence, so the *I* does not cohere; thus it can be profoundly and irreversibly moved by random environmental factors. Tolstoy is deadly serious about chance. This fact has led Gary Saul Morson to suggest that *War and Peace*, that unclassifiable work, is closer to satire than to any other genre. Its target, he proposes, "is all forms of thinking that would explain away the randomness, the asystematicity and 'unstorylike' character of history and psychology." Tolstoy's greatest works all explore this ruthless radical contingency, and his successful heroes learn how to build a life within it. In each of these protagonists the absence of an ultimate coherence to the self, along with Tolstoy's failure to endorse a strategy of explanation, constitutes a sort of freedom and terror that Dostoevsky could not have envisioned for his characters.

DONNA TUSSING ORWIN

[Children and Peasants in *Anna Karenina*: From Nature to Culture]†

In the 1860s, before turning to *War and Peace*, Tolstoy had set up and run a peasant school on his estate and published the journal *Iasnaia Poliana*, in which he had set forth his own theory of education. In the flagship article, entitled "Education for the People" [*O narodnom obrazovanii*] and published in January 1862 in *Iasnaia Poliana*, he concluded that the one criterion of pedagogy must be freedom. As he put it in this particular context, the pupil must be able to reject what he knows will not satisfy him. The student knows instinctively what good and evil are, because "the consciousness of good and evil, independent of the will of any one human being, lies in all of humankind and develops unconsciously together with history." Although Tolstoy wrote of history

† From Donna Tussing Orwin, *Tolstoy's Art and Thought, 1847–1880* (Princeton: Princeton University Press, 1993), pp. 144–47. © 1993 by Princeton University Press. Reprinted by permission of Princeton University Press.

here, he was not promoting what he disdainfully called elsewhere "the religion of progress." In *War and Peace*, he went on to assimilate "real" history to nature. The consciousness of good and evil is also, therefore, natural, and in another article in *Iasnaia Poliana*, "Who Should Be Teaching Whom to Write: Should We Be Teaching the Peasant Lads, or They Us?" [*Komu u kogo uchitsia pisat', krestianskim rebiatam u nas ili nam u krestianskikh rebiat*], written after mid-October 1862, he could write that "Man is born perfect" and that the purpose of education was either to maintain or to return to that natural perfection.

In the 1870s Tolstoy took up pedagogy again and published his *Primer* [*Azbuka*] in 1872. Accordingly, he published another article entitled "Education for the People" [*O narodnom obrazovanii*] in *Notes of the Fatherland* [*Otechestvennye zapiski*] in 1874. It is most enlightening to compare the principles of this article with those expounded in *Iasnaia Poliana* in 1862. The later article referred the reader to the earlier ones for the author's theory of education and claims that that theory remained the same. In the later article, however, Tolstoy nowhere reasserted the natural goodness of man. He, instead, summed up the results of his educational experiments in the 1860s as "the sole criterion of pedagogy is freedom, the sole method—experience." In the later article, moreover, he no longer illustrated the idea of natural goodness by contrasting, as he had in "The Iasnaia Poliana School in November and December," the purity of the peasant boys with the debased condition of their parents. (I refer to the lyrical scene in which he walks the boys home through a beautiful winter night and peers into the ugly huts to which they are returning.) Instead, he praised peasant culture and the values it inculcated, and he relied on parents to know what their children should be learning.

In the eleven years between the two articles entitled "Education for the People" nature had ceased to be an absolute standard for good for Tolstoy. A trend away from nature and toward moral freedom is visible in all the writing of this decade, in the pedagogical writing that precedes *Anna Karenina*, in various philosophical fragments, and in the drafts to the historical novel on Peter the Great that Tolstoy worked on for many years but never completed. In a related development the peasant, as the embodiment not of nature but of tradition and convention, emerges in Tolstoy's writing as the repository of moral truth. Whereas in *War and Peace* the peasant way is one lesson joined with others in Pierre's soul, in *Anna Karenina* the narod[1] have become the only moral way. As Tolstoy perceived a split between nature and moral goodness, he turned from nature to culture—and peasant culture became his new standard for morality.

The new critical attitude toward nature and also the latter's residual

---

1. The [common] people [*Editor*].

goodness are reflected in the role of children in *Anna Karenina*. Here, as in *War and Peace*, children figure as innocent and pure, but prone to basic human weaknesses. What is different in the two novels is the narrator's attitude toward those weaknesses. Petia Rostov and Serezha Karenin are both shown to love sweets, for instance. Petia's sweet tooth is portrayed sympathetically. One of the most touching moments in the novel comes when Denisov, looking at the corpse of his young friend, remembers it. It is one instance of the vitality that also sends him on his reckless ride to death; nonetheless, we love the vitality in him as we love it in ourselves. Tolstoy's attitude toward vitality was more critical in *Anna Karenina*, and so even in children it is no longer shown as simply good. Like his Uncle Stiva, Serezha finds that he cannot resist forbidden fruit: he takes a peach the way Stiva would steal rolls (or cheat on his wife). Serezha, however, unlike Stiva, is not corrupt. He cannot point, as Stiva does in the opening episode of the novel, to the "reflexes of the brain" to excuse his misbehavior. Serezha knows that he has been naughty and expects his mother to punish him. This is proof that conscience is as active as the voices of desire in Serezha's healthy, innocent soul. When Anna does not scold him, Serezha is "confused" as well as happy. He needs to be punished in order to have his own moral sense confirmed in him. He is not naturally sinful, as St. Augustine saw himself to be when as a child he stole fruit. He is pure and innocent, but naturally weak and prone to impulse.

Anna fails to punish Serezha because, knowing herself to be guilty of a greater sin, she is more concerned that he love and forgive *her* than that she do what is best for *him*. In the next chapter, Anna herself cries "all out, as children who have been punished do." She has judged herself and is unhappy the way a Liza Merkalova, also compared to a child, can never be. When she judges herself, Anna is behaving like a responsible adult disciplining a child. Even as she judges, however, she knows that "she," the she who acts, cannot change her ways. Small wonder that when called on to act, as she sits weeping, she feels herself "dividing in two." Child and adult in her, vitality and morality or moral reason, are parting company.

Children in *Anna Karenina* are also seen as capable, in an innocent way, of the pride and consequent love of distinguishing themselves that are Levin's weaknesses. These are what Tolstoy called spiritual, as opposed to bodily vices. When Levin is condemning the excessive pride of philosophers, he uses an example from the behavior of Dolly's children to make his point. The children are trying to cook raspberries over candles and to pour milk into their mouths like a fountain. Their mother reprimands them by telling them that they are destroying what others have prepared for their nourishment. Remembering this incident, Levin reflects that philosophers are like children. Philosophers rely for their happiness on truths they have learned from others and, out of the need to distinguish themselves, they invent tortuous ways to arrive at these same truths.

In *War and Peace,* either chance comes to the rescue of foolish children (like Natasha in love with Anatole), or children like Petia die as part of a mysterious and harmonious scheme of balance in the universe. In *Anna Karenina,* children need adults, human wisdom, to correct them. Again I refer to a shift in emphasis, not a complete change in ideas. In *Anna Karenina,* human beings in their natural state are not simply moral. Happiness still comes from nature, but morality, especially the higher morality of self-sacrifice, is transmitted through tradition. And whereas in *War and Peace* tradition itself—present, for instance, in Platon Karataev's characteristic use of folk sayings—perfects nature, in *Anna Karenina* it corrects nature.

Tolstoy explored this theme in the drafts to the historical novel on the Petrine period that he attempted in the seventies. He did not claim there that children were evil. At birth they are "pure and without sin" but ignorant of the essential truth that will keep them that way. The need for belief is one of two natural responses—the other being "desires and passions"—to the natural fear of death, a fear that is coeval with the consciousness of individual life that appears already in very young children. Tolstoy no doubt adopted this idea from Pascal with whom he became enamored around the beginning of 1876. In the famous section of the *Pensées* entitled "Diversions," Pascal argues that the proof that human beings are fundamentally unhappy lies in the fact that all of them, even kings, seek diversions rather than confronting the reality of their lives, and especially the reality of "inescapable death and disease." Following Pascal, Tolstoy wrote in the drafts to the Petrine novel that people could either try to forget death, as it was natural for children to do, by busying themselves with "desires and passions," or they could look for a meaning in life that would not be destroyed by death, a meaning supplied by faith.

And here at last is where the peasants come in. They alone of all the Russian people possess this faith and transmit it from generation to generation. They are different from other Russians because they still retain what other Russians lost at the time of Peter. Russian Christianity permeates every aspect of their lives. At the end of the 1870s, Tolstoy remarked in his diary that Peter should have taken the same view of the West as the peasants did to this day: that Russia needed Western technology without Western beliefs. The beliefs were so important, so much the basis of a uniquely Russian solution to the philosophical questions of life, that Tolstoy agreed with the peasants that it would be better to reject Western science if it eroded traditional beliefs. These beliefs were the product of a culture, not of nature or of one individual. As Tolstoy remarked while he was preparing his primer in the early 1870s, the wisdom of the Russian people, expressed in folklore, was spread all over

Russia. If you collected all the proverbs together, you would have this wisdom.

This explains the attitude that, according to Tolstoy, peasants took toward the education being offered them by the Westernized upper classes. In "Education for the People" (1874), Tolstoy claimed that the peasants wanted to limit the curriculum in public education to Russian, Church Slavonic, and mathematics. This policy would allow students to advance in other fields and would limit the interference of outsiders to narrowly practical matters.

Tolstoy agreed with the peasants that they possessed moral truths that needed protection from desecration by upper class do-gooders. As he wrote in a letter to Strakhov in early 1876, the peasants had less analysis, less science, than the educated classes, but a more healthy religious, that is, synthetic, view of the world.

Tolstoy made fun of educational theorists who called their peasant pupils "savages" [dikari] and thought that they themselves knew the answers to the deepest philosophical questions. Adequate answers to those questions were, in fact, already enshrined in peasant culture, and the peasants understandably resisted the efforts of narrow rationalists to reform it.

[Moral Freedom: Schopenhauer and Levin][1]

Tolstoy's acquaintance with the philosophy of Arthur Schopenhauer was one big reason for the shift in emphasis in Tolstoy's writing from nature to culture in the 1870s. As early as 1868 Tolstoy began to read the German philosopher. He spent the summer of 1869 reading all of Schopenhauer's works. At the end of the summer he wrote Fet:

> Do you know what the past summer has been for me? Constant ecstasy at Schopenhauer and a series of spiritual pleasures which I have never before experienced. I've ordered all his works and I've read them and am reading them (I've read through Kant too) . . . I don't know if I'll ever change my opinion, but right now I'm convinced that Schopenhauer is the greatest genius of all. You say that he's written a little on philosophic subjects? What do you mean, a little? This is the whole world in an unbelievably clear and beautiful exposition. I've begun to translate him. How about you taking up a translation? We could publish together. Reading him, I can't comprehend how his name could have remained unknown. There's only one explanation, the one that he often repeats; namely, that the world is made up mostly of idiots.

Although his exposure to Schopenhauer's philosophy changed Tolstoy forever, his initial infatuation soon gave way to a more nuanced rela-

1. Orwin, *Tolstoy's Art and Thought*, pp. 150–52, and 176–78.

tionship. He spent the 1870s coming to grips with this powerful new influence, and the novel *Anna Karenina* may be understood as part of his struggle. Tolstoy found Schopenhauer irresistibly familiar. Like Tolstoy, he was the type of metaphysical idealist who identified "ultimate reality with the Will, and not with Reason." Eikhenbaum shows that Tolstoy borrowed his argument on the relationship of determinism and freedom of the will in the second epilogue of *War and Peace*, written in 1869, from *The Two Fundamental Problems of Ethics*. In this work Schopenhauer, like Tolstoy in *War and Peace*, both acknowledged the existence of determinism in the physical world, and nonetheless defended the possibility of free will in the spiritual world. Schopenhauer also resembled Tolstoy (and Rousseau) in his reliance on reason. He gave philosophy a privileged position, because he did not regard all aspects of thinking as expressions of will. (Here is where Nietzsche parted company with Schopenhauer.) Schopenhauer believed in ultimate standards—Platonic Ideas as he understood them—which gave reason real authority and independence from the passions.

Although Schopenhauer's teaching helped Tolstoy resolve a central problem of his early thought (the relation of freedom and necessity), it differed from Tolstoy's early understanding in ways that created a crisis for the writer of the beginning of the 1870s. In the first place, Schopenhauer insisted on the tension, indeed the antipathy, between the natural freedom of man and the possibility of morality. *Natural* freedom, in the strict sense in which Schopenhauer understood it, is a product of will. It is purely a negative concept, signifying the *absence* of law, or reason. This freedom, far from being happiness, makes us miserable. "Our existence has no foundation on which to rest except the transient present. Thus its form is essentially unceasing motion, without any possibility of that repose which we continually strive after." Life, "in the desire for which our essence and existence consists," has no positive content according to Schopenhauer. This is proved by the phenomenon of boredom; if life were positive, "mere existence would fulfill and satisfy us." So much for the "sentiment of existence" of savage man which for Rousseau was more satisfying than any feeling civilized man could know. In order to have any real, extended existence, this sentiment, in Schopenhauer's analysis, would have to be based on some law in organic nature, some stable point that does not in fact exist. So much, too, for Goethean "living reason," at least as it may be understood to provide a foundation for the "sentiment of existence."

For Schopenhauer, in contradistinction to Tolstoy and Rousseau, man is naturally bad.[2] The following passage reads like a refutation of

2. Here Schopenhauer agrees with Pascal, who speaks of nature as corrupt (Pascal, *Pensées*). By this Pascal means, following standard Christian doctrine, that human beings as a result of the Fall have become selfish. Here, too, his opinion jibes with that of Schopenhauer, though Pascal was a Christian and Schopenhauer was not. Schopenhauer may have been the matchmaker who brought Tolstoy and Pascal together.

Rousseau's account of human history in the *Second Discourse,* where he had claimed that evil began only with the beginnings of human society:

> He who is capable of thinking a little more deeply will soon perceive that human desires cannot begin to be sinful simply at that point at which, in their chance encounters with one another, they occasion harm and evil; but that, if this is what they bring about, they must be originally and in their essence sinful and reprehensible, and the entire will to live itself reprehensible. All the cruelty and torment of which the world is full is in fact merely the necessary result of the totality of the forms which the will to live is objectified, and thus merely a commentary on the affirmation of the will to live. That our existence itself implies guilt is proved by the fact of death.

Natural man is "sinful" *because* he is free: he is completely without reason and is not governed by reason from without. As a result, he lives entirely for himself in a kind of Hobbesian war of all against all. It is useful to compare Schopenhauer's teaching on this point with that of the Savoyard Vicar. Schopenhauer regarded the *Profession of Faith* as the "prototype of all rationalism," which he criticizes for taking, not reason, but "theism and optimism" as its "presuppositions." Schopenhauer will be more reasonable than the so-called rationalists. As an atheist he sees no necessary correspondence, implicit in the Vicar's arguments and especially in the natural setting he chooses for his profession of faith, between order in nature and morality. The Savoyard Vicar strives to prove that the conscience is natural. Schopenhauer declares that one fundamental condition for morality, the freedom to be reasonable and therefore moral, must be outside of nature: "It is metaphysical; in the physical world it is impossible." *Moral* freedom for Schopenhauer, then, in contradistinction to Rousseau, is freedom *from* nature, freedom *from* life.

Schopenhauer and Rousseau would both agree that man is naturally selfish. What Schopenhauer denies in Rousseau's, and especially the Savoyard Vicar's account, is the existence of any natural law, either negative or positive, that holds human selfishness in check. To put the Schopenhauerian view in Rousseauist terms, man is naturally all expansion, no unity. And, unlike the Savoyard Vicar, Schopenhauer does not see expansiveness as moral or reasonable in any way. For him Olenin's "web of love" would have been just another weapon in the arsenal of the lover of glory. And there could be no divine purpose behind the slaughter of war. Man is naturally sinful because he wants to expand to the greatest extent possible at the expense of his neighbor.

For all this, Schopenhauer is not rejecting the possibility of morality. On the contrary, as Tolstoy understood when he borrowed the Scho-

penhauerian position on freedom and necessity, Schopenhauer put morality on a firmer footing by insisting, in the first place, on natural man's
complete freedom from natural law. Precisely because we are creatures
of will, not of order, who can, nonetheless, choose order, we can be
held responsible for our actions. We can *make* ourselves moral. This is
a second, and positive, freedom, the freedom to conform to law. Tolstoy
defines moral freedom in precisely this way in his notebook on 25
October 1868, when, according to an American visitor to his estate, he
was already enthusiastically reading Schopenhauer: "What does freedom
consist in? In a correspondence with eternal laws." Because this new
reasonable freedom is not natural to human beings, however, it leads
us eventually to reject life, understood as the action of the will, for
"real," that is, reasonable existence. Schopenhauer argues that his philosophy represents the true meaning of Christianity. It "demonstrates
theoretically the metaphysical foundation of justice and charity" in the
denial of self, "the denial of the will to live" which denial is "the true
soul of the New Testament . . . the spirit of asceticism." Reason leads
eventually to the "thing in itself, the will to live . . . present whole and
undivided in every single being" and hence not destroyed by the death
of an individual. We can be just and compassionate because we are,
essentially, the same will to live as everyone else. Through reason, we
see ourselves from an objective, not a particular point of view. We see
ourselves as the idea of the will to live, not a particular and unself-
conscious manifestation of it. Reason leads us out of our natural selves,
out of natural selfishness, out of nature. It leads us from the seeming
variety of appearance to the sameness of law.

Like Tolstoy, and perhaps more than Rousseau, Schopenhauer was
concerned to defend the foundations of morality. Schopenhauer's moral
philosophy grew out of Rousseau's teaching on compassion but was both
more radical and more systematic than Rousseauian morality. In *On
the Basis of Morality*, which was first published (in 1841) as part of *The
Two Fundamental Problems of Ethics*, Schopenhauer acknowledged his
debt to Rousseau, "undoubtedly the greatest moralist of modern times."
Like Rousseau, Schopenhauer understood pity, and morality altogether,
as a product of comparison, and therefore of reason.

> What distinguishes a moral virtue from a moral vice is whether the
> basic feeling towards others behind it is one of envy or one of pity:
> for every man bears these two diametrically opposed qualities within
> him, inasmuch as they arise from the comparison between his own
> condition and that of others which he cannot help making; one or
> other of these qualities will become his basic disposition and de-
> termine the nature of his actions according to the effect this com-
> parison has on his individual character. Envy reinforces the wall
> between Thou and I: pity makes it thin and transparent; *indeed, it*

*sometimes tears the wall down altogether, whereupon the distinction
between I and Not-I disappears.*

These lines could have been written by Rousseau or, for that matter,
by the later Tolstoy. They show clearly that Schopenhauer understood
the connection between Rousseauian *amour propre* and compassion.
They differ from the Rousseauist and the Tolstoyan teaching only at
one point in the lines that I have emphasized. Since pity for Rousseau
was based on the fact that we have bodies and are therefore physically
distinct beings, "the distinction between I and Not-I" could never completely disappear. Unlike Rousseau, however, Schopenhauer was a tho-
roughgoing subjectivist: for him the whole phenomenal world is a
creation of the brain, and the body is an objectification of particular
aspects of the will. The body, therefore, exist though it may, need not
stand in the way of a complete union of self and nonself.

Schopenhauer believed that the will to live, taken as a whole, had a
moral function. He made his argument for morality, however, at the
expense of the morality, and especially the possible happiness, of the
individual. The natural desire for individual happiness was selfish and
sinful, according to him, and therefore must be abandoned. If this proved
impossible, then the individual must yearn for, indeed do all he could
to bring about, his own death, even by suicide.

Tolstoy embraced Schopenhauer because the philosopher's more systematic thought gave structure to his own ideas. Like his teaching on freedom, Schopenhauer's teaching on compassion would have appealed to
Tolstoy because it set the concept of compassion on a firmer theoretical
footing. This clarification of thought, however, came at a steep price.
The draught that Tolstoy gulped down so eagerly during the summer of
1869 contained a hidden poison that threatened to destroy all his happiness. As Sigrid McLaughlin has discerned, Schopenhauer's attack on the
life of the individual as incorrigibly selfish and sinful at the core dealt a
potentially mortal blow to Tolstoy's more Rousseauist, optimistic view.

* * *

Since nothing but matter exists and everything happens according to
predetermined physical laws, the life of the body, which Stiva lives to
the fullest, is the only life possible. His body operates according to laws
over which he has little, often no, control. At times parts of his body
—that conditioned smile, for instance, when he confronts Dolly—even
do things not in the interest of the whole Stiva's response in these cases
is simply to go with the flow. Like his sister he has both physical grace
and a remarkable sensitivity to nuances of feeling. He would never have
made Vronsky's unforgivably awkward move that breaks Frou-Frou's
back. He is perfectly at home in the aimless flux of nature as envisaged
by ancient epicureans and modern materialists alike.

The fashionable determinism that Stiva introduces into the novel in a comic vein takes on darker tones in the story of his sister and of Levin. It is important to keep in mind, however, the extent to which Tolstoy himself believed in the power of both routine and outside influence over the human soul. Stiva's foolish smile recalls the inappropriate smile on Pierre's face at his father's deathbed, or, for that matter, the funny incident in Tolstoy's very first surviving work of fiction, the so-called "History of Yesterday," in which the narrator's feet convey him out the door when he still has something to say to his hosts. Constant motion in nature translates in human beings into the constant and often irresistible influence of feelings, sensations, and memories, Chernyshevsky's dialectic of the soul.

This state of being, moreover, when acknowledged by the individual, creates compassion for others whom the individual understands to be subject to the same whims as himself. As in Dickens and in Sterne, an understanding of the power of impulse over reason is related to an attitude of compassion toward human weakness. Levin is insufficiently compassionate in the symposium because he has not yet come to grips with this fact of human nature. In contrast to his attitude at the restaurant, Levin's final reflections, which end the novel, begin with an affirmation of his human weakness: "I will get angry at Ivan the coachman just as before, I will quarrel as before, I'll blurt out my thoughts inopportunely, as before there will be a wall between the holy of holies of my soul and others, even my wife, just as before I'll blame her for my fear and repent of it."

"That's the way the world is made": Stiva's response to Levin's confession of past sin in the symposium receives its ultimate vindication in these lines. By the end of the novel, Levin has accepted the fact, humiliating for mind and soul, that he has a body, which to a great extent goes its own way as part of a larger and seemingly random chain of causes and effects.

Levin, however, goes on in his final reflections equally to affirm the existence in himself of the "sense of the good which I have the power to insert into it [life]." Acceptance of the body is a good and necessary thing, then, but living simply for the body is not. The peak of Stiva's spirituality is a fleeting compassion which vies in him with other feelings. He lives only for physical pleasure. What Stiva totally lacks is moral freedom, the freedom to make moral choices among competing influences. Tolstoy's defense of the variety of life and its beauty, as developed in the letter to Strakhov, is based on the existence it implies of a freedom that makes both good and evil possible. But because the exercise of *moral* freedom depends ultimately on the moral sense that Levin possesses, Tolstoy's own position in the letter actually combines the points of view of Stiva and Levin. Thus Levin, in contrast to Stiva, regrets his sins, quoting famous lines from Pushkin's poem "Remembrance" [*Vospominanie*].

Stiva's conclusion, that the variety of life is a good thing, is correct, but his reason for drawing that conclusion—merely that it makes life beautiful and charming—is not. In making Stiva the champion of mere beauty, Tolstoy may indeed be taking issue with the aestheticism of his friends in the fifties, and in the process pointing out the connection between it and vulgar epicureanism. Living for the body, Stiva pities, but he does not judge either himself or others. Since he lives for pleasure, relegating his conscience to the status of other voices in his soul, he is not truly free, that is, free to follow moral law. Here he differs from his sister, who inhabits the same moral world as Levin. To appreciate the moral value of Stiva's defense of variety, therefore, one must step out of the symposium to compare Levin with Anna.

Anna Karenina was much criticized by contemporaries as containing two novels, one about Anna and the other about Levin. When the publisher Katkov used this excuse to cut off publication of the novel in The Russian Herald [Russkii vestnik] at the end of part 7, after Anna's suicide, Fet came to Tolstoy's defense. In an unpublished response to Katkov's decision—a decision actually made for political reasons—Fet argued that "the inner, artistic link of Levin with Karenina stares you in the face throughout the whole novel." He jokingly suggested that to make his intention absolutely clear, Tolstoy should have entitled his novel Karenina, or the Adventures of a Lost Lamb, and the Stubborn Landowner Levin, or the Moral Triumph of a Seeker after Truth. The novel can only end with part 8, where the parallel and contrast between the lives of the two characters is completed. Fet crosses t's and dots i's for the philistine reader who does not comprehend the dramatic structure of the novel.

In order to encourage the reader to compare Anna and Levin, Tolstoy made them alike in certain fundamental ways. Although they meet only once in the course of the novel, and then only toward its end, they are spiritually akin. Both share an openness to influence and change that makes them potentially moral. It is important to note in this context that Levin makes his first appearance in the novel not as the moralist in the symposium, but as a skater famous for his skill and strength. Like Anna and Stiva, then, Levin has physical grace. Like Anna and unlike various intellectuals in the novel, he also has the ability to change his mind, even to the point of seeming illogical. Sergei Ivanovich criticizes his brother for "a mind although quick enough, nonetheless subject to the impressions of the moment and hence full of contradictions." Levin and Anna are in touch both physically and spiritually with the illogical forces that govern life from minute to minute. Both differ from the two Alekseys, Karenin and Vronsky, in that they do not, cannot, lock themselves into a set of rules that would shield them from natural flux. It is precisely in the midst of the "krugovorot" [whirlwind], the wild snowstorm on the way back to Petersburg, that Anna has her first chance consciously to reject Vronsky. "Oblivion" [the rejection of moral consciousness] beckons her, "and she could as she willed [*po proizvolu*] give in to it or restrain herself." Real choices only present themselves when, for better or for worse, we step outside the house of rules we have built for ourselves or that others have built for us.

At the same time and on the other hand, Levin and Anna are alike in that they both feel the influence of and need for moral law. They cannot simply go with the flow. The Petersburg fast set live quite comfortably in the "whirlwind" of passions that eventually sweeps Anna to her death.

Betsy explains Anna's problem to her: "You see, it is possible to look at one and the same thing tragically and make a torture of it, and to look at it simply and even merrily [*veselo*]. Perhaps you're inclined to look at things too tragically." Anna's response, which follows immediately, links the tragic with the moral: " 'How I wish I could know others as I know myself,' said Anna seriously and thoughtfully. 'Am I worse than others, or better? Worse, I think.' " Anna is worse than Betsy and the others only because, unlike them, she makes moral judgments about herself. She is a tragic heroine, unlike the comic Stiva, because she inwardly acknowledges the choice between good and evil. This similarity between Anna and Levin sets up the contrast that Fet observed. Both live morally: one chooses evil and dies, while the other chooses good and lives. This choice is possible only when both freedom and moral law exist. Drama, for Tolstoy, was therefore ultimately a didactic genre, in which, as he told P. A. Sergeenko in 1900, conflicting sides speak their pieces fully and as forcefully as possible, but "at the same time the main, basic thought is felt everywhere."

In the symposium, Levin initially takes the side of law against freedom. Recollection in the middle of the conversation of his own past moral struggles makes him realize that he is somehow mistaken in his simple moralism. He eventually learns Stiva's lesson, that to live means to be tempted and often to fall. *Anna Karenina* teaches that the imperfection of human beings imposed on them by their bodies is necessary in a free and yet moral universe. Tolstoy has taken the atheist Schopenhauer's point about the irrational and hence fundamentally evil nature of human individuals and made it part of a budding theology.

Characters in *Anna Karenina* are necessarily imperfect, but they are capable of moral choices. Moral choice is the lynchpin around which *Anna Karenina* turns. Corresponding to this shift in emphasis from what Mirsky calls the "vegetable" (in *War and Peace*) to the "moralistic" (in *Anna Karenina*), the Goethean "metaphysics of opposites," still the skeleton of a living work of art, also evolves to acquire a moral function. Within the human soul, the opposites become choices for good or evil available to human beings by which they confirm or do not confirm their humanity and moral freedom.

Leo Tolstoy: A Chronology

1828	Tolstoy is born on his father's estate, Yasnaya Polyana, near Tula, eighty miles south of Moscow.
1830	Tolstoy's mother dies. (Tolstoy is brought up by an aunt.)
1837	Tolstoy's father dies.
1844	Tolstoy enters the University of Kazan; studies first oriental languages, later law.
1847	Leaves the University of Kazan without having graduated; lives on his estate, Yasnaya Polyana.
1851	Goes to the Caucasus; obtains commission in the army; participates in skirmishes with mountain tribesmen.
1852	Completes *Childhood*, published in *Sovremennik (The Contemporary)*.
1854	Is transferred to Sevastopol; participates in the Crimean War.
1855–56	*Sevastopol Sketches*.
1855	Leaves army; goes to Petersburg; famous for the *Sevastopol Sketches*; lives at Yasnaya Polyana.
1857	Visits Western Europe; founds school for children at Yasnaya Polyana.
1860–61	Visits Western Europe.
1861	Tolstoy's brother Nikolai dies of tuberculosis.
1862	Marries Sofia Bers, a neighboring aristocrat.
1863	*The Cossacks*.
1863–69	*War and Peace*.
1873–76	*Anna Karenina*.
1877–85	Much religious and moral writing, little artistic work.
1880–82	*A Confession*, describing his religious doubt, despair, and conversion.
1886	*The Death of Ivan Ilich*.
1890	*The Kreutzer Sonata*.
1891	Organizes famine relief in rural areas.
1896–1904	*Hadji Murad*.
1897	*What Is Art?*
1910	In October Tolstoy leaves Yasnaya Polyana to live in a monastery.
1910	On November 22 Tolstoy dies in the railroad station in Astapovo.

Selected Bibliography

This bibliography does not include those works from which the excerpts above have been taken.

Bayley, John. *Tolstoy and the Novel*. London: Chatto and Windus, 1966.
Berlin, Isaiah. "The Hedgehog and the Fox." *Russian Thinkers*. New York: Viking, 1978. Pp. 22–81.
———. "Tolstoy and Enlightenment." *Encounter* (February 1961): 29–40.
Bloom, Harold, ed. *Leo Tolstoy*. New York: Chelsea House Publishers, 1986.
Christian, R. F. *Tolstoy: A Critical Introduction*. London: Cambridge U Press, 1969.
Eikhenbaum, Boris. *Tolstoy in the Seventies*. Trans. Albert Kaspin. Ann Arbor, MI: Ardis, 1982.
Feuer, Kathryn. "Stiva." *Russian Literature and American Critics*. Ed. Kenneth Brostrom. Ann Arbor, MI: U of Michigan, 1984. Pp. 147–57.
Gifford, Henry. *Tolstoy*. New York: Oxford UP, 1982.
Goldenveizer, A. B. *Talks with Tolstoy*. Richmond, 1923.
Gorky, Maxim. *Reminiscences*. New York, 1895.
Gustafson, Richard F. *Leo Tolstoy, Resident and Stranger: A Study in Fiction and Theology*. Princeton: Princeton UP, 1986.
Heldt, Barbara. "Tolstoy's Path to Feminism." *Terrible Perfection: Woman and Russian Literature* (Bloomington: Indiana UP, 1987).
Howells, William Dean. *My Literary Passions*. New York, 1895.
Jackson, Robert Louis. "Chance and Design in *Anna Karenina*." *The Disciplines of Criticism: Essays in Literary Theory, Interpretation, and History Honoring Rene Wellek*. Eds. Peter Demetz, Thomas Greene, and Lowry Nelson, Jr. New Haven: Yale UP, 1968. Pp. 315–29.
Jones, Malcolm, ed. *New Essays on Tolstoy*. New York: Cambridge UP, 1978.
Leavis, F. R. "*Anna Karenina*: Thought and Significance in a Great Creative Work." *Anna Karenina and Other Essays*. London: Chatto and Windus, 1967. Pp. 9–32.
Lukacs, Georg. "Tolstoy and the Development of Realism." *Studies in European Realism*. New York, 1964.
Mandelker, Amy. "A Painted Lady: *Ekphrasis* in *Anna Karenina*." *Comparative Literature* 43, no. 1 (winter 1991): 2–18.
———. *Framing Anna Karenina: Tolstoy, the Woman Question, and the Victorian Novel*. Columbus: Ohio State UP, 1994.
Mann, Thomas. "*Anna Karenina*." *Essays of Three Decades*. New York: Alfred A. Knopf, 1948. Pp. 176–88.
Matlaw, Ralph, ed. *Tolstoy: A Collection of Critical Essays*. Engelwood, NJ: Prentice-Hall, 1967.
Maude, Aylmer. *The Life of Tolstoy*. London, 1930. 2 vols.
McLean, Hugh, ed. *In the Shade of the Giant: Essays on Tolstoy*. Berkeley, CA: U of California P, 1989.
Morson, Gary Saul. "Prosaics and *Anna Karenina*: Eleven Theses on Anna." *Tolstoy Studies Journal* 1 (1988): 1–12.
Muchnic, Helen. "Lev Nikolaevich Tolstoy." *An Introduction to Russian Literature*. New York, 1964.
Poggioli, R. *The Phoenix and the Spider*. Cambridge, MA: Harvard UP, 1957. Pp. 1–108.
Price, Martin. "Tolstoy and the Forms of Life." *Forms of Life: Character and Moral Imagination in the Novel*. New Haven: Yale UP, 1983. Pp. 178–203.
Redpath, Theodore. *Tolstoy*. London, 1960.
Schultze, Sydney. *The Structure of Anna Karenina*. Ann Arbor, MI: Ardis, 1982.
Silbajoris, Rimvydas. *Tolstoy's Aesthetics and His Art*. Columbus, OH: Slavic Publishers, 1991.
Stenbock-Fermor, Elisabeth. *The Architecture of Anna Karenina*. Lisse: Peter de Ridder, 1975.
Steward, David H. "*Anna Karenina*: The Dialectic of Prophecy." *PMLA* (June 1964): 266–82.
Thorlby, Anthony. *Anna Karenina*. New York: Cambridge UP, 1987.

Trilling, Lionel. *"Anna Karenina." The Opposing Self.* New York, 1955. Pp. 66–75.
Wasiolek, Edward. *Tolstoy's Major Fiction.* Chicago: Chicago UP, 1978.
———. *Critical Essays on Tolstoy.* Boston: G. K. Hall, 1986.
Wellek, René. *"Tolstoy (as critic)." A History of Modern Criticism,* 3. New Haven, 1965.
Wilson, A. N. *Tolstoy.* New York: W. W. Norton, 1988.